The Bhagavadgita Original Commentary

Unveiling the Gita's Secrets

Translation & Commentary by

Jayaram V

Published by
Pure Life Vision LLC
New Albany, Ohio

The Bhagavadgita Original Commentary: Unveiling the Gita's Secrets

Published and Distributed Worldwide by Pure Life Vision LLC., USA.
www.PureLifeVision.com
First edition 2025
Page Count 818

Library of Congress Publisher Cataloging-in-Publication Data

V, Jayaram (Vemulapalli, Jayaram)
The Bhagavadgita Original Commentary: Unveiling The Gita's Secrets
Earlier Edition: Bhagavadgita: Unveiling The Gita's Secrets, 2024
Translation and Commentary by Vemulapalli, Jayaram (V, Jayaram)
LCCN: 2024936720
ISBN-10: 1-935760-27-0
ISBN-13: 978-1-935760-27-6

Printed in the United States of America
10 9 8 7 6 5 4 3 2 1
First Edition 2025

About the Author

Jayaram V has authored over 3000 articles and 16 books, which include such notable works as Brahman, The Awakened Life, An Introduction to Hinduism, Bhagavadgita: Unveiling Gita's Secrets, Essays on the Bhagavadgita, Brahman, The Awakened Life, Hinduism, an Introduction, Selected Upanishads, Brihadaranyaka and Chandogya Upanishads, Shiva Sutras: Mystic Knowledge Explained, The Hindu Caste System, etc. His writings are appreciated all over the world for their originality and quality of information, and his analysis and interpretation of ancient texts. Jayaram V has studied Hinduism and related religions for over 40 years and writes regularly about various aspects of Hinduism, Buddhism, Jainism, spirituality, yoga, and self-improvement. Through his writings, he brings out the knowledge found in the ancient texts, their hidden symbolism, and the significance of various key concepts found in them, and interprets them objectively with modern insights and without sectarian biases. His scientific and spiritual background helps him examine the subjects analytically with an open mind and maintain objectivity in his writings and interpretations. He combines the mundane and finite aspects of life with the mystical and transcendental without losing sight of their spiritual and practical value in today's world. Inspired by Swami Vivekananda, Sri Aurobindo, and several other spiritual masters of the past and present, he founded Hinduwebsite.com in 2000 to counter negative propaganda and share authentic information about Hinduism and related religions. He believes in religious tolerance and the fundamental freedom of everyone to choose their faith or belief system according to their nature, needs, and preferences. He believes that atheism is also a part of one's spiritual journey. His efforts have helped make ancient Hindu texts more accessible to the world audience and appreciate the teachings found in them. His work has helped bring the wisdom of India's oldest religious and spiritual traditions to people around the world and educate and inspire them. You can explore more of his writings on Jayaramv.com and Hinduwebsite.com.

Contents

Preface 9
Author's Note 11
01 – Arjuna Vishada Yoga 13
02 – Sāmkhya Yoga 50
03 – Karma Yoga 131
04 – Jnāna Karma-Sannyāsa Yoga 191
05 – Karma-Sannyāsa Yoga 243
06 – Atma Samyama Yoga 278
07 – Jnāna Vijnāna Yoga 332
08 – Akshara Brahma Yoga 366
09 – Rājavidya Rājaguhya Yoga 400
10 – Vibhuti Yoga 440
11 – Visvarupa Darshana Yoga 486
12 – Bhakti Yoga 536
13 – Kshetra Kshetrajna Vibhāga Yoga 560
14 – Gunatraya Vibhāga Yoga 601
15 – Purushottama Yoga 632
16 – Daivāsura Sampadvibhāga Yoga 654
17 – Shraddhā Traya Vibhāga Yoga 687
18 – Moksha Sannyasa Yoga 723
The Greatness of the Bhagavadgita 815

BOOKS BY Jayaram Vemulapalli (JAYARAM V)

Shiva Sutras: Mystic Knowledge Explained, 2024

The Hindu Caste System, 2025

Sacred Numbers of Hinduism, 2025

The Awakened Life: Spiritual Knowledge from India's Sacred Traditions, 2024

Brihadaranyaka Upanishad, Revised 2024

Chandogya Upanishad, Revised 2024

Introduction to Hinduism, Second Edition, 2024

Brahman, Second Edition, 2025

Selected Upanishads

Think Success: Essays on Self-help

Being the Best: Practical Advice for Peace and Happiness

Thoughts and Quotations

Sadhana Panchakam - The Fivefold Spiritual Practice

The Bhagavadgita: A Complete Translation, 2011

The Bhagavadgita: A Simple Translation, First Edition, 2011

Essays on the Bhagavadgita, 2012

The Bhagavadgita: A Simple Translation, Second Edition, 2024

The Bhagavadgita: Unveiling the Gita's Secrets, 2024

The Bhagavadgita Original Commentary: Unveiling the Gita's Secrets, 2025

The Essential Bhagavadgita: Its Philosophy and Doctrine, 2025

Preface

The author, Jayaram V, has been studying and working on the Bhagavadgita since the beginning of this millennium. He has written several articles on its teachings and concepts, published a book titled Essays on the Bhagavadgita, as well as a series of articles on the scripture's knowledge and wisdom with the aim of completing at least 365 of them. He published his first translation of the scripture at Hinduwebsite.com in 2002. It was a free translation into simple English. Many people appreciated it. At least one person even published it in print without our permission. Jayaram published his second translation with an elaborate commentary in 2010. He wrote the commentary, letting his mind flow freely and interpreting the concepts in the slokas as he understood them without any reference to past works. He did not consult anyone or refer to any particular work while writing it. However, while working on the Bhagavadgita Wisdom Series for Hinduwebsite.com, he felt that it needed improvements in many respects.

Therefore, in 2020, he began a new commentary, which took three years to complete. This time, he studied various commentaries, especially by classical writers like Shankara and Madhava, to ensure that he understood all the concepts and points of view. Since he wrote it afresh with new insights, we decided to publish it as a new work rather than a revision of the previous edition. The first version of this was published in June 2024 under the title Bhagavadgita: Unveiling the Gita's Secrets. It has now been republished with a few corrections under the new title: The Bhagavadgita Original Commentary: Unveiling the Gita's Secrets. To avoid confusion and ensure the integrity of each edition, we have withdrawn both the previous two commentaries entirely from the market before introducing this one.

This new commentary is one of the most comprehensive and scholarly works on the Bhagavadgita ever attempted. By saying that, we are not undermining the work of previous masters or the efforts they made in spreading the knowledge and wisdom of Lord Krishna. They are brilliant, each presented from a particular philosophical or theistic perspective to help the Lord's pious devotees find their way to peace and happiness. We do not have any intention of replacing them. This is a humble effort from our side in this age and time to spread this immemorial teaching of Lord Krishna and do our part.

This work stands out because it is presented from a broader perspective without limiting its scope to a particular sect, teacher tradition, or philosophy. The author interpreted it as an Upanishad and a scripture on Yoga and Dharma. We believe it will help all those spiritual people who want to improve their lives, thinking, and actions through Krishna's teachings and grace, cultivating discernment, discipline, duty, and devotion.

For the benefit of our readers who may not be familiar with Indian culture, Jayaram provided detailed descriptions of certain words, beliefs, and practices. This is to ensure that everyone, regardless of their background, can fully appreciate the depth and richness of the Bhagavadgita's teachings. In some cases, he repeated the same concepts to ensure that the commentary for each sloka is complete and readers can understand them easily without backtracking.

In a voluminous work like this, there are bound to be spelling mistakes despite our best efforts. We are thankful to Shri C. Ratna Kumar for reviewing the whole scripture, correcting spelling mistakes, and giving valuable suggestions.

Publisher

July 15, 2025

Author's Note

Hinduism recognizes the Brahmasutras, the Upanishads, and the Bhagavadgita as the three great works that guide humans on their journey to the final liberation (prastanatraya). Anyone who wants to understand the historical, spiritual, and philosophical aspects of India's religious development or their contribution to the emergence of present-day Hinduism or to the civilization that is uniquely Indian should study them. They are useful even for those who want to practice spirituality, yoga, or simple devotion with discernment and with the right knowledge and awareness. I previously translated 15 Upanishads with explanatory notes, including the large ones, Chandogya and Brihadaranyaka Upanishads. I also wrote extensively and published many articles on the wisdom of the Upanishads and Bhagavadgita. This work, my second on the Bhagavadgita, provides the readers with an in-depth commentary of all the 600 slokas, some from different perspectives.

This work has helped me understand myself better. It has led me to realize that I must acknowledge my divine nature and do my best to give precedence to it and strengthen it. If God exists in me as my very Self, it is proof enough that he exists in all and the universe also. Therefore, our spiritual effort should be to realize and express this divine nature through our thoughts and actions until it becomes our natural state (sahaja svabhavam) and elevates our consciousness so that, at some point, it reflects the Lord and becomes one with him. It is my conviction that true liberation (Moksha) is but liberation from the identities or from that nature and consciousness in us which are the sources of all our troubles, desires, attachments, and suffering arising from them. We are closer to God when we are calm, renounce our identities, and set our minds free from the modifications to which they are subject. We actualize the divine qualities mentioned in this scripture to the extent we are free from their opposites.

When I started working on the Bhagavadgita, I did not know that the scripture presented a God-centric worldview and put God at the center of everything, including liberation. According to it, nothing happens without God's intervention or his will. That led me to wonder whether we have any freedom or free will at all, and if he decides everything, why should we suffer from karma? Then, as I started working on the verses, it dawned on me that the divine will is not distinct or separate from the individual will. To think that individual will is separate from that of the Lord or that you are different from him is the delusion, or Maya, to which all humans are subject. It was probably why Lord Krishna spoke in the first person on and off while speaking about Brahman in the second person at other times. Once we accept this fundamental premise, everything taught in this scripture falls into place. God is not different or separate from you. He is working through all his manifestations individually, collectively, and universally. All their actions arise from him and because of him. Call him by whatever name - he is the Lord of all and the Self in all (sarva bhutatma), and the right way to worship him is by surrendering our egos, desires, and delusions and living and acting as if he is responsible for all our actions. By this consecration, the devotee must set himself free from himself and all consequences.

The Bhagavadgita has been a source of inspiration for many people since ancient times. It continues to be so even today. It is a book of divine solutions for human problems. If you set aside your habitual thinking and read it with an open mind, you will find many solutions to your day-to-day problems. To those who want to be free from the encumbrances of life, it shows how they may achieve it without subjecting themselves to the rigors of sannyasa or denying themselves or the Lord in them the enjoyments of mortal life. You can live freely and fearlessly when you acknowledge the Lord in you and make him an inseparable part of your life and consciousness. Indeed, this relationship between man and the Lord is excellently portrayed in the Bhagavadgita itself by presenting Arjuna as the troubled human (nara) and Lord Krishna as the all-knowing, all-pervading, Supreme Lord, whom you can choose as your teacher, guide, and leading force.

I have to admit that I was not alone while working on this. Lord Krishna worked through me, and, therefore, I consider that this is his work only. He opened my mind so that I could see the full import of his teaching. He helped me endure three years of hard work. I hope he will step into your life also and be your guide, master, teacher, inspiration, witness, and support in all your actions. I hope that he will speak to you through this work and inspire and guide you on your spiritual journey of self-discovery.

This book was published last year under the title Bhagavadgita: Unveiling the Gita's Secrets. This is now republished with the new title to ensure that the title reflects the nature and subject of the work. In this new edition, I have made spelling and grammatical corrections and changed the title to include "Original Commentary," which I believe clarifies the purpose. Otherwise, everything remains the same. Readers should note that the pronouns used for God sometimes start with a capital letter and sometimes with a lowercase letter (as in the case of Him or His) for clarity.

I am grateful to Lord Krishna for being my guide, teacher, and inspiration throughout this karma yoga and jnana yajna, which I now dedicate to Him with the utmost devotion.

Jayaram V

July 15, 2025

01 – Arjuna Vishada Yoga

Arjuna's State of Sorrow

Sloka 1

dhṛtarāṣṭra uvāca
dharmakṣetre kurukṣetre samavetā yuyutsavaḥ
māmakāḥ pāṇḍavāś caiva kim akurvata sañjaya

dhṛtarāṣṭra = dhrtarashtra; uvāca = said; dharmakṣetre =in sacred field, in the field of righteousness; kurukṣetre = kuruksetra; samavetā = gathered, assembled; yuyutsavaḥ = raring to fight; māmakāḥ = my sons; pāṇḍavāś = Pāndavas; ca = and; eva = certainly; kim = what; akurvata = doing; sañjaya = O Sanjaya.

Dhritarashtra said, "In the sacred field of Kurukshetra, O Sanjaya, what are my sons and Pāndavas doing, having assembled and raring to fight? "

At the time of the Mahābhārata war, Dhritarashtra was ruling Hastinapur. He was visually impaired from birth, because of which he was sidelined for succession, although he was the eldest son. Instead, his brother Pandu was chosen. The decision hurt him and left him nursing the wound for the rest of his life. He married Gandhari, who gave birth to 100 sons and a daughter. They were called Kauravas after the name of their clan or kingdom. His brother Pandu married a princess named Kunti, through whom he had five sons, who were known as Pāndavas after his father's name. When Pandu died due to a curse, Dhritarashtra became the king. Both the Kauravas and Pāndavas grew up under his protection. They were trained in the art of warfare, weaponry, and martial arts by Dronacharya. When they reached adulthood, Dhritarashtra wanted his eldest son, Duryodhana, to be the successor. However, the elders in the court suggested that Dharmarāja, the eldest son of Pandu, was the rightful heir. Dhritarashtra agreed reluctantly. However, Duryodhana and his brothers disliked this decision and began plotting against the Pāndavas to eliminate them. The seeds of the Kurukshetra were sown thus. In time, the differences grew irreconcilably, and war became inevitable.

The Bhagavadgita is a part of the epic Mahābhārata. It appears in the sixth section, called Bhīshma Parva. If you want to know the events that led to the Kurukshetra war or what happened in it, you may read the epic Mahabharata or one of its abridged versions. Its translations are available in many languages in print and digital copies. Dhritarashtra is an excellent example of how families are ruined when elders ignore their moral duties and obligations and succumb to selfishness and evil temptations. Although he possessed excellent skills and knowledge, he did not put them to proper use.

Due to desires and delusion, he allowed his children to plot against the Pāndavas and deny them their legitimate right to rule. Thus, in many ways, due to selfishness and filial love, he allowed the rivalry between the cousins to go out of control and made the war inevitable. He could have prevented it if he had controlled his children and acted justly and impartially in his duties as the guardian and upholder of Dharma and the protector of all.

In this verse, Dhritarashtra wanted to know from Sanjaya what was happening on the battlefield of Kurukshetra after his sons and the Pāndavas gathered there with their armies and stood facing each other. Sanjaya appears in the Bhagavadgita because, due to his visual impairment, Dhritarashtra wanted to know, through a clairvoyant, the events on the battlefield in real-time from his palace at Hastinapur. Therefore, he sought the help of his guru, Veda Vyasa, who sent his student Sanjaya to help him after granting him clairvoyance. Although the Bhagavadgita is a sacred dialogue (samvada) between Lord Krishna and Arjuna, it is composed as a conversation within the conversation between Sanjaya and Dhritarashtra. Hence, it is considered a scripture composed from memory (smriti) rather than hearing directly from God (shruti). Since Sanjaya was remotely watching them in real-time and conveying the information to the king, the knowledge of the Bhagavadgita was received not only by Arjuna but also by Sanjaya and Dhritarashtra.

The three recipients represent how God transmits spiritual knowledge to his devotees. Arjuna represents the direct method. It is not frequent, but God uses it in exceptional circumstances to communicate with his exclusive devotees or divine souls when circumstances warrant. Sanjaya represents the second method, the intuitive or psychic method. He uses it to communicate with his pure devotees who possess discerning wisdom and achieve perfection in self-control and jnana yoga. The king represents the third method, the indirect method, by which the Lord communicates with his imperfect devotees through enlightened masters or other instruments when they develop an interest in knowing themselves, worshipping him, or achieving liberation. The three methods also represent the three ways in which human beings receive divine knowledge in the transcendental (turiya), dream or trance (svapna), and wakeful (jagrata) states of human consciousness. It is said that apart from them, Hanuman and sage Vyasa also overheard the conversation. Hanuman heard it while sitting on Arjuna's chariot as their emblematic flag bearer. Sage Vyasa was said to have received it just as his disciple, Sanjaya, through clairvoyance.

A great deal of symbolism is hidden in the Bhagavadgita. For example, it is said that the Mahābhārata war symbolizes life itself. The battlefield of Kurukshetra, which is mentioned here as dharmaksehtra (field of Dharma), represents the human body. The battle between Pāndavas and Kauravas represents the battle between good and evil, which goes on in everyone's mind, life, and the world. Pāndavas represent the five senses held in check by the five restraints: Kauravas, evil thoughts and intentions under the influence of the five chief evils; Dhritarashtra, the deluded and impure lower nature; Sanjaya, the intelligent mind; Arjuna, the higher nature, and Lord Krishna, the Self or the Supreme Self.

Sloka 2

sañjaya uvāca
dṛṣṭvā tu pāṇḍavānīkaṃ vyūḍhaṃ duryodhanas tadā
ācāryam upasaṅgamya rājā vacanam abravīt

sañjaya = Sanjaya; uvāca = said; dṛṣṭvā = having seen; tu = but; pāṇḍavānīkaṃ = Pandava's army; vyūḍhaṃ = battle formation; duryodhanas = Duryodhana; tadā = then ācāryam = teacher; upasaṅgamya = went near; rājā = king; vacanam = words; abravīt = spoke.

Sanjaya said, "Having seen the numerous battle formations of the Pandavas' army, King Duryodhana then went near his teacher (Dronacharya) and spoke these words.

Sanjaya began his narration with Duryodhana, probably to please the King since he was eager to know what his son was doing on the battlefield. The king thought that the odds were in their favor since the Kauravas had a larger army, and most of the renowned warriors were on their side, obligated by duty, friendship, or political alliance. Duryodhana was leading their side. Hence, he surveyed the battle formations of the Pāndavas to assess their strength and plan his strategy. He approached Dronacharya, his guru, to alert him. Drona was the royal teacher who taught the art of warfare and military strategy to both Kauravas and Pandavas. However, his heart was with the Pandavas while he was duty-bound to support Duryodhana. Hence, the latter had some doubts about his loyalty. Those familiar with the epic Mahābhārata know that Duryodhana was envious of the Pāndavas and spared no effort to destroy them and deny them their right to rule the kingdom. He was also unhappy with their success and popularity.

In Sanskrit, Duryodhana means one who is difficult to fight. His original name was Suyodhana, meaning a great fighter. He had a diverse nature, with many great and evil qualities. Hence, he was a mixture of opposites, with many strengths and weaknesses. He was a true friend to those he liked and an arch-enemy to those he disliked. He made Karna, his close friend, a king and granted him a kingdom to elevate his social status as a warrior king and spite the Pandavas. Because of extreme passions such as anger, pride, and envy, he repeatedly ignored the advice of the wise ones and elders in the family and the Court, making any reconciliation with his cousins impossible. Even Lord Krishna's attempts to settle their differences proved futile because of his petulance. Duryodhana personifies rajasic nature, which induces extreme passions. We will discuss it later. According to our shastras, it is within the right of a warrior king or prince to forcefully usurp another kingdom. Hence, Duryodhana was in his own right to fight the Pāndavas, but he tried to do it selfishly and egoistically, ignoring the advice of Lord Krishna, the Supreme Being. Hence, despite favorable circumstances, he failed in the end.

Sloka 3

paśyaitāṃ pāṇḍuputrāṇām ācārya mahatīṃ camūm
vyūḍhāṃ drupadaputreṇa tava śiṣyeṇa dhīmatā

paśya = look; etāṃ = the; pāṇḍuputrāṇām = Pāndavas; the sons of Pandu; ācārya = teacher; mahatīṃ = great; camūm = military might; vyūḍhāṃ = formation; drupadaputreṇa = by the sons of Drupada; tava = your; śiṣyeṇa = disciple; dhīmatā = intelligent.

O great teacher, look at the military might of the Pāndavas' army, arrayed by your intelligent disciple and son of Drupada.

In all, 18 akshauhinis (divisions) participated in the Kurukshetra war, eleven on the Kauravas' side facing the west and seven on the Pandavas' side facing the east. According to one estimate, an akshauhini is a large military division consisting of 21,870 chariots, the same number of elephants, 65,610 horse riders, and 109,350 soldiers. Bhīshma, the Kuru family's eldest scion and Mother Ganga's son, initially led the Kauravas' army. He had the gift of remaining alive and invincible as long as he wished. On this occasion, he stood at the forefront of the eleventh division, facing the Pāndavas' army. He was a great warrior with impeccable character, impartial to all his grandchildren but with special affection toward Arjuna. Like Drona, he was reluctant to fight on behalf of the Kauravas but agreed as he was bound by an oath to protect the Kuru kingdom. However, as a condition for his cooperation, he insisted that Karna should not be on the battlefield as long as he was in command. Ultimately, it proved disadvantageous to the Kauravas since the combination of Bhīshma and Karna would have been formidable for the Pāndavas. Dhrishtadyumna, the son of Drupada, commanded the Pandavas' army. He was a brother of Shikhandi and Draupadi (the wife of the Pāndavas) and a disciple of Drona. The three were born for specific reasons traceable to their past lives. Draupadi was born to destroy the Kuru race. Dhrishtadyumna was born to kill Drona, with whom his father had a long feud. Shikhandi was born to avenge Bhīshma for his actions in her past life. Thus, karma, fate, and divine will bring the warring factions to the battlefield. Duryodhana was aware of Drona's relationship with Drupada. Hence, instead of mentioning Dhrishtadyumna directly by his name, he called him Drupada's son.

Sloka 4

atra śūrā maheṣvāsā bhīmārjunasamā yudhi
yuyudhāno virāṭaśca drupadaś ca mahārathaḥ

atra = here; śūrā = heroes; maha = great; iṣvāsā = archers; bhīmārjuna = Bhima and Arjuna; samā = equal to yudhi = in fighting; yuyudhāna = Yuyudhana; virāṭaśca = virata also drupadaśca = Drupada also; mahā = great rathaḥ = charioteer.

Here in this army are great heroes and archers, equal to Bhima and Arjuna in fighting, also like Yuyudhāna, Virata, and the great charioteer, Drupada.

Sanjaya was narrating to Dhritarashtra what Duryodhana was saying to Drona about the heroic fighters on the Pāndavas' side. By mentioning their names, he probably wanted Drona to stay firm and take his fighting seriously without succumbing to feelings and emotions. A true commander-in-chief does not underestimate his enemy. He ensures that his side will stay strong and fight until the end. Duryodhana did the same. Although his army was superior in strength and he had great fighters like Bhīshma and Drona on his side, he wanted Drona to fight with his full might and not spare his enemies, even if some were his disciples in the past. Hence, he reminded him that great warriors like Bhima and Arjuna, known for their excellent fighting skills and feared by most, were fighting on the opposite side.

He specifically mentioned Yuyudhāna, Virata, and Drupada. Each was a skillful warrior and led a division of the Pāndavas' army. Yuyudhana's other name was Satyaki. He belonged to the Vrishni clan of the Yadavas, to which Lord Krishna also belonged. He survived the Kurukshetra war and died years later at the hands of a few assailants when he insulted them in a state of intoxication. Virata ruled two provinces, namely Matsya and Virata. An entire section in the Mahābhārata is named after him. He gave shelter to the Pāndavas when they were exiled and married his daughter, Uttara, to Arjuna's son, Abhimanyu, who died in the Kurukshetra war, fighting valiantly against great warriors such as Bhishma and Drona as they joined forces to kill him in a concerted attack to save themselves from his ferocity.

Drupada's name is mentioned in the previous verse also. He was Panchala's king and originally a friend of Dronacharya, but later became an arch-enemy due to his arrogance. In retaliation, Drona defeated him in a battle, assisted by Pāndavas and Kauravas, and forced him to surrender and cede half of his kingdom. He obtained three children through a sacrifice (yajna): Dhrishtadyumna, Draupadi, and Shikhandi. They were born to avenge their enemies from their previous lives. Dhrishtadyumna was born to kill Drona since he humiliated his father and took half of his kingdom. Draupadi was born to destroy the Kuru clan since they fought with her father and helped Drona to shame him, and Shikhandi was born to ensure the destruction of Bhīshma since he wronged her in her past life. Drupada is an excellent example of how events shaped by one's actions, fate, and acts of God gather force in time and lead to grave consequences and suffering for oneself and others.

Sloka 5

dhṛṣṭaketuś cekitānaḥ kāśirājaś ca vīryavān
purujit kuntibhojaś ca śaibyaś ca narapuṅgavaḥ

dhṛṣṭaketuś = Dhristaketu; cekitānaḥ = Cekitana kāśirājah = king of Kasi; ca = also; vīryavān = heroic; purujit = Purujit; kuntibhojah = Kuntibhoja; ca = and śaibyah = Saibya; ca = also; narapuṅgavaḥ = Notable among men.

And there are great fighters such as Dhristaketu, Cekitana, the king of Kasi, the heroic Purujit, Kuntibhoja, and Saibya, the most notable ones among men.

Several acclaimed warriors fought on the Pāndavas' side in the Mahābhārata war. They were hardened by many battles and earned recognition for their fighting skills and heroic victories. They joined the Pāndavas at the behest of Dharmarāja, who sought their help. According to the Mahābhārata, a few days before the war preparations began, and when it became certain that a truce would not materialize, Dharmarāja, the eldest of the Pāndavas, summoned his close allies to his camp and requested them to join him and fight for them. They agreed because they had been witnessing the feud between the two groups for some time and knew which side was clearly wronged. Some agreed to help because they were related through kinship and marriage, or the Pandavas helped them fight their enemies.

Five warriors are mentioned in this verse. Dhristaketu was one of the five Kekaya brothers who had a similar history to that of the Pāndavas, as their brethren also betrayed them. He was the son of Shishupala, who was then king of Chedi. He led the armies of Chedis, Kasis, and Narushas in the Kurukshetra War. Chekitana was his son. In the Kurukshetra War, he fought many renowned warriors, including Dronacharya, and rescued Nakula (Arjuna's brother) from the hands of Duryodhana. However, on the eighteenth day of the war, he died at the hands of Duryodhana, fighting heroically. Purujit was a Yadava prince. He was the son of Lord Krishna through Jambavathi. Kuntibhoja was the adopted father of Kunti, the mother of the Pāndavas. Saibya was also a Yadava warrior from the Vrishini clan, just like Lord Krishna, and was probably his son through his wife, Saibya. He was an archer and fought in the Kurukshetra war on behalf of the Pāndavas.

Sloka 6

yudhāmanyuś ca vikrānta uttamaujāś ca vīryavān
saubhadro draupadeyāś ca sarva eva mahārathāḥ

yudhāmanyuh = Yudhamanyu; ca = and; vikrānta = mighty; uttamaujāh = Uttamauja; ca = and; vīryavān = very powerful; saubhadro = son of Saubhadra; draupadeyāh = the sons of Draupadi; ca = and; sarva = all; eva = certainly; mahārathāḥ = great charioteers.

There are also Yudhamanyu, the mighty Uttamauja, the sons of Subhadra and Draupadi, who are all certainly great charioteers.

The Kurukshetra war lasted for eighteen days, in which almost all the 18 akshauhinis (divisions) perished, leaving a few to witness the destruction it caused. Everyone who fought died or lost someone dear to them. Yudhamanyu, Uttamauja, and the children of Subhadra and Draupadi also perished, leaving their mothers devastated and heartbroken. Yudhamanyu and Uttamauja were Panchala princes and brothers of Draupadi. In the war, they served as guards to protect Arjuna's chariot wheels from enemy attacks. Being great charioteers, they also fought in the war against many warriors, including Dronacharya and Duryodhana. In the end, they were killed by Asvatthama, the son of Drona, on the night of the last day of the war when they were asleep in the Pandavas' camp. Draupadi had five sons through her husbands: Prativindhya, Sutasoma, Shrutakarma, Shatanika, and Shrutasena. They were also killed by Asvatthama on the same night in a cowardly fashion while they were asleep, leaving Draupadi in inconsolable grief. Subhadra, Lord Krishna's half-sister, was married to Arjuna. They had a son named Abhimanyu, who was mentioned before. He also died fighting bravely on the battlefield, leaving his parents and relatives grief-stricken.

Sloka 7

asmākaṃ tu viśiṣṭā ye tān nibodha dvijottama
nāyakā mama sainyasya saṃjñārthaṃ tān bravīmi te

asmakam = our; tu = but; visistah = especially powerful; ye = those; tan = them; nibodha = just take note; be informed; dvija-uttama = the best of the twice born; nayakah = leaders; mama = my; sainyasya = of the army; samjna-artham = for identification; tan = them; bravimi = I am speaking; te = you.

Superior among the twice-born, let me also tell you about the most distinguished leaders of my army so that you will be able to locate them and distinguish them during the battle.

War is a collective effort. Success depends on how commanders motivate and inspire their soldiers. They should know their strengths and weaknesses and how to effectively harness their skills to defeat the enemy or launch surprise attacks. It is not sufficient to have brave soldiers and great warriors. The commander should know how to safeguard or help them when they need protection or support. Until now, Duryodhana explained to Drona the might of the Pāndavas' army and their distinguished warriors. Now, he wanted to apprise him of the notable warriors on their side. He did it to help Drona know where they were stationed so that when needed, he could summon them for reinforcement or plan a concerted attack against the enemy and cause significant damage. He addressed him as 'dvijottama' (superior among the twice-born) because he was a Brahmana by birth, although a Kshatriya by profession. In the Vedic caste hierarchy, Brahmanas are superior to Kshatriyas and Vaishyas, although all three are considered twice-born. A few warriors on Kaurava's side could match Arjuna or Bhima's in the art of warfare. Dronacharya was the best among them since they were his students, and he knew their strengths and weaknesses. Bhishma and Karna were equally excellent and could tilt the balance to their side. However, God was not on their side since they fought for Duryodhana and supported adharma.

Sloka 8

bhavān bhīṣmaś ca karṇaś ca kṛpaś ca samitiñjayaḥ
aśvatthāmā vikarṇaś ca saumadattis tathaiva ca

bhavan = yourself; bhismah = Bhisma; ca = also; karnah = Karna; ca = and; krpah = Krpa; ca = and; samitim-jayah = always victorious; asvatthama = Asvatthama; vikarnah = Vikarna; ca = as well as; saumadattih = the son of Somadatta; tatha = and as; eva = certainly; ca = and.

You, Bhīshma, Karna, Kripa, the ever-victorious in battle; Aswaththama, Vikarna, and Somadatta's son.

Volumes can be written about the warriors who fought in the Mahābhārata war on both sides. They were legends in their own right, born with a purpose. One can learn a lot from them and the Mahābhārata about ethical conduct, human nature and relationships, the role of God in our lives, and the conflict between good and evil. The ones mentioned here were great heroes. However, due to fate, circumstances, or choice, they chose the wrong side and fought for an evil person like Duryodhana. Each had an excellent reputation and great qualities. In the end, they perished since they could not win against the will of God, who, as we will learn later, decided their fate well in advance. They serve as good examples of how men of valor and virtue are often forced to take the side of evil because of karma, duty, fate, and circumstances (daivikam) beyond their control.

Of all the warriors who appear in the epic, Bhīshma stands tall, next only to Lord Krishna in character, conduct, and virtue. He was the eldest, uncle to Dhritarashtra, grandfather to Kauravas and Pāndavas, and mentor to all in the family. He is the only one who appears in the epic from the first chapter until his death on the battlefield. He accepted the role of the commander-in-chief of the Kauravas' army as an obligatory duty since he pledged to protect the Kuru kingdom until his last breath. However, he put a condition that he would fight if only Karna stayed out of the battlefield. He did it partly because he disliked Karna's haughtiness and partly because he did not want the Pāndavas to fight two invincible opponents simultaneously. He also told Duryodhana that he would not kill his grandchildren under any circumstances but would not mind slaying as many soldiers and generals as he could. Thus, Bhīshma fought the war on his terms and tried to balance his affections, but still sided with the Kauravas and invited his own death.

Karna was born to Kunti through Surya, the sun god, before her marriage to Pandu when she was still a maiden. Fearing that it would ruin her reputation, she abandoned him immediately after he was born. A childless couple known as Sutas, who were charioteers and poets by profession, adopted him. He grew up to become a valiant fighter with many radiant qualities of the sun god himself. Due to circumstances, he sided with the Kauravas against the Pandavas and remained loyal to Duryodhana, who granted him a kingdom and elevated his social status as a Kshatriya. He became the supreme commander of the Kaurava army on the sixteenth day of the battle after Dronacharya's death and died the next day in the hands of Arjuna. Kripacharya was the royal priest of the Kurus. His sister Kripi was married to Drona. He was a sage and a warrior and earned the epithet Chiranjeevi since he was gifted with the boon of immortality from birth. He survived the Mahābhārata war and became Parikshit's teacher and mentor, the last surviving member of the Pāndava lineage. Ashwatthama was Dronacharya's only son. He became the last supreme commander of the Kauravas in the final hours of the war after the deaths of Salya and Duryodhana. He was also a great warrior, but his discernment was clouded by his hatred for the Pāndavas, which led him to kill Draupadi's five children and several others in a dastardly fashion when they were asleep. Vikarna was the only virtuous Kaurava who repeatedly questioned his brothers' judgment and criticized them for their evil actions. He criticized Dusshasana for his shameful conduct when he dragged Draupadi by her hair and tried to disrobe her in front of everyone in the court. However, he stood with them in the war, being a brother and bound by his brotherly duty, and assisted Drona against Drupada. Somadatta's sons were Bhurisravas and Sala. Their father ruled Vahilka, a small province in northwestern India. They were cousins to both

Pāndavas and Kauravas but supported Duryodhana in the war for strategic reasons.

Sloka 9

anye ca bahavaḥ śūrā madarthe tyaktajīvitāḥ
nānāśastrapraharaṇāḥ sarve yuddhaviśāradāḥ

anye = others; ca = also; bahavah = many; surah = heroes; mad-arthe = for my sake; tyakta-jivitah = sacrifice their lives; nana = many; sastra = weapons; praharanah = equipped with; sarve = all of them; yuddha = battle; visaradah = skillful, excellent or outstanding.

Also, many other heroes, all equipped with weapons and skillful in warfare, are willing to lay down their lives for my sake.

Surā means a hero, a god, a deity, or one who is born with a divine nature or powers (daivāmsam). Suras are not gods but godlike, radiating divine virtues and cheerful dispositions. They possess light and knowledge and are filled with joy and pleasure. However, just like other mortals, they are also bound to samsara, karma, duty, and fate. Asurās are their brothers with contrasting qualities. They are beings of darkness and ignorance without light (a + sura) and oppose the forces of truth and righteousness. Bhīshma, Drona, Karna, and many others on the side of the Kauravas descended from gods and possessed divine qualities. They represented the best of human nature. Although they fought on the side of the Kauravas in the Mahābhārata war, they were still suras because their actions did not spring from their inherent nature (svabhava) but from circumstances. They supported Duryodhana, bound by duty. They followed the Vedic way of life, following the Vedas and performing sacrifices as true karma yogis for the sake of God. Their decision to support the Kauravas exemplifies situations where people are compelled by fate or circumstances to act against their best judgment and face the consequences with stoical indifference.

Human beings are composite beings. You cannot put them in rigid categories such as good and evil. They are a mixture of light and darkness due to the interplay of the gunas, circumstances, fate, and karma. Duryodhana had a demonic nature (asura prvritti) but possessed many virtues. However, his otherwise distinguished character was overshadowed by his evil qualities, which drove him into a self-destructive mode. Yuddha-visāradah means the one who is proficient and skillful in warfare. The warriors whom Duryodhana cited here excelled in the art of warfare. They fought many wars and possessed skillfulness (kausalam) in using and neutralizing the most destructive weapons. Some could destroy the Earth itself, invoking the most destructive forces. Therefore, Duryodhana acknowledged their presence and willingness to sacrifice their lives for him.

Sloka 10

aparyāptaṃ tad asmākaṃ balaṃ bhīṣmābhirakṣitam
paryāptaṃ tvidam eteṣāṃ balaṃ bhīmābhirakṣitam

aparyaptam = insufficient, limited; tat = that; asmakam = of ours; balam = strength; bhisma = by Bhisma; abhiraksitam = well protected; paryaptam = sufficient, unlimted; tu = but; idam = all these; etesam = of the Pāndavas; balam = strength; bhima = by Bhima; abhiraksitam = well protected.

Insufficient is our strength, well protected by Bhīshma, but the strength of the Pāndavas' army, which is well protected by Bhima, is sufficient.

Duryodhana had eleven military divisions, while the Pāndavas had only seven. Kauravas were led by Bhīshma, who was invincible and possessed the gift to die of his own will, as and when he wished. Pāndavas primarily relied upon themselves and the blessings of Lord Krishna. They were led by Bhima, who was a great warrior and possessed the strength of several elephants. The five Pāndavas were themselves equal to several armies. Therefore, although the Kauravas had a numerical advantage in many areas, they did not have enough warriors who could withstand the might of the five brothers. Hence, Duryodhana was not very happy about the strength of his army, which Bhishma led. Duryodhana knew that Lord Krishna was on the Pāndavas' side and would help them with his knowledge and foresight, although he promised not to fight directly for them. He was also skeptical of Bhishma's commitment to battle since he had a soft corner for the Pandavas, his grandchildren, whose courage and conduct he admired. Besides, Duryodhana knew that Bhishma was not happy with the Kauravas' behavior. He was also skeptical of Dronacharya, who had a special affection for Arjuna. Hence, he was not delighted with the situation and could not think positively about his side or the generals supposed to fight for him. If an army commander has little confidence in his warriors, it is likely reflected in his leadership and lowers their morale. These words were also prophetic since it was what happened in the end. Pāndavas completely wiped out his army. The words 'aparyāptaṃ' and 'paryāptaṃ' are interpreted differently in some translations, meaning unlimited and limited. They entirely change the meaning of the verse. If we use them, they suggest that Duryodhana felt the strength of his army under the command of Bhishma was unlimited, while that of the Pandavas was limited. This interpretation is also justified since Duryodhana had a larger army and brave warriors like Karna on his side, who were equal to the Pāndavas in many respects.

Sloka 11

ayaneṣu ca sarveṣu yathābhāgam avasthitāḥ
bhīṣmam evābhirakṣantu bhavantaḥ sarva eva hi

ayanesu = in the strategic places; ca = also; sarvesu = all; yatha-bhagam = as planned; avasthitah = standing, placed; bhismam = to Bhisma; eva = certainly; abhiraksantu = provide protective cover; bhavantah = until the end; sarve = all; evahi = firmly.

Placing yourselves in strategic places, as planned, all of you shall firmly provide protective cover to Bhīshma until the end.

In the Kurukshetra war, Bhīshma was the Kauravas' commander-in-chief for the first ten days of the 18-day war. He led the eleventh division, which stood at the forefront, facing the Pāndavas' army directly. On the first day of the war, Duryodhana decided to use Bhishma's might to launch an offensive attack on the enemy and break their morale, inflicting heavy losses. Therefore, he asked Dronacharya to place warriors around him and protect him from all sides until the fight lasted. In the Bhīshma Parva, the Mahābhārata states that on the first day, as the war progressed, five Kaurava warriors, namely Durmukha, Kritavarma, Kripa, Salya, and Vivimsati, surrounded Bhīshma and formed a defensive shield. They protected him from all sides while he went on fiercely attacking Pandava's army with blazing arrows and slew many charioteers and soldiers until the night fell. Those who survived the attack retreated in great haste to their camp.

Sloka 12

tasya sañjanayan harṣaṃ kuruvṛddhaḥ pitāmahaḥ
siṃhanādaṃ vinadyocchaiḥ śaṅkhaṃ dadhmau pratāpavān

tasya = his; sanjanayan = increasing; harsam = joy, happiness; kuru-vrddhah = grand old man of kurus (Bhisma); pitamahah = the grandfather; simha-nadam = lion's roar; vinadya = sound, noise; uccaih = very loudly; sankham = conchshell; dadhmau = blew; pratapa-van = the valiant.

Then, to increase his happiness, valiant Bhīshma, the grand old sire of Kurus and his grandfather, roared like a lion and blew his conch.

War is a serious effort. It is not a pleasant place to be in it or see it from far or near. When it begins, those who participate in it face anxious moments. They would not know how it would end and whether they would survive and return to their families. In those crucial moments, the commanders and generals who lead the troops must show courage and confidence through their words and actions to inspire them and boost their morale. Duryodhana wanted a clear indication from his grandfather that, even though he was reluctant to fight against his grandchildren, the Pandavas, he would still give his best and would not spare them. On his part, Bhīshma had no such confusion. He knew he was bound by duty, and as a true Kshatriya, he had to give his best irrespective of who stood on the other side. Throughout his life, he fought many battles. This was no different. Therefore, he roared like a lion and blew his conch to put fear in the Pandavas' army. By blowing the conch, he conveyed to Duryodhana that he was ready to do his duty and would not let his affection for his grandchildren interfere with his actions. The sounding of conches during wars was an ancient Indian practice. Renowned warriors kept conches, gave them specific names, and blew them to mark important events or declare their presence in the wars.

Sloka 13

tataḥ śaṅkhāś ca bheryaś ca paṇavānakagomukhāḥ
sahasaivābhyahanyanta sa śabdas tumulobhavat

tatah = thereafter; sankhah = conches; ca = also; bheryah = kettle drums; ca = and; panava-anaka = trumpets and drums; go-mukhah = horns; sahasa =

suddenly; eva = certainly; abhyahanyanta = all at once; sah = that; sabdah = sound; tumulah = tumultuous; abhavat = resulted.

Then, many conches, large drums, small drums, kettle drums, and horns were all blown suddenly at once, and the resulting sound was tumultuous.

Sloka 14

tataḥ śvetair hayair yukte mahati syandane sthitau
mādhavaḥ pāṇḍavaś caiva divyau śaṅkhau pradaghmatuḥ

tatah = thereafter; svetaih = by white; hayaih = horses; yukte = yoked; mahati = in a great; syandane = chariot; sthitau = seated, ensconced; madhavah = Krishna; pandavah = Arjuna; ca = also; eva = certainly; divyau = divine, heavenly, celestial; sankhau = conchshells; pradadhmatuh = sounded.

Then, seated in a grand chariot, which was yoked to white horses, Krishna and Arjuna also blew their divine conches.

This is where we hear about Lord Krishna and Arjuna for the first time in the scripture. Since it is presented from the perspective of Sanjaya, who narrated the events to Dhritarashtra, the initial attention was on Duryodhana and his actions. We do not hear about Lord Krishna and Arjuna since Sanjaya did not see them present on the battlefield. For those who have not read the Mahābhārata or know the context in which Lord Krishna delivered the Bhagavadgita discourse, here is a brief explanation of how it happened and how Lord Krishna became the charioteer for Arjuna. It is said that before the war began, both Duryodhana and Arjuna went to Dwaraka, the capital of Lord Krishna's kingdom, to secure his support. When they met him, he gave them the option to choose either him or his vast army of elephants, charioteers, horse riders, archers, and foot soldiers. He told them clearly that if they chose him, he would not take part in the fighting since he had enmity with none and all were equal to him, but would give moral and spiritual support. He put the option before Arjuna first because when they arrived, he saw Arjuna first. When they came, he was sleeping in his chamber. Arjuna came and sat at his feet, and Duryodhana at his head, while they waited for him to wake up. When he woke up, he first saw Arjuna. Hence, he asked him to choose first. Arjuna wanted him on his side as his mentor and charioteer, and to give mental and spiritual support. His decision surprised Duryodhana, who expected him to choose his army and felt that he had made a tactical error by choosing him instead of his army. Therefore, he happily agreed to take his army, thinking that it would strengthen his might and make him formidable. Although it was a good military decision and increased the chances of his victory, it was not a good decision. By that decision, he put more faith in himself and put God on the other side, giving the Pandavas a clear advantage. Being egoistic and deluded, he thought that having a bigger and stronger army improved the odds of his victory. Arjuna had chosen wisely. He secured the support of Lord Krishna and brought him to their side. By that, he vastly improved their chances of following his counsel and winning the war.

Although Lord Krishna agreed to support the Pāndavas morally and spiritually, he kept his promise to Duryodhana and did not carry any weapons or participate in the actual fighting. He remained on the chariot as an impartial witness to the drama that unfolded, giving timely advice to Arjuna whenever needed. In the end, the arrangement proved detrimental to the Kauravas since they ignored the role of God in their chances of victory. Staying neutral and without unleashing any weapons or arrows or fighting, he strengthened Pandava's morale and gave them tactical advice in crucial moments, helping them win against heavy odds. In real life, too, it is necessary to seek the Lord's help and keep him on our side. If he is on your side, you will not have to worry about anything since he will take charge and guide you in the right direction. He may not participate directly in your struggles and daily battles, but will remain in the background as your mentor and supporter, and will stay with you until the end. Having him on your side is better than having a whole army behind you.

Sloka 15

pāñcajanyaṃ hṛṣīkeśo devadattaṃ dhanañjayaḥ
pauṇḍraṃ dadhmau mahāśaṅkhaṃ bhīmakarmā vṛkodaraḥ

pancajanyam = Pancajanyam; hrsika-isah = Krishna; devadattam = Devadattam; dhanam-jayah = Arjuna; paundram = Paundra; dadhmau = blew; maha-sankham = big or great conchshell; bhima-karma = mighty deeds; vrka-udarah = perrson with great hunger.

Krishna blew (his conch) Panchajanyam, Arjuna, the Devadatta, and Bhima of mighty deeds and voracious stomach, the great Paundra.

Panchajanyam, Devadattam, and Paundram were the names of the conches (shankham) belonging to Lord Krishna, Arjuna, and Bhima. In ancient India, nobles and warriors carried conches to the battlefield to announce their presence and readiness for the war or declare their solidarity with the king they served. Some conches were given specific names to distinguish them and their significance. People believed them to possess magical powers or bring luck. Some were acclaimed as divine conches. Apart from conches, warriors often took musical instruments or musicians with them to the battlefield to create loud sounds, boost fellow participants' morale, or frighten their enemies. They also used them to signal important events, such as the beginning or the end of a day's war. Besides warriors, priests and householders used conches for religious purposes and kept them in their homes for worship. Even today, conches are revered as holy objects and used in religious worship (puja) in many households and temples. They are used to invite gods to the place of worship or drive away evil spirits and negative vibrations. They are also valued in Buddhist worship as one of the eight sacred objects. Many Hindus keep them and other objects, such as saligramas (fossilized conch shells or seashells), for luck or worship. Some consider them to represent serpent deities (nagas) symbolically. The water poured from them is believed to be sacred and purifying, like the water from a sacred river. Their sounds symbolize Brahman's power to awaken gods, just as the sounds from the Vedic mantras awaken the deities presiding over them. The

Supreme Brahman was initially associated with the sounds (nada) hidden in the sacred syllables of the Vedas. Although he is not ritually worshipped as a deity, he is regarded with the highest esteem as the Supreme Self and the Lord of sacred sounds. People believe that when mantras are chanted, the sounds arising from them travel through space (akasa) and draw the gods' attention in heaven. On hearing them, they visit the ritual place and accept the offerings to nourish themselves. Thus, conches are prized in Hinduism since they are considered purifiers and bring good luck.

Sloka 16

anañtavijayaṃ rājā kuntīputro yudhiṣṭhiraḥ
nakulaḥ sahadevaś ca sughoṣamaṇipuṣpakau

ananta-vijayam = Anantavijayam; raja = the king; kunti-putrah = the son of Kunti; yudhisthirah = Yudhisthira; nakulah = Nakula; sahadevah = Sahadeva; ca = and; sughosa-manipuspakau = Sughosa and Manipuspaka.

King Yudhishtira, the son of Kunti, blew Anantavijayam, and Nakula and Sahadeva, Manipushpaka and Sughosha.

Anantavijayam, Manipushpaka, and Sughosha were the names given to the conches belonging to Yudhishtira, Nakula, and Sahadeva. Yudhishtira was the eldest of the Pāndavas and the legitimate heir to the throne of Hastinapur before he was tricked into losing everything and going into exile with his brothers. Hence, Sanjaya called him the king (Raja). The Pāndavas were five, born to two mothers. They are called Pāndavas after their father Pandu, who died before they were born. Although they are known by their father's name, they were born through the divine power of the gods since Pandu died before he consummated his marriage with the queens. According to the epic, his first queen, Kunti, gave birth to three children through a secret power she secured from sage Durvāsa, who taught her how to invoke the gods and obtain children from them. When King Pandu died prematurely due to a curse, Kunti used her secret powers and gave birth to Yudhishtira, Arjuna, and Bhima by invoking Yama, Indra, and Vayu. Then, she taught the same knowledge to Mādri, Pandu's second queen, and helped her give birth to Nakula and Sahadeva by invoking the twin Asvins. Thus, the five Pāndavas were born with the powers of five gods, which made them almost invincible with exceptional physical strength and mental brilliance.

Sloka 17

kāśyaś ca parameṣvāsaḥ śikhaṇḍī ca mahārathaḥ
dhṛṣṭadyumno virāṭaś ca sātyakiś cāparājitaḥ

kasyah = an epithet for the king of Kasi; ca = and; parama-isu-asah = the great archer; sikhandi = Sikhandi; ca = also; maha-rathah = great charioteer; dhrstadyumnah = Dhrstadyumna; viratah = Virata; ca = also; satyakih = Satyaki; ca = and; aparajitah = undefeated or invincible.

The King of Kasi, the great archer Shikhandi, the great charioteer Dhrishtadyumna, Virata, and the invincible Satyaki.

Kāśya means the king of Kashi (Varanasi). At the time of the Mahābhārata war, Kāshi was ruled by Abibhu, the son of Mahābāhu. He and his two sons died in the war fighting for the Pāndavas. Virāta was Matsya's ruler. During their exile, the Pandavas served in his court for a year in disguise. Later, he married his daughter Uttara to Abhimanyu, Arjuna's son, and strengthened his alliance with them. Shikhandi was a princess named Amba in her previous birth. She was born to Drupada as Shikhandini, a princess, but subsequently changed her gender so she could participate in the Kurukshetra war as a man and fight Bhishma, whom she vowed to kill and avenge the wrong he caused her in her past birth. Bhīshma, who was gifted to die by his own will, was well aware of her background and her resolve to kill him. Before the war, he narrated her story to the Kauravas and suggested to them how his end might come. As the legend goes, long before Pāndavas and Kauravās were born, when Bhīshma was still a young prince, he abducted a young princess named Amba from her palace to marry her to his brother Vichitravirya. When he forcefully brought her to his court, against her wishes, she told him that she was already in love with another prince named Sālva, and so she should be set free. Upon knowing it, Bhīshma relented and allowed her to return to Sālva. However, when she went to Sālva, he refused to accept her feeling that the abduction had tarnished her name. Amba went back in humiliation to Bhīshma and requested him to marry her or ask his brother to marry her, since no one would accept her. Bhīshma told her that he could not marry anyone because he vowed to practice celibacy for life, while his brother refused to marry her since she was in love with another prince.

Thus, rejected, wronged, and humiliated by the three men for no fault of her own, she approached Parasurama, Bhīshma's guru, and sought his help. Upon hearing her story, he tried to persuade Bhīshma, but he refused to oblige. Angered by his insolence, Parasurama challenged him to a fight and tried to force him to surrender, but Bhishma remained invincible and unyielding. As their fight ended in a stalemate, Parasurama left, advising Amba to pray to Lord Shiva and seek his help. Amba then did severe penance (tapas) for several years on the banks of Yamuna with great resolve and obtained a boon from Lord Shiva. He assured her that she would be able to fulfill her wish and avenge Bhīshma in her next birth. As he foretold, Amba was born in her next life as a daughter of Drupada. However, since her parents desired a son, they named him Shikhandi and groomed her as a prince. When she reached marriage age, they married her to a princess, hiding her gender. The princess was aghast when she learned that her husband was a female. When she reported it to her father, he became angry and began preparations for a war. Upset by these developments, Shikhandi ran away in humiliation to a nearby forest to end her life. There, she met a Yaksha, who agreed to exchange his manhood with her temporarily and change her into a man.

Thus, Amba, reborn as Shikhandini, became Shikhandi in male attire by circumstances and waited for her turn to kill Bhishma. When the Mahābhārata war took place, she stood in Arjuna's chariot before him, knowing that Bhīshma would be reluctant to fight with Arjuna, seeing a woman standing in the way. When he saw her in Arjuna's chariot, he knew that his end had approached, and Death came to him in her form. Therefore, having lived for a long time and completed all his duties and vows, he decided to give up fighting and let Arjuna do the rest. Mortally wounded by many arrows, he fell into his chariot and was swiftly carried away by his helpers from the battleground. He remained alive for several days, waiting for an auspicious time on a bed made of arrows and with Arjuna's arrows still stuck in his body. Before dying, he requested all his grandchildren to stop fighting and make peace, which they promptly ignored. Bhisma will be remembered as long as the Mahābhārata is remembered. He was such an exceptional character.

Sloka 18

drupado draupadeyāś ca sarvaśaḥ pṛthivīpate
saubhadraś ca mahābāhuḥ śaṅkhān dadhmuḥ pṛthakpṛthak

drupadah = Drupada; draupadeyah = the sons of Draupadi; ca = and; sarvasah = all; prthivi-pate = O lord of the earth; saubhadrah = the son of Subhadra; ca = also; maha-bahuh = very strong; sankhan = conchshells; dadhmuh = blew; prthak prthak = each separately.

O Lord of the earth, Drupada, the sons of Draupadi, and the mighty son of Subhadra also blew their conches separately.

Drupada was the king of Panchala at the time of the Mahabharata war. He participated in it mainly to avenge Drona, who captured him in the past in a war with the help of Kauravas and Pāndavas and forced him to cede half of his kingdom for insulting him. For Drupada and his three children, Shikhandi, Draupadi, and Dhrishtadyumna, that wound never healed. They vowed to avenge it. They also had other issues to settle with the Kurus, and the war offered them a great opportunity to resolve them. Thus, they played a significant role in the events leading to the Mahābhārata war and were instrumental in causing large-scale destruction. Shikhandi was responsible for Bhīshma's death. Draupadi intensified the rivalry between her husbands and the Kauravas and made it irreconcilable. She was also responsible for the death and destruction of Dusshasana and Duryodhana at the hands of Bhima for insulting and attempting to disrobe her in front of everyone in the royal court. Dhrishtadyumna was responsible for Drona's death. According to the epic, he manifested from a sacrificial fire to fulfill his father's wish to kill Drona and succeeded in killing him on the fifteenth day of the war, hours after his father lost his life while fighting Drona.

Sloka 19

sa ghoṣo dhārtarāṣṭrāṇāṃ hṛdayāni vyadārayat
nabhaś ca pṛthivīṃ caiva tumulobhyanunādayan

sah = that; ghosah = roar, din, noise; dhartarastranam = of the sons of Dhrtarastra; hrdayani = hearts; vyadarayat = shook, startled, disturbed; nabhah = the sky; ca = also; prthivim = the earth; ca = also; eva = certainly; tumulah = tumultuous; abhyanunadayan = reverberating.

That tumultuous roar reverberating through the sky and the earth certainly shook the hearts of Dhritarashtra's sons.

On the battlefield, no one will feel happy seeing the enemy in better spirits. Kauravas were disheartened by the morale and fervor of the Pandavas' army despite their numerical disadvantage. They had an army of seven divisions, while the Kauravas had eleven. A large portion of the latter's army came from Lord Krishna, who agreed to give them his entire army in exchange for himself. Therefore, the Kauravas had every reason to feel confident about their strength and chances of victory. However, the sound of the conches coming from the Pandavas frightened them and made them worried. We have seen (in verse 10) that Duryodhana had his doubts about his army when he felt that it was insufficient (aparyāptam).

Sloka 20

atha vyavasthitān dṛṣṭvā dhārtarāṣṭrān.h kapidhvajaḥ
pravṛtte śastrasaṃpāte dhanur udyamya pāṇḍavaḥ

atha = thereupon; vyavasthitan = situated; drstva = watching; dhartarastran = the sons of Dhrtarastra; kapi-dhvajah = with the flag of Hanuman mounted on his chariot; pravrtte = disposed; sastra = arrows; sampate = ready to come down; dhanuh = bow; udyamya = taking up, getting ready; pandavah = the son of Pandu (Arjuna).

Thereupon, having observed that arrows were about to fly down from the sons of Dhritarashtra and taking up his bow, the son of Pandu, whose flag atop the chariot bore the image of Hanuman...

Saṃpāte means falling, descending, or being ready to collide. Arjuna noticed the war was about to begin, and arrows were ready to fly. Everyone was battle-ready. At that moment, he must have realized that once the fighting began, no one would be able to change their minds or withdraw from the battlefield. All attempts to negotiate peace between them also failed. Therefore, there was no chance of a truce either. In those days, once warriors entered the battlefield and began fighting, it was a do-or-die situation for them. Their code of conduct proscribed them from withdrawing from the battlefield in the middle, except under extraordinary circumstances when they surrendered or were fatally wounded. Arjuna was a brave warrior. On that fateful day, he faced the same dilemma common to most soldiers when they realized that their lives were at stake and the war would leave many wounded and dead, leaving permanent scars for their families that would never heal. Are wars necessary? Can they be avoided? What will happen to the families and children of those who die in it? Is the decision to fight wars and kill people justified at all, especially when they are waged for selfish, egoistic, or evil reasons?

Arjuna must have felt similar doubts assailing him as he looked at the two armies standing in the middle of the battlefield. Sanjaya subtly conveyed Arjuna's mental state in one word, 'udyama', when he lifted his bow and prepared for the battle. Udyama means to rise, prepare, or stand up with effort. From a philosophical perspective, it denotes a riotous, restless, and uncontrollable state of mind due to churning and disturbing thoughts. Thus, we have to presume that as Arjuna stood up to start fighting, strong emotions welled up in him, and he was about to lose his poise and control.

Arjuna's chariot was mounted with a flag that bore the image of Hanumān. Hence, Sanjaya used the word 'dhvajah.' In the Kurukshetra war, the Pāndavas used Hanuman's image for their emblem. They did it because Bhima, who was the supreme commander of the Pāndavas' army, was Vayu's son, and so was Hanuman. He was still alive when they met him by chance in a forest. During the encounter, he requested them to use him as their emblem so he could personally witness the war. Pandavas happily agreed since he was a great devotee and personified many divine and auspicious qualities. Thus, the Pandavas were twice blessed. They had Lord Krishna on their side and Hanuman atop their chariots.

Sloka 21

hṛṣīkeśaṃ tadā vākyam idam āha mahīpate
senayor ubhayor madhye rathaṃ sthāpaya mecyuta

Hrisikesam = to Krishna; tada = that; vakyam = speech, words, sentence; aha = said; mahipate = O lord of the earth; senayoh = armies; idam = this; ubhayoh = two, both; madhye = between; ratham = chariot; sthapaya = stop; me = my; acyuta = Achyuta.

O Lord of the Earth, he spoke these words to Lord Krishna, "O Achyuta, stop the chariot between the two armies."

This verse is important for two reasons. First, the dialogue (samvad) between Lord Krishna and Arjuna begins from here. Second, it involves all four characters and both their conversations: one between Sanjaya and Dhritarashtra and the other between Arjuna and Lord Krishna. It starts from where the previous one ended and continues to the next. Sanjaya used two epithets in his utterance, Hṛṣīkeśa for Lord Krishna and Mahīpate for Dhritarashtra, while Arjuna used Achyuta to address Lord Krishna. Hṛṣīkeśa means lord of the senses. Mahīpati means lord of the earth, which aptly describes King Dhritarashtra. Achyuta means firm, strong-willed, imperishable, strong-minded, or standing on firm ground. It offers a contrasting picture of Arjuna and Krishna. Arjuna was about to lose control and become mentally distressed and unstable, while the Lord was always stable and in control, and even a devastating war like the Mahabharata war would not unsettle him.

Sloka 22

yāvad etān nirikṣehaṃ yoddhukāmān avasthitān
kair mayā saha yoddhavyam asmin raṇasamudyame

yavatas = all or as as many as; etan = all these; nirikse = see, take a look; aham = I; yoddhu-kaman = raring to fight; avasthitan = standing, present; kaih = with whom; maya = by me; saha = with; yoddhavyam = fight; asmin = in this; rana = war, battle; samudyame = exertion, work hard.

So that I may see all these men who are standing here, raring to fight, and against whom I have to exert myself in this war.

If you study the Mahābhārata, you will know that Arjuna did not come to Kurukshetra for the first time, and he knew the size and strength of both armies well in advance. Preparations for the war began long before it started and went on for days and weeks as armies came from different parts of India. Arjuna must have visited them and had many discussions with the generals in his camp to discuss strategy and draw the battle plans, since a war of that magnitude required careful planning and preparation. On one occasion, he even assured Dharmarāja when he began worrying about the size of Duryodhana's army, saying that victory would be theirs no matter who fought on the other side. However, on that fateful day, he would react differently since destiny would unsettle his mind and draw Lord Krishna's attention to set the stage for his discourse.

Sloka 23

yotsyamānān avekṣeham ya etetra samāgatāḥ
dhārtarāṣṭrasya durbuddher yuddhe priyacikīrṣavaḥ

yotsyamanan = those who will be fighting; avekse = let me see; aham = I; ye = who; ete = those; atra = here; samagatah = assembled; dhartarastrasya = son of Dhrtarastra; durbuddheh = evil minded; yuddhe = in the battle; priya = pleasing; cikirsavah = wishing.

Let me also see those who have assembled here, wishing to please Dhritarashtra's evil-minded son in the battle.

The war symbolizes the eternal conflict between good and evil forces on earth as well as in creation. Dharmarāja personifies discernment and righteousness despite many personal flaws, while Duryodhana symbolizes delusion and sinful nature. His brothers (except for one) were equally evil-minded and did their best to exterminate the Pāndavas. When they failed, they invited them to play a dice game and used trickery to steal their kingdom and exile them. When they returned, they denied their right to the kingdom, refused to negotiate, and made the war inevitable. Hence, Arjuna rightly called Duryodhana, the architect of all these troubles, the evil-minded (durbuddhi) son of Dhritarashtra. The epic describes that when Duryodhana was born, ominous signs appeared everywhere, portending the birth of an evil being. Wise men in the court advised his father to abandon him, fearing that he might bring calamity upon the family and the kingdom. Dhritarashtra ignored their advice and doted on him, hoping to see him on the throne and fulfill his lifelong wish. Therefore, he was reluctant to act against his evil intentions and his ambition to be the sole heir. Subsequent events proved how he lost control and allowed the destruction of his whole family, little realizing that the fire he allowed to grow would eventually engulf and destroy everything he cherished. Arjuna wanted to see those who joined Duryodhana against their judgment and the principles of Dharma.

Sloka 24

evam ukto hṛṣīkeśo guḍākeśena bhārata
senayor ubhayor madhye sthāpayitvā rathottamam

sanjayah = Sanjaya; uvaca = said; evam = thus; uktah = told, spoken, addressed; hrsikesah = Hrisikesa; gudakesena = by Gudakesa; bharata = O Bharata; senayoh = of the armies; ubhayoh = of both; madhye = in between; sthapayitva = station; ratha-uttamam = the finest chariot.

Sanjaya said, "O, Bharata, thus spoken by Gudakesa, Hrisikesha stationed their excellent chariot between the two armies."

An archer like Arjuna must be skillful and focused to counter the enemies and hit the targets accurately. Arjuna was the best marksman of his time, better than Bhishma and Drona in archery. He perfected his skills through relentless practice, resolve, and discipline. He could not have achieved it without mastering his senses. Therefore, the title guḍākeśa, meaning the lord and conqueror of sleep with well-trained senses, perfectly fits him. The epithet is also used for Lord Shiva since he has control over the mode of tamas, which induces sleep, slothfulness, negligence, and a lack of self-control and discipline. Kurus descended from the Vedic tribe of Bharatas, who lived in northwestern India before they broke into several small groups and dispersed. The legendary Bharata was their ancestor. The Bharatas are mentioned in the Rigveda as one of the tribes that took part in the Battle of Ten Kings and emerged victorious. Since Dhritarashtra descended from this tribe, Sanjaya addressed him as Bharata.

Sloka 25

bhīṣmadroṇapramukhataḥ sarveṣāṃ ca mahīkṣitām
uvāca pārtha paśyaitān samavetān kurūn iti

bhisma = Bhisma; drona = Drona; pramukhatah = facing, in front of; sarvesam = all; ca = also; mahi-ksitam = rulers of the earth; uvaca = said; partha = O Partha); pasya = behold; etan = all of them; samavetan = assembled; kurun = kurus; iti = thus.

In front of Bhīshma, Drona, and all the rulers of the earth, Krishna said, "O, Partha, see all the Kurus who are assembled here."

Lord Krishna stopped the chariot in the middle of the two armies and asked Arjuna to see all the Kurus who assembled on the Kauravas' side in a battle formation behind Duryodhana. He particularly mentioned Bhīshma and Drona since they were commanding troops and were placed at strategic locations to launch the initial attack and inflict maximum damage. Duryodhana also placed many warriors around them to provide them with a defensive shield and protect them from a counterattack. Hence, Arjuna could see them clearly from where his chariot was stationed.

Sloka 26

tatrāpaśyat sthitān pārthaḥ pitṛn atha pitāmahān
ācāryān mātulān bhrātṛn putrān pautrān sakhīṃs tathā

tatra = there; apasyat = saw; sthitan = standing; parthah = Arjuna; pitrn = fathers; atha = also; pitamahan = grandfathers; acaryan = teachers; matulan = maternal uncles; bhratrn = brothers; putran = sons; pautran = grandsons; sakhin = friends; tatha = also, too.

There, as they stood, Arjuna saw fathers, besides grandfathers, teachers, maternal uncles, brothers, sons, grandsons, friends...

Arjuna did not see the warriors arrayed on the battlefield. He saw people who could be fathers, grandfathers, teachers, maternal uncles, brothers, grandsons, friends, and relations to someone somewhere. He saw in them relationships they might have formed and become attached to. The human side of war is the most difficult to ignore when you are on the battlefield and know that soon, most of them will die, leaving their close relations in great grief.

Sloka 27

śvaśurān suhṛdaś caiva senayor ubhayor api
tān samīkṣya sa kaunteyaḥ sarvān bandhūn avasthitān

svasuran = fathers-in-law; suhrdah = amiable, good hearted; ca = also; eva = certainly; senayoh = of the armies; ubhayoh = of both api = including; tan = all of them; samiksya = saw; sah = he; kaunteyah = Arjuna; sarvan = all kinds of; bandhun = relatives; avasthitan = standing in position.

Fathers-in-law and also amiable people in both armies. After Arjuna saw all kinds of relatives standing in their respective positions.

Perceptions do matter. The mind draws its conclusions when it sees certain things. On those occasions, both reason and emotions influence our thoughts, depending upon the situation and our state of mind. Arjuna did not see those who stood on the Kauravas' side as enemies or warriors but as humans like him, who assembled there bound by their duty to fight for their side. Each of them was someone's father, grandfather, brother, friend, teacher, son, grandson, etc. Their actions would bring a lot of grief to them and their relations. This is one of the broader ramifications of a war. It will hurt many people, even those who do not participate in it or have nothing to do with it.

In life, relationships matter. They are the most apparent attachments we form on earth. They define us. They are also the most difficult to overcome since they fulfill our need for security, love, comfort, and belongingness. Without them, life would be empty and lonely. Through them, we feel validated, approved, accepted, and assured. Therefore, we cannot take them lightly, especially when we know that soon we will be parting from them one way or the other. Thus, Arjuna saw the human side of the war in the large assembly of men. He saw people drawn into violent conflict and ready to sacrifice their lives for a cause that was probably of no consequence for most of them.

Sloka 28

kṛpayā parayāviṣṭo viṣīdann idamabravīt
dṛṣṭvemaṃ svajanaṃ kṛṣṇa yuyutsuṃ samupasthitam

krpaya = by compassion; paraya = great; avistah = overcome, filled with; visidan = with sadness; idam = thus; abravit = spoke; dṛṣṭva = see; mama = my; svajanaṃ = own people; kṛṣṇa = O Krishna; yuyutsuṃ = ready to fight; samupasthitam = gathered.

Overcome with great compassion and filled with sadness, Arjuna spoke thus," O Krishna, seeing my kin gathered here ready to fight."

Arjuna felt compassion and grief when he saw men who assembled there as humans who performed various roles in their lives as fathers, grandfathers, friends, sons, etc. A warrior knows the plight of other warriors even when they fight on the other side, especially when they are thrown together by fate in a consequential and catastrophic war like the Kurukshetra War. He himself was a husband, father, friend, and brother to others who loved him. Therefore, he could empathize with the warriors who stood there and the destruction that was awaiting them. He felt sad, knowing that most of them would be dying soon. War is not a pleasant activity. No one rejoices when it unleashes its fury. No one truly wins without suffering. In ancient times, wars were even more brutal since people fought in close proximity, facing each other and surrounded by many from all sides, where chance played dice, and the fighting armies faced a do-or-die situation. Few could escape unscathed in that melee of swords, maces, arrows, spears, and daggers. The fighting lasted until one side won or surrendered. Arjuna felt compassion because he knew the warriors who gathered there to support them had no stake in the war except as allies, friends, and well-wishers. They came to help, bound by bonds of friendship, relationship, or kinship, even though they could have stayed away under some pretext. They had families, children, and dependents who needed them and depended upon them. If they died, they would leave many in great grief. Hence, he was overcome by compassion and filled with sadness.

Sloka 29

sīdanti mama gātrāṇi mukhañ ca pariśuṣyati
vepathuś ca śarīre me romaharṣaś ca jāyate

sidanti = shaking; mama = my; gatrani = limbs; mukham = mouth; ca = also; parisusyati = parched.; vepathuh = trembling of the body; ca = also; sarire = on the body; me = my; roma-harsah = hairs standing on end; ca = also; jayate = is taking place;

My limbs are shaking, my mouth is parched, my body is trembling, and the hair on my body is standing on end.

We are all humans. However strong, brave, or intelligent we are, there will be moments when we feel crumpled and crushed by fate or circumstances or by inimical forces who seem to challenge our hopes and dreams or our courage and convictions. Those moments are crucial because, on such occasions, we find our strength and character and prove our mettle. However, our initial reaction in most cases would be rather weak and shaky or confusing as we experience anxiety and uncertainty, and fail to foresee or grasp the enormity of the situation. Arjuna faced such a moment on that day as he stood on the battlefield and was overwhelmed by strong emotions. Although he knew and planned for the war with his brothers, he forgot the warrior in him when he stood there and felt the full weight of the war and its implications. He panicked as he realized that nothing good would come out of that war, and while they might win a kingdom and some glory, both sides would be left with many losses and troublesome memories. His reaction should not be mistaken for cowardice. He was a brave warrior, but had a human side. Like a true Kshatriya, he had humanity and compassion. We know from the Mahabharata that he had an impeccable record as a fighter who won many wars but was never cruel or violent toward the vanquished. He was Indra's son, born with a godly nature. Unknowingly, he even fought Lord Shiva and stood his ground. Therefore, we cannot say he reacted due to fear or cowardice. What caused his grief was probably the conviction that the war would hurt many and lead to irreparable loss for the warriors on both sides. He did not want to be the cause of it, responsible for the death of many, or the cause of suffering to their families and relations.

Sloka 30

gāṇḍīvaṃ straṃsate hastāt tvak caiva paridahyate
na ca śaknomy avasthātuṃ bhramatīva ca me manaḥ

gandivam = Gandivam; sramsate = slipping; hastat = from the hands; tvak = skin; ca = and; eva = certainly; paridahyate = burning; na = nor; ca = and; saknomi = am I able; avasthatum = stand; bhramati = reeling; iva = as; ca = and; me = my; manah = mind;

Gandivam is slipping from my hands, my skin is burning all over; I am not able to stand, and my mind is reeling.

Gandivam was Arjuna's celestial bow forged in heaven by gods and gifted to him. It initially belonged to Brahma, Indra, and Varuna in the same order. Varuna gifted it to Arjuna at Agni's request. Once, Agni grew weak and requested Krishna and Arjuna to help him gain strength. Both obliged and went to the Khāndava forest. Arjuna unleashed many arrows and burned the entire forest to nourish him. In that fire, all the creatures, plants, and animals became food for Agni. Pleased by their actions, he granted Arjuna the bow. The Pāndavas subsequently built their capital city on the land where the forest existed and named it Khandavaprastha. Gandivam was a magical bow with special powers. With it, Arjuna could unleash arrows in quick succession with the energy of hundreds of bows. It was also heavy and unwieldy. Only Arjuna and Lord Krishna had the strength and skill to use it. Along with the bow, Varuna also gifted him two quivers. They had the unique power to supply him with endless arrows. The bow and the quivers served him well in the wars he fought and made him invincible. However, on that particular day, Arjuna felt weak and could not hold the bow as his hands shook, and he could not think or stand firmly.

Sloka 31

nimittāni ca paśyāmi viparītāni keśava
na ca śreyonupaśyāmi hatvā svajanam āhave

nimittani = bad omens; ca = and; pasyami = I foresee; viparitani = inauspicious, the opposite; kesava = O Kesava; na = not; ca = and; sreyah = good; anupasyami = foresee; hatva = by killing; sva-janam = kin, own people; ahave = in the battle, fight;

And I see inauspicious omens, O Keshava. Nor do I foresee any good from killing my kin in the battle.

Arjuna saw ill omens and inauspicious signs as he was overwhelmed with negative thoughts and emotions. He even forgot his purpose and duty as a Kshatriya and felt no good would result from that war or killing his cousins and other relations who stood with them. In a disturbed state of mind, it is human for anyone to temporarily lose reason and think irrationally or exaggerate outcomes. Arjuna experienced the same as he could not see any good coming out of the war or his actions. He was certain that his relations and many would die in that battle and felt its foreboding in the bad omens he saw. In that commotion, he addressed Lord Krishna as Keshava, meaning the long-haired one. The epithet is associated with Lord Vishnu and Lord Krishna and is used in prayers and invocations by devotees to neutralize evil omens and adversity.

Sloka 32

na kāṅkṣe vijayaṃ kṛṣṇa na ca rājyaṃ sukhāni ca
kiṃ no rājyena govinda kiṃ bhogair jīvitena vā

na = notr; kankse = desire; vijayam = victory; krsna = O Krsna; na = not; ca = and; rajyam = kingdom; sukhani = happiness thereof; ca = and; kim = what; nah = to us; rajyena = kingdom; govinda = O Govinda; kim = what; bhogaih = enjoyment; jivitena = living.

I do not desire victory, O Krishna, nor kingdom, nor the joy of having it. Of what use, O Govinda, kingdom or enjoyment or even living?

At that moment, Arjuna thought, "I do not need this victory. I do not want the kingdom, nor do I see any advantage in having it or enjoying it." He wondered what good living or enjoying served if one had to fight a war and kill people and relations for it. In life, we often suffer from guilt, despair, and self-doubt when our morale is low, and we are overwhelmed with negative thoughts, passions, and emotions. On such occasions, we feel helpless, unable to avoid or escape from the conditions life or circumstances impose upon us. We wonder how we can cope with the situation or manage the emotional turmoil. When life throws seemingly insurmountable problems and challenges at us, we react as mere mortals and vulnerable weaklings. These kinds of experiences leave lasting impressions on our minds and stay in our consciousness for a long time. They even change our thinking, behavior, and actions. In some situations, people lose faith in themselves. They give up their battles or compromise with circumstances. Only a few hardened ones recover from the initial shock and move on with resolve, perseverance, and renewed faith in God. In some instances, shaken by the intense surge of sadness and despair (samvega) arising from such experiences, people turn to spirituality to resolve their suffering or renounce worldly life to escape from it or explore its causes and resolution. Arjuna went through a similar internal churning. He felt no joy at the thought of achieving victory, glory, or the prospect of ruling a kingdom. He was on the threshold of weighing the consequences of the war he did not so seriously think before. It was a momentous occasion for him and the world since his suffering and reaction would be immortalized as it would set in motion the discourse of the Bhagavadgita and help all those who go through similar life-altering experiences. Suffering is a punishment as well as a blessing and gift from God. For the right-minded and the rightly resolved, it teaches important lessons, opening their eyes to the wisdom and truths not discernible before.

Sloka 33

yeṣām arthe kāṅkṣitaṃ no rājyaṃ bhogāḥ sukhāni ca
ta imevasthitā yuddhe prāṇāṃs tyaktvā dhanāni ca

yesam = for whom; arthe = sake kanksitam = desired; nah = our; rajyam = kingdom; bhogah = enjoyment; sukhani = happiness; ca = and; te = they; ime = these; avasthitah = stand, arrayed; yuddhe = in the battle; pranan = lives; tyaktva = renouncing; dhanani = riches; ca = and;

Those for whose sake (we) desire the kingdom, enjoyment, and happiness, they stand (here) in the battle, renouncing their lives and riches.

Arjuna was a householder. In his opinion, he was meant to perform duties for his and his family members' enjoyment and happiness. Therefore, he wondered what was the point of honoring his Kshatriya dharma when it involved killing and maiming those he was supposed to protect and honor. He had this confusion because he did not know the true meaning of Dharma and the purpose and importance of obligatory duties. Lord Krishna would subsequently explain why duties are needed and why one should perform one's duties, irrespective of their merits or demerits. A warrior's primary duty is to fight and do his part on the battlefield, irrespective of its moral or personal implications, and without worrying about its wider consequences. Yet, it is normal and human for warriors to experience such anxious thoughts when they are in the thick of war, and death and destruction are inevitable.

Sloka 34

ācāryāḥ pitaraḥ putrās tathaiva ca pitāmahāḥ
mātulāḥ śvaśurāḥ pautrāḥ śyālāḥ sambandhinas tathā

acaryah = teachers; pitarah = fathers; putrah = sons; tatha = thus; eva = even; ca = and; pitamahah = grandfathers; matulah = maternal uncles; svasurah = fathers-in-law; pautrah = grandsons; syalah = brothers-in-law; sambandhinah = relatives; tatha = as well as.

Teachers, fathers, sons, and thus even grandfathers, maternal uncles, fathers-in-law, grandsons, brothers-in-law, and other kinsmen.

Relationships are also mentioned in verses 26 and 27. The double emphasis suggests how desires and attachments cause human suffering.

Sloka 35

etān na hantum icchhāmi ghnatopi madhusūdana
api trailokyarājyasya hetoḥ kiṃ nu mahīkṛte

etan = all these; na = never; hantum = for killing; icchami = do I wish; ghnatah = being killed; api = even; madhusudana = O Madhusudana; api = even if; trai-lokya = of the three worlds; rajyasya = of the kingdoms; hetoh = for the sake; kim = what to speak of; nu = only; mahi-krte = for the sake of the earth.

I do not wish to kill them, O Madhusudana, even if they may (kill me), not even for the lordship of the three worlds. Then what to speak of the earth?

Arjuna saw those he was supposed to fight and kill to win the war. It was not that he did not think previously about the death and destruction arising from the war. Most likely, the thought that he would not see those relations again after the war must have depressed him. He did not see in them enemies, though they were, but only relationships, the people he knew and grew up with from an early age. In that emotional state, he concluded that he would not wish to kill them, not even for the lordship of the three worlds, and he would rather be killed by them than kill them. His reaction was typical of human reactions in irrational and emotional states. Once you are emotionally disturbed and decide not to do something, you will invent all the reasons and justifications to defend your decision. You will be in denial and find excuses to reinforce your conviction, even if it does not make sense to the people around you. Arjuna was in a similar situation. He forgot that those relations he wanted to avoid killing were also bound by their duty and would not spare him or his brothers on the battlefield if they had a chance to kill them. As we learn from the Mahabharata, as the war progressed, his relations and even elders in the family mercilessly and unfairly killed his son, Abhimanyu, surrounding him from all sides against the then rules of warfare. On the final day of the war, Aswatthama, Drona's son, killed Arjuna's sons through Draupadi in a dastardly fashion when they were sleeping. Once, Kauravas tried to kill all Pandavas cunningly by inviting them to a lac house and setting it on fire when they were asleep. In that thick of emotions, Arjuna forgot such incidents and took pity on the people who did not deserve any pity. We often ignore such hard facts of life when we succumb to desires and attachments. Due to his attachments, Arjuna temporarily forgot the circumstances that brought them to the battleground. He ignored the ordeals they went through due to the evil schemes his cousins hatched and the failure of the elders in his family to render justice. Although Kauravas personified evil and caused them much suffering and pain, because of his good nature, he did not wish to kill them or fight them. However, duty does not give scope for human weaknesses. It demands righteous actions.

Sloka 36

nihatya dhārtarāṣṭrān naḥ kā prītiḥ syājanārdana
pāpam evāśrayed asmān hatvaitān ātatāyinaḥ

nihatya = by slaying; dhartarastran = the sons of Dhrtarastra; nah = our; ka = what; pritih = pleasure; syat = will there be; janardana = O Janardana; papam = sin; eva = certainly; asrayet = take shelter; asman = us; hatva = by killing; etan = all these; atatayinah = aggressors.

By slaying Dhritarashtra's sons, what pleasures will be ours, O Janardana? Sin will certainly abide in us if we kill these aggressors.

Arjuna's lopsided logic continues. He was in denial and thinking irrationally, having lost perspective and discernment. He forgot that as a Kshatriya, his duty was to protect and defend his side from enemy attacks and support his king. He forgot that a Kshatriya would not incur sin but attain glory and heaven if he defeated and killed his enemies on the battlefield, but infamy would await him if he neglected his duty. He was thinking of the suffering that would result from his action but not the suffering his enemies might cause by killing them. He had this turmoil because he focused on the result or the fruit of his actions rather than his obligatory duty. His ignorance resulted from his ignorance and delusion about himself, his duty, and his actions. He addressed Lord Krishna as Janardana because he was in a state of sorrow and wanted him to address it. Janārdana means he who causes suffering to evil people, not the righteous ones. Arjuna was a righteous person. Hence, he wanted Lord Krishna to spare him from suffering. Janārdana also means he to whom people (jana) cry in pain (arthana) in troubled times. We may, therefore, conclude that Arjuna turned to him to alleviate his suffering.

Sloka 37

tasmān nārhā vayaṃ hantuṃ dhārtarāṣṭrān svabāndhavān
svajanaṃ hi kathaṃ hatvā sukhinaḥ syāma mādhava

tasmat = therefore; na = not; arhah = right, authority, deserving; vayam = we; hantum = to kill; dhartarastran = the sons of Dhrtarastra; sa-bandhavan = relations; sva-janam = own people; hi = certainly; katham = how; hatva = by killing; sukhinah = happy; syama = become; madhava = Madhava.

Therefore, we do not have the right to kill Dhritarashtra's sons and our relations, who are our own people. Certainly, O Madhava, how can we be happy by killing (them)?

Arjuna reached the illogical conclusion that he had no right to kill Dhritarashtra's sons and other relatives fighting on the opposite side. He wondered how he could be happy doing it. One could see that Arjuna lost his reason and judgment. He forgot his obligatory duty and focused on the results of his actions rather than on the duty-bound actions he was meant to perform as a Kshatriya. True, from a moral perspective, wars are not at all justified. However, when they become inevitable due to evil people, the righteous ones are obligated to fight. Arjuna was a good human being. Therefore, he thought about the moral consequences of the war. Even the very name of Arjuna means the one who does not inflict cruelty upon others. Because of his good nature, he felt the anguish. However, we should remember that he was a Kshatriya by birth, nature, and duty. He was born to participate in the Kurukshetra war to fulfill the aims of Dharma and assist Lord Krishna in destroying evil, protecting Dharma, and restoring order and regularity in the world, which at that time was in chaos. All the events in his life were meant to bring him to this point and serve the Lord, who incarnated upon earth in a human body to restore order. However, at that crucial moment, his emotions swayed him, and he forgot the distinction between Dharma and Adharma and who was on God's side and who was against it. He was right to call his cousins our people (svajanam) because they were related, but wrong to ignore his duty to God and worry about the consequences of his actions. As we will learn later, inaction is not a solution to any problem, and Arjuna was leaning toward it. Life does not always happen according to our expectations. Sometimes, it puts you against yourself and expects you to make the right choices without becoming lost in confusion and delusion. In ambiguous situations, you must remember your duty to yourself and God and stay on the side of Dharma. On that occasion, Arjuna should have thought from the perspective of his obligatory duty and his moral imperative (righteousness) as God's true soldier on earth to serve the aims of creation. He should have remembered that his first duty was to protect and defend his king, Dharmarāja, his supreme commander and brother, and the Lord himself, who was standing before him in a human form, rather than his relations on the other side, who were destined to be killed and destroyed.

Sloka 38

yadyapyete na paśyanti lobhopahatacetasaḥ
kulakṣayakṛtaṃ doṣaṃ mitradrohe ca pātakam

yadi = if; api = certainly; ete = they; na = do not; pasyanti = see; lobha = greed; upahata = destroyed; cetasah = mind, heart, soul; kula-ksaya = destruction or decline of the family; krtam = done; dosam = impurity, defect; mitra-drohe = betraying one's friends; ca = also; patakam = great sin;

Even though they, with their hearts and minds destroyed by greed, do not perceive the great sin of destroying their own family and betraying their own friends.

At that time, the family was uppermost in Arjuna's mind. He thought they all belonged to the same joint family, with Dhritarashtra as its head. He grew up in that family until he reached adulthood and obtained his education from elders like Bhishma and Vidura and teachers like Dronacharya and Kripacharya. Therefore, he was unhappy to find himself in a situation where he had to fight members of what he considered his family and elders. However, as we know, he was not thinking rationally. Even in that state, he remembered that their minds were destroyed by evil passions such as greed and envy but was still unwilling to fight them. He had this difficulty because he had set opinions about morality and immorality and was subject to desires, attachments, and expectations. He thought like a householder and focused on his relationships, even though they were dysfunctional and troublesome, rather than on his purpose as a Kshatriya and his obligatory duties.

Arjuna said that the Kauravas' minds (chetasa) were destroyed by greed and envy. Chetasa means mind or that which is filled with chetana or chaitanya, meaning consciousness, movement, sentience, or awareness. Another related word is 'chitta' (mind-body consciousness), which is mentioned in the Yogasutras of Patanjali as the seat of modifications (vrittis) due to impurities. When the chitta is pure, one discerns correctly, does not experience perceptual or cognitive errors, and makes the right decisions. When it is impure, the result is passion, delusion, confusion, mental afflictions, etc. Hence, in the classical yoga tradition, there is much emphasis on purifying the mind and body to achieve truth, purity, stability, tranquility, and self-absorption. Kauravas lacked discernment since their minds were filled with evil passions. Therefore, as Arjuna argued, while they would not see any sin in destroying their friends and relations, he would not commit the same sin since he was free from such evil passions and possessed discernment.

Sloka 39

kathaṃ na jñeyam asmābhiḥ pāpād asmān nivartitum
kulakṣayakṛtaṃ doṣaṃ prapaśyadbhir janārdana

katham = why; na = not; jneyam = known; asmabhih = by us; papat = from sins; asmat = from these; nivartitum = stop, put an end; kula-ksaya = the destruction of the family; krtam = by doing so; dosam = sin, impurity, blemish; prapasyadbhih = by those who can see; janardana = Janardana.

But why do we, who know the sin that arises from the destruction of the family, not stop doing it to avoid the sinful blemish, O Janardana?

Arjuna argued that since the Kauravas lacked discretion and their minds were filled with evil passions, they would not care whether their family members died in the war and would kill anyone in their greed to usurp the kingdom. For them, winning the kingdom mattered, and to achieve it, they would not mind destroying anyone who came in their way. However, he had no desire for the kingdom or the riches that came with it. Hence, he had no reason to resort to evil. Arjuna was aware of the doctrine of karma and the sinful consequences arising from evil actions. He knew that harming one's relations would result in sin. However, his knowledge of karma was limited, and he did not know well when actions produced sin. He will come to know them later when Lord Krishna teaches him the secrets of karma yoga. Though delusional, Arjuna's questions and statements are relevant since they would set the stage for the entire discourse of the Bhagavadgita.

Sloka 40

kulakṣaye pranaśyanti kuladharmāḥ sanātanāḥ
dharme naṣṭe kulaṃ kṛtsnam adharmobhibhavaty uta

kula-ksaye = with the destruction of the family; pranasyanti = perish, come to an end, disintegrate; kula-dharmah = caste duties; sanatanah = eternal; dharme = law, lawful; naste = is destroyed; kulam = family; krtsnam = entire, whole; adharmah = lawlessness, adharma; abhibhavati = overwhelms; uta = it is said.

With the destruction of the family, caste duties are destroyed, and the eternal Dharma is destroyed. The whole family succumbs to adharma.

Here, Arjuna reasoned why he did not want to be the cause of his family's destruction and, thereby, the destruction of Dharma. He argued that if his family was destroyed and if in any way he caused it, there would be no one to perform obligatory duties, such as protecting the women in the family and offering daily sacrifices to gods, ancestors, etc. When such duties were neglected, which were obligatory to him and his caste (kula-dharma), his family would fall into evil ways due to the sin that would accrue from it. His argument was right as far as family duties are concerned. However, he forgot that he no longer belonged to his erstwhile family, who abandoned him and his brothers. If they failed to perform their duties, the onus was on the elders in that family, not on him or his brothers. They were in no way responsible for the Kauravas or their families. He also forgot that as a Kshatriya, he had an obligatory duty towards his brothers, wives, and children, apart from his social and religious duties and obligations toward his fellow warriors who were supporting them, his king, and God himself.

Here, Arjuna spoke about Dharma without a proper understanding of it. Dharma has several meanings. In a limited sense, it means moral, religious, or obligatory duty. In a broader sense, it has multiple meanings: essential nature, primary function, distinguishing quality or property, religion, religious teachings, divine laws, God's eternal duties, virtue, morality, justice, a deity named Dharma, code of conduct, moral obligation, righteous actions, etc. In the Vedic way of life, Dharma precedes all the aims of life since discipline, duty, virtue, and allegiance to God are the foundation of peace and happiness. Hence, Dharma comes first in the four chief aims of human life (purusharthas), the other three being Artha, Kama, and Moksha. God is the creator, upholder, and promulgator of Dharma. Because of his self-imposed obligation to uphold Dharma only, he performs his chief functions: creation, preservation, concealment, destruction, and revelation. The householder's Dharma arises from his eternal Dharma only since its purpose is to ensure the order and regularity of the world. Since we are obligated to serve God, we are morally and existentially obligated to uphold His Dharma by performing our duties upon the earth. Since they are modeled on his duties and arise from them, the obligatory duties we are meant to perform are also considered eternal (sanātana). Whether it is family, society, the world, or creation itself, order and regularity arise only when human beings sincerely practice their Dharma. When they uphold it, peace and order prevail in the world. When they are neglected, the institutions, traditions, customs, duties, and principles that depend upon them or arise from them, including marriage and family customs and traditions, fall into evil hands, and chaos will result. Therefore, for humans, God's Dharma comes first through their Dharma.

Sloka 41

adharmābhibhavāt kṛṣṇa praduṣyanti kulastriyaḥ
strīṣu duṣṭāsu vārṣṇeya jāyate varṇasaṅkaraḥ

adharma = irreligiousness; abhibhavat = predominance, prevalence; krsna = O Krishna; pradusyanti = defiled, become impure; kula-striyah = family women; strisu = women; dustasu = fall into evil ways; varsneya = O descendant of Vrshni; jayate = arise, takes place; varna-sankarah = intermixture of castes.

With the ascendence of adharma, O Krishna, family women become impure, and when they fall into evil ways, O descendent of Vrshni, the intermixture of castes arises.

Arjuna said that when adharma prevailed, which meant when men of the household perished and the household had no one to perform the family's obligatory duties, the women in the family would have depended upon others to perform sacrifices or make offerings and become vulnerable to outside influences. Interactions with outside men and dependence upon them might have led to many complications, including amoral relationships, disrepute, and rumors. If the sacrificial fires were not lit, or the house was unclean or unfit for the gods' visitation, they would stop visiting that house and granting the wishes of its inhabitants. If they did not receive regular offerings of food, they would be displeased and stop protecting the people and cattle in it. Without protection from men and gods, the women and the girl children in the house would be vulnerable to outside threats from evil people.; They might take advantage of them, forcefully carry them away, sell them into slavery, keep them in captivity, or force them to do domestic work. It would result in the corruption of the women's chastity and intermixture of castes since those men might be outcastes or belong to different castes.

This was Arjuna's line of argument and justification to avoid killing his relatives. In his time, it probably made sense since the world then revolved around men, and women had little or no freedom or protection without men in the family protecting them. Arjuna was neither irrational nor narrow-minded. His world reflected the moral and social values of his time. From today's perspective, it may look odd, but we must remember that he lived in a very different world. There were no welfare states, no gender equality, and no police or laws to protect people. Even if some laws existed, their enforcement depended upon the sagacity of the kings and their administrators. Arjuna made these arguments not because he distrusted his women or questioned their loyalty. He expressed them due to his concern for their safety and welfare. He lived at a time when caste purity, family lineage, honor, and reputation mattered most. People's lives and honor depended upon them. They determined the laws of inheritance, eligibility for education, suitability for marriage, and children's future. Therefore, we should look at Arjuna's words and sorrow from a historical, spiritual, or philosophical perspective rather than attributing our current standards and values.

Sloka 42

saṅkaro narakāyaiva kulaghnānāṃ kulasya ca
patanti pitaro hy eṣāṃ luptapiṇḍodakakriyāḥ

sankarah = inter mixture; narakaya = hell; eva = certainly; kula-ghnanam = destroyers of family; kulasya = of the family; ca = also; patanti = descend to hell, decline, ruined; pitarah = ancestors; hi = certainly; esam = of them; lupta = become violated, neglected; pinda = sacrificial offerings to departed souls; udaka = water; kriyah = sacrificial acts.

With the intermixture of castes, the destroyers of the family and the family also descend to hell. Neglected, their ancestors fall down as they do not receive the sacrificial offering of food, water, and the fruit of sacrificial acts.

To understand this, we need to know the concept of the afterlife and rebirth in the Vedic religion, which is still valid in Hinduism. According to the Vedas, individual souls go to the ancestral heaven or the eternal heaven after death. Those whose karmas have not fully fructified go to the former, and those who have completely exhausted them through yoga, self-purification, or divine grace go to the latter. Existence in the ancestral heaven is temporary but permanent and inexhaustible in the eternal heaven. The embodied souls that go to the ancestral heaven return after exhausting some karma to take another birth. Their stay in that world depends upon their karma and the offerings they receive from their descendants on earth. The sacrificial food they receive through the offerings nourishes their causal bodies and prolongs their stay in the ancestral heaven. Thus, householders on earth have a moral and filial obligation to nourish their ancestors through sacrificial offerings and keep them happy. It is their obligatory duty, Dharma. Through that, they must ensure the transmigration of their ancestors and the continuity of their family lineage. If they fail to do it, they will be doing a disservice to themselves and their ancestors and incur sin. By neglecting their obligatory duties, they will not only disrupt their transmigration but also that of their ancestors. Deprived of the sacrificial food, the souls in the ancestral world lose their causal bodies quickly and fall to earth through the rain to take another birth.

Arjuna spoke these words with similar beliefs in his mind. He was worried that if evil people influenced women or carried them away due to the absence of men in the household, and if it resulted in the intermixture of castes, the lineage of his family would be disturbed since the children born from it would belong to another lineage, and even if they made the offerings, the original ancestors would not receive them since they were not their true descendants. As a result, they would be emaciated and quickly fall to the earth without exhausting their allotted karma to face the prospect of taking birth in unrelated families and living in difficult conditions. Arjuna must have thought of such possibilities as he weighed the consequences of killing his family members and relations in the war.

Sloka 43

doṣair etaiḥ kulaghnānāṃ varṇasaṅkarakārakaiḥ
utsādyante jātidharmāḥ kuladharmāś ca śāśvatāḥ 1.43

dosaih = because of such misdeeds; etaih = these; kula-ghnanam = destroyers of the family; varna-sankara = admixture of castes; karakaih = perpetrators of; utsadyante = causes devastation; jati-dharmah = obligatory social duties; kula-dharmah = obligatory family or caste duties; ca = and; sasvatah = permanently.

Because of the misdeeds of these destroyers of family and perpetrators of the admixture of castes, obligatory social duties and family traditions are permanently destroyed.

The destroyers of the family (kulaghnās) are those who kill men in the war and disrupt their households, hurting their families and spiritual destinies. Perpetrators of the admixture of castes (varna-sankara-kārakas) are those who harm women and widows when their men die in the war, and they are forced to live without adequate protection, means of livelihood, and family support. Without men performing obligatory duties, supporting gods and others, and protecting women and children, jāti-dharma and kula-dharma are permanently destroyed. Jāti refers to an entire ethnic group, tribe, or members of a community who practice the same faith and are bound by history, genealogy, bloodlines, geography, and tradition. Kula refers to the family and the caste duties that arise from it. They will fall into disrepair if a large number of men are killed in wars.

The order and regularity of the world depend upon how responsibly people live and do their part in preserving and upholding Dharma at various levels. In the Vedic tradition, householders have obligatory personal duties (svadharma), which are meant for their material and spiritual well-being. They have social obligations (jāti-dharma), which are intended to ensure the order and regularity of the world and society. They have family duties (kula dharma) to ensure peace, prosperity, and happiness for all family members and their ancestors' transmigration. These duties are obligatory, which means they cannot be ignored or neglected. These duties make life predictable and orderly in an otherwise unpredictable and uncertain world. They must be performed not only for worldly reasons but also as an obligatory service or sacrifice to God, the upholder of all. If we are duty-bound, disciplined, and live in a predictable and organized way, we can expect predictable and controllable outcomes and manage our lives accordingly. When the members of a community (jāti) follow the same set of standardized principles and values and do their part, taking responsibility for their actions, life will be more orderly, predictable, and peaceful. When people live for themselves, without consideration for others or their spiritual welfare, chaos and confusion will follow. This is the simple principle of Dharma implied in Arjuna's words. When evil grows and Dharma is neglected, things will go out of control, and everyone will suffer from evil consequences.

Sloka 44

utsannakuladharmāṇāṃ manuṣyāṇāṃ janārdana
narake niyataṃ vāso bhavatīty anuśuśruma

utsanna = destroyed, ruined, uprooted; kula-dharmanam = of the family traditions; manusyanam = of such people; janardana = O Janardana; narake = in hell; niyatam = certainly, inevitably; vasah = abode; bhavati = it so happens; iti = thus; anususruma = heard from the masters.

I happened to hear from the masters, O Janardana, that the place of the people who destroy their family dharma is inevitably in hell.

Arjuna said those who destroy or disregard their family duties would suffer in hell. Now, how can anyone disregard family duties? First, you can do it by not performing them; second, by performing them wrongly; third, by performing them against tradition and approved practice; and fourth, by practicing those prohibited by the scriptures or not suggested by them. We will learn later that when obligatory duties are performed with desires and expectations or for selfish reasons, they produce sinful karma and cause suffering. Lord Krishna would address these problems with Arjuna later while teaching him the secrets of karma yoga and karma-sannyasa yoga. Between birth and death, a householder is obligated to perform many duties for himself, his family, and society. He has to ensure that everyone in the family is fed and cared for, including his family deities (kula devatas), gods, and ancestors. Then, he must feed spiritual people, beggars, etc., who do not cook for themselves and depend upon others for food, animals, and other creatures. Apart from these daily sacrifices, he must perform other sacrifices as ordained by the Vedas, avoiding those declared sinful or prohibited. He has to ensure that his children and dependent children are initiated and educated early in religious duties, taught family traditions, encouraged to learn the scriptures, and brought up with good moral values. Other duties include giving gifts to Brahmanas, hosting sacrifices, practicing austerities, treating guests with honor, living virtuously, respecting parents, teachers, elders, etc. He is also expected to maintain good standing in society and live virtuously.

These duties are obligatory, which means they cannot be avoided. According to Arjuna, if men die in the war, they cannot perform these duties, whereby their families would decline, and the world would also suffer. Then, the sin of destroying the kula-dharma of the deceased would fall on those who kill them. This is one of the justifications used by Arjuna to argue that he would rather avoid fighting than kill his relations and family members so that he would not be tainted by the sin of destroying their families and family duties. Indeed, Arjuna was ignoring his most important obligatory duty as a Kshatriya: fighting for his king and the people he was meant to protect from the evil Kauravas. According to our shastras, killing any living being is a mortal sin, especially killing a human being. However, it should not be confused with killing enemies on the battlefield. It is an essential duty under Kshatriya dharma. In his disturbed state of mind, Arjuna forgot about it.

Sloka 45

aho bata mahat pāpaṃ kartuṃ vyavasitā vayam
yad rājyasukhalobhena hantuṃ svajanam udyatāḥ

aho = alas; bata = how unfortunate it is; mahat = great; papam = sins; kartum = committing; vyavasitah = decided; vayam = we; yat = so that; rajya = kingdom; sukha = pleasure; lobhena = out of greed; hantum = to kill; sva-janam = own people; udyatah = preparing, getting ready.

Alas, how unfortunate it is that we decided to commit the great sin of killing our own people out of greed for the pleasures of the kingdom.

Neither Arjuna nor his brothers desired the kingdom for enjoyment or egoistic pride. They claimed their right to the throne because Dharmarāja was the lawful and rightful heir to the throne. He had an obligatory duty to claim it for himself and all those who follow him as the rightful heirs. He also had a duty to God and his subjects as the upholder and protector of Dharma. Arjuna forgot these facts and blamed himself and his brothers for desiring the kingdom as if they had a selfish desire to enjoy the pleasures of ruling it. He also forgot that they were victims of injustice and were not responsible for the war. The war became inevitable only after they exhausted all avenues. Duryodhana adamantly refused to grant them even five villages and refused to negotiate with them. Thus, they were forced into this situation by the Kauravas, not because they had any intention to wage war and kill them. Since Arjuna was disturbed and lost his discernment, he became remorseful and blamed himself and his brothers for the situation in which they found themselves.

Sloka 46

yadi mām apratīkāram aśastraṃ śastrapāṇayaḥ
dhārtarāṣṭrā raṇe hanyus tan me kṣemataraṃ bhavet

yadi = even if; mam = unto me; apratikaram = merciful, without being vengeful; asastram = unarmed; sastra-panayah = armed with weapons; dhartarastrah = the sons of Dhrtarastra; rane = in the battle; hanyuh = may kill; tat = that; me = mine; ksema-taram = better; bhavet = become.

It is much better if the sons of Dhritarashtra, armed with weapons, kill me when I am unarmed and not in a retaliatory mood to fight.

In desperation, Arjuna thought that it would be better if the Kauravas killed him with their weapons when he was unarmed and not in a retaliatory mood to fight. Troubled by such irrational thoughts and negative emotions, he forgot the purpose of the war, the circumstances that led to it, and his duty and obligation to uphold his Kshatriya dharma, if not for his sake but for the sake of his family, his king, and the future of his descendants. He also forgot about the role of God and fate in the lives of humans and erroneously thought that the problem would go away if he ended his life. He did not weigh the fact that giving up his life in a meek surrender was a mortal sin, several times more sinful than killing his enemies on the battlefield. He should have thought that no one could solve problems by avoiding them or running away from them. If problems are not addressed immediately, they gain strength and grow into even bigger problems. Inaction does not solve any problem. It just makes things worse. In a normal situation, Arjuna would have thought rationally and remembered these truths of life. He would have realized that even if he withdrew, the Kauravas would go ahead with their plans and fight them. They would be even emboldened if a warrior like him withdrew from the battlefield without fighting.

Sloka 47

sañjaya uvāca
evam uktvārjunaḥ saṅkhye rathopastha upāviśat
visṛjya saśaraṃ cāpaṃ śokasaṃvignamānasaḥ

Translation

sanjayah = Sanjaya; uvaca = said; evam = thus; uktva = saying; arjunah = Arjuna; sankhye = in the the battle; ratha = chariot; upasthe = situated on; upavisat = sat down again; visrjya = setting aside; sa-saram = along with arrows; capam = the bow; soka = by sorrow; samvigna = distressed, disturbed; manasah = within the mind.

Said Sanjaya," Having spoken thus, Arjuna sat down in his chariot, setting aside his bow and arrows, with his mind distressed by sorrow."

After expressing his grief and moral confusion, Arjuna sat down in the chariot in distress, laying down his bow and arrows, which devotees usually do after they pray to God for help, troubled by the problems life imposes upon them. The first chapter of the Bhagavadgita is introductory. It sets the stage for the rest of the discourse. Its title, "Arjuna's Vishada Yoga," meaning Arjuna's state (yoga) of sorrow (vishadam), signifies the importance of suffering and misery in human life and how it is the first stage in the spiritual transformation and liberation of any human being. Life is full of suffering because it is meant to open our eyes to the harsh realities of mortal life and remind us of our ultimate purpose: liberation from the limitations and impurities we are subject to. The Bhagavadgita symbolically conveys that suffering and sorrow will open our eyes and lead to our enlightenment and liberation through successive states (yogas) of self-awakening and purification. Suffering tests our limits of endurance. It pushes us to the edge of our patience and tolerance, exposes our limitations, vulnerabilities, and frustrations, and forces us to look for help and solace within ourselves by taking refuge in the Lord, who lives in us as our very Self. Suffering (dukkha) or sorrow (vishada) is inherent and inevitable in our lives for a reason. It arises from our faults, failures, and inability to discern truths and abide by our essential nature. When we discern its causes, we mend our ways and find its solution.

We suffer to the extent we are deluded and ignorant and deviate from our duties and core nature, and to the degree we are unwilling to change our paths or learn from our faults and mistakes. People respond differently when life takes strange turns due to forces beyond their control, and their suffering is aggravated by self-inflicted failures, clouded thinking, and judgment. Some try to resolve it on their own with faith in themselves; some turn to God or a supernatural entity or power for help, while some try to do both, unable to know which one is better. Arjuna belonged to the last category. When he was overwhelmed with sorrow at the thought of killing his relatives, his initial reaction was fear and confusion. He wanted to escape from it by withdrawing from the battlefield without fighting. However, he did not act on that impulsive thought. Instead, as a true devotee, he shared his deepest thoughts and moral fears with Lord Krishna, who was present with him in the chariot on that occasion, witnessing his confusion and suffering. He was fortunate to have the Lord himself to share his feelings and find solace. Lord Krishna responded with love and compassion and imparted to him the sacred knowledge of achieving liberation by performing actions with knowledge and discernment, and without suffering from their sinful consequences. That supreme knowledge, the secret of secrets, forms the core subject of this sacred scripture, one of the most significant scriptures ever composed on earth and still relevant to our lives even today. However, let us not believe for a moment that we do not have the same opportunity that Arjuna had. The Lord is present in us as our very Witness and the charioteer of our minds and bodies. He is always willing to listen to our thoughts, prayers, and supplications. We can also approach him and seek his guidance. For that, we need to look within with faith and wait for the answer.

Conclusion

iti srīmadbhāgavadgītāsupanisatsu brahmavidyāyām yogasāstre srikrisnārjunasamvāde arjunavisādayogo nāma prathamo 'dhyayah

iti = thus; srīmadbhāgavadgītā = in the sacred Bhagavadgita; upanisatsu = in the Upanishad; brahmavidyāyām = the knowledge of the absolute Brahman; yogasāstre = the scripture of yoga; srikrisnārjunasamvāde = the dialogue between Sri Krishna and Arjuna; arjunavisādayogo nāma = by name Arjuna's sorrow; prathamo 'dhyayah = first chapter.

Thus ends the first chapter, named Arjuna Vishada Yoga (Arjuna's State of Sorrow), in the Upanishad of the sacred Bhagavadgita, the knowledge of the Absolute Brahman, a treatise on Yoga, which contains the dialogue between Arjuna and Lord Krishna.

02 – Sāmkhya Yoga

The Yoga of Knowledge About the Self and the Body

Sloka 1

sañjaya uvāca
taṃ tathā kṛpayāviṣṭam aśrupūrṇākulekṣaṇam
viṣīdantam idaṃ vākyam uvāca madhusūdanaḥ

sanjayah uvaca = Sanjaya said; tam = to him; tatha = thus; krpaya = with compassion; avistam = entered, possessed, overwhelmed, overpowered; asru-purna = full of tears; akula = distressed; iksanam = eyes; visidantam = unhappy, sad; idam = this; vakyam = words; uvaca = spoke, said; madhu-sudanah = Madhusudana.

Sanjaya said, "Thus overwhelmed with compassion, Madhusudana spoke these words to him whose eyes were tearful, and (who was) distressed and unhappy."

In the first chapter, we saw how fate and circumstances drew good-hearted people like Arjuna into difficult situations and subjected them to suffering and moral dilemmas. When Arjuna entered the battlefield, sitting in the chariot driven by Lord Krishna, and saw both armies, he was conflicted and distressed, thinking that he would be responsible for the death of his friends, elders, and relations. He was not a coward because he did not worry about his death, but the death of others. Therefore, he wanted to abandon his duties and withdraw from the war. He even argued that he would rather live on alms than kill his relations. Obviously, he was confused about his obligatory duties and moral and social responsibilities. He was swayed by worldly desires, attachments, and mistaken notions about karma, sin, and obligatory duties. Arjuna is not alone in this predicament. We also face similar dilemmas in our lives. Our morals are relative. Therefore, we cannot always be certain of what we should or should not do and whether we are thinking correctly or making the right decisions. We are conflicted because we are bound to our desires and attachments and see our problems from the narrow perspective of our egos without realizing our spiritual nature or oneness with the Supreme Lord. We understand this better when we study the Bhagavadgita and realize why it is necessary to realize our spiritual nature and perform our duties as a sacrificial offering to the Lord who lives in us as our very Self. In the second chapter, we are introduced to this core doctrine of the Bhagavadgita. Some people consider it a summary of the whole scripture.

The first chapter of the Bhagavadgita is about the importance of mind-altering experiences of sorrow and suffering, which change our perspective about life and death and turn to God or a supernatural deity for support, solace, protection, and solutions. The second chapter is about beginning that journey and how we can cultivate the right knowledge and wisdom to live righteously and explore our spiritual nature without becoming attached to transient things and shunning desires and attachments. Arjuna's suffering and sorrow (vishadam) symbolize the confusion and the struggle we experience almost continuously due to duality, desires, delusion, etc. We are constantly exposed to them and vulnerable to them. It also shows how, in the face of difficulties and conflicting situations, we lose discrimination, reason, and foresight and suffer from agonizing mental conflicts, confusion, and self-doubt. The outward suffering results from the inward modifications (vrittis) of the mind, which is fickle by nature due to the impurities and gunas (modes). As long as they are active, no one can escape suffering or the cycle of births and deaths. Thus, human suffering is mostly self-inflicted due to the imperfect and impure nature of our existence. We will find a permanent escape from it only through our spiritual nature and with divine help.

From this scripture, we also realize that suffering is a great teacher who imparts to us valuable lessons, although somewhat slowly and painfully, as a part of life's correcting mechanism. Suffering opens our eyes to the reality of our existence and the need to escape from it by cultivating proper knowledge and wisdom and avoiding the conditions and factors which lead to it. Due to divine grace, karma, or some other cause, the knowledge or awareness to resolve it dawns upon us either by itself or through an independent, external source such as a person, teacher, or experience. In Arjuna's case, God intervened directly and opened his eyes. When he suffered from a surge of emotions at the prospect of fighting and killing his relations, he wavered and lost his nerve. Lord Krishna responded with love and compassion and showed him the righteous path to perform actions without incurring sinful karma. They had known each other for a long time. Arjuna was his relation, devotee, and close friend. They also went on many joint expeditions before, including the one when they burned the Khāndava forest to help Agni and build a new capital city on the cleared land for Dharmaraja's newly acquired kingdom. Therefore, the Lord took pity on him and, through a long discourse, offered him a permanent solution to resolve his suffering. He taught him the secret (Upanishadic) knowledge and technique (yoga) of performing actions intelligently and harmlessly to avoid sin and achieve liberation. It would permanently set him free from confusion, doubts, and ignorance.

Sloka 2

śrībhagavān uvāca
kutas tvā kaśmalam idaṃ viṣame samupasthitam
anāryajuṣṭam asvargyam akīrtikaram arjuna

sri-bhagavan uvaca = said the Supreme Lord; kutah = from where; tva = to you; kasmalam = dejection, disgraceful; idam = this; visame = critical situation; samupasthitam = entered, settled; anarya = ignoble, ignominious, dishonorable; justam = practiced by; asvargyam = unworthy of heavenly life; akirti = infamy; karam = causing; arjuna = O Arjuna.

The Supreme Lord said, "From where did this dejection befitting ignoble people descend (upon you) at this critical moment, O Arjuna, which is unworthy of heavenly life and the cause of infamy?"

Lord Krishna reminded Arjuna that it was not the appropriate time to waver or suffer from self-doubt and conflicts. The fate of the war and many people depended upon him. Therefore, it was not appropriate for him to lose courage and withdraw. His reaction was unworthy of a warrior and heavenly life, which dutiful and noble warriors attain. Asvargyam means not fit for heavenly life. Kasmalam means any weakness, sadness, or impure thought. Anārya means not befitting a noble person (Arya) or a person of noble birth. By using these words, Lord Krishna mildly chided Arjuna for losing his heart and becoming weak at a crucial moment when his brothers were waiting for him on the battlefield. He cautioned him that his actions would bring him infamy (akirti). Arjuna spoke about the consequences of killing his relatives in the war. In response, Lord Krishna reminded him of the consequences of withdrawing from the war.

The law books stipulate that a Kshatriya must serve his king and lay down his life if necessary. It is his sacred and obligatory duty. He owes that to the king he serves. He must be strong and courageous and should not be afraid of causing death or destruction of the enemy. He must be willing to die for righteous causes if his king or circumstances warrant. He must do so even if his king pursues aggression unjustly. It is not up to him to decide whether the war is justified or not. His duty is to obey the king or the commander's orders and serve. Arjuna belonged to this heroic tradition of ancient warriors who entered the battlefields with two aims: to secure victory or die in that effort. By that, they attained the path of the warriors (viragathi) that led to the warriors' heaven (virasvargam). At the same time, those who turned their backs on their enemies or ran away from the battlefield would have to live in ignominy and lose the chance to attain heavenly life. By reminding him of these consequences and appealing to his pride and reputation, Lord Krishna wanted him to overcome his grief and prepare for the war. Bhagavadgita's central theme is that one should perform obligatory duties selflessly without worrying about the results or consequences. Arjuna's grief on the battlefield created a favorable environment for Lord Krishna to elaborate on that idea and teach him the secrets of attaining liberation through karma, jnāna, sannyāsa, and bhakti yogas.

Sloka 3

klaibyaṃ mā sma gamaḥ pārtha naitat tvayyupapadyate
kṣudraṃ hṛdayadaurbalyaṃ tyaktvottiṣṭha paraṃtapa

klaibyam = cowardliness, mental weakness, timidity; masmagamah = do not succumb; partha = Partha; na = not; etat = this; tvayi = to you; upadyate = suit, appropriate; ksudram = lowly, mean, base, vile; hrdaya = heart; daurbalyam = weakness; tyaktva = leave aside; uttistha = get up; param-tapa = O chastiser of the enemies

O Partha do not succumb to cowardliness. It does not suit you. Shake off this lowly weakness of your heart, and stand up, O chastiser of the enemies.

Wars are fought mostly in the minds of the warriors rather than on the battlefield. Those who do not have the courage and conviction cannot win. A warrior's mental or emotional state is far more important than his skills. We know from history that sometimes small and ill-equipped armies win against large and well-trained armies if they are strongly motivated to defend themselves. Lord Krishna wanted Arjuna not to succumb to cowardliness and shake off his mental or emotional weakness (hridaya daurbalyam). Traditional commentators of the Bhagavadgita, such as Shankara and Bhaskara, suggested that Lord Krishna identified Arjuna's problem as the weakness of his heart rather than his mind and subtly dealt with it using appropriate words. He addressed him as Partha to remind him of his birth as a warrior and his connection with Indra, the supreme commander of gods and hero of many heavenly battles. He used 'tvai' to remind him that he fought well with Maheswara (Lord Shiva) himself in the past. He addressed him as Parantapa to remind him of his reputation as a great warrior and destroyer of enemies. By equating his emotional weakness with lowliness, he appealed to his pride and encouraged him to stand up to his reputation and fight. He knew Arjuna well. Therefore, he could read his mind and respond appropriately.

Sloka 4

arjuna uvāca
kathaṃ bhīṣmam ahaṃ sāṅkhye droṇaṃ ca madhusūdana
iṣubhiḥ pratiyotsyāmi pūjārhāv arisūdana

arjunah uvaca = Arjuna said; katham = how; bhismam = to Bhisma; aham = I; sankhye = in the battle; dronam = to Drona; ca = and; madhu-sudana = Madhusudana; isubhih = with arrows; pratiyotsyami = repulse, counter attack; puja-arhau = venerable, qualified for woship; ari-sudana = slayer of enemies.

Arjuna said, "O Madhusudana, how am I going to attack venerable Bhīshma and Drona in the battle with my arrows, O slayer of enemies?"

Arjuna felt that fighting Bhishma and Drona with his arrows was disrespectful and against tradition. They were renowned warriors with impeccable character and conduct. Bhishma was his grandfather, and Drona was his teacher (guru). According to the same law books, both are considered equal to fathers. Further, Drona was a Brahmana. The law books hold that killing a Brahmana for any reason is a mortal sin. Therefore, Arjuna had a genuine concern, and he raised the same here. While expressing it, he used two epithets for Lord Krishna: Arisudana and Madhusudana. Arisudana means slayer of enemies, and Madhusudana means slayer of evil people. By using them, he conveyed that a slayer of enemies and evil people like him should know better who deserved to be killed on a battlefield. Bhishma and

Drona were neither enemies nor evil. Pandavas had enmity with Kauravas, not with these elders. Lord Krishna would answer this question later while explaining the importance of desireless actions (nishkāma karma) in discharging obligatory duties (dharma) without worrying about sinful consequences.

The scriptures are not unanimous. They contain a diversity of opinions (nana matam), which can be confusing to a novice or one who lacks discernment. Ashtavakra said one should become indifferent to the scriptures due to this problem and remain established in the Self. However, a householder like Arjuna cannot ignore scriptural opinions and become a recluse. He has to respect the code of conduct as prescribed by tradition or scriptures. Arjuna would not have had this confusion if he had the discernment to distinguish right from wrong. In making decisions, the context is also important. Arjuna ignored the context. He did not weigh all the factors to know whether it was appropriate to attack Bhishma and Drona. True discernment arises when one is free from ignorance, egoism, delusion, desires, and attachments. If one cultivates it by overcoming them, one does not need any scripture or teacher. His intelligence becomes his teacher and shows him the way to a solution through a maze of conflicting morals, values, and situations. Arjuna will soon learn the importance of discerning wisdom from Lord Krishna.

Sloka 5

gurūn ahatvā hi mahānubhāvān śreyo bhoktuṃ bhaikṣyam apīha loke hatvārthakāmāṃstu gurunihaiva bhuñjjīya bhogān rudhirapradigdhān

gurun = teachers; ahatva = not killing; hi = certainly; maha-anubhavan = elderly people; sreyah = highest good, appropriate; bhoktum = eating; bhaiksyam = begging; api = even; ihaloke = in this world; hatva = killing; artha = wealth; kaman = pleasure; tu = but; gurun = teachers; iha =here, this; eva = certainly; bhunjiya = enjoying, eating; bhogan = food, enjoyments; rudhira = blood; pradigdhan = stained.

In this world, not killing teachers and elders is the highest good. Eating alms obtained through begging is certainly better than enjoying bloodstained wealth and pleasures.

Arjuna was not afraid of the war. He had an emotional problem with fighting and killing his teachers and elders due to his beliefs and values about relationships, morality, and immorality. He studied the law books and knew his duties as a householder. The war presented him with a moral dilemma (dharma sankatam) he never faced before. The wars he fought before were with those who were enemies. In this particular war, he was presented with the difficult choice of fighting Bhishma, Drona, and other elders in his family who were not his enemies but well-wishers. In Hinduism, Dharma (duty), Artha (wealth), Kama (enjoyment), and Moksha (liberation) constitute the four chief aims of human life, especially for a householder. In this verse, Arjuna alluded to all four. He wondered how far it was appropriate to pursue wealth and pleasure when they conflicted with duty and liberation and whether immoral actions such as killing one's teachers or relations would ever lead to peace and happiness here and hereafter. He probably thought that pursuing wealth and pleasure (artha and kama) should not conflict with his religious and moral beliefs, values, and duties. He was right to think so because Artha and Kama should be pursued according to the principles of Dharma without ignoring the aim of Moksha. The only problem was Arjuna did not consider all aspects of Dharma and his duty as a warrior.

Such conflicts are bound to arise if you follow the scriptures without discernment. According to the law books, respecting teachers and elders is the norm and obligatory for everyone. However, if the duty demands and the cause is righteous, a Kshatriya has to fight anyone, be it a teacher, elder, or close relation. Bhīshma fought with his teacher Parasurama when the latter intervened to support Amba. Lord Rama fought with Bali even though the latter had no personal enmity with him. Drona fought with his friend, Drupada, and took half his kingdom to avenge an insult. He also unjustly demanded the righthand thumb as fee (guru dakshina) from Ekalavya for treating him as his guru and using his image for inspiration to practice archery. It is difficult to judge such actions as moral or immoral without considering the circumstances and the factors that influence them. Arjuna was not using his best judgment to draw the right conclusions. He let his heart be swayed by emotions and irrational thoughts. Therefore, he could not assess the situation with clarity. With clouded intelligence, he even concluded that he would be better off becoming a beggar and living on alms than fighting in the war. He did not see that his svadharma (essential duty) as a Kshatriya was more important and imperative for his life and destiny than resorting to the paradharma (another's duty) of a beggar. Lord Krishna would teach him later the distinction between the two and why he should stick to his essential dharma even if he found it inferior or problematic.

Sloka 6

na caitadvidmaḥ kataran no garīyo yad vā jayema yadi vā no jayeyuḥ
yān eva hatvā na jijīviṣāmas tevasthitāḥ pramukhe dhārtarāṣṭrāḥ

na = not; ca = and; etat = this; vidmah = do know; katarat = which one; nah = for us; gariyah = more improtant; yat = that; va = either; jayeyu = be conquered; yadi = if; va = or; (yadiva = otherwise); nah = us; jayema = conquer; yan = those; eva = certainly; hatva = by killing; na = not; jijivisamah = desire to live; te = all of them; avasthitah = standing; pramukhe = in front, arrayed, facing; dhartarastrah = the sons of Dhrtarastra.

Nor do I know which one is more important for us - to conquer them or to be conquered by them. Even all these sons of Dhritarashtra, by killing whom we certainly do not wish to live, are now standing in front of us.

Arjuna admitted his confusion here. His confusion was partly due to our relative morals and values, which change according to circumstances. What is right from one perspective appears wrong from another. Killing an enemy on a battlefield is justified, but from an ethical perspective, intentionally killing a living being is considered sinful. Renouncing worldly life and living on alms seems better than fighting a war and killing one's relations.

However, it is unjustified if the war is for a righteous cause and if the one making the decision is a King or a Kshatriya. A householder has the permission to renounce worldly life and take up sannyasa, but he cannot do so if he wants to abandon his duties and responsibilities and leave his dependents in a lurch. Therefore, one should think carefully before taking any action. Our actions should not hurt others and produce unintended consequences. If it is about fighting a war, one has to see whether it is obligatory. If it is not obligatory, one must see who will be hurt more by it. Bhishma, Drona, and others Arjuna mentioned, were honorable people but were supporting the evil Kauravas. According to our lawbooks, those who support evil actions (adharma) or do not knowingly oppose them are also evil (adharmis) even if they are not evil. By sparing them, Arjuna would have harmed the righteous people who were fighting on his side for a righteous cause. Arjuna did not weigh these factors. He thought by simply avoiding his obligatory duties (karma) and restoring them to inaction (akarma), he would solve the problem. He did not know the distinction between action and inaction, and that inaction was not the right solution to avoid sin. He would learn about it later from Lord Krishna.

Sloka 7

kārpaṇyadoṣopahatasvabhāvaḥ pṛcchāmi tvāṃ dharmasaṃmūḍhacetāḥ yac chreyaḥ syān niścitaṃ brūhi tan me śiṣyastehaṃ śādhi māṃ tvāṃ prapannam

karpanya = meekness, wretchedness, miserliness; dosa = impurity; upahata = afflicted with, struck by; sva-bhavah = inherent nature, natural state, condition, disposition; prcchami = I am asking; tvam = you; dharma = duty; sammudha = deluded, confused; cetah = in citta, mind; yat = what; sreyah = better; syat = may be; niscitam = decidedly, clearly; bruhi = tell; tat = that; me = to me; sisyah = disciple; te = yours; aham = I am; sadhi = instruct; mam = me; tvam = to You; prapannam = surrendered, fallen at someone's feet.

With my nature afflicted by the impurity of meekness and my mind confused about the duty, I am asking you to tell me clearly which is better. I am your disciple. Instruct me. I have surrendered to you.

Arjuna was confused about duty (dharma) because he lacked proper knowledge. He suffered from a moral conflict between his duty as a Kshatriya and his values as a human being and a family man because he was conditioned by certain morals, values, and norms. He was confused about fighting certain relations because of the bonds he formed with them. He rationalized his fears according to his conditioned beliefs and learned knowledge, which most people do when they are swayed by passions and emotions. In this, he was not alone. These are symptoms of ignorance, attachments, egoism, and delusion to which most people are subject. His arguments could have been right in different circumstances, but not when he had an enormous responsibility on his shoulders to win the war. However, even in that suffering and confusion about duty and morality (dharma-sammudha), he admitted that he was afflicted with the weakness of his heart (kārpanyam), and very appropriately made a life-altering decision. He humbly surrendered to Lord Krishna and sought his advice.

When in distress, we have two main choices. We can try to resolve our problems on our own using our knowledge and best judgment, or ask others to help us. It is much better if we take the Lord into confidence and surrender to him, seeking his guidance. The first one is the worldly approach followed by most people. They rely upon their egos, limited knowledge, and intelligence to solve their problems. The second one is the spiritual approach, followed by those who believe in God or his manifestations, such as a guru, a god, or an enlightened master. Arjuna followed the spiritual approach. Like a true devotee, he turned to Lord Krishna and sought his help. Many people cannot put themselves entirely in the hands of God and wait for a solution. It requires courage, conviction, and unwavering devotion. Only a few people resort to it. Arjuna opted for it.

God assures his devotees in many scriptures that he will not abandon those who approach him and pray to him with faith, love, and devotion. He may help them in four principal ways, just as he transmitted the knowledge of the Bhagavadgita to four devotees according to their devotion and commitment. He taught it directly to Arjuna, who was his dearest devotee; psychically to Sanjaya, who was his saintly devotee; indirectly through another person to Dhritarashtra, who was his deluded devotee, and through the knowledge preserved in the scriptures to all those who are his ordinary devotees with mixed faith. Arjuna knew Lord Krishna and had faith in him and his knowledge and wisdom. In ancient times, two conditions were needed for spiritual teachers in India to accept new disciples. Arjuna satisfied both. He approached Lord Krishna as a disciple (sishya) and requested him to tell him what he should do. He proved his keenness and devotion by saying he surrendered (prapanna) to him. His actions proved that he possessed faith, character, devotion, purity, and resolve, and was qualified to receive the secret knowledge of the Bhagavadgita.

Sloka 8

na hi prapaśyāmi mamāpanudyād yac chokam ucchoṣaṇam indriyāṇām avāpya bhūmāv asapatnam ṛddhaṃ rājyaṃ surāṇām api cādhipatyam

na = not; hi = certainly; prapasyami = I see; mama = my; apanudyat = may dispel; yat = that; sokam = sorrow, grief; ucchosanam = heat; indriyanam = in the senses; avapya = obtaining; bhumau = on the earth; asapatnam = unrivalled; rddham = rich, prosperous; rajyam = kingdom; suranam = over the divinities; api = even; ca = and; adhipatyam = suzerainty, sovereignty, dominion, rule.

I do not see that obtaining a prosperous kingdom upon earth and even lordship over the divinities would dispel my sorrow or the heat in my senses.

Arjuna said that gaining a prosperous kingdom or establishing sovereignty over the gods would not free him from sorrow if he engaged in bloodshed and killed his relations in the war. He saw no better alternative or possibility than avoiding the war and his duties. Our responses to the problems and circumstances in our lives depend upon our state of mind and our predominant thoughts and emotions. In deeply disturbed states, we feel exasperated by conflicting thoughts, desires, fears, and expectations. When the mind is paralyzed by exaggerated fears, even a small problem appears insurmountable and unsolvable. Arjuna was in no mood to foresee any positive outcome from the war since his mind was frozen by fear and anxiety, and his thoughts were induced by desires and attachments. He made himself miserable with faulty reasoning and irrational thoughts and concluded that nothing would dispel his sorrow and lift his spirits unless he withdrew from the battlefield.

His desire to shun wealth and the lordship of heaven stemmed from his desire to avoid performing his difficult and painful duties, not because he developed a sudden spiritual awareness and became adept in detachment and dispassion or self-restraint and renunciation. He could not resolve or reconcile his conflicting desires and attachment to certain values and notions. He experienced grief because he focused on the results or the fruit of his actions (karma-phalam) rather than his duty (dharma). He could not control his emotions or achieve mental stability because he took refuge in his ego and thought like a mere mortal with a physical body and mind. At this stage in the Bhagavadgita, he personified an ignorant and deluded devotee who was driven by attraction and aversion and performed actions with the desire to enjoy their fruit. Therefore, we should not take his claims seriously as the outpouring of an awakened yogi or philosopher but as the outbursts of a troubled mind, ignorant of his purpose and spiritual nature. However, from a spiritual perspective, he did not sink into a tamasic morass. He gave up fighting with himself and looked to Lord Krishna for proper guidance and knowledge. Soon, his decision would open his mind to an ancient and forgotten wisdom that would lift his spirits, heal his mind, and lead him on the path to eternal freedom, peace, and happiness.

Sloka 9

sañjaya uvāca
evam uktvā hṛṣīkeśaṃ guḍākeśaḥ paraṃtapaḥ
na yotsya iti govindam uktvā tūṣṇīṃ babhūva ha

sanjayah uvaca = Sanjaya said; evam = tin this manner; uktva = having said; hrsikesam = unto Hrisikesa; gudakesah = Gudakesa; parantapah = terror of the enemies; na=not; yotsye = shall fight; iti = thus; govindam = to Govinda; uktva = having said; tusnim = silent; babhuva = became; ha = certainly.

Sanjaya said, "Having spoken in this manner to Hrisikesha, Gudakesa said to Govinda, 'I will not fight,' and became silent."

In the Bhagavadgita, Lord Krishna represents the eternal Lord, Narayana, and Arjuna represents Nara, the ignorant and deluded human who has the potential to become an exclusive devotee but is not ready yet. Arjuna was undoubtedly a great warrior, but his mind was riddled with desires, passions, and attachments. Although he had the best education and was proficient in the scriptures, he was ignorant about his essential nature as the

Self and his purpose in life. If this were not the case, he would not have needed the teaching from the Lord for his deliverance. His words and actions betrayed his delusion and lack of true knowledge. His suffering conveyed his attachment to fixed notions about sin, suffering, family, and relationships. He came to the battlefield with a desire to win the war, but after entering the battlefield, he was conflicted by other desires. Fearing that his desire to win the war would conflict with his desire to protect his family and relationship and bring him a bad reputation, he decided to withdraw from the battlefield and escape from his duties. He had these conflicting thoughts because he did not know how to reconcile his conflicting desires and attachments, and lacked the knowledge that sin would not arise from actions but from desires and attachments.

He was unaware that he would not be able to escape from karma through inaction, since it would also produce karma if it resulted from desires. Like most worldly people, he assumed responsibility for his actions and did not see God as the doer and recipient of all actions. He lacked the discernment to know that obligatory duties must be performed as a sacrifice to God without desiring their fruit. Having surrendered himself to the Lord and said he would not fight, he fell silent. It meant his ego gave up struggling and complaining and yielded itself to divine intervention. Sometimes, it is better to stop struggling, yield to silence, and pray. When the ego falls silent, the mind stops churning, and the heart is filled with faith and devotion, solutions may emerge from the depths of our own being and help us move in the right direction. For Arjuna, it happened on the battlefield. The Lord responded to him with compassion and helped him know the path to achieve peace and tranquility without worrying about the consequences arising from his actions.

Sanjaya used two epithets for Lord Krishna and one for Arjuna. They are relevant to the context here. Parantapa means he who causes intense agitation or disturbance among the enemies. Hrisikesha means the lord of hrisika or sense organs. Gudakesa means lord of gudaka or slothfulness. Govinda means a cow keeper or the keeper of light rays. These epithets are relevant to the discussion here. Who is fit to teach divine knowledge? The one who has the right knowledge (Govinda) and is the master of the senses (Hrisikesha). Who is fit to receive it? The one who is completely silent and mentally alert (Gudakesa).

Sloka 10

tam uvaca hṛṣīkeśah prahasann iva bharata
senayor ubhayor madhye visidantam, idam vacah

tam = to him; uvaca = said; hrsikesah = Hrisikesa; prahasan = playfully, lightheartedly; iva = thus, in this manner; bharata = Bharata; senayoh = of the armies; ubhayoh = of both; madhye = in the middle; visidantam = grief stricken; idam = these; vacah = words.

O Bharata, to him (who was) thus grief-stricken between the two armies, Hrisikesha playfully said these words in this manner.

Lord Krishna watched Arjuna lose his courage and descend into chaos. Until now, he had listened to him without showing any response. He read Arjuna's mind and knew instantly that his fears were unfounded and his reasoning was faulty. He realized that Arjuna entered the battlefield without giving much thought to the moral implications of the war or his impending fight with the Kauravas and other relations, including those he held in high esteem. He felt the enormity of the situation only after watching both armies. As the gravity of the situation dawned upon him, he overreacted and exaggerated his fears without putting the problem in perspective. Fear, anxiety, and self-doubt are common when we face difficult choices. When life takes a different turn against our expectations, we feel confused and overwhelmed, and lose balance. The same happened to Arjuna. Fear and worry due to desires and expectations paralyzed him into inaction. He lost his reason and discernment. He worried about the consequences of fighting his relations, but did not consider the consequences of not fighting them. He also thought of himself and his actions, ignoring that his brothers and several others were also involved in the war, and their fate depended upon it. He did not think that if he withdrew, they would be harmed more than the harm he might inflict upon his relations on the other side by fighting them.

Hence, Lord Krishna reacted calmly to Arjuna's overwhelming emotions. He did not agree with him, sympathize with him, or console him. Instead, he responded with a smile and playful words, subtly conveying to him that it was not a serious problem at all and he was overreacting. He saw Arjuna's sorrow from the divine perspective as Nature's play and the expression of an ignorant, egoistic, and deluded mind. He knew how people would react under the influence of egoism, desires, and delusion in the face of ambiguity, uncertainty, and conflicting situations. Therefore, he saw his plight as the symptoms of a conflicted and deluded mind and spoke to him lightheartedly to lift his spirits and remind him that there was a war waiting for him and he should focus on it rather than worry about those who were already doomed. For him, the war and the death, destruction, and violence that were to follow it were already destined because he had already willed it to happen to cleanse the earth. Therefore, Arjuna had no choice but to be a part of it and do his duty. Hence, as the Knower of all, detached and perfectly balanced within himself and as the upholder of Dharma, who was equal to the dualities of life, he spoke to Arjuna gently in a lighthearted manner.

Sloka 11

śrībhagavān uvāca
aśocyān anvaśocas tvaṃ prajñāvādāṃś ca bhāṣase
gatāsūn agatāsūṃś ca nānuśocanti paṇḍitāḥ

sri-bhagavan uvaca = Sri Bhagavan said; asocyan = not to be grieved for; anvasocah = you are grieving; tvam = you; prajna-vadan = wise arguments; ca = and; bhasase = speak; gatasun = the dead, the life that has passed; agatasun = the living, life that has not yet passed; ca = also; na = not; anusocanti = grieve; panditah = knowledgeable people, wise ones.

The Supreme Lord said, "You are grieving for those who should not be grieved for. You have put forth wise arguments, but the wise ones who know do not grieve for the dead or the living."

Arjuna feared that if he fought the war, he would have to kill those close to him whom he respected. He saw them as physical entities rather than as spiritual entities having an eternal Self. He forgot or did not know that the Self in them was eternal and indestructible, and even if he killed them, they would still be alive in a different world. Therefore, there was no real reason for worry at all. Secondly, he grieved about transient relationships. For the one who is established in the Self, relationships do not matter. He does grieve for them when they are alive or when they are dead. He knows that the Self is independent, self-existent, and eternally free from attachments and relationships. In other words, Arjuna worried about transient matters like death, destruction, honor, and reputation, ignoring his eternal, indestructible, and unchanging existence in which none of them mattered. Hence, Lord Krishna said that those who had the right knowledge and knew the real nature of our existence would not feel sorry for what was lost or gained. They would remain undisturbed because they would regard gain and loss as the play of Maya and know that nothing was really gained or lost.

It is difficult for worldly people to believe in their spiritual selves, ignoring their minds and bodies, or remaining indifferent to the vicissitudes of life. For them, the physical body is real because they can see it and feel it. It represents them to the world. Denying it means denying themselves and their very identities. They cannot feel the same about the Self because it remains hidden behind the commotion of the mind and senses and the veil of ignorance and delusion. Thereby, they fall into the trap of Maya and accept their physical selves as their real selves. If at all they acknowledge it, it is because the scriptures say so, or someone they respect might have told them. In rare cases, people see it directly through a personal experience and realize its existence. It is why, as in Arjuna's case, they accept physical suffering as real and react, whether it is their suffering or that of others. The situations may be different, but the responses are almost identical. People worry about things they should not. When someone dies, they grieve, and when someone is born, they rejoice. Due to attraction and aversion, they go through emotional ups and downs, ignoring that, in the end, nothing matters. All the values, beliefs, worries, attachments, hobbies, habits, conflicts, friendships, and relationships to which they cling do not matter in the end. Death ends all that and creates a temporary respite for the Self to begin anew in a new body with a new life and circumstances.

Sloka 12

natv evāhaṃ jātu nāsaṃ na tvaṃ neme janādhipāḥ
na caiva na bhaviṣyāmaḥ sarve vayam ataḥ param

na = not; tu = indeed; eva = and; aham = I; jatu = a time; na = not; asam = existed; na = not; tvam = you; na = not; ime = these; jana-adhipah = rulers of the people; na = not; ca = and; eva = certainly; na = not; bhavisyamah = exist in future; sarve = all; vayam = we; atah param = here after.

There was never a time when I did not exist, neither you nor all these kings. Also, we will not cease to exist in the future after we depart from here.

Lord Krishna told Arjuna that there was never a time when he and others did not exist, and there would never be. All beings, irrespective of whether they are human or nonhuman, possess eternal and indestructible selves, and they are eternal and indestructible. Although our scriptures repeatedly affirm this, and they might have heard it several times, many people do not believe that they possess an eternal Self or accept it without skepticism. The Self cannot be perceived or seen because it is not an object the senses can perceive. Hence, most people remain skeptical or do not believe in it. They accept their bodies, egos, names, and forms as real since they can experience or cognize them. When someone dies, they grieve, and when someone is born, they rejoice, although, from a spiritual perspective, they should do the opposite. Most people also do not believe in rebirth or the afterlife because they cannot recollect them or their existence in other worlds.

The wise ones acknowledge these limitations. They rely on the testimony of the scriptures and self-realized yogis and take refuge in faith, accepting the existence of the Self as an indisputable fact. They know that without having faith in the Self, no one can achieve liberation or self-realization. The Self remains hidden behind the commotion of the mind, the senses, and the veil of ignorance and delusion. It does not come to the surface because it is passive and makes no effort to help in your exploration. You have to find it by suppressing and silencing your mind and ego and merging into it. Here, Lord Krishna removed any doubt we may have about our spiritual nature. He clearly stated that we are eternal, immutable, and imperishable. The Upanishads declare the same. They declare that the Self exists in all as the witness and the Lord. Its essential nature is pure consciousness, which can be experienced in transcendental states when a yogi withdraws his mind and senses, overcoming the illusion of duality and diversity created by the mind and senses.

If you see yourself as an immortal Self and believe in it without doubt, you will have a different perspective on life and your existence. With its help, you will find your inner sanctuary where you can experience peace and tranquility. Withdrawing into that, you can remain undisturbed by the impermanence and instability of the world. Abiding in that, you will gradually cultivate detachment towards your mind, body, and the world and remain engrossed in the Self with undivided attention. This is the first lesson that initiates learn when they withdraw their minds and senses into themselves and contemplate upon the Self for their transformation and purification. They become aware of their higher or spiritual nature, which remains hidden beneath the objective mind. It is by knowing it as eternal and indestructible and becoming established in that awareness that a person becomes the twice-born (dvija). This is the first step to true awakening on the path to self-realization and liberation. Very aptly, at the very beginning of his discourse, Lord Krishna planted this idea in Arjuna's mind. He wanted him to know that he was an immortal Self who would never cease to exist. He would not have to worry about sinful consequences if he engaged in a righteous war. He did it to stop Arjuna from worrying about the destruction of the body or the death of his relations. The Self in them would not be affected by them. Hence, he should not worry unnecessarily.

In this verse, Lord Krishna used three words: aham (I), vayam (we), and ime (these). One may use his statement to conclude that the Supreme Self and the individual selves are eternally different, a belief held by the school of Dvaita. However, we cannot definitively say other possibilities do not exist. The Bhagavadgita does not explicitly support any of the Vedantic schools, although they interpret it according to their beliefs and perspectives. The starting point of any spiritual practice in Hinduism is believing and acknowledging that your spiritual Self is the Lord in you and your true identity. Whether He is the same as the Supreme Lord or different will be known only when one attains oneness and enters His absolute state of pure consciousness.

Sloka 13

dehinosmin yathā dehe kaumāraṃ yauvanaṃ jarā
tathā dehāntaraprāptir dhīras tatra na muhyati

dehinah = indweller of the body, jivatma; asmin = in this; yatha = as; dehe = in the body; kaumaram = childhood; yauvanam = youth; jara = old age; tatha = In the same way; deha-antara = another body; praptih = obtain, attain; dhirah = the steadfast ones, the firm-minded; tatra = in such matters; na = not; muhyati = deluded.

Just as the dweller of the body passes from childhood to youth to old age, in the same manner, he obtains another body. Therefore, in such matters, the steadfast ones do not get deluded.

Death does not end your existence. You are an eternal Self dwelling in a perishable body. This is an important lesson we can learn to cultivate endurance, detachment, and equanimity. The person in the body (behind) lives on after death. Just as he remains intact while passing through different phases of his life, he remains intact even after he passes through death, minus the body that sheltered him. Although he goes through the different phases of his life as the person enjoying his life's numerous experiences, he will remain the same. When he leaves the body, he experiences death and survives in a subtle form, without his gross body. Since he does not carry many memories with him, and the memories he carries also decay over time, he does not remember much about his past lives. His current life is but one life in a series of lives he lives, and it goes on until he is tired and works for his liberation.

According to our beliefs, each jiva possesses two bodies: the outer gross (sthula) body and the inner subtle (sukshma or linga) body. They are further divided into five bodies called koshas (sheaths): the food, breath, mental, intelligent, and bliss bodies. Of them, the physical body constitutes the gross body (sthula sariram), and the rest constitute the subtle body (sukshma sariram). The gross body perishes with death, but the residue of the subtle body containing his past life impressions (samskaras) accompanies the

Person as his causal body (karana sarira). They serve as the seed for his next life and his essential nature.

If you firmly believe that you are an immortal Self subject to rebirth, you will think differently about yourself, the world, and others, and view your problems from a broader perspective. You will not feel disturbed by difficulties in your life or want to escape from them as Arjuna felt. You will take them in your stride with patience and understanding and live responsibly, ensuring that you will not become a problem for yourself. Hence, Lord Krishna emphasized the importance of cultivating this awareness at the beginning of the discourse. He reminded Arjuna and all of us that we should always remember that we are eternal selves and not physical entities who are subject to birth and death. Ignorant people ignore it and remain attached to their bodies. They experience suffering due to the modifications arising in them. The wise cultivate detachment from their bodies and remain indifferent. They see births, deaths, and modifications as happening to their bodies, not to them. Therefore, they do not grieve for the life that is gone or yet to be gone, or react to the suffering that arises from their bodies.

Sloka 14

mātrāsparśās tu kaunteya śītoṣṇasukhaduḥkhadāḥ
āgamāpāyinonityās tāṃs titikṣasva bhārata

matra =matter, material world, sense objects; sparsah = contact, touching; tu = indeed; kaunteya = Kaunteya; sita = cold; usna = heat; sukha = pleasure; duhkha = pain; dah=giving, producing; agama = coming; apayinah = going; anityah = impermanent; tan = these; titiksasva = bear with, tolerate; bharata = Bharata.

Indeed, contact with material objects, O Kaunteya, gives rise to cold and heat, pleasure and pain. (They) come and go, are impermanent. Bear with them, O Bharata.

Cold and heat, or pain and pleasure, are dualities or pairs of opposites. They are also impermanent. We experience them when we interact with the objects or when we are separated from them. In the process, we go through many conflicting experiences - happy when we meet someone we love and unhappy when we part with them, happy when we eat tasty food and unhappy when we are not allowed to eat it, and so on. The same is the case with the dualities such as heat and cold. Depending upon circumstances, they produce conflicting emotions and mental states. For example, in winter, we desire warmth and avoid cold, and in summer, we desire cool air and shade and avoid the sun and hot temperatures. These responses arise from attraction and aversion or likes and dislikes. They are, in turn, induced by desires and attachments.

The pairs of opposites serve a definitive purpose in our lives. They teach us that if we want to grow spiritually and break the chains that bind us to our fears and anxieties, we must transcend them and accept life in its totality. Lord Krishna implied the same idea in this verse. He suggested that we have to go through life without being troubled by the pleasant and unpleasant aspects of our experiences, since they come and go and do not last forever. We must accept them as temporary conditions and bear with them or remain indifferent. We cannot escape from life or from duties and obligations because they are difficult, painful, or troublesome. We should keep working and performing our duties, if not for ourselves, for others.

Although heat and cold and pain, and pleasure are dualities, they are not the same. Hence, they are mentioned separately. Heat and cold produce a wide range of feelings and sensations in different conditions. For example, cold produces pain and discomfort in the freezing cold, but happiness and comfort in the summer heat. The opposite is true with heat. The same is not the case with pain and pleasure. Pain always produces pain, and pleasure always produces pleasure. Their intensity may vary, but their basic propensity does not change. Even when the body is cut under anesthesia, the nerves experience pain, although the mind may not receive their sensations, and the body does not feel the pain. The distinction between the two types of dualities is important. It means that the same conditions do not always produce the same effects, and we should not go by external conditions and causes to resolve our problems. The same situation or external factors may produce happiness in some and sorrow in others. For example, Arjuna felt grief at the thought of fighting in the war. Duryodhana might have felt differently as he was eager to kill his enemies and achieve victory. Therefore, the solution to human suffering does not lie in mitigating its external causes or conditions. It may provide temporary relief, but not a lasting one. The solution lies within oneself, which is independent of the dualities and apparent causes. We will learn about it in the next sloka.

Sloka 15

yaṃ hi na vyathayanty ete puruṣaṃ puruṣarṣabha
samaduḥkhasukhaṃ dhīraṃ somṛtatvāya kalpate

yam = whom; hi = certainly; na = not; vyathayanti = trouble; ete = these; purusam = person; purusa-rsabha = best among men; sama = equal; duhkha = pain, sorrow; sukham = pleasure, happiness; dhiram = firm, stable, resolute; sah = he; amrtatvaya = for liberation, eternal life; kalpate = fit, qualified.

The one whom these do not trouble, that person, O best among men, who is equal to pleasure and pain, and firm, he is fit for immortality.

Who is fit for liberation? The answer is that one who is not troubled by the external causes and conditions and is equal to the dualities. The world exerts a lot of influence on us through the attachments we form. Those invisible bonds limit your freedom and happiness, and do not let you be free. You may think that you are free, but if you think of the bonds you formed with the world through numerous relationships, likes, and dislikes, you will realize how deeply you are entangled with it and how difficult it would be to free yourself from them. If you envision them as strings, you will feel like a puppet in the hands of invisible forces. Indeed, we all are prisoners of the things we seek and the relationships we cherish. We are bound by the things we love and hate. We are chained to the world and its influences of our own volition until we cut off the bonds. Now, how can you regain your freedom? It is by cutting off those bonds and becoming indifferent to the dualities.

In this verse, Lord Krishna said that those who were not troubled by the pairs of opposites and remained equal to them were fit for liberation. Liberation or immortality is not possible when the mind and body are bound by desires to external objects. Suffering cannot be mitigated by avoiding or escaping from the world, from duty, or from difficult situations, as Arjuna wanted to do. It can be done only by cultivating equanimity and sameness towards the dualities, accepting and treating the conditions of life with sameness and indifference. Mental stability (dhiram) is the foundation of all spiritual and yoga practices. It is the highest virtue. It is best achieved when we cultivate tolerance (titiksha) towards the vagaries of life, knowing them to be fleeting. We need to firm up mentally and suppress the modifications of our minds through yoga to experience peace and self-absorption. In this verse, Lord Krishna addressed Arjuna as the best among men (purusharsabha) to remind him that the best among men were men of stability and inner strength, who, unlike him, were not troubled by the dualities of life or tried to escape from difficult conditions. Through self-effort, they overcome attraction and aversion.

There are two commonly practiced methods to deal with pain and suffering. The first one is by controlling the factors or causes that produce or prolong them. When they cannot control them, they try to avoid them, run away from them, or distract their minds from the painful reality. This is the worldly way, which is effective but not always. It addresses the causes but not the suffering or one's vulnerability to it. The second one is by self-restraint, detachment, and indifference to endure life as it happens, controlling one's desires and attachments. This is the spiritual approach. It is more effective and lasting. In this verse, Lord Krishna spoke about it and said that those who become equal to pleasure and pain and are firm and resolute are fit for liberation. If you want a lasting solution to your suffering and sorrow, you must restrain your mind and become indifferent to or equal to pleasure and pain. We cannot control the world or the circumstances, but we can regulate our thoughts, desires, attachments, actions, and responses. We also cannot run away from the world or live in denial of our problems or suffering because wherever we go, the world follows us, and reality stares at us. Therefore, we must learn to tolerate the conditions in which we find ourselves and use them as opportunities to achieve inner freedom and detachment from things that tend to disturb us or exert influence over us.

Sloka 16

nāsato vidyate bhāvo nābhāvo vidyate sataḥ
ubhayor api dṛṣṭo.antas tv anayos tattvadarśibhiḥ

na = not, never; asatah = of the nonexistent; vidyate = is; bhavah = existence, state, being; na = not; abhavah = does not exist; avidyate = is not; satah = of the existent; ubhayoh = of the two; api = also; drstah = seen; antah = concluded, determined; tu = indeed; anayoh = of them; tattva = the essence of That; darsibhih = by the seers.

The unreal has no true existence; the real has no non-existence. Thus, the seers, who have seen the reality of That, reached the conclusion about the two.

The distinction between reality and unreality, existence and nonexistence, or being and non-being is explained in this verse. Before we explain the meaning of this verse, let us know the definition of Sat and Asat. Sat (the real) is eternally true, real, and existent. Asat is what is not Sat, or everything that is not Sat. These meanings may be misleading or confusing to some if they try to understand them from a purely mental perspective. The distinction between the real and unreal needs to be understood from a universal and eternal perspective. Shankaracharya interpreted that both the causes and effects are Asat. Although perceived through the senses, they are unreal because they do not exist permanently. Madhavacharya interpreted them as righteous and unrighteous deeds and bhava and abhava as happiness and misery, respectively.

What we consider Sat is always universally real or true, irrespective of time, place, or conditions. It does not qualify as Sat if it is intermittently, relatively true, or real. In other words, Sat is the reality of absolute truths, which are always true, independent, and self-existent. Whatever is not absolutely true or real is Asat. Sat never ceases to exist or comes into existence because it is eternally present without a beginning or end, and modifications. Anything that does not fall under this definition is Asat. If something happens intermittently or comes and goes, like heat or cold, or pain or pleasure, it does not qualify as Sat because it is not eternally existent. For example, you do not consider a dream real because it might have felt real when it happened. It is not real in a true sense because it did not happen in your wakeful state and exists in your memory as a dream. You also cannot recreate or recollect it precisely as it happened. You may remember it, but that does not make it real. Also, one shall not be confused by the fact that the unreal (Asat) may temporarily appear as Sat (real) in a deluded state due to mistaken notions, and the Sat may temporarily remain hidden and become imperceptible to our senses, as in the case of the Self or Brahman. Shankara said that any object, such as a clay pot, is unreal (asat) because it did not exist before it was created or after it was destroyed.

Simply because you cannot perceive Sat, it does not mean that it does not exist, or because you perceive Asat, it does not mean that it exists. The only criterion to decide whether something qualifies as Sat is whether it is eternally and unchangeably existent (bhava). According to the Vedas, the distinction between Sat and Asat is represented by the Self and the body at the most fundamental level. At the highest level, they are represented by Brahman and his creation or manifestation, respectively. The world, the body, and the materiality they represent are Asat because they are effects produced by causes. They have a beginning and an end but do not eternally exist. The supreme reality of Brahman is eternal and immutable, but everything else, including His creation, is unreal or illusory.

Similarly, the absolute Brahman is Sat. However, from Isvara downwards, all his manifestations, including the highest gods, are Asat since they have a beginning and an end and last for the cycle of creation. Some may argue that the highest gods are also Sat. However, it depends upon how you view them. Whether it is a god or a human, any being with names and forms (which are transient) is unreal. However, their essence may be true since it is Brahman only.

Sat represents Brahman's absolute, eternal, pure, and infinite reality, which exists by itself and in itself. It is also the purest and blemishless reality (shuddha tattva), which appears as Atman or the individual Self in beings (jivas) and as the Supreme Self in the Supreme Being, who is also known as Saguna Brahman or Isvara (Lord of the Universe) in creation. Asat is devoid of suddha sattva or the eternal divine essence. Sat may pervade Asat, but the two remain distinct and never unite. Brahman, the personification of Sat, pervades Asat, just as He pervades our minds and bodies, but He does not exist in them. The whole creation exists in Him as His projection, but He does not exist in it.

Sat is not to be mistaken with sattva, which is a mode of Nature. Our minds and bodies contain sattva along with the other two gunas. However, sattva has no direct relationship with Sat. It is just a poor reflection of Sat in the field of Nature. Hence, it has the name sattva, or that which reflects the purity of Sat. When you have the predominance of sattva, you will cultivate nearness to Sat and experience it. The phenomenal world and all the modifications of Nature arise in the brilliance of the Pure Consciousness as temporary formations. They are mere reflections without any real substance. Therefore, the objective reality, along with all the objects and phenomena in it, which we experience in our minds and bodies as states (bhavans), such as aging and death, or as pairs of opposites (dvandva), such as heat and cold or as impermanent realities (tattvas), is strictly unreal. They are nonexistent because they are false (mithya), inconsistent, and impermanent, just like the images appearing on a film screen or in a mirror.

In our consciousness, Asat comes into existence when we pay attention, when our mind and senses perceive it, when the Self exists in the body as the witness and enjoys it, or when the duality of subject and object arises in the internal organ (antahkarana) due to the activity of the senses. Perceptions arise from Asat and exist in the mind as formations. They are Asat since they are impermanent and subject to modifications. They cease to exist when the internal organ changes from one state to another or retreats into resting mode (abhava). Since they are mere formations or projections with a beginning and an end, subject to change and impermanence, we cannot say they qualify as Sat. On the contrary, the Self is permanent, stable, and immutable. It does not depend upon any agent or instrument for its existence. It is eternally real and always exists, whether it is perceived or not.

Tattva (tat + tva) Darshana is the vision of That (Tat) Supreme Reality or Brahman as perceived through oneness. Tattva jnana is the knowledge of his reflection (form) in the field of Nature. The seers who have seen the essence of Brahman have the knowledge and discretion to identify the real from the unreal because they know how things appear and disappear in consciousness and how truth exists eternally and immutably beyond the mind and the senses. They know that the Self (bhava) is the cause, while any experience (anubhava) is the effect. They also know that the phenomenal world is made of several tattvas, but the Self is made of only Sat, described by some as shuddha sattva. Knowers of the Self are known as seers because they experience the essence of Brahman (Sat) and see the appearance of things (Asat) by controlling the modifications of their minds and transcending the pairs of opposites.

Sloka 17

avināśi tu tad viddhi yena sarvam idaṃ tatam
vināśam avyayasyāsya na kaścit kartum arhati

avinasi = indestructible; tu = but; tat = that; viddhi = know; yena = by whihc; sarvam = the whole universe; idam = this; tatam = pervaded; vinasam = destruction; avyayasya = of the unchangeable; asya = of this; na=not; kascit = anyone; kartum = to do; arhati = is able.

Know that to be indestructible by which all this is pervaded. None can do the destruction of that unchangeable One.

Lord Krishna wanted Arjuna not to worry about the destruction he might cause in the war because the Self was indestructible. Even if someone died by his arrows, he should know that the Self in that person would remain unscathed. The Self is Sat. It is the indestructible, immutable, eternal, and supreme reality that pervades all. We identify it as Brahman or Atman. It is eternally and continuously permanent, fixed, and constant whether it is present in the jivas (beings) as the embodied Self or in the universe as the Supreme Self or the Supreme Reality, or beyond them as the unknown (nigudha) and the unmanifested (asambhuta). Avyaya means that which is not liable to change, diminish, expend, or does not expand or constrict. It is the nature of things (Asat) to grow, change, wither, age, diminish, wilt, or fade, whereas Sat is not subject to such modifications. It is always complete, unyielding, constant, all-pervading, and independent of time and space. In contrast, the objective or the not-self reality is Asat and depends upon them for existence. Even at the time of the final dissolution (pralaya) of all the worlds, Sat is immutable and indestructible. The Vedas affirm that it is always as it is, is always complete, and remains full even if you take something out of it or add something to it. Our essential nature is Sat, while our bodies are Asat. If we abide in Sat, we cultivate nearness with it and become dissolved in it. However, if we are drawn to Asat and become involved with it, the fact that it is impermanent and unstable will subject us to modifications and suffering.

Sloka 18

antavanta ime dehā nityasyoktāḥ śarīriṇaḥ
anāśinoprameyasya tasmād yudhyasva bhārata

anta-vantah = have an end; ime = these; dehah = bodies; nityasya = eternal; uktah = said; saririnah = the embodied; anasinah = indestructible; aprameyasya = unprovable, immeasurable, unknowable; tasmat = therefore; yudhyasva = fight; bharata = Bharata.

These bodies of the embodied Self, which is said to be eternal, indestructible, and unknowable, have an end. Therefore, O Bharata, fight.

The Self in the body is eternal (nitya) and indestructible (anasina). Although both words suggest the eternal and immutable nature of the Self, there is a subtle difference between them. Nitya means continuous, uninterrupted, perpetual, or without any break. It is a positive word. Anasinah means devoid of destruction or immune to destruction. It is a negative word. According to Shankaracharya, the two words have been used here to juxtapose the state of the Self to the two types of destruction to which beings or their bodies are usually subject: complete and partial. In the first, the bodies are destroyed wholly without any residue left, as in the case of their destruction by fire. In the second type, parts of the body may die or wither away or change due to disease or starvation, whereby the original healthy body is lost or destroyed or ceases to exist and is not the same as the previous one. The Self is not subject to these types of destruction. It is also said to be aprameya, which means it is unknowable or immeasurable or without a knower, object, basis, or cause (prameya). In other words, the Self cannot be measured, known, or proven to others by any independent means. It is self-evident, self-knowable, self-accomplished, or known by itself (svatah siddha) without the mediation of any external or internal agent such as the senses, the mind, intelligence, or the internal organ. Thus, it being Sat, the Self is indestructible and different from the body, which is Asat. Eventually, the body will be destroyed due to age, disease, natural events, fate, or acts of God. Therefore, Lord Krishna advised Arjuna to fight and not worry about the death or destruction he might cause in the war. This was the first reason or justification he gave to Arjuna why he should fight.

Sloka 19

ya enaṃ vetti hantāraṃ yaś cainaṃ manyate hatam
ubhau tau na vijānīto nāyaṃ hanti na hanyate

yah = he who; enam = this; vetti = knows; hantaram = the killer, slayer, destroyer; yah = he who; ca = and; enam = this; manyate = thinks; hatam = killed; ubhau = both; tau = they; na = not; vijanitah = know; na = not; ayam = this; hanti = kills; na = not; hanyate = is killed.

He who knows this as the killer and he who thinks this as the one killed, both of them do not know that this does not kill and cannot be killed.

In this verse, he gives the second reason why Arjuna must fight. The Self does not perform or participate in any actions and is not subject to death or destruction. Therefore, anyone who thinks that the Self is the agent of any action or is subject to the actions of any other agent is ignorant. The Self neither causes anything to happen nor is it affected by any cause. It is eternal, independent, and self-existing. According to the Vedas, the Self does not engage in any action, nor can it be propelled into action by anything else. It remains passive in the being and witnesses the actions and modifications of the mind and body without taking part in them and without being tainted by them. It neither approves nor disapproves nor judges anything. It cannot be killed because it is Sat, which is eternal and indestructible. When the body is destroyed, it leaves the body but remains unchanged. However, this does not mean we have the license to kill the jivas indiscriminately. Wanton destruction of life simply because the Self is indestructible is not permitted by our shastras. It is also not approved by the code of conduct they prescribe, according to which non-injury (ahimsa) is the highest virtue to which all other virtues lead. Without practicing nonviolence, we cannot engage in righteousness (Dharma) or achieve liberation.

However, the principle of nonviolence does not hold well on the battlefield when a warrior is called to fight. On that occasion, he has an obligatory duty to fight and follow his king's or commander's commands. When fighting becomes obligatory, he should not worry about causing death or injury to others or being killed or injured by them. He should remain steadfast in his duty, knowing that death and destruction are for the body, not the Self. This knowledge or awareness should help him overcome any anxiety, guilt, or fear of sin he may experience while fighting. The physical self (or the ego self) engages in actions due to desires and attachments. It is also the physical self that is subject to the actions of other agents. The Self supports the body but does not participate in its activities. The ego, which is but a reflection (pratibimba) of the Self in the mirror of Prakriti (Nature), takes control of the mind and body and propels them into action. It should not be mistaken for the Self. One should live with the mind firmly established in the Self, knowing the distinction between the two and that all actions and modifications happen in the body, with the body acting as their agent, in which the Self does not participate.

Sloka 20

na jāyate mriyate vā kadācin nāyaṃ abhūtvā bhavitā vā na bhūyaḥ
ajo nityaḥ śāśvatoyaṃ purāṇo na hanyate hanyamāne śarīre

na = not; jayate = born; mriyate = dies; va = either; kadacit = at any time; na = not; ayam = this; abhutva = not existed in the past; abhavita = not exist in future; va = or; na = not; bhuyah = the state of becoming; ajah = unborn; nityah = eternal; sasvatah = permanent; ayam = this; puranah = the most ancient; na = never; hanyate = is killed; hanyamane = being killed; sarire = body.

This one is not born, nor does it ever die. At no time was it nonexistent in the past, nor will it be nonexistent in the future, nor will it become existent again. Unborn, eternal, permanent, and ancient, this is not killed when the body is killed.

The eternal and indestructible nature of the Self is repeated in this verse to contrast it with the impermanent and changeable nature of the body, using the six states of distortions or transformations (bhava vikaras) to which Nature and the gross body are subject because unlike the Self, which is indivisible and without parts, they are divisible and made up of parts. The six transformative states to which beings are subject are (1) birth (jayate), (2) the current state of being (asti), (3) growth (vriddhi), (4) change (viparinama),

(5) decay (apakshaya), and (6) death (mrityu) or destruction (nasyati). The phenomenal world also has these six vikaras, which are illusory, temporary, and unreal and arise due to the modes (gunas) and Nature's primordial parts or categories (tattvas) from which all animate and inanimate forms arise in the Field of Prakriti. They do not exist in the Self, which is one, eternally constant, and free from modifications and transient states. The Self also does not exist in them while living in the beings as their indweller. The body is nonexistent before birth and will be nonexistent again after death. It comes into existence when it is born and then exposed to various modifications and states of being, such as growth, aging, sickness, death, etc. All material things are subject to these six distortions (vikaras), but the Self is not subject to them. The body's impermanence is mentioned twice in this verse with two verbs, mriyate and hanyate. According to Shankaracharya, they are not repetitive or synonymous. Mriyate alludes to the mortality of the body, and hanyate to the destructibility of the body. The Self is free from both of them.

Sloka 21

vedāvināśinaṃ nityaṃ ya enam ajam avyayam
kathaṃ sa puruṣaḥ pārtha kaṃ ghātayati hanti kam

veda = knows; avinasinam = indestructible; nityam = eternal; yah = who; enam = this self; ajam = unborn; avyayam = inexhaustible; katham = how; sah = he; purusah = person; partha = O Partha; kam = whom; ghatayati = cause to kill; hanti = kill; kam = whom.

Whoever knows that this Self is indestructible, eternal, unborn, and inexhaustible, how can that person, O Partha, kill or cause to kill?

The previous verse explained that the eternal and indestructible Self would not perform any actions, nor would it cause any action to be performed by others. We also learned that the Self is not subject to transitional states (bhava vikaras) of impermanence, change, and destructibility. It is free from desires, obligation, dependence, qualities, or functions, does not perform actions or cause others to perform them, is independent, self-existent, and unlimited by time or space. From that, it naturally follows that the Self is passive and does not engage in actions by itself or through any agencies (upadhis). It is neither an agent of actions nor the cause of actions by other agents. Thus, what is stated in this verse is a logical conclusion of what we learned before about the Self. The Self does not participate in the modifications of Nature, nor does it cause them. These words of Krishna also contain the hidden message that actions have no bearing upon the enlightened ones. Being the knowers of the Self, neither Arjuna nor Krishna would incur sin if Arjuna fought his enemies or Krishna encouraged him to do so. Since Krishna taught Arjuna about the Self, Arjuna was also qualified as an enlightened one. The meaning of "how can that person…kill or cause to kill" is how can that person, who knows the Self is indestructible, kill the Self? He knows that with the body's death, the Self does not die.

If you think you are a physical being and view life from a material perspective, you will not appreciate this idea. You will be disturbed by the modifications of your mind and body, such as aging, death, sickness, fear, anger, etc. However, if you think you are an eternal soul, fear of death will not disturb you. You will regard it with detachment as a modification in which the Self (you) does not participate. Those who know the Self discern that they do not participate in any actions of the mind and body, knowing that they act according to their natural propensities (prakriti dharma). They also practice nonviolence, the foremost of all virtues, as an obligatory duty. Traditional commentators of Patanjali's Yogasutras, such as Vyasa, opined that nonviolence is the root of all other virtues, and they are subservient to it. However, they agree it should not hamper anyone from performing their ordained duties. If you take up the duty of protecting and upholding your dharma, circumstances may force you to fight for your sake, for God, or for those you love. Thus, although nonviolence is the highest ideal, it should not be an obstacle for a warrior or a knower of the Self to perform his duties. Gods such as Lord Vishnu, Lord Shiva, or even Mother Kali perform their duties in this manner and exemplify karma yoga.

When they engage in wars with the demons and slay them with great fury, they are not consumed by violent passions or viciousness. They do it with equanimity and sameness, even though outwardly, they may appear fierce as a part of their duties to protect and uphold Dharma or instill fear in them. Even if they are forced to kill the evil ones in a battle, they do so without anger and vengeance and with a nonviolent attitude since they know that the fury that they unleash upon them is for the welfare of the world and whatever destruction they cause is confined to the bodies which are impure, perishable and renewable. Violence has no place in their consciousness or essential nature. Through their duties, they exemplify that nonviolence is the culmination of attaining purification and perfection (siddhi) in karma yoga. At the same time, they convey that one must not be afraid to perform duties for Dharma's sake. In the mortal world, only great souls, who are blemishless and self-restrained, exemplify it through their actions. Lord Parasurama is considered an incarnation of Lord Vishnu. He lived like a sage and exemplified the highest virtues. At the same time, he fought many battles to restore Dharma and destroyed all the Kshatriya kings of his time who fell into evil ways.

Sloka 22

vāsāṃsi jīrṇāni yathā vihāya navāni gṛhṇāti naroparāṇi
tathā śarīrāṇi vihāya jīrṇāni anyāni saṃyāti navāni dehī

vasamsi = clothes; jirnani = torn, worn out; yatha = just as; vihaya = discards; navani = new; grhnati = accepts; narah = a person; aparani = various, several different; tatha = in that way; sarirani = bodies; vihaya = discards; jirnani = worn out, aged; anyani = another; samyati = obtains, gets, receives, accepts; navani = new; dehi = the embodied.

Just as a person discards worn-out clothes and wears several different ones, in the same manner, the embodied Self discards the aged and worn-out bodies and obtains new ones.

This is one of Bhagavadgita's most widely discussed, debated, and quoted verses in which the idea of the transmigration of the Self, which forms the core of Hindu beliefs, is affirmed. With some variations, it is also a core belief of Buddhism and Jainism. The body is compared to a cloth worn by the Self. Just like a cloth, it is subject to wear and tear. The comparison ends here. While you can wear as many clothes as you wish, you can wear only one body in each life. Maybe people may develop a new technology a hundred years from now to discard an old body and wear a new one in the same life. Current scientific and technological developments indicate that we are slowly moving in that direction. Some people want to preserve their bodies after death so they can return to life if a new technology is developed. While we do not know the full implications of these developments and how one can revive and regenerate a worn-out body, we know that Nature has already incorporated a similar mechanism through rebirth to ensure the continuity of the jivas upon the earth without breaking them down mentally and physically and without disrupting the natural flow of life.

After stating previously that the Self was eternal, indestructible, and not an agent of action or the cause of action, in contrast to the body, which was perishable and mutable, Lord Krishna now said that the body was just a covering or a clothe for the Self, which it would wear and discard in each life during its transmigration from one birth to the next. Thus, he contrasted the body's impermanence with the Self's permanence. Many scholars of the Bhagavadgita frequently quote the verse in support of rebirth or transmigration of souls. It is also ideal for contemplation to cultivate detachment towards the body and abide in the Self. The Upanishads suggest that by thinking, "Not this, not this," while contemplating upon the body, one can become detached from it and realize the true nature of Brahman.

By bringing up the subject of reincarnation of the Self, Lord Krishna addressed the doubts and concerns raised by Arjuna about killing his opponents on the battlefield. Through these assuring words, he clarified that death and decay were for the body but not for the Self, and it was natural for each of the jivas to assume a new body in each birth and start a new life afresh with renewed vigor and a unique opportunity to unchain itself from samsara. The idea that the transmigration is for the embodied one only, but not for the liberated Self, is made amply clear by the word "dehi." The use of aparani (various or different) indicates that the Self may live in many different kinds of bodies during its existence on Earth.

According to the Vedas, the souls that return to the earth from ancestral heaven may take birth as humans, animals, or other creatures according to their karma. Those who perform their duties and live virtuously take birth in good families and favorable circumstances. The vilest ones may not qualify for rebirth and languish in the lowest hells for a long time until their sins are cleansed. Human birth is rare and attained after several births and deaths. The Vedas also affirm that rebirth is for those who fail to cleanse their karmas. Those who do so will attain liberation and never return to the earth. They remain forever in the immortal world of Brahman.

Sloka 23

nainaṃ chindanti śastrāṇi nainaṃ dahati pāvakaḥ
na cainaṃ kledayanty āpo na śoṣayati mārutaḥ

na = not; enam = this, he; chindanti = cut, divide, pierce; sastrani = weapons; na = not; enam = this; dahati = burn; pavakah = fire; na = never; ca = and; enam = this; kledayanti = soak, moisten; apah = water; na = not; sosayati = dries; marutah = wind.

Weapons cannot cut or pierce this; fire cannot burn this; water cannot wet this; and wind cannot dry it.

The indivisibility, indestructibility, immateriality, and immutability of the Self, its superiority and invincibility over the elements of Nature, and its distinction from the body, which is made of these elements, are reemphasized in this verse, using the agents that can potentially harm or destroy the body, namely weapons, fire, water, and wind. The Self is whole and indivisible. Hence, it cannot be cut into pieces by any weapon. Since it has no parts or elements, it is not subject to decay or decomposition. Since it is indestructible, it cannot be destroyed by the elements such as fire, water, and wind. Since it is immaterial, the elements have no power to control it. These statements reemphasize that the Self remains intact even when the body is destroyed, divided, burned, drowned, or blown away. It does not undergo any change due to any of these causes while wandering from one body to another. In other words, transmigration is for the Self, and transformation is for the body. Also, during transmigration, the Self remains unaffected.

Sloka 24

acchedyoyam adāhyoyam akledyośoṣya eva ca
nityaḥ sarvagataḥ sthāṇur acaloyaṃ sanātanaḥ

acchedyah = impervious, impenetrable; ayam = this; adahyah = incombustible; ayam = this; akledyah = insoluble; asosyah = unparchable; eva = certainly; ca = and; nityah = eternal; sarva-gatah = all-pervading; sthanuh = constant, fixed; acalah = immovable; ayam = this; sanatanah = perpetual, everlasting.

This is impenetrable, incombustible, insoluble, and undryable. Certainly, this is eternal, all-pervading, constant, immovable, and everlasting.

Eight distinct attributes (upadhis) of the Self are mentioned in this verse. Each of them is complementary to denote the eternal and indestructible nature of the Self. While these statements are seemingly repetitive, Lord Krishna wanted to reemphasize the immortality and indestructibility of the Self against the known agents of destruction to ensure that Arjuna clearly understood the nature of the Self without doubts. Sometimes, we must repeat the same information in various ways to reinforce it in the listener's mind and clear all doubts and questions about it. This verse affirms that the eternal Self is immune to the elements and forces of Nature and cannot be destroyed by any known methods or means. They have no power over it and cannot transform or destroy it. Therefore, he said it is impenetrable, insoluble, and cannot be dried or destroyed. It is also all-pervading. Yet, unlike wind, which moves everywhere, it remains fixed and immovable. In other words, although it is spread everywhere (sarvagatah), it is eternally true (sat), fixed (sthanu), and does not change with time or place, now or in the future. It is also invisible, while it is the seer, the witness in the body. We do not know how it looks or where it exists in the body or the universe. Whatever information we have about it is from the scriptures. Therefore, there is every possibility that we may not understand what it is unless our teachers and scriptures clearly describe it with necessary examples and clarifications. Lord Krishna did the same here since he wanted Arjuna to understand the nature and reality of the Self and overcome his ignorance and delusion about death and destruction.

Sloka 25

avyaktoyam acintyoyam avikaryoyam ucyate
tasmād evaṃ viditvainaṃ nānuśocitum arhasi 2.25

avyaktah = unmanifested, invisible; ayam = this; acintyah = unreachable by thought, incomprehensible; ayam = this; avikaryah = unchangeable; ayam = this; ucyate = said to be; tasmat = therefore; evam = thus, like this; viditva = knowing well; enam = this; na = not; anusocitum = grieve, repent; arhasi = deserve.

Unmanifested is this; unreachable by thought is this; unchangeable is said to be this. Therefore, knowing well, thus, this is not fit to be grieved.

In the previous verse, Lord Krishna described a few upadhis (attributes) of the Self, stating that it was indivisible, unburnable, insoluble, undryable, eternal, all-pervading, etc. Here, he added a few more to highlight its immortal, immutable, and imperishable nature. He said that the Self was unmanifest or unexpressed, unthinkable, and unchangeable. He used these descriptions of the Self to convince Arjuna that he should not worry about the death and destruction of the bodies on the battlefield since the souls in them were eternal, indestructible, and impervious to our actions. The Self does not appear in samsara and cannot be seen because it is immaterial and transcendental and is neither an object nor a subject nor a connecting link. Hence, although it is all-pervading, it is unmanifest, cannot be seen, and is beyond the mind's and senses' grasp. Second, it is entirely detached from the mind. Hence, it is also unthinkable, inconceivable, and indescribable. You can only speak about it in symbols or metaphors and discern his presence through actions. Next, it is also not subject to any bhava-vikaras or modifications of state, nature, or condition. Therefore, it is unchangeable (avikarya). However, without his presence in the body, they do not happen.

These attributes suggest that the Self is eternally as it is. Neither worldly events nor your thoughts nor your actions will impact it. If you are steeped in your mind-body awareness and identify yourself with your physical nature or name and form, you will not grasp the true meaning of these statements. To truly understand them, you must center yourself in your higher nature and acknowledge your pure Self as your true identity. Then only you will know what they mean.

It should be clear by now that the Self is unlike anything we know in the physical world and belongs to a different realm or dimension. You cannot reach, touch, or influence it with your actions, thoughts, words, prayers, magic, or mantras. You cannot draw it into any equation or relation or involve it in your schemes, designs, or enjoyments. It is your silent witness when you are steeped in duality, but yourself when you overcome it and attain oneness. It serves as your inmost support and the highest ideal or goal. Although it is beyond your reach, its presence in your body facilitates the transcendental state of oneness through self-absorption. At the same time, you should not mistake it for something other than you.

The Self is you only in utter silence. You are the Self. This is the truth, although it may seem confusing because you think of it with duality. Your mind and body, and all their parts or divisions, are meant to serve you since you are their lord. Although they are connected to you through your body, you are beyond their grasp. They do not know that you exist, but they perform their functions to facilitate your existence. You do not belong to them, anything here, your body, or this world. As the pure Self from the highest realm, as pure consciousness and Brahman himself, you are beyond the gods. These words have been repeated by every jnani and in every age. At this stage in your life, you may not understand or accept it, but someday you will, and that day will be significant in your life. Those who have realized it and abide in that thought have better chances of attaining oneness and entering the Supreme Reality. They will not incur sin even if they engage in actions since, by that thought alone, they wash away all sins.

The Self in the body should not be confused with Isvara, the Lord of the Universe and the Supreme Controller. He possesses a universal body, filled with the finest shaktis and supreme qualities, which, unlike in our case, is always under his inviolable control. He is different from you, but the Self in both may be the same. He is also not subject to samsara and is different from the jivas. The worlds and all the beings are part of his body only. They constitute his lower nature or the gross body, while their souls or selves constitute his higher nature or subtle body. Different from them is his pure Self, whose nature is pure consciousness, just as the Self in us. They exist in him, partaking in his essential nature until they fully merge in him. Therefore, while the Self is passive and inactive, the Lord is active and responsive due to his association with Prakriti. Your prayers and supplications will not move the Self in him or you, but the Lord will.

Sloka 26

atha cainaṃ nityajātaṃ nityaṃ vā manyase mṛtam
tathāpi tvaṃ mahābāho naivaṃ śocitum arhasi 2.26

atha = if, otherwise; ca = and; enam = this; nitya-jatam = born continuously; nityam = eternally; va = or; manyase = think; mrtam = dies; tatha api = even; tvam = you; maha-baho = O mighty-armed one; na =not; evam = thus; socitum = grieve, lament; arhasi = deserve.

Otherwise, if you think that this is born continuously or dies constantly, even then, O mighty armed one, this is not to be repented for.

In this verse, Lord Krishna used a counterpoint to address the incongruity of the human intellect in making sense of the essential nature of the Self, which was beyond the grasp of the mind and the senses. In the previous verse, he declared that the Self was incomprehensible to human thought (achintyam). That incomprehensibility can lead to speculation, confusion, arguments, and counterarguments. Therefore, ancient scholars used various approaches and counterarguments to support or refute their standpoints or those of others. For example, some schools of ancient India believed that the Self was neither eternal nor indivisible nor indestructible but a temporary formation or aggregation of parts that imparted to the being its individuality, consciousness, and egoism (anavatva). Buddhism does not accept that souls are eternal or indestructible. It believes in the transmigration of subtle or causal bodies (the not-self), rather than eternal souls, from one birth to another until they are dissolved into nothingness through the practice of Dharma. The Chārvakas or the Lokāyatas were atheists who believed that the Self of a being died along with the body at the time of death, and it neither transmigrated to another body nor survived death. For them, death was salvation. Lord Krishna adopted a counterview that was probably prevalent in his time, according to which beings eternally and repetitively went through numerous births and deaths without ever attaining liberation or a permanent escape from samsara. He might have done it to convince Arjuna that even if he assumed that the Self passed through many births and deaths or died along with the body at the time of death, there was no need for lamentation because in the natural order of things that which died would be reborn in the next life and that which was born in this life would die anyway at some point.

Sloka 27

jātasya hi dhruvo mṛtyur dhruvaṃ janma mṛtasya ca
tasmād aparihāryerthe na tvaṃ śocitum arhasi

jatasya = For the one who is born; hi = indeed, surely; dhruvah = certain; mrtyuh = death; dhruvam = certain; janma = birth; mrtasya = for the dead; ca = and; tasmat = therefore; apariharye = that which is unavoidable; arthe = regarding; na = not; tvam = you; socitum = lament; arhasi = deserve.

For the born, indeed, death is certain, and for the dead, birth is certain. Therefore, regarding that which is unavoidable, you should not grieve.

We may not know anything about the Self because it is invisible, ungraspable, and unthinkable. However, we know that whoever is born here is bound to die someday. None can escape death. It is an irrefutable fact, at least for now, because we do not know what new inventions and technologies may be available to prolong the lifespan of beings on Earth in the future. When we know that death is inevitable and cannot be avoided, what is the use of worrying about it? We should accept it and get on with our lives. Although we know that we are bound to die someday, we are conditioned by the world to live in denial of it and live with such optimism as if death is not going to happen to us. The right thing to do is to make the best use of our time on earth and focus on our essential goals to achieve peace and happiness, improve our character and conduct, and prepare for the next life or liberation. Lord Krishna said that Arjuna should not worry about the deaths on the battlefield since it was an inevitable fact of war and life on earth.

While we know that everyone is bound to die, we are unsure whether those who die will be reborn. For us who depend upon the mind and senses for knowledge and evidence, it is a possibility, a belief, or an illogical assumption. Our scriptures suggest that when we are unsure about transcendental truths and have no personal experience or factual evidence, we should look for corroborating evidence in the scriptures, which contain the words of God, and accept them as verbal testimony (sabda pramana). For ages, the Vedas have been considered the words of God and the final say in ascertaining metaphysical truths. They affirm that the bound souls depart from here to the ancestral world upon death. After exhausting their karma, they take another birth when they return from there. They also explain the whole process of the journey of the souls to the next world and their return and rebirth. It is true that although Hindus believe in rebirth, most of them lament the death of their friends and relatives. It is one of the incongruent tendencies that betray our ignorance, weak faith, or the lack of it. In an ideal world, we would have accepted birth and death as the two facets of life and responded to death with equanimity or the awareness that the soul had temporarily escaped from samsara and suffering.

Sloka 28

avyaktādīni bhūtāni vyaktamadhyāni bhārata
avyaktanidhanāny eva tatra kā paridevanā

avyakta = unmanifested; adinin= in the beginning; bhutani =beings, elemental selves; vyakta = manifested; madhyani = in the middle; bharata = Bharata; avyakta = unmanifested; nidhanani = upon destruction; eva = also; tatra = then, for that; ka = what; paridevana = lamentation, complaint, wailing.

Beings are unmanifest in the beginning, manifest in the middle, and O Bharata, are unmanifest again in the end upon their death. Then, where is the reason to grieve?

All living beings have a beginning and an end; they appear and disappear at each birth. One should not grieve for the loss of mortal life because the life that is gone will return in another form. Instead, one should rejoice that life is eternal and the Self has no birth and death. This is the essence of this verse. The Self exists eternally on the scale of infinity. It exists before life forms come into existence and after they all die. It exists forever, through all cycles of creation, unchanged and undiminished.

However, the same is not true about life or a jiva's beingness or its whole persona. Life on Earth and probably elsewhere is a temporary phenomenon both at the cosmic level and at the level of each individual. It is an aberration from the perspective of eternity because it does not exist everywhere or forever, and appears only under certain circumstances and ideal conditions. In contrast, the Self is all-pervading and eternal. Brahman, the Supreme Self, is always unmanifest, indestructible, and fixed. His cosmic manifestation as Isvara, the Cosmic Being (Purusha), who is identified with Lord Brahma in the Vedas and with Lord Vishnu and Shiva in the Puranas, is also all-pervading. However, he is active for the duration of each time cycle only. He, too, like the beings, appears and disappears. The material universe is his body or beingness, with Brahman as his Self. He appears at the time of creation and goes into resting mode at dissolution. So is the case with life on earth.

Life does not exist and is impossible when Isvara is asleep, and Prakriti in him remains undifferentiated and dormant. As the Creation Hymn in the Rigveda declares, in the beginning (when Brahman alone existed and was unmanifest), there was nothing whatsoever, neither the sky, the earth, the heavens, nor the divinities. That One alone existed, immersed in itself and all by itself, without qualities and dualities. Everything manifested from That One Supreme Self, including Isvara and all the beings. Beings will become nonexistent again when they achieve liberation or when Isvara withdraws them into himself. Thus, beings come and go. The birth and death, or the coming and going, of mortal beings are natural, cosmic processes. There is no point in worrying about them because the natural order of life on earth can neither be stopped nor prevented.

At the individual level, we see the movement of the souls through the revolving door of transmigration. They come and go as objects in a magic show. They exist on Earth for a while and disappear. If you think calmly, nothing is truly destroyed in this process except names and forms. Of the Purusha and Prakriti, the source of all this diversity, Purusha remains unaffected during these changes at the cosmic level as well in each being, while Prakriti undergoes modifications. In the end, they withdraw everything into themselves. The seers and the sages are aware that the disappearance of names and forms is a transient phenomenon, just as the rising and falling of the waves upon the surface of an ocean. Now, imagine if we start worrying about each wave as it rises and falls. There will be no end to our sorrow. Lord Krishna, therefore, advised Arjuna not to worry about the coming and going of the individual souls since they are untouched by mortality or modifications.

For the living beings, the manifested ones, birth follows death, and death follows rebirth as certainly as dawn follows dusk. Impermanence, instability, and destruction are inherent in mortal life. At its best, their existence in jivas or association with the manifested Prakriti (sambhuta) is a temporary phenomenon or a passing phase in the journey of souls upon earth. It is similar to the dream state, which lasts for a while and disappears as if it never happened. Philosophically, therefore, there is no justification for grieving for that (the body), which does not last and does not matter in the end. Know that you are currently in your manifested state. Your life is short. Someday, you will become unmanifested again and await your rebirth. Therefore, before it happens, make the best use of your life and work for your transformation and liberation, taking refuge in God.

Sloka 29

āścaryavat paśyati kaścid enam āścaryavad vadati tathaiva cānyaḥ
āścaryavac cainam anyaḥ śṛṇoti śrutvāpy enaṃ veda na caiva kaścit

ascarya-vat = as amazing, wonderful; pasyati = see; kascit = one; enam = it or this; ascarya-vat = amazing; vadati = speak; tatha =similarly; eva = indeed; ca = and; anyah = another; ascarya-vat = as wonderful or amazing; ca = and; enam = this; anyah = others; srnoti = hear; srutva = having heard; api = even; enam = this; veda = do know; na = never; ca = and; eva = at all, certainly; kascit = anyone.

One beholds it as wonderful; similarly, indeed, another speaks of it as wonderful, and another hears of it as wonderful. Yet, having heard, no one knows it at all.

This verse speaks about the incomprehensibility or the unknowability of the transcendental Self with intellectual effort or through the senses. Even those pure ones (sattvikas) who worship and marvel at him do not know him. This is the essence. Usually, we learn about material things by seeing, sensing, studying, or knowing them through inference, imagination, comparison, etc. About the Self, all our methods of knowing and grasping are useless because the Self exists by itself and is detached from everything in creation. In the state of duality, it is unknowable and ungraspable for the human mind. You may know about it in a state of unity or Self-absorption (samadhi). Still, you cannot recreate that experience in your wakeful state, just as you cannot remember anything that happens when you are deeply asleep. You may have a vague idea of how you perceived the Self when you entered the transcendental state (turya) by chance or effort, but you may find it difficult to articulate, remember, or understand it. A limited intelligence cannot comprehend an absolute and infinite truth, just as you cannot fit an ocean inside a small bottle or an earthen jar. You may grasp its essence but not its entirety or immensity.

In the Upanishads, we hear that even the seers who realized it by themselves or the students who learned about it from teachers recognized the difficulty of knowing the Self through intellectual means. The Self is not an object that can be objectified and studied as a model or concept; it is beyond the mind and senses. Therefore, it cannot be known objectively or logically. To know it, one needs to subdue the senses and empty the mind of all thoughts and opinions, leaving no trace of egoism, pride, envy, attachment, desires, etc. When the mind is completely still and free from all attachments, impurities, modifications, and latent impressions, one comes within the proximity of the Self in purity and experiences oneness, which may be permanent or temporary. Even then, the experience may remain vague and incomplete if the transformation is incomplete or the surrender is insincere. The Yogasutras state that the Self can be known by meditating upon it as Aum. Since everyone cannot silence the mind or enter samyama (concentrated meditation), only a few people attain the knowledge of the Self or oneness with it. The rest must be satisfied with what they learn about Him from the scriptures or their teachers.

Sloka 30

dehī nityam avadhyoyaṃ dehe sarvasya bhārata
tasmāt sarvāṇi bhūtāni na tvaṃ śocitum arhasi

dehi = the indweller of the body; nityamavadhyah = can never be slaughtered; ayam = this; dehe = in the body; sarvasya = in all; bharata = Bharata; tasmat = therefore; sarvani = all; bhutani = living beings; na = not; tvam = you; socitum = worry, grieve; arhasi = deserve.

This eternal indweller of the body who dwells in the bodies of all can never be slain, O Bharata. Therefore, it is not fit for you to grieve for any living being.

Once again, Lord Krishna drew a clear distinction between the body and the Self to remind Arjuna that he should not worry about the death of any living being because its indweller, the Self, was imperishable. Therefore, he implied that it would be delusional to worry about the death and destruction of anyone who might die in his hands on the battlefield. The body serves the soul as its vehicle or a cloth. Therefore, one should not become attached to it or cry when the Self departs from it. The thought of death should not disturb anyone who knows the distinction between the body and the Self. We already discussed that it is ignorance to cry when someone dies. Those who know that death is for the body but not for the Self should not at all grieve for the death of anyone. They should rejoice in the awareness that the soul is on its way home. The Self is immortal, and death is a phase in its passage into another existence or dimension, from where it will surely return one day. Therefore, devotees who worship gods and believe in the scriptures should accept birth and death as natural and recurring events in the transmigration of souls. When they see someone dead or dying, be it human or any other living being, they should pray for their liberation or safe return to the earth. They should have the same attitude towards themselves as well.

Sloka 31

svadharmam api cāvekṣya na vikampitum arhasi
dharmyād dhi yuddhāc chreyonyat kṣatriyasya na vidyate

sva-dharmam = one own duty; api = also; ca = indeed; aveksya = considering; na = not; vikampitum = to tremble, waver, hesitate; arhasi = deserve; dharmyat = with regard to duty; hi = in fact, indeed; yuddhat = than fighting; sreyah = better; anyat = no other; ksatriyasya = of a ksatriya, warrior; na = not; vidyate = is, exists.

Further, looking to your duty also, you should not tremble. Indeed, with regard to duty, nothing else is better for a warrior than fighting.

So far, Lord Krishna had debated why Arjuna should fight on moral and spiritual grounds and not worry about the death or destruction he might cause, since the Self is indestructible. In this verse, he extended the same argument, but from a worldly perspective, saying a warrior had no better duty (Dharma) than fighting. In this and the subsequent seven verses, he explained why Arjuna must fight to uphold his obligatory duty. Having discussed the metaphysical aspects of life and death and the eternal nature of the Self, he reminded him that for a Kshatriya, there was no better Dharma or duty than fighting. When called upon to fight, he should not be afraid of upholding his Kshatriya Dharma.

Some people wrongly interpret that the Bhagavadgita promotes violence and encourages people to fight wars or indulge in acts of violence. It is untrue. Since Arjuna was the subject and the occasion was war, one may get the impression. Bhagavadgita's primary focus is on duty, devotion, and selfless actions, not violence or war. The Kurukshetra War was chosen as the background because it is a part of the Mahabharata and appears in the section that deals with the war. Secondly, from a human perspective, fighting in a war is one of the most challenging and unpleasant tasks or duties one can imagine. Wars illustrate the violence and brutality inherent in human conflicts where force is involved. They also create many moral dilemmas since they cannot easily be justified or judged as moral or immoral. Further, life is also a war, and we fight battles every day, though not of the violent kind. The knowledge and wisdom found in it can be suitably applied to our daily lives and struggles.

Hence, the background chosen for the discourse is very appropriate to illustrate the importance of upholding one's obligatory duties, however difficult or unpleasant they may be. The scripture also clarifies that events such as the Kurukshetra war happened due to divine will, and humans are mere role-players in it. Its primary focus is on selfless duty, sacrifice, and devotion to God. All the yogas mentioned in it are meant to prepare humans to represent these eternal values. Warriors do not have the license to kill anyone, but when called upon to do so, they must perform their duties for their side or the king they serve without wavering. According to the principles of Dharma, self-defense is also an obligatory duty. The law books approve it. Everyone has the duty and the right to protect themselves, their families, and their dependents from aggression and external threats. Even tiny organisms have a right to life. However, the law books prohibit violence for violence's sake or hurting and harming others with selfish or evil intentions. In Hinduism, nonviolence is the highest virtue. As the adage goes, nonviolence is the foremost duty (ahimsa paramodharamah) of everyone.

Sloka 32

yadṛcchayā copapannaṃ svargadvāram apāvṛtam
sukhinaḥ kṣatriyāḥ pārtha labhante yuddham īdṛśam

yadrcchaya = happening by fate, chance or coincidence; ca = and; upapannam = happened; svarga = heaven; dvaram = door; apavrtam = open; sukhinah = happy; ksatriyah = warrior; partha = Partha; labhante = get, obtain, attain; yuddham = war; idrsam = like this.

Happy are the warriors, O Partha, who obtain (a chance to fight in) a war such as this, which presents itself by fate and opens the doors of heaven (for them).

Those who love their work feel happy whenever they have an opportunity to excel. They keep an open mind and face life's challenges with courage. A righteous war is an opportunity for warriors like Arjuna to prove their courage and fighting skills. When an opportunity to fight arises fortuitously (yadrcchaya), they readily use it to prove their mettle and qualify for heaven. Lord Krishna reminded Arjuna that the Kurukshetra war offered him an opportunity to excel in his duty and fulfill his obligation to the people who depended on him for support or protection. Circumstances beyond his control brought him to the battlefield. He should not throw away that opportunity and fail in his obligatory duty. Even though he had to fight his relations on the other side, he should fight since his duty was to protect his side and ensure victory. This is an important lesson for all, not just warriors. When opportunities arise to excel in our professions, we should take them up. Chance plays an important role in our lives. Much of what happens to us happens due to chance or random events rather than what we wish to happen. Many events in our lives happen due to chance only. Therefore, when tough situations arise against our wishes or expectations, we should deal with them with discernment. If we are attentive, they also teach us many valuable lessons.

Sloka 33

atha cet tvam imaṃ dhārmyaṃ saṅgrāmaṃ na kariṣyasi
tataḥ svadharmaṃ kīrtiṃ ca hitvā pāpam avāpsyasi

atha = now, here, so also; cet = if; tvam = you; imam = this; dharmyam = righteous, dutiful; sangramam = battle, fighting, war; na = not; karisyasi = fight, do; tatah = then; sva-dharmam = own duty; kirtim = fame, reputation; ca = and; hitva = thrown away; papam = sin; avapsyasi = gain, incur, attain.

Now, if you do not fight this righteous war, then you will be casting away your duty and reputation and incur sin.

Previously, in the first chapter, Arjuna was anxious about three consequences that might arise if he fought in the war: death and destruction, dishonor and decline of the family, and sinful karma. Here, Lord Krishna told him that if he failed to uphold his duty as a Kshatriya, he would face similar consequences. By not fighting in the war which presented itself to him by chance and abandoning his duty, he would lose an opportunity to attain heaven, throw away his reputation, and incur sin. According to the Vedic Dharma, a warrior must fight when needed or when called upon. In Arjuna's case, it was his essential duty (svadharma) since he was born as a Kshatriya. He was supposed to fight in that righteous war (dharmyam) for righteous reasons to uphold Dharma and destroy the evil Kauravas. Therefore, a lot was at stake. If he avoided it, he would incur the triple sin of abandoning his essential duty and a righteous war as a Kshatriya and upholder of Dharma, and not protecting those he was bound to protect. Further, it would displease the gods who bestowed upon him several boons in the past and granted him special weapons, expecting that he would use them for righteous causes. If he fought and won, Dharma would prevail, and they would continue to receive nourishing offerings from devotees.

Sloka 34

akīrtiṃ cāpi bhūtāni kathayiṣyanti tevyayām
saṃbhāvitasya cākīrtir maraṇād atiricyate

akirtim = infamy; ca = and; api = besides; bhutani = people, beings; kathayisyanti = speak about, narrate; te = of your; avyayam = endlessly, ceaselessly; sambhavitasya = for a respectable person; ca = and; akirtih = dishonor; maranat = death; atiricyate = worse than.

Besides, people would endlessly speak about your infamy, and for a person of repute, dishonor is worse than death.

Worldly people value others' approval and opinions about themselves more than they value their own. They like to be respected, approved, appreciated, accepted, and perceived positively. Renunciants are indifferent to worldly opinions, name and fame, honor and dishonor, or praise and criticism. They look upon the values, opinions, or whatever arises from or is aggravated by desires and egoism as trivial. Hence, they give them up and practice sameness. It does not matter to them how they are perceived, honored, or ignored. Arjuna was a householder (grihastha). He had many virtues. At the same time, he was driven by the same values, desires, aspirations, and expectations as most worldly people. Therefore, he would naturally value his reputation, public image, and how people perceived or treated him. Knowing that, Lord Krishna appealed to his vanity to remind him that for a warrior, dishonor was worse than death, and if he abandoned the war and left the battlefield, he would have to live with that reputation forever, and it would follow him everywhere. By mentioning 'bhutani' (beings), he also hinted that he would face disgrace in this world and other worlds, and the stain of cowardice would follow him to the next world.

Sloka 35

bhayād raṇād uparataṃ maṃsyante tvāṃ mahārathāḥ
yeṣāṃ ca tvaṃ bahumato bhūtvā yāsyasi lāghavam

bhayat = because of fear; ranat = from the battle; uparatam = withdrawn; mamsyante = will think; tvam = of you; maha-rathah = great charioteers; yesam = by whom; ca = and; tvam = you; bahu-matah = thought higly; bhutva = having been; yasyasi = will go; laghavam = small, insignificant.

Great charioteers will assume that you withdrew from the battlefield due to fear, and you will become small and insignificant to those who think of you highly.

In the first chapter, Arjuna argued that not killing teachers and elders was the highest good, and he would prefer to live on alms than enjoy bloodstained food. He was concerned about the sin of killing great warriors and close relations, and going to hell. In the previous verse, Lord Krishna told him what people might think if he abandoned his duty and left the battlefield. Here, he told him that even those teachers and elders, such as Bhīshma and Drona, he wanted to save would not appreciate him if he withdrew and left without fighting. They would not think of him kindly or forget his ignominious action. He would fall in their esteem, and his reputation would be damaged forever. Since Arjuna valued other people's opinions, Lord Krishna cleverly used them to convince Arjuna to rethink his decision. Arjuna had to weigh which was more damaging to his reputation, fighting in the war and doing his duty, or abandoning it and earning a bad reputation forever. Situations like this also arise in our lives where each alternative leads to some unhappy or undesirable consequence. In difficult and ambiguous situations, when we experience moral dilemmas or where our desires and duties conflict, we are forced to make hard choices without knowing what might happen. Here, Lord Krishna suggested that on such occasions, one should go by what his duty or obligation to God and others demands. If the duty demands, one should perform it, irrespective of the moral or social implications.

Sloka 36

avācyavādāṃś ca bahūn vadiṣyanti tavāhitāḥ
nindantas tava sāmarthyaṃ tato duḥkhataraṃ nu kim

avacya = improper, unspeakable; vadan = words; ca = and; bahun = many; vadisyanti = will say; tava = your; ahitah = ill-wishers, enemies; nindantah = defame, blame, denigrate; tava = your; samarthyam = power, force, ability; tatah = than; duhkha-taram = very painful; nu = of course; kim = what.

Your enemies will say many improper and impolite words, defaming your power and ability. What can be more painful than this?

As a successful person, Arjuna had many enemies. The Kauravas despised him and his brothers from an early age because they could not defeat them, eliminate them, or force them to give up their claim to the throne. They envied the fact that Bhishma, Drona, Vidura, and many others in the court respected them, secretly supported them, and wished them success. They also envied the close relationship Arjuna had with Lord Krishna, whom they feared. So did Karna, who set his eyes on Arjuna and wanted to target him when the war began. Lord Krishna, therefore, cautioned Arjuna that his enemies would take advantage of his action and defame him if he withdrew from the battlefield, interpreting it as an act of cowardice. It would be painful to watch them making fun of him, calling him a coward, or questioning his prowess and bravery. They would be delighted to see his reputation smeared by his willful actions and make it look even worse.

Sloka 37

hato vā prāpsyasi svargaṃ jitvā vā bhokṣyase mahīm
tasmād uttiṣṭha kaunteya yuddhāya kṛtaniścayaḥ

hatah = by getting killed; va = or; prapsyasi = you will gain; svargam = heaven; jitva = by winning; va = or; bhoksyase = enjoy; mahim = the earth; tasmat = therefore; uttistha = stand up, get up; kaunteya = Kaunteya, son of Kunti; yuddhaya = for the battle; krta = act, fight; niscayah = determination.

If you are killed, you will attain heaven. Otherwise, you will enjoy the Earth by winning. Therefore, O Kaunteya, stand up to fight with determination.

Lord Krishna suggested to Arjuna that he consider the rewards of fighting. In the previous verses, he told him that not fighting would result in the loss of his image, reputation, and heavenly rewards. Even his relations, whom he was hesitant to fight, would not appreciate his action if he left the battlefield. Here, he suggested the rewards of fighting in victory as well as defeat. If he lost fighting, he would attain heaven, but if he won, he would enjoy the riches of the earth. Therefore, even if he considered the rewards, he would be better off fighting than leaving the battlefield. Heavenly life and the enjoyment of riches on earth are most cherished by Kshatriyas since their lives are uncertain, and their fate hangs between life and death in each war. Therefore, Lord Krishna cleverly used them to draw his attention. Although he encouraged Arjuna to perform his obligatory duty as a Kshatriya to enjoy its rewards, he would later teach him not to perform actions for worldly rewards but to sacrifice them to the Supreme Lord to avoid their consequences. Here, he focused on convincing him to stay and fight. He would begin his main discourse from the next verse onward.

Sloka 38

sukhaduḥkhe same kṛtvā lābhālābhau jayājayau
tato yuddhāya yujyasva naivaṃ pāpam avāpsyasi 2.38

sukha = happiness, pleasure; duhkhe = sorrow, pain; same = alike, same; krtva =treating; labha-alabhau = gain and loss; jaya-ajayau = victory and defeat; tatah = then; yuddhaya = for the fighting; yujyasva = prepare, get ready; na = not; evam = thus; papam = sin; avapsyasi = incur, obtain, gain.

Treating alike happiness and sorrow, gain and loss, victory and defeat, you shall prepare to fight. Then, you will not incur sin.

How should Dharma be practiced? With sameness and equanimity, and without worrying about the results. Dharma should be practiced for the sake of Dharma, not for spiritual or material rewards. This is one of the core teachings of the Bhagavadgita. Desires and expectations create karma and lead to suffering. They should be shunned because they create dependence and bind us to the world. Actions must be performed as an offering to God without seeking any personal gains out of them. We will learn more about this in the coming verses. The practice of Dharma is the means, not an end in itself. It should be practiced to serve the aims of God and achieve liberation while living as his loyal devotees and dutiful householders. In a simple sense, Dharma means moral duty or obligation arising from your essential nature (sahaja svabhava) and the roles you play as a father, mother, husband, student, etc., or from the relationships you build or the professions you choose. We tend to become emotionally involved with our duties and actions due to desires and expectations, which results in mental distress and emotional instability. In the end, all that striving leads us nowhere. It may temporarily nourish our egos but takes away a few years of our lives and opportunities to be peaceful and contented, leaving us inwardly unhappy, dissatisfied, unfulfilled, and spiritually empty.

In this verse, Lord Krishna suggested to Arjuna that although there were earthly and heavenly rewards of fighting the war, which he explained in the previous verses, in the end, they were inconsequential. He said he should not focus on them but on doing his duty as a warrior without worrying about the moral and material consequences that might arise from them. He also said that he should fight, treating alike the dualities of victory and defeat, loss and gain, or happiness and sorrow with the attitude of sameness and equanimity. The subsequent verses elaborate on performing actions with sameness and stability. In ancient India, many ascetic traditions suggested equanimity towards the pairs of opposites as the best solution to mitigate the problem of human suffering. They preached that peace could be experienced only when the mind, the seat of instability, was stabilized by arresting all the modifications that stirred in the mind in wakefulness, sleep, dreams, imagination, memory, thinking, perceptions, and so on. The classical yoga of Patanjali, with which the original Samkhya philosophy was closely aligned, prescribed a similar approach, which is why this chapter is titled Samkhya Yoga. Although the Samkhya Yoga of the Bhagavadgita derives its name from them, it differs from both schools in many respects.

Sloka 39

eṣā te'bhihitā sāṅkhye buddhir yoge tv imāṃ śṛṇu
buddhyā yukto yayā pārtha karmabandhaṃ prahāsyasi

esa = this; te = to you; abhihita = spoken, declared, imparted; sankhye = Sankhya; buddhih = wisdom, intelligence; yoge = yoga; tu = but; imam = to this; srnu = listen; buddhya = concerning wisdom; yuktah = endowed, filled with; yaya = by which; partha = Partha; karma-bandham = the bondage of karma; prahasyasi = release from.

This teaching (which has been) imparted to you (so far) is Samkhya; but (now) listen to the Yoga of Wisdom, O Partha, endowed with which you will be released from the bondage of action.

Although traces of Samkhya and Yoga philosophies (Darshanas) of Hinduism are found in the Samkhya Yoga of the Bhagavadgita, they are not the same. The original Samkhya and Yoga are distinct philosophical systems that developed over a long time, each with a history of its own. The Samkhya Yoga of the Bhagavadgita is a foundational doctrine that forms the basis for other yoga systems in the scripture. However, you can see that it was derived mainly from the teachings of the Samkhya and Yoga schools only. Hence, the common name. Some of the similarities between the two are about the individual Self (purusha), functions of Nature (Prakriti), the triple modes (gunas), devotion to the Self, the nature of the mind and senses, purification of the mind and body, withdrawal of the mind and senses, contemplation, self-absorption, devotion to the Self, emphasis upon detachment, renunciation, desireless actions, etc. As rational philosophies, Samkhya and Yoga occupy a place of honor in the evolution of Hindu thought. However, they do not believe in the existence of a Supreme God or his role in the creation and liberation of jivas. In contrast, the Samkhyayoga of the Bhagavadgita is theistic, which puts the Supreme Lord (Isvara) at the center of everything. He is the source, support, subject, and goal of all devotees. In the context of the scripture, Samkhya Yoga means the knowledge that illuminates the eternal and indestructible Self and distinguishes it from the objective realm and the field of Prakriti.

Lord Krishna stated here that he would speak about Buddhi Yoga or the Yoga of intelligence. Buddhi is translated differently as intelligence, rational mind, the higher mind, or discerning mind. While knowledge of the Self is essential for purification and liberation, we must cultivate discernment and know the difference between truth and falsehood and between the body and the Self to arrive at it. Buddhi is the highest faculty or tattva in our bodies, which gives us the ability to think rationally and intelligently and make wise decisions. The great Buddha focused on cultivating pure intelligence to achieve nirvana. He did not go beyond it and ignored the Self since he did not want to speculate upon an abstract concept that he thought could not be known or could not have served any purpose in alleviating human suffering. He wished to find rational and practical means to overcome suffering since, according to him, it should be the immediate goal or concern. Hence, he taught the vehicle of pure intelligence (bauddhayana), which can be corroborated through the human experience without confusing the mind with abstract notions.

Hinduism believes that Buddhi is the highest faculty of the physical Self. However, it is not the ultimate reality (tattva). Beyond the physical Self is the real Self, which is eternal and transcendental. The Bhagavadgita holds a similar opinion. Buddhi gives us the power of reasoning and discrimination, whereby we know right from wrong and the difference between the Self and the not-self. We also become aware of the distinction between knowledge and ignorance and between actions that bind us and actions that liberate us. As the highest principle of Nature, which is found in the human body, it reflects the brilliance of the Self just as the moon reflects the light of the Sun. With the help of buddhi yoga, we can let the light of the Self in us shine through our consciousness (antahkarana) and discern the truths about ourselves and our existence, free from ignorance and delusion.

Lord Krishna wanted Arjuna to cultivate discriminatory intelligence through buddhi yoga and sharpen his thinking and judgment to know how to perform his duty without suffering from the moral and mental conflicts he experienced earlier. In life, the right knowledge is necessary to perform actions and avoid mistakes, be it the performance of duties, completing a task, or achieving liberation. We need to know what is right and what is important, and the ability to distinguish them so that we will not be trapped by our thinking and imagination and remain bound to samsara. Having taught the knowledge of the Self, Lord Krishna now turned his attention to the importance of performing actions with wisdom and the correct discrimination.

Sloka 40

nehābhikramanāśosti pratyavāyo na vidyate
svalpam apy asya dharmasya trāyate mahato bhayāt

na = not; iha = here, in this; abhikrama = effort; nasah = loss; asti =is; pratyavayah = harm, sin, setback; na = not; vidyate = there is; svalpam = little; api = even; asya = of this; dharmasya = of this dutifulness; trayate = saves, protects; mahatah = great; bhayat = fear of mortal life.

In this, there is no loss of effort, no harm. Even a little of this dutiful practice can save one from the Great Fear.

The knowledge of the Bhagavadgita (samkhya) and its practice (yoga) will always lead you incrementally in the right direction toward liberation. Even if you stumble on the path or leave your effort in the middle, no harm will come to you. At any time in your life, you can pick up where you left off and continue without facing any negative consequences. If you stop or fail, it may delay your progress, but it will not hamper you from reaching your ultimate goal of liberation or freedom from worry and anxiety. It is not the same with worldly knowledge or worldly actions. For example, if you do not know how to fix a car, you cannot start it. You will not have a good harvest if you only do a little farming. The knowledge and practice of the Bhagavadgita are different. Even a little knowledge and a little practice will be helpful. Whatever you sow in the practice of Yoga, you will reap. The Lord himself gave this assurance in this verse. No harm will arise if you ignore it or practice it imperfectly, inconsistently, or incompletely. On the contrary, if you succeed in practicing it even a little (svalpam), it can save you from the fear of bondage or death or the suffering which arises from them.

In these words, Lord Krishna assured Arjuna that he should listen to him carefully and pay attention to what he would speak about the Yoga, which would help him overcome all his fears and anxieties. The whole of the Bhagavadgita is a treatise on Samkhya Yoga only. The Samkhya part deals with the nature of the Self, the Supreme Self, Prakriti, Jiva, or the body. They exist in their respective dimensions and make life possible on Earth. Through the knowledge of Samkhya, we gain an understanding of the distinction between them and realize our true purpose, which is oneness or union with the eternal Self. The Yoga part deals with the various means (yogas) through which that union or oneness is attained.

Thus, the second chapter of the Bhagavadgita is a summary of the entire scripture. Verses 16-30 contain the knowledge of the Self and its distinction from the body, and the subsequent ones deal with the methods to realize it. The first part, or the Samkhya part, deals with the knowledge of the Self, and the second part, or the Yoga part, encompasses all the yogas that Lord Krishna recommends to control the mind and body and realize the Self. Therefore, the name Samkhya Yoga should not be mistaken for a yoga system like karma, jnana, or sannyasa yogas. It should rightly be called the yoga of knowledge about the Self and the body, with two parts. The first part, or the Samkhya part, deals with the Self, the body, and their distinction, and the second part, or the Yoga part, with the methods to realize the Self and achieve oneness.

The words spoken by the Lord in this verse should be encouraging for any initiate who wants to study the Bhagavadgita and put the knowledge (samkhya) into practice (yoga) without worrying about the results. It is comforting even for worldly people. If they study the Bhagavadgita and practice it even a little, they will still be better off than not practicing it. Practicing jnana, karma, and sannyasa yogas while performing their household and professional duties, they can live freely without feeling anxious about death, rebirth, or samsara.

Sloka 41

vyavasāyātmikā buddhir ekeha kurunandana
bahuśākhā hy anantāś ca buddhayovyavasāyinām

vyavasaya-atmika = resolute; buddhih = discriminating intelligence; eka = only one; iha = in this; kuru-nandana = scion of the Kurus; bahu-sakhah = various branches; hi = indeed; anantah = endless; ca = and; buddhi= mind; avyavasayinam = without determination.

The discriminating intelligence of the resolute-minded is one-pointed, O scion of the Kurus, whereas endless with many branches indeed is the discriminating intelligence of the irresolute.

This verse shall be read in conjunction with the previous one in which Lord Krishna said that no effort in the practice of Yoga would be lost, and even a little practice could save one from the great fear of bondage and death. Here, he hinted that firm and resolute intelligence was needed to succeed. Intelligence will be steady and stable if the mind and senses are firmly controlled and not allowed to wander. Intelligence (buddhi) is the higher mind or faculty of the internal organ (antahkarana). It differs from the lower mind or the memorial mind (manas), although both are often used interchangeably. It is Prakriti's highest reality (tattva) in humans, which is responsible for critical and rational thinking. When it is pure and unwavering, one develops clarity, discernment, and freedom from delusion. If it is impure, one becomes deluded and confused. When combined with the right knowledge and purity of thought, free from desires and attachments, one develops the discernment to make wise decisions.

Lord Krishna termed well-developed intelligence as vyavasāyātmikā buddhi. What does it mean? It means purified and firmed-up intelligence that is strong and steady and is not confused, swayed, or distracted. It also means cultivated or curated intelligence, free from impurities and the influence of desires and attachments. It blooms when the mind is plowed correctly, watered, and seeded with the right knowledge and effort. You attain it through the persistent practice (vyavasaya) of Yoga, when you withdraw your mind and senses from worldly things and remain inwardly focused upon the Self (atma). An adept yogi's resolute intelligence, purified by the fire of knowledge and watered with devotion in the field of righteousness, helps him abide in self-control, sameness, equanimity, and devotion.

His resolute intelligence remains like a rock in the ocean of turbulence. It stays firm amidst the mind's modifications. Even if it is temporarily disturbed, it regains its balance and strength and returns to its tranquil state. The opposite is the case with those whose minds are impure and untrained. Their senses pull them in different directions, keeping them restless, distracted, and deluded. The difference between the two types of intelligence is similar to a field that is well cultivated (vyavasaya) and fenced from all sides, and one that is left uncultivated (avyavasaya) or undeveloped and left open. The idea is that you should know clearly what you intend to do and work resolutely until you realize it. For that, you must think with discernment, without being swayed by desires and attachments, outside influences, or egoistic concerns, and find the right way to reach the intended goal. Otherwise, you will be pulled in different directions, influenced by your desires and natural propensities.

Whether choosing a scripture, a teacher, a path, a technique, or a solution, your discernment must be your guide, and your knowledge and wisdom must be your aids. Even then, mistakes may happen. Hence, the wise ones offer their decision to God and leave the result to him. Whatever happens, they accept it as divine will. If mistakes happen, they learn from them and move on. Resolute intelligence should not be mistaken for stubbornness. The firmness of the mind arises from faith, devotion, knowledge, and intelligence, whereas stubbornness arises from selfishness, egoism, ignorance, and delusion. The wise ones are not easily swayed because they know and are sure of what they know because they discern well, and their minds are not swayed by their senses or desires; the ignorant ones also hold their ground, but it is because they are delusional, egoistic, and driven by desires and attachments. Their intelligence remains clouded. Therefore, they go by whatever seems convenient or serves their purpose.

Sloka 42

yām imāṃ puṣpitāṃ vācaṃ pravadanty avipaścitaḥ
vedavādaratāḥ pārtha nānyad astīti vādinaḥ

yam= all; imam = these; puspitam = flowery; vacam = words; pravadanti = speak; avipascitah = people with poor discernment; veda-vada-ratah = delight in the discussion of the Vedas; partha = Prtha; na = not; anyat = other; asti =is; iti = thus; vadinah = declare.

All these people with poor discernment speak flowery words (and) take delight in the discussion of the Vedas, O Partha, declaring that there is nothing else other than this.

The phrase "All these people" refers to those who lack discernment and self-knowledge but possess the knowledge of the Vedas. According to them, by knowing the Vedas, everything is known, and nothing else needs to be known, and by performing sacrifices and rituals as ordained by them, one can fulfill the ultimate purpose of life. It may be a reference to the Mimansikas of the Mahabharata period. In the early days of the Vedic religion, Mimansa, or the philosophy associated with Vedic ritualism, was predominant. The Mimansikas believed that the Vedas were the ultimate in knowledge and inviolable, and rituals were the answer to every problem and need. For them, nothing else (nānyat) mattered. Although they made offerings to gods, because the Vedas said so, they believed that the gods were instrumental and that all the benefits and rewards accrued from the sacrifices (yajnas). They also did not believe in a Supreme God. They emphasized studying the Vedas and performing sacrifices strictly as ordained by them to fulfill the four aims of human life. They also considered the Vedas the final authority on all matters, and their testimony indisputable. In their value system, Dharma meant practicing Vedic rituals and the code of conduct strictly as prescribed by the tradition. Their lives revolved around the Vedas and sacrifices rather than God. It is more likely they practiced the early versions of karma yoga, performing sacrifices as their obligatory duty to fulfill their desires and attain heavenly life.

Today, we do not have Mimansikas, but people who practice rites and rituals to fulfill their desires or believe in superstitious practices. They worship gods, worship plant and animal spirits, and visit temples, but do not worship the Lord in them, practice spirituality, or work for their liberation. We also find many intellectuals, atheists, nihilists, materialists, rationalists, etc., who possess intellectual knowledge, speak flowery words, and excel in their professions. However, they do not give much importance to righteous conduct or spiritual knowledge. Some even argue that religions hinder progress and distract people from the real problems of the world. They are karma yogis who live for themselves and perform actions to fulfill their desires and egoistic needs rather than serve God or the aims of creation. You will also find many intellectuals who believe in God with some skepticism and lean more toward materialism. Someday, they may turn to God and become his true devotees, but they are not yet ready for self-discovery. According to the Bhagavadgita, they may have knowledge but do not possess the wisdom to know the distinction between the Self and the not-self. In other words, knowledge does not necessarily lead to true wisdom or self-knowledge.

Special Note: The Mimansa we spoke about here is currently known as Purva Mimansa to contrast it with the Uttara Mimansa, also known as Vedanta, a later development. Both schools acknowledge the supremacy and inviolability of the Vedas. The basis of Mimansa was Jaimini's Mimansa Sutras (4th century BCE). Its central focus is Dharma and the practice of different rituals and sacrifices found in the Vedas.

Sloka 43

kāmātmānaḥ svargaparā janmakarmaphalapradām
kriyāviśeṣabahulāṃ bhogaiśvaryagatiṃ prati

kama-atmanah = mind filled with lustful desires; svarga-parah = heaven as the highest goal; janma-karma-phala-pradam = birth as the fruit of actions.; kriya-visesa = special rites and rituals; bahulam = various; bhoga = enjoyment; aisvarya = wealth; gatim = attaining, obtaining; prati = for the sake of.

Minds filled with lustful desires, heaven as the highest goal, birth as the fruit of karma, they engage in various special rites and rituals for the sake of attaining wealth and enjoyment.

In the previous verse, Lord Krishna spoke about those who lacked discernment but spoke flowery words and took delight in the knowledge of the Vedas as if nothing else mattered. In this, he spoke about those who were filled with passions and desires and engaged in various rites and rituals, desiring wealth and enjoyment and holding heaven as the highest goal and birth as the fruit of karma. The description also most likely refers to the ancient Mimansikas or ritualists. The Mimansikas believed in the Vedas only and nothing else. They took delight in studying them, discussing them, and practicing the rites and sacrifices ordained by them. Of the four parts of the Vedas, they dutifully followed the ritual portions (karmakanda), ignoring the knowledge portion (jnanakanda), believing that through sacrifices and rituals, they could fulfill the four aims of human life: Dharma, Artha, Kama, and Moksha. They were not interested in knowing the Self or worshipping the Supreme Lord since they believed that the sacrifices fulfilled all human needs and aspirations. Hence, they did not practice any yoga or spiritual methods to attain liberation. For them, liberation (Moksha) meant securing a place in heaven by performing sacrifices and rituals and living strictly according to the Vedas.

We should not use these verses to construe that Lord Krishna was opposed to practicing sacrifices and domestic rituals or seeking wealth and enjoyment. He did not undermine the importance of attaining the four chief aims of human life through sacrifices. This and the previous verses are not against ritual practices or worldly enjoyment. They speak about the narrow-minded approach of some who, due to lack of knowledge and discernment, preoccupy themselves with rites and rituals (karmakanda) for worldly ends, ignoring the ultimate purpose, liberation. They serve as the background to introduce karma sannyasa yoga, which he will explain later. Even today, you will find people who engage in ritual practices to fulfill their worldly desires. With their minds filled with desires (kama atma), they engage in desire-ridden actions, ignoring their spiritual well-being.

Religiosity and religious duties are important for householders in Hinduism since they must serve gods, ancestors, and others with sacrificial food as an obligation to the Lord of creation. These duties are necessary for our spiritual transformation and progress. However, at some stage, they must be renounced to pursue liberation, the highest and ultimate purpose (paramartha) of human life. According to the Vedic Varnashrama Dharma, a householder must spend the first half of his life studying the Vedas to acquire both ritual and spiritual knowledge to perform obligatory duties, such as daily sacrifices, domestic rites, occasional sacrifices, and sacraments (samskaras). In the second half, he should gradually withdraw active duties, renounce worldly life, and use his spiritual knowledge to engage in contemplative practices (Yoga) with liberation as the sole aim.

In Hinduism, Dharma (duty), Artha (wealth), Kama (pleasure), and Moksha (liberation) are the chief aims of human life for householders. These aims are mutually complementary and prescribed by the Vedas to ensure that people lead a wholesome life, serve God and his creation, and earn his grace through selfless actions. The Upanishads, such as Isa and Chandogya, also emphasize ritual and spiritual approaches for householders to achieve liberation. Therefore, although ritual knowledge is considered inferior, householders have an obligatory duty to practice sacrificial rites and to ensure the order and regularity of the world. However, they should not be considered an end in themselves. They are necessary to serve God, but it is not human life's sole aim or purpose. Lord Krishna will speak about this later.

Sloka 44

bhogaiśvaryaprasaktānāṃ tayāpahṛtacetasām
vyavasāyātmikā buddhiḥ samādhau na vidhīyate

bhoga = enjoyment; aisvarya = wealth; prasaktanam = intense desire, obsession; taya = by that; apahrta= stolen, lost, carried away; cetasam = mind; vyavasaya-atmika = resolute, one pointed; buddhih = discriminating intelligence; samadhau = setting; na = not; vidhiyate =become fixed, established.

With an intense desire for enjoyment and wealth, the mind being lost by that, the setting of the intelligence, which is resolute and one-pointed, does not become well established.

Again, in this verse also, Lord Krishna probably referred to the beliefs and practices of the Mimansikas or ritualists of the Mahabharata period, conveying that discernment would not be well established if people were consumed by desires and attachments and engaged in desire-ridden actions to pursue wealth and worldly enjoyment. Since their minds remain restless and drawn out and are swayed by the impurities of egoism, desires, and delusion, worldly people who engage in desire-ridden actions do not possess one-pointed, resolute intelligence (vyavasāyātmikā buddhi). Without stable and firm intelligence, one cannot think clearly, analytically, or rationally, avoid making mistakes, discern truths without cognitive distortions, or cultivate sameness undisturbed by desires and dualities. To possess unwavering intelligence that is not swayed by desires, emotions, attraction, and aversion, one must restrain the mind and senses, overcome desires, and practice self-control. In this effort, the mind ridden with impurities is the most formidable obstacle. Sacrificial duties are meant to uphold Dharma, nourish gods, ancestors, etc., and fulfill one's obligation to the Creator God. It is possible only when one restrains the mind and senses, overcomes the impurities, and performs selfless actions as a sacrifice.

Sloka 45

traiguṇyaviṣayā vedā nistraiguṇyo bhavārjuna
nirdvandvo nityasatvastho niryogakṣema ātmavān

trai-gunya = regarding the triple gunas; visayah = topic, subject matter; vedah = Vedas; nistraigunyah = resolve the gunas; bhava = be; arjuna = Arjuna; nirdvandvah = without the pairs of opposites; nitya-sattva-sthah = ever established in sattva; niryoga-ksemah = without concern for acquisitions and possessions; atma-van = imbued with the self.

The triple gunas are the subject matter of the Vedas. O Arjuna, you shall resolve the triple gunas to be free from duality, to remain ever established in purity, to stay indifferent to acquisition and possession, and to remain ever-absorbed in the Self.

In this verse also, Lord Krishna repudiated the popular notion of his times that the Vedas were all about sacrifices and sacrificial duties, which the

Mimansikas held. He countered it, saying that they also contain the knowledge of the triple gunas or modes, namely Sattva, Rajas, and Tamas, and how to remain ever-absorbed in the Self. The gunas pervade all the worlds in existence and are present in all animate and inanimate objects. Even the divinities, from the highest to the lowest, possess them. They are responsible for our basic propensities and essential nature. In combination with the elements and aspects of Prakriti, they create the duality and diversity of creation. Since they induce desires and attachments, jivas experience attraction and aversion and dualities such as heat and cold or pain and pleasure. As they engage in desire-ridden actions, beings incur sinful karma, bondage, and suffering. When the gunas are active, one cannot experience equanimity or sameness since the mind and senses remain restless and unstable, pursuing sense objects and worldly enjoyments. Hence, Lord Krishna advised Arjuna to resolve them and overcome duality (nirdvanda), cultivating purity, detachment, and indifference to pleasures and establishing his mind in the Self.

Apart from resolving the gunas, Lord Krishna advised Arjuna to cultivate eternal purity (nitya sattva) and remain established in it. Eternal purity is not attained by suppressing rajas and tamas and cultivating the predominance of sattva. It is achieved by completely suppressing and transcending all the gunas, including sattva. In the initial stages, one may cultivate sattva to establish the mind in the Self, but eventually, one has to transcend all the gunas to become a true nirvana. It is because sattva also belongs to the domain of Nature and induces desires and attachments. Therefore, only when a yogi transcends all the gunas and, thereby, all desires and attachments does he truly become free from attraction and aversion and from the desire to acquire and possess things (niryoga-kshema). In that desireless and stable state, his intelligence becomes unwavering and one-pointed, his mind becomes stable and silent, and he becomes firmly established in the eternal purity of Self (atmavan). Thus, in this verse, Lord Krishna clearly stated that liberation or self-realization would not arise from our preoccupation with the Vedas or their superficial knowledge and instructions. One should focus on self-purification rather than ritual knowledge by transcending the gunas and abiding in the purity of the Self to overcome impurities and become eternally pure.

Sloka 46

yāvān artha udapāne sarvataḥ saṃplutodake
tāvān sarveṣu vedeṣu brāhmaṇasya vijānataḥ

yavan = as much; arthah = purpose; uda-pane = well, reservoir, pool; sarvatah = everywhere; sampluta-udake = water in a flood or deluge; tavan = so much; sarvesu = all; vedesu = in the Vedas; brahmanasya = of a Brahmana or one who has realized Brahman; vijanatah = one who knows.

As much purpose the water in a well serves when there is a deluge, so much do all the Vedas for a Brahmana who has the knowledge (of Brahman).

Tavan means so much, and yavan means as much. They are used for comparison. If you are not thirsty, you do not need to drink water. If there is a deluge and water is all around, why would you look for the water in a well? Similarly, when you have the oceanic knowledge of the Self, why will you look to the Vedas or any scriptures for limited knowledge? The knowledge of the Vedas is compared here to the water in a well, and the knowledge of the Self to a deluge. For a yogi who renounces the world, only self-knowledge matters. He may study the Vedas, but would eventually know the Self through self-realization. The knowledge found in the Vedas is limited compared to the knowledge one gains through oneness or absorption in the Self. Hence, why would an enlightened Brahmana who knows Brahman depend upon the Vedas or any scripture? Having realized Brahman as his very Self and reached the end of a long journey, he would remain contended and satisfied within himself. He knows that just as a well is useful to quench thirst when there is no water nearby, the Vedas are useful to those who have no other means to acquire knowledge and evolve spiritually. For the knowers of Brahman, they are of little use except for teaching or validation.

Lord Krishna did not question the supremacy of the Vedas in this verse. He implied that they are not useful to the knowers of Brahman. The Vedas are considered his manifestation in word or sound form. However, they are not the same as him. They are useful to the ignorant ones but not to the knowers of the Self who possess resolute intelligence (vyavasāyatmika buddhi) and are eternally pure (nitya sattvas) and free from dualities (nirdvanda). By these words, he repudiated the Mimansikas' belief that the knowledge of the Vedas was all that one needed to practice rituals and sacrifices (karma kanda) and attain wealth and enjoyment here and a heavenly life in the next life. Ritualists like them show little interest in knowing the Self or attaining liberation to escape from samsara. They are inclined to practice sacrifices to fulfill their desires rather than knowing the Self and achieving liberation. The Vedas contain the knowledge of Brahman. However, it is not the same as the knowledge that arises independently and spontaneously in transcendental states. They represent Brahman just as an image represents a person or an object. They may help you understand and conceptualize him intellectually, but they are not useful to know him truly without duality and division. However, the liberated yogis (nityamuktas) do not disrespect the Vedas or sacrificial duties. They may still practice rituals and sacrifices and encourage the study of the Vedas for the welfare of others or to set an example.

Sloka 47

karmaṇyevādhikāraste mā phaleṣu kadācana
mā karmaphalahetur bhūr mā te saṅgostv akarmaṇi

karmani = toactions; eva = only; adhikarah = right; te = your; ma = never; phalesu = to the fruit; kadacana = at any time; ma = never; karma-phala = fruit of actions; hetuh = cause, purpose, reason; bhuh = become; ma = do not; te = your; sangah = attachment; astu = have; akarmani =inaction.

Your right is to actions only, but never to their fruit. Never let the fruit of your actions be the cause (of your actions), nor should you have an attachment to inaction.

This is one of the most well-known and frequently quoted verses from the Bhagavadgita. It contains the essence of karma-sannyasa yoga and contains two important instructions. The first one is that we have the right to perform actions but not to enjoy their fruit. It means the desire for the fruit of action should never be the reason why we should perform actions. The second one is that we should not develop an attachment to inaction. Thus, it suggests how one should perform actions to avoid sinful consequences (karma phalam) that may arise from them. In the previous verses, Lord Krishna stated that the Vedas and Vedic sacrifices were of little consequence to those who possessed the knowledge of the Self. Here, he clarified that actions (and thereby the Vedas) were still important for those who engaged in householder duties and had not yet attained self-knowledge. They have a right to perform their sacrificial duties, but without the desire or expectation to benefit from them or earn rewards from them. In the context of the Vedas, karma primarily means any actions and, in a certain sense, all obligatory duties. They can be performed without desires (nishkama) or with desires (kamya karmas). Sinful consequences arise from the latter.

The sacrificial rituals ordained by the Vedas for householders constitute the ritual part (karmakanda). These rituals are divided into three categories: obligatory, optional, and prohibited. Householders cannot avoid obligatory duties. They must perform them without desires since they are meant to discharge them from their karmic debt to gods, ancestors, and others and to serve God and his aims of creation. The optional ones are not compulsory, but householders may perform them to fulfill their desires. Hence, they are known as desire-ridden actions (kamya-karmas). The prohibited ones should not be performed at all since they produce sinful karma. In this verse, Lord Krishna clearly states that actions should not be performed, desiring to enjoy their fruit. It means one should perform all obligatory duties without desires. As for the kamya karmas, they should avoid them, perform them without selfish desires, or perform them for the sake of others. At the same time, he also said that one should not abandon any action or resort to inaction (akarma) with the desire to avoid sinful consequences. He especially mentioned it because Arjuna wanted to avoid the sinful consequences of fighting in the war through inaction. Karma is also of several types. The obligatory duties are usually known as karma or baddha karmas. The prohibited ones are known as vikarma, and inaction is known as akarma. When desires are involved, they all produce sin and bind people.

Hence, Lord Krishna told Arjuna, who was worried about the consequences of his actions on the battlefield, to focus on his actions without desiring their fruit. The desire to enjoy riches and pleasures or avoid pain and suffering, which was the main theme of Arjuna's arguments earlier, should never be the reason why one should perform or not perform any action. It should be because the Supreme Lord ordained them as obligatory for Kshatriyas like him through the Vedas. This is a perfect commonsense approach to the problem of karma. It is also logical and realistic. If you engage in actions due to selfish or egoistic desires, you will be responsible for them and their consequences. You will own the actions and their fruit, but if you perform them without desires and as a sacrifice to God and as his loyal and dutiful servant, you will earn his love and mercy and remain untouched by the actions. In worldly life, people perform many actions with the desire to enjoy their fruit. Those desires make them responsible for their actions and bind them to samsara. Hence, if one wants to perform actions but avoid the consequences, one should take the poison of desire from one's actions and remain free. In worldly life, desires are the foundation for success and happiness. In spiritual life, they are considered an obstacle and the source of suffering and bondage.

The profound wisdom hidden in this verse makes sense even from a practical point of view. We have control (adhikara) over our actions but not over their outcomes (karma phala). The outcome is not in our hands (except the most routine ones) since it depends upon many factors that are mostly out of our control. If we focus on the results that are not under our control, we are bound to experience many conflicting feelings and emotions and remain restless and unstable. Arjuna experienced them as he thought of the consequences of killing his relations and elders, although he did not know yet what was going to happen. Therefore, it makes sense to perform actions and leave the result to God. It holds well even for spiritual actions. A yogi should remain indifferent and free from desires while engaged in contemplative or devotional practices. He should be free from even the thought or the desire to achieve liberation or oneness, or nearness to the Lord. Whether he is engaged in action or inaction, he should not let any attachments or desires influence him. If he is free from desires, he is already free, even if he is not.

Sloka 48

yogasthaḥ kuru karmāṇi saṅgaṃ tyaktvā dhanañjaya
siddhyasiddhyoḥ samo bhūtvā samatvaṃ yoga ucyate

yoga-sthah = established in yoga; kuru = perform; karmani = actions; sangam = attachment; tyaktva = renouncing; dhananjaya = Dhananjaya; siddhi = gain, success; asiddhyoh = failure, loss; samah = equal; bhutva = becoming; samatvam = sameness or equality; yogah = yoga; ucyate = is called.

Established in yoga, perform actions, renouncing attachment, O Dhananjaya, and becoming equal to success and failure. Sameness or equanimity is called yoga.

This verse contains another important instruction regarding actions. It says actions should be performed by renouncing attachment to their fruit, treating success and failure or gain or loss equally, with sameness. Sameness is the auspicious state one attains through karma-sannyasa yoga or by renouncing the desire for the fruit of actions. Hence, Lord Krishna defined yoga as sameness. Arjuna felt sorrow (vishadam) because he was attached to particular outcomes from the war and his actions. Lord Krishna advised him to renounce them. Established in yoga means established in sameness. How should actions be performed? By giving up desires and attachments, and becoming equal to all the outcomes. Sameness means remaining indifferent and not feeling disturbed by the results of actions.

By defining Yoga as a state of sameness, he also clarified its meaning and purpose. He had already spoken to Arjuna about Samkhya (self-knowledge). Here, he turned to Yoga and defined it as the state or condition that manifests when we perform actions, renouncing attachment to their fruit. In the Bhagavadgita, the word yoga is used in different contexts to refer to a state or condition, to a method, technique, or practice, and to a philosophy or system of knowledge. All meanings are valid. Yoga as a state or condition has been defined differently by different scholars. In the Bhagavadgita, Lord Krishna defined it differently in different contexts, as we will notice later. However, in their final essence, they all mean the same. Here, he said that by establishing the mind in the practice of Yoga, renouncing desires and attachments, and becoming equal to success or failure in actions, a yogi should attain the supreme state (Yoga), which is sameness. Sameness means freedom from desires, likes, and dislikes. In that state, you will treat all the happenings in your life without choice or preference and accept them or endure them as divine will. It is attained only by withdrawing the mind and senses from the sense objects and cultivating detachment by suppressing desires and attachments. Gain and loss, or success and failure, are the fruit of our actions. They should not be why we should perform actions, but to discharge our duties and obligations, which we owe to God and others. When actions are performed as a duty or sacrifice to him, offering him their results, we are delivered from their consequences.

Patanjali defined Yoga as the cessation of the modifications (vrittis) of the mind. In his definition, he described it as a system of techniques to attain peace and equanimity. He focused on the methods or practices, which he called limbs (angas), and suggested that their practice would lead to the highest state of self-absorption (samadhi) or oneness with the Self. Although they seem different, they point to the same state of perfection. When the modifications of the mind are suppressed, one attains sameness only. When sameness is attained, the mind rests in peace, free from modifications, and becomes absorbed or dissolved in the Self. Thus, although both definitions appear different, they point to the same ideal condition: freedom from the disturbances or modifications of the mind, which leads to sameness and self-absorption or union with the Self.

Sloka 49

dūreṇa hy avaraṃ karma buddhiyogād dhanañjaya
buddhau śaraṇam anviccha kṛpaṇāḥ phalahetavaḥ

durena = by far; hi = verily; avaram = inferior; karma = action; buddhi-yogat = discerning intelligence; dhananjaya = Dhananjaya, conqueror of wealth; buddhau = of intelligence; saranam =refuge; anviccha = seek; krpanah = the little-minded, pitiable, wretched, poor, needy, miserly; phala-hetavah = for the fruit of actions.

Far inferior, verily, is karma (yoga) to buddhi-yoga (discerning intelligence), O Dhananjaya. Seek refuge in intelligence. The pitiable ones, who are devoid of judgment, seek the fruit of action.

Karma yoga means ritually performing actions or duties, which the Vedas prescribe for householders. In the philosophy of Mimansikas, they are entitled to enjoy the rewards flowing from the yajnas, and performing them without desires is not obligatory. In their worldview, the yajnas are meant for humans to seek enjoyment and fulfillment through them. Lord Krishna said that desire-ridden actions would produce sin, and there were better approaches to practicing karma yoga to avoid it. Merely performing duties to fulfill one's desires as ordained by the Vedas, which the Mimansikas practiced, is far inferior to the actions performed by wise ones with intelligence and discretion and without the desire to enjoy their fruit. If you have to choose between practicing karma yoga with desires and practicing it with intelligence and without desires, you must choose the latter. With purified intelligence, you will know how to avoid the poison of karma hidden in your actions rather than avoiding actions or resorting to inaction. With the discernment thus gained, you will know which actions will produce karma and rebirth and which ones will lead to evenness and liberation.

In pursuing liberation, buddhi (intelligence) is your internal guru and spiritual guide. For a yogi, it is the sole support, apart from God. The journey of liberation is a lonely journey where you must rely upon your intelligence to find your way in the darkness of delusion and ignorance. Even to practice your teacher's instructions, you need intelligence to analyze, understand, or assimilate them. Therefore, yogis who cultivate discerning wisdom take shelter in their wisdom rather than their actions to purify themselves and progress on the path. They know the distinction between karma yoga and karma-sannyasa yoga. In karma yoga, you perform your obligatory duties as ordained by the shastras, like the Mimansikas. In karma-sannyasa yoga, you perform them intelligently like skillful yogis without desires, using your discerning wisdom and knowing which actions should be performed and which should be avoided.

Those who take refuge in desire-ridden actions or depend upon them rather than their discriminating intelligence (buddhi) for frivolous enjoyment deserve pity because they remain bound to samsara due to their lack of judgment and wisdom. They may secure a good life in the next birth, but not liberation. Kṛpaṇā means poor, pitiable, small-minded, or wretched. It refers to those who suffer due to their ignorance and delusion. They are poor and pitiable, not necessarily because they lack worldly wealth, but because they do not possess the right knowledge and judgment, and do not choose wisely what is good for them or their liberation. Due to ignorance, they think merely performing their obligatory duties through karma yoga and following the scriptures will ensure liberation or a good birth in the next life. They miss a rare chance to arrest the formation and accumulation of karma and achieve liberation through self-knowledge (Samkhya) and spiritual practice (Yoga).

In worldly life, we perform actions due to desires or with the expectation of rewards. Attraction and aversion drive our motivation. Modern management methods focus on motivating people with rewards and punishments to maximize their potential and productivity. They appeal to their needs and desires to control them and keep them motivated, leaving many unhappy and stressed. In spiritual life, the rules are different. You are not supposed to seek rewards or approval for your effort, not even the reward of liberation. Instead, you must purify your intelligence and give up desires and possessions to cultivate detachment and sameness and progress quickly, avoiding mistakes and the fruit of karma.

Sloka 50

buddhiyukto jahātīha ubhe sukṛtaduṣkṛte
tasmād yogāya yujyasva yogaḥ karmasu kauśalam

buddhi-yuktah = the one endowed discriminating intelligence; jahati = gives up, rejects, casts off; iha = here, in this world; ubhe = both; sukrta-duskrte = good and bad deeds; tasmat = therefore; yogaya = for the sake of yoga; yujyasva = get ready, be prepared; yogah = yoga; karmasu = in doing karma, in performing actions; kausalam = skillfulness, cleverness.

The one who is endowed with discriminating intelligence gives up both good and bad deeds. Therefore, be prepared for the sake of Yoga (to give up desire-ridden actions). Yoga is skillfulness in action.

In this verse, Lord Krishna stated the advantage of having discerning intelligence. Giving up good and bad deeds does not mean giving up all actions. It only means giving up the desires hidden in them or the desire for their fruit. Earlier, we heard that yoga meant sameness or equanimity. Here, we are told that yoga is skillfulness in action. There is no contradiction here. Both meanings are interrelated and point to the same supreme state of choiceless awareness (Yoga). Skillfulness arises from the wisdom that the desire for the fruit of actions should not be why one should engage in actions or avoid them. The wise ones perform both good and bad deeds if they are a part of their obligatory duties. The word kausalam is frequently used in conjunction with intelligence (buddhi) as dexterity, sharpness, cleverness, or skillfulness (buddhi-kausalam). When a yogi is endowed with it, he knows how to find his way out of any situation. He knows what to do, how and when to do it, and how to deal with the consequences that arise from it. In Yoga, it means he knows how to perform actions intelligently to overcome their sinful consequences.

The yogi endowed with intelligence (buddhi yukta) and skillfulness in actions gives up attachment to good and evil deeds. Having overcome attraction and aversion, he treats all actions and circumstances equally with sameness. Thereby, even if he performs them, he is untouched by their purity or impurity. Dexterity or mastery of the mind (buddhi kausalam) arises from the absence of desires or excellence in practicing detachment and renunciation. When it is firmly established, one attains skillfulness in actions. Through that, the mind stabilizes in sameness and equanimity. Thus, buddhi yoga is the foundation of karma yoga. Hence, Lord Krishna advised Arjuna to take shelter in it while practicing karma yoga. Those who practice both yogas attain sameness (samatvam) and remain steadfast in success and failure. Since they offer the fruit of their actions to God, they earn neither sin nor merit.

The verse also states that the discerning yogi gives up good and bad deeds. It does not mean he gives up actions as such. He gives up the desire to perform those which produce merit (punyam) or shy away from those which produce sin (papam). Both types of actions bind us. Therefore, the intelligent yogi treats them equally with sameness and performs them neither desiring the good nor avoiding the bad. The idea is that one should dutifully perform actions without judging them and without desires and expectations, irrespective of their moral or ethical implications. It is not up to us to decide whether actions are good or bad. We have to perform them with sameness and indifference as long as we are obligated to perform them as our duty. War has its moral implications, but a warrior has an obligation to fight wars as his duty, even if it is against his principle of nonviolence. He cannot be a judge of the moral basis of his duties. Since Arjuna refused to fight on ethical grounds, Lord Krishna advised him to give up his desire to avoid sin and perform his duty intelligently without worrying about the consequences. He also implied that devotion to intelligence was better than devotion to desire-ridden actions.

Sloka 51

karmajaṃ buddhiyuktā hi phalaṃ tyaktvā manīṣiṇaḥ
janmabandhavinirmuktāḥ padaṃ gacchhanty anāmayam

karma-jam =born out of actions; buddhi-yuktah = with equanimity and discernment; hi = indeed; phalam = fruit, result; tyaktva = renounce, give up; manisinah = great among humans; janma-bandha = bondage to birth; vinirmuktah = liberated; padam = exalted state, position; gacchanti = go; anamayam = painless, healthy, auspicious, wholesome.

Endowed with discernment, the wise ones among humans renounce the fruit born of actions. Released from their bondage to birth, (they) reach the auspicious state, which is free from pain and suffering.

Endowed with intelligence (buddhi), which gives discernment and skillfulness in action (kausalam), the intelligent ones perform actions without expectations, giving up the desire for their fruit (karmaphalam). By that renunciation, they remove the causes of karma and bondage and reach the boundless state of the Self (anamayam), which is auspicious, blissful, wholesome, and painless. This is the essence.

When you have intelligence, which is pure and untainted by desires, you know right from wrong and see things clearly without judgment and without being swayed by your likes and dislikes. You know how to escape from the bonds of life (janma bandham) and samsara without abandoning your obligatory duties. With this attitude, the wise ones among men attain the highest state of liberation, even while practicing their obligatory duties through karma yoga. Madhavacharya counted as wise men (buddhi-yuktas) three types of virtuous people: those who practice their obligatory duties in the service of God through karma yoga, those who gain insight into the shastras through study, and those who directly perceive the Truth of Samkhya through renunciation. They are all qualified to attain liberation by renouncing the fruit of their actions.

'Anama' means without a name. "Anamayam" is the condition, realm, or state that is free from names and forms, in contrast to our world of names and forms. It also means that which is devoid of evil or delusion (ayomayam). It also means the condition or state that is healthy, sound, painless, deathless, eternal, absolute, etc., which is often associated with the pure state of Brahman, Shiva, or Vishnu. In the context of this verse, buddhi means intelligence that is endowed with discernment (kausalam) and sameness (samatvam) and that does not choose but accepts all conditions without judgment, attraction, or aversion. It is a state beyond duality in which one is not disturbed by the pairs of opposites. The wise among men, who have knowledge and discrimination, neither choose their actions nor seek the fruit of their actions according to their merit or demerit. They perform actions without expectations because they know it is the root of the problem and is responsible for our suffering and bondage.

Sloka 52

yadā te mohakalilaṃ buddhir vyatitariṣyati
tadā gantāsi nirvedaṃ śrotavyasya śrutasya ca

yada = when; te = your; moha = delusion; kalilam = dense, turbidity, confusion; buddhih = discriminating intelligence; vyatitarisyati = transcend, go beyond; tada = then; ganta asi = shall go; nirvedam = dispassion, indifference, disinterest; srotavyasya = what should be heard; srutasya = has been heard; ca = and.

When your buddhi crosses the turbid mire of delusion, then you will attain indifference to what has been heard and what should be heard.

This is a reaffirmation of the same idea from verse 46. When flood water is all around, what is the need for well water? When a yogi discerns the knowledge of the Self through pure intelligence, why would he have to depend upon the Vedas (what has been heard) to know what he already knows? The words "śrotavasya" and "śrutasya" refer to the knowledge of the śrutis or the Vedas, particularly the knowledge of the sacrifices. For example, śrautakarma refers to Vedic rites. It may also refer to the ritual knowledge (found in the Samhitas, Brahmanas, and Aranyakas) one learns from teachers or scholars. The Vedas are known as śruti, 'the heard ones,' because in ancient times, when there was no written script, students used to learn them from their teachers through hearing, and their students, in turn, learned from them through hearing. Thus, the oral tradition continued for centuries, and the Vedas became known as the scriptures, which were learned through hearing. They continued this tradition for various other reasons. One of them was to limit the knowledge to a few groups or communities and preserve their purity and secrecy.

Ritual knowledge of the Vedas helps householders fulfill their desires, nourishing gods through sacrifices and securing their blessings. It also helps them pursue the chief aims of human life, namely Dharma, Artha, and Kama. However, once they gain the knowledge of the Self, they give up desires and attachments, become indifferent to their pursuit, and focus solely on pursuing liberation (moksha), the highest and ultimate aim (paramartha). A deluded person goes by the appearance of things. He accepts perceptual knowledge as true knowledge, which he gains through his mind and senses, and fails to discern the hidden and imperceptible Self. Because of his limited knowledge, he focuses on worldly enjoyment, pursuing his immediate needs and desires, thereby delaying his liberation. The world is a turbid mire of delusion (kalilam), in which jivas are stuck due to ignorance, egoism, desires, and delusion. Just as you cannot see things in the darkness, you cannot know the truth of things when your mind is filled with the darkness of delusion. When we lack discernment, we do not know what is truly good or harmful to us. It is especially true because our values are relative and depend upon circumstances. Success in worldly life is considered a failure in spiritual life since worldly success prolongs suffering and delays liberation. We can break this pattern through self-purification and resolute intelligence.

Sloka 53

śrutivipratipannā te yadā sthāsyati niścalā
samādhāv acalā buddhis tadā yogam avāpsyasi

sruti = the Vedas; vipratipanna = conflicting ideas; te = your; yada = when; sthasyati = remains; niscala = stable and firm; samadhau = self-absorption; acala = immovable, unshakeable; buddhih = intelligence; tada = then, that; yogam = yoga; avapsyasi = you will attain.

When your intelligence, which is troubled by the conflicting statements of the Vedas, becomes stable and firm in self-absorption, then you will attain yoga.

A karma yogi who overcomes confusion and delusion due to well-developed intelligence (vyavasayātmika buddhi) and is endowed with discerning wisdom (buddhi yukta) is not confused by the conflicting statements of the Vedas. He realizes his folly and engages in karma-sannyasa yoga, offering the fruit of his actions to God, whereby he attains mental absorption (samadhi) and abides in Yoga, which Lord Krishna previously described as the state of sameness (samatvam) and skillfulness (kausalam) in actions. Thus, a karma yogi bound to samsara due to desire-ridden actions becomes a karma-sannyasa yogi when he attains pure and unwavering intelligence (achala buddhi) and gives up desires.

In this verse, as in some previous ones, you will find Lord Krishna's repudiation of the Mimansa belief that the Vedas are inviolable and their words are final. If they are inviolable and indisputable, they must consistently assert truths, which is not always the case. The Vedas cover a wide range of subjects and approaches and contain a variety of practices and beliefs, which can be confusing to beginners. The Samhitas, Brahmanas, and Aranyakas of the Vedas, which contain the knowledge of rituals (karmakanda), are meant for householders (grihasta) who must perform sacrifices and rituals as their obligatory duty. By performing them and making sacrificial offerings, they must fulfill their obligation to gods, ancestors, etc., and ensure the order and regularity of the world (rta).

In them, you will find beneficial rituals meant for the world's welfare and for granting health, wealth, and happiness. At the same time, they also recommend rituals for casting spells, deluding, and harming others. Some rituals are intended to revive people from debilitating illnesses, and some to destroy enemies. They also prescribe animal sacrifices to appease gods and charms to bewitch and control people. At the same time, they also reveal the higher knowledge of the Self. In the Aranyakas (Forest books) and the Upanishads, you will see a definite shift in their emphasis from gaining material rewards through sacrifices to attaining liberation through spiritual knowledge. They also emphasize the need to renounce rituals to know the Self, stating that ritual knowledge is inferior to spiritual knowledge.

However, although the ritual (karma kanda) and spiritual (jnana kanda) aspects of the Vedas are seemingly contradictory, for the discerning mind, they are complementary. The rituals and sacrifices instill discipline, sacrificial attitude, and selflessness in the early part of householders' lives and prepare them for liberation. They advise householders to perform obligatory duties in the first half of their lives and prepare for liberation in the second half, leading a life of contemplation and renunciation. Thus, although the Vedas contain conflicting statements and offer conflicting approaches and schools of philosophy, they ultimately point to the same goal of liberation. To those who are endowed with intelligence (buddhi yuktas), they reveal the secret knowledge of practicing karma-sannyasa yoga to perform their obligatory duties and escape from the sin arising from their actions. Purified thus, they can attain the auspicious state of yoga (sameness and serenity) and skillfulness in actions even while performing them.

The ninth chapter of the Ashtravakra Samhita also contains a similar instruction from sage Ashtavakra, who says, "After seeing the diversity of opinions among great seers, saints, and spiritual people, who will not cultivate indifference to learning and attain peace? The wise one gains the knowledge of the pure Self through dispassionate indifference, sameness, and intelligence, and overcomes the cycle of births and deaths." According to the sage, the key to self-realization is to know without confusion that what happens in the body happens to it, not to the Self. When he renounces desires, he finds himself everywhere.

Sloka 54

arjuna uvāca
sthitaprajñasya kā bhāṣā samādhisthasya keśava
sthitadhīḥ kiṃ prabhāṣeta kim āsīta vrajeta kim

arjunah uvaca = Arjuna said; sthita-prajnasya = of one who has stable intelligence; ka = what; bhasa = language, definition, description; samadhi-sthasya = of the state of self-absorption; kesava = Kesava; sthita-dhih = the stable minded one; kim = what; prabhaseta = may speak; kim = how; asita = sits; vrajeta = walks; kim = how.

Arjuna asked, "What is the language of the sthitha-prajna, O Kesva, who is established in samadhi? How does the stable-minded one speak, sit, or walk?"

This is the first of the sixteen questions Arjuna asks in the whole discourse. His question indicates that he recovered from his sorrow and confusion and was ready to listen to him and learn from the secret of attaining a stable mind and performing actions without being tainted by them. He wanted to know what language (bhasha) a stable-minded person who was established in samadhi (sameness) spoke and how he performed his daily tasks, such as speaking, sitting, or walking. Before going into further details, let us understand the meaning of sthithaprajna. Sthita means stable, static, or firm. Prajna means intelligence. Sthithaprajna means stable intelligence that is free from modifications, egoism, desires, attachments, and delusion. The person who possesses it is also known as the same. A sthithaprajna is not subject to doubt and confusion or disturbed by desires and attachments. Sthitaprajnas are endowed with highly developed intelligence (buddhi yuktas). They possess astute wisdom (buddhi kausalam) and know with firm insight (achala buddhi) the truths of the Vedas and other scriptures. They know definitively what they should or should not do in any given situation, whether it is performing their obligatory duties or practicing yoga to achieve liberation. Since they overcome desires and delusions, attain mental clarity, and are equal to dualities, their discernment is not affected by external or internal factors.

You may come across mentally brilliant intellectuals, but not true sthithaprajnas whose mental brilliance is not swayed by desires and attachments. Hence, Arjuna was curious to know how they lived. Prajna is the intelligence of the pure mind lit by the radiance of the Self. When the mind comes under its control, it becomes stabilized and free from distractions and modifications. Sameness is samadhi (sama+adhi), which means being equal (sama) to the dualities and having control (adhi) over them. Samadhi has multiple meanings. However, the quality of sameness is implied in all cases. It is known as self-absorption in the Yogasutras, sameness in the Bhagavadgita, and mental absorption in the Yogacara school of Buddhism. People who attain it may still experience physical or mental pain and suffering since it is the nature of the body to experience natural states. However, they endure it and do not show any outward reaction. They may also react to external events and empathize with other people's suffering and emotional reactions, but their responses remain subdued and controlled. Whatever they do, whether speaking, sitting, walking, or listening, they do so with indifference and without judgment and personal involvement.

We have already learned that buddhi yoga is superior to karma yoga, and karma-sannyasa yoga is the fruit of their combined practice. When you purify and stabilize your intelligence, you will realize that desires, not actions, are the root causes of karma and bondage, and by renouncing the fruit of your actions, you can set yourself free and attain the auspicious and stainless state of oneness. Thus, although we frequently hear about karma yoga, jnana yoga, or bhakti yoga, their foundation is buddhi yoga only. It is superior to all yogas since no one can effectively practice yoga without it. Buddhi yoga is about cultivating discerning intelligence (prajna) with which you can find your way, cutting through the web of attachments (karma bandhas) that arise from your actions. It helps the initiates overcome confusion through discernment, control their minds and bodies through self-restraint (atma-samyama), and stabilize their minds in the Self with evenness and exclusive devotion.

The Samadhi of Patanjali's Yogasutras is not the same as that of the Bhagavadgita. The former refers to the pure state of self-absorption or indistinguishable oneness that is free from duality and division. It is the same as the transcendental state of Turya, which is mentioned in the Mandukya Upanishad. The samadhi Lord Krishna mentioned here arises in the yogis when they practice self-purification through karma-sannyasa yoga, cultivate knowledge through jnana yoga, and discerning wisdom through buddhi yoga. It refers to the undisturbed and even state of mind (samatvam), free from desires and disturbances. Unlike the samadhi of Patanjali, it is a conscious and wakeful state in which karma yogis perform their actions with knowledge and awareness but without the modifications of the mind, desires, and expectations.

In classical yoga, samadhi is the ultimate discipline (anga) of the eightfold practice, in which one is not conscious of the mind and body but self-aware, and in which the distinction between the knower and the known disappears along with objectivity and perceptual awareness. Since the mind and senses do not participate in it, it is difficult to remember or translate it into words. Hence, it is described as exceedingly far (atita) and indescribable. The Yogasutras also mentions different states of samadhi, which yogis may experience when they go beyond concentration and meditation depending upon their level of awareness and depth of absorption. In the lower states, they retain some degree of duality and mental awareness, but in the higher ones, they disappear, leaving them in a subjective state of unified awareness. These states should not be mistaken with the awareness that arises in the mentally stable karma yogis (sthitaprajnas) who perform actions intelligently, with discerning wisdom and resolute and stable intelligence.

Sloka 55

śrībhagavān uvāca
prajahāti yadā kāmān sarvān pārtha manogatān
ātmany evātmanā tuṣṭaḥ sthitaprajñas tadocyate

sri-bhagavan uvaca = the Supreme Lord said; prajahati = renounces; yada = when; kaman = desires; sarvan = all types; partha = Partha; manah-gatan = happening or arising in the mind; atmani = in the Self; eva = alone; atmana = by the Self; tustah = satisfied; sthita-prajnah = stable person; tada = then; ucyate = is said, called.

The Supreme Lord said, "Renouncing all types of desires which arise in the mind, O Partha, whoever remains satisfied in the Self by

the Self alone, he is called (sthithaprajna) a person of stable intelligence."

The distinguishing features of the stable-minded one (sthithaprajna) are described here. Lord Krishna said that he who renounces all desires and remains satisfied within himself and by himself is called a sthithaprajna. In other words, the stable-minded one does not depend on the external world, his own body, or anything for happiness or fulfillment. Having realized that the Lord (the Self) resides in him and he is complete within himself, he does not desire anything. Knowing that the Lord in him presides over his mind and body, and all actions arise from him, he performs them as a sacrifice to him, renouncing the desire for their fruit. Realizing his essential nature as the pure Self through the pursuit of knowledge (jnana yoga), he becomes a true karma-sannyasa yogi, becoming himself an offering in the sacrifice of life. He gives up all desires (sarva kama prajahati), meaning he gives up all passions and desires that are induced by the triple gunas, explicitly prohibited by the scriptures, and will lead to bondage. He remains satisfied in the Self by the Self (atmani eva atmana) means he gives himself to the Lord, renounces all desire, conditions, and expectations, and accepts everything that happens to him as the Lord's will. Because of his unwavering faith in him, he remains confident, calm, and self-assured with the firm conviction that the Lord will take care of him and lead him in the right direction, irrespective of the circumstances and what happens or does not happen.

Having overcome attraction and aversion and cultivated detachment and indifference, the stable-minded one finds little pleasure in worldly things. He remains contended within himself, knowing that he shares an extraordinary relationship with the Lord, who resides in him as his very Self, companion, protector, and guide. The verse clearly states that by giving up desires, he does not fall into misery or depression since he knows that desires lead to bondage and suffering and reduce joy, peace, and happiness. He feels happiness (tushti) because he draws it from within himself from his blissful Self. The Lord who lives in him as his very Self is complete and perfect (purnam). His essential nature is truth, intelligence, and bliss (sat-chit-ānanda). Therefore, if you acknowledge him as the deity who is worthy of your worship and if you are one with him in thought and deed, you will be complete and perfect and remain satisfied and content within yourself. If you know that the Lord is in you as your very Self and you are always one with him, no matter who you are or where you live, what else do you need? Shri Shankaracharya suggested that one may find these characteristics in those (vidvat sannyasins) who renounce the world after achieving discerning wisdom (vyavasayātmika buddhi) and knowing without confusion the difference between the Self and the not-self. They are also found in those (vividisa sannyasins) who renounce the world and practice yoga but have yet to cultivate that wisdom. Sarvakama means all types of desires, without exception, including the desire for liberation. Manogatan means within the mind.

This verse does not say that desires do not arise in the mind of a stable person. It only says that he renounces (prajahati) them. A renunciant or a stable-minded one does not act on his desires. He endures them and remains indifferent to them and all dualities, overcoming attraction and aversion. The mind and the body are instruments of Nature and vulnerable to modifications. The body needs proper care, rest, and nourishment. They are the basic biological and physiological needs necessary for our survival and cannot be ignored by anyone, including advanced yogis. The body will crave food and water if you starve it for a few days. It will perish if it is starved continuously. Therefore, it is not that all desires will die if one attains perfection. Some natural functions in the stable-minded yogis will still remain under Nature's control. What sets them apart is how they respond to them. They cannot prevent the aging, sickness, or death of their bodies, but they know how to prepare for them and endure them. In other words, as Ashtavakra said, they may experience desires and cravings just as any human being, but they know that it is their bodies, not they, that are craving and remain indifferent.

Sloka 56

duḥkheṣv anudvignamanāḥ sukheṣu vigataspṛhaḥ
vītarāgabhayakrodhaḥ sthitadhīr munir ucyate

duhkhesu = in sorrow; anudvigna-manah = undisturbed; sukhesu = pleasure; vigata-sprhah = who is free from desires; vita = free from; raga = attachment, passion, attraction; bhaya = fear; krodhah = anger; sthita-dhih = stable and firm minded; munih = a sage; ucyate = is called.

He, who is undisturbed in sorrow, indifferent and uninvolved in pleasures, free from desires, and is without passions, fear, and anger - he is called sthitadhi, a sage with a stable and firm mind.

Three qualities of a yogi (sthithaprajna), whose mind is stable and firm and who is established in sameness, are stated here. The first is that his mind is undisturbed by pain or sorrow. We are conditioned to react to external situations, especially if they are painful or disturbing. The tranquil one unconditions himself from the learned and habitual responses of his mind and body and remains established in the Lord (the Self) in him with equanimity as if the world and external events have no control over him. If any pain or sorrow arises in him due to external factors, he remains undisturbed, thinking that they are happening to his mind and body but not to him or the Lord in whom he is firmly established.

Dukha means any physical or mental suffering that may arise due to internal (adhyatmika) or external causes (adhibhautika) or acts of God (adhidaivika). The suffering from acts of God may arise due to our past actions (karma), actions of those who are affected by our actions, or the forces and causes that are beyond our control. They cannot easily be resolved since one cannot anticipate them, prevent them, or ascertain the true causes to neutralize them. The stable-minded yogi is free from emotional exuberance (anudvigna mana) amidst sorrow since he withdraws his mind into the Lord and remains detached from his body as if it has an existence of its own. In adverse circumstances, he worships the Lord in him with firm faith and devotion, attributes all his life's happenings and problems to his inviolable will, and leaves their resolution to him. According to the Yogasutras, our suffering is created by ignorance (avidya), egoism (asmita), passions and attachments (raga), hatred (dvesha), and clinging to life (abhinivesa). These are absent in the yogi who excels in buddhi yoga and conquers desires and attachments with discerning wisdom. Those who are attached to pleasures (sukha) and repelled by sorrow (dukha) cannot escape from fear and anxiety since they cannot anticipate how long their pleasures will last or when sorrow and suffering arise and trouble them. The steady ones are not disturbed since they neither seek pleasures nor avoid sorrow, but remain equal to them.

The second quality is indifference to the enjoyment and creature comforts (sukham). The yogi, who is established in equanimity (sthitadhi), is always contented and satisfied within himself due to the absence of desires and his devotion and faith in the Lord, who is present in him as his Self. He establishes a strong, internal, inseparable, devotional relationship with him and looks to him to take care of his welfare and his problems and rescue him from samsara. Amid pleasures, he shuts down his mind and senses and remains uninvolved and indifferent as if he is unconscious, unconcerned (vigatasprha), or absent. He neither craves nor enjoys worldly pleasures. At the same time, if fate or circumstances bring him into their midst, he remains aloof and dispassionate, as if he is detached from the body and it has an existence of its own.

The third quality is freedom from passions (raga), fear (bhaya), and anger (krodha), which arise due to attraction and aversion, and lack of discernment. They, in turn, arise from the modes of rajas and tamas. They distort our perception and understanding. The stable yogi who has resolute intelligence attains that state by suppressing the modes of rajas and tamas fully and thereby subdues all passions and emotions. Hence, he remains free from attraction and aversion and all the passions to which ordinary humans are vulnerable.

"Sthita" means stable, and "dhira" means firm or wise. "Sthitadhir" is the one who remains stable and firm, undisturbed by pain or pleasure. The phenomenal world is characterized by dualities and impermanence, which are responsible for the instability, sorrow, and suffering of the deluded who become involved with them. The yogi whose mind is steady and fixed (sthithadhir) is neither drawn to nor repelled by the world. Since he overcomes all desires and attachments through self-purification and remains detached from his mind, body, and the world through renunciation, he becomes a passive witness. He sees all happening in him and outside as the play of the Lord in him. By overcoming the longing for life, he overcomes the fear of death, which is the worst of all fears, and with it, all other fears and evil passions, such as anger or envy. Thus, discernment, faith, devotion to the Lord as oneself, and freedom from desires are essential to becoming a sthithaprajna or a sthitadhi.

Sloka 57

yaḥ sarvatrānabhisnehas tattatprāpya śubhāśubham
nābhinandati na dveṣṭi tasya prajñā pratiṣṭhitā

yah = who; sarvatra = everywhere; anabhisnehah = without attachment or affection; tat = that; tat = that; prapya = achieving; subha = pleasant, auspicious, bright; asubham = unpleasant, inauspicious, impure; na = not; abhinandati = welcomes, appreciates; na = nor; dvesti = dislikes or hates; tasya = of his; prajna = discriminating wisdom; pratisthita = firmly fixed.

He who is unattached everywhere, who neither welcomes the auspicious nor detests the inauspicious upon attaining it, that person's discriminating intelligence is firmly fixed.

Anabhisneha means freedom from affection, attachments, parental bonds (nabhi), friendship (sneha), or relationships of any kind. The firm and stable-minded yogi (sthitadhi) does not entertain any attachments toward his parents, brothers, teachers, name, fame, etc., and remains indifferent to everything and everyone everywhere. He is free from all sides, which means he is wholly unentangled and uninvolved in all respects everywhere, from everyone and everything. Hence, he does not allow even the desire for liberation or attachment to his guru to influence him. Since he worships the Lord in him as his sole support, identifies with him, and remains satisfied within himself, he develops complete detachment from the external world and its influences. To have a relationship, you need a subject and an object, with desires or attachments acting as the connecting links. Although the stable-minded yogi may experience duality and dwell upon subject and object relationships, he renounces all attachments, fixing his mind on the Lord as his very Self, and remains aloof and detached from the objectivity he experiences in his consciousness. Seeing the Lord in him as the all-pervading supreme reality and the only relationship worth keeping and renouncing all worldly things and relationships, he becomes the dweller of oneness (kevalin).

Qualities such as detachment, desirelessness, dispassion, sameness, and egolessness are the defining marks of an enlightened yogi. In Sanskrit, a wise person is known as dhira, which means one who is wise, firm, and resolute. The stability arises from the absence of desires and attachments. Indeed, if you overcome desires and attachments, you are already free, and nothing will disturb you. Wisdom (intelligence) is of different types, such as emotional or social intelligence. Spiritual intelligence, or the wisdom that arises from knowing or contemplating the Self, is above all and encompasses all. It arises from the spiritual knowledge and awareness one acquires through study and from inner purity, stability, and firmness of the mind established through yoga. When your mind is pure, stable, and firm, you can see through the veil of delusion (maya) and discern things with greater clarity and intelligence. An untrained and impure mind is usually deluded and unstable. Therefore, it can easily be misled, confused, or distracted. In contrast, the mind of a wise person (sthithaprajna) is stable, one-pointed, and undisturbed. You cannot confuse, distract, or unsettle him. Since he remains indifferent and detached toward all dualities, opinions, beliefs, and actions, and sees the Lord in him as the Lord in all, he remains in peace and harmony with the rest of the world. Having attained a pure mind and overcome impurities, he can read others and empathize with them or help them without expecting anything in return. Even if disturbed by unusual situations, he quickly regains his balance and control and abides in sameness. Knowing that the world is impermanent and illusory, and pleasure and pain are transitory, he renounces it as the source of misery and abides in thoughts of the Self (God) with firm faith.

Sloka 58

yadā saṃharate cāyaṃ kūrmoṅgānīva sarvaśaḥ
indriyāṇīndriyārthebhyas tasya prajñā pratiṣṭhitā 2.58

yada = when; samharate = fully, completely; ca =and; ayam = this one; kurmah = tortoise; angani = limbs; iva = just as; sarvasah = from all sides, wholly; indriyani = the senses; indriya-arthebhyah = from the sense objects; tasya = his; prajna = discriminating intelligence; pratisthita = becomes firmly established.

When this one fully withdraws his senses from the sense objects, just as a tortoise completely withdraws its limbs from all sides, his discriminating intelligence is firmly established.

Commentary

When a stable-minded person (sthitaprajna) withdraws his sense organs wholly from the sense objects, he finds peace and stability within himself. The qualifier 'wholly' or 'from all sides' is relevant. Mental stability does not arise from half-hearted attempts. A devotee must entirely withdraw his senses, both physically and mentally, in order to experience peace and stability and abide in the Lord, his Self, because the interaction between the senses and the sense objects distracts and disturbs the mind. When that connection is fully cut off through withdrawal, the mind becomes calm and tranquil. We are programmed by Nature to look to the world and become involved with it through our senses to fulfill our needs and desires. Our dependence upon them is such that we cannot imagine our lives without them. They are responsible for our thinking, actions, desires, and the latent impressions (samskaras) we carry to the next birth. Because of them, we remain outwardly drawn and attached to sense objects and rarely look within ourselves to know who we are or become mindful of our feelings and sensations.

The outgoing nature of our senses is responsible for the modifications of our minds and the resultant suffering and bondage. Therefore, withdrawing the senses from the world is necessary for stabilizing the mind and intelligence. It is also required for concentration, meditation, and self-absorption. The senses are the organs or the extensions of the mind. Just as the limbs of a tortoise facilitate its movements, the senses facilitate the mind's movements, perceptions, and understanding. However, they must be withdrawn and restrained since they keep the mind restless and deluded. Withdrawal of the senses is known in Yoga as pratyahara. It is one of the eight limbs of classical yoga. The senses indulge in seizing, grasping, taking away, removing, attracting, and holding the sense objects. Collectively, they are known as "hara." Samhara is the opposite. It means not grasping, not seizing, and not taking away, which is characteristic of the state of withdrawal of the senses. When we restrain the senses, we set in motion the withdrawal process, which ultimately leads to concentration, self-absorption, and self-realization.

Samhara also means destroying or killing. In this sense, withdrawing the senses is a destructive process in which you temporarily immobilize the senses to end the modifications, restlessness, and the outgoing nature of the mind.

However, one cannot achieve lasting peace or mental stability by merely withdrawing the senses from the world. As soon as the control is lifted, the senses will revert to their outgoing mode and disturb the mind. We withdraw our senses, fully or partially, when we are busy, lost, distracted, resting, dreaming, or asleep. However, it does not lead to lasting control over the senses since we temporarily distract them from their habitual actions. Liberation requires a permanent solution, for which we have to identify and resolve the root causes of the mind's instability so the senses can be tamed, restrained, withdrawn, and kept under control by will. For that, one must resolve the modes and overcome desires and attachments through self-purification.

Sloka 59

viṣayā vinivartante nirāhārasya dehinaḥ
rasavarjaṃ rasopy asya paraṃ dṛṣṭvā nivartate

visayah = sense objects; vinivartante = turn away, recede; niraharasya = without food, abstaining, fasting; dehinah = of the embodied; rasa-varjam = leaving aside or excepting the taste; rasah = taste; api =even that; asya = of his; param = supreme transcendental; drstva = upon seeing; nivartate = ceases, falls away.

Sense objects recede from the embodied one who abstains from food, excepting their taste. Even that taste falls away from him when he sees the supreme transcendental Self.

By merely studying the scriptures or withdrawing the senses from sense objects, one does not gain knowledge of the Self. One should not only withdraw and restrain the senses from the objects but also overcome the desire (taste) for the pleasures and sensations they create, including the memories associated with them. Only then does the yogi of resolute intelligence abide in the Self without duality, confusion, and delusion. What does "He sees the supreme, transcendental Self" mean? It means he abides in the witness consciousness and discerns the Lord in him as his very Self. By seeing him in the transcendental state and becoming established in him without duality, he discerns that the Lord is his Self, distinct from his mind and body, indifferent and detached from all sides and in every respect. Thereby, he reaches the firm realization that he does not have to look for him outside but within himself. This is the essence of this verse.

Thus, withdrawing the mind and senses from sense objects (pratyahara) should not be limited to mere physical withdrawal. It must be practiced at every level until the gunas are subdued and the craving for sense objects is gone. There is an important saying that whatever you do, be it devotion to God, studying the scriptures, or practicing buddhi yoga, must be sincere and complete and must match your thoughts, words, and actions ('manasa vacha karmana'). The same holds true in this practice also. The sense organs are fifteen: the five organs of action, the five sense organs, and the five subtle senses or tanmatras, which correspond to the five perceptual sensations (sound, touch, smell, taste, and form). To achieve perfection in pratyahara and cultivate sameness, one has to withdraw and restrain all fifteen senses. However, withdrawing and silencing the subtle senses is more challenging since they are active not only when the senses dwell upon sense objects but also when the mind remembers the sensations they create in dreams or imagination. Therefore, even if you withdraw the sense organs from sense objects, the five subtle senses (tanmatras) may remain active and keep producing desires and subtle sensations from memory to disturb you. The problem disappears when the yogi sees the Lord in his body as himself or as his pure Self in a transcendental state.

It is why when people fast and abstain from food, they may still crave food and cannot stop thinking about it. Thus, withdrawal or physical separation of the senses from worldly objects does not guarantee stability, equanimity, or even-mindedness. To be a true sthithaprajna and experience sameness (samadhi), the yogi must control all parts of his internal organ (antahkarana), including the subtle senses. The tanmatras cease to disturb the mind only when he successfully withdraws the senses from the sense objects and cultivates detachment at all times, from all sides and everywhere (sarvatra). Only then would he remain undisturbed amidst sorrow, indifferent amidst pleasure, and free from passions, anger, and fear. When the mind is freed from desires and drawn into the Lord, his Self, and when the mind and senses are fully and firmly withdrawn from external objects into him, only then sameness and resolute intelligence (sthithaprajna) are firmly established in the yogi. In that transcendental state, he discerns the Lord as himself or as his Self without duality or confusion. As he firmly establishes his mind and intelligence in the knowledge and conviction arising from that realization, all notions of desires, dependence, and relationships disappear. Attaining kaivalya (aloneness), he remains contended within himself and by himself, disturbed by neither sorrow nor happiness.

The taste for sense objects lingers in some people and extends to their next birth. When it happens, they find it difficult to overcome certain habits, desires, and natural tendencies, the cause of which they cannot easily fathom. For the same reason, even highly advanced yogis may have trouble controlling past-life habits, tendencies, or behaviors they inherit. For example, some spiritual teachers develop unhealthy habits such as smoking, eating tasty foods, or having a preference for certain types of enjoyment, such as wearing expensive clothes or traveling in luxurious cars, which are usually shunned in spiritual circles and attract public displeasure and controversy.

Sloka 60

yatato hy api kaunteya puruṣasya vipaścitaḥ
indriyāṇi pramāthīni haranti prasabhaṃ manaḥ

yatatah = while striving, endeavoring; hi = indeed; api = even; kaunteya = Kaunteya, son of Kunti; purusasya = of the person; vipascitah =learned, wise, discerning person; indriyani = the senses; pramathini = turbulent, unsteady;

haranti = take away, steal, carry away, snatch away; prasabham = forcibly; manah = the mind.

Indeed, even while striving, O Kaunteya, the turbulent senses forcibly carry away the mind of even a wise and discerning person.

As we stated in the preceding commentary, due to karma or past life impressions, even mahatmas succumb to temptations and seduction if they do not fully subdue their minds or control their senses. To establish firm control, one should withdraw the senses from sense objects and suppress all the lingering desires and memories associated with them. It is achieved only through sustained and unrelenting practice. Rajas and tamas are the major obstacles in this effort. They resist any attempt to suppress them until the last. Hence, until resolute intelligence (vyavasayātmika buddhi) is firmly established, the gunas are resolved, and the mind and senses are firmly controlled, even mahatmas and great yogis are vulnerable to desires and modifications. An aspirant may have trained his senses, studied the scriptures, perfected his spiritual practice, and cultivated discernment. However, he may still feel upset by small things until he completely conquers his mind and body through regular practice. Many people fail because it requires superhuman effort and cannot be achieved through self-effort only. Even with an exalted and purified mind and mental brilliance, he may still need the Lord's grace and protection to overcome deeply ingrained desires and habitual thoughts.

The difficulty is complicated by the fact that the mind and senses are always in contact with the world. We are never separate from the world, even when we are asleep or have withdrawn our senses. The world is an integral part of our consciousness. We cannot easily withdraw from it or its pervasive influence. The mind and body are not different or separate from the world. Just as the body is made up of the food we eat, our minds are made up of the perceptual knowledge and accumulated memories we gather from the world. Through them, the world becomes internalized in us and conditions our desires, thinking, and actions. Hence, as the previous verse suggests, even if we withdraw the senses from sense objects from the world, the taste for worldly enjoyment lingers on in our minds and keeps disturbing us. Hence, even the Mahatmas have to struggle to detach themselves from it and establish their minds in contemplation without interruptions. The sense organs are like coiled serpents. They spring into action at the slightest provocation and resist all efforts to control them. It is their nature to run in all directions like wild horses, disturbing you even when you are lost in your thoughts. Hence, restraining the mind and senses is the most difficult part of cultivating self-control, sameness, and equanimity. This problem can be resolved with divine help and devotional practice, as suggested in the next verse.

Sloka 61

tāni sarvāṇi saṃyamya yukta āsīta matparaḥ
vaśe hi yasyendriyāṇi tasya prajñā pratiṣṭhitā

tani = of them; sarvani = all; samyamya = restraining; yuktah = established; asita = remains restful or seated, sits; mat-parah = Me as the supreme; vase = in control; hi = certainly; yasya = whose; indriyani = senses; tasya = of him; prajna = wisdom, higher intelligence; pratisthita = firmly established or stabilized.

Having restrained them all and sitting restfully established in yoga, he should remain with his mind drawn to Me. He whose senses are under firm control, certainly his intelligence is firmly established.

Here, tani (them) refers to the senses. According to this verse, restraining his mind and senses, the yogi must sit restfully with his mind fixed on the Lord, who dwells in him as his Self. If he controls his senses, his mind and intelligence become firmly established in the Lord, and he can engage in uninterrupted concentration and meditation. Through that constant and repetitive practice, he gradually dissolves his identity and discerns the Lord in him as his pure Self without duality or division. The ignorant ones fix their minds upon images, names, and forms with duality and delusion. They think the deity they worship is external to them and make him offerings as if he is a separate entity. They may please the deity and fulfill their desires, but do not attain liberation, pure consciousness, or oneness. Driven by their egos and desires, they see duality and diversity instead of oneness within themselves or outside. They rest their minds and their deluded intelligence in multiple identities and distinctions, and prefer to be known by them. The rational ones think that intelligence is everything. They take refuge in their knowledge and wisdom or intellect rather than their spiritual nature and engage in desire-ridden actions to pursue desires and goals they think are logically justified for peace and happiness. The wise ones with discerning wisdom (buddhi yuktas) acknowledge their spiritual nature. They fix their minds with exclusive devotion and concentration upon the Lord, who dwells in them as their very Self. They take refuge in their higher nature, worship the Lord internally, and try to overcome the duality and division.

As this verse implies, when you restrain your mind and senses through samyama (self-restraint), you become stable-minded, a sthithaprajna. However, the skillful yogi (buddhi yukta), endowed with all the right qualities and fit to achieve liberation, cannot restrain his mind or senses entirely by himself. For that, he has to take refuge in the Lord and contemplate upon him inwardly, keeping his mind and senses under control until he achieves the tranquil state of sameness and oneness. He has to abide by the thought that his pure Self is none other than the Supreme Self and translate that thought into reality by silencing his mind and senses. In this verse, Lord Krishna used the word samyama to mean self-restraint or, more specifically, restraint of all gross and subtle senses (tani sarvani). When a yogi succeeds in that effort, his conviction grows, and his knowledge and intelligence become firm and stable.

Samyama means control of the mind and senses. Self-control (atma samyama) is an arduous and comprehensive effort involving all the organs in the body, especially the mind and senses. It is the foundation for all other yogas, without which neither the senses nor the mind can be restrained or established in the contemplation of the Self. In classical yoga, samyama is defined as restraining the mind and body from worldly things to practice concentration (dharana) and meditation (dhyana) and enter the tranquil states of self-absorption (samadhi). Here, it means restraining the mind and senses from external objects and stabilizing the mind in the Lord (the Self) through contemplation and devotion to attain firmness, sameness, and oneness.

Sloka 62

dhyāyato viṣayān puṃsaḥ saṅgas teṣūpajāyate
saṅgāt sañjāyate kāmaḥ kāmāt krodhobhijāyate

dhyayatah = thinking, meditating, dwelling upon; visayan = sense objects; pumsah = of the person; sangah = attachment; tesu = in them (sense objects); upajayate = arises, is born, originate; sangat = attachment; sanjayate = develops; kamah = desire; kamat = from desire; krodhah = anger; abhijayate = arises, is born, produced.

Thinking of sense objects, one develops an attachment to them. From the attachment is born desire, and from desire arises anger.

Thinking of sense objects, one develops attachments. From attachments arise desires and passions (anger, envy, etc.). Under their influence, one sinks into evil. When actions are performed with selfish intentions and attachments, it leads to sinful karma, bondage, and suffering. The concept is simple. Those who are attached to the world, think of the world, become involved with the world, and desire to possess and enjoy the world remain in the world, birth after birth, until they give up desires and attachments. However, those who renounce the world, worldly desires, and all worldly things and establish their minds in the Lord within them go to him and escape from birth and death.

The senses are primarily responsible for our involvement with the world, which leads to bondage and delusion. They are responsible for the duality and objectivity we experience in our minds, whereby we do not readily acknowledge our spiritual nature or pay attention to the Lord who dwells within us. We look out to the world for our joys and pleasures, and ignore the eternal source of happiness that always dwells in us as long as we breathe. Thereby, we miss a great opportunity to look within and realize our divine nature and oneness with the Lord. Thus, this verse explains how the senses contribute to our existential misery and emotional instability. You become restless when you run after them into the objective world and seek things that promise to make you happy or fulfilled. The truth is that the senses lack intelligence of their own. They rely upon you. However, when you are subject to desires, attachments, attraction, and aversion, they become your masters and control your movements and actions and, thereby, your destiny, binding you to worldly objects and not letting you be free. The idea of ownership and doership also arises for the same reason as we come to accept that if we seek and strive for worldly things, we gain more of them, and thereby, we can secure our lives and happiness. Once we develop an attachment to them, we do not let them go. When desires are obstructed for any reason, we experience varied emotions, particularly anger, fear, and frustration. Anger is one of the evilest passions. It temporarily impairs our thinking and judgment, whereby we lose control and act without forethought or discernment, which will lead to unhappy consequences. The next verse explains how attachment contributes to the loss of discriminating intelligence (buddhi nāsanam).

Sloka 63

krodhād bhavati saṃmohaḥ saṃmohāt smṛtivibhramaḥ
smṛtibhraṃśād buddhināśo buddhināśāt praṇaśyati

krodhat = from anger; bhavati = arises, develops; sammohah = confusion, stupefaction, delusion; sammohat = from confusion or delusion; smrti = of memory, law books; vibhramah = muddle, error, doubt, wrong; smrti-bhramsat = from loss of memory; buddhi-nasah = destruction of intelligence; buddhi-nasat = upon destruction of intelligence; pranasyati = left to perish or lose, be lost.

From anger arises confusion; from confusion, muddled memory; from muddled memory, the loss of discriminating intelligence, and upon the destruction of intelligence, one is left to perish.

Anger is a destructive passion. It destroys reason, memory, and discernment. Hence, from the earliest times, it has been declared in the scriptures as one of the evilest of passions (maha patakas). This verse describes how anger leads to self-destructive behavior by causing confusion, loss of memory, and muddled thinking. In worldly life, anger creates many problems for those who are prone to anger frequently. Since anger is mostly directed at others and anger attracts more anger, angry people usually end up alone or miserable, surrounded by many unhappy and disgruntled people who resent them, avoid them, or wish to harm them. Spiritual people suffer even more if they cannot control it, since it keeps them disturbed and becomes a major obstacle to attaining peace and equanimity. It is indisputable that anger is problematic in worldly life and spiritual practice. It impairs reason, memory, balance, emotions, perceptions, understanding, and all cognitive functions that are responsible for normal human behavior. Even advanced yogis may lose control over their minds due to surging anger and act irrationally and hurt themselves or others with their thoughts and actions. When spiritual people succumb to it, they waste away their spiritual energies and delay their chances of attaining liberation or obtaining a good life in their next birth. It is also difficult to control it since it is triggered by many factors, especially the desire to control and prevail over others or fulfill one's desires at any cost. Hence, angry people are seldom liked or appreciated. Dealing with them is like walking on eggshells.

In this verse, Lord Krishna aptly described anger as the destroyer of life. As he stated, the first consequence of anger is confusion, stupefaction (sammoha), or loss of clarity. In that confusion caused by anger, people temporarily lose touch with reality, reason, propriety, and balance and suffer from temporary memory loss (smritivibhrama). They forget who they are, why they are angry, how their words and actions may affect others, or the consequences that may arise. With that, they also suffer from the loss of judgment or discernment (buddhi nasa) and act irrationally or thoughtlessly, speaking unspeakable things or doing what they would generally prefer to avoid, such as hurting and harming others, speaking untruths, exaggerating or falsifying facts, making false accusations, seeking vengeance, or seizing things from others unlawfully. Such thoughtless actions can lead to their spiritual downfall since they produce sinful consequences for their actions and for hurting and harming others.

Sloka 64

rāgadveṣavimuktais tu viṣayān indriyaiś caran
ātmavaśyair vidheyātmā prasādam adhigacchati

raga = attraction; dvesa = aversion; vimuktaih = released; tu = but; visayan = sense objects; indriyaih = with the senses; caran = moving; atma-vasyaih = under own control; vidheya-atma = a self-disciplined person; prasadam = peace and tranquility; adhigacchati = attains.

Free from attraction and aversion, restraining his senses under his firm control when they move among sense objects, the self-disciplined person attains peace and serenity.

Attraction and aversion (ragadvesha) are why the senses move restlessly among the sense objects. When a yogi overcomes them through self-control (atmavasa), his senses cease to have a reason or cause to wander wildly or uncontrollably. Once he controls them through self-restraint, his mind falls in line and surrenders to his will. Then, with firm resolve and resolute intelligence, he attains peace and clarity through stable and firm intelligence (sthithaprajna), which is mentioned in verse 61. Thus, this verse affirms that a yogi or devotee who is self-disciplined and who keeps his senses free from attraction and aversion and under his firm control attains peace and stability. Anger arises from desires; desires arise from attachments, and attachments gain strength when the senses repetitively interact with sense objects due to attraction and aversion. Therefore, logically, it makes sense that by controlling desires through self-discipline and freeing the senses from attraction and aversion, one can control the mind and achieve peace and serenity (prasadam). A word-for-word literal translation of this verse is difficult to understand because of the way it is composed. However, this is the essence of it.

It states that peace and serenity are possible when a yogi brings his senses (indriya) under his control (atma vasih), overcoming attraction and aversion to sense objects (vishayas) with self-control (vidheya atma). Attraction and aversion are the mind's natural reactions or responses to external objects. They are caused by attachments, desires, likes, and dislikes. They are our minds' natural responses or reactions to the dualities of life or the pairs of opposites. In worldly life, we learn from experience and interaction to seek things we like and avoid those we dislike. We instinctively turn away from those that are painful or repulsive and are drawn to those that are pleasing or agreeable. We prefer happiness to sorrow and seek things that make us happy, even though we know that what produces happiness initially may eventually end up producing sorrow and suffering. On the surface, it seems a clever strategy to look for happiness and pleasure in the things and situations that promise to produce happiness and fulfillment and reduce or resolve suffering. However, in life, we do not always succeed in getting what we want or avoiding what we do not want. Since we cannot foresee far, we do not know how our actions and choices will turn out or what fruit and consequences they will produce. Nothing lasts forever, be it happiness or sorrow. Hence, the discerning ones with stable intelligence practice self-control, restrain their minds and senses, and overcome attraction and aversion, the twin causes of our restlessness or mental instability, and become indifferent to the dualities of life.

Sloka 65

prasāde sarvaduḥkhānāṃ hānir asyopajāyate
prasannacetaso hy āśu buddhiḥ paryavatiṣṭhate

prasade = in serenity; sarva = all; duhkhanam = sorrows; hanih = destruction, removal, eradication; asya = of his; upajayate = arise, happen, follow; prasanna = serene, pleasant cetasah = mind, person; hi = indeed; asu = soon; buddhih = discriminating intelligence; pari = from all sides, sufficiently, firmly; avatisthate = firmly established.

In that serenity, the end of all his sorrows happens for him. Indeed, the discriminating intelligence of that serene mind is firmly established (in the Self) from all sides.

Commentary

From this and the previous verse, it logically follows that attraction and aversion (raga dvesha) are the root causes of our suffering. Once they are resolved, the senses fall silent, discriminating intelligence arises firmly, and the mind, free from sorrow, attains serenity and sameness (samatvam) and becomes firmly established in the awareness that the Lord dwelling in the body is indeed his very Self. Peace or serenity (prasadam) prevails from all sides as he becomes absorbed in that awareness with self-control, with his mind and senses withdrawn and detached from the dualities of life and himself freed from attraction and aversion (raga dvesha vimukti). In serenity, all his sorrows end, his senses and mind become restful in the contemplation of the Lord, and he abides in sameness (samadhi) with stable intelligence (sthithaprajna). In that state, he remains satisfied in himself and by himself (atmani atmana, 5.55). Tushti (contentment) and prasadam (serenity) are not attained by escaping from sorrows, distracting the mind from problems, or pursuing happiness and enjoyment through desire-ridden actions. These approaches are problematic. Practically, they are not viable solutions because one cannot wholly remove suffering from life by addressing the superficial causes that seem to produce it.

To overcome suffering permanently or on a lasting basis, one has to address its root causes: desires, attachments, and the natural, outward movement of the senses toward sense objects. They have to be controlled or silenced. Even then, some suffering remains, which cannot be avoided since the body is subject to the pain and suffering arising from natural causes such as injury, aging, or sickness. Even advanced yogis and enlightened masters cannot escape from it and have to endure it with the years of equanimity, sameness, and endurance they cultivate. Hence, if lasting peace and happiness are the aims, one must find them within oneself, overcoming attraction and aversion, controlling desires, and restraining the mind and senses, rather than finding them outside in the world or the things one desires. By nature, the Lord who dwells in us is indestructible, peaceful, fixed, and serene. When we discern him with pure intelligence, establish our minds in his contemplation with unwavering devotion, and withdraw mentally from the impermanent world with detachment, we open ourselves to attaining permanent peace and happiness through oneness with him. In short, the Lord can be discerned and attained without duality or division only by those whose minds and senses are silent and withdrawn into him, whose intelligence is firm and stable (sthithaprajna), and who are free from desires, attachments, attraction, and aversion.

Sloka 66

nāsti buddhir ayuktasya na cāyuktasya bhāvanā
na cābhāvayataḥ śāntir aśāntasya kutaḥ sukham.

na= not; asti = there is; buddhih = discriminating intelligence; ayuktasya = the unrestrained or uncontrolled; na = not; ca = and; ayuktasya = unsteady, uncontrolled; bhavana = concentration; na = not; ca = and; abhavayatah = one without concentration; santih = peace; asantasya = for the one without peace; kutah = where is; sukham = happiness.

For the unrestrained one, there is no discriminating intelligence, and for that unrestrained one, no concentration (either). For that one who is without concentration, there is no peace, and for the one who is without peace, how can there be happiness?

One attains serenity (prasada) when the senses are restrained from their natural, outward movement and withdrawn into the mind, the mind into intelligence, and intelligence into the Self. Without stable and firm intelligence (sthithaprajna) acting as the controller, it is not possible for the one who lacks self-control to withdraw his mind and senses and abide in the Lord with peace and tranquility. A yogi who is endowed with pure intelligence and can fix his mind upon any object without distractions is a yukta, the yoked one. He is fit to plow his mind and harvest sameness, peace, and happiness. Ayukta is the opposite. His mind is not cultivated and tamed, and his intelligence is not bright enough to discern the Self or stabilize his thoughts. He lacks the purity and wisdom to control his mind and draw his attention and devotion to himself.

This verse declares that real happiness arises from within when the mind and senses are restrained and discriminating intelligence (sthithaprajna) is firmly established. When the mind is yoked with stable and resolute intelligence, the skillful yogi discerns the Lord in him and concentrates on him without interruptions. With uninterrupted concentration (bhavana) and exclusive love and devotion, he merges his identity in the Lord, his Self, offering himself or his dual identity as a sacrifice. Thus, self-control (atma-samyama) is the key to practicing exclusive devotion (ananya-bhakti) and attaining the Supreme Being without duality, delusion, or division. We will learn more about it in the final chapters of this scripture.

When the mind is stabilized through withdrawal, concentration, and meditation, peace and serenity follow. From peace arises firmness and happiness. Bhavana is translated by many as meditation or concentration. Literally, it also means feeling or a state of mind. In the context of this verse, it may refer to all these and the state of samyama, described in classical yoga as the simultaneous practice of devotional concentration, meditation, and sameness or self-absorption. With discriminating intelligence, the mind becomes steady. When it is steady, it can be drawn and stabilized in the Lord, who dwells inside as the Self. When it is saturated with the thoughts of love and devotion for him (Isvara pranidhana), the yogi experiences tranquility and sameness (samadhi).

An unsteady person who is caught in the phenomenal world is devoted to the attractions of the world. His mind and senses wander in different directions, seeking things propelled by desires. With his mind drawn out into the world and his senses running wildly, he does not feel the need to look within himself, find the Lord who dwells in him, and experience devotion for him or union with him. Even if he practices concentration or devotional worship, his mind will distract him and lead him toward his desires and natural propensities. A steady mind is, therefore, vital to practicing concentration, meditation, and devotion and experiencing peace and happiness through union with the Lord who dwells within all.

Contrary to popular opinion, meditation does not lead to a steady mind. The restraint of the senses leads to it and to uninterrupted concentration and meditation, whereby one experiences peace and devotion to the Lord. The path of devotion is not easy to practice. As we learn from this verse, true devotion arises in a yukta, whose mind and senses are restrained and who is firmly established in intelligence. Thus, the serene mind (prasada) is not the cause but the effect of self-purification and transformation through the sustained practice of buddhi, jnana, karma-sannyasa, and bhakti yogas.

Sloka 67

indriyāṇāṃ hi caratāṃ yan manonuvidhīyate
tad asya harati prajñāṃ vāyur nāvam ivāmbhas

indriyanam = of the senses; hi = for; caratam = wandering, moving; yat = that one; manah = mind; anuvidhiyate = obediently follows, in obedience; tat = that; asya = of him; harati = carries away, takes away; prajnam = wisdom or understanding arising from discriminating intelligence; vayuh = the wind; navam = a boat; iva = like; ambhasi = on the water.

For, the mind which obediently follows the wandering senses, that (mind) of him carries away his wisdom as wind (carries away) a boat on the water.

An intelligent mind should control the senses, not the other way around. A karma yogi endowed with pure discernment (suddha buddhi) is supposed to be the lord (Indra) of his mind and senses and wield his natural power of reasoning, analysis, and judgment (buddhi) to restrain them, perform his obligatory duties as ordained for him, without desiring their fruit. However, he will remain restless and deluded if he lets his mind and senses wander everywhere and induce him to perform the same duties with desires and attachments. As this verse states, self-control is vital to cultivate unwavering intelligence. The unruly senses, without a master, will cloud the mind with modifications and disturbances and impair its ability to think and discern clearly. A restless mind, with its intelligence covered by impurities, is the seat of evil thoughts, ignorance, delusion, desires, attachments, and sinful karma. Wisdom arises from intelligence, and intelligence shines in a person whose mind is pure, calm, and illuminated by knowledge and devotion. A steady mind endowed with pure intelligence must practice concentrated meditation (samyama) upon the Self to attain self-absorption.

Thus, more than education, discipline, and self-control are necessary for a striving yogi to practice virtues and achieve liberation. Present-day education does not teach people how to control and purify their minds and bodies or cultivate reason and intelligence to distill their experience and knowledge, which are essential for building character, righteous conduct, and mental brilliance (prajna). It has many repercussions since most people are not equipped to make the right decisions about their lives or problems with clarity and discernment. A wandering mind, aided by unruly senses and drawn to the things of the world, which are impermanent in themselves, remains restless, driven by desires, passions, and attachments. In that state, it is difficult to stay calm, experience peace and stability, practice meditation and concentration, or think of God. Therefore, controlling and restraining the senses and drawing the mind to the chosen purpose with discernment is paramount. In the next verse, Lord Krishna confirms the same.

Sloka 68

tasmād yasya mahābāho nigṛhītāni sarvaśaḥ
indriyāṇīndriyārthebhyas tasya prajñā pratiṣṭhitā

tasmat = therefore; yasya = whose; maha-baho = O mighty-armed one; nigrhitani = withdrawn, restrained; sarvasah = in all respects; indriyani = the senses; indriya-arthebhyah = from the sense objects; tasya = of him; prajna = discriminating intelligence; pratisthita = firmly established.

Therefore, O mighty-armed, he whose senses are withdrawn in all respects from the sense objects, his discriminating intelligence is firmly established.

Since a wandering mind carries away one's wisdom and discernment, a yogi must restrain his senses from sense objects and stabilize his mind through self-purification (resolving the gunas) to cultivate discernment and firm intelligence. When his mind is stable, his senses are withdrawn, and his intelligence is firm, he will discern the Lord who dwells within him as his Self and overcome his duality and delusion. Mental clarity arises only when the mind is pure and free from desires and attachments. When the mind is free and pure, intelligence also becomes sharp and one-pointed. The yogi, who wishes to cultivate both, must practice self-control, withdrawing his mind and senses and holding them firmly within himself. Only he who can do it without interruptions and disturbances can establish his mind in the Lord and experience oneness or sameness. With a serene mind, with his thoughts firmly established in him with discernment and devotion, he experiences samadhi or sameness.

Sarvasah means always, in all places, from all sides, and in all respects. It means that a wise person (dhira) should always control his mind and senses fully and firmly in all circumstances, not occasionally or according to his convenience. He should not let up or let his mind and senses wander and disturb serenity. A disturbed mind cannot possess resolute intelligence or discern truths. With a distracted mind and unruly senses, one cannot think clearly, discern truths, stay calm and composed, or focus on goals, free from worry and anxiety. Hence, a skillful yogi practices self-control persistently. Even when he is moving among the sense objects or interacting with other people, he remains in control and does not let his thoughts or actions disturb his peace or internal connection with the Lord. This is the essence of this teaching.

Sloka 69

yā niśā sarvabhūtānāṃ tasyāṃ jāgarti saṃyamī
yasyāṃ jāgrati bhūtāni sā niśā paśyato muneḥ

ya = that which; nisa = night; sarva = all; bhutanam = for the beings; tasyam = in that; jagarti = wakeful; samyami = the self-restrained; yasyam = in which; jagrati = awake; bhutani = beings; sa = that is; nisa = night; pasyatah = sees; muneh = the silent seer.

That which is night for all beings, in that the self-restrained one remains awake; that in which the beings are awake, that is night for the silent seer.

This is another important verse from the Bhagavadgita, which describes the consciousness of an awakened yogi who is free from delusion and ignorance. Worldly people are wakeful (active or actively engaged) in the presence of sense objects and objective reality, but asleep in the presence of the Self or the Supreme Reality. The wise ones are asleep (passive or inactive) in the presence of sense objects and worldly pleasures, but awake in the presence of the Self. The difference is that worldly people do not restrain their senses and let them wander freely among the sense objects, while the wise ones control them and withdraw them into themselves so that they can remain absorbed in the contemplation of the Self. This is the essence.

The day is symbolic of our active involvement with the world. The night represents our withdrawal from it. When worldly people are awake and their senses are engaged, that is the day for them. During that time, they remain actively involved with worldly objects and things, ignoring the consequences that may arise from them. Due to the lack of discernment, they do not follow their higher purpose or liberation or acknowledge the Self, which is hidden in them and represents their higher nature. Instead, they engage their minds and senses to fulfill their desire for material things and worldly possessions or pursue the triple aims of dharma, artha, and kama. When their senses are withdrawn, and they fall asleep, it is the night for them. During that time, they remain passive or inactive and ignorant of their physical and spiritual nature. Thus, when it is the day and their senses are active, they pursue desires and desire-ridden actions. When it is night and they are inactive, they fall asleep and abide in darkness, overcome by tamas, and are ignorant of everything.

In contrast, the seers who control their minds and senses and possess stable intelligence (prajna) remain inactive, indifferent, detached, and disinterested when they are awake and active and when their senses are engaged in their natural outward movement (prvritti). Amidst worldly people or worldly objects, they restrain their minds and become passively apathetic as if they are asleep or unconscious (vigatasprha). Due to self-control and resolute intelligence, they do not participate in the activities of their minds and senses and remain indifferent to the world and its ways. Since they know the ways of maya, they are not tempted or repelled by the attractions and aversions of the world. When their senses are in the outgoing mode (prvritti), they keep their minds in the inward mode (nivrtti). Therefore, amidst worldly enjoyments, they act as if they are asleep. When their minds and senses are withdrawn, and in the inward mode (nivrtti), they remain actively awake, contemplating upon the Self. Thus, what ordinary people consider the day in which their minds and senses are awake is the night for the seers, and vice versa.

Munih means a sage or hermit who practices silence (maunam). He silences his mind, senses, thoughts, and desires to abide in the Self. He pursues liberation as the sole aim, renouncing the world, suppressing his desires and attachments, and remaining absorbed in concentration and contemplation. Amidst worldly pleasures, when ordinary people are active and awake, he remains passive and inactive as if asleep.

From a philosophical or symbolic perspective, for the jivas, samsara is the night where they suffer, and the immortal world is the day where they are ever awake and blissful. Ignorance of the Self is the night, and awareness of it is the day. Performing desire-ridden actions to fulfill desires is the night, and controlling them to pursue liberation is the day. The deluded mind is the night, and pure consciousness is the day. Karma is the night, and becoming free from karma is the day. Knowledge is the day, and ignorance is the night. Delusion is the night, and discernment is the day. Thus, you can see that the day for the wise ones (yuktas) is the night for worldly people. The wise ones know when and where to be active or inactive. In contrast, the ignorant ones are active, where they are supposed to be inactive, and vice versa. They are asleep to the supreme reality of the Self, which they cannot discern due to their clouded intelligence. Thus, these two types of people offer contrasting scenarios.

Samsara is a long night for the jivas who are stuck in the mortal world, where Death, the god of the Night, rules. When they escape from him and achieve final liberation, they enter the world of Brahman, which is the eternal day of light and bliss for all liberated beings. The wise ones know the distinction between true knowledge (vidya) and false knowledge (avidya). They are not confused or carried away by the promises of ritual knowledge (avidya) or the allurements of spiritual powers or worldly wealth. In the darkness of samsara, they find their way with the help of their knowledge and intelligence, while others remain stuck in it, chained by their karma and fate.

The Mandukya Upanishad describes four states of consciousness, namely the wakeful (jagrat), dream (svapna or taijasa), deep sleep (susupti), and transcendental (turiya) states. According to tantra or siddha yoga, ordinary people remain awake in the wakeful state but asleep in the other three. In contrast, self-realized siddhas who attain the supreme knowledge (vidya) of pure consciousness (sahaja yoga) remain awake in all four states. They withdraw their minds and senses but remain in the transcendental state of oneness, seeing the world as their projection. Harnessing the awakened energies (chaitanya shaktis) in them, they enter the pure state of self-knowing (sahaja vidya) by gradually bringing the transcendental consciousness of the turiya state into the other three and soaking them with it. Thus, a truly enlightened yogi who has realized his Self remains awake even in deep sleep, which is not possible for ordinary people. Since he remains centered on the Self and sees it as the ever-wakeful, supreme reality, appearances no longer delude him, whether his mind and body are asleep or awake, and whether it is day or night.

Sloka 70

āpūryamāṇam acalapratiṣṭhaṃ samudram āpaḥ praviśanti yadvat
tadvat kāmā yaṃ praviśanti sarve sa śāntim āpnoti na kāmakāmī

apuryamanam = Ever full to the brim; acala-pratistham = unmoving, steadfast, firmly established; samudram = the ocean; apah = waters; pravisanti = enter; yadvat = as; tadvat = so; kamah = desires; yam = to whom; pravisanti = enter; sarve = all; sah = that person; santim = peace; apnoti = attained; na = not; kama-kami = pursuer of desires.

Just as water from all sides enters the ocean, which is always full but unmoving, even so are desires which enter the person who has attained peace, not the one who is a pursuer of desires.

Just as water that flows from all rivers and waterways into an ocean has little effect upon the size and movements of the ocean, so is the consciousness of the yogis who attain peace and equanimity and abide in the sameness. They are undisturbed or little affected even when their senses constantly bring sense perceptions from all sides because they subdue their desires, establish their minds in contemplation, and remain satisfied within themselves and by themselves. The symbolism should not be taken literally because oceans are not static. Many activities, currents, and movements happen deep inside them, although outwardly and from far away, the ocean may look calm and stable. However, we know that the ocean is not affected by the waters that flow into it constantly from the rivers, creeks, etc. A stable-minded yogi (sthithaprajna) who abides in sameness is also not moved by what happens or does not happen or whatever impressions the senses may bring. Neither desires nor dualities influence him because he is the silent hermit (muni) whose mind is quiet and whose desires are asleep. In contrast, worldly people who cannot restrain their desires are easily disturbed by what happens or does not happen.

Desires play an important role in the lives of worldly people. They are responsible for their bondage and suffering. However, desires have no power over the yuktas, who are endowed with steady intelligence (sthithaprajna) and practice detachment, firmness, and sameness. A yogi who cultivates indifference and one-pointed intelligence passively witnesses the coming and going of sense objects and desires but does not act upon them or surrender to them. His consciousness (samprajnata) is like an ocean, which is complete, unmoving, and unchanged. Being full to the brim, it does not need anything and does not seek anything to fulfill itself. Ordinary people look to the world for fulfillment, and self-realized yogis look within themselves for undisturbed peace and happiness.

The world consists mainly of those who enjoy pursuing desires (kamakamis) rather than liberation (mokshagamis). Nature intends the world to be this way since liberation is against its design, which is to bind the souls to samsara and continue the cycle of creation. A worldly person who is bound by desires serves the interests of Nature. His mind is like the water of a small lake or pond, which overflows when it is flooded with the outpouring of heavy rains. Similarly, a worldly person is easily overwhelmed with desires and expectations. He is unfit for liberation since he cannot cultivate discernment or detachment, but only a yogi who attains peace by overcoming desires. When he erases the boundaries of his consciousness through sameness and abides in the tranquility and pure consciousness of the Self, he remains unmoved even while desires enter him because, in him, all desires dissolve as soon as they enter. Desire-ridden thoughts may still enter him because of past karmas, residual memories, and latent impressions, but they fail to move him into action or create ripples in his consciousness.

Sloka 71

vihāya kāmān yaḥ sarvān pumāṃś carati niḥspṛhaḥ
nirmamo nirahaṃkāraḥ sa śāntim adhigacchhati

vihaya = having renounced; kaman = all desires; yah = who; sarvan = all; puman = the person; carati = moves about; nihsprhah = without longing, passion or desires; nirmamah = without the sense of ownership; nirahankarah = without egoism; sah = he; santim = peace; adhigacchati = attains.

That person attains peace, who, having renounced all desires, moves about without longing, without the sense of ownership, (and) without egoism.

The Bhagavadgita is not opposed to happiness and fulfillment through enjoyment or worldly life but recommends the ideal of enjoying life without desires, attachments, egoism, ownership, seeking, and striving. It supports attaining the four aims of human life (dharma, artha, kama, and moksha) by selflessly serving the aims of God and performing his duties upon the earth as a sacrifice. When the impurities mentioned above are absent, a yogi can move freely in samsara without being bound. In a very material sense, freedom from desires is liberation by itself, which is also the essence of sameness and firmness. The same idea is reflected in this verse. It says that when desires are renounced, and the mind with discriminating wisdom is firmly established in the Self, it leads to the flowering of virtues in God's devotees, such as the absence of seeking and striving (nihsprhah), ownership, the sense of mine (nirmama), pride and egoism (nirahankara). With purity and intelligence firmly established, they experience the state of sameness and undisturbed peace (santih).

Nirmama means not having mamatvam or the feeling of ownership (me and mine), which is an obstacle to liberation. In its opening verse, the Isa Upanishad explains why we should refrain from entertaining the notion of ownership, doership, and egoism. It declares that the whole creation belongs to Brahman, and he is its rightful owner, inhabitant, and lord (Isvara). If we think and act as if we are the owners of anything in this world and take pride in it, we will incur the sin of stealing what does not belong to us and incur karma. Therefore, it suggests that human beings should perform their obligatory duties as an offering to God and wish to live here for a hundred years. Nirmama is not exactly egoism but an offshoot of it. One of the most dominant and powerful desires that drives us into materialism is the desire to live and enjoy life. It is described in Yoga as the longing for life (abhinivesa), which manifests either as an attraction to the promise of life or as the fear of death. Without it, it is difficult to continue upon the earth and keep the morale high since life is so full of problems and hardships, making it logically not worth living.

The longing for life keeps our hopes alive and gives us the justification to participate in samsara despite its impermanence, instability, and the inevitability of death and suffering. It is present in all living beings, including lower life forms. Even monks who renounce worldly life experience it until they attain perfection in discernment, detachment, and renunciation, at which stage their longing and seeking end. With desires and attachments suppressed, they live as if they are lifeless and dull (nihsprhah). Egoism or ahamkara is the desire to preserve and perpetuate one's identity in multiple ways and fulfill one's desires at the expense of others. It manifests in our consciousness in various forms, resulting in desire-ridden actions, attachments, delusions, and bondage.

Sloka 72

eṣā brāhmī sthitiḥ pārtha naināṃ prāpya vimuhyati
sthitvāsyām antakālepi brahmanirvāṇam ṛcchati

esa = this; brahmi = highest, Brahman; sthitih = state; partha = Partha; na = not; enam = this; prapya = having attained; vimuhyati = is deluded; sthitva = thus established; asyam = in this; anta-kale = end time, last stages of life; api = also; brahma-nirvanam = union, dissolution or absorption into Brahman; rcchati = attains.

This is the highest state, O Partha; having attained this, one does not become deluded. Thus, established in this one, at the end of life, one attains Brahma Nirvana, absorption in Brahman, the Supreme Self.

The pure consciousness that discerns the indwelling Lord is without desires, longing, ownership, and egoism. It does not seek even the bare minimum necessities of life but accepts unconditionally what is obtained from others, without seeking, as divine providence. Such is the highest state of liberation, Brahma Nirvana, or eternal freedom to which all the yogas lead. It is also the absolute state of Brahman, considered the supreme Goal (parandhama) of all devotees and seekers of liberation. Brahman represents the absolute, supreme reality from which everything manifests and into which everything is withdrawn. It is the ultimate state of perfection and completeness, which is pure, eternal, infinite, complete, transcendental, self-existent, self-knowing, inexhaustible, indestructible, and incomparable. There is nothing higher or other than Brahman. He is beyond the mind and senses, ungraspable and indescribable. Even gods do not know him and will not attain him unless they take birth as humans.

When a yogi attains it, he becomes a living embodiment of Brahman. He contains within himself the indivisible and indescribable state of pure consciousness, the light of which radiates through his mind and body and his words, conduct, and actions. His voice becomes the voice of reason and wisdom. His actions reflect the will of God as he dissolves himself in it and is no longer guided by his ego or duality. When he departs from here, he leaves forever, never to return. Nirvana means putting out, extinguishing, dissolving, or ending all becoming and being, seeking and striving, embodiment, samsara, dependence, individuality, separation, distinction, and duality. In Nirvana, beingness is dissolved as the mind and senses fall silent. Only the Self remains as the one, eternal, indivisible, and all-pervading reality. For seekers of liberation, it is the highest state and goal. Having attained that, nothing else remains to be attained, and one is never deluded again.

Conclusion

iti srīmadbhāgavadgītāsupanisatsu brahmavidyāyām yogasāstre srikrisnārjunasamvāde sāmkhyayogo nāma dvitiyo 'dhyayah

Translation

iti = thus; srīmadbhāgavadgītā = in the sacred Bhagavadgita; upanisatsu = in the Upanishad; brahmavidyāyām = the knowledge of the absolute Brahman; yogasāstre = the scripture of yoga; srikrisnārjunasamvāde = the dialogue between Sri Krishna and Arjuna; sāmkhyayogo nāma = by name Samkhya Yoga; dvitiya = second; adhyayah = chapter.

Thus ends the second chapter, named Samkhya Yoga in the Upanishad of the sacred Bhagavadgita, the knowledge of the Absolute Brahman, a treatise on Yoga, which contains the dialogue between Arjuna and Lord Krishna.

03 – Karma Yoga

The Yoga of Action

Sloka 1

arjuna uvāca
jyāyasī cet karmaṇas te matā buddhir janārdana
tat kiṃ karmaṇi ghore māṃ niyojayasi keśava

arjunah = Arjuna; uvaca = said; jyayasi = superior; cet = if; karmanah = to action; te = your; mata = thought, opinion; buddhih = discriminating intelligence; janardana = Janardana; tat = then; kim = why; karmani = in action; ghore = horrible, awful, hideous, terrible; mam = me; niyojayasi = engaging me; kesava = O Kesava.

Arjuna said, "O Janardana, if, in your opinion, discriminating intelligence is superior to actions, then why are you engaging me in hideous actions, O Kesava?"

Arjuna's question in this verse reflects the confusion any initiate would experience in the early stages of learning about karma yoga from his teacher. In the previous chapter, Lord Krishna spoke to him about different yogas and approaches to attain the serenity of the mind. The knowledge he taught can be overwhelming even to advanced students since he introduced many concepts and yogas while speaking about Samkhya Yoga. He taught him the importance of self-knowledge (jnana) and intelligence (buddhi) in the life of a householder. However, it appears he had not yet fully grasped the connection between actions and intelligence or between karma yoga and buddhi yoga. In the last chapter, Lord Krishna said (2.49) that karma yoga was far inferior to buddhi yoga. At the same time, he advised Arjuna to perform his duties as a warrior. Therefore, Arjuna could not correlate the two contradictory statements. He heard that intelligence was superior to actions, but could not understand why he had to perform actions instead of practicing buddhi yoga. He also did not fully grasp the Lord's statement (2.50) that yoga meant skillfulness in actions and that skillfulness would arise from knowledge and discernment. He also did not understand the true meaning of renunciation or how to practice it as a karma yogi. He understood that actions should not be abandoned but must be performed. However, he did not understand with what attitude they should be performed or why discernment was needed to perform them.

The Vedas classify sacrificial actions (karmakanda) into three kinds: obligatory (nitya), prohibitory (nishiddha), and optional (kamya). The first ones must be performed by all householders, meaning they cannot avoid or neglect them without incurring sin. They should also be performed without desires as a duty, obligation, and sacrifice to God. The second ones are prohibited for all. They should not be performed at all since they produce sinful consequences. The third ones are optional, which means householders can perform them to fulfill their desires through rituals and sacrifices, offering food to the gods to appease them. Since they are performed to fulfill desires or attain desired ends, they invariably produce sin and bind people to samsara. Even obligatory actions produce sin if performed with desires, egoism, and selfishness. However, duties ordained by the Vedas as obligatory and performed with a sacrificial attitude for the sake of others or the Supreme Lord improve one's chances of attaining liberation or a good birth in the next life. They produce sin only if neglected or performed with desires or against established procedures. Hence, tradition advised householders to study and cultivate discernment and the knowledge of the Vedas to practice karma yoga skillfully and avoid sin.

Knowledge and intelligence are the foundation of all yogas. They are essential for renunciants (sannyasis) who give up desires and worldly life, seekers of knowledge (jnanis) who study the scriptures and pursue self-knowledge, and householders (grihastas) who practice karma yoga to perform obligatory duties and discharge their karmic debt to gods and others. With knowledge and discernment, renunciants will know what they should renounce; knowledge seekers will know which knowledge they should cultivate, and karma yogis can discern which actions will produce sin and which ones will not, so they can perform them intelligently to avoid sin. Previously, Arjuna used his moral judgment and concluded that fighting and killing his relatives in the war was sinful and would ruin his reputation. He was unaware that he could fight skillfully with knowledge and intelligence and avoid the sin he feared would ruin his family and reputation. Since he still needed the knowledge to grasp the significance of karma yoga and its connection to buddhi yoga, he wanted to know why Lord Krishna asked him to perform the unpleasant task of fighting when he could have practiced buddhi yoga and achieved liberation or peace and happiness.

Sloka 2

vyāmiśreṇeva vākyena buddhiṃ mohayasīva me
tad ekaṃ vada niścitya yena śreyoham āpnuyām 3.2

vyamisrena = mixed, ambiguous, conflicting; iva = as it is; vakyena = statements; buddhim = understanding arising from discriminating intelligence; mohayasi = confused, bewildered; iva = as; me = my; tat = therefore; ekam = one; vada = please tell; niscitya = with clarity or certainty; yena = by which; sreyah = highest good; aham = I; apnuyam = may attain.

"With conflicting statements, you seem to be confusing my understanding. Therefore, please tell me clearly that (path) by which I may attain the highest good."

A student may feel confused when he is introduced to a new subject. If he does not pay attention or listen properly when the teacher teaches him, lacks interest, or the subject is new to him, his confusion will increase further. It was unlikely that Arjuna was inattentive or disinterested. Indeed, he was troubled by the prospect of fighting his close relations and causing bloodshed. However, he also requested Lord Krishna, with great humility, to guide him. He put his doubts and confusion before him, treating him like a friend, and consulted him for a solution. Arjuna exemplifies a troubled devotee who prays to God for solutions and looks to him for inspiration and guidance. He was also pure in his heart, had faith in the knowledge and wisdom of Lord Krishna, and was eager to know the consequences of fighting and killing his relations on the battlefield. He possessed some knowledge of the scriptures and his duties, but lacked the right knowledge that would set him free from doubts and confusion and strengthen his resolve to fight.

Therefore, we cannot say that he was not listening or inattentive. He was confused because he could not comprehend the importance of various yogas, which Lord Krishna briefly mentioned in the second chapter, and how they would fit into his problem and resolve his sorrow and indecision. It is also possible that the author of the scripture purposely interjected this situation into the conversation to reinforce the teaching and ensure that those who study it gain clarity and understanding. The second chapter is very comprehensive and, in a way, summarizes the entire discourse. Therefore, first-time listeners may have trouble understanding and grasping its essentials. The scripture contains the knowledge and practice of so many yogas that its essential teaching may still elude us even after reading it several times. Many scholars (including this writer) admit that with each reading, their understanding of it improves. Knowledge of the various yogas may not confuse an adept who knows the scripture by heart, since he can discern their relative importance and see how they can aid the initiates in their practice. Arjuna needed that understanding. Further, he was still in a despairing mood and reluctant to fight. He did not see the connection between buddhi yoga and karma yoga and was unsure which of them he should follow. Hence, he made the right call and asked the question. By asking the question, he also conveyed that he was attentive, interested, and willing to learn from Lord Krishna so he could overcome his sorrow and perform his duty.

Sloka 3

śrībhagavān uvāca
lokesmin dvividhā niṣṭhā purā proktā mayānagha
jñānayogena sāṅkhyānāṃ karmayogena yoginām

sri-bhagavan uvaca = said the Supreme Lord; loke = in the world; asmin = this; dvi-vidha = two kinds of; nistha = discipline, steadfastness, faith; pura = in the past; prokta = declared; maya = by Me; anagha = sinless one; jnana-yogena = by the yoga of knowledge; sankhyanam = for the wise men of knowledge; karma-yogena = yoga of action; yoginam = for the practitioners of yoga.

The Supreme Lord said, "O sinless one, two types of disciplines were declared by Me in this world in the past: jnana yoga for the samkhyas and karma yoga for the (karma) yogis.

By addressing Arjuna as anagha, meaning the sinless one, Lord Krishna indicated that this knowledge was fit for sinless people or those trying to overcome sin through righteous actions. Nishta refers to any sustained and resolute practice, discipline, or application to achieve any intended goal or overcome any obstacle. Here, it denotes the two spiritual disciplines or yogas: jnana yoga (the yoga of knowledge) and karma yoga (the yoga of action). Although there is a fine distinction between jnana and samkhya yogas, they are used synonymously here to denote the path of knowledge. The classical Samkhyavadins used to pursue the knowledge of Samkhya and practice the eight limbs of Yoga. Many ascetic traditions of ancient India followed the same pattern. Jnana yoga refers to the system of yoga in which a yogi pursues spiritual knowledge through self-study, scriptures, spiritual teachers, or contemplation to overcome ignorance and delusion and achieve self-realization. Samkhya yoga is a type of jnana yoga only, with its particular emphasis on cultivating knowledge and intelligence to distinguish and detach the Lord (Self) in the body from its tattvas and absorb the mind in his contemplation to attain oneness, sameness, or self-absorption. In the Bhagavadgita, both the jnana and samkhya yogas are often used synonymously.

Jnana yoga and karma yoga are two divergent traditions of Hinduism, each with a long history. In jnana yoga, knowledge is the means, and in karma yoga, karma or actions. In the days of the Vedic tradition, Karma yoga was probably practiced by Mimansikas (ritualists) who were preoccupied with rituals and sacrifices, and jnana yoga was practiced by Vedantins (spiritualists) or forest dwellers who studied and taught the Upanishads and practiced some form of asceticism, away from worldly people. The Mimansa school believed that performing yajnas (sacrificial ceremonies) was vital to enjoying peace and happiness and that humans should perform them as ordained by the Vedas to uphold Dharma and enjoy life on earth. Therefore, they focused on acquiring the ritual knowledge of the Vedas and performing sacrifices (karmakanda), giving no importance to the knowledge of the Self or the practice of contemplative methods. According to them, householders were obligated to perform sacrifices as ordained by the Vedas to fulfill their desires and ensure the welfare of all. They did not believe in God or the idea of final liberation. They thought that by practicing karma yoga and performing yajnas, householders could achieve the four aims of human life and secure a place in heaven or a good life in the next birth.

Jnana yoga seems to have become popular with the development of Upanishadic knowledge and the internalization of the Vedic rituals. It formed the basis for the emergence of contemplative practices and mental worship (manasa puja), which subsequently became integral to all spiritual and yoga traditions. It was practiced by those who learned the secrets of the Upanishads, renounced worldly life, and led contemplative lives, pursuing liberation and inquiring into the nature of existence or their consciousness. They relied upon the knowledge portions of the Vedas (jnanakanda) as found in the Upanishads (Vedanta) and some Brahmanas and Aranyakas, which they considered the higher knowledge (vidya) compared to the ritual knowledge found in the Samhitas and Brahmanas, which they equated with ignorance (avidya) or lower knowledge. Their ultimate goal was liberation (moksha) or oneness with the indwelling Lord, who was beyond their minds and senses. They internalized sacrificial rituals, inventing yogic and contemplative practices that corresponded with the aspects of yajnas, and relied upon them to purify their minds and bodies and discern the Self in them, which they believed represented the highest and absolute reality. They equated the Self in them with Brahman or Isvara and the organs in their bodies with the gods of heaven, who needed to be nourished and energized through internal offerings of food and self-purification. According to them, salvation was possible only by knowing and becoming one with the Lord (Self) in them, for whom the mind, body, and senses existed and performed their duties. They did not give much importance to sacrificial rituals, which, according to them, played a limited role in the life of a householder up to a certain age and ensured them a place in heaven and a better life in their next birth. According to them, the ultimate goal (paramartha) of human life was attaining liberation (Moksha) from our sorrowful and death-ridden world by renouncing worldly enjoyments and taking up sannyasa to practice self-purification and establish the mind in the Self.

Both approaches are currently grouped under Mimansa Darshana (philosophy). The ritual school is known as Purva Mimansa, and the spiritual school is known as Uttara Mimansa. The Purva Mimansa school is almost extinct. However, its remnants can still be seen in the prevailing ritual traditions of Hinduism, in Smartaism, the Samskaras, Grihya Sutras, tantras, and temple worship. It is difficult to find pure ritualistic schools nowadays or ritual puritans, although rituals are still widely practiced in Hinduism. However, Vedanta is still prevalent in different forms in the philosophical and sectarian traditions of Hinduism, such as Shaivism, Vaishnavism, and Shaktism. It is also difficult to find pure karma yogis or jnana yogis today. Hindu spiritual practices draw from both yogas, apart from other ancient schools such as Samkhya and Yoga philosophies. The Bhagavadgita reflects the effort of the Vedantic seers to unite and integrate these two divergent paths (jnana and karma) into a composite system and bring renunciation into the mix. In this verse, Lord Krishna declared that he taught these two yogas in the remote past, samkhya yoga for the seekers of knowledge and karma yoga for the men of actions. As we have discussed before, in the context of the Bhagavadgita, Lord Krishna used the word Samkhya to refer to the knowledge of the Self, and that of Yoga to denote the techniques or the methods of practice, which result in the direct perception of the Self or of the knowledge which is acquired through study and contemplation. However, when he used both words together (as samkhya yoga), he meant it to be jnana yoga only. Samkhya means the teaching regarding the knowledge of the Self. Yoga means a set of methods and practices to validate that knowledge. However, samkhya yoga is a form of jnana yoga with aspects of both Samkhya and Yoga.

It is true that the original Samkhya and Yoga Schools of Hinduism, which are included in its six philosophies (Darshanas), are different from the Samkhya and Yoga teachings of the Bhagavadgita. The original Samkhya School of Kapila did not believe in the Supreme God, Creator (Isvara), or even gods. However, it acknowledged eternal souls (purushas) who were bound to samsara when they dwelt in the jivas and eternally free when they attained liberation. It viewed the mortal world as a work in progress whose structure, function, existence, and continuity were entirely governed by the natural laws of Prakriti or Nature. She was responsible for all the causes and effects that manifested in existence without the intervention of any other force or will. She was also not entirely independent but bound by her laws. Hence, she exercised no will and created nothing new since the effects that were to manifest were already latent in their causes as ideas or potencies. Prakriti brought them forth mechanically and spontaneously without any conscious or intelligent effort.

In contrast, the Bhagavadgita holds that Brahman is the supreme and absolute reality, both existent and nonexistent. Isvara is his highest manifestation. He is the creator and controller of all. In all actions, his will is involved directly (in pure souls) or indirectly (in impure and deluded souls). Creation is an intelligent process, which is willed and initiated by him as a part of his duty (Dharma) as the Supreme Controller and the source of all. Prakriti manifests his will and brings forth worlds and beings acting as his dynamic force. She is also responsible for samsara, maya, and keeping the beings in the mortal world bound to their nature until their liberation or the end of the world. She is not a blind automaton but an active and intelligent force responsible for their delusion, illumination, bondage, and liberation. However, she is not independent but bound to the will of Isvara. Thus, the Bhagavadgita's Samkhya philosophy differs from that of Kapila's Samkhya in many respects. It upholds Brahman as the Supreme Reality and Isvara as his highest manifestation, who, together with Prakriti, is responsible for the fivefold functions of creation, preservation, destruction, concealment, and revelation. In all these functions, only his will is the driving force.

The Samkhya yoga (path of self-knowledge) of the Bhagavadgita is meant for yogis or sannyasis, who want to achieve liberation by knowing the Lord (who dwells in them as their Self and support) through study, inquiry, discernment, and contemplative practices. For that, they renounce worldly life and contemplate upon him, withdrawing their minds and senses into themselves and cultivating detachment, indifference, and sameness. By developing discernment, knowing the distinction between the Lord in them (the Self) and his creation (body or the not-self), and opening their minds to his transcendental presence within themselves rather than to his impermanent, projected, or superimposed self (the mind and body or the world), they eventually stabilize their minds in him and attain the supreme yoga (brahma yoga) of oneness. Since knowing the indwelling Lord (antaratma) as one's true Self is central to this path, it is known as the path of knowledge (jnana yoga) or self-knowledge (samkhya yoga). Traditionally, it is meant for those who take up sannyasa without becoming householders (grihastas) or for householders who become sannyasis before or after discharging their obligations. Tradition encourages householders to renounce the world only after discharging their obligatory duties, since such duties are essential to ensure the orderly progress of the world.

The path of action (karma yoga) is meant for householders (grihastas) who want to pursue the goal of liberation in a roundabout way without abdicating their other goals (purusharthas), duties, and responsibilities. Their duties (dharma) arise from Brahman only, for whom the whole universe is but an abode (griha) in which a small part (amsa) of him manifests and resides as gods, worlds, and beings, with him acting as the sole support. He is its ultimate owner and dweller (grihasta). His will is inviolable and drives all the individual wills that manifest in the jivas with different intensities according to their spiritual purity. It manifests fully in those who are completely pure and have fully subdued the gunas. The idea is that since Isvara, the Supreme Lord, is the source of all and his will determines the initiation and outcome of all actions, movements, and happenings, we are not supposed to take any credit for them, including our actions and the consequences arising from them. They should be offered to him only, because since he is their cause, their responsibility or results also rest with him.

However, within karma yoga, you will find two approaches: an inferior method in which one performs actions with desires and attachments, and a superior one in which one performs them without desires. In the former case, karma yogis incur karma (for exercising their will and owning the actions) and keep transmigrating through the cycle of births and deaths. However, in the latter case, when they perform them without desires and offer the fruit of their actions to God, surrendering their will and egos, they become free and achieve liberation. The first is the way of the Mimansikas, and the second is that of the Vedantins, who pursue knowledge, cultivate discernment, and consecrate their lives to God through actions. It is the ideal path for worldly people who want to follow the example of the Supreme Lord in their lives and perform his duties for his sake to ensure the order and regularity of the world without claiming anything for themselves. By doing his work, without desire and expectations, serving him with love and devotion, and offering him all they have, including ownership and doership, they clear their karmic debt and attain liberation. When they perform actions for Isvara rather than for themselves, all the consequences arising from their actions (the fruit of karma) accrue to God but not to them. Thus, karma yoga of the selfless kind, which we will learn later, is ideal for those who want to perform their obligatory duties and earn God's grace.

Both karma and jnana yogas are equally effective and can potentially lead yogis and devotees on the sunlit path to eternal freedom. They are also mentioned in several scriptures, including the Upanishads. Ideally, karma yoga is suitable for householders who pursue the four aims of human life, namely Dharma (duty), Artha (wealth), Kama (pleasure), and Moksha (liberation) through sacrificial actions. They serve gods and others by performing their obligatory duties and earning merit, peace, prosperity, and happiness. With the superior strategy of accumulating merit and avoiding sin, they either secure a place in heaven and a good birth in the next life or achieve liberation. Jnana yoga is ideal for those who renounce worldly life and practice self-purification to absorb their minds in the contemplation of the Self and attain oneness. They are not obligated to perform obligatory duties and uphold Dharma since they renounce worldly life.

However, although this verse implies that karma and jnana yogas are distinct and different, they are also complementary. As we will subsequently learn from the Lord, jnana yogis need to be karma yogis and vice versa. Those who renounce the world still need to perform actions to maintain their bodies and observe their vows of renunciation. Those who engage in obligatory duties need the knowledge to know rules and restraints, scriptural knowledge, methods of self-purification, code of conduct, the distinction between the Self and the not-self, or between reality and unreality, etc. Hence, ideally, seekers of liberation should practice both yogas to cleanse themselves and overcome obstacles.

Indeed, the Vedic tradition itself upholds the idea. Both approaches are mandatory in the practice of the varnashrama dharma, which ensures that those who are born in a higher caste or practice the Vedic tradition must learn Dharma in their childhood by studying the scriptures before they take up household duties. Endowed with that knowledge, they should progress through the remaining phases of human life. Thus, knowledge and intelligence (without which one cannot grasp the knowledge or apply it intelligently) are superior to actions. Memorial knowledge (smriti) is necessary to know the duties (dharma) one needs to perform and how to perform them correctly. Knowledge of the Self is acquired through self-study or by approaching a teacher with a humble request to reveal the secrets of the Self.

It is said that the continued practice of karma yoga lays the foundation for self-purification and prepares the householders to practice jnana yoga and acquire the knowledge of the Self. According to the Varnashrama Dharma, householders should begin their lives as karma yogis, and later in their lives, they should turn to jnana and sannyasa yogas to attain liberation. Thus, although karma and jnana yogas are seemingly different, they must be practiced together for liberation. The Isa Upanishad affirms it, declaring that those who only worship the knowledge of sacrifices enter blinding darkness, and those who only worship the knowledge of the Self end up in greater darkness. However, he who has the knowledge of the Self and sacrifices and practices them together intelligently crosses the world of death through the knowledge of sacrifices and attains immortality through the knowledge of the Self.

Sloka 4

na karmaṇām anārambhān naiṣkarmyaṃ puruṣośnute
na ca saṃnyasanād eva siddhiṃ samadhigacchati

na = without; karmanam = from actions; anarambhat = by not doing; naiskarmyam = freedom from actions; purusah = person; asnute = attain; na = nor; ca = also; sannyasanat = giving up, renunciation; eva = only; siddhim = freedom from actions; samadhigacchati = attain.

A person does not attain naishkarmya siddhi by abstaining from actions, nor does he attain freedom from actions by merely giving them up.

The importance of karma yoga to attain freedom from actions and their fruit is affirmed in this verse. Naiskarmya siddhi means freedom from all karmas and their fruit. It also means freedom from the duty or obligation to practice nitya karmas (obligatory duties), a householder is ordained to practice as a service or debt to God. Since karma also means the fruit of karma (karma phalam), it also refers to the state in which actions do not produce karma. When a person attains naishkarmya siddhi, he is free from the obligation to carry out any duties and responsibilities and not burdened by karma, whether he performs them or not. However, that state is not easily attained.

For that, a karma yogi has to ensure that his actions do not bear fruit. As Lord Krishna stated here, freedom from actions (duties) and their fruit (karmaphalam) is not attained by abandoning or renouncing actions but by performing them. Therefore, no one should consider giving up actions to achieve naishkarmya siddhi. One has to perform them in such a manner that they do not bear fruit and lead to bondage. The teachings of the Bhagavadgita are meant to attain this noble state only. Freedom from karma arises only when one renounces desires and attachments completely and performs actions without desiring their fruit.

This verse refers to two divergent schools of opinion, probably prevalent in the Mahābhārata times, about how to escape sin and the bondage arising from actions (karma bandha). One was by doing nothing or leading a passive life, avoiding all willful actions and obligatory duties, and making no conscious effort to take control of anything or attain anything. The other was renouncing worldly life to escape duties and obligations and living an idle life in seclusion. The first one was practiced by sects such as the Ajivakas, who were fatalists and believed that since everything was predetermined, there was nothing anyone could do to change the course (niyati) of one's life or the progression of the world. Therefore, they resigned to their fate and went through life passively without exerting themselves or trying to achieve anything. The second method was practiced by those who took the vows of renunciation (sannyasa) to escape from personal problems, duties, and responsibilities. They were namesake ascetics or renunciants who lived in seclusion to escape from the burdens of this world (samsara) rather than from the cycle of births and deaths (samsara). They donned the robes to avoid their householder duties or family responsibilities.

Apart from them, there were Mimansikas, the ritualists, who believed that since human beings were meant to perform sacrificial duties until the end, one should not seek freedom from actions (karmakanda) at all as long as one lived on earth. In other words, they ruled out the possibility of attaining freedom from actions (naishkarmya siddhi) and the fruit of actions. According to them, human beings were born to perform sacrificial actions following the Vedas, and their actions produced either sinful or sinless karma, depending upon whether they followed the injunctions of the Vedas. They did not believe in permanent liberation from duties or samsara but only in a temporary escape from the mortal world in a subtle body to heaven, where they stayed until their subtle bodies withered and returned to the earth to take another birth.

Lord Krishna refuted these approaches. According to him, naishkarmya siddhi cannot be attained by abstaining from actions or renouncing them. Also, it cannot be achieved by practicing karma yoga according to the Vedic injunctions and performing sacrifices and obligatory duties to fulfill one's desires. These approaches are ineffective since they do not address the problem of karma or bondage, which arises from desire-ridden actions. The right approach is to cultivate knowledge and discernment to resolve the problem of karma permanently, knowing how actions produce karma, how they should be performed intelligently, and what should and should not be renounced while performing them.

Sloka 5

na hi kaścit kṣaṇam api jātu tiṣṭhaty akarmakṛt
kāryate hy avaśaḥ karma sarvaḥ prakṛtijair guṇaiḥ

na = not; hi = because, for; kascit = anyone; ksanam = moment; api = even; jatu = even; tisthati = exist, remain; akarma-krt = actionless, inactive, without performing action; karyate = made to do; hi = indeed; avasah = without their own accord or active involvement; karma = actions; sarvah = all; prakrti-jaih = born of Prakriti or Nature; gunaih = modes.

Because not even for a moment can anyone remain without performing actions. Indeed, all are helplessly made to perform actions by the modes born of Nature.

In the early Vedic tradition, when Mimansa was the dominant school, karma originally meant karmakanda or sacrificial rituals and obligatory duties householders were obligated to perform according to the Vedas to ensure their happiness here and hereafter. The first two portions of the Vedas, namely the Samhitas and Brahmanas, contain the knowledge of sacrifices and how to perform them. In the Bhagavadgita, Lord Krishna followed the expanded meaning of karma to include all natural and mundane actions such as eating, breathing, walking, thinking, dreaming, sleeping, etc., including inaction. According to it, karma means any desire-ridden action that has the potential to bear fruit and produce consequences. The law applies not only to human beings but also to all other living beings. Jainism and Buddhism also follow a similar definition. From this perspective, karma means any willful or natural action or inaction arising from one's gunas or essential nature, which produces binding consequences. Lord Krishna said that no one can remain free from performing actions even for a moment. Driven by desires and attachments induced by their essential nature, they helplessly perform actions and revolve in the cycle of births and deaths until they attain naishkarmya siddhi.

The expanded definition of karma is very pragmatic. It also makes sense since it expands the scope of karma. If we accept the restricted definition of karma from a purely Vedic perspective, it should be applicable only to a few whom the Vedas ordain to perform sacrificial duties. The rest, maybe 98% of humans, do not have to worry about their actions or consequences. However, we can see that birth, death, and rebirth are common to all living beings. Karma must be an inescapable fact of our existence since all actions produce consequences. Every action creates ripples in the stream of life and touches others. Even science acknowledges the butterfly effect. Everyone engages in actions driven by the gunas born of their nature. It is true even for the sannyasis who renounce worldly life. They also perform actions to maintain their bodies and observe vows of renunciation. Even the practice of Yoga, be it karma, jnana, or bhakti yoga, is karma only. Karma also arises from our thoughts, words, and intentions. Thus, no one can escape from the force of Nature and avoid actions entirely or escape from karma. Even ascetics who renounce worldly life and live austerely have to perform actions to control and purify their minds and bodies. Hence, avoiding karma is almost impossible unless we resolve its root causes rather than evading actions. In the following few verses, Lord Krishna will explain how one may practice karma yoga and achieve naishkarmya siddhi, or freedom from actions. Karma yoga is necessary to perform actions and escape from the consequences of actions.

Sloka 6

karmendriyāṇi saṃyamya ya āste manasā smaran
indriyārthān vimūḍhātmā mithyācāraḥ sa ucyate

karma-indriyani = organs of action; samyamya = controlling; yah = who; aste = remains; manasa = by the mind; smaran = recollecting, remembering; indriya-arthan = sense objects; vimudha = deluded; atma = soul; mithya-acarah = false or deceitful practitioner; sah = he; ucyate = is called.

Controlling the organs of action, he who keeps remembering sense objects in his mind, that deluded soul is a false practitioner.

In the second chapter, Lord Krishna emphasized the importance of controlling the mind and senses to cultivate discerning intelligence (prajna) and attain peace and serenity (prasada) through jnana and buddhi yogas. He said that when a yogi fully withdrew his senses from sense objects, just as a tortoise withdrew its limbs, his intelligence (prajna) would be fully established. With his mind and senses firmly restrained and intelligence perfected, he would control anger, delusion, etc., and overcome attraction and aversion to stabilize his mind in the Self and attain serenity, equanimity, and freedom from sorrow. Thus, self-control is the key to attaining intelligence, peace of mind, and self-realization. He reaffirmed the same idea here about actions and freedom from actions. Mere restraint of the body's physical organs is ineffective in attaining naishkarmya siddhi, or freedom from karma. One has to withdraw the mind and senses from sense objects and perform actions with equanimity and without any desire to stabilize the mind in contemplation and attain freedom from karma.

Comparatively, it is easier to control the body, but when it comes to the mind, it resists any attempt to control it. It remains restless and distracted when the senses are active and busy among sense objects. They must be withdrawn and silenced to restrain the mind and experience peace and stability. Your mind is the last bastion of Nature, where you encounter the fiercest battle with the demons who reside there. Unless you reclaim it from her subduing the gunas, you will not find peace and stability. Residual desires, attachments, and past life impressions, which you accumulate through successive births and deaths, linger in the back of your mind and disturb your thoughts. They do not let you establish your mind in the Lord who dwells in you. Even if you renounce the world, your habitual mind persists in memory and troubles you. Its influence is so tenacious that many people fail to continue and return to worldly life. To achieve perfection and reach the end of that path, a seeker should be true to himself, know his progress, and his natural tendency to delude himself.

Self-control is essential for success in all yogas. Without it, one cannot practice karma, jnana, or sannyasa yogas without interruptions and delays. The yogi should firmly establish his mind in the indwelling Lord with exclusive devotion and consecrate his actions to him without expectations. If his mind remains deluded and keeps wandering among sense objects, he cannot overcome his desires and attachments and stabilize his mind in his contemplation or offer him his sacrificial actions. He must resolve these problems by purifying his mind and body through desireless actions (nishkama karma) and cultivating resolute intelligence. In this verse, Lord Krishna suggested that it would not be possible for a yogi to overcome delusion or escape from karma by merely restraining the organs of action and remaining physically inactive. Superficially restraining the body without corresponding inner purity and self-control is but a delusional and false practice (mithyachara). It leads to neither liberation nor self-control nor inner purity.

One can say the same about renunciation. What is the point of renouncing the world if the mind is repeatedly drawn to worldly pleasures and enjoyments? The body, mind, and senses must be completely withdrawn and controlled (samyama) in all respects to remove all traces of desire for sense objects. Even after that, latent desires persist in the consciousness and keep coming to the surface until they are fully suppressed. The scriptures identify fifteen sense organs (indriyas), namely the five organs of action (karmendriyas), five organs of knowledge (jnanedriyas), and five organs of sensory perceptions (tanmatras). A yogi has to withdraw them all to achieve perfection. He may start with the organs of action. However, until the subtle senses are also suppressed and immobilized, he will not establish complete control over the inner demons.

Sannyasa (renunciation) is not an act of taking initiation from a guru and wearing orange robes to escape life's burdens. It must be practiced with pure intentions, free from delusion, doubt, and self-deception. For that, one should give up everything and become empty, including the selfish desire to live or achieve liberation. The surrender must be complete so that the aspirant lives according to the will of God, putting his ego at his feet. It is also not easy to give up the world. Even if you avoid the company of worldly people and worldly objects, it follows you wherever you go. Even if you leave it and hide in a cave in the Himalayas, it follows you there as your past and keeps recreating itself in your thoughts and dreams. Therefore, you have to make your mind a cave and shut it from all sides to prevent distractions. True renunciation is the renunciation of desires and attachments. We will learn more about it from Lord Krishna in the subsequent verses. Self-control (samyama) must be practiced at all levels, beginning with the senses.

Self-deception and hypocrisy are the works of Maya. Worldly people take comfort in them to find acceptance and approval, fulfill their desires, or achieve success. Those who excel in them are more successful in worldly life since the world goes by appearances rather than truths. We are conditioned to hide the truth about ourselves rather than reveal it. Hence, practicing truthfulness in this world is rather complicated and impractical. A seeker of truth cannot follow such worldly ways. He has to remove the masks he wears and remain honest and truthful to himself and others in all respects. To achieve perfection on the path of liberation, he must honor truth, respect truth, practice truth, and stand for truth. Truthfulness is an important prerequisite and one of the five restraints (yamas) recommended by classical yoga and many spiritual traditions. Truthfulness means one should not hold back any truth, except in extraordinary circumstances where it may endanger one's life, but set it free. If we are truthful, our perceptions will not deceive us. Our intelligence will reveal to us secrets that ordinary people cannot perceive. If we take refuge in truth, truth will guide us and protect us. In this verse, Lord Krishna suggested that one should practice self-restraint truthfully and sincerely without deluding oneself. Otherwise, whoever practices the withdrawal of the senses but keeps thinking about material things should be reckoned a hypocrite and a practitioner of falsehood.

Sloka 7

yas tv indriyāṇi manasā niyamyārabhaterjuna
karmaindriyaiḥ karmayogam asaktaḥ sa viśiṣyate

yah = he who; tu = but, however; indriyani = the senses; manasa = the mind; niyamya = restraining; arabhate = begins, practices; arjuna = Arjuna; karma-indriyaih = organs of actions; karma-yogam = yoga of action; asaktah = without attachment; sah = that one, he; visisyate = special, better, stands apart, distinguished.

However, he who practices karma yoga (the yoga of action) with the karmendriyas (the organs of action), O Arjuna, restraining his senses with his mind, without attachment, that one is special.

The deluded karma yogi, who is insincere and lacks self-control and who is mentioned in the previous verse, is contrasted here with the true karma yogi, who controls his organs and performs actions without desires and attachments. This one is distinguished because he is not swayed by desires and has better discipline and discernment than the false practitioners (mithyacharas), even if they possess excellent knowledge or appear to be sincere, pious, and appealing. Perfection in karma yoga is not determined or achieved by worldly knowledge, lineage of gurus, or caste distinctions. They may matter in worldly life, but in spiritual life, truth only matters. To excel in karma yoga or any yoga, the yogi must overcome all desires and attachments and cultivate resolute intelligence. Then only, he will be considered a true practitioner (sadachari).

The organs of action (karmendriyas) are meant for physical actions. They should not be restrained but put to the right use to practice obligatory duties, restraining instead the mind and senses. In other words, one should restrain the internal organ (antahkarana) while letting the organs or actions perform their natural functions. This is the essence of this verse. We have already learned in the previous verses why self-control is essential in actions. One should not wish to achieve liberation through inaction because it is practically impossible. No one can remain inactive even for a moment. Further, a householder must perform his obligatory duties and should not escape from them in the name of renunciation. A householder's path to liberation is only through freedom from actions and their consequences (naishkarmya siddhi), achieved by performing his obligatory duties without desires and attachments. He must offer the fruit of their actions to the

Supreme Being. This is the path laid out for him by the Vedas. Whoever performs karma yoga in this manner is assured of a safe passage to the immortal world. He is better than the deluded renunciants (kapata sannyasis) and false practitioners (mithyachara) who act according to their desires and attachments.

True karma yoga is not just about performing obligatory duties to achieve desired ends, as some schools of Vedic religion used to believe. It is also not about making the right choices or evading sinful karma by performing daily sacrifices (nitya karmas) and avoiding the sinful kamya karmas or prohibited karmas. True karma yoga requires uncompromising self-control. One must perform all actions, be they nitya karmas or kamya karmas, as a sacrifice without desires and expectations. With the right knowledge and discernment, a karma yogi should resolve his karma and bondage without abandoning his duties and obligations. If the situation demands, he must be willing to perform the most difficult actions, even if they are against social or moral norms or scriptural injunctions. In other words, perfection in karma yoga rests upon performing actions righteously and selflessly with discernment (buddhi yoga) and right knowledge (samkhya or jnana yoga). By addressing the causes that produce karma, a karma yogi should take the poison of karma and the suffering that follows out of his actions and attain naishkarmya siddhi.

The Vedas explain why desire-ridden actions lead to bondage. It rests upon the justification that we own nothing in this world. The world does not belong to us. We are here as guests in the world owned and inhabited by the Lord. Therefore, we should live here as guests only, sacrificing the ownership and doership of our actions to him. As God's true representatives, we have the right to enjoy life by following his will, but not by pursuing our goals through desire-ridden actions. Since we are living in his world, we are also obligated to work for him and do his work upon earth, performing his duties as if they are our own, without seeking any benefit. Through that selfless service and sacrifice, we must discharge our karmic debt. This is the essence of karma yoga and why the Vedas ordain sacrifices for householders.

Sloka 8

niyataṃ kuru karma tvaṃ karma jyāyo hy akarmaṇaḥ
śarīrayātrāpi ca te na prasidhyed akarmaṇaḥ

niyatam = ordained, obligatory; kuru = perform; karma = duties; tvam = you; karma = action; jyayah = superior; hi = cetainly; akarmanah = without actions, inaction; sarira = bodily; yatra = continuation, journey, maintenance; api = even; ca = and; te = your; na = not; prasiddhyet = will not be possible; akarmanah = without action.

You have to perform the actions that have been ordained for you. Certainly, action is superior to inaction, and without actions, even the continuation of the body will not be possible.

What actions are we supposed to perform? Those that arise from God or the injunctions of the Vedas. Why are actions superior to inaction? Because through actions only can we overcome karma. Maintaining the body or living on earth will not be possible without actions. Inaction is not a solution to the problems we face, including the problem of bondage. Nothing is achieved by doing nothing. It is by action only that we gain happiness here and hereafter. However, according to our scriptures, we must choose actions that are connected to our duties and obligations or to the personal Dharma we practice on earth. As humans endowed with intelligence and self-awareness, we have several duties and responsibilities on earth toward ourselves, others, gods, and the Supreme Lord himself. We cannot avoid them without suffering from the sin of neglecting them. Without performing actions, we cannot even keep ourselves alive. Our bodies need nourishment and care. For that, we have to perform several actions such as eating, sleeping, walking, resting, etc. They also produce karma since the desire to live is inherent to them. Even ascetics who practice austerities, renouncing worldly life, cannot remain inactive or free from karma. They perform several actions to keep themselves alive and pursue liberation. Although the body is impure and an instrument of Maya, we must keep it alive and in good health to achieve our spiritual and material goals. Hence, no one can live without performing actions or incurring the karma they produce.

Life is a God-given gift. It should not be sacrificed or forsaken. Our first duty is toward our bodies and then toward God, others, and the world. By serving them selflessly through desireless actions, we are expected to enjoy life here and hereafter. Thus, irrespective of our personal choices and spiritual goals, we should not neglect our duties, especially those that are obligatory. In the past, they were determined by caste rules or the law books (Dharma shastras). Nowadays, we do not follow those criteria to choose our professions or occupations, or way of life. One way to resolve this is by knowing to whom we owe our existence and serving them. For example, we are indebted to our parents, elders, teachers, siblings, children, and those who help us, support us, protect us, serve us, employ us, teach us valuable lessons, or enrich our lives in a significant way. We have an obligation to serve our gods, ancestors, seers, sages, animals, and other creatures that keep the world revolving. We have to keep the world safe, live righteously and virtuously, and support righteous causes. The Bhagavadgita says that these duties arise from God. Hence, they must be honored to keep your side of the promise. You may consider the Supreme Lord as your role model and decide your duties. You may also draw inspiration from great people, saints, and sages, and follow their example. The karma yoga of the Bhagavadgita is ideal for householders and essential for preserving life on earth and attaining peace and happiness here and hereafter. You can elevate it further by adding the best aspects of jnana and sannyasa yogas without renouncing the world.

Sloka 9

yajñārthāt karmaṇonyatra lokoyaṃ karmabandhanaḥ
tadarthaṃ karma kaunteya muktasaṅgaḥ samācara

yajna-arthat = for the sake of sacrifice; karmanah = action; anyatra = otherwise; lokah = the world; ayam = this; karma-bandhanah = bound by actions; tadartham = for That; karma = actions; kaunteya = O son of Kunti; mukta-sangah = free from attachment; samacara = do, perform.

For the sake of yajna (sacrifice) only is karma. Otherwise, this world is bound by karma. It means, O son of Kunti, you must perform karma (actions) free from attachment.

Yajna means any sacrificial or devotional ritual, action, offering, or worship. Each sacrifice involves a sacrificer, an offering, and an object of sacrifice, usually a deity or the Supreme Lord. In the Vedic tradition, it refers to ritual sacrifices such as fire, soma, or horse sacrifices mentioned in the Vedas and performed according to prescribed methods. The Bhagavadgita expands its meaning to include all actions, including mundane actions, which are performed as a sacrificial or devotional service to God or as an obligatory duty to serve him and his creation. It also equates the yajna concept with God himself as the giver (data) of all. Yajna (ya + jna) means that which leads you (ya) toward the attainment of supreme intelligence (jna) or by which the supreme intelligence (Brahman) manifests. In other words, any selfless action in which you willingly give away something of your own or consecrate to God becomes a yajna or a sacrificial action. If you consecrate yourself to God and spend your life to serve him, then your whole life becomes a continuous yajna. By the sacrifice of your separate identity, duality, separation, and delusion as a jiva, you burn your impurities and enter the Supreme consciousness of your pure Self. The idea is justified because we owe our existence to the Supreme Lord. He helps you in numerous ways through several fellow humans, gods, his manifestations, shaktis, and other entities. Your whole existence depends upon him and his creation. Hence, you owe him a lot of karmic debt that you must repay through sacrificial actions. If you perform them with desires, you will incur more karmic debt and remain bound to samsara until everything is squared off. Thus, depending upon how you perform actions, sacrifices open the doors to eternity or suffering and rebirth.

Here, karma is equated with yajna. This is the original Vedic definition of karma. All Vedic sacrifices are collectively known as karma, and that part of the Vedas dealing with them is karmakanda. Yajnas have a great significance in Vedic Dharma, especially in the Mimansa school, which holds that the Vedas are eternal, inviolable, and uncreated, and the yajnas which they prescribe have the potency by design to fulfill our wishes and grant liberation or heavenly life, without even the involvement of an external entity such as God. The Bhagavadgita accepts the idea in essence but rejects the notion that they have their own potency independent of God. It affirms that God created yajnas for the welfare of the world, and householders must serve him and his creation through them. The spirit of yajna must be reflected by the discerning souls through sacrificial actions, performing them without any desires, expectations, or attachments so they can discharge their karmic debt and attain the Supreme heaven. Any action or sacrifice becomes impure or pure by the presence or absence of desires, attachments, or selfishness, even if the Vedas recommend them. By elevating all actions as sacrifices, the scriptures introduce the idea of divine life or God-centered living.

For householders who are not inclined to renounce worldly life, karma yoga is the best option to perform their obligatory duties and all actions as sacrifices and worship the Lord through them as if they are engaged in continuous devotional service. When you spend your life serving the Lord through the duties and actions he ordained for you, sacrificing to him all the benefits and good tidings that accrue from them, then actions will not taint or bind you. The fruit of such deeds will accrue to him rather than to you, and you will be free. This is the essential practice of karma yoga, primarily meant for householders. By taking upon themselves the duty of serving the Lord through their duties and actions (dharma), they will serve him and live freely in his name with the assured feeling that they do not have to worry about any consequences. Thus, the Bhagavadgita uplifts karma yoga to a higher level, transforming all actions into sacrificial actions (yajnas) and imparting to them the purity of detachment and renunciation.

Karma yoga is a simple and straightforward solution to resolve sin for the jivas who are caught in samsara and obligated to pursue the four aims of Dharma, Artha, Kama, and Moksha to uphold God's creation. Its message is clear and simple. Consecrate your life as a sacrifice (yajna) to the Supreme Lord. Let him be the judge and the witness. Focus on your actions without worries and anxiety, letting go of everything. By that sacrifice and giving up doership and ownership, you transfer the burden of your life and actions to him and put yourself entirely into his hands. Thus, karma yoga of the higher kind becomes your protector. It builds a protective shield around you and keeps you free from the impurities of samsara. Since our morals are relative and we do not know how our actions will end up, karma yoga is the best antidote to the uncertainty and the poison of karma hidden in our actions. Through its practice, a pious soul can serve God devotedly, setting aside his selfish desires, egoistic notions, and judgments and performing his actions sacrificially with indifference and detachment. The next verse explains why it is necessary to perform actions for the sake of God.

Sloka 10

sahayajñāḥ prajāḥ sṛṣṭvā purovāca prajāpatiḥ
anena prasaviṣyadhvam eṣa vostv iṣṭakāmadhuk

saha = along with; yajnah = sacrificial rituals; prajah = human beings; srstva = having created; pura = in the remote antiquity; uvaca = said; praja-patih = Brahma, the creator of beings; anena = by this; prasavisyadhvam = grow and multiply; esah = certainly; vah = your; astu = let it be; ista = what is desired; kama-dhuk = the giver or fulfiller.

In remote antiquity, having created human beings along with sacrificial rituals, Brahma Prajapati declared, "By this only you shall grow and multiply. Let it be your fulfiller of desires and wishes."

According to this verse, Brahma (a manifestation of Brahman) created humans along with yajnas and told them to nourish the gods and fulfill their desires and wishes through them. In the Vedic conception of life upon earth, yajnas are the means for householders to attain peace and happiness and earn sinless karma by nourishing gods and others with sacrificial food. Thus,

Vedic sacrifices have a social and spiritual dimension. They connect humans with gods and other beings and instill in them the spirit of service, selflessness, mutual dependence, and cooperation. Life thrives in creation due to sacrificial actions that promote harmony and cooperation between various categories of beings. If all the jivas, especially gods and humans, live selfishly for themselves, imagine what will happen. Creation or existence thrives on interdependence. That is true about life on Earth also. Neither gods nor humans can live by themselves. They have to help each other. The same principle applies in the case of the relationship between humans, plants, and animals. They have to depend upon each other for their welfare and the world. Plants and animals sacrifice their lives for humans, and humans must sacrifice their desires and selfishness to engage in sacrificial actions and nourish gods, other humans, plants, and animals. This is the order of the world.

Brahma is the creator god. At one time, he was worshipped as the highest deity of the Vedic pantheon before Shiva and Vishnu gained prominence. Kshatriyas of those times regarded him as their chief deity, lord of people (Prajapati), philosopher king, teacher, guardian, revealer of secret knowledge, and ruler of gods. They placed him in their esteem higher than Indra. For them, he personified the ideal of kingship, purity of knowledge and wisdom, sagacity, and excellence in delivering justice and protecting the worlds. Vedic hymns extol him as the highest manifestation of Brahman and call him variously Purusha, Prajapati, etc. According to them, after he manifested or woke from a long slumber lasting billions of years, he created the worlds and populated them with beings of various kinds. The Upanishads describe him as the first teacher of gods, humans, and demons, to whom he revealed the knowledge of the Vedas, the Self, and liberation. In the long history of Hinduism, he gradually lost prominence, probably due to the decline of the original Kshatriya clans, the intermixture of Kshatriyas due to wars and conquests, and the rise of sectarian traditions. The Vedas also mention at least two incarnations of Brahma, which were later ascribed to Vishnu.

This verse echoes the sentiment of the Mimansikas that Vedic rituals are meant for the welfare of humans and the fulfillment of their desires and wishes. However, it disagrees with their belief that Vedic sacrifices are eternal, self-existing, uncreated, and unalterable, and everything we need to know or achieve is possible through them only. In this verse, Lord Krishna clearly states that in remote antiquity, Brahma Prajapati created humans and the yajnas so that they could fulfill their desires through them. As we discussed earlier, the school of Mimansa does not acknowledge the Supreme Lord, Isvara, or the idea that the yajnas are meant to serve him or the aims of creation without desires and attachments. According to them, the yajnas have no higher purpose other than serving as the means or instruments to fulfill desires.

In the Vedic parlance, yajna means a deity (yajna devata) as well as a sacrificial ritual. They have a hidden purpose: to connect humans with gods and animals and facilitate cooperation and sacrifice. The sacrifices are elaborate rituals that must be performed precisely and strictly according to established procedures. It means they must be performed under the supervision and through the mediation of experienced priests. In complex rituals, several priests participate to perform different functions. The Rigveda mentions at least seven priests: hotr, potr, nestr, agnidh, prasastr, adhvaryu, and brahman. Each yajna is performed at the behest of a host (yajamana) who desires to perform it for specific ends. He bears all the costs and organizes the resources required to perform the ceremony. The priests fix an auspicious date for the occasion. Some yajnas may take months or even years. Some may also require more than one yajamana due to the costs and the duration involved. Gods and humans participate in them as guests. The offerings are made first to Agni, the fire god, by dropping them in the sacrificial fire. The underlying belief is that Agni is the mediator between humans and gods. He accepts the offerings and distributes them among the gods according to their preordained share.

The ultimate presiding deity of all the Vedic yajnas is Brahman only, and he is the silent and passive witness (sakshi) and the ultimate enjoyer of all sacrifices. The yajnas are meant to fulfill desires by nourishing the gods and seeking their help or intervention in return. Apart from them, offerings are also made in some sacrifices to ancestors and others. Some yajnas are obligatory, and some are optional. The optional ones are meant to fulfill desires. According to Vedic beliefs, yajnas are ordained for humans because gods and ancestors cannot make food for themselves, and they have to receive nourishment through the yajnas from humans only. The gods, in turn, cause the rains to fall and make the earth fertile so humans can have plenty of harvests and food. Thus, yajnas link heaven and the earth and bring gods and humans together to coexist in peace and harmony, helping and nourishing each other.

Many present-day Hindus put more faith in sacrificial rituals or nourishing gods. However, they do not understand their true significance or know their obligation to nourish the gods, ancestors, and others. They do not know how they contribute to their peace and happiness, and how they should be practiced for their material and spiritual well-being. Most people practice them rather mechanically due to fear of sin, vanity, social compulsions, family tradition, or to ward off bad luck or adversity. Rituals and sacrifices may not be suitable for all. However, as the Bhagavadgita and several Upanishads affirm, we cannot ignore their importance in Hinduism or to human life. They have a special place in our spiritual and religious development. In Vedic cosmology, sacrificial rituals are considered the source of everything, including creation, preservation, destruction, procreation, conception, birth, marriage, healing, protection, death, etc. The Rigveda proclaims that worlds originated from a cosmic sacrifice performed by Brahma in which he used parts of his own body as the sacrificial material. From that sacrifice, it says, emerged the whole diversity of worlds, beings, laws, divisions, time, dualities, tattvas, gunas, gods, goddesses, and so on. All the Vedic rituals are modeled on that universal sacrifice. Since they originated from the highest Lord in heaven, they are considered sacred and auspicious. Some sacrifices are also meant to seek expiation from the gods to absolve people from sin, adversity, or faults in performing rituals. The contemplative practices of yoga are internalized yajnas only in which the body serves as the sacrificial pit, the mind as the priest, senses as the guests, all the thoughts, words, mantras, and actions as offerings, and intelligence or knowledge as the sacrificial fire. They also have a higher purpose, hidden symbolism, and a special place in the order of things. The orderly movement of seasons, time, celestial objects, or creation's rhythm (rta) depends upon them. Karma yogis, who are devotees of God, are obligated to perform them. Through them, only human life progresses from one stage to another and culminates in transmigration or liberation.

Thus, Vedic sacrifices have a special place in Hindu rituals and spiritual practices. They are essential for the traditional householders to perform their duties and ensure order and regularity. Those who do not want to practice ancient rites and rituals but pursue liberation should still take the idea of yajna and integrate it into their actions and way of life. They have to elevate all their actions into sacrifices by renouncing desires so they can cleanse their karma and attain liberation.

Sloka 11

devān bhāvayatānena te devā bhāvayantu vaḥ
parasparaṃ bhāvayantaḥ śreyaḥ param avāpsyatha

devan = gods, devas; bhavayata = you nourish; anena = with this; te = those; devah = gods, devas; bhavayantu = nourish; vah = you; parasparam = mutually, each other; bhavayantah = nourishing; sreyah = good; param = the highest, supreme; avapsyatha = you should obtain.

Nourish the gods with this (sacrifice), and those gods shall nourish you. Thus, by nourishing each other, you will obtain the highest good.

Bhāvayatana means respectful and devotional service or worship. Here, Lord Krishna advised Arjuna to worship the gods devotionally and serve them through yajnas and with the offerings of food so that they will be impressed by it and reciprocate by granting him his wishes and helping him do his duties and uphold his duty (dharma) as a warrior. The Vedas encourage actions that facilitate cooperation between gods and humans through sacrifices. Humans have the obligatory duty to perform them to nourish the gods and others. Gods have the obligatory duty to help them in return by granting them their wishes and protecting them from their enemies, life-threatening situations, and evil ones. When gods are pleased with the humans who perform sacrifices, they reciprocate with benevolent actions such as granting boons, precipitating rains, preventing accidents and natural calamities, relieving pain and suffering, ensuring victory against enemies, protecting wealth, farmlands, cattle, etc., and granting them knowledge, strength, name and fame, peace, prosperity, children, and so on.

In the Vedic worldview, gods in heaven and humans on earth exist in a symbiotic relationship. They are codependent and cannot exist without each other, and neither can they neglect their duties without attracting perilous consequences. The gods depend upon humans for nourishment, and humans, in turn, depend upon them to achieve their principal aims of Dharma, Artha, and Kama. They may also help them in liberation, but they usually do not, since they dislike the idea of permanently losing those who nourish them through sacrifices. In this mutually beneficial relationship, both have an obligation to uphold the divine laws and ensure world order, whereby the wheel of life, karma, time, and Dharma keep moving as ordained by the Supreme Being. Nourishing each other through sacrifices and cooperation, they ultimately attain the highest good in their respective spheres. Divinities grow in strength and brightness while humans attain peace, happiness, and the fulfillment of their desires.

Karma yoga does not prohibit householders from performing Vedic yajnas. It, however, instructs them to perform them as a service or duty instead of using them to fulfill selfish desires. From this perspective, people should perform sacrifices to nourish gods and others and enjoy whatever good they may derive from them without asking. If nothing good or beneficial follows from them, they should still not complain but keep doing their duties. The original intent of the Vedas, which is to promote mutual dependence and cooperation between gods and humans, is still relevant for karma yogis and should be honored by them. However, as the Bhagavadgita suggests, they should do it as a duty or as a token of reverence and service to the gods and compassion for others rather than solely to fulfill their selfish desires and accept with detachment and indifference whatever manifests from their sacrifices as the fruit (prasada), gift, or remains of the sacrifice.

This is the essence of karma yoga of the higher kind, also known as karma-sannyasa yoga, which we will learn later. If any benefits arise from sacrificial actions, worshippers have the right to enjoy them without any consequences if they do not have the intention to enjoy them or take advantage. Any action, even mundane, becomes a sacrifice when offered to God or dutifully performed to serve others rather than fulfill selfish desires. For example, if you offer food to the gods before eating it, that action becomes a sacrifice and gives you the right to enjoy it. So are all physical and mental actions you perform to nourish the gods who reside in your body as the presiding deities of your organs. You can transform any action into a sacrifice by remembering the Lord while performing it or mentally making offerings to the gods. When actions are performed in this manner, you will succeed in stopping the flow of sinful karma. Therefore, in the next verse, Lord Krishna suggests that a devotee must perform sacrifices as duty and service. By nourishing the gods of heaven, he avoids the sin of stealing the rewards of a sacrifice.

Sloka 12

iṣṭān bhogān hi vo devā dāsyante yajñabhāvitāḥ
tair dattān apradāyaibhyo yo bhuṅkte stena eva saḥ

istan = desired; bhogan = enjoyments; hi = indeed; vah = to you; devah = gods, devas; dasyante = confer; yajna-bhavitah = nourished by the sacrifices; taih = by them; dattan = what has been given; apradaya = without giving; ebhyah = to them; yah = who; bhunkte = enjoys; stenah = thief; eva = certainly; sah = is he.

Indeed, nourished by the sacrifices (you perform), the gods confer upon you desired enjoyments. He who enjoys what has been given by them without giving them in return is certainly a thief.

According to the Vedas, gods are responsible for many auspicious happenings on Earth. They ensure that the earth is green, rains fall, rivers flow, seasons move, lands produce crops and vegetables, cattle give milk, and humans enjoy wealth, health, progeny, food, water, air, peace, prosperity, and happiness. They also protect us from evil, sickness, and calamities as a part of their obligatory duty to uphold Dharma. Therefore, it becomes the householders' duty as upholders of Dharma to reciprocate and serve them with the offerings of food through sacrifices. Whoever enjoys their blessings without nourishing the gods with offerings is a thief and incurs sin because he does not repay the karmic debt he owes to the gods and keeps the portion of food due to them with himself.

The relationship between the gods and humans is mutual. Both have an obligation to each other for their mutual welfare. Humans depend upon gods for peace and happiness, and gods depend upon humans for sacrificial food. According to the Vedas, this is how the Creator God intended them to live. He made gods and humans depend upon each other so that their debt to each other is squared off. The gods reside not only in the higher realm of the macrocosm but also as the presiding deities of the organs and faculties in our bodies. They facilitate various functions and keep the life breath (prana) flowing. As the lords of our inner universe, they ensure the health and well-being of our bodies and protect them from sickness, premature death, and harm. Therefore, the law books (Dharma shastras) enjoin humans to offer them sacred food through sacrificial rituals and external worship, and all the objects of the mind through internal sacrifices or mental worship. Many devout Hindus follow the principle verbatim and offer food and water to the gods during their daily sacrifices, morning and evening prayers, and before they eat food. Through these offerings, they avoid the sin of neglecting the gods and eating for themselves.

The body is a world in itself and a ritual place where we have an opportunity to perform the sacrifice of life through mundane actions. Any action becomes a sacrifice when it is offered to the gods or God as a token of reverence and gratitude. Thus, every action in our daily lives, such as eating, breathing, sleeping, enjoying, thinking, speaking, etc., can be transformed into an act of sacrifice by consecrating it to the indwelling Lord and the deities in the body. If you offer it to the Lord who dwells in you as your Self, you will simultaneously offer it to all the deities in the universe and your body. From birth until death, life is one continuous sacrifice (yajna). For a devotee who has consecrated his life to the Supreme Being, every action in it is a sacrificial action and an opportunity to practice karma yoga. Conception is a sacrifice. Birth is a sacrifice. Initiation (upanayana) is a sacrifice. The pursuit of knowledge is a sacrifice. Marriage is a sacrifice. Procreation is a sacrifice, even cremation, in which the body is finally offered to the fire as the last sacrifice (antyeshti). The gods in our bodies participate in these sacrifices as witnesses and recipients of the offerings. Therefore, it makes sense that when you eat food every day, you offer it to them before you eat it. By that, you keep squaring off the debt you owe to them.

Vedic sacrifices are meant to serve not only the gods but also other entities. The recipients of the sacrifices are broadly classified into five classes, namely Brahman (the Self) and his manifestations, gods (devas), ancestors (pitrs), birds, animals, insects, etc., and beings of the spirit world (bhutas), and people who depend upon others or live on alms (manushyas). By letting us serve them, these five classes of beings help us earn merit (punya) and neutralize any sin that arises from our daily actions. This is the law of compensation or karma, which allows human beings to redeem themselves from their faults and sinful actions. Karma yoga is based upon this principle only. Do your actions for the sake of Dharma, and you will earn the blessings of the gods and reap the rewards of life. By doing good, being good, and making sacrifices, one earns the right to enjoy life and escape from sinful karma. This is the law ordained by God to protect humans from sin and selfishness and gods from hunger and pride.

Sloka 13

yajñaśiṣṭāśinaḥ santo mucyante sarvakilbiṣaiḥ
bhuñjate te tv aghaṃ pāpā ye pacanty ātmakāraṇāt

yajna-sista = what is left of the sacrifice; asinah = those who eat; santah = the pious; mucyante = are freed; sarva = all kinds of; kilbisaih = from sins; bhunjate = incur; te = those; tu = but; agham = sin; papah = sinners, unholy people; ye = those who; pacanti = cook; atma-karanat = for themselves

The pious, who eat what is left of a sacrifice, are freed from all kinds of sins, but those evil ones, who cook food for themselves, certainly eat sin.

In this and the previous verses, Lord Krishna explained the importance of performing sacrifices and giving offerings to the gods and others to avoid or neutralize the sin that may arise from desire-ridden actions. His teachings are primarily about karma yoga in the traditional sense and how householders may avoid that sin through sacrifices and sacrificial offerings. Karma yoga is the practice of making sacrificial offerings to gods and others through obligatory duties and enjoying the remains of the sacrifice as the reward. It differs from jnana and karma-sannyasa yogas, where a karma yogi transcends desires and the duality of merit and sin (punya and papa) with awareness and consecrates his actions to God, offering him their fruit and wishing nothing for himself. In karma yoga, a householder may perform sacrifices and obligatory duties to fulfill his desires and enjoy whatever merit may accrue. By serving gods through sacrifices and upholding Dharma, he wishes to fulfill the four aims of his life, namely dharma, artha, kama, and moksha. While, from a spiritual perspective, it is not the best alternative, from the perspective of obligatory duties, it is a worthy path that teaches humans to live responsibly and do their part in serving God and his creation.

The Vedas recognize the importance of sacrificial actions in squaring off the debts a householder owes to others and neutralizing the evil or the sin that may arise from his actions. It is impossible to live on earth without incurring sin, interacting with evil things, or causing inconvenience, hurt, and harm to other living beings. We are surrounded by sin arising from the impurities of the world; we live in sin, committing sinful actions, and we are filled with sin due to the impurities in our minds and bodies. We cannot avoid sinning even from simple actions such as cooking or eating food. Imagine how much destruction and disturbance happen when crops and vegetables are planted in the fields until they reach our homes through various agencies, besides the destruction that happens when we prepare them for cooking and eating. Even those who are vegetarians engage in violence since they cannot secure food without harming plants, trees, fruits, and vegetables. Even while cooking food, many microorganisms die due to heating, cleaning, or cooking.

Thus, we cannot avoid hurting and harming others in our struggle for survival. On top of that, if we hoard things due to fear or greed and do not pay a fair price for the items we purchase, we incur more sin. Manusmriti identifies five instances where human beings invariably and repeatedly engage in some form of violence or destruction and incur sin: the cooking fire, grinding stone, mortar and pestle, water tank or pot, and broom. Hence, they are called the five slaughterhouses (panchasuna). By those actions alone, humans cannot escape from sin or attain heavenly life or liberation. The Vedas (and the Bhagavadgita, which follows them) recognize this problem and suggest that all actions should be performed as sacrifices without desiring their fruit. Sacrifice (tyagam) itself means giving up selfishness. People should not forget it when they perform sacrifices or make offerings.

Sloka 14

annād bhavanti bhūtāni parjanyād annasaṃbhavaḥ
yajñād bhavati parjanyo yajñaḥ karmasamudbhavaḥ

annat = from food; bhavanti = come into existence; bhutani = beings; parjanyat = from Parjanya, rain god; anna = food; sambhavah = is created; yajnat = from the sacrifice; bhavati = arise; parjanyah = rains; yajnah = sacrifice; karma = obligatory duties; samudbhavah = origin.

From food, beings come into existence; from Parjanya (cloud or rain god) is created food; from sacrifice arise rains; and yajna has karma as its origin.

In Vedic symbolism, food stands for what we eat and for the materiality of the whole manifestation. In the macrocosm, it stands for the manifested Nature (sambhuta) or the creation illuminated by Brahma (Viraj). According to the Upanishads, food is an aspect of Brahman only, and all that exists on earth is also food for the Lord of Death (Kala), who manifests from Brahman at the beginning of creation and rules the mortal world as the great devourer. He creates and devours things to facilitate change, impermanence, death, and rebirth. Food is also the creator and preserver of life. The gross physical body is known as the food body (annamaya kosa) because it is formed by food only. Part of the food we eat transforms through digestion into sperm (retas) in males and eggs (anda) in females, and through their union, life continues. Thus, food is the source of birth, death, and renewal of life on earth.

The second part of the verse alludes to the fact that rain produces food. It is true because, without rain, food cannot be produced, and without food, life cannot be sustained or continued. The Earth sustains life because of rainwater. According to the Vedas, rains are caused by Parjanya, the solar deity (Aditya), who presides over clouds. They suggest that he remains active and causes rain to fall as long as he is nourished and strengthened through the yajnas with sacrificial food. Thus, in Vedic cosmology, rain and clouds have a direct connection with sacrifices. Science offers a different explanation for the causes of rainfall or how the planet sustains life. However, it does not explain why weather and precipitation vary from region to region and why the planet does not have uniform weather. According to the Vedas, the seemingly random processes behind the weather phenomena are controlled by gods who have vast powers to manipulate the forces of Nature. Their actions depend upon their relationship with the people in the region and their collective karma. Rains will fall if Dharma prevails in the region and the gods are happy. While such beliefs may look absurd to modern minds, in the past, people believed them and prayed to gods for rain. Sometimes, their prayers were answered.

The last part of the verse says that yajnas originated from karma. It is true because, according to the Vedas, karma means sacrificial actions (karma kanda) only, which humans are expected to perform upon the earth as their obligatory duty. They are obligatory for ignorant people who are deluded and do not possess the knowledge of the Self or the inclination to work for their liberation. For such people, the Vedas prescribe obligatory duties and sacrifices through which they can serve the Creator. It is the first step in the spiritual evolution of humans. It is the best form of devotional service that Lord's devotees can perform when they do not have access to the knowledge of the scriptures or the means to know or practice it. The Vedas made certain duties obligatory for humans for a reason. If they are not obligatory, householders will ignore them or neglect them, which will result in the decline of Dharma and the rise of evil. Without food, the gods will grow weak and cannot protect humans or control natural phenomena. The result is chaos and calamities such as floods, epidemics, and famines. Therefore, worldly people must understand the importance of sacrifices and obligatory duties in the order and regularity of the world and their liberation.

Sloka 15

karma brahmodbhavaṃ viddhi brahmākṣarasamudbhavam
tasmāt sarvagataṃ brahma nityaṃ yajñe pratiṣṭhitam

karma = work; brahma = Brahma; udbhavam = originated; viddhi = know; brahma = Brahman; aksara = the Imperishable; samudbhavam = manifested; tasmat = therefore; sarva-gatam = all-pervading; brahma = Brahman; nityam = eternally; yajne = in sacrifice; pratisthitam = situated.

Know that karma originated from Brahma, and Brahma originated directly from the imperishable Brahman. Therefore, the all-pervading Brahman is eternally established in all acts of sacrifice.

Sacrificial duties (karma) originated from Brahma because their source is the ritual portion (karmakanda) of the Vedas, whose source is Brahma only. Brahma originated from Akshara, which is a reference to the imperishable Brahman. Therefore, Brahman is the ultimate presiding deity of all the sacrifices. We must read this verse in conjunction with the previous one to understand how sacrifices originated from Brahman and how he is established in them. For that, we have to read these verses backward.

Brahman, the imperishable Supreme Self, created Brahma. Brahma revealed the Vedas to humans. Rituals and obligatory duties (karmakanda) originated from the Vedas. Humans must perform their duties through sacrifices (yajnas) since only through them can they communicate with the gods and nourish them. Through that relationship, the welfare of heaven and the earth is guaranteed. Sacrifices ensure rainfall. From rain, food is born, and from food, all beings come into existence, since food is also the source of reproductive material. Through food, the gods become strong and protect the world.

According to the Vedas, the formless Imperishable (Akshara) Brahman is the highest and absolute reality. He is the transcendental Supreme Self whose essential nature is truth, pure consciousness, and bliss. His highest, manifested aspect in the field of Nature is Isvara, the universal Lord, known as Purusha and by several other names. As the source of all and the cause of everything, he presides over the entire creation as its controller and supreme enjoyer. Another manifestation of Brahman in the dynamic field of Prakriti is Prajapati Brahma, described in the Vedas as the Golden Egg (Hiranyagarbha) and the World Soul. If Isvara is Brahman's reflection in the mode of Sattva, Brahma is his reflection in the mode of rajas. Brahma is the creator god. His consort is Saraswathi, the goddess of knowledge. Brahma has days and nights; his day stretches for billions of years, spanning one creation cycle. At the beginning of each day, he brings forth all the beings and the entire creation in stages. When gods, humans, and demons are manifested, he reveals to them the knowledge of the Vedas. He makes it obligatory for humans to perform sacrificial rituals as ordained by the Vedas to nourish the gods.

The Vedas exist eternally in the highest realms of creation. In the mortal world, Brahma reveals their knowledge first to the seven seers, who then pass it on to their progeny with the instruction to pass it on to others and preserve it for the world's welfare. Since the knowledge of the Vedas is orally transmitted to humans in each creation cycle through a long series of teachers starting with Brahma, they are known as shruti (the heard ones), apaurusheya (not human in origin), and sabdabrahma (Brahman in word form). Brahma ordained humans to perform sacrifices as their moral duty to attain peace and happiness upon earth and liberation or heavenly life upon their departure. The purpose of sacrifices is to nourish the gods, the earth, and other beings. By that, humans earn meritorious karma (punya) and secure a better life in the next birth.

Thus, we have a clear hierarchy, starting with sacrificial acts at the bottom and ending with Brahman at the top. Brahman created Brahma, who revealed the Vedas. The Vedas contain the knowledge of the sacrifices to be practiced by householders to uphold the eternal Dharma. Indeed, the purpose of the Vedas is to let humans know the duties of the Creator and perform them upon the earth as their own duties to serve him and repay their karmic debt. All the obligatory duties, collectively known as Dharma, arise from Brahma and, thereby, from Brahman only. As his loyal and devoted servants (Bhagavatas), householders must perform them upon earth to ensure the orderly progression of the world. Thus, Brahman is eternally established in Vedic sacrifices (karmakanda), and through them, humans can realize

Brahman, who resides in them as their indwelling Lord. People will not incur sin if they perform them as an obligation, sacrifice, or service to him, but they do when they perform them to fulfill their desires. This is the basis for karma yoga.

Sloka 16

evaṃ pravartitaṃ cakraṃ nānuvartayatīha yaḥ
aghāyur indriyārāmo moghaṃ pārtha sa jīvati

evam = thus; pravartitam = moving; cakram = wheel; na = not; anuvartayati = follows; iha = here, in this; yah = who; agha-ayuh = sinful life; indriya-aramah = indulging or abiding in the senses; mogham = in vain; partha = Partha; sah = he; jivati = lives.

He who does not follow here the wheel thus moving, whose life is sinful, indulging in the senses, in vain, O Partha, he lives.

The wheel (chakra) mentioned in this verse refers to the chain of events described in the previous two verses connecting Brahman to sacrifices and how life originates from them. We may also consider it the Wheel of Dharma, which, in turn, moves the wheels of karma, samsara, and creation. In the Vedic vision of the world, existence depends upon sacrifices because the ultimate source of all is Brahman, who is eternally established in them. They are collectively known as Dharma, or a set of sacred duties. As Isvara, the Lord of the universe, and as Brahma, the creator god, he created food and life through personal sacrifice and set an example for others to follow. He also set the Wheel of Creation in motion through a sacrifice, which he moves continuously through sacrificial actions (eternal duties) for the sake of the world. The wheel (chakram) can be variously interpreted as the world, time, creation, dharma, karma, life, or any revolving phenomenon. All these are cyclical and forward-moving and revolve around the axis of Brahman. They are all facilitated by sacrificial actions only. The earth and heaven exist because of the interdependence between gods and humans, and the earth produces food and sustains life because of the sacrificial duties performed by humans. If this cycle is disrupted, chaos will follow.

Therefore, humans should follow the example of Brahman and perform their duties selflessly to keep the wheels of their lives moving. Instead of letting their senses wander freely and pursuing selfish desires, they must follow the laws of Nature as ordained by God and perform their duties with discernment so they can keep moving the wheel of Dharma and keep their side of the promise until they escape from samsara. The senses distract people from discerning their true nature or performing their duties without delusion, desires, and egoism. They do not let them cleanse themselves, cultivating virtues and nearness to the Lord who resides in them. Those who give in to them and do not perform their duties or uphold God's eternal laws disrupt the wheel of life and keep revolving in the cycle of births and deaths.

Obligatory duties are prescribed in the scriptures for householders, while renunciants (sannyasis) are exempted from them. Karma yoga is primarily meant for deluded worldly people who do not study the scriptures or know their true nature. It is also a sacrifice only since it involves service and duty for the sake of others. Karma yogis who perform their obligatory duties (karmakanda) and pursue the four aims of human life for happiness here and hereafter are also the Lord's devotees, even if they do not practice devotional worship or bhakti yoga. It is a purifier that leads people on the path of Dharma and prepares them for further progress toward liberation. Since householders go through the turbulence of life, bearing the burdens of their duties, drinking from the cup of suffering, and delaying their liberation, their Dharma (grihastha dharma) is considered the best of Dharmas. In the next verse, Lord Krishna explains why renunciants (sannyasis) are exempted from obligatory duties.

Sloka 17

yas tv ātmaratir eva syād ātmatṛptaś ca mānavaḥ
ātmany eva ca saṃtuṣṭas tasya kāryaṃ na vidyate

yah = who; tu = but; atma-ratih = delights in self; eva = only; syat = remains; atma-trptah = satisfied by self; ca = and; manavah = human being; atmani = in the self; eva = only; ca = and; santustah = happy, contended; tasya = for him; karyam = duty; na = no; vidyate = arising from the Vedas.

But he who delights in the Self only is satisfied by the Self and happy within the Self, for that human being, duty does not arise from the Vedas.

In this verse, the Bhagavadgita radically departs from the Mimansa beliefs regarding karma and duty. Lord Krishna clearly stated that obligatory duties do not apply to those who renounce worldly life and pursue liberation. Karma yoga is appropriate for householders who want to perform their duties in devotion to God and pursue the four aims of Dharma, Artha, Kama, and Moksha. The Vedic tradition encouraged householders to take up sannyasa in old age after fulfilling their obligatory duties. However, they did not prohibit people who wanted to do it early without fulfilling their obligations and took the vows of sannyasa to pursue liberation. The Mimansa school probably did not appreciate the practice of householders renouncing sacrificial duties and family responsibilities to achieve liberation without fulfilling their obligations. According to them, human beings were born to uphold yajnas as ordained by the Vedas and fulfill the chief aims of human life through them. They held that all the material and spiritual rewards flowed from the yajnas, not from God or any supernatural being. Therefore, they approved renunciation as an outlier and disruptive practice, ideal for people in the last phase of their lives to secure a better life in the next birth.

The Bhagavadgita is theistic. It accepts some ideas of the Mimansa regarding sacrifices and obligatory duties, but refutes their beliefs regarding the Supreme Being. It acknowledges him as the creator, controller, and source of all and offers different options (yogas) to householders to achieve liberation. Of them, karma yoga is an adjunct or a foundational practice that sets the stage for worldly people to evolve spiritually. It recommends it for those who want to pursue the four aims of human life through sacrificial duties as a service to the Lord and prepare themselves for purification and liberation. At the same time, it offers alternative approaches to those who want to pursue knowledge and liberation through study, contemplation, renunciation, and devotion. In this verse, Lord Krishna explicitly states that the duties ordained by the Vedas do not apply to those who take delight in the Self and are satisfied within themselves. The appropriate paths for them are jnana yoga, sannyasa yoga, or jnana karma-sannyasa yoga. The last one can be practiced by householders also if they are interested in pursuing knowledge and duty simultaneously.

In other words, karma yoga is suitable for those who do not have the resolve to control their desires and engage in desire-ridden actions to pursue Dharma, Artha, and Kama rather than liberation or the knowledge of the Self. Through karma yoga, they can perform their obligatory duties and secure a place in heaven or attain good birth in the next life. However, it does not guarantee them eternal freedom from samsara. While karma yogis are bound to their duties and responsibilities, those who practice jnana yoga and sannyasa yoga can renounce them and pursue liberation only. On these paths, they are bound by their vows of renunciation and are obligated to perform actions that are necessary to observe their vows and keep their bodies alive. Although jnana yoga is a distinct path, it is hard to find pure jnana yogis. Most yogis pursue knowledge to cultivate discernment, understanding, and self-awareness. Householders can practice jnana and karma-sannyasa yogas to improve their knowledge and chances of liberation. Karma yoga is the most effective when it is practiced in conjunction with jnana, buddhi, karma-sannyasa, atma-samyama, and bhakti yogas.

Three essential qualities are mentioned in this verse to practice renunciation and abide in the Self: atmarati, atmatrpta, and atma santushta. They arise when yogis restrain their minds and senses, suppress their desires and attachments, and become indifferent to the world and dualities. For those who practice karma yoga, the Vedas are the source of knowledge, peace, and happiness. Duty is their support, and heaven is their goal. For those on the path of jnana and sannyasa yogas, the Self or the indwelling Lord is the goal and support. Knowledge, intelligence, serenity, and freedom are the rewards. When they practice these yogas, their effort is sustained by their purity, faith, resolve, and devotion to persevere and overcome obstacles. The Mundaka Upanishad extols renunciation as the best path in the following words, "Indeed, breath is this one who shines in all. The knower who discerns him does not indulge in far-fetched discussions. Absorbed in his play, delighting within himself, this practitioner of kriya yoga is superior among the knowers of Brahman."

Sloka 18

naiva tasya kṛtenārtho nākṛteneha kaścana
na cāsya sarvabhūteṣu kaścid arthavyapāśrayaḥ

na = not; eva = at all; tasya = for him; krtena = by performing duty; arthah = purpose, object of desire, interest; na = not; akrtena = without performing duty; iha = in this world; kascana = whatever; na = no; ca = and; asya = for him; sarva-bhutesu = in all living beings; kascit = any; artha = object; vyapasrayah = dependence, taking shelter.

For him, there is no purpose or interest at all in performing the duty or not performing it. For him, there is no dependence whatsoever on any object or on any living being.

Householders have a purpose or interest in performing or avoiding actions. They depend upon gods and the world for their survival and fulfillment. Renunciants have none since they have no obligatory duties and have no dependence upon anyone or anything. At most, they depend upon the Lord who dwells in them. They are indifferent to the ways of the world, its rules and laws, or expectations, or the conditioning it imposes upon people. Since they want to cut all bonds and break free from samsara, they resolve to control their desires and remain detached and free from the world and its myriad influences. With no prescribed duties, obligations, compulsions, or expectations, they live freely, unburdened by the weight of the world. They also take vows not to depend upon anything or anyone except the Supreme Lord, the indwelling Lord, or both. Why do renunciants have to live like this? Why do they have to give up desires, attachments, and dependence? It is because they want to cultivate likeness or sameness with Brahman or with the Lord in them, who is eternally free, independent, self-existing, self-knowing, and self-abiding. Hence, as the starting point, they follow his example and live like him, free in all respects and from all sides.

A yogi who renounces the world and contemplates upon the Self, free from desires and dependence, naturally remains delightful, satisfied, and contented within himself. Since he overcomes desires and duality, how can he be interested in doing or not doing anything, or what need is there for him to depend or not depend upon anyone or anything? As the duality between him (not-self) and the Lord who dwells in him as his Self disappears, with the former becoming inconsequential and unappealing, he becomes complete, self-satisfied, and self-existent. He perceives everything with detachment, indifference, and sameness as empty and the play of Maya. Having become desireless and independent and dissolved his mind in the reality of his pure Self, he remains indifferent and unaffected by what happens or does not happen. His indifference to external events does not arise from inattentiveness or lethargy but from contentment, fulfillment, and happiness from within (atmarati, atmatripti, and atmasantushti), as mentioned in the previous verse. Having taken shelter (vyapasrayah) in the Lord who dwells within him and knowing him as himself, he does not take shelter in anything else, be it knowledge, duty, worldly pleasures and possessions, gods, or lesser manifestations of God.

As Lord Krishna said before, why would anyone look for water in a well when there is a flood of water everywhere? When a yogi finds the Lord in him, attains sameness, and becomes equal to all, what else would he need to complete or complement himself? Everything becomes equal when you have them or do not need them. That is the natural state of a yogi who excels in sannyasa. By overcoming his desires and finding fulfillment and contentment within himself, he remains mentally stable, self-absorbed, and equal to all. He shows no interest in the performance or the nonperformance of any duty or action. Because he is detached, egoless, and free from desires in oneness with the Self in him, he does not depend upon or seek to profit or gain from his knowledge, wisdom, any special powers he may have, or worldly actions. Therefore, he has no compulsion to perform duties, and no one can fault him for doing or not doing them. For the renunciant, who regards the Lord in him as his sole object of veneration and his only goal, devotion becomes his sole support and reason to live. However, since he is not bound by anything, he can still, by choice, participate in actions or even sacrificial duties to set an example or encourage others to participate in them. In the next verse, Lord Krishna emphasizes this.

Sloka 19

tasmād asaktaḥ satataṃ kāryaṃ karma samācara
asakto hy ācaran karma param āpnoti pūruṣaḥ

tasmat = therefore; asaktah = without attachment, disinterested, indifferent; satatam = always; karyam = obligatory; karma = work, duty, actions; samacara = perform; asaktah = disinterest; hi = certainly; acaran = performing; karma = work; param = the Supremet; apnoti = attains; purusah = a person.

Therefore, always perform your obligatory work without attachment. Certainly, by performing actions without attachment, a person attains the Supreme Self.

Lord Krishna said, "Arjuna, only renunciants can avoid duties and live freely without a worldly purpose or obligation. They are not bound by anything. You are a householder, not a sannyasi. Therefore, you must perform your duties without desires and expectations to attain liberation. There is no other way." This is the essence of this verse.

By practicing karma yoga and performing sacrificial duties to serve God, a householder may avoid the sin of selfishness and attain a better life in the next birth. He may achieve the first three aims of human life: Dharma, Artha, and Kama. He may also attain purity (sattva suddhi) through yoga. However, he will not attain liberation (moksha). Some karma yogis may attain liberation due to God's grace or the merit they might have accumulated in past births, but it does not happen in all cases. Karma yoga is meant to keep the wheel of life running and ensure fulfillment for householders. Hence, by its very design, it precludes the possibility of anyone escaping from samsara. Liberation is more likely when they practice karma yoga on the path of knowledge and renunciation, giving up desires and attachments and cultivating purity and sameness. Therefore, householders who want to achieve liberation should practice the higher form of karma yoga, taking refuge in the Self or the Supreme Self. Through selfless and desireless actions, with detachment and with their minds absorbed in the Lord who dwells in them or creation, they should consecrate their lives to him and qualify for liberation or the supreme state (para) of oneness, sameness, or aloneness (kaivalya).

Arjuna was a householder. As we noticed in the first chapter, he was still a householder, subject to desires and attachments. Therefore, Lord Krishna rightly advised him to practice karma yoga with detachment and disinterest or indifference (asakti), without worrying about the future and the reputation of his family or the sinful consequences of his actions. Sannyasa frees you from petty worries and problems. When you are detached, disinterested, and indifferent, you will not be drawn to particular choices or outcomes of your actions. You will accept whatever happens or falls in your way as divine providence and perform your actions without expectations. For the householders, the best option is to practice karma yoga with knowledge, discernment, detachment, and renunciation, and enjoy both worlds. By that, they will not only escape from sinful karma but also from samsara.

Sloka 20

karmaṇaiva hi saṃsiddhim āsthitā janakādayaḥ
lokasaṃgraham evāpi saṃpaśyan kartum arhasi

karmana = through work; eva = only; hi = for; samsiddhim = equanimity, sameness; asthitah = attained; janaka-adayah = Janaka and others; loka-sangraham = welfare of the world; eva = and; api = also; sampasyan = for the sake of; kartum = do your duty; arhasi = you should.

Through work only, sameness was attained by (king) Janaka and others. For the welfare of the world only, you are required to do your duty.

Samsiddhi (sama + siddhi) means the state of sameness or perfection in sameness. As we noted earlier, in the Bhagavadgita, Lord Krishna equated it with samadhi, or the highest goal, while defining yoga. The Lord abides in sameness. Hence, he sees all as equal. Just as the sun shines equally upon the earth, he showers his grace upon all equally. However, just as the sunlight falls upon only those who come into its direct light, his grace falls upon those devotees who come into his light directly through exclusive devotion. Those who surrender to him and worship him exclusively and unconditionally have better chances of earning his grace and protection. According to this verse, samsiddhi is attained by yogis when they give up desires and practice karma yoga with knowledge, discernment, detachment, and devotion. It affirms that karma yoga should not be taken lightly or treated as inferior to jnana and sannyasa yoga. If you practice it with proper knowledge and the right attitude, it will lead you to liberation.

Those who conquer their desires and attachments and give up desire-ridden actions, seeking and striving, attain that supreme quality. They treat the pairs of opposites, such as pleasure and pain or happiness and sorrow alike, with sameness and indifference. They remain contented within themselves, with their minds absorbed in the Self and undisturbed by what happens or does not happen. As this verse implies, sameness arises when you practice karma yoga with detachment, as Janaka and others did. Those great ones practiced jnana yoga but acquired sameness through karma yoga only because the latter teaches you to face reality and learn from your life's experiences. Knowledge improves your discernment and helps you know your true identity, while actions let you test your knowledge, learn from your actions, and become wiser. Ordinary people react to situations because of desires, attraction, and aversion. The yogi who conquers desires and excels in karma yoga remains equal in all situations, just like the Lord in him.

Therefore, as this verse implies, to attain sameness (samsiddhi), you should not renounce actions but perform them dutifully with detachment and indifference, conquering desires. When you are established in karma yoga without judgment, choices, or preferences, it will eventually lead to sameness (samatvam) or choiceless awareness in which you are untroubled by the outcomes of your actions or the fear of the unknown or uncertainty. King Janaka was a warrior (Kshatriya) king who ruled a large kingdom in the early Vedic period. He lived an exemplary life and became a symbol of ideal kingship. He is frequently mentioned in the Upanishads as a patron of Vedic saints and scholars, whom he used to invite to his court and generously grant them gifts of land and cattle in recognition of their knowledge and erudition. As a philosopher king, he practiced both jnana and karma yogas, pursuing knowledge to abide in the Self while performing his royal duties as a karma yogi. In his old age, he renounced his kingly duties and retired to the forests to attain liberation. Hence, Lord Krishna reminded Arjuna that even great ones like King Janaka cultivated sameness through karma yoga, performing their duties with detachment for the welfare of the world.

Sloka 21

yadyad ācarati śreṣṭhas tattad evetaro janaḥ
sa yat pramāṇaṃ kurute lokas tad anuvartate

yadyad = whatever; acarati = does; sresthah =superior, distinguished, great; tattat = that that; eva = only; itarah = other; janah = people; sah = he; yat = whatever; pramanam = example, standard; kurute = sets; lokah = the world; tat = that; anuvartate = follows.

Whatever a superior person does, that alone other people (do). Whatever example or standard he sets, the world follows that.

Sannyasa is not obligatory for anyone. It is always a voluntary choice. This is true even for those who practice the Vedic varnashrama dharma, according to which householders may retire to forests and take up sannyasa in the third and fourth stages of their lives after they fulfill their obligatory duties. You take up sannyasa if you develop apathy towards the world or worldly things, or are vexed by the emptiness in your life, or by the lack of meaning and purpose. Alternatively, something in you wakes you up and jolts you out of your mental torpor, pushing you to break free from the weight of the world and explore truths about yourself and your existence. It happens rarely to a few when they reach a saturation point in their relationship with the world or with themselves. Therefore, those who do not want to take up sannyasa do not have to feel despair. They can practice karma yoga with detachment and sameness as the best alternative. King Janaka, like many others, had no obligation to renounce worldly life and take up sannyasa. Therefore, he chose karma yoga as the next best alternative to set an example for others. He took up sannyasa and retired to the forests only in his old age. Like him, Arjuna also had no moral or spiritual obligation to take up sannyasa. Therefore, Lord Krishna suggested to him that he could follow the same ideal and set an example for others to follow.

People prefer to follow those who stand apart and achieve exemplary success or possess extraordinary talents and skills. They draw inspiration from them and accept them as their role models. We follow God because he personifies the best, brightest, perfect, and most exalted qualities in the universe. He is vishesha (special), para (transcendental), and parandhama, the highest goal or ideal for yogis and devotees to follow. Anyone who possesses a spark of that greatness (mahatvam) attracts attention because he reminds people of that supreme state. We know that the world's best and brightest minds influence and inspire people to learn from their example. As their admirers develop an imaginary and illusory relationship with them, accepting them as their inspiring role models, they listen to them, adopt their values, and model their lives on their example. However, that influence works for the better or the worse, depending on what examples the role models set and what qualities they exemplify.

Role models with questionable moral values or character can be a bad influence. It can happen even with spiritual gurus. When they set a bad example due to some weakness or controversial action, it is a great loss to society because, in doing so, they disrupt the lives of many and contribute to the confusion of values, loss of faith, and moral decadence. This was equally true in ancient times as it is now. People with superior achievements and exceptional talents carry a great responsibility. They must set an example for those who look to them for guidance and inspiration. By quoting the example of King Janaka, Lord Krishna reminded Arjuna that he should be a good role model and set a good example. By performing his actions with detachment, he should inspire others to perform their duties and uphold Dharma. If he left the battlefield without fighting, other warriors might follow his example and stop fighting or performing their obligatory duties using the same logic he used.

Sloka 22

na me pārthāsti kartavyaṃ triṣu lokeṣu kiṃcana
nānavāptam avāptavyaṃ varta eva ca karmaṇi

na = no; me = for me; partha = Partha; asti = there is; kartavyam = duty to do; trisu = in the three; lokesu = worlds; kincana = whatsoever; na = not; anavaptam = not gained; avaptavyam = to be gained; varte = engage; eva = also; ca = and; karmani = in obligatory duty.

For me, O Partha, there is no duty whatsoever that needs to be done in the three worlds, nor is there anything not gained that needs to be gained. Yet, I also engage in obligatory duties.

Here, Lord Krishna spoke of his self-example, how he performs his duties even though he has no set duties and gains nothing from them. By that, he implied that he, too, practices karma yoga to set an example. An incarnation of God is the best example the world can have. He personifies divinity, teaches us how the Creator would live upon the earth, and what example he would set if he were ever born into a human body. Thus, his incarnations are the best role models anyone can have. In each incarnation, he personifies certain qualities from which humanity can learn and improve itself.

The three worlds mentioned in this verse are the earth (bhur), the middle world of ancestors (bhuva), and the heavenly world of gods (suvah). The Vedas identify them as the Earth, the Moon, and the Sun, respectively. The Earth is the world of Death, where mortals live. The sphere of the moon is where departed souls temporarily stay to exhaust their karma before they return to the Earth to take their next birth. The sphere of the sun (suryalok) is the world of immortals. It is the final destination of liberated beings who depart from here, never to return. This threefold universe was the original model of the Vedic cosmology before a more complex structure emerged, with the commingling of numerous ideas borrowed freely from other traditions. The improved cosmic version envisaged a vast universe consisting of seven worlds of light above and seven worlds of darkness below, with the Earth standing in the middle.

The second part of the verse may also be translated alternatively as 'nor is there anything not gained or gained.' I followed the standard approach of many scholars, including Sri Shankaracharya, as 'nor is there anything not gained that needs to be gained.' It conveys the completeness and perfection of the Supreme Lord and the absence in him of desires, wants, needs, or expectations for fulfillment. Isvara, the Supreme Being, has no responsibilities because he is complete and perfect in himself. There is nothing in the world that he wants or needs for any reason because he already has everything. We seek things for different reasons because we are imperfect and incomplete, always looking for something to feel good or be happy. Our desire for things arises due to our fears, inadequacies, and the need for security and comfort. People also seek things due to lust, anger, pride, greed, or envy, which are completely absent in the pure consciousness of the Self. In the supreme consciousness of the Lord, these are absent.

Hence, in the state of nonduality, Lord Krishna said that while he had no specific duties or obligations and no need to gain anything to complete himself, he still performed obligatory duties. He explained the reason in the next verse. By stating it, he suggested that we also should perform our duties even if we do not gain anything from them. Now, one may ask what duties the Supreme Lord of the universe performs. The scriptures attribute five main functions to him: creation, preservation, concealment, destruction, and revelation. He performs them through his fivefold (panchanana) manifestations to create and uphold the worlds he creates. As the Supreme Lord of all, he creates worlds and beings, activating Prakriti. Once they manifest in the field of Prakriti as his projections, he acts as the upholder of his eternal duties and directs Prakriti to preserve them through her various agencies. At the end of the cycle of creation, he withdraws them all, including Prakriti, into himself and goes into a deep sleep, which lasts for billions of years. However, technically speaking, as the source of all, the Supreme Lord is responsible for all actions. He dwells in all as their Self. His will drives all the jivas into action. However, due to the impurities, it is driven in the jivas by desires, egoism, etc., and is not as effective as his pure and absolute will.

Sloka 23

yadi hy ahaṃ na varteyaṃ jātu karmaṇy atandritaḥ
mama vartmānuvartante manuṣyāḥ pārtha sarvaśaḥ

yadi = if; hi = indeed; aham = I; na = not; varteyam = abide, exist, continue doing; jatu = always; karmani = in duty; atandritah = unwaveringly or undistracted; mama = My; vartma = path; anuvartante = follow; manusyah = people; partha = O Partha; sarvasah = in every way, everywhere.

Indeed, if I do not always abide by doing my duty unwaveringly, people will follow my path in every way, O Partha.

Previously, Lord Krishna told Arjuna that whatever good examples the best of humans (shreshta) set, the world tends to follow them. The Supreme Lord is the best of the best (athishreshta) example for anyone to follow. He personifies the best and the highest qualities, perfections, and excellences one can imagine. Hence, there can be no better example than him for us to follow. If he remains inactive and neglects his duties, people will take inspiration from that and neglect theirs. The Lord is the upholder of Dharma. His devotees take inspiration from him and follow his example in their lives, practicing virtues and upholding Dharma. If any righteousness (dharma) is left in the world today, it is because they believe in him and would like to obey his laws and earn his grace rather than disobey them, incur sin, and suffer from the consequences. Some people may practice morality due to their personal beliefs, even if they do not believe in a Supreme Being or follow His words. It is possible if you develop humanity, compassion, empathy, universal friendliness, and selflessness. The Buddhists exemplify that. However, most people derive their inspiration from the scriptures, which contain the words God conveyed through numerous messengers, teachers, prophets, divinities, and incarnations. For them, he represents the highest ideal and the best example to mold their character and conduct. We have yet to reach a stage where the world does not need any ideals for inspiration or practice. Until then, the values that are enshrined in our scriptures and are purportedly upheld by God himself are the best examples for the world to follow. The Supreme Lord personifies the best of all virtues, perfections, and manifestations. He still inspires millions of devotees to follow his example and preserve whatever virtue is left in today's world. Because of him, we still have some semblance of humanity, morality, the good old order, and regularity (rta). Without him providing inspiration and setting an example, the world will fall into confusion and chaos. This is stated in the next verse.

Sloka 24

utsīdeyur ime lokā na kuryāṃ karma ced aham
saṃkarasya ca kartā syām upahanyām imāḥ prajāḥ

utsideyuh = be destroyed; ime = these; lokah = worlds; na = do not; kuryam = perform; karma = duty, actions; cet = if; aham = I; sankarasya = intermingling of castes; ca = and; karta = the perpetrator; syam = would become; upahanyam = cause harm; imah = these; prajah = people.

These worlds will be destroyed if I do not perform actions. I will be the perpetrator of the confusion of castes and cause considerable harm to these people.

If the Supreme Lord does not perform his duties as the upholder of all, the Wheel of Creation will collapse, and existence will end. One of God's primary duties is to uphold Dharma, establishing and preserving the order and regularity (rta) of the world. Therefore, if he does not perform them, the world will fall into chaos, and the social and moral order he regulates will perish. When he created the mortal world, he established a social order consisting of four classes of humans according to their essential nature and laid down laws for their conduct, duties, and norms. To the extent they follow the duties arising from their nature, which is, in turn, regulated by their karma, the order and regularity of the world will prevail.

The caste system is not flawless. In the past, it enabled many to perpetrate social evils and violence upon others in the name of God and the scriptures. Although the principle of creating a fourfold division of society was noble in its conception and formulation, its true intent and purpose surfaced in its implementation as it declined into a system of inequality, discrimination, and injustice, resulting in suffering and oppression for the multitude. People in the ancient world might have had reasons for creating and enforcing a rigid caste system. However, in the long run, it harmed many, who were deprived of their basic right to live freely with self-respect and choose their vocations according to their natural talents and potentials. The evil of the caste system still prevails in many communities and continues to be a divisive and disturbing factor.

The idea underlying the caste system is inherent in the karma doctrine. It is based on the belief that human beings are born with certain basic tendencies, characteristics, or essential nature, which form the basis for their actions, existence, and conduct upon the earth in their current lives. By expressing their essential nature and performing their actions accordingly, they should aspire to evolve mentally and intelligently, using their circumstances and natural endowments arising from their karma or previous births. Through trial and error, through successes and failures, they should chisel their personas and destinies on the path to perfection. This is the underlying justification. However, it should not be used to create an unjust and unequal society. While it is true that birth initially limits the possibilities of success and achievement in life, people should have the freedom to use opportunities and improve their lot. The rigid caste system does not permit that. They should have opportunities to grow and improve their karma. It must be up to them to make use of their circumstances and inherent talents to grow materially and spiritually without any obstructions from other beings who have their karma to manage and are no different in the eyes of God. These choices should not be imposed upon them or made for them without their consent by external agencies or institutions. If they do, they should then take responsibility for their karma and lives.

Sloka 25

saktāḥ karmaṇy avidvāṃso yathā kurvanti bhārata
kuryād vidvāṃs tathāsaktaś cikīrṣur lokasaṃgraham

saktah = with attachment; karmani = actions; avidvamsah = the ignorant; yatha = as; kurvanti = perform; bharata = Bharata; kuryat = act; vidvan = the learned ones, knowledgeable ones; tatha = thus; asaktah = without attachment; cikirsuh = desiring to; loka-sangraham = welfare of the world.

O Bharata, just as ignorant people perform actions with attachment, the learned ones must act without attachment, desiring the welfare of the world.

Knowledge and learning help seekers make intelligent choices and live responsibly, avoiding the mistakes ignorant people make. This verse explains how knowledge and wisdom are relevant to karma yogis and how they can elevate their practice and make a difference to them and the world. Due to desires and attachments, ignorant people perform actions for selfish reasons, ignoring their duties and obligations to God and others. The learned ones (vidvans) who acquire knowledge by studying the scriptures or serving a guru do the opposite. They use their knowledge to practice karma yoga, perform actions without attachment, and live for the sake of Dharma. Thus, they serve God and Dharma by renouncing desires and doing their part in fulfilling the aims of creation as he intended. They perform actions without any selfish intentions, even the desire to avoid karma or escape from samsara. Knowing the distinction between their physical and spiritual selves and between what binds them and what sets them free, they pursue the four chief aims of human life with detachment and renunciation. The learned ones (vidvans) who are mentioned here are not renunciants (sannyasis) or liberated souls (muktas) but ordinary householders who acquire knowledge through study and perform their duties just as King Janaka did without desires and attachments. Endowed with that knowledge and wisdom, they serve God and his creation with unwavering devotion. What sets them apart from ignorant devotees is that they are knowledgeable, dutiful, selfless, and remain satisfied within themselves (atmatrupta). Through their actions and conduct, they set an example to others and inspire them without disturbing them. This is explained in the next verse.

Sloka 26

na buddhibhedaṃ janayed ajñānāṃ karmasaṃginām
joṣayet sarvakarmāṇi vidvān yuktaḥ samācaran

na = not; buddhi-bhedam = mental conflict; janayet = cause; ajnanam = among the ignorant; karma-sanginam = attachment to action; josayet = make them do; sarva = all; karmani = duties; vidvan = learned; yuktah = skillfully, in an appropriate manner; samacaran = performing, practicing.

Without causing confusion or mental conflicts to the ignorant ones (who are) attached to their actions, the knowledgeable one should encourage them to perform all their duties, (while) performing his duties skillfully.

The learned karma yogis do not confuse or cause mental conflicts in others with their knowledge or erudition. They set an example, performing their duties while encouraging others to perform theirs. Lord Krishna says that those who have knowledge and discernment and practice karma yoga should not confuse ignorant ones by teaching them what they cannot comprehend. Instead, they should lead by example and encourage them to practice Dharma for the welfare of the world. If they ask them to cultivate discernment or practice karma yoga with detachment and renunciation, they may not understand or become confused and conflicted (buddhi bhedam). Hence, they should be allowed to progress at their own pace on the path of karma yoga, doing what they are naturally inclined to do and following the methods with which they are comfortable. Instead of putting pressure on them, they should be motivated through self-example, showing them how to serve others and participate in God's work. It is better than lecturing others on what they should or should not do, especially when they are not ready and do not possess the knowledge, motivation, or purity.

People do not change easily because of their circumstances and past life influences. They may have their problems, priorities, and responsibilities peculiar to their circumstances. Since they are also products of their karma, they cannot easily overcome their predominant desires, habits, attitudes, and past life impressions. Therefore, transforming them would be like sculpting a raw stone. They should be given time and opportunity to acquire the right knowledge and progress on the path at their own pace. Therefore, Lord Krishna rightly suggested that the wise ones should lead the ignorant ones by example rather than confusing them with the knowledge or methods and practices they do not understand. In verse 21, he said that the ignorant ones tend to follow the best minds. Therefore, they should be led by example. He conveyed the same idea here, though differently, suggesting that it is the best way to transform them.

Karma yoga is easier to practice because it does not impose too many conditions upon its practitioners. One has to practice obligatory duties and serve God and his creation to excel in it and qualify for a better life in the next birth. Jnana yoga and sannyasa yoga are comparatively difficult since they demand perfection, purity, and control over the mind and body, which require persistent practice. Karma yoga is the first step. Its continued practice will prepare the ignorant ones to transition slowly into karma-sannyasa yoga with knowledge and discernment. From there, they can gradually advance into still higher stages to attain samadhi or sameness. Spiritual transformation is a slow and steady process. One should not try to hasten it or pull the higher shaktis who facilitate it without preparation.

Sloka 27

prakṛteḥ kriyamāṇāni guṇaiḥ karmāṇi sarvaśaḥ
ahaṃkāravimūḍhātmā kartāham iti manyate

prakrteh = of Prakriti, Nature; kriyamanani = actions are performed; gunaih = by the qualities; karmani = actions; sarvasah = all types of; ahankara-vimudha = deluded by ego; atma = jivatma, the embodied self; karta = doer; aham = I; iti = thus; manyate = thinks.

All types of actions are performed by the gunas of Prakriti (Nature). Deluded by the ego, the embodied Self thinks thus, "I am the doer."

The gunas (modes) are pervasive and responsible for our actions and essential nature. One cannot escape their influence until they are neutralized, suppressed, or transcended. Therefore, this teaching is important to overcome desires and practice self-control and uninterrupted meditation. If you identify yourself with your mind and body, you will assume that you are the source of your actions and that everything in your life happens because of you. You fall into this delusion because of the influence of the triple modes: sattva, rajas, and tamas. They are responsible for all our actions. By creating desires and attachments and inducing the jivas to engage in desire-ridden actions, they bind them to samsara. Yogis overcome them, cultivating discernment and constantly remembering that the gunas active in their bodies are responsible for their desires and actions, and they are not their cause. On the surface, you may think that you are in control of your life and responsible for your actions. This conviction arises because of egoism, ignorance, and delusion, which convince you that you are a mere physical being and are responsible for your life and actions. As this verse affirms, the delusion that you are the doer of your actions arises because of the gunas. We will learn more about them in the subsequent chapters.

The word guna is translated in English as mode, quality, energy, or natural propensity. There is no equivalent word for it in English since the concept is unique to the faiths and philosophies of India. The gunas represent behavioral and personality modes or natural propensities to which we are prone. They exist in animate and inanimate things and impart to them properties, qualities, actions, and tendencies. Sattva represents purity, equanimity, and propensity for pleasure. It is represented by the color white. Rajas represents passions, attachments, and propensity for passions, pride, assertiveness, dominance, egoism, and restlessness. It is represented by the color yellow. Tamas represents ignorance, delusion, aggression, indiscretion, and the inclination to indulge in wickedness, perversion, defiance, and destructive nature. The color black symbolizes it.

Our actions are induced by desires and attachments. They are, in turn, induced by the gunas. Thus, the gunas are the root cause of our suffering, rebirth, and all that happens to us in the physical world. They are responsible for our inherent nature, thinking, attitude, behavior, personality traits, tendencies, and actions. They influence our conduct, natural disposition, the choices we make, the goals we pursue, the relationships we build, and the gods we worship. The Paingala Upanishad states that all the diversity in creation arises from them because of their admixture with the five elements (fire, water, earth, air, and space) in different permutations and combinations. Since they are present in the whole creation, no one can truly escape from their influence. Even gods, including Brahma, Vishnu, and Shiva, are subject to them. Brahman is beyond them (gunatita). However, his manifestations, or reflections in Nature, are subject to them. The higher tattvas of Nature, namely the mind (manas), ego (aham), and intelligence (buddhi), are also subject to them. Therefore, they cannot be taken lightly. Without resolving them, one cannot overcome the impurities of the mind and body or withdraw the mind and senses into the Self to practice self-restraint (atma samyama) and exclusive devotion. The individuality or the personality of each being, arising from its name and form (nama rupa), is also shaped by them. Because of them only, the deluded one thinks that he is the doer (karta) and the source of his life and destiny. Thereby, he assumes ownership and doership and remains bound.

Sloka 28

tattvavit tu mahābāho guṇakarmavibhāgayoḥ
guṇā guṇeṣu vartanta iti matvā na sajjate

tattva-vit = the knower of the nature of things, a person of knowledge; tu = but; maha-baho = mighty-armed one; guna-karma = gunas and actions; vibhagayoh = divisions; gunah = the modes; gunesu = in the modes; vartante = are, exist; iti = thus; matva = having thought; na = not; sajjate = becomes attached.

But, O mighty-armed one, the knower of tattvas and the division of actions arising from the gunas, does not become attached, thinking thus, 'The gunas are in the gunas.'

The knower of the tattvas (tattvavid) is the one who has a good knowledge and understanding of the aspects of Nature, how the mind and body evolve, and how the gunas pervade them and influence one's desires, thinking, and actions. He knows that actions arise and subside in the mind and body due to the gunas, and he is not in them or in the actions they induce. Thereby, he remains unattached and undisturbed. When you know that the body is an aggregate of the tattvas and gunas and you are not in them or their actions and movements, you will become mentally detached from them. Knowing that you are not your mind and body, you detach yourself from them and their actions and remain centered in the awareness that you are distinct from them, not in them, and not responsible for their actions.

The expression, "guna gunesu vartante" or "the gunas tend to be in the gunas," means that the senses, propelled by the gunas, move among the objects of similar nature possessing the same gunas. They are attracted to objects of similar nature and repelled by those in which they are absent or not predominant. Thus, sattva drives beings to seek or interact with sattvic things, rajas with rajasic things, and tamas with tamasic things. Hence, Lord Krishna said that the gunas are in other gunas. Those who think thus do not become attached to the desires or the actions they induce. Although the gunas are only three, their permutations and combinations produce a variety of states, conditions, behavioral tendencies, and propensities. Therefore, it isn't easy to classify beings and things strictly according to their gunas. However, by knowing which gunas are predominant and which of them influence our thoughts and actions, we can work for our self-purification. In this regard, the knowledge that they induce desires and drive the jivas towards the things in which they are predominant is helpful.

Thus, for example, sattvic people develop a taste for sattvic food, which promotes sattva; rajasic people prefer rajasic food, which strengthens rajas, and tamasic people take pleasure in tamasic food, which leads to the predominance of tamas. One can see the same tendencies playing out in relationships, choices, and habits. It is why spiritual people are advised to spend time in the company of holy people or like-minded sattvic people and strengthen their sattvic nature. One cannot ignore their influence in the books we read, the movies we watch, the habits we cultivate, or the professions we choose. These activities reinforce the gunas that are already predominant in us. Thereby, they make it increasingly difficult to overcome our desires, habits, and attachments. While they complicate our lives, on the positive side, they make our lives and actions more predictable and manageable. Knowing our essential nature and predominant modes, we can make wise decisions to reach our goals.

Gunakarma vibhagayoga means the division of actions according to the gunas. Just as with other things in Nature, the actions they induce can be divided into three: sattvic, rajasic, and tamasic actions. Sattvic actions lead to positive thinking, purity, spirituality, friendliness, peace, and happiness. Devotion to God arises spontaneously when sattva predominates. Knowledge and intelligence also shine when it is predominant. Rajasic and tamasic modes lead to impurities such as passions, egoism, wild desires, negativity, extreme thinking, delusion, and ignorance. The yogis who know how the modes act and induce actions do not feel disturbed by them. They withdraw their minds and senses into themselves and practice self-control to subdue the gunas and weaken their influence.

Sloka 29

prakṛter guṇasaṃmūḍhāḥ sajjante guṇakarmasu
tān akṛtsnavido mandān kṛtsnavin na vicālayet

prakrteh = of Nature; guna-sammudhah = deluded by the gunas; sajjante = become attached; guna-karmasu = in guna related activities; tan = those; akrtsna-vidah = those with incomplete knowledge, the ignorant; mandan = poor intellect; krtsna-vit = the all-knowing one, the knower of all; na = not; vicalayet = disturb.

Deluded by the gunas of Prakriti, the ignorant one becomes attached to the actions induced by them. Those who possess complete knowledge shall not disturb those of poor intellect with little knowledge.

In the second chapter, we learned that attachment to actions arises due to the repeated interaction of the senses with sense objects. It leads to desires, from desires to attachments, from attachments to passions, and from passions to delusion. This is the chain reaction arising from the gunas that results in bondage and suffering. The deluded ones take credit for their actions and desire to enjoy their fruit, believing that "I have done this action. I have put so much effort, resources, and energy into it. Therefore, I have the right to enjoy whatever I may gain from it." Hence, in the same chapter, Lord Krishna said that with desire-ridden minds, heaven as the highest goal, and birth as the fruit of their actions, the deluded ones engage in various sacrificial rituals to attain wealth and enjoyment. This is the attitude of karma yogis who are deluded by the gunas and perform their duties to enjoy happiness here and a better life in the next birth.

In this verse, he referred to them as the ignorant ones (mudhas) who develop an attachment to their actions induced by their gunas. The ignorance he alluded to is the reference to the ignorant notion that the mind and body constitute one's absolute self, and all actions arise from it. Deluded by that misapprehension, the ignorant ones assume ownership and doership of their actions and become bound to samsara. In contrast, he said that the all-knowing wise ones (krutsnavid), who know that the gunas are responsible for their actions and they are not in them, renounce ownership and doership of their actions and perform them without attachment and without desiring their fruit. Thus, he described the simple karma yogis of little knowledge and poor intellect, who live and act for themselves as the ignorant ones, and those who perform actions without desires and sacrifice them to the Lord as the all-knowing wise ones, and advised the latter not to disturb the former. He gave the same advice in verse 26.

The idea is that the ignorant ones should be allowed to pursue the four aims of human life and evolve gradually. They should be allowed to progress steadily from birth to birth according to their nature and at their own pace. Each householder is connected to several people and beings through his karma. Many lives depend upon him. The world still needs people like them to ensure its continuity. Therefore, they should not be pushed to be other than who they are. It is not in the interests of Dharma or the order and regularity of the world to interfere with their destinies and upset or uproot their lives. When the time is ripe and they are ready, the Lord will ensure that they know the truth and find the right way to perform their duties and progress further. It is why, in Hinduism, spiritual teachers do not initiate everyone. They initiate only those who are ready and prepare them for the journey incrementally. In ancient times, Upanishads were taught to students only after they were observed closely and found to be fit enough. They sat near their teachers so that others would not listen. Hence, their teachings came to be known as the Upanishads, meaning "sitting nearby."

Sloka 30

mayi sarvāṇi karmāṇi saṃnyasyādhyātmacetasā
nirāśīr nirmamo bhūtvā yudhyasva vigatajvaraḥ

mayi = to Me; sarvani = all; karmani = actions; sannyasya = renouncing; adhyatma = in the Self; cetasa = fixing the mind; nirasih = without desires or expectations; nirmamah = without egoistic ownership; bhutva = by remaining; yudhyasva = fight; vigata-jvarah = without feverish agitation.

Renouncing all actions to Me, establishing your mind in the Self, free from desires and the thoughts of 'me and mine,' you must fight without feverish agitation.

In this verse, Lord Krishna suggested how a karma yogi should perform actions the right way and with the right attitude. He said that by renouncing desires and attachment to all actions, remembering that he is the pure and immortal Self (or Brahman), and stabilizing his mind in that thought, he should perform actions without feverishness (vigatajvara) induced by anxiety, fear, or worry. Until the Kurukshetra war, Arjuna was a simple karma yogi like many householders. He knew how to perform his actions dutifully, befitting a warrior, and live righteously in the pursuit of the four aims of human life. He was unaware of the Lord who dwelt in him as his pure Self or his essential duty and obligation to him. Lord Krishna introduced him to that knowledge and the importance of performing actions by renouncing desires. He taught him the essential practice of buddhi yoga and karma-sannyasa yoga to discern the Self from his mind and body and practice his obligatory duties without confusion, doubt, fear, or worry.

Renunciation of action (karma sannyasa) does not mean you have to renounce actions, but their ownership, doership, and the desire to enjoy their fruit, and sacrifice them to the Supreme Lord, who is the true source, owner, and doer of all actions. In short, you must consecrate your life and actions to him as a sacrifice, without desires, doing your part and playing your role as the upholder of his eternal Dharma upon the earth. You reach this stage when you are free from egoism, desires, and delusion and possess the knowledge and discernment that your mind and body are mere instruments meant to serve the aims of Dharma, and the Lord whom you worship as the upholder of all also resides in you as your very Self. By that consecration, you transform every action of yours into an act of worship, devotion, and sacrifice, and your life itself into a continuous devotional service. Then, actions will not taint you but lead you toward the ultimate goal. Therefore, if a karma yogi wants to progress, he must transcend his desires and selfishness and serve the Lord as his dutiful and humble Bhagavata.

Nirāśa means freedom from desires and expectations (āśa). It also refers to the state of indifference. Nirmama means freedom (nir) from 'mama,' the egoistic thought or feeling of me and mine. Vigatajvaram means without the agitated or feverish state of distress, worry, anxiety, or agitation. Adhyatma chetasa means the mind filled with the awareness of the Self, or the mind which is fully established in the Self without duality. By that constant awareness, whether you are engaged in actions or not, you will gain control over your mind and senses and experience peace and equanimity even when you perform actions or your senses are drawn to sense objects.

The difference between karma yoga and karma-sannyasa yoga is that in karma yoga, you perform your duties to fulfill your desires while also serving the Lord and taking responsibility for the consequences that arise from them. In karma-sannyasa yoga, you renounce desires and attachments, ownership and doership, and perform those duties as a sacrifice to him without desiring their fruit. By that act of sacrifice, you will escape from karma. Thus, karma-sannyasa yoga gives you the freedom to live fearlessly and remain untainted by the mortal world. It lets you be a part of God's creation and serve him without having to give up your regular life as a householder. Sri Madhavacharya said that in this effort, you must renounce desires and all false notions regarding the Self. While you renounce the desire to enjoy the fruit of your actions, you may still wish to cultivate knowledge, purity, and devotion since they are positive intentions that do not violate the code of conduct.

Sloka 31

ye me matam idaṃ nityam anutiṣṭhanti mānavāḥ
śraddhāvantonasūyanto mucyante tepi karmabhiḥ

ye = those; me = my; matam = teachings, doctrines; idam = this; nityam = always, constantly; anutisthanti = practice, follow; manavah = human beings, people; sraddha-vantah = with great faith; anasuyantah = without envy, indignation; mucyante = are freed; te = they; api = also; karmabhih = from actions.

Those people who constantly practice My teachings with great faith and without envy are also delivered from actions.

Those who constantly practice these teachings with faith and without envy also achieve liberation, just as those who practice karma-sannyasa yoga, renouncing all actions to him and establishing their minds in him. There is no contradiction here. Whether you practice karma-sannyasa yoga or follow the teachings of Lord Krishna with regard to actions, they are practically the same and lead to the same end, which is freedom from karma and samsara. Here, he emphasized faith, constant practice, and freedom from envy. You cannot practice any teachings or philosophy for a long time with faith and sincerity unless you believe in it and accept it wholeheartedly without doubts and confusion. If that knowledge flows from a teacher, you must believe in him unconditionally and accept his guidance with full and unwavering faith.

Anutishthati means constant practice. It has the same meaning as abhyas or regular practice. Through practice only, we achieve perfection and excellence. Freedom from karma in this verse does not mean freedom from actions but from their fruit. Actions mean all actions: those that are obligatory, those that are not obligatory, and those that are prohibited. In other words, a karma-sannyasa yogi does not have to worry about whether his actions are righteous or not if they are a part of his duty. He can perform any actions that he is required to perform without incurring sinful karma. Freedom from envy (anasuyantah) means not having any negativity, bitterness, jealousy, or ill will towards the teacher for his knowledge, wealth, status, excellence, or popularity. The word may have also been used here to represent all the evil passions, such as lust, anger, fear, greed, etc., which keep people deluded and sinful. It means those who wish to achieve liberation should be free from all evil passions that are natural to deluded minds.

In this verse, Lord Krishna spoke in the first person, as 'Me' or 'I' or 'Mine.' Whenever he does it, we have to infer that he was speaking from an exalted state of nonduality in oneness with Brahman or the Supreme Lord himself. Most people do not understand this concept since they cannot see beyond duality and division. The Lord dwells in everyone. When you are one with him and dissolve your mind in him, indeed, it is the Lord who speaks through you in oneness. Now, it does not mean Lord Krishna was not the Supreme Lord. He was, indeed. However, in his incarnated state, he too must have experienced duality and spoken sometimes as Krishna, the person, and sometimes as Krishna, the Lord of the universe. When he delivered the Bhagavadgita, he must have spoken from the most exalted state of his consciousness as the Lord of the universe. Whatever may be the truth, Hinduism acknowledges that anyone who enters the nondual state of oneness with the Supreme Lord would speak in the first person as the Lord himself. If he does not, then he would be negating or denying his very state of oneness or liberation. In the purest state of self-awareness, which is free from duality, delusion, and division, for all purposes, the devotee becomes the Lord himself. It is why we worship enlightened masters and equate them with God, saying, "gururdevobhava." We leave that debate to the wise ones and focus on the message that the Lord delivered. The supreme reality of Brahman, which Lord Krishna represented or personified in the scripture, is free from duality, diversity, or divisions. It is an indistinguishable and purest state of oneness without boundaries.

Special note: Gururdevobhava means the teacher is verily God.

Sloka 32

ye tv etad abhyasūyanto nānutiṣṭhanti me matam
sarvajñānavimūḍhāṃs tān viddhi naṣṭān acetasaḥ

ye = those who; tu = but; etat = this; abhyasuyantah = out of envy; na = do not; anutisthanti = follow; me = My; matam = teaching, doctrine; sarva-jnana = knowledge of the all-knowing Self; vimudhan = bewildered, confused, deluded; tan = they; viddhi = know; nastan = ruined; acetasah = without discriminating intelligence, without mindfulness.

But those who, out of envy, do not follow My teaching, know them to be confused about the knowledge of the all-knowing Self, ruined and lacking in discriminating intelligence.

Those who do not renounce desire-ridden actions, do not establish their minds in the indwelling Lord, and do not overcome desires and the thoughts of 'me and mine' should be considered deluded, confused, and lacking in discerning wisdom. They are ruined because they fall into lower hells or remain stuck in samsara. The light of purity and divinity in them will gradually fade, clouded by impurities, and they will slowly descend into the darkness of egoism, ignorance, sensuality, desires, passions, and evil thoughts. Drawing out their minds, following their senses, and embracing the world, they bring ruin upon themselves, performing desire-ridden actions and accumulating sinful karma. Lord Krishna already advised his devotees not to confuse them with their knowledge or wisdom but to leave them to their fate. At best, they may inspire them by setting an example.

The teachings of the Lord are found in many scriptures, especially in the revelatory ones (shrutis). Enlightened masters (gurus) and learned ones (vidvans) also channel them through their teachings and exemplary conduct. God's devotees should, therefore, read scriptures every day, follow the example of seers and sages, and keep their minds soaked with the knowledge of the all-knowing Self (Sarvajna). Scriptures such as the Bhagavadgita, which contain his teachings, should not be kept in the house and worshipped superficially. They must be studied and practiced sincerely with faith and discernment. One may honor the seers and sages, but more important than that is honoring them by exemplifying their virtues and teachings through one's conduct.

Divine knowledge constantly flows to us from the higher realms and unexpected sources. We will receive them if we keep our hearts and minds open. It is not necessary that God has to manifest upon the earth and personally impart to us the sacred knowledge of liberation. His teachings and messages flow to us continuously through many channels. If we are receptive and open our hearts and minds, we will receive them and learn from them. Many people are not attuned to receiving divine knowledge since their minds are filled with worldliness, egoism, and delusion. They are lost in the quagmire of instant gratification and sensuality, which do not let them know their true nature or turn to spirituality to see the world with stable intelligence (prajna). This verse does not say that those who do not follow the teachings of the Supreme Being will be punished. The Lord does not punish anyone. All punishments arise from karma. They are self-inflicted. We reward and punish ourselves through our actions, choices, likes, and dislikes. Our essential nature plays a vital role in this. Lord Krishna speaks about it in the next verse.

Sloka 33

sadṛśaṃ ceṣṭate svasyāḥ prakṛter jñānavān api
prakṛtiṃ yānti bhūtāni nigrahaḥ kiṃ kariṣyati

sadrsam = accordingly; cestate = acts; svasyah = his own; prakrteh = Nature; jnana-van = a wise person; api = even; prakrtim = nature; yanti = follow; bhutani = living beings; nigrahah = restraint or suppression; kim = what; karisyati = can do.

Even a wise person acts according to his nature. All beings follow their nature. What can restraint or suppression do?

Whether intelligent or ignorant, people act helplessly according to their essential nature (svabhavam) as determined by their gunas. Those who are ready can be taught to achieve liberation through self-purification. However, the deluded ones who are not ready cannot be taught to cultivate discernment or achieve liberation since their essential nature would not allow them to change. You cannot stop wise people from pursuing liberation or worshipping the Lord in them. Similarly, you cannot stop the deluded ones from engaging their minds and senses in the pursuit of worldly pleasures and desire-ridden actions. It is only possible through stupendous effort and divine intervention. This is the summary.

If wise people act according to their inherent nature and cannot go against it, what about common people who are ignorant and do not have the knowledge of the Self or resolving karma? In other words, we cannot go against our essential nature without a paradigm shift in our consciousness and the transformation of our minds and bodies. Nature prevails as long as we are not ready, awakened to the reality of the Self that dwells in us, and do not accept it as our guiding light. Even the Supreme Lord does not seem to interfere with her methods and mechanisms. Bound by the same principle, his manifestations or projections in creation also act according to their nature.

While this appears to contradict the notion that God is Supreme and Lord of the Universe, it makes sense to believe that he lets Nature not only execute his will according to the laws that are already set in motion but also manage all her creative processes diligently. By that, she makes sure that everything stays in its place and follows its nature, and creation does not fall into disorder and chaos.

Thus, as this verse states, we are bound to our essential nature and cannot go against it despite our best efforts. We cannot also prevent it from doing what it intends to do and manifest our destinies. We may tame it partially through yoga and austerities and act against its influence, but in the process, we may experience a lot of resistance, pain, and suffering. If we let up control even for a while, we will revert to our old habits. We are products of our past. Through many births and deaths, we have reached this stage in our evolution and possess our respective natures. We cannot just transform them. It requires persistent effort, commitment, firm faith, and a lot of good karma. The problem is further complicated by the fact that the gunas keep reinforcing our inherent nature through habitual and repetitive actions. Caught in the cycle of births and deaths, we become products of our past and prisoners of our essential nature, which we can neither control nor suppress, and from which we cannot easily escape without acquiring the right knowledge and earning divine grace. We have to live with what we create and precipitate as the fruit of our actions within ourselves and our lives, live with it, and endure it until it dissipates.

For these reasons, self-purification and transformation take time and involve considerable effort. It is also why Lord Krishna previously advised Arjuna not to confound the ignorant and the deluded and let them improve naturally or through example. Even if they are inclined somehow, their essential nature would not let them change quickly. However, we can overcome this problem and lay the foundation for a new beginning and a better future through karma yoga or karma-sannyasa yoga. By performing actions and doing our duties according to our nature and consecrating them to God with detachment and indifference, we can escape from their consequences and cultivate purity. However, for that to happen, we must give up egoistic effort, desires, and expectations and leave the result entirely to God.

Sloka 34

indriyasyendriyasyārthe rāgadveṣau vyavasthitau
tayor na vaśam āgacchhet tau hy asya paripanthinau

indriyasya = of the senses; indriyasya arthe = in the sense objects; raga = attraction; dvesau = aversion; vyavasthitau = established, organized; tayoh = their; na = not; vasam = influence, control; agacchet = should (one) come; tau = they; hi = certainly; asya = his; paripanthinau = obstacles on the path, stumbling blocks.

Attraction and aversion to sense objects are established for the sake of the sense organ. One should not come under their influence. Certainly, they are major obstacles on the path (to liberation).

Nature established attraction and aversion in the jivas to facilitate sense activity and keep them bound to the world. Attraction for the sense objects draws them out, and aversion draws them in. Attraction results in positive attachments, and aversion leads to negative attachments. Both keep the mind restless and agitated. Those who pursue liberation should not be swayed by them or allow their minds and senses to wander. They must withdraw them and restrain them so that they can establish their minds in peace and stability. The first step to achieving it is to know that attraction and aversion are responsible for the movement of the senses and the mind's instability, delusion, and disturbance.

Attraction and aversion (raga dvesha) strengthen in the jivas due to repeated interaction between the senses and sense objects. The gunas play an important role here. They induce the senses to interact with objects in which they are predominantly present and avoid those in which they are absent. Thus, they arise in the jivas mainly due to the gunas and their tendency to establish dominance. Desires arise when the senses repeatedly interact with objects of similar nature, which the mind or the jiva finds agreeable or disagreeable. They are attracted to things that produce agreeable or pleasant sensations and repelled by those that produce disagreeable, unpleasant, or painful sensations. All jivas act in this manner. The gunas influence their likes and dislikes. Sattvic people seek sattvic things, rajasic ones, rajasic things, and tamasic ones, tamasic things. This is the way of Nature (prakriti svabhavam). She controls our destinies, behaviors, and natural propensities through attraction and aversion and keeps us bound to the mortal world. The outgoing nature of the mind and senses (prvritti) also arises because of them only. Therefore, the practice of self-control must begin with the senses by withdrawing them into the mind and keeping them under control. When the senses are withdrawn and inactive, the mind relaxes and dissolves into silence.

Another important take from this is that seekers of liberation should not act or pursue things according to their likes and dislikes but according to their discernment only, doing what is necessary to remain in control and practice self-purification. They should not allow themselves or their senses to be swayed by desire, emotions, or attachments. Ignorant people pursue desires and act according to their likes and dislikes. They develop attachments and become selective in their choices and actions, which prevents them from living freely. The right approach is to perform actions that are necessary or relevant to one's duties and obligations and serve God, the world, and others, transcending attraction and aversion.

Sloka 35

śreyān svadharmo viguṇaḥ paradharmāt svanuṣṭhitāt
svadharme nidhanaṃ śreyaḥ paradharmo bhayāvahaḥ

sreyan = superior; sva-dharmah = one's own duty; vigunah = inferior gunas, defective, devoid of merit; para-dharmat = duty of another; svanusthitat = better suited, well formed; sva-dharme = one's own duty; nidhanam = death; sreyah = better; para-dharmah = duty of another; bhaya-avahah = brings or invites fear and danger.

Svadharma (one's own duty) is better even if it is rooted in inferior gunas than paradharma (another's duty), which is well-formed and better suited. It is better to die performing your own duty. Another person's duty brings fear and danger.

In the previous verse, Lord Krishna said that attraction and aversion are obstacles to liberation. Here, he provided the reason. If you follow your likes and dislikes, you will perform only those duties you like and avoid those you dislike. You may also choose duties that you are not supposed to do just because they are convenient, more profitable, or to your liking. Since those decisions arise from your desires, egoism, or selfishness, they will produce karma. Hence, he suggested that everyone must stick to their duties (svadharma) that arise from their essential nature rather than someone's duties (para dharma) to which they are attracted or develop a liking. He also said that performing another's duties brings fear and danger since the person who does that may not know how to perform them or perform them incorrectly and land himself or others in trouble. Further, when you try to do another's duties, your essential nature may not cooperate with you and prevent you from completing them.

Therefore, he suggested that one should stick to the duties that are natural or agreeable to one's essential nature and serve the Lord. You will then be in harmony with yourself and excel in your actions. The idea which is presented here is simple. You must be true to yourself and choose the actions that suit you. By being yourself and living naturally, you will be in a better position to manifest your destiny, talents, and uniqueness and fulfill your obligations without conflicts and confusion. If you try to be another person, you will not only be unhappy, ineffective, and restless but also incur the sin of failing in your duties or neglecting the ones you were supposed to follow.

Many people lead unhappy lives because they go against their essential nature and try to follow someone. Due to vanity or delusion, they try to imitate those they admire or live like them. As this verse affirms, it is not a wise choice. If you choose professions that are inconsistent with your inborn talents and aspirations or your knowledge and skills, you will not be happy or fulfilled, and most likely end up as a failure. Your present life is a continuation of your past lives. You have to fulfill your destiny shaped over several lives. You cannot do it unless you express your inherent talents and deepest aspirations or the predominant thoughts you inherited from your previous births. You will also experience resistance, obstacles, and conflicts in reaching your spiritual goals as you struggle to reconcile your goals and actions with your spiritual ideals.

In ancient times, caste laws regulated people's lives, duties, and conduct. They determined how they should live, what roles they should play, and which code of conduct they should follow for the order and regularity of the world. This was especially true in Vedic times when the kings had the obligatory duty to protect their subjects, follow the Vedic Dharma, and enforce the laws among their subjects as prescribed by the Dharma Shastras (law books). Family heads, village heads, and local rulers also enforced similar laws. Hence, people had no confusion. They knew what was expected of them, what would attract retribution and punishment if they violated the laws or their caste rules, and adhered to their respective duties and professions.

Today, those rules do not apply since the ancient social order has been replaced by a constitutionally guaranteed modern legal system in almost all countries based on the principles of fairness, equality, and freedom. We are now guided by egalitarian principles and social and professional standards, which give us considerable freedom to make decisions for ourselves and live according to our best hopes and aspirations. We can choose our professions and occupations according to our skills and talents and decide how to regulate our lives, conduct, and behavior, or meet our obligations. Therefore, the task of choosing duties according to one's svadharma becomes complicated. Hindu householders who follow the traditional way of life still have many duties and obligations to themselves, others, and God. For the sake of Dharma and their spiritual well-being, they cannot ignore them. Castes may not be as important. However, the duties that arise from one's essential nature or the profession or occupation one chooses are still important. Devout Hindus should choose such duties that fit into their lifestyles and professions or agree with their essential nature, deepest aspirations, natural talents, or skills. In doing so, they should remember the principles that serve as the pillars of Hindu Dharma.

Sloka 36

arjuna uvāca
atha kena prayuktoyaṃ pāpaṃ carati pūruṣaḥ
anicchann api vārṣṇeya balād iva niyojitaḥ

arjunah uvaca = Arjuna said; atha = then; kena = by what; prayuktah = induced; ayam = this; papam = sin; carati = commit; purusah = a person; anicchan = against will; api = even; varsneya = O Varsneya, descendent of Vrsni tribe; balat = by force; iva = as if; niyojitah = compelled.

Said Arjuna, "Then, O Varshneya, induced by what does this person commit sin against his will as if he is compelled to do so?"

Arjuna wanted to know what caused a person to sin against his own will. Previously, he heard from Lord Krishna that he (Isvara) was the source of all actions. Then, he heard from him that people incurred sin due to desires, attachments, and other causes such as delusion, ignorance, gunas, essential nature, etc. In the previous verse, he heard that one should not come under the influence of attraction and aversion since they were major obstacles to liberation. Hence, he wanted to know what made one act according to his nature, as if he were compelled to do so. We see in the world how people are driven by their predominant desires, beliefs, thoughts, and habits. Under their influence, they commit unthinkable acts and sabotage themselves as if they have no power or control over themselves and are helplessly driven to act against their best interests. Sometimes, they also lose control and give in to their passions and emotions despite their best intentions and act emotionally or impulsively against their best judgment. Even if they know or have learned that they are spiritual beings with a soul, they act as if they are mere physical beings with no soul and no spiritual possibilities, such as rebirth or liberation.

It is natural for animals, birds, insects, and other creatures with fewer senses and tattvas to be driven by their inherent nature, fate, circumstances, or acts of God. We cannot say the same about ourselves since we are endowed with higher faculties and can discern truths, learn from observation and experience, and improve ourselves through practice. The question, then, is how far we are controlled by the forces of Nature, God's will, or our own will, thoughts, and actions. Are we condemned to live according to our fate, or do we have some freedom to change our lives and escape from certain outcomes? Probably, the truth lies somewhere in between these two possibilities. It seems our lives are controlled by fate, circumstances, God, and our and others' actions and decisions. Recent research suggests that our minds and bodies are already predisposed to act in certain ways due to genetic, biological, and neurological factors, and that free will may be an illusion.

In ancient India, a school of fatalists known as Ajivakas believed that everything in life was predetermined by fate, from which there was no escape. They argued that free will was an illusion, and human beings had no choice but to live their lives to fulfill their predetermined destinies right from birth, which unraveled according to a prearranged order (niyati). If fate willed that a person should sin, he would because there was no escape from it. Thus, they lived passively, resigning themselves to their fates and hardly resisting whatever happened to them. Opposed to them were the believers in karma who held that our actions shaped our lives and destinies. They believed that beings were subject to the law of cause and effect, and people reaped rewards and punishments according to the actions and choices they made, assuming ownership and doership and exercising their free will. They also believed that karma could be resolved through various means, suppressing desires, praying to gods, or engaging in pious actions and acts of purification. The doctrine of karma is based on the premise that people can change their lives and destinies through willful and intelligent actions within the freedom granted by the natural laws or the Creator's will. Whether they want to live independently and egoistically or surrender to him and let him take care of their lives and liberation is a personal choice that will lead them to different ends.

The Bhagavadgita accepts the doctrine of karma with God as the Supreme Controller. It identifies desires, passions, and attachments as the root causes of sinful karma and suggests that we can overcome suffering by knowing and addressing the causes of our suffering and bondage. The gunas induce desires, passions, and attachments. They lead to sinful actions, karma, and rebirth. Hence, by renouncing desires, subduing passions, giving up doership and ownership of actions and possessions, offering our actions and their fruit to the Supreme Lord, and acknowledging him as the source of all, we can escape from karma and attain liberation. The karma doctrine puts our lives back into our hands, cautioning, at the same time, not to live selfishly for ourselves or succumb to wild passions but to serve God and his creation, living responsibly and dutifully and taking refuge in him.

Sloka 37

śrībhagavān uvāca
kāma eṣa krodha eṣa rajoguṇasamudbhavaḥ
mahāśano mahāpāpmā viddhy enam iha vairiṇam

sri-bhagavan uvaca = said God Supreme; kamah = desire; esah = this; krodhah = anger; esah = this; rajah-guna = the mode of rajas; samudbhavah = is born, arises; maha-asanah = great devourer; maha-papma = great sinner, evil doer; viddhi = know; enam = this; iha = here in this world; vairinam = the enemy.

The Supreme Lord said, "This lust, this anger, which is born of rajoguna, is a great devourer and great sinner. Know that in this world, it is the enemy."

Here, Lord Krishna confirmed that people commit sin against their will as if they are helpless and compelled to do so due to lust, anger, and similar passions that arise from rajas. In a general sense, Kama means all desires and, in a particular sense, lust. Shankaracharya identified it with desires and declared it as the enemy since desire is the root of all evil. In this context, it may mean lust if we consider that it is mentioned along with anger, another evil passion. Lust is the most powerful of all passions and difficult to control. When it is thwarted, it turns into anger and destabilizes the mind. Thus, kama turns into krodha, and together, they devour the mind and intelligence and drive people to engage in unspeakable acts. The evil passions are chiefly five: kama (lust), krodha (anger), bhaya (fear), mada (pride), and matsarya (envy). In some lists, fear is replaced with greed (lobha). They are known as the five chief mortal sins (pancha maha patakas). They all produce sinful desires. When they are thwarted, they produce anger. Lord Krishna stated that the root of all passions is rajoguna. However, lust, anger, or rajas cannot be considered the devourer, sinner, or enemy in all cases since they are active only in specific situations and do not consume everyone's mind as much as desires. Therefore, the great devourer and the enemy of all is none but desire. From this perspective, kama means desire only.

Of the three gunas, sattvaguna represents purity, rajoguna represents passions, and tamoguna represents ignorance and perversion. The last two gunas are considered impurities. Mahasan means a voracious eater whose hunger is never satisfied. Coincidentally, the Lord of Death (Kala) is also a great devourer. He devours everything upon the earth, including kama and all other passions. As stated in the Shrimad Bhagavatam (9.19.13), desires cannot be satisfied by appeasement or fulfillment. Just as by adding ghee, fire is intensified; by satisfying desires, desires are intensified. Controlling lustful desires and thoughts is much more difficult. Even great yogis succumb to them and sink into ignominy. Hence, kama (desire) is rightly called a great devourer, which devours virtue, wisdom, and knowledge and makes people ignorant and delusional, a great sinner since it induces people to commit various sins through desire-ridden actions, and an arch enemy since it deludes people and prevents them from knowing themselves and attaining liberation. According to our scriptures, the enmity between two kingdoms or countries can be resolved by four conciliatory methods, namely amity or friendship (sama), generosity or charity (dana), discord or division (bheda), or force or coercion (danda). However, these standard methods of statecraft (rajaniti) are ineffective against desires and passions. They can be controlled only by neutralizing the triple gunas, their root causes, through a holistic spiritual effort.

Sloka 38

dhūmenāvriyate vanhir yathādarśo malena ca
yatholbenāvṛto garbhas tathā tenedam āvṛtam

dhumena = by smoke; avriyate = covered, enveloped; vahnih = fire; yatha = as; adarsah = mirror; malena = by impurities; ca = and; yatha = as; ulbena = by womb; avrtah = is covered; garbhah = fetus; tatha = so; tena = by that; idam = this; avrtam = is enveloped.

Just as fire is covered by smoke, a mirror by impurities, and a fetus is enveloped by the womb, so is by that (desire) this one is enveloped.

Smoke, a layer of dust, and the womb symbolically represent the mild, moderate, severe, or extreme types of impurities caused by desires and passions. They cloud the beings' consciousness and intelligence and increasingly involve them with sense objects and worldly pleasures. Sattva induces milder, nontoxic impurities arising from the desire and attachment to pleasure and happiness. Rajas is responsible for moderate or semi-toxic impurities caused by selfish desires and passions, such as lust, anger, envy, etc. Tamas is responsible for the most severe and toxic impurities induced by egoism, delusion, and ignorance. These impurities envelop the internal organ (antahkarana) and keep the jivas in varying states of ignorance and bondage. The milder impurities are not problematic and do not interfere much with one's thinking and actions. Just as smoke dissipates easily as the fire catches up, a karma yogi can burn them easily through self-restraint and self-purification, practicing his duties, and cultivating knowledge and discernment.

The moderate and semi-toxic impurities caused by rajas are comparable to the layer of dust that accumulates on the surface of a mirror. Just as dust accumulates gradually on the mirror due to negligence, these impurities accumulate slowly in one's consciousness due to intense desires and passions. They distort and delude one's thinking, perceptions, reality, stability, and balance. They cannot be wiped away easily and require considerable effort. However, rajasic people still have a chance to overcome them, cultivating knowledge and discernment (samprajnata), and performing their duties without desires and attachments. The impurities arising from tamas are the most difficult to resolve. Just as the fetus is enveloped in darkness inside the womb and the womb does not let any light enter it, these impurities form a thick layer around the mind and intelligence and do not let any light enter them. As a result, the beings in whom they are active remain deluded and ignorant and do not show any interest in their spiritual nature or working for their liberation. They give themselves to animal passions, distorted thinking, and self-destructive behavior and refuse to see any good in worshipping God, performing sacrificial duties, or righteous actions. From this, we can conclude that desires and passions should be controlled before they become persistent and troublesome.

Sloka 39

āvṛtaṃ jñānam etena jñānino nityavairiṇā
kāmarupeṇa kaunteya duṣpūreṇānalena ca

avrtam = enveloped; jnanam = wisdom, knowledge; etena = by this; jnaninah = of the wise; nitya-vairina = constant or eternal enemy; kama-rupena = in the form of desire; kaunteya = Kaunteya, son of Kunti; duspurena = insatiable; analena = by the fire; ca = like, and.

O Kaunteya, wisdom is enveloped by this constant enemy of the wise ones in the form of desire, which is like an insatiable fire.

Shankaracharya stated that desire was the 'constant enemy 'of the wise but not the ignorant. According to him, wise people know from the beginning that desires are problematic and that giving in to them results in sinful consequences. They know that desires can overwhelm even the disciplined ones at any time if they are careless. Therefore, they see desire as their constant enemy (nitya vairina) and always remain guarded, practicing self-restraint and keeping their minds withdrawn and absorbed in the Self. The Puranas contain many instances where seers and sages like Vishwamitra succumbed to lustful passions and fell from their spiritual heights. Hence, the wise ones remain guarded from all sides and do not let the fire of passion and desire burn them. The ignorant ones lack that discernment or foresight due to ignorance or carelessness. They realize it only after chasing desires and passions and burning themselves. Some may not realize it at all and continue to indulge in them, resulting in their downfall.

Lord Krishna described desire, especially lustful desire, as insatiable because it cannot be weakened or put down through fulfillment or enjoyment. With each attempt to satisfy it, it only gathers strength and intensity and consumes the mind and body. The wise ones know it. Therefore, they starve it through self-restraint, austerity, celibacy, detachment, renunciation, etc., and weaken it until it becomes weak and ceases to be troublesome. The three types of impurities, mild, moderate, and severe, arise from desires and attachments only. They cloud the mind and intelligence. Hence, Lord Krishna drew our attention to desire, describing it as the constant enemy that deludes and distracts those who want to escape from the mortal world forever.

Sloka 40

indriyāṇi mano buddhir asyādhiṣṭhānam ucyate
etair vimohayaty eṣa jñānam āvṛtya dehinam

indriyani = the senses; manah = the mind; buddhih = the discriminating intelligence; asya = of this; adhisthanam = the seat; ucyate = said to be; etaih = by these; vimohayati = deludes; esah = of this; jnanam = wisdom; avrtya = enveloped; dehinam = the embodied.

The senses, the mind, and intelligence are said to be the seat of this. Through them, it deludes the one in the body, veiling the wisdom.

The senses, the mind, and intelligence are the strongholds of desires. It is from where they rule the jiva, induced by the gunas, and determine his fate and the course of his life. The senses (indriyas) are fifteen, namely the five organs of action, the five organs of perception, and the five sense perceptions (tanmatras) or sense experiences (seeing, listening, smelling, touching, and tasting). Manas is the memorial mind. It is where objects of the mind (memories, perceptions, sensations, etc.) are stored. It is different from intelligence (buddhi), which is responsible for the higher faculties of the mind, including the executive functions, intuition, cognition, reasoning, etc. Hence, they are separately mentioned. The mind stores memories associated with desires and desire-ridden actions, which reinforce attraction and aversion, and attachment to certain desires and senses objects. Buddhi is the thinking or the logical mind responsible for reasoning and discernment. It uses the knowledge stored in the manas to decide which actions to pursue and which ones to avoid. If the buddhi is veiled, we cannot think properly, realize our true nature, or make intelligent decisions, just as a person cannot think clearly when confused, disturbed, or intoxicated. Desires and lustful thoughts affect the functioning of all the organs in the body, except breath, and delude the jivas (embodied souls) by compelling them to engage in desire-ridden actions and incur sinful karma. Because of them, the jivas cannot escape from samsara.

Sloka 41

tasmāt tvam indriyāṇy ādau niyamya bharatarṣabha
pāpmānaṃ prajahi hy enaṃ jñānavijñānanāśanam

tasmat = therefore; tvam = you; indriyani = senses; adau = in the beginning; niyamya = by restraining; bharata-rsabha = the best among the Bharatas; papmanam = sin; prajahi = slay, control; hi = indeed; enam = this; jnana = knowledge; vijnana = higher knowledge; nasanam = destroyer.

Therefore, O best of the Bharatas, restraining the senses in the very beginning, slay the cause of sin, which is indeed the destroyer of knowledge and wisdom.

Desires are the root cause of sin and suffering. They destroy knowledge and wisdom, whereby beings engage in desire-ridden actions indiscriminately, become deluded, and accumulate sin. They exert their influence mainly on the senses, the mind, and intelligence, and keep the beings restless. Hence, if you want to control them, you have to begin with the senses by withdrawing them into the mind, the mind into intelligence, and everything into the Self. When all three are under control, desires begin to lose strength, and the mind becomes tranquil. In this verse, Lord Krishna suggested two methods to control desires: withdrawing and restraining the senses and beginning it at the very starting point (adi), the point of contact. He might have implied that the restraint must begin from the very early stages of spiritual practice for self-purification. He advised Arjuna to control his senses because controlling them is easier than controlling the mind or intelligence. Since they keep the mind restless and unstable, it also makes sense to restrain them first so that the mind and intelligence can be controlled and stabilized with the senses withdrawn and detached from the external world.

Desire (kama) is described here as the cause of sin and the destroyer of knowledge and wisdom. The state in which people engage in sinful actions is indeed the sinful state of ignorance and delusion only. It is also the state of egoism, attachments, bondage, and suffering. Their root cause is desire, which destroys the knowledge and wisdom of embodied souls and keeps them bound to the mortal world. In a worldly sense, jnana refers to the accumulated knowledge that arises from the information stored in the mind (manas) as memories, perceptions, and impressions. Vijnanam is the wisdom or the processed knowledge that arises from buddhi (intelligence) due to thinking, reasoning, and discretion. Jnanam is the memorial knowledge that accumulates in the manas through learning, perceptions, and memories. It is like a storehouse of information that helps us know and remember things. Vijnanam refers to the empirical knowledge that arises from learning and thinking when buddhi or intelligence processes the memorial knowledge available in the manas and uses it to solve problems, draw conclusions and inferences, or learn from application, practice, and experience. However, in the spiritual context, as Shankaracharya defined, jnanam refers to the knowledge of the Self, which is learned or secured from the study of the scriptures or the teachings of a guru. Vijnanam refers to the cognitive knowledge gained through practice, understanding, observation, or personal experience.

Sloka 42

indriyāṇi parāṇy āhur indriyebhyaḥ paraṃ manaḥ
manasas tu parā buddhir yo buddheḥ paratas tu saḥ

indriyani = senses; parani = superior; ahuh = say; indriyebhyah = to the senses; param = superior; manah = the mind; manasah = to the mind; tu = also; para = superior; buddhih = discriminating intelligence; yah = one who; buddheh = to the intelligence; paratah = superior; tu = but; sah = he.

(They) say that the senses are superior; superior to the senses is the mind; superior to the mind is the discriminating intelligence; the one superior to the discriminating intelligence is He.

This verse suggests that to control desires, one must restrain the senses since they are the starting point of contact with the external world, and through that contact, they incite desires and attachments and keep the mind restless. The senses are also first in the hierarchy of the tattvas of the internal organ (antahkarana). The Katha Upanishad contains a verse (1.3.10) which states that the senses are superior to the gross body, the mind is superior to the senses, the buddhi is superior to the mind, and the Self is the highest. However, some texts go beyond them and state that higher than the individual Self (Atman) is the manifested Self (vyakta) or Isvara, and higher than the manifested Self is the invisible and unmanifested Brahman (avyakta). Higher than Brahman, there is nothing. He is the highest, the absolute, and the ultimate. The superiority and inferiority of the bodily parts may arise due to the difficulty in controlling them and their sphere of influence in controlling our actions and liberation. It may also be due to the relative status of the deities who control them.

According to the Vedas, the body is a miniature cosmos and a playground of Prakriti where various deities reside in the organs and control their actions in return for the nourishment they receive as offerings through the sacrifice of bodily functions such as breathing, eating, and drinking. Just like the world, the body has denser and subtler aspects. Some organs are dense and gross, while some are subtler and subtlest. Therefore, the tantras divide the deities and the organs in the body into gross, subtler, and subtlest. The gross ones are easier to control than the subtlest ones, where yogis may have to invoke divine help to achieve higher standards of purity and perfection to overcome the forces of maya. The sense organs, representing the devas in Indra's heaven, fall into the middle category. They are also not equal and have a hierarchy according to their importance. The organs of perception (jnanendriyas) are superior to the organs of action (karmendriyas), and the subtle senses (tanmatras) are superior to the organs of perception. Higher than the senses are the mind, the ego, and intelligence. Above intelligence is the eternal and indestructible Self, which is other than, different from, and superior to all the tattvas of Prakriti.

Why are the organs of perception superior to the organs of action and other bodily parts? It is because they are controlled by superior gods who preside over them. Further, they have mobility and extensibility with which they can effortlessly connect the mind to the rest of the world and travel far and wide, bringing valuable information about the world and objects, which helps the beings in their survival and enjoyment. They also protect jivas from harm by alerting them to perceived threats. Most importantly, they serve the body's higher organs, namely the mind, the ego, and intelligence, by helping them in their tasks. Thus, the senses are certainly superior to the gross organs in the body, which are fixed to the body and have little mobility. The mind is superior to the senses because it is their lord. They serve him while he controls them. It can travel farther than the senses with imagination or memory. Symbolically, it is compared to Indra, the lord of the heavens, while the senses are compared to the deities who serve him as his deputies. In Vedic terminology, the mind (manas) represents the memorial mind, which acts as the receptacle of all the information that flows into it as perceptions, thoughts, memories, sensations, feelings, emotions, instincts, etc. In short, the memorial mind is a repository of accumulated, objective knowledge. If the senses are like rivers, which flow into an ocean, the mind is like an ocean into which all sensory information constantly flows. Just as an ocean is undoubtedly far superior to the rivers that flow into it, the mind is superior to the senses into which information from them flows.

However, the mind can do nothing independently since it has no self-induced light. It is a passive organ that holds our consciousness as a vessel under the control of the ego and intelligence. Higher than the memorial mind and ego is the thinking mind or intelligence (buddhi), which uses the memorial knowledge of manas for decision-making. In the body, it is the highest tattva and is responsible for thinking, reasoning, analysis, decision-making, discretion, etc. Without buddhi, we must live by the blind force of Nature, instinct, habit, chance, or fate. Intelligence is superior to the memorial mind because it shines the light it receives from the Self upon all the parts of the internal organ (antahkarana) and uses the available knowledge, perceptions, and information to discern things and make intelligent choices or decisions. When clouded by impurities, it does not discern the Self, know its existence, radiate any light, and remains bound to the limited self or the ego. However, upon becoming pure and discerning the Self, the light of the Self radiates through it, which helps the yogis discern truths and progress on the path of liberation with knowledge and wisdom (jnanam and vijnanam). Only when intelligence is pure and unblemished, yogis discern the Self and attain stable intelligence (samsiddhi) and freedom from karma (naishkarmya siddhi).

Like the memorial mind, intelligence is also not self-illuminated. Its light comes from the Lord within, the highest reality in the body, who shines by himself. Higher than all the tattvas of Prakriti, including intelligence, he does not depend upon anything since he is self-illuminated, self-existent, self-knowing, self-supporting, indestructible, and eternal. He is not a tattva, but some schools describe him as having a self-luminous body made of the purest tattva (shuddha tattva). Although he exists in the jivas as the indwelling Lord, he is not of this world and is not subject to the modes of Nature or their modifications. Although he resides in all, amidst the organs and modifications of the body, he is immutable and free from impurities, death, and decay. Since he is beyond the senses, the mind, and the intelligence and acts as their support, and since he is free and exists by himself, he is considered the lord of the body (Isvara) and the highest (param) of all. Thus, you can see that the relative importance of the organs in the body, or their hierarchy, just as the pantheon of gods in the universe, depends upon their subtlety and nearness to the Lord within and the light they receive from him. The densest parts do not receive any light. The subtle ones receive some, and the subtlest ones receive the most. Hence, the tattvas which are mentioned last are considered superior.

Sloka 43

evaṃ buddheḥ paraṃ buddhvā saṃstabhyātmānam ātmanā
jahi śatruṃ mahābāho kāmarūpaṃ durāsadam

evam = thus; buddheh = to discriminating intelligence; param = beyond, higher, superior; buddhva = by knowing; samstabhya = stabilizing; atmanam = the mind; atmana = by intelligence; jahi = slay; satrum = the enemy; maha-baho = O mighty-armed one; kama-rupam = the form of desire; durasadam = formidable.

Thus, knowing Him who is beyond or higher than intelligence, stabilizing the mind by intelligence, O mighty-armed one, slay the formidable enemy in the form of desire.

The first step to suppressing desires is withdrawing the senses from worldly objects into the mind, meaning shutting them down and not letting any perceptions enter. The next step is stabilizing the mind with discernment or intelligence, meaning not letting it wander or think of any worldly things.

The third step is knowing or discerning the Lord, who dwells within as the Self, and establishing the mind in his contemplation, meaning to practice constant remembrance and concentrated meditation (nidhdhyasa) on the Lord until the mind loses all body, worldly, and objective awareness. When the mind rests in Him completely without duality or division, all impurities, including desires and attachments, dissolve automatically. Thus, in this verse, Lord Krishna suggested that by knowing how desires and disturbances arise, the yogi should practice self-control and stabilize his mind and intelligence in the contemplation of the Self to overcome the formidable enemy called desire.

Desire is the arch enemy because it is a force of maya, and its purpose is to keep us deluded and bound to the mortal world until the end of creation. It is formidable because it cannot be neutralized by the usual means worldly people use to make peace with their enemies (sama, dana, bheda, and danda). If you try to placate, it grows stronger. If you try to resist, it grows even stronger. Since the senses act according to desires and reinforce them constantly, the control must begin with them. "Samstabhya atmanam atmana" means stabilizing the mind by intelligence. In other words, you must practice meditation on the Self intelligently with awareness, knowing how desires and modifications arise and subside and how you can detach yourself from them and remain established within. In some commentaries, 'samstabhya atmanam atmana' is translated as controlling the lower self by the higher self or the lower nature by the higher nature. The meaning is almost the same. However, since this verse continues from the previous one, the reference seems to be to the tattvas (mind and intelligence) rather than to the lower and higher selves.

Conclusion

iti srīmadbhāgavadgītāsupanisatsu brahmavidyāyām yogasāstre srikrisnārjunasamvāde karmayogo nāma tritiyo 'dhyayah

iti = thus; srīmadbhāgavadgītā = in the sacred Bhagavadgita; upanisatsu = in the Upanishad; brahmavidyāyām = the knowledge of the absolute Brahman; yogasāstre = the scripture of yoga; srikrisnārjunasamvāde = the dialogue between Sri Krishna and Arjuna; karmayogo nāma = by name karma yoga; tritiya = thirdd; adhyayah = chapter;

Thus ends the third chapter, named Karma Yoga (The Yoga of Action) in the Upanishad of the divine Bhagavadgita, the knowledge of the Absolute, a treatise on Yoga, which contains the dialogue between Arjuna and Lord Krishna.

04 – Jnāna Karma-Sannyāsa Yoga

The Yoga of Knowledge About Renunciation of Actions

Sloka 1

sri-bhagavan uvaca
imaṃ vivasvate yogaṃ proktavān aham avyayam
vivasvān manave prāha manur ikṣvākavebravīt

sri-bhagavan uvaca = the Supreme Lord said; imam = this; vivasvate = to Vaivasvata; yogam = yoga; proktavan = taught; aham = I; avyayam = imperishable; vivasvan = Vivasvat; manave = to the first-born Manu; praha = taught; manuh = Manu; iksvakave = to King Iksvaku; abravit = taught.

The Supreme Lord said, "I taught this imperishable yoga to Vaivasvat. Vaivasvat taught it to Manu. Manu taught this to King Iksvaku."

The yoga, which has been taught in the previous two chapters, which leads to the knowledge of the Self and resolution of karma through karma yoga and which requires the practice of obligatory duties and renunciation of desires, is imperishable (avyayam), just as the Vedas are. This chapter contains the knowledge of karma-sannyasa yoga by which one can engage in 'nivritta karma' or actions and duties that cease to produce consequences. It has become a trend nowadays to treat yoga as a physical exercise and a secular discipline. Yoga has always been an integral and essential part of Hinduism and, to some extent, Buddhist and Jain traditions. It is practiced in various forms by all sects of Hinduism and by several ascetic traditions that have become extinct. The word yoga has been found in many ancient texts, including the Upanishads and the Tantras. It has several meanings: a discipline, philosophical system, method or technique, path, state or condition, union, fastening, and goal.

The source of this yoga is not Patanjali, as some claim, but the Supreme Lord (Isvara) himself, as affirmed here by Lord Krishna. Patanjali compiled the knowledge of yoga that existed in his time into a scripture. Many techniques and concepts of yoga, which have been practiced for centuries in the esoteric traditions of Hinduism, are unknown to the common people and probably even to Patanjali. They have been kept in secrecy for several reasons. One of them is that the sacred knowledge of the scriptures and liberation must be transmitted through adept gurus only. This has been a valid reason for a long time when there were no other means by which knowledge could be acquired. In today's world, you have a choice to learn knowledge through a guru as well as self-study (svadhyaya) or by even watching a television program or documentary. You do not have to learn it only under the guidance of a guru, especially when we know that true gurus are hard to find and please. If you have a genuine aspiration to know, knowledge will come to you with the blessings of God. He will create opportunities for you to learn and progress.

The yoga that is central to the teachings of the Bhagavadgita is karma yoga, and the scripture is meant primarily for the householders who practice it as a part of their Dharma. The knowledge concerning the Self, intelligence, self-control, renunciation, and devotion is an adjunct to achieving perfection in its practice. That perfection is attained by renouncing desires. The title of this chapter is jnana karma-sannyasa yoga, meaning the knowledge of karma yoga that should be practiced with renunciation. The difference between karma yoga and karma-sannyasa yoga is that in the latter, you add renunciation to the practice of karma yoga to make it sin-proof and arrest the formation of karma arising from actions. In karma-sannyasa yoga, you do not renounce actions but desire-ridden actions or desires in your actions. This chapter deals with the knowledge of it. Hence, the title. Karma-sannyasa yoga is not a different yoga. It is an advanced form of karma yoga only practiced with knowledge, discernment, and renunciation to resolve the problem of karma by ensuring that obligatory duties are performed to serve God and the aims of creation rather than to fulfill one's desires.

In this verse, Lord Krishna stated that he first taught the knowledge to Vaivasvat, who is mentioned in the Vedas as the sun god and one of the twelve solar deities (Adityas). He, in turn, revealed it to Manu, who is regarded in Vedic texts as the progenitor of the human race. According to our tradition, in each cycle of creation, the earth is ruled by several Manus. They rule for the duration of a manvantara, during which they give birth to a new human race. Each manvantara lasts for 307.62 million years and is divided into 71 cycles of four yugas: Krita, Treta, Dvapara, and Kali yugas. Cumulatively, each cycle for a total duration of 4.32 million years. At the end of each yuga, the life upon earth will be recycled and recreated. At the end of 71 such cycles, the presiding Manu departs, and a new Manu takes over to bring forth a new race of human beings. It is said that 14 Manus will rule the earth in each cycle of creation, presiding over a particular human race during their reign for a total of 4.32 billion years, or 1000 cycles of four yugas. It constitutes a day (Kalpa) in the life of Brahma, the creator god.

The lifetime of the present universe is said to be 100 Brahma years, at the end of which the Lord of the universe will dissolve it, and a new universe will emerge to continue the creative cycle. Each Manu who appears during the day of Brahma bears a different name. The present Manu's name, by coincidence, is also Vaivasvat. He taught the knowledge of yoga to King Ikshvaku, the founder of the solar (Ikshvaku) dynasty of Kshatriya kings. According to Matsya Purana, King Ikshvaku was a direct descendent of the present Manu at the time of the great deluge. These timelines illustrate the antiquity of yoga and how the Supreme Being transmitted its knowledge to the people on Earth. The knowledge of yoga is imperishable because it eternally resides in the highest heaven and is revealed to humans at the beginning of creation by him or his manifestations.

Sloka 2

evaṃ paramparāprāptam imaṃ rājarṣayo viduḥ
sa kāleneha mahatā yogo naṣṭaḥ paraṃtapa

evam = thus; parampara = regular succession; praptam = having received, gained, obtained; imam = this; raja-rsayah = the saintly kings; viduh = knew; sah = this; kalena = in the course of time; iha = here; mahata = great; yogah = yoga; nastah = lost; parantapa = destroyer of foes.

Thus, having received the knowledge through regular succession, the saintly kings knew this (yoga), but O destroyer of the foes, over time, this great yoga was lost in this world.

A few conclusions emerge from this verse. The first one is that the knowledge of yoga was traditionally passed on through a succession of gurus or spiritual teachers, and when that chain was broken, the knowledge was lost. The second one is that, just as with everything else in this world, knowledge of yoga also suffered decay in the remote past and was lost to humanity. Impermanence is not confined to material things only. Death, decay, and destruction can happen to knowledge also for various reasons. History proves that it happened several times in the past and afflicted not only the sacred knowledge but also the institutions and spiritual guardians who were expected to uphold it. Another important point is that when sacred knowledge is lost, the Lord of Creation may reintroduce it to restore and preserve Dharma or revive the lost teachings. It is one of his chief functions, which he accomplishes mostly through his incarnations. Sometimes, he may also do it through associate gods, demigods, enlightened masters, spiritual messengers, partial incarnations, etc.

Another important conclusion from this verse is that the original teachers of karma yoga were philosopher kings (raja-rishis). The same was true about the knowledge of the Upanishads. The founders of Jainism and Buddhism were also Kshatriyas only. References to the early Kshatriya teachers can be found in the Upanishads themselves, which suggest that rulers of that period possessed the secret knowledge of the Self and liberation, often accepted Brahmanas as students, and taught them. In ancient India, Kshatriya kings played an important role in preserving the sacred knowledge of Brahman, apart from performing their obligatory duties as rulers, while Brahmanas took care of ritual knowledge and social order. Kings like Janaka acted as the guardians and upholders of Dharma, encouraging debates and discussions, financing religious ceremonies, supporting priestly families by donating wealth and gifts, and taking a personal interest in disseminating religious and spiritual knowledge. They also protected it from rival traditions by guarding its institutions. Unfortunately, with the decline of Kshatriya kings in the later Vedic period, the secret knowledge of yoga was also lost.

Sloka 3

sa evāyaṃ mayā tedya yogaḥ proktaḥ purātanaḥ
bhaktosi me sakhā ceti rahasyaṃ hy etad uttamam

sah = that; eva =indeed; ayam = this; maya = by Me; te = to you; adya = today; yogah = yoga; proktah = taught; puratanah = greatly ancient; bhaktah = devotee; asi = you are; me = My; sakha = friend; ca = and; iti = because; rahasyam = secret; hi = for; etat = this; uttamam = great, utmost.

Indeed, that yoga of great antiquity has been taught to you by Me today because you are My devotee and friend. It is the utmost secret.

Historically, in India's religious and spiritual traditions, knowledge was taught to those who were found to be qualified and worthy enough by their teachers. The idea was not to confuse those who were deluded and not ready. The gurus relied on two important criteria: family background and suitability. They ascertained the first one by inquiring about their lineages (gotras) and family names, and the second by observing them and testing them while they lived under their supervision. Of the two, eligibility or suitability mattered the most. Satyakama Jabala was one such example. His teacher initiated him into the secret knowledge of the Upanishads, even though he came from a humble background and was unaware of his family's lineage. In his case, his teacher relied upon his conduct and devotion to knowledge. Here, Lord Krishna said that he was teaching the knowledge of karma-sannyasa yoga to Arjuna because of his devotion and friendship. Arjuna was a close friend of Lord Krishna, besides being a relation. He spent considerable time with him, even during his exile, and earned his trust, loyalty, and friendship. Further, as a devotee, he showed humility, readiness, and willingness to learn from him with devotion and follow his advice.

By mentioning these traits, Lord Krishna also conveyed to his devotees that anyone who has love and devotion to him and is free from enmity or envy towards him is well-qualified to receive the knowledge. It is also an instruction for the teachers of the Bhagavadgita that they should consider similar criteria while selecting and initiating students. From this, one can discern that caste and family background are not as important as devotees' conduct, purity, and readiness. In the eyes of God, all are equal and eligible for liberation if they are worthy enough to receive his teachings. In this verse, Lord Krishna also stated that the yoga he would be teaching was of great antiquity. It meant that the utmost secret knowledge of karma-sannyasa yoga, which he imparted to Arjuna, was not new but had a long history and a long lineage of teachers.

Sloka 4

arjuna uvāca
aparaṃ bhavato janma paraṃ janma vivasvataḥ
katham etad vijānīyāṃ tvam ādau proktavān iti

arjunah uvaca = Arjuna said; aparam = later; bhavatah = Your; janma = birth; param = earlier; janma = birth; vivasvatah = of Vaivsvat; katham = how; etat = this; vijaniyam = may I to understand; tvam = You; adau = in the beginning; proktavan = taught; iti = thus.

Arjuna said, " Your birth was later. Vaivasvata's birth was earlier. How may I understand this, that You taught (him) in the beginning?"

Vaivasvat appeared at the beginning of creation, long before Lord Krishna incarnated and the Mahabharata war occurred. Hence, Arjuna had genuine doubt and could not reconcile the Lord's statement that he taught the same yoga to Vaivasvat in remote antiquity. It may also be that this question was introduced in the scripture to clear any doubts devotees may have about Lord Krishna's divinity and status as the world teacher. Sri Shankaracharya commented that Arjuna purposefully asked it, knowing well the divine birth of Lord Krishna, to demolish the opinion of the ignorant ones that he was an ordinary person. By that, he wanted the world to know that Lord Krishna was but the omniscient and omnipotent Supreme Lord.

However, this explanation is not fully convincing. If he had been fully conversant with the omniscience and omnipotence of Lord Krishna, a long discourse would not have been needed to convince him to fight, or the need to show him his universal form would not have arisen. Probably, Arjuna knew Lord Krishna's divine origin and mystic powers vaguely but was unaware of his identity as the supreme godhead or the extent of his powers and manifestations. It happens to us also. For example, we draw our conclusions when we meet spiritually enlightened yogis or teachers. We may conclude that they are different or special, but we do not know how enlightened they are or what level of consciousness they possess. We go by appearances and make assumptions about the people we meet in our lives. Often, we do not recognize the significance of people who appear in our lives at crucial times to teach us important lessons or provide guidance. When great souls live amongst us, people do not readily recognize them or discern their spirituality. Even when they acknowledge them, doubts persist in their minds, and they walk past them, wasting an opportunity to learn from them. They may even look down upon them or talk disparagingly about them. History shows that it happened several times to seers and saints, even to the Buddha and Mahavira, and those human proclivities happen even now. It is common knowledge that eminently spiritual people and enlightened masters are ignored by even those who live in their vicinity or belong to their families. In contrast, others travel thousands of miles worldwide to visit them, seeking their guidance and blessings.

Sloka 5

śrībhagavānuvāca
bahūni me vyatītāni janmāni tava cārjuna
tāny ahaṃ veda sarvāṇi na tvaṃ vettha paraṃtapa

sri-bhagavan uvaca = the glorious Bhagavan said; bahuni = many; me = my; vyatitani = have gone by; janmani = births; tava = of yours; ca = and; arjuna = O Arjuna; tani = those; aham = I; veda = know; sarvani = all; na = not; tvam = you; vettha = know; parantapa = O destroyer of the foes.

The Supreme Lord said, "Many births of mine and those of yours have gone by, O Arjuna. I know them all, but you do not know, O destroyer of the foes."

Arjuna did not know his previous births or Lord Krishna's. Hence, he asked Lord Krishna how he taught Vaivasvat, who existed long before them. From a human perspective, one can understand it. Very few people remember their past lives. Even their memories will be vague, and it will be difficult to determine whether they are true or imaginary. Although people may learn from scriptures about rebirth and transmigration of souls, they will not readily accept them due to a lack of proof. Even saintly people do not seem to possess complete knowledge of their past births, while they may speak about them. People may receive vague impressions of their past births in meditation, dreams, and regressive hypnosis. However, it is difficult to be convinced by such experiences since we do not know whether they are induced by imagination or accurate recollection.

In a way, it is good that we do not remember our past lives. The emotional burden of remembering them would be enormous and difficult to manage. Nature has done an excellent job by limiting our memory to our current births and not letting us lose our sanity by remembering and enduring the painful memories of our past lives. It would have also been difficult to manage the repressed or subconscious memories of those births, apart from managing the complex relationships we might have formed over several lives. However, it is different in the case of Lord Krishna, who is a complete and direct manifestation of Brahman in a mortal body. As the knower of the past, present, and future and omniscient pervader and the knower of all (Sarvajna), it would not have been difficult for him to recollect his past incarnations and past cycles of creation or tap into any knowledge of the past and present he wanted to recollect. Being the self-existing, self-knowing, and all-knowing Supreme Lord, he would have known his and others' past births. Hence, he said that many of their births had gone by, and that he knew them, although Arjuna did not know.

The concept of rebirth in Hinduism is as old as the Vedas. It is mentioned even in the Upanishads. They declare that upon death, human beings may go to the ancestral heaven, which is controlled by gods, or to the immortal heaven of Brahman, which is above all the worlds, even that of gods. Those who go to the ancestral heaven return to the earth upon exhausting some of their karma and take rebirth, while those who enter the immortal world of Brahman never return. The ultimate goal of human life is to attain immortality through liberation, which is not possible for all. Most humans and other jivas remain bound to samsara and keep going through repeated births and deaths according to their deeds. Only after innumerable births and deaths do they make a conscious effort to attain permanent liberation. While we can understand why Arjuna was born several times in the past, we do not understand why Lord Krishna, who is Narayana himself and is unborn and immortal, took several births. The answer is provided in the next verse.

Sloka 6

ajopi sann avyayātmā bhūtānām īśvaropi san
prakṛtiṃ svām adhiṣṭhāya saṃbhavāmy ātmamāyayā

ajah = unborn; api = although; san = I am; avyaya = imperishable; atma = self; bhutanam = living being; isvarah = the Lord; api = although; san = I am; prakrtim = Prakriti, Nature; svam = my own; adhisthaya = presiding over; sambhavami = I take birth; atma-mayaya = by my own power of maya.

Although I am unborn and imperishable, although I am the Lord of all beings, presiding over my own Nature, I manifest by my own power of Maya.

Although I am unborn, free from births and deaths, indestructible, and although I rule over the worlds as the Supreme Lord, presiding over my own Nature, which is made up of the gunas and the tattvas, which depends upon me since I am its sole support and by which the world is deluded and bound to samsara, I manifest upon the earth by my own mystic powers to carry out my duties as the protector and upholder of Dharma. This is the essence. In the previous verse, Lord Krishna said that he and Arjuna had many births in the past. Here, he distinguished himself by saying that he takes birth by his will, controlling and directing his nature, unlike Arjuna or others who are bound to Prakriti and whose births are determined by their fates and karmas.

This and the following verses explain how and why the Supreme Being, the highest Isvara, Brahman, manifests on the earth in a physical form as a living being. The Lord of all is unborn, yet sometimes he takes birth in a mortal body. Here is another paradox about Brahman that is confusing to an ignorant and deluded person but makes sense from the all-encompassing perspective of a discerning mind. The idea that the Lord of the universe takes birth in a physical form in the mortal world is peculiar to Hinduism. In messianic religions, it is a messiah or a prophet who brings God's messages or instructions from the eternal heaven to the mortal world. The underlying assumption in such religions is that God does not have to take birth in a mortal body to reform this world. He can do it in many other ways. In our tradition, we also believe that God works his miracles and communicates with us in numerous ways through scriptures, messengers, dreams, and numerous manifestations. However, sometimes, he also incarnates to accomplish specific tasks of restoring and renewing human faith and righteousness, since this is an impermanent world, and things decay over time.

When jivas are reborn, they remain under the control of Nature. In the case of divine incarnations, it is different. They incarnate with complete control over Prakriti, presiding over her and retaining their complete and absolute control. As a result, all his potencies either manifest or remain latent in them. Therefore, even if they incarnate as humans or in some other form, they still retain their potencies and omniscience. The deluding force of Maya also remains under their control. Since the deluding force of Maya remains under their control from the beginning, they possess the power to perform miracles and superhuman acts or acts of magic to enthrall people. Incarnations are not bound to their bodies. They remain detached and free from the impurities of the world. Hence, they are not tainted by their actions. However, once born, they do not interfere with the natural processes of their minds and bodies. They willingly go through aging, sickness, and death like other jivas, letting Nature perform her usual tasks.

An incarnation is not a mere appearance of God or an illusory phenomenon. He is a true manifestation with a name, form, and definite purpose. He may continue to manifest before his close devotees in the same form even after he ends his incarnation and retires from the earth. It is why the incarnations of the Supreme Lord are worshipped in Hinduism with the same respect and reverence as himself. The purpose of each incarnation is to restore balance in the mortal world and protect Dharma. It is his obligatory duty to maintain the order and regularity (rta) of the world because gods and beings of other worlds depend upon it. He assumes these responsibilities for the sake of creation, although there is nothing he needs to accomplish or gain. He explains it in the next verse.

Sloka 7

yadā yadā hi dharmasya glānir bhavati bhārata
abhyutthānam adharmasya tadātmānaṃ sṛjāmy aham

yada yada = whenever; hi = surely; dharmasya = duty and virtue; glanih = decline; bhavati = there is; bharata = Bharata; abhyutthanam = increase, ascendence; adharmasya = vice and evil; tada = then; atmanam = by myself; srjami = manifest; aham = I.

O Bharata, whenever there is a decline of virtue and ascendance of evil, then surely, I manifest by Myself.

The concept of avatars or incarnations is unique to Hinduism. Avatar means descent, manifestation, advent, or restoration. Generally speaking, any great soul or distinguished person with divine qualities is considered an Avatar or a manifestation of God. However, in Vaishnavism, Avatar refers to the full or partial manifestation of Lord Vishnu in the mortal world in physical forms. He may incarnate through a womb or directly. The Puranas list ten full Avatars of Lord Vishnu. Of them, the last one, Kalki Avatar, is portended to happen at the end of the current epoch. The main difference between an incarnation and a manifestation is that in the incarnation, he assumes a body, whereas in the manifestation, he appears as a divinity with a name and ethereal form. Vaishnavism also reveres the images and idols of Lord Vishnu or his manifestations, installed according to traditional rites, as his incarnations, known as Arcas. Life is breathed into them, and their power is continuously augmented and increased through rituals and devotional worship by devotees. An incarnation should not be mistaken for a jiva. Jivas are born under the control of Prakriti. An incarnation appears by his own power with his potencies and is not bound to Nature. Even if he assumes a body that may look like an ordinary body to the world, and even if he is born through a womb, he possesses divine powers (Yoga Maya) and uses them to accomplish his aims on earth.

Thus, each Avatar is entirely divine, pure, blissful, and fully conscious. This is confirmed by Lord Krishna in the last part of this verse in the following words, "tadātmānaṃ sṛjāmy aham," which means, "I create or manifest My form by Myself." However, this does not always happen with his manifestations. Sometimes, he may partially incarnate and assume a semi-divine body or manifest an aspect of himself as an associate deity or enlightened being for specific purposes, in which he may suppress some or all of his original potencies. The Avatar is usually an epochal event, which happens once or twice in each epoch (yuga), while numerous partial incarnations and associate divinities may manifest in each epoch. It is also said that when an incarnation appears upon earth to restore Dharma and revive the earth, numerous other deities and great souls also take birth to assist him in his duties. In each Avatar, he removes the most potent evils from the earth and reintroduces the lost teachings of eternal wisdom to revive Dharma.

Therefore, the incarnation of God or Isvara should be regarded as an exceptional event and a part of his duties to preserve life on earth. His main duties are creation, preservation, and destruction. Shaivism ascribes two other functions: concealment and revelation. As the Creator, he manifests the worlds by revealing, concealing, expressing, and suppressing his immense powers. As the preserver, he upholds them through his divine law (dharma) and inviolable will. As the destroyer, he destroys our ignorance and delusion to facilitate our spiritual rebirth and liberation. At the end of each cycle of creation, he withdraws everything into himself and rests. In between, whenever there is a decline of Dharma, he incarnates to restore order and righteousness. He protects the weak, promotes virtue, enforces the divine laws, revives sacred teachings, and destroys evil. All religions identify God as the protector and preserver of the whole existence. In Hinduism, we take this concept a step further, holding that in exceptional circumstances, when time is running out, he will incarnate, if necessary, and take control. However, incarnations do not happen spontaneously. They are already built into the cycle of creation and happen when the time comes. Since he is omniscient and knows the past, present, and future, he knows well in advance when he should incarnate and what specific duties he must perform.

The primary purpose of an incarnation is to restore Dharma. At the most basic level, Dharma means a set of obligatory duties expected of each living being who lives on earth. At the highest level, it means the divine laws, which define the standards for our moral and religious duties and virtuous conduct. From this perspective, Dharma encompasses morality, virtue, and religiosity; universal laws that ensure order, discipline, and continuity; moral and religious duties that connect humans to gods and pave the way for their mutual protection and peaceful coexistence; divine knowledge, wisdom, righteousness, and the way of life which lead humans on the path to liberation. In short, it means living like God himself on earth and performing his duties as our obligatory duties to fulfill the aims of creation. It also means natural function, quality, or propensity. For example, the dharma of fire is to glow and burn, and water is to flow and drench. The basic dharma of a human being is to be humane, rational, and dutiful, and serve gods, humans, and others through sacrificial actions. Religion, basic good, godliness, essential nature, and moral obligation are its other popular meanings. God is the upholder of Dharma. It is his primary duty as an upholder of the world. His incarnation serves as a great example for humans to follow in his footsteps and live like him, exemplifying the best of human nature, character, and conduct.

Special note: The concept of Avatar is absent in Saivism.

Sloka 8

paritrāṇāya sādhūnāṃ vināśāya ca duṣkṛtām
dharmasaṃsthāpanārthāya saṃbhavāmi yuge yuge

paritranaya = for the protection; sadhunam = of the pious, good, virtuous; vinasaya = for the destruction of; ca = and; duskrtam = the wicked; dharma = moral laws and religious duties; samsthapana-arthaya = for the sake of establishing; sambhavami = manifest myself, come into being; yuge yuge = from time to time.

For the protection of the pious people and the destruction of the wicked, and for the sake of establishing the Dharma, I manifest myself (upon earth) from epoch to epoch.

An incarnation of God (avatar) is his most direct and personal involvement in the happenings on earth, which gives his devotees an opportunity to see him physically, live in his company, and earn his blessings or grace. His coming to the earth is an ominous sign that epochal events are about to happen. It does not happen frequently, but once or twice in a millennium or two, when things go out of control and divine intervention is required. It is said that if a few saintly people (sadhus and mahatmas) fervently pray to him with exclusive devotion to restore order and normalcy or save the planet, he listens to them and incarnates. Some people consider Lord Krishna an incarnation of Lord Vishnu. It is also the most popular belief. However, there is a section of devotees who strongly believe that he is Isvara, or the Supreme Lord of the universe, and appeared on earth as his own incarnation. Some go a step further and declare that Lord Vishnu, as the preserver of the worlds, is his aspect or manifestation, and as the Supreme Being, he is an Avatari, the source of all incarnations. These outlier beliefs are prevalent in some Vaishnava sects that revere Lord Krishna as the self-existent Lord Supreme (svayam bhagavan). They also believe that he incarnated several times to help humankind, not just ten times.

Irrespective of who incarnates, one cannot deny the possibility that divine incarnations must be numerous. Even if we assume he incarnates once or twice in every yuga and about ten or twelve in every cycle of four yugas (chaturyuga), one can imagine how many incarnations must happen in a day of Brahma, spanning 14 manvantaras, 1000 chaturyugas or 4000 yugas. The main incarnations (Yugavataras) in the current time cycle are said to be 10 or 12, not counting many that are not included in the main list. For example, Chaitanya Charitamrta (20.246), the biography of Chaitanya Mahaprabhu, mentions six types of Krishna's incarnations: Purnavataras or Purushavatars (the incarnations of Vishnu as an aspect of Krishna), Gunavataras (incarnations personifying the triple modes of Nature), Lilavataras (incarnations that display Krishna's grandeur and divine play), Manvantaravataras (the incarnation of Manus in each manvantara), Yugavatäras (incarnations to mark the beginning or end of each epoch), and Saktyaveçavataras (incarnations endowed with the power of Shaktis).

Sloka 9

janma karma ca me divyam evaṃ yo vetti tattvataḥ
tyaktvā dehaṃ punarjanma naiti mām eti sorjuna

janma = birth; karma = actions; ca = and; me = My; divyam = divine; evam = thus; yah = who; vetti = knows; tattvatah = essentially truly, correctly; tyaktva = leaving; deham = the body; punarjanma = rebirth; na = never; eti = come; mam = to Me; eti = come; sah = he; arjuna = O Arjuna.

He who, thus, knows My divine birth and My actions truly and essentially would never have rebirth upon leaving his body. He comes to Me, O Arjuna.

In this verse, Lord Krishna assures us that he, who truly knows his divine births and actions, would be liberated from the cycle of births and deaths and, upon death, reaches him only. You will know others only when you spend time with them or try to know them. You will not do that unless you have some interest in doing it. In the case of a divine person such as Lord Krishna, you will not know him unless you have faith and devotion and engage your mind in that pursuit. Those who study the Bhagavatam, Bhagavadgita, Mahabharata, or Puranas and spend time in His contemplation stand to possess that knowledge. They should know Him not only through study and learning but also, in essence (tattvatah), which is possible only through oneness or self-absorption. In other words, those who know His life and works and know Him as the Supreme Lord of the universe and the Self of all (sarvabhutatma) and experience His state of pure and absolute consciousness through self-realization stand a better chance of achieving liberation.

Further, those who correctly know His divine births (incarnations) and duties follow His example and perform their duties indifferently and without desires. Thereby, they improve their chances of achieving liberation. His divine births are numerous. Even if you know one correctly, it is sufficient. If you contemplate Him, His manifestations, and His achievements, it will cleanse you and qualify you for liberation. In other words, knowing the births of the Supreme Lord and his deeds upon earth is a transformative experience. It is an austerity by itself and eventually leads to liberation. When that devotee departs from here, he will attain Him and become liberated from births and deaths. Some scholars say that "divya" refers to the transcendental or immaterial nature of His births in which Prakriti plays no role. While it may be true, for the devotees who are lost in the thoughts of the Lord, such nuanced distinctions do not matter. The very memory of His divine personality, births, and deeds can produce ecstatic and purifying devotion in them and cleanse them of their past sins.

Lord Krishna qualified his statement with tattvatah. It means knowing Him through His tattva or essence. Tattvas and gunas belong to the domain of

Prakriti. They do not exist in the Self. However, the Self is also often described as a pure tattva, in contrast to the Prakriti tattvas, which are impure. It cannot be known objectively, unlike Nature's tattvas, but only through self-knowing, absorption, or oneness in which the faculties of the mind and intelligence do not participate. The supreme reality of Brahman is very different from the objective reality we experience through our minds. The former is free from the duality of the subject and object or the knower and the known. In the latter, only the subject exists, and the duality between the subject and object disappears. Hence, it is not the same as knowing the objective reality through the mind and senses.

Since Brahman is indeterminate and nothing can be said about Him definitively, the Upanishads describe Him as Tat, meaning That. Tat is the transcendental reality of Brahman that is beyond our minds and senses. What is within our reach is tvam, meaning this. Tat is the subject, and tvam is the object. Tat is the knower, and tvam is the known. Tattvajnanam is the combined knowledge of Tat and tvam or Brahmatattva or Krishnatattva, and Prakriti tattvas. Krishnatattva is pure, eternal, indestructible, and immutable, but Prakriti tattvas are impure, destructible, and mutable. Together, they represent the dualities of Brahman and his creation, the Self and the Body, Purusha and Prakriti, and so on. In the transcendental state of oneness, tvam disappears, and Tat only remains. How do we arrive at the supreme knowledge of the Self or the Lord? This is explained in the next verse.

Sloka 10

vītarāgabhayakrodhā manmayā mām upāśritāḥ
bahavo jñānatapasā pūtā madbhāvam āgatāḥ

vita = free from; raga = passion; bhaya = fear; krodhah = anger; mat-maya = fully absorbed in Me; mam = to Me; upasritah = taking refuge; bahavah = many; jnana = self-knowledge; tapasa = austerity, penance; putah = purified; mat-bhavam = My state; agatah = attained.

Free from passion, fear, anger, fully absorbed in me, taking refuge in me, many, purified by the austerity of self-knowledge, attained My State.

Here, Lord Krishna explained how to attain his state. He mentioned freedom from passion, fear, and anger, establishing and absorbing the mind in him, taking refuge in him, and purifying the mind and body with the austerity of knowledge and wisdom. Vitaraga means freedom from passions or attraction and aversion (ragadvesha). Matmaya means becoming absorbed in My thoughts or the awareness that I am the all-pervading Supreme Self. 'Mam upasrita' means taking refuge in Me, thinking of Me only, and depending upon Me as the sole support. It also means not worshipping or making sacrifices for any other gods. Jnana tapas means practicing austerities to purify the mind and intelligence while pursuing self-knowledge. It may also mean focusing solely on acquiring self-knowledge rather than any other knowledge. 'Mat bhava' means 'My Supreme State,' which is indestructible, unchanging, indistinguishable, and free from all impurities, dualities, divisions, and limitations. Thus, jnanis and karma yogis can attain liberation through self-knowledge by contemplating upon the indwelling Self as the Lord and purifying their minds and intelligence.

Liberation can be achieved by various means. In the previous verse, Lord Krishna suggested that a devotee could become forever free from rebirth by knowing his births (incarnations) and actions. In this verse, he suggested that liberation could be attained through self-purification by the following means.

1. Becoming free from passions such as fear and anger through detachment, self-control, and renunciation
2. Surrendering to God with devotion, absorbing the mind in his thoughts, taking refuge in him, and performing sacrifices for him only
3. Purifying the mind and body with jnana tapas, or the austerity of knowledge and wisdom

As we will learn later, knowledge, devotion, and the practice of karma yoga are helpful if they are practiced along with self-control to overcome desires and attachments. Passions such as fear and anger arise due to the impurities of egoism, desires, attachments, and delusions. The gunas also induce them. When they are removed through self-effort and by taking refuge in God, the mind becomes tranquil and free from modifications. In that tranquil state, one becomes filled with devotion instead of passion, faith instead of fear, compassion instead of anger, and sameness instead of attraction and aversion.

The scriptures suggest various austerities for purifying the mind and body and attaining the highest purity. In this verse, Lord Krishna suggested the austerity of knowledge (jnana tapas). It means you must acquire knowledge, and with that knowledge, you must practice penances and self-control, withdrawing your internal organ from worldly objects and concentrating upon the Self to burn the impurities of your mind and body and cultivate purity, discernment, and mental brilliance. When you are firmly established in it with unwavering devotion, you enter the supreme state of oneness. Tapas is a transformative practice, more ancient than Yoga, in which physical energies are transformed into subtle heat (tapah) to dissolve bodily impurities. In the body, it shines as vigor (tejas), and in the mind, as mental brilliance (medhas). The rewards of karma yoga vary according to sincerity, devotion, loyalty, and commitment. There are different rewards for those who worship many gods to fulfill their desires and those who worship the Supreme Being exclusively and selflessly with knowledge, purity, and discernment. This is explained next.

Sloka 11

ye yathā māṃ prapadyante tāṃs tathaiva bhajāmy aham
mama vartmānuvartante manuṣyāḥ pārtha sarvaśaḥ

ye = who; yatha = in whatever; mam = to Me; prapadyante = they approach; tan = them; tatha = in the same manner; eva = even; bhajami = reward; aham = I; mama = My; vartma = path; anuvartante = do follow; manusyah = human beings; partha = Partha; sarvasah = in every way, in all respects.

In whatever (manner) they approach Me, in the same manner, I reward them, O Partha. Human beings follow My path in every way.

The Supreme Lord has no favorites but loves his devotees as much as they do and rewards them suitably according to their faith and devotion and how they approach him. Your devotion determines his response. He grants the wishes of karma yogis who worship him to fulfill their desires. He grants knowledge and wisdom to jnana yogis to cultivate discernment and find him within themselves through contemplative means. To the renunciants, he gives strength and fortitude to withstand the rigors of renunciation and find peace and tranquility within themselves. However, if they worship him exclusively without desires and attachments, establishing their minds in him, he liberates them from samsara and keeps them closer to him. The Supreme Being is like a mirror. He reflects your thoughts, desires, and attitudes by granting you whatever you desire or wish. He will not decide what to give you or influence what you should want or choose for yourself. That responsibility rests with you. It is up to you how you approach him, whether with love and devotion or desire. Whatever desire, want, wish, or need you express to him with conviction, he will manifest that for you if your aspiration is sincere, your faith is strong, and your devotion is free from conflicts and doubts. Even sinners are redeemed if they sincerely aspire, seek forgiveness, and change their ways.

Hidden in this verse is the subtle message that the Lord does not favor or prefer certain groups, nations, and religions. He is not saying here that if you follow this religion, that prophet, scripture, or guru, you will be liberated or helped. He is not saying that you must follow him and obey him or fear him for him to fulfill your wishes. He clearly said that he would not impose any conditions upon his devotees. He would reciprocate the manner in which they worship him or approach him. They have to knock on his door with love and devotion, expressing their wish, and they will be rewarded. He will not decide the reward. You must seek that by stating clearly what you want or need without doubt or confusion, or you must let it go if liberation is your aim.

Those who blame God for not getting what they want should remember these words. If their prayers are unanswered, they must look within themselves to see what is coming in the way and what they need to correct. A lot depends on the devotees in their relationship with the Lord. If they are confused, confusion will prevail. If they are uncertain, uncertainty will manifest; if they fear him, their fear of him will grow and intensify; if they approach him as a friend, he will reciprocate as their friend; if they treat him as their guru and worship him with devotion, he will become their teacher and grant them knowledge and discernment. He may not do it personally, directly, or instantly, but he makes sure that the wishes are granted. He reciprocates the actions and wishes of even those who detest him, envy him, or disbelieve in him by manifesting their negativity. He strengthens the faith of atheists in his nonexistence by becoming completely silent. Our Puranas illustrate that he grants boons to evil people if they worship him with devotion. However, he does not stop them from destroying themselves with those boons if they wish to misuse them.

The Lord is the path as well as the destination. Devotees who practice jnana, karma, and sannyasa yogas with exclusive devotion attain ecstatic union with him. Wise men on the path of knowledge attain knowledge of the Self and enter pure consciousness to become dissolved in oneness. Householders on the path of karma yoga experience fulfillment in their lives and lay the foundation for a better life in the next birth or attain liberation from the cycle of births and deaths. All these people who spend their lives in his service and variously worship him eventually end up in the highest heaven as his closest associates and devotees. God is the manifesting power who would not deny any request and is always willing to help his worshippers in whatever way they approach him. He is the giver and the benefactor who rewards his devotees, whether good or bad, according to their desires, thoughts, fears, and aspirations. Since there are no limits to what you may ask and what he may give, you must be careful about your prayers and wishes because what you seek may affect your karma. If your intentions are clouded, you may also pay the price.

Sloka 12

kāṃkṣantaḥ karmaṇāṃ siddhiṃ yajanta iha devatāḥ
kṣipraṃ hi mānuṣe loke siddhir bhavati karmajā

kanksantah = desiring; karmanam = of actions; siddhim = success; yajante = perform sacrifices; iha = here, in this world; devatah = the divinities; ksipram = quickly; hi = indeed; manuse loke = in the world of human beings; siddhih bhavati = success achieved; karma-ja = born of sacrificial actions.

Desiring success in actions, they perform sacrifices for the divinities in this world. Indeed, success is quickly achieved in the world of human beings through sacrificial actions.

In the following few verses, Lord Krishna explains how he rewards his devotees according to their faith and devotion, or how they worship him. In this verse, he said that those who perform sacrifices for the gods, desiring success, will achieve success through them. Here, the expression 'desiring success' (kanksha) is important. It limits their rewards. They will fulfill their wishes and achieve success in attaining Dharma, Artha, and Kama, but not Moksha. The Lord ordained sacrifices and duties for householders. Therefore, he rewards them for their devotion to duty by helping them attain their desired ends through the gods they serve and obtain a good life in their next birth.

Sacrificial rituals are made to produce quick results. If this is not the case, people would not be attracted to them or perform them. If people do not perform them, gods, ancestors, and others who depend upon them for food will not receive nourishment and will grow weak. Ancestors will return to the earth quickly as their causal bodies perish. Seers and sages fail to spread the knowledge of Dharma or support their students. Evil gains strength. Gods grow weak due to a lack of nourishment and fail to control natural calamities or protect the world from evil. Thus, sacrifices are necessary to keep the world going. Through them, gods and humans achieve their respective ends, uphold Dharma, and ensure the welfare of all. Therefore,

God rewards suitably those who engage in sacrificial duties and nourish others. He helps them since they are devoted to their duties and uphold the eternal Dharma he established on earth. However, he does not grant them liberation since they are more interested in other aims, instead of Moksha.

The Vedas recognize three types of sacrificial rituals: nitya, naimitta, and kamya. Nitya karma are daily sacrifices. They are obligatory and must be performed by householders. Hence, they are also known as baddha karmas or bound duties. Naimitta karmas are also obligatory duties that must be performed on special occasions to mark events such as birth, initiation, marriage, festivals, the onset of seasons, etc. Kamya karmas are optional and meant to fulfill desires. Since desires are involved, they produce sinful karma. Ideally, karma yogis should perform obligatory duties and avoid kamya karmas. The Vedas prohibit certain actions and sacrifices known as Nishiddha karmas. They are meant to harm, hurt, or control others and are performed with evil intentions. Hence, they are prohibited. From a spiritual perspective, knowledge of sacrifices and rituals is considered ignorance (avidya) or inferior knowledge. They help householders achieve Dharma, Artha, and Kama, but not Moksha, since those who perform them with desires remain bound to samsara. Ideally, householders should perform all sacrifices, duties, and actions without desiring their fruit. Then, they will qualify for liberation.

Sloka 13

cāturvarṇyaṃ mayā sṛṣṭaṃ guṇakarmavibhāgaśaḥ
tasya kartāram api māṃ viddhy akartāram avyayam

catuh-varnyam = the four castes; maya = by Me; srstam = created; guna = quality; karma = action; vibhagasah = division of; tasya = of that; kartaram = the creator; api = although; mam = Me; viddhi = know; akartaram = non-doer; avyayam = inexhaustible.

The four castes are created by me based on the division of actions arising from the gunas. Although I am the creator of that (division of castes), know Me as the non-doer and imperishable.

Castes are exclusive to Hinduism. In the ancient Vedic order, duties were assigned to families according to them. Householders who desired to reap the rewards of sacrifices were obligated to perform them according to their castes and continue their family traditions and occupations. From the reference to the world of men (mānuṣe loke) in the previous verse, we have to presume that the caste system is meant for humans only. However, Brihadaranyaka Upanishad (1.4.11) projects castes into gods also and suggests which gods are ideal for worship for different castes.

In this verse, Lord Krishna stated that he established the fourfold caste (varna) system based on the fourfold division of actions as determined by the gunas or the essential nature. It confirms that the caste system was originally intended to divide obligatory duties among humans according to their gunas to ensure that they performed their duties according to their essential nature and fulfilled the aims of the eternal Dharma. It also confirms that the birth of a person was not intended to be the criterion to determine caste. Gunas may influence actions and, thereby, the birth of a person. However, there is no guarantee that sattvic parents will give birth to sattvic children or that their children will naturally be inclined to take up their duties or professions. Birth does not determine a person's essential nature. It may also change after a person is born. People will be happier and peaceful when they have an opportunity to express themselves and follow their aspirations and inclinations. In Vedic times, people believed that the souls that returned from the ancestral heaven took birth in the same families from which they departed. A father who died and returned from that world took birth in the same family and continued the same family tradition, inheriting the same duties from his parents. These beliefs justified the birth-based caste system but are difficult to accept in the present-day world.

Actions and gunas are interrelated, and the predominance of gunas depends upon karma or past births. Therefore, it makes sense that the fourfold social divisions were originally established to provide a blueprint of social order for humans to choose their duties and professions according to their essential nature. Sattvic people are fit for religious and spiritual duties, teaching, counseling, or duties that require detachment, dispassion, virtue, knowledge, and wisdom. Rajasic people are well-qualified for duties that require courage, strength, passion, heroic qualities, leadership, initiative, perseverance, and so on. People in whom rajas and tamas predominate are fit for agriculture, business, trade, and commerce, and the fourth group, in whom tamas and rajas predominate, are fit for manual duties and serving others. This fourfold division of humanity is found in all communities worldwide. It is a natural order that does not require enforcement through laws, scriptures, or institutions. Nature will take care of it and enforce it internally since it is difficult for people to act against their essential nature. If they do, at some point, they will find it too difficult to continue and make peace with themselves by following their natural inclinations.

In the second part of the verse, Lord Krishna said that although he created the system, he is not a part of it and should be known as the non-doer and imperishable. As the Supreme Lord of all, he is not subject to the natural laws that govern the world and the jivas. He is beyond and without the gunas (gunatita, nirguna). Although all actions and duties arise from him only, and he performs several duties, he does not participate in them through desires or egoistic involvement. Caste distinctions and divisions arise in the Field of Prakriti. The Self that dwells within the bodies is the same in all. It is not bound to the values and distinctions we create in the world.

Sloka 14

na māṃ karmāṇi limpanti na me karmaphale spṛhā
iti māṃ yobhijānāti karmabhir na sa badhyate

na = not; mam = Me; karmani = actions; limpanti = taint; na = not; me = my; karma-phale = fruit of actions; sprha = desire; iti = thus; mam = Me; yah = who; abhijanati = know; karmabhih = by action; na = not; sah = he; badhyate = bound.

Actions do not taint Me, nor do I have the desire for the fruit of actions. He who knows Me thus is not bound by actions.

In the previous verse, Lord Krishna said that although he performed actions such as creating the fourfold social order, he was the inexhaustible non-doer. Here, he explained the reason. Actions do not taint him because he performs them without desires and attachments. There is no craving in him, nor any trace of egoism or ownership. He performs actions to keep the triple worlds going without any desires or attachments, nor does he have any interest in their outcome. Gain or loss does not make any difference to him because he is complete in himself. Since he performs actions without desires and expectations, he is not bound to them. In the verse, he also said that he who knows him in this manner is not bound by his actions. It means by knowing that the Supreme Lord is his very Self, how he performs actions with detachment and disinterest, and identifying with him, whoever performs actions in the same manner remains unbound by his actions. When we follow his example and perform actions, establishing our minds in his contemplation and thinking, "Actions do not taint me, and I do not have the desire or attachment to the fruit of my actions, "we are also not tainted by our actions.

The title of the chapter is Jnana Karma-Sannyasa Yoga, which means either the knowledge of karma-sannyasa yoga or the practice of karma yoga with knowledge and renunciation. Both meanings are appropriate and justified. Karma means both actions and the fruit of actions, and Karma yoga means the yoga of actions or duties. Karma-sannyasa yoga means the yoga of the renunciation of actions, in which you do not renounce actions (karma) but the fruit of your actions (karma or karma-phalam). Thus, this chapter is about how to avoid the fruit or the karmic consequences (karma) arising from your actions (karma) or karma yoga practice. Karma-sannyasa yoga is an advanced form of karma yoga only in which you renounce desires and attachments while performing your duties to avoid their karmic consequences. The Supreme Lord personally exemplifies it through his duties of creation, preservation, and destruction, and sets an example for humans to follow. In this verse, he introduced this idea, suggesting how we can renounce desires and expectations about our actions and arrest the flow of karma to attain oneness with him.

Actions do not taint us when they are performed without desires, ownership, doership, delusion, and egoism. The idea is easier to grasp but difficult to follow. The impurities take time to dissolve since the forces of maya remain active in our bodies and do not easily let us be free from them. The Bhagavadgita gives us hope, stating that if we focus on duties rather than desires, follow the Lord within rather than the mind and senses, and practice self-restraint, we will gradually overcome the problem. It imparts a new meaning to sannyasa and brings a fundamental shift in our understanding of it. True renunciation is the renunciation of desires rather than actions. Karma-sannyasa yoga combines the best aspects of the three fundamental yogas: jnana, karma, and sannyasa yogas. It is best suited for householders who want to perform their obligatory duties without renouncing their families or duties and achieve liberation.

Sloka 15

evaṃ jñātvā kṛtaṃ karma pūrvair api mumukṣubhiḥ
kuru karmaiva tasmāt tvaṃ pūrvaiḥ pūrvataraṃ kṛtam

evam = thus truly; jnatva = knowing; krtam = performed; karma = actions; purvaih = ancient; api =even; mumuksubhih = seekers of liberation; kuru = perform; karma = actions; eva = even; tasmat = therefore; tvam = you; purvaih = by the ancient; purva-taram = in the past ages; krtam = performed.

Knowing thus truly, actions were performed even by the ancient seekers of liberation. Therefore, even you (too) perform actions as were performed by the ancient ones in the past ages.

At the beginning of this chapter, Lord Krishna said that he taught this (karma-sannyasa) yoga in the remote past to Manu and others, and he was teaching it again since it had been lost to the world over time. Here, he said that this ancient yoga was practiced by ancient yogis such as King Janaka with dispassion and detachment for self-purification or to serve others. They did not renounce actions but the fruit of their actions. Hence, as a householder, he should also follow their example and perform his actions without desires and expectations. After encouraging him to practice the karma-sannyasa yoga, Lord Krishna will explain in the following verse the knowledge (jnana) associated with it to help him understand why it is necessary to perform actions, renouncing desires, and how this yoga is more beneficial and ideal than karma yoga. He already said that wise ones like King Janaka set an example to inspire others. Therefore, he asked him to follow their example and perform actions.

Sloka 16

kiṃ karma kimakarmeti kavayopy atra mohitāḥ
tat te karma pravakṣyāmi yaj jñātvā mokṣyaseśubhāt

kim = what is; karma = action; kim = what is; akarma = inaction; iti = thus; kavayah = wise, prudent, intelligent, sensible; api = even; atra = about; mohitah = confused, bewildered; tat = that; te = you; karma = action; pravaksyami = I shall explain; yat = which; jnatva = knowing; moksyase = will be liberated; asubhat = from the inauspicious or misfortune.

Even the prudent ones are confused about what action is and what inaction is. I shall explain to you that (kind of) action, by knowing which you will be liberated from this inauspicious (one).

Even the prudent ones (kavis) who were well versed in the Vedas are confused about karma (action) and akarma (inaction) because the Vedas define them differently. Karma yogis should know them to decide whether they would like to engage in desire-ridden actions or renounce desires and the fruit of their actions to escape from samsara. Hence, Lord Krishna said he would explain the difference to Arjuna so that he could be free from the cycle of births and deaths and attain liberation. In a mundane sense, karma means any action performed by the mind and body or the various organs, and akarma means not performing any action, doing nothing, or remaining idle. This simplistic approach creates the mistaken notion (moha), even among the wise ones (kavi), that one can escape from karma through akarma (inaction) by avoiding sinful actions or not performing them. Under this deluded notion, some people take up sannyasa to escape from family duties and responsibilities. In the following discussion, we will understand why it is not correct.

The Vedas have a different approach to karma and akarma. For them, karma means all righteous, lawful, or duty-bound actions (dharma), and akarma means all actions that are unrighteous, unlawful, or not duty-bound (adharma). All the obligatory duties that are ordained for householders and cannot be avoided or neglected by them constitute karma, or duty-bound or righteous actions that promote Dharma. All the optional sacrifices, which are desire-ridden and known as kamya karmas, and all the prohibited actions, which are tainted by evil and known as nishiddha karmas, are considered akarma or not duty-bound and lead to Adharma. Although desire-ridden actions and sacrifices (kamya-karmas) are unrighteous, unlawful, and not necessary for practicing Dharma, the Vedas do not prohibit them. Householders have the option to perform them or not perform them. Those who desire to go to the ancestral heaven and obtain a good birth in the next life may practice them at their own risk, along with their obligatory duties in the pursuit of Dharma, Artha, Kama, and Moksha. However, the Vedas discourage everyone from performing the prohibited sacrifices (nishiddha karmas) since they are not only unrighteous, unlawful, and not duty-bound but also evil and lead to mortal sin.

The Bhagavadgita approaches duty-bound actions (karma) and not duty-bound actions (akarma) from the perspective of desires. According to it, all actions performed as a sacrifice or offering without desires and without desiring their fruit constitute righteous and duty-bound actions (Dharma), and all actions where desires are involved are not duty-bound (Adharma). It expands the scope of karma to include all obligatory (nitya karmas), optional (kamya karma), and prohibited (nishiddha karmas) sacrifices, and all physical, mental, and bodily functions such as thinking, speaking, eating, sleeping, breathing, etc. Thus, from the perspective of the Bhagavadgita, actions (karma) are duty-bound (Dharma) or not duty-bound (Adharma), depending upon whether desires are involved. The same criterion applies to inaction also. Inaction is righteous (Dharma) or unrighteous (Adharma), depending upon whether desires are involved. If a person intentionally avoids action to escape from the consequences of his actions or for some other reason, it is sinful and will produce sinful karma.

From these definitions, one can see that even the wise ones, who are well-grounded in the knowledge of the Vedas, may feel confused about the meaning of karma and akarma, or action and inaction. For a karma yogi, these distinctions matter since they perform kamya karmas and other desire-ridden actions in addition to their obligatory duties. However, for karma-sannyasa yogis who renounce desires and the desire for the fruit of actions, they do not matter. For them, all actions are lawful, even the prohibited actions, since they perform them as a sacrifice to God without desires or intentions and without desiring the fruit of their actions. The ancient yogis knew that both actions and inaction produced sinful consequences and bound the jivas if desires were involved. Therefore, they practiced karma-sannyasa yoga and escaped from the inauspicious and sin-ridden mortal world. Lord Krishna said that he would teach Arjuna the same knowledge that was lost, and by knowing which, he would be liberated from the cycle of births and deaths.

Sloka 17

karmaṇo hy api boddhavyaṃ boddhavyaṃ ca vikarmaṇaḥ
akarmaṇaś ca boddhavyaṃ gahanā karmaṇo gatiḥ

karmanah = of actions; hi = indeed, certainly; api = truly; boddhavyam = learn, know; boddhavyam = should be known; ca = also; vikarmanah = wrong action, prohibited actions; akarmanah = inaction; ca = and; boddhavyam = should be known; gahana = difficult, impenetrable, thick, dense; karmanah = of actions; gatih = the way or path.

Indeed, one must truly learn about actions, learn about wrong actions, and learn about inaction. The path of action is difficult to know.

The path of action is difficult to know because one has to know the distinction between action, inaction, and wrong action. Without that knowledge and discernment, it is hard to foresee which actions bind and which ones do not, and in what circumstances. Actions become sinful or sinless depending upon the attitude and knowledge with which they are performed. Karma yogis who practice karma kanda as ordained by the Vedas must be conversant with the Vedas, with the sacrifices and the procedures they should follow, the nature of karma that arises from them, and how they can neutralize it to escape from sinful consequences. Without knowing any of it, they can still escape from the consequences of their actions if they know how to neutralize the karma that arises from their sacrifices or actions through karma-sannyasa yoga.

Although the Bhagavadgita is a Vedantic scripture, sometimes it must be studied and interpreted in the context of the Mimansa philosophy (also known as Purva Mimansa), which was probably the original and the oldest philosophy of the Vedic religion. Since Mimansa derived its authority exclusively from the Vedas, it also probably remained unchallenged for a long time until other schools of philosophy and theistic traditions emerged in Vedism to challenge its position on various concepts. These developments also explain why the early Vedic gods such as Brahma, Indra, Agni, and Varuna, the main deities of sacrificial ceremonies, lost their prominence and yielded their place to deities such as Vishnu, Shiva, and Skanda along with the rise of bhakti or devotion. In bhakti, sacrificial rituals were replaced with contemplative and devotional practices, which gradually led to the popularity of yoga.

We can see in the Bhagavadgita an attempt to reconcile the agreeable aspects of the Mimansa with Vedanta (also known as Uttara Mimansa), discarding the atheistic and nontheistic aspects of the former and keeping those that agree with the Vedas and established Vedic practices. Hence, we find a two-pronged approach in it. On the one hand, it repudiates those aspects of Mimansa with which the Vedanta school disagrees. On the other hand, it accepts the beliefs of Mimansa, which fit into its theistic worldview with God as the center and circumference of everything. It agrees with the basic premise of Mimansa that human beings are obligated to perform sacrificial actions as ordained by the Vedas for the order and regularity of the world and to fulfill their chief aims in life. It agrees with the karma yogis who perform their obligatory duties and pursue desire-ridden actions also to attain Dharma, Artha, and Kama. However, it offers them a better solution, suggesting that they can avoid the sinful consequences of their actions and escape from samsara by renouncing desires and the desire for the fruit of their actions and offering it as a sacrifice to the Supreme Lord. It also affirms that he is the ultimate recipient of all the sacrifices, and he is also the one who liberates beings from samsara. Karma yoga was probably a Mimansa concept. Karma-sannyasa yoga is an advanced version of it, which might have gained popularity along with the rise of Vedanta and the Upanishadic teachings.

Mimansa holds that the power or the potency to grant a worshipper's wishes is inherent in the sacrifices (yajna), and the gods are mere agents bound by the yajnas to assist the worshippers in return for the nourishment they receive. According to the school, one should focus on performing actions according to established procedures without worrying about results, since results are guaranteed if procedures are followed. With such beliefs in the sacred power of the yajnas, the Mimansa posed a great challenge to the Vedism's theistic traditions, which believed in an intelligent and self-existent creator God and a cosmos ruled by numerous deities. In the Bhagavadgita, we find a middle approach and an attempt to establish a common ground so that devotees can benefit from the best practices of both schools.

We find a similar attempt in this verse also. For example, the Mimansikas divided actions into three: karma (lawful or righteous action), vikarma (crooked or evil action), and akarma (unlawful or unrighteous action). According to them, karma means performing duties and sacrificial rituals (karma kanda) ordained by the Vedas for various purposes according to the established procedures and instructions (vidhi). Vikarma means duties and sacrifices that are ordained but performed against approved procedures (avidhi), duties and sacrifices that they do not prescribe, and those they explicitly prohibit (nishiddha). In their worldview, akarma meant not performing the obligatory duties at all, which were supposed to be performed by the householders according to the established social norms. Thus, for the Mimansikas, karma means whatever sacrifices the Vedas approve. Vikarma means whatever sacrifices are performed against their injunctions and approved practices, and akarma means not performing the sacrifices they ordain for householders. The first one leads to peace and happiness here and hereafter—the other two lead to suffering and sinful consequences.

The Bhagavadgita gives a slightly different interpretation. It rejects all desire-ridden actions (be it obligatory duties, desire-ridden sacrifices, or prohibited actions) as sinful and unlawful (Adharma) and recommends karma-sannyasa yoga as the solution. According to the Mimansa schools, karma, vikarma, and akarma produce different results: sinless, sinful, and mixed. Bhagavadgita holds that if desires are involved, they all produce sin and lead to bondage and suffering only. When desires are involved, karma (action) and akarma (inaction) produce suffering, and vikarma even more. Hence, it suggests that one should cultivate the right discernment and navigate through life on the path of karma-sannyasa, performing actions with the right knowledge, discernment, and detachment without desiring their fruit. Karma yogis who are ignorant of the Self and lack discernment may engage in desire-ridden actions while performing obligatory duties. By that, they will attain heaven and a good life in the next birth, not liberation. Karma-sannyasa yoga neutralizes all actions and arrests the flow of karma since it involves performing actions without the poison of desires. Thus, as we learn in the next verse, every action becomes inaction when desires are absent.

Sloka 18

karmaṇyakarma yaḥ paśyed akarmaṇi ca karma yaḥ
sa buddhimān manuṣyeṣu sa yuktaḥ kṛtsnakarmakṛt

karmani = in action; akarma = inaction; yah = he who; pasyet = perceives; akarmani = in inaction; ca = and; karma = action; yah = who; sah = he; buddhiman = wise; manusyesu = among people; sah = he; yuktah = adept who established in yoga; krtsna-karma-krt = although performs actions.

He who perceives inaction in action and action in inaction - he is wise among people. He is an adept who is firmly established in yoga, although he performs actions.

This verse can be interpreted in different ways from different perspectives. Therefore, the following explanations require attention. Before going into it, we will discard the Vedic notions of karma and akarma and revert to our mundane definitions of them as action and inaction. The traditional interpretation is that the wise one who knows the Self and has discernment sees the inactive Lord in the actions that are driven by desires and passions. In contrast, he sees the active Lord in those who renounce desires and attachments and perform them without desiring their fruit. In other words, when an ignorant person lacking in knowledge and discernment is active and engages in desire-ridden actions, assuming ownership and doership, the Lord remains passive in him and makes him responsible for the karma which arises from his actions. However, when a yogi who possesses knowledge and discernment renounces desires and attachments and practices karma-sannyasa yoga, the Lord becomes active in him and frees him from all karma as if he has been inactive or not performed any actions at all.

When you are uninvolved, detached, and indifferent in your actions and offer them to the Lord, you are inactive even if you have been active since the Lord assumes the doership and ownership and absolves you of the karma produced by them. Karma does not accrue to you from those actions, even if you have been the doer and even if such actions are obligatory, not obligatory, or prohibited. This is inaction in action. It is also naishkarmya siddhi (freedom from all karma), which we will discuss later. However, when you are passionately involved in your actions or attached to them due to desires and attachments, and assume doership and ownership, you become responsible for them. Since you have not relinquished doership and ownership for such actions, God remains passive and lets you take the active role. He will let you assume their ownership or doership and accumulate karma for all the actions you perform or do not perform willfully. Those who indulge in it will not achieve naishkarmya siddhi (the state of inaction in action). This is the situation with most people, including karma yogis. They engage in sacrifices and desire-ridden actions due to egoism, desires, and passions.

Karma means actions that produce consequences. However, inactivity (akarma) can also produce consequences if desires are involved. For example, if you willfully neglect your obligatory duties and remain idle, you will incur sinful karma for neglecting them. You will also incur sinful karma if you are idle and your mind is filled with desire-ridden thoughts. Thus, karma and akarma do not refer to physical activity, inactivity, or sacrifices. They are distinguished by the consequences they may or may not produce. In this verse, Lord Krishna spoke about karma in akarma (action in inaction) and akarma in karma (inaction in action). They are certainly confusing for those who have yet to understand the karma doctrine. They know that actions produce consequences, but wonder how inaction also produces them.

In this regard, we can envisage four scenarios. 1. You perform actions and incur karma; 2. You perform actions but do not incur karma; 3. You are idle but incur karma, and 4. You are idle but do not incur karma. These four situations arise due to the presence or absence of desires and attachments. From this, evidently, you do not have to perform actions to produce karma. It is sufficient if your mind is active due to desires and attachments. The mind also produces karma, just like the body. As long as your ego is active and driven by passions and desires, you are active whether you are active or inactive and awake or asleep.

Sri Shankaracharya interpreted karma and akarma using the Self and the body. He stated that ignorant people do not perceive the difference between action and inaction because of delusion. Since they mistake the body for the Self, they assume that the Self is active when the body is active. When it is inactive, they assume that the Self is inactive. The truth is that the actions of the mind and body pertain to the mind and body only. The Self does not participate in them. It is the passive witness. The wise ones know that actions pertain to the physical self, and inaction pertains to the spiritual Self. The latter remains inactive when the body is active. This is inaction in action. The body is also active even when resting, since the mind remains active and keeps producing thoughts. This is action in inaction. Sri Madhavacharya, the proponent of Dvaita (dualism), offered a different explanation. According to him, the case of inaction in action arises when a wise person sees the absence of his independent activity and God as the independent, active agent. He sees action in inaction when he sees that the Lord is active in the dream and deep sleep states when his mind and body are resting or inactive.

The duality of action and inaction arises when the mind is filled with impurities, and one engages in desire-ridden actions with that impure mind. The distinction of karma, akarma, and vikarma applies to humans since they are not independent agents but depend upon their minds and bodies (Prakriti) to perform their actions. These distinctions disappear when ownership and doership are passed on to God, an independent Agent who is not subject to karma or bondage due to his actions or inaction. Therefore, when the senses are active and moving among sense objects, the wise one in whom desires and attachments are absent knows that the gunas are active among the gunas, and he is not in them. When he performs actions, he knows that his mind and body are engaged in actions, and he is not. Thus, he remains free from karma, seeing his inaction in the actions of his senses or mind and body. Similarly, when you renounce your ego and abide in the Self without distinction or duality, by that very act of sacrifice, your actions cease to produce karma. This is also inaction in action. The case of action in inaction may also arise when you instigate others to perform desire-ridden actions. Even though you are inactive, you will have a share in the sin that arises from it.

Thus, in karma-sannyasa yoga, the meaning of action and inaction depends upon the presence or absence of the causes of karma, especially desires and attachments. A wise person who is skillful in yoga (yukta) knows this and remains stable in both situations. Through self-restraint and detachment, he transcends the duality of action and inaction and that of attraction and aversion and remains free from the consequences of his selfless actions. The purpose of karma-sannyasa yoga is to achieve the supreme state of inaction in action.

Sloka 19

yasya sarve samārambhāḥ kāmasaṃkalpavarjitāḥ
jñānāgnidagdhakarmāṇaṃ tam āhuḥ paṇḍitaṃ budhāḥ

yasya = whose; sarve = all; samarambhah = undertakings; kama = desire; sankalpa = intentions, decisions; varjitah = free from, devoid of; jnana = knowledge; agni = fire; dagdha = burnt away; karmanam = actions; tam = him; ahuh = call; panditam = learned; budhah = the wise.

He whose all undertakings are free from desire-ridden intentions, whose actions are burnt in the fire of knowledge, the wise ones call him a pandita.

He whose actions are free from the desire for their fruit, whose ignorance is burnt in the fire of knowledge whereby he realizes that the Supreme Lord is the independent Agent and doer of all actions and thereby refrains from assuming ownership and doership, the wise ones call him a Pandita, meaning he who excels in the knowledge of karma-kanda (sacrifices) and jnana-kanda (Brahman and Atman) of the Vedas. This is the essence.

Kama means desires. Sankalpa means intention, decision, or determination. Kama sankalpa indicates desire-ridden intention. Investing in a business to earn money for personal profit is a kama sankalpa. So is performing a sacrifice to seek boons or achieve personal gain. The Vedic tradition views desire as problematic and selfishness as an evil quality. However, since desires are at the root of selfishness, they are considered the prime problem. Actions must be free from kama sankalpa. Only then will they not produce karma phalam (fruit of actions) and bind the beings. Most resolutions (sankalpas) people make have desires as their roots. When they put them into action, they will suffer from the consequences. The wise ones (panditas) know it. Therefore, they burn their actions in the fire of knowledge. "Jñānāgni dagdha karmāṇa" means they purify their actions by removing desires from them with the knowledge that actions that are performed without seeking their fruit do not produce karma or lead to bondage. They do not renounce actions but the desires and attachments in their actions. They renounce kama sankalpa rather than karmakanda and keep performing their duties as sacrificial offerings to God. Through selfless and desireless actions, they help others, serve gods, or keep their bodies alive. They may also perform such actions to cleanse their past karmas or burn their latent impressions (samskaras), which persist even in advanced stages of progress. Actions performed in this manner set them free since they arise from sacrifice rather than desires.

A pandita is a knowledgeable person with purified intelligence and mental brilliance who performs actions skillfully without desiring their fruit and abstains from prohibited actions. Since he is well-versed in the knowledge of the Vedas, he knows not only the precepts and injunctions (vidhi) that one should follow but also the actions and methods that are prohibited (nishedha). Having burned his desires in the fire of knowledge, he excels in karma-sannyasa yoga and sets the standards for others.

Sloka 20

tyaktvā karmaphalāsaṅgaṃ nityatṛpto nirāśrayaḥ
karmaṇy abhipravṛttopi naiva kiṃcit karoti saḥ

tyaktva = having given up; karma-phala-asangam = association or attachment to the fruit of actions; nitya = always; trptah = content, satisfied; nirasrayah = depending on nothing; karmani = in actions; abhipravrttah = engaged; api =also; na = not; eva = even though; kincit = anything; karoti = does; sah = he.

Having given up attachment to the fruit of his actions, always content, depending upon nothing, even though he is engaged in actions, he does nothing at all.

Knowing the difference between action in inaction and inaction in action with the wisdom that actions should be free from desire-induced thoughts and one should not desire their fruit, an adept yogi (yukta), endowed with that knowledge practices karma-sannyasa yoga, giving up both attachment and association with the fruit of his actions. Thereby, he does nothing at all, even if he engages in actions.

'Karma phala sanga' means association with the fruit of actions. An adept karma-sannyasa yogi gives up desires and attachments to the fruit of his actions and all manner of associations (sanga) with it. In other words, he does not attach himself to any action he performs or its outcome. For example, if he wishes someone to be happy, he does not desire to share their happiness or expect to be appreciated, but remains aloof and away if possible. He shows no particular interest in any action or its outcome since he is ever content within himself and satisfied with himself. His happiness or contentment does not depend upon external conditions or factors. Therefore, he remains detached from everything. Having given up desires, attachments, and associations with the fruit of his actions, he also exemplifies inaction in action. Hence, although he engages in various actions, it is as if he has not performed any actions at all.

We learn from this verse that three conditions are necessary to escape from the consequences of actions: 1) giving up desires and attachment to things, especially to the fruit of actions, 2) feeling contentment within oneself, and 3) cutting off dependence from all sides and letting go of egoism, attachments, and delusion. The first condition leads to the second, and the first and second lead to the third. Mental freedom is the basis for spiritual freedom or liberation. Without being mentally free, you cannot qualify to be spiritually free. Nirasrayah means having no shelter or not taking refuge in anything. An adept karma-sannyasa yogi (yukta) does not seek happiness or comfort in worldly things. He takes shelter within himself and remains content within himself. Dependence upon external things for comfort, peace, or happiness is a form of mental slavery. In search of happiness and fulfillment, we depend upon many things and take refuge in many things, such as name, fame, family, status, caste, community, nationality, etc. Instead of setting us free, they increase our dependence upon them. The knowledgeable ones (panditas) know it. Therefore, they burn their desires and passions in the fire of knowledge and sever their connection (sanga) with the fruit of their actions. They do not give up actions because they know it is impossible and impractical for anyone to refrain from actions, even for a moment.

Sloka 21

nirāśīr yatacittātmā tyaktasarvaparigrahaḥ
śārīraṃ kevalaṃ karma kurvan nāpnoti kilbiṣam

nirasih = without desire or expectation; yata = controlled; citta = mind; atma = body; tyakta = giving up; sarva = all; parigrahah = possessions; sariram = body; kevalam = only; karma = actions, functions; kurvan = doing so; na = not; apnoti = acquires, incurs; kilbisam = sin.

Without desire or expectation, with the mind and body under control, giving up all possessions, performing only body-related functions, even while performing actions, he incurs no sin.

All the practices mentioned in this verse are interrelated. Niraśir (nir + aśa) means having no desire, hope, or expectation. It refers to the state of mind that does not look at the world with hunger or thirst for things or fulfillment. The state of desirelessness arises when you are completely satisfied or fully in control of your mind and body. Chittatma shall be interpreted here as the mind and body or the beingness. The Self cannot be controlled. What can be controlled is the physical being or the personality made up of the mind and body. Chitta is mainly translated as the mind or consciousness. However, in the yoga tradition, chitta is more than the ordinary mind or its consciousness. It extends beyond the mind and body into the surrounding akasa (space). One may call it the mind-body consciousness, including the aura surrounding it, of which the mind (manas) is just a part.

The control of beingness (cittatma) requires a holistic approach in which you gradually gain control of the tattvas and gunas through self-restraint and self-purification. According to classical yoga, the purity of perceptions depends upon the presence of sattva in the chitta. A pure chitta reflects the luminosity of the objects with unobscured clarity. When the impurities of rajas and tamas enter it, it becomes impure, opaque, and vulnerable to misapprehension, confusion, and delusion. Just like a dust-covered mirror poorly reflects objects, an impure chitta fails to reflect the truth of things correctly and suffers from modifications (chittavrittis), afflictions (kleshas), desires, and delusion, which in turn result in distorted thinking, lack of judgment, discernment, and understanding. Classical yoga recommends various techniques to suppress these modifications and impurities and purify the consciousness so that one may discern the Self and become absorbed in it.

This verse suggests that the best way to purify the cittatma is by giving up desires and possessions. Parigraha means a possession or whatever one can grasp (grahya) with the mind or the senses. Technically, all the material objects found in the objective realm are graspable by the senses. The mind may also be drawn to the mental objects or perceptions the senses create in it through constant interaction. Aparigraha, meaning not seeking or coveting possessions, is recognized as one of the five cardinal virtues of many spiritual traditions, along with nonviolence, truthfulness, non-stealing, and celibacy. It arises due to the predominance of sattva and the absence of greed (nirlobha), egoism (nirmama), and desires (nirasa). When the mind is pure and filled with sattva, all desires disappear.

The verse also states that the yogi should perform body-related functions (kevalam sarira-karma) only without desires and attachments. It is mentioned here probably because wasting away the body through austerities and self-mortification was one of the cardinal practices of the Vedic Sannyasa Ashrama and some ascetic traditions of ancient India. The Bhagavadgita prohibits such extreme practices. It encourages yogis to nourish their bodies and give them proper rest to ensure their health and continuity. The body is the abode of the gods, who need to be regularly nourished to keep them active and content. If they are unhappy or angry, they can cause obstructions and prevent them from achieving their intended goals. Hence, Lord Krishna specifically stated that one should perform body-related functions not out of desire but as an obligatory duty to keep oneself alive and nourish the gods and Shaktis presiding over the organs in the body. In the next verse, he explains how they can remain unattached and free from sin, even while performing actions such as begging, seeking alms, or looking for possessions (parigraha) such as a begging bowl, a staff, or clothing to cover and protect their bodies.

Sloka 22

yadṛcchālābhasaṃtuṣṭo dvandvātīto vimatsaraḥ
samaḥ siddhāv asiddhau ca kṛtvāpi na nibadhyate

yadrccha = unintentionally, by chance or coincidence; labha = gain; santustah = contended; dvandva = pairs of opposites, duality; atitah = transcending; vimatsarah = free from envy; samah = same, equal; siddhau = in success;

asiddhau = failure; ca = and; krtva = while performing actions; api = even, although; na = not; nibadhyate = is bound.

Content with what is obtained by chance, transcending the pairs of opposites or the dualities, free from envy, the same in success and failure, he is not bound even while performing actions.

This and the previous verses are not meant for householders but for the renunciants who give up worldly life and live in seclusion to attain liberation. Householders may also practice them without giving up their duties, but renouncing all desires and attachments. An adept yogi endowed with knowledge and discernment and established in karma-sannyasa yoga goes about his work indifferently, surrendering his will to the will of God and accepting whatever fate befalls him. If he is a householder, he sincerely performs his duties and accepts the results that arise from them, remaining equal to success and failure. Amidst dualities and uncertainties, he remains the same, adapting to the impermanent world's changing conditions and circumstances or remaining indifferent. If he renounces worldly life and takes the vows of sannyasa, he practices contemplation upon the Self and avoids self-mortification. He nourishes his body as an obligatory duty to keep it alive and serve the Lord. When he seeks alms, he is content with what he obtains or does not obtain by chance, remaining indifferent amidst the dualities of heat and cold, success and failure. Since he practices sameness and contentment, he is free from envy when he sees people who are better or more successful than him or have earned the Lord's grace. By cultivating detachment, desirelessness, equanimity, sameness, and contentment, which arise from his pursuit of knowledge (jnana) and practice of karma-sannyasa yoga, he remains untainted by his actions. His actions do not produce the poison of sin and suffering or lead to karma and bondage. When he performs actions, he thinks his body is engaged in actions and is not involved with them. Thus, renouncing egoism, ownership, and doership, he is inactive although he is active.

This verse emphasizes living an active life without seeking, striving, and desiring. He who attains perfection in karma-sannyasa yoga lives his life as a sacrifice, performs his actions as a sacrifice, and worships God with a sacrificial attitude. He is not disturbed by circumstances, success, or failure, and remains contented with what happens by chance or coincidence or does not happen, accepting them as God's will. He lives like a true sannyasi, giving up desires and desire-ridden actions and flowing with life, neither rejecting nor resisting what life throws at him. The hidden meaning of sannyasa is to live without egoistic striving, zeal, or exertion (ayasa) and with no particular aim or intent. A sannyasi gives up egoistic desires, choices, and effort and lives freely, letting God choose his path. The same idea is reflected in this verse. Renunciation is a way of life that is exactly opposite to how worldly people live. It is a life of freedom in which worry, anxiety, and the burdens of worldly life lose their poisonous strength to overwhelm the mind and produce suffering.

Sloka 23

gatasaṅgasya muktasya jñānāvasthitacetasaḥ
yajñāyācarataḥ karma samagraṃ pravilīyate

gata-sangasya = gone attachments; muktasya =of the liberated; jnana-avasthita = established in knowledge; cetasah = mind; yajnaya = for the sake of sacrifice; acaratah = performs; karma = actions; samagram = all; praviliyate = dissolved or destroyed.

(He) whose attachments are gone, who is liberated, whose mind is established in knowledge, who performs actions for the sake of sacrifice, all (his) actions are completely dissolved.

This is the essence of karma-sannyasa yoga. Through these perfections, the skillful yogi attains liberation. His attachments dissipate because he overcomes desires. He is liberated because he is not bound to material things, dualities, and the distinction between dharma and adharma, or between karma and akarma, or vikarma. His mind is established in the knowledge gained through study, contemplation, and self-absorption. He performs actions as a sacrifice to God since he knows it is the best way to remain free from karma. His actions are completely dissolved since he relinquishes ownership and doership and offers them to him without expectations.

Mukti, in this context, means freedom from a being's engagement and involvement (sanga) with the mortal world in the initial stages and permanent freedom from samsara (the cycle of births and deaths) in the final stages. Without the first, the second stage cannot be attained. Freedom from all things is first experienced in the internal organ (antahkarana) as one becomes a yukta (a yogi endowed with skill and wisdom) and later in the Self as jivanmukta, a free soul in a mortal body. When that liberated person departs from his body, he is completely freed from the field of Prakriti, never to return. Liberation is for the Self, not for the body or the mind. It arises due to a paradigm shift in one's consciousness as the impurities are gradually removed. It is achieved first by knowing, through samkhya yoga, the Self and its distinction from the body and the awareness that the Self does not participate in the desire-ridden actions of the mind and the body. With that knowledge and discernment gained through jnana yoga, he learns the supreme reality of the Self, the causes of bondage, the nature of suffering, and the means to overcome it. In the next stage, he cultivates detachment and dispassion and resorts to karma-sannyasa yoga, performing his actions as a sacrifice and in service to God. Finally, having purified himself through karma-sannyasa yoga and giving up dualities, desires, and seeking and striving, he stabilizes his mind by contemplating upon the Self and practicing exclusive devotion and self-control.

Thus, this verse neatly sums up the progress of an ordinary householder who practices karma yoga and worships his gods to fulfill his desires into an adept yogi or renunciant who gives up desires and attachments and dissolves his karma in the fire of duty, knowledge, and devotion, performing his actions without desiring their fruit and offering them to God as a sacrifice with devotion. A liberated karma-sannyasa yogi, free from duality, desires, envy, and expectations, is neither bound to his actions through desires and attachments nor to the consequences that may arise from them because his actions are induced by neither the gunas nor desires but by his obligation to serve God and his creation. Since his actions are purified by devotion, detachment, renunciation, and sacrifice, he remains pure even while engaged in them. The scriptures vouch for it. The fruit of such actions accrues to God, the source of all. When karma is performed as a sacrificial offering to him, it becomes akarma as its fruit is automatically dissolved in the fire of sacrifice.

Sloka 24

brahmārpaṇaṃ brahma havir brahmāgnau brahmaṇā hutam
brahmaiva tena gantavyaṃ brahmakarmasamādhinā

brahma = Brahman; arpanam = the act of offering; brahma = the Supreme Brahman; havih = oblation of clarified butter; brahma = Brahman; agnau = sacrificial fire; brahmana = by brahman; hutam = the pouring; brahma = Brahman; eva = surely; tena = by him; gantavyam = attained, reached; brahma = Brahman; karma = actions; samadhina =associates, joins, unites, establishes.

The act of offering is Brahman; the oblation of clarified butter is Brahman; the burnt offering is poured into the fire of Brahman by Brahman. Brahman is surely attained by him who firmly unites Brahman with actions.

Brahman is the hidden power behind all movements and actions. Because of him, the worlds move, planets revolve in their respective orbits, seasons happen regularly, time moves at a set pace, and life happens. He is the universal power or energy that energizes the sacrificial mantras and manifests the wishes of the worshippers. Because of him, sacrificial fires burn, oblations and offerings reach gods and ancestors, stars glow, day and night happen, and the sun and the moon brightly shine. In obeisance to him, everything happens as ordained. Therefore, we should not assume ownership, agentship, or doership of anything, and as the Isa Upanishad declares, we should wish to live here by offering our actions to him. One of the earliest beliefs of the Vedic tradition was that Brahman was the power hidden in all movements and movements within movements. It still holds good, although subsequently, they identified that power as Prakriti, the force of Brahman. The energy in your body is not yours. It belongs to Brahman, and you should accept that, surrender to that idea, and live accordingly.

A karma-sannyasa yogi knows that Brahman is the mover of all actions and that the jiva (being) is a mere instrument. Therefore, he renounces doership and duality and attributes every movement and action of his mind and body to Brahman only. He sees him everywhere and in everything: in the yajnastala (ritual place or the body) of sacrifice, in the act of offering, in the offering itself, in the fire into which that offering is poured, and in the object and subject of that offering. In other words, he sees, or rather firmly accepts with conviction, that Brahman is the source of all things, the cause of all actions, and the purpose and intent of all sacrifices. When he firmly harmonizes his actions with Brahman and dissolves dualities and divisions within himself, seeing only Brahman in everything, he realizes that Brahman is his very Self. When Brahman becomes the doer of your actions and your life's purpose and foundation, your ego is automatically dissolved. With that, the delusion of separation or the duality between the worshipper and the worshipped disappears.

One may also read in this verse the hidden message that a devotee can achieve oneness with Brahman through both knowledge and actions on the path of karma-sannyasa yoga, with his mind filled with knowledge, wisdom, devotion, and faith. No further effort is required if he sees that union or oneness without duality and as perfect and indivisible. By seeing Brahman in all aspects of his actions and decisions (sankalpa) and practicing karma-sannyasa yoga as a devotional service and sacrifice, he can make the very act of living a continuous offering of duty and devotion to the eternal, and in the process, dissolve all notions of separation to achieve oneness with him. By separating or detaching his egoistic self from his actions and putting Brahman at the center of them as the true Agent, he can set himself free from karma and bondage. A yogi reaches this stage only upon attaining purity through the continuous practice of karma-sannyasa without duality, division, attachment, or delusion. In that state, he sees Brahman everywhere and in everything, and in himself, others, his actions, and others' actions.

The first step to overcoming duality and delusion and absorbing the mind in the Self is to acknowledge that you are not a Jiva but Shiva, the eternal Self, and actions arise in the field of Prakriti, not in you. You have the obligation to perform actions as an offering, but not for their fruit. You are not the owner of your body, the prana that flows in it, the thoughts that arise in your mind, or the actions you perform, but a dweller of the body, the pure Self, and Brahman himself. If you think that you are a jiva and an agent and doer of your actions, you become responsible and accountable for them, but when you identify with Brahman, the eternal Self, and acknowledge him as the doer, the deed and the beneficiary of the deed, you will attain oneness with him and permanently establish sameness in you. The Lord lives in you as your pure Self. You become the Lord when you realize the truth without duality.

Sloka 25

daivam evāpare yajñaṃ yoginaḥ paryupāsate
brahmāgnāv apare yajñaṃ yajñenaivopajuvhati

daivam = a divinity, God; eva = only; apare = other, some; yajnam = yajna or sacrifice; yoginah = yogis; paryupasate = worship; brahma = Brahman; agnau = in the fire of; apare = some others; yajnam = sacrifice; yajnena = by the sacrifice; eva = even; upajuhvati = pouring.

Some yogis worship yajna as a divinity in itself. Others perform the sacrifice by pouring the sacrifice into the fire of Brahman.

This verse refers to the two basic methods of sacrificial worship: deva yajna and brahma yajna. One refers to the ritualistic belief that the sacrifice is a deity through whom one can communicate with gods, propitiate them, and fulfill their wishes. The other is the spiritual belief that Brahman or the Self is the sacrifice into which worshippers pour their knowledge, breath, thoughts, and actions to purify themselves and attain liberation. One is external, and the other is internal. One is practiced by karma yogis, and the other by karma-sannyasa yogis. The former was probably held by the Mimansikas and the latter by the contemplative traditions of the Vedanta schools. Mimansa was an orthodox Brahmanical tradition that rested heavily upon ritual knowledge of the Samhitas and Brahmanas. It was also the foremost of the Vedic philosophies (Darshanas), which promoted the supremacy of the Vedas and the centrality of Vedic knowledge and rituals in the practice of Dharma.

The Vedanta philosophy was derived from the Aranyakas, Upanishads, and some Brahmanas. Vedic seers internalized the Vedic sacrifices (yajna) into contemplative, austere practices to harness the energies of the mind and body and transform them into spiritual fire (tapah) to control the elements and the tattvas or achieve liberation or oneness with Brahman. They poured their desires, individualities, impurities, devotion, knowledge, and faith into that fire as offerings. The idea of yoga as a contemplative and spiritual practice gradually emerged from such earlier efforts. As stated in the previous verse, followers of the Vedanta equate yajna and all actions associated with it with Brahman. They perform internal sacrifices for the sake of Brahman only, seeing him as the source and support, pouring their thoughts, actions, and energies as oblation into the fire of Brahman.

Both approaches are considered the same at the highest level because deva yajna ultimately culminates in brahma yajna only, Brahman being the ultimate recipient of all sacrifices to whichever gods you may offer them. Brahman is the seeker or the worshipper. Brahman is the support, and Brahman is the goal. In deva yajna, karma yogis make offerings to gods as an obligatory duty to propitiate gods (devas) and seek their help to fulfill their desires. In Brahma yajna, karma-sannyasa yogis who overcome their ignorance and delusion recognize Brahman as the source of all and perform sacrifices for him only, without desiring their fruit. By removing desires from their actions and offering them to the Supreme Lord as a sacrifice, they purify their actions and become free from karma and samsara. Those who renounce worldly life and take up sannyasa also engage in karma-sannyasa yoga only when they engage in bodily actions to keep themselves alive and contemplate upon him without desires. They offer themselves and their actions to the Self or the Supreme Being as the sacrificial offering, pouring their impurities (upajuhvati) in the fire of Brahman to achieve sameness or oneness (samadhi). Thus, all is Brahman, and nothing ever belongs to anyone.

Sloka 26

śrotrādīnīndriyāṇy anye saṃyamāgniṣu juvhati
śabdādīn viṣayān anya indriyāgniṣu juvhati

srotra-adini = ears etc.; indriyani = senses; anye = others; samyama = of self-restraint; agnisu = in the fires; juhvati = pour; sabda-adin = sound etc.; visayan = sense objects; anye = others; indriya = of the senses; agnisu = in the fire; juhvati = pour.

Some offer sense organs beginning with their ears into the fires of self-restraint; others pour sound and similar sense objects into the fire of the sense organs.

Sacrifice means offering something ritually or spiritually. In ritual sacrifices, we offer food to the divinities by pouring it into the sacrificial fire. In spiritual sacrifices, we offer the food we consume and mental objects, such as thoughts, feelings, desires, attachments, sense objects, etc., to the divinities in the body by offering them to the internal fires or to God himself, who represents them all. By those sacrifices, we nourish the gods and keep them active in their respective spheres. Internal sacrifices are possible because inside the body is considered a ritual place (yajnastala) or sacrificial pit (yajnakunda). Inside it, many types of fires dwell, which are fueled by prana and play an important role in keeping the body healthy, alive, and active. They are considered manifestations of prana only. The fires remain lit as long as the body is alive and the offerings are poured into them. When those offerings are made with desires, the fires become tainted and produce sinful consequences, but when they are made as offerings to God, they remain pure and cleanse the mind and body, which results in the cessation of karma.

Two types of internal sacrifices are mentioned here, which have been practiced on the path of liberation by householders and renunciants since the Vedic times. Many ascetic groups and successive teacher traditions (guru paramparas) practice them even today. Both are meant to purify the mind and the body and establish the predominance of sattva, peace, equanimity, and stability. In the first method, a practitioner restrains his organs of perception (jnanedriyas), namely ears (srota), skin (tvaca), eyes (casksu), tongue (jivha), and nose (ghrana), and withdraws them into himself to control their movements, just as the tortoise withdraws its limbs. By withdrawing them thus, which is a symbolic offering of the senses to the fires of self-restraint (samyamagni) or austerity (tapasagni), he temporarily burns the connection between the mind and the perceptual world and withdraws it into himself. Each sense organ requires a different type of restraint. Hence, the plural 'fires' is used in this verse. Through their continued practice, his mind is gradually detached from the external world and stabilized in the contemplation of the Self. In the process, the impurities and the sinful karma that arise from the contact between the senses and the sense objects are also burnt.

In the second method, the practitioner goes a step beyond and also restrains his subtle senses (tanmatras), namely hearing (sabda), touching (sparsha), seeing (rupa), tasting (rasa), and smelling (gandha). These subtle feelings arise when the senses come into contact with the sense objects. By disconnecting the sense impressions (vishaya) from the senses and pouring them into the fires of sense organs (indriyagni), he suppresses the modification of the mind and experiences peace and equanimity. Sense perceptions are difficult to control since even after silencing the senses, the memories of previous perceptions may still disturb the mind and one's concentration. The Yamas and Niyamas help yogis control and suppress them. In traditional yoga, the restraint of the mind and senses is usually accompanied by breath control (pranayama). Breath is the fire of the sense organs (indriaygni) because it fuels them and their activities. By controlling the five types of breaths (prana, apana, vyana, udana, and samana), one can also control the sense organs. Hence, in many yogic systems, samyama (restraint) of the mind and body is practiced in conjunction with yamas, niyamas, breath control (pranayama), and withdrawal of the senses (pratyahara).

Sloka 27

sarvāṇīndriyakarmāṇi prāṇakarmāṇi cāpare
ātmasaṃyamayogāgnau juvhati jñānadīpite

sarvani = all; indriya = senses; karmani = activities; prana-karmani = activities of the vital breaths; ca =and; apare = others; atma-samyama yoga = atma-samyama yoga; agnau = in the fire of; juhvati = pour, offer; jnana-dipite = ignited by knowledge.

Others pour all the activities of the senses and the activities of the vital breaths into the fire of atma-samyama, ignited by knowledge.

The senses are fifteen, and the vital breaths are five. In a deluded person, his senses, mind, ego, and other parts of the internal organ pour offerings into the fires of desires, delusion, and egoism, which lead to sin and suffering. In a karma-sannyasa yogi whose mind is lit by wisdom (jnana dipti), his restraints become offerings into the fires of atma-samyama (self-restraint). Restraining the sense organs is the first step to self-restraint or the restraint of the mind and body. It is more effective than the previously discussed sacrifices involving the senses and sense objects, in which only partial restraint is achieved. In atma-samyama, the entire internal organ (mind, intelligence, consciousness, and ego), the five breaths, and the fifteen senses are restrained and absorbed in the Self. Therefore, it is more advanced and integrated than the previously mentioned practices for self-purification and liberation.

Atma samyama requires total mind and body control. It is achieved in the advanced stages when a yogi is free from desires, attachments, and other impurities, having withdrawn his senses, regulated his breaths, controlled his mind and intelligence, and absorbed them in the contemplation upon the Self. According to Classical Yoga, samyama means concentrated meditation that leads to self-absorption (samadhi), in which the yogi controls the three internal limbs of yoga (antarangam), concentration (dharana), meditation (dhyana), and mental absorption (samadhi). It is practiced in different stages of equanimity and awareness to dissolve the mind-body awareness and enter the purest state of nonduality or oneness. Its sustained practice may lead to the manifestation of many mystic powers (siddhis) in the yogi, such as the knowledge of the past and future, knowledge of the languages of all creatures, invisibility, knowledge of death, telepathy, purity, ability to listen to subtle sounds that travel in akasa (space), and so on. Restraint of the senses, vital breaths, mind, and body is critical to the practice of atma-samyama because, without it, one cannot stabilize the mind in the Self or achieve sameness or oneness, which, according to the Bhagavadgita, is samadhi. It is also critical to suppress desires and attachments, cultivate discernment, and transcend the gunas.

Sloka 28

dravyayajñās tapoyajñā yogayajñās tathāpare
svādhyāyajñānayajñāś ca yatayaḥ saṃśitavratāḥ

dravya-yajnah = sacrifices with material wealth; tapah-yajnah = sacrifices with austerities; yoga-yajnah = sacrifices with yoga; tatha = in the same manner; apare = others; svadhyaya = self-study; jnana-yajnah = sacrifice of knowledge; ca = and, on the other; yatayah = the yatis, self-restrained ascetics; samshita = prepare, organize, resolve; vratah = through strict vows and austere penances.

In the same manner, others perform dravya yajnas or tapo yajnas, or yoga yajnas, while the self-restrained yatis who prepare themselves through strict vows and austere penances practice svadhyaya-jnana yajnas.

This verse describes four types of sacrifices: dravya yajnas, tapo yajnas, yoga yajnas, and jnana yajnas. Dravya yajnas are material sacrifices practiced in the standard conventional form with the offerings of food to gods and gifts to Brahmanas or in other forms such as charity, philanthropy, charitable works, etc. Any sacrificial action that you selflessly perform without expectations, using wealth or material things as a devotional offering, is a dravya yajna. Tapo yajna is any spiritual practice you perform with rigorous penances, austerities, and contemplative practices to discipline your mind and body and transform their physical and mental energies into spiritual energy (tapah) for self-purification. Fasting, celibacy, observing silence, indifference to pain and pleasure, and contemplation are the conventional means by which one can practice it.

Yoga yajna involves practicing one or more yogas, such as ashtanga yoga, raja yoga, hatha yoga, kriya yoga, bhakti yoga, karma yoga, jnana yoga, etc. The purpose of yoga yajna is to dissolve the duality of the mind's consciousness in oneness and absorb it in the pure consciousness of the eternal Self. Yati means any wise person, devotee, sage, or ascetic who practices self-restraint and cultivates wisdom through knowledge and self-purification. They sacrifice ignorance and delusion in the fire of knowledge on the path of jnana-yoga to acquire self-knowledge and discernment. They dissolve their impurities, desires, and attachments in the fire of self-knowledge (svadhyaya jnana yajna), studying the scriptures, such as the Upanishads, or following the teachings of their gurus.

In Hinduism, Life is a sacrificial duty in which you can transform any action into a sacrifice and take out the poison of karma from it by performing actions without desires and offering their fruit to the Supreme Being. Sacrifice means anything you offer, use, spend, or give up with or without desires. It does not have to be a sacrificial ritual. Any action or effort that involves giving and receiving or offering and accepting, with a result or effect, can be counted as a sacrifice. Thus, all actions are sacrifices. Eating, breathing, walking, sleeping, speaking, etc., are sacrifices only. Hinduism accepts this model of life as a sacrifice and perceives it in every aspect of a jiva's existence on Earth. It even accepts sacrifice as the source of creation, which the Vedas confirm. Since sacrifice is the way of life and all aspects of existence are associated with it, Hinduism is known as a way of life. For a devout Hindu, life is a continuous service to God and his creation, in which every action is an offering. Those who perform them with selfish desires incur evil karma and suffer from their consequences, while those who perform them without desiring their fruit are liberated.

You can transpose the idea of sacrifice on your life and action and make your living a continuous offering to the Supreme Lord, or you can waste it away fulfilling your desires and enjoying worldly pleasures. The choice is yours. Even today, devout Hindus live dutifully, consecrating their lives to the service of God. Material sacrifices give you an opportunity to serve gods and others and pay your karmic debt. Mental or spiritual sacrifices in which you renounce all selfish notions and cultivate the attitude of giving help you overcome impurities and unburden yourself from the turbulence of the mind. According to the Brihadaranyaka Upanishad, Brahma advised humans to practice dana (charity) since selfishness is inherent to human nature, and most people do not think beyond themselves and their families. The sacrifice of austerity is a more intense form of divine worship in which you sacrifice your bodily comforts to practice self-control and suppress your desires. In the sacrifice of yoga, you burn latent impressions and the impurities of your mind and body in the fire of sattva. In the sacrifice of self-study (svadhyaya), you offer your ignorance, delusion, and egoism to the fire of sacred knowledge to qualify for self-realization.

Sloka 29

apāne juvhati prāṇaṃ prāṇepānaṃ tathāpare
prāṇāpānagatī ruddhvā prāṇāyāmaparāyaṇāḥ 4.29

apane = in apana; juhvati = offer, pour; pranam = in prana prane = prana; apanam = in apana; tatha = in the same manner; apare = others; prana = prana; apana = apana; gati = movement; ruddhva = restraining; prana-ayama = pranayama, breath control; parayanah = devoted to, absorbed in, adhering to.

Similarly, others who are devoted to the practice of breath control pour Prana into Apana and Apana into Prana, restraining the movements of Prana and Apana.

The sacrifice of breath is made in the sacrificial pit of the body by restraining and pouring the incoming and outgoing breaths (prana and apana) into each other. The practice is known as kumbhaka. The spiritual traditions of India recognize five types of vital breaths: prana, apana, samana, udana, and vyana. Prana is the outgoing breath. Apana is the incoming breath. Samana is the breath that circulates in the middle part of the body. Udana is the breath that circulates in the vocal cords and is responsible for speech. Vyana circulates freely and pervades the body. Together, the five breaths are known as vital breaths and collectively as Prana, the subtle energy that sustains the life of a jiva. According to the Vedas, the body is alive as long as the five breaths circulate in it. It becomes lifeless when the indwelling Lord departs from it, along with the breaths and other divinities. The Upanishads describe him as the breathing one and equate breath (Prana) with the Self. Breath is the fire (Agni) in the body that nourishes all the organs. They depend upon breath and cease to function as soon as the breath leaves the body. Further, unlike the other organs, breath is not vulnerable to desires and selfishness. One may engage the mind or the body due to desires, but breath is a natural activity that is not induced by the gunas, desires, or attachments, or affected by evil thoughts and intentions. Hence, it is considered a purifying agent with which one can purify and control the mind and body and attain peace through breath control (pranayama).

Prana means the air we breathe and the energy that flows or circulates in the body through subtle channels (nadis) and energy centers (chakras). The air we breathe is the outward and visible aspect of it. The subtle energy that flows in the body arises from the food we eat and is further energized and purified by the air we breathe. In the yoga tradition, pranayama is practiced in different ways. Puraka is practiced by inhaling and filling the lungs with breath for a few seconds. Rechaka is practiced by emptying the lungs during exhalation and holding them empty for a few seconds without air. In Kumbhaka, one holds the breath after inhaling and exhaling. It may be practiced independently or in conjunction with Puraka and Rechaka. It is also practiced by breathing through the two nostrils alternatively, one at a time, and holding the breath each time it is exhaled or inhaled. Bhastrika is the practice of inhaling and exhaling in quick succession and short bursts. In Ujjai, breathing is done through the throat and diaphragm, which is good for clearing the throat and strengthening the vocal cords.

In the previous verse, Lord Krishna mentioned dravya yajnas, tapo yajnas, and yoga yajnas. In this verse, he mentioned Pranayama separately as a sacrifice by itself. It may be because Pranayama, as a technique of purifying or stabilizing the mind and body, might have developed independently and was later included in Ashtanga Yoga as one of its limbs. The Upanishads mention Prana vidya, or the knowledge of breaths and their use in the purification of the mind and body, as one of the Brahma Vidyas meant for studying and realizing Brahman. By controlling breath movements and arresting mental modifications (chittavrittis), a yogi can stabilize his mind and improve his practice of concentration, contemplation, and samyama, which will lead to self-absorption (samadhi) or oneness with the indwelling Self.

Sloka 30

apare niyatāhārāḥ prāṇān prāṇeṣu juvhati
sarvepy ete yajñavido yajñakṣapitakalmaṣāḥ

apare = others; niyata = restraining, limiting; aharah = food; pranan = vital breaths; pranesu = in the vital breaths; juhvati = offer; sarve = all; api = also; ete = these; yajna-vidah = knowers of sacrifice; yajna = sacrifices; ksapita = cleansed; kalmasah = impurities.

Others, restraining food, offer their vital breath into the vital breath. All these are knowers of sacrifice, with their impurities cleansed by sacrifices.

This verse speaks of the highest form of sacrifice: prana yajna, self-sacrifice, or the sacrifice of life. Alternatively, it may also mean offering the senses to the vital breaths or withdrawing the senses (pratyahara) into the mind through breath control (pranayama). In the Upanishads, breath is often used interchangeably to denote breaths (prana) and sense organs (indriya). Technically, offering life breaths into life breaths (pranan pranesu juhvati) means giving up or returning prana to its source. If you read it in conjunction with "niyata aharah," it means giving up life by fasting or limiting the intake of food gradually. Self-mortification through slow starvation is an extreme form of self-sacrifice. It is prescribed in the Vedas for those who took the vows of sannyasa and entered the last phases of their lives. Some ascetics outside the Vedic fold also practiced it in ancient India as the final act of giving up the last impurity, the body itself, to free the pure Self.

The Vedic Varnashrama Dharma prescribed four sets of duties for householders in the four phases of their lives, namely brahmacharya (young, celibate student phase), grihastha (adult householder phase), vanaprastha (midlife retirement phase), and sannyasa (old-age renunciation phase). Students had to practice celibacy and study the Vedas to know their duties and responsibilities. Householders had to perform obligatory duties to uphold and ensure the order and regularity of the world by serving God. After fulfilling their obligations, they were supposed to retire to the forests and contemplate upon their lives and the knowledge they gained from the scriptures, or to spend their time in the company of seers and sages. In the last phases of their lives, they had the option to give up everything, take up the vows of renunciation (such as not using fire, not cooking food, not living under a roof, etc.), and live like recluses to achieve liberation.

Those who took sannyasa had the option, at least in theory (since we do not know how many really practiced it), to practice self-mortification in stages by gradually limiting food and water intake and starving themselves. We do not know when this practice was discontinued. It was most likely an outlier form of sacrifice in which the body became an offering (bhakti) to the Lord of Death. Those who practiced it offered their emaciated bodies to the elements: fire, water, and earth, their breaths to the air, and their souls to ether as the final act of self-giving, emptying, and self-purification. Self-mortification is not currently practiced in Hinduism. The Buddha practiced a version of it and discarded it, describing it as extreme, painful, not fit for the Middle Way, and not useful for overcoming suffering. However, some Jain monks still practice a modified version of it.

Sloka 31

yajñaśiṣṭāmṛtabhujo yānti brahma sanātanam
nāyaṃ lokosty ayajñasya kutonyaḥ kurusattama

yajna-sista = remains of the sacrifice; amrta-bhujah = eat the life sustaining food; yanti = go, reach; brahma = Brahman; sanatanam = eternal; na = not;

ayam = this; lokah = world; asti = there is; ayajnasya = those who do not perform sacrifices; kutah = where; anyah = the other; kuru-sat-tama = O best amongst the Kurus.

Those who eat the life-sustaining remains of the sacrificial food go to the eternal Brahman. This world is not for those who do not perform sacrifices. Then, where is the question of the other worlds, O the best among the Kurus?

The Bhagavadgita upholds sacrificial actions and various types of sacrifices (yajnas) mentioned before. They play an important role in the liberation of beings and in ensuring the order and regularity of the world. Life is a continuous sacrifice, and every action in it can be transformed into a sacrificial offering to the eternal (sanatana) Brahman. Yajnas do not mean ritual sacrifices (dravya yajnas) only. As Lord Krishna explained in the previous six verses, a sacrifice is a devotional offering in which one can offer wealth, thoughts, sense objects, breaths, desires, comfort, enjoyment, etc., to overcome desires and attachments or cleanse oneself. The idea behind an act of sacrifice (yajna) is that one should enjoy life after paying all the karmic debts one owes to God and his creation. By right, the first share of the gains of your actions shall go to him if you want to enjoy peace and happiness and be free from karma and bondage. Anyone content with the remains of his sacrificial actions is guaranteed a higher world or immortality. Hence, Lord Krishna compared the remains of sacrificial food (yajnasista) to Amrit, the heavenly nectar which is supposed to grant immortality to mortal beings. The implication is that by performing sacrifices and offering their fruit, whether they are thoughts, words, riches, actions, duties, or rituals, and enjoying what is left of them, one keeps collecting Amrita and qualifies for liberation.

Sacrifices lead to liberation only when they are performed without desiring their fruit. Those who perform them dutifully as prescribed by the Vedas with desires and attachments, seeking rewards for themselves, attain the world of ancestors (pitrloka) or the world of gods upon death according to the merit they accumulate. However, when their karma is exhausted, they would return to the earth to take another birth. If they continue to perform obligatory duties, birth after birth, in the form of sacrifices and uphold their religious duties (dharma), with the merit they gain from such actions, they will eventually overcome their ignorance and delusion, practice karma-sannyasa yoga, and attain the highest world of Brahman. Thus, those who perform sacrifices in one way or another secure a place in this world or a higher world, but those who sacrifice everything to God without any desire or expectation will attain the immortal heaven. Those who do not perform any sacrifices or duties and live solely for themselves will not enter any of the higher worlds. Weighed down by their sinful actions, wasting away their human birth, they will fall into the lower worlds of darkness and deny themselves the chance of taking birth as humans.

Sloka 32

evaṃ bahuvidhā yajñā vitatā brahmaṇo mukhe
karmajān viddhi tān sarvān evaṃ jñātvā vimokṣyase

evam = thus; bahu-vidhah = various types; yajnah = sacrifices; vitatah = spread out, extended; brahmanah = Brahman; mukhe =in the face; karma-jan = to be born of actions; viddhi = know; tan = then; sarvan = all; evam = thus; jnatva = knowing; vimoksyase = be liberated.

Thus, various kinds of sacrifices spread out in the face of Brahman. Know them all to be born of action. Knowing thus, you will be liberated.

Brahman is the source of the Vedas. They are considered Brahman in sound form (shabda brahma). Hence, they are revered as Brahman himself. Since they contain methods to invoke his power or attain him through various sacrifices and contemplative practices, their knowledge is considered inviolable and final in ascertaining metaphysical truths or resolving philosophical disputes. The Vedas are four: Rigveda, Yajurveda, Samaveda, and Atharvaveda. Each is divided into four parts: Samhitas, Brahmanas, Aranyakas, and Upanishads. The Samhitas contain invocations to various gods. The Brahmanas contain the procedural aspects of the rituals. The quality and efficacy of the sacrifice depend upon how closely and precisely they are followed. The Aranyakas, or the Forest Books, contain the mystic and symbolic knowledge associated with the rituals. Finally, the Upanishads, the end part of the Vedas (Vedanta), contain the knowledge of Brahman and liberation. Of the four parts of each Veda, the first two are known as karma kanda, the ritual or the action part. They are used to practice conventional sacrifices such as the dravya yajnas or fire sacrifices. The last two parts are known as jnana kanda, the knowledge part, which is used to practice internal rituals such as tapo yajna, yoga yajna, prana yagna, svadhyaya-jnana yajna, etc. This division of the Vedas into these two parts only holds well in most cases, but not all, since some Upanishads are derived from Brahmanas also.

All the sacrifices arose from the actions (karma) of Brahma, the creator god. They are meant to help humans perform sacrificial duties and attain peace and happiness. Knowing their purpose and performing actions without desires, humans can achieve liberation. The sacrifices can broadly be divided into ritual and spiritual types. Through them, one can achieve the four paramarthas or the chief aims of human life, namely Dharma (moral and religious duties), Artha (wealth), Kama (pleasures), and Moksha (liberation). The ritual sacrifices are meant for householders to perform their obligatory duties. The spiritual ones are meant for the seekers of liberation or those who want to cleanse themselves. Karma (action) is the basis of all these sacrifices because they involve physical and mental actions and produce consequences (karma phalam). Even in contemplative practices, one has to engage the mind, the senses, breaths, intelligence, etc. Hence, by saying that the sacrifices are all born of action, Lord Krishna conveyed to Arjuna that sacrifices are rooted in action, and even those who renounce worldly life cannot avoid them. Therefore, the best way to perform them is by doing one's duty without desires and attachments.

Sloka 33

śreyān dravyamayād yajñāj jñānayajñaḥ paraṃtapa
sarvaṃ karmākhilaṃ pārtha jñāne parisamāpyate

sreyan = better; dravya-mayat = using materials; yajnat = sacrifice; jnana= knowledge; yajnah = sacrifice; parantapa = O destroyer of enemies; sarvam = all, everywhere; karma = actions; akhilam = everywhere, in the whole world; partha = Partha; jnane = in knowledge; parisamapyate = culminate.

Better than dravya yajnas is jnana yajna, O destroyer of enemies. Everywhere in the whole world, O Partha, all actions culminate in knowledge.

Jnana yajna (the sacrifice of knowledge) is better than Dravya yajna (the sacrifice of material things). Why is it so? It is because knowledge is the foundation of all ritual and spiritual sacrifices (yajnas) and yogas. With the right knowledge, one can serve God better by performing sacrifices through the offering of food (dravya yajnas) and discerning him within oneself through the offering of surrender, renunciation, and devotion (jnana yajnas). Knowledge makes a karma yogi a better karma yogi, a jnana yogi a better jnana yogi, and a devotee a better devotee. Through knowledge and discernment, a seeker will quickly progress toward his intended goal of finding the Lord within himself and resting in him with devotion. Further, all actions and material sacrifices culminate in knowledge because, through observation and experience, and by knowing how actions produce sinful consequences, one learns important lessons, becomes wiser in thinking and conduct, and practices karma-sannyasa. Knowledge is also the basis of all actions, yogas, and yajnas. Be it karma yoga, jnana karma-sannyasa yoga, or bhakti yoga, one must cultivate the right knowledge to excel in them.

From the perspective of Dharma, material sacrifices are worthy since they promote the aims of Dharma and contribute to the welfare of the world and being. However, from the perspective of liberation, knowledge is more important. On the path of liberation, material sacrifices are considered inferior because they do not lead to immortality but to transmigration and rebirth. Material sacrifices are usually performed by priests who are well-versed in them. The host of the sacrifices (yajamana) does not have to know them. It is sufficient if he follows the instructions of the priests and performs the sacrifice without knowing the meaning of the mantras or their purpose. However, householders must pursue all four aims. The Isa Upanishad encourages people to pursue both material and spiritual goals to avoid self-destruction, stating that those who worship knowledge of sacrifices enter into blinding darkness, and into greater darkness enter those who worship knowledge of the Self alone. He who knows both crosses death and attains immortality.

To cultivate faith and devotion and achieve liberation, householders must perform their obligatory duties and acquire the right knowledge (vidya), which is found in the knowledge portion (jnana kanda) of the Vedas. By performing ritual sacrifices and practicing Dharma, they can purify themselves and qualify for a better life in the next birth. However, by pursuing knowledge, they can overcome ignorance and delusion and permanently escape from the cycle of births and deaths. Ignorance means not knowing your spiritual nature as a pure being untainted by sin or mental modification, the causes of your bondage and liberation, and the methods or yogas to attain liberation. Delusion means mistaking your physical self (mind and body) or your ego for your true Self. You can overcome them by acquiring the right knowledge (jnanam) through self-study (svadhyaya) and the grace of God or a guru. Therefore, in whatever manner you may begin your existence on earth, at some stage, you must eventually realize the importance of knowledge and pursue it for your material and spiritual progress, peace, and happiness. Through jnana yoga only, a karma yogi excels in karma-sannyasa, atma-samyama, and bhakti yogas. Through knowledge only and knowing their spiritual nature, they have the chance to advance from ego-driven animal nature (pasutvam) to self-driven divine nature (daivatvam).

Studying the scriptures, participating in spiritual discussions, listening to the words of enlightened masters, contemplating upon Brahman, and pursuing the study of Brahman (brahmavidya) are a few examples of how one may practice the sacrifice of knowledge (jnana yajna). You practice it by pouring the right knowledge (vidya) into your consciousness to improve your actions, cultivate discernment, cleanse yourself, and realize your true self or Brahman. In that sacrifice, you are the sacrificer, your internal organ (antarangam) is the sacrificial pit, the impurities such as egoism, desires, etc., faith (shraddha), devotion (bhakti) and aspiration are the sacrificial materials, the pure consciousness of the resplendent indwelling Lord is the fire and the knowledge (vidya) which arises from it is the fruit of the sacrifice (yajna phalam). The Vedic rituals have both material and spiritual aspects. Material sacrifices are usually performed to appease gods and obtain rewards from them. The spiritual sacrifices, where knowledge is essential, lead to internalizing the ritual practice and its elevation into tapo yajna or yoga yajna.

Sloka 34

tad viddhi praṇipātena paripraśnena sevayā
upadekṣyanti te jñānaṃ jñāninas tattvadarśinaḥ

tat = that; viddhi = know, realize; pranipatena = prostrating, falling at one's feet, obeissance; pariprasnena = by asking questions; sevaya = by rendering service; upadeksyanti = give initiation; te = to you; jnanam = knowledge; jnaninah = the knowledgeable; tattva = truth; darsinah = the seers.

Know that by falling at the feet, asking questions, and doing service. The enlightened ones, the seers of truth, initiate you into knowledge.

This verse explains how a student or a householder should approach an enlightened master (jnani) to acquire the right knowledge to perform his obligatory duties and pursue liberation on the path of karma-sannyasa yoga. Knowledge of the Self, mentioned here as That (tat), is necessary to engage in actions with the right awareness and attitude to avoid sinful karma and escape from samsara. The verse states that one should not approach anyone but a truly knowledgeable teacher who has witnessed the Lord dwelling in his body and possesses the knowledge of the sacrifices, tattvas, and gunas, and the spiritual knowledge of Brahman and liberation. In other words, the teacher should be well-versed in the ritual (karma) and spiritual (jnana) knowledge of the Vedas, the truths of Brahman and the Self, and the methods and techniques to attain liberation. This was especially important in ancient times when there were no other means to acquire esoteric knowledge, since all knowledge was taught orally. Students learned the scriptures from their parents and elders or from qualified and enlightened gurus who lived in seclusion or remote forests and were not easily available.

In ancient India, it was customary for students to approach renowned teachers and spend considerable time earning their trust and confidence through righteous conduct before they were admitted and initiated. There were some exceptions to this rule. For example, if the student belonged to a higher caste and the teacher came from a lower one, the teacher had the obligation to accept the student if he or his family had no personal blemishes. Teachers spent considerable time testing the character and conduct of their students, paying attention to their merits and family history before admitting them and initiating them on the path of knowledge. There were fewer restrictions on teaching the ritual portions of the Vedas, Vedangas, Sutras, and Shastras to qualified students. However, the Upanishads, which contained the secret knowledge of the Self or Brahman, were taught only to a few students who were interested in knowing the Self and working for their liberation. Upanishad means "sitting near." They were so-called because their knowledge was considered confidential and taught in person to the students when they gathered near their teachers. While the students chanted the Vedic hymns loudly to memorize them, they contemplated and memorized the Upanishadic verses silently or meditatively so that they remained a secret to the uninitiated. Further, teachers who knew the Upanishads were rare, and rarer still were those who knew all the important Upanishads and their meanings.

Even today, it is difficult to find enlightened masters who teach the knowledge of liberation. If you find one, you should consider yourself lucky and not waste the opportunity, since receiving initiation from an enlightened master is the fruit of your meritorious karma and does not frequently happen. How can a student acquire knowledge from him? An enlightened teacher will not be interested in teaching for monetary or material rewards. He does not care whether the student is rich or poor. By nature, he remains indifferent and equal to those who approach him for knowledge and admits them only if he finds them worthy enough. It is up to the student to impress him and learn from him.

Here, Lord Krishna suggested that the student who wants to acquire knowledge of the ritual and spiritual sacrifices or liberation should prostrate at the feet of his teacher, ask questions, and do service. Pranipata means prostrating on the ground with face downward and stretching both hands toward the deity or the object of veneration and joining them. Students have to do it before the teachers as a mark of respect, obedience, egolessness, and humility, and to show them they are eager to learn from them. In Hinduism, spiritual gurus are treated with utmost respect since they help their students purify themselves and attain liberation. Since they are also believed to be knowers of Brahman, they are considered Brahman's personifications. The salutation is just the introductory part. It does not convey much about the student since every student would do the same when approaching a teacher, hoping to impress him and find his acceptance or approval. Once students are admitted into the fold, they must prove their worthiness and readiness at each step until the end. They should ask questions to show that they are learning, inquisitive, and interested in learning further. They must serve the teacher by working in his household or serving him personally to prove that they are willing to perform their obligatory duties and serve others selflessly as students and grown-ups. The law books prescribe many rules and restraints for teachers and students to practice their respective Dharmas as karma yogis or karma-sannyasa yogis.

Sloka 35

yaj jñātvā na punar moham evaṃ yāsyasi pāṇḍava
yena bhūtāny aśeṣeṇa drakṣyasy ātmany atho mayi

yat = that; jnatva = by knowing; na = not; punah = again; moham = delusion; evam = in this manner; yasyasi = fall into; pandava = O Pandava; yena = by which; bhutani = all living beings; asesani = without exception; draksyasi = you will see; atmani = in the Self; atho = and, so also; mayi = in Me.

Knowing that, you will not again fall into delusion in this way, O Pandava; by that (knowledge), you will see all beings without exception in yourself and in Me.

Once you wake up from a dream, you will not fall into that dream again. Once you realize your true nature, you will not fall into mistaken notions about yourself. The undeluded will not be deluded by Maya. Once the Self awakens, it remains awake forever. In that expanded vision of knowing and understanding, everything becomes an extension or projection of the Self, and the awakened one will see all in himself. This is the essence. The delusion (moham) to which this verse refers is the mistaken notion that you are a physical being with a name and form. It arises due to egoism, attachments, and other impurities which are induced by the play of maya, and which create the deluded notion of duality, division, and the feeling that you are separate and distinct from others and from the rest of creation. Such deluded notions are destroyed only when you enter the supreme state of pure consciousness under the guidance of an enlightened master after subjecting yourself to rigorous self-transformation. In that state, which is infinite, indestructible, all-pervading, and all-encompassing, you will see yourself in all and all in you. You will realize that the same Lord who dwells in you as true Self and in whom you have dissolved your dual identity also exists in all as their very Self. It is an irreversible state. It means you will not fall into delusion again or consider yourself a physical being.

This verse may convey the impression to some that the individual Self (Atman) and the supreme Self (Brahman) are different. Followers of Dvaita (dualism) and Vishistadvaita (qualified dualism) do interpret it that way, with slight variations in their interpretation. However, its true meaning is that in the state of self-realization, first, you will realize that you are the eternal, indestructible, and all-pervading pure Self. At the same time, you will also realize that the same nature or pure consciousness in which you are fully absorbed is everywhere, and there is no other reality beyond your experience of oneness. The supreme state of pure consciousness is one without a second, whether it exists in you, in the world, or others. The vision of oneness, which comes with the realization that beyond the apparent nature, modifications, and disturbances of your mind, body, and senses, and in the deepest silence of your being, is hidden your true nature, and it is eternally the same, indestructible, and indivisible everywhere. The truth of it is vouched for in the Upanishads and confirmed by several seers and masters from their personal experience. It is the same vision that leads to such profound expressions as "I am Brahman (aham Brahmasmi)," "You are That (tatvamasi)," or "I am Shiva (Shivoham)." Not all schools of Hinduism agree with this view. They hold that the Lord in the body and the Lord of the universe may share the same consciousness, but are not the same. It is perfectly justified because the supreme state of Brahman is incomprehensible and indeterminate. Therefore, no one can ever be certain what the absolute state of Brahman is or is not. We can only vouch that the apparent reality is diverse, impermanent, and divisible.

Sloka 36

ced asi pāpebhyaḥ sarvebhyaḥ pāpakṛttamaḥ
sarvaṃ jñānaplavenaiva vṛjinaṃ saṃtariṣyasi

api = even; cet = if; asi = are; papebhyah = of the sinners; sarvebhyah = of all; papa-krttamah = sinner, the doer of sinful deeds; sarvam = all; jnana-plavena = by the raft of knowledge; eva = alone, only; vrjinam = the ocean of sin, misery or wickedness; santarisyasi = cross over.

Even if you are the worst sinner of all sinners, you will cross the ocean of impurities by the raft of knowledge alone.

Sin invariably accrues from our actions when we are subject to delusion and ignorance and perform our actions with egoism, desires, and attachments. Without the right knowledge and discernment and without knowing the causes of bondage and suffering and their solution, it is impossible to avoid sin or escape from it while living in this world. Just as it is impossible for the fish in an ocean to avoid water, the beings of this world cannot remain free from the impurity of sin. Sin arises from even mundane actions such as speaking, breathing, eating, sleeping, drinking, walking, cooking, and bathing. All the jivas are caught in the cycle of birth, death, and rebirth. Due to the play of maya and the influence of the gunas, they cannot avoid being tainted with impurities.

Vrujina has multiple meanings and refers to all the impurities to which we are subject, such as sin, misery, wickedness, deceit, guile, etc. Sin is their cause, and sin is their consequence. Our world is surely a vrujina, which is why it is difficult for the beings who are caught in it to escape from it. Yet, Lord Krishna assures us that there is no need to lose hope or feel despair.

Even the worst of sinners can escape from the world with the help of transcendental knowledge. Through jnana yoga, when they acquire knowledge and overcome their ignorance and delusion, they can stabilize their minds in the indwelling Lord described as the Self and become fully absorbed in him without duality. By that, they can safely cross the impure ocean of sin, suffering, physicality, and mortality and reach the immortal realm of blissful, pure consciousness where neither sin nor causes of sin exist. How this happens is explained in the next verse.

Sloka 37

yathaidhāṃsi samiddhognir bhasmasāt kuruterjuna
jñānāgniḥ sarvakarmāṇi bhasmasāt kurute tathā

yatha = just as; edhamsi = wood; samiddhah = blazing; agnih = fire; bhasmasat = to ashes; kurute = reduces; arjuna = O Arjuna; jnana-agnih = the fire of knowledge; sarva-karmani = all actons; bhasmasat = to ashes; kurute = reduces; tatha = similarly.

Just as a blazing fire reduces wood to ashes, O Arjuna, in the same manner, the fire of knowledge reduces to ashes all karma.

With the right knowledge, a karma yogi realizes what is holding him down and preventing him from attaining liberation from suffering and rebirth. He realizes that to burn his impurities, he must perform his obligatory duties without desires and offer their fruit to the Supreme Lord, who is the source of all actions. By that sacrifice, he cleanses himself and attains immortality. Thus, knowledge helps him burn all his karma, renders him sinless (anagha), and sets him free. That knowledge must be gained by the karma yogi through study, observation, philosophical inquiry, serving a spiritual master, and providence. However, knowledge alone is not helpful unless one renounces desires and practices karma-sannyasa yoga, performing desireless actions with discernment and offering their fruit to God as a sacrifice. By that sacrifice of desires, actions, and attachments in the fire of knowledge and wisdom, he attains perfection in his practice and qualifies for liberation. By practicing karma-sannyasa yoga with knowledge and discernment, he burns all his sinful karmas that have not yet been fructified and attains purity (sattva), tranquility, and sameness. What remains, in the end, is the prarabdha karma, or the karma that accrues from previous lives and becomes one's fate at birth for the current life. One has to exhaust it by letting it bear fruit or by earning God's grace.

The idea is also corroborated by the Yogasutras of Patanjali, which suggests that if we want to be free from karma, we must burn all the latent impressions (purva samskaras) in our consciousness. They act as the seed of our next birth and future actions. Without resolving them, one cannot be free. In the fourth chapter of the scripture (4:28), Patanjali states that the sense of egoism and the notion of I prevail even in those in whom discriminating awareness (viveka) arises because of the activities of the latent impressions, which are persistent and difficult to erase. If we want to be completely free from the consequences of our actions and escape from the cycle of births and deaths, we should burn those that are latent in our consciousness and inherited from past lives, and the newer ones that may form in this life.

Elaborating on it, Patanjali states that if one persists on the path of yoga, and as one enters into deeper states of meditation (dhyana) and self-absorption (samadhi), the sin-bearing latent impressions are gradually replaced or obstructed from bearing fruit by rtambhara prajna (wisdom-bearing) samskaras and nirodha (preventive) samskaras. Although such samskaras are pure by nature, having the ability to stabilize the mind and restrain the sin-bearing and outgoing latent impressions (vyuttana samskaras), they still lead to consequences and future births. To be eternally free, a yogi must resolve all types of latent impressions, which is possible only when he is fully dissolved in the seedless state of self-absorption (nirbija samadhi), where the indwelling Lord (Isvara) eternally shines without a second and without any movement or otherness. His mere touch or contact (brahma sparsha) makes one eternally pure and free, even in the embodied state.

Sloka 38

na hi jñānena sadṛśaṃ pavitram iha vidyate
tat svayaṃ yogasaṃsiddhaḥ kālenātmani vindati

na = not; hi = indeed; jnanena =to knowledge; sadrsam = comparable; pavitram = sacred, pure; iha = here, in this world; vidyate = is; tat = that; svayam = by itself; yoga = yoga; samsiddhah = perfected, ready, prepared; kalena = in course of time; atmani = in himself; vindati = knows, realizes.

In this world, there is nothing comparable to or as sacred as knowledge. That person who has skillfully attained perfection in yoga will realize the Self in time.

Knowledge distinguishes the ignorant and the deluded from the wise. It determines one's quality of life, actions, and progress in any endeavor. Hence, there is nothing comparable to it in this world. The knowledge mentioned here is the right knowledge acquired through study, observation, or learning with a pure, stable, and intelligent mind. Through the right knowledge, a karma-sannyasa yogi dispels false notions about the Self and actions and practices karma-sannyasa yoga, which will quickly lead him toward liberation. He will not achieve liberation immediately but in due course (kalena) since he has yet to exhaust the prarabdha karma of his previous lives, which will take time to resolve. Karma-sannyasa yogis who attain naishkarmya-siddhi, purity, and perfection are liberated only after they depart from here.

The importance of knowledge in achieving liberation from samsara is incomparable because nothing improves the practice or the possibilities of attaining a goal as knowledge does. It is the foundation of all skillful actions, yogas, and also their fruit. It is sacred (pavitram) because its source is not in this world but in heaven. Also, it neutralizes sins by letting us know how they arise and how they can be neutralized. If separation (viyoga) from the Self is the cause of our suffering, union with it (yoga) is the source of our liberation, in which knowledge is the connecting and revealing link, and duty and devotion are the driving forces.

True knowledge is purifying, uplifting, and liberating. It comes to us in two ways: learning from study and experience. The first one is gained by studying scriptures through self-study (svadhyaya) or learning from enlightened masters. The teachers may come to you in various guises in real life, in dreams, or meditative states and help you open your mind to higher knowledge. Experience is also a great teacher, which teaches you many valuable lessons if you are open to them and willing to learn from them. Knowledge gained from them helps the determined yogis cultivate discernment, overcome delusion and attachment to their physical bodies (deha bhava), develop the spiritual awareness (atma bhava) that the Lord in them represents their true Self, and realize that through contemplation and purification practices, they can find him and dissolve their duality and delusion in him. Knowledge of the body, tattvas (tattva jnanam), gunas, and obligatory duties helps them practice self-restraint and withdraw their minds and senses from sense objects to overcome desires and attachments and establish their minds within themselves. With the help of knowledge thus gained, they can eventually attain freedom from karma (naishkarmya siddhi).

Samadhi yoga means the state of sameness and equanimity (samsiddhi) attained by overcoming the duality of attraction and aversion and freedom from desires and attachments. It is attained by the persistent practice of karma-sannyasa yoga aided by knowledge (jnana), discernment (buddhi), self-control (atma samyama), and devotion (bhakti). For that also, knowledge is the foundation.

Sloka 39

śraddhāvāṃl labhate jñānaṃ tatparaḥ saṃyatendriyaḥ
jñānaṃ labdhvā parāṃ śāntim acireṇādhigacchati

sraddha-van = a faithful aspirant; labhate = gains; jnanam = knowledge; tat-parah = intent on, exclusively devoted to; samyata = controlled; indriyah = organs of action and perception; jnanam = knowledge; labdhva = attained; param = supreme; santim = peace; acirena = quickly, without delay, soon; adhigacchati = attains.

A faithful aspirant, who is intent and eager (to know) and has control over his senses, gains knowledge. Having gained knowledge, he quickly attains supreme peace.

Anyone who seeks knowledge of any kind requires these three qualities: shraddha (having faith), jnana tatparah, and samyata. Shraddha means having firm faith, without doubt, uncertainty, aversion, envy, reservation, condition, or disinterest. It strengthens your resolve to practice yoga despite obstacles and difficulties. Jnana tatpara, meaning the eagerness to know, learn, or acquire knowledge, is necessary to explore known avenues of knowledge and overcome doubt, confusion, and ignorance. Samyata means restraining, subduing, or controlling the mind and senses. By restraining the mind and senses, you can control your instinctual behavior, desires, and attachments and practice concentration and contemplation without distractions and disturbances.

These three criteria are also necessary to gain the true knowledge of the transcendental kind, which is free from duality and perceptions and which burns away all the latent impressions and the resultant karma. It arises when you excel in your practice with faith, intense aspiration, and control over your thoughts and desires, and attain perfection. Having gained the right knowledge, with your mind firmly stabilized in contemplation, free from desires and disturbance, you will attain samadhi yoga, or the state of peace, tranquility, sameness, and oneness. Faith is the foundation of all the yogas on the path of liberation. With faith comes strength and determination to persevere and reach the goal. Through inquisitiveness (jnana tatpara), you persevere and continue the practice. Through self-restraint, you strengthen your faith and resolve further. Controlling disturbing thoughts and desires or any weaknesses, you remain established in the Self with unwavering devotion. When you strengthen these qualities and perfect your practice, you will attain samadhi yoga, and the lamp of transcendental self-knowledge quickly shines in you. Just as darkness is instantly (acirena) removed when a lamp is lit, the light of the Lord flows uninterruptedly in your consciousness and dispels all traces of vestigial darkness. Thus, the three (faith, self-control, and knowledge) are interrelated and presented here in the same order of their relative importance.

Sloka 40

ajñaś cāśraddadhānaś ca saṃśayātmā vinaśyati
nāyaṃ lokosti na paro na sukhaṃ saṃśayātmanaḥ

ajnah = one lacking in knowledge, ignorant; ca = and; asraddadhanah = one without the wealth of faith; ca = and; samsayatma = doubting mind; vinasyati = perishes; na = not; ayam = this; lokah = world; asti = there is; na = not; parah = next world; na = not; sukham = happiness; samsayatmanah = skeptic.

The ignorant one without knowledge, without the wealth of faith, and with a doubting mind perishes. For the skeptic, there is neither this world nor the next world nor happiness.

The faithful aspirants (shraddhavan) who possess the three qualities, shraddha, jnana tatpara, and samyata, quickly attain liberation by gaining the right knowledge (jnanam) through unwavering practice. However, the ignorant ones (ajnani), who lack faith and interest to learn and are assailed by doubts, do not go far. Due to the lack the resolve and the determination to practice yoga or achieve liberation, they remain stuck in the mortal world, birth after birth. They do not achieve lasting peace and happiness here or in the next world. To be born as a human being in this world is an excellent opportunity to cultivate purity and discernment, know the Lord who dwells in us, and achieve liberation. Even gods do not have that privilege. Ignorant people do not realize the value or purpose of human life and waste the opportunity. They do not find it worthwhile to overcome their ignorance and delusion, practice self-control, study the scriptures, or cultivate knowledge and faith. They may still possess some knowledge and faith, but not enough to overcome doubts or stabilize their minds in the thoughts of the Self. With vacillating faith and skepticism and accumulating sinful karma from desire-ridden actions, they remain unhappy and restless, bound to the cycle of births and deaths. The skeptic will not find eternal happiness and fulfillment in this world or the next because both worlds are subject to impermanence. Only those who cultivate knowledge and faith and overcome the dualities succeed in stabilizing their faith and achieving liberation. The rest remain ignorant and bound. It is Nature's way of ensuring that the jivas are bound to her laws and serve her aims. By design, they are induced to remain ignorant, impure, delusional, and subject to her play of maya. Hence, only a few succeed in breaking free from her control and achieving liberation.

Sloka 41

yogasaṃnyastakarmāṇaṃ jñānasaṃchinnasaṃśayam
ātmavantaṃ na karmāṇi nibadhnanti dhanaṃjaya

yoga = yoga; sannyasta = renounced; karmanam = actions; jnana = knowledge; sanchinna = dispelled or destroyed; samsayam = doubts; atma-vantam = conquered the Self; na = not; karmani = work; nibadhnanti = do not bind; dhananjaya = O Dhananjaya.

Actions do not bind that person, O Dhananjaya, who practices karma-sannyasa yoga, whose doubts have been dispelled by knowledge, and who is in control of himself.

The yogi, who overcomes ignorance and doubts by cultivating the right knowledge of performing the actions the right way with self-control, is not bound by his actions. He does not accumulate sin as he dissolves his identity in the Lord who dwells in him, renounces all desires and attachments, passes on ownership and doership, and the fruit of all his actions to him, whether they are righteous or unrighteous. For him, actions cease to produce sinful consequences since he removes the poison of sin from his actions by renouncing the desire for the fruit of his actions rather than the actions. This chapter is called Jnana Karma Sannyasa Yoga, which means the practice of karma yoga with knowledge and renunciation. Kama yogis perform actions to fulfill their desires. They possess the knowledge of rituals (karma-kanda) and their duties to pursue Dharma, Artha, and Kama, but not the knowledge of the Self (jnana-kanda) or liberation (Moksha). Karmay yogis become karma-sannyasa yogis and advance on the path of yoga when they acquire the right knowledge to discern the Self in them and perform actions without incurring sin. They acquire the knowledge through jnana yoga, learning from self-study, teachers, or self-inquiry, and cultivate discernment through buddhi yoga. They practice austerities and self-control to subdue their minds and bodies so that they are not troubled by desires or the instability of their minds and senses. In that pursuit, faith and self-control are important. As we learned before, karma-sannyasa does not mean renouncing actions but renouncing the fruit of actions only. Karma means both actions and the fruit of such actions. Karma sannyasa yogis renounce the latter and sacrifice them to the Lord in them without expectations. Through that sacrifice and renunciation, they cleanse themselves and become conquerors of their minds and bodies (atmavanta).

Sloka 42

tasmād ajñānasañbhūtaṃ hṛtsthaṃ jñānāsinātmanaḥ
chittvainaṃ saṃśayaṃ yogam ātiṣṭhottiṣṭha bhārata

tasmat = therefore; ajnana-sambhutam = born out of ignorance; hrt-stham = in the heart; jnana = knowledge; asina = by the sword; atmanah = of the self; chittva = crush, smash, cut into pieces; enam = this; samsayam = doubt; yogam = yoga; atistha = becoming firmly established; uttistha = stand up to fight; bharata = O descendant of Bharata.

Therefore, crush this doubt of yours, which is born out of ignorance and entrenched in your heart, with the sword of self-knowledge, and become firmly established in yoga, O Bharata.

The doubt that Lord Krishna wanted Arjuna to overcome was about actions and the death he might inflict upon his close relations through them. Hence, he could not decide whether he should fight or withdraw from the battlefield. His doubt was born out of ignorance about actions and the Self. Lord Krishna advised him that he had the right to perform actions only and that he should renounce the fruit of his actions to God, who is the source of all actions. By that sacrifice, he would not incur any sin. He also told him that death was for the body but not for the Self. Hence, he should fearlessly fight without worrying about the consequences. In the last three verses, he emphasized the importance of faith (shraddha). In the last two, he also spoke about practicing self-restraint and overcoming doubts about the Self with the help of knowledge. He knew that Arjuna's confusion and sorrow were mainly due to his ignorance and lack of discernment. He knew that Arjuna's doubt and ignorance could be dispelled if he cultivated the right knowledge, faith, and discretion. Faith is the antidote to doubt, and self-control is the antidote to the weakness of the mind. Both are reinforced by the right knowledge or the knowledge of the Self and discernment. Hence, he advised him to crush the doubt that arose in him due to ignorance with the sword of knowledge and fight with faith and resolve, firmly established in karma-sannyasa yoga.

Conclusion

iti srīmadbhāgavadgītāsupanisatsu brahmavidyāyām yogasāstre
srikrisnārjunasamvāde jnānakarmasanyāsayogo nāma caturdho 'dhyayah

iti = thus; srīmadbhāgavadgītā = in the sacred Bhagavadgita; upanisatsu = in the Upanishad; brahmavidyāyām = the knowledge of the absolute Brahman; yogasāstre = the scripture of yoga; srikrisnārjunasamvāde = the dialogue between Sri Krishna and Arjuna; jnānakarmasanyāsayogo nāma = by name yoga of knowledge with renunciation of action; caturtha = fourth; adhyayah = chapter.

Thus ends the fourth chapter, named Jnana Karma-Sannyasa Yoga in the Upanishad of the divine Bhagavadgita, the knowledge of the Absolute, a treatise on Yoga, which contains the dialogue between Arjuna and Lord Krishna.

05 – Karma-Sannyāsa Yoga

The Yoga of Renouncing the Desire for the Fruit of Action

Sloka 1

arjuna uvāca
saṃnyāsaṃ karmaṇāṃ kṛṣṇa punar yogaṃ ca śaṃsasi
yac chreya etayor ekaṃ tan me brūhi suniścitam

arjunah uvaca = Arjuna said; sannyasam = renunciation; karmanam = of actions; Krishna = O, Krishna; punah = again; yogam = yoga; ca = and; samsasi = you praise; yat = which; sreyah = is better; etayoh = of these two; ekam = one; tat = that; me = to me; bruhi = please tell; suniscitam = decisively, clearly.

Meaning

Arjuna said, "O Krishna, you praise renunciation of actions, and again yoga (of action). Of these two, which one is better? Please clearly tell me."

Commentary

Traditional sannyasa yoga involves renouncing worldly life, desires and attachments, and obligatory duties. Karma-sannyasa involves renunciation of desires and attachments only. The former is practiced by those who give up worldly life and take up sannyasa. The latter is by those who possess the knowledge of the Self and discernment and perform their obligatory duties, renouncing the desire for their fruit. Arjuna wanted to know which was better, karma yoga or sannyasa yoga. He was still confused and undecided about whether to fight or abandon his duties and live on alms. Karma-sannyasa yoga is a hybrid between karma yoga and sannyasa yoga, containing the best aspects of both. His question shows that he had yet to fully grasp the true meaning of karma-sannyasa or the difference between karma yoga and karma-sannyasa yoga. Karma yoga is ideal for the ignorant and deluded, who cannot overcome their desires and attachments or are not inclined to cultivate the right knowledge, faith, self-control, and discernment. By engaging in obligatory duties and desire-ridden actions, they will enjoy the twin fruits of entering ancestral heaven and securing a better life in the next birth. Their chances of attaining liberation or overcoming sin and suffering are very limited.

However, karma-sannyasa yoga is ideal for them if they are willing to give up desires and cultivate the right knowledge and discernment to perform their actions as a sacrifice to the Supreme Lord. Neither sannyasa nor karma yoga is suitable for householders who want to pursue the ultimate goal of liberation. However, by combining them and practicing karma-sannyasa, they can improve their chances. In karma yoga and karma-sannyasa yoga, householders must perform their obligatory duties. In the traditional sannyasa, the renunciants do not have that obligation. When they take the vows of renunciation, they can give up their obligatory duties and worldly life and live a secluded life, practicing contemplation, austerities, and self-control to subdue their minds and bodies and burn their impurities in the knowledge of the Self. The Bhagavadgita defines true renunciation (sannyasa) as the renunciation of desires, not duties and obligations.

Thus, karma-sannyasa yoga is a better alternative for householders who possess knowledge and wisdom and are not merely interested in pursuing the four aims of human life to secure a better life in their next birth. By combining the best aspects of jnana, karma, and sannyasa yogas, they can elevate all their actions into sacrifices and attain liberation quickly. This path is known as Karma-Sannyasa Yoga. Knowledge, discernment, and self-control are its support. If it is practiced in conjunction with faith and devotion, it is even better. This yoga has been explained in some detail in the previous chapter and will be elaborated further in this chapter. It should not be mistaken for traditional karma or sannyasa yogas, but as an advanced practice that combines the best practices of jnana, karma, buddhi, sannyasa, and atma-samyama yogas. The terminology can be confusing if you have yet to grasp the meaning and purpose of sannyasa in karma yoga. Arjuna's question reveals that he had yet to grasp the essential practice of karma-sannyasa yoga and how it differs from karma and sannyasa yogas.

Sloka 2

śrībhagavān uvāca
saṃnyāsaḥ karmayogaś ca niḥśreyasakarāv ubhau
tayos tu karmasaṃnyāsāt karmayogo viśiṣyate

sri-bhagavan uvaca = the Supreme Lord said; sannyasah = renunciation; karma-yogah = yoga of action; ca = and; nihsreyasa-karau = lead to liberation; ubhau = both; tayoh = of the two; tu = however; karma-sannyasat = of renunciation of action; karma-yogah = yoga of action; visisyate = excels.

The Supreme Lord said, "Renunciation (of actions) and the yoga of action both lead to liberation. Of the two, however, the yoga of action excels over the renunciation of action."

Traditional Sannyasa yoga involves the renunciation of worldly (householder's) life and obligatory duties such as daily and occasional (nitya and naimittika) sacrifices ordained for householders and living in seclusion to pursue liberation. It differs from karma yoga, which is meant for householders and involves performing duties as ordained by the Vedas. According to them, as karma yogis, householders must perform their obligatory duties (nitya karmas) without desires. However, they may also perform some sacrifices (kamya karmas) to fulfill their desires in the pursuit of Dharma, Artha, and Kama. When karma yogis perform their duties without desires, they become karma-sannyasa yogis. As we learned before, karma-sannyasa does not mean renunciation (sannyasa) of duties (karma) but only the renunciation of desires that propel actions and the fruit of such actions. Therefore, it should rightly be called karmaphala-sannyasa yoga.

However, karma-sannyasa is also appropriate since yogis must renounce all desires, whether they are engaged in actions or not. Since actions are performed without desires, it is also known as nishkama karma yoga. Although different, both karma-sannyasa yoga and sannyasa yoga will lead to liberation. Shankara felt that Lord Krishna declared karma yoga to be better than sannyasa because sannyasa is more difficult and painful to practice. The chances of failure in sannyasa are also higher. Although Lord Krishna compared karma yoga with sannyasa in this verse, we must presume that he meant it to be karma-sannyasa yoga since this chapter is about it. Further, in the Bhagavadgita, karma yoga and karma-sannyasa yoga are often used interchangeably since karma-sannyasa yoga is an advanced version of karma yoga only.

Sannyasa is the right solution when one develops a distaste for worldly life and obligatory duties and decides to live as an ascetic or renunciant (sadhu or sannyasi) in seclusion away from worldly people. Renunciants practice self-control and self-purification on the path of liberation. They renounce all desires, observe their vows, rules, and restraints (yamas and niyamas), and practice austerities as ordained for them to stabilize their minds in contemplation and devotion. Karma yoga is suitable for householders who are content with performing their duties and pursuing the four aims of human life, living virtuously. Karma-sannyasa yoga is superior since it brings the spirit of renunciation into karma yoga and improves the chances of karma yogis attaining liberation. As the name implies, it is ideal for those who cultivate knowledge and discernment, recognize their spiritual nature, and remain detached, renouncing doership and ownership of their actions. Knowing that actions arise and subside in their minds and bodies, which belong to Prakriti, they neither participate in them nor take responsibility for them. Endowed with that wisdom, they perform duties selflessly and indifferently, without desires, attachments, egoism, and delusion, offering their fruit to God.

Here, Lord Krishna firmly declared that karma yoga is better than sannyasa yoga because renunciants do not contribute much to the world. They work for their liberation and remain indifferent to the world. In contrast, karma yogis serve God and his creation and play a vital role in ensuring the order and regularity of the world. Through their duties and actions, they preserve the world and family lineages, propagate Dharma, contribute to the creation and circulation of wealth, and, through sacrifices and procreation, ensure the transmigration of souls. They also serve the renunciants who approach them for food, gods, ancestors, and others through sacrifices. Thus, they play an important role in preserving and upholding Dharma and the world. Hence, the householder's Dharma (grihasta dharma) is considered superior to all other Dharmas, and karma yoga is superior to all other yogas. The world will not survive if householders renounce their duties and take up sannyasa. Therefore, it is not surprising that Lord Krishna declared karma yoga as superior to sannyasa. He also stated previously that he preferred to engage in karma yoga to set an example and inspire humans to follow the same. Although he has no desires, duties, or the need to achieve anything, he still performs his duties as a karma yogi and upholds his creation. Lastly, both karma yoga and sannyasa yoga are meant for those who have not attained liberation. The liberated ones have no duties, although they may engage in actions since they attain naishkarmya siddhi (freedom from karma) through nishkama karma (desireless actions).

Sloka 3

jñeyaḥ sa nityasaṃnyāsī yo na dveṣṭi na kāṅkṣati
nirdvandvo hi mahābāho sukhaṃ bandhāt pramucyate

jneyah = should be known; sah = he; nitya = always; sannyasi = renunciant; yah = who; na = never; dvesti = hates; na = not; kanksati = desires; nirdvandvah = free from dualities and pairs of opposities; hi = in fact; maha-baho = O mighty-armed; sukham = is easily, comfortably; bandhat = from bonds; pramucyate = is liberated.

He who neither hates nor desires should be known as the one who is ever engaged in renunciation. Indeed, free from dualities and pairs of opposites, O mighty-armed, he is liberated easily from all bonds.

Here, Lord Krishna defined a nitya-sannyasi as someone who is ever engaged in sannyasa through the renunciation of obligatory duties and worldly life or the renunciation of desire-ridden actions and their fruit (karma-sannyasa). The former involves renouncing duties, desires, and attachments, and the latter only desires or desire-ridden actions (kamya karmas). The traditional sannyasis shun worldly life and live in seclusion, practicing austerities, self-purification, self-control, contemplation, meditation, etc. Karma-sannyasis perform their obligatory duties with devotion while renouncing desires and attachments. They engage in selfless actions without desiring their fruit and offer them to the Supreme Lord as a mark of their devotion. A nitya sannyasi who practices either of the two yogas overcomes attraction (raga) and aversion (dvesha) through self-restraint, renunciation, and detachment. Therefore, he neither hates nor desires anything or anyone. Free from passions and emotions, and knowing that the Lord who dwells in him is his very Self and that all actions arise and subside in Prakriti in which neither participates, he stabilizes his mind and cultivates sameness and equanimity. Establishing his mind within himself and suppressing the gunas, desires, and attachments that arise from them, he quickly cultivates indifference or sameness towards the dualities, such as heat and cold or pain and pleasure.

Thus, giving up desires and attachments is important to achieving freedom from attraction and aversion, overcoming dualities, and suppressing the modifications of the mind. Whether one practices sannyasa or karma-sannyasa, the ultimate aim is to become detached from the lower nature of Prakriti and remain established in the higher nature of the Self, which is pure consciousness. If you conquer desires, you conquer the world within you and all its impurities that arise due to your constant interaction with the external world. By that, sannyasis on both paths escape from samsara. Since they do not accumulate new karma and their prarabdha karma keeps exhausting itself, they remain on a fast track to achieving liberation and freedom from births and deaths. Whether they live in seclusion or the midst of people, they abide by sameness and remain indifferent to the world and its dualities, unconditionally accepting what life offers, neither complaining about what they do not have nor escaping from the obstacles and difficulties fate (vidhi) puts before them. Finding the Lord within them and meditating on him, they live with stoical indifference even amidst the chaos of life. Having entered that pure state of freedom, they are easily liberated from their past and present karmas.

Sloka 4

sāṃkhyayogau pṛthag bālāḥ pravadanti na paṇḍitāḥ
ekam apy āsthitaḥ samyag ubhayor vindate phalam

sankhya = samkhya yoga; yogau = yoga; prthak = distinct, different; balah = the young, immature, the underdeveloped, the ignorant; pravadanti = say; na = but not; panditah = the learned ones; ekam = one; api = even; asthitah = being established, gaining mastery; samyak = properly, completely; ubhayoh = of both; vindate = gets; phalam = the fruits.

Children, not the wise ones, say Samkhya and Yoga are distinct. Established firmly, even in one with mastery, one obtains the fruits of both.

In this verse, Samkhya refers to the knowledge of the Self (atma vidya). Yoga refers to the practice of karma yoga or karma-sannyasa yoga with the knowledge gained from Samkhya. We have already proposed that the Samkhya Yoga of the Bhagavadgita refers to the combined practice of Samkhya and Yoga rather than the yoga of knowledge only. The Samkhya and Yoga of the Bhagavadgita have many similarities with the classical Samkhya and Yoga Darshanas of Hinduism, whose history dates back to the later Vedic period and which were undoubtedly pre-Buddhist. Followers of the Samkhya school pursued the knowledge of Purusha and Prakriti, the nature and influence of the gunas, karma, and liberation of the individual soul. Since it was a purely speculative philosophy with no applied aspect attached to it, ancient Samkhyas used the knowledge of Samkhya to practice the methods of classical Yoga to attain liberation. The practitioners of Yoga relied upon the knowledge of Samkhya for the same purpose since they had no independent philosophy of their own. Hence, the name Samkhya became historically associated with Yoga. As was the case in ancient times, the traditional Samkhya and Yoga Darshanas complemented each other just as Nyaya and Vaishesika or Purva and Uttara Mimamsas. However, the Samkhya of the Bhagavadgita differs from the original Samkhya in some respects, which we have already discussed in the previous chapter. The scripture expands the scope of Yoga to integrate several yogas (karma, jnana, buddhi, atma-samyama, sannyasa, and bhakti) around the central practice of karma-sannyasa and recommends it for householders to achieve union with the Self.

In the first verse of this chapter, Arjuna wanted to know which one was better between sannyasa and karma yoga. Lord Krishna replied that karma yoga was better than sannyasa. Here, he said that it did not matter which one was better. By having mastery over even one of them, one can achieve liberation.

Traditional Samkhyas practiced renunciation, endowed with discernment and the knowledge of the Self. They also practiced Classical Yoga, renouncing desires and attachments to realize the indwelling Self (Isvara) through contemplative and transformative practices. Hence, here, he referred to sannyasa as Samkhya while suggesting even that is as good as the other if one practices it perfectly. However, we can safely assume that the word 'yogau' in this verse does not refer to Classical Yoga. It refers to karma-sannyasa yoga only. Ignorant karma yogis engage in desire-ridden actions (kamya karmas). In contrast, the enlightened ones (the karma yogis who study the Vedas and discern the Self) perform desireless actions (nishkama karma) in devotion to the Lord who dwells in them, offer him the fruit of their actions, and absolve themselves of all sins. Through the yoga of desireless actions and sacrificial duties, they burn the impurities of their minds and bodies and attain liberation. Thus, the intent and purpose of nitya sannyasis and karma-sannyasis are the same, while their methods differ. Mastery in either of them is sufficient to attain liberation. Hence, he said that Samkhya yoga and Karma yoga are not different, and one can attain the fruit of both by gaining mastery in at least one.

Sloka 5

yat sāṃkhyaiḥ prāpyate sthānaṃ tad yogair api gamyate
ekaṃ sāṃkhyaṃ ca yogaṃ ca yaḥ paśyati sa paśyati

yat = whatever; sankhyaih = by yoga of knowledge; prapyate = obtained; sthanam = goal, destination, place; tat = that; yogaih = yoga; api = also; gamyate = reached; ekam = one; sankhyam = knowledge; ca = and; yogam = action; ca = and; yah = one who; pasyati = sees; sah = he; pasyati = sees.

Whatever goal is attained by samkhya yoga, that one is also reached by (Karma) yoga. He sees (truly) who sees both samkhya and (karma) yoga as one.

Whatever state is attained by the yogis who give up obligatory duties and practice renunciation (sannyasa) on the path of samkhya yoga is also attained by those who practice karma-sannyasa without renouncing their obligatory duties. Knowledge and renunciation of desires and attachments are the foundation for both. In sannyasa, one renounces desire and desire-ridden action. In karma-sannyasa also, the yogis do the same. Both discern their spiritual nature and establish their minds in the Self, withdrawing from the external world and its distractions. The main difference is that karma-sannyasis perform their obligatory duties while traditional sannyasis observe vows of renunciation and perform duties that are necessary to maintain their bodies and pursue liberation. Another difference is that samkhya yogis who practice renunciation may attain liberation in the embodied state and become jivanmuktas (liberated jivas) while still alive. In contrast, karma-sannyasa yogis will attain liberation only after they depart from here. Both engage in nishkama karma (desireless actions) only and renounce the fruit of their actions. Both establish their minds with devotion in the thoughts of the Lord, who resides in them as their Self. Thus, in both yogas, the end is the same: absorption in the Self, oneness or nonduality, sameness, freedom from impurities, and liberation from sin and samsara. They pursue different paths, but their goal is the same: to overcome the impurities of the mind and body through self-purification and escape from samsara. To accomplish it, they restrain their minds and senses, giving up desires and attachments.

Sloka 6

sannyäsas tu mahābāho duḥkham āptum ayogataḥ
yogayukto munir brahma nacireṇādhigacchati

sannyasah = renunciation; tu = but, however; maha-baho = O mighty-armed; duhkham = hard, difficult; aptum = attin; ayogatah = without yoga; yoga-yuktah = engaged in yoga; munih = the silent one, an ascetic person; brahma = Brahman; na cirena = quickly, sooner; adhigacchati = attains.

Renunciation is hard to attain, O mighty-armed, without yoga. Engaged in (this) yoga, a silent renunciant attains Brahman quickly.

Sannyasa and Karma-sannyasa are both good. However, sannyasa is difficult to practice. Renunciants will progress quickly if they practice karma-sannyasa while observing their vows and practicing self-control. Thus, renunciation (sannyasa) can be practiced the hard way by simply observing the vows of renunciation and following the methods and instructions of the teacher or tradition, or the easier way by practicing karma-sannyasa while observing them as a sacrifice and passing on the fruit of actions to the Lord who dwells as the Self with devotion. The goal of renunciation, which Lord Krishna mentioned here as difficult to attain, is oneness or union with the Self through sameness and restraint of the senses. He mentioned these two in the discourse while defining yoga.

Perfection in renunciation is hard to attain since the munis, the silent ones, who practice it must silence not only their speech, mind, and senses but also their desires and attachments, suppressing the gunas and not letting them influence their thoughts and actions. They must cultivate freedom from desires and sameness through austerities and self-control, overcoming attraction and aversion, and remaining the same to the dualities such as pleasure and pain, happiness, and sorrow. It is not an easy task unless they take refuge in the silence of the Self within themselves and remain established in it with perseverance. The mind is naturally fickle, unstable, and subject to modifications. It can quickly derail any effort to control or silence it. Hence, only a few ever attain perfection in sannyasa and achieve liberation. As they engage in self-purification and transformation, many demons awaken in their minds and unleash chaos, potentially affecting their physical and mental health. If they succumb to temptations and fail to control themselves, they also suffer from the twin consequences of breaking their vows and engaging in sinful karma. Hence, Lord Krishna rightly said that it is difficult to attain perfection in renunciation (sannyasa). Even a momentary lapse can make the recluses (muni) vulnerable to evil thoughts and demonic influences. The gods also do not cooperate with them since they give up sacrificial duties and deny them their daily nourishment. We learn from the Puranas that, displeased by their efforts to surpass them, the gods may put many obstacles in their path and try to discourage and distract them from their goal.

In contrast, karma-sannyasa is comparatively less painful and easier to practice. Since karma-sannyasa yogis take refuge in God and offer their actions to him without desiring their fruit, they earn his grace and live in his continuous protection. By surrendering to him unconditionally and practicing exclusive devotion, with their minds absorbed in his thoughts, they become dearer to him and attain him quickly. The gods also do not interfere with their progress since they receive from them their share of the sacrifices and remain contented. If the karma yogis stumble on the path or fail to control their desires and attachments, they will still earn the merit of upholding Dharma and keep progressing. As the Lord declared before, there is no failure on this path. Karma yogis who falter and fail in this life can always begin from where they left off in their next birth. Since they serve the Lord and do his work, practicing self-control and exclusive devotion, they enjoy his attention, love, and protection. Through their sacrifices and devotion, they also awaken the higher maya-shaktis in them, who will assist them in their purification and transformation and protect them from the deluding maya-shaktis. Thereby, they quickly attain liberation.

Hence, the Lord suggested that the silent ones (munis) should do the same. If they take refuge in him and practice karma-sannyasa when engaged in actions, they will attain Brahman quickly. Like karma yogis who pursue liberation, they should also pursue knowledge (jnana), cultivate discernment (buddhi), withdraw their senses and minds, practice self-control (atma-samyama), and engage in contemplative practices to stabilize their minds and, with faith and devotion, remain established in the Lord who dwells in them. The practice of sannyasa involves the renunciation of desires. It is the central aspect of sannyasa. Therefore, it should not be difficult for the renunciants to perform their bodily functions without desires and offer their fruit to them. Instead of starving their bodies and emaciating them with extreme ascetic practices, which was the norm in many renunciant traditions of the past, they should nourish the gods in their bodies through karma-sannyasa with detachment and without desires and selfishness. By that sacrifice, they will quickly gain control over themselves and attain oneness. The main difference between sannyasa and karma-sannyasa is that, unlike the karma yogis who practice karma-sannyasa, renunciants give up their household duties and family responsibilities and leave their homes, families, and worldly people to achieve liberation. It produces karma since it is an act of selfishness. It is also an act of Adharma since those who give up duties and responsibilities do not uphold their Dharma and incur the same sin as those who neglect them. They may not easily overcome those sins without practicing karma-sannyasa or establishing their minds in the Self with devotion and surrender.

Sloka 7

yogayukto viśuddhātmā vijitātmā jitendriyaḥ
sarvabhūtātmabhūtātmā kurvann api na lipyate

yoga-yuktah = skillful in yoga; visuddha-atma = pure natured; vijita-atma = master of the mind and body, self-subdued; jita-indriyah = conqueror of the senses; sarva-bhuta-atma = all living beings; bhuta-atma = the embodied self; kurvan api = even when engaged in work; na = not; lipyate = tainted.

He, who is skillful in (karma-sannyasa) yoga, pure-natured, master of the mind and body, conqueror of the sense organs, whose Self becomes the Self of all living beings, is untainted even when engaged in actions.

Karma-sannyasa is the shield that protects yogis from sin and suffering, whether they practice sannyasa yoga, jnana yoga, or karma yoga. It is the antidote to the poison of karma, which afflicts all beings on earth. Since humans habitually engage in desire-ridden actions and cannot remain idle, they cannot be free from sinful karma. Therefore, practicing karma-sannyasa yoga in conjunction with any other yoga method or practice is the best option for them to remain free from the impurities arising from their actions and attain liberation. Skill or mastery in any yoga and freedom from sin and suffering arise from karma-sannyasa only, since whatever method or yoga one practices should be practiced without desires, so they do not produce any consequences. Perfection in karma-sannyasa leads to pure nature (vishuddha atma) with subdued gunas, mastery of the mind and body (vijitatma), control of the senses (jitendriya), and the realization that the Self that dwells within is the same (Self) in all, and he is the Lord that one should worship. Madhavacharya commented that this verse contains four references to the association of the Self (Atman) with the four aspects of existence: Nature, the mind and body, the individual Self, and the Supreme Self, respectively.

Renunciation does not entail a life of inaction. For an aspiring yogi, it is a transformative and cleansing practice that requires karma-sannyasa as the balancing and sustaining force to deliver its promise of liberation. Even the most reclusive sannyasis have to perform actions to keep themselves alive and continue practicing their vows to attain pure nature, control their minds, bodies, and senses, and realize the Lord who dwells in them as their Self. Therefore, the best way to achieve liberation is not by abdicating duties, be they household duties or bodily functions, but by renouncing desires and desires for the fruit of such actions. Karma-sannyasa yoga is considered the best solution because it can be incorporated into any practice, method, path, or yoga. By practicing it, yogis of all backgrounds can work for their liberation without using painful and coercive methods to control their minds and bodies and without upsetting their lives or the balance of their minds and bodies. It does not impose too many conditions and restrictions and is comparatively easier to practice without the limitations of time, place, or environment. The toughest part of karma-sannyasa is overcoming desires and attachments, which is also the case with sannyasa. However, by remembering the Lord as the doer (karta) of all actions while performing them, be they household duties or devotional or contemplative practices, karma yogis can achieve the results even if they have not completely suppressed their desire. Those who practice sannyasa do not have that advantage unless they also practice it while performing their actions or observing their vows and leaving the results to the Lord they worship.

A skillful karma yogi who attains perfection in his practice of karma-sannyasa yoga knows how to let go of everything without the obligation to give up the world or his duties. Instead of giving up actions, he gives up ownership, doership, attachments, egoism, and delusion. Perfection (siddhi) in karma yoga arises from serving others through one's duties, and excellence in karma-sannyasa arises from knowledge, discernment, self-control, devotion, and renunciation of desires. These practices help yogis purify themselves and attain the selfless and desireless state of equanimity and sameness, subduing their passions and desires, resolving the gunas, restraining their minds and senses, and overcoming attraction and aversion.

Lord Krishna mentioned here three types of yogis who practice karma-sannyasa yoga on the path of karma, jnana, sannyasa, or bhakti yogas: the pure-natured soul (vishuddhatma), the master of the mind and body (vijitatma), and the controller of the senses (jitendriya). They refer to the three stages in reverse order in which yogis attain perfection and purification before they enter the fourth stage, the liberated state (sarvabhutatma). Thus, jitendriya (conquering the senses) is the first stage, vijitatma (conquering the mind and body) is the next, and vishuddhatma (attaining the pure or divine nature) is the third stage. In the final stage, they become liberated, having attained the highest purity, self-control, perfection, and oneness with the Self. In that state of oneness, they realize that the same Lord who dwells in them also resides in all as the Self of all (sarvabhutatma). With that realization, they take their practice of karma-sannyasa even a step higher by serving others, knowing that serving others and his creation is the same as serving him.

Sloka 8

naiva kiṃcit karomīti yukto manyeta tattvavit
paśyañ śṛṇvan spṛśañ jighrann aśnan gacchan svapañ śvasan

na = not; eva = indeed; kincit = anything; karomi = I do; iti = thus; yuktah = skillful or adept yogi; manyeta = thinks; tattva-vit = one who knows the truth about tattvas of the mind and body; pasyan = seeing; srnvan = hearing; sprsan = touching; jighran = smelling; asnan = eating; gacchan = walking; svapan = dreaming; svasan = breathing.

While seeing, hearing, touching, smelling, tasting, walking, dreaming, and breathing, the skillful yogi who knows the truth about the tattvas of the mind and body thinks thus, "I do nothing."

This and the following verse refer to the practice by which a sannyasi or a karma yogi who is skillful in karma-sannyasa yoga and knows the truth about the tattvas of the mind and body enters the first stage of perfection in his practice and becomes a conqueror of the senses (jitendriya). With the knowledge acquired through studying the scriptures or listening to the guru, he discerns the distinction between himself and his mind and body or between the Self and the not-self. This awareness is the key to excelling in karma-sannyasa yoga, restraining the mind and senses, and remaining uninvolved in their actions. Knowing that he is not his mind and body but the pure and essential Self, which is independent and indestructible, he sees himself as inactive while they are engaged in actions. When his senses move among sense objects, he remembers that the gunas are moving among the gunas, and he is not causing them to act. When desires arise, he watches them passively and quietly without acting upon them. Remaining passive, mindful, uninvolved, and detached while performing actions and thinking he is a mere instrument doing God's work, he attains the supreme state of inaction in action and freedom from karma (naishkarmya siddhi).

Thus, the true practice of karma yoga or sannyasa, which is essential to excel in karma-sannyasa or selfless actions, depends upon the perception or the conviction that one is neither the doer nor the owner of anything, and the right to perform actions and avoid karma arises from giving up all desires and attachments and offering the fruit of actions to the true support, the Lord within, who is also the Lord of all and to whom all this belongs. The knower of the tattvas and their actions (tattvavid) knows that the senses, mind, ego, intelligence, and the organs in the body are propelled by their nature and act according to the gunas in them. Detaching himself from his mind and body, giving up their ownership and doership, and subduing his desires and passions, he distances himself from his physical nature and remains indifferent to what happens to him or to the actions he performs. Cultivating the thinking and awareness that he is not his mind and body and that actions arise in them due to the gunas, he develops witness consciousness and excels in nishkama karma yoga. In the Ashtavakra Samhita (9.7) as well, we find a similar teaching, which says, "The moment you realize that the modifications of the elements arise and subside within the elements only, you are at once liberated from bondage and abide in your true Self."

Sloka 9

pralapan visṛjan gṛhṇann unmiṣan nimiṣann api
indriyāṇīndriyārtheṣu vartanta iti dhārayan

pralapan = speaking; visrjan = releasing; grhnan = grasping; unmisan = opening; nimisan = closing; api = even; indriyani = the senses; indriya-arthesu = with sense objects; vartante = are engaged; iti = thus; dharayan = holding.

While speaking, releasing, grasping, opening, closing, he thinks, 'The senses are engaged with the sense objects.'

The karma yogi and sannyasi who understand the nature of the tattvas and their functions (tattvavid) and who are skillful (yukta) in practicing karma-sannyasa with discernment know that true renunciation does not mean giving up obligatory duties and worldly life to live as a recluse. Sannyasa, for a karma yogi, truly means giving up desire-ridden actions and performing nishkama karma as a sacrifice to the Supreme Lord who dwells within, thinking that actions arise and subside in the Field of Prakriti, and he is not their source. Seeing himself inactive amidst the actions of his mind and body, and thinking that what happens in them happens in them but not in him, he does not incur karma even though he is engaged in them. By purifying his physical self and detaching himself from it, he witnesses the activities of his senses and other organs with disinterest and indifference. Thus, becoming a witness to his mind and body, renouncing desires, attachments, ownership, and doership, he transforms his life into a continuous service and sacrifice to the Supreme Lord, remaining inactive and passive amidst activity, and exemplifies the glorious state of inaction (akarma) in actions (karma). This is the height of karma sannyasa, a mark of excellence and skillfulness, which is attained by vishuddhatmas who achieve purity by subduing their gunas, vijitatmas who master their minds and bodies by conquering desires, and jitendriyas who withdraw their senses into themselves to restrain them and experience peace and equanimity.

Sloka 10

brahmaṇy ādhāya karmāṇi saṅgaṃ tyaktvā karoti yaḥ
lipyate na sa pāpena padmapatram ivāmbhasā

brahmani = Brahman; adhaya = by dedicating, placing, offering; karmani = actions; sangam = attachment; tyaktva = giving up; karoti = performs actions; yah = who; lipyate = is tainted; na = not; sah = he; papena = by sin; padma-patram = lotus leaf; iva = like; ambhasa = in the water.

By offering all actions to Brahman and giving up attachment, whoever performs actions is not tainted by sins, just like the lotus leaf in the water.

This is the essence of karma-sannyasa or skillfulness in karma yoga. Renouncing desires, attachments, and the fruit of his actions, the karma yogi becomes a pure soul (vishuddhatma). Realizing that desires and desire-ridden actions are the sources of karma and bondage, he performs actions as a sacrifice. Mentally detaching himself from his mind and body and controlling them, cultivating nearness to the Self (Brahman) who dwells in him, offering him all his actions with devotion, and identifying himself with him without duality, he remains untouched by the impurities of the world and his actions. He relinquishes the ownership and doership and offers the fruit of his actions to the Lord in him as a mark of his surrender, devotion, and egolessness. By that consecration and sacrifice, he remains pure, untainted by any sin or merit which may arise from them. Hence, whether he engages in karma, akarma, vikarma, dharma, or adharma, he remains sinless and pure amidst the play of Maya and the gunas, just as a lotus leaf that floats in water is untouched by its impurities.

Brahman is the lawful owner and inhabitant of this universe. All that is here belongs to him and is created by him. He is the source of all actions and manifestations. Therefore, we are supposed to live here as his true representatives, servants, or devotees and perform our actions for him as a sacrifice. As the Isa Upanishad declares, one should wish to live for a hundred years on earth by offering all actions to him. We cannot assume ownership or doership of anything unless we want to bear the burden of our sins and samsara. Nothing belongs to you. You do not create anything new that does not already exist in the universe in some form. All this is the domain of Brahman only. He pervades all, is hidden in all, and moves all. The idea behind karma-sannyasa yoga is that if you assume responsibility for your actions, you also become responsible for their consequences. However, if you perform them as an offering to Brahman without selfish intentions and pass on the ownership and doership to him, he takes responsibility for them and sets you free.

If we live selfishly for ourselves and perform actions to fulfill our desires, we cannot achieve oneness or sameness. We remain stuck in samsara since taking credit and ownership of what does not belong to us is sinful. Brahman is the provider, the sustainer, and the support. The air we breathe, the food we eat, the water we drink, and the energy we use arise from Prakriti, and Prakriti belongs to him only. Therefore, a karma yogi should live as if the world is an extension of himself and he is engaged in the sacrifice of life for the sake of Brahman, who represents that oneness and must offer all his actions to him. It is as if by offering your whole being, your life, and your actions, you perform a sacrificial duty or a devotional service to pay your debt and return to him what is due to him. When you relinquish desires and attachments along with the ownership and the doership of all actions that arise from your mind and body, which belong to him rather than to you, you become free from the weight of karma, rebirth, and suffering. You will be like a lotus leaf without being tainted by the impurities of the world or the consequences of your actions.

Sloka 11

kāyena manasā buddhyā kevalair indriyair api
yoginaḥ karma kurvanti saṅgaṃ tyaktvātmaśuddhaye

kayena = with the body; manasa = with the mind; buddhya = with the intelligence; kevalaih = only, merely, exclusively; indriyaih = with the senses; api = even; yoginah = yogis; karma = actions; kurvanti = perform; sangam = attachment; tyaktva = giving up; atma = self; suddhaye = for the purification.

With the body, mind, intelligence, and even with sense organs, the yogis perform actions, giving up attachments for self-purification.

This verse refers to karma-sannyasa yogis on any path who practice nishkama karma without desiring the fruit of their actions. They give up desires and attachments, and practice karma-sannyasa for self-purification when they use their bodies, minds, intelligence, and senses to perform actions such as austerities, restraints, withdrawal of senses, concentration, meditation, etc. The ego is not included in the agents of actions in this list because they surrender it to the Supreme Lord and do not let it interfere with their actions. The use of api (even) in connection with the senses conveys that they do not use them for enjoyment but for self-restraint. Restraining the senses and not letting them wander freely is also an action or an austerity. Yogis must practice it for self-purification, controlling their desires and attachments. Engaging in such actions and purifying themselves, they must subdue their gunas, minds, and bodies and become pure souls (vishuddhatma). Actions do not taint them or bind them because they consecrate them to Brahman, who dwells in them as the very Self, desiring nothing. As a result, the organs and tattvas of their bodies, such as the mind, intelligence, and senses, which bind ignorant and deluded people, remain subdued and cease to be troublesome as agents of Maya.

Skillful yogis control their minds and bodies by controlling themselves and not letting the world invade them and disturb them. When their organs perform actions, they remain indifferent, knowing that actions are performed by Prakriti, which belongs to God and not to them. Thus, remaining indifferent to their actions, not assuming ownership and doership, the karma-sannyasa yogis of any path achieve the pure state of inaction in action, meaning even if they performed actions, it is as if they have not performed any action at all. Thus, becoming witnesses to their actions, renouncing desires, ownership, and doership, they engage in nishkama karma to purify themselves with detachment and without becoming involved with the world or their physical nature.

The physical self is the seat of Maya and the field of Prakriti. It is filled with impurities, which incite egoism, ignorance, delusion, desires, and passions and bind the jivas to samsara. By knowing that only the senses move among the sense objects and he is not a part of them, a yogi becomes a conqueror of his senses (jitendriya). By discerning that only his intelligence, mind, and body perform actions, and he is not in them, he becomes a conqueror of his physical self (vijitatma). Further, by remaining detached and indifferent to all his actions, becoming a witness to them, and offering them to Brahman who dwells in him, the pure Self (vishuddhatma) enters his pure state without duality and realizes that he is the Self of all (sarva bhutatman).

Sloka 12

yuktaḥ karmaphalaṃ tyaktvā śāntim āpnoti naiṣṭhikīm
ayuktaḥ kāmakāreṇa phale sakto nibadhyate

yuktah = adept or skillful yogi; karma-phalam = fruit of karma; tyaktva = giving up; santim = peace; apnoti = attains; naisthikim = resolute practice, firmness, resoluteness; ayuktah = the unskillful yogi; kama-karena = impelled by or driven by desires, impelled by desire; phale = in fruit; saktah = eager, drawn, interested; nibadhyate = is bound, becomes responsible.

The skillful yogi, giving up the fruit of karma, attains peace with his resolute practice. The unskillful one, driven by desires and drawn to the fruit of his actions, becomes bound.

The verse describes the difference between a skillful and resolute (naisthika) karma-sannyasa yogi and a deluded and unskillful (ayukta) karma yogi. Endowed with knowledge and discernment, the karma-sannyasi engages in nishkama karma without desires and offers the fruit of his actions to God, thinking that actions arise from Prakriti (his mind and body) and that Prakriti does not belong to him but to God. By that renunciation of ownership and doership or agency (kartrtvam), he attains peace (liberation) and avoids sin. In contrast, the deluded karma-yogi, lacking in knowledge, discernment, and control, engages in desire-ridden actions (kamya karmas), thinking he is the agent of his actions and the fruit of such actions rightfully belongs to him. Taking responsibility for his actions and their results, he becomes bound.

Lord Krishna distinguished here between yogis who renounce desires and attachments and perform their actions with knowledge and discernment and the deluded ones who, being drawn to the fruit of their actions, perform them with desires and suffer from the consequences. Both perform actions, but they lead to different ends. Actions do not bind skillful yogis even if they perform optional (kamya) karmas or prohibited (nishiddha) karmas or perform karma, akarma, or vikarma, since they desire nothing from them. In contrast, the unskilled ones (ayukta) perform them to secure their lives or achieve something. They certainly eat sin by being selfish, claiming and enjoying what does not belong to them, and not offering it to the Lord to whom it truly belongs. Hence, they incur karma even if they practice Dharma, live morally, worship gods, help others, or perform righteous actions.

The resolute karma-sannyasi attains two kinds of peace by giving up attachment to the fruit of his actions: mental peace and lasting peace. The first one arises in the conquerors of the senses (jitendriyas) and conquerors of the mind and body (vijitatmas) who withdraw their minds and senses into themselves and remain established in the indwelling Self. Since they are unattached to their minds and bodies and renounce the fruit of their actions, they are not disturbed by success or failure or what happens or does not happen and remain peaceful, contented, and indifferent. They live with the conviction that the Supreme Lord, who dwells in all and controls all, will look after their well-being and decide what is good for them. The lasting peace, which is indestructible and immutable, arises when they gain complete mastery over their minds and bodies, enter the Supreme State of Brahman, and attain oneness, realizing that the Lord in them is also the presiding deity in all. The peace that follows from that realization is permanent, transcendental, self-existent, natural, and independent of external causes. It is attained by pure souls (vishuddhatmas) who realize the Lord in them in the state of non-duality as the Sarva-Bhutatma (the Self of all). The first kind of peace is temporary, while the second one is permanent and indestructible.

Since desires and attachments are hard-coded in our consciousness due to the presence of the gunas and since the karma accumulated in the previous lives is not yet fully exhausted, practicing karma-sannyasa yoga in the early stages of any path is difficult and painful and bound to result in repeated failures. Karma yogis who want to advance from traditional karma yoga to karma-sannyasa yoga have to battle hard to overcome conditioning, desires, and attachments and conquer their minds and bodies. Even the renunciants, jnana yogis, and bhakti yogis have an uphill task since it requires a complete reorientation in their thinking and attitude. It is easier to take vows of renunciation, but difficult to observe them. It is easier to pursue and acquire knowledge, but difficult to put that knowledge into practice without desires and expectations. Bhakti yoga seems to be easier, but it is not. Pure and unwavering devotion arises only when the mind is pure and completely free from egoism, delusion, desires, etc. Worship is also an act of karma and sacrifice, and must be free from desires and attachments. Only then does the devotee earn divine grace.

It is indisputable that without becoming skillful in karma-sannyasa through perseverance, none can achieve perfection in any yoga or attain oneness. Karma-sannyasa is not an end in itself but the means to practice any yoga on the path of liberation. It must be the basis for all actions in all yogas. One should, therefore, perfect it with skill and knowledge to succeed on any path.

Naistikam means firm, resolute, fixed, or final. Traditionally, it was used in connection with a religious student who continued to stay with his spiritual teacher even after completing his studies and taking a lifelong vow to practice celibacy. Its use here indicates that the practice of nishkama karma requires a completely dedicated and resolute effort, free from the impurities of egoism, selfishness, desires, and delusion.

Sloka 13

sarvakarmāṇi manasā saṃnyasyāste sukhaṃ vaśī
navadvāre pure dehī naiva kurvan na kārayan

sarva = all; karmani = actions; manasa = mentally; sannyasya = renouncing, giving up; aste = remains; sukham = in happiness; vasi = the self-controlled; nava-dvare = nine gates; pure = in the city; dehi = the embodied; na = not; eva = indeed; kurvan = performing actions; na = not; karayan = causing action.

Mentally renouncing all actions, firmly in control, the embodied one remains happily in the city of nine gates, neither performing actions nor causing them.

A yogi, who remains firmly established in the indwelling Self without duality, as the Lord himself, remains happy and blissful within the body, neither performing actions nor causing them to happen, even though his mind and body perform them. He renounces all actions, meaning he does not attach himself to them or desire their fruit. When they are performing actions, he thinks that Prakriti is responsible for them, and he is not in Prakriti. When desires arise, he thinks the gunas are responsible for them, and he is not in the gunas. When his senses are active, he thinks that the gunas are moving among the gunas through them. Thus, he becomes indifferent to what happens or does not happen within himself or in the world. He remains in firm control, meaning he restrains his mind and senses and remains on guard without letting any deluding or egoistic thoughts and desires enter his mind and disturb his peace and equanimity. Even if they do, he remains aloof, attributing them to his nature rather than to himself. He stays happily in the city of nine gates, which means he severs all connections with his body and lives in it as a tenant rather than its owner. He neither performs actions nor causes them, which means he renounces ownership and doership and does not consider that he is their cause. When he performs obligatory duties, he thinks that Prakriti is the agent and he is a mere witness, and their fruit belongs to the Supreme Lord, who is the source of all. Thus, he becomes a kevala (loner without attachments) and a nimittamatra (a mere catalyst or instrument).

A yogi on the path of liberation gives up desires and attachments to his physical identity, name, and form. By mentally separating himself from his mind and body, he becomes a witness to them rather than their owner and agent. Becoming firmly established in his spiritual nature, he looks upon his physical self (mind and body) with indifference as the agent of Prakriti, which acts according to its essential nature. For a yogi, his body is a physical construct formed by the association of tattvas and organs in which he lives temporarily to engage in God's work and fulfill his aims of creation. He becomes an inhabitant of his body (dehi) rather than a physical entity (jiva) who uses the body to fulfill desires or achieve selfish aims. For the indwelling Lord, the body is a vehicle. It has no independent existence of its own. Therefore, it cannot also be the independent agent of any action. All actions arise in the Field of Prakriti due to the gunas. The wise ones know this. Therefore, they do not involve themselves in their actions and remain aloof.

True renunciation is an attitude, a thought process, which is to be practiced spiritually in the mind (adhyatmika) while practicing any yoga, observing rules and restraints, or keeping the vows. The attitude of renunciation must be present in all actions and permeate every aspect of a yogi's conduct and consciousness, whether he pursues knowledge, practices renunciation, performs obligatory duties, or worships the Lord with devotion. To succeed in that effort, he must overcome the impurities through self-purification. Karma-sannyasa is also a purifier. Hence, one must begin practicing it in the early stages of any yoga and keep practicing it in all actions. It is indeed difficult to control one's desires and attachments and give up ownership and doership. The mind does not fall in line easily. It keeps churning out habitual thoughts until it is fully cleansed. Therefore, it would be unrealistic to presume that yogis do not experience desires. Even if they have progressed on the path, they may still experience them when their bodies rebel and crave food, water, or comfort. When those desires manifest, they should remain on guard, indifferent, and passive until the disturbances subside. It is a constant battle between nature and the seeker's resolve. Those who persevere eventually cross the threshold and make peace with themselves.

Sloka 14

na kartṛtvaṃ na karmāṇi lokasya sṛjati prabhuḥ
na karmaphalasaṃyogaṃ svabhāvas tu pravartate

na = not; kartrtvam = doership; na = not; karmani = actions; lokasya = of the world; srjati = creates, causes; prabhuh = the Lord; na = not; karma-phala = fruit of actions; samyogam = union, association connection; svabhavah = by essential or inherent nature; tu = indeed; pravartate = happen, occur, come into existence.

The Lord causes neither doership nor actions for the world nor the union between actions and their fruit. They happen according to the essential nature.

The Lord (prabhu) in this verse means the Creator or the Lord of the Universe. Although he created the world and beings, he has not endowed the jivas with the doership or the power to act independently. He does not determine what actions they should or should not perform. He also does not determine the fruit of their actions or what results or effects should arise from their actions. He does not unite effects with their causes, meaning he does not fructify any actions. Actions and their consequences arise from the jivas' inherent or essential nature according to the modes (gunas) and laws she governs under the will of the Supreme Lord. The Vibhu who dwells in the body as the embodied Self also does not confer doership on the jivas. He does not cause any actions to happen or not happen. He neither participates in the jiva's actions nor ensures what results should arise from them. They all happen in the Field of Prakriti according to the essential nature as determined by the gunas that are specific to each jiva. Jivas are bound to their bodies and perform actions according to their essential nature. That said, neither the Jivas nor Prakriti has any independence. They are also subject to the will of the Supreme Lord, meaning they are bound to the laws he established. He alone can change them or change someone's life, fate, or destiny if he decides to do so. He alone can rescue the jivas from the turbulent world of samsara or alter the reality, causes, and effects if he decides.

Neither the jivas nor the Self in them have any control over the results (fruit) arising from their actions or what has been destined by Fate or the laws of the Universe. In other words, jivas cannot escape from karma or the consequences of their actions or alter the course of their lives without divine intervention. The jivas have the power to perform actions but not to choose them. If they do, they will incur sin. They cannot determine the results that arise from their actions or desire them for selfish enjoyment. Since actions arise from the essential nature in the Field of Prakriti, the jivas should not participate in them with desires or the desire for their fruit. Instead, they should relinquish doership and be content with performing actions, leaving the results to him only. By that renunciation, they will escape from karma. We do not know whether the Self and the Supreme Self are two entities or the same. We presume that whether they are different or the same, they seem to perform different functional roles. In the jivas, the Lord remains passive and lets Prakriti do her duties, while in creation, he remains active and directs Prakriti to act according to his will and the laws he established.

Thus, humans should not view themselves as agents of their actions or masters of their fate, or think and act as if they have the power to act independently against the will of the Supreme Lord. Since the Lord is the source of all, whether directly or through Prakriti, they should live in gratitude to him and serve him by performing their duties selflessly as ordained by him to cleanse themselves and discharge their karmic debt. Being aware that they have no independent existence or freedom from suffering and rebirth, they should control their minds and bodies, overcome desires and attachments, and subdue their essential nature with the help of God, who is both the Self and the Supreme Self. As Lord Krishna stated here, all actions in the jivas arise from their essential nature, which is formed by the gunas and past life karmas. Therefore, one should focus on purifying it through self-control, detachment, and renunciation.

The Bhagavadgita envisions Prakriti as God's inseparable and dependent force. At the highest level, she is the Primal Force and God's eternal companion. However, there is no unanimity about this. Different schools describe her differently as eternal, equal, dependent, or independent, and free or under the control of Isvara. The Bhagavadgita describes her as the dependent force of the Lord and the material or instrumental cause of all actions, movements, and manifestations under his inviolable will. All causes and effects in the jivas arise and subside in her, while the Lord remains passive in the jivas as the embodied Self and active as the Lord of Creation. Although actions in the jivas arise from their essential nature, since he is their ultimate source, yogis should offer their actions to him only to escape from karma and bondage. By performing actions without desires and attachments and renouncing the fruit of such actions, they can subdue their essential nature and attain oneness with the Lord who dwells in them. Through that union, they attain liberation.

Sloka 15

nādatte kasyacit pāpaṃ na caiva sukṛtaṃ vibhuḥ
ajñānenāvṛtaṃ jñānaṃ tena muhyanti jantavaḥ

na = not; adatte = accepts; kasyacit = anyone's; papam = sin; na = not; ca = and; eva = even; su-krtam = good deeds; vibhuh = the Lord; ajnanena = by ignorance; avrtam = enveloped; jnanam = knowledge; tena = by that; muhyanti = deluded; jantavah = the living beings.

The Lord accepts neither the sins nor the good deeds of anyone. Knowledge is enveloped by ignorance. By that, the living beings are deluded.

Vibhu in this verse means either the jiva (who thinks that he is the master of his life and destiny) or the embodied Self in the jiva, without whom the jiva cannot exist. Neither of them has the power to accept the merit of good deeds or condone the sins of sinful actions. Neither of them can connect the causes to their effects, control, alter, or void the results arising from actions, or possess the power to act independently and cancel the consequences of any action. That power rests solely with the Supreme Lord of the Universe, who, through Prakriti, controls all this. However, he does not help or interfere as long as the jiva is bound to ignorance, egoism, and delusion, lacks discernment and self-control, and binds himself to samsara through desire-ridden actions. The Supreme Lord rescues him from samsara, the impurities of his mind and body, and the sins of his past only when the jiva overcomes his ignorance and delusion, discerns the Lord in him, and practices karma-sannyasa, knowing that all actions arise in the Field of Prakriti and that he is not their cause and does not have the right to enjoy their fruit.

This is an important teaching to cultivate discernment, renunciation, and self-control to neutralize Prakriti's deluding and binding influence and escape from samsara. If we become involved with the world and perform actions under the influence of the gunas or the desires and attachments they induce, we remain bound. The deluded and ignorant ones are left to their fate. Neither our limited knowledge and intelligence, Prakriti, the Lord who resides in us as the Self, nor the Supreme Lord of the Universe, who presides over the whole creation, helps them or interferes with their lives. Lord Krishna already said they should not be confused with the knowledge they cannot understand. Due to delusion and egoism, ignorant people may think that they can take care of their lives and destinies and, through self-willed actions, they can ensure their success and happiness, achieve their goals, or fulfill their desires. They may also think that by worshiping gods, performing sacrifices, and engaging in good deeds, they can neutralize their sins and attain liberation. All these measures are useful to improve karma, but ineffective in permanently resolving bondage and suffering. It is achieved only by practicing karma-sannyasa, renouncing desires, attachments, ownership, and doership, and offering all actions along with their fruit to the Supreme Lord with devotion and detachment.

The Lord in the body (vibhu) has no duties, obligations, or functions. However, the Lord of the Universe (Isvara) performs several functions. He is the Supreme Controller and source of all. He personally takes care of those who take refuge in him and worship him with exclusive devotion. If they earn his grace, he may also cleanse their karma and absolve them of all sins. Although all actions arise from Prakriti, he is the ultimate controller and source of all. Therefore, the assertions made in verse about Vibhu, the embodied Self or jiva, do not apply to him. If this is not the case, there will be no need to worship him or practice karma-sannyasa, offering all actions to him.

Although the Lord in the body remains passive and does not perform any functions, a yogi can transcend Prakriti and attain liberation by establishing and absorbing his mind in his pure Self or consciousness. In other words, although the Self is passive, it is the witness and the doorway to reach Brahman and his immortal realm. Just as devotees attain the Lord by worshipping his images with exclusive devotion, yogis can attain him by establishing their minds in the Self through unwavering devotion and self-absorption. The embodied Self in the jiva never engages in action in the bound or the liberated state. A liberated sannyasi or yogi, while practicing karma-sannyasa and radiating the Self, may create the impression that the Lord in him is engaged in actions. However, in truth, even in him, actions arise from his Prakriti (mind and body) only. The Self does not participate in them and remains passive and detached like a lotus leaf in water, untouched by the impurities of the world.

Sloka 16

jñānena tu tad ajñānaṃ yeṣāṃ nāśitam ātmanaḥ
teṣām ādityavaj jñānaṃ prakāśayati tat param

jnanena = by knowledge; tu = but; tat = that; ajnanam = ignorance; yesam = of whom; nasitam = destroyed; atmanah = of the Self; tesam = their; aditya-vat = like the sun; jnanam = knowledge; prakasayati = illuminates, shines forth; tat param = that Supreme Reality.

But those in whom that ignorance is destroyed by the knowledge of the self, their knowledge, like the sun, illuminates that Supreme Reality.

The knowledge that you are the eternal Self and not responsible for the sins or the good deeds of your mind and body is the knowledge (jnana) that destroys delusion and ignorance. In ignorant humans, that knowledge is enveloped by the delusion (moha) that they are physical beings with names and forms and are responsible for their actions. They do not perceive the Self. Hence, for them, the not-self or the body represents indisputable reality. Ignorance is the natural state of all the jivas who are subject to the triple impurities of egoism, attachments, and delusion. They assume the ownership and doership of their actions, thinking that they are responsible for the causes and effects that manifest through them in their lives. It binds them. Human beings have the unique privilege of overcoming it by acquiring the right knowledge about their spiritual nature and their distinction from Prakriti, which represents their lower nature. The knowledge of the Self dispels the darkness of egoism, delusion, and other impurities and illuminates their consciousness. Illuminated by that and discerning the Self hidden in them through the conquest of the mind and senses, the awakened karma yogi realizes that he is not the cause of his actions or the movements of his mind and body and has no control, ownership, or relationship with the fruit of his actions. Knowing that actions arise from his essential nature in his mind and body, not in him, he renounces them and the desires that propel them, offering them as a sacrifice to the Lord in him. With that knowledge and conviction, performing his actions without desires, he excels in karma-sannyasa and sets himself free.

Thus, bondage arises due to ignorance and freedom when that ignorance is dispelled by knowledge and discernment. Both happen in the field of Maya or Prakriti, in which the Self does not participate except as an enjoyer or witness. Here, knowledge means the awareness that you (the pure Self) are not your mind and body, you are not the cause or the controller of your actions, and you do not participate in them or their fruit. Ignorance is believing that you can control your life and destiny or overcome suffering and bondage through desire-ridden actions. If you have that knowledge, you are fit to achieve liberation. You will not need any further knowledge. Seeing inaction in action and becoming inactive amidst activity by restraining your desires and offering the fruit of your actions to the Supreme Lord, you will achieve the supreme goal of naishkarmya-siddhi (freedom from karma). Illuminated by that knowledge, your consciousness becomes dissolved in the pure consciousness of the Self.

Sloka 17

tadbuddhayas tadātmānas tanniṣṭhās tatparāyaṇāḥ
gacchanty apunarāvṛttiṃ jñānanirdhūtakalmaṣāḥ

tat-buddhayah = those whose intelligence is fixed in that; tat-atmanah = those who have That as their Self; tat-nisthah = those who firmly set their minds upon attaining That; tat-parayanah = those who are intensely devoted to That as their goal; gacchanti = attain; apunah-avrttim = state of non-return; jnana = knowledge; nirdhuta = cleansed; kalmasah = impurities.

Those whose intelligence is fixed in That, those who regard That as their Self, those who are intent upon attaining That, those who are intensely devoted to That, go to the state of irreversible non-return, with their impurities washed away by knowledge.

According to this verse, a karma yogi must fix his mind firmly in the knowledge and awareness that he is the eternal Self, distinct and different from his mind and body, and he does not participate in their actions or their results. Establishing himself firmly in that oneness and knowing that actions arise and subside in the Field of Prakriti, and he (the Self) is not their cause or effect, he must offer them to the Lord as a sacrifice. Having cultivated that abiding pure awareness and attitude, he must practice karma-sannyasa without desires, attachments, ownership, and doership. Those who are intensely devoted to this knowledge and its practice will ultimately enter the irreversible state of transcendence and oneness. Even if their minds and senses are active, they remember their connection with the Self and keep reinforcing it. Tad means That. The Upanishads use this gender-neutral word to refer to the Self, or Brahman, representing the Supreme Reality, whose nature is pure consciousness that is devoid of egoism, attachments, and delusion. It is different from the physical self (this), the beingness, or the not-self, which is enveloped by ignorance, egoism, desires, and other impurities.

Tad is your divine nature or pure Self, which is self-existent, self-illumined, and unlike your physical self, which is dependent and has no independent illumination. It is that part of your consciousness beyond your known personality and awareness, but remains hidden in it as the witness and the enjoyer. When you cultivate detachment and become established in it with devotion, you will progress from a state of ignorance to the irreversible and highest state of pure knowing. Thus, this verse describes how karma yogis attain the supreme state of liberation through successive stages, transitioning from ignorance to knowledge, darkness to light, and mortality to immortality through the renunciation (sannyasa) of desires and attachments. They are 1) cultivating the awareness of the Pure Self through discernment, 2) becoming firmly established in it, 3) strengthening the resolve to attain liberation, and 4) cultivating exclusive devotion. When the yogi excels in them, he will reach the final stage of oneness or union with the Self, which is irreversible.

Sloka 18

vidyāvinayasaṃpanne brāhmaṇe gavi hastini
śuni caiva śvapāke ca paṇḍitāḥ samadarśinaḥ

vidya = knowledge; vinaya = gentle behavior, subdued conduct; sampanne = endowed with; brahmane = on a brahmana; gavi = on the cow; hastini = on the elephant; suni = on the dog; ca = and; eva = even sva-pake = lowly person, an unclean person who cooks dog meat and eats it; ca = and; panditah = the learned ones; sama-darsinah = look equally.

The learned ones who are endowed with the right knowledge and subdued conduct look equally upon a brahmana, a cow, an elephant, a dog, and even a lowly and unclean person.

This verse describes how learned ones who are endowed with the right knowledge and subdued conduct practice sameness and look upon all with an equal eye. Shankara commented that the Brahmana, the cow, the elephant, and the dog mentioned in this verse represent the pure and impure states of the four classes of people. With the knowledge of the Self, the erudite ones look upon them equally with humility and consideration. Sameness is the hallmark of excellence in karma-sannyasa. It is the culmination of all yogas, which indicates that one has attained or is on the verge of reaching the irreversible state of liberation. A karma yogi attains it when he is free from desires and attachments, overcomes attraction and aversion, and practices karma-sannyasa, remaining firmly established within himself in a pure state without duality. When he excels in karma-sannyasa and dissolves his impurities, he attains oneness and realizes that the Lord in him, with whom he has merged, is the same Self (sarva bhutatma) in all. In that state of oneness and sameness (samadhi), seeing himself as the witness in all and of all, he does not feel superior or inferior to anyone or anything. Establishing himself in sama-darsana (the vision of sameness), from that vantage, he treats all, the high and the low, the pure and the impure, as equal or as he would treat himself.

By nature, we are judgmental. We tend to compare, contrast, and categorize things and people to make sense of them and the world. Our thoughts, opinions, feelings, and judgments arise from our beliefs, desires, attitudes, likes, and dislikes, which are, in turn, determined by the gunas that shape our essential nature. The learned ones (panditas) know through discernment that the apparent diversity of the manifest world is but an interplay of the gunas or modes and that hidden behind them and pervading through them is the eternal Self, which is the same in all. It may remain hidden in different classes of jivas, but it is the same. With that realization, they experience the unity of all creation and develop sameness towards all, seeing the same Self in all and everywhere. They may acknowledge outward distinctions and diversity, but will not let it influence their thinking or attitude towards the world or the people and things with whom they interact. Firmly established within themselves in oneness, remaining uninvolved, detached, passive, and peaceful, they treat all beings with the same respect and reverence as if they are the different faces of the same Supreme Reality.

Learning and knowledge (pandityam) should improve human behavior, attitude, character, and conduct. It should broaden the mind and make people look upon the world with tolerance, inclusiveness, and compassion. Knowledge should make people more sympathetic and merciful since everyone in the mortal world suffers and is hopelessly driven to engage in actions by the modes of Nature. But unfortunately, our education system does not teach people to cultivate sameness or good values. It does not help you much to see the world with an equal eye or see the underlying unity or oneness with the whole world. Instead, it makes people see its diversity and how they are wedged against it. That feeling of separation and smallness (anavatvam) makes them even more competitive, selfish, ambitious, and aggressive, which is why the world is perpetually riddled with class conflicts, wars, envy, anger, greed, and strife. A truly learned person is like a silent sage (muni) who sees the oneness of the whole existence, overcomes selfishness, sees himself in all, and exemplifies karma-sannyasa even in thinking and attitude. He consciously remains silent because he knows that all thoughts, opinions, judgments, and attitudes arise and subside in the field of Prakriti (kshetra), and he is neither responsible for them nor should assume ownership or feel pride. Seeing the presence of oneness everywhere and in everyone and knowing that duality and diversity, including the diversity of opinions and appearances, belong to the domain of Nature, he remains equal to everything.

Sloka 19

ihaiva tair jitaḥ sargo yeṣāṃ sāmye sthitaṃ manaḥ
nirdoṣaṃ hi samaṃ brahma tasmād brahmaṇi te sthitāḥ

iha = here in this world; eva = itself; taih = by them; jitah = conquered; sargah = rebirth, creation, succession of life; yesam = whose; samye = in sameness; sthitam = established; manah = mind; nirdosam = without defects, impurities; hi = alone; samam = equal to all; brahma = Brahman; tasmat = therefore; brahmani = in Brahman; te = they; sthitah = are established.

In this world itself, rebirth is conquered by those whose mind is established in sameness. Brahman is free from impurities and equal to all. Therefore, they are established in Brahman only.

Those who establish their minds in Brahman, realize him as their very Self in oneness. They see themselves in all, see that oneness as all-pervading, and treat everyone as equal, knowing that Brahman, who represents that oneness and sameness, is pure amidst the impurities of all existence and untainted and undisturbed in all living beings. For them, the distinction of Brahmana, Kshatriya, or Sudra does not arise, nor the distinction between humans and animals. They see the diversity through their senses but feel their underlying unity, oneness, and sameness in their hearts. However, the ignorant ones who do not realize Brahman see the jivas but not the Self in them, which connects them all. Therefore, they look upon people as pure, impure, noble, not noble, superior, inferior, etc., not knowing that their spiritual nature and connection with God, which unites them all at a deeper level, is untainted, even if their bodies are pure or impure. Therefore, they judge people according to their birth or social status, ignoring that they all possess the same divine spark and manifest from the same Supreme Lord.

Thus, this verse speaks about the vision of sameness (sama darsana) cultivated by self-realized yogis who conquer rebirth and attain union with Brahman even while living on earth in the embodied state. Endowed with knowledge (vidya) and humility (Vinaya), and established in oneness, they look upon everyone, from the highest to the lowest, with sameness or equality. They attain the auspicious state of nonduality, sameness (samsiddhi), and freedom from karma (naishkarmya siddhi), overcoming the impurities of their minds and bodies and practicing karma-sannyasa, knowing that they neither participate in actions nor cause them to happen. Established firmly in the witness consciousness, with indifference, and without involvement, and seeing the same Self in themselves and others, they treat everyone equally as the manifestation of the Supreme Lord. The vision of sameness does not arise in them as an idea, concept, or moral necessity but as a natural extension of their oneness with Brahman, as they feel connected to everyone and the whole world through him and see the diversity of creation as an extension or projection of him.

Sarga means rebirth, the order of creation, or the orderliness of the worlds. Birth, aging, death, afterlife, and rebirth: this is the order (sarga) of creation and life upon earth. This world, the higher worlds of light, and the lower worlds of darkness constitute the order of the cosmos. It is a part of Rta, the natural rhythm of the manifest universe, which ensures the orderly progression of life, time, celestial bodies, seasons, duties, functions, laws, etc. Sarga is also the path by which individual souls ascend or descend into the other worlds, according to their actions and individual merits. All living beings are subject to these cycles within the cycle of creation. However, those liberated from the impurities (dosha) of Nature and fully established in Brahman are not bound to them, just as they are not bound to the cycle of births and deaths. Having attained sameness upon the earth and disconnected forever from the field of Prakriti, they attain oneness with Brahman when they depart from here and reach the world of immortality.

Sloka 20

na prahṛṣyet priyaṃ prāpya nodvijet prāpya cāpriyam
sthirabuddhir asaṃmūḍho brahmavid brahmaṇi sthitaḥ

na = not; prahrsyet = rejoice; priyam = the pleasant; prapya = gaining; na = not; udvijet = feeling unhappy, disturbed, agitated; prapya = gaining; ca = and; apriyam = what is unpleasant; sthira-buddhih = stable mind; asammudhah = without being deluded; brahma-vit = the knower of Brahman; Brahmani = in Brahman; sthitah = established.

Neither rejoicing upon gaining the pleasant nor feeling disturbed upon gaining the unpleasant, the stable-minded yogi and the knower of Brahman, who is free from delusion, remains established in Brahman.

The idea of gain and loss or pleasure and pain exists in those who are steeped in diversity and cannot see their connection to the all-pervading Supreme Lord and their eternal oneness with him. An ignorant person who identifies with his mind and body sees only diversity and duality. He considers that the physical self is the true self and reacts to pleasant and unpleasant experiences according to circumstances, thinking they are happening to him and he is responsible for them. His happiness and sorrow depend upon his perceptions and experiences, and his egoistic notions about them. The knower of Brahman overcomes the delusion and attachment to his body and abides in oneness. Therefore, when pleasant and unpleasant experiences or sensations arise in his body, he remains indifferent and does not react, knowing that they arise and subside in his body, not in him. He remains undisturbed and equal to all the modifications that arise in them. Having attained oneness with Brahman and established in pure consciousness through the continued practice of karma-sannyasa, renouncing desires and the fruit of his actions, and reaching the ideal state of inaction in action, he becomes the eternal non-doer. He sees the dualities of the impermanent world as the play of maya and the nature of life on earth (prakriti svabhavam). Since he sees Brahman in all and identifies himself with the all-pervading supreme reality, he sees the world with the vision of oneness (sama darsana). When you develop all-inclusive self-awareness, overcoming attraction and aversion and suppressing your desires and attachments, you will remain satisfied within yourself, untroubled by what happens or does not happen, and witness the world as a manifestation of Brahman without becoming involved with it and without judgment and reaction. Detachment is the foundation of this undisturbed vision.

Sloka 21

bāhyasparśeṣv asaktātmā vindaty ātmani yat sukham
sa brahmayogayuktātmā sukham akṣayam aśnute

bahya-sparsesu = in external contacts; asakta-atma = disinterested; vindati = finds; atmani = in himself or in his self; yat = that which; sukham = bliss; sah = he; brahma-yoga = supreme state of Brahman; yukta-atma = adept yogi; sukham = bliss; aksayam = inexhaustible; asnute = enjoys.

Disinterested in contacting the external sense objects, he finds within himself that supreme bliss. Thus, firmly established in the supreme state of Brahman, the stable-minded adept yogi enjoys inexhaustible bliss.

Becoming detached from his body, its gunas, and natural propensities, and cultivating distaste for worldly objects, he finds pure happiness in himself, independent of external things. Firmly established in sameness (samadhi) through yoga and practicing self-control and exclusive devotion, with his mind firmly fixed on the infinite oneness of Brahman, he experiences unending peace and harmony.

Deluded people do not experience the bliss of oneness because they remain established in duality and diversity and feel as if they are oppressed or threatened by the world. They remain restless, fearful, anxious, and uncertain about their future as they identify with their physical nature and take responsibility and ownership of what happens or does not happen to them. The outgoing nature of their senses prevents them from overcoming their attachment to external objects and their own bodies and from seeing their hidden connection with the whole existence. The karma-sannyasi who realizes that there is no permanent joy in the external world or in interacting with sense objects, which produce mostly pain and suffering, withdraws his mind and senses into himself, enters the boundless inner silence, and realizes his pure state as the all-pervading pure consciousness. Uniting with it, dissolving his impurities, he enjoys unending bliss. Attaining the highest and absolute state of Brahman in the flawless and seedless (nirbija) samadhi, with his internal organ completely purified, he enters the absolute state of Brahman and becomes fully absorbed in oneness in which the not-self becomes silent, subdued, and immaterial. He realizes that when he silences everything in him, the world becomes one, and he is indistinguishable from it at the deepest level below its apparent commotion and chaos.

These statements convey that if you want to enjoy the supreme bliss of your true Self, you must withdraw your mind and senses from pain-producing sense objects and become a passive witness to the play of Maya within yourself and in the world. When you are silent, indifferent, uninvolved, and unattached, subduing your mind and body, suppressing your desires and ego, and excelling in karma-sannyasa and pure devotion, you enter the supreme state of Brahma Yoga, where you will experience peace and oneness.

Sloka 22

ye hi saṃsparśajā bhogā duḥkhayonaya eva te
ādyantavantaḥ kaunteya na teṣu ramate budhaḥ

ye = those; hi = indeed; samsparsa-jah = born from contact with sense objects; bhogah = enjoyments; duhkha = suffering and sorrow; yonayah = causes, sources; eva = indeed; te = they are; adi = beginning; anta = end; vantah = they have; kaunteya = O son of Kunti; na = not; tesu = in them; ramate = take pleasure, indulge; budhah = wise person, discriminating person.

Indeed, those enjoyments that are born from contact with sense objects are causes of suffering and sorrow. They have a beginning and an end, O son of Kunti. A wise person does not take pleasure in them.

All sensory pleasures and enjoyments are fleeting and produce pain and suffering over time since they induce attachments through attraction and aversion and produce lasting consequences. Therefore, the wise ones cultivate indifference and do not enjoy them. They have a beginning and an end because they continue only as long as the senses are in contact with sense objects and disappear once the contact is lost. Their fleeing nature makes people restless and unhappy and, to their detriment, causes them to look for the same experiences repeatedly in search of permanent happiness. Since they are impermanent and produce suffering, wise people do not enjoy them. Instead, they seek lasting peace and happiness through union with the blissful Self, knowing that the bliss of the Self is self-existent, without a beginning and end, and does not depend upon external causes. Sensual pleasures and enjoyments keep the mind restless and unsteady, producing mental modifications (citta vrittis) and habitual thought patterns. A disturbed mind, which is caught in dualities and sense pleasures, experiences disturbances (viksepas) such as disease (vyadhi), idleness (styana), doubt (samsaya), carelessness (pramada), sloth (alasa), lack of detachment (avirati), confusion (bhranti), and instability caused by egoism (anavastitatva). Hence, Yogasutras (2.15) state that for a yogi who has knowledge and discrimination, everything here is suffering because all perceptions and experiences either lead to or arise from karma, pain, latent impressions (samskaras), the triple gunas, and mental modifications. They keep the mind and body impure and unsteady. Continuous indulgence in sensory pleasures also leads to mental afflictions (kleshas) such as ignorance (asmita), egoism (asmita), attachment (raga), aversion (dvesha), and longing for life (abhinivesa). They, in turn, lead to karma and further suffering.

Sloka 23

śaknotīhaiva yaḥ soḍhuṃ prāk śarīravimokṣaṇāt
kāmakrodhodbhavaṃ vegaṃ sa yuktaḥ sa sukhī naraḥ

saknoti = able to do, can; iha = here; eva = itself; yah = he who; sodhum = withstand, tolerate; prak = before; sarira = body; vimoksanat = death, departing; kama = lust; krodha = anger; udbhavam = source, produced from;

vegam = rushing flood of impulse; sah = that; yuktah = skillful yogi; sah = he; sukhi = happy; narah = human being.

He who can withstand in this world itself, before departing from the body, the rushing flood of an impulse born of anger and lust, that skillful yogi is a happy human being.

Kama also means desires. However, since it is associated with anger (krodha), the meaning of lust is appropriate here. Lust and anger arise only when the body is alive and before one departs from this world. They do not arise after one's death. Therefore, Lord Krishna specifically said, 'before departing from the body.' In the short span of life, if we succeed in overcoming passions and desires, we will be happy human beings. Passions and desires like anger and lust are powerful maya shaktis. They are especially active in impure bodies. When they arise with intensity, it is difficult even for the most experienced yogis to control them, remain uninvolved and detached from them, or not act upon them. As the Puranas indicate, even sages such as Vishvamitra or Parasara succumbed to them and created consequences for themselves and others. Kama and krodha are traditionally regarded as the foremost of the five chief evils, namely lust, anger, pride (mada), greed (lobha), and envy (matsarya). Due to their deluding nature, they have the power and strength to derail the practice of even the most advanced yogis. Unless one is firmly established in karma-sannyasa yoga and cultivated sameness and detachment, it is difficult to remain indifferent and detached from them. True happiness (sukham) arises only when they are firmly controlled. Passions arise from the primitive brain, which is also the source of natural urges, instincts, and impulses that are difficult to control. Therefore, humans cannot easily control the rushing flood of passions and emotions without cultivating the predominance of sattva through self-purification and transformation and practicing karma-sannyasa until perfection is attained. When the yogi sees the same Self in all and experiences oneness, desires and passions automatically subside.

Sloka 24

yontaḥsukhontarārāmas tathāntarjyotir eva yaḥ
sa yogī brahmanirvāṇaṃ brahmabhūtodhigacchati

yah = who; antah-sukhah = internally happy; antah-aramah = internally restful and blissful; tatha = so also; antah-jyotih = ligh within; eva = has; yah = anyone; sah = that; yogi = practitioner of yoga; brahma-nirvanam = absorption in Brahman; brahma-bhutah = Supreme Being; adhigacchati = attains.

He who is internally happy, internally restful and blissful, and who has light within, that practitioner of yoga attains Brahman and becomes absorbed in him.

The self-realized karma-sannyasi remains uninvolved and disentangled from his mind, body, and external world. He derives his happiness, peace, and joy from within himself, performing actions to keep his body alive without desires and attachments. Even if his senses move among the sense objects, they do not produce desires or passions since the maya shaktis in him remain subdued. Thus, free from the gunas and their influence, the external world, and its objects, he rests his mind in silence and finds peace and happiness within himself, mentally detached from his past, present, name, and form. Antah sukha means inborn happiness, which is independent of external circumstances or contact with sense objects. Self-induced happiness is the natural state of a self-realized person, irrespective of the conditions that produce various emotional states in deluded people. It does not arise from having things and enjoying them but from the spiritual state of inner freedom (from dualities), oneness, and sameness, which arise from the direct experience of Brahman within, without any intermediary agent. Whether asleep or awake, the liberated yogi is aware of the presence of the Self within and its universal presence in all things he perceives. He feels connected to the whole universe through his pure and tranquil Self. Therefore, he is always happy and self-satisfied.

Antah aramah means internally restful. The yogi rests his mind and senses in the silence and tranquility of his pure nature and dissolves his conditioned self, which is the source of duality and disturbance. Whether active or inactive, his mind is always engaged in devotion and restful in the thoughts of the Supreme Lord or the silence of his consciousness. Therefore, he is always peaceful, untroubled by dualities, fear, or anxiety, or having or not having anything. Arama also means the blissful condition or enjoyment. A yogi experiences bliss within himself due to his connection with his pure nature and absorption in oneness. He is always blissful and restful since he never forsakes his connection with the consciousness that represents oneness and the Lord of the Universe, who personifies it. Even though he lives in the body and is physically distant, he internally enjoys an inseparable connection with the Supreme Lord. Through the invisible bond of exclusive devotion and mutual love, he shares his blissful consciousness in the unified state (yoga) of oneness.

Antah jyotih means inner light. The liberated yogi is self-illumined. The light of pure consciousness radiates from his pure Self and lights up his antahkarana (internal organ) and body, which are purified by skillfulness and perfection in yoga. The light is not a reference to the physical light but to the incorruptible intelligence, discernment, and pure self-knowing, which manifests in yogis when they subdue passions and emotions and experience uninterrupted silence, oneness, or nonduality. The knower of Brahman is self-illuminated because unified consciousness arises in him spontaneously in the natural state of self-knowing (sahaja vidya) due to self-absorption, in which the mind and senses remain subdued and silent. In him, the pure state of undivided Self only prevails, giving no scope for duality, division, or separation. That light of Brahman's pure consciousness illuminates his consciousness in the wakeful, dream, deep sleep, and transcendental states. It manifests outwardly as mental brilliance (medhas), psychic powers, and physical vigor (tejas or varchas).

In this context, yogi means a karma-sannyasa yogi who achieves union with Brahman, having discharged his duties and attained sameness (samasiddhi) and freedom from karma (naishkarmya siddhi), overcoming desires and attachments. Brahmabhuta means the Cosmic Being, Isvara, or the Universal Lord. He is the manifested Brahman with qualities and materiality or beingness. The material universe is his cosmic body, supported by the unmanifested Brahman serving as his Cosmic Self (Hiranyagarbha) and passive witness. He is Brahman's reflection in the field of Nature, possessing the highest purity and supreme powers, with Nature serving as his dynamic energy under his control. Therefore, although he is embodied, unlike the embodied souls, he is eternally free and not subject to karma or rebirth. Brahma-nirvana means the dissolution of physical nature and absorption of the individual Self in the Supreme Self without a trace.

Sloka 25

labhante brahmanirvāṇam ṛṣayaḥ kṣīṇakalmaṣāḥ
chinnadvaidhā yatātmānaḥ sarvabhūtahite ratāḥ

labhante = gain, attani; brahma-nirvanam = dissolution or absorption in Brahman; rsayah = the seers; ksina-kalmasah = with their impurities greatly diminished; chinna dvaidhah = duality destroyed; yata-atmanah = in control of themselves; sarva-bhuta = all living beings; hite = welfare; ratah = engaged.

With their impurities greatly diminished, their duality destroyed, themselves under firm control, wishing the good of all living beings, the seers attain Brahma Nirvana, dissolution in Brahman.

The blessed state of the karma-sannyasa yogis, who achieve Brahman Nirvana or absorption in Brahman, is described here. In Brahma nirvana, you see nothing but Brahman everywhere and in all. The world disappears and, along with it, duality, division, and separation. What remains is the same Self, the state of oneness pervading all. The blessed yogis achieve it by destroying their impurities, overcoming duality and delusion, practicing self-control, and wishing for the welfare of all. The rishis are the radiant sages whose internal organs are lit by the light of pure consciousness from the Self within (antar jyoti) and who are well qualified to attain the blessed state of Brahma Nirvana. This verse describes how they dissolve their individuality in Brahman and attain that indestructible oneness. It mentions four processes through which it happens. It begins with the removal of impurities. They are greatly diminished and cease to be a problem when the yogis cultivate the knowledge of the Self, subdue their minds and bodies, transcend the gunas, and overcome desires and passions. Through karma-sannyasa, they neutralize their karma, and through exclusive devotion, they earn the grace of the Lord. With their impurities destroyed mostly, they become pure souls (vishuddhatmas). The impurities are mainly induced by rajas and tamas. However, from a spiritual perspective, even sattva is an impurity only since it also induces desires and attachments of the benign kind. Hence, the verse refers to the diminished state of impurities, not destruction. They can be neutralized through karma-sannyasa by offering actions to the Lord.

Duality is destroyed when the yogis transcend attraction and aversion and cultivate sameness towards the pairs of opposites, such as heat and cold or pleasure and pain. The duality of the Self and the not-self, or the subject and object, persists because of the activity of the senses. When one withdraws from them and abides in the Self, overcoming attachment to the physical self and worldly objects, it disappears. When one attains the pure consciousness of Brahman and becomes dissolved in it, the duality between the individual Self (Atman) and the Supreme Self (Brahman) disappears. In the transcendental state of self-absorption, only the oneness of Self remains without a second, and it extends in all directions from the stoical silence of the seer's mind. However, according to Madhavacharya, the proponent of Dvaita, the duality the seers overcome is not the fundamental duality between Atman and Brahman but the wrong notion that the Self is other than what it is. For the dualists (dvaitas), their duality prevails even after liberation. Self-control is foundational to all yogas and disciplines. It is attained by restraining the mind and senses, cultivating detachment and indifference, and establishing the mind with resolve in the Self. The fourth condition mentioned here is wishing for the welfare of all. When yogis realize that the same Self resides in all, they make peace with everything and enter the harmonious state of enduring love and compassion. For them, nonviolence ceases to be a practice or restraint and becomes a natural state and way of life.

Sloka 26

kāmakrodhavimuktānāṃ yatīnāṃ yatacetasām
abhito brahmanirvāṇaṃ vartate viditātmanām

kama = lust; krodha = anger; vimuktanam = freed; yatinam = the ascetics who practice self-restraints; yata-cetasam = minds under control; abhitah = everywhere, near; brahma-nirvanam = absorption in Brahman; vartate = is, exists, happens; vidita-atmanam = having known the self.

For the self-restrained ascetics who are freed from lust and anger, who keep their minds under control, and who have known the self, absorption in Brahman is possible everywhere and in all situations.

When you see the whole existence as one, pervaded by the same silence and pure awareness that extends from you, like the light that radiates from the sun, you understand what all-pervading means and how the seers can remain absorbed in Brahman everywhere. In the context of this verse, 'abhitah' means readily, near, everywhere, quickly, or from all sides. The verse suggests that karma yogis, who discern the Self and firmly control their minds, desires, and passions to attain him, quickly achieve absorption in the unified consciousness of the Self or Brahman (Brahma Nirvana) wherever they are. Since they attain the indestructible state of oneness or pure consciousness, they remain in that state everywhere and in all situations. Vidtatmanam means knowing from within that the pure Self one discerns beneath layers of surface consciousness and the total silence of successive contemplative states is the indistinguishable and indestructible true Self that is distinct from the physical self. Knowing the Self through study or hearing does not immediately lead to absorption in it. Cultivating the discernment between the two selves, a karma yogi has to practice karma-sannyasa to purify himself and engage his mind in the contemplation of Brahman or the pure Self, practicing dhyana yoga. It is explained in the following two verses and the next chapter.

Sloka 27

sparśān kṛtvā bahir bāhyāṃś cakṣuś caivāntare bhruvoḥ
prāṇāpānau samau kṛtvā nāsābhyantaracāriṇau

sparsan = the sense objects; krtva = Keeping; bahih = outgoing; bahyan = outside, external; caksuh = gaze, eyes, vision; ca = and; eva = certainly; antare = between; bhruvoh = the eye brows; prana-apanau = prana and apana breaths; samau = equal; krtva = doing so; nasa-abhyantara = within in the nostrils; carinau = moving.

Keeping the sensations arising from external sense objects external, fixing his gaze between the eyebrows, controlling and balancing the incoming and outgoing breaths as they pass through the nostrils...

This verse is incomplete and has to be read in conjunction with the subsequent one. The instructions given here apply to munis (karma-yogis and sannyasis), who engage in contemplative practices, restraining themselves and their bodily actions. Muni means the silent recluse who renounces the world, silences his desires, speech, mind, senses, and other organs in the body, and leads a contemplative life, with his mind withdrawn and established within himself or in oneness. He may be a jnana yogi, a karma yogi, a sannyasi, or a bhakti. However, he must invariably practice karma-sannyasa while performing actions because it is the best way to resolve karma and past life samskaras.

In this verse, you will find three yogic methods that are common to many yoga schools, including the Ashtanga Yoga of Patanjali, namely the withdrawal of the mind and senses (pratyahara), concentration (dharana), and breath-control (pranayama) by balancing the outgoing (prana) and incoming breaths (apana). During contemplation (dhyana), some fix their gaze between the eyebrows, traditionally believed to be the location of the inner Self (atman). Some do it by concentrating on the nostrils or the outgoing and incoming breaths. Pratyahara means withdrawing the senses from the sense objects into the mind and the mind into the Self. According to this verse, the muni should withdraw his mind from the sensations and perceptions arising from the contact of his senses with the sense objects and remain established in contemplation. Thus, keeping the external objects externally (bahirbahya), not thinking about them, and not letting them disturb his mind, he should practice restraint, detachment, contemplation, and exclusive devotion. Through these methods, the mind becomes tranquil, and one gradually enters a deeper state of pure consciousness where all dualities and divisions disappear, and only pure self-awareness remains without any other notion or awareness.

There is a strong connection between breath and the mind. Breath slows down when the mind is tranquil. It becomes quick and erratic when the mind is disturbed or restless. This common knowledge, which anyone can experience, has been used for centuries by yogis to control their minds by regulating their breathing patterns. Those who are skillful in yoga know how to control their minds and senses and experience peace and tranquility using various breathing techniques. Some yogis even succeed in holding their breath for a long time in meditation and remain breathless for extended periods.

Sloka 28

yatendriyamanobuddhirmunir mokṣaparāyaṇaḥ
vigatecchābhayakrodho yaḥ sadā mukta eva saḥ

yata = restraining, controlling; indriya = senses; manah = mind; buddhih = intelligence; munih = the silent one; moksa = liberation; parayanah = intently devoted; vigata = free; iccha = desire; bhaya = fear; krodhah = anger; yah = one who; sada = forever; muktah = liberated; eva = even; sah = he.

Restraining his senses, mind, and intelligence, the silent sage, intently devoted to liberation, freed from desires, fear, and anger, is forever liberated.

Restraining his internal organ, freeing himself from desires and passions, intent upon liberation, and detaching himself from all external sensations and keeping them external, the muni practices uninterrupted contemplation (dhyana) and attains liberation. A muni is a reclusive ascetic or a hermit who renounces the world and lives in isolation, practicing the silence of the highest kind. He may have attained the silence and purity of his mind and body through karma, jnana, or sannyasa yogas. When he is free from desires and passions and is satisfied within himself, with his mind engaged in devotion and contemplation, he enters the deepest silence of his mind. There, absorbed in himself without duality and division, he experiences the unified consciousness of his pure state, where the whole existence seems to be an extension of his own consciousness. As oneness or the state of nonduality becomes his natural state through the uninterrupted silence of his mind and senses, he exemplifies sameness, equanimity, and freedom from judgment, delusion, and egoism. Devoted to liberation (moksha parayana) and the Supreme Lord (bhakti parayana), he eventually enters the indestructible silence of oneness in the depths of his own being, where nothing can ever disturb him or subject him again to duality, division, separation, or rebirth.

Sloka 29

bhoktāraṃ yajñatapasāṃ sarvalokamaheśvaram
suhṛdaṃ sarvabhūtānāṃ jñātvā māṃ śāntim ṛcchati

bhoktaram = the enjoyer; yajna = yajnas, sacrifices; tapasam = tapas, penances and austerities; sarva-loka = all worlds; maha-isvaram = the Supreme Lord; su-hrdam = good-hearted companion, friend; sarva = all; bhutanam = of living beings; jnatva = thus knowing; mam = Me; santim = peace; rcchati = attains.

Knowing me as the enjoyer of sacrifices and austerities, the Supreme Lord of all the worlds, and the good-hearted companion of all living beings, he attains peace.

Peace is the permanent state of the supreme Brahman. Unified consciousness is the absolute state of Brahman, in which the division of this and that or I and you does not exist. He is pure consciousness without qualities, boundaries, attributes, modifications, movements, or the division of subject and object. Therefore, those who attain Brahman also attain eternal peace and indeterminate oneness. Peace in an earthly sense means freedom from suffering, duality, and modifications of the mind, but in the spiritual sense means freedom from samsara, fulfillment, completeness, independence, or self-existence. We already know that the Supreme Lord is the source, support, subject, object, and enjoyer of all sacrifices. On the path of karma-sannyasa yoga, all actions are transformed into sacrifices when a karma yogi offers them to the Lord selflessly without desiring their fruit. While ignorant karma yogis perform them as their obligatory duty, expecting divine rewards, those endowed with knowledge and discernment perform them without desires and attachments to express their devotion and commitment and attain freedom from karma (Naishkarmya Siddhi). By pouring their actions and impurities into the fire of knowledge, devotion, and renunciation, they attain liberation or the supreme state of absolute and eternal peace.

Brahman is also described here as the Supreme Lord of all the worlds (sarva-loka Maheswara) and an affectionate, good-hearted companion (suhrdaya). It is comforting to know that the Supreme Lord of all, who is by nature indifferent and free from desires and attachments, is also an affectionate friend of all and wholeheartedly helps them without expecting anything in return. Standing as their inner witness (antrayami) and consuming the fruit of their actions, he helps them achieve liberation or manifests their thoughts and desires according to their faith and devotion. In whatever way they approach him, he reciprocates their love, devotion, and faith, or the lack thereof, becoming a friend to those who look upon him as a friend and an enemy to those who envy, detest, or distrust him. Therefore, it is up to his devotees and the humans on earth how they approach him, regard him, or worship him. The Self within us is passive, but the Lord of the Universe is the supreme controller of all, who reciprocates our love and devotion and responds to our calls for help. He never deserts those who are pure, self-restrained, and exclusively devoted. However, if liberation is the aim, you can reach him through the pure Self in you only. It is the doorway to the immortal heaven. The path that leads to it is oneness or sameness.

Conclusion

iti srīmadbhāgavadgītāsupanisatsu brahmavidyāyām yogasāstre srikrisnārjunasamvāde karmasanyāsayogo nāma pancamo 'dhyayah

iti = thus; srīmadbhāgavadgītā = in the sacred Bhagavadgita; upanisatsu = in the Upanishad; brahmavidyāyām = the knowledge of the absolute Brahman; yogasāstre = the scripture of yoga; srikrisnārjunasamvāde = the dialogue between Sri Krishna and Arjuna; karmasanyāsayogo nāma = by name the yoga of renouncing the desire for the fruit of action; pancama = fifth adhyayah = chapter.

Thus ends the fifth chapter named Karma Sannyasa Yoga (The Yoga of Renouncing the Desire for the Fruit of Action) in the Upanishad of the divine Bhagavadgita, the knowledge of the Absolute, a treatise on Yoga, and the debate between Arjuna and Lord Krishna.

06 – Atma Samyama Yoga

The Yoga of Contemplation With Self-control

Sloka 1

śrībhagavān uvāca
anāśritaḥ karmaphalaṃ kāryaṃ karma karoti yaḥ
sa saṃnyāsī ca yogī ca na niragnir na cākriyaḥ

sri-bhagavan uvaca = the Supreme Lord said; anasritah = without depending or attachment; karma-phalam = fruit of action; karyam = obligatory duties; karma = actions; karoti = performs; yah = he who; sah = he; sannyasi = renunciant, renouncer; ca = and; yogi = yogi; ca = and; na = not; nih = without; agnih = fire; na = nor; ca = and; akriyah = without obligatory duties.

The Supreme Lord said, "He who engages in actions to perform obligatory duties, without attachment to the fruit of such actions - he is a sannyasi and a yogi; not the one who does not keep the sacred fires and does not perform obligatory duties."

Since we are now in the sixth chapter, let us briefly review what we learned. The Bhagavadgita is primarily meant for householders like Arjuna, who live like sannyasis (renunciants) but practice karma yoga to perform their obligatory duties. Karma yoga without renunciation of desires does not guarantee liberation. Hence, householders should overcome their ignorance and delusion, know their spiritual nature, and practice karma-sannyasa yoga, cultivating knowledge and discernment, overcoming desires and attachments, and offering the fruit of their actions to the Supreme Lord. Karma-sannyasa combines the best of sannyasa and yoga. Hence, yogis who want to achieve liberation should invariably practice it. It is also vital to practice jnana yoga, bhakti yoga, classical yoga, dhyana yoga, or traditional sannyasa. Success in these yogas depends upon self-control and renunciation of desires. In this chapter, we learn the importance of atma samyama yoga, or the yoga of self-control. It involves the restraint of the mind and senses or the mind and body, and contemplation of the Self. It is the closest to the classical yoga of Patanjali. Its continued practice leads to oneness, sameness, or samadhi. Hence, it is also known as samadhi yoga.

Having revealed the knowledge of the Self and the importance of performing selfless actions and establishing the mind within oneself to attain sameness (sama-darshana) and freedom from karma (naishkarmya siddhi), Lord Krishna next focused his attention on the importance of stabilizing the mind in the Self and attaining Brahma Nirvana or oneness through karma-sannyasa, atma-samyama, and dhyana yogas. This and the next five chapters reveal to us the Knowledge of Brahman, the Supreme Lord, and how to absorb the mind in his contemplation and attain his absolute state of indivisible, indestructible oneness. Oneness or nonduality is the ultimate goal of sannyasa and yoga. When you have it, you have peace, stability, and freedom from karma and suffering.

In this verse, Lord Krishna described a karma-sannyasi as a true sannyasi and yogi. He juxtaposed the two divergent practices of Indian spirituality, sannyasa and yoga, and presented them as the two sides of the same practice that leads to liberation. He said that a true sannyasi and yogi performs his obligatory duties without attachment to their fruit. He becomes a sannyasi by giving up desires and attachments and a yogi by practicing karma-sannyasa and establishing his mind in sameness with stability or steadfastness. From his previous teachings, we may conclude that cultivating knowledge, discernment, self-control, renunciation, and devotion is crucial to achieving perfection in both. For further emphasis, he added that those who engage in desire-ridden actions (kamya karmas) or abandon their duties cannot be considered true renunciants or yogis. Thus, he implied that to achieve liberation, one must be a sannyasi and a yogi at the same time. He becomes a sannyasi by renouncing desire and a yogi by achieving sameness through the yogic practices of withdrawal of the mind and senses, cultivating discernment, breath control, dharana, dhyana, etc.

According to Shankaracharya, Lord Krishna's words in this verse apply to householders only, not to those who practice the traditional sannyasa, renouncing sacred fires, obligatory duties, and worldly enjoyments. Madhavacharya felt that it applies to everyone. According to him, even though the traditional sannyasis renounce sacred fires and obligatory duties, they still keep their internal fires alive through austerities and perform their actions by renouncing desires. Along with renunciation, they also practice yoga to stabilize their minds in the Self and attain oneness. Whatever the truth, sannyasa and yoga are most effective when they are practiced together. They reinforce each other and help the yogis and sannyasis alike attain samadhi quickly.

The title of the chapter is Atma Samyama Yoga. It follows jnana (samkhya) yoga, karma yoga, and karma-sannyasa yoga. Its practice with knowledge, discernment, and renunciation leads to the knowledge of Purusha and Prakriti and their distinction, which is discussed in the next chapter. The purpose of atma samyama yoga is to control the mind and body (Prakriti) and attain oneness with the Self (Purusha). By mere contemplative practices, none can attain knowledge or liberation. Dhyana is one aspect of the yoga practice. To practice it uninterruptedly, one must possess the right knowledge about oneself, cultivate discernment, overcome desires, attachments, and other impurities, and establish the mind in the pure awareness of the Self. Pure and exclusive devotion arises when the yogi who is also a sannyasi (or a sannyasi who is also a yogi) worships the Supreme Lord with self-control, contemplation, and devotion and realizes that the Lord who pervades and controls all this also exists in him as his very Self. By dissolving himself in him, he attains the indivisible, indestructible state of Brahman. By yoga, we mean all the yoga practices mentioned in this scripture. By renunciation, we mean the renunciation of desires and attachments. When they are practiced together, one attains freedom from samsara.

What marks true renunciation is the attitude of indifference and detachment, or the state of desirelessness and egolessness, not the outward practices of wearing a robe, growing hair, giving discourses, or attracting devotees and followers. There must be a fundamental shift in awareness, thinking, approach, priorities, and choices. Whether one is a householder (yogi) or a sannyasi, both are considered sannyasis only if desires and attachments are absent in them and they perform actions without desiring their fruit. Appearances can be deceptive. Hence, people often fall into the trap of believing the namesake gurus and sannyasis, whose actions betray their selfishness, egoism, and desires. One becomes a sannyasi by the attitude of renunciation, which is better defined as the absence of desires and attachments rather than outward actions. A true renunciant does not renounce actions but desires and attachments only. His every action is a sacrifice and an offering to the Supreme Lord, who pervades all this and exists in all as the true Lord. He keeps his inner fires alive through devotion, restraint, and contemplation.

For the householders in ancient times, sannyasa was also an obligatory duty (ashrama dharma) in the last phase of their lives. After completing their grihastha dharma and family obligations, they were ordained to take up sannyasa and pursue Moksha or liberation, the fourth aim of human life after Dharma, Artha, and Kama. The occasion was marked by taking vows, giving up the use of fire, and living in secluded places or wandering from place to place. Although they gave up using fire, cooking food, or living under a roof, they kept alive their internal fires (tapa) through austerities and renunciation. In the last phases, they gave up taking water and food and gave up their lives. That was the traditional form of sannyasa practiced by Vedic people during the sannyasa ashrama. However, numerous ascetic groups also practiced renunciation in ancient India. They followed different traditions, beliefs, and practices, but renunciation was common to them. Lord Krishna suggested that even householders and yogis could practice sannyasa by giving up desires and attachments.

Sloka 2

yaṃ saṃnyāsam iti prāhur yogaṃ taṃ viddhi pāṇḍava
na hy asaṃnyastasaṃkalpo yogī bhavati kaścana

yam = what; sannyasam = renunciation; iti = thus; prahuh = they call; yogam = yoga; tam = that; viddhi = know; pandava = O son of Pandu; na = not; hi = indeed; asannyasta = without giving up; sankalpah = desire, intention; yogi = yogi; bhavati = becomes; kascana = anyone.

What they speak of as renunciation, know that as yoga, O Pandava. Indeed, without renouncing intentions, none can become a yogi.

In the verse, Lord Krishna drew a parallel between pure sannyasa and karma-sannyasa. In pure sannyasa, the ascetic gives up sacred fires, obligatory duties, and desire-ridden thoughts and intentions. In karma-sannyasa, a householder does not give up his duties or sacred fires but renounces desire-ridden thoughts and intentions, especially the desire for the fruit of his actions, which he offers to the Supreme Lord as a sacrifice. Common to both practices is renouncing desire-ridden thoughts and intentions. Essentially, the foundation of sannyasa and karma-sannyasa is the same since desires and desire-ridden thoughts and intentions are renounced in both. This is confirmed in the second part of the verse, which states no one can become a yogi without renouncing desires or intentions. In other words, to become a true karma-sannyasa yogi, a householder must renounce all desire-ridden thoughts and intentions like a sannayasi but should not renounce his obligatory duties. To be a true sannyasi, the yogi must renounce desires, attachments, and duties, but should continue to perform his bodily actions without desires and attachments and give up the fruit of his actions.

Thus, whether one is a householder on the path of karma yoga or a renunciant on the path of sannyasa yoga, the attitude of renunciation, or renunciation of desires and attachments, is the foundation of both practices. Only those qualify as karma-sannyasa yogis who have a distaste for worldly life and do not entertain desire-ridden thoughts and intentions while performing actions or otherwise. Since they renounce desire, they also do not desire the fruit of their actions. In the second chapter (verse 48), Lord Krishna defined yoga as equanimity or sameness (samatvam). Here, he defined it as the renunciation of desires. Both definitions are interrelated. Sameness or equanimity arises only when desires and attachments are renounced. A karma yogi who practices renunciation neither entertains any thought of performing desire-ridden actions nor seeks the fruit of his actions. He remains untainted, whether he performs obligatory duties (nitya karmas), prohibited actions (vikarma), actions that are normally considered sinful (kamya karma), or remains inactive and silent (akarma).

Sankalpa means giving shape to thought, intention, or desire through conscious and willful effort. Since desires are involved, it has the potential to produce karma and bind the doer. Karma yogis who desire liberation do not indulge in them. Renouncing desires and attachments and endowed with knowledge and discernment, they transition from karma yoga to karma-sannyasa yoga. Even renunciants (sannyasis) who give up worldly life and obligatory duties must practice karma-sannyasa while performing actions to maintain their bodies or keep their vows. Whether a yogi practices karma-sannyasa or pure sannyasa, he has to renounce desires and attachments, including the desire for the fruit of his actions. Even for the practice of self-control (atma-samyama), contemplation (dhyana), or exclusive devotion (bhakti), one has to renounce desire-ridden thoughts and intentions. Thus, renouncing desire-ridden thoughts and intentions is central and foundational to achieving perfection in other yogas.

Sloka 3

ārurukṣor muner yogaṃ karma kāraṇam ucyate
yogārūḍhasya tasyaiva śamaḥ kāraṇam ucyate

aruruksoh = of the one who aims to progress; muneh = muni, ascetic, sage; yogam = the state of yoga; karma = actions; karanam = the cause, means; ucyate = is said to be; yoga = atma samyama yoga; arudhasya = in control, well established; tasya = his; eva = certainly; samah = even mindedness; karanam = the means, cause; ucyate = is said to be.

For the sage who wishes to attain yoga, action is said to be the means. For the one who is well-established and in control of yoga, serenity is said to be the means.

Until one attains perfection in yoga, one must keep practicing it by performing actions without desires and attachments and offering the fruit of such actions to the Supreme Lord. Once he attains perfection and peace, he should remain established in peace and serenity or sameness. Obligatory duties are the means for those who wish to attain perfection in karma-sannyasa yoga by giving up desires and attachments. However, once they attain perfection in it, sameness or serenity is the means. Sannyasa may mean karma-sannyasa or pure sannyasa. In either case, one should not abandon actions. They must be performed without desiring their fruit, which requires the practice of withdrawal and self-control (atma-samyama). Once success is achieved in conquering desires and performing desireless actions (nishkama karma), the yogi must concentrate on keeping his mind and body under control (atma-samyama) and become established in equanimity or sameness, for sameness is indeed the culmination of karma-sannyasa yoga. In karma-sannyasa yoga, you have to perform obligatory duties. In sannyasa yoga, you have to give up duties and desires to practice equanimity, self-control, and sameness, living as a recluse. Both yogas are complementary on the path of liberation since the ultimate goal is Brahma yoga or oneness with Brahman. Perfection in the former facilitates progress in the latter.

For a karma-sannyasa yogi, karma (action) is the means to overcome desire-ridden thoughts and intentions in his works, while for the sannyasa yogi who has given up worldly life and obligatory duties, the practice of serenity or even-mindedness is the means, which is attained through self-control, equanimity, contemplation, and devotion. In the previous verse, Lord Krishna said that what people called yoga was but renunciation (yaṃ saṃnyāsam iti prāhur yogaṃ). He also said that renunciation meant renunciation of desires in actions, not actions themselves. Accordingly, renunciation is central to both yogas. In both yogas, one has to practice sannyasa (renunciation of desires) only. In the former, one practices it while performing his duties (Dharma) with devotion and discipline. In the latter, one practices it while observing his vows of sannyasa, restraining his mind and senses (atma samyama), and contemplating upon the Self with devotion (dhyana). In the former, one renounces desire only, while in the latter, one gives up duties and desires. Both are stages in the spiritual progress of a householder as he practices varnashrama dharma and advances from karma yoga to sannyasa yoga through karma-sannyasa. Knowledge (jnana) is the foundation for both, and renunciation and self-control are the support.

Hence, when a householder fulfills all his obligations and reaches the final stage of sannyasa, he must have already disciplined and purified himself enough and overcome attraction and aversion to qualify as a sannyasi with qualities such as detachment, discernment, purity, and sameness or serenity. Once he takes up sannyasa, he would be ready to practice self-control and meditation to stabilize his mind in the Self within and cultivate equanimity or sameness towards the pairs of opposites, such as pain and pleasure, heat and cold, etc. Thus, for a householder (yogi), karma yoga is the means to achieve self-purification and progress on the spiritual path until he enters the life of retirement (vanaprastha) as a recluse (muni) and prepares for the fourth and final phase, the sannyasa ashrama. In that phase, he renounces dharma and karma (duties) and practices self-control (atma-samyama) to attain the pure state of sameness, tranquility, equanimity, and self-absorption. It is true that nowadays, no one practices varnashrama dharma, but that was ideal when the Bhagavadgita was originally composed. However, those ideals are still relevant, and a householder can still take inspiration from them and practice karma-sannyasa until he is ready to give up worldly life.

Sloka 4

yadā hi nendriyārtheṣu na karmasv anuṣajjate
sarvasaṃkalpasaṃnyāsī yogārūḍhas tadocyate

yada = when; hi = only, truly; na = not; indriya-arthesu = for sense gratification, or sense objects; na = not; karmasu = in actions; anusajjate = is attached; sarva-sankalpa = all desires or intentions; sannyasi = he who has renounced; yoga-arudhah = established in yoga; tada = then; ucyate = is said to be.

Truly, when a sanyasi who has renounced all desires and intentions is not attached to sense objects or actions, he is said to be well established in yoga.

When does even-mindedness become the focal point of sannyasa yoga? When a yogi becomes a master (yogarudha) of karma-sannyasa yoga, achieving perfection in it, and qualifies to practice pure sannyasa. When is he considered to have achieved such a mastery? The answer is given in this verse. It is when he renounces all desire-ridden thoughts and intentions, does not engage in any actions for sense gratification, and is unattached to sense objects or his actions. Desires and attachments arise from thoughts and intentions (samkalplas). Hence, they should be restrained and controlled. However, the yogi may still engage in actions but renounce attachment, doership, attraction and aversion, egoism, ownership, and desire for their fruit. Restraining his mind and senses, he should think that he is NOT the agent or the cause of his actions and renounce all notions of individuality and involvement, attributing them to the Supreme Lord. Thus, renunciation means renunciation of desires and attachments, not actions. As Lord Krishna emphasized before, the attitude of renunciation is important and must permeate the yogi's consciousness. He must remain mentally detached from everything, becoming the witness self to his mind, body, and world around him. Only then does he qualify to be called a sarva samkalpa sanyasi (the renunciant of all desires and intentions).

Sloka 5

uddhared ātmanātmānaṃ nātmānam avasādayet
ātmaiva hy ātmano bandhur ātmaiva ripur ātmanaḥ

uddharet = uplift, redeem, deliver; atmana = by oneself; atmanam = oneself; na = not; atmanam = the self; avasadayet = debase, degrade; atma = oneself; eva = surely; hi = for; atmanah = one's own; bandhuh = kin, relation, friend; atma = the Self; eva = surely; ripuh = enemy; atmanah = one's own.

Uplift yourself by yourself; do not debase yourself. Surely, you are your own kin and truly your own enemy.

This verse can be translated in various ways, but the idea is the same. The first part says you must depend upon yourself, supporting your spiritual practice with self-effort and without degrading yourself with desire-ridden thoughts, intentions, and actions. The second part says that you are your best friend or your worst enemy in this yoga. For the yogi who restrains himself and practices renunciation, fully suppressing his desires and attachments, his lower self (mind and body) acts as his best friend. The Opposite is the case with the deluded one who lacks purity and self-control and engages in desire-ridden actions. Your mind and body become your friend or enemy, depending on your purity or impurity. They must be aligned with your spiritual goals. Self-control (atma samyama) is crucial to achieving this goal and being in harmony with yourself and with your goal of liberation. The be a pure soul (vishuddhatma), one must be a conqueror of his senses (jitendriya) and conqueror of his mind and body (vijitatma). Only then does the karma yogi have the chance to become skillful in yoga (yoga yukta) and the master of yoga (yogarudha). Your positive thoughts uplift you and lead you toward your goal, and your negative thoughts obstruct you and lead to your downfall. In worldly life also, the same principle applies. To be successful in any field, your actions must match your thoughts, goals, and intentions. It is even more important on the path of liberation because it is a solitary journey that happens entirely within yourself and by yourself.

A seeker of liberation is always a lonely traveler. He may have friends and well-wishers, but his journey is his alone, in which the ultimate goal is also aloneness (kaivalya) only, and his success and failure depend upon his thinking and actions. Even if you have a guru, he will show you the path but not walk with you. You have to make the effort yourself to achieve sameness or oneness, overcoming all dependencies and attachments and enduring hardships and suffering. You become your best friend when you perform your obligatory duties, avoid evil actions and conduct, and engage in self-control and contemplation with your mind fixed on the Supreme Lord. You harm yourself when you ignore your spiritual well-being and let your mind and senses run wildly, seeking enjoyment and gratification of desires. Thus, on the path of liberation, you are your friend or enemy, depending upon your goals, thoughts, intentions, conduct, actions, and attitude.

Sloka 6

bandhur ātmātmanas tasya yenātmaivātmanā jitaḥ
anātmanas tu śatrutve vartetātmaiva śatruvat

bandhuh = kin, friend; atma = the self; atmanah = by self; tasya = of him; yena = by whom; atma = the self; eva = very; atmana = of self; jitah = conquered; anatmanah = for one who has not conquered oneself; tu = but; satrutve = with enmity or hostility; varteta = acts, behaves; atma eva = very self; satru-vat = as an enemy.

Of him, who has conquered himself by himself, he is the friend of himself, but for him who has not conquered himself, he verily acts with hostility as an enemy of himself.

This verse emphasizes the importance of self-control (atma-samyama), which is vital to attain perfection in sannyasa and karma-sannyasa. In the previous verse, Lord Krishna stated how a yogi on the path of aloneness would uplift or degrade himself through his thoughts, intentions, and actions. In this verse, he suggests how a person will become his own friend or enemy depending on whether he practices self-control or not. This verse may confuse some, just as the previous one, due to the use of atmana or atma, which refers to both the person and the Self. The idea is the same. The yogi must restrain his physical Self from worldly pleasures to conquer desires, delusion, attachments, egoism, and other impurities and stabilize his mind in concentration and contemplation to experience serenity and sameness. The Self does not participate in any actions. It remains aloof, uninvolved, and indifferent amidst the dualities and impurities of samsara, witnessing everything as its own extension and seeing no separation or division. The mind and body must be aligned with it so that oneness or sameness becomes one's natural state. Therefore, the effort must come from you, the jiva, to purify your mind and body and align them with your pure Self. It is up to you to practice self-control, cleanse yourself, and work for your liberation. You must develop peace and harmony within yourself and feel connected to the rest of the world through the all-pervading oneness. Human life is an excellent opportunity because it gives us self-awareness, knowledge, and intelligence to regulate our lives and solve our problems, including the problem of bondage and suffering. Unfortunately, many people do not utilize that opportunity and spend their lives in frivolous activities. They pursue mundane goals that may give them temporary happiness, but keep them divided and conflicted and put them against themselves. Lost to desires and passions, they become their worst enemies, sabotaging their chances of attaining peace and happiness. They will be better off if they listen to themselves and engage in karma-sannyasa to redeem themselves.

Sloka 7

jitātmanaḥ praśāntasya paramātmā samāhitaḥ
śītoṣṇasukhaduḥkheṣu tathā mānāpamānayoḥ

jita-atmanah = who has conquered his mind and body; prasantasya = who is peaceful, tranquil; parama-atma = Supreme Self; samahitah = united, devoted to, established; sita = cold; usna = heat; sukha = in happiness; duhkhesu = in distress; tatha = also; mana = honor; apamanayoh = and dishonor.

The peaceful and serene conqueror of the mind and body, devoted to the Supreme Self, remains the same in cold and heat, pain and pleasure, and honor and dishonor.

Commentary

The friend of the Self, the tireless karma-sannyasa yogi, conquers his mind and senses, overcoming attraction, aversion, desires, and attachments. With his mind firmly established in the Self, with unwavering devotion, he performs his actions without desiring their fruit as an offering to the Supreme Lord. He attains serenity and sameness, treating the pairs of opposites such as cold and heat, pain and pleasure, or honor and dishonor alike. In the first verse of this chapter, Lord Krishna stated that a true karma-sannyasi performs actions without desiring their fruit. In the next verse, he said that true renunciation means giving up desire-ridden thoughts and intentions (samkalpas). In the third one, he said that for those who want to attain yoga, action is the means, and for those who attain it and master it with self-control, the serenity of the mind. In the fourth one, he said that whoever renounces his desires and intentions and is detached from sense objects is well-established in yoga.

One can see a pattern in these descriptions. Renunciation of desires (sannyasa) with self-control (atma samyama) is foundational to achieving mastery in yoga. When a yogi controls the outgoing tendencies (pravritti) of his mind and senses and withdraws them into himself (nivritti), cultivating distaste for worldly pleasures and sense objects, he quickly becomes a peaceful and serene conqueror of his mind and body (jitatman, vijitatma, or jitendriya). The verse also mentions another important attribute, steadfast devotion to the Supreme Self. By establishing his mind in the Self with steadfast devotion (samahita), with his senses firmly restrained and desires subdued, the master of yoga (yogarudha) becomes detached from all objectivity and attains supreme peace and sameness.

Sloka 8

jñānavijñānatṛptātmā kūṭastho vijitendriyaḥ
yukta ity ucyate yogī samaloṣṭāśmakāñcanaḥ

jnana = knowledge; vijnana = wisdom arising from knowledge; trpta = contented, satisfied; atma = person, soul, being; kuta-sthah = firmly established in the highest; vijita-indriyah = master of the senses; yuktah = one who is united with God; iti = thus; ucyate = said to be; yogi = yogi; sama = equal, same; lostra = dirt, lump of clay; asma = stone; kancanah = gold.

The one who is content with knowledge and wisdom, firmly established in the highest, master of the senses, that yogi is said to be skillful and well established in yoga, who regards a lump of clay, stone, and gold as the same.

Jñāna-vijñāna-tṛptātmā means the contended soul who is satisfied with the knowledge and wisdom he gained from the scriptures or learned people or from his guru through study, observation, discernment, and learning, and clarified all his doubts and questions about the Self and liberation. It means he confidently knows what needs to be done to reach his goal of liberation and does not suffer from doubts and uncertainty. Kutasta means one who is firmly established in the highest aspect or reality, like a star in the sky (kuta) or one who has reached the heights of his progress, which is a reference to his nearness or oneness with the expansive and infinite pure Self and his state of tranquility, just as the sky. The karma-sannyasa yogi who practices self-control (atma samyama) and withdraws from the world remains seated within himself as the witness, remaining indifferent to the actions of his mind and body. Therefore, he is also mentally stable. Vijitendriya means one who restrains and keeps his senses under firm control. He does it by cultivating detachment and suppressing his gunas and desires. It is also an aspect of self-control only.

These practices or accomplishments make the yogi a yukta who is yoked to the Self or the Supreme Self. It also means one who is skillful or an expert in karma-sannyasa yoga through atma samyama (self-control), whereby he overcomes attraction and aversion to the dualities of life, such as heat and cold or pleasure and pain, and remains equal to all. Everything, be it a lump of gold, stone, or clay, is the same for him since he places no value upon material things and treats them equally. Contentment (tripti) is a state of mind that arises from freedom from desires and expectations or attraction and aversion. It corresponds with the state of sameness attained through self-purification and self-control. The yoked one (yukta) is content with his knowledge, wisdom, situation, nearness to the Self, and devotion to the Lord. Contentment is difficult for humans since there is no end to their desires, wants, needs, and expectations. True contentment arises when one is satisfied with whatever one has or does not have, even amidst adverse conditions.

Sloka 9

suhṛnmitrāryudāsīnamadhyasthadveṣyabandhuṣu
sādhuṣv api ca pāpeṣu samabuddhir viśiṣyate

su-hrt = well-wisher, kind-hearted; mitra = friend; ari = enemy; udasina = indifferent, unconcerned; madhya-stha = mediators; dvesya = haters; bandhusu = relations; sadhusu = saints; api = also; ca = and; papesu = sinners; sama-buddhih = same discernment or judgment, impartial; visisyate = he excels.

He excels who has the same regard for well-wishers, friends, enemies, disinterested people, mediators, haters, relations, saints, and also sinners.

Interestingly, Lord Krishna spoke about maintaining sameness towards friends and foes, standing in the middle of a battlefield, and simultaneously asking Arjuna not to lose his heart and resort to fighting. Standing on one side were enemies representing evil, and on the other were friends and relations united in the interest of righteousness. Friends, well-wishers, professional soldiers, mediators, pious people, elders, and onlookers were on both sides. Krishna spoke about equal-mindedness. Yet, he also advised Arjuna to fight. Does it mean that there is a contradiction in his statements? No, he wanted Arjuna to fight in the war as his obligatory duty, with detachment, without expectations, and ill will toward his foes. He wanted him to practice karma-sannyasa and do his part as a Kshatriya, with sameness and equanimity as a service to Dharma and the Supreme Lord. In short, one should not avoid duties and obligations, whatever the difficulties may be. Judgment, fear, and other emotions arise from having desires, attachments, attraction, and aversion. Therefore, a warrior like Arjuna should restrain his mind and senses to be free from them and fight without involving himself in the outcome or the actions.

Madhavacharya distinguished the people who are mentioned in this verse. The well-wishers (suhrid) are always good-hearted. Their good nature does not depend upon conditions and circumstances. Friends (mitra) are those who reciprocate friendliness and help their friends in need. Their friendship is conditional. Enemies (ari) are those who cause harm and destruction. They are motivated by enmity and hostility. Their enmity is also conditional. The indifferent ones (udasina) are neither friends nor foes because they may be strangers, preoccupied with themselves or their problems, or simply disinterested in what happens around them. However, they may potentially become friends or foes depending on circumstances. The mediators (madhyastha) are neither friends nor foes but neutral because they have no stakes in the problem or the conflict, do not know much about it, or may benefit from staying neutral. They can be helpful or problematic. The haters are definitely inimical, vengeful, or envious, waiting for an opportunity to strike, hurt, or harm. They are the opposite of the good-hearted ones. They hold grudges and are, therefore, more dangerous. Blood relations (bandhus) are different. They have a mutual moral obligation toward each other and have to help each other whenever the situation demands it. These relationships are sustained by familial bonds rather than likes and dislikes, desires, and attachments. The saints (sadhus) love unconditionally and universally. You may find in them a well-wisher, a friend, a relation, or a teacher. However, their help or support is not guaranteed as they are also disinterested and indifferent. The enemies are more intense than haters, more distrustful, and even more dangerous.

A saint may have disciples, rivals, critics, enemies, friends, and relations. He may be understood or misunderstood by others. His teachings may be followed or misinterpreted. People may dig out unsavory events about his past to defame him. If he is a self-realized yogi (yukta), he remains equal to them without showing anxiety or concern to defend himself or strike against his opponents. The attitude of equanimity in a saintly person is not an affected trait but the spontaneous outcome of his natural state of detachment, absence of judgment, inner stability, and union with his inner Self. An equal or impartial attitude towards all denotes freedom from attraction and aversion. In the third verse of this chapter, Lord Krishna declared that for a karma yogi who wishes to achieve perfection, action (karma) is the means, and for a karma-sannyasa yogi, sameness. This verse speaks about the yogi who has attained that perfection.

The world is filled with diverse people. Some are friends and well-wishers; some are enemies and ill-wishers; some do not care what happens to you; some try to be neutral and keep their distance; some hate you whatever you do or however friendly you try to be, and some are pious with their minds and hearts filled with the thoughts of God and love for all humanity. Then, some sinners do not foresee the consequences of their actions and engage in self-destructive behavior. It is natural for us to judge them differently according to their conduct or our perceptions. Ignorant and deluded people go by their thinking and judgment, and cannot be equal to all. They are prone to misjudge people or draw wrong conclusions about them, which is problematic since it can lead to further complications in their relationships, perceptions, and personal conduct. Sameness arises from oneness with the Self. A karma-sannyasa yogi who practices atma-samyama (self-control) and is free from desires and attachments attains oneness. Therefore, he is pure, non-judgmental, and sees the same Self in all. Therefore, he remains equal to all.

Sloka 10

yogī yuñjīta satatam ātmānaṃ rahasi sthitaḥ
ekākī yatacittātmā nirāśīr aparigrahaḥ

yogi = a yogi; yunjita = concentrate; satatam = always, constantly; atmanam = upon Self; rahasi = in a secret or a solitary place; sthitah = staying, sitting; ekaki = alone; yata-citta-atma = with mind and the body under control; nirasih = without desires; aparigrahah = without material possessions.

A yogi should always concentrate on the Self, staying in a secret or solitary place, alone, with his mind and body under firm control, without desires, and without seeking material possessions.

Restraining the mind and senses and controlling desires through atma samyama, the yogi should then practice dhyana yoga or meditation on the Self. This verse mentions six requirements for a yogi or a sannyasi who practices self-control on the path of sannyasa or karma-sannyasa. First, he should always concentrate on himself and within himself. By abiding in himself, he will gradually overcome his attachment to his name, form, and physical identity and realize that beneath his physical nature is hidden a deeper and enduring nature that is undisturbed by the commotion of the mind or desires.

Second, he must avoid contact with others and live in a solitary or secret place. Shankaracharya states that he should not live or stay with anyone, even with a fellow renunciant. In the past, yogis and ascetics used to dwell in abandoned homes, ruins, caves, mountains, mangroves, forests, etc., to avoid interacting with worldly people and focus on self-purification. Karma-sannyasa yogis who have not abandoned their duties may have to find a suitable place within their surroundings to practice dhyana.

Third, he must stay alone. This is to avoid attachments and relationships. The ultimate aim of sannyasa yoga is to achieve oneness or aloneness (kaivalya) by establishing the mind within oneself and avoiding all distractions. The state of liberation is the state of aloneness. The Self is eternally independent, alone, and without a second. Therefore, a yogi must cultivate the attitude of aloneness and feel comfortable living in seclusion. The yogi who meditates upon his divine Self (the purest aspect of him) with exclusive devotion is never alone. When he has awareness of his mind and body, he lives in the contemplation of his pure consciousness, and when he is in samadhi, he lives within himself with no other thought or awareness.

Fourth, he must firmly control his senses, mind, and body (yata cittatma) and withdraw them into himself. Chitta means the mind or mind-body consciousness, and atma refers to the physical body. Through self-control (yatatma), the yogi who practices renunciation and detachment overcomes desires and attachments and attains peace and equanimity. Through meditation and withdrawal, he gradually loses awareness of his mind and body and remains established in his pure Self or pure consciousness. Fifth, he must be free from desires (nirasi). It means he must relinquish desires and attachments and practice karma-sannyasa yoga with detachment, renouncing the fruit of his actions. When desires subside, the mind becomes tranquil, and the yogi descends into the depths of his witness consciousness, overcomes duality or otherness, and enters the state of aloneness or oneness.

Lastly, he must give up all material possessions and keep only those necessary for his survival and practice, such as a staff, a begging bowl, a cloth to cover his body, a vessel for drinking water, a necklace of beads (rudrakshas) for contemplation, etc. He should also refrain from staying in sheltered homes, enjoying luxuries and comforts, accepting gifts, or the hospitality of worldly people unless he has attained liberation. Possessions are burdensome. The less a yogi has, the better for him.

The law books prescribe a strict code of conduct for the ascetics and recluses, who renounce worldly life and take the vows of sannyasa. They instruct them not to change their residence during the rainy season, not to enter any village except to seek alms, and not to wear any clothing except to cover their nakedness. They should abandon all forms of desire for tasty food and eat only detached plant parts, not be alone with the opposite sex, and not give in to temptations. The idea is that they should be simple and austere in their conduct, endure hardships with indifference, and practice self-denial, self-control, detachment, sameness, and indifference, with their minds firmly fixed in the deepest silence within themselves until they find the pure Self, shining by itself and extended everywhere.

Sloka 11

śucau deśe pratiṣṭhāpya sthiram āsanam ātmanaḥ
nātyucchritaṃ nātinīcaṃ cailājinakuśottaram

sucau = in a clean; dese = place, location or area; pratisthapya = having established, stationed, set up; sthiram = firm; asanam = seat, base, support; atmanah = of his own; na = not; ati = very; ucchritam = high; na = not; ati = very; nicam = low; caila-ajina = cloth and deerskin; kusottaram = kusa grass.

In a clean place, having established a firm seat of his own, neither very high nor very low, covered with cloth, deerskin, and kusa grass...

This and the following two verses contain a standard method of active meditation (dhyana) with self-control (atma-samyama) on the path of sannyasa or karma-sannyasa. Yogis and ascetics have been practicing this method in India for centuries. In the past, those who renounced worldly life and took vows of renunciation used to retire to forests and solitary places to practice self-purification and attain liberation. The method is still followed today, with suitable adaptations. The first condition stated here is that the place should be clean and free from dirt, leaves, ants, snakes, biting insects, scorpions, and other harmful creatures. Even today, cleanliness (suci) has a great significance in Hindu ritual and spiritual practices because it is equated with godliness, with the belief that the best way to sanctify a place to invite gods or keep away evil influence is to keep it clean and free from impurities such as meat, foul smells, stale food, etc.

In yoga, cleanliness has a much greater significance. Yoga and ascetic traditions of Hinduism recognize the importance of external cleanliness (bahya suddhi) and inner cleanliness (atma suddhi) in self-purification. They equate cleanliness with auspiciousness (subhasuci), peace, and prosperity. The underlying belief is that mental and spiritual purity cannot be attained without physical purity and cleanliness. Uncleanliness is a characteristic of tamasic people. The law books also provide additional guidelines for the ascetics to ensure cleanliness externally and internally. For example, they suggest that the place where they practice yoga or austerities should be free from moisture, dirt, insects, pollutants, strong smells, ants, snakes, and similar pests. They have to avoid places such as cremation grounds, burial grounds, places where animals were slaughtered or subjected to cruelty, places defiled with human and animal waste, or places haunted or frequented by evil people or dangerous animals.

The second condition is that the ground upon which meditation is practiced shall be elevated but not too high or too low. If the ground is too high, the yogi may fall off or roll down in a trance or deep meditation and hurt himself. If it is too low, it can become damp with rainwater and attract ants, snakes, scorpions, and other harmful creatures. The third condition is that the yogi has to prepare a firm seat with cloth, deerskin, and sacred grass known as kusa or darbha. The materials should be used in reverse order. First, the ground must be covered with kusa grass, then deerskin should be spread on it, and finally, a cloth should be put on both. These materials help the yogi sit comfortably, relax, and concentrate his mind. They also serve as a buffer between the yogi's body and the earth and prevent the spiritual energy generated in meditation from becoming discharged into the ground, since the earth readily absorbs all energies from the objects that come into contact with it.

Sloka 12

tatraikāgraṃ manaḥ kṛtvā yatacittendriyakriyaḥ
upaviśyāsane yuñjyād yogam ātmaviśuddhaye

tatra = thereupon; eka-agram = one pointed, single minded; manah = mind; krtva = doing so; yata-citta = controlling the mind; indriya = senses; kriyah = movements, activities; upavisya = sitting on; asane = on the seat; yunjyat = execute; yogam = yoga practice; atma = heart; visuddhaye = for clarifying.

Thereupon, sitting on that seat, with single-minded concentration, keeping the movements of his mind and senses under firm control, he should practice the yoga for self-purification.

After establishing a firm seat in a clean place and covering it with kusa grass, deerskin, and cloth, the yogi should sit cross-legged in a lotus position on it and practice meditation, restraining and withdrawing his mind and senses into himself. In that relaxed state, he should meditate on the Self or Supreme Self with unwavering concentration. At this stage, he should spend his time mostly in meditation until he stabilizes his mind and gains a firm grip on his spiritual nature. Simultaneously, he should practice self-restraint, austerities, and karma-sannyasa to purify his mind and body, subduing desires, passions, and attachments so that his mind and senses will not revert to their habitual ways. Ekagracittam means one-pointedness. It is attained only when the world becomes inconsequential to the yogi for all purposes and ceases to distract or ensnare him with desire-ridden thoughts and intentions induced by the gunas. Until he succeeds in it, he has to keep practicing meditation (dhyana) with self-control (atma-samyama) by withdrawing his mind and senses from external objects, overcoming desires and attachments, and contemplating upon the Self or the Supreme Lord with exclusive devotion. The mind is, by nature, fickle and unstable due to its outgoing nature (prvritti) and habitual movements, hardened by years of involvement with worldly life due to the influence of the gunas. Therefore, it requires perseverance and determination to subdue the gunas and the mind through detachment, renunciation, distaste for worldly objects, and exclusive devotion.

Sloka 13

samaṃ kāyaśirogrīvaṃ dhārayann acalaṃ sthiraḥ
saṃprekṣya nāsikāgraṃ svaṃ diśaś cānavalokayan

samam = straight; kaya-sirah = body and head; grivam = neck; dharayan = holding; acalam = stable, without moving; sthirah = still; sampreksya = fixing his gaze, looking intensely; nasikagram = tip of the nose; svam = own; disah = directions; ca = and; anavalokayan = not looking around.

Holding his body, head, and neck straight, stable, and still, fixing his gaze firmly (as if) on the tip of his nose and not looking around in other directions.

We may make yoga a simple spiritual practice or a complicated ritual. We may use a few techniques to discipline and purify our minds and bodies, or become involved with celebrity teachers, difficult postures, elaborate routines, and advanced techniques, forgetting the actual goal. Yoga should be practiced for a few important reasons, mainly to transform our physical nature and become free from it. When we succeed in the first, we attain the second. The first one involves cultivating sattva, stabilizing the mind through withdrawal, and suppressing the gunas and the desires and attachments they induce. The second practice requires renunciation, constant meditation, and concentration, becoming established in the oneness of the Self and detaching oneself mentally from the mind-body awareness, renouncing the identity that arises from it.

Freedom from Nature (Prakriti) from all sides arises when the modifications of the mind and body, and the dualities and the impermanence of the world cease to trouble us. When yoga is practiced with increased emphasis on body postures and health benefits, it proves counterproductive. It increases desires and attachments and draws and distracts the yogis from knowing the real purpose of yoga or cultivating detachment, stability, and inwardness. Yoga has many short-term benefits, such as good health, relaxation, and improved body posture. They are important. However, yoga's ultimate purpose is self-purification and liberation. When yoga is practiced for whatever reason, that purpose should be at the back of a yogi's mind and should not be forgotten.

This verse suggests the standard practice of holding the body, the head, and the neck in a straight line, remaining focused on the Self, and keeping the mind and senses under control. By holding them in a straight line, yogis will have better posture, comfort, control, and stability. Further, when they are straight, kundalini energy can flow easily from the base of the spine to the head region through the middle chakras and the neck. Although the verse suggests that the yogi has to fix his gaze upon the tip of his nose, Shankara suggested that the yogi should fix his gaze as if he is looking at the tip of his nose while focusing on the Self only because it is the real purpose. By concentrating his gaze on his nose and his attention on the Self, he has to practice meditation with self-control and without distractions.

Sloka 14

praśāntātmā vigatabhīr brahmacārivrate sthitaḥ
manaḥ saṃyamya maccitto yukta āsīta matparaḥ

prasanta = tranquil, peaceful, placid; atma = soul; vigata-bhih = without fear; brahmacari-vrate = practicing celibacy, brahmacharya; sthitah = abiding, established; manah = mind; samyamya = controlling; mat = absorbed in me; cittah = mind, consciousness; yuktah = balanced; asita = let him remain seated; matparah = devoted to Me.

The peaceful and tranquil soul, without fear, firmly established in the practice of celibacy, controlling his mind, his mind absorbed in Me, balanced, let him remain seated, devoted to Me.

Although Sanskrit is closely associated with Latin and Greek, certain words in Sanskrit are difficult to translate into European languages like English, French, or German because their meanings and the beliefs and practices associated with them are uniquely Indian. Therefore, translating them into foreign languages is an uphill task. At best, we may find words closest to them in meaning and use them. The word "citta" (or chitta) is one such word. Although loosely translated in English as mind or consciousness, it has a broader meaning and requires additional context to explain its true import. The word is central to the Yoga philosophy and an important concept of Hindu philosophy. Without knowing it, one cannot truly understand the purpose of yoga or even liberation. As Patanjali succinctly puts it, yoga aims to arrest the modifications of citta and stabilize it in the Self.

While it seems simple, citta is not just the mind or consciousness. It is physical awareness or mind-body consciousness arising from the contact of the mind and body with the external world. It is the sum of all thoughts, memories, emotions, feelings, sensations, intuition, intelligence, egoism, and the auric or astral field surrounding the body. It is the repository of our perceptions, feelings, dreams, memories, past life impressions, objectivity, duality, and subtle body experiences. According to the yoga tradition, it is a transparent substance suffused with the light of sattva that can mold itself according to the forms it perceives and create replicas in the consciousness as impressions or mental objects we experience as perceptions. When it is permeated by the influence of the three gunas and the desires and attachments they induce, it suffers from fluctuations and disturbances like water inside a boiling pot. However, when the rajas and tamas are removed, and sattva predominates, it becomes stable and reflects the radiance of the Self and the objects one perceives. In yoga practice, aspirants aim to cleanse their citta and stabilize it in the contemplation of the Self so that it dissolves quickly in pure consciousness without leaving any residue. When the mind is pure, perception and cognition improve without perceptual errors and logical distortions.

This verse explains how a karma-sannyasi or sannyasi should practice atma-samyama (control of the mind and body), cultivating the six requirements to attain that goal: tranquility, fearlessness, celibacy, control of the mind (samyama), absorption in the Self, and devotion. Peace or tranquility arises when the yogi renounces the desire for the fruit of his actions and offers it to Brahman. By renouncing desires and attachments, he cultivates sameness. While performing actions, he thinks that his mind and senses are engaged in them, and he is not their cause. By giving up desires and attachments, he subdues the gunas and suppresses the modifications (vrittis) of his citta to attain serenity. Fearlessness arises when he realizes that he is the pure and indestructible Self and longs for liberation, giving up his attachment to his mind, body, name, and form. Knowing that he is the pure Self and surrendering his care to the Supreme Lord, he is no more troubled by the prospect of Death or the uncertainties of life.

Brahmacharya, or celibacy, is an important austerity, recommended as an essential practice and prerequisite in all spiritual traditions to attain purity or cultivate sattva. Without it, one cannot stabilize the mind in contemplation or achieve absorption in Brahman. Samyama means restraint, control, or tying up. In classical yoga, samyama is practiced by restraining the mind and senses and drawing the mind to the Self through concentrated meditation. It gradually results in the dissolution of the mind in the pure consciousness of the Self. By that, he overcomes duality and abides in oneness. In the previous chapter, Lord Krishna explained (verse 25) how seers attain absorption (Brahma-nirvana) through self-purification and self-control. Matcitta means keeping the mind engaged in the devotional contemplation of the Supreme Lord. Devotion to the Supreme Lord is an important prerequisite to achieving liberation in bhakti sampradayas. Those who seek liberation should cultivate exclusive devotion to the Lord to earn his grace. Through self-control, they should cultivate the nearness to Him and earn His grace, putting themselves at His feet and becoming an offering.

Sloka 15

yuñjann evaṃ sadātmānaṃ yogī niyatamānasaḥ
śāntiṃ nirvāṇaparamāṃ matsaṃsthām adhigacchati

yunjan = concentrating, united with; evam = thus; sada = ever, constantly; atmanam = mind established in the Self; yogi = yogi; niyata-manasah = disciplined mind; santim = peace; nirvana-paramam = supreme state of liberation; mat-samstham = abode, presence; adhigacchati = attain.

United thus continuously with the Self, the yogi, whose mind is restrained and controlled, attains the supremely peaceful state of liberation, (after that) My abode.

The yogi who practices dhyana with self-control (atma-samyama) unites his mind with the Self and dissolves it in him through concentration and contemplation. He soaks his mind with the thoughts of the Self and remains in control without letting his mind and senses wander freely or pursue desires. Through that disciplined effort, he draws his mind into the Self, removing all the distinctions and barriers that stand between them, and lets his consciousness slowly lose itself in the pure consciousness of the Self without duality and objectivity. Thereby, he achieves oneness with the pure state of the Self, which is otherwise ungraspable, unknowable, and impenetrable to the ordinary mind. Through the constant practice of atma-samyama and dhyana, aided by detachment, devotion, renunciation, and desireless actions (nishkama karma), he attains Brahman and freedom from karma (naishkarmya siddhi) and sameness (samsiddhi). He becomes a jivanmukta, a liberated, pure soul in a living body. He is no longer tainted by the actions he performs or does not perform.

When he departs from here, he attains the immortal world of Brahman. For a human being, the dissolution of his physical nature in the pure consciousness of Brahman (Brahma-nirvana) is a rare achievement. It is attained only in rare cases when all the impurities of the mind and body are completely resolved. Union with the Self is attained only in the purest state when the mind falls into utter silence without any objectivity or duality. The result is nirvana, the transcendental state of absolute freedom, which is beyond the reach of the mind and senses. Nirvana means the permanent ending or torching of all the causes that keep the jiva bound to samsara. For the yogi who attains it, there is no rebirth or further involvement with Nature. For him, it is freedom from all limitations, mortality, and earthly life. A yogi who attains it while living is known as a jivanmukta. Although he is liberated and karma does not accrue to him, he may still have to resolve the yet-to-be-exhausted, old prarabdha karma. Upon departing from here, he goes directly to the immortal world of Brahman.

Sloka 16

nātyaśnatas tu yogosti na caikāntam anaśnataḥ
na cātisvapnaśīlasya jāgrato naiva cārjuna

na = not; ati = excessively, voraciously; asnatah = one who eats; tu = but; yogah = yoga; asti = is; na = not; ca = and; ekantam = at all; anasnatah = who does not eat; na = not; ca = and; ati = excessively, for too long; svapna-silasya = who sleeps; jagratah = who remains awake; na = not; eva = ever; ca = and; arjuna = O Arjuna.

O Arjuna, yoga is not for the one who eats voraciously, nor for the one who does not eat at all; not for the one who sleeps for too long, nor for the one who remains awake.

Whether it is in sleeping, eating, speaking, or any other activity, moderation and balance are important. They are even more important when one practices yoga to practice self-control or achieve liberation. Yogis must not resort to extreme practices in their zeal to achieve quick results or pull the higher Shaktis into the body for cleansing before one is ready. Extreme measures in any aspect of life produce pain and suffering and may result in unintended consequences. We can survive dualities such as heat and cold, but not extreme dualities such as freezing or boiling temperatures. Therefore, Nature always forces us to find the middle ground, adapt ourselves to tolerable circumstances, and live within our means. We learn this lesson very early in childhood when we cross our limits and experience pain and discomfort. To live comfortably, we must respect the limitations Nature imposes upon us and avoid harming or hurting our bodies to achieve our material or spiritual goals. The body is a gift and should be treated as such. Our goals should be realistic and moderate, and so should our actions. Progress in spiritual practice is not achieved through extreme practices as much as by practicing moderation in our actions to overcome impurities, desires, and passions. Moderation is necessary even in self-control (atma-samyama) to avoid self-harm, suffering, and cruelty to ourselves. Therefore, one should practice yoga for self-purification with discernment and balance. The mind cannot be stabilized with harsh measures. Sameness is difficult for those who ignore the limits of their tolerance. Some ascetic sects of Hinduism recommend extreme methods of yoga, austerities, and observances for self-purification. Traditional sects prohibit them as outlier practices. In this verse, Krishna rightly advised Arjuna to practice moderation and avoid extremes. In the following verse, he explains the reasons.

Sloka 17

yuktāhāravihārasya yuktaceṣṭasya karmasu
yuktasvapnāvabodhasya yogo bhavati duḥkhahā 6.17

Yukta = sensible, balanced, moderate; ahara-viharasya = in eating and enjoyment; yukta = sensible, balanced, moderate; cestasya = in thinking or in mind; karmasu = in actions; yukta = balanced, moderate; svapna-avabodhasya = sleeping and waking; yogah = yoga; bhavati = happens, becomes; duhkha-ha = destroyer of sorrow.

He who is sensible in his eating and enjoyment, who restrains his mind in actions, (and) whose sleeping and waking are balanced, for him, yoga becomes the destroyer of his sorrows.

In this context, yoga particularly means the practice of atma-samyama (self-control) on the path of karma-sannyasa or sannyasa yoga. In the Bhagavadgita, it is difficult to define yoga since its meaning changes in the context of the particular. The scripture does not even tell you clearly what yoga you should practice. It presents various yogas and leaves the rest to your discretion. We believe that the central theme of the Bhagavadgita is karma-sannyasa yoga, and the rest, jnana (samkhya), buddhi, atma-samyama, sannyasa, bhakti, etc., are adjuncts to assist those who are engaged in performing their obligatory duties. In a general sense, yoga may encompass all the practices mentioned in this scripture. Whatever the truth, yoga as a system of spiritual practice helps us control and purify our minds and bodies, subduing the influence of the triple gunas. It helps the yogi discern how suffering arises due to a lack of control and attachment to material things, names, and forms, and how peace and equanimity can be attained by renouncing them and cultivating detachment and indifference. By establishing an unwavering and strong devotional connection with the Self through contemplation and self-purification and disassociating from his physical self and identity through renunciation, the self-controlled yogi who practices contemplation uninterruptedly can become established in oneness within himself and attain oneness with Brahman (Brahma nirvana).

Atma-samyama yoga is difficult to practice since it demands uncompromising effort in self-purification. To be free from the modifications of the mind and remain indifferent to them, you have to go against your essential nature to control it. In doing so, you will face many problems and heavy resistance from within yourself. Your mind will unleash chaos and inner demons when you try to control it to discourage, forcing you to revert to your old habits and worldly ways. Many fail, finding it difficult to cope with the fury unleashed by their minds and bodies and the deluding Maya shaktis that inhabit them. It is natural and expected because the lower nature does not easily give up its control or surrender itself willingly to the higher nature. Yogis who know that the poison of suffering arises from their effort to control their natural tendencies (prvritti) and behavior endure it and remain undisturbed. For them, yoga becomes a learning and improving process. Learning valuable lessons from their experience, they move on toward the goal.

This verse suggests five restraints to achieve self-control through balance and moderation: restraint in eating, enjoyment, actions of the mind and senses, sleeping, and waking. Controlling sleeping and waking means the yogi should control his sleeping and waking hours, sleep and wake up at fixed times, and give his mind and body proper rest. Self-control involves practicing restraints (yamas) without violating them, especially nonviolence (ahimsa), and following niyamas (observances) at all times.

Suffering is natural to all living beings, and no one can fully resolve it. One can endure suffering, but cannot prevent it or escape from it. Some physical pain and suffering persist even after liberation since the body of a liberated yogi is also subject to the same natural laws, such as aging, sickness, and death. However, he responds to it with indifference or equanimity, without letting it control him. Through yoga, self-purification, renunciation of desires, and self-control, yogis learn to endure their suffering and continue their practice without overdoing it. It is common knowledge that you cannot control the world or its causes of suffering, but can only control yourself, your thoughts, actions, desires, attachments, or how you perceive and respond to suffering. The purpose of self-control (atma-samyama) is the same. It teaches you to remain undisturbed amidst disturbances, restrain your mind and senses amidst distractions and temptations, and practice nonviolence, restraint, moderation, and compassion towards yourself and others, seeing the same Self in all and everywhere.

Sloka 18

yadā viniyataṃ cittam ātmany evāvatiṣṭhate
niḥspṛhaḥ sarvakāmebhyo yukta ity ucyate tadā

yada = when; viniyatam = restrained, controlled; cittam = the citta; atmani = in the Self; eva = only; avatisthate = established; nisprhah = without desire or craving; sarva = all; kamebhyah = passions and pleasures; yuktah = adept, skilled, established, harmonized; iti = thus; ucyate = is said to be; tada = then.

When the mind is controlled and established in the Self only, without desires and craving for objects, then he is said to be an adept yogi.

The yogi who has perfected his practice of atma samyama yoga, controlling his mind and establishing his thoughts in the Self, remains tranquil, content within himself, and free from desires and cravings. He is called a yukta because he has mastered self-restraint, become skillful in meditation, and harmonized his physical and spiritual nature. Since he controls his mind and body and subdues the gunas, he is said to be indifferent (nisprhah), without desires and cravings. Firmly established in equanimity, he exemplifies the virtues of self-control, detachment, renunciation, and equanimity. The consciousness (citta) of a yukta is like a placid lake, and it is tranquil because it is freed from the influence of the ego and the triple gunas.

As long as the mind fluctuates and produces desire-ridden thoughts and impressions, we cannot say that the yogi has mastered his mind or skillfulness and become a yukta, even if he practices dhyana, samyama, karma-sannyasa, or nitya sannyasa, because his mind still produces modifications and karma and keeps him unstable and bound. To be free from the world, he must arrest all formations and modifications of his mind, rest in himself, and find peace in the resting ground of his pure consciousness, which is without duality, distinction, or otherness. Perfection in self-control is achieved when the mind is freed from external and internal influences through its practice with firm faith, resolve, and devotion, and established fully in oneness and sameness.

To establish the mind in the oneness of the Self and achieve perfection in equanimity, the yogi must also overcome past life samskaras (latent impressions), neutralize his gunas, and remove the last remnants of his past associations and unresolved troublesome memories. When he overcomes these barriers and dissolves his mind in the contemplation of the Self, he enters the deeper states of mental absorption and experiences self-absorption. Firmly established in it through repetitive practice as the witness Self, undisturbed by what happens or does not happen, removing all traces of formations and disturbances from his consciousness until nothing is left and imbuing his wakeful consciousness with the thoughts of the Self, he becomes the silent one (muni) who abides in oneness and sees himself in all.

Sloka 19

yathā dīpo nivātastho neṅgate sopamā smṛtā
yogino yatacittasya yuñjato yogam ātmanaḥ

yatha = as; dipah = a lamp; nivata-sthah = windless place; na = not; ingate = flickers; sa upama = that metaphor, example; smrta = comes to mind, remembered; yoginah = about the yogi; yata-cittasya = whose citta is under control; yunjatah = practicing; yogam = yoga of self-control; atmanah = within the Self.

Just as a lamp in a windless place does not flicker - that metaphor is remembered about the yogi whose mind is under control and who practices the yoga of self-control, established in the Self.

In the absolute silence of the mind, nothing moves, and nothing exists except the indivisible and indistinguishable pure consciousness of the Self and the subjective experience of oneness. It is because the mind either ceases to be a barrier to self-knowing or becomes completely tame and silent. A yogi who excels in self-control arrests the movements of his mind by will. Like the light of a lamp or candle in a windless place, his mind does not waver at the sight of worldly objects or disturbing scenes. The yogi who attains such perfection and control can suppress any thought or desire at will. He remains undisturbed, like a lamp protected from wind, because he is firmly established in the Self (Atman) and endures dualities and disturbances of samsara, without any desires or cravings for external things and with sameness and indifference. Hence, he is known to other yogis as skillful (yukta), stable (sthitadhi), silent (muni), resolute (dhira), and firmly intelligent (sthithaprajna). The unwavering mind arises from the continued practice of atma-samyama aided by contemplation (dhyana), renunciation of desires (karma-sannyasa), and devotion (bhakti). It is the culmination of a long effort.

Patanjali also states in the Yogasutras that a yogi achieves self-absorption (samadhi) through controlled meditation (samyama) after achieving perfection in the other seven limbs of yoga. By restraining and controlling the movements of his mind and senses, he attains samadhi in stages according to the sattva he cultivates. Breath control, withdrawal of the senses, concentration, and meditation are the beginning steps in classical yoga. Samyama is an advanced stage in which years of practice culminate in liberating the mind from modifications. Although the metaphor of a lamp in a windless place describes the state of the yogi who is well established in the Self, it does not completely justify his condition because if the lamp is brought into a windy place, it will flicker. A yogi who has mastered his mind and body will remain undisturbed in all circumstances, like the shining sun. The winds of adversity or the temptations of worldly life do not trouble him. He will remain serene and calm when he is alone or in the company of others, and whether the conditions are favorable or unfavorable.

Sloka 20

yatroparamate cittaṃ niruddhaṃ yogasevayā
yatra caivātmanātmānaṃ paśyann ātmani tuşyati

yatra = in that state of stillness; uparamate = withdrawing, ceasing, abstaining; cittam = the citta; niruddham = restrained; yoga-sevaya = by the service or practice of yoga; yatra = in that; ca = and; eva = only; atmana = in the Self; atmanam = the self; pasyan = by seeing; atmani = in the self; tusyati = remains satisfied.

That (state) in which the mind is withdrawn and restful, restrained by the practice of yoga, in that (state), seeing the Self by the self, he remains satisfied within himself only.

When the yogi who practices celibacy and moderation in eating and sleeping and contemplates upon the Self with unwavering concentration and devotion, living in solitude, ever contended and equal to all, withdrawing his mind and senses into himself and conquering desires and attachments through renunciation, his mind becomes one-pointed, transparent like a crystal and stabile like a flame in a windless place. In that state of equanimity and silence, with the mind becoming purified and transparent by sameness and self-absorption, he directly perceives the Self as his real nature. That perception is not physical or mental with the duality of the knower and the known, but metaphorical to denote a realization or a remembrance of the pure state of consciousness hidden in everyone.

Except for a few fortunate ones, yogis attain this state through stages. In the early stages, the self-restrained renunciant (sannyasi) abides in witness consciousness and experiences peace and stillness, but some objectivity remains. According to the Yogasutras, this stage of the samadhi is known as samprajnata samadhi or bija samadhi because seeds (bija) of duality, some awareness (prajna), and objectivity still persist in the consciousness. As he perseveres in the practice, he succeeds in removing the remaining residual impurities of past life impressions and latent desires and attains the pure, stateless, and objectless (asamprajna) samadhi in which all objectivity disappears and only the knower remains within himself and by himself in the stillness of his pure consciousness. It is what we understand as turya or the nondual state of oneness.

In this verse, yatra (that state of stillness) refers to this state of consciousness only, in which the yogi discerns in the silence of his mind the purest state of himself as his true Self. It is the most auspicious (parama pavitram), blissful, and supreme (parama yogam) state of consciousness. Hence, when the yogi finds himself within himself, he experiences abiding stillness and rapture and remains gladdened by it. Yogis do not attain it if they do not subdue the gunas and suppress the modifications of the mind caused by them. Under the influence of deluding shaktis, the ego uses all possible ploys to resist and prevent its dissolution in the oneness of the Self, does not easily give up, and resurfaces in various guises to keep the yogi mentally disturbed and distracted. Hence, the mind or the ego that controls it is often compared to Ravana with ten heads. If it is not controlled, it creates an objectified and illusory version of samadhi as a diversion to remain in control and keep deluding the yogi. Hence, yogis must remain on guard and strive to attain excellence in self-control and renunciation to become established in yoga (yukta) with tranquil minds (niyatamanas).

Sloka 21

sukham ātyantikaṃ yat tad buddhigrāhyam atīndriyam
vetti yatra na caivāyaṃ sthitaś calati tattvataḥ

sukham = happiness, bliss; atyantikam = endless, infinite, supreme; yat = which; tat = that; buddhi = intelligence; grahyam = realized, grasped; atindriyam = beyond the senses, transcendental; vetti = knows; yatra = wherein; na = not; ca = and; eva = surely; ayam = this; sthitah = situated; calati = moves, deviates; tattvatah = truth, reality.

That infinite and supreme bliss, which is grasped by intelligence but beyond the senses, having become established (in that), he no longer deviates from (its) truth.

When desires, attachments, and gunas are fully suppressed, and when the mind becomes still through meditation and self-control, the yogi realizes the infinite oneness of the Self and the happiness that flows from it. He grasps it through wakeful discernment in the silence of turya within himself, not through his senses since it does not arise from the contact of the senses with sense objects. It happens internally within himself due to the dissolution of his duality in the oneness of the Self and his subjective experience of rapturous aloneness without a second. It is grasped by intelligence because it is the highest and the nearest tattva in the body to the Self, and when it is pure, it allows the light and bliss of the Self to radiate through it uninterruptedly. A yogi experiences the blissful state of the Self only when there are no impurities in him, and his lower nature is completely subdued. The ignorant ones cannot experience it because, in them, the Self (one's pure consciousness) remains enveloped by a thick cloud of impurities. United with the Self, without any barriers in between, the pure mind reflects the purity and intelligence of the Self in all four states of consciousness. Hence, the yogi who attains oneness within himself is never separate from the Self and does not deviate from the truth or the consciousness it reflects. Truth, bliss, and perfection, the supreme qualities of the Supreme Lord, become permanently established in him when his individuality and consciousness are completely dissolved.

Early commentators of the Yogasutras, such as Vacaspati Misra and Vijnanabhikshu, described the blissful (ananda) condition which arises in yoga through samyama as one of the advanced states of stateful (samprajnata) samadhi, short of the final or the most excellent state in which there is no awareness of even that bliss. In this state, a yogi frequently falls into rapturous trances because of the predominance of sattva and intense devotion. While it is a good sign that he has progressed on the path and is nearer the supreme goal, it can also be a source of distraction, especially if he becomes attached to it and wishes to experience it repeatedly. Therefore, he should be on guard and treat these experiences with indifference. Formations, objectivity, duality, and subtle sensations and feelings in the consciousness disappear only in the final state of objectless self-absorption (asamprajnata samadhi) or seedless (nirbija) samadhi. The distinction between these two types of samadhi is subtle and difficult to theorize. Even those who experience it do not know exactly what they have gone through.

The intuitive awareness (samprajnata) of the ecstatic state of self-absorption within oneself arises in intense concentration (samyama), in which the mind and the senses do not participate. The yogi experiences a vague objectivity in that state. It is difficult to say how much of that experience he can bring back into his wakeful state or recollect it clearly. Awareness of the blissful nature of the Self arises in intelligence (buddhi) because, among the constituents of Nature, only it can reflect the brilliance and the purity of the Self. In that state, the yogi may have a vague recollection of the blissful state, as if he has gone through a transcendental dream state. According to some commentators, in this state of samadhi, which is incomplete but almost nondual, there is no real or direct experience of oneness with the Self. The experience arises due to nearness rather than oneness, while the mind is not yet ready for complete dissolution. It is as if you are standing on the edge of an infinite ocean, and you can feel its depth and incredible power, but you have not yet decided to enter it. Whatever the perception of that experience, a yogi who reaches that state of purity and transcendence will not show much interest in the objective experience of his wakeful consciousness. Not even the greatest wonders upon earth will distract him from the truth he just realized or is about to realize.

Sloka 22

yaṃ labdhvā cāparaṃ lābhaṃ manyate nādhikaṃ tataḥ
yasmin sthito na duḥkhena guruṇāpi vicālyate

yam = which; labdhva = gaining, obtaining; ca = and; aparam = another; labham = gain; manyate = thinks; na = not; adhikam = better, greater, superior; tatah = than, ; yasmin = in which; sthitah = being established; na = not; duhkhena = sorrow, suffering; guruna = greatest, heaviest; api = even; vicalyate = disturbed, vexed, troubled.

By obtaining which one does not think of another gain better than that, and becoming established in which one is not disturbed by even the most troubling sorrow.

Two defining characteristics of an adept yogi, self-absorbed and united within himself, are described here. Firstly, he does not think of any further accomplishment or gain since he obtained the best and highest, his union with the Self. Second, he remains undisturbed by the heaviest sorrows because he is free from attraction and aversion and blissfully established within himself with sameness and equanimity. He also accepts everything as divine will. Since he is free from desires, has attained unified consciousness, and sees the Self in all, he does not think of securing any further gain to complete or complement himself. Because of delusion and selfishness, the ego reacts differently to the dualities, such as loss and gain or happiness and sorrow. With his ego subdued and his desires and attachments gone, he does not have to prove himself or impress others by performing or not performing any actions. Knowing that he is complete and independent within himself and is one with Brahman, he remains silent, established in sameness, satisfied within himself, and does not look to the world for fulfillment. Once you experience the highest and the best, you will not think of gaining anything else. The fact is that behind the superficial consciousness and beyond the silence of the deep mind is pure consciousness, which represents our essential nature and truth. However, since we are not yet established in it, we keep looking for happiness and gratification outside ourselves. When the yogi becomes united with the eternal Self and perceives it everywhere and within himself in a state of unity, what else will he need? Further, since he is blissfully established within himself, he is untouched by the heaviest sorrows.

Sloka 23

taṃ vidyād.h duḥkhasaṃyogaviyogaṃ yogasaṃjñitam
sa niścayena yoktavyo yogonirviṇṇacetasā

Tam = that; vidyat = be it known; duhkha = pain and suffering; samyoga = union, contact, association; viyogam = disconnection, separation; yoga = yoga; samjnitam = called, named, sah = that yoga; niscayena = with resolve; yoktavyah = should be practiced; yogah = yoga; anirvinna-cetasa = without depressed mind.

Separation from the union with pain and suffering that shall be known and called yoga. That yoga shall be practiced with resolve, without a depressed mind.

Separation from union with pain means separation from attachment to the body, which is the source of pain and suffering. When a yogi becomes detached from it and abides in the Self, he becomes free from pain and sorrow. In other words, yoga means separation from the union with the mind and body and union with the Self. One should practice this yoga with determination and equanimity, without negativity and despair, which arise when one practices detachment and renunciation.

The word "tam" in this verse refers to the exalted state of the yogi, described in the previous three verses (20-21). Let us recall the predominant aspects of that highest state (yoga) in which the yukta abides.

1. With his mind withdrawn and restful and becoming the witness, the yogi remains happy and satisfied within himself.
2. Grasping the infinite and supreme bliss of the Self with his intelligence and becoming established in it, he does not deviate from the truth of the blissful Self.

3. Having realized that he obtained the best and the highest and that nothing can be gained further, he remains undisturbed by even the most troublesome sorrows.

This exalted, supreme state arises because the yogi is permanently separated from his previous, karma-driven, egoistic connection with his physical self and the pain and suffering that arise from it. This permanent separation through detachment from the mind and body, which are the seats of pain and suffering, and the simultaneous, blissful union with the Self in the state of self-absorption, is called yoga or the supreme state. In other words, the state of samadhi, absorption in oneness or union with the Self, is called yoga because, in that state, there is the simultaneous separation of the seer from sorrow (body) and union with bliss (the Self).

Yoga is not only a union with a unified consciousness of the Self, truth, and bliss (satchidananda) but also a disunion from the mundane and objective reality of the mind and the suffering that arises from it. Yoga removes the impurities from the mind and body and lets the purity of the Self reflect in it. In the previous verses, we heard that the mind becomes established in the pure Self through atma samyama yoga, and unlimited peace and sameness arise from uninterrupted meditation (dhyana yoga). The same idea is represented here in the assertion that yoga is dissociation from union with pain and suffering, but in a roundabout way.

Yoga is the union with peace and happiness and disunion from sorrow (dukkha), which is the predominant theme of mortal life. Life is full of suffering, and we are aware of it. We turn to religion, liberation, or spiritual life to escape permanently from suffering, having realized that we cannot escape from it physically, mentally, or with the help of material things, enjoyment, or distractions. Suffering does not exist in the Self but only in the jivas who are subject to Nature's tattvas and gunas. Because of this, the jivas are constantly exposed to dualities, impermanence, and modifications. The jivas' association with Nature is in itself a form of bondage to samsara. It is also the source of sorrow and suffering as Nature subjects them to impurities and keeps them bound to their nature. The mind and the body, which constitute the Field of Nature, are in themselves seats of pain and suffering. Through yoga, we can become detached from them and stop responding to the suffering they create.

Sloka 24

saṅkalpaprabhavān kāmāṃs tyaktvā sarvān aśeṣataḥ
manasaivendriyagrāmaṃ viniyamya samantataḥ

sankalpa-prabhavan = induced by desire-ridden thoughts and intentions; kamam = desires; tyaktva = giving up; sarvan = all; asesatah = completely without any desires remaining, completely; manasa = in the mind; eva = only, itself; indriya-gramam = the assembly of sense organs; viniyamya = controlling, restraining; samantatah = equally from all sides.

Giving up all desires that are induced by desire-ridden thoughts and intentions, completely without any desires remaining, restraining

within the mind the entire group of sense organs from all sides equally...

The yogi who strives to attain disunion from the pain-producing mind and body and union with the blissful Self should first eliminate all desires and attachments from his mind, subduing the gunas and restraining his senses from all sides. "Sankalpa prabhava kamam" means desires induced by desire-ridden thoughts and intentions (sankalpa). Desires, desire-ridden thoughts and intentions, and the memories and habits associated with them will disappear only when the mind and body are fully controlled and subdued, neutralizing the gunas and practicing detachment and renunciation. Self-restraint (atma-samyama) is, therefore, important in yoga. Without it, the yogi cannot control the habitual actions and reactions of his mind and body, subdue his desire and passions, or establish peace within himself. To achieve samyama (balance and control), he must withdraw his mind and senses from all sides into himself and meditate attentively on the Self or the Supreme Lord without losing control or letting them wander or interact with the objects. Even if they do momentarily, he should withdraw them and persist in his practice until they are firmly restrained and silenced. When not meditating, he should be indifferent to any sensations or perceptions they produce. Without that, he will not attain serenity, cross the deep silence within him, and experience oneness. It is especially important when the yogi falls into deeper and restful states of mental absorption (bija samadhis), becomes too distant from his physical self, and temporarily loses control over it. In short, the yogi must achieve complete self-mastery in all four states of consciousness. He should restrain his subtle and gross senses and stop them from producing any feelings, sensations, or sense impressions so that the thoughts, images, latent impressions (samskaras), or other mental objects do not arise in his consciousness, whether he is awake or asleep, and keep producing modifications and karma. How it should be done intelligently is explained in the next verse.

Sloka 25

śanaiḥ śanair uparamed buddhyā dhṛtigṛhītayā
ātmasaṃsthaṃ manaḥ kṛtvā na kiṃcid api cintayet

sanaih-sanaih = gradually, step by step; uparamet = should withdraw; buddhya = with the help of discriminating intelligence; dhrti-grhitaya = with firm control and resolve; atma-samstham = entirely in the Self; manah = mind; krtva = fixing or placing; na-kincit = nothing; api = whatsoever; cintayet = thinking of.

Gradually, step by step, let him withdraw with discriminating intelligence with firm control and resolve, entirely fixing his mind in the Self, thinking of nothing else whatsoever.

The yogi must withdraw his senses gradually, step by step, first from the external objects, then from his mind and memory, until they are completely withdrawn from all objectivity and are arrested within himself. The mind is a memory bank. Even if you shut down your senses completely, you may still perceive mental images, sounds, tastes, or smells, which may still trigger desires and attachments or attraction and aversion and disturb you. Therefore, the yogi must withdraw his mind further into himself until it ceases to be a problem and rests in itself. Controlling fifteen senses simultaneously is like riding and controlling fifteen horses at a time. Hence, patience and intelligence are required. The Ashtanga Yoga of Patanjali recognizes this problem. Hence, Patanjali suggests a systematic and step-by-step guide to establishing firm control over the mind and body and entering the seedless state of self-absorption (nirbija samadhi). Although a yogi may start practicing the eight limbs simultaneously, it will take a long time to achieve self-purification and excel in them. In the early stages, much of his time goes into observing rules and restraints (yamas and niyamas), breath control (pranayama), and postures (asanas), and in the final stages, into the withdrawal of the senses (pratyahara), concentration (dharana), and meditation (dhyana). Samyama (control and balance) takes an even longer time until the mind becomes fully absorbed in itself and the yogi attains oneness or sameness. The first four limbs are primarily meant to purify the body, and the last four are for purifying and stabilizing the mind. In karma-sannyasa, the yogi must begin by performing duties without desiring their fruit. In the later stages, he must internalize that habit to practice renunciation and overcome all the disturbing aspects of his mind and body through self-control, meditation, and devotion. Through persistent self-control, subduing his mind and body, and resolving desires and attachments, he must attain naishkarmya-siddhi (freedom from karma), sama-buddhi (sameness), atma-samstha (absorption of the mind in the Self), and oneness (Brahma-nirvana).

Sloka 26

yato yato niścarati manaś cañcalam asthiram
tatas tato niyamyaitad ātmany eva vaśaṃ nayet

yatah yatah = for whatever reason and in whichever way; niscarati = keeps wandering; manah = the mind; cancalam = shaking, restless; asthiram = unstable; tatah tatah = from all such causes; niyamya = restrain; etat = it; atmani = own; eva = only; vasam = control; nayet = should bring.

For whatever reason and in whichever way the restless and unstable mind keeps wandering, let him restrain it from that and bring it back under his control only.

Even after years of practice, a yogi's mind tends to wander from thought to thought and memory to memory or object to object. Controlling it and establishing it in a particular mode or condition is probably the toughest of all tasks in yoga. A yoga practitioner may initially feel disturbed by this habitual nature of his mind and take it as a sign of weakness. The verse suggests that he should carefully pay attention to the causes that distract his senses and withdraw them, knowing that it is the nature of the senses to seek objects repeatedly that are illusory and induce passions and desires. He can do it effectively by becoming a passive witness to the movements of his mind and remaining detached and uninvolved. Attraction and aversion, attachment, desires, relationships, duality, delusion, ignorance, the triple gunas, and lack of discrimination are some of the causes that keep the mind and senses restless. In dhyana, a yogi should pay attention to them and stay in control with sameness and equanimity. It is a well-known adage that external events and conditions do not disturb us, but our attitude and responses. It can be practiced in all aspects of life, whether one is engaged in yoga or mundane activities. A yogi should pay attention to his habitual thoughts and responses to external events and change them suitably to control himself. Withdrawing his mind and senses constantly into himself, restraining them whenever they revert to their outgoing mode, he must persevere until he attains self-mastery.

Sloka 27

praśāntamanasaṃ hy enaṃ yoginaṃ sukham uttamam
upaiti śāntarajasaṃ brahmabhūtam akalmaṣam

prasanta = placid, tranquil; manasam = mind; hi = alone, only; enam = this; yoginam = to the yogi; sukham = happiness; uttamam = supreme, the highest; upaiti = comes; santa-rajasam = subdued passions; brahma-bhutam = the Supreme Self; akalmasam = without impurities.

Supreme happiness comes to the yogi, whose mind is placid, whose rajasic passions have been subdued, who has attained the Supreme Self, and who is free from impurities.

Supreme happiness is the natural state of the yogi who attains the Supreme Brahman by removing his impurities through nishkama karma, self-control, and devotion and becomes a jivanmukta (a liberated soul in a living body). He attains serenity as he withdraws his mind and senses into himself, step by step, and restrains them with resolve, fixing his mind upon the Self and constantly meditating until he is fully absorbed in himself. Whenever his mind wanders, he brings it back under his control and continues his effort to find his ultimate Self and become fully established in it. Through self-purification and self-control, he overcomes the desires and passions induced by rajas that disturb his mind. By overcoming desires, attraction, and aversion (raga and dvesha), he overcomes duality and delusion and abides in sameness. Self-transformation is an arduous and time-consuming process. It cannot be accomplished unless the yogi burns his impurities and latent impressions (purva samskaras) through the sacrifice of sannyasa, pouring them into the fires of knowledge, austerity, renunciation, self-control, and devotion. The qualities necessary for attaining liberation, such as detachment, egolessness, dispassion, compassion, nonviolence, non-stealing, devotion, humility, truth, etc., are interconnected. They support, complement, augment, and reinforce each other. To achieve skillfulness in yoga, the yogi must cultivate them through karma-sannyasa or nishkama karma, whether he practices the sacrifice of duty, knowledge, wisdom, self-control, meditation, or devotion. Only then will he attain supreme happiness through disunion (viyoga) from the body and union (samyoga) with the serene Self.

Sloka 28

yuñjann evaṃ sadātmānaṃ yogī vigatakalmaṣaḥ
sukhena brahmasaṃsparśam atyantaṃ sukham aśnute

yunjan =fixing his mind; evam = thus; sada = always; atmanam = within himself; yogi = yogi; vigata = freed from; kalmasah = impurities; sukhena = easily; brahma-samsparsam = direct contact with Brahman; atyantam = highest; sukham = happiness; asnute = attains.

Thus, fixing his mind always within himself, the yogi who is freed from all impurities easily attains supreme bliss arising from direct contact with Brahman.

Supreme happiness or bliss (atyanta sukham) arises in a yogi when he comes into direct contact with his pure Self (the deepest part of him that is free from duality, division, modes, qualities, or modifications) and becomes absorbed in it through self-control (samyama). In an objective-subjective state of mixed self-absorption, he feels proximity to it through his higher mind (buddhi) and purified nature. However, in a purely subjective state, where all dualities and impressions disappear completely, and the mind and senses surrender and recede into complete silence, he experiences it as his natural state without delusion or confusion. The pure Self has the same essential nature as Brahman, which is infinite bliss. Hence, in principle, union with one's pure Self (Atman) is the same as union with the Supreme Brahman, the Universal Self. During intense moments of concentration, a yogi may have a direct vision of his pure Self as other than himself and enter a rapturous state, or he may become absorbed in him and experience the same state. Transcendental experiences are difficult to categorize and generalize. As the paths to God are many, so are the experiences. Only the yogis who advance this far on the path of yoga know their true nature. However, to avoid confusing others, they seldom speak about them. Hence, we cannot be sure how the seers experience direct contact with Brahman and how it translates into cognizable memory.

Brahmasparasam, which means contact with Brahman (God Reality), is a beautiful expression. A yogi or sannyasi may establish contact with Brahman in various ways. Sometimes, he may be certain about the experience or have a vague idea or memory of it, as if he has woken up from a dream. For example, in deep sleep states, we abide in the void or pure consciousness, but we have no awareness of it because the experience happens outside our minds and senses. This is the encounter of the first kind between the mind and the pure Self, where the mind is silent and unaware of its continuous and hidden connection with the supreme Self and its dependence upon him. Sometimes, we come to know about his presence deep within ourselves in wakeful consciousness through intuitive means. For example, when our prayers are heard and answered, they touch the deepest core of our being and reach the inner deity. In tender moments of compassion also we may also feel his universal presence or the oneness of life as we empathize with others' suffering and feel something in us being moved by it. Our faith is sustained upon the belief that we can establish a silent but effective communion with the supreme God and experience oneness with him in a subjective state.

When we perform sacrifices and awaken the invisible power of Brahman to communicate with various divinities and seek their blessings, we know that we can elevate our thoughts to the heavenly realm through the power of prayers augmented with faith. This is the encounter of the second kind, where you realize the presence of God by the results that manifest from your devotional and sacrificial actions.

In the third kind of encounter, we feel the presence of God in our hearts and minds, in a dream state or a deeper state of subtle duality. In moments of intense devotion and love, we feel the direct presence of the Supreme Being and do not doubt it for a second. This is the encounter of the third kind, where you feel the presence of the Lord within yourself mentally and emotionally, and your conviction grows. The fourth kind of encounter is the spiritual kind, described here and experienced by yogis in an absolute state of self-absorption. The last and the fifth kind of encounter happens only when exceptionally pure and liberated souls leave their bodies and depart from here to the world of Brahman, never to return. The pure Self of the adept yogi who is liberated thus either becomes absorbed in the absolute consciousness of the Supreme Self or eternally lives in his presence as a free soul (nitya mukta), maintaining an inseparable inner connection with him through his consciousness. Both schools have their own following in Hinduism and find acceptance in the schools of Vedanta.

Sloka 29

sarvabhūtastham ātmānaṃ sarvabhūtāni cātmani
īkṣate yogayuktātmā sarvatra samadarśanaḥ

sarva-bhuta-stham = in all beings; atmanam = the Self; sarva = all; bhutani = beings; ca = and; atmani = in the Self; iksate = he sees; yoga-yukta-atma = adept yogi well established in yoga; sarvatra = everywhere; sama-darsanah = the vision of sameness.

Seeing the Self in all beings and all beings in the Self, the adept yogi who is well-established in yoga sees everything with the vision of sameness.

In an objective world characterized by diversity, it is impossible to see sameness everywhere. It becomes even more difficult when we perceive the world through our senses and let our egos control our thoughts and actions. Through renunciation and self-control, an adept yogi practices nishkama karma, subdues his ego, mind, and senses, and becomes absorbed in the consciousness of his pure Self. In that state of self-absorption, he sees himself in all and all in himself. When a person is in love, he sees his love everywhere and in everyone, as his mind is repeatedly drawn to that feeling and the memories associated with it. A devotee who is exclusively devoted to God sees him everywhere and in himself, with his mind absorbed in his thoughts. A yogi who attains oneness or sameness remains indifferent to the duality and diversity of the world. His sameness does not arise from the delusion or imagination of the mind. It arises from the purity of his mind and as a consequence of becoming an adept yogi (yuktatma). It manifests naturally when he dissolves his mind and lower nature in the infinite Self and becomes a pure soul.

In pure consciousness, the Self alone shines with subjective awareness and no otherness. Duality, division, and objectivity disappear, and the yogi attains unified consciousness and sees himself in all. When love and devotion dissolve all barriers created by the lower nature, he sees everything as an extension of himself. Until he purifies himself and achieves liberation, the yogi should shun the world and stay away from worldly enjoyment. However, upon attaining liberation, he can move freely since he is no longer affected by the world or its attractions and distractions. Having consumed the poison of samsara like awakened Shiva, he returns to it, keeping his mind and body fully subdued, and continues to practice nishkama karma. With the pure consciousness of the Self firmly established in him, he experiences the omnipresence of Brahman and sees the whole universe pervaded by him. He sees his consciousness stretching infinitely, pervading and enveloping everything and everyone.

On the spiritual path, egoism is the biggest obstacle to overcoming duality and individuality. Once it is removed, the yogi's consciousness fills the whole universe as all the barriers put up by it dissolve, leaving the Self to shine as the lonely seer by himself and within himself. A self-realized yogi has no ego. Even if it exists rudimentarily, it remains free from attachments and desires. His subdued ego and restful mind enable him to connect to others without the natural barriers put up by Nature. He can empathize with others, read their minds, or feel their feelings without exchanging words. He may also foresee their past, present, and future, how they are affected by their karma, or how it may fructify in the future due to the actions they performed in their past or past lives. In the tranquil state of sameness, his intelligence goes beyond the appearance of things to discern their essence as they are or in oneness without distortions.

Sloka 30

yo māṃ paśyati sarvatra sarvaṃ ca mayi paśyati
tasyāhaṃ na praṇaśyāmi sa ca me na praṇaśyati

yah = he who; mam = Me; pasyati = sees; sarvatra = everywhere; sarvam = all things; ca = and; mayi = in Me; pasyati = he sees; tasya = for him; aham = I; na = not; pranasyami = cease to exist; sah = he; ca = also; me = to Me; na = nor; pranasyati = ceases to exist.

He who sees Me everywhere and sees all things in Me, I do not cease to exist for him, and he does not cease to exist for Me.

The deluded one sees the world as the world and himself as a jiva or physical being, distinct from others, having an existence of his own, and made to live for himself. That very thinking makes him desire things to complete himself. A liberated yogi (yuktatma) sees the world filled and his whole being filled with the presence of the Supreme Lord. He sees Himself in all and everywhere. His seeing is not affected by desires, attachments, or circumstances but arises from the unity or oneness he experiences within himself and feels its inseparable connection to the whole existence. His inner experience of his unified consciousness translates itself into supreme devotion to the Lord, who personifies it. There is no relationship as such in that bonding since the duality of subject and object does not exist in it. It is always the Self, the subject. Therefore, the devotee who has attained oneness is never separate from the Lord or the Lord from his devotee. They abide in the same consciousness, with an invisible bond connecting them inseparably through it and helping the devotee sustain himself until he departs from the body. We do not know what happens after that, whether he continues to exist as an immortal soul or merges into him completely like a water drop that falls into the ocean and disappears completely. Whatever the truth, the yogi who attains oneness with the Self or with Brahman never wavers in his devotion and is never forsaken by the Lord.

The duality of union and separation is a fact of our physical existence. They do not exist in the unified consciousness of the Self or the yogi who attains it and enjoys the same consciousness as the Supreme Brahman. The liberated yogi sees Him as himself everywhere and in everything. He does not think that by attaining that state, he has achieved or attained anything, as he realizes that the consciousness that he was seeking was but his natural and deepest Self all along, and that he was oblivious of it because he was stuck in samsara and enveloped by its impurities. Yogis will experience it only when they renounce everything that arises in them from the world and enter the deepest part of their consciousness, where the world does not exist and only the seer remains. In that exalted state, the yogi experiences oneness with the Lord rather than duality and sameness rather than a relationship. He finds himself in an indistinguishable state from the Lord and realizes that the Lord he has been worshipping with unwavering devotion has been within himself all along as his pure Self.

Devotion brings God and His devotee together and cements their relationship. It is strengthened to the extent that the devotee cultivates purity, nearness, and sameness with God. When he becomes pure and transparent like a crystal, he attains samāpatti, or the ability to radiate the purity of his soul. Therefore, unwavering devotion is the key to attaining perfection in the yoga of liberation. When you are deeply in love with God, you see Him in yourself and feel his presence wherever your mind and senses go. When you are emotionally drawn to Him, you will not bear the thought of separation from Him, even for a moment. In this state, which is essentially a fervent emotional state, you may not transcend the duality or achieve complete liberation. However, if your devotion is strong and pure, you will eventually cross the threshold and experience the divine presence of Brahman, the supreme reality, in everything and everywhere.

A devotee of pure mind and heart, who has no ego and no hankering, is never separate from the object of his love, which is God, and God never forsakes him because their bond is unique and irreversible. This is an assurance of God. Once you form a bond with Him, having forsaken all other bonds, you are never lost to Him, nor is He lost to you. A deluded one may be lost to Him because of the barriers between them, but not a devotee who has attained His pure consciousness. If the deluded one happens to be an atheist, the Lord may cease to exist for him to fulfill his egoistic desire to see Him as nonexistent, but He never does that for a devotee who resides in His heart.

Sloka 31

sarvabhūtasthitaṃ yo māṃ bhajaty ekatvam āsthitaḥ
sarvathā vartamānopi sa yogī mayi vartate

sarva-bhuta-sthitam = dweller of all being; yah = he who; mam = to Me; bhajati = worships; ekatvam = oneness; asthitah = established, situated; sarvatha = always; varta-manah = present condition; api = however, whatever; sah = that, he; yogi = yogi; mayi = in Me; vartate = lives, exists, behaves, acts.

He who worships Me as the dweller of all things, always established in oneness, that yogi exists in Me, however he may live.

A yogi who worships the Supreme Lord as the dweller of all (sarva bhutatma) and constantly engages his mind in Him, established in oneness and with no other thought or desire, is never lost to Him. He enjoys his grace and protection, even if he does not adhere to the prescribed code of conduct. Hence, as this verse suggests, through oneness and pure devotion, a devotee can achieve the same goal as a yogi through karma-sannyasa or sannyasa. However, for that, he must practice self-control, cultivate purity, knowledge, and discernment, and worship the Lord exclusively established in oneness through contemplation. However, it is much better if a yogi stabilizes his mind and practices both karma-sannyasa and devotion simultaneously. Controlling his mind and body, performing actions for the sake of God, and engaging his mind constantly in His thoughts, he can practice both the yogas. He can strengthen devotion through the three Vedantic practices: hearing (sravanam), remembering (mananam), and contemplation (nidhidhyasana). It does not matter whether he worships the Lord internally or exclusively, but his devotion must be pure and his actions must be free from desires and delusion.

Thus, if you restrain yourself, remain established in the oneness of the Self, and worship the Lord selflessly, your actions will not taint you, and the Lord will not forsake you. Consecrating your life, possessions, and your mind and body to God is the ultimate sacrifice and the highest form of sannyasa. By that, you will exemplify the ideal of self-sacrifice, which is at the heart of both karma-sannyasa and devotion. By giving up attachment to your mind and body and subduing your ego, duality, and delusion, you will let God live in you and become the enjoyer and controller of your life and actions. A true devotee who has given himself to pure devotion is never separate from God. He lives in God just as God lives in him. His mind remains established in His thoughts and does not waver. Since he performs actions in His name and lets Him be the sole enjoyer of their fruit, it does not matter how he lives or what actions he performs.

A devotee who realizes that God dwells in all treats His creation with the same devotion, respect, and consideration. He harbors no ill will against others or causes them any harm. Compassion and nonviolence arise in him naturally as he sees himself or the Lord in all and empathizes with their suffering. Seeing Him or himself as the Self of all, he transcends his likes and dislikes and treats others with sameness, accepting them as God's numerous forms and faces. The world becomes a temple for him, and he becomes a true Bhagavata, the servant (dasa) of God. His very living becomes a continuous form of worship and adoration through his devotion, and his actions become sacrificial offerings in the fire of renunciation. Whether he is engaged in obligatory duties (karma), inaction (akarma), or prohibited actions (vikarma), sin will not attach to him since he is established in Him without duality and lives for Him only.

Sloka 32

ātmaupamyena sarvatra samaṃ paśyati yorjuna
sukhaṃ vā yadi vā duḥkhaṃ sa yogī paramo mataḥ

Translation

atmaaupamyena = using the self as the standard; sarvatra = everywhere; samam = equally; pasyati = sees; yah = he who; arjuna = O Arjuna; sukham = happiness; va = or; yadi =whether; va = or; duhkham = sorrow, distress; sah = that; yogi = yogi; paramah = supreme; matah = considered.

Meaning

Holding himself as the standard for comparison, whoever sees equality (of all) everywhere, whether in happiness or sorrow, O Arjuna, that one should be considered a supreme yogi.

Commentary

Atmaupamayena means using oneself as the standard to view others or understand them. A self-realized yogi who sees himself or God in all considers everyone as himself or God, treats them the same way he would like to be treated, and holds them with the same esteem as he holds himself. He sees them as the numerous faces of the Supreme Isvara rather than as individual entities. Knowing that God dwells in all and they experience the same feelings and dualities, such as pain, pleasure, happiness, heat, and cold, he practices restraints such as nonviolence, truthfulness, non-possession, and non-stealing so that he will not be the cause of any disturbance or suffering for others. According to Shankara, he feels their pain and suffering just as he feels his own and, therefore, does not hurt or harm anyone.

The apparent diversity is the play of Maya, which the deluded ones accept as real and act accordingly. They do not see others as equal but as different. They do not see the God who dwells in them but their apparent names and forms. Due to desires and delusion, they care more for themselves than for others and seek their own happiness and fulfillment, ignoring how their actions may affect others. The yogi who abides in sameness exemplifies their opposite qualities. He sees the underlying unity of all rather than their diversity. He radiates love and compassion that arises from his oneness and serves others through nishkama karma as if he is serving the Lord. Through his selfless actions, he exemplifies the truth that serving others is serving the Lord. The mind sees diversity. The Self sees unity. Duality arises from the surface consciousness. Oneness arises from the indivisible pure consciousness. If you reject the objective reality of your mind, become detached and indifferent to it, and see the world from the unified consciousness of the Self, even notionally, you will have a different perspective about what you see in others or how you connect to them or empathize with them. Then, the all-pervading Self (sarva bhutatma) becomes the focal point of your worldview and the measure (upamana) of things.

This verse refers to that exemplary devotee who sees the Lord everywhere and in all with oneness and considers everything as his own play (lila) and himself a player or actor in it. Purified by his devotion and restraint, he perceives the Lord in himself and others, the world as his play, and all that exists in it as his projections or appearances. He becomes a witness to it, knowing that the same Lord stages that drama to enthrall himself, enacting all roles, performing all actions, and going through all experiences. A yogi who develops that vision of unity, equality, and inclusiveness is considered the best of yogis because he achieves sameness, nonduality, and union with his pure consciousness.

Sloka 33

arjuna uvāca
yoyaṃ yogas tvayā proktaḥ sāmyena madhusūdana
etasyāhaṃ na paśyāmi cañcalatvāt sthitiṃ sthirām

Translation

arjunah uvaca = Arjuna said; yah = which ayam = this; yogah = yoga; tvaya = by You; proktah = described, spoken, spoken; samyena = by sameness; madhu-sudana = O Madhusudana, slayer of Madhu; etasya = of its; aham = I; na = do not; pasyami = see; cancalatvat = due to restlessness of the mind; sthitim = state or condition; sthiram = stability or constancy.

Meaning

Said Arjuna, "O Madhusudana, this yoga, which was declared by you as sameness, I am not seeing its stability or constancy due to the restless state of mind."

Commentary

Arjuna wanted to know how the mind could be stabilized and sameness could be achieved since it was unstable and restless by nature and subject to modifications. In the previous verses, Lord Krishna explained to him the importance of restraining his mind and senses, overcoming attraction and aversion, and practicing detachment and renunciation to achieve sameness. He told him how a yogi who became the conqueror of the senses (jitendriya), mind, and body (vijitatma) and saw the Self as the Self of all (sarva bhutatma) would be equal to dualities such as heat and cold or pleasure and pain and treat a lump of gold or a piece of clay with the same indifference. He further said that the yogi who was established in oneness and worshipped him as the dweller of all beings would exist in him always, and whoever saw all things equally in happiness and sorrow should be considered the best yogi. Arjuna felt that even if the best of the yogis succeeded in controlling their minds, they would naturally become unstable or restless as soon as their minds fell into their usual modes. Therefore, he wondered whether it would be possible at all to stabilize the mind and abide in sameness or equanimity. Sameness is the culmination of a long and persistent practice. For that, one has to overcome many obstacles and excel in karma-sannyasa and atma-samyama. One attains it only after a prolonged practice and after earning divine grace. Therefore, Arjuna wondered whether sameness could be achieved at all through self-control, even after all the practice, since the mind was naturally restless and unstable.

Sloka 34

cañcalaṃ hi manaḥ kṛṣṇa pramāthi balavad dṛḍham
tasyāhaṃ nigrahaṃ manye vāyor iva suduṣkaram

Translation

cancalam = fickle, unsteady, restless; hi = surely; manah = mind; krsna = O Krsna; pramathi = turbulent; bala-vat = strong; drdham = obstinate, stong,; tasya = its; aham = I; nigraham = control; manye = think; vayoh = of the wind; iva = like; su-duskaram = difficult.

"Surely, O Krishna, the mind is fickle, turbulent, strong, and obstinate. I think it is as difficult to control as wind."

Arjuna compared the mind to the wind to reiterate his argument that it was unstable and turbulent by nature and difficult to control. He mentioned its four characteristics, saying it was fickle, turbulent, strong, and obstinate. Chanchalm means constantly moving from point to point and seldom in the same place. The mind is fickle, just like the wind. It keeps wandering due to desires and attachments and does not settle for long on anything. It is so common even for yogis to be lost in thoughts or reverie. Pramati means feeling easily disturbed, irritated, afraid, annoyed, troubled, tormented, or affected by events and circumstances. The turbulent state of mind is caused by attraction and aversion, desires and attachments, and passions induced by the triple gunas. The mind is also strong (balavat), meaning it does not easily give up, surrender, or yield, and is difficult to control or restrain. Drdham means obstinate, uncontainable, incorrigible, not amenable to reason. It is well known that the mind has set modes and habitual ways that are difficult to change or overcome. Some habits last for a lifetime and extend to the next life through the causal body. These qualities make practicing self-control (atma-samyama), concentration, and meditation difficult. Only a few yogis ever succeed in it.

However, as Sri Aurobindo said, while the mind is an obstacle up to a point, it is also a friend and facilitator if you know how to control and attune it. Although considered an obstacle in spiritual practice, it is also the most impressive organ in the body that sets us apart from other living beings and gives us exceptional powers to know ourselves, solve problems, and work for our improvement and liberation. It is also the most difficult to control since it is not easily amenable to discipline or restraint. It is fickle and unstable like the wind due to the influence of the triple modes and the activity of the senses. They are responsible for the impurities (dhosa) such as ignorance, egoism, desires, attachments, and delusion, which aggravate its instability. It is also the seat of suffering due to mental modifications (vrittis) and afflictions (kleshas), which keep it restless.

Patanjali listed mental instability (anvastitatvam) as one of the chief causes of the mind's turbulence. The others are disease (vyadhi), idleness (stayana), doubt (samsaya), negligence (pramada), laziness (alasya), lack of detachment (avirati), mistaken perceptions (bhranti darsana), and failure to ground the mind in concentration (alabda bhumikatva). These disturbances, which are responsible for its instability, are caused by the impurities in the consciousness (citta), which can only be eliminated through purification. According to him, they also lead to secondary disturbances (viksepas), such as pain and suffering (dukha), dejection or frustration (daurmansyam), trembling of the body (angam ejayatva), and unsteady breathing (prasvasa). A yogi can remove them and stabilize his mind by practicing concentration on a single object (eka tattvam), cultivating virtues such as friendliness and compassion, regulating the incoming and outgoing breath, using sense objects as support (visayavati) in contemplation, sleeping and dreaming, overcoming desires, etc. The mind is stable, clean, and transparent like a bright diamond when it is without impurities.

Sloka 35

śrībhagavān uvāca
asañśayaṃ mahābāho mano durnigrahaṃ calam
abhyāsena tu kaunteya vairāgyeṇa ca gṛhyate

sri-bhagavan uvaca = the Supreme Lord said; asamsayam = undoubtedly; maha-baho = O mighty-armed one; manah = mind; durnigraham = difficult to control; calam = restless; abhyasena = by repeated practice; tu = however; kaunteya = O son of Kunti; vairagyena = distaste, detachment, indifference, aversion, renunciation; ca = and; grhyate = tamed, held in control.

Meaning

The Supreme Lord said, "O mighty-armed, without doubt, the mind is restless and difficult to control. However, O son of Kunti, through regular practice and vairagya, it can be tamed.

Lord Krishna replied that although the mind is restless and difficult to control, sameness can still be attained through the regular practice (abhyasa) of self-restraint and detachment (vairagya). However, he did not specify what he meant by regular practice (abhyasa). Going by the context, we have to assume that he was referring to the regular practice of karma-sannyasa yoga with devotion, meditation (dhyana), and self-control (atma samyama) to cultivate detachment, indifference, and sameness. The word "vairagya" has multiple meanings. In mundane life, it refers to the state of despair in which one loses hope and passion and develops aversion (virakti) to the previously attractive things. In spirituality, it refers to the absence of desires and passions for worldly life and material things, which is characteristic of viragis (bairagis) or those who are free from attraction and aversion (raga and dvesha). It arises from the consistent practice of detachment, renunciation, austerities, and self-control. Vairagya is central to all renunciant traditions because, without it, one cannot overcome desires, develop a distaste for worldly things, or practice renunciation to subdue the gunas.

The mind is comparable to the water in a turbulent lake, which is always in a state of flux and easily disturbed or ruffled by the things that enter it or the wind that blows over it. If you want to control it, you have to control its four propensities mentioned by Arjuna, namely fickleness (chanchalam), turbulence (pramati), unyielding strength (balavat), and stubbornness (drdham). They must be overcome through withdrawal, concentration, desirelessness, desireless actions, self-control, and meditation. As one practices karma-sannyasa yoga, with knowledge, discernment, devotion, self-control, and meditation, the mind falls in line and yields to silence and equanimity. Alternatively, you may practice meditation and worship with unwavering devotion to the Lord who dwells in you as your Self and controls everything as the Lord of all, seeing him within yourself and everywhere until you overcome duality and are firmly established in oneness. Some engage in devotional activities such as singing, dancing, praying, chanting, remembering his names and forms, listening to his glories, etc., to strengthen their devotion and establish their minds firmly in his contemplation. All these approaches are helpful in stabilizing the mind, cultivating dispassion and renunciation, and establishing the mind in the Self without duality.

In the first chapter (1.12) of the Yogasutras, we find a similar observation about controlling the mind. It states that a yogi can stop and counter (nirodha) the mind's modifications (vrittis) with regular practice (abhyasa) and dispassion (vairagyam). Probably, this two-pronged approach was popular in ancient India to practice self-control. Patanjali defines abhyasa (1.13-14) as diligent effort (yatana) in concentration. The mind becomes firmly established in the Self when concentration is practiced uninterruptedly (nirantaram) for a long time (dirgha-kalam) with devotion (satkarasevita). In the next verse (1.15), Patanjali defines dispassion (vairagyam) as controlled consciousness attained by overcoming the craving for sense objects, whether real, perceived, or imagined. He also states that indifference to the modes is more important than renunciation. Thus, both the scriptures uphold abhyasa and vairagya as effective techniques for taming the mind. Therefore, if liberation is the goal, one must practice self-control relentlessly and uncompromisingly, withdrawing and arresting the fickleness of the mind and senses and holding them steady. Restraining them thus and practicing karma-sannyasa or nishkama karma, devotion, and renunciation, the yogi should strive for perfection in atma-samyama, dhyana, and sannyasa to achieve oneness.

Sloka 36

asaṃyatātmanā yogo duṣprāpa iti me matiḥ
vaśyātmanā tu yatatā śakyovāptum upāyataḥ

asamyata-atmana = by a person who lacks self-control; yogah = the state of yoga; dusprapah = difficult to obtain; iti = so, thus; me = My; matih = opinion; vasya-atmana = one who has control over his mind; tu = but; yatata = strives hard; sakyah = possible; avaptum = to achieve; upayatah = by means.

Yoga is difficult to attain by him who does not control himself, so is My opinion. However, it can be attained by a person who strives hard to control himself by (these) means.

The yoga the Lord was referring to in this verse is the yoga of sameness, stillness, or oneness, or seeing him everywhere as the Self of all, attained through the persistent effort to control the internal organ (antahkarana). In the previous verse, he suggested that although it was difficult to control the mind, it could still be achieved by abhyasa (regular practice) and vairagya (distaste). In this verse, he restated the same, saying that one could control it through repeated effort (yatata). Whether in mundane life or yoga, persistent effort (yatata) is necessary to reach the chosen goal. However, while deluded people strive with desires and passions to attain their desired ends, the yogis who are established in dispassion (vairagya) and renunciation (karma-sannyasa) do it without desires and expectations, offering the fruit of their actions to the Supreme Lord, seeing him in all as the Self of all. They engage in persistent practice (abhyasa) to follow their vows of renunciation and practice the restraints (yama) and rules (niyama) to cleanse themselves without desiring their fruit. These practices are necessary to tame their minds and senses, subdue the gunas, and harness pure energies or higher Shaktis in the contemplation of the Lord. For that, they must strengthen the three qualities, faith (sraddha), fear of sin (bhayam), and devotion (bhakti), which are foundational for perfection in it. Their intention to practice self-control must also be pure and selfless. For example, demons (danavas or rakshasas) also practice austerities with rigorous self-control to secure boons from the gods for evil purposes. They predictably misuse their powers and bring trouble upon themselves and others. Self-control is meant to purify and stabilize the mind in contemplating the Lord as the Self of all to achieve liberation through oneness or sameness. It is the means, not an end. In the following verse, the Lord states that if intentions are pure, failure in yoga will not lead to sinful consequences or one's downfall.

Sloka 37

arjuna uvāca
ayatiḥ śraddhayopeto yogāc calitamānasaḥ
aprāpya yogasaṃsiddhiṃ kāṃ gatiṃ kṛṣṇa gacchati

arjunah uvaca = Arjuna said; ayatih = an unrestrained yogi; sraddhaya = with faith; upetah = endowed with, possessed of; yogat = from yoga; calita = wandering, agitated, shaken; manasah = mind; aprapya = without gaining; yoga-samsiddhim = success, perfection or sameness in yoga; kam = what; gatim = goal, destination; krsna = O Krsna; gacchati = goes.

Arjuna said, "The unrestrained yogi who is endowed with faith but has not attained perfection in yoga due to (his) wandering mind, in which direction, O Krishna, does he go?"

Arjuna wanted to know what happens to a yogi who has faith but does not attain liberation or perfection in his practice due to the lack of self-control and failure to restrain his wandering mind. Success is not guaranteed for everyone who strives for liberation because of the mind's instability and turbulent nature, and because of the wayward senses. Previously, Lord Krishna himself acknowledged this in verses 35 and 36, saying that perfection in yoga was difficult to attain but could be achieved by a yogi who controlled his mind with persistent practice and cultivated a distaste for worldly pleasures. Arjuna wanted to know what happens to the yogi who has faith in the Lord, but does not strive enough to control himself, and where he would go, whether to the ancestral heaven or the immortal heaven. Would he attain liberation or continue to revolve in samsara?

The mind's outgoing tendency (prvritti) is very strong. Even after years of practice, it may revert to its habitual ways even if the yogi strives hard. The Puranas show how, even after a prolonged practice of austerities, many seers and sages fall for temptations and fail in their austerities. As long as the gunas are active and exert influence, desires and attachments remain the main drivers of actions. Yogis who practice self-control (atma-samyama) and contemplation (dhyana) face two hurdles. First, they must suppress the modes (gunas) and their influence. Second, they must resolve their karma through nishkama karma and devotion to God. Both require a perseverant effort since, to transcend the gunas and desires, they must control their essential nature and deep-rooted tendencies, especially those that might have been inherited from their past lives. It is as challenging as swimming against the flow of a turbulent river flooded by heavy monsoon rain. Hence, failure is common and frequent on the path of liberation. Only a few succeed in the first attempt.

In karma-sannyasa, yogis are not supposed to think of the result or the consequences. Here, Arjuna asked a question about the result of failure in yoga. One may wonder whether it is justified. One should indeed perform actions without desiring their fruit and without expectations. However, knowing the consequences of failure in yoga is not sinful or prohibited. Teachers have an obligation to let their students know what may happen to them if they fail or falter in their practice. This question is relevant to the discourse since it addresses an important concern. It will help the yogis to prepare themselves for all eventualities and focus their attention on the practice.

Sloka 38

kacchin nobhayavibhraṣṭaś chinnābhram iva naśyati
apratiṣṭho mahābāho vimūḍho brahmaṇaḥ pathi

kaccit = does he; na = not; ubhaya-vibhrastah = fallen from both; chinna = torn, broken; abhram = cloud; iva = like; nasyati = perishes; apratisthah = without a firm ground or resting place, unstable; maha-baho = O mighty-armed; vimudhah = deluded; brahmanah = Brahman; pathi = on the path.

"O mighty-armed, would he not perish like a broken cloud, having fallen from both, without a firm ground or resting place, and deluded on the path of Brahman?"

A cloud fragment broken from a larger cloud will gradually dissipate and disappear. Arjuna compared it to the yogi who failed in meditation and self-control. He wanted to know whether that yogi would perish without a proper resting ground (stable mind). He thought that having failed on both counts (ubhaya-vibhrastah) to restrain his mind and body and establish his mind in the Self, the yogi would fail to earn God's grace, which is necessary for liberation, and remain deluded and broken. He probably assumed that by giving up worldly life and failing to achieve liberation, the yogi would deny himself happiness here and hereafter. Hence, he wanted to know the fate of that yogi. According to Shankaracharya, the twin failures refer to the failures in practicing karma and jnana yogas. The discussion is about self-control and the topic is the fickle and stubborn nature of the mind, which Lord Krishna said could be controlled through the twin practice of abhyasa and vairagya. Hence, we may presume that Arjuna was referring to the twin practices of karma-sannyasa and atma-samyama. Dhyana (meditation) is an important practice of atma-samyama only.

Sloka 39

etan me saṃśayaṃ kṛṣṇa chettum arhasy aśeṣataḥ
tvadanyaḥ saṃśayasyāsya chettā na hy upapadyate

etat = this is; me = my; samsayam = doubt; krsna = O Krsna; chettum = dispel; arhasi = qualified, enlightend; asesatah = completely; tvat = than You; anyah = other; samsayasya = of the doubt; asya = of this; chetta = dispeller, remover; na = never; hi = certainly; upapadyate = is to be found.

Surely, O Krishna, you are the most qualified to dispel my confusion without further doubt. Certainly, no one else will ever be found who can clarify it.

Doubt (samsayam) may arise due to a lack of faith or proper knowledge. In Arjuna's case, it must be due to a lack of knowledge since he had unwavering faith in Lord Krishna. Otherwise, he would not have chosen him as his charioteer or sought his advice when he decided not to fight. He also expressed it by saying that no one other than him would be able to clear his doubt. A student must have complete confidence in his teacher. He must be motivated by his faith rather than his desires, fear, or doubt. Faith strengthens his interest, willingness, curiosity, determination, and attention. When a student or disciple trusts his teacher with complete faith, he learns quickly without doubting what he has learned and without looking to others for confirmation. This is especially true about the knowledge that cannot be validated by any means other than verbal testimony from an authoritative source. Lord Krishna was the Supreme Lord. Therefore, there would be no better testimony than His words. We do not doubt that Arjuna knew the value of an authoritative testimony like Lord Krishna. Therefore, he asked Him this question with complete faith and humility, surrendering his ego, pride, and ignorance.

Sloka 40

śrībhagavān uvāca
pārtha naiveha nāmutra vināśas tasya vidyate
na hi kalyāṇakṛt kaścid durgatiṃ tāta gacchati

sri-bhagavan uvaca = the Supreme Lord said; partha = O son of Partha; na = not; eva = surely; iha = here in this world; na = not; amutra = in the next world; vinasah = downfall, destruction; tasya = for him; vidyate = there is; na = not; hi = surely; kalyana-krt = performs auspicious actoins; kascit = anyone; durgatim = towards misfortune, hardship, adversity; tata = O dear, My son; gacchati = falls, lands, goes.

The Supreme Lord said, "O Partha, certainly there is no downfall for him in this world and the next. My son, surely, no one who performs auspicious deeds falls into misfortune."

This verse affirms the karma doctrine. Good actions lead to good ends, although the rewards may take time to manifest. Even karma yogis who perform righteous actions without desiring their fruit must let their karmas exhaust. If they deviate from the path, it will delay their liberation. Life is uncertain. Therefore, yogis strive until the end without losing control. The karma that has already accrued from their pious deeds and yoga practice will yield its fruit in due time. Meanwhile, assuming that the yogi who strayed from the path did not sabotage himself further through mortally sinful actions, we can safely predict that he has a good chance of recovering from his failure if he starts practicing yoga again. His progress may be delayed, but it will not be denied. Thus, while good deeds lead to good karma, there are no negative consequences for not performing them. God's devotees may earn merit according to their devotion and yoga practice, but will not be punished if their devotion or practice falters in the middle. However, it will prolong their bondage and affect their next birth. Thus, a devotee or yogi who has strayed from his path is not punished by anyone but by himself.

In the Bhagavadgita, we discern three types of karma: righteous actions (sakama karma), evil actions (dushkama karma), and selfless or desireless actions (nishkama karma). Good actions lead to purity, light, and liberation. Evil actions result in impurity, darkness, and suffering. Selfless actions free him from his sins and improve his chances of attaining liberation. Although the law of karma is universal, and jivas accrue karma according to their actions and intentions, there is no loss of whatever purity or karmic good (punya) has already been earned for leaving yoga in the middle or failing in it. Whatever merit has already accrued to the yogi remains. We find this assurance from Lord Krishna in this verse. No one accrues sin for discontinuing spiritual practice. However, by doing so, they will risk their future. By addressing Arjuna as tata (beloved or my son), Lord Krishna also implied that this observation applies to all his devotees who are like his children and worship him with faith and devotion.

However, it isn't easy to foresee when and how karma will manifest in a jiva's existence or in what form. This uncertainty about how karma unravels can be unsettling for many when they see evil people enjoying a good life and good people suffering from difficulties and adverse conditions. In worldly life, it looks as if good deeds go unnoticed, and evil deeds are amply rewarded. It is not the fault of karma or the failure of divine justice. It is because karma takes time to fructify. Besides, the lives of all the jivas in the world are interconnected. A person's life and destiny are determined not only by his actions but also by the actions of others, including those of Nature. Further, we cannot be certain that a good life is always a reward for good deeds or that a life of suffering is a punishment for sins. There may be other hidden factors since, in spiritual life, success and failure do not have the same meaning as in worldly life. The good life may be a trap to delude and distract, and the adverse life may be a gift to help the suffering one overcome past failures and improve. Without practicing karma-sannyasa and living righteously, no one can escape from sinful actions.

As Lord Krishna promised here, what is certain is that no one who performs good deeds ever falls into misfortune. Good deeds, such as renunciation, austerities, contemplation, etc., produce good conditions in this life or the next. Lord Krishna clearly assured here that there is no ruin or downfall for his devotees who are pure in their minds and hearts and engage in righteous actions. Their rewards may not immediately be visible or known, but their good actions will surely lead them in the right direction (sugati). There is no suffering (durgati) for the pious who perform good deeds (sukrtam) and no heavenly life for the wicked who engage in evil actions (dushkrtam).

Sloka 41

prāpya puṇyakṛtāṃ lokān uṣitvā śāśvatīḥ samāḥ
śucīnāṃ śrīmatāṃ gehe yogabhraṣṭobhijāyate

prapya = having attained; punya = righteous, meritorious; krtam = deeds, actions; lokan = worlds; usitva = having dwelt; sasvatih = long time, countless; samah = years; sucinam = of the pious; sri-matam = of the prosperous; gehe = in the house of; yoga-bhrastah = the yogi who has stumbled on the faith; abhijayate = is born.

Having attained the worlds of those who perform righteous deeds and dwelt there for a long time, the yogi who stumbles on the path of yoga is born in the house of the pious and the prosperous.

What happens to a person after death depends upon his actions and the karma he accumulated in his current life and all his past lives. Therefore, his destiny is rather complicated and cannot be predicted clearly. Generally, those who perform good deeds go to the ancestral world, enjoy their stay there, and return to the earth to take another birth. They enjoy the bhogas (enjoyments) of various kinds in their current lives as the rewards for their pious deeds. After departing from here, some advanced souls and siddhas may continue to evolve in the higher heavens, spending time near their beloved gods and developing even more skills and perfections. After spending a long time in those worlds, they return to the world as enlightened masters, saints, and gurus and engage in pious deeds to help others or spread the spiritual knowledge of liberation. The karma yogis who perform their obligatory duties while they are alive go to the ancestral world. They stay there until their due time. When they return, they enjoy better opportunities to continue their journey and evolve further. The karma-sannyasis, who give up their practice in the middle and fail to achieve naishkarmya siddhi or samsiddhi or resolve their prarabdha karma, enjoy a similar fate. They can start from where they left off and advance further. In all these cases, a good rebirth is guaranteed for the righteous ones. For the liberated yogis, there is no rebirth, but for the fallen ones, the path of liberation is still open if they wish to return. Liberation is a personal journey in which everything hinges on the seeker's knowledge, faith, devotion, wisdom, and commitment.

With the debts of his karma unpaid, the yogi who has fallen in his yoga practice (yoga-brashta) returns to the mortal world to perform his obligatory duties. If he continues on the path of karma yoga, he will reap the fruit of his sacrificial actions and progress further. If he advanced well on the path in his previous life, he may take birth in the house of a pious and prosperous family in favorable and auspicious circumstances. What happens to him after that depends entirely upon what he will do in his current life. If he continues to practice yoga, he will progress. If he makes mistakes or falters again, he will delay his liberation and may find himself in even more difficult situations. Spiritual recovery is a complex process that requires more effort and personal care than the recovery of the mind and body. Therefore, yogis should not abandon their practice in the middle due to desires or temptations. Since human life is difficult to attain and no one can predict how life will take a turn in the future, they should make the best use of their opportunity to practice yoga and achieve liberation. The good thing is that there is no destruction for them if they fail. They can always return to complete their journey and escape from samsara. Even a little practice of yoga brings good rewards.

Sloka 42

athavā yoginām eva kule bhavati dhīmatām
etad dhi durlabhataraṃ loke janma yad īdṛśam

athava- = or; yoginam = of yogis; eva = even; kule = in the family of; bhavati = is born; dhi-matam = of great wisdom and intelligence; etat = such; hi = indeed; durlabha-taram = rare or difficult to attain; loke = in this world; janma = birth; yat idrsam = the one like this.

Or he is born in a family of yogis of great wisdom and intelligence. Indeed, a birth such as this one is rare or difficult to attain in this world.

The yogi who fails in his practice may be born into a pious and wealthy family or a family of poor yogis or seers. According to Shankara, the latter birth is rarer and more difficult to obtain than the former one. Therefore, it should be considered a blessing. Hindu scriptures mention the names of many great souls who were born in families of pious people, seers, and sages. Atri was one of the seven great seers of Hinduism (saptarishis). He had three sons: Durvasa, Dattatreya, and Patanjali. Bharadwaja was sired by sage Brihaspati, the son of Rishi Angiras. Parasurama, considered an incarnation of Vishnu, was born of Jamadagni and Renuka. Sage Jamadagni was himself a descendant of another great seer, Bhrigu. Prahlada, the great devotee of Vishnu, was born to Hiranyakasipu, a demon who belonged to the lineage of sage Kashyapa. (He did not take birth in a family of holy men or pure sages, but in a family of demons because he was destined to be instrumental in the destruction of Hiranyakasipu). Svetaketu was the son of Uddalaka Aruni, a renowned seer of the Upanishads, from whom he learned the knowledge of Brahman. The Upanishads also mention another Svetaketu, the son of Gautama.

Thus, the circumstances surrounding the birth of humans play an important role in shaping their destiny, which is, in turn, determined by their past karma. This is amply illustrated in the biographies of many seers and sages. When you engage in good deeds, you create favorable circumstances for your future and next life. However, it does not always have to happen in all cases since spiritual requirements for a yogi's transformation may vary. Sometimes, they may be born in ordinary circumstances but eventually reach their goal through self-effort. For example, Satyakama Jabala was born of a maid and an unknown father, but, due to his truthfulness, secured the secret knowledge of Brahman from his teacher, Gautama, and became a great sage. Maitreya was a housewife who learned the same knowledge from her husband, Yajnavalkya, before he retired to the forests, renouncing worldly life. To be born into a family of sages or yogis is rare because most of them practice celibacy and do not marry or live as householders.

Sloka 43

tatra taṃ buddhisaṃyogaṃ labhate paurvadehikam
yatate ca tato bhūyaḥ saṃsiddhau kurunandana

tatra = there; tam = that; buddhi-samyogam = united with buddhi; labhate = becomes, gains; paurva = of previous; dehikam = bodily existence; yatate = he strives; ca = and; tatah = than before; bhuyah = seriously; samsiddhau = perfection in equanimity or sameness; kuru-nandana = O son of Kuru.

O Son of Kuru, there he becomes united with the intelligence of his previous bodily existences and strives more seriously than before for perfection in equanimity.

Some achievements and perfections of past lives are carried forward from one birth to another. This is confirmed in this verse. When the time is ripe, a yogi who has fallen on the path in his past life may reconnect to his failed cause and revive his practice to pursue liberation again. People are often fed up with their worldly lives and suddenly decide to explore spirituality. They leave everything behind and go in search of meaning and purpose. It is probably because of such reasons. Gautama Buddha's parents did their best to keep him busy and prevent him from becoming a monk, as astrologers predicted at the time of his birth. When the time came, he left everything behind and went in search of answers for human suffering. From his early childhood, Shankaracharya was driven by an intense desire to pursue knowledge and uphold Dharma. Many seers and saints were drawn to spirituality early in their lives. It was as if a mysterious force drove them to look within themselves and pursue self-knowledge. We cannot say they turned to spirituality because they failed to attain liberation in their past births, but it could be one reason.

The Yogasutras (3.55) declares that when the purity of discriminating intelligence is equal to that of the Self, one attains liberation. Therefore, if a person has attained purity up to a certain level in one life, he has a chance to increase it further and bring it to perfection in the next. If he stumbles somewhere along the path, he still has a chance to redeem himself either in this life or the next by starting from where he left off. Krishna rightly referred to the intelligence of previous births while speaking about the prospects of a fallen yogi born in a family of ascetics. Buddhi or intelligence is responsible for discriminative discernment (viveka khaki), which illuminates the lamp of knowledge (jnana dipti). It arises in the mind and the body due to the predominance of sattva, when both are purified, and the impurities of rajas and tamas are greatly reduced through yoga. Sattva is responsible for the mind's brilliance, lucidity, and stability. When sattva is predominant in the consciousness, the mind acts like a pure jewel, taking the form of the objects before it is placed, without discoloration. This state is described in yoga as samapattih.

Liberation depends upon a person's purity and intelligence. The practice of various yogas increases the predominance of sattva (purity) and, thereby, the buddhi (discriminating intelligence) of the yogi and his chances of liberation. Circumstances favor the yogi born in a family of pious people to cultivate sattva and purify his intelligence until it reflects the brilliance of the Self without any hindrances. At the time of death, neither memories nor intelligence nor the mind of a being accompanies the Self. Only dominant memories and latent impressions (samskaras) accompany him as his causative mind (karana-citta). In the journey of the Self, it becomes the blueprint for his next life. In the case of a yogi, it determines when and how he may reconnect to his half-finished goals and, in what circumstances, regain his purity and intelligence.

Everyone is not fortunate enough to succeed on the path, even after reconnecting to the residual memories of their past lives. One needs to work hard without distractions and excel until perfection (samsiddhi) is attained. Hence, the word 'yatata' is specifically mentioned in this verse, which further states that perfection in equanimity or sameness (samsiddhi) arises from perfection in atma samyama yoga. With that, the mind becomes placid and is no longer distracted. There are no certainties in yoga or on the path of liberation, but only possibilities. Liberation depends upon a yogi's effort (abhyasa) in self-purification, self-control, and renunciation (vairagya). At the same time, depending upon circumstances, karma may aid or hinder that effort. Therefore, one should not take any chances while practicing yoga for liberation.

Sloka 44

pūrvābhyāsena tenaiva hriyate hy avaśopi saḥ
jijñāsur api yogasya śabdabrahmātivartate

purva = past life; abhyasena = practice; tena = by that; eva = for surely; hriyate = is attracted; hi = surely; avasah = uncontrollably; api = even against himself; sah = he; jijnasuh = the inquisitive aspirant or seeker; api = also, further; yogasya = of yoga; sabda-brahma = the sounds of the Vedas; ativartate = surpasses, goes beyond.

Surely, by that practice in his past life, he is uncontrollably drawn (to yoga) even against himself. Further, the inquisitive aspirant of yoga goes beyond the words or sounds of the Vedas.

Due to the way the transmigration matrix works and how Maya clouds the consciousness, humans do not remember much about their past births. Even those who remember them possess only vague and disconnected memories. Therefore, when a yogi who failed in his previous life is reborn, he may not be interested much initially in spiritual matters or yoga practice. However, when the time comes, and if he has not committed any grave sins or deviated from the path by engaging in adharma, his past life impressions (purva samskaras) kick in. Against his own interests and inclinations, he will irresistibly be drawn to spiritual knowledge and start practicing yoga again. Persisting in his newfound interest, he will soon go beyond book knowledge and attain oneness. If he has been studying the Vedas or practicing Vedic rituals until then, he would graduate into spiritual knowledge and focus on knowing the Self. By withdrawing into himself and practicing atma-samyama, he goes beyond the ritual knowledge of words and sounds of the Vedas to discern the hidden Self and dissolve himself in it.

Past life impressions drive many events that unfold in our lives, sometimes against our wishes. They shape our lives, our dominant desires, and our irresistible actions. Even the curiosity (jignasa) or the aspiration to know something, such as yoga, scriptures, or the Self, arises from past life impressions only. In the process, he may internalize the Vedic rituals as a contemplative practice and go beyond the sounds of the Vedic hymns and his initial conditioning to practice introspection and spiritual discipline. Internalizing Vedic practices into yoga and contemplation makes sense only to those familiar with Vedic symbolism and the ritual significance of the Vedas. Sabda Brahman means Brahman in the form of sounds or words. The Vedic hymns are considered Brahman in sound form. Force or energy hidden in the sound vibrations is one of Brahman's numerous manifestations as Isvara. Brahman means that which expands, goes forth, or moves infinitely in all directions. The Vedas are also known as Brahman because the sounds arising from their chanting contain the infinite power of Brahman. In the later Vedic period, these aspects of Brahman were identified as Prakriti.

It is believed that when the Vedic hymns and mantras are loudly and correctly chanted, the power of Brahman hidden in them as their presiding deities becomes unleashed and moves upwards through space (akasa) toward heaven, where the gods reside. When they hear them, they descend to the sacrificial place or the source of those chants to participate in the sacrifice, accept the offerings, and grant the worshippers their wishes and prayers. Thus, the Vedas serve both gods and humans. Through them, gods receive nourishment, and humans fulfill their desires and ascend to heaven after death. Karma-sannyasa yogis go a step further. They may perform obligatory duties according to the Vedas to serve God's creation rather than fulfill their desires. Hence, they have better chances of achieving liberation. Karma yogis who practice sacrificial rituals have heaven as their destination. However, those who renounce desires and attachments and practice karma-sannyasa or sannyasa go beyond the ritual knowledge of the Vedas, attain the knowledge of Brahman, and escape from samsara.

Sloka 45

prayatnād yatamānas tu yogī saṃśuddhakilbiṣaḥ
anekajanmasaṃsiddhas tato yāti parāṃ gatim

prayatnat = striving, effort, exertion, endeavor; yatamanah = subdued mind; tu = indeed; yogi = yogi; samsuddha = cleansed; kilbisah = of all sins; aneka = several, many; janma = births; samsiddhah = perfection in equanimity; tatah = thereby; yati = goes; param-gatim = highest world of Brahman.

Indeed, striving with a subdued mind, cleansed of all sins, the yogi who has attained perfection in equanimity over many births thereby goes to the highest (world of Brahman).

Despite facing many failures, hardships, and obstacles through several births and deaths, the persevering yogis eventually succeed in attaining sameness (samsiddhi) and go to the highest, immortal world. Some commentators translate Yatamana as striving, but it is incorrect because it is preceded by a similar word (prayatna) with approximately the same meaning. Its correct meaning is restrained or subdued mind (yata + manas), which is the hallmark of an atma samyama yogi. This verse contains three essential truths about yoga. The first one is perfection in yoga (samsiddhi). It arises from purity (sattva), which in turn arises from self-control (samyama) and self-cleansing (samsuddhi). As we have discussed before, the mind (citta) and intelligence (buddhi) have to be illuminated with the purity of sattva by cultivating it and fully suppressing the other two modes. The second truth is that perfection in yoga is a slow and gradual process attained through several births and repeated attempts (prayatnam). Buddhist scriptures vouch that the Buddha attained enlightenment after taking innumerable births in various forms. Even in his last birth, he had to strive hard and explore several options before receiving enlightenment. The same is true about several seers and sages, and even Indra, who is said to have practiced austerities for thousands of years to impress his teacher Brahma before he received enlightenment. The third truth is that repeated and perseverant yoga practice leads to the highest goal (paramagati), which is liberation or the immortal world of Brahman. It means that liberation is not immediately guaranteed for a fallen yogi, even if he returns to yoga and continues his practice. He has to attain perfection and purity, which may take several births, provided he stays on the path and makes no mistakes. The verse also implies that subduing the mind (yatamanas) is necessary for success on the path. Without it, the yogi cannot transcend duality and division and experience oneness with the Self. These verses give hope to the yogis who fail or falter on the path that they need not despair. As the scripture affirms, they can safely return to the path and continue the effort from where they discontinued. The good karma they earned in their past lives will not go to waste and will help them. However, they should not take liberation for granted, even if they have advanced on the path.

Sloka 46

tapasvibhyodhiko yogī jñānibhyopi matodhikaḥ
karmibhyaś cādhiko yogī tasmād yogī bhavārjuna

tapasvibhyah = practitioners of tapas or austerities; adhikah = higher, greater, superior; yogi = the yogi; jnanibhyah = pursuers of jnana or knowledge; api = also, even, in addition; matah = regarded, considered; adhikah = higher, greater, superior; karmibhyah = men of actions or obligatory duties; ca = and; adhikah = higher, greater, superior; yogi = the yogi; tasmat = therefore; yogi = yogi; bhava = just become; arjuna = O Arjuna.

A yogi is higher than the practitioners of tapas (austerities), even higher than the pursuers of jnana (knowledge), and much higher than men of karma (duties). Therefore, O Arjuna, you should become a yogi.

According to this verse, a karma-sannyasa yogi who practices contemplation with devotion, controlling himself and renouncing desires and attachments, is better than the renunciants who practice austerities (tapah), seekers of knowledge (jnana), or karma yogis who perform duties to fulfill their desires. This verse refers to four traditional approaches of yoga, namely the path of austerities (tapas), knowledge (jnana), obligatory duty (dharma-karma), and renunciation with knowledge, devotion, contemplation (dhyana), and self-control (atma samyama). Of them, Krishna declares the last one to be the highest or the best because other practices are integrated into it. Their combined practice prepares the yogis to attain oneness or absorption in the Self. Pursuing knowledge, cultivating discernment, and practicing austerities such as penances and obligatory duties are the early steps. They are like the yamas and niyamas of classical yoga. Through them, the yogi, who is also a householder, becomes purified and develops an interest in knowing the Self. Studying the scriptures and pursuing the right knowledge (jnana), he discerns the pure Self as his true Self, develops the will and the resolve to overcome desires and attachments, and subdues his modes (gunas), mind, and senses. Withdrawing them into himself, renouncing desires, attachments, and the fruit of his actions, he engages in the contemplation (dhyana) of the Supreme Lord as his Self with supreme devotion until he achieves perfection in sameness (samsiddhi), nearness, and oneness or liberation.

Tapah is the most ancient ascetic spiritual discipline mentioned in the Vedas and the Puranas. Vedic seers and sages practiced it to accumulate heat (tapa) in their bodies and attain purity, perfection, and spiritual powers. According to Vedic beliefs, tapah leads to increased power and vigor. It manifests in the body as heat (tapa) and in the mind as mental brilliance (medha) and equanimity. The practice may also result in the onset of several supernatural powers. However, the spiritual power (tapo shakti) may dissipate if it is misused, overused, or abused. In other words, a yogi who practices austerities and attains powers and perfection must always practice self-control (atma samyama) and never take his power for granted. He must restrain himself and lead an austere life to preserve the powers he has already gained and replenish them, if necessary, through further effort. If he falters, he may lose all of it. Further, the mere practice of tapah does not guarantee liberation or purity, especially if practiced with desires or to impress gods and obtain boons from them. According to the Puranas, sometimes demons also practice tapah to secure boons and powers from the gods. Once they gain them, they misuse them and perish. Hence, austerities are not considered the best option to achieve liberation. Paingala Upanishad (4.16) declares that a yogi might perform austerities standing on one leg for a thousand years but would not deserve one-tenth of the merit gained from concentrated meditation. However, austerities are useful to yogis to control their minds and bodies and overcome desires and attachments.

Jnana yoga, the pursuit of knowledge, may seem superior, but knowledge alone will not dispel our ignorance or lead to enlightenment. Knowledge gives us discernment and improves our intelligence. It teaches us right and wrong, how to perform obligatory duties, practice the righteous code of conduct, uphold Dharma, or reach a cherished goal. It is useful and effective only when we put that knowledge into proper practice without losing control, making mistakes, or deviating from the path. Hence, discipline and self-control are vital to attain perfection in any effort. Hence, Lord Krishna correctly identified atma-samyama yoga as higher than the other three. Knowledge is of different kinds, and we need discernment to identify the right knowledge. For example, knowledge can be perverse or polluted with the impurities of the maya and lead the yogi in the wrong direction, making his liberation a distant goal. According to the Puranas and even the Upanishads, the evil ones also pursue knowledge, mainly of a perverted and tamasic kind. They believe that the body is the true Self, and the eternal Self is nonexistent. Therefore, they do not believe in the afterlife, heaven, or liberation. Knowledge without purity, discipline, and self-control is even dangerous. It is an obstacle to self-purification and enlightenment. Intellectual knowledge gained through listening, study (abhyasa), and observation (darsana) is also problematic if it strengthens egoism, delusion, passions, desires, etc. Hence, on the path of liberation, one should pursue the right knowledge with self-discipline, discernment, equanimity, detachment, and renunciation, and perform actions without desires.

Practicing obligatory duties as karma yogis is an important starting point for householders in their journey towards liberation. By performing the triple karmas (nitya, naimitta, and kamya), following the prescribed procedures, and avoiding the prohibited ones, they may secure a place in heaven or the ancestral world on the path of karma yoga. They may gain peace and happiness here and hereafter, but will not attain final liberation. Hence, karma yoga should be regarded as the starting point of a yogi's journey toward liberation. As Lord Krishna explained in this chapter, devotees should renounce desires and attachments and pursue liberation by cultivating the right knowledge and discernment, establishing their minds in the Self or the Supreme Self with devotion and concentration, and practicing karma-sannyasa yoga to perform all their actions. Through that austere path only, they will attain perfection.

Sloka 47

yogināmapi sarveṣāṃ madgatenāntarātmanā
śraddhāvān bhajate yo māṃ sa me yuktatamo mataḥ

yoginam = among the yogis; api = however; sarvesam = all; mat-gatena = devoted to Me; antah-atmana = with his mind; sraddha-van = with faith; bhajate = worships; yah = who; mam = Me; sah = he; me = by Me; yukta-tamah = most skilful yogi; matah = regarded.

However, among all the yogis, the one who worships Me with unwavering faith, with his mind devoted to Me, he is regarded by Me as the most skillful yogi.

When contemplation is practiced with self-control, faith, and devotion to the Supreme Lord (Isvara paridhana), established in sameness or even-mindedness, it becomes even more effective. Devotion is the culmination of knowledge, purity, and perfection achieved through the yogas we have discussed so far. The next eight chapters of the Bhagavadgita deal with devotion, which develops in skillful yogis (yuktas) as the cumulative effect of all the previous practices (yogas) discussed. The consistent practice of austerities, karma, jnana, sannyasa, dhyana, and samyama leads to ananya bhakti or exclusive devotion. It brings the karma yogi, now a self-disciplined renunciant and devotee, closer to his goal of oneness with the Self or the Supreme Self. Therefore, we may regard this verse as an introduction to the yoga of devotion. By uniting the mind and body with the Lord, who is the Self, through renunciation, self-control, and devotional contemplation, yoga becomes elevated and sanctified by the power of devotion and self-surrender. Since the Lord is worshipped internally and continuously as one's pure Self or the Supreme Self, devotion also leads to nearness (samipya) and oneness (kaivalya) to him through the dissolution of all the impurities that accumulate around him in the embodied state from numerous births.

According to devotional traditions (bhakti sampradayas), mental stability is quickly achieved by those who surrender to the Lord in them or the Supreme Lord and fix their minds upon him with unwavering devotion, restraining their minds and senses and removing the duality and division. When a devotee treads the path of devotion with the innocence of a childlike pure mind, pouring his senses, mind, ego, and desires into the fire of renunciation, the Lord takes full responsibility for his life and liberation. He becomes his guardian, teacher, protector, and upholder, and neutralizes any karma that may arise from his actions. When the yogi fixes his mind upon the Lord with intense devotion and concentration, considering him his very Self, he enters the pure state of oneness. Satisfied in himself by himself, he seeks nothing else except oneness with the Self and the bliss of union that pervades him. In the Vedic symbolism, devotion to the Lord is envisaged as an internalized Vedic sacrifice or an inner ritual of concentration, meditation, and self-control (samyama) in which symbols, images, thoughts, prayers, feelings, and sacred syllables (Aum, etc.) or sayings from the scriptures are used as pourings in the fire of devotion.

The Vedas recognize Isvara, the Supreme Being, as the true liberator. As the Lord and Controller of all, he liberates those who worship him with unwavering faith (sraddha). In the Bhagavadgita itself, the Lord has assured that he takes care of those devotees who worship him with complete faith and devotion. He is not lost to them; they are not lost to him, and both are connected internally through identical, pure consciousness. Thus, devotion cements the perfection attained through other yogas and improves the chances of reaching the final goal. Svetasvatara Upanishad says that the only way to achieve liberation is by knowing God, "I know the Supreme Purusha of golden color beyond the darkness. By knowing him alone, one transcends death. There is no other path for going there."

Devotion to God may express itself spontaneously in many ways. A yogi may express it by fixing his mind internally upon his pure Self (Atman) or externally upon the Supreme Self (Brahman) or the Supreme Lord (Isvara). Alternatively, he may concentrate upon the Supreme Lord as his very Self, seeing no distinction between the two. Of the two approaches, the second approach is better since it facilitates the withdrawal of the mind and senses, the removal of duality and division, and the absorption of the mind in the Self. Through that nearness and identification, the Lord becomes an integral part of the yogi's consciousness and remains constantly in his thoughts until their duality and division dissolve permanently. The Yogasutras (1.23) suggests that devotion (Isvara pranidhana) to the Self (the inner Lord) is the best means to attain liberation. Patanjali does not acknowledge any supreme entity other than the Self and thus precludes the possibility of any duality between the Self and a Supreme Lord of the universe. Recognizing the Self as the Lord, he identifies devotion to Isvara (the Self) as a significant aspect of Kriya yoga (2.1) and Isvara pranidhana as one of the five niyamas (2.32). Patanjali further states that Isvara, the inner Lord, is free from impurities and obstacles. The yogi should repeatedly chant Him as Aum and meditate upon its meaning. When he perseveres in it, he develops a special awareness (pratyak cetana) and attains freedom from the obstacles that interrupt self-absorption (antarayas). It results in the dissolution of the duality (samadhi).

Conclusion

iti srīmadbhāgavadgītāsupanisatsu brahmavidyāyām yogasāstre srikrisnārjunasamvāde ātmasamyamayogo nāma shasto 'dhyayah

iti = thus; srīmadbhāgavadgītā = in the sacred Bhagavadgita; upanisatsu = in the Upanishad; brahmavidyāyām = the knowledge of the absolute Brahman; yogasāstre = the scripture of yoga; srikrisnārjunasamvāde = the dialogue between Sri Krishna and Arjuna; ātmasamyamayogo nāma = by name yoga of contemplation with self-control; shatah = sixth; adhyayah = chapter;

Thus ends the sixth chapter, named Atmasamayama Yoga (the Yoga of Contemplation with Self-control) in the Upanishad of the divine Bhagavadgita, the knowledge of the Absolute, a treatise on Yoga, which contains the dialogue between Arjuna and Lord Krishna.

07 – Jnāna Vijnāna Yoga

The Yoga of the Knowledge About the Lord and Creation

Sloka 1

śrībhagavān uvāca
mayy āsaktamanāḥ pārtha yogaṃ yuñjan madāśrayaḥ
asaṃśayaṃ samagraṃ māṃ yathā jñāsyasi tac chṛṇu

sri-bhagavan uvaca = the Supreme Lord said; mayi = to Me; asakta = devoted, interest, aspiration; manah = mind; partha = O Partha; yogam = yoga; yunjan = practicing; mat-asrayah = take refuge in Me; asamsayam = without any doubt, undoubtedly; samagram = completely in all aspects; mam = to Me; yatha = as much as; jnasyasi = you will know; tat = that; srnu = listen.

The Supreme Lord said, "With your mind drawn to Me, practicing yoga, taking refuge in Me, listen, O Partha, how you will know Me in all respects without any doubt."

Knowing the Lord in all respects (samagram) and without any doubt is necessary to cultivate faith and devotion and establish the mind in his contemplation. Hence, this and the next few chapters aim to help his devotees know his opulence and manifestations to stabilize their minds in him. We can divide the 18 chapters of the Bhagavadgita into three parts of six chapters each. The first six chapters contain the knowledge of the Self and the various yogas to attain him. The next six chapters deal with the knowledge of the Supreme Lord, his opulence, and manifestations. The final six chapters reveal the knowledge of Prakriti, her tattvas, gunas, their functions, and purification. The knowledge of the Self and the Supreme Self is considered true knowledge (jnana). Knowledge of Prakriti, God's creation, and his numerous manifestations constitutes material knowledge (vijnana). The former is attained through oneness, and the latter is attained through knowledge and intelligence.

Although jnana and vijnana are translated as knowledge in popular usage, from a philosophical perspective, they are different and serve different purposes. For example, jnana is self-existent, eternal, independent, and indestructible, acquired through direct knowing, inference, or scriptures like the Vedas. Vijnana is acquired through the cognitive functions of the mind and senses, such as perception, observation, thinking, reasoning, inference, study of the scriptures, etc. The knowledge contained in the Vedas is known as direct knowledge because they were not created from the mind but from direct known. Scriptures created with the help of the mental faculties are known as smritis, memorial works. When you study any scripture, its knowledge becomes vijnana. However, when you realize the truths in them without the mind and senses participating in it, the knowledge so acquired becomes jnana. When it is translated into a teaching or a scripture by the self-realized one for the benefit of others, it becomes vijnana again. A yogi needs both types of knowledge to cultivate discernment between the Self and the not-self and between the essential and nonessential knowledge to stabilize his mind in the contemplation of the Self. Until knowledge becomes self-evident, it is vijnana. When it becomes self-evident, it is jnana.

In this verse, Lord Krishna gave Arjuna three specific instructions before teaching him the knowledge of his greatness: he should draw his mind to the Supreme Lord, restrain his mind and senses, and take refuge in him. Asakti means having interest, inclination, fascination, enthusiasm, curiosity, favorable intent, loving devotion, etc. It is hard to learn anything if you do not have an interest or inclination (asakti) in the teacher or his teaching. Learning also requires concentration and attention, for which one has to restrain the mind and senses and draw them to the source of knowledge. It also depends on interest. In this context, yoga means the yoga of self-control required to listen with total concentration, faith, and devotion. Taking refuge in him means surrendering the mind and ego to the Lord with complete faith and without doubt. When you have these three, you will be open to receiving the knowledge and assimilating it.

Sloka 2

jñānaṃ tehaṃ savijñānam idaṃ vakṣyāmy aśeṣataḥ
yaj jñātvā neha bhūyo.anyaj jñātavyam avaśiṣyate

jnanam = higher knowledge; te = to you; aham = I; sa = along with; vijnanam = worldly knowledge; idam = this; vaksyami = will explain; asesatah = in full, without any remains; yat = which; jnatva = knowing; na = not; iha = in this world; bhuyah = again; anyat = nothing else; jnatavyam = knowable; avasisyate = remains to be known.

I will fully explain to you this knowledge of the Lord along with the knowledge of his creation, by knowing which nothing else remains to be known in this world.

Here, we will dwell further on the distinction between jnana and vijnana to ensure they are properly understood. The distinction between jnana and vijnana is vague. Sometimes, they are used interchangeably. In general usage, vijnana is mere book knowledge or knowledge that arises from listening, reading, or seeing. Jnana is knowledge that arises from understanding, intelligence, analysis, etc. In spiritual terms, jnanam means knowledge of the Self, which arises internally from self-knowing, meditation, intuition, pure intelligence, etc. Vijnanam is the knowledge of the mind, the body, the world, and other material things, which arises mentally, cognitively, or intuitively from perceptions, thinking, reasoning, observing, understanding, etc.

In Vedic philosophy, jnanam refers to the knowledge of the truth (Sat) or the supreme and absolute reality represented by Brahman or the Supreme Self. Hence, it also refers to the knowledge of the Self (atma jnanam). Knowledge of Brahman and the Self is also known as the right knowledge or higher knowledge (vidya). The Upanishads describe it as true knowledge or superior knowledge since it leads to enlightenment and liberation. Vijnanam is the knowledge acquired through the mind's cognitive functions, such as learning, perception, observation, understanding, analysis, discernment, etc. It includes the knowledge of God's creation or Nature (Prakriti), her tattvas and gunas, divisions, and functions.

In the context of the Vedas, jnanam refers to the knowledge contained in the Aranyakas and Upanishads, known as the knowledge portion (jnana kanda). Vijnanam refers to the knowledge of the Samhitas and Brahmanas, known as the ritual portion (karma kanda). We may also categorize jnanam as the knowledge of the Self and vijnanam as the knowledge of the not-self (mind and body). In literature, revelatory knowledge (sruti) constitutes jnanam and intellectual and memorial knowledge vijnanam. In yoga, jnanam is the knowledge of the Self, and vijnanam is the knowledge of the means to attain it. Devotional traditions define jnanam as the knowledge of the Supreme Self or Brahman and vijnanam as the knowledge of Isvara (manifested Brahman), his names, and forms. Currently, in popular usage, all spiritual and religious knowledge constitutes jnanam, and all scientific and empirical knowledge is vijnanam.

A self-realized yogi possesses direct knowledge of the Self (jnanam). However, when he imparts it to others, it becomes learned knowledge (vijnanam) for them. With jnanam, we become aware of Brahman's transcendental states and the supreme truth through personal experience. With vijnanam, we learn about the objects, the nature of reality, the worlds, elements, and the constituent parts (tattvas) of Nature and the material world through observation, learning, and study of the scriptures. We may also regard jnanam as the knowledge of the Self (atma-jnanam) and vijnanam as the knowledge of the mind and the body. In popular usage, jnanam is spiritual knowledge, and vijnanam is scientific knowledge. Both of them are relevant and important to our lives. They also remove ignorance and purify the mind and intelligence. Knowledge of Brahman (Purusha) and knowledge of the world (Prakriti) complement each other. Eventually, they culminate in discriminating wisdom (viveka khyati) and skillfulness. In short, when a yogi has both types of knowledge, he becomes a wise and learned person (pandita). Through vijnana, he attains jnana, the firsthand knowledge of the Self. Through vijnana, he realizes how his mind and body are subject to impurities and how he can cleanse them to abide in the Self. Therefore, both are important in the pursuit of liberation. The Isa Upanishad cautions those who pursue only jnanam or vijnanam, suggesting that both are necessary to achieve liberation and escape from the sinful world.

Sloka 3

manuṣyāṇāṃ sahasreṣu kaścid yatati siddhaye
yatatām api siddhānāṃ kaścin māṃ vetti tattvataḥ

manusyanam = of men; sahasresu = among thousands; kascit = a rare one; yatati = strives; siddhaye = for perfection, for success or accomplishment; yatatam = of the striving ones; api = even; siddhanam = of the perfected, of the accomplished; kascit = a rare one; mam = Me; vetti = knows; tattvatah = in truth.

Among thousands of men, a rare person strives for perfection (in yoga); even among the perfected ones who strive (for liberation), a rare person knows Me in truth.

The most austere, disciplined, and ardent practice of yoga may not lead to self-realization or the knowledge of the transcendental Self (jnanam) because success depends upon many factors, including one's karma and fate. When a yogi takes a solemn vow (samkalpa) to practice any yoga and attain liberation, many factors conspire to help or obstruct him. At the very outset, he must deal with the heavy resistance arising from within himself, from his mind and body, which are vulnerable to the forces of Maya and difficult to control. Then, he has to deal with the forces of Nature, circumstances, the value system enforced by society or the world, and disapproval from his friends and family. Even advanced yogis are not immune to these problems. They have to strive hard and face numerous difficulties to control their minds and bodies and achieve perfection in their practice. The path of liberation is indeterminate, and success is uncertain. It is like finding your way through a pathless land where the landscape changes every moment. There are no set ways to follow any instructions or methods you can naively rely on. Some methods may be initially promising but do not necessarily deliver the promise. What works for one does not necessarily work for another. At each stage of progress, the yogi has to tread cautiously to avoid making mistakes or falling into the traps set by his mind and delaying his progress. Even with the guidance of a guru, success may remain elusive.

Hence, in the second chapter (verse 48), Lord Krishna advised yogis to cultivate sameness (samatvam) by remaining equal to success and failure. Here, he reiterated that even among the perfected yogis (siddhas), only the rare ones succeed. True knowledge (jnanam) is difficult to attain because it arises only in the absence of egoism, attachments, and delusion when the mind is free from modifications and fully self-absorbed. Only those who achieve nearness to Brahman through selfless actions, purity, and sameness, with their egos, desires, and gunas subdued and silenced, can achieve that rare distinction. The knowledge of the Self is unattainable as long as the mind is bound to the objective reality or driven by desires and attachments or the influence of the gunas. The yogi must possess the knowledge (vijnana) to overcome these obstacles. He must practice karma-sannyasa to attain sameness, as affirmed by Lord Krishna previously in the third chapter (verse 20). In several verses, the Kena Upanishad explains the inscrutability of knowing Brahman. Using an allegorical tale involving Brahman and the gods (Indra, Agni, and Vayu), it illustrates (3.1-12) how even they do not know much about him or his supreme state. Although Indra spent considerable time knowing Brahman from his teacher, Brahma, he could not recognize him when he appeared before him as a celestial spirit (yaksha). Maybe it was this experience that prompted him to approach Brahman and learn about the Self.

Sloka 4

bhūmir āponalo vāyuḥ khaṃ mano buddhir eva ca
ahaṃkāra itīyaṃ me bhinnā prakṛtir aṣṭadhā

bhumih = earth; apah = water; analah = fire; vayuh = air; kham = space; manah = mind; buddhih = intelligence; eva = also; ca = and; ahankarah = ego; iti = thus; iyam = this; me = My; bhinna = division; prakrtih = Nature; astadha = eightfold.

Earth, water, fire, air, space, mind, intelligence, and so also ego; this is the eightfold division of My Nature.

After promising to teach Arjuna transcendental (jnana) and material knowledge (vijnana), Lord Krishna listed the eightfold division of his physical nature. It constitutes vijnana. Brahman's material aspect, manifestation, or creation is described in the Vedas as Endless (ananta), Cosmic Egg (brahmanda), First (adi), srishti, sarga, etc., personified as Purusha (the Cosmic Being), or Isvara (the Lord of the Universe). It encompasses his numerous names, forms, powers, and manifestations collectively known as Prakriti, meaning the natural state or what is found in creation in its original (sahaja) state or condition. The forms and manifestations of Brahman are numerous. They arise from the embodiment of the Cosmic Self by Prakriti or his materiality. Their forms are made up of finite realities or divisions known as tattvas (axioms, realities, archetypes, principles), in which the Self remains as the support, witness, and enjoyer, untouched and distinct from them. The Self represents the higher nature, and the materiality represents the lower nature. The tattvas are impure and sources of bondage. The infinite reality or the highest reality (parama tattva) of Brahman is pure (suddha) and indefinable. Considering our previous definition of jnana and vijnana, we may conclude that the knowledge of Nature and her tattvas should be construed as vijnana or the knowledge of his body, material manifestations, or beingness.

Knowledge of this world, the material universe, our minds, and bodies also falls under the category of vijnana only. This knowledge is essential to practice self-control and subdue the gunas. In a jiva, the physical body is the field of Nature in which the Self dwells as a passive witness. By knowing the tattvas and their functions and characteristics, we know how Nature exerts her influence and binds the beings, and how we can be free from her entrapment. In creation, Prakriti represents Brahman's dynamic force or aspect. She is the source of all actions, movements, and happenings. The Puranas describe all the manifestations arising from their union as the names (nama), forms (rupa), and energies (Shakti) of Isvara, the Supreme Lord. Here, Lord Krishna described the divisions of his differentiated Nature (sambhuta), which constitutes a minuscule aspect of his undifferentiated aspect in which both Purusha and Prakriti remain in an indistinguishable, unmanifested (asambhuta) state. Isvara, the Supreme Lord, personifies the union between the Manifested Brahman (the Self) and his Manifested Force Field or Prakriti. Since he has materiality (the body), he is also known as the Supreme Being (Mahadeva). The jivas are also created in the same way. The Self that resides in them represents Purusha, and their bodies represent Prakriti, her tattvas, and the force field. Unlike some schools of Hinduism, the Bhagavadgita regards Prakriti as the dependent aspect of Brahman and Isvara, in whom both are present, as the efficient and material cause of creation.

Samkhya school identifies 23 tattvas; these eight tattvas plus 15 senses: five organs of action (karmendriyas), five organs of perception (jnanendriyas), and five sensations (tanmatras) associated with them. The Self is not a part of the tattvas, although some schools describe it as a pure tattva. Of the 23 tattvas, the senses, the mind, the ego, and the intelligence constitute the internal organ (antahkarana). Of them, the mind (manas) and ego (aham) are considered the higher tattvas, and intelligence (buddhi) the highest. They manifest only in higher organisms having three or more senses. Intelligence is considered the highest tattva and closest to the Self in its essential nature. In the body of the Supreme Lord, it is known as the great part (Mahat). Reason and discernment arise from intelligence only. The schools of Shaivism recognize additional tattvas, known as Shiva and Shakti tattvas, and increase their number to 36. They consider them higher than all the tattvas, including the mind, ego, and intelligence. The tattvas are divisions of the not-self, the materiality, objective reality, or the otherness of Purusha or Brahman, which extend from him as his creation, projection, reflection, or superimposition. They arise as Prakriti's modifications, not Purusha's, who is immutable. Hence, they are not in Brahman, and Brahman is not in them. They exist in Prakriti (the body) only.

Sloka 5

apareyam itas tvanyāṃ prakṛtiṃ viddhi me parām
jīvabhūtāṃ mahābāho yayedaṃ dhāryate jagat

apara = inferior, lower; iyam = this; itah = than this; tu = but; anyam = other; prakrtim = nature; viddhi = know; me = My; param = higher, superior; jiva-bhutam = the Self or soul of all living beings; maha-baho = O mighty-armed; yaya = by which; idam = this; dharyate = is upheld, supported; jagat = the world.

O mighty-armed one, inferior (Nature) is this; but know other than this is My higher Nature, the Self of all living beings, by which this world is supported.

In his manifested state, Brahman has two aspects: his lower nature, which is made of the tattva, gunas, and the impurities they induce, and his higher nature, which is represented by his pure Self and which acts as the Self of all living beings (jiva-bhutam) in the entire creation. All the divine qualities of Isvara and his pure manifestations, which arise from his association with Prakriti, also constitute his higher nature. As the Self of all, Isvara, the manifested Brahman, supports the whole creation. The body cannot survive for a minute without him. The same is true about the whole creation or the body of Isvara. It dissolves when Brahman, the supreme Self, withdraws himself from it. Some schools believe that Atma (individual Self) and Paramatma (Supreme Self) are distinct entities. Atma is the witness Self, and Paramatma is the Supreme Controller or Isvara. Madhavacharya viewed the individual Self (Atman) as a part of the Lord's lower nature. It is consistent with the view held by the school of dualism (Dvaita). For our discussion, we hold the individual Self and the Supreme Self as one. Their duality is an illusion or delusion arising from ignorance and egoism. In the jivas, he remains embodied and bound to Prakriti. Upon liberation, the duality disappears.

The lower nature is mostly mechanical and is the effect rather than the cause of creation. The Self is both cause and effect. The Supreme Self is the cause, and the individual Self is the effect. Some schools of Hinduism, however, believe that the Individual Self is eternal and uncreated. Therefore, it is also without a cause. However, being passive and immutable, it will not produce any effects. Brahman's higher nature, apart from the Self, appears in all his highest manifestations. His highest manifestations are Isvara, the Lord of Creation; Hiranyagarbha, the World Soul; Viraj, the not-self, world, or the objective reality; and Purusha, the embodied Self. In the bound jivas, the last one remains hidden, enveloped by impurities. In the liberated jivas, he shines through the divine qualities that manifest in them. In the jivas, the mind and body constitute the not-self (anatma) or the lower nature. The Self and the divine qualities that appear in yogis due to self-purification and suppression of gunas constitute the higher nature. In the macrocosm, the Self and the not-self (creation) constitute the body or the universal form (murtham) of the Supreme Lord (Isvara). What exists beyond Isvara or the manifested form of Brahman is the unmanifested (avyakta) Brahman, also known as the formless (amurthim). They are also known as saguna and nirguna.

The dualistic and semi-dualistic schools recognize different types of souls according to their purity and state of liberation: divine souls (devatmas) and eternally free souls (nitya muktas) that are never subject to samsara, liberated souls (muktas) that have attained liberation, bound souls (baddhas) that are in different states of bondage and ignorance, and, finally, impure or demonic souls that will never be free even if they are born in the mortal world. According to these schools, the material universe and the various types of individual selves constitute the Universal Being (Purusha) or the living Self (jivabhutam). Pervading the lower and higher Nature are the gunas (modes), namely sattva, rajas, and tamas. The higher nature is predominantly sattvic, and the lower nature is predominantly rajasic and tamasic. The inert matter, which is made up of one or more of the five elements, is mostly unconscious and inanimate (acetana). It is formed by the admixture of gunas and elements in different permutations and combinations. The lower and higher tattvas, in combination with the gunas, impart different forms, potencies, qualities, consciousness, and awareness to the jivas according to their role in creation. In the higher beings, such as Devas (gods), Gandharvas, Yakshas, and Kimpurushas, who inhabit the celestial worlds, the higher tattvas remain permeated with different degrees of light, intelligence, and purity, with the predominance of sattva. In contrast, they are covered with different degrees of darkness, delusion, and other impurities in the beings of the lower worlds. In some, such as microorganisms and lower life forms, they are not even present. In human beings, the purity and nature of tattvas depend upon their spiritual evolution. Since only humans have the opportunity for self-transformation and purification, only they are qualified to achieve liberation. In them, the higher nature becomes self-evident only through self-purification.

Sloka 6

etadyonīni bhūtāni sarvāṇīty upadhāraya
ahaṃ kṛtsnasya jagataḥ prabhavaḥ pralayas tathā

etat = these; yonini = origin, source; bhutani = living beings; sarvani = all; iti = thus; upadharaya = know, understand; aham = I; krtsnasya = whole, entire; jagatah = world; prabhavah = origination, manifestation, creation; pralayah = dissolution; tatha = and, also.

Know that all beings have their origin in these. Therefore, I am the source of creation and the dissolution of the whole world.

In the last two verses, Lord Krishna stated that the tattvas and gunas in the body constitute his lower Nature and the Self, his higher Nature. He spoke here as Isvara, the Lord of all creation, in whom both higher and lower natures exist in their purest form. His lower nature is the eightfold division of Prakriti. His higher nature is the Self, which supports all creation and the qualities that manifest in his pure creations. He did not specifically mention whether the Self means the individual Self (Atman) or the Supreme Self (Brahman) or whether there is any distinction between him and his two natures. Those who believe in the Dvaita philosophy hold that the Supreme Self constitutes the Lord's higher nature, and the individual Self, the tattvas, and the modes his lower nature. In contrast, Advaita does not recognize any distinction between the individual Self and the Supreme Self and holds that the same Self appears in all beings as the Self of all (sarva bhutatma). Hence, according to them, Prakriti represents his lower nature, and the Self and associated qualities represent his higher nature.

Whatever the truth, based upon these descriptions, we can identify three basic aspects of all existence: 1) absolute Brahman, known as Nirguna Brahman, who is without Nature or any association; 2) the Manifested Brahman or Isvara, who possesses higher and lower nature and acts as the Lord of the universe; and 3) creation which arises from Isvara's Nature as a projection or extension and dependent reality. We may also describe them as Brahman (the Pure Self), Isvara (the Cosmic Self), and Prakriti (Nature, world, or the not-self). The second part of the verse affirms that Brahman, not Prakriti, is the source of all creation and dissolution. Prakriti acts as an instrument or aspect of Isvara and manifests his will. We may presume that Prakriti manifests creation according to his will. At the time of dissolution, she withdraws them into Isvara and ends creation. Isvara then goes into a sleep mode that lasts billions of years. The relationship between Purusha and Prakriti is a contentious matter in Hinduism. Some schools hold that Prakriti is an independent and eternal entity and the source of all creation, while the Self remains a passive witness. According to them, she is the creator, preserver, and destroyer.

The classical Samkhya School offers a different explanation. According to Isvarakrishna, one of its early proponents, creation is essentially an act of Nature (Prakriti) in which the individual Self plays no role other than passively remaining in the background as a mere witness. It serves as a catalyst or a trigger point for Prakriti. She performs all actions and contains all causes and effects. With her tattvas and gunas, she builds an alternate reality around the individual selves and binds them to samsara. The Samkhya school does not recognize or envisage any role for God in this. It is a materialistic and nontheistic philosophy that holds that individual souls (jiva bhutam) and Nature exist eternally without a beginning and an end, and souls have an opportunity to escape from Prakriti through yoga practice and attain liberation.

Some schools of Vedanta believe that Purusha is the efficient cause and Prakriti is the material cause. The Bhagavadgita holds that the Supreme Lord is both the efficient and material cause. He is also the cause of all causes and controller of all, and Prakriti is his dynamic and dependent force only. Unlike the classical Samkhyas, who hold Prakriti as a blind and mechanical force, the scripture regards her as an instrument of Isvara, the Supreme Lord, manifesting creation intelligently according to his will. This verse affirms that Isvara is both the efficient and material cause of creation. Everything emanates from him. He is the cause, the source (yoni), and the support of everything. However, he does not exist in them. In the end, he withdraws them all into himself.

Sloka 7

mattaḥ parataraṃ nānyat kiṃcid asti dhanaṃjaya
mayi sarvam idaṃ protaṃ sūtre maṇigaṇā iva

mattah = than I; para-taram = higher; na = not; anyat kincit = nothing else whatsoever; asti = there is; dhananjaya = O Dhananjaya, conqueror of riches; mayi = on Me; sarvam = all; idam = this; protam = is threaded, strung; sutre = thread; mani-ganah = a string of pearls; iva = like.

There is nothing else whatsoever that is higher than Me, O Dhananjaya. All this is threaded upon Me as pearls strung on a thread.

The previous verse taught us that the supreme Lord is the source of all creation. Here, we are told that he is also its support. The different aspects of creation (worlds and beings) rest upon Para Brahman, the supreme Lord, like pearls strung on a thread. Brahman is the sutradhar, the architect and director of all creation, in which he is the player, controller, and witness on a stage that rests within him only. As the individual Self, he is the witness; as the jiva, he is the player and the witness; and as the Supreme Lord, he is the player, the witness, and the controller of all. By creating the objects, he enthralls himself through his senses, and by becoming the subject, he enjoys all that he witnesses. The whole creation is by him, for him, with him, and within him. He is also the highest. There is nothing else beyond him other than him. Nothing else is equal to or comparable to him, except probably his highest manifestations. As the support of everything, he is not only the creator and destroyer but also the preserver and upholder. Everything that exists in creation is permeated by him as well as enveloped by him. He holds the whole creation like the pearls on a string, the pearls representing his lower nature and the string his higher nature. He is, therefore, the threading Self

(Sutratman), the thread holder (sutradhari), who unites everything and holds them together as their support.

Sloka 8

raso.aham apsu kaunteya prabhāsmi śaśisūryayoḥ
praṇavaḥ sarvavedeṣu śabdaḥ khe pauruṣaṃ nṛṣu

rasah = taste; aham = I; apsu = in the water; kaunteya = O son of Kunti; prabha asmi = I am the brilliance; sasi-suryayoh = in the moon and the sun; pranavah = the sacred syllable Aum; sarva vedesu = in all the Vedas; sabdah = sound; khe = in space, ether; paurusam = manliness, virility; nrsu = in man.

I am the taste in the water, O son of Kunti; I am the brilliance in the sun and the moon; the sacred syllable Aum in all the Vedas; the sound in space and manliness in the man.

Apart from being the creator and supporter of all things in creation, Isvara, the manifested Brahman, is also the essence or taste (rasa) of things, without which they will not be distinguishable. His essential nature or higher nature is reflected through the qualities that manifest in the things and beings according to their purity and divinity. Their natural states are suppressed when impurities are present and become distinguishable when they are removed. Although Prakriti is different from him, her qualities and states arise due to his presence only. Thus, he is the taste in water, brilliance in the sun and moon, the power and sanctity of the sacred syllable Aum, the sound that travels in the silence of space, and the manliness of men. In other words, because of him, water is water, the sun is the sun, the moon is the moon, aum is aum, the sound is the sound, and man is the man. He imparts to them their essential qualities, but does not exist in them. They manifest or are reflected in Nature since he is established in Prakriti and pervades all creation.

Sloka 9

puṇyo gandhaḥ pṛthivyāṃ ca tejaś cāsmi vibhāvasau
jīvanaṃ sarvabhūteṣu tapaś cāsmi tapasviṣu

punyah = pure, sacred, sweet; gandhah = fragrance; prthivyam = in the earth; ca = and; tejah = brilliance; ca = and; asmi = I am; vibhavasau = in fire; jivanam = life; sarva bhutesu = in all living beings; tapah = austerity; ca = and; asmi = I am; tapasvisu = ascetics who practice austerities.

I am the pure fragrance in the earth and the brilliance in the fire; I am the life in all living beings and the austerity of the ascetics.

The agreeable qualities, such as the fragrance of the earth and the brilliance of fire, arise due to the presence of the Lord in Nature. He does not mix with Nature, but his very presence becomes known through the qualities that manifest in the world as a reflection of his higher nature. Disagreeable qualities, such as foul odors or darkness, arise in things and beings when he is absent, or his presence is obstructed by impurities. Agreeable smells, tastes, flashes of brilliance, sacred syllables, harmonious sounds, etc., radiate from him and manifest in the purest aspects of Prakriti when they are unhindered.

Life exists only when he is present in the jivas as their support. Thus, in the theistic vision of the Bhagavadgita, the Supreme Lord is not a mere passive witness to the play of Maya. That is just one of his roles or manifestations as the embodied Self. However, as the Supreme Controller and Lord of the Universe, he is the cause of all material and efficient causes. All the effects also arise and subside in him as the waves in an ocean. Nature is his dependent entity and works according to his will. As the individual Self, he is the witness, but as the Supreme Lord, he is the controller, director, and sutradhar (stage manager) of the whole play of creation. The materiality and dynamism of manifested things arise in the domain of Nature because of the Lord's will only. His higher and lower natures perform distinct functions. His lower nature is responsible for materiality, and His higher nature is responsible for all the excellent qualities and perfection that manifest in creation. All the positive, bright, and beautiful aspects of creation manifest from him only. An ignorant person may see the beauty and symmetry of objects, but not see the power of God manifesting in them. However, a self-realized yogi sees them as different manifestations of the same eternal Truth.

Sloka 10

bījaṃ māṃ sarvabhūtānāṃ viddhi pārtha sanātanam
buddhir buddhimatām asmi tejas tejasvinām aham

bijam = the seed; mam = Me; sarva-bhutanam = of all living beings; viddhi = know; partha = O Partha; sanatanam = eternal; buddhih = intelligence; buddhi-matam = of the intelligent; asmi = I am; tejah = brightness; tejasvinam = of the brightest; aham = I am.

Know Me, O Partha, as the eternal seed of all living beings. I am the intelligence of the intelligent, (and) I am the brightness of the brightest.

The Supreme Lord is the seed (the cause) of all living beings. He is the one who endows them with power and vitality to procreate and prosper upon the earth. As the Upanishads declare, at the beginning of creation, he divided himself into male and female, desiring company, and began multiplying through them. Although he compared himself to a seed, he is not a seed in the ordinary sense. Natural seeds are subject to modifications and degeneration during their germination and growth. Unlike them, the Lord, as the eternal seed (sanatana bijam), is not subject to any modifications or transformation. Whatever modifies, he is its cause and controller while he remains unchanged. He is responsible for creation, preservation, and destruction, but remains immutable. Things emerge from him, partaking of the qualities he imparts to them through Nature, while as the Self of all, he remains without qualities and attributes.

The Aitareya Upanishad declares that Brahman is pure intelligence (prajnanam brahma). Where Brahman is, there is intelligence. The natural state of Brahman is pure consciousness filled with self-existent pure intelligence. In Nature, his intelligence is reflected in the faculty of buddhi or the higher mind, which is responsible for intelligent thinking, reasoning, and discernment. A yogi cultivates nearness to Brahman in proportion to his purity, intelligence, and mental brilliance (tejas). When he is filled with the radiance of sattva, he becomes enlightened and gains knowledge of the Self (atma-jnanam) and the wisdom to escape from bondage. Tejas has many meanings: sharpness, luster, vigor, brilliance, splendor, courage, majesty, dignity, and so on. However, it should be considered mental brilliance since it is associated with intelligence. The luster and vigor of the body also arise due to the predominance of sattva and the presence of the Self.

Sloka 11

balaṃ balavatāṃ cāhaṃ kāmarāgavivarjitam
dharmāviruddho bhūteṣu kāmo.asmi bharatarṣabha

balam = physical strength; bala-vatam = of the strong; ca = and; aham = I am; kama = passion; raga = attachment; vivarjitam = devoid of; dharma-aviruddhah = not against moral obligations and religious duties; bhutesu = in all beings; kamah = desire asmi = I am; bharata-rsabha = O great among the Bharatas.

And I am the physical strength of the strong, devoid of passion and attachment. I am the desire in all living beings, which is not against moral injunctions and religious duties, O great among the Bharatas.

The verses from 8-11 are good starting points for meditating on Isvara, the Supreme Lord of the Universe, and establishing the mind in him. You can remember him when you discern his qualities hidden in Nature: when you taste water, see the brilliance of the sun and the moon, listen to the sound of the sacred syllable Aum or chants of the Vedas, smell the fragrance of the earth, practice austerities, watch the brilliance of fire or marvel at the intelligence of the mind. Anything imbued with his divine presence is fit for contemplation and concentration, and engaging the mind in his thoughts strengthens devotion.

These verses remind us not to take pride in our good qualities or achievements because they come from God only. The strength of the strong and all righteous intentions arise from him only. He is the source of all physical and mental strength among the beings that are devoid of passions such as pride or anger. All the positive, brighter, and good qualities and actions manifest in Nature because of him, while their opposites manifest when he remains concealed. The strength (balam), which manifests because of him, is of the sattvic type and free from passions and attachments. With physical strength, one can indulge in both moral and immoral actions. Hence, to clarify, Lord Krishna says that the strength he represents is free from desires and passions. According to Shankara, kama is the desire for what is absent, and raga is the passion for what one already has. Since God is complete and perfect, he is free from both. While Brahman is devoid of desires, he is the source of desires in all beings, which are not against the injunctions of Dharma. He also states that the Lord represents the strength needed for survival, procreation, and continuity, but not indulging in wicked actions.

This verse also states that Isvara is the source of kama (sexual desire) in all living beings. It means kama is not evil, but lust is. In the Vedic tradition, Kama is one of the four aims (purusharthas) of human life, the other three being Dharma, Artha, and Moksha. In Hinduism, householders are permitted to pursue these aims, including kama, without engaging in adharma (evil) or prohibited actions. In a broader sense, kama includes all desires. One may apply the same principle to them also. The law books clearly distinguish between desires that can be pursued and those that must be avoided. They recognize the importance of desires in the preservation of the worlds. Even gods engage in desire-ridden actions, sometimes against Dharma, and suffer from consequences. Thus, a householder may pursue legitimate desires such as the desire for progeny, name and fame, wealth, divine blessings, good health, peace, happiness, the welfare of the world, the good of all, and so on. However, he should not pursue them for selfish ends and offer the fruit of his actions to God, the source of all desires.

Sloka 12

ye caiva sātvikā bhāvā rājasās tāmasāś ca ye
matta eveti tān viddhi na tv ahaṃ teṣu te mayi

ye = these; ca = and; eva = indeed; sattvikah = sattva; bhavah = mode or state; rajasah = rajas; tamasah = tamas; ca = and; ye = those; mattah = sprung from Me; eva = only; iti = thus; tan = them all; viddhi = know; na = not; tu = however, but; aham = I; tesu = in them; te = they; mayi = in Me.

Indeed, these, having the mode of sattva, and those of rajas and tamas know them all to have sprung from Me only. However, I am not in them. They are in Me.

All things in the Field of Prakriti that contain one or more of the triple gunas arise from the Supreme Lord through her. He is their efficient and material cause. This is a direct refutation of the view held by the classical Samkhya schools that Prakriti is an independent reality and source of all the tattvas, gunas, and material things. Lord Krishna also states that he is not in them, which means they exist separately as dependent realities. He is not in them means he does not partake in their nature, or they do not partake in his essence. He pervades them but is not mixed up with them. They exist for him, in him, and because of him, but have no direct connection with him. The jiva, things, and the whole creation manifest from him as a projection and exist in him, but separately. He knows them, but is unknown to them. They depend upon him, but he is independent of them. Yet, he is the creator, supporter, and destroyer of all that manifests. It means creation does not have the purity, divinity, independence, constancy, continuity, or transcendence of Brahman. Whatever brightness, divinity, or purity manifests in them is due to his presence in them as the imperishable, eternal, independent, and distinct reality. Thus, while he is the source of the tattvas and the triple gunas, they do not partake in his purity, immutability, effulgence, or intelligence. They may reflect him, but do not contain him. Although he is united with Nature, he is inherently separate and distinct from her, just as oil and water are separate even when they are mixed.

Sloka 13

tribhir guṇamayair bhāvair ebhiḥ sarvam idaṃ jagat
mohitaṃ nābhijānāti mām ebhyaḥ param avyayam

tribhih = triple, three; guna-mayaih =filled with gunas; bhavaih = states or modes; ebhih = by these; sarvam = whole; idam = this; jagat = world; mohitam = deluded; na abhijanati = do not know; mam = Me; ebhyah = beyond these; param = higher; avyayam = inexhaustible.

Filled with these triple modes and the states (they induce), this whole world is deluded and does not know Me, who is higher and beyond them and inexhaustible.

The world is enchanted by the power of Maya, whereby the jivas mistakenly perceive the objective reality as real, unaware of the supreme reality, which is beyond them and the perceptible world. Isvara, the Lord of the universe, is the enchanter (mayavi) who casts his net of Maya by triggering the gunas present in the primal Nature (mula prakriti) in the beginning stages of creation when she becomes active in creation. Propelled by his power, the gunas permeate all beings and things in various permutations and combinations and subject them to different states of attachment, ignorance, and delusion. The pervasive influence of the gunas extends to all the jivas, whereby they remain ignorant and deluded in varying degrees and bound. In creation, the modes are responsible for the diversity. In the jivas, they are responsible for desires, attachments, mental instability, modifications, and afflictions. They are also responsible for desire-ridden actions and their consequences. Because of them, we experience impermanence, instability, conflicting thoughts, emotions, and desires, from which suffering follows.

The gunas compete with each other for predominance and, in the process, induce in us three impure states (bhavas) or modes of being: delusion (absence of discernment), passion (absence of sameness or stability), and ignorance (absence of knowledge). Shankara identified the three states (bhavas) as physical love, hatred, and attachment. The three states arise in different intensities from the triple gunas according to their predominance. Sattva produces positive states; rajas, mixed states; and tamas, negative states. They produce diverse types of mixed states when they are found together in different proportions. The gunas also tend to attract things of similar nature and repel those of dissimilar nature. Thus, sattva propels us to seek objects that are predominantly sattvic, rajas that are predominantly rajasic, and tamas that are predominantly tamasic. Depending upon which of them prevails in us, we engage in actions and accumulate karma, which, in turn, leads to bondage. The imperishable Supreme Lord (the Self) is not subject to the gunas since he is beyond and separate from Nature. However, his purity, divinity, and intelligence may become reflected in the tattvas and gunas, just as pure fragrance spreads through the air or sunlight is reflected on the surface of the water, inducing specific states and characteristics in us. Hence, in the jivas, especially humans, divinity can be perceived only through character, conduct, and actions. The Self is always elusive to the mind and senses because they cannot truly grasp that which is imperceptible and transcendental.

Sloka 14

daivī hy eṣā guṇamayī mama māyā duratyayā
mām eva ye prapadyante māyām etāṃ taranti te

daivi = divine; hi = indeed; esa = this; guna-mayi = imbued with the gunas; mama = My; maya = maya, enchanting or deluding power; duratyaya = difficult to overcome; mam = to Me; eva = alone; ye = those; prapadyante = surrender and take refuge, surrender; mayam etam = this delusion; taranti = transcend; te = they.

Indeed, this, My divine Maya, which is imbued with the gunas, is difficult to overcome. Those who surrender and take refuge in Me alone - they transcend this delusion.

This verse clearly states that the delusion (maya) induced by the divine (daivi) Maya Shakti, who is the beloved of the Supreme Lord and whom she serves with utmost dedication, can be overcome only by taking refuge in him and earning his love and grace through devotion. It means that one cannot achieve liberation by individual effort alone. One needs God's help in addition to individual effort. All the yogas, karma, jnana, atma-samyama, dhyana, sannyasa, etc., are effective when they are practiced with exclusive devotion and karma-sannyasa. By surrendering and taking refuge in him only, devotees engaged in various yogas can overcome their delusion and duality induced by the gunas and attain liberation. However, one cannot cultivate exclusive devotion or unconditionally take refuge in God without purity. It is possible only when they practice the yogas and cultivate self-control, purity, and stability of the mind. Hence, they are equally important until liberation is attained.

The triple gunas, namely sattva, rajas, and tamas, tend to wield their influence by inducing desires and desire-ridden actions. They strengthen attachment to worldly things in the jivas by creating attraction and aversion and keep their senses in their outward mode, driving them to repeatedly seek things that are agreeable and avoid those that are disagreeable. They also create the delusion that the visible and perceptible reality is real and the ignorance that by seeking sense objects and worldly enjoyments through the pursuit of Dharma, Artha, and Kama, one can secure peace and happiness. In that pursuit, they engage in desire-ridden actions and experience delusion, bondage, and suffering.

According to Yogasutras, we can cultivate indifference to sense objects (visaya vitrnasya) by practicing renunciation (sannyasa) and dispassion (vairagyam). Simultaneously, we can also fix the mind upon the Self (Isvara) or the sacred syllable Aum, cultivating devotion (Isvara pranidhana) and developing direct awareness of our spiritual nature. Thus, to overcome the influence of the gunas and the problem of delusion and bondage, Patanjali suggests the twin approach of practicing dispassion or indifference to sense objects and the gunas and taking refuge in Isvara. Here, Lord Krishna recommends the second approach, suggesting that one can overcome the gunas and their influence by taking refuge in him only.

Brahman, the eternal Self, is beyond the gunas (guntatita) and free from their influence. He is also their Lord and Controller. Maya is his dependent aspect. Therefore, by seeking refuge in him, rather than appeasing Maya, a devotee can become free from her influence and the impurities she creates. When you take refuge in the Lord, meditating on him as your Self without duality, he becomes your shield, and the lower maya-shaktis cease to exert their deluding influence. In their place, the higher Shaktis awaken and purify your mind and body, and let the light from the Self shine through. You can facilitate that process by surrendering to the Lord and letting His Shaktis do their work without interruption or interference.

Sloka 15

na māṃ duṣkṛtino mūḍhāḥ prapadyante narādhamāḥ
māyayāpahṛtajñānā āsuraṃ bhāvam āśritāḥ

na = not; mam = to Me; duskrtinah = evil doers; mudhah = foolish, deluded; prapadyante = take refuge; nara-adhamah = most depraved human beings; mayaya = by maya; apahrta = carried away, stolen; jnanah = knowledge; asuram = demonic; bhavam = nature; asritah = abide, take refuge.

The evil doers, the deluded ones, and the most deprived of human beings do not take refuge in Me since, with their knowledge being carried away by my Maya, they take refuge in demonic nature.

Dushkarma is essentially selfish karma. Those who are selfish by nature and engage in selfish actions are dushkritas. They engage in adharma (dushkarma), perform desire-ridden and selfish actions, and ignore the code of conduct that is conducive to peace and happiness. They are foolish and deluded (mudha) because they lack discernment, ignore the Lord, and defy their spiritual nature. They are the most depraved (naradhama) because they take refuge in their evil nature (asurabhavam) and engage in evil and inhuman actions. Since their knowledge is carried away by delusion (maya), they do not take refuge in the Lord or consider liberation their chief aim. Deprived of their humanity and divinity, they are but asuras (demons) in human bodies and enemies of the Supreme Lord.

According to our scriptures, humans have the same form as Purusha, the Cosmic Being. However, their divinity, potencies, and purity remain suppressed by the impurities created by the gunas. Hence, they are predisposed to an evil nature and vulnerable to the influence of Maya and the triple gunas, which subject them to desires, selfishness, duality, and delusion. Because of them, humans experience egoism, passions, desires, and attachments. Therefore, they are oblivious to their spiritual nature and remain predisposed to their lower nature. To realize their divine potential and abide in their spiritual nature, they must overcome the gunas by renouncing desires, practicing self-control (atma samyama), and performing actions as a sacrifice. Exclusive devotion arises in them when they attain purity through spiritual effort over several lifetimes. When they reach perfection and take refuge in the Supreme Lord with supreme devotion, they earn his grace and attain liberation. However, only a few out of millions of humans succeed in achieving liberation, performing desireless actions (nishkama karma) and attaining sameness (samsiddhi), freedom from karma (naishkarmya siddhi), and selfless and exclusive devotion (ananya bhakti).

At the other end of the spectrum are the evildoers, the most depraved humans (naradhamas). They do not worship God. With the predominance of rajas and tamas, deluded by egoism and attachments, they take refuge in worldly things such as wealth, power, status, family name, etc., and bring ruin upon themselves. They may worship the Lord to fulfill their desires or seek powers to harm someone. They are similar to the asuras in their nature and actions. The Asuras are a special class of beings who live in the demonic worlds. According to the Puranas, they are also Brahma's children. Due to the impurities clouded by the darkness of tamoguna, they mistake their physical selves for their real selves and take refuge in their demonic nature. They also keep fighting with the gods for the same reasons and take wicked pleasure in troubling the Lord's devotees. It is said that in the remote past, they used to live in a distant world, but nowadays they exist very much in humans as a part of their essential nature due to the influence of Kaliyuga.

When human beings nourish their evil nature through evil thoughts, desires, and actions, they develop evil tendencies (asura pravritti) and join the ranks of Asuras in human bodies. Through their evil actions, they strengthen their evil nature, nourish the Asuras, and become their instruments in spreading adharma. In this age of darkness (Kaliyuga), pure souls are rare. It is said that as time progresses, the world will become increasingly unrighteous, unspiritual, evil, and chaotic. As human beings turn to materialism and pursue material goals, ignoring their spiritual concerns, they will become more vulnerable to demonic influence and indulge in evil actions, making it harder for them to achieve peace and equanimity or work for their liberation.

Sloka 16

caturvidhā bhajante māṃ janāḥ sukṛtinorjuna
ārto jijñāsur arthārthī jñānī ca bharatarṣabha

catuh-vidhah = four types of; bhajante = worship; mam = Me; janah = people; su-krtinah = people who earned merit through sinless action; arjuna = O Arjuna; artah = the unhappy and distressed people; jijnasuh = those who are curious and inquisitive; artha-arthi = those seeking material wealth; jnani = the wise ones who possess the knowledge of the self; ca = and; bharata-rsabha = O greatest among the Bharatas.

Four types of people who earned sinless karma through good actions worship Me, O Arjuna, the greatest among the Bharatas, the unhappy and distressed people, the curious ones who seek knowledge, the seekers of material wealth, and the wise ones who possess self-knowledge.

Here, Lord Krishna states four types of devotees who worship him with devotion arising from their righteous actions (sukrita) and meritorious karma (punya). They are those in distress, the curious ones who want to know, the seekers of wealth, and the knowers of the Self. He mentioned them in the order of their merit, the first being the commonest and the last the rarest. The distressed ones are those who might have faced some form of adversity, such as sickness, a calamity, or the loss of someone or something. The curious ones (jijnasa) are those who want to know the secrets of the Self or liberation, in which ordinary people are disinterested. Most people fall into the third category, especially in today's world. They worship God, seeking wealth and material comforts. The jnanis are those who possess the knowledge of the Self and take refuge in God to abide in oneness. You can also see that they are all devotees of God and uphold Dharma. Hence, they are also the most qualified to receive his help and protection. Spiritually, they are better than those who scorn God, doubt his existence, or ignore their obligatory duties and the code of conduct expected of humans. As he stated before, evildoers do not worship God at all since their wisdom is carried away by the deluding power of Maya and their demonic nature. If at all, they worship him, it is for an ulterior or wicked purpose.

Devotion to God does not arise in everyone, nor does the curiosity to explore the knowledge of the Self. It arises only due to the good deeds (sukrita) performed in the past. Most people turn to God seeking material or personal rewards (phalakama) such as a heavenly life, relief from pain and suffering, knowledge, or material wealth. Their devotion is mixed with varying degrees of impurities such as desires, egoism, delusion, and selfishness. Only those who possess sattva and are free from evil develop true devotion to the Lord. The yearning and the inclination to worship him with selfless devotion arise in them in proportion to their good karma and the predominance of sattva. They reach this state after many births and persistent practice of yoga. As they develop a distaste for worldly life and material rewards due to their good karma, they turn to the Lord with selfless love, worshipping him with supreme devotion and remaining content within themselves. Materialistic people worship material things such as wealth, name and fame, success, good health, freedom from suffering, etc. Their love for God is secondary. If they worship God, it is primarily to fulfill their desires. For them, God is the means, not an end. They may succeed in their effort since God does not discriminate against anyone and may grant their wishes. However, selfish rewards may have their consequences even if they arise from God. For example, the Puranas illustrate how the evil asuras who obtain boons from the gods suffer the worst fate when they cross their limits and indulge in evil actions. Pure devotion does not seek anything except the love and nearness of God or oneness with the Self. It manifests only in the purest of the pure.

Sloka 17

teṣāṃ jñānī nityayukta ekabhaktir viśiṣyate
priyo hi jñāninotyartham ahaṃ sa ca mama priyaḥ

tesam = Of them; jnani = the wise one; nitya-yuktah = ever connected to me in yoga; eka bhakti = devoted to the One only; visisyate = excels; priyah = dear; hi = surely; jnaninah = the knower of the Self; atyartham = supremely, highly; aham = I am; sah = he is; ca = and; mama = to Me; priyah = dear.

Of them, the wise one excels, who is ever connected to me in yoga and devoted to Me only. Surely, I am supremely dear to the wise one, and he is dear to Me.

A yogi who constantly practices the yoga of self-control (atma samyama) with steadfast devotion, knowledge, and wisdom, who is ever connected to the Supreme Lord through contemplation and self-absorption, and whose mind cannot be disturbed by any desire or distraction, Lord Krishna says that the wise one is the dearest to him. He attracts his love and attention through the devotion of the purest kind, which is not afflicted with desires, selfishness, or egoism. He worships him as his very Self and the Self of all and sees no distinction between them. The wise one, a jnani, is not necessarily an erudite scholar who studies the scriptures and knows them thoroughly. He may or may not be a scholar of worldly wisdom (vijnani), conversant with the ways of the world or the nature of things. He is not distinguished by them but by his pure and unconditional devotion. He earns God's love through the purity of his love and devotion. Most importantly, he practices self-control, practices nishkama karma as a sacrifice, worships him with exclusive devotion, and remains ever connected to him through contemplation or self-absorption. Therefore, he is far superior to all other devotees and much closer to God. Love and admiration are mutual between God and his devotees, who exemplify these excellent qualities. They earn his love because they are ever absorbed in his devotion and, through that, are ever connected to him.

Here, we do not want to speculate on whether the individual Self and the Supreme Self are the same or different. We believe that they are the same or essentially the same and enjoy an internal and inseparable connection. Those who know the Supreme Lord through oneness do not feel any distinction between them. They experience oneness with him and see him universally in all and everywhere. Seeing him thus, they cultivate universal love and friendliness towards the whole creation. They experience oneness with him internally and see his footprints everywhere externally. Thereby, they are never separate from him or disconnected from him. To reach this state of oneness or perfection on the path of liberation, a yogi must diligently practice karma-sannyasa yoga with self-restraint, devotion, discernment, and detachment, renouncing all desires and attachments. According to Patanjali, constant devotion to God (Isvara pranidhana) results in the realization of the singular consciousness (pratyak cetana adhigama), which further leads to oneness with Isvara's pure consciousness and freedom from all mental disturbances (antarayabhavas). In that state of union, there is no distinction or duality between the Self and this devotee of pure wisdom (jnani) who attains him. He is lost forever in an ocean of love and infinite bliss.

Sloka 18

udārāḥ sarva evaite jñānī tv ātmaiva me matam
āsthitaḥ sa hi yuktātmā mām evānuttamāṃ gatim

udarah = generous, noble, exalted; sarve = all; eva = surely; ete = these; jnani = the wise one, the knower of the Self; tu = but; atma eva = like My very Self; me = My; matam = opinion; asthitah = fixed, situated; sah = he; hi = firmly;

yukta-atma = absorbed in the Self; mam = to Me; eva = certainly, surely; anuttamam = the highest goal; gatim = goes, reaches.

All these are indeed noble and exalted, but the knower of the Self, in My opinion, is like My very Self; fixed firmly, absorbed in himself, he certainly reaches Me, the highest goal.

All the Lord's devotees are noble and generous because they practice sacrificial duties for the welfare of others and serve God and his creation as their obligatory duty. They respect the code of conduct prescribed by the scriptures and the sacred suggestions found in them. They may worship him with or without desires, but rise above themselves and their selfish nature through service and devotion. Thus, every devotee who serves the Supreme Being and others is noble and exalted, even if his devotion is tinged with certain impurities. Devotion by itself elevates him into an exalted state and brings him closer to his goal. If he keeps practicing it, it will gradually lead him farther up the path of spiritual evolution. If you have devotion and can sustain it and strengthen it through yoga, you can be sure of finding the eternal resting ground within yourself. It may not happen in one life, but you will surely progress in the right direction.

Nobility or gentleness (udara svabhavam) arises from sattva's predominance. Only a few who are predominantly sattvic turn to God and become his devotees. It is the most striking aspect of the wise ones or the knowers of the Self (jnanis). They are his best devotees because they are pure, love him unconditionally as their very Self, and make the highest sacrifice, giving up egoism, desires, and attachments and dissolving in him their lower nature and all the associated identities. Therefore, devotees who are pure and worship him are dearer to the Supreme Lord. However, still dearer are those who come nearest to him in purity and divinity and worship him exclusively with no other thought.

Lord Krishna already assured that he would personally care for the welfare of his devotees who worship him with single-minded devotion. When a devotee empties impure himself from his mind, silences his selfish desires and egoistic cravings, and contemplates upon him with exclusive devotion, he takes care of his liberation also. Hence, the wise ones give up everything and meditate upon him with concentration and devotion. They put complete trust in him, give up desire-ridden thoughts and intentions, and endure suffering that may arise from their practice without complaining. They exemplify indifference and sameness with their minds firmly withdrawn and established within themselves. Yogis of such caliber are rare to find since they live in seclusion and avoid public places and the company of worldly people. However, they do not escape from the attention of the Lord or his love. He reciprocates their love and devotion and treats them as if they are not different from Him. When they depart from their bodies, they go directly to the immortal world of Brahman and become eternally free.

Sloka 19

bahūnāṃ janmanām ante jñānavān māṃ prapadyate
vāsudevaḥ sarvam iti sa mahātmā sudurlabhaḥ

bahunam = many; janmanam = births; ante = at the end; jnana-van = the wise one, the knower of the Self; mam = to Me; prapadyate = surrender, takes refuge; vasudevah = Vasudeva; sarvam = all; iti = thus; sah = such; maha-atma = great soul; su-durlabhah = very difficult to find.

At the end of many births, the wise one surrenders to Me, knowing thus, "Vasudeva is all." Such a great soul is very difficult to find.

When a yogi worships Vasudeva as his very Self and realizes through a profound inner experience that he is also the Self of all (sarva bhutatma) and pervades all (sarvam), he becomes firmly established in that realization. After that, he remains established in that thought and exemplifies it, whether engaged in contemplation, mundane actions, or worship. He attains that realization after passing through many births and deaths when the impurities accumulated in him dissolve, and his mind stabilizes in sameness. Liberation takes time. It is a long and arduous process that happens over several lives. If it were easy, everyone would be a seer. In the divine order of things, causes may take time to manifest effects. No one can predict events such as the birth of a baby, the flowering of a plant, or the germination of a seed, but we can be sure that they can happen if the causes and conditions that produce them are present. Lord Krishna presents here the conditions that will lead a great soul (mahatma) to the realization that Vasudeva is all.

When you read the Isa Upanishad, you will know that its seers attained perfection. Through their inner realization, they saw Brahman pervading all and being the source of all and declared affirmatively that all is inhabited by the Lord only (isavasyam idam sarvam). It dawns upon a yogi who becomes absorbed in the Self and attains oneness, dissolving his lower nature and all the accompanying notions of separation, distinction, and delusion. When you know that everything here belongs to the Supreme Lord, and he is all, you will reflect that in your thinking and actions. You will live with humility and gratitude and exemplify that truth, knowing you cannot claim ownership or doership of anything and that you earn the right to live here by performing your obligatory duties and offering their fruit to him. If you constantly remember it, live with a sacrificial and selfless attitude, and do not become involved with the world or its impurities, you will live freely, untainted by sin.

Madhavacharya and Shankaracharya interpreted 'Vasudeva sarvam' differently. The former felt that it meant Vasudeva was the cause of all, and he was the absolute, perfect Being. The latter thought that it meant Vasudeva was the Self of all. The declaration that 'Vasudeva is all' is true both materially and spiritually since Prakriti is Brahman's dependent aspect and is a part of him. Both are present in Isvara, the Lord of the Universe. His body, or the whole creation, is Prakriti, and his consciousness, or the Self, is Brahman. All the jivas have the same configuration. Therefore, the statement that Vasudeva is all is literally true. He is without a second. There is nothing besides him. 'Vasudeva is all' means all this belongs to the Brahman, is made up of Brahman, supported by the Brahman, and dissolves in Brahman. It also means there is nothing else besides him. The conviction that the Supreme Self is all (sarvam), the source of all, the upholder of all, and the inhabitant of all arises after many births when the mind dissolves in the Self. A yogi reaches that firm conclusion through the persistent practice of karma-sannyasa, atma-samyama, dhyana, and bhakti yogas when he attains oneness and enters that absolute reality.

Sloka 20

kāmais tais tair hṛtajñānāḥ prapadyantenyadevatāḥ
taṃ taṃ niyamam āsthāya prakṛtyā niyatāḥ svayā

kamaih = by desires; taih taih = various; hrta = taken away, carried away, stripped of, deprived; jnanah = with their knowledge; prapadyante = worship, surrender; anya = other; devatah = deities, gods; tam tam = such and such, various; niyamam = observances, rules, instructions; asthaya = following; prakrtya = by nature; niyatah = forced, ordained, constrained; svaya = by their own.

Those whose knowledge is carried away by various desires worship other deities, following various observances forced by their own nature.

This and the following two verses tell us how important it is to worship the one Supreme Lord rather than numerous divinities. Jnanis, the knowers of the Self, who know that Vasudeva is all, worship him exclusively. They do not especially worship any other divinity since they know that they all represent him only, and he is all. However, those who do not know his opulence and omniscience and are still evolving spiritually worship different gods to fulfill their desires. They do not see that by worshipping the one Supreme Lord, they would be worshipping all. Therefore, they worship each of them differently according to their desires. They may even spend time arguing about which of them is better or superior. In Hinduism, we have a choice. If you worship Isvara or any god as if he is Isvara, you will eventually attain liberation. On the contrary, if you worship them individually as independent gods, you will not attain liberation.

Thus, ideally, devotees should worship the One Lord only or any deity which they may envision as Him, since all the divinities in their purest and highest aspect are but Brahman alone. Instead, if they worship various deities and engage in rites, rituals, sacrifices, penances, etc., seeking heaven, wealth, health, progeny, etc., they may succeed in fulfilling their desires, but they cannot escape from rebirth. Some devotees worship both the Universal Deity and other gods. Even they do not attain liberation unless, at some point, they worship him exclusively without desires. The devotees' essential nature, as determined by their gunas, influences their choices and methods. If it envelops their knowledge and discernment, they will worship many deities, including gurus, babas, village deities, spirits, animals, trees, etc., vainly hoping to secure a better life here and hereafter. It may also determine which gods they should worship. For example, Brihadaranyaka Upanishad (1.4) classifies gods according to their gunas. Thus, ignorant devotees may choose several gods for their worship according to their gunas or desires. They may also do it out of their anxiety, not to miss out on anything. Whatever the choice, the result will be the same. They accumulate karma due to desires and remain bound and deluded.

Sloka 21

yo yo yāṃ yāṃ tanuṃ bhaktaḥ śraddhayārcitum icchati
tasya tasyācalāṃ śraddhāṃ tām eva vidadhāmy aham

yah yah = whoever; yam yam = whichever; tanum = form; bhaktah = devotee; sraddhaya = with faith; arcitum = worship; icchati = wishes, desires; tasya = of his; tasya = of that; acalam = firm, steady; sraddham = faith; tam = him; eva = surely; vidadhami = stabilize, strengthen; aham = I.

Whoever devotee wishes to worship with faith, whatever form, I surely strengthen that firm faith of his (in that form).

Here, Lord Krishna did not say that all devotees should worship him only. Instead, he said that in whatever way they worshipped him, he would strengthen their faith in that direction. Since he is all, it does not matter who they will choose for their worship. Ultimately, he receives all offerings. Therefore, he remains neutral and helps them according to their faith and devotion. This is an important revelation that distinguishes Hinduism from other religions. Devotion to a particular deity is fundamentally a matter of personal choice since it depends upon devotees' karma and their evolution. If they are drawn to particular deities, it may be because the deities represent or reflect their essential nature. Since karma shapes people's lives and destinies on earth, God would like to stay out of such decisions. However, he may help them if they pray to him and fervently appeal to him for help or guidance.

Thus, your faith depends upon your inherent nature, which is, in turn, influenced by your karma or what you reap. Due to a lack of knowledge and discernment, most people grope in darkness and stumble many times before they find direction and discernment and see things clearly. True discernment arises after many births due to a great inner churning and awakening as one cultivates distaste for worldly enjoyments and engages in self-inquiry and spiritual exploration. In this verse, Lord Krishna clearly states that he will strengthen the faith of his devotees according to their devotion and inherent nature, but not according to his will. Whichever deity they choose or the method of worship they follow, he will strengthen their faith in them and allow them to grow spiritually and naturally at their own pace.

In the previous verse, he already drew a clear distinction between those who worshipped him and those who worshipped numerous deities, demigods, and others. Here, he clearly conveyed that he played no part in their choice and would not insist that they should worship him only. It does not mean that it is okay to worship numerous gods to fulfill one's desires. It also implies that no one should interfere with the faith of others. If they are worshipping other gods, you have no business compelling them to follow your path. You may teach the right knowledge and the importance of discernment, but you are not supposed to enforce it against others' will.

From this verse, we can discern that God is a compassionate being who does not interfere with the choices of people. He lets them live according to their preferences and priorities or inherent nature and reap both positive and negative consequences that may arise from them. Without being judgmental or vindictive, he lets the world evolve spiritually, accepting the diversity of people's thinking and choices as the norm. We have the freedom to experiment with our faith or our methods of worship as a part of our learning and transformative process, and find our way toward light and immortality. In other words, whether you worship the highest God or the smaller deities, it too happens due to the will of God only, who, out of compassion and love, gives us the freedom to make our choices. Finally, one should not interpret this verse to mean that only those who worship Lord Krishna attain liberation. It means all those who worship Isvara, the Lord of the Universe, or the absolute Supreme Self.

Sloka 22

sa tayā śraddhayā yuktas tasyārādhanam īhate
labhate ca tataḥ kāmān mayaivaḥ vihitān hi tān

sah = he; taya = with that; sraddhaya = faith; yuktah = endowed; tasya = that; aradhanam = worship; ihate = aspires, wishes, desires; labhate = gains, obtains; ca = and; tatah = from it; kaman = desires; maya = by Me; eva = only; vihitan = as decreed; hi = very; tan = those.

Endowed with that faith, he aspires to worship that form and gains from it those very desires that are decreed by Me only.

Endowed with the faith that arises from his essential nature, a devotee chooses his deity (or deities) and worships him to fulfill those desires that the Lord himself induces through Maya, his deluding force to keep the jivas bound. Thus, in the vision of the Bhagavadgita, God is all-powerful and responsible for bondage as well as liberation. He determines through karma, Dharma, or by himself which deities we should worship, which methods of worship we should follow, and which desires we should seek through rituals and sacrifices. Whether one worships a god, goddess, demi-god, spirit, or local deity, he is the cause of our actions and the desires that connect the devotees to their deities. Whatever form devotees choose to worship with faith and devotion, he stabilizes their faith in that form and fulfills the desires they seek through that worship. Thus, the power to grant desires rests not with the deities that people worship but with the Supreme Lord. The divinities people worship are his manifestations only. They perform specific duties as ordained by him to uphold creation. Just as we have obligatory duties, they, too, have their obligatory duties. Since he is the ultimate source of all, and they perform the duties he ordains, even they derive their power and divinity from him only.

Therefore, whether we worship him directly or indirectly through other deities, he is the one we all worship, although the effects may not be the same. It means that while worshipping the lower gods may not be an appropriate choice, a devotee's effort will not be futile if he worships them. Even in such inferior methods of worship, the Lord remains hidden in the divinities and ensures that their prayers are heard and answered. As is the source of all sources, cause of all causes, and as the witness Self of all, he watches his devotees progress from one stage to another and evolve spiritually. He receives all the prayers and offerings even when they do not worship him directly. Devotees may worship any deity in the early stages of their spiritual practice. Still, as their faith strengthens and their desires are fulfilled over time, they will eventually cultivate the right knowledge, discern the correct path, and worship the Lord only to attain liberation. Hence, in whatever way a devotee's spiritual journey may begin, as in the case of a river, he will eventually reach the oceanic state of Brahman only.

Sloka 23

antavat tu phalaṃ teṣāṃ tad bhavaty alpamedhasām
devān devayajo yānti madbhaktā yānti mām api

anta-vat = has an end, limited, perishable; tu = but; phalam = fruit; tesam = of theirs; tat = that; bhavati = is; alpa-medhasam = who are of poor intelligence; devan = gods, divinities; deva-yajah = worshipers of gods, divinities; yanti = go; mat = My; bhaktah = devotees; yanti = come; mam = to Me; api = only.

However, the fruit of those who are of poor intelligence is limited and has an end. The worshippers of gods go to the gods. My devotees come to Me only.

To avoid confusion or misunderstanding, the Lord clarifies that the rewards of worshipping the lower gods are limited. Therefore, they should choose wisely whom they want to worship. Those who worship him go to him and attain liberation. However, those who worship gods, demigods, or others go to the lesser realms where they reside, stay there for a limited time, and return to the earth to take another birth. Here, he categorically stated that if we worship the Supreme Self, we will achieve final liberation and never return. However, if we worship the lesser gods, we will reap the rewards of our devotion and attain a better life in the next birth, but we will remain bound to samsara. While the Lord does not force anyone to worship him, the object of our worship and our intentions directly affect our spiritual destinies. If we worship lower gods to fulfill our desires, we have to accept the consequences of engaging in desire-ridden actions and bear the burden of karma. In worldly life also, your success depends upon your goals. In these matters, discernment is essential. He already said that only the knowers of the Self, after innumerable births, realize that Vasudeva is all and take refuge in him. Due to a lack of intelligence and discretion, others remain caught in the web of samsara and delay their liberation.

Devotion (bhakti) to the Supreme Lord arises due to self-purification through the persistent practice of various yogas and renunciation of desires. When desires are suppressed, the senses are withdrawn, impurities such as egoism and delusion are removed, the gunas are subdued, the mind is filled with the thoughts of the Supreme Being as one's pure Self, exclusive devotion in its purest form arises naturally in the devotees. Through that devotion, he connects to the Lord and earns his grace and protection. In this sacred journey, knowledge (jnanam), purity, and devotion (bhakti) complement each other and propel the devotees to the cherished goal. Devotion becomes elevated according to purity and the right knowledge. When the mind is pure and free from delusion, the mind attains stability, equanimity, and sameness, and devotion becomes one-pointed. A devotee who is pure, detached, and established in sameness may not be erudite and may not possess intellectual or scriptural knowledge. Yet, he is far superior to an erudite scholar (pandita), who is bound to desires and attachments and pursues knowledge and devotion for worldly gains. His spiritual rewards remain limited as he is stuck in the web of Maya and keeps returning to the earth, birth after birth. Therefore, if liberation is the aim, a devotee must worship the Supreme Lord only and firmly establish him in his mind. He may worship other gods, but must acknowledge them as the Lord himself and remember him only.

Sloka 24

avyaktaṃ vyaktim āpannaṃ manyante māmabuddhayaḥ
paraṃ bhāvam ajānanto mamāvyayam anuttamam

avyaktam = does not manifest, non-beingn; vyaktim = manifested, being; apannam = become, gain, obtain, reduced to; manyante = think; mam = Me; abuddhayah = ignorant people lacking in discerning intelligence; param = supreme; bhavam = state; ajanantah = without knowing; mama = of My; avyayam = immutable, inexhaustible, imperishable; anuttamam = most exalted, the best, the highest.

Ignorant people who lack discriminating intelligence think of Me, who does not manifest (in a material body) as manifested, without knowing My supreme state, which is inexhaustible and the highest.

God does not manifest Himself. What manifests in His creation is the body, His materiality. The Self has no birth or death. Ignorant people mistake the body for the Self and fall into delusion. Here, Lord Krishna says that ignorant people, who lack discernment and proper knowledge and do not know Brahman's supreme and imperishable state, believe that the Lord takes birth like the jivas and has a beginning and an end. They mistake him for his forms and ignore the Self or his absolute essence, whose nature is pure consciousness and which is eternal, indestructible, and immutable. The knowledgeable ones know that the supreme Brahman is pure Self and has no materiality. He is pure consciousness in the manifested state as well as the unmanifested state. Therefore, he should not be mistaken for a being even if he assumes a form or incarnates in a mortal body. When one worships him, one should always remember that he is pure Self or Supreme Self.

The Vedas validate these statements. The Self (Atman) does not manifest. It does not have a body. It does not take birth. Even in the embodied state, it remains immutable, unmanifest, and untainted through births and deaths. It is the same with the Supreme Self (Brahman). He is always unmanifest, without corporeality and materiality in his pure state. Even when he manifests creation, he does not engage in physical actions except through Prakriti, his primal Nature. The material universe, which arises from him through Prakriti, is a projection or superimposition. It is distinct and separate from him and should not be mistaken for him. Although it exists because of him, and he pervades and supports it, he does not exist in it or is imbued with its qualities or materiality. The world or material universe is comparable to his body, but he is not connected to it, attached to it, or bound by it. He is its support since it cannot exist without him.

The wise ones are aware of this. They do not mistake him as a being or a god with a body, or worship his names and forms. Instead, they consider him the infinite, eternal, and indestructible Supreme Reality or pure consciousness and meditate on him accordingly to become absorbed in his thoughts and transcend their minds. Even if they worship an image of the Lord, their devotion is not to the form or the name but to His Pure Self. They practice dhyana (contemplation) with self-control (atma-samyama) and exclusive devotion. Withdrawing from the visible, perceptible, and objective reality, which includes this world, their minds, and bodies, they meditate on him as their very Self, thinking of him as the inexhaustible, highest, transcendental, pure consciousness. Absorbing their minds in that thought, they gradually enter his pure state and become dissolved.

One may worship the names and forms or the numerous manifestations of the Supreme Lord, but always with the awareness that they are his superficial aspects and do not represent him or his pure Self. Although the Supreme Lord is invisible, formless, and unmanifest, the scriptures and devotional traditions (bhakti sampradayas) approve of image worship because it is the best way to draw and silence the mind. Besides, it is difficult for humans to worship the unmanifest Brahman or connect to him with concentration and unwavering devotion. Therefore, in the early stages, images and mental objects are allowed for the initiates in meditation and ritual worship to stabilize their minds and cultivate devotion. However, as they progress, they should withdraw from them and focus on the subtle aspects of their consciousness, such as feelings and emotions, or subtle sounds, and finally rest their minds in the contemplation of the Self. This method is recommended because one cannot attain oneness or sameness (samadhi) if the mind is active and attached to names and forms or mental objects. The images, names, and forms of the Supreme Beings are the means to practice devotion, concentration, contemplation, and purification, but not an end in themselves.

Sloka 25

nāhaṃ prakāśaḥ sarvasya yogamāyāsamāvṛtaḥ
mūḍhoyaṃ nābhijānāti loko mām ajam avyayam

na = not; aham = I; prakasah = shine light, reveal, illuminate; sarvasya = all; yoga-maya = deluding power; samavrtah = covered, enveloped; mudhah = deluded; ayam = this; na = not; abhijanati = know; lokah =the world; mam = Me; ajam = unborn; avyayam = inexhaustible.

Veiled by My deluding power, I do not illuminate the whole world. (Hence), this deluded world does not know Me, the unborn and inexhaustible.

Lord Krishna says here that he does not illuminate everything, the minds of everyone, or the whole world. It is limited by our ignorance, knowledge, and impurities. Like the sun, he is always self-illuminated but remains concealed in most due to the veiling power of Maya. Shankara defined yoga maya as the deluding power arising from the union of the triple gunas. It arises from the will of the Lord himself. Things become visible in this world when there is light. When light is withdrawn, they become invisible. The Self cannot be perceived with physical light or the senses because it is eternally unmanifested and invisible. It can only be discerned through the illumination of the mind by intelligence (buddhi). None of the tattvas, including intelligence, are self-illuminated. Their illumination comes from the Self only. To the extent it is pure, it radiates the light of the Self. Since everyone is not equally pure, the purity of their intelligence also varies. When it is filled with impurities, people remain deluded and ignorant of the Self since it remains veiled and cannot be discerned. This is the summary.

Although he said he does not illuminate all, it does not mean he is partial and selective. As the Self of all, he is present in everyone and radiates the same effulgence equally. However, in the impure minds where the gunas and maya shaktis are active, he remains invisible or indiscernible since they obstruct his light and do not let it spread far, just as thick clouds obstruct the sun and do not let its light spread on the earth. He becomes self-evident only when the consciousness is pure, free from the influence of the gunas and the desires they induce, and his light is uninterruptedly reflected or radiated through it. Those whose minds are filled with impurities due to the deluding nature of the gunas and their influence cannot perceive the Self and remain ignorant of it. In other words, the Supreme Lord is not directly responsible for our purity, knowledge, or ignorance. Just as a mirror covered with dust or soot cannot reflect objects truly and accurately, a mind filled with impurities does not allow the light of the Self to shine through. Therefore, one has to cultivate purity to engage the mind in contemplation and discern the Lord, who is seated in all and radiates equally. The Lord's deluding power can be removed only through self-purification, cultivating discerning intelligence (viveka khyati).

Sloka 26

vedāhaṃ samatītāni vartamānāni cārjuna
bhaviṣyāṇi ca bhūtāni māṃ tu veda na kaścana

veda = know; aham = I; sama = equally; atitani = past; vartamanani = present; ca = and; arjuna = O Arjuna; bhavisyani = future; ca = also; bhutani = living beings; mam = Me; tu = but; veda = knows; na = not; kascana = anyone.

I know the beings of the past, the present, and the future equally, O Arjuna, but no one knows Me.

The deluding power (yoga maya) of Prakriti obstructs his illumination from spreading into our bodies or the world, just as dark clouds prevent the sun's illumination from spreading out. Hence, beings who are subject to delusion and ignorance cannot discern him or know him. One may learn about him through the scriptures or from others, but that knowledge is insufficient to know him without confusion. The Supreme Lord will always be a great mystery and an utmost secret for ignorant and deluded people drawn to materialism and worldly enjoyment. They cannot be sure what he is or is not. Even self-realized yogis who attained liberation do not know him fully, except perhaps in the transcendental state of oneness. Since he is limitless and no one can fathom his beginning or end, the human mind cannot comprehend his dimensions or hidden states. The material universe, which is a manifestation of the Supreme Self and which we can consider his body, is equally indescribable, unfathomable, and incomprehensible since it is also too vast, diverse, and complex to fit into our imagination or understanding. We may learn a few things about it, but we cannot fully grasp its true dimensions.

The Upanishads and the Puranas point to this difficulty. The Kena Upanishad illustrates how gods such as Indra, Vayu, and Agni had little knowledge or awareness of him and did not recognize him when he met them in disguise as a Yaksha. In the Creation Hymn, the seers of the Rigveda express the difficulty of knowing him, his actions, origin, the creation of the worlds, or the extent of his limits. If it was the case with the knowers of Brahman, one can imagine the difficulty deluded humans would have in knowing him. Our knowledge of Brahman and the absolute, eternal Reality he represents is derived mainly from scriptures, speculation, and inference. However, the Scriptures contain conflicting statements and create confusion and ambiguity. Hence, we have so many philosophies and interpretations about him and his creation.

These limitations arise because the Lord of the Universe does not illuminate everyone equally. They do not exist in him because he is fully illuminated. He is the knower of all, including the past, the present, and the future of all. He knows what may or may not happen, how creation will progress from one epoch to another, and how it will end. He knows all the gods, goddesses, and beings of the higher and the lower worlds, what they may do, or what may happen to them. Even though his light does not spread everywhere due to his Maya, he knows what lurks in those shadows and how they may trouble the world. In the incarnated state also, he retains his omniscience. However, he may not show it unless it is required.

Time (Kala) is one of Isvara's highest manifestations. He creates Time to create the illusion of movement, impermanence, and the beginning and end of things and to set in motion the cycle of creation, the order of the worlds (rta), and their progression (niyati) from one phase to another. As the knower of all, he is not subject to the limitations of time, place, knowledge, power, or intelligence. The divisions of past, present, and future do not exist in him. They are limited to his creation and manifestations and are meant to facilitate his fivefold duties: creation, preservation, destruction, suppression, and expression. Time creates the illusion of change, movement (prvritti and nivrtti), impermanence, knowledge, ignorance, duality, birth, death, and destruction. He is also timeless, eternal, and fixed. Hence, he is free from ignorance and confusion.

Sloka 27

icchādveṣasamutthena dvandvamohena bhārata
sarvabhūtāni saṃmohaṃ sarge yānti paraṃtapa

iccha = attractions, like, desire; dvesa = aversion, dislike, hatred; samutthena = arising from, produced from, born out of; dvandva = twofold, dual; mohena = by the delusion; bharata = O Bharata; sarva bhutani = all beings; sammoham = into illusion, confusion, bewilderment; sarge = birth, procreation, creation; yanti = go, fall; parantapa = O destroyer of enemies.

Due to the delusion of duality arising from attraction and aversion (to sense objects), O Bharata, all beings fall into confusion from birth, O destroyer of enemies.

The delusion of duality (dvandva moha) arises from attraction and aversion due to the activity of the senses under the influence of the gunas. Because of it, beings experience the dualities of subject and object, heat and cold, happiness and sorrow, etc. They also develop mistaken notions about themselves and others, about God and his creation, and their relationship with him. Because of the delusion, they accept their bodies as real and fail to discern the Self in them or identify with Him. Thereby, they fall into confusion, engage in desire-ridden actions, and pursue wrong aims. The jivas are born with this delusion from birth. They are conditioned by it. Their experiences and perceptions keep reinforcing it. Hence, they cannot easily overcome it or discern any truth that does not fit into their conditioned thinking or reasoning. Living amidst the dualities and accepting them as real and permanent, they seek pleasure in pain and happiness in sorrow and suffer from confusion and bewilderment.

This is the natural propensity of all living things, from humans to the tiniest creatures endowed with one or more senses. Drawn to pleasures and repelled by pain, making choices in the false hope of seeking fulfillment or prolonging happiness, and lacking self-control and mental stability, they experience modifications and afflictions. Making attraction and aversion the basis of their actions and decisions and seeking happiness and freedom from sorrow and afflictions through desire-ridden actions, they prolong their suffering and bondage. This is the way of life on Earth. It is how Nature intended us to live in this world so that she can keep the cycle of creation moving forward and keep things and beings under her firm control. Hence, it is difficult even for yogis to escape from her iron claws. Since Isvara is the cause of it, the solution also lies with him. As Lord Krishna will suggest in the next verse, one has to overcome the delusion by surrendering to him, taking refuge in him, and cultivating sameness towards all dualities. As he stated before, sameness (samatvam) is the highest yoga. The delusion of dualities disappears only when one attains it.

Sloka 28

yeṣāṃ tv antagataṃ pāpaṃ janānāṃ puṇyakarmaṇām
te dvandvamohanirmuktā bhajante māṃ dṛḍhavratāḥ

yesam = whose; tu = however; anta-gatam = has come to an end; papam = sin; jananam = people; punya = pious; karmanam = actions; te = they; dvandva = duality; moha = delusion; nirmuktah = freed from; bhajante = worship; mam = Me; drdha-vratah = with strong resolve, determination.

However, those people of pious actions, whose sins have come to an end, who are freed from delusion, worship Me with strong resolve.

Since the Lord himself causes delusion and bondage through Prakriti, he also provides the solution to those who strive for it. Devotees who want to escape from samsara should engage in pious actions (punya karma) through karma-sannyasa and worship him with exclusive devotion to resolve their sinful karmas and cultivate sameness. Thus, although all beings are born with delusion arising from attraction and aversion, his devotees have the chance to overcome it with his help. Having cultivated discernment and realizing that the Lord is the cause, support, and solution for their bondage and suffering, they can strive for liberation with strong resolve. 'Yesam tv anagatam papam jananam' means those for whom sins have become a thing of their past. Nothing lasts forever in this world, even the delusion that arises from birth. After many births and deaths, some jnanis come to their senses due to the good deeds performed in the past and strive for liberation, taking refuge in the Lord and worshipping him exclusively. Through sustained devotional and contemplative practices, they overcome dualities, attractions, and aversions and enter the pure state of Brahman. Only those whose sins have ended and whose minds and bodies are purified with the suppression of the gunas are truly qualified for it.

From this, we can conclude that egoistic striving will not lead the devotee anywhere. He needs to secure divine grace through desireless actions (nishkama karma), a stable mind (nischala manas), and stainless devotion (nishkala bhakti). If the Lord is satisfied with him, he will carry him across the ocean of samsara, becoming his boat, the boatman, the paddle, the sails, and the wind. If you are inclined to acquire spiritual knowledge and believe in the possibility of liberation, if you perform actions without desires and attachments, if you can restrain your mind and senses and withdraw them into yourself to cultivate sameness, if pure devotion comes to you naturally due to self-purification, and if you worship God in any form exclusively with unwavering faith and without desires, you will progress on the spiritual path and reach the supreme Goal. You will find this assurance in the Bhagavadgita from the Lord himself.

Sloka 29

jarāmaraṇamokṣāya mām āśritya yatanti ye
te brahma tad viduḥ kṛtsnam adhyātmaṃ karmacākhilam

jara = old age; marana = death; moksaya = for deliverance, liberation; mam = in Me; asritya = by taking refuge; yatanti = strive, endeavor; ye = those who; te = they; brahma = Brahman; tat = that; viduh = know; krtsnam = whole, total, entire; adhyatmam = self-knowledge; karma = actions; ca = and; akhilam = all.

Those who strive for liberation from old age and death by taking refuge in Me, they do know that Brahman, the whole self-knowledge, and all about karma.

Brahman is the support and the refuge for knowing Brahman. That is why exclusive devotion is so important. There is no other way. When you wake up from a dream, you know you have been through an altered reality or consciousness and returned to the reality of wakeful consciousness. Except for the experience of the dream, nothing much changes for you. Life goes on normally, although some dreams may linger in memory or disturb you temporarily. For the jiva also, the life of duality and delusion is an altered state of reality that lasts for several lifetimes but is never permanent. Even though the embodied Self passes through many births and deaths, it remains immutable and is not changed by its existence in samsara. Even the worst adversities and nightmarish conditions do not disturb its pure state. Its untainted existence in the impure bodies of the mortal world is but a temporary phase on the scale of eternity. However, from the perspective of the jiva in whose body he resides, it may look like an eternity. Deluded humans search for solutions to the problems of aging and death through physical means. They may temporarily delay or hide aging or death, but cannot escape from them.

Indeed, in this world, no one can overcome impermanence, death, or morality through physical means. At least, the world is not there yet, and currently, spiritual solutions are the only means to find solace and comfort from the thoughts of mortality, death, and aging. They are facts of life that must be lived through with stoical calmness, knowing that the Lord in us, who is our very Self, is eternal and indestructible, and by taking refuge in him, we can cross the river of death. Only a few reach that conclusion without doubt and succeed in attaining immortality. Physically, we are born to die. We start dying from the moment we are born. We may spend a lifetime trying to ignore it or live in denial, but the thought always remains in the background and reveals itself in moments of fear, danger, or insecurity.

When we are young, we do not bother much about death. When we see others dying, we may temporarily feel depressed or philosophical, but soon recover from the depressing thoughts and move on. As we become older, the thoughts of death begin to assail our minds and disturb our peace. It is why, in the Vedic tradition, sannyasa (renunciation) is prescribed for householders when they retire from active duties. Those who renounce their worldly duties, desires, names, and forms, take refuge in Brahman and view death as the door to transcendence and eternal life, are most qualified to earn his love and attain liberation. Practicing renunciation, observing their vows, and stabilizing their minds in devotion, they resolve their sins, acquire the knowledge of the Self, and attain the Supreme State of Brahman

Sloka 30

sādhibhūtādhidaivaṃ māṃ sādhiyajñaṃ ca ye viduḥ
prayāṇakālepi ca māṃ te vidur yuktacetasaḥ

sa-adhibhuta = presiding lord of the elements; adhidaivam = presiding lord of the divinities; mam = Me; sa-adhiyajnam = presiding lord of all sacrifices; ca = and; ye = those who; viduh = know; prayana kale = at the time of departing from here; api = even; ca = and; mam = Me; te = they; viduh = know; yukta-cetasah = with their minds yoked.

Those who know Me as the Adhibhuta, Adhidaiva, and Adhiyajna know Me even at the time of departing from here with their minds yoked (to Me).

Those who know that Brahman is the Lord of the physical realm, the Lord of the spiritual realm, and the Lord of all sacrifices know that he is also the support for every devotee's attainment of liberation. Therefore, by establishing their minds in him and devoting themselves exclusively to him, they attain liberation.

Adhi means the Lord or the presiding and controlling deity. Bhuta refers to the objective world (the not-self), which is made up of the five elements and other Prakriti tattvas. Adhidaiva means Lord of the divinities, the subtle worlds, and the entire spiritual realm. It refers to the Self or the Supreme Self. The divinities reside in the organs of the body, such as the mind, speech, the senses, heart, breath, digestive organs, etc., as their presiding deities. The Self is their Overlord. Adhiyajna means the presiding deity of all the yajnas (sacrifices) or actions. Although devotees invoke various deities in the sacrifices and make offerings to them to propitiate them, Brahman is the presiding deity of all yajnas and the ultimate recipient of all sacrificial offerings. All the offerings made to the gods by them ultimately reach him only. Thus, Brahman is the Lord of all. He is the Lord of the physical, subtle, and transcendental realms. He presides over our minds and bodies as well as all the world, from the highest to the lowest and from the grossest to the subtlest.

Devotees can use this information to meditate on him and stabilize their minds. They can practice mananam (remembering) or nidhidhyasanam (contemplation), envisioning him as the Lord of their bodies (Adhibhuta), minds (Adhidaiva), and actions (Adhiyajna). Thus, with their minds yoked to him (yukta chetasa), they can remain ever-absorbed in his contemplation with steadfast devotion and cultivate equanimity and sameness. If they practice it uninterruptedly, they can also remember him at the time of death as Adhibhuta while leaving the body. They can remember him as Adhidaiva when separated from the body and as Adhiyajna when they see their bodies being cremated. When the soul departs from the mortal world for the mid-region, the presiding deities (devas) of the organs offer him salutations, knowing him as the Adhidaiva, and bade him farewell to return to their source. Upon entering the immortal world of Brahman, the Self remembers he is the offering in the sacrifice of liberation, and Brahman presides over it as the Adhiyajna, the Lord of Sacrifices. Remembering that he achieves the final union.

The knowledge that Brahman is the source of all and the Lord of all realms, physical, mental, spiritual, and all actions and movements, is transformative. It helps the yogis remember him and meditate on him constantly, whether they are engaged in mundane actions or yoga. Through regular practice and seeing him as the all-pervading Supreme Self (sarvavyapai) and the Self of all (sarvataryami), they can strengthen their faith and devotion and dissolve their minds in his contemplation. Those who envision Brahman in this manner with devotion and purity realize the truth stated in the Isa Upanishad, "All this is for the habitation of the Lord (isavasyamidam sarvam)." After that, they will never forsake him, and he will not forsake them. With their steadfast minds absorbed in his thoughts, they remain yoked to him even at the time of their death and enjoy his support and protection during their journey to the highest heaven. Scholars and intellectuals may suffer from occasional forgetfulness or confusion about the knowledge they possess. However, those who are free from the delusion of duality and know the Self as the Lord, or the Lord as the Self, overcome ignorance and duality and establish an inseparable connection with him.

Conclusion

iti srīmadbhāgavadgītāsupanisatsu brahmavidyāyām yogasāstre srikrisnārjunasamvāde jnānavijnānayogo nāma saptamo 'dhyayah

iti = thus; srīmadbhāgavadgītā = in the sacred Bhagavadgita; upanisatsu = in the Upanishad; brahmavidyāyām = the knowledge of the absolute Brahman; yogasāstre = the scripture of yoga; srikrisnārjunasamvāde = the dialogue between Sri Krishna and Arjuna; jnānavijnānayogo nāma = by the name the yoga of the knowledge about the lord and creation; saptama = seventh; adhyayah = chapter.

Thus ends the seventh chapter, named Jnana Vijnana Yoga (The Yoga of the Knowledge About the Lord and Creation) in the Upanishad of the divine Bhagavadgita, the knowledge of the Absolute, a treatise on Yoga, and the debate between Arjuna and Lord Krishna.

08 – Akshara Brahma Yoga

The Yoga of Imperishable Brahman

Sloka 1

arjuna uvāca
kiṃ tad brahma kim adhyātmaṃ kiṃ karma puruṣottama
adhibhūtaṃ ca kiṃ proktam adhidaivaṃ kim ucyate

arjunah uvaca = Arjuna said; kim = what; tat = that; brahma = Brahman; kim = what; adhyatmam = the inner Self; kim = what; karma = karma; purusa-uttama = O Supreme Person; adhibhutam = the elemental self; ca = and; kim = what; proktam = is said to be; adhidaivam = the divine self; kim = what; ucyate = is said to be.

Arjuna said, "What is that Brahman? What is the Adhyatma? What is karma, O Supreme Being? What is declared as Adhibhuta, and what is said to be Adhidaiva?

As the title suggests, the eighth chapter of the Bhagavadgita is primarily about the imperishable Brahman. According to the Vedas, Brahman is the highest, absolute, eternal, indestructible, indefinable, indescribable, and ultimate reality. He is sometimes personified as the Supreme Lord and sometimes as the Self, Pure Self, Supreme Self, pure consciousness, or the Absolute Reality. He is the Self (Adhyatma), the source of all actions and movements (karma), the Lord of Creation (Adhibhuta), and the Lord of all divinities (Adhidaiva). These are all his manifestations only.

In this and the next verse, Arjuna asked seven questions concerning Brahman, the Supreme Being. Although we often refer to Brahman as a Being or deity, in his absolute state, he represents the Highest Reality (Sat), which is true in itself and by itself, and from which everything differentiates to create the illusion of diversity and multiplicity. The one Self becomes many by projecting an alternate reality (the other Self) in the field of Prakriti. Thus, he has both real and unreal and manifested and unmanifested aspects or dimensions. As the unchanging, eternal, supreme reality, he is the source and support of all creation. Since he represents all and is the sum of all realities and dimensions manifesting from him, he cannot be defined into a specific category, name, or form. He is without genders, names, forms, attributes, or modes. Yet, in his manifested aspects, he appears with them and deludes himself.

Brahman is the presiding deity or the overlord (adhipa) of all existence. Since he is the creator, preserver, and destroyer of all, everything arises from him and subsides in him. He has three fundamental dimensions: the physical, mental, and supramental. They are also called the gross, subtle, and subtler and distinguished as the Adhibhuta, Adhidaiva, and Adhyatma, respectively. Adhibhuta refers to the physical realm or the material universe, which is perceptible or graspable in wakeful consciousness through the senses. It is impermanent, subject to modifications, and includes the earth and the subterranean worlds. Adhidaiva refers to the mental, astral, or subtle realms. They can be known through scriptural knowledge or the mind and intelligence in restful, meditative, dream, or intuitive states. The worlds of gods, subtle beings, and ancestors, who inhabit the mid and the heavenly regions, are ruled by him. Adhyatma refers to the metaphysical realm or the Supreme Reality of Brahman. It is beyond the mind and senses and cannot be known except through transcendental states. It is the realm of pure consciousness, which is the subtlest of the subtle and is ungraspable, indescribable, unlimited, self-existent, fixed, complete, infinite, eternal, and blissful. Only Isvara, the highest manifested aspect of Brahman, who goes by several names, has a direct and continuous connection with it and presides over it. Brahman's highest and purest manifestations and those who attain oneness (such as the freed souls and gods of higher planes) and partake in Isvara's higher nature and absolute consciousness belong to this realm and remain connected to him through it.

In the human body, the gross material body represents the realm of Adhibhuta. The mind and intelligence represent the realm of Adhidaiva, and the transcendental Self represents the Adhyatma. The gross, subtle, and subtler parts are present in all creation. Hence, the whole manifestation is considered the body of Isvara, pervaded and supported by Him. Thus, we can see that just as each individual being has a physical body, a subtle body, and the inner Self, Brahman, the universal Cosmic Reality, whose nature is said to be truth, bliss, and consciousness (sachidananda), has also material, divine, and eternal dimensions. In the previous chapter, Lord Krishna distinguished jnana (knowledge of the Self or his higher nature) from vijnana (knowledge of the body or his lower nature). The knowledge of Adhibhuta and Adhidaiva constitutes Vijnana, and the knowledge of the Adhyatma constitutes Jnana. Both types of knowledge are necessary to cultivate discernment and absorb the mind in the Supreme Self.

Sloka 2

adhiyajñaḥ kathaṃ kotra dehesmin madhusūdana
prayāṇakāle ca kathaṃ jñeyosi niyatātmabhiḥ

adhiyajnah = Lord of the sacrifices; katham = how; kah = who; atra = here; dehe = in the body; asmin = this; madhusudana = O Madhusudana; prayana-kale = at the time of departure; ca = and; katham = how; jneyah = be known; asi = you; niyata-atmabhih = by the self-restrained.

"O Madhusudhana, who is the Lord of the sacrifices in this body and how; and at the time their departure from this world, how should you be known by the self-restrained yogis?"

In this verse, Arjuna asks three questions: who is the Lord of the Sacrifices in the body, how is he the Lord of the Sacrifices, and how should self-restrained yogis know him? He wanted to know, in a jiva, who performs the sacrifices, who receives those offerings, and how Lord Krishna should be known. Should he be known as the sacrificer or the Lord of the sacrifices?

In the Vedic symbolism, all the obligatory functions of the mind and body, such as eating, walking, sleeping, breathing, digestion, thinking, remembering, etc., are considered internal sacrifices. They are meant for the enjoyment of the Self in the body. He is the Lord in the body, and all actions of Prakriti are meant for him only. Hence, they should be consecrated to him only. Performing actions in this manner is the duty of every human on earth. It is their obligatory duty (Dharma). By performing actions in this manner, they can avoid any sin arising from their actions and remain sinless. In the development of the Upanishadic thought, the Vedic seers stumbled upon the idea of sacrifice as the basis of all actions and all existence. They saw that the idea or the design of sacrifice was hidden in all natural functions and movements, including the activities of the mind and body. They perceived that the impetus to perform actions did not arise from the jivas but from God himself through his dynamic force or Prakriti, and whatever materials or energies were used in such actions belonged to him only. Therefore, they concluded that no one should claim ownership or doership of any action. They should be considered offerings in the greater sacrifice of life or creation and consecrated to him only. The idea of karma-sannyasa, or the renunciation of desires in actions, is also linked to this.

The Vedic tradition rests on the belief that creation itself began with an act of sacrifice. Brahman used parts of himself as the sacrificial material to perform it, and from that, all the beings and worlds emerged as the remains of the sacrifice. In its worldview, the order and regularity of creation and all the divine laws established by the Supreme Lord depend upon human actions. If they perform actions selflessly and sacrificially, there will be peace, prosperity, and happiness. If they perform them selfishly or with evil intentions, there will be chaos and disorder. Thus, the Vedic seers envisioned sacrificial actions as the basis for establishing divine order on Earth. They felt that the knowledge of sacrificial duties and actions gave them an opportunity to consecrate their thoughts and actions to the Supreme Lord as an offering and escape from samsara.

The Upanishadic seers of Vedanta went a step further and suggested that even the most mundane actions, such as eating, sleeping, breathing, digestion, intercourse, procreation, etc., should be performed with the same attitude so they could be elevated into sacrificial actions, and a just and orderly life and world could be established on earth. The Upanishads internalized the Vedic sacrifices. They conceptualize the human body as a sacrificial pit and the food, water, air, pleasure, pain, etc., consumed by the being (jiva) as offerings to nourish the divinities that reside in the organs so they can work efficiently. By the same analogy, one may presume that all the activities performed by the mind and body are sacrificial actions. Their ultimate recipient is the Lord, who resides in all beings as their very Self. Since he is also the Lord and upholder of all, he should be considered the Lord of all sacrifices (Adhiyajna) in the body and outside. What this means is that householders who renounce worldly life to become sannyasis may abandon sacrificial rituals but should never abandon sacrificial actions. They should continue to perform karma-sannyasa in all stages of human life.

Thus, the Vedic religion upholds sacrifice as a way of life in which humans have an opportunity to consecrate their lives, thoughts, and actions to the Supreme Lord as an offering to avoid the sin of living selfishly and ignoring their obligations to him. Through their selfless actions, they can live for him and perform his duties as their own to escape from sin, samsara, and the pains of mortality. By consecrating themselves to this higher cause, devotees can transform their thoughts and actions into selfless offerings and their living into a continuous and lifelong sacrifice on the path of karma-sannyasa. Thus, by cultivating discernment and performing actions intelligently, they can avoid the sin of engaging in desire-ridden actions. The Chandogya Upanishad (3.16) compares the whole life as a sacrifice, declaring that the first twenty-four years are the morning libation, the next forty-four years are the midday libation, and the next forty-eight years are the third libation. It further states (3.17) that when a person restrains himself from pleasures, it constitutes the initiatory rites. He joins the upasada (salutary) ceremonies when he eats and drinks. He joins the chants and recitations when he laughs, eats, and indulges in sexual pleasure. When he practices austerities, charity, virtue, nonviolence, and truthfulness, they amount to giving gifts to the priests. In this sacrifice of life, death is the final sacrifice (antyeshti), in which the body is sacrificed to Agni as an offering to the gods to facilitate the journey of the soul to the next world. A similar idea is found in the Isa Upanishad.

Sloka 3

śrībhagavān uvāca
akṣaraṃ brahma paramaṃ svabhāvodhyātmam ucyate
bhūtabhāvodbhavakaro visargaḥ karmasaṃjñitaḥ

sri-bhagavan uvaca = the Supreme Lord said; aksaram = imperishable; brahma = Brahman; paramam = the highest and absolute, transcendental; svabhavah = independent or essential nature; adhyatmam = the presiding Self, related to the inner Self; ucyate = is called; bhuta-bhava = the physical state, beingness; udbhava-karah = the cause of the origin; visargah = offering, pouring, emission, giving away, oblation; karma = actions; samjnitah = is called.

The Supreme Lord said, "The imperishable is Brahman. He is the highest and absolute. In them who act according to their independent nature, he is called the Adhyatma, the presiding Self. The sacrificial offering, which causes the origin of things and beings, is called karma."

In this, the Lord replied to Arjuna's first three questions:" What is that Brahman? What is the Adhyatma? What is karma?" He defined Brahman as the imperishable, highest, and absolute. Brahman means one who is unsurpassable or without limits. He represents the unchanging, eternal, supreme reality. The same Brahman manifests as the Self (Adhyatma) in all the jivas who act according to their nature. Although Brahman is described as a deity, in reality, he represents the highest, indestructible, infinite, and absolute state of existence or supreme reality in contrast to ours, which is impermanent, unstable, divisive, diverse, and subject to duality and delusion. Brahman is also compared to the sky or the infinite space (akasa) in which everything rests. In that absolute and infinite reality, the whole creation manifests as an outpouring, separation, emission, reflection, projection, or superimposition (visarga).

Arjuna's second question was about the individual Self. Lord Krishna told him that in the living beings (jivas), who act according to their nature, Brahman is known as Adhyatma, the presiding Self. Bhuta-bhava refers to all beings (bhutas) and all physical or material states or conditions (bhava). Brahman, in his manifested aspect as Isvara (the lord of the universe), is the ultimate cause of their existence. Svabhava is the essential nature of all things and beings, as determined by Prakriti's gunas (modes) and tattvas. The presiding deity in all the jivas is the Self (adhyatma), which is an aspect of Brahman only. He is also known as Isvara or Atman. In creation, Brahman manifests as Isvara, the Lord of all. Prakriti is his dynamic or active principle. Adhyatma means inner Self, related to the Self or the presiding Self. These meanings are used interchangeably in the scriptures to describe the nature of Brahman and Atman and their relationship. Madhavacharya defined Adhyatma as the body (atmanam adhi) or that which is attached to the Self.

In this verse, karma is defined as the sacrificial offering responsible for the origin (udbhava) of jivas and their transmigration from one birth to another. Although all actions are now considered karma, in the early Vedic tradition, it referred to sacrificial actions or the obligatory duties that human beings were expected to perform as their essential duty (dharma). The idea of karma-sannyasa, or performing actions renouncing desires, came much later. The Vedas caution people to avoid the sinful consequences of performing actions with desires and attachments. Sacrificial actions are meant to serve God and creation by nourishing gods, ancestors, humans, etc., and ensuring the welfare of the triple worlds. Thus, in Hinduism, the concept of karma is rooted in the idea of sacrifice and selfless service. Karma does not exist in the absolute and universal Self, but only in the Lord's creation, as a moving and dynamic force, sustained by his will and enforced by Prakriti.

While his creation is subject to karma, he is not subject to it because his actions are free from desires and attachments. The Vedas proclaim Creation as a sacrificial act of Brahman in his manifestation as Purusha (the Cosmic Being), in which he brings forth all the beings and the worlds at the beginning of each cycle of creation. According to the Purusha Sukta of the Rigveda, in the beginning, the worlds emanated from Purusha (the cosmic person) due to a sacrifice performed by the most ancient gods of the highest heaven. Acting as priests, they used parts of Purusha's body for the offering to perform the cosmic ritual. Descriptions like these in the Vedas support the view that the Supreme Being is both the efficient and the material cause of Creation. Prakriti serves him as his dependent entity to manifest his will.

Sloka 4

adhibhūtaṃ kṣaro bhāvaḥ puruṣaś cādhidaivatam
adhiyajñoham evātra dehe dehabhṛtāṃ vara

adhibhutam = physical manifestation which represents all beings and objects; ksarah = perishable, exhaustible; bhāvah = existence, state, nature; purusah = Purusa, the Cosmic Person; ca = and; adhidaivatam = Supreme Being, Godhead, Isvara; adhiyajnah = the Lord of the sacrifices; aham = I am; eva = certainly; atra = in this; dehe = body; deha-bhrtam vara = O best of the embodied.

Adhibhuta is the perishable existence. Adhidaiva is Purusha, the Cosmic Person, and I am certainly Adhiyajna in the body, O best of the embodied.

This verse describes the three functional manifestations of Brahman in the gross, subtle, and transcendental realms of creation. Adhibhuta is the material universe consisting of all the worlds, beings, and objects. It exists in both gross and elemental forms. By nature, it is impermanent and perishable. It exists in Brahman, but Brahman does not exist in it. Hence, it does not contain the characteristics of Brahman, such as eternality, self-existence, self-knowing, indestructibility, purity, or infinity. However, Brahman's higher nature may manifest in it as qualities. It is another name for Nature (Prakriti) and her manifestations. In humans, the physical body constitutes Adhibhuta. Since it is perishable by nature, it is subject to aging, sickness, and death.

Adhidaiva is the manifested Brahman in the field of Prakriti. He is variously known as Saguna Brahman, the universal Self (visvatma), the Cosmic Person (Purusha), the golden germ (Hiranyagarbha), the universal Lord (Isvara), and so on. Purusha is the Cosmic Being who manifests in the world in association with Prakriti. In Hinduism, the name is used to refer to the individual Self as well as the Cosmic Self. Purusha is symbolized in the Vedas as the sun. Purusha itself means the one who rises in the East (the sun) and fills the world with his radiance, the one who lives in the city (pura) of nine gates, the one who resides in the Sun, and the one who nourishes the body and fills it with prana (breath). In the beings, he represents the illumination of the body and its tattvas.

Adhiyajna also refers to the Self (jivatma) in the jivas. He is given the name because the Self is also the presiding deity of all actions, perceptions, knowledge, and intelligence arising in them. Since all actions and movements in the jiva are meant for his enjoyment, he is described as the final recipient or the lord of sacrifices. In this role, as the witness, he facilitates their existence and watches over all the actions they perform with or without desire. As the inner Lord and enjoyer, he receives all the offerings made by the organs in the body, including the sense objects brought in by the senses. Some schools hold that the Self (atma) and the Cosmic Self (Paramatma) are different. The Self is the witness, and the Cosmic Self is the Lord of the Sacrifices and all the organs in the body.

At the cosmic level, Adhibhuta represents Isvara's physical universe or lower nature, which is often symbolized as his material body. Adhidaiva represents his higher nature or divine body, consisting of all souls and divinities. Each god or goddess is an aspect of Isvara only and is endowed with an essential nature (svabhavam) specific to their functions. In their functional role, they are subordinate to Isvara, but in their purest aspect, they are the same. They uphold the divine laws (dharma) and represent Isvara's functional roles in the sacrificial ritual of creation, preservation, destruction, etc. In humans, the elemental body represents Adhibhuta; the subtle body or the internal organ (antahkarana), the Adhidaiva; and the embodied Self (dehatma), the Adhiyajna. What binds them is karma.

Sloka 5

antakāle ca mām eva smaran muktvā kalevaram
yaḥ prayāti sa madbhāvaṃ yāti nāsty atra saṃśayaḥ

anta-kale = at the the time of death; ca = and; mam = Me; eva = only; smaran = remembering; muktva = giving up; kalevaram = the body; yah = he who; prayati = departs; sah = he; mat-bhavam = My State; yati = attains; na = not; asti = there is; atra = here; samsayah = doubt.

And at the time of death, he who gives up the body and departs, remembering Me only, attains My State (of consciousness). There is no doubt about this.

This is an important revelation. If a person remembers the Supreme Lord at his death, he will promptly attain his absolute state and achieve liberation. This is affirmed in the Vedas and other scriptures also. The karma doctrine also supports it. It is also one of the basic tenets of Hinduism. Many Hindus believe that whatever humans remember at the time of death, they attain that immediately or in the next life. If they remember the Supreme Lord, they will attain him. If they remember their children, they will be born again in the same families. If they remember worldly things, they will attain worldly things. If they remember relations, friends, enemies, or lovers, they may take birth in their families or become their relations, friends, enemies, or lovers in their next lives. The Puranas suggest that if they think of animals, they may be reborn as animals. On the other hand, if they remember the Supreme Being in the last moments of their lives, they attain his Supreme State, even if they engaged in sinful actions in the past.

Therefore, devotees are advised to restrain themselves and establish their minds and intelligence in pious thoughts or the Supreme Lord. If they train their minds and remember him constantly, they have better chances of remembering him at the time of their death and attaining him. Although this seems an easy solution, without proper training, remembering the Lord in the final moments of one's life is not easy. For that, devotees must practice self-discipline and absorb their minds in his thoughts through devotional activities such as hearing (sravanam), remembering (mananam), chanting (japam), singing (bhajan), and meditating (nidhidhyasana). Their chances of liberation also improve if they live in the last phases of their lives amidst God's devotees and serve them, or live in a spiritual environment, a sacred place such as Kashi, or near an enlightened guru. Devotional activities such as hearing (sravanam), remembering (mananam), chanting (japam), singing (bhajan), and meditating (nidhidhyasana) also help greatly to train the mind and remember God constantly. If the mind is constantly drawn to his thoughts, free from desires and attachments to worldly things, it will be easier to remember him, even amidst distractions or at the time of death.

Sloka 6

yaṃ yaṃ vāpi smaran bhāvaṃ tyajaty ante kalevaram
taṃ tam evaiti kaunteya sadā tadbhāvabhāvitaḥ

yam yam = whatever; va = or; api = verily; it may be; smaran = thinking or remembering; bhavam = state, entity, condition; tyajati = one gives up; ante = in the end; kalevaram = the body; tam tam = that and that; eva = only; eti = it attains; kaunteya = O son of Kunti; sada = ever, always; tat = that; bhava = state; bhavitah = absorbed, engrossed.

Whatever state one remembers in the end, while giving up the body, that and only that one attains, O son of Kunti, being ever absorbed in that state.

Just as a devotee attains the Supreme Lord by remembering him at the time of death, a person attains whatever he thinks or remembers or whatever state of mind he holds while leaving his body. Therefore, a person's state of mind (smaran bhavam) or the memories, thoughts, feelings, and emotions that prevail in his consciousness at the time of his death are important. They determine the course of his afterlife and transmigration. Our mental and emotional states, natural propensities, likes and dislikes, habitual thoughts, predominant desires, and attachments arise from our essential nature as determined by the gunas that are predominant in us. Therefore, devotees must focus on controlling their minds and thoughts by purifying themselves and their essential nature. They must resolve their impurities and impure thoughts by suppressing rajas and tamas.

Bhāvam means any state, condition, feeling, emotion, or entity. Bhava is what is or the state of being. Anubhavam is the state of mind that arises from the experience of bhava (being). From bhavam (the state of being) arises anubhavam (experience or the state of having been), and from anubhavam arises memorial knowledge, latent impressions, predominant desires, and habitual thoughts. They play an important role in shaping one's essential nature and, thereby, one's predominant thoughts, memories, and states of mind (bhāvam), even at the time of death. Your experiences control your thoughts, attitudes, relationships, and actions. It is, therefore, necessary to practice self-control, cultivate discernment, and stay free from the negativity, troublesome memories, and hurtful feelings that assail your mind. If a person is constantly drawn to certain habitual thoughts or desires or indulges in certain emotional states, his mind will most likely remain preoccupied with them even at the time of his death. This is a potential problem because the final thoughts, emotions, or memories at the time of a person's death become the seed for his next life. Hence, as one nears death, one should avoid the company of evil people and keep the mind stable, pure, and free from negative thoughts, passions, desires, and emotions. For that, one has to purify and restrain the mind and body, practicing karma-sannyasa and other yogas.

Life is full of suffering, regrets, failures, disappointments, and unhappy memories. If we habitually dwell upon them, we will not have peace and stability, and most likely end up dying unhappily. Therefore, before it is too late, we must resolve the impurities and make peace with ourselves to keep our minds filled with positive thoughts and memories. One must cleanse the mind of evil passions like lust, anger, pride, envy, fear, greed, etc., renounce desires and attachments, and remain peaceful and contented. Evil begets evil in this life and the next. One should, therefore, practice restraint, cultivating detachment, equanimity, and sameness. By letting go of everything, withdrawing the mind and senses, engaging the mind in concentration and contemplation, and controlling one's thoughts and emotions even at the time of death, one can attain the Supreme State.

Sloka 7

tasmāt sarveṣu kāleṣu mām anusmara yudhya ca
mayy arpitamanobuddhir mām evaiṣyasy asaṃśayaḥ

tasmat = therefore; sarvesu kalesu = at all times; mam = Me; anusmara = remember, think; yudhya = fight; ca = and; mayi = to Me; arpita = offering; manah = mind; buddhih = intelligence; mam = Me; eva = only, alone; esyasi = you will attain; asamsayah = undoubtedly.

Therefore, remembering Me at all times, you shall fight. With your mind and intelligence offered to Me, you will undoubtedly attain Me only.

Here, Lord Krishna says: I told you clearly that whatever people remember at the time of death, they attain that. Therefore, Arjuna, you should do your duty of fighting, constantly remembering Me only. If you do that, without any doubt, you will attain Me. Thus, the Lord advised Arjuna to remember Him while fighting instead of worrying about his relations or the consequences. By that, if he dies on the battlefield, he will attain Him only without incurring any sin. This is the essence.

The paths to liberation or the Supreme State of Brahman are many. Lord Krishna suggested karma-sannyasa for householders and jnana and sannyasa for others in the Bhagavadgita itself. He advised householders to practice karma-sannyasa in conjunction with jnana, buddhi, atma-samyama, dhyana, and bhakti yogas. Householders may also attain liberation through other paths, but it is difficult. Knowledge, devotion, discernment, self-restraint, and renunciation are primarily meant for attaining perfection or skillfulness in karma-sannyasa through self-purification (atma suddhi), freedom from sinful karma (naishkarmya siddhi), and steadfastness in contemplation, sameness, and equanimity. In addition to the main yogas, our scriptures suggest a few other solutions to achieve liberation, such as remembering the Lord at the time of death, chanting specific mantras, or performing specific rituals and devotional practices. Of them, remembering God at the time of death is the most popular. Lord Krishna himself suggested it in the previous verses. On any typical day, a person may think of numerous things, but in the final moments of his life, his mind will bring up only the most predominant thoughts, memories, and desires. They will determine his fate in the next world and his next birth. Therefore, it is necessary to prepare the mind through self-control.

Since the human mind has the power to manifest predominant thoughts and desires, one should be careful about what one thinks. Our thoughts and actions are greatly influenced by our likes and dislikes, arising from attraction and aversion, desires, and attachments. They are, in turn, influenced by the gunas. Because of them, we are repeatedly drawn to the same objects, experiences, and attractions in life and engage in habitual thoughts. The wise ones know it. Hence, they practice self-control and restrain themselves, absorbing their minds in the contemplation of the Self. They steer their minds in the right direction and make them their allies in their journey of liberation, rather than a problem or an obstacle. By constantly remembering the Lord in all places and situations and keeping their minds in a devotional mode, the great yogis control their minds while performing actions. They do the same at the time of their death to ensure that they will attain Brahman. By intuiting the place and time of their death through regular practice (abhyasa), they prepare themselves for the final moments to enter the state of self-absorption and dissolve their minds in it. Therefore, through proper training and control, anyone who constantly thinks of God in all situations will remember him even at the time of death and attain him only.

Sloka 8

abhyāsayogayuktena cetasā nānyagāminā
paramaṃ puruṣaṃ divyaṃ yāti pārthānucintayan

abhyasa = practice; yoga = yoga; yuktena = endowed with skillfulness; cetasa = by the mind; na anya-gamina = undistracted, not moving or going in other directions; paramam = supreme; purusam = Person, the Being; divyam = effulgent, divine; yati = attains; partha = O Partha; anucintayan = by constantly meditating, recollecting.

Endowed with skillfulness in the practice of yoga, with the mind not going in other directions, by constantly meditating, O Partha, one attains the transcendental Supreme Purusha.

In this verse, Lord Krishna describes how, without letting the mind wander in different directions and by constantly meditating on the Supreme Being, one can attain him. Purusha is the Supreme Lord who resides in the creation and all beings as the inner Lord and fills them with his radiance. One attains him through contemplation only, controlling the mind and its movements. The verse describes the practice (abhyasa) itself as yoga because any practice or method is yoga if the aim is liberation (Moksha). The regular practice of any yoga will eventually lead the devotees to the highest goal. If the mind is not restrained and established in contemplation through persistent practice (abhyasa), it will remain distracted and drawn to other things. With a disturbed and restless mind, it will be difficult to remember the Lord in crucial moments or at the time of death. Hence, as this verse also suggests, one must tame the mind and absorb it in contemplation through self-control (atma-samyama) and constant remembrance (anuchintana). By that, one overcomes the gunas and their influence, restrains the outgoing mode (pravritti) of his mind and senses, and keeps them from wandering in different directions (anyagami).

Similar ideas are also found in the Yoga texts. For example, in the Yogasutras, Patanjali suggests that a yogi should stabilize his mind by constantly meditating upon Isvara (the inner Self) as Aum. By constantly repeating it and meditating upon its meaning, he should become free from distractions, detached from his mind and body, and attain the witness consciousness (pratyak cetana). The Self (Purusha) is the means and the end for the mind. By using him as the object of meditation, the yogi should control his mind and senses and suppress the modifications of his mind to enter the supreme state of self-absorption.

Perfection in the skillful practice of yoga is quickly attained if one perseveres in attaching the mind to the thoughts of the Self as the Supreme Lord. As this verse suggests, through meditation only, one enters the pure state of the Self and attains oneness. The mind is an obstacle until you control it fully. After that, it becomes your ally and support to attain liberation. Through constant meditation and self-restraint, it becomes pure, stable, and transparent with the predominance of sattva. Purified, it lets the brilliance of Purusha, who is hidden in you, radiate through it as mental brilliance (medhas) and physical vigor (tejas). As it radiates in you, through you, and from you, others will notice it, feel drawn to it, and experience affinity and love. With your mind remaining absorbed in the contemplation of the Lord as your very Self, many higher energies (maya shaktis) also awaken and become active in you. Unlike the deluding, lower maya shaktis, they assist you in your transformation and purification and lead you in the right direction toward the Supreme Goal. If you persevere in the abhyasa of yoga and mirror the Self in your consciousness, they will let you enter pure consciousness and experience oneness.

Sloka 9

kaviṃ purāṇam anuśāsitāraṃ aṇor aṇīyāṃsam anusmared yaḥ
sarvasya dhātāram acintyarūpaṃ ādityavarṇaṃ tamasaḥ parastāt

kavim = omniscient seer, sage, poet; puranam = the most ancient; anusasitaram = the Lord of the universe; anoh = the smallest, atom; aniyamsam = smaller than; anusmaret = always thinks, meditates upon; yah = he who; sarvasya = of all; dhataram = the upholder; acintya = inconceivable; rupam = form; aditya-varnam = of the color of the sun, golden hued; tamasah = of the darkness; parastat = beyond.

He who constantly meditates upon the Omniscient Seer, Ancient of all, Lord of the Universe, smaller than the smallest, upholder of all, of inconceivable form, golden-hued like the Sun, and beyond the darkness.

This and the following verse tell us how to meditate on the Supreme Lord at the time of death to attain liberation. It is very difficult to be conscious and in control at the time of death. However, through practice, as the yogis who enter samadhi do, one can gain control and remain conscious. The Supreme Being is described here as the all-knowing seer, the most ancient Lord of the universe, smaller than the smallest, supporter of all, whose form is ungraspable by the mind, golden-hued, and beyond the darkness. The Svetasvatara Upanishad (1.3) declares that those who meditate on Brahman (dhyana yoga) will find His Supreme Reality hidden in their essential nature (svaguna) induced by the modes (gunas). Divine qualities manifest in us if we meditate upon him in this manner with utmost concentration and purity. Brahman is beyond our intellectual grasp. He is imperceptible to the senses and incomprehensible to the mind and its faculties. He cannot be known objectively or in duality. However, such descriptions are useful as a starting point to fix our minds upon that Supreme Reality with firm control (samyama) and experience it subjectively in the silence of our consciousness.

Brahman is described here as the all-seeing or all-knowing seer because he is the Universal Self, who dwells in all as their witness (sakshi) and pervades the whole creation. He is not in them, but he knows them all since he is their source. Therefore, he is aptly described as the all-knowing, wise seer. Since he is imperishable and not subject to the divisions of time, he knows the past, present, and future of everything that manifested and is yet to manifest. As the eternal Self, he is the most ancient, who existed before all things that ever manifested, even before this creation and all the creations that manifested before it. He will remain unchanged and unmoved even if all his creations cease to exist. Therefore, he is also known as the one without a beginning or an end,

According to the Rigveda, Brahman, in his manifestation as Isvara, produced all the worlds and beings out of his Nature (Prakriti), desiring the company of a second. As the Lord of the universe, he rules over his perishable Nature (pradhana) and the imperishable Hara. He is not bound by the limitation of size, place, position, time, knowledge, strength, or potency. Hence, he is described as the smallest of the small, hidden in the subtlest of things, and the largest of all. He is Dhatar, the preserver and supporter, who upholds the mutable, immutable, manifested, and unmanifested aspects of creation. Supporting all, he ensures their order and regularity, keeping them in their respective spheres and controlling their movements and properties according to their nature. The whole creation depends upon him, but he is independent and self-existent and does not depend upon anything. He is also golden-hued since, like the sun, which symbolizes his physical nature, he radiates his golden effulgence in all things where sattva predominates. He is beyond darkness because he is only seen like the morning sun at the end of darkness, or when darkness recedes. Darkness arises in the perishable world only when he withdraws himself or remains concealed behind the veil of impurities, just as the sun remains invisible behind dark clouds. The next verse suggests that he who meditates on Brahman, thus, at the time of death, will forever escape from samsara.

Sloka 10

prayāṇakāle manasācalena bhaktyā yukto yogabalena caiva
bhruvor madhye prāṇam āveśya samyak sa taṃ paraṃ puruṣam upaiti divyam

prayana-kale = at the time of death; manasa = with mind; acalena = unwavering; bhaktya = in devotion; yuktah = engaged; yoga-balena = by the power of yoga; ca = and; eva = surely; bhruvoh = between the eyebrows; madhye = in; pranam = prana, life breath; avesya = fixing; samyak = firmly completely; sah = he; tam = that; param = Supreme; purusam = Brahman; upaiti = attains, achieves; divyam = divine.

At the time of death, with an unwavering mind, engaged in devotion and fixing the life breath firmly between the eyebrows by the power of yoga, he attains Brahman, the Supreme and divine.

This verse explains how sages, seers, and adept yogis attain oneness with Brahman at the time of their death. You may have heard of instances where self-realized ones, yogis, gurus, babas, and other pious people foresee their impending death and prepare for it, choosing a place and time to enter yoga samadhi and leave this world peacefully. When the time comes, they go into meditation and leave their bodies with their minds established in the Lord. However, it is not easy for unprepared minds to remember him or the Self in the final moments of their death. Only those who gain control over their minds and bodies through yoga have better chances of remaining in control in those crucial final moments. As their end time nears, they fill their minds with devotional thoughts and remain steadfast with unwavering minds (achala manas). By focusing their attention on the Lord and holding their breaths between their eyebrows through firm concentration, they attain the Supreme Brahman. Others must be very fortunate to do it consciously without self-control and without attaining perfection in concentrated meditation (samyama). Only adept yogis manage to leave their bodies consciously, gathering the life energies (prana shakti) flowing in their nadis, fixing their minds between their eyebrows, and remembering the Self or Supreme Lord.

Ordinary people cannot do it since they do not possess the premonition to foresee their death until the last. When death approaches, they go through conflicting emotions or remain unconscious, semiconscious, depressed, or remorseful. Hence, prior preparation and perfection in yoga are required to steady the mind and keep it focused and fixed on the Lord. This verse suggests a few conditions that may lead to it. Firstly, it says that the mind must be stable and unwavering. It is possible only when it is free from attachments, desires, passions, and other impurities. Secondly, it says that one must be engaged in pure devotion at the time of death. Exclusive devotion arises only when one overcomes desires and passions and the influence of the gunas. Thirdly, it suggests that the yogi must fix the breath between his eyebrows with the power of yoga (yoga balam). Without perfection or skillfulness, none can control the five breaths (pranas) or hold them between the eyebrows. Hence, a yogi must excel in various yogas and purify himself to possess that power. With the strength thus gained and with an unwavering mind, and concentrating all his attention upon his breath, he must hold it between his eyebrows, just below the highest chakra, from where the Self can quickly escape from the body, accompanied by the deities presiding over the breaths and the organs. Only then can he attain liberation and leave the world permanently.

Sloka 11

yad akṣaraṃ vedavido vadanti viśanti yad yatayo vītarāgāḥ
yad icchanto brahmacaryaṃ caranti tat te padaṃ saṃgraheṇa pravakṣye

yat = that which; aksaram = imperishable; veda-vidah = knower of the Vedas; vadanti = declare; visanti = enters; yat = that which; yatayah = the self-restrained ascetics; vita-ragah = devoid of passions; yat = that which; icchantah = desiring; brahmacaryam = celibacy; caranti = practice; tat = that; te = to you; padam = word; sangrahena = in summary, briefly; pravaksye = I will explain.

That which the knowers of the Vedas declare as imperishable, that which the self-restrained ascetics who are devoid of passions enter, desiring which brahmacharya is practiced, that word I will briefly explain to you.

If you only read this verse, you may not know what Lord Krishna was referring to. By the description of it, you may guess that he was alluding to Brahman or the supreme state of Brahman. However, if you read it with the following two verses, you will realize that the reference is to the mystic syllable Aum (or Om). The second part of this verse is also found in the Katha Upanishad (1,2.15), in which Lord Yama explains the significance of Aum to young Naciketa in the exact words, "Desiring which they practice celibacy, that word I will briefly explain to you." Scholars often use this verse to suggest that the Bhagavadgita was composed later than the later-day Upanishads, such as the Katha Upanishad, and probably during the later Vedic period when the Mahabharata was expanded into its current format.

The Vedas and the Upanishads proclaim that Aum represents Brahman in the auditory or vocal form. It is widely used as a mystic symbol of Brahman in ritual chanting, in the chanting of sacred mantras, and in practicing yoga, meditation, and devotional and tantric rituals. Some devotees also keep it in their homes or worship it as an icon or symbol of mystic power to purify their minds and living spaces, ward off evil powers, or improve their luck. The Vedas declare it as the imperishable sound inherent in space (akasa) or in creation as the vibratory force of Brahman. He is its presiding deity. The word or the sound of Aum elevates anything associated with it, be it a mantra, written word, writing, speech, or any action. Ascetics and yogis use it in their meditation and concentration to restrain and stabilize their minds and senses in Brahman. By meditating upon it, they enter the tranquil states of samadhi.

Aum is described here as padam, meaning any word. Padam has several meanings. However, in the Vedic tradition, it means any word of the Vedas. The Mimansikas held that every word in the Vedas was sacred, eternal, indestructible, inviolable, and divine. Of them, they found that the sounds of certain words and syllables produced more powerful effects than others during chanting. Aum was the foremost among them. In ritual and spiritual practices, it can be used alone, in combination with other sacred syllables such as Aim, Hreem, Kleem, etc., or as a prefix to other sounds or words. The use of Aum in contemplative and mystic practices has a long history in

India's spiritual traditions, especially in the Yoga and Tantra traditions. Its significance is affirmed by several Upanishads, Tantras, and by Patanjali in the Yogasutras. In the first section (1.27) of the Yogasutras, Patanjali suggests that Aum should be used to fix the mind upon the inner Self. Many Upanishads extol its mystic importance and equate it with Brahman, declaring it as the doorway by which yogis enter the supreme state of Brahman.

This verse states that desiring the imperishable Aum (Brahman), self-restrained ascetics practice brahmacharya, which in this context does not mean celibacy only, but the worship of Brahman with self-control or the devotional contemplation of Brahman with an unwavering mind. Madhavacharya defined brahmacharya as "the sending of the mind to Brahman, or the devotion of the mind and all the senses to the Lord." Since brahmacharya (devotion to Brahma) cannot be practiced without self-control (atma samyama) and since controlling sexual desires and passions is the most difficult part of it, brahmacharya is usually understood as celibacy. One may contemplate upon the Self or Brahman in any manner, but worshipping him as Aum, alone or in association with other sacred syllables or words, is the standard practice according to many Upanishads, Yoga, and Tantra shastras.

Sloka 12

sarvadvārāṇi saṃyamya mano hṛdi nirudhya ca
mūrdhny ādhāyātmanaḥ prāṇam āsthito yogadhāraṇām

sarva-dvarani = all the openings of the body; samyamya = having controlled; manah = mind; hrdi = in the heart; nirudhya = having restrained, confined, held back; ca = and; murdhni = on the top of the head; adhaya = having fixed; atmanah = one's own; pranam = life breath; asthitah = firmly established; yoga-dharanam = in the concentration by yoga.

Having controlled all the openings of the body, restrained the mind within the heart, and fixed the life breath in oneself on the top of the head, firmly established in concentration by yoga...

This and the following verse refer to a few important practices of atma-samyama yoga as well as classical yoga, which were most likely practiced by many ascetic traditions of ancient India while contemplating upon Aum to stabilize their minds. The practice is helpful to achieve purification and self-control, establish the mind in the Lord as the Self, and achieve the highest goal, which is indestructible and which ascetics free of passions attain by practicing brahmacharya. The body is often described as the city of nine gates, which refers to the nine openings in the body: the two ears, one mouth, two nostrils, two eyes, the anus, and the genitals. If left to themselves, they can destabilize the mind and body and cause impurities, suffering, and afflictions. Therefore, yogis aim to control them through various techniques. They control the mouth and anus by limiting the food intake, and nostrils by rolling the tongue back towards the soft palate and closing the nasal cavity (known as khechari mudra) or by reducing their breathing to the minimum, to the point where they stop breathing and hold the breath inside. They control the other openings in the body (eyes, ears, and genitals) by withdrawing the mind and senses and cultivating indifference to sense impressions and material things.

The mind is fickle by nature. However, it can be tamed and stabilized through the regular practice (abhyasa) of dispassion or detachment (vairagya). The practice consists mainly of pratyahara, or restraining and withdrawing the senses into the mind and the mind into the Self. This verse speaks of restraining the mind in the heart (hṛdi nirudhya). It may mean restraining and withdrawing the mind into the higher nature, intelligence, or the Self. As suggested here, fixing the prana (life breath) on the top of the head requires the combined practice of pranayama (breath control) and dharana, or concentration. By pranayama, one lifts the prana upwards through the body's energy channels (nadis), which extend from the heart region to the head region. By practicing controlled and concentrated meditation (samyama), the yogi must concentrate his life breaths in the head region and restrain his mind deep within himself in equanimity. Its sustained practice culminates in samadhi.

Concentration (yoga dharana) means fixing the mind in one place (desa-bandha). The Mahābhārata and some ancient texts on yoga identify various places (desas) in the body where the mind can be fixed during concentration (dharana), such as the navel, the heart, the tip of the nose, and the light in the head. To fix the mind in the Self (heart) without distractions and disturbance, one must overcome desires and passions, practice detachment and indifference, suppress the gunas, and remain firmly established in sameness and equanimity. Most yogis practice concentration (dharana) by fixing their minds upon a physical or mental object, name, form, memory, image, symbol, sensation (anubhuti), thought, or a sacred syllable or sound like Aum. It is difficult to concentrate on formless (Nirguna) Brahman. Hence, one may choose specific objects such as a mantra, a mystic diagram (yantra or mandala), a syllable, or the image of a deity.

Sloka 13

aum ity ekākṣaraṃ brahma vyāharan mām anusmaran
yaḥ prayāti tyajan dehaṃ sa yāti paramāṃ gatim

Aum = Aum, the sacred syllable; iti = thus; eka-aksaram = indestructible monosyllable; brahma = Brahman; vyaharan = chanting, reciting; mam = Me; anusmaran = remembering; yah = whoever; prayati = departs; tyajan = discarding, abandoning; deham = the body; sah = he; yati = sage, adept yogi, ascetic; paramam = supreme; gatim = state, goal, destination.

Contemplating upon Brahman, reciting the indestructible, monosyllable Aum, and thus remembering Me, whosoever departs from here discarding the body that adept yogi attains the supreme Goal.

These practices help the yogis control their minds or establish them in the thoughts of the Lord at the time of their departure from this world. Lord Krishna already stated that whatever a person remembered in the final moments of his life, he would attain only that. Here, he said that to attain liberation, the highest goal, one should discard the body while reciting the indestructible Aum and remembering Brahman.

The Vedas recognize Aum as the most sacred syllable. It is sacred because it represents Brahman in sound form (sabda brahma) and possesses the power to purify and grant liberation to those who chant it or meditate on it with concentration, either alone or in association with other sacred words, syllables, or the names of the Lord. Since it contains the force of Brahman, it is chanted in prayers and rituals along with other mantras with the belief that it will awaken the deities in chants to carry the prayers and supplications to heaven through space (akasa) and invite the divinities to the ritual place. In the Vedas, Brahman is equated with space, the medium of sounds, and the force that moves all sounds and sound vibrations through it to their respective destinations. Speech is a form of sound only. Through it, we communicate with others, with gods, and other celestial beings. Through the sounds of speech, mantras, and ritual chants, we augment our powers, extend our reach, communicate our desires, and fulfill them. Since Aum is Brahman in sound form, it helps us to connect to him through speech as well as thoughts.

Aum is also known as Pranava. It consists of three letters, A, U, and M, each letter representing a particular aspect of Brahman, his creation, or state of consciousness. Some believe that it was the first primal sound that manifested in creation and awakened Prakriti to set in motion all her energies (shaktis), functions, and actions. The sound of Aum is similar to the sound of breath. One can hear it in meditation. Hence, it is also known as the sound of breath (Pranava nada). Aum is also considered the manifest form of the unmanifest, primal, inner sound (antarnada), which is not a sound at all but an unformed, subtlest, unheard, silent, and transcendental sound with infinite reach and potency. Since Aum is its manifested form, one can attain it through chanting or meditating on Aum. In their deep meditative states, Yogis hear the transcendental sound of Aum (para nada) through their subtle senses and, through that, enter the state of supreme consciousness.

Much symbolism is also associated with Aum and its constituent parts. Hence, it is used in the meditative practices of almost all yogic traditions, including those belonging to Jainism and Buddhism. Because of its spiritual significance, it is frequently mentioned in the Samhitas and the Upanishads as a deity in itself, having the power to purify the mind and the body and liberate the Self from the control of Nature. While the Isavasya Upanishad starts with the declaration that all this is for the habitation of the Lord (isavasyamidam sarvam), the Mandukya Upanishad begins with the words, "Aum, this syllable is all this (aum it etad aksaram idam sarvam)." It adds that all that is the past, the present, and the future, and all this is Aum only, and whatever is beyond them is also the same syllable Aum.

The same Upanishad explains its symbolic significance as Brahman having four states of consciousness in his manifested aspect, namely the wakeful state, the dream state, the deep-sleep state, and the transcendental state. The first three states are represented by the letters A, U, and M, respectively. Syllable Aum itself represents the transcendental state. The Maitri Upanishad explains how we can reach the soundless state of transcendence with the help of the sacred sound of Aum. As Lord Krishna suggested here, when Aum is chanted in conjunction with the name of the Lord, it becomes even more powerful. Many Hindu traditions, including classical yoga, share a similar view.

Sloka 14

ananyacetāḥ satataṃ yo māṃ smarati nityaśaḥ
tasyāhaṃ sulabhaḥ pārtha nityayuktasya yoginaḥ

ananya-cetah = without thinking anything else; satatam = constantly; yah = he who; mam = Me; smarati = remembers; nityasah = uninterruptedly; tasya = for that; yogi; aham = I am; su-labhah = easy to attain; partha = O Partha; nitya = constantly; yuktasya = accomplished and well-established; yoginah = reverent yogi.

Without any other thought, continuously, every day, whoever remembers me, for that one, O Partha, who is accomplished and ever established in My remembrance, I am easy to attain.

This verse stipulates the method or the practice to attain the highest goal: union with the Supreme Lord, dissolving individuality. For that, one has to remember him as one's Self and meditate on Aum every day (nityam), constantly, uninterruptedly (satatam), exclusively, and without any other thought, interest, or attachment (ananya chetah). The verse affirms that for the one who is well accomplished and established in remembering the Lord as one's Self, liberation or union with him is easy (sulabha). When remembering or meditating becomes a regular practice (abhyasa), the Lord himself will strengthen his faith and devotion, remove the obstacles, and make his goal easier. This is the essence.

The ultimate purpose of yoga is liberation or attaining the supreme state of Brahman. In this verse, Lord Krishna explains how it can quickly be done. Devotion is of several types. The lower forms of devotion are mixed with the impurities of egoism, ignorance, desires, and selfishness. Devotees who engage in them practice desire-ridden actions (kamya-karmas) to fulfill their desires by pleasing gods and practicing Dharma. They yield beneficial results, but not liberation. In the higher forms of devotion, the impurities disappear as one resolves the gunas and attains purity. Of them, the highest form of devotion, which is exemplified here, is the single-minded devotion (kevala bhakti), in which the mind is continuously filled with the thoughts of God, so much so that there is no scope for any other thought to enter the mind (ananya chetah). Devotees who practice it engage in selfless actions (nishkama karma).

Although practicing it is not simple or easy, the message is simple: attach your mind to the Lord through constant remembrance and meditation, and the Lord will guide you to the highest goal. The path of liberation is the path of pure and uninterrupted devotion to God. However, a lifetime of effort may not be enough to achieve that state since the human mind is inconsistent and difficult to control. To achieve success in it, you must turn your attention inward from the mundane aspects of the world to the divine presence of the

Lord in you. Withdrawing your senses, mind, and thoughts from the world and turning to God with devotion, you must fill your mind with his thoughts. When your mind is unburdened by the desires and attachments to worldly life and is filled with the glorious chant of Aum, only then does it become illuminated with his light. Ordinary people are drawn to material things and think of the Lord only when they need something to fulfill themselves. Only a few succeed in transcending their desires and, through the constant remembrance of His names, forms, or glories, they seek none but Him alone. The doors of the immortal world automatically open to him as he absorbs his mind in his contemplation. Self-control and exclusive devotion are the foundation for it. What happens to such a yogi upon attaining that goal is explained in the following verse.

Sloka 15

mām upetya punarjanma duḥkhālayam aśāśvatam
nāpnuvanti mahātmānaḥ saṃsiddhiṃ paramāṃ gatāḥ

mam = to Me; upetya = having reached, approached; punarjanma = rebirth; duhkha-alayam = house or place of miseries; asasvatam = impermanence; na = not; apnuvanti = obtain, attain; maha-atmanah = great souls; samsiddhim = perfection of sameness or oneness; paramam = highest; gatah = attained.

Having reached Me and attained the highest perfection of sameness (samsiddhi), the great souls do not obtain rebirth (in samsara), which is impermanent (and) the house of miseries.

Those who enter the immortal House of God (devalayam) attain eternal life and never return to take another birth in this world or anywhere else. Eternal life is permanent and supremely blissful, unlike mortal life, which is impermanent and filled with miseries and suffering (dukkha). Punar-janma means rebirth. However, in this context, it may mean rebirth in samsara, a world of miseries (dukhalayam) where rebirth and suffering are the norms.

The Self has no rebirth or death. Hence, whoever escapes from samsara through the union with the Supreme Lord is forever freed from it. The mortal world is a house of miseries since the beings in it are caught in the cycle of births and deaths (samsara) due to the play of Maya and the nature of the tattvas and gunas, which are impure and impermanent and induce desires and attachments. While ordinary people may regard pain and pleasure as inseparable aspects of life and try to overcome pain and suffering through desire-ridden actions, skillful yogis (yuktas) are disinterested in temporary solutions. For them, existence in samsara is suffering in itself. They see the mind, body, and the world as the main sources of suffering and instability. Therefore, they try to resolve the causes of suffering by suppressing the gunas, which are responsible for impurities, desires, attraction, aversion, etc. Becoming equal and indifferent to all the dualities and disturbances through renunciation and detachment and concentrating on the Lord as their very Self, they attain freedom from karma (naishkarmya siddhi), sameness (samsiddhi), lasting peace, and stability.

There is no suffering for the Self, even when he is bound to the body and Maya. He is eternally blissful, pure, and immutable. The suffering is only for the beings (jivas) since they are subject to impurities and impermanence. When they are purified, and the transformative functions (parinama-karma) of the gunas in them are resolved, they return to their original inactive or subdued state (pratiprasava), letting the beingness of the jiva dissolve in the Self. Self-absorption or union with the Self is the highest state of perfection, which is attained by rare individuals. Patanjali described it as dharma-megha samadhi, meaning absorption in the cloud of virtues or ecstasy. In that state, the embodied Self (jivanmukta) remains indifferent to everything, including the omniscience or omnipotence of the Self. While classical yoga holds Isvara, the inner Self, as a mere witness who does not actively participate in the liberation process but facilitates it by his mere presence, the Bhagavadgita holds that Isvara, as the Self of all, plays an active role in the liberation of his devotees and rewards them according to their faith, devotion, and purity.

Sloka 16

ā brahmabhuvanāl lokāḥ punarāvartinorjuna
mām upetya tu kaunteya punarjanma na vidyate

ābrahma bhuvanah = including the world of Brahma; lokah = worlds; punahravartinah = recurring, recreated again and again; arjuna = O Arjuna; mam = to Me; upetya = after coming; tu = but; kaunteya = O son of Kunti; punah janma = rebirth; na = not; vidyate = there is.

The worlds, including the world of Brahma, are recreated again and again, O Arjuna, but after coming to Me, O son of Kunti, there is no rebirth.

While Brahman is imperishable, inexhaustible, and indestructible, his creation is temporary and impermanent. It has a beginning and an end. Even modern science acknowledges that billions of years later, this universe will end. However, it will not vouch for its recurrence, although it hypothesizes the possibility. According to our scriptures, all the worlds, except Brahman's immortal realm, are subject to rebirth and recurrence. They are created repeatedly in each cycle of creation, and the beings who inhabit them are also subject to rebirth. The gods have longer lifespans but are also withdrawn at the end of each creation and brought forth again at the beginning of the next. If Brahman is like the sky, his creation is like the clouds and cosmic objects that constantly appear and disappear in its vast space. If Brahman is an ocean, his creations are like the waves that appear and disappear on its surface. Just as days and nights or seasons have beginnings and ends and recurring phases of change, the worlds have a beginning and an end and are subject to order and regularity (rta) and recurring cycles of creation and destruction. They are created at the beginning of each cycle of creation and withdrawn at the end. Invoking his deluding power (maya), the one Supreme Lord, Isvara, manifests his nature variously in different forms and roles in the worlds and realms he creates. Only those free souls (muktas) liberated from samsara or eternally free (nitya muktas) exist permanently in the realm of Brahman. They are not subject to transience, change, rebirth, or mortality.

Sloka 17

sahasrayugaparyantam ahar yad brahmaṇo viduḥ
rātriṃ yugasahasrāntāṃ te.ahorātravido janāḥ 8.17

sahasra = thousand; yuga = yugas, great epochs; paryantam =up to, extends as far as; ahah = day; yat = that; brahmanah = of Brahma; viduh = they know; ratrim = night; yuga = great epochs; sahasra-antam = at the end of thousand; te = that; ahah-ratra = day and night; vidah = understand; janah = people.

Those who know that the day of Brahma lasts as long as a thousand great epochs and the night as long as a thousand great epochs, they know the Day and Night of Brahma.

The lengths of days and nights are relative to the places or the worlds where they happen. Our great seers intuited it long ago in the formative period of our civilization. They knew that time was relative to the world in which it happened. However, it is incorrect to say that they knew the theory of relativity. They believed that the higher and lower worlds of gods, celestial beings, ancestors, spirits, and demons lasted longer than the mortal world, and time moved there slowly. Our months and years are like moments or minutes in their worlds. According to Vishnu Purana, a year of mortal beings, consisting of two ayanas of six months each, is equal to a day and night of the gods. The first six months, known as uttrayana (northern solstice), are considered the day. The next six months, known as the dakshinayana (southern solstice), constitute their night. Twelve thousand such years in the world of gods, each consisting of 360 of their days, are equal to one Mahayuga (Great Epoch) in our world.

Each Great Epoch is divided into four yugas (epochs): Kritayuga, Tretayuga, Dwaparayuga, and Kaliyuga. Their duration varies. Kritayuga is the longest, and Kaliyuga is the shortest. The four yugas span thousands of human years, during which the world witnesses many epochal events, incarnations of God, the progressive decline of Dharma, destruction and renewal of numerous life forms, many catastrophic wars and conflicts between good and evil, and the coming and going of great beings and human races. Each great epoch is followed by an interlude lasting as many centuries as millenniums in its duration. A thousand such great epochs constitute a day of Brahma. During this period, fourteen Manus would rule the earth. With the birth of each Manu, many divinities and seven great seers (rishis) also appear on earth to perform specific tasks. At the end of each Manu's reign, he and the rest are withdrawn by the Lord into himself. The reign of each Manu lasts for 852,000 divine years or 306.72 million human years. Fourteen times constitute a day of Brahma.

At the end of each day of Brahma, all the worlds, elements, objects, divinities, and beings are dissolved into an ocean of undifferentiated primal existence. During this period of dissolution, which may last for thousands of years, the liberated souls (mahatmas) reside in the bosom of Brahma, who goes into a long sleep for a thousand great epochs, resting on the mighty ocean of consciousness. A combined day and night of Brahma is known as a Kalpa. 360 Kalpas constitute one year of Brahma. A hundred such years constitute the lifespan of each Brahma. The first fifty Brahma years constitute the ascending period, and the second fifty years the descending period. In the infinite time and space of Brahman, who is eternal and inexhaustible, countless Brahmas appear and disappear as bubbles upon the ocean of pure consciousness, spanning billions of Brahma days and nights, with endless cycles of creation, preservation, and destruction. Such is the vastness of creation and the glory of the manifestations of Brahman. From this, one can conclude that nothing is permanent, even Brahma or Isvara, except the Supreme Brahman. However, according to the Dvaita and Vishistadvaita schools, Isvara, the immortal gods of the highest realms, the immortal souls, and the liberated souls exist eternally along with the Supreme Brahman. They have no rebirth.

Sloka 18

avyaktād vyaktayaḥ sarvāḥ prabhavanty aharāgame
rātryāgame pralīyante tatraivāvyaktasaṃjñake

avyaktat = the unmanifested; vyaktayah = manifested things; sarvah = all; prabhavanti = come into existence; ahah-agame = at the dawn of the day; ratri-agame = at the approach of night; praliyante = they dissolve; tatra = in that; eva = only; avyakta = the unmanifested; samjnake = which is known as.

From the unmanifested, all the manifested things come into existence at the dawn of the day. At the approach of night, they all dissolve in that only, which is known as the unmanifested.

The unmanifested (avyakta) Brahman is not a nonexistent state. It should not be confused with nonexistence (abhava), which the Vaisheshikas named as a category to describe the nature and characteristics of substances (padarthas). It is not the absence of Brahman either. It is the absolute Brahman representing an undifferentiated, indeterminate state that is yet to be manifested (vyakta) or materialized. In other words, existence does not spring from nonexistence. The Supreme Self or the pure consciousness of Brahman does not participate in it. It arises from the existing but unmanifested (asambhuti) primal Nature (Mula Prakriti) as a modification or formation due to Nature's inherent properties and functions. Some scholars tend to equate the unmanifested as Brahman and the manifested as Nature. Their argument is justified because Nature is but an inseparable aspect of Brahman only. However, since Brahman is imperishable and immutable, it makes sense to consider the manifest (vyakta) and the unmanifest (avyakta) as the different states of Nature, with the pure Self or Supreme Self acting as the support for both. When Brahma is asleep during his night, Nature remains unmanifested (asambhuta), but when he is awake at the dawn of his day, it manifests (sambhuta).

Before creation manifests from the Creator (Brahma or Isvara) as a projection or formation, Nature remains undifferentiated and unformed, consisting of undifferentiated energies, latent causes, effects, possibilities, and potencies. Some schools of Hinduism describe the state as the primal Nature (pradhana). In that primal state, which is without divisions and distinctions, the triple gunas also remain indistinguishable and in equilibrium. From that unmanifested state (avyaktam), several basic realities or primal organs called tattvas manifest, which act as the basic building blocks. Along with them, the triple modes (gunas), namely sattva, rajas, and tamas, also manifest and become active. The permutations and combinations of the tattvas and gunas produce diverse objects, worlds, and beings. Among the tattvas, intelligence is the first to manifest in creation. In the world, it manifests as the supreme intelligence (Mahat), which ensures order and regularity, and an intelligent creation. In humans, it becomes the discriminating intelligence (buddhi), responsible for the faculties of reason and discernment.

References to the unmanifested are also found in the Upanishads. For example, the Katha Upanishad states (2.3.8) that the unmanifest exists beyond the senses, the mind, the intelligence, and the great individual Self (mahan-atma). Beyond the unmanifest is the all-pervading Supreme Person, the Universal Being, without parts (alinga). By knowing him, one enters eternal life. The Svetasvatara Upanishad (1.8) also contains a reference to the unmanifest, which states that Isah, the Lord, supports all existence, which is a combination of the destructible and the indestructible, as well as the manifest and the unmanifest. The individual Self, not being the Lord, is bound to the manifest, as it becomes the enjoyer of the sense objects. According to Vishnu Purana, the other entities that manifest along with Prakriti are Purusha (the Cosmic Male), Kala (Time), and Vyakta (visible substance). Together, these four are responsible for the manifestation of the trinity of gods, the worlds, all the divinities, beings, objects, and phenomena. According to some schools of Hinduism, the unmanifest (Prakriti) is self-existent and eternal; according to others, it is the power of Brahman, which he unleashes at the beginning of each cycle of creation.

Sloka 19

bhūtagrāmaḥ sa evāyaṃ bhūtvā bhūtvā pralīyate
rātryāgamevaśaḥ pārtha prabhavaty aharāgame

bhuta-gramah = the multitude of beings; sah = that; eva = very; ayam = this; bhutva bhutva = having taken birth again and again; praliyate = become dissolved; ratri = night; agame = at the approach of; avasah = helplessly; partha = O Partha; prabhavati = they manifest; ahah agame = upon the arrival of the day.

That very multitude of beings, having taken birth again and again, becomes dissolved helplessly at the approach of the night (of Brahma). O Partha, upon the arrival of the day, they manifest again.

Beings are brought forth at the beginning and withdrawn at the end of each cycle of creation. Avasa means without control or without one's involvement. In other words, at the end of creation, all beings are withdrawn into Brahman without their involvement. They reappear again when a new cycle of creation begins. Although outwardly, beings (bhuta-gramah) seem to be participating in it, they follow the natural cycles of birth and death, bound to Prakriti. The Self in them does not participate in any of these modifications. It also remains untainted by the impurities of the jivas or the mortal world. Of the multitude of beings, some embodied souls (jivatmas) are bound forever, and some achieve liberation, while the rest remain in various stages of spiritual progress according to their deeds. When they are finally withdrawn at the end of Brahma's Day, which spans over 1000 great epochs or 14 Manvantaras, everything disappears into a temporary state of inactivity. It remains latent or in suspended animation for the next 1000 Mahayugas. Dissolution is not the end of everything but a temporary prelude to the next cycle of creation. Creation and dissolution are the two sides of the Lord's projected reality, which arises in him through Prakriti. It is incorrect to assume that Brahman has the twin states of wakefulness and sleep. They are the aspects of the Supreme Lord as Isvara, the Lord of the universe, who manifests from Brahman with dynamic force (Prakriti) and is described in the early compositions of the Vedas as Brahma or Purusha and subsequently as Vishnu or Shiva. Each Day of Brahma is a period of activity, and each Night is a period of inactivity. These divisions, days, and nights do not exist in Brahman but in his Creation only. Creation is thus a repetitive and cyclical process in which the Supreme Being participates both as the subject and the object, or as the Creator and the created, without undergoing any change. The changes happen only in the domain of his Nature or materiality. Creation arises from him in the field of Nature as a projection or an alternate reality. However, it does not contain his essence, although he pervades it, resides in it, and supports it. Apart from this, there is another aspect of Brahman, which is described in the next verse.

Sloka 20

paras tasmāt tu bhāvonyovyaktovyaktāt sanātanaḥ
yaḥ sa sarveṣu bhūteṣu naśyatsu na vinaśyati

parah = distinct; tasmat = from that; tu = but, yet; bhavah = being, state; anyah = another; avyaktah = unmanifested; avyaktat = from the unmanifested; sanatanah = eternal; yah = who; sah = that; sarvesu = all; bhutesu = beings; nasyatsu = destroyed; na vinasyati = not destroyed.

Distinct from that unmanifested is yet another eternal unmanifested, that which is not destroyed when all the beings are destroyed.

Here, Lord Krishna spoke of two unmanifested realities or states and drew a clear distinction between them, using the word 'tu' (but). One refers to the unmanifested primal Nature (Mula Prakriti or Adi Shakti), and the other to the unmanifested Brahman, also known as Nirguna Brahman or Avyakta Brahman. Although Nature has a physical state or materiality in creation, which is perceptible to the senses, it has a pure state that does not participate in creation. It acts as the revealing and liberating force of Shakti in association with Brahman rather than as a deluding power. The unmanifested Prakriti (asambhuti) is made up of the purest (shuddha) sattva and is forever associated with the pure state of Brahman, which is pure consciousness. Together, they create the divine state of Sacchidananda or Truth, Consciousness, and Bliss, which yogis experience in samadhi. In Tantra, it is referred to as the Natural State (sahaja vidya) or the highest goal. Unmanifested (avyakta) in this verse may refer to the unmanifested Prakriti (asambhuta) or the multitude of beings in their withdrawn state in the interlude between two cycles of creation.

Prakriti has a pure, unmanifested state and several manifested states, or as many as necessary to manifest diversity in creation. The unmanifested state of Prakriti is immutable and indestructible. In contrast, the manifested ones are mutable and destructible and subject to renewal and regeneration, as is evident from the descriptions given by Lord Krishna in this chapter. Brahman, too, has manifested states. They arise due to his association with Prakriti, in which he remains immutable. In association with Prakriti, he manifests as Isvara, Purusha, Kala, Hiranyagarbha, Viraj, and so on. In them also, he remains immutable, while Prakriti remains active as the executress of his inviolable will. Some accounts describe them as Brahman's reflections in the field of Prakriti with varying degrees of dynamism and purity. Whatever the process, beings come into existence only due to the association of Brahman with the manifested Prakriti. Thus, for example, Isvara, Narayana, Paramesvara, or Sadashiva is Brahman in association with the purest of sattva (shuddha sattva), Brahma with rajas, Vishnu with sattva, Shiva with tamas, and so on. Beings manifest due to the admixture of elements with various permutations and combinations of the triple gunas. Thus, while the manifested Nature is subject to modifications, the supreme Brahman remains indestructible, invisible, immutable, and formless even when he participates in creation.

The Katha Upanishad (1.3.11) also refers to the unmanifest in these words, "Beyond the Great One (Mahat) is the unmanifest (avyaktam). Beyond the unmanifest is the Universal Self. Beyond It, there is nothing higher. It is the end of the journey and the final goal (para gatih)." The truly unmanifest has no ego, sense of self, divisions of Nature, or the admixture of gunas. The scriptures describe the state as that in which there was neither day nor night, neither sky nor earth, neither darkness nor light nor any other thing, save only One, invisible, unknown, and incomprehensible. In the beings or the embodied state, the unmanifest state or reality is equal to the deep sleep state or the transcendental state of absolute bliss. According to some, the unmanifest represents the state of the perfect union between the unmanifested Brahman (Sada Shiva) and the unmanifested Nature (Para Shakti). It should not be mistaken as nothingness or emptiness (shunyam) but a pure and indeterminate state which is neither beingness nor non-beingness, neither existence nor nonexistence, and does not fit into any known categories of description. According to others, it is but the source of all sources, which can be considered an intermediary state of latency in which everything remains indeterminate and indefinite. Shankara described the unmanifested as the night of Brahma, when everything remained suspended, waiting for the spark of desire to ignite it. It is when the great Lord goes into sleeping or resting mode and wakes up after a thousand yugas or billions of years.

Sloka 21

avyaktokṣara ity uktas tam āhuḥ paramāṃ gatim
yaṃ prāpya na nivartante tad dhāma paramaṃ mama8.21

avyaktah = unmanifested; aksarah = indestructible; iti = thus; uktah = it is described; tam = which; ahuh = they extol; paramam = the highest; gatim = Goal; yam = which; prapya = gaining; na = never; nivartante = return; tat dhama = that sacred abode; paramam = supreme; mama = Mine.

Unmanifested, the indestructible, thus it is described, which they extol as the highest Goal, by gaining which one never returns. That supreme sacred abode is Mine.

The unmanifest (avyakta) is indestructible (akshara) because it always remains unmanifest. If it becomes manifest (vyakta), it cannot be considered eternal, indestructible, or fixed. It is the highest goal (paramagati) because, beyond it, there is nothing to be found or achieved. Whoever attains it attains oneness without a second and never returns. They achieve infinity, immortality, indestructibility, perfection, self-existence, eternal freedom, and fulfillment.

There is no unanimity among various schools of Hinduism about what happens to the embodied Self when it attains liberation. According to Advaita (nondualism), when yogis attain the highest goal, the illusion of separation or duality between the individual Self (Atman) and the Supreme Self (Brahman) disappears, and Brahman alone remains. It is like when a pot is broken, the space in it becomes indistinguishable from the space around it. According to Vishistadvaita (qualified nondualism), upon liberation, the liberated souls experience internally the same consciousness as Brahman and keep an inseparable connection with him while remaining in the immortal world as pure souls ever enjoying the love of the Lord. Followers of Dvaita (dualism) believe that the liberated souls remain distinct and separate from the Lord after liberation, and the duality between them is permanent and everlasting. In this verse, the word 'ahuh' (they) refers not only to the yuktas and muktas who realized Brahman but also to the scriptures, which are considered the standard (pramana) in establishing metaphysical truths that cannot be validated by other means.

The Upanishads describe Brahman as the highest, Supreme Being, indestructible and transcendental. Strictly speaking, Brahman is everything. Since the primal Nature is an inseparable part of him, he is both the destructible and the indestructible, the Creator and the created, the manifested and the unmanifested, being and non-being, known and unknown, with form and without form, and so on. Scholars are not unanimous about how creation manifests from Brahman. We have many speculative theories according to which he brings forth the worlds by assuming various forms in association with Prakriti, during which the latter may arise from him as a projection or superimposition, or reflection and envelop the souls, subjecting them to various impurities and the play of maya.

Just as there are no limits to his powers and methods, there are no limits to his creative methods. Since Brahman is without a second and is all this, He must manifest creation out of Himself using part of His own body or materiality. This is the consensus opinion among most scholars. The Vedas describe it as a great sacrifice. While Brahman is indestructible and immutable, his manifested creations and forms, such as Isvara or Viraj, are subject to modifications since they are associated with Nature and have a beginning and end. Beyond them is the unmanifested Brahman, which remains constant and eternally immutable. Even the gods cannot fathom him since he is above all. However, he is attainable for his ardent devotees in the highest states of self-absorption. When they enter that pure unified consciousness, they become free from the cycle of births and deaths. The next verse suggests how that highest state can be achieved.

Sloka 22

puruṣaḥ sa paraḥ pārtha bhaktyā labhyas tv ananyayā
yasyāntaḥsthāni bhūtāni yena sarvam idaṃ tatam

purusah = Purusha; sah = That; parah = the Highest, Supreme; partha = O Partha; bhaktya = by devotion; labhyah = attained, achieved; tu = indeed; ananyaya = unwavering; yasya = whom; antah-sthani = established within; bhutani = all beings; yena = by whom; sarvam = all; idam = this; tatam = extended, spread out, pervaded.

That Supreme Being (Purusha), O Partha, is indeed attained by exclusive devotion only, in whom all beings are established and by whom all this is pervaded.

The importance of devotion is explained in this verse. Lord Krishna described the Supreme Being as Purusha and confirmed that he is attainable only through exclusive devotion (ananya bhakti). It means the Supreme Reality of Brahman is attained by his pure devotees only, whose minds are filled with the thoughts of the Supreme Lord, who have no other aim or interest and are exclusively and unwaveringly dedicated and devoted to him. Unwavering devotion is the royal road to liberation. There is no better path or alternative. All the yogas described in the scripture are meant to lead the devotee toward this highest ideal. They are meant to help the yogis in the early stages cultivate purity, discernment, mental stability, and sameness so that they can establish their minds in exclusive devotion and earn the Lord's love and affection. Lord Krishna affirmed that liberation is attained through unwavering devotion only. All yogas must eventually lead the yogis to the path of pure devotion.

Ananya bhakti means devotion, which is one-pointed, undivided, and free from desires and selfishness. Devotees seeking liberation must remain exclusively devoted to the Supreme Lord, choosing any name or form that suits them without any other thought or distraction. Brahman is described here as Purusha. It means the devotee must worship the Lord (Supreme Self) as one's very Self and dedicate himself to him. Purusha (pur+usha) means the light which arises and shines from the East. It is a reference to the sun. In the Vedas, Brahman is compared to the sun and its rays to his creation. Just as the sun's light pervades the earth, the light of Brahman pervades and illuminates his whole creation. He shines from above as well as from within all. He pervades and supports the whole creation from within and without

Nature as the embodied Self and the Supreme Self. Hence, the Svetasvatara Upanishad (1.16) compares him to the butter which pervades the milk. Purusha also means the Lord (Isa), who resides in the city (pura) of nine gates, a reference to the human body. One should worship him as the Supreme Being only, withdrawing the mind and senses and abiding in his thoughts with supreme devotion. Since he is the self of all, he is attainable to those who strive to reach him through pure and unwavering devotion.

Sloka 23

yatra kāle tv anāvṛttim āvṛttiṃ caiva yoginaḥ
prayātā yānti taṃ kālaṃ vakṣyāmi bharatarṣabha

yatra kale = that time when; tu = now; anavrttim = do not return; avrttim = return; ca = and; eva = also; yoginah = of yogis; prayatah = departing; yanti = after going forth; tam kalam = that time when; vaksyami = I will declare; bharatarsabha = O best of the Bharatas.

O best of the Bharatas, I will now declare that time when departing, the yogis do not return, and that time when going forth, they return.

Lord Krishna is now going to describe the time during which liberated yogis travel to the immortal world of Brahma by the path of light, never to return, and the time during which bound karma-yogis travel by the path of semi-darkness to the ancestral world to return to the earth to take another birth. Yogis who practice karma-sannyasa, self-control, and exclusive devotion are guaranteed liberation. In contrast, the fate of others depends upon their karma and external factors such as the time of their departure from here.

In Hinduism, Time (Kala) is a manifestation of Brahman. He is also the Lord of Death who presides over the paths by which beings travel to different worlds upon their death and according to their deeds. Time becomes auspicious or inauspicious depending on place, time, and circumstances (desa, kalamana, paristhiti). Certain times are auspicious and favorable when the planets are properly aligned and the gods have the upper hand. Inauspicious moments are those when the planets are improperly aligned and when evil forces have an advantage. Therefore, people are advised to pay attention to time, place, and circumstances while performing their tasks. The Vedic almanac provides detailed information about which times are auspicious and which ones are inauspicious so people can decide when to perform their sacrificial duties and important tasks.

According to the karma doctrine, everything happens due to the causes and effects set in motion by one's previous actions. Fate is the fruit of karma only. It can be offset by factors such as others' actions, deities' intervention, or the Lord's grace. However, since the events are already set in motion by fate, no one can determine the place and time of one's death. At the same time, the immortal world is guaranteed for those who attain liberation, and rebirth is certain for those who are still bound to samsara. Adept yogis who attain perfection (siddhi) in yoga may possess the intuitive knowledge of their past, present, and future and foresee the time and place of their death or how they would depart from here. It may help them prepare for their final journey, choosing the time and place of their death and preparing for their final departure. Ordinary people do not have that advantage. They have to wait for their final departure to the next world according to their fate and karma.

Sloka 24

agnir jotir ahaḥ śuklaḥ ṣaṇmāsā uttarāyaṇam
tatra prayātā gacchanti brahma brahmavido janāḥ

agnih = fire; jyotih = light; ahah = day; suklah = the waxing period of the moon, the bright fortnight, new moon to full moon; sanmasah uttara-ayanam = the northern solstice; tatra = by that path; prayatah = having departed; gacchanti = attain; brahma = Brahman; brahma-vidah = who are knowers of Brahman; janah = persons.

Fire, light, daytime, the waxing period of the moon, the six months when the sun is in the northern hemisphere, having departed by that Path, people who are knowers of Brahman attain Brahman.

This verse describes how the liberated souls travel from the earth to the immortal heaven located in the sun. The journey takes about a year or a day in the life of the gods. The objects mentioned here refer to the phases through which they pass and the deities who preside over them. The first deity mentioned is Agni, the fire god. He presides over the cremation fire and releases the embodied Self from the body along with the bodily fires (breaths). He is a manifestation of Brahman and the presiding deity of the time during which the bodies of the deceased are cremated and the liberated souls depart from the body. Agni, light, daytime, the waxing period of the moon, and the first six months of the year are aspects of Kala (Time). He is a Brahman's manifestation only. When the liberated soul departs from the body, with the help of Agni, he travels to the mid-region (antariksha) or the space between the earth and the sun, assisted by the sunlight (Jyoti) during the daytime (Ahah). If the liberated person dies in the night in darkness when there is no sunlight, his soul waits until the sun appears in the sky to reach the mid-region. From there, he travels upwards toward the moon if it is the waxing period of the moon (Shukla Paksha). If it is the waning period of the moon (Krishna Paksha), he waits until the waxing period arrives. From there, if the sun is in the northern hemisphere and the time falls in the first six months of the year (Saṇmāsā Uttarāyaṇam), he travels upwards further through space toward the sun. If the sun is still in the southern hemisphere and the time is in the second six months of the year, he waits until the auspicious period arrives and the sun is properly aligned. Finding the right time, he travels for the next six months toward the immortal heaven, which is located at the center of the sun. Having reached it, he either merges with the Supreme Self or stays there forever as a liberated soul.

The Brihadaranyaka Upanishad (6.2.14-15) also describes this journey. It states that when the body of a liberated person is consigned to the funeral flames, his internal fire becomes the fire, fuel the fuel, smoke the smoke, flame the flame, coal the coals, sparks the sparks. In other words, the elements of the body revert to the elements in Nature, which is their source. In that fire, the gods make an offering, out of which arises the person (purusha) with a luminous light color (bhasvara varna). The person is the Self, held within the body and subjected to the laws of Nature. It further states that those who know this and those who meditate in the forests on Brahman with faith pass into the light. From that light, they pass into the day, from the day into half-month (paksha) of the waxing moon, and from there into the northern hemisphere when the sun shines brightly. From there, the liberated Self travels to the world of gods, from the world of gods to the sun, and from the sun to the region of lightning. Then, a mind-born son of Brahma (Brahma manasa putra) goes to this region and leads it to the world of Brahman. That liberated Self will live forever, and there is no return for it.

As we can see, contrary to popular opinion, the phases mentioned here do not necessarily correspond to the time of death but to the period during which the Self passes from one phase to another. For example, daytime in the eastern hemisphere may be night in the western hemisphere. They refer to the time ideal for the transition of the Self from one point to another. Therefore, if the time is not conducive, the liberated souls will wait for the right moment. Thus, if a liberated yogi dies in winter when it is night or when the sun is not in the northern hemisphere, it does not mean that he will not attain the immortal world. It means he must wait for the right time at each entry point to go to the next. In other words, his journey may be delayed by a few more months, but it is not hindered.

The world of Brahman also exists in each of us. We enter it daily in a deep sleep, unaware of it. This is explained in the Chandogya Upanishad (3.2), which states that just as those who walk over a field do not know the treasures that are lying underneath, even so, all beings who go day after day into Brahman do not know him or find him. What are the means to reach that world of Brahman? The Upanishads declare that one can attain it by study, sacrifices, meditation, austerities, yoga, morality, and celibacy. In the Kausitaki Upanishad as well, we find a description of the journey of the souls through different planes. It states the obstacles, celestial beings, and various phenomena they encounter as they travel from one phase to another until they reach the highest seat of immortality.

Sloka 25

dhūmo rātris tathā kṛṣṇaḥ ṣaṇmāsā dakṣiṇāyanam
tatra cāndramasaṃ jyotir yogī prāpya nivartate

dhumah = smoke; ratrih = night; tatha = also; krsnah = the waning period of the moon, the dark fortnight from full moon to new moon; sat-masah daksina-ayanam = the southern solstice; tatra = by that path; candra-masam = the world of moonlight; jyotih = rays, light; yogi = the mystic; prapya = gained; nivartate = returns.

Smoke, night, the waning period of the moon, the southern solstice, or the six months when the sun is in the southern hemisphere- by that path, the yogi attains the moon's rays and reaches the world of the moon.

This verse describes the journey of the souls to the ancestral world, the planes through which they pass, and the deities who preside over them. The deities (aspects of Kala) who assist the bound souls to the ancestral world are Dhuma, Ratri, Krishna Paksha, and Sanmāsa Dakshināyaanam. From this, one can see that Agni does not assist the souls bound to the ancestral world. He assists the liberated souls only, purifying their bodies before releasing them into the air. In the case of the bound souls, this duty is performed by Dhuma (smoke).

Bound souls, destined for rebirth, travel to the ancestral world only. Those who indulge in mortal sins are consigned to the underworld of Yama. While the sun symbolizes Brahman and his immortal world, the moon symbolizes the ancestral world, a temporary resting place for the souls until their next birth. The sun represents permanence and constancy, while the moon symbolizes impermanence and instability because of its waxing and waning. The objects, spheres, or the time through which the souls travel on this journey are not pure but possess a mixed nature. Hence, they are not bright or pure but half-bright or gray. This path awaits those who engage in desire-ridden actions and incur sinful karma. In the ancestral world, they will stay to serve the gods through the offerings of the casual bodies and purify themselves. After paying their dues and exhausting some of their karma, they will return to the earth to continue their existence in the moral world. The ancestors' path is not the best since it does not liberate the souls from samsara or suffering. However, it is not the worst either, since it offers another chance for the bound souls to redeem themselves and attain liberation.

The Brihadaranyaka Upanishad (4.2.16) also describes the Southward Path, which leads to the ancestral world. It states that those who perform sacrificial offerings, charity, and austerity pass into the smoke (that arises from the burning wood during their cremation). From there, they pass into the mid-region at night and travel in space for fifteen nights during the moon's waning period until the new moon day. There, they wait until the sun enters the southern solstice. From then on, they travel in a southerly direction, guided by the southbound sun for six months until they reach the ancestral world. Its physical location is uncertain, although it is presumed to correspond to the physical moon. In the ancestral world, their causal bodies become food to the gods. Their stay in that world depends upon their karma. When their departure time is due, they become earthbound and fall into the mid-region (space) through the moon's rays. From there, they enter the air; from the air, they enter rain and fall to the earth. They enter the earth through the rain and, from there, through the rainwater, into plants and animals. Through them, they become part of the food eaten by humans. Through food, they enter the fire (semen) of males. From there, through sexual intercourse, they enter the fire (wombs) of females, where they grow their bodies and reenter the world through rebirth. The Vedas also describe a third and inferior path that awaits those who neglect their sacrificial duties and indulge in evil actions. Because of their extreme nature and perverted actions, they do not qualify for human birth. Instead, they enter the subterranean worlds and are born as insects, moths, and other biting creatures.

It is important to remember that the journey of the souls to the immortal world of Brahman or the ancestral world depends upon what the jivas remember in the final moments of their death. While immortality is guaranteed for the liberated souls, rebirth is guaranteed for karma yogis, who uphold Dharma and perform their obligatory duties as householders. However, due to their delusion and desire-ridden actions, they do not attain perfection in samadhi (sameness) or freedom from karma (naishkarmya siddhi).

Sloka 26

śuklakṛṣṇe gatī hy ete jagataḥ śāśvate mate
ekayā yāty anāvṛttim anyayāvartate punaḥ

sukla = white; krsne = black; gati = paths; hi = surely; ete = these two; jagatah = of the world; sasvate = eternal; mate = considered; ekaya = by the one; yati = an ascetic, the self-restrained; anavrttim = not return; anyaya = by the other; avartate = return; punah = again.

White and black, these two, are thought to be the only eternal paths of the world; by the one, a self-restrained yogi goes, not to return, and by the other, he returns again.

Only two paths are available to the jivas in the mortal world after death: a bright path, meant for the illuminated souls, which is a one-way ticket to immortality, and a dark path, meant for the impure jivas, which is a two-way ticket to the ancestral world and back. The Paths are eternal, which means they continue in every cycle of creation with no other option or alternative. The bright path is also known as Devayana, the path of the gods or the path of the liberated souls who have attained divinity or oneness with the Lord. The dark path is known as Pitryana, the path of ancestors, or the path that leads to the ancestors, or where the departed souls meet their ancestors and stay with them until their return. The bright path is attained by achieving perfection (siddhi) in yoga or remembering the Supreme Lord at death. The other path is reserved for karma yogis who do not attain perfection or fail in their efforts. Lord Krishna stated in the sixth chapter (6.40) that there is no downfall for the yogis who do not attain perfection on the path of liberation. If they fail, they can still return to the path in their next birth and continue from where they left off. Rebirth offers an opportunity for all bound souls to redeem themselves. They are born again with the lessons they learned in their previous lives. However, due to the deluding power of Maya, only a few succeed in correcting their faulty ways and past mistakes and attaining liberation.

These two paths also have symbolic significance. In the body, the sun and the moon are represented by the Self and intelligence (buddhi), respectively. The Self, like the sun, is self-effulgent. Intelligence has no illumination of its own. Just as the moon relies on the sun for light, intelligence relies on the Self for illumination. The path to the knowledge of the Self (jnana) through self-absorption or union with it is the bright path to eternal freedom or the world of immortality. The path to the knowledge of the Self or the world (vijnana) through intellectual means is the dark path, which ensures a place in the ancestral world and a better life in the next birth, but not liberation. The waxing moon, whose brightness gradually increases during the fifteen days of the month, represents the increasing purity and intelligence of the yogi, who cultivates discernment and acquires knowledge of the Self through studying the scriptures and yoga practice. Although he is better than most deluded people, he is still imperfect and bound to samsara. He keeps returning to the world, birth after birth, until he attains perfection and union with the Self.

Sloka 27

naite sṛtī pārtha jānan yogī muhyati kaścana
tasmāt sarveṣu kāleṣu yogayukto bhavārjuna

na = not; ete = these two; srti = paths; partha = O Partha; janan = knowing; yogi =yogi; muhyati = deluded; kascana = whosoever; tasmat = therefore; sarvesu kalesu = at all times; yoga-yuktah = firmly established in yoga, or absorbed in yoga; bhava = be, remain; arjuna = O Arjuna.

Knowing these two paths, O Partha, no yogi whosoever is deluded. Therefore, O Arjuna, at all times, remain firmly established in yoga.

"Yoga yukto bhava" means becoming a skillful master of yoga. One attains skill and mastery in yoga through steadfast and persistent practice. "Sarva-kaleshu" means always. In other words, the yogi should become a master of yoga by practicing it continuously and persistently until he attains the goal. Lord Krishna said that when a yogi knows the two paths, the bright path and the gray path, he is no longer deluded. Why? It is because, after knowing them, he knows which path leads to liberation and sees no reason why he should opt for the lesser alternative that leads to repeated births and deaths. Therefore, he will strive for liberation only by practicing yoga persistently and attaining mastery. Knowledge of the two paths is thus important. When the yogi has the wisdom to know which path leads to liberation and immortality, he will focus on establishing his mind in the Self and stabilizing it. Worldly pleasures and enjoyments cease to attract him as he realizes that they lead to suffering and bondage. Equipped with that knowledge and discernment, he engages in yoga with steadfast devotion and faith. Whether he is a householder, a seeker of knowledge, or a renunciant, and whether he follows the path of jnana, karma-sannyasa, or sannyasa, the yogi should know the difference between these two paths with supreme faith. Knowing this, he should worship the Supreme Lord continuously with exclusive devotion and without desires and attain perfection in samsiddhi (sameness) and naishkarmya siddhi (freedom from karma), earn his grace to escape forever from the mortal world.

Sloka 28

vedeṣu yajñeṣu tapaḥsu caiva dāneṣu yat puṇyaphalaṃ pradiṣṭam
atyeti tat sarvam idaṃ viditvā yogī paraṃ sthānam upaiti cādyam

vedesu = from study of the Vedas; yajnesu = sacrificial rituals; tapahsu = austerities; ca = and; eva = surely; danesu = giving alms, charity; yat = that; punya-phalam = the fruit of good deeds; pradistam = implied; atyeti = surpasses, goes beyond; tat = those; sarvam idam = all this; viditva = knowing; yogi = the yogi; param = supreme; sthanam = place; upaiti = achieves; ca = also; adyam = first, foremost, primal, ancient.

Knowing all this, the yogi goes beyond the fruit of the good deeds that accrue from the study of the Vedas, sacrificial rituals, austerities, and charities and attains the highest place, which is also the foremost.

Knowing that good deeds such as the study of the Vedas and performing sacrificial rituals, austerities, and charities lead to the ancestral world and rebirth only, the karma yogi gives up desires and attachment to the fruit of his actions and transcends from karma yoga to karma-sannyasa yoga. He realizes that he should engage in desireless actions (nishkama karma) to perform his obligatory duties and pursue Dharma, Artha, Kama, and Moksha with utmost devotion, offering the fruit of his actions to the Supreme Lord. The knowledge also opens his eyes to the truth that he should not settle for a lesser path of performing sacrificial duties to secure a good life in the next birth, but should aim for liberation only by becoming a master of yoga (yoga yukta). Thus, in this verse, Lord Krishna clearly instructs his devotees to aim for liberation rather than practicing karma yoga to fulfill their selfish desires. The Brihadaranyaka Upanishad also declares that liberation should be the goal for humans in this prayer to the Lord: "Lead me from the unreal to the real; from darkness to light; and from death to immortality." The unreal is this world, and the real is the immortal world of Brahman. Darkness refers to ignorance, and light to knowledge and enlightenment. Death refers to impermanence and the cycle of births and deaths, and immortality refers to the supreme state of eternal life and liberation. When one pursues the path of light through yoga, consciousness expands from stage to stage until it transcends all barriers and becomes unlimited and indivisible. For those who remain on the path of darkness, their consciousness remains limited, bound to the ego, delusion, and other impurities, and subject to change and divisions.

Conclusion

iti srīmadbhāgavadgītāsupanisatsu brahmavidyāyām yogasāstre srikrisnārjunasamvāde askharabrahmayogo nāma ashtamo 'dhyayah

iti = thus; srīmadbhāgavadgītā = in the sacred Bhagavadgita; upanisatsu = in the Upanishad; brahmavidyāyām = the knowledge of the absolute Brahman; yogasāstre = the scripture of yoga; srikrisnārjunasamvāde = the dialogue between Sri Krishna and Arjuna; akṣarabrahmayogo nāma = by the name the yoga of Imperishable Brahman; ashtama = eighth; adhyayah = chapter.

Thus ends the eighth chapter, named Akshara Brahma Yoga (The Yoga of Imperishable Brahman) in the Upanishad of the divine Bhagavadgita, the knowledge of the Absolute, a treatise on Yoga, and the debate between Arjuna and Lord Krishna.

09 – Rājavidya Rājaguhya Yoga

The Yoga of Sovereign Knowledge and Mystery

Sloka 1

idaṃ tu te guhyatamaṃ pravakṣyāmy anasūyave
jñānaṃ vijñānasahitaṃ yaj jñātvā mokṣyaseśubhāt

sri-bhagavan uvaca = the Lord Supreme said; idam = this; tu = now, and, indeed; te = to you; guhya-tamam = the utmost secret; pravaksyami = I will speak; anasuyave = who is not envious; jnanam = spiritual knowledge; vijnana = material knowledge; sahitam = together; yat = which; jnatva = knowing; moksyase = you will be liberated; asubhat = from the inauspicious and impure or sinful.

The Supreme Lord said, "Now, I will speak to you, who is not envious of Me, this utmost secret, the knowledge of Myself and My material Nature together, knowing which you will be liberated from the inauspicious and sinful state."

Lord Krishna said that he would deliver the utmost secret knowledge. It is the utmost secret because it is about himself and his creation. That knowledge is exclusive to those who are devoted to him and worship him, not to those who envy him or despise him. Those who know it are forever liberated from the inauspicious and sinful mortal existence. Liberation is granted only to those who earn the grace of the Supreme Lord through exclusive devotion through worship or contemplation. It may be recalled that in chapter seven, Lord Krishna spoke about the knowledge of his higher and lower nature. He referred to them as jnana and vijnana. In the eighth chapter, he explained Adhidaiva, Adhibhuta, etc., and how to contemplate upon him since that knowledge is essential for understanding this chapter. This chapter is believed to be a continuation of the previous two chapters. In this, he reveals jnana and vijnana: knowledge about himself and the knowledge about his creation and manifestations. He described life upon earth as impure and inauspicious (asubham) because it is antithetical to the Self and filled with Death and delusion (maya). The Self in the jivas is immortal, pure, perfect, blemishless, and resplendent. From the perspective of the pure and auspicious Self, which Lord Krishna represents as Isvara, all that he projects in creation with the help of Prakriti is impure and sinful.

For liberation and a proper understanding of oneself, both jnana and vijnana are essential. Jnana is the knowledge of Brahman or the Self. Vijnana is the intellectual knowledge of the world, Nature, God's creation, and his numerous manifestations. (We will learn about his manifestations in the next chapter.) Any knowledge attained through self-knowing in a state of oneness is jnana. Any knowledge learned or acquired through the mind, senses, and intelligence is vijnana. Scriptural knowledge gained intellectually, perceptually, or cognitively through the mind, senses, and experience is also vijnana only. However, these distinctions are not definitive since scriptural and spiritual aspects of knowledge are also considered jnana by many scholars. The knowledge accumulated in the mind (vijnana) is helpful to know the world, to perform obligatory duties, and to pursue the four aims of human life, Dharma, Artha, Kama, and Moksha. Jnana is attained first through studying scriptures or learning from a spiritual teacher, validated further through self-knowing or direct knowing (pratyaksha) in which neither the mind nor the senses participate. Those who pursue jnana have better chances of reaching Brahman's realm by the bright path of immortality, while those who pursue vijnana will most likely end up in the ancestral heaven by the gray path of rebirth.

Jnana and Vijnana also refer to the knowledge of Isvara's higher and lower natures. They pertain to the knowledge of the Self (atma jnana) and the body (svarupa jnana) in the beings. Both types of knowledge are essential for the bound souls to liberate themselves from the impure and inauspicious (asubham) mortal world. The Isa Upanishad encourages devotees to cultivate both types of knowledge, suggesting that those who pursue only one will have no peace or happiness. However, those who know both enjoy life here, cross death with the help of knowledge, and attain eternal life through direct knowing. Vijnana is necessary to practice yoga, cultivate discernment, know the Self as one's true identity, and develop detachment from the physical self. It is helpful to progress from karma yoga to karma-sannyasa yoga and from pursuing Dharma, Artha, and Kama to pursuing Moksha. When one attains perfection, one gains jnana or the knowledge of the Self. Thus, material knowledge prepares us for the rigors and hardships of spiritual life. The knowledge of the Self leads us to the world of Brahman through the sunlit path of immortality, which was described in the previous chapter.

Sloka 2

rājavidyā rājaguhyaṃ pavitram idam uttamam
pratyakṣāvagamaṃ dharmyaṃ susukhaṃ kartumavyayam

raja-vidya = sovereign knowledge; raja-guhyam = sovereign secret; pavitram = purifying, sacred, sanctifying; idam = this; uttamam = the best, excellent, supreme; pratyaksa = directly; avagamam = knowable; dharmyam = has dharma as the basis, righteous; su-sukham = blissful; kartum = doable, or practicable; avyayam = inexhaustible.

This is sovereign knowledge, sovereign secret, purifying, supreme, directly knowable, rooted in Dharma, blissful, practicable, and inexhaustible.

Although we may distinguish jnana and vijnana, for the seeker of liberation, they both refer to the knowledge of Brahman only. Both are essential to practicing yoga and achieving liberation. In this verse, Lord Krishna described the knowledge of Brahman as sovereign (raja-vidya), secret (guhya), purifying or uplifting (pavitram), excellent or the best (uttamam), knowable (avagamam), righteous (dharmyam), conducive to bliss or happiness (susukham), practicable and endless or inexhaustible. It is sovereign because it is the knowledge of the supreme Brahman, who is the first, the highest, and the foremost. It is secret because it is beyond the mind and senses and revealed only to those whom the Lord chooses. That knowledge removes sin, neutralizes karma, sanctifies those who attain it, and elevates them to the supreme state of pure consciousness. Hence, it is sacred, liberating, uplifting, and purifying. It is the best because no other knowledge has the illumination to free people from delusion, egoism, desire, attachments, etc., and lead them to the immortal world by the sunlit path. However, although it is secret and transcendental, it is not unknowable. One can attain it through direct knowing by dissolving oneself in oneness through devotion and yoga practice. It is righteous because it is drawn from Brahman and the Vedas, is rooted in Dharma, and promotes Dharma through duties and righteous conduct. Only virtuous people who follow righteous conduct as prescribed by the scriptures and practice Dharma without desires and attachments qualify for it. Since they experience unending bliss and happiness upon liberation, it is bliss-producing. The knowledge is not theoretical, rhetorical, or speculative but rooted in reality. Anyone can practice it and realize Brahman. Hence, it is rightly described here as doable or practicable (kartum). Finally, it is infinite, all-encompassing, inexhaustible, indeterminate, and cannot be known fully. Hence, it is avyayam, meaning there is no limit to what you can know or learn from it.

Sloka 3

aśraddadhānāḥ puruṣā dharmasyāsya paraṃtapa
aprāpya māṃ nivartante mṛtyusaṃsāravartmani

asraddadhanah = insincere, devoid of faith; purusah = people; dharmasya = righteous teaching; asya = of this; parantapa = O killer of the enemies; aprapya = without attaining; mam = Me; nivartante = return; mrtyu = mortal, death; samsara = cycle of births and deaths; vartmani = path, cycle.

People who have no faith in this righteous teaching, O destroyer of the enemies, without attaining Me, return to the cycle of births and deaths.

In the last two verses, Lord Krishna told Arjuna that he would teach him the sovereign and secret knowledge by knowing which, he would be delivered from the inauspicious state of bondage to death and rebirth. He taught him because Arjuna had faith and devotion. A student should have faith (sraddha) in the teacher and his teaching, especially when he pursues liberation. Those who lack it will keep moving in circles and remain stuck in samsara. In this verse, Lord Krishna implied that impure and sinful people who lack faith would not attain him. Divine help is necessary to cultivate purity and attain liberation or enter his absolute state of oneness. Brahman is Vidya, pure knowledge and consciousness. He is not separate from his teaching. He is the teaching, the Vedas (shruti), the Way, and the Goal. Therefore, it is his inviolable will, manifested as divine laws, which grants humans liberation or bondage. One such law is that even a little impurity or association with Nature or its gunas prevents a seeker from attaining liberation.

Sraddha means having faith, interest, diligence, curiosity, inclination, and enthusiasm. Asraddha means carelessness, disbelief, negligence, and irreverence. Faith is necessary to believe in spiritual or metaphysical knowledge. Without it, one cannot practice yoga, establish the mind in the thoughts of the Lord, and attain liberation or union through direct knowing (pratyaksha avagama). The Vedas are helpful as the verbal proof (shabda pramana) to introduce us to the metaphysical knowledge of the Self or Brahman. However, if faith is lacking, it will not ignite aspiration or yearning in the devotee to pursue liberation. If you show even a little interest, inclination, and faith (sraddha), the Lord will reciprocate and strengthen your devotion and determination or show you the way. If you keep it alive in your heart, he will ensure that you progress in the right direction.

On the path of liberation, faith sustains your effort. It gives you the strength and determination to endure suffering and adversity and remain steadfast on the path. In weak moments and difficult circumstances, the devotee with firm faith perseveres against them. Unwavering faith is the foundation for unwavering devotion (ananya bhakti). Both arise only when the mind and body are pure with the predominance of sattva and free from desires, passions, and attachments. They are interrelated and sustain and reinforce each other. They do not manifest in deluded people even if they know the scriptures, worship the Lord, or practice yoga. Hence, it is vital to cultivate pure devotion through self-purification and selfless actions (nishkama karma), surrendering yourself to the Supreme Lord, your very Self, and letting him be the guide, the teacher, and the support.

Sloka 4

mayā tatam idaṃ sarvaṃ jagad avyaktamūrtinā
matsthāni sarvabhūtāni na cāhaṃ teṣv avasthitaḥ

maya = by Me; tatam = pervaded; idam = this; sarvam = all, whole; jagat = material universe; avyakta-murtina = unmanifested form; mat-sthani = exist in Me; sarva-bhutani = all beings; na = not; ca = and; aham = I; tesu = in them; avasthitah = exist.

All this material universe is pervaded by My unmanifested form. All beings exist in Me, but I do not exist in them.

The first part of the verse states that the invisible, indivisible, unmanifested, and pure Brahman pervades the universe. He is avyakta (unmanifested) because he is self-existent, complete, independent, and without associations, formations, causes and effects, and attachments. In the second part, Lord Krishna affirms that although creation exists in him, he does not exist in it. To understand this paradoxical statement, we have to understand the pure state of Brahman himself and his relationship with the creation that manifests from him. We can use the analogy of space to explain it. Just as space exists everywhere, contains all, and pervades all, it is not in the things and is not an integral part of any object. They are not made of space. The same is true with Brahman. He is not in his creation, although he pervades it. It manifests from him as a projection, formation, or superimposition. In some schools, it is considered his material body. In his unmanifested aspect, Brahman is invisible, absolute, formless, eternal, indestructible, and free from materiality since the primal Nature remains in him in an indeterminate, inactive, and unmanifested (asambhuta) state.

In his manifested state, Brahman appears with modes (saguna) as Isvara, the Lord and controller of the universe. Along with him, Prakriti becomes manifested (sambhuta) with her modes and tattvas as his dynamic force and the executress of his inviolable will. Together, they represent the fundamental duality of the whole existence. With the assistance of Prakriti and her modes and tattvas, he manifests numerous forms and worlds and resides in them as their witness Self. Although the whole creation exists in him like a dream or a spider's web, and although he pervades it and supports it, he remains independent and detached. "Na aham tesu" (I do not exist in them) means he is not a part of the materiality of creation or the corporeality of the jivas. He has no direct contact with Prakriti, the universe, or the jivas, although he resides in them as their support, without any support for himself. They are entirely made up of the matter, energy, tattvas, and gunas of Prakriti. She exists in him as a dependent reality and in the jivas as their projected reality, but he does not exist in either. While creation is filled with impurities and subject to impermanence and change, he remains untouched and immutable.

Sloka 5

na ca matsthāni bhūtāni paśya me yogam aiśvaram
bhūtabhṛn na ca bhūtastho mamātmā bhūtabhāvanaḥ

na = not; ca = and; mat-sthani = dwell in Me; bhutani = beings and things; pasya = see, perceive; me = My; yogam = state; aisvaram = majestic, supreme, royal; bhuta-bhrt = I am the upholder of all beings and things; na = not; ca = but; bhuta-sthah = present in the material things; mama = My; atma = Self; bhuta-bhavanah = indweller of beings.

Beings and things do not dwell in Me, nor can anyone perceive my supreme opulent State! I am the Upholder of all beings and things, but I am not present in them. My (eternal) Self is where all beings dwell.

This verse contains three important aspects of the Supreme Lord: bhutabhrat, bhutastah, and bhuta-bhavana. "Bhutas (beings, elements, and things) do not dwell in Me "means they are not part of the Lord's essential nature or unmanifested aspect, which is pure consciousness. Beings cannot perceive his supreme state (yoga aisvaryam) because he is beyond their minds and senses. He is bhutabhrat, the supporter of all, because they all arise from him and subside in him. He is not in them (bhutastah) means he is not a part of their bodies or essential nature. He is always distinct from them, just as space is distinct from the objects it pervades. They do not arise from him but from Prakriti. In other words, he is not an integral part of their bodies but pervades them as an independent, detached, and distinct entity. The jivas are made up of tattvas and gunas. The Self is without modes (Nirguna). He is not a part of them and does not exist in them. The tattvas and the gunas belong to the domain of Nature.

However, Lord Krishna followed up with another statement that all beings dwell (bhuta-bhavana) in him only. In other words, he creates, supports, houses, and nourishes all the beings, but would not let his pure consciousness or unmanifested aspect be touched or tainted by them. Similarly, he remains untouched by their impurities or actions while he dwells in them as their embodied Self. He dwells in the jivas but has nothing in common with them. He does not partake in their nature or perish with them. As the embodied Self, he transmigrates passively and independently from one birth to another but does not actively participate in it as the cause or the effect. Thus, as this verse states, although all beings exist in Brahman, they are not part of his supreme state. Although he exists in them as their indwelling Self, he is NOT a part of their essential nature (prakriti svabhavam).

The distinction between the Self and the not-self (the body) is permanent in the jivas. They exist separately in their own spaces, but both are required for the jivas to exist. The body (and the mind) is called the not-self because it is distinct from the Self. The Upanishads also state the same. They declare that Brahman is present in all as their inner Controller, but beings do not know him. They cannot perceive him because he is transcendental. He is not the senses, but they cannot work without him. Since he is distinct and detached from Nature, he is untouched by its modifications. Therefore, in the midst of impermanence, he remains permanent and fixed. Amid death and destruction, he remains indestructible. This knowledge is useful to cultivate detachment from the mind and body and become established in the Self.

Sloka 6

yathākāśasthito nityaṃ vāyuḥ sarvatrago mahān
tathā sarvāṇi bhūtāni matsthānīty upadhāraya

yatha = justas; akasa-sthitah = existing in the space; nityam = always; vayuh = wind; sarvatra-gah = travels everywhere; mahan = mighty, great; tatha = in the same manner; sarvani = all; bhutani = things and beings; mat-sthani = situated in Me; iti = thus; upadharaya = you should know.

Just as the mighty wind travels everywhere existing in space, in the same way, all things and beings are situated in Me. Thus, you should know.

All things and beings (sarva bhutastam) are situated in Brahman, but without any connection. Just as space is untouched by wind or unaffected by its movements or properties, Brahman supports and contains all but is untouched by them, their nature, or actions. Both space and wind are elements (bhutas). They exist in Brahman but do not reach him. Among the elements, space (akasa) is compared to Brahman because it has many attributes that can be used to describe the latter and contrast it with the things it contains, such as the clouds or the earth itself. Like Brahman, space is invisible, infinite, indescribable, and ungraspable. However, we should use this analogy for understanding without stretching it too far. In the objective world, space is comparable to Brahman, but it is not the same as Brahman.

All five elements (pancha bhutas), including space, belong to the domain of Prakriti. Brahman is beyond them, does not exist in them, and is untouched by them.

Sloka 7

sarvabhūtāni kaunteya prakṛtiṃ yānti māmikām
kalpakṣaye punas tāni kalpādau visṛjāmy aham

sarva-bhutani = all things and being; kaunteya = O son of Kunti; prakrtim = Prakriti, Nature; yanti = enter, go; mamikam = My; kalpa-ksaye = at the end of the kalpa or time cycle, the day of Brahma; punah = again; tani = them; kalpa-adau = at the beginning of the time cycle, kalpa; visrjami = I create, project, bring forth; aham = I.

O son of Kunti, at the end of each time cycle, all things and beings enter my Prakriti. Again, at the beginning of each time cycle, I bring them forth.

The first part of the verse contains two important declarations: 1. Prakriti is a dependent aspect of the Supreme Lord and is under his control; 2. At the end of creation, he withdraws beings into his Nature, not into himself. Thus, in this verse also, he maintains the clear distinction between him and Nature and between him and his creation. The second part of the verse affirms the cyclical nature of creation. While there are divergent theories in Hinduism about the relationship between God and his creation, there is a unanimous opinion about the cyclical nature of creation. In Hinduism, creation is considered cyclical and repetitive. Nothing is eternal or indestructible in existence except God himself. He also enforces order and regularity (rta) of the whole creation through the laws (dharma) he establishes to ensure that it proceeds predictably to its predetermined end. The current theories of astronomy also favor the view that the universe may have recurrent cycles of expansion and contraction, just as the theories of creation found in the Hindu texts. Carl Sagan, the famous astronomer, observed that Hinduism is the only tradition that supports the idea that the cosmos is subject to infinite deaths and rebirths.

Kalpa is a day and night in Brahma's life, equivalent to roughly 8.64 billion years. The creation of the phenomenal world begins at the start of the day and continues until the night, spanning over 4.32 billion years, roughly equivalent to the lifetime of the planet Earth. It is dissolved at night, and a new Earth manifests in the next Kalpa. Prakriti is the sum of all the energy and matter in the material universe and its subtle dimensions. Brahman represents pure consciousness in which Prakriti exists as a distinct and dependent entity. It is through her that the inactive Brahman becomes active and controls creation. Just as in the Bhagavadgita, some schools of Vedanta consider Prakriti to be a dependent aspect of Brahman and Isvara. They think that he is both the material and efficient cause of creation. However, according to others, she is eternal and autonomous from Brahman and acts independently. They consider Brahman the efficient cause and Prakriti the material cause. Both speculative philosophies find their validation in the Vedas.

Sloka 8

prakṛtiṃ svām avaṣṭabhya visṛjāmi punaḥ punaḥ
bhūtagrāmam imaṃ kṛtsnam avaśaṃ prakṛter vaśāt

prakrtim = Nature; svam = My; avastabhya = under control; visrjami = I bring forth; punah punah = repeatedly again, again; bhuta-gramam = the mulitude of things and beings; imam = this; krtsnam = the whole; avasam = helplessly; prakrteh = by Nature; vasat = held under its control.

Holding My Nature under control, I repeatedly bring forth the multitude of things and beings who are powerlessly held by Nature under its control.

In the Bhagavadgita, God is viewed as the Supreme Controller. This view is not universally accepted in Hinduism. However, since the Bhagavadgita is a theistic scripture of Vedanta, we must accept God as the controller of all to understand its teachings. As the Lord of Creation, he ensures that Nature acts according to his will and fulfills the aims of creation. If she holds beings under her powerful control and helplessly binds them to the mortal world, it is because of his will only, but not otherwise. Madhavacharya commented that God has the power to act on his own. If he executes all actions through Prakriti, it is due to his gift and guidance to her. In other words, he has power and can act with or without her, but by his own volition, he lets her do her duty in creation.

Bhagavadgita describes Nature as His dependent force. Nature manifests things and words according to His will, and they, in turn, remain under her control. Thus, we have a hierarchy or a line of command in the whole existence, starting with him at the top, Nature in the middle, and all created things at the bottom. All inanimate objects form the lowest rung. Although in the embodied state, as the Self of all, he remains inactive and passive, at the highest level, as the Supreme Lord, he is the creator, preserver, destroyer, and controller of all. He also intervenes in creation, if necessary, through manifestations and incarnations. As the Self, he may remain detached and indifferent, but as Isvara, he ensures the orderly progression of each cycle of creation. As the upholder of Dharma, he sets an example by performing duties like a true karma-sannyasi with detachment and indifference and without desires and passions. However, if Dharma declines and evil ascends, he incarnates upon earth to restore order. We see the same idea being affirmed several times in the scripture. Within her field, Nature holds the fort and keeps the beings under control, subjecting them to the play of maya and the cycle of births and deaths. However, if the Lord chooses, he intervenes and grants liberation to the devotees he deems worthy. Most importantly, he is the source of Prakriti's powers, modes, and tattvas. Therefore, she cannot perform her duties without him, just as the body cannot survive without the Self.

The Vedas hold a similar view. They suggest that Brahman is the Supreme Controller, who brings forth the worlds and beings through a supreme sacrifice. He is the One Magician (mayavi), who spreads the net of illusion, rules with his sovereign powers, and remains immutable and indestructible while things appear and disappear in the field of Nature. Drawing forth from his own Nature, he weaves the worlds and beings like a spider. The Svetasvatara Upanishad states that Prakriti is maya (illusion), and Brahman is the wielder of maya. Because of him, beings are held helplessly under its control by Nature. He is the One (ekam) in whom all things dissolve in the end and manifest again at the beginning. As the Protector, he keeps all the worlds in balance and chaos at bay. As the one God, he rules over the mutable matter (pradhana) and all the embodied souls.

Sloka 9

na ca māṃ tāni karmāṇi nibadhnanti dhanaṃjaya
udāsīnavad āsīnam asaktaṃ teṣu karmasu

na = not; ca = and; mam = Me; tani = these; karmani = actions; nibadhnanti = bind; dhananjaya = O conqueror of riches; udasina-vat = indifferent, passive; asinam = remaining; asaktam = disinterested, unattached; tesu = those; karmasu = actions.

And these actions do not bind Me, O conqueror of riches, (as I am) seated in those actions as if indifferent and detached.

According to traditional commentators, God is not indifferent to creation or the created beings. However, since he has no particular interest or involvement in anything due to the absence of ego, desires, etc., and remains detached, it appears as if he is indifferent and aloof. Since he is independent of all causes and effects, he is not bound by them. Besides, he is the Lord of Prakriti also. Hence, Prakriti has no power over him. Even the schools of Vedanta, which hold that Prakriti is an independent and eternal entity, agree that Isvara is not bound by his actions and remains untainted in the beings and creation. The classical Sankhya school also agrees that individual selves (purushas) are not tainted by the action of Nature or the jivas. Prakriti performs actions rather mechanically, like a preprogrammed automaton, and manifests the effects already hidden in their causes. However, the embodied souls in the jivas remain passive and indifferent, untouched by them. The school also holds that effects are not independent of causes. Nature does not produce any new effects or causes but manifests only those that are already hidden in preexisting causes. However, causes may produce different effects or results due to the intervention of other causes. The school also does not acknowledge God as the source of all but considers Prakriti the sum of all causes, effects, energies, tattvas, gunas, actions, and movements.

The Bhagavadgita does not concur with such atheistic notions of Samkhyavada or that Nature, rather than God, is solely responsible for all manifestations. Instead, it holds that God is an active principle and the ultimate cause of all causes. Since he is the supreme controller, Nature dutifully performs all actions according to his will rather than mechanically. Although he may appear to be indifferent and detached, he performs all actions through Prakriti without becoming involved with them and ensures the order and regularity of his manifested realities. As these verses affirm, Nature is not a blind force or an independent entity but is bound to God's will and executes it intelligently. He remains seated amidst the tattvas and gunas in the jivas and witnesses the play of Maya as if indifferent and detached. That indifference is a mere illusion, a part of his play. By remaining indifferent, he sets an example for his devotees of the right way to live in this world, practicing karma-sannyasa yoga. By following his example, they can enjoy life here and liberation hereafter.

Sloka 10

mayādhyakṣeṇa prakṛtiḥ sūyate sacarācaram
hetunānena kaunteya jagad viparivartate

maya = under My; adhyaksena = supervision, watchful observation; prakrtih = Nature; suyate = manifests; sa = with; cara-acaram = moving and the nonmoving things; hetuna = because anena = of this; kaunteya = O son of Kunti; jagat = the whole world, manifest universe; viparivartate = revolves.

Under My control, Nature manifests the moving and the nonmoving. Because of this only, O son of Kunti, the whole world revolves back and forth.

In this verse, Lord Krishna reaffirms that he is Isvara, the Lord and Supreme Controller of all creation. Any object, such as a piece of cloth or an image, does not manifest by itself or on its own. There must be a cause, an action, and a result. It must first exist in the consciousness of its creator as an idea or concept. Then, it must be created, crafted, and transformed into reality through intelligent and willful action. A similar process must happen at the cosmic level for creation to manifest. According to these statements of the Bhagavadgita, the Supreme Being is the source of all creation. It revolves back and forth because of him only. Prakriti does not manifest anything by herself. He gives her the impetus to manifest the whole creation hidden in his consciousness as a seed. Under his direct control and supervision (adhyakshena) and following his will, she dutifully manifests the moving and nonmoving aspects of creation as he intends or wills. At the end of it, again under his lordship and control, and as he wills, she withdraws them into herself. Outwardly, he may appear to be uninvolved or indifferent, but he is the one who sets the stage, remains behind the screen, and directs Prakriti to enact his play.

Thus, the Bhagavadgita envisions a unipolar universe, with God serving as the Supreme commander and controller (adhyaksha) and Prakriti as his dutiful and loyal assistant or executress. In its vision of the universe, Isvara is the grand wizard (mayavi), the source and supporter of all, while as a dependent force, Nature does not act on her own but according to his will only. However, for good order and to ensure that the cycle of creation revolves as intended, in the field of Prakriti and the jivas, he acts as if he is indifferent, uninvolved, and passive as the witness Self (sakshi). As the source of all, he is the efficient and the material cause of all existence, the ultimate cause of all, or the cause of all causes, while Nature is the apparent, instrumental cause. Together, they make the whole existential reality at the cosmic and individual levels possible.

In this model of creation presented by the Scripture, as the Supreme Lord and the Self of all, Brahman represents the three components of every action or manifestation, assisted by Prakriti: karta (doer), kriya (the process or action), and karma (the result or fruit). Brahman is pure consciousness, with dormant, indeterminate, and unmanifested (asambhuta) Prakriti. Isvara is Brahman with active and manifested Prakriti (sambhuta) as his dynamic, dependent force. In the projected reality of creation, he conceals himself, supporting and pervading it from within, enveloping it from the outside, and letting Prakriti execute his will unhindered.

Sloka 11

avajānanti māṃ mūḍhā mānuṣīṃ tanum āśritam
paraṃ bhāvam ajānanto mama bhūtamaheśvaram

avajananti = disregard, disrespect; mam = Me; mudhah manusim = foolish people lacking in intelligence; tanum = body; asritam = residing; param = supreme, transcendental; bhavam = state, nature; ajanantah = not knowing; mama = My; bhuta = beings; maha-isvaram = the supreme Lord of.

Foolish people who lack intelligence disrespect Me when I reside in the physical body, not knowing My Supreme State as the Supreme Lord of all beings.

Who are the foolish people (mudha manus) who disrespect God? Those who do not worship him as the highest and supreme Controller of all creation (sarvesvara) or as the Self of all (sarva bhutatma). They are mudha (foolish) because they lack the intelligence or the discernment to know that he resides in them as their very Self and that they owe their existence to him. What is his Supreme State (param bhavam) that they do not know? It is his transcendental, eternal, fixed, indestructible, invisible state as the Creator and Lord of all beings (bhuta mahesvara). Due to these twin misconceptions or ignorant notions, they regard themselves as mortal beings and treat the Lord with contempt, indifference, or disrespect. When he appears amidst them as an incarnation, they mistake him as an ordinary mortal being just like them and demand proof of his powers, divinity, or lordship.

The disregard for God may arise in two ways: 1. when they ignore the existence of the Self in them, and 2. when they ignore the existence of the Lord of the Universe. Both situations arise due to impurities like egoism, delusion, and ignorance. In the first instance, they discount their spiritual nature and act as mere physical beings, attributing their existence and continuity to chance or random causes, engaging in desire-ridden actions to satisfy their selfish desires and animal passions, and thinking that death is the end of all and that there is no afterlife, rebirth, heaven, or liberation. They extend the same attitude to others and treat them carelessly as mere physical entities. In the second instance, they deny his existence, opulence, lordship, or his role as the creator, preserver, and destroyer of all. Disrespect for the Lord may manifest in some as perverted notions about him, his powers, and his creation. They extend the same contempt and disregard to the knowledge of the scriptures or the words of enlightened masters, seers, and saints, casting aspersions on them or their truthfulness. With perverted beliefs and ignorant notions, they neglect their obligatory duties, pursue material goals, assume ownership and doership, and bring ruin upon themselves.

Avajānanti means to despise, show contempt, disrespect, or have a low opinion. Disrespect or contempt for God manifests numerously in humans. For example, treating God as a mere being, not recognizing his supreme nature, criticizing him for one's failures or sinful actions, or feeling anger, envy, or enmity towards him are some of the disrespectful or contemptuous attitudes. Other forms of disrespect are ill-treating or ridiculing the Lord's devotees, disturbing their worship or devotional activities, passing judgments on their actions or actions of God, disrespecting the scriptures, images, or symbols of divinity, desecrating temples and religious places, engaging in prohibited or sinful actions that are explicitly prohibited by the scriptures, etc. Treating him as a mere idol, image, or living entity with a mind and body, invoking him to hurt and harm others, and expecting him to be a partner in evil actions are also disrespectful, attitudes only arising from ignorance and delusion.

These attitudes and behaviors manifest in humans due to impurities such as egoism, ignorance, delusion, desires, etc., and due to the lack of purity, self-control, faith (sraddha), fear of sin (bhayam), and devotion (bhakti). Devotion manifests in humans according to the gunas. To be free from negative attitudes towards the Supreme Being, one must cultivate purity and discernment and overcome desires, egoism, and delusion. Exclusive and pure devotion will not arise without establishing your mind in the contemplation of the Lord, who is present in you as your very Self.

Sloka 12

moghāśā moghakarmāṇo moghajñānā vicetasaḥ
rākṣasīm āsurīṃ caiva prakṛtiṃ mohinīṃ śritāḥ

mogha= vain, fruitless, futile, useless; asah = hopes; mogha-karmanah = useless rites; mogha-jnanah = futile knowledge; vicetasah = deluded, mindless, senseless, confused; raksasim = demonic; asurim = evil; ca = and; eva = surely; prakrtim = nature; mohinim = deceitful; sritah = take shelter.

With vain hopes, useless rites, and futile knowledge, the deluded and mindless ones take refuge in the demonic, evil, and deceitful nature.

The deluded and demonic ones engage in vain hopes, meaning what they wish for or hope to accomplish through their actions will not happen because they are unrealistic and delusional about themselves and their strengths and abilities. For example, in their greed to earn excessive wealth, they may resort to shortcuts or evil actions, ignoring the consequences that may arise from them. In their eagerness to destroy or control others due to lust, anger, pride, or envy, they may engage in forbidden rites and rituals (mogha karma) and bring ruin upon themselves. Their knowledge is futile because they do not pursue the right knowledge due to the lack of discernment, make mistakes, and fail to reach their material and spiritual goals.

A devotee's mind should be filled with devotion and thoughts of God only. He must have allegiance to him only and worship him exclusively with liberation as his goal. He should treat everything that does not lead to his goal or strengthen his devotion to the Lord as worthless or inconsequential.

Accordingly, the deluded ones who are mentioned by Lord Krishna in this verse are ill-qualified for liberation, self-purification, or pure devotion. From a spiritual perspective, vain hopes are hopes for material things that are transient and produce karma, pain, and suffering. A true devotee hopes for liberation by securing God's love, nearness, and mercy. Deluded people hope for material things, riches, and comforts by engaging in desire-ridden actions. True devotees engage in obligatory duties for the welfare of the world, but not for themselves. They practice kama-sannyasa, offering the fruit of their actions to the Supreme Lord. In contrast, the deluded ones perform them for selfish and egoistic purposes, thinking they can attain peace and prosperity through them. They practice kamya karmas rather than selfless actions (nishkama karma) with the desire to benefit from them. Their knowledge is futile and confusing because it does not lead to austerity, virtue, liberation, or self-purification. Instead, it leads them deeper into worldliness, strengthens their desires and attachments, and prolongs their suffering and bondage. If they continue on this downward path, they may end up becoming tools in the hands of evil.

Human nature is divine, demonic, or mixed. We will learn about them in Chapter 16 from Lord Krishna. For now, it is sufficient to know that human beings may become divine or demonic according to their thoughts and actions. The asuras are the elder brothers of the gods and humans. Egoistic and perverted, due to the predominance of tamas, they are forever in conflict with the divinities and beings of light. Because of delusion, they take refuge in their demonic nature and indulge in evil actions, disregarding the consequences. The rakshasas are another group of evil beings who are cruel and pitiless by nature. They take pleasure in violent and destructive actions, oppressing and harassing others, inflicting pain and suffering upon God's devotees, creating chaos and confusion, or disrupting the natural order of things. Those who seek liberation should stay away from evil influences and take refuge in the Lord as their very Self.

Sloka 13

mahātmānas tu māṃ pārtha daivīṃ prakṛtim āśritāḥ
bhajanty ananyamanaso jñātvā bhūtādim avyayam

maha-atmanah = great souls; tu = but; mam = o Me; partha = O Partha; daivim = divine; prakrtim = nature; asritah =take refuge; bhajanti = devotional worship; ananya-manasah = without any distraction; jnatva = knowing Me; bhuta adim = the source of all beings; avyayam = inexhaustible.

But the great souls, O Partha, taking refuge in My divine nature, worship Me only without any distraction, knowing Me as the inexhaustible source of all beings.

The deluded ones take refuge in demonic nature, ignore the Lord, and despise him, unable to recognize his opulence or divinity. However, the great souls (mahatmas) take refuge in him as their very Self and worship him only, knowing that he is the inexhaustible source and the Self of all. In truth, there are no great souls (mahatmas) or evil souls (duratmas). The Self is always pure and resplendent, whether in humans, animals, or pure or impure beings, since it is untouched by the impurities of Prakriti even in the embodied state. Mahatmas are pure souls, dearer to God, and ever engaged in contemplation and exclusive devotion. They are great (maha) not because the Self (atma) is any different in them in size, purity, or illumination but because through detachment, devotion, and desireless actions (nishkama karma), they cultivate nearness to God and take refuge in his higher nature. They absorb their minds in his contemplation and devotional worship through prayers, studying scriptures, singing devotional songs (bhajans), remembering his names, listening to his glories, etc. Knowing that the Supreme Lord is the imperishable source of all beings and developing a distaste for perishable things, they worship him, seeking liberation as their final goal with single-minded devotion, sameness, and equanimity. As they fill their hearts with exclusive devotion and absorb their minds in his thoughts without any distraction, suppressing the gunas and desires, they enter the silence of the Self and attain oneness. Only the great ones are capable of unwavering devotion without any trace of selfishness, egoism, or delusion. Whether asleep or awake, their minds are always established in the thoughts of God. They quickly attain liberation by overcoming duality and delusion and resolving their karma through desireless actions. Such pious souls are rare since only a few reach that stage after several births. Therefore, meeting and learning from them in person is a great blessing and a rare opportunity.

Sloka 14

satataṃ kīrtayanto māṃ yatantaś ca dṛḍhavratāḥ
namasyantaś ca māṃ bhaktyā nityayuktā upāsate

satatam = always; kirtayantah = singing praise; mam = Me; yatantah = striving; ca = and; drdha-vratah = penances with firm vows; namasyantah = offering salutations; ca = and; mam = Me; bhaktya = with devotion; nitya-yuktah = ever absorbed yogis; upasate = worship.

Always singing My praise and striving for Me through penances with firm vows and offering Me salutations with devotion, the ever-absorbed yogis worship Me.

This verse describes how pious souls, the great ones (mahatmas) or the ever-absorbed yogis (nitya yuktas), express and exemplify their exclusive devotion in various ways. They always sing his praise and glories (satatam kirtayanta) through devotional songs and prayers (bhajans and kirtans). It means they have no ill will, contempt, or negativity towards the Lord. Through penances, austerities, and strict vows (drdha vrata), they prove their love, devotion, self-control, sacrifice, commitment, and firm faith (sraddha). Prostrating before his images and remaining ever-absorbed in his contemplation, they exemplify surrender, loyalty, reverence, and egolessness. The pious souls entertain no thought other than the thoughts of God. They are attracted to nothing but the knowledge or matters concerning the Lord. They depend upon none but the Lord alone. Even the prospect of liberation does not interest them as much as their love and devotion for him. The ever-active pure devotees (nitya yuktas) practice nitya bhakti or ananya-bhakti, renouncing all desires and attachments and putting themselves at the feet of the Lord. They excel in bhakti yoga, the most excellent of all yogas, and the royal path to liberation. However, pure devotion is difficult to attain. It is usually experienced after attaining purity and excellence in all other yogas. One reaches it through karma, jnana, and sannyasa yogas. Only a few succeed in it. There are many levels of devotion. True devotion arises only when there is a complete absence of desires and all notions of egoism and materiality. Devotion can also be practiced or expressed in other ways, which are explained in the next verse.

Sloka 15

jñānayajñena cāpy anye yajanto mām upāsate
ekatvena pṛthaktvena bahudhā viśvatomukham

jnana = knowledge; yajnena = by the sacrifice; ca =and; api = alone; anye = others; yajantah = sacrificial worship; mam = Me; upasate = adoring, meditating; ekatvena = as one; prthaktvena = as distinct; bahudha = as many; visvatah-mukham =with faces everywhere.

Others worship Me by the sacrifice of knowledge alone, meditating upon Me as One, as distinct, and as many with numerous faces everywhere.

All are God's devotees only. Some despise him and take refuge in their demonic nature. They ignore their spiritual well-being and pursue vain hopes, useless rites, and futile knowledge. Some great souls (mahatmas) take refuge in his divine nature, practice firm vows, austerities, and penances, and worship him with exclusive devotion and self-discipline. They exemplify exclusive devotion (ananya bhakti). In this verse, the Lord mentioned those who practice the sacrifice of knowledge. They worship him according to their knowledge and understanding as one indivisible Self, as different from creation, and as a deity with numerous names, forms, and manifestations. They all exemplify the various shades of jnana yoga.

The Vedic knowledge is centered on or around the idea of sacrifice (yajna). The most commonly known sacrifices are the sacrificial rituals performed by householders as karma yogis. In them, they make offerings to the gods as their obligatory duty to express gratitude or fulfill their desires. Some sacrifices are ordained by the Vedas as obligatory, and some as optional. The Vedas also recognize other types of sacrifices in which various objects or things are really or symbolically sacrificed to the Lord for self-purification, such as the sacrifice of knowledge (jnana), the body (bhuta), materials (dravya), chants (mantra), breath (prana), etc. As the Bhagavadgita states, sacrifices are useful to achieve Dharma, Artha, and Kama. However, to achieve Moksha, the Ultimate Goal, the karma yogi must perform them without desires and attachments, and their fruit must be offered to God as a sacrifice.

In Jnana yajna, devotees offer (sacrifice) their minds, intelligence, and senses to know the Self. They engage them in the study, listening, observation, and contemplation with self-control, detachment, and renunciation. In this approach, knowledge is offered to the organs in the body (the senses, mind, and intelligence) to achieve self-purification, stabilize the mind in the Self, and achieve equanimity, detachment, and sameness. Symbolically, jnana yajna is an internalized form of Vedic ritual in which knowledge and intelligence are poured into the fire of consciousness that is kindled in the pit of the internal organ to burn the impurities of the mind and body and achieve purity and mental brilliance. The Upanishads suggest various ways, known as Brahmavidyas, in which the Supreme Self is internally meditated upon and realized as breath, the senses, mind, intelligence, the Self, pure consciousness, and so on.

This verse suggests that yogis practice the sacrifice of knowledge by worshipping or meditating upon Brahman in three ways. In the first method, they perceive him as their very Self or as the one, indivisible, indistinguishable, pure, and absolute Supreme Reality. The Advaitavadins (nondualists) uphold this view. They meditate upon the Supreme Lord as their very Self and the Self of all, withdrawing from the illusory world. According to them, Brahman is the only reality, and the rest, including the individual Self (Atman), is an illusion or projection. They hold that duality and diversity are deluded notions that arise in our minds due to the influence of Maya and the presence of impurities. When they are removed, we overcome delusion and attain oneness.

In the second approach, Brahman is worshipped as distinct from the inner Self. The followers of Dvaita hold this view. According to them, the Supreme Self (Brahman) and the individual Self (Atman) are eternally different, although both are everlasting, indestructible, and fixed. Their distinction remains even after the jivas achieve liberation. Individual souls are also distinct and different from each other. Thus, according to the school, duality is the defining principle of creation. As the Supreme Being (Isvara), Brahman is the creator, upholder, and destroyer of all. He watches over everyone as their controller, protector, and upholder. His opulence is unlimited, and his will inviolable. Everything in creation depends upon him and his grace.

In the third approach, which is a variation of the Dvaita, devotees worship the Supreme Lord and his numerous manifestations(vibhutis), aspects (amsas), incarnations (avatars), and emanations. They see the Lord as different from them and revere his numerous manifestations as if they are different from each other, ignoring their underlying unity or oneness. It is practiced by those who are deluded, ignorant, and lack discernment. Karma yogis who perform sacrificial rituals and worship gods and demigods with offerings also fall into this category.

Sloka 16

ahaṃ kratur ahaṃ yajñaḥ svadhāham aham auṣadham
mantro.aham aham evājyam aham agnir ahaṃ hutam

aham = I; kratuh = kratu; aham = I; yajnah = yajna; svadha = svadha; aham = I; aham = I; ausadham = medicinal herb; mantrah = mantra, sacred chant; aham = I; aham = I; eva = certainly; ajyam = fuel, melted butter; aham = I; agnih = fire; aham = I; hutam = burnt offering.

I am kratu (Soma ritual), I am Yajna (sacrifice), I am svadha (benediction), I am ausadham (medicinal herb), I am mantras (sacred chant), I am ājyam (melted butter, ghee, or oil), I am Agni, and I am hutam (burnt offering purified by fire).

In this verse, Lord Krishna directly refuted the Mimansa doctrine that yajnas are the supreme source of all manifestations and God has no role in it, stating that he is their source and support and represents every aspect of them. The previous verse is about the sacrifice of knowledge (jnana yajna). This one concerns the ritual proper (karma yajna) and its constituent parts. Lord Krishna declared here that he represents the Vedic sacrifice and all its aspects, be it a traditional Agnistoma Sacrifice, Soma Sacrifice, or a symbolic sacrifice such as a devotional service or meditation. In the Vedic conception of creation, life itself is a great yajna, and every action we perform in it is either an independent sacrifice or part of the great sacrifice of life. The Vedas describe that the world was created as the fruit of a great sacrifice performed by the Cosmic Being (Purusha) at the beginning of creation. In that sacrifice mediated by the ancient gods as priests, he used parts of himself as the sacrificial offerings to produce the worlds, beings, laws, and the order (rta) of things. Since then, human beings have been following the same formula to manifest things, invoke gods, or fulfill their desires. Since he created the Yajna out of himself, he is invariably present in every aspect of it, as the host of the sacrifice, the sacrificed material, the priest, the chants, the fruit, and the remains of the sacrifice.

Although outwardly sacrifices (yajnas) may look like devotional or magical rituals, they are replete with hidden symbolism. In the internalized form of the yajna or the sacrificial ritual, we use parts of our minds and bodies or our energies and faculties as offerings to the Supreme Lord for self-purification or self-realization. Thereby, a devotee's actions become sacrificial actions, and his life transforms into a continuous offering in the fire of devotion. Creation itself is envisaged in the Vedas as an act of sacrifice. So are all our daily actions and mundane tasks, such as breathing, eating, sleeping, walking, and speaking. The scriptures envision the world as a sacrificial place in which Brahman performs numerous sacrifices (actions) through the beings, with himself acting as the upholder (yajna bhrta), the priest, the offering, the offered, and the witness. He is the source of all sacrifices (karmic actions) and sacrificial food (energy). He is also the yajna bhokta, the ultimate recipient and enjoyer of all actions and sacrificial offerings. Therefore, if we do not relinquish ownership and doership and offer the fruit of our actions to him, we will become responsible for our actions, incur karma, and remain bound.

Now, to the terminology used in this verse. Knowledge of the sacrifices and the ritual terminology is found in the Srauta and Grihya Sutras. Yajna means any sacrificial action, rite, or ritual ordained by the Vedas and the Smritis (law books). Each sacrifice consists of three important components: dravya (sacrificial material), devata (deity), who is invoked or receives the offering, and tyaga (the act of sacrifice). In this verse, Lord Krishna said that he represents all three. The materials and the utensils (ayudha) used in them depend upon the type of sacrifice and the deities involved. Kratu is a type of yajna only, in which fire is not used. The offerings (dravyas) made in them, such as the Soma juice or the methods used to perform them, were probably unconventional and not originally approved by the first three Vedas. They are also shorter in duration compared to elaborate and complicated sacrifices, such as some fire sacrifices, horse sacrifices (asvamedha yajna), and coronation sacrifices (rajasuya). Svadha is a benediction or utterance originally made in connection with the offerings of food (pinda) and water (tarpana) made to ancestors to ensure their well-being in the ancestral heaven and safe return from there. It may also be used in connection with some other rituals.

Aushadham means any medicinal plant, herb, or substance used to prepare medicine. More specifically, it may refer to the herbs used in performing soma rituals to improve life and longevity, magical rituals to cure diseases, snake bites, etc., or remove impurities (dhosas) and evil influences. It is also said that aushadham stands for all types of food since it has medicinal value and serves as a medicine. Mantra means any vehicle of sacred thought, word, text, utterance, sound, or syllable, packed with the power of Brahman to manifest things or fulfill desires. They are of various types and are found in the Vedic hymns (Rics, Yajus, Samans, and Nigadas). The mantras are the heart of the Vedic rituals. When uttered properly and in unison, they create powerful vibrations and awaken the deities who preside over them. Ajyam is the melted butter, ghee, or oil poured into the sacrificial fire. Hutam is also an offering, a burnt offering purified by fire. It may consist of food grains, pieces of meat (symbolic or real), or any solid substances dropped into the sacrificial fire. They are collected at the end of the sacrifice and consumed by the worshippers as the remains of the sacrifice.

Sloka 17

pitāham asya jagato mātā dhātā pitāmahaḥ
vedyaṃ pavitram oṃkāra ṛk sāma yajur eva ca

pita = father; aham = I; asya = of this; jagatah = universe; mata = mother; dhata = supporter; pitamahah = grandfather; vedyam = to be known; pavitram = sacred, pure; om-kara = symbol of Aum; rk = the Rg Veda; sama = the Sama Veda; yajuh = the Yajur Veda; eva = certainly; ca = and.

I am the Father, Mother, Supporter, Grandfather of this universe, the One to be known, the sacred one, the symbol of Aum, surely the Rigveda, Sama Veda, Yajurveda, and...

This verse mentions the first three Vedas only. Atharvaveda, the fourth one, is not mentioned. However, Shankaracharya suggested that the word 'ca' at the end of the verse implied the inclusion of Atharvaveda. Originally, the Vedas were only three: Rigveda, Samaveda, and Yajurveda. Atharvaveda was subsequently added, maybe due to the influence of outlier cultures the migrating Vedic tribes met during their eastward and southward migration into the plains of India. This verse suggests that some portions of the Bhagavadgita were probably composed before the fourth Veda was widely accepted as a part of the Vedic litany, and its status as a Sruti was fully established. In this verse, Lord Krishna describes himself as the Father,

Mother, Supporter, Grandfather of this universe, the One to be known, the sacred one, the symbol of Aum, and the triple Vedas. As the Supreme Purusha, the creator and source of all, he is the Universal Father. As the Supreme Mother, the womb of all existence, he is the Universal Mother. He is the supporter (dhata) because everything rests in him while he rests upon none. His materiality supports the whole manifestation while he nourishes all beings with food, prana, and energies. He is the grandsire (pitamaha) because he is the first, foremost, before all, and the ancestor of all beings and human races. As the father of Isvara, Hiranyagarbha, Viraj, Brahma, and other gods, he is surely the Universal Grandfather of all. He is the One to be known through the Vedas (vedyam) because by knowing him only, beings (jivas) attain liberation. He is sacred and auspicious (pavitram) because he is without impurities, free from any association or attachment. One becomes pure and resplendent like him by knowing him, attaining him, or by his mere touch or glance. He has the form of Aum because by meditating upon him as Aum, yogis attain the supreme state of pure consciousness. He is the triple Vedas because Brahman is their subject, object, cause, support, and purpose. The purpose of these descriptions is to remind his devotees that they should practice exclusive devotion, with no other thought, connection, or interest, renouncing their families, attachments, and relationships.

Sloka 18

gatir bhartā prabhuḥ sākṣī nivāsaḥ śaraṇaṃ suhṛt
prabhavaḥ pralayaḥ sthānaṃ nidhānaṃ bījam avyam

gatih = goal; bharta = the husband; prabhuh = Lord; saksi = the witness; nivasah = the abode; saranam = the refuge; su-hrt = the friend or well-wisher; prabhavah = the origin or source; pralayah = dissolution; sthanam = the foundation; nidhanam = the source of riches, treasure chest, storehouse; bijam = the seed; avyayam = imperishable.

I am the Goal, Husband, Lord, Witness, Abode, Refuge, Friend, Origin, Dissolution, Foundation, Source of all wealth, the Imperishable Seed.

In this verse, Lord Krishna lists 12 of his divine attributes. They are ideal for contemplation. Gati means goal or direction, or movement. Brahman is the highest goal (paramartham) for devotees and seekers of liberation. He is the one to whom all actions should be offered, for whom all actions are performed, and to whom all devotees are attracted. Ignorant people choose Dharma, Artha, and Kama as their goals and remain bound, but those who choose him as the highest goal attain him only. He is also the ultimate goal of the whole creation, since it will eventually dissolve in him only. Bharta means a husband or one who supports and nourishes. The Supreme Lord nourishes and supports all creation. As Isvara, Prakriti's Supreme Lord and husband, he creates, controls, supports, and destroys all manifestations with his indomitable will. Hence, the role of the husband (bharta) fits him perfectly. In Shaivism, Lord Shiva is described as Pati, the husband or the lord of all creation. He is the witness (sakshi) because, as the Self of all, he witnesses all that happens or does not happen without participating in them while controlling all existence from outside. He is the Abode (nivasa) because the whole creation exists in him. The material universe is meant for his habitation only. Hence, devotees extol him as Srinivasa, the Supreme Dweller of the heart of Lakshmi (materiality). He is also the ultimate refuge (saranam) for saints, sinners, and devotees alike, who protects them, within and without, from evil-doers. All things and beings in creation arise from him and subside in him like waves upon an ocean. Hence, he is the origin and dissolution of everything. He is the best companion and well-wisher (suhrt) anyone can have since he readily and selflessly helps those who approach him and pray to him in the hour of need or in times of adversity. He is the ground (sthanam) or the foundation on which everything rests. All this belongs to him, rests in him, and depends upon him. He is Lord of Opulence (Bhagavan) and the source of all abundance. Hence, he is the treasure chest (nidhana). He is the imperishable seed (bija) because, unlike the ordinary seeds that disintegrate or transform into saplings while germinating, he remains inexhaustible, immutable, and indestructible even while serving as the seed of all existence.

Sloka 19

tapāmy aham ahaṃ varṣaṃ nigṛṇhāmy utsṛjāmi ca
amṛtaṃ caiva mṛtyuś ca sad asac cāham arjuna

tapami = provider of the heat; aham = I; aham = I; varsam = rain; nigrhnami = stop, restrain; utsrjami = send down; ca = and; amrtam = immortality; ca = and; eva = certainly; mrtyuh = death; ca = and; sat = existence, being; asat = nonbeing, non-existence; ca = and; aham = I; arjuna = O Arjuna.

I am the source of heat, I restrain and release rain, and O Arjuna, certainly I am immortality and death, existence, and non-existence.

Brahman is the source of light and heat. In the macrocosm, he is the source of heat from the sun and other self-luminous bodies. In the beings, he is the source of the physical and spiritual heat (tapas) arising from sattva, which keeps the beings alive and safe from Death. The heat produced from austerities and yogic practices cleanses the mind and body and leads to immortality, but that produced due to impurities causes fever, sickness, and death. He is also the Lord of the rains, having the power to restrain or release the waters from rain-bearing clouds. Weather gods, such as Indra, Vayu, Varuna, Maruts, and the Rudras, follow his will only. At the highest level, he is the eternal, Supreme Self and the Lord of Immortality who grants liberation to the embodied souls. In the mortal world, he is the Lord of Death (kala), who devours everything as his food and keeps the mortal beings chained to the cycle of births and deaths.

Sat and Asat are relative terms. They are variously translated as existence and nonexistence, being and non-being, and manifested and unmanifested. Brahman is invisible and imperceptible, but cannot be nonexistent since He is eternal and immutable. What is said to be nonexistence is a type of existence, or a state of Brahman, which is unknown and imperceptible to the human mind and intelligence since it is beyond their grasp and knowing. However, nonexistence is possible in the mortal world. Whatever happened and disappeared, did not happen, or is not found in the world, is nonexistent.

Shankara interpreted Asat as the past and future, which are currently nonexistent. Most scholars agree that in the macrocosm, Asat is Nirguna Brahman, who is unknown and about whom nothing can be said with certainty. He is unreal or untrue (Asat) because his existence cannot be validated by any means. Sat is Saguna Brahman, who manifests in the field (kshetra) of Prakriti with modes, qualities, names, and forms. His subtle form is imperceptible and nonexistent for the human mind, but the opposite is true about his material manifestations since they are within reach of the mind and senses. The two words also denote the two primary states of Brahman, namely the presence or absence of individuality and beingness. In human beings, Sat refers to the wakeful state of the mind in which one experiences duality and separation, and asat to an indeterminate state, such as the deep sleep state, in which nothing is experienced. The indeterminate state is said to be the original state of Brahman, which is beyond all descriptions and comprehension. The gods (and perhaps even the wakeful Brahman himself) are unaware of the Supreme State of Brahman.

Sloka 20

traividyā māṃ somapāḥ pūtapāpā yajñair iṣṭvā svargatiṃ prārthayante te puṇyam āsādya surendralokaṃ aśnanti divyān divi devabhogān

trai-vidyah = the knowers of the triple Vedas; mam = to Me; soma-pah = drinkers of soma; puta papah = purified of sins; yajnaih = with sacrifices; istva = worshiping; svah-gatim = the goal of heaven; prarthayante = pray for; te = they; punyam = good karma, merit; asadya = having reached; sura-indra = of great god Indra; lokam = the world; asnanti = enjoy; divyan = celestial; divi = divine; deva-bhogan = heavenly pleasures.

The knowers of the triple Vedas, drinkers of Soma, purified of their sins, worship Me with sacrifices, praying for the heavenly goal. Having reached the world of the great god Indra (by virtue of) good karma, they enjoy divine and heavenly pleasures.

In this verse, Lord Krishna mentioned the third type of devotee. In verses 13 and 14, he mentioned the great souls (mahatmas) who worship him with exclusive devotion (ananya bhakti). In verse 15, he mentioned those who pursue knowledge and contemplate upon him variously as one, distinct, and many. Here, he mentioned karma yogis who worship him with obligatory duties, desiring heavenly life to enjoy heavenly pleasures. Their devotion is inferior since it is tinged with desires. However, since they cleanse their sins by performing their obligatory duties as ordained by the scriptures and accumulate meritorious karma, they attain the heaven of Indra as they wish and enjoy heavenly pleasures. Upon returning from there, they will attain a good birth in their next life and continue their journey. It is not the best option, but it is certainly better than the existence obtained by those mentioned in verse 12, who fall into the lower hells due to their sinful actions and evil nature.

In the previous Chapter (8:26), Lord Krishna described two eternal paths, which he called white and black. By following the first, he said the departed souls would attain Brahman and never return, but by the second, they would return to take another birth. In this verse, he spoke about the second path reserved for the karma yogis, who ascend to the heaven of Indra, performing virtuous deeds (punya kriya) such as studying the triple Vedas, drinking Soma juice, and performing sacrificial rituals. When people perform such actions with selfish desires or intent, they do not achieve liberation. Instead, they accumulate merit (punyam) and earn the right to ascend to Indra's world and enjoy heavenly pleasures. As Lord Krishna previously stated, such gains are temporary since, after exhausting their merit, they return to the earth to take another birth.

The Vedic texts are not unanimous about what happens to karma yogis (bound souls) after they depart from here. Some passages in them suggest that they would ascend to the ancestral heaven (pitrlok), and some suggest that they would attain the world of gods (devlok) or Indra (Indralok). This verse supports the latter view. Some accounts suggest that warriors ascend to the warriors' heaven (virsvarg) upon their death on the battlefield. While the Vedas mention the immortal world of Brahman as the highest world and the destination of liberated souls, Shaiva and Vaishnava texts mention it as Kailasa and Vaikuntha, respectively. They may be speaking of different heavens or the same heaven with different names. The earliest Vedic hymns identify subterranean worlds, the earth, the mid-region inhabited by celestial beings, the ancestral world, Indra's heaven, and the immortal world of Brahman.

Sloka 21

te taṃ bhuktvā svargalokaṃ viśālaṃ kṣīṇe puṇye martyalokaṃ viśanti evaṃ trayīdharmam anuprapannā gatāgataṃ kāmakāmā labhante

te = they; tam = that; bhuktva = having enjoyed; svarga-lokam = heavenly world; visalam = vast; ksine = being exhausted; punye = their good karma; martya-lokam = mortal world; visanti = reenter, fall down; evam = thus; trayi = in the three Vedas; dharmam = religious duties; anuprapannah = following sincerely; gata-agatam = going and coming, death and rebirth; kama-kamah = desiring enjoyments; labhante = they attain.

Having enjoyed that vast heavenly world, with their good karma exhausted, they reenter the mortal world. Thus, following the religious duties prescribed by the three Vedas, desiring enjoyment, they attain the state of going and coming.

Heavenly life is not forever. It is a temporary reward earned by people for their good deeds (punya karma) to enjoy a brief respite in heaven from the suffering that is inherent in mortal life. Those who live piously and perform their obligatory duties according to the code of conduct prescribed by the scriptures earn that reward. Once their good karma is exhausted, they return to the earth to take another birth. It is like a deposit we put in the vaults of heaven to earn a passage into it. This verse explicitly states that only good karma (punyam) is exhausted during the stay in Indra's world. It means we cannot easily get rid of sinful karma (papam). It must be exhausted through suffering in samsara or a lower world. People should be aware of this and avoid sinful actions to the extent possible. Further, one should not take heavenly life for granted because there are no guarantees. People may still go to hell due to the karma accumulated over several lives, even if they earned the fruit of good karma in this life. Afterlife in the ancestral or Indra's heaven is a resting period that provides the jivas with a temporary respite from the suffering they experience in samsara. It is like a pleasant dream at the end of which one must return to the reality of the mortal world and the difficulties one must face. It does not resolve all karma, especially sinful karma. It only exhausts your good karma and leaves you with less good karma and more bad karma at the start of your next life. Therefore, liberation is always the best option, in which you square all your karma and arrest its further formation through karma-sannyasa, renunciation of desires, and desireless actions (nishkama karma). One should permanently escape from transmigration or the state of going and coming.

Sloka 22

ananyāś cintayanto māṃ ye janāḥ paryupāsate
teṣāṃ nityābhiyuktānāṃ yogakṣemaṃ vahāmy aham

ananyah = without any other; cintayantah = thoughts; mam = Me; ye = who; janah = people; paryupasate = worship everywhere; tesam = their; nitya = at all times, always; abhiyuktanam = absorbed in devotion; yoga-ksemam = wellbeing and safety; vahami = take care; aham = I.

Those people who worship Me everywhere and at all times without any other thoughts, ever absorbed in devotion, I take care of their well-being and safety.

In this verse, Lord Krishna has assured that he would take care of the welfare of all those who dedicate their minds and bodies to him and worship him exclusively all the time, with their minds absorbed in his thoughts. In general usage, yoga-kshema is translated as peace and happiness. In a philosophical sense, yoga is translated as the attainment of what one does not have, and kshema as having the assurance or security of what one already has. Madhavacharya defined them as such. According to him, the Lord grants liberation and secures immortality for his devotees who worship him without desires and attachments, but grants Indra's heaven for those who engage in sacrifices and worship him to fulfill their desires. According to Shankara, since exclusive devotees worship him without desires and attachments, the Lord secures and guarantees their yoga (liberation) and kshema (immortality) for them.

These words of Lord Krishna may lead to the erroneous conclusion that the Supreme Lord is partial to his purest devotees. The Lord is impartial and equal to all. He treats all beings equally as their Father, Mother, and Grandfather, according to the laws he ordains, whether they worship him or have devotion to him or not. Similarly, he ignores or remains indifferent towards the deluded and ignorant ones who hate him, dislike him, disbelieve him, disrespect him, do not worship him, show hostility to him, or assume doership and ownership of their actions. He is equal to all. He lets them live according to their nature if they desire worldly things, enjoy the fruit of their actions, or wish to claim ownership and doership of their actions. However, he cares for those who approach him, surrender to him, take refuge in him, make sacrifices to him, worship him, sing his praises, meditate on him, or offer the fruit of their actions to him. To those who worship him exclusively with purity, faith, and unwavering devotion, he takes personal responsibility for their lives and grants them liberation and immortality.

In other words, you can move the Lord with pure devotion and unconditional allegiance. Otherwise, he remains equal to all but indifferent, unmoved, and impassive like a statue or idol in a temple. Through unconditional surrender and exclusive devotion, you can draw his attention, melt his stone-like heart, and earn his love. When his devotees approach him with devotion, he listens to their prayers and supplications and responds according to their faith, devotion, and resolve. If they perform sacrifices and make him offerings, wishing to fulfill their desires, he grants them their desires and ensures a place for them in heaven. If they engage in desireless actions (nishkama karma) through karma-sannyasa, practice self-discipline, and worship him with exclusive devotion, for them, he opens the doors of liberation and ensures their safe journey to the immortal world or the highest heaven. In this verse, by using the word 'vahami,' he clearly stated that he would personally carry the burden of looking after his pure devotees' needs and well-being, not through another agency.

The Mother of Sri Aurobindo Ashram once used the analogy of kittens in a speech to exemplify true surrender. She said that without any hesitation, the kittens give themselves up completely to their mother's care and let her carry them to safety by holding their necks with her teeth. The kittens would not know what would happen to them or where she would carry them. Yet they would trust her completely out of love and let her do her work. Ananya bhaktas do the same. They trust the Lord completely and let him take care of their yoga and kshema without any fear, doubt, or anxiety. They surrender to him and worship him with unwavering faith, not knowing what would happen to them and whether he would take care of them. That kind of blind trust and devotion is difficult for most humans in whom the ego is still active. Yet, some devotees exemplify it by silencing their egos and developing exclusive faith and devotion. This verse is meant for them. They do not complain if their prayers are unanswered or if they are put to great suffering due to their prarabdha karma. They endure suffering, accept all outcomes as the will of God or the fruit of their karma, continue to worship him exclusively with unwavering devotion, and wait patiently for the Lord to fulfill his promise of liberation and immortality.

Sloka 23

yepy anyadevatābhaktā yajante śraddhayānvitāḥ
tepi mām eva kaunteya yajanty avidhipūrvakam

ye = those; api = even; anya = other; devata = divinities; bhaktah = devotees; yajante = worship; sraddhaya anvitah = endowed with faith; te = they; api = also; mam = Me; eva = only; kaunteya = O son of Kunti; yajanti = worship; avidhi-purvakam = ignorantly or in an inappropriate manner.

Even the devotees who worship other divinities endowed with faith - they also, O son of Kunti, worship Me only (although) inappropriately.

All the divinities are Brahman's manifestations only. In their highest and absolute aspect, they are Brahman only. Those who worship them also worship Brahman since their offerings are ultimately received by him only. However, if they worship them as different gods or lesser gods, their yoga-kshema is not guaranteed by him. Some overenthusiastic devotees of Lord Krishna interpret this verse to mean that only Lord Krishna should be worshipped, and worshiping other deities such as Lord Shiva, Vishnu, or Brahma is inappropriate. While they are free to do so, they cannot claim that only Lord Krishna is the Supreme Lord and others are inferior. Brahman has no absolute name. The name Brahman itself is not a name. It refers to the highest, formless, invisible, eternal, indestructible, State or Supreme Reality from which everything manifests. Brahman means one who cannot be surpassed, who is limitless, and who is always ahead of all so that no one can ever know his beginning or end. In the Vedas, Brahman is revered as the Supreme Self and the ultimate recipient of all offerings, but not revered directly as a deity. Only his forms or manifestations are worshipped. In the cosmic hierarchy, they belong to different levels or spheres, but any of them can be worshipped as Brahman or the Supreme Being. According to the Mahabharata and Puranas, Lord Krishna is an incarnation of Lord Vishnu, or Narayana, in his role as the Supreme Lord. According to some Vaishnava sampradayas, he is none other than the Supreme Lord, who manifested upon earth to restore Dharma and teach people the secrets of devotion and liberation. These are sectarian views that entered mainstream Hinduism in the last few centuries. What is meant in this verse is that one should worship Brahman or the Supreme Self, who goes by different names but is always one and only. All the divinities we revere in Hinduism are but his manifestations only. They can be worshipped as the highest Supreme Lord or as individual deities. The former approach is common in Hinduism's sectarian traditions, namely Shaivism, Vaishnavism, Shaktism, and Ganapatya. The latter is an inferior approach practiced in popular and polytheistic methods of worship. It produces an inferior result and leads to rebirth.

Sloka 24

ahaṃ hi sarvayajñānāṃ bhoktā ca prabhur eva ca
na tu mām abhijānanti tattvenātaś cyavanti te

aham = I am; hi = indeed; sarva = of all; yajnanam = sacrifices; bhokta = enjoyer; ca = and; prabhuh = the Lord; eva = even; ca = and; na = not; tu = but; mam = Me; abhijananti = know; tattvena = in eternal aspect, in reality; atah = therefore; cyavanti = fall; te = they.

I am indeed the enjoyer and the Lord of all sacrifices, but they do not know Me in truth. Therefore, they fall.

Although people worship him and make offerings to him, they do not truly know him, his supreme reality, his relationship with other gods, or the fact that they can overcome bondage and attain immortality by attaining him. Hence, they keep falling into samsara, birth after birth. This is the essence.

Lord Krishna, as Brahman, is the Supreme Lord and the ultimate enjoyer of all our sacrifices and actions. Since he is the indweller of all, including the gods, the lord of sacrifices (Adhiyajna), and the ultimate enjoyer (bhokta), he participates and enjoys all the sacrificial offerings people make to Agni, Indra, Soma, etc. People do not know him because he is invisible, unknown, indescribable, transcendental, and remains hidden from the mind and senses. As he described in a previous verse, he is the sacrificer, the sacrificed, the facilitator of the sacrifice, the remains of the sacrifice, and the ultimate recipient of all sacrificial offerings. Therefore, the most appropriate way to perform sacrifices is to recognize the truth (tattva) of all the deities and remember Brahman as the hidden divinity in them while worshipping them or making them sacrificial offerings. Only true devotees who overcome desires and attachments and cultivate discernment know that the gods are his manifestations only but not equal to him. Therefore, they worship the Supreme Lord only and make their offerings to him, even when they perform the traditional sacrifices as prescribed by the Vedas. They perform sacrifices and duties like karma yogis, but make offerings to Brahman only without desiring their fruit. Since they see the Supreme Lord in the whole creation, including all gods and beings, and are constantly engaged in exclusive devotion, acknowledging no other god, they earn his love and grace and quickly attain liberation.

Sloka 25

yānti devavratā devān pitṛn yānti pitṛvratāḥ
bhūtāni yānti bhūtejyā yānti madyājinopi mām

yanti = achieve; deva-vratah = the worshipers of divinities; devan = to the divinities; pitrn = to ancestors; yanti = go; pitr-vratah = worshipers of the ancestors; bhutani = to spirit world; yanti = go; bhuta-ijyah = worshipers of spirits; yanti = go; mat = My; yajinah = devotees; api = only; mam = to Me.

The worshippers of the divinities go to the divinities; the worshippers of the ancestors go to the ancestors; the worshippers of spirits go to the spirit world. My devotees come to Me only.

Our minds play an important role in creating our future. What we think mostly, we become. Our predominant thoughts sow the seeds of our future and our destinies. As they are strongly etched in our consciousness due to our repetitive thinking, they become our latent impressions (samskaras) and sources of our karma and our becoming and being. Only those yogis achieve oneness or the highest self-absorption (dharma mega samadhi) when they overcome the impurities of their minds and bodies, resolve the gunas and karma through exclusive devotion, and enter the pure consciousness of Brahman. Only they can burn the seeds of rebirth and the impurities of egoism, attachments, and delusion.

Previously, Lord Krishna stated that whatever people remembered at the time of death, they would go to them only. The mind has the power to manifest its most predominant thoughts and desires. Therefore, at the time of their death, people will most likely remember their beloved deities or dear ones and attain their worlds. Those who worship perishable gods go to their perishable worlds and remain in their company until the end of Kaliyuga. Those who are attached to ancestors (pitrs) and worship them or make their offerings go to them and stay there until their good karmas are exhausted. Those who are into worshipping spirits (bhutas) join them in the spirit world and return when their next birth is due. However, the knowers of Brahman, who are forever absorbed in his thoughts and devotion, attain his immortal realm and remain there forever.

Therefore, one must remember these words of Lord Krishna, worship the Supreme Lord only, and refrain from worshipping gods, ancestors, spirits, demigods, local deities, nature gods, village deities, etc. Polytheism, or worshipping numerous gods, is an important aspect of popular Hinduism and is accepted as a legitimate but inferior practice. It is ideal for beginners and ignorant people to practice karma yoga so they can gradually purify themselves and divert their attention from Dharma, Artha, and Kama to Moksha. They may worship the gods through sacrifices and make offerings to them to fulfill their desires and enjoy worldly pleasures. The tradition approves the practice for worldly people as preparatory for their spiritual purification and transformation. However, those who desire liberation should purify their minds and bodies through study(svadhyaya), withdrawal of the mind and senses, detachment, discernment, renunciation (karma-sannyasa), and self-control. They should worship or meditate exclusively upon the Supreme Lord with unwavering devotion until they attain sameness or oneness (samadhi).

Sloka 26

patraṃ puṣpaṃ phalaṃ toyaṃ yo me bhaktyāprayacchati
tad ahaṃ bhaktyupahṛtam aśnāmi prayatātmanaḥ

patram = a leaf; puspam = a flower; phalam = a fruit; toyam = water; yah = whoever; me = to Me; bhaktya = with devotion; prayacchati = offers; tat = that; aham = I; bhakti-upahrtam = offer made in devotion; asnami = accept; prayata = pious, holy, pure; atmanah = of the soul.

Whoever offers Me with devotion a leaf, a flower, a fruit, water, I accept that offer of the pure soul made in devotion.

Here, the Lord tells us that he will readily accept whatever devotees offer to him, be it a leaf, flower, fruit, or just water. He specified only two conditions. The devotees must be pure souls or have a pure heart (prayata atmana). Second, they must offer it lovingly out of pure devotion (bhakti-upahrtam). If these two conditions are met, it does not matter how they conduct the worship or what offerings they make. In other words, it is not the value of the sacrifice but the attitude with which it is given. Sacrificial rituals (yajnas) are complex. One has to follow elaborate procedures and require the assistance of one or more officiating priests. Even then, mistakes can happen, and one has to perform expiatory rituals to avoid sinful consequences. Such difficulties do not arise in the worship of the Supreme Being. He accepts whatever you offer him, in whichever way you choose, as long as your heart is pure and you make the offering with pure devotion (suddha bhakti), without selfish desires and intentions.

The word 'bhakti' is used twice in this verse to emphasize its importance. Devotion, which is pure and exclusive, will neutralize the faults and mistakes of a devotee since the Supreme Lord is ever-forgiving, friendly, and compassionate. He will accept whatever you offer him wholeheartedly in exclusive devotion, with a pure heart and mind. Thus, the true test of worship is whether you unconditionally love God and worship him as your very Self with an unwavering mind. There must be a direct, heart-to-heart connection with him without the mediation of any intermediaries. Some traditions hold that liberated souls live in the immortal world near the Lord, establishing a heart-to-heart connection with him and enjoying the same bliss and consciousness internally.

The four objects mentioned in this verse (leaf, flower, fruit, and water) are standard offerings in Hindu ritual worship. He mentioned them to convey that the offerings do not have to be special, and no special arrangements need to be made to procure them. Devotees can offer him what is readily available and convenient. They can even make a symbolic mental offering as an alternative if nothing is available. A similar idea is found in the Srimad Bhagavatam (4.31.21), in which Narada declares that Sri Hari does not accept the service of ill-minded people who are deluded by their knowledge, wealth, and high birth, or disrespect his devotees who worship him exclusively. In the same scripture, Lord Krishna states that while he accepts the smallest gifts from his devotees, the best offerings from the insincere ones do not please him.

According to the Vedas, God made humans and gods to depend on each other mutually. Humans can make food, but do not have adequate powers over Nature's forces. They cannot make the rains fall or the seasons change. In contrast, the gods have power over the elements and natural forces. They can make the rains fall or the seasons change, but they cannot make food for themselves in heaven. Humans enjoy food, peace, and happiness due to the gods' actions and intervention. Hence, the Vedas make it obligatory for humans to cook food and offer it to them first through sacrifices before eating it. By that reciprocation, they will discharge themselves from the karmic debt they owe to the gods. The gods discharge their debt to humans by fulfilling their desires and keeping the earth green. Hence, in the Vedic rituals, the emphasis is not on the purity of the heart or devotion but on whether the gods and humans fulfill their mutual obligations by helping each other by performing their obligatory duties. Devotion is secondary in ritual sacrifices. The emphasis is on the purity of intention, pronunciation, and procedure, and the proper selection of mantras, materials, ritual types, and their specific order. In devotional worship, the emphasis shifts from external to internal and from ritual procedures to spiritual purity and devotion. The Lord does not require any nourishment. He does not depend upon anyone. By nature, he is not easily pleased with rituals and procedures that are devoid of devotion, purity, or personal connection. He is pleased by pure devotion, which is free from desires and expectations.

Sloka 27

yat karoṣi yad aśnāsi yaj juhoṣi dadāsi yat
yat tapasyasi kaunteya tat kuruṣva madarpaṇam

yat = whatever; karosi = you do; yat = whatever; asnasi = you eat; yat = whatever; juhosi = sacrificial offering you make; dadasi = you give as charity; yat = whatever; yat = whatever; tapasyasi = austerities you perform; kaunteya = O son of Kunti; tat = that; kurusva = do; mat = to Me; arpanam = offer.

Whatever you do, whatever you eat, whatever sacrificial offering you make, whatever you give as a charity, whatever austerities you perform, O son of Kunti, offer that to Me.

When you perform an action, think that God is working through you and performing that action. When you eat, think that he is responsible for that food and eating it through you. When you perform a sacrificial ritual, austerity, or domestic ritual, think that he is performing it through you, it is for him and by him, and he is the offering and the object of that offering. Whatever charity you give, remember that he gives that through you and gives that to himself, since he also resides in the being who receives it. Hence, you should not claim any reward, gain, ownership, or doership from your actions. Let that offering or action be for God, by God, and with God. By that supreme sacrifice, you will be free from karma and samsara.

In karma-sannyasa yoga, householders are advised to offer God the fruit of their obligatory duties as ordained by the Vedas. In this verse, Lord Krishna stated that his devotees should offer him whatever they do, eat, offer to the gods, give as charity, or the austerities they perform. In other words, one must dedicate everything one has, and whatever one is, to the Lord as a mark of devotion, sacrifice, surrender, and renunciation. By offering ownership and doership, devotees become free from their obligation to God and the consequences of their actions. In that uninterrupted sacrifice of their lives and actions, through the continuous offering of their love and devotion, and absorbing their minds in the continuous worship of the Lord, they exemplify exclusive devotion, selfless actions (nishkama karma), and earn his love and grace.

Devotees can offer their actions to God in different ways. They can offer them before, after, or while they are performed. They can do it explicitly while performing each action or implicitly by remembering him or thinking of him when they perform them. It is better to surrender their egos to the Lord as an offering and let him become the true controller of their lives and actions. By letting go of their wills, identities, desires, and attachments, and through renunciation, they can empty themselves and let the Lord fill them with his radiance and loving awareness. The idea is simple. When you surrender your ego to God, consecrate your life to him, and offer him your actions as a token of your devotion and surrender, you elevate karma-sannyasa yoga to a higher level. You infuse your thoughts and actions with supreme devotion, letting him live through you and manifest your destiny according to his will. By surrendering your ego, you become empty or nonexistent while he fills that emptiness with his supreme presence and power. If your offerings are pure, selfless, and free from desires and attachments, the Lord will readily accept your offerings. He already promised his devotees that he would accept anything given to him sincerely and with a pure heart.

The Isa Upanishad declares that all this belongs to the Supreme Lord. Hence, in the mortal world, we should perform actions, acknowledging and remembering this truth. Whatever happens here, every thought we think and every action we perform happens because of him. He is the source of all. We live in him and depend upon him. Therefore, we cannot truly claim anything here as ours, although it is human nature to live with desire and expectations and seek love, belongingness, ownership, appreciation, and enjoyment. These attitudes bind us to samsara. However, by making little adjustments to our thinking and outlook, we can bring God into our lives and transform our thoughts and actions into sacrificial actions. Sacrifice is the road to freedom and happiness. It is the basis of sannyasa, karma-sannyasa, surrender, and selfless devotion. Through sacrifice, we become empty, unburden our karmas, and free ourselves.

Sloka 28

śubhāśubhaphalair evaṃ mokṣyase karmabandhanaiḥ
saṃnyāsayogayuktātmā vimukto mām upaiṣyasi

subha = good, auspicious; asubha = evil, inauspicious; phalaih = fruit; evam = thus; moksyase = you become liberated; karma bandhanaih = bondage caused by actions; sannyasa = renunciation; yoga = yoga; yukta-atma = with the mind established; vimuktah = liberated; mam = to Me; upaisyasi = will attain, come.

Thus, you become liberated from the bondage caused by the fruit of both good and bad actions. With your mind established in the yoga of renunciation and being liberated, you will come to Me.

In the previous verse, Lord Krishna suggested that you should offer to him whatever you do, whatever you eat, whatever sacrificial offering you make, whatever you give as charity, and whatever austerities you perform. We also understood why it is necessary. When you offer your actions to him as a sacrifice, knowing that he is the source and cause of all, you transfer your burden of karma to him and earn his mercy, support, and protection. It is the best way to escape from the wheel of karma and samsara. When you renounce the fruit of your actions and offer them to the Supreme Lord, actions will not bind you, whether you perform ordained or prohibited actions. It does not mean God is showing any special favors to his devotees. He is equal to all but makes sure that people are rewarded according to their actions. If they live for themselves, they will be responsible for their actions. If they live selflessly, then God will take care of them and lead them on the path of liberation. Therefore, it is up to you how you want to live your life. If you want to escape from samsara, you must renounce desires, live selflessly as a true devotee, become a truth Bhagavata, and serve him with exclusive devotion.

From this verse and the previous ones, one can see that, in the Bhagavadgita, sannyasa yoga takes precedence over all other yogas. Other yogas, namely karma, jnana, atma-samyama, and bhakti yogas, become effective when they are practiced by renouncing desires and attachments. Renunciation (sannyasa) of desires is the key to attaining sameness or perfection in samadhi. Whether one practices karma, jnana, bhakti, or any other yoga, the desires hidden in our thoughts and actions must be renounced. Devotion is of several kinds. The purest devotion manifests in us only when we are filled with pure love, free from desires and attachments. Some believe that by the mere practice of devotion, one can cultivate detachment and renunciation. They encourage devotees to engage in devotional activities, suggesting that those actions eventually lead to exclusive devotion. While it may be true, here Lord Krishna explicitly advised Arjuna to practice nishkama karma (desireless actions) by offering his actions to him so that his mind would be established in renunciation, and he would attain him only. Therefore, one should follow his instruction and overcome desires through renunciation to attain perfection in any yoga.

Sloka 29

samohaṃ sarvabhūteṣu na me dveṣyosti na priyaḥ
ye bhajanti tu māṃ bhaktyā mayi te teṣu cāpy aham

samah = equal; aham = I am; sarva-bhutesu = to all being; na = none; me = to Me; dvesyah = hateful; asti = is; na = none; priyah = dear; ye = those; bhajanti = worship; tu = yet; mam = to Me; bhaktya = in devotion; mayi =exist in Me; te = they; tesu = in them; ca = also; api = certainly; aham = I.

I am equal to all beings. None is hateful to Me, none is dear. Those who worship Me with devotion - they exist in Me, and I exist in them.

I am equal to all beings, which means all beings are the same to me. I have no favorites. His statement, "None is hateful to Me, and none is dear," means I am indifferent, unattached, unemotional, and uninvolved; I am free from likes and dislikes and do not harbor any feelings towards anyone; therefore, all are the same to me. However, he also says that those who worship him with devotion, He exists in them, and they exist in Him. It means devotion is important, and through devotion, a devotee can draw His attention. Although He is equal to all and detached from everything, an irresistible connection forms between Him and His devotees, and He responds to them according to their devotion. Thereby, He lives in their hearts just as they live in His.

Does this mean that God is partial to his devotees? The answer is No. The Lord mirrors all and responds to them according to their devotion. As he already said, he responds to them in whatever way they approach him. Jivas are bound to their nature and karma. Their devotion also depends upon them, and so is his response. He treats them according to their karma, faith, purity, and predominant nature. As the Lord of the Universe who protects and upholds Dharma, he implements all the laws equally and impartially and rules the universe without discriminating against anyone.

The absolute state of Supreme Brahman is complete, perfect, independent, and all-inclusive. It does not exclude anything or reject anything in particular because nothing can exist by itself or outside. He personifies the choiceless and desireless state of completeness, purity, perfection, and fulfillment. Some traditions may claim that God is partial to his devotees and supports them in their fight against nonbelievers or those who despise him. Therefore, they act as if they have a God-given right to indulge in wars and violence in his name. This is delusional. The Supreme Being is without a second. He is not in competition with anyone. No one can equal him or compete with him. Therefore, it is wrong to believe that he expects humans to punish others for their beliefs. The Lord does not despise or discriminate against anyone, even the worst sinners. He actively helps those who constantly remember him and worship him with devotion, but remains passive and indifferent toward those who worship material things or lesser gods to fulfill their selfish desires. He may help when people pray with devotion, but does not harm if they do not. Thus, he impartially implements the laws he sets in motion and lets our actions and devotion determine our fate. His devotees are never lost because it is one of the laws he enforces dutifully. Similarly, the sinners are never ignored if they reform and return to the virtuous Path.

As the Vedas proclaim, Brahman is the Supreme Lord of all and Creator of the whole manifestation. He is comparable to the sun, who shines upon all equally when they come into his light. Whoever seeks his light receives warmth and love, but whoever shies away from it remains in darkness. Therefore, it is not God but our thoughts and actions that create the difference. If we want to secure his help or earn his love and attention, we must uphold Dharma and follow the laws with which he governs the world and our lives and destinies. We may learn them from life, experience, observation, study, or others. Knowing which laws and actions lead to liberation and which ones lead to bondage and suffering, we must cultivate discernment and engage in righteous actions to ensure that we do not punish ourselves with our indiscretions.

True devotees of God are constantly absorbed in his contemplation. They are never separate from him because they surrender to him and dissolve their egos, sense of separation, and duality in him. By their thoughts and acts of devotion, they overcome duality and attain oneness, whereby they remain in him, and he remains in them without distinction. Others who cannot overcome their egos, desires, or identities remain bound, ignorant, and deluded. There is no otherness in Brahman. It exists only in our minds because of our delusions. Only when you drop your name and form and all the layers of protection and security you build around yourself do you qualify for God's true love. When you cultivate purity to the extent that you cannot reflect anything but the radiance of your pure Self and devotion to him, he becomes a part of your life and consciousness. Until then, you remain bound to your mind, body, and limited individuality.

A yogi who follows the path of knowledge is as qualified to attain liberation as a true devotee who practices unconditional devotion. In the journey of liberation, you first travel by the path of knowledge to reach the state of true devotion. When you truly know him as your very Self, you become devoted to him and dissolve in him. Therefore, remember that Brahman does not punish anyone in particular for not following him or not surrendering to him. We punish ourselves through our egoistic and desire-ridden thoughts and actions, and to the extent we fail to abide by His Dharma and follow His laws.

Sloka 30

api cet sudurācāro bhajate mām ananyabhāk
sādhur eva sa mantavyaḥ samyag vyavasito hi saḥ

api = even; cet = if; su-duracarah = a person of very evil conduct; bhajate = worship; mam = Me; ananya-bhak = single minded devotion; sadhuh = good, pious; eva = surely; sah = he; mantavyah = to be considered; samyak = rightly; vyavasitah = decided, determined, resolved; hi =for; sah = he.

Even if a person of very evil conduct worships Me with single-minded devotion, surely, he is to be considered pious because he has rightly resolved.

The significance of exclusive devotion (ananya bhakti) in the redemption of sinners is explained in this verse. It has two important messages. One, the Supreme Lord maintains an unbroken connection with his devotees, who are exclusively devoted to him. Two, because of their unwavering devotion, their relationship remains intact even if they suffer moral degradation or fall into evil ways. In other words, a kevala bhakta who has fallen into evil ways still has a chance for redemption if his devotion to him is intact and undiminished, and he resolves to persevere in it. He enjoys divine protection from the Lord through exclusive devotion, even if his conduct is questionable. Even if he is not a kevala bhakta previously but cultivates exclusive devotion and worships him with an unwavering mind, he still has a chance to redeem himself and qualify for liberation.

Thus, one can see that in yoga or on the path of liberation, unwavering devotion to the Supreme Lord takes precedence over everything. Character, conduct, virtue, morality, or righteousness are important for progress on the path, but exclusive devotion triumphs over them. There can be many reasons for a person's sinful actions. It can be due to karma, divine causes, or the times in which we live. It can also be a part of God's play. In contrast, one does not become an exclusive devotee by mere providence. Kevala bhakti is the fruit of intense self-effort, mostly against circumstances and providence. Sustaining it is even more difficult, especially when one falls into evil ways. Therefore, due credit must be given to the exclusive devotee who falters on the path and falls into evil ways (suduracara) but whose devotion to the Supreme Lord remains undiminished and who still worships him with unwavering devotion (ananya bhakti). He should still be considered a good person (sadhu) because his heart and mind are still filled with pure devotion, and he is still under God's protection. Hence, as this verse affirms, moral conduct may not compensate for the lack of devotion, but pure devotion can neutralize the ill effects of moral turpitude and evil nature.

This distinction is limited to the kevala bhaktas, whom Lord Krishna described in verse 22 of this chapter as those who are ever absorbed in his devotion and worship him everywhere and always without any other thought. He also assured in the same verse that he would take care of their well-being and protection (yoga kshema) because they are always absorbed in his thoughts and do not think of themselves. Here, he reiterated that assurance, stating that even if they temporarily deviated from the path of righteousness, they would still be considered his devotees because the seed of devotion is still alive in them and because they are still connected to him internally with their minds absorbed in him. They might have abandoned the righteous path, but not their exclusive devotion to him. He previously said there was no loss on the path of liberation, and those who falter in this life could return and restart from where they left off. In the next verse, he confirms that they would never perish because they would quickly recover from their evil ways and attain liberation.

A pure devotee (mahatma) never loses his connection with the Supreme Being, even if he is pierced by evil. He is still his devotee and has a chance for redemption since the Lord is especially forgiving towards his kevala bhaktas, even if they temporarily lose their way. Just as a father forgives his errant children, he forgives those whose minds are fully established in him, even if they have temporarily fallen into evil ways due to circumstances. Since they have not forsaken him and their devotion is undiminished, he will not forsake them. He knows that the world is mired in Maya, and even the best of his devotees may suffer from delusion and temporary lapses in their conduct. He is pleased if they still worship him and remain devoted to him despite their transgressions, since, as he said before, they are in him, and he is in them. Hence, he keeps the door of liberation open for them and protects them. Exclusive devotees only enjoy this protection and assurance from the Supreme Lord. According to the Epics and the Puranas, many demonic beings, such as Kamsa and Ravana, secured liberation despite their evil conduct because of their exclusive devotion. Putana, a demoness who died in the hands of Lord Krishna, also attained liberation because, in her previous birth, she was a devotee of Maha Vishnu. Here, the word ananya bhakti is important. Those who despise God or envy him have no such luck. Divine protection is guaranteed if devotees are rightly resolved to worship the Lord exclusively. Their unwavering allegiance and devotion to him protect them from harm, even if they fall into evil ways.

The use of 'samyak vyavasitha' confirms it. Samyak means right, fitting, apt, or appropriate. Vyavasita means resolve, decision, determination, etc. The resolve to worship the Supreme Being arises from the right knowledge and right discernment induced by sattva (purity). Ordinary people worship numerous gods according to their convenience or desires, but true bhaktas worship only the Supreme Lord, seeking nothing in return. There is no place in them for any other deity or thing. By nature, they do not indulge in evil actions or fall into sinful ways. They do not willingly harm anyone since they renounce the world and overcome desires and attachments. However, in rare circumstances, they may engage in evil actions because of their own karma or unresolved evil disposition (asura prvritti) or divine providence, as in the case of Jaya and Vijaya, Lord Vishnu's doorkeepers. This verse assures such unfortunate souls that they would still be protected if their resolve to worship him exclusively was intact.

The verse also leads to another conclusion. Those who fall into evil ways and commit mortal sins may still have a chance to redeem themselves by returning to God and cultivating exclusive devotion. They can overcome their evil nature and earn the Lord's love by cultivating ananya bhakti, remembering him always. Evil people (suduracara) cannot easily establish undistracted devotion to the Supreme Being. However, there is no better option for them to escape from the consequences of their evil actions or prolonged suffering in the lower worlds than following the path of pure devotion. One of the blessings of mortal life is that it offers us many choices to improve ourselves through self-effort. We have the intelligence and discernment to learn from our mistakes and failures and improve our chances of liberation. Even a vile and evil person has an opportunity to worship Isvara with single-minded devotion and save himself. As deluded souls caught in the play of Maya and forced by circumstances, we are bound to make mistakes and deviate from our spiritual goals. However, through pure devotion, we can still turn to God to save ourselves.

Sloka 31

kṣipraṃ bhavati dharmātmā śaśvacchāntiṃnigacchhati
kaunteya pratijānīhi na me bhaktaḥ praṇaśyati

ksipram = promptly, quickly; bhavati = becomes; dharma-atma = pious soul, a person of righteous conduct; sasvat-santim = everlasting peace; nigacchati = attains; kaunteya = O son of Kunti; pratijanihi = know for certain; na = never; me = My; bhaktah = devotees; pranasyati = perish.

Very quickly, he becomes a person of righteous conduct and attains everlasting peace; O son of Kunti, know for sure that My devotee shall never perish.

A kevala bhakta who turns into a duratma (evil person) quickly becomes a dharmatma (righteous person) and attains everlasting peace if he continues to worship him with exclusive devotion and rightly resolves to return to the righteous path and engage in righteous conduct, renouncing desires and desire-ridden actions. Knowledge, righteousness, and renunciation of desires are helpful in achieving self-purification, but devotion is required to earn the Lord's love, support, and redemption if necessary. Through devotion only, one can overcome the evil nature or its consequences. The Bhagavadgita makes God a partner in the devotees' effort to achieve liberation. Without him, their journey will be difficult and uncertain. Without devotion (bhakti) and his support, as these teachings suggest, wicked people (duratmas) have no hope. Through devotion only, they can overcome their evil nature, become righteous ones (dharmatmas), and cross the ocean of samsara. Lord Krishna stated here that devotees who worship him with undisturbed, supreme devotion achieve liberation even if they do not abide in righteous conduct, provided they repent for their evil actions and mend their ways. As they intensely worship the Lord with unwavering devotion and seek his forgiveness, he reciprocates their devotion and helps them escape from the mire of samsara. In other words, the devotees of the Supreme Beings who take refuge in him and practice exclusive devotion (kevala bhakti) do not perish for temporary lapses in their judgment or conduct. The Lord protects them and sets an example for other devotees so they do not lose hope and continue their practice, knowing that he will ensure their well-being (yoga kshema) and liberation. By using the word 'pratijanihi,' meaning proclaim loudly or know for certain, Lord Krishna conveyed to Arjuna not to worry about the moral consequences of killing his relations or elders in the war, such as Bhishma or Drona. He also implied that he readily forgives evil people if they are exclusively devoted to him and repent of their ways, but not those who hate him and are not devoted to him.

Sloka 32

māṃ hi pārtha vyapāśritya yepi syuḥ pāpayonayaḥ
striyo vaiśyās tathā śūdrās tepi yānti parāṃ gatim

mam = Me; hi = surely; partha = O Partha; vyapasritya = by taking shelter; ye = who; api = even; syuh = becomes; papa-yonayah = sinful wombs; striyah = women; vaisyah = vaisyas; tatha = and; sudrah = sudras; te api = even; yanti = go; param = highest; gatim = Goal.

Surely, O Partha, by taking shelter in Me, even those who are born from sinful wombs, women, Vaishyas, and Sudras, even they reach the highest Goal.

In this verse, Lord Krishna further amplified the idea that evil people (duratmas) would be saved from their wickedness if they practiced single-minded devotion to him, emptied their minds of all evil thoughts, and became pure souls (mahatmas). He promised to rescue those born in adverse circumstances if they took refuge in him and worshiped him, suggesting that he would even make an exception to their karma in such rare cases. While through good karma, people can secure a good life in the next birth, through exclusive devotion, everyone, even those with a history of sinful karma, can seek redemption and achieve liberation. Prahlada was born into a family of demons. Yet, he exemplified pure devotion to Lord Vishnu and was rescued by him from his father's cruelty, who despised the Lord and treated his devotees with contempt. Many Hindu sages and saints were born into underprivileged families, but it did not hinder them from practicing pure devotion and achieving liberation.

Some scholars often use verses such as these to justify the Hindu caste system. Just as the Mahābhārata, of which it is a part, the Bhagavadgita underwent several alterations and iterations after it was originally composed in the remote past. Therefore, we should not invent excuses to rationalize some of its assertions about castes, social order, women's condition, etc., knowing that it is not a shruti and, in certain aspects, it reflects the beliefs and conditions in which it was composed rather than indisputable truths. While people may have caste prejudices, the Lord does not treat them according to their status, caste, or gender. He previously affirmed that all are equal to him, and none is hateful or dearer. He also said that whoever worships him with devotion lives in his heart, and he in theirs. In this verse, he stated that he would liberate all his devotees who take refuge in him and worship him, irrespective of their birth or caste.

This verse shows that, spiritually, exclusive devotion to the Lord far outweighs all other yogas. It will purify them, remove their defects (dhosas), and neutralize their evil nature, sinful karma, and any sin that may accrue due to their living in adverse circumstances and amidst impure people. A devotee who worships the Lord exclusively with unwavering devotion is far superior to all other classes of human beings, irrespective of caste, birth, status, or achievement. In the esteem of the Lord, devotion to him far outweighs all the riches in the world and all other material or spiritual considerations. The Lord's exclusive devotees enjoy a special relationship with him. He promptly rescues them from the evils of the world, even if they temporarily succumb to evil nature due to the play of Maya. They live in his protection and contemplation, just as he lives in them as their witness.

Sloka 33

kiṃ punar brāhmaṇāḥ puṇyā bhaktā rājarṣayas tathā
anityam asukhaṃ lokam imaṃ prāpya bhajasva mām

kim = how much; punah = again, repeated; brahmanah = brahmanas; punyah = meritorious, virtuous; bhaktah = devout; raja-rsayah = saintly kings; tatha = and; anityam = transient; asukham = sorrowful, joyless; lokam = world; imam = this; prapya = gained, obtained; bhajasva = worship; mam = Me.

How much can then be repeated about the virtuous Brahmanas and the devout saintly kings? Having gained this impermanent and sorrowful world, you should worship Me.

If the most sinful and ignorant people can attain the goal of final liberation through exclusive devotion and by taking refuge in the Lord, what else can further be said about those pious and pure Brahmanas and kings who attain these exalted positions because of their past karma, and who still lead virtuous and holy lives and who are exclusively devoted to him even while living in an impermanent and sorrowful world filled with Maya? They must have secured favorable circumstances in this life due to their pious acts and devotional service to the Lord in their past births, and they will surely enjoy his protection and attain liberation since they are exclusively devoted to him. Following their example, the Lord says Arjuna should also worship him exclusively. This verse describes the world as an impermanent, joyless, or sorrowful place (anityam asukhaṃ lokam). Those who attained it are already unfortunate, even though some, like the pious Brahmanas and the dutiful kings, may be better placed than others. Because of their past karma and pious actions, they are all already qualified to earn the Lord's mercy and compassion. Therefore, if they take a little initiative and worship him with exclusive devotion, they will readily earn his love and protection. Having entered this sorrowful world by the quirk of fate or their past sins, humans should strive to escape from it by taking refuge in the Lord, the only place of comfort and peace available to them in this sad and dreary world. Lord Krishna explains how one may do it in the following verse.

Sloka 34

manmanā bhava madbhakto madyājī māṃ namaskuru
mām evaiṣyasi yuktvaivam ātmānaṃ matparāyaṇaḥ

mat-manah = with your mind absorbed in Me; bhava = be; mat = to Me; bhaktah = devoted; mat = to Me; yaji = make sacrifices; mam = to Me; namaskuru = salutations; mam = to Me; eva = certainly; esyasi = come; yuktva

= being absorbed; evam = thus; atmanam = within the Self; mat-parayanah = Me as the supreme Goal.

With your mind absorbed in Me, be devoted to Me; make sacrifices to Me; (and) offer Me salutations. You will certainly come to Me, absorbed thus in the Self, with Me as your Supreme Goal.

There is no distinction between the Self and the Supreme Self. One should contemplate upon the Self as the Lord. That way, one can simultaneously practice contemplation and devotion to him. If you treat him as if he is different from you, which many devotees do, you may experience devotion through duality, seeing the Lord as someone other than you or different from you. In so doing, you may miss the true experience of sameness or oneness (samadhi). In this verse, Lord Krishna mentioned six supreme requirements or practices necessary to excel in exclusive devotion. They are man-mana bhava, mat bhakti, mat yaji, mam namaskaram, atmanam yukta, mat parayanah.

Manmana bhava means absorbing the mind in the contemplation of the Supreme Lord with exclusive devotion. For that, the mind must be filled with the thoughts of the Supreme Lord only and should not be distracted by any other thought or object. When an exclusive devotee meets other people, he sees the Lord only in them and remembers him rather than them or their distinctions. Whatever he perceives in the objective realm draws his mind to the thoughts of the Lord and keeps him engaged in his contemplation.

Mat bhakti means to remain supremely devoted to the Lord, remembering his name, singing his greatness, extolling his virtues, contemplating his forms and manifestations, listening to his glories, and spending time in the company of other devotees. Kevala bhaktas do not take pleasure in reading the scriptures or engaging in fruitless conversations to gain intellectual knowledge. They are forever drawn to the Lord's thoughts and remain absorbed in them.

Mat yaji means worshipping him mentally or ritually and exclusively as a true bhakta, dasa (domestic help), friend (sakha), or Bhagavata (servant of God) through sacrifices, devotional worship, austerities, charity, prayers, devotional service, visiting or serving in the temples, making offerings, serving the Lord's devotees, etc. Kevala bhaktas do not worship gods and demigods. They worship the Supreme Lord only, even when they worship them.

'Mam namaskaram' means offering salutations by folding and joining the hands, prostrating before the Lord's images or statues with humility, love, and selfless devotion, or circumambulating his abodes (temples) or sacred places that are associated with his incarnations and manifestations. Humility is an important aspect of devotion. One cannot truly surrender to the Lord or practice pure devotion without humility.

Atmanam yukta means to remain firmly established in the Self, withdrawing the mind and the senses. Exclusive devotees are bhakti yuktas excelling in unwavering devotion. They envision him everywhere as the omnipresent Lord and cultivate a reverential attitude toward everything. Their minds are never separate from his thoughts. They cultivate nearness to him, envisioning him as their very Self, and remain absorbed in that idea without duality or division. By that, they form an emotional connection with him and remain drawn to him.

'Mat parayana' means always looking to him as the goal or the final destination. The Lord personifies the ultimate state of freedom and self-existence. By attaining him, one is free forever. Therefore, he is considered the ultimate or the highest goal (paramartha), by attaining which nothing else needs to be achieved. He is the goal, the object of liberation, and the purpose of human life.

Those who excel in these six virtues are exalted devotees (Bhagavata). No one is dearer to the Lord than them. They exemplify pure devotion and self-sacrifice, the ultimate sacrifice. In ancient times, bhaktas used to sacrifice themselves as a token of their unconditional devotion and to become pure by liberating themselves from the last vestige of impurity, the body itself. Some used to self-immolate themselves in the fire. Nowadays, in the age of Kaliyuga, symbolic self-sacrifice is sufficient. It means one should mentally give up all the baggage one carries within oneself, such as one's identity, family, belongings, ownership, doership, pride, individuality, etc. By offering them to the Lord in the fire of pure devotion, the devotee disentangles himself from the world to remain centered in the supreme state of kevala bhakti.

To become absorbed in the pure consciousness of Brahman and attain oneness through exclusive devotion, devotees have to let go of desires and passions, which strengthen egoism and delusion. To cultivate the highest purity and absorb their minds in the purity of the Self, they must remove the barriers that hold them back and prevent them from attaining oneness. Kevala bhakti means there must be no place in the heart and mind of a devotee for anything other than the Supreme Lord, not even the thoughts of himself or anything that he owns, claims, defends, protects, or desires. When he is thus free from all the attractions and diversions, having completely given himself up to the Supreme Lord from all sides with complete faith and trust, he qualifies to enter the purest form of self-absorption (samadhi) and dissolves into oneness. In that pristine state of indistinguishable consciousness, he will let the pure brilliance of the Self shine through him, without any cloud of obstruction or interference, just as the sun radiates its light in a bright and clear sky.

If your mind is active and defensive or possessive, you cannot achieve union with the Self. If you hold on to anything other than the Lord or remain attached to your physical identity or name and form, you cannot attain the supreme state of indistinguishable nonduality and union with the Lord. Only the purest devotees attain it. When they find the Lord within themselves, they will find him everywhere and be one with him. Through that unadulterated, unconditional, and natural state of unified consciousness, they will free themselves from the impurities that hold the deluded ones in ignorance, delusion, and bondage.

Conclusion

iti srīmadbhāgavadgītāsupanisatsu brahmavidyāyām yogasāstre srikrisnārjunasamvāde rājavidyārājaguhyayogo nāma navamo 'dhyayah

iti = thus; srīmadbhāgavadgītā = in the sacred Bhagavadgita; upanisatsu = in the Upanishad; brahmavidyāyām = the knowledge of the absolute Brahman; yogasāstre = the scripture of yoga; srikrisnārjunasamvāde = the dialogue between Sri Krishna and Arjuna; rājavidyārājaguhyayogo nāma = by name yoga of sovereign knowledge and sovereign mystery; navama = ninth; adhyayah = chapter.

Thus ends the ninth chapter, named Rājavidyā Rājaguhya Yoga (the Yoga of Sovereign Knowledge and Mystery) in the Upanishad of the divine Bhagavadgita, the knowledge of the Absolute, a treatise on Yoga, and the debate between Arjuna and Lord Krishna.

10 – Vibhuti Yoga

The Yoga of Divine Manifestations

Sloka 1

śrībhagavānuvāca
bhūya eva mahābāho śṛṇu me paramaṃ vacaḥ
yat tehaṃ prīyamāṇāya vakṣyāmi hitakāmyayā

sri-bhagavan uvaca = The Divine Lord said; bhuyah = again; eva = indeed; maha-baho = O mighty-armed; srnu = listen, hear; me = to My; paramam = most profound, supremely important, essential; vacah = words; yat = which; te = to you; aham = I; priyamanaya =who is deeply interested; vaksyami = speak; hita-kamyaya = wishing your welfare.

The Supreme Lord said, "O mighty-armed, listen to My most profound and important words which I will speak to you, wishing your welfare, and which will surely delight you."

In the seventh to the ninth chapters, Lord Krishna revealed the mysteries, the mystic and abstract knowledge of the imperishable Supreme Brahman, his essential nature, his lordship and opulence, and his sovereign status as the source and support of all, and the importance of worshipping him and meditating on him instead of gods, demigods, and others. In this chapter, he will further reinforce that knowledge, describing his numerous manifestations in Prakriti. These chapters help devotees cultivate a broader understanding of the Lord, establish their minds in his contemplation, and cultivate exclusive devotion. While the knowledge in the previous chapters helps them understand Brahman subjectively as the all-pervading and enveloping omniscient, transcendental Lord, the source and support of all, and see him within themselves as their very Self, the knowledge in this chapter will help them envision him objectively, contemplate upon his manifestations, and feel his presence around them.

Both types of knowledge are essential to knowing and meditating on the significance and opulence of the Supreme Lord and strengthening one's faith, resolve, and devotion. Lord Krishna wanted to teach this supreme knowledge to Arjuna to help him see the play of God everywhere and in everyone while performing his warrior's duty on the battlefield. He wanted him to fight with faith and supreme devotion as an offering and obligation to Dharma, taking refuge in him and remaining exclusively devoted to him. This verse presents some difficulties for a translator due to its construction. Lord Krishna told Arjuna to listen to his words, which were profoundly important since they would help him discern the presence of Brahman in the manifested world and understand his importance. He said it would be for his good (hitam) only since it would help him cultivate devotion and feel assured by his presence around him. He also said that Arjuna would be pleased to hear those sweet words (priyamana) since he knew that devotees are always fond of listening to the words about the glories and greatness of the Supreme Lord who lives in their hearts and minds.

Sloka 2

na me viduḥ suragaṇāḥ prabhavaṃ na maharṣayaḥ
aham ādir hi devānāṃ maharṣīṇāṃ ca sarvaśaḥ

na = not; me = My; viduh = know; sura-ganah = the multitude or assembly of gods; prabhavam = origin, supreme power; na = not; maha-rsayah = great seers; aham = I am; adih = first, the root, the source; hi = certainly; devanam = of the gods; maha-rsinam = of the great seers; ca = and; sarvasah = in all respects.

The multitude of gods do not know My origin, nor do the great seers. I am certainly the first among the gods and the great seers in all respects.

A father knows the birth of his children, but the children do not know their father's birth. They may hear about it from their father or others. The Supreme Lord is the father of all and before all. There is none other than him. Therefore, who can know his origin or where he came from? We may speculate about him, but we cannot be certain of our knowledge about him. As he stated here, not even the assembly of gods and great seers know his origin or his 'prabhava,' meaning origin, greatness, power, glory, or radiance, because he is their creator. They manifest from him much later. It does not mean that they do not know him at all. Just as children know about their father vaguely through multiple sources, they may possess some knowledge of Brahman but do not know him fully or the extent of his powers, glory, and opulence.

The Vedas suggest that even the most eminent gods know little about him. The Kena Upanishad describes an incident in which Indra, Agni, and Vayu had a chance encounter with Brahman, who appeared before them as a Yaksha. Not knowing who he was, they tried to demonstrate their powers to him but failed. When he disappeared, goddess Uma manifested in the sky and revealed to him who he was. Thus, the gods exist because of him but do not know him, just as the organs in the body exist because of the Self but do not know him at all. Of all the gods, only Indra (the mind) learned about the Self from Brahma (intelligence), with great difficulty, through speculation, trial, and error.

The great seers may realize or experience the Supreme Reality of Brahman through contemplation and self-absorption. However, since their knowledge is limited to their experience, they cannot fathom what is unknowable, ungraspable, indescribable, and infinite. The mind and senses have limited reach. Hence, even in the objective realm, they cannot fully grasp the mysteries and the extent of his creation. The physical universe is so vast, complex, and diverse that no extent of scientific study, inquiry, or understanding will help us know its depth and dimensions. We may speculate about it and know certain aspects, but only partially. Even though we live in it, perceive it through our senses, and are enveloped by it from all sides, the material universe is largely a mystery, just as Brahman is. If this is the case with the physical universe, one can imagine the problem in comprehending Brahman's supreme reality, which is beyond our reach. He is unknowable because he cannot be objectified or grasped in a state of duality.

Brahman is certainly the most mysterious Being. Nothing can be said about him with certainty since he contains all possibilities and dualities within himself. He represents all dualities and contradictions, the known and the unknown, the real and the unreal, and the manifested and the unmanifested. The Upanishads reflect the difficulty. The Kena Upanishad states that Brahman is other than the known and above the known. Those who think they know him may know him, but little, and those who think they do not may probably know him. The multitude of beings caught in the web of samsara either do not know him or do not know that they do not know. Brahman is unknowable because he is the earliest of all, the source of all, and beyond all. Therefore, no one knows him until they attain him.

Sloka 3

yo mām ajam anādiṃ ca vetti lokamaheśvaram
asaṃmūḍhaḥ sa martyeṣu sarvapāpaiḥ pramucyate

yah = who; mam = Me; ajam = unborn; anadim = without a beginning; ca = and; vetti = knows; loka maha-isvaram = Supreme Lord of the worlds; asammudhah = undeluded; sah = he, that; martyesu = among the mortals; sarva-papaih = from all sins; pramucyate = is freed.

Whoever knows Me as the unborn, without a beginning, and as the Supreme Lord of the worlds, that undeluded one among the mortals is freed from all sins.

Whoever (yah) means great souls (mahatmas), adept yogis (yuktas), wise ones (jnanis), devotees (bhaktas), etc., who are devoted to the Supreme Lord, worship him, do not despise him, and have the wisdom to know who he is. Unborn (ajam) means not subject to birth or rebirth like the jivas, gods, etc. Anadi means without a beginning or eternally existent. Maheswaram means not just a lord (Isvara) of some realm but the Great Lord or the Lord of the Lords. They know him thus because they are undeluded (asammudha). They are freed from sin because they practice desireless actions (nishkama karma) through karma-sannyasa, acknowledge him as the doer and owner of all, and offer him the fruit of their actions.

The Supreme Lord is unborn and eternal. The testimony of the Vedas validates it. Hence, we accept it as an eternal truth. Although he occasionally reincarnates upon earth, he is still unborn because birth and death are for the body, not for the Self. All other gods, except the Supreme Self, have a beginning and an end. The Supreme Lord (Maheswara) manifests them at the beginning of creation and withdraws them into himself in the end. Therefore, they are incomparable to him and cannot be considered eternal. Knowing him thus, a discerning devotee does not worship gods and demigods. He fixes his mind upon him with single-minded devotion (kevala bhakti) and strives to attain him. The deluded ones (mudha) do not know him or his essential nature because of impurities. They worship material things, gods, demigods, etc., and pursue Dharma (sacrifices), Artha (wealth), and Kama (pleasure) to fulfill their desires and escape from suffering. They remain bound and sinful without the right knowledge and awareness, ignoring their own spiritual nature, engaging in desire-ridden actions, and living for themselves with vain hopes, actions, and knowledge.

Sloka 4

buddhir jñānam asaṃmohaḥ kṣamā satyaṃ damaḥśamaḥ
sukhaṃ duḥkhaṃ bhavobhāvo bhayaṃ cābhayam evaca

buddhih = intelligence; jnanam = knowledge of Brahman; asammohah = freedom from delusion; ksama = forgiveness; satyam = truthfulness; damah = control of the body; samah = control of the mind, equanimity; sukham = pleasure; duhkham = pain, sorrow; bhavah = existence, birth; abhavah = non-existence, death; bhayam = fear; abhayam = fearlessness; eva = even; ca = and.

Intelligence, knowledge, freedom from delusion, forgiveness, truthfulness, control of the body, control of the mind, pleasure, pain, birth, death, and even fear and fearlessness...

This verse has to be read in conjunction with the next. In these two verses, the Lord explained the qualities manifesting from his higher nature to Arjuna. In his absolute and eternal state as Brahman, the Supreme Lord (Isvara) is the source of all. Therefore, although he stated that certain qualities manifested from him, it does not mean that other qualities or their opposite ones do not arise from him. He particularly mentioned these for the benefit of his devotees so that they could contemplate them and cultivate them to achieve purity and nearness to him.

As the transcendental Supreme Self, in his absolute state as Brahman, the Supreme Being is free from qualities, dualities, modes, desires, limitations, and emotional states. Therefore, in his pure state, he is called Nirguna Brahman (Brahman without qualities and modes). He is also without names and forms (nirakara) and said to be unmanifested (asambhuta). However, the Saguna Brahman, with qualities and modes, manifests from him with higher and lower nature as the Supreme Lord and Creator of all. He casts the net of delusion and unleashes Prakriti to produce duality, diversity, names and forms, and different states of existence and inexistence (bhava and abhava). He creates worlds and beings by manifesting and concealing them in different states and with the admixture of gunas and tattvas. The qualities mentioned here are intelligence, knowledge, freedom from delusion, forgiveness, truthfulness, control of the bodily organs, control of the mind, happiness (or pleasure), sorrow, birth, death, fear, and fearlessness. Most of them are self-explanatory. We will focus on the important ones.

Intelligence (buddhi) is the highest tattva of Nature. It is the closest to Brahman's pure intelligence (prajna) but inferior to it, and common to both humans and gods. It gives us the ability to recognize and distinguish things, names, and forms, and make sense of experiential reality. Damah and samah are the twin aspects of self-control (atma-samyama), without which one cannot stabilize the mind or control desires. Through dama (restraint of the body and bodily organs), we achieve sama (equanimity). One may note that the dualities of pleasure and pain or happiness and sorrow arise from the Supreme Lord only. Both open our eyes to the reality of samsara and strive for liberation. Fear of God, sin, and retribution help us to practice dama and sama. Fearlessness helps us resist evil and the demons of our minds and stabilize them. Thus, these qualities are interrelated and complementary. For example, with discerning intelligence, one acquires knowledge of the Self. With the knowledge of the Self, one controls the mind and body and overcomes egoism, fear, and delusion to excel in forgiveness, truthfulness, etc.

These qualities lead to the realization of Brahman or Self, but they do not exist in him. They may manifest in his aspects and projected forms in Nature. Although they arise from him and manifest in his manifestations, he is unaffected by them. So is the embodied Self. It remains untouched by the actions and modes of the mind and body or their impurities. In many ways, the Supreme Reality of Brahman is antithetical to His creation and manifestations. If Brahman is the Self, His creation is the not-self. If Brahman is indistinguishable and unexpressed (asambhuta), His manifestations are distinguishable and distinct (sambhuta).

The absolute Brahman does not create the worlds or participate in them, except maybe as the witness Self. The Supreme Lord (Isvara), who manifests from himself in union with Prakriti (sambhuta), is the source of all that exists and manifests. He is the wielder of Maya and the source of dynamism, activity, beingness, and awareness, which beings (jivas) experience as real. Both good and evil arise from him only. We experience pain and pleasure, or fear and fearlessness, because of him only. He is the source of the chit-shakti or the consciousness infused with dynamism and awareness (chaitanyam), where the sense objects leave their impressions, and the gunas exert their influence to create different states of being (bhava), beingness, and modifications. As the all-pervading and all-encompassing Supreme Self, Brahman watches over us while we pass through the cycle of births and deaths numerous times, carrying the burden of our impurities, moral failings, and sinful karma. Just as we create dreams in our sleep, the Supreme Lord, Isvara, creates the worlds and beings in his surface consciousness and watches them over as their Lord, witness, and enjoyer.

Sloka 5

ahiṃsā samatā tuṣṭis tapo dānaṃ yaśoyaśaḥ
bhavanti bhāvā bhūtānāṃ matta eva pṛthagvidhāḥ

ahimsa = nonviolence; samata = equanimity; tustih = contentment; tapah = austerity; danam = charity; yasah = fame; ayasha = infamy, disrepute; bhavanti = happen; bhavah = states; bhutanam = in living beings; mattah = because of Me; eva = only; prthak-vidhah = different types.

Nonviolence, equanimity, contentment, austerity, charity, fame, infamy, these different types of states arise in beings because of Me only.

This verse mentions seven additional qualities that manifest in the jivas from the Supreme Lord (Isvara). Of them, only one, ayasha, is negative. Nonviolence (ahimsa) means not injuring anyone mentally, verbally, or physically. It is considered the virtue of virtues since all other virtues lead to it only. Violence is inherent in the very process of our living and being. It is impossible to live in this world without hurting or harming anyone. Without exception, everyone engages in violence and destruction to secure daily necessities such as food, water, clothing, or shelter. Therefore, practicing nonviolence, which is difficult, is essential to purify and stabilize the mind in contemplating the Lord and escaping from samsara.

Equanimity or sameness (samata) means being equal to the pairs of opposites. It arises from detachment and the absence of desires, likes, and dislikes. By overcoming them, an adept yogi remains equal, indifferent, and undisturbed amidst the dualities of pain and pleasure, happiness and sorrow, or heat and cold. Tushti means being contented or satisfied with whatever one has. It is one of the distinguishing qualities of a kevala bhakta, which saves one from the evil passions of lust, anger, pride, greed, envy, etc. Contentment also arises from the absence of desires and attachments. Tapah refers to the practice of austerities with self-restraint, including nonviolence, sameness, and brahmacharya, which preserves and augments the fire or heat in the body (tapah) and channels it through subtle channels (nadis) to produce spiritual power, mental brilliance, and physical vigor. Charity (dana) is prescribed for humans since, through selfless giving, they can overcome selfishness, which is deemed an evil quality by the law books. The Lord personally exemplifies it by generously granting boons to his devotees and fulfilling their wishes. Yash (fame) and ayash (infamy) are opposites that manifest in humans due to their actions or their prarabdha karma. Therefore, fame may not arise due to virtue (dharma) or infamy due to evil (adharma).

These twenty qualities, which should be construed as illustrative since there are countless others, arise from the Supreme Being only. They exist in Prakriti and creation but not in Brahman, the Supreme Self. Just as the sweetness or sourness of a fruit does not exist in the tree that produces it, the qualities mentioned in these verses manifest in creation but do not exist in the absolute state of the Creator. This distinction is important because we should not mistake divinity for the divine. Divinity is a temporary projection, just as the names and forms. The divine is eternal, without modes and qualities. A devotee must cultivate them since they stabilize the mind in exclusive devotion to attain sameness with the Lord. However, they should remain fixed on liberation, the ultimate aim (paramartha). True liberation is liberation from everything, including our relative qualities, values, and morals. They are necessary to cultivate purity and overcome delusion, but are not an end in themselves. They manifest in us according to our actions, devotion, and prarabdha, but do not accompany us to the world of immortality.

Sloka 6

maharṣayaḥ sapta pūrve catvāro manavas tathā
madbhāvā mānasā jātā yeṣāṃ loka imāḥ prajāḥ

maha-rsayah = the great seers; sapta = seven; purve = before; catvarah = four; manavah = Manus; tatha = and; mat-bhavah = born of Me; manasah = from My Mind; jatah = were born; yesam = of whom; loke = on the world; imah = these; prajah = beings.

The seven great seers and the four Manus before them were born out of My Mind; from them were born all these beings of the world.

Lord Krishna delivered the discourse of the Bhagavadgita in the unified state of pure consciousness in which the duality of subject and object does not exist. In that state of indistinguishable oneness, nonduality, or unified self-consciousness, he spoke through the silence of his surface consciousness as one indivisible Self without duality, divisions, and distinctions. In that state, specific to incarnations and Brahman's highest manifestations, the deity remains firmly established in himself, without objectivity, duality, or otherness, and communicates as the Lord himself, without the interference of physical or mental noise. In samadhi, an adept yogi (yukta) enters the pure consciousness of the Self and becomes absorbed in it without duality. The knowledge that arises from it will be vague and indistinct. At best, it can be construed as mental absorption or deep silence. However, an incarnation does not have such limitations. He can enter his supreme consciousness by mere will and communicate from there as and when he chooses. He can shut it down and act as a normal being if necessary. This is the distinction. Hence, in the scripture, you will find Lord Krishna often speaking himself as the Supreme Lord and often as Lord Krishna, the person or a friend of Arjuna.

Being an incarnation who is ever established in the unified pure consciousness of the Supreme Self, when Lord Krishna said that all these great beings were born from him, we have to presume that he was referring to himself as the pure and resplendent Isvara, the Creator. He was speaking as Isvara, from Isvara's perspective, and with Isvara's consciousness. He was not channeling Isvara, which some yogis may appear to do in a trance. He was communicating with Arjuna as Isvara himself in a wakeful state, with his human faculties receding into the background and falling silent. If you are absorbed in the pure consciousness of the Self and can remain awake without duality and delusion, you may enter that state. However, it is beyond human capability. Lord Krishna is the manifested form. Isvara is his essential and unmanifested cosmic form, and Brahman is the transcendental Self, supporting both. This is the most plausible reason why Lord Krishna sometimes spoke to Arjuna as the Supreme Lord and sometimes as Krishna himself.

The Vedas do not say that the seers and Manus were born from Lord Krishna. According to them, they originated from Brahma, the creator god, and one of the trinity gods. Whether it is Lord Krishna, Brahma, Vishnu, or Shiva, they are Brahman in their highest and absolute aspect, and Isvara, the Creator and the Lord of the universe, in their manifested aspect. Hence, in popular

Hinduism, we venerate them as distinct deities, but in sectarian traditions, we venerate them as Brahman or the Supreme Lord. In the latter case, the fivefold functions of Isvara (creation, preservation, concealment, revealing, and destruction) are ascribed to them also.

The Vedas proclaim that the seven rishis and the four Manus originated from Brahma, who is but a manifestation of the Supreme Lord only. It is said that at the beginning of each Kalpa, which is equal to a day in the life of Brahma, the seven great seers (sapta-rishis) manifest from his mind. Since they are born from his mind, they are also known as Brahma's mind-born sons (manasaputras). Some accounts mention nine seers instead of seven, namely Bhrigu, Pulastya, Pulaha, Kratu, Angiras, Maríchi, Daksha, Atri, and Vaśishtha. Each played an important role in introducing the Vedas, establishing the Vedic tradition, and connecting the gods with humans through sacrifices. Being Brahma's mind-born sons, they passed on the knowledge of the Vedas from Brahma to humans to preserve the Sanatana Dharma. They are still revered in Hinduism as the deities of their respective lineages (gotras).

The Manus are the progenitors of human races in each time cycle. Although this verse refers to only four Manus, other scriptures mention six to fourteen of them. They appear in each cycle of creation in succession to rule the earth and introduce different human races. The reign of each Manu is known as a Manvantara, spanning millions of years. The current Manu, Vaivasvata, is the seventh in the line. After him, seven more Manus would rule the earth until the end. According to Vishnu Purana, each Manu springs from the mind of Brahma by himself as his replica. Therefore, they are also known as self-created (Svayambhu) Manus. They are also known as Prajapati Manus since they rule the world as the Lords (pati) of all beings (praja).

Sloka 7

etāṃ vibhūtiṃ yogaṃ ca mama yo vetti tattvataḥ
sovikampena yogena yujyate nātra saṃśayaḥ

etam = this; vibhutim = supreme powers, forms or manifestations; yogam = supreme state; ca = and; mama = My; yah = he who; vetti = knows; tattvatah = in truth, in reality; sah = he; avikampena = steadfast, unwavering, without wavering; yogena = in yoga; yujyate = united, absorbed, joined; na = not; atra = of this, regarding this; samsayah = doubt.

He who knows in truth My supreme powers, forms and manifestations, and supreme state, through unwavering and steadfast yoga, becomes united (with Me). Of this, there is no doubt.

Knowledge of the Supreme Lord is essential to cultivate exclusive devotion and achieve liberation. In pursuing liberation, we explore that knowledge until we experience it directly. In this verse, Lord Krishna said that whoever knows his powers and manifestations and his supreme state (yogam) as the infinite, Great Lord (Mahesvara) will undoubtedly unite with him. How shall he be known? We read in the previous verses that he should be known as the unborn, without a beginning and end, Lord of the worlds, creator of great seers and Manus, etc., and the source of qualities such as intelligence, knowledge, freedom from delusion, nonviolence, forgiveness, and so on. Knowing this, he said his devotees (kevala bhaktas) should meditate upon him with their minds absorbed in him, practicing unwavering devotion (kevala bhakti) with self-control (atma samyama) and renunciation (sannyasa). This chapter helps us know and meditate on his greatness and opulence, speak about him, emulate him, and strengthen faith and devotion.

Vibhuti means might, power, splendor, or greatness. It also refers to God's supreme powers, forms, qualities, and states, which even the divinities and seers may not know fully. His opulence, power, and splendors manifest as reflections in the gunas, Prakriti, and our minds and bodies when unhindered by samsara's impurities. They appear in us to the extent that we are pure and cultivate divine qualities. The Lord illuminates us just as the light of the Sun radiates in the world and the objects upon the earth according to their purity and inherent properties. In the incarnations, they manifest fully, which deluded people do not perceive and treat the Lord in them as a human being.

The powers of the Supreme Being are numerous and infinite. The Epics and the Puranas describe eight sovereign powers (ashta aisvaryas). They manifest fully in his highest manifestations and partially in his lower ones. They are 1. the power to become small or subtle (anima); 2. the power to grow large (laghima); 3. the power to attract, gain, or become heavy (prapti or garima); 4. the power to fulfill desires or manifest will (prakamya); 5. the power to grow in strength, splendor or size (mahima); 6. the power to command lordship or sovereignty (ishita); 7. the power to delude or overpower (vasitha), 8. and the power to control and suppress desires (kamavasayitha). They denote his omniscience, omnipresence, omnipotence, and his inviolable will. The Bhagavadgita also lists many attributes of Isvara, the Supreme Lord. We find some of them in the following verses.

Sloka 8

ahaṃ sarvasya prabhavo mattaḥ sarvaṃ pravartate
iti matvā bhajante māṃ budhā bhāvasamanvitāḥ

aham = I; sarvasya = of all; prabhavah = source, origin; mattah = because of Me; sarvam = all; pravartate = acts, moves, issues forth; iti = thus; matva = knowing; bhajante = worship mam = Me; budhah = the wise; bhava-samanvitah = filled with emotion or devotion.

I am the source of all, because of Me, everything acts according to nature. Knowing Me thus, the wise worship Me filled with devotion.

Lord Krishna delivered these messages in the unified state of consciousness as the Supreme Lord himself. Here, he declared himself as the material and the efficient cause of all creation. The devotees who worship him exclusively with unwavering devotion know that they owe their existence to him; their actions arise from him, and he cares for them. They know that he is the cause of all that happens to them and ensures their peace and happiness (yoga kshema) if they take refuge in him and worship him with gratitude and devotion, renouncing ownership and doership and offering their actions without desiring their fruit. To know that the Lord is the source of all is wisdom and humility, and to think that "I am the source of all and everything happens because of me" is a delusion. The former leads you nearer to the goal of liberation, and the latter farther away into bondage and suffering.

The second part of the verse suggests that the wise ones who overcome desire and delusion, acquiring the right knowledge from scriptures, self-study, and teachers, worship him with full devotion, acknowledging him as the giver and granter of all. The Vedas proclaim that the source of all is One, and the One becomes many. The Upanishads repeatedly affirm this. The classical Samkhya school does not recognize Brahman as the creator. According to them, all things arise in Nature and from Nature, except the individual souls, which are eternal, unborn, and indestructible. Just like many schools of Vedanta, the Bhagavadgita refutes this argument and recognizes the Supreme Lord, Bhagavan, as the source of all and Prakriti as his dependent reality. Since the wise ones with purified intelligence (buddhi) know this, they are not deluded.

If you are drawn to the names and forms of the material world, you cannot stabilize your mind in contemplation or worship the Supreme Lord, who is beyond all names and forms and distinctions. Egoistic acts of devotional service should not be confused with pure devotion in which no distinction remains between oneself and the Supreme Self. In the heart of a true devotee, the sense of separation does not exist; only Brahman exists. Therefore, only the wise ones succeed on the path of exclusive and unadulterated devotion. Pure devotion arises from the intense longing to join the Supreme Lord and live in his company. A devotee becomes a kevala bhakta only through purity, knowledge, discernment, detachment, self-control, and the will of God. Knowing that the world is God's creation, filled with his presence, he remains equal to dualities and disturbances as providence. His heart flutters with intense emotion when he thinks of Krishna, worships him fervently, or hears his names and descriptions. He seeks nothing but oneness and nearness to him.

Sloka 9

maccittā madgataprāṇā bodhayantaḥ parasparam
kathayantaś ca māṃ nityaṃ tuṣyanti ca ramanti ca

mat-cittah = mind absorbed in Me; mat-gata-pranah = senses or life-breaths devoted to Me; bodhayantah = trying to know; parasparam = among themselves; kathayantah = speaking ca = and; mam = Me; nityam = always; tusyanti = contented; ca = and; ramanti = delightful, take delight; ca = and.

With their minds absorbed in Me, their life-breath dedicated to Me, knowing (about Me) from one another and always speaking about Me, they remain contented, taking delight in Me.

With their minds absorbed in Me means with their minds engaged in Krishna's thoughts and contemplation; with their prana devoted to Me means devoting their senses, life breaths, or energies to his worship and devotional service; knowing about Me from one another means spending time or living in the company of like-minded devotees; always speaking about Me, means speaking about Krishna only with no other distraction or avocation. Drawn to him thus, his exclusive devotees remain contented, dedicating their lives and energies to his contemplation and devotion, without desiring sense objects and seeking nothing but his company or presence.

Thus, this verse describes how the wise ones devotionally worship Lord Krishna, the Supreme Lord, through various means and become increasingly purified by their devotion. Their contentment arises from the satisfaction that they have the Lord's protection, and he decides what is good for them. Material comforts, worldly riches, and pleasures do not give them as much comfort or satisfaction since they develop a distaste for them and yearn to cultivate nearness and oneness with the Lord. True devotees engage their minds in the constant contemplation of the Lord and dedicate their lives to his service. The thoughts of Krishna and devotion to him consume their minds, and they are not tired of speaking about him, contemplating him, or remembering him, since it compensates for all the troubles they endure in their lives.

The people you love most do not escape from your thoughts. You express that love and longing in various ways through your thoughts, actions, relationships, interests, likes, and dislikes. You are not tired of seeing, interacting with, or spending time with them. You are drawn to them due to desires and attachments, or because you find yourself in them, or aspects of you. Love or devotion of this kind, common among people, is inferior, selfish, conditional, and does not last long. Exclusive devotion to the Supreme Lord is its opposite. It may begin with desires and expectations, but in some, it ascends to the next level and becomes selfless, sacrificial, and pure, in which the impurities of egoism, desires, and delusion yield to the soul's aspiration to unite with its source. In them, it transforms into a spontaneous outpouring of unconditional and unwavering love, admiration, and devotion.

For exclusive devotees, devotion is a way of life. They offer themselves as a sacrifice to the Supreme Lord and lead a divine-centered life, emptying themselves, making themselves humble and insignificant, and putting themselves at his mercy and will. They worship him through their minds, speech, and actions (manasa, vaca, karma). Their unending devotion to him fills their hearts and minds and pours out as love for humanity and all the things in which his sacred presence is felt. The Yoga Vashista declares that the Supreme Lord should be worshipped with neither the mind nor the body nor material substances but with pure consciousness, meditating upon him as pure consciousness devoid of qualities, objectivity, and duality.

Sloka 10

teṣāṃ satatayuktānāṃ bhajatāṃ prītipūrvakam
dadāmi buddhiyogaṃ taṃ yena mām upayānti te

tesam = to them; satata-yuktanam = always absorbed or engaged; bhajatam = in devotional worship; priti-purvakam = to My satisfaction; dadami = I give; buddhi-yogam = discerning wisdom, discriminating intelligence; tam = that; yena = by which; mam = to Me; upayanti = come; te = they.

To those who are ever absorbed in devotional worship to My satisfaction, I give them discerning wisdom by which they come to Me.

There must be a spark of exclusive devotion in the devotees. If they keep it alive, the Lord will take care of the rest. If they continue their effort, he will intensify their devotion, grant them knowledge and wisdom, and reveal the resplendence of the pure Self. If your mind is exclusively devoted to the Lord, you will eventually be absorbed in him and attain oneness. This is the message and the promise.

Thus, in this verse, the Lord suggests how his devotees can earn his love and mercy and attain liberation through their devotion. They must worship him exclusively to his satisfaction (priti purvakam). If they can fulfill that part, he will take care of their welfare (yoga-kshema) as he promised before and their liberation, as he stated here. The Lord does not merely sit and enjoy the devotion and dedication of his devotees. He also reciprocates and rewards them by reciprocating their love, devotion, and sacrifice. He helps them overcome their impurities and progress on the path until they reach his immortal world from which there is no return. He shows them the way, leads them in his direction by giving them discernment, and helps them attain oneness. Thus, we find here the assurance that those singularly devoted to him are assured of a permanent escape from samsara. They can attain the highest yoga through unwavering devotion (kevala bhakti) and by earning his love and mercy.

The Bhagavadgita envisages Krishna as the Supreme Controller. He is responsible for everything, including your delusion and devotion. At the same time, his responses depend upon your actions or effort. Previously, Lord Krishna stated that his pure devotees were never lost to him, and he was not lost to them. The bond between them is one of unconditional love. Once the devotee surrenders to him unconditionally and remains established in his devotion with unwavering faith, the Lord takes him into his protection and leads him to the final goal. His devotion arises from his essential nature and karma, but whether he reaches the final goal of liberation or not depends upon the Lord's will and grace. His devotion to the Lord must be pure and selfless and not induced by desires or the expectation of liberation. It must arise from his heart's longing to attain the Supreme Lord and become dissolved in his pure and absolute state. Great devotees like Ramakrishna Paramahamsa, Mirabai, or Chaitanya exemplified that longing and devotion. They were so lost in their love and devotion to the Lord that they forgot about their welfare and suffering. Their devotion was unhindered by the problems and obstacles they faced. Their lives and actions show us that through exclusive devotion, humans can attain the Supreme Lord, and their devotion to him gives them the strength to endure their suffering and the obstacles they face on the path.

Sloka 11

teṣām evānukampārtham aham ajñānajaṃ tamaḥ
nāśayāmy ātmabhāvastho jñānadīpena bhāsvatā

tesam = for them; eva = only; anukampa-artham = out of mercy, for the sake of compassion; aham = I; ajnana-jam = born out of ignorance; tamah = darkness; nasayami = remove, destroy; atma bhavasthah = residing in them as their own Self; jnanadipena = by the lamp of knowledge; bhasvata = shining, glowing, luminous.

Only out of mercy for them, established in them as their very Self, I remove their darkness born out of ignorance by the glowing lamp of knowledge.

Lord Krishna said that he removes the darkness of ignorance from his devotees by lighting the lamp of knowledge in them out of mercy or compassion. He takes pity on them because he resides in them as their Self and witnesses their undiminished and undisturbed devotion despite their suffering. Thus, in this verse, he confirmed that the knowledge gained through exclusive devotion and his grace is more effective than that gained through intellectual effort. His words also convey that humans can secure his help through exclusive devotion to achieve liberation. It means those who practice jnana, karma, and sannyasa yogas do not enjoy that privilege unless they take refuge in him and become his exclusive devotees. Without devotion, they may probably achieve liberation. However, it may take time and involve much suffering, hardship, and uncertainty since they have to depend solely upon themselves and their prarabdha. The straight path to liberation is through exclusive devotion only.

Lord Krishna's words may give the impression that he is partial to his devotees and ignores others. It is not true. In the previous chapter, he said (9.22) that when people are exclusively devoted to him, ever absorbed in him, and worship him without any other thought, he becomes responsible for their welfare. He also said (9.25) that those who worshipped him with faith would attain him, but those who worshipped others would reach them only. In another verse (9.29), he said that although he was equal to all beings and no one was particularly hateful or dear to him, his devotees existed in him, and he existed in them. He further said (9.30) that if an evil person worshipped him with single-minded devotion, he would surely consider him pious because he made the right decision. In other words, he takes responsibility for their liberation also. He helps them because they become so helpless, vulnerable, and dependent that he cannot ignore them. As they surrender their will to him and take refuge in him, they become his personal responsibility.

Therefore, devotion to the Supreme Lord is important, whether you pursue jnana, karma, or sannyasa yoga. At some point, all yogas must culminate in pure and selfless devotion. His mercy shines equally upon everyone, just as the sun shines equally upon all. However, if someone stays in the shade or darkness, he cannot blame the sun for his situation. The same analogy applies to those who do not want to take refuge in him or worship him with devotion. They cannot blame him if they do not want to relinquish control. If they want to earn his love and mercy, they must give themselves up, take refuge in him, and surrender to him with unwavering devotion. However, self-effort (karma) is also important since pure devotion does not arise without attaining perfection in other yogas. Devotees must cultivate exclusive devotion through obligatory duties, the pursuit of knowledge, renunciation of desires, selfless actions (nishkama karma), self-control, devotional worship, surrender, and contemplation. Those who pursue desire-ridden actions cannot practice true devotion. It manifests only when the mind is empty, except for the thoughts of the Lord.

Sloka 12

arjuna uvāca
paraṃ brahma paraṃ dhāma pavitraṃ paramaṃbhavān
puruṣaṃ śāśvataṃ divyam ādidevam ajaṃ vibhum

arjunah uvaca = Arjuna said; param = supreme; brahma = Brahman; param = supreme; dhama = abode, goal, light; pavitram = pure and sacred; paramam = most; bhavan = you; purusam = person, being, purusa; sasvatam = permanent; divyam = divine; adi-devam = the first among the gods; ajam = unborn; vibhum = the mightiest, the greatest, omnipotent.

Arjuna said, "You are the supreme Brahman, the supreme Abode, the purest and most sacred Being, the Eternal, Divine, the Foremost God, the Unborn, the Mightiest."

In this verse and the following four verses, Arjuna extolls Lord Krishna with great devotion, acknowledging him as the Supreme Brahman in human form and pleads to tell him about his divine manifestations. Brahman represents the highest, supreme reality. Although he is often spoken of as a Being, he truly represents pure consciousness or absolute Reality, also known as unified consciousness or Krishna consciousness. The Upanishads refer to it as That. Prakriti, his physical aspect, remains suppressed in him but becomes active in his manifestations. Brahman means that which expands or goes forth indefinitely so that it is unsurpassable and always remains ahead of everything else. The Vedas extol him as the supreme deity, the high priest, the silent witness, the source of all, and the ultimate recipient of all sacrifices and offerings. All the divinities of the Hindu pantheon are his aspects or manifestations only.

Para or param means the highest, the absolute, the greatest, transcendental, different, distinct, beyond, excellent, and supreme. Dhama means abode, light, goal, or place. The word parandhama is usually associated with Brahman or his transcendental and absolute state. Lord Krishna as Brahman is Parandhama, the Supreme Goal of all those who seek liberation and the Supreme Abode of all liberated souls. Upon realizing him within themselves as their Self through self-absorption or oneness, they reach his world (dhama) and remain there forever as eternally free souls. Pavitram means pure, auspicious, holy, sacred, sinless, etc. As Brahman, Lord Krishna is supremely pure (parama pavitram), and auspicious because no evil or impurity can ever taint him, pierce him, exist in him, or approach him. Further, by coming into contact with him through devotion and surrender, even the most sinful ones are freed from their sins and become pure. His touch (brahmasparsa) or glance purifies and liberates even the sinful ones. The absolute Krishna is also eternal and permanent (sasvatam) because he is indestructible and immutable. He is Purusha, the Cosmic Being who arises from himself as the foremost Lord of creation and manifests worlds and beings. The material universe is his body, and all the individual souls constitute his higher Nature. He is Adi Deva, the foremost (primal) God, because he is before all the divinities who manifest from him. Since he is without a beginning and an end, he is called the unborn (ajam). He is Vibhu, the mightiest, wealthiest, strongest, and omnipotent Lord. There are no limits to his powers, potencies, abundances, and manifestations. As a part of his great play (lila), he pervades all and assumes many forms.

Sloka 13

āhus tvām ṛṣayaḥ sarve devarṣir nāradas tathā
asito devalo vyāsaḥ svayaṃ caiva bravīṣi me

ahuh = speak; tvam = of You; rsayah = seers; sarve = all; deva-rsih = the divine seers; naradah = Narada; tatha = also; asitah = Asita; devalah = Devala; vyasah = Vyasa; svayam = personally, yourself; ca = and; eva = even; bravisi = saying; me = to Me.

"All the seers, divine seers, Narada and so also Asita, Devala, and Vyasa speak of You thus; and (now) even You also are personally saying (this) to Me."

Arjuna said that he heard all the seers, divine seers, Narada, and others speaking of Lord Krishna as the Supreme Brahman, the supreme Abode, the purest, the most sacred Being, etc., and he heard the same from Lord Krishna himself. Thus, he was left with no doubt about his lordship, glory, and opulence. What he heard from the seers and sages, or their works, was verbal testimony (shabda pramana). For most of us, it is the most reliable source of proof to ascertain metaphysical truths. However, Arjuna also heard Lord Krishna vouching for it personally. Hence, he needed no further proof of his lord or his teaching.

Rishi means enlightened seer, singer of sacred hymns, a ray of light, saintly person, sage, etc. Rishis take birth in the mortal world as humans and become enlightened through self-effort. Devrishis are a step above them. They are not born but created by Brahma from his consciousness at the time of creation, along with the Manus and mind-born sons (manasaputras). Therefore, they possess divine powers and self-born or inborn knowledge of Brahman and the Vedas. In each cycle of creation, Brahma channels the knowledge of the Vedas to the world through them. The four divine seers mentioned here are also mentioned in the Mahābhārata. They are well known for their unconditional and exclusive devotion to Lord Narayana and their role in spreading the sacred knowledge of the Self and liberation.

Narada was a great devotee of Lord Narayana. He was given the supernatural power of attainment (prapti) with which he can be anywhere and in any part of the universe in an instant as he wishes and wills. Not much is known about Asita. It is said that Asita and Narada spread the knowledge of the Mahābhārata to the gods and ancestors. Asita disseminated it in the ancestral world, while Narada did so in Indra's heaven. According to one legend, Devala was born on earth as Ashtavakra (the sage with eight deformities) because of a curse. His discourse on the importance of knowing the Self and attaining oneness with it to King Janaka is well known as the Ashtavakra Gita. Vyasa is the most famous of all the four sages. He is considered a partial incarnation or emanation of Lord Vishnu and credited with the authorship of the epic Mahābhārata and the eighteen Puranas.

Sloka 14

sarvam etad ṛtaṃ manye yan māṃ vadasi keśava
na hi te bhagavan vyaktiṃ vidur devā na dānavāḥ

sarvam = all; etat = that, this; rtam = true; manye = think, accept, consider; yat = which; mam = Me; vadasi = You have told; kesava = O Kesava; na = not; hi = surely; te = Your; bhagavan = blessed Lord; vyaktim = personality, manifestation; viduh = know; devah = the gods; na = not; danavah = the danavas, demons.

" O Kesava, I consider all that which you have told me to be true. Surely, O Blessed Lord, neither devas nor danavas know Your manifestations."

Arjuna expressed his faith in the words of Lord Krishna and accepted them wholeheartedly as true. He acknowledged that even the seers and the divine seers did not know his manifestations. He was convinced that Lord Krishna was indeed none other than the Supreme Lord, the Manifested Brahman, Adi Purusha. Faith is necessary to cultivate exclusive devotion. Liberation rests on faith since it is vital to cultivate devotion and secure the Lord's love and mercy. A student must have faith and trust in his teacher and his teachings. He must be inquisitive, humble, open-minded, and willing to learn. Like a true devotee, Arjuna accepted Lord Krishna's words about his opulence and greatness as true (rtam). Thereby, he showed his readiness to learn further about the Lord and his manifestations. Rtam means indisputable, divine truth or law, or the very personification of truth. By using that word, Arjuna affirmed his conviction in what he heard. Earlier, Lord Krishna told him that neither the gods nor the seers knew his origin, and only those who knew his manifestations and powers would reach steadfastness in yoga. Arjuna agreed, reiterating that neither the devas nor the danavas knew his true personality or manifestation (vyaktitvam) as the Supreme Lord. Vyakta means that which appeared, manifested, expressed, evolved, or developed. Isvara, the Supreme Lord or Purusha, manifested from Brahman. He is the vyakta (manifested) from the avykta (unmanifested). His personality is vyakti (the person). Since he is before all, no one knows his origin or the extent of his powers and greatness. Divine seers such as Narada, Asita, Devala, and Vyasa might have spoken about him, but they also do not know him well.

Sloka 15

svayam evātmanātmānaṃ vettha tvaṃ puruṣottama
bhūtabhāvana bhūteśa devadeva jagatpate

svayam = Yourself; eva = alone; atmana = by Yourself; atmanam = by Yourself; vettha = know; tvam = You; purusa-uttama = O Supreme Being or Person; bhuta-bhavana = Creator of beings; bhuta-isa = Lord of beings; deva-deva = O God of gods; jagat-pate = O Lord of the worlds.

"Only Yourself know Yourself by Yourself, O Supreme Being, O Creator of beings, Lord of beings, God of gods and the Lord of the worlds."

What is without a beginning and an end, and before all, cannot be known by means other than itself. That which is infinite cannot be known except in a state of unity and oneness. Hence, only Brahman, who fits that description, knows about himself and his manifestations. Others may know him but little. Since he is self-existent and self-knowing, knowledge of him exists within him only. Others have no access to it. The mind and senses play no role in that knowing. Whatever is known through them is a reflected truth, but not the truth itself. Brahman knows himself by himself and within himself because knowing implies the duality between the knower and the known. Since he is beyond the mind and senses, duality and objectivity do not exist in him except as an illusion or projection. The truth (rtam) of Brahman is his absolute and indivisible pure consciousness that pervades all this and extends beyond. His manifestations that are subject to duality, divisions, and modes also do not know him unless they are centered in his absolute state.

Even the objective universe and all its objects are projections of this unitary cosmic consciousness. In their essential nature, beneath their names and forms and distinguishing features, they are projections or reflections of that pure consciousness only. The illusion of their existence as objects floating in the cosmic space is created by the objectivity arising from our perceptions and the duality of the mind. When the mind becomes silent and the ego withdraws in complete submission, the duality disappears, and one realizes the essential nature of existence as pure, indivisible reality infused with and sustained by consciousness. Consciousness is everything. Consciousness becomes everything. The transition of things from one state into another arises from the disturbances of the cosmic mind (citshakti). Those caught in them cannot go beyond the empirical experience unless they enter that inner realm of peace and tranquility where consciousness remains pure and stable. The awareness of pure consciousness arises in us in subjective, transcendental states only when our minds are silent and free from disturbances. However, it exists eternally in its pristine and absolute state in Brahman or Krishna's absolute state. Neither effort and movement nor dualities and divisions of time and other things exist in it. However, they manifest in his self-manifestation as Isvara and his creation, which we perceive as the objective reality or the not-self.

Sloka 16

vaktum arhasy aśeṣeṇa divyā hy ātmavibhūtayaḥ
yābhir vibhūtibhir lokān imāṃs tvaṃ vyāpya tiṣṭhasi

vaktum = tell; arhasi = please be kind enough; asesena = in full, without any remainder; divyah = divine; hi = surely; atma = self, own; vibhutayah =

manifestations; yabhih = by which; vibhutibhih = manifestations; lokan = worlds; iman = these; tvam = You; vyapya = pervading; tisthasi = being established.

"Please be kind enough to tell Me, without leaving out anything about your divine manifestations by which manifestations you pervade these worlds, established in them."

Arjuna wanted to know Lord Krishna's divine manifestations from himself, since he alone knew them inherently and independently. The Supreme Lord manifests worlds and beings and, becoming established in them, pervades them all. He is the intelligence of the intelligent, the virtue of the virtuous, the strength of the strong, the beauty of beautiful creations, the devotion of devotees, the austerity of ascetics and renunciants, and the courage of warriors. When many such supreme qualities appear in their full intensity in a person or object, we recognize that as a divinity or a divine manifestation. When they are fully or partially absent due to his concealment or withdrawal, we identify those objects as undivine, dark, and evil. Thus, everything is a manifestation of the Lord alone, in which he manifests or conceals glories (vibhutis) in different degrees to create the illusion of diversity we experience as the perceptual or objective reality. His manifested reality is other than him, although it arises from him. Hence, it is known as the not-self.

A person becomes divine or demonic by the expression or concealment of divine nature due to the play of Maya and karma. When tamas and rajas predominate in him, the Lord's glories become suppressed, but when sattva prevails, they manifest to the extent he is pure. Thus, divine and demonic nature manifests in creation due to the expression or suppression of God's vibhutis or divine qualities. When impurities envelop consciousness, the radiance of the Self does not light the internal organ. When they are dissolved, the Lord shines forth and becomes self-evident through intelligence, speech, senses, qualities, knowledge, character, actions, etc. When people endowed with his supreme nature live amongst us, we venerate them as saints, seers, and great souls.

Brahman is the all-knowing, all-containing, and all-pervading Supreme Reality. His absolute and unmanifested state is the indivisible and indistinguishable oneness or unified consciousness that no one can fathom or comprehend. In his manifested state as Isvara, he unleashes his power and glories (vibhutis). He manifests worlds and beings in which he resides as their indwelling Self while pervading, enveloping, and supporting them from within and without, and within himself as their Supreme Lord, controller, and upholder. However, since he remains concealed in most by his power of maya, he remains mostly unknown and incomprehensible. Through the qualities that manifest from him in creation or the objective reality, we can discern his presence and his footprints. In the brilliance of the rising sun, the beauty of a flower, the innocence of a newborn, or a myriad of other things that dazzle us with beauty and perfection, we can discern his hidden presence and the game of hide and seek he plays with us as a part of his unending play. They manifest in humans as mental brilliance, purity, excellence, extraordinary skills, godliness, beauty, majesty, grace, joy, perfection, strength, saintliness, courage, supernatural powers (siddhis), etc.

It is humanly impossible to maintain oneness with everything when the mind is wakeful and active. In the objective realm, duality and division persist when the mind and senses are in their outgoing mode. Because our surface consciousness is ridden with impurities, duality, and objectivity, we cannot perceive the Self or the pure, indivisible, and transcendental consciousness, which remains hidden in us as our ultimate reality. The Supreme Lord has the manifesting power as well as the pervading power. He unites the knower with the known and the known with the unknown and beyond. Since he envelops and pervades the worlds and things he creates, he simultaneously knows the truth (rtam) of things subjectively, objectively, and from different perspectives, with a unified, holistic vision that is impossible for humans or gods.

Arjuna wanted to know the manifestations of the Supreme Lord from the Lord himself, since he was the only one who could speak about them with greater authority and personal knowledge. By now, he was convinced that Lord Krishna was the true manifestation of the Supreme Brahman and possessed knowledge of everything in its pristine state. To the human mind, the Supreme Being is unknowable and imperceptible. He alone has the power to reveal them to us and help us know his greatness, opulence, and glories.

Sloka 17

kathaṃ vidyām ahaṃ yogiṃs tvāṃ sadā paricintayan
keṣu keṣu ca bhāveṣu cintyosi bhagavan mayā

katham = how; vidyam = know; aham = I shall; yogin = O Yogi; tvam = You; sada = constant; paricintayan = meditation; kesu = in what; kesu = in what; ca = and; bhavesu = states, manifestations; cintyah asi = You should be contemplated; bhagavan = O blessed Lord; maya = by Me.

"How may I know you, O Yogi, by constantly meditating, and upon which and which manifestations You should be contemplated by Me, O Blessed Lord?"

The unknowable supreme Brahman is not ideal for contemplation or worship since the mind cannot settle on that which is incomprehensible, imperceptible, and invisible. However, his manifestations are fit for contemplation and worship due to their association with names and forms and the materiality of Prakriti. Therefore, Arjuna wanted to know which of the Lord's manifestations were ideal for the purpose. While asking, he used two epithets: Yogin and Bhagavan. The Supreme Lord is not an ordinary yogi. He is the source of all yogas and yoga shastras. Hence, he is also known as the First Yogi (adi yogi), the Perfect Yogi (siddha), and the Lord of Yoga (yogisvara). He is also the Supreme Yogi (Parama Yogi) who controls the entire creation, is ever established in supreme yoga (oneness), and possesses magical and supernatural powers with which he performs his five functions: creation, preservation, suppression, expression, and destruction. Bhagavan means the lord of love, loveliness, beauty, excellence, majesty, prosperity, reproductive organs, happiness, passion, and dispassion. The blessed Lord has these supreme qualities, powers, and abundances. As the all-pervading Supreme Being, he is found everywhere and in everything. Although he is present in all and everything is worthy of contemplation, his power and presence, or his divine qualities, do not equally manifest in all due to the presence of impurities. Therefore, from a devotional perspective, one should choose those aspects that are worthy of veneration and contemplation and where one might feel His sacred presence and nearness (samipyam).

Sloka 18

vistareṇātmano yogaṃ vibhūtiṃ ca janārdana
bhūyaḥ kathaya tṛptir hi śṛṇvato nāsti memṛtam

vistarena = in detail; atmanah = your; yogam = divine state; vibhutim = divine manifestations; ca = and; jana-ardana = O Janardana; bhuyah = again; kathaya = tell me; trptih = satisfaction; hi = certainly; srnvatah = listening, hearing; na asti = there is no; Me = my; amrtam = immortal, sweet, liberating.

"Please tell me again in detail your Supreme State and manifestations, O Janardana. Certainly, there is no end to my satisfaction in listening to your sweet and liberating words."

Arjuna said, "Please tell me, O Janardana (remover of people's miseries and tormentors), your yoga (state, connection with the world, supreme reality, etc.), and vibhutis (powers, manifestations, opulence, glory, greatness, sovereignty, etc.), for I can go on listening to them endlessly since there is no end to my happiness when you speak about them. Your words are nectar-like and help devotees like me to contemplate your greatness and glory and attain immortality through ecstatic self-absorption."

The supreme state of Brahman (yogam) is unknowable to the mind and senses. He is known objectively through his manifestations and qualities that appear in association with Prakriti. Yogis contemplate them to attain Brahman and experience his supreme state. Arjuna wanted to know them in detail to meditate on them and stabilize his mind in devotion. It is the standard practice of yoga. Through dhyana, the mind is silenced and dissolved in the object of contemplation. In that pure state of oneness, the essence of the object is realized. Therefore, the names, forms, glories, and attributes of the Supreme Lord are ideal for contemplation and self-absorption (samadhi).

Like a true devotee, Arjuna told Lord Krishna that there was no end to the happiness he would enjoy while listening to his glories and manifestations. He was already convinced that Lord Krishna was indeed the Lord of the universe (Isvara) in his manifested aspect and Brahman in his unmanifested, absolute aspect. He also heard seers and divine seers speaking about him. Now, he wanted to know directly from himself the extent of his opulence and sovereignty. True devotees who exemplify kevala bhakti (exclusive devotion) often fall into a trance-like condition and become ecstatic when they hear about Krishna's glories, deeds, and names. They are instantly drawn to any conversation where devotees congregate and speak about it. Hanuman is considered the foremost devotee of Lord Rama. He exemplified exclusive devotion. It is said that even today, wherever Lord Rama's devotees assemble or participate in devotional activities, he presents himself and enjoys their company and conversations. Arjuna expressed a similar level of devotion to Lord Krishna when he told him that he would never be tired of listening to his glories and nectar-like, liberating words. By expressing it, he proved himself to be a kevala bhakta in the making.

Sloka 19

śrībhagavān uvāca
hanta te kathayiṣyāmi divyā hy ātmavibhūtayaḥ
prādhānyataḥ kuruśreṣṭha nāsty anto vistarasya me

sri-bhagavan uvaca = the Belssed Lord said; hanta = yes; te = to you; kathayisyami = I will tell or describe; divyah = divine; hi = verily; atma-vibhutayah = My manifestations; pradhanyatah = principal, chief, primary; kuru-srestha = O the best of the Kurus; na asti = there is no; antah = end; vistarasya = extent, expansiveness, vastness, reach, sway; me = My.

The Supreme Lord said, "O best among the Kurus, I will tell you My chief manifestations that are truly divine. There is no end to my expansiveness."

The manifestations of Krishna, the Supreme Lord, are infinite. They are also divine (divya) because they radiate his glory and opulence. Evil does not manifest in them since they are endowed with supreme qualities. However, evil does manifest in beings when the Lord's higher nature remains concealed in them by a veil of impurities. Just as darkness arises from the withdrawal of light, evil manifests when the radiant power and opulence of the Lord remain concealed or withdrawn. Everything in creation, from a blade of grass to an intelligent being or divinity (deva), is infused with the presence of the Supreme Being, but he does not radiate his glory equally in all. He gives reigns to Prakriti and lets her manage the diversity in creation. Prakriti exists in him and depends upon him, but he does not exist in her. Accordingly, beings exist in him and depend upon him, but he does not exist in their essential nature or depend upon them. Since his manifestations are numerous and a lifetime may not be sufficient to describe them, the Lord said that he would reveal only the important ones to Arjuna. By addressing Arjuna as Kuru Shrestha, the best among the Kurus, he also conveyed why he chose him for the purpose.

Sloka 20

aham ātmā guḍākeśa sarvabhūtāśayasthitaḥ
aham ādiś ca madhyaṃ ca bhūtānām anta eva ca

aham = I; atma = Self; gudakesa = O Gudakesa; sarva-bhuta = all beings; asaya-sthitah = situated within in the heart; aham = I am; adih = beginning; ca = and; madhyam = the middle; ca = and; bhutanam = beings; antah = end; eva = truly; ca = and.

O Gudakesa, I am the Self residing in the heart of all beings. I am truly the beginning, the middle, and the end of all beings.

In his absolute state, Lord Krishna is the Supreme Self or Brahman. He resides in the hearts of all beings as the individual Self (Atman or the embodied Self (jivatma) and in creation as the Supreme Lord (Isvara), and watches over both indifferently from a distance as the Supreme Self (Paramatma). As the source and support of all, he is responsible for the creation, preservation, and destruction of all beings (jivas). The individual Self is Gudakesa, the conqueror of sleep, because he is always awake and needs no rest. Anyone can be considered a Gudakesa, who is pure, who is awakened spiritually, and who knows that the Self is different from the physical self. Gudaka means sleep, and Isa means the lord or master. Gudakesa means lord of sleep. Sleep also symbolizes inertia or tamas. By addressing Arjuna as Gudakesa, Krishna implied that he was imparting the knowledge to a deserving devotee who removed the darkness of tamas from his mind and body, who is fully yoked to single-minded devotion and is ready to wake up to the absolute reality of his pure consciousness.

Since the Self is eternally free from impurities, it is always awake and pure, even in the embodied state. It is always in the transcendental state (turiya), unlike the body, which is subject to wakefulness, dreams, and sleep. Thus, whether the mind is asleep or awake, the Self is always an absolute master of sleep (Gudakesa). So is a self-realized yogi. He remains awake when others are asleep, while his mind is asleep to the desires and attractions to which others' minds are awake. By gradually soaking his wakeful consciousness (jagrat) with the transcendental state of turiya, overcoming the duality that separates him from the rest, and conquering egoism, desires, and delusion, he gradually becomes awake to the reality of himself. The state of oneness, or nonduality, becomes his natural state or condition (sahaja) as he establishes his mind firmly in the Self with equanimity and attains pure consciousness. Thus, only the individual Self, if it is different from Brahman, can enter his absolute state, and only a self-realized yogi who is ever awake with pure consciousness is considered a Gudakesa.

Lord Krishna said that he lives in the heart of all beings (āśayasthita). Asaya means a chamber or a reservoir, a reference to the heart region in the body. However, Shankaracharya thought it meant the internal organ (antahkarana), also the seat of latent impressions or past-life memories. In some Upanishads, the Self is described as situated in the body's inner chamber (asaya) or the heart. The Svetasvatara Upanishad describes Brahman as the dweller of the heart in the beings (bhuta-guhasaya). Although he is the size of a thumb, he is the lord of all (maha prabhu) with a universal form of immense proportions and numerous forms. According to Katha Upanishad, the Self is "difficult to be seen (gudham), deeply hidden (anupravistam) and set in the cave of the heart (guhatitam)," knowing which a wise man transcends the duality of joy and sorrow. Brahman, the absolute Krishna, is the Creator of all. He is also the preserver, protector, and destroyer. Thus, He is the beginning, the middle, and the end of all his manifestations, while He is without a beginning and an end. For Him, the whole universe (sarvam idam) is an asaya which He inhabits and envelops.

Sloka 21

ādityānām ahaṃ viṣṇur jyotiṣāṃ ravir aṃśumān
marīcir marutām asmi nakṣatrāṇām ahaṃ śaśī

adityanam = among the Adityas; aham = I am; visnuh = Vishnu; jyotisam = among the shining ones; ravih = the Sun; amsu-man = radiant; maricih = Marici; marutam = of the Maruts; asmi = I am; naksatranam = among stars; aham = I am; sasi = the moon.

Among the Adityas, I am Vishnu; among the shining ones, I am the radiant Sun; among the Maruts, I am Marichi; among the stars, I am the moon.

The Adityas are solar deities mentioned in the Vedas as the sons of Aditi, who is also known as the Primal Goddess and the mother of all divinities. Their number varies in the scriptures from seven to twelve. Their names also vary. The Puranas mention twelve Adityas: Dhata, Mitra, Aryama, Rudra, Varuna, Surya, Bhaga, Vivasvan, Pusa, Savita, Tvastr, and Vishnu. In some lists, we find the names of Yama, Surya, and Indra. The Vedas describe Vishnu as a friend of Indra and the god of three strides. He became a prominent Vedic deity by the time of the Puranas, which extol him as Brahman himself and as the Preserver and Lord of Vaikuntha. The god of three strides subsequently became Vamana, an incarnation of Maha Vishnu who, with his two strides, covered the earth and heavens and, with his third, sent Bali, the demon king, to the nether world.

Marīchi, probably mentioned here as a Marut, may not be the same divinity mentioned in the Puranas as a divine seer (sapta rishi) born from Brahma's mind. According to the legends, he was the father of Kashypa. His name appears in the epics also. The Marīchi described here may be the leader of Maruts, the gods of commonality, also mentioned in the Vedas as the wind and storm gods. At times, they are also identified with Rudras, another group of storm gods. The Maruts and Rudras are said to be active before and during storms and gales and play an important role in renewing the earth and its vegetation. Their number varies. According to the epic Ramayana, they are 49, all born to Diti, divided into seven groups of seven each, namely Avaha, Pravaha, Vivaha, Paravaha, Udvaha, Samvaha, and Parivaha. The stars are numerous. However, Vedic astronomy recognizes 27 principal star regions or systems, which appear along with the moon on each specific day in the lunar calendar. Since they appear near the moon, each bears a specific name. Technically, the moon is not a star but a semi-luminous world ruled by Lord Soma, where the ancestors of humans await their next birth. It is considered a star here because it shines in the night sky in the company of the stars.

Although Lord Krishna particularly identified specific deities as his manifestations, it does not mean that other divinities in each group did not manifest from him or do not contain his divinity. They are also his manifestations only. However, comparatively, his qualities and effulgence appear more profoundly in the specifically mentioned deities. Thus, in Vishnu, divine qualities appear more profoundly than in all other Adityas. According to the Vaishnava schools, he is the purest of all gods and is made up of the purest sattva (suddha sattva), in which Brahman radiates the qualities of higher nature in their purest state. Thus, each of the manifestations mentioned here and in subsequent verses radiates divine qualities more profoundly than his counterparts and enjoys a superior status in the hierarchy of the Lord's creation.

Sloka 22

vedānāṃ sāmavedosmi devānām asmi vāsavaḥ
indriyāṇāṃ manaś cāsmi bhūtānām asmi cetanā

vedanam = among the Vedas; sama-vedah = the Sama Veda; asmi = I am; devanam = among the gods; asmi = I am; vasavah = Indra; indriyanam = among the senses; manah = the mind; ca = and; asmi = I am; bhutanam = among the beings; asmi = I am; cetana = liveliness.

Of the Vedas, I am the Samaveda. Of the gods, I am Indra. Among the sense organs, I am the mind, and among the beings, I am liveliness.

The Vedas are four. Of them, the Rigveda was the earliest. The other three are Yajurveda, Samaveda, and Atharvaveda. In the Vedic tradition, they constitute the core literature. They are considered Sruti (the heard ones) because they were heard from the transcendental realm and preserved for posterity by the divine seers or the mind-born sons of Brahma. According to the Vedic beliefs, the Vedas exist eternally in the highest realm of Brahman. At the beginning of each cycle of creation, they are revealed to humans through Brahman and the seven divine seers (sapta rishis). In turn, they reveal them to their disciples. From then on, the knowledge is passed on to successive generations of students by the descendants of the seers. Since they exist eternally in the realm of Brahman, the knowers of the Self may know them in transcendental states. However, such knowing may not translate into memorial knowledge due to the natural barriers between the mind and the Self. The knowledge of the Sruti, which is eternal and self-existent, is known only to the Self by the Self. The seven seers (sapta rishis) rendered them into cognizable verbal sounds since they were the mind-born sons of Brahma and were created for the specific purpose of establishing the eternal Dharma upon the earth.

Of the four Vedas, Lord Krishna declared the Samaveda as his manifestation. It does not mean the other three Vedas are not. For upholding the Dharma, the four Vedas are equally sacred and important. However, Samaveda is particularly mentioned because its hymns are better suited for singing due to their metrical nature. Hence, the Veda is regarded as one of the earliest sources of India's classical musical tradition. The hymns of the Samaveda are known as Samans, hymns set to different melodies and sung by Udgatri priests during the sacrificial ceremonies. Although Samans are mostly copied from the Rigveda hymns (Riks), in the Samaveda tradition, they are set to particular melodies and sung during invocations. Hence, during sacrificial ceremonies, when they are sung in unison by priests, they fill the environment with rhythmic vibrations and add to the solemnity of the occasion. The Veda also played an important role in the development of the Vedic philosophy. The Vedanta School derives its doctrine partly from the Chandogya and Kena Upanishads associated with it.

Lord Krishna also declared Indra, the lord of the heavens, as one of his manifestations. He called him Vasava, one of his epithets meaning the Self or a heavenly being. Indra was the most prominent deity after Brahma in the early Vedic tradition. The Vedas extol him as a warrior god who slew the demons, released the waters in the clouds held captive by them, and nourished the earth with rains. In the human body, the senses and the five breaths symbolically represent the divinities, and the mind, their lord, represents Indra. Hence, the mind is rightly called the king of the senses. As Lord Krishna stated here, in the beings, he manifests as chetana, translated variously as consciousness, intelligence, activity, or the liveliness of the living beings. Without chetana, the worlds and beings would be lifeless (achetana). Hence, it is rightly equated with the Self (or God), without which creation would be without dynamism and liveliness.

Special note: Although the Bhagavadgita was also heard from Lord Krishna, it is not considered a Sruti because it forms part of the Mahabharata, which is a smriti, a memorial work. Further, it was composed by Veda Vyasa from his memory after hearing the discourse indirectly and clairvoyantly through Sanjaya.

Sloka 23

rudrāṇāṃ śaṃkaraś cāsmi vitteśo yakṣarakṣasām
vasūnāṃ pāvakaś cāsmi meruḥ śikhariṇām aham

rudranam = of the Rudras; sankarah = Lord Siva; ca = and; asmi = I am; vitta-isah = Kubera, the lord or treasures; yaksa-raksasam = among the Yaksas and Raksasas; vasunam = of the Vasus; pavakah = Pavaka; ca = and; asmi = I am; meruh = Meru; sikharinam = of the mountains; aham = I am.

Of the Rudras, I am Siva; among the Yakshas and Rakshasas, I am Kubera, the lord of treasures; of the Vasus, I am Pavaka; and of the mountains, I am Mount Meru.

The Rudras are eleven gods of the Middle World who become active before the onset of storms and tempests and create turbulence. According to Vamana Purana, they were born to the sage Kashyapa and Aditi. In the Vedas, they are associated with Rudra, a manifestation of Shiva, the Supreme Lord of Saivism. Rudra was popular even during the Vedic times as a healer, howler, snake charmer, and lord of Death. Symbolically, in the microcosm, the Rudras represent the five senses, five breaths, and the mind or its modifications. Some accounts describe them as the subjects or companions of Rudra.

The Yakshas are supernatural spirits of a subterranean world or a group of beings who live below the ground and protect hidden treasures, lakes, ponds, etc. They are known for their knowledge and intelligence and are depicted as kind and cruel. They may also appear to humans and gods in various disguises to trick them or test them. According to the Kena Upanishad, Brahman appeared to the gods in the guise of a Yaksha to test their strength and teach them a lesson. In the Mahabharata, after they lost their kingdom and wandered in the forests, the Pāndavas met a Yaksha guarding a lake. He wanted them to answer his questions before drinking water from the lake. Only Dharmaraja answered them wisely. Therefore, even today, the phrase 'yaksha prasna' (difficult questions) is commonly used in many Indian languages, meaning difficult or too many questions.

Lord Kubera is the lord of the Yakshas and the richest among all the divinities and beings in all the worlds. He often lends money to gods and charges them interest. He is also a friend of both Lord Vishnu and Lord Siva, besides being the brother of Ravana, the demon king of the Ramayana. The Rakshasas (demons), who stand further down in the cosmic hierarchy and prefer to inhabit dark and demonic worlds, are the brothers of Yakshas and arch-enemies of the gods (devas). The Vasus are elemental gods who represent weather and other phenomena. Initially, they were described as the attendant divinities of Indra, but in the subsequent descriptions, they became associated with Vishnu. They are also mentioned in the Brihadaranyaka Upanishad and the Mahābhārata. Bhīshma was one of the eight Vasus, born on earth due to a curse by sage Vashista. Mount Meru, or Sumeru, is the sacred mountain revered equally in Hinduism, Buddhism, and Jainism as the center of the universe, upon which all the divinities and celestial beings rest.

Sloka 24

purodhasāṃ ca mukhyaṃ māṃ viddhi pārthabṛhaspatim
senānīnām ahaṃ skandaḥ sarasām asmi sāgaraḥ

purodhasam = of the priests; ca = and; mukhyam = foremost, renown; mam = Me; viddhi = know; partha = O Partha; brhaspatim = Brhaspati; senaninam = among commanders of the armies; aham = I am; skandah = Skanda; sarasam = among the great lakes; asmi = I am; sagarah = the ocean.

O Partha, among the chief priests, know that I am Brihaspati; among the commanders of armies, I am Skanda; and among the great lakes, I am the ocean.

Many Vedic sacrifices are performed by single priests, but in the complex ones, such as an Agnihotra or a Rajasuya, many priests participate to perform diverse functions. The Brahman priest serves as their head priest. As a part of his duty, he must ensure that the sacrifice is conducted according to the prescribed procedure and that the remains of the sacrifice are properly distributed. At the end of the ceremony, he is also obligated to perform expiatory functions to neutralize the sins arising from the mistakes or omissions made by the priests, the hosts, or the invitees. In ritual terminology, he symbolizes Brahman as the overseer, silent priest, witness, or guardian of the Vedic injunctions. In the Vedas, Brahman is also extolled as the Highest Priest of all, who not only keeps a watch over the sacrifice of creation after initiating it but also ensures its proper progression and completion.

Lord Krishna says that among such head priests, he is Brihaspati, also known as Brahmanspati, Purohita, and Angirasa. He is the teacher and head priest of the gods, officiates as the royal priest of Indra, and, in difficult times, gives counsel to the gods. In Vedic astronomy, he represents Jupiter. His name is associated with an ancient law book (Dharma shastra) and a sutra text. The Rigveda describes him as the priest of the heavens, without whom sacrifices are incomplete. In the Vedic hymns, he is praised as the leader of the hymns, the sweet-tongued deity whom both gods and mortals oblige and obey.

Skanda is the younger son of Siva and the brother of Lord Vinayaka. He goes by many names, such as Kartikeya, Murugan, Kumara, Subramanya, Shanmukha, Ayyappa, etc. He is a warrior deity and the commander-in-chief of Shiva's armies. Historically, he is one of the most ancient deities of Hinduism, as corroborated by numismatic evidence. He is also worshipped outside India in countries where Hinduism spread during the incursions of Indian kings into the Far East. According to the Shaiva Puranas, Skanda helped the gods several times by fighting vigorously and valiantly against demons and evil beings. In one battle, he slew Tarakasura, one of the arch-villains of the gods and humans.

Sloka 25

maharṣīṇāṃ bhṛgur ahaṃ girām asmy ekam akṣaram
yajñānāṃ japayajñosmi sthāvarāṇāṃ himālayaḥ

maha-rsinam = among the great seers; bhrguh = Bhrgu; aham = I am; giram = of the sounds; asmi = I am; ekam = one; aksaram = syllable Aum; yajnanam = of the sacrifices; japa-yajnah = sacrifice of chanting; asmi = I am; sthavaranam = of the immovable things; himalayah = the Himalayas.

Among the great seers, I am Bhrigu; among the sounds, I am the one (supreme) syllable Aum; of the sacrifices, I am the sacrifice of Japa; and among the immovable things, I am the Himalayas.

The seven great seers are mentioned in several ancient texts. However, their names vary. They are said to be born in each age of Manu (manvantara). Many hymns in the Vedas are attributed to them. The name of Bhrigu does not appear in many lists except in the Krishna Yajurveda. However, his name appears in several Puranas. In some accounts, he is mentioned as a divine seer born from the mind of Brahma. In this verse, Lord Krishna declared him as one of his manifestations. It may be because he was born with the knowledge of Time (Kala), composed the Bhrigu Samhita, and is considered the father of Vedic astrology. Lord Parasurama, an incarnation of Lord Vishnu, was born to Jamadagni, one of Bhrigu's descendants. According to the Puranas, Bhrigu was one of the Prajapatis (rulers and protectors of creation) appointed by Brahma. He is also credited with the authorship of some portions of the Manusmriti.

Aum is the most auspicious of all the sacred syllables, representing Brahman, the four worlds, and the Vedas. It has three letters (a+u+m), followed by the fourth, silence, and is considered a manifestation of Brahman in sound form (sabda Brahman). Taittiriya Upanishad (1.8.1) extols Aum in the following words, "This Aum is Brahman. This Aum is all this. This word, which is Aum, invokes obedience...Uttering Aum, the Adharvayu priest responds with praise. Uttering Aum, the Brahman priest indicates approval. Uttering Aum, the Agnihotri priest gives permission (to the sacrificer) to make offerings (in the fire sacrifice). A Brahmana says Aum when he was about to begin the recitation (of the Vedas), wishing, 'May I attain Brahman.' Thus (wishing) he attains Brahman."

The Katha Upanishad states (2.15 & 16), "That attainable goal which all the Vedas declare, for that which all the austerities are said to be, desiring which celibacy is practiced, I will speak to you in brief of that goal. Aum, it is. Indeed, this syllable is Brahman only. This syllable is the most supreme. By knowing this syllable, whatever is desired is fulfilled."

Aum is the most sacred syllable in Buddhism, Jainism, and Sikhism as well. The Yogasutras declare that by meditating upon Isvara as Aum, one can overcome the afflictions of the mind and stabilize it in the Self.

Japa means continuous and repetitive chanting of any sacred name or syllable. It is practiced to stabilize the mind and cultivate exclusive devotion. In sacrificial ceremonies, the hymns are chanted or sung loudly, whereas in Japa, the names of God or mantras, or sacred syllables, are uttered silently. Of the various forms of sacrifices (yajnas), Lord Krishna declared the sacrifice of Japa (japa-yajna) as his manifestation. It may be because Japa combines the powers of speech and mind, meditation and concentration, and sacrifice and devotion to augment devotional fervor and establish the mind in the Lord. In practice, it is closest to mananam, which is a form of mental japa only.

The Himalayas are the tallest mountains in the world, closest to the heavens, where gods, seers, ascetics, and sages live and practice austerities. It is also the seat of Kailash, where Shiva resides with his family and exclusive devotees.

Sloka 26

aśvatthaḥ sarvavṛkṣāṇāṃ devarṣīṇāṃ ca nāradaḥ
gandharvāṇāṃ citrarathaḥ siddhānāṃ kapilo muniḥ

asvatthah = asvattha; sarva-vrksanam = among the trees; deva-rsinam = among the divine seers; ca = and; naradah = Narada; gandharvanam = among the gandharvas; citrarathah = Citraratha; siddhanam = among the perfect yogis; kapilah munih = Kapila Muni.

Among the trees, I am the Asvattha tree; among the divine seers, I am sage Narada; among the Gandharvas, I am Chitraradha; and among the perfect yogis, I am sage Kapila.

Asvattha is the sacred tree of creation, described in the Katha Upanishad as Brahman, with its roots in heaven and its branches spread below everywhere in the manifested worlds. It is compared to the banyan tree (Ficus benghalensis) or the pipal tree (Ficus religiosa), commonly found in India and revered as a sacred tree. It is often compared to a family tree or a genealogy tree. It also symbolizes the whole of humanity since all beings belong to one universal family, divine family, or the Lord's family (vasudaika kutumbam). The tree is extolled in many other texts.

Lord Krishna mentioned Narada, a divine seer, as his manifestation. The divine seers (deva rishis) are higher than the great seers (maharishis). They are born directly from the mind of Brahma with his knowledge, purity, and intelligence. Hence, they belong to the celestial sphere and possess omniscience. Narada means the giver of wisdom. He is the most prominent divine seer because of his exemplary devotion to Lord Vishnu and his ability to travel in the three worlds at will, for which he earned the epithet of the triple-world traveler (trilokasanchari). He is also mischievous and takes pleasure in meddling in others' affairs and creating conflicts between them for fun. He is credited with the authorship of the Narada Bhakti Sutras.

The Gandharvas are celestial beings who live in the middle region between Indra's heaven and the earth. They are exceptionally talented in music and other art forms and are known for their beauty and grace. The name is also associated with the Gandhara region, Gandhara art, and some northwestern tribes of ancient India. Gandhari, the wife of King Dhritarashtra, was from that region. Chitraradha was a prominent Gandharva mentioned in the Ramayana and the Mahābhārata. He had a fortuitous encounter with Ravana and fearlessly prevented him from entering the heavens. Sage Kapila is credited with the founding of the Sankhya School and the authorship of Kapila Sutras, which expound the doctrine of the Samkhya philosophy, different from the Samkhya Yoga of the Bhagavadgita. He is mentioned in the Bhagavata Purana as a devotee and an incarnation of Lord Vishnu and in the Mahābhārata as a great yogi who spoke on the virtue of nonviolence.

Sloka 27

uccaiḥśravasam aśvānāṃ viddhi mām amṛtodbhavam
airāvataṃ gajendrāṇāṃ narāṇāṃ ca narādhipam

uccaihsravasam = a horse named Uccaihsravas; asvanam = among the horses; viddhi = know; mam = Me; amrtam = elixir or life; udbhavam = born from; airavatam = Airavata; gaja-indranam = kingly elephants; naranam = among human beings; ca = and; nara-adhipam = the king.

Among the horses, Know Me as the Ucchaisravas, which was born from the elixir of life, as Airavata among the kingly elephants, and as their ruler among humans.

Ucchaisravas is a superiorly fine horse with wings and seven heads. Airavata is a mighty elephant with multiple tusks. Both are spotlessly white and serve as Indra's vehicles in wars and peaceful times. According to the legends, they emerged from the milky ocean (kshirasagaram) when the gods and demons churned it for the elixir of life (Amrit). Lord Krishna mentioned them as his manifestations, probably because they emerged from the milky ocean where Maha Vishnu resides and share his qualities, such as immortality and purity. Narādhipa means ruler or sovereign of naras (humans). In ancient India, a king or a sovereign was considered a divine entity and a direct descendent of God himself or a divinity such as the Moon or the Sun. As a divine entity, he is supposed to function as the ordainer, protector, and upholder of divine laws (dharma) upon the earth and enforce them for the welfare of all. Many rulers in ancient India used to trace their lineage from the gods of repute to command respect and obedience. The three manifestations mentioned in this verse, Ucchaisravas, Airavata, and the rulers upon earth, represent divine qualities such as purity, lordship, majesty, strength, and swiftness. In the Vedas, Brahman is described as a horse, an elephant, and the Lord of all.

Sloka 28

āyudhānām ahaṃ vajraṃ dhenūnām asmi kāmadhuk
prajanaś cāsmi kandarpaḥ sarpāṇām asmi vāsukiḥ

ayudhanam = of the weapons; aham = I am; vajram = the thunderbolt; dhenunam = among the cows; asmi = I am; kama-dhuk = the Kamadhenu; prajanah = progenitors; ca = and; asmi = I am; kandarpah = Kandarpa; sarpanam = of the serpents or snakes; asmi = I am; vasukih = serpent Vasuki.

Of the weapons, I am Vajra. Of the cows, I am Kamadhenu. Among the progenitors, I am Kandarpa, and among the serpents, I am Vasuki.

All the deities of the Hindu pantheon are warrior deities. As the protectors and upholders of Dharma, they often participate in fierce battles against evil forces. Therefore, almost all Hindu deities carry one or more weapons for protecting and upholding Dharma and the pious ones, and destroying the wicked. Their weapons are also unique and powerful, with distinct names to denote their strength and distinction. Some symbolism is also associated with them. In the Vedic pantheon, as the lord of the heavens, Indra wields the mightiest weapon, the thunderbolt known as Vajra. It is called Vajra because it is indestructible and has the brilliance and power of a pure diamond. According to the Vedas, he slew many demons with it, including Vrtasura, a fierce demon who imprisoned the rain waters and sun rays. Symbolically, lightning represents the spark of mental brilliance and flashes of pure intelligence that appear in one's consciousness in exalted moments of divine ecstasy or deep trance. In the Kena Upanishad, we learn that seers often envision Brahman as lightning in deeper meditative states. At one time, Indra enjoyed the status of a Supreme Lord. His prominence declined in the later Vedic age, along with that of Brahma and several other Vedic gods.

Kamadhenu is the name of the celestial cow, known for its ability to grant wishes and fulfill one's desires. Hence, the name Kamadhenu. She possesses wings and is considered the mother of all earthly cows. Just like Ucchaisravas and Airavata, she too is said to have emerged from the Milky Ocean during its churning. Puranic accounts mention different sages, such as Vashista or Jamadagni, as the owner of the sacred cow. Kandarpa is an epithet of the cupid god, Manmatha. He is the inveterate divine tempter who invokes lustful thoughts in gods and humans alike. He once tried his tricks on Lord Shiva and got burnt. Although the Supreme Lord is free from desires and attachments, he is the source of all desires. Therefore, Lord Krishna identified Kandarpa, the god of love and lust, as one of his manifestations. Vasuki was a mighty serpent king. Gods and demons used him to churn the oceans and produce Amrit (the elixir of life). His name also appears in the Buddhist literature. He is considered a manifestation of Ananta or Adishesha in the mortal world.

Sloka 29

anantaś cāsmi nāgānāṃ varuṇo yādasām aham
pitṛṇām aryamā cāsmi yamaḥ saṃyamatām aham

anantah = Ananta; ca = and; asmi = I am; naganam = among the naga snakes; varunah = Varuna; yadasam = of the water divinities; aham = I am; pitrnam = of the ancestors; aryama = Aryama; ca = and; asmi = I am; yamah = Lord Yama; samyamatam = of the controllers; aham = I am.

I am Ananta among the Nagas, and Varuna among aquatic gods. Of the ancestors, I am Aryama, and of the controllers, I am Lord Yama.

In the previous verse, Lord Krishna said that among the serpents (sarpas), he was the mighty serpent, Vasuki. Here, he stated that among the Nagas, he was Ananta. Although the Sarpas and Nagas are serpentine beings, they are different. Sarpas are earthly creatures who live in the subterranean earth and guard the treasures of the earth. The Nagas are celestial serpents who possess divine qualities and are usually associated with gods and celestial beings. Ananta, meaning endless, is the name of a giant celestial serpent of countless hoods, described in the Puranas as Adishesha (the eternal remainder). Symbolically, he represents primal Nature or the entire materiality of Brahman in its undifferentiated aspect. According to the Puranas, Lord Vishnu rests upon his mighty coils in the milky ocean and keeps an attentive gaze upon the entire creation as its Preserver. Hence, Vishnu is also known as Anantasayana (he who rests upon Ananta). Ananta shares the qualities of infinity and stability of the mighty Brahman. Varuna is one of heaven's mightiest and just gods. The Vedas describe him as the upholder and enforcer of morality, divine laws, and justice. He is associated with rains, water bodies, karma, and Dharma in the hymns. Aryama is either an Aditya (solar deity) who controls the movements of time or the progenitor of the Vedic Aryas. The latter description seems more appropriate since Lord Krishna described him here as an ancestor. Yama means control or restraint, as in the Yamas of classical yoga. In the Vedic pantheon, Lord Yama is a manifestation of the Lord of Death and is well known for his impartiality, self-control, and sense of justice. He rules the underworld and awards punishments to the deceased beings according to their sins. He is also popular and revered in Buddhism.

Sloka 30

pralhādaś cāsmi daityānāṃ kālaḥ kalayatām aham
mṛgāṇāṃ ca mṛgendrohaṃ vainateyaś ca pakṣiṇām

prahladah = Prahlada; ca = and; asmi = I am; daityanam = among the demons; kalah = time; kalayatam = record keepers; aham = I am; mrganam = of the animals; ca = and; mrga-indrah = the king of animals, lion; aham = I am; vainateyah = Vainateya; ca = and; paksinam = of birds.

I am Prahlada among the demons, and I am Time among the keepers of time. Among the animals, I am the lion, the king of animals, and among the birds, Vainateya.

Prahlada was an exemplary devotee of Lord Vishnu. Although he was born among the daityas, who were cruel and evil by nature, he became an exclusive devotee of Lord Vishnu with abiding faith, much to the displeasure of his father, Hiranyakashipu, who wanted him to worship him rather than Lord Vishnu. When Prahlada did not relent in his devotion, his father subjected him to cruel punishment and torture. Much to his annoyance, Prahlada endured the suffering and continued to worship Lord Vishnu with exclusive devotion. One day, unable to tolerate his son's continued devotion and control his anger, he wanted him to prove that Lord Vishnu was indeed an omniscient and omnipresent Lord who would readily respond to his devotees' calls and help them. Pointing to a pillar in his palace, he wanted Prahlada to prove whether, through devotion, he could make Lord Vishnu emerge from it instantly. When Prahlada prayed to Lord Vishnu, he burst through the pillar with a roar in the incarnation of Narasimha, a half-lion and half-human being, and slew Hiranyakashipu with his bare hands. The legend proves that the Supreme Lord reciprocates the love of his devotees and fervently keeps his promise to protect and care for them.

Kala is one of the highest manifestations of the Supreme Lord. Kala means both Time and Death. He is the Lord of the mortal world, where everything is food for him through impermanence, death, and decay. The lion symbolizes divine qualities such as royalty, sovereign power, majesty, invincible strength, and ferocity. Hence, among the animals, it is truly considered a divine manifestation with superior strength and majesty. Vainateya is an epithet of Garuda, the divine eagle, the king of birds, who serves as Lord Vishnu's majestic vehicle. Since he was born to Vinata, he is known as Vainateya (or Vainateya). He personifies agility, swiftness, foresight, devotion, dutifulness, loyalty, surrender, and selfless devotion. The Garuda Purana is named after him. Symbolically, he also represents the individual Self (atman), which is inseparably connected from within to the Supreme Self and experiences the same consciousness.

Sloka 31

pavanaḥ pavatām asmi rāmaḥ śastrabhṛtām aham
jhaṣāṇāṃ makaraś cāsmi strotasām asmi jāhnavī

pavanah = the wind; pavatam = of the purifiers; asmi = I am; ramah = Lord Rama; sastra-bhrtam = among the wielders of weapons; aham = I am; jhasanam = among the fish; makarah = makara; ca = and; asmi = I am; srotasam = among the rivers; asmi = I am; jahnavi = Jahnavi.

Of the purifiers, I am the wind. Of the wielders of weapons, I am Lord Rama. Among the fishes, I am Makara, and among the rivers, I am Jahnavi.

Pavana means the wind god or Vayu. He is a purifier because he sweeps away turbulent clouds, pollutants, harmful insects, and foul odors from the air and cleans the earth, the mid-region, and the sky with his swift movements. The same wind moves in us as breath (prana) and purifies and energizes our minds and bodies. By moving constantly, he makes sure that the rains fall, the earth yields crops, and we do not suffocate due to lack of air. Wind also carries sounds and facilitates communication between distinct classes of beings, including gods and celestial beings, through speech, prayers, and sounds. Brahman Himself is a great purifier. His very touch (brahmabhuta sparsa) is purifying and liberating. Anyone who experiences it is instantly liberated. Another quality of Brahman is its invincible power and supremacy. These qualities are reflected in Vayu and Lord Rama, an exemplary warrior prince and an incarnation of Lord Vishnu, and the slayer of Ravana. He wielded the mighty Bow of Shiva and broke it with one hand. His mighty arrow is known as Rama's arrow (Ramabanam). Once unleashed, it is irrevocable and invincible and hits the target without fail. Only Lord Rama can withdraw it. His devotees still believe he is active in the earth's consciousness and keeps a watch over them as their protector and upholder of Dharma. Thus, lord Rama is rightly declared here as a manifestation of Brahman. Some commentators think the name Rama in the verse may refer to Rama or Parasurama. The latter was also a great warrior and wielder of the mighty axe with which he exterminated many Kshatriya kings.

The Supreme Lord of all creation represents unity in diversity. He has innumerable forms and goes by numerous names. His diversity is well represented in some of his manifestations, such as the Makara, a mighty sea dragon and a mythical creature with the body of an elephant, the tail of a fish, and bodily parts that seem to have been drawn from different creatures. It is the vehicle of Mother Ganga and is often associated with Manmadha, the cupid god. It is also the astrological sign of Capricorn in the Zodiac.

Jahnavi is an epithet of Ganga, revered by Hindus as the most sacred of all the rivers on earth, with its origin in the heavens. According to the Puranas, when Ganga descended upon earth, its turbulence angered sage Jahnu, who gulped its waters and held her captive. Later, at the request of the gods, he released her and let her flow on the earth. Since he swallowed her and later let her emerge from his mouth and flow again, Ganga is also known as Jahnavi. In Hindu symbolism, the river represents the pure consciousness of Brahman, whose very touch removes all sins and ensures the liberation of beings.

Sloka 32

sargāṇām ādir antaś ca madhyaṃ caivāham arjuna
adhyātmavidyā vidyānāṃ vādaḥ pravadatām aham

sarganam = of creations; adih = beginning; antah = end; ca = and; madhyam = middle; ca = and; eva = certainly; aham = I am; arjuna = O Arjuna; adhyatma-vidya = atma vidya, knowledge of the Self; vidyanam = of vidyas, branches of knowledge; vadah = fair argument; pravadatam = debaters; aham = I am.

O Arjuna, of the creations, I am the beginning, the middle, and the end. Of the branches of knowledge, I am the knowledge of the Self. Among the debaters, I am the fair argument.

In a previous verse, Lord Krishna declared that he was the beginning, the middle, and the end of all existence because he is eternal and before all. In that verse (verse 20), he said it in reference to the jivas who are subject to birth and death. Here, he said the same about all his creations. They may be creations of all worlds and beings or innumerable objects, states, conditions, dimensions, and realities that arise and subside in each time cycle or on each day of Brahma that lasts for billions of years. Brahman is the only constant and eternal reality in the whole universe. He is always ahead of others and expands infinitely. Hence, he is known by the name Brahman, the ever-expanding one. Everything else comes and goes. Some worlds or planes may last longer than others, but in the end, all disappear into the vast unknown of Brahman. From the beginning to the end of all creation, he remains immutable and imperishable, serving as the witness, enjoyer, and Lord of all, while the worlds he witnesses appear and disappear as waves or bubbles upon an ocean. He is the creator (beginning), preserver (the middle), and destroyer (the end) of the worlds and beings he creates. A part of him watches silently the dance of life within himself, while the other part becomes actively involved with it, enjoying its sweet and bitter fruit. Thus, the One, Supreme Brahman, becomes all this and acts as the subject and object of his creation, appearing in numerous forms and performing numerous roles and functions. In the Bhagavadgita, we worship that absolute Supreme Lord as Krishna.

Vidya means knowledge or that which is to be known. There are many types of Vidyas. Some are considered inferior or this-worldly, and some are superior or otherworldly. Of all the Vidyas or branches of learning, the knowledge of Brahman (Brahma Vidya) or the knowledge of the Self (Atma Vidya) is considered the highest because it leads to enlightenment and liberation, while the rest lead to attachment, delusion, and bondage. Here, Lord Krishna identified himself with the knowledge of the Self because the Self is Brahman only, and without knowing it, one cannot attain the pure consciousness of Brahman or the Self. The Self is the door to liberation and the immortal world of Brahman from which one never returns to take another birth. As the Katha Upanishad declares, it is only through the yoga of self-knowing or self-realization (adhyatma yoga) that a wise person (dhira) leaves behind both joy and sorrow.

Lord Krishna said that among the debaters, he was 'vada,' meaning an argument or point of view. There can be no debate without an argument or viewpoint. It is the subject or the focus of any debate. It is also the meeting ground of diverse thoughts and opinions (vada-vivada), just as Brahman, who represents the diversity of creation and the meeting ground of opposites. However, arguments can be logical, illogical, truthful, false, fair, or perverse. Of them, Lord Krishna declared the fair argument (vada), which is rooted in truth, as his manifestation. Debates and discussions played a significant role in the development of Hindu philosophical systems. Scholars of rival faiths and philosophies debated in public or in the presence of kings to outdo each other and establish the superiority of their doctrines or standpoints.

Sri Shankaracharya, who participated in many debates to proclaim the superiority of Advaita, described three types of debate prevalent in ancient India: Vada, Jalpa, and Vitanda. Vada is an enlightened form of debate in which the participants present their respective points with an open mind in search of truth. In Jalpa, participants present different viewpoints and try to justify their arguments and win, using unfair means, if necessary, such as falsifying information or unfairly attacking their opponents. If this tactic is used by only one party in a debate or discussion, it is called Vitanda, a perverse argument. Sattvic people present fair and truthful arguments (vada) based on facts and reason to explore truths; rajasic people resort to unfair arguments (jalpa) based on passions, emotions, and assumptions to win, and tamasic people use perverse arguments (vitanda) with little regard to facts, reason, or established norms to force their opinions and beliefs upon others.

Sloka 33

akṣarāṇām akārosmi dvandvaḥ sāmāsikasya ca
aham evākṣayaḥ kālo dhātāhaṃ viśvatomukhaḥ 10.33

aksaranam = among the letters; akarah = the first letter A; asmi = I am; dvandvah = dual compound, dvandva samasa; samasikasya = among the samasas, compound words; ca = and; aham = I am; eva = surely; aksayah = inexhaustible, unending; kalah = time; dhata = creator; aham = I am; visvatah-mukhah = faces in all directions.

Among the letters, I am the first letter, A(अ), and among the samasas (compound words), dvandva. I am indeed the inexhaustible Time, Kala; I am the creator (Brahma), with faces in all directions.

As Brahman, Lord Krishna is first in everything and everywhere. As the Primal Being (Adi Purusha), he is before all, the beginning of all, and the most ancient. Since he is the first (prathama) and foremost and the source of all sounds, letters, and languages, he rightfully represents the first letter of any alphabet. It is with the first letter in the alphabet that we begin our education and our journey into the world of knowledge and devotion and, eventually, into the world of immortality. The first letter of the Sanskrit alphabet, अ, also figures prominently in many attributes of Krishna, such as Adi, Anadi, Ananta, Asesha, and the sacred syllable, Aum. It is also the first letter that newborn babies learn to utter as they start vocalizing sounds to communicate with their mothers.

Samasa is a grammatical term that refers to the conjunction of words in a dual compound in which two nouns are joined. In Sanskrit, depending upon how the compound words are formed by joining the nouns, four types of samasas are distinguished: dvandva, tatpurusa, avyayibhava, and bahuvrihi. In dvandva, two independent nouns are brought together to form a compound word in which both nouns retain their respective meanings and stand in their own right even after joining them. Thus, for example, when two nouns, sukham (pleasure) and dukham (pain), are joined to form the compound word, sukhadukham or 'sukham ca dukham,' their original meanings are not lost. Thus, the dualities characteristic of the Lord's creation are well represented by dvandva samasas. Each of the nouns used in them represents the immutability of his absolute state, which is always the same whether he appears as the Supreme Self, the individual Self, the embodied Self, or the Cosmic Self. Just as the nouns in a dvandva, in creation also, the dualities coexist as distinct phenomena complementing each other, such as day and night or life and death. Together, they make existence possible. Life is a combination of dualities, just as the nouns in a dvandva. Each jiva formed by the union of Prakriti and Purusha, or the body and the soul, also exemplifies dvandva. Thus, the dual compound (dvandva samasa) rightly represents the whole manifestation, which arises as a perfect union between the Supreme Lord and his creation or between his two aspects, Purush and Prakriti, in which they retain their distinction.

Kala (time) is one of the Supreme Lord's earliest and highest manifestations. In his absolute state, he is eternal, immutable, inexhaustible, and without division, direction, or movement. We may even say that he does not exist. However, in creation, he has forms, movements, divisions, and direction. He moves back and forth, repetitively or cyclically, according to purpose and circumstances. Although the past and present may seem to disappear into an unknown void, they are never lost but are duly recorded by the guardians of Fate and divine justice to enforce karma and transmigration. In Hinduism, Kala is also revered as the Lord of Death. In the mortal world, none can escape Kala (Death) or his manifestations: impermanence, destruction, aging, sickness, death, and decay. Eventually, all things and beings meet their end according to their nature, fate, or karma. Therefore, the Vedas proclaim that Kala, the Lord of Death, rules this world. In the last part of the verse, Lord Krishna stated that among the creators, he was Brahma. As the Supreme Brahman, he is the creator of several Brahmas in many creations. In each creation, Brahma is the firstborn and the first creator god. He is also considered a manifestation of Brahman only. In each time cycle, he creates worlds and beings and sets in motion the cycle of creation. He has four faces in four directions. Hence, he is described here as the 'visvatah-mukhah.'

Sloka 34

mṛtyuḥ sarvaharaś cāham udbhavaś ca bhaviṣyatām
kīrtiḥ śrīr vāk ca nārīṇāṃ smṛtir medhā dhṛtiḥ kṣamā

mrtyuh = death; sarva-harah = all ending, removing; ca = and; aham = I am; udbhavah = origin; ca = and; bhavisyatam = of what happens in future; kirtih = fame; srih = beauty; vak = speech; ca = and; narinam = in women; smrtih = memory; medha = intelligence; dhrtih = fortitude; ksama = patience.

I am the all-ending Death, and I am the origin of what happens in the future. In women, I am fame, beauty, speech, memory, intelligence, fortitude, and patience.

As far as the mortal world is concerned, death is the end of everything that manifests from Nature in the jiva, namely the not-self consisting of the ego, desires, attachments, memories, possessions, names, forms, tattvas, gunas, etc. Therefore, Death is rightly described here as the all-devouring and all-ending (sarva hara) divine manifestation. Death shares with Isvara his destructive function. As the Destroyer, he is the ultimate cause of death, decay, and destruction of things and beings in the mortal world. His destruction has the twin purpose of ending and renewing life. Through them, he keeps the cyclical nature of existence in motion. As the Lord of Death, he consumes things and beings to destroy what is undesirable and preserve and renew what is obligatory for the order, regularity, and continuation of the world. He also helps in our spiritual progress, consuming our impurities and past sins according to our karmas to open our eyes to the truths of our existence and essential nature. When we continue to cling to the world and wallow in darkness and delusion, he manifests in our lives to end our striving and hankering and give us another opportunity in another life. He also ensures balance by limiting our time on earth in each life and the burdens we can carry. Imagine how oppressive it will be if we have to live forever. The life of Bhīshma is a case in point. In a way, we are blessed with mortality because we do not have to suffer forever from life's burdens or keep accumulating sins with no chance to escape from samsara.

In death, we find a temporary break from our current lives and circumstances and find another opportunity through rebirth to start afresh with the lessons we learn and the knowledge we gain. In this regard also, the Lord plays an important role. Through death, he deconstructs our lives and reconstructs them through rebirth. He puts us on a new journey, using our past deeds (karma) as the basis, concealing the memories of our past lives, and giving us a fresh chance to start all over again with a fresh mind and body. Thus, through creation, preservation, destruction, renewal, and regeneration, he ensures that life continues upon the earth in an orderly manner, unimpeded by the memories from past lives. In his unmanifested aspect, he is devoid of qualities (nirguna), but in his manifested aspect as Isvara, he reflects many. They do not exist in him, and he does not exist in them. They arise from his Nature (Prakriti) due to his presence and remain confined to his Nature only. They also manifest in us according to the degree to which we are pure and divine and reflect the Self in us. Without them manifesting in us, we cannot realize our divinity or purity or attain oneness with the Self.

In this verse, Lord Krishna mentioned the most sublime and divine qualities found in virtuous women due to the predominance of sattva. They are the footprints of the Supreme Lord that manifest in them as they advance spiritually, purifying themselves and filling their hearts and minds with devotion. Kirti, meaning name and fame, is a double-edged sword. It may be earned through righteous means or dubious means. Hence, it should be considered a divine quality only when it is earned through righteous means. Sri means beauty, auspiciousness, wealth, and prosperity, which are considered the qualities of Goddess Lakshmi. The power of speech (vak) comes with knowledge, virtue, education, upbringing, and refinement. The other qualities mentioned here are directly related to the mode of sattva. They manifest when a person is predominantly pure and virtuous.

Sloka 35

bṛhatsāma tathā sāmnāṃ gāyatrī chandasām aham
māsānāṃ mārgaśīrṣoham ṛtūnāṃ kusumākaraḥ

brhat-sama = the Brhat-sama; tatha = also, and; samnam = of the Sama chants; gayatri = the Gayatri; chandasam = of meters; aham = I am; masanam = of months; marga-sirsah = Margasirah, November-December; aham = I am; rtunam = of the seasons; kusuma-akarah = flowering season, spring.

I am Brhatsama of the Sama chants and Gayatri among the meters. Of the months (of the year), I am Margasira. Of the seasons, I am the flowering season.

In a previous verse, Lord Krishna said that among the Vedas, the Samaveda was his manifestation. In this verse, he particularly identified the Brhatsama of the Samaveda as his manifestation. The hymns of the Samaveda are known as Samans. They are known for their metrical form and their ability to invoke devotion to the gods. The Brihat Saman is addressed to Indra, the lord of the heavens, who is also deemed a manifestation of the Supreme Brahman only. Brhati is derived from the same root word 'Brh' (as in Brahman), meaning expanding, going forth, or uplifting. The expansive and uplifting quality of Brhatsama is a divine quality of Brahman as Isvara, the ultimate presiding deity of all the Vedas and Vedic mantras. He is also the source of the power that carries the sacred sounds of the Brihat Saman through the space to Indra's heaven when auspicious minds chant them. Carrying forth the prayers of priests and devotees across space to the heavens and beyond, he connects them with the deities of the higher realms and secures their relationship.

The same is true about the sacred Gayatri chant from the Rigveda (3.62.10), composed in the meter having the same name. The chant is an invocation to the god Savitur, a solar deity of a higher realm (subtle mind) and a manifestation of Brahman only. Since the sacred mantra can invoke the higher energies of the mind and body and illuminate the internal organ with the brilliance of multiple suns (Adityas), it is considered one of the most powerful and auspicious prayers of the Vedas. Margasira is the ninth month of the lunar calendar, from about the middle of December to the middle of January, and is considered the most auspicious month of the year. According to the Vaishnava tradition, Lord Vishnu himself is its presiding deity. Since it is an auspicious month, several festivals are celebrated, including the Vaikunta Ekadashi, which falls on the 11th lunar day of the month. On that day, devotees observe penance and worship Lord Vishnu in homes and temples. Gita Jayanti is also celebrated on the same day since Lord Krishna is said to have delivered the Bhagavadgita to Arjuna on the battlefield of Kurukshetra on that day only.

Kusumakara means the flowering season or spring, also known as Rituraja or the king of seasons. It is the favorite season of Lord Krishna since he is primarily a pastoral deity who lived in Gokul amidst Nature as a child. Spring is divine because the world appears in its best colors during this period, decked with the abundance of Nature, as life in many forms regenerates and radiates Nature's beauty and God's splendor. The world becomes filled with beauty, vitality, fertility, harmony, happiness, peace, prosperity, diversity, music, hope, vigor, and vibrancy. It also coincides with the onset of the harvest season and the beginning of many Hindu festivals. The famous festivals, Holi and Vasant, are celebrated during this season only.

Sloka 36

dyutaṃ chalayatām asmi tejas tejasvinām aham
jayosmi vyavasāyosmi sattvaṃ sattvavatām aham

dyutam = dice play, gambling; chalayatam = among the deceptions and trickeries; asmi = I am; tejah = brilliance, brightness, radiance; tejasvinam = of the brilliant or radiant; aham = I am; jayah = victory; asmi = I am; vyavasayah

= resolve, strenuous effort; asmi = I am; sattvam = purity, sattva; sattva-vatam = of the pure nature; aham = I am.

Of the deceptions and trickeries, I am the dice play; the brilliance of the brilliant I am; victory I am; resolve I am; I am the purity of the pure nature.

Qualities such as dexterity, intelligence, radiance, supremacy, strength, purity, and gentleness reflect the Lord's presence in creation. They are the visible signs of his omnipresence and omniscience, although he remains hidden and concealed. They manifest in the purity of things and remain concealed amidst impurities. Concealment is also a function of the Supreme Lord, just as creation, preservation, and destruction. Just as darkness manifests when the sun is absent or concealed, evil qualities manifest when impurities conceal the effulgence of the Self. In other words, divine qualities manifest when Krishna's higher nature is unimpeded, and negative qualities appear when his maya shaktis reign supreme. The Self always reflects divine qualities only. Their evil counterparts manifest only when he is veiled and concealed by the play of Maya. Thus, in creation, evil is the absence of divinity.

Lord Krishna stated that of the deceptions, he is gambling or dice play. In gambling, one must rely on luck, chance, trickery, or deception to win. Those who conceal their deception without being caught enjoy a clear advantage against those who play honestly. The Supreme Being is also a master of illusions and trickery (mayavi) since he casts the net of delusion upon all and plays dice with their lives, subjecting them to the vagaries of fate and uncertainties. However, his trickery is selfless and has a divine purpose. As the Concealer, he obscures the truths of the Supreme Reality from the mortal beings and deludes them into believing the real as unreal and the unreal as real. He also keeps them bound to samsara by concealing their omniscience and omnipresence from themselves. Life on earth is a game of chance, in which we do not know what will happen or how our actions may bear fruit. Hence, we also lack control over its course.

The remaining qualities mentioned here bloom in Nature due to the predominance of sattva. They manifest according to the purity of a person or object. Since Krishna is pure intelligence and the source of light, he is the brilliance of the brilliant and the effulgence of the effulgent. All the divinities partake in his nature. Being the Lord of all with inviolable will, he is invincible and victorious in all endeavors. Hence, he personifies the victory of the righteous kind. He also grants victory to those who pray to him or uphold Dharma. Vyavasaya means resolve, strenuous effort, or persevering with determination. It is essential to achieve success in any effort or complete any task. Lord Krishna himself is the beginning, middle, and end of every manifestation. It means he completes all tasks. Because of him only, his devotees and yogis succeed in achieving liberation.

Sloka 37

vṛṣṇīnāṃ vāsudevosmi pāṇḍavānāṃ dhanaṃjayaḥ
munīnām apy ahaṃ vyāsaḥ kavīnām uśanā kaviḥ

vrsninam = of the Vrsnis; vasudevah = Vasudeva Krishna; asmi = I am; pandavanam = of the Pāndavas; dhananjayah = Arjuna; muninam = of the hermits; api = and; aham = I am; vyasah = sage Vyasa; kavinam = of the omniscient seers; usana = Usana, Sukracharya; kavih = the omniscient.

Of the Vrishnis, I am Vasudeva Krishna; of the Pāndavas, Arjuna; among the hermits, I am Vyasa; and among the omniscient seers, I am the omniscient Usana.

Vrishnis belonged to an ancient clan of Yadavas, said to have descended from Vrishni, the son of Satvata, grandson of Yayati, and a descendant of Yadu of the Yadu-Turvasa tribe. They lived in the Gangetic Valley before migrating to Dwaraka (on the west coast) after fighting a war with Jarasandha. In the Mahābhārata war, they fought on the side of the Kauravas to honor the agreement reached by Lord Krishna with both sides. A few decades after the war, the entire tribe perished due to internal conflicts and civil unrest, coinciding with the conclusion of Lord Krishna's incarnation. Vasudeva is an epithet of Lord Krishna since his father was Vasudeva. It is also an epithet of Lord Vishnu. Symbolically, it means the deity (deva) who dwells (vāsa) in all. As the individual Self and the all-pervading Self, Brahman is the indweller of all living beings and the whole creation.

Muni refers to a special type of ascetics, seers, sages, or hermits who live in seclusion and observe physical and mental silence (maunam) as an austerity (tapas) to practice self-control and purification. By restraining their speech and the movements of their minds and bodies, they silence their desires and attachments and establish themselves in the witness consciousness. Here, Lord Krishna declared that among such hermits, he was Vyasa or Veda Vyasa, also known as Krishna Dvaipayana. He is considered an aspect or a minor incarnation of Lord Vishnu and credited with the authorship of the Mahābhārata, the Puranas, Brahma Sutras, and several hymns of the Vedas. He was also the grandfather of the Pāndavas and Kauravas since he fathered Dhritarashtra, the father of Kauravas, and Pandu, the father of Pandavas.

Kavi means the one who knows the past, the present, and the future. Kavi also means the creator who has full knowledge of his creations. In this verse, Lord Krishna said that among the kavis (divine seers), Usana was his manifestation. The Usana to whom Krishna referred in this verse was the sage Sukracharya. He was the principal teacher of the demons and was known for his proficiency in Vedic astrology. He was the son of Bhrigu, also known as Kavi, the father of Vedic astrology, whom Lord Krishna identified as his manifestation in the previous verse.

Sloka 38

daṇḍo damayatām asmi nītir asmi jigīṣatām
maunaṃ caivāsmi guhyānāṃ jñānaṃ jñānavatāmaham

dandah = law or the rod of punishment; damayatam = of the punishers; asmi = I am; nitih = lawful conduct, morality, right behavior; asmi = I am; jigisatam = of those who seek victory; maunam = silence; ca = and; eva = verily; asmi =

I am; guhyanam = of secrets; jnanam = knowledge; jnana-vatam = of the knowers; aham = I am.

Of the punishers, I am the law or rod of punishment. I am the lawful conduct of those who seek victory, and verily, I am the silence of the secrets. I am the knowledge of the knowers.

Punishments arise from karma only, and punishment is the fruit of sinful karma or conduct. Most of the time, you may not know why and how punishments may manifest from past sins. Your punishment may arise from your actions, fate, or your responses to others' actions, in which you assume responsibility for your actions and do not renounce desires, ownership, and doership. The Lord of the Universe neither judges, punishes, nor rewards anyone. He may rescue his exclusive devotees from samsara and forgive even the gravest sinners if they practice devotion, taking refuge in him. The punishment usually arises from the laws he establishes or ordains through the law books (Dharma shastras) or the judgment of the guardians, such as the kings, rulers, and administrators who have an obligation to uphold, protect, and enforce them for the sake of Dharma, order, and regularity. They determine punishments according to the severity of each case. Hence, the Lord aptly declared himself the punishing rod (the means) of each punishment. The administrators of justice are the punishing hands. The laws themselves, which guide them in their decisions, represent the punishing rod. The power to punish the offenders arises from the Lord only and flows through them.

He also stated that he was the righteous or the lawful conduct of those who were victorious. What it means is that he represents only those victories that are achieved through righteous means or lawful conduct. In other words, in the completion of tasks, the means are as important as the ends. The goal must be righteous, and the actions to achieve it must also be righteous. Only then can we expect the Lord to support us. He obviously does not support or participate in the victories won through evil or dishonesty. It also means he stands with those who fight for righteous causes and pursue righteous ends with righteous means. Victory does not always mean gaining or winning. Victories are also achieved through losing, giving, giving up, sacrifice, endurance, and abiding faith. If a person achieves victory through dishonest means or by sacrificing his moral or ethical values, it is not deemed a real victory but a spiritual defeat. A person who fights for righteous causes without sacrificing his aims, moral values, or righteous conduct is deemed a winner even if he loses the battle. In the battle of life, sometimes we win, sometimes we lose. However, irrespective of what happens, we must maintain our basic morality and sense of justice. Success and failure, victory or defeat, are relative terms—their meaning and value change according to the methods used. Methods and outcomes become irrelevant when one practices karma-sannyasa yoga. One may also conclude from this that Lord Krishna wants his devotees to pursue the four aims of human life through righteous and selfless actions without forsaking Dharma or discernment.

The verse also states that the Lord is the knowledge of the knowers. Knowledge means the right knowledge, which purifies and liberates beings from bondage and suffering. It may arise from the study of scriptures, the teachings of spiritual masters, observation, contemplation, or direct knowing. The all-knowing Supreme Brahman personifies self-existent, eternal, and indestructible pure knowledge. Hence, knowledge reigns supreme in the knowers of Brahman.

Sloka 39

yac cāpi sarvabhūtānāṃ bījaṃ tad aham arjuna
na tad asti vinā yat syān mayā bhūtaṃ carācaram

yat = whatever; ca = and; api = also; sarva-bhutanam = of all beings; bijam = the seed; tat = that; aham = I am; arjuna = O Arjuna; na = not; tat = that; asti = there is; vina = without; yat = which; syat = can exist; maya = by Me; bhutam = thing; cara-acaram = moving and unmoving.

And whatever the seed of all beings is, that also I am. O Arjuna, there is nothing, moving or unmoving, which can exist without Me.

The Supreme Lord is the beginning, middle, and end of all creations, including the creation of all beings. He is also their seed or source. While life appears to arise from the union of male and female reproductive materials outwardly, beings are filled with life (prana) only when the Self enters the embryos. Therefore, he is indeed the source of all life on Earth. The very existence of the jivas depends upon His presence in them. You also play a similar role in your life or in your little creation called life or consciousness. For example, if you do not exist, your world does not exist. If your senses are completely withdrawn, the world disappears into a void. The world may have its independent existence, but it does not manifest in your consciousness unless you illuminate it with your senses. This may create the illusion that you are indeed making everything happen with your thoughts and actions or with your mind and body, and that you are the source of your life and the reality you experience between birth and death, even if it lasts for a while.

The right approach is that you should not claim ownership or doership of your life or actions. It is because the world does not belong to you, and the power and the intelligence to create your life, any life, or anything, or perform any action arises from the Lord only. He is the source of all actions and their outcomes. Therefore, we must pass on the fruit of our thoughts and actions to him only and consider him to be the sole Creator of all. He is the source and support of all that manifests in the whole creation. Even Prakriti serves him only and manifests his will. Without him, she remains inactive and undifferentiated. As the Supreme Controller and Lord of all, he energizes and illuminates every action, manifestation, and movement. He is the ultimate cause of the creation, preservation, evolution, and destruction of all things and beings. Through his association with Prakriti, he upholds all this by himself.

In the mortal world, life arises due to the presence of the Self in matter. Forms appear because of the admixture of gunas and tattvas and the gradual development of higher evolutes, namely the mind, the ego, and intelligence. Together, they create the liveliness (jivatvam), existence (asthitvam), and distinct qualities (jiva lakshnam) of the jivas and their diversity (bhinnatvam), with varying degrees of individuality and self-awareness, shaped by karma and other forces of Nature. As the Self enters the deeper layers of Nature and her tattvas and is enveloped by her impurities, he becomes bound to names and forms and a limited consciousness. From then on, his existence in the jivas as the embodied Self depends upon the jiva's actions. Bound to the mortal body and the mortal world, he remains indifferent, witnessing the jiva engaging in desire-ridden actions due to egoism, attachments, dualities, delusion, and suffering from their consequences. He escapes from it only through liberation. In this journey, also, the Lord is the cause and the solution.

Sloka 40

nāntosti mama divyānāṃ vibhūtīnāṃ paraṃtapa
eṣa tūddeśataḥ prokto vibhūter vistaro mayā

na = nor; antah = end; asti = there is; mama = My; divyanam = divine; vibhutinam = manifestations; parantapa = O conqueror of the enemies; esah = this; tu = however; uddesatah = as an illustration; proktah = spoken; vibhuteh = manifestations; vistarah = vast, expansive; maya = by Me.

There is no end to my divine manifestations, O conqueror of the enemies. However, this description of (My) endless manifestations is spoken by Me as an illustration.

The Supreme Lord represents the limitless supreme reality, which is eternal and fixed. There are no limitations to his opulence, power, and glory. His infinite power manifests in infinite ways. Even the descriptions of his manifestations mentioned here are only a few and illustrative in the endless ocean of his creation. They reveal his supreme nature and endless power. We may never know or recognize most of them because our minds have a limited capacity to fathom the secrets of creation or recognize those with which they are not familiar. His manifestations appear and disappear in the vast spaces of the universe. Some may not happen in our universe or time, and some may belong to different worlds and planes of consciousness beyond our understanding. The seers and sages who are mentioned in this chapter belong to past ages and lost civilizations. We have yet to learn when and how they disappeared into the depths of history and how many others were lost to history, forgotten, or erased from the annals of the earth. We do not know or cannot foretell how many more divine manifestations may appear in this world in the future to uphold Dharma and ensure the progress of our civilization. However, we can always discern his footprints in all the luminous objects of the world that radiate his supreme qualities. Wherever we find beauty, harmony, peace, love, perfection, excellence, sweetness, strength, courage, and intelligence, we know that they are but the telltale signs of his presence only amidst us. The best of everything everywhere and in all things represents him only. The most excellent of what we think, own, create, see, hear, touch, feel, and relate to also arise from his reflection in our consciousness. By knowing his manifestations and cultivating his purity and intelligence to discern them and their significance, we experience reverential devotion towards the whole existence. We become aware that we live in his creation, surrounded by his unmistakable presence and protection, and we are a part of his sacred manifestations.

Sloka 41

yad yad vibhūtimat sattvaṃ śrīmad ūrjitam eva vā
tat tad evāvagaccha tvaṃ mama tejoṃśasaṃbhavam

yat yat = whatever; vibhuti mat= endowed with glory; sattvam = truth, object; sri-mat = beauty and prosperity; urjitam = energy; eva = for certain; va = or; tat tat = all that; eva = only; avagaccha = know; tvam = you; mama = My; tejah = power; amsa = part of; sambhavam = manifests.

Whatever object is endowed with beauty, prosperity, and energy, know for sure that all that manifests as a part of My Power only.

The beauty and splendor of the world attract our senses and fill us with positive emotions. We respond instinctively to all the bright and beautiful things we see or experience. By nature, we seek peace and prosperity. We revere those who personify divinity and divine qualities. We do so because we are naturally drawn to the power and glory of the Supreme Being. We may not see him directly, but we see his footprints everywhere and are automatically drawn to his hidden presence in the world. The world is filled with his power and magic, yet in our eagerness, we seek miracles and further proof of his existence. His discernable signs of presence are truth, perfection, beauty, prosperity, order, regularity, discipline, power, energy, strength, heroism, courage, compassion, etc. They remind us that we live in his world, in his presence, under his watch, surrounded by and supported by him, and we draw our nourishment from his benevolence and opulence. One of the reasons we are advised to contemplate upon the Self is that it will strengthen our divine nature and our resolve to grow in his image. We may seek him in temples, sacred places, and the divinities we worship, but in reality, the world is his one vast temple, and we are his numerous devotees, serving him in our peculiar ways with devotion or delusion. The beauty and incredible power of his creations are self-evident everywhere, but we tend to ignore them in our eagerness to pursue our material and selfish goals. If your heart is devoted to Isvara Brahman and your mind is absorbed in his thoughts, you will instantly feel his presence in and around you. You may not notice the Lord, but he will notice you and lead you gently to the doors of liberation.

Sloka 42

athavā bahunaitena kiṃ jñātena tavārjuna
viṣṭabhyāham idaṃ kṛtsnam ekāṃśena sthito jagat

athava = however; = or; bahuna = extensively; etena = this; kim = what; jnatena = knowing; tava = you; arjuna = O Arjuna; vistabhya = uphold and pervade; aham = I; idam = this; krtsnam = whole, all; eka = one; amsena = fraction; sthitah = remain; jagat = world.

However, O Arjuna, what does it do to you knowing my many manifestations? I uphold and pervade this whole world with a fraction of Myself.

This is what Lord Krishna intended: "However, O Arjuna, I can keep on describing my numerous manifestations. There is no end to them. Therefore, there is no use in knowing them further. Your knowledge of them will always be incomplete, even if I keep describing them. Just know that I pervade and uphold this whole creation (which is also vast and immeasurable) by a fraction of Myself."

The manifestations of Krishna as the Supreme Lord are numerous. Knowing them all is not only humanly impossible but also not very useful for liberation. However, it is not without its rewards. Devotees can use the knowledge to practice contemplation upon his opulence and cultivate devotion or develop an emotional connection with him. As Lord Krishna said before, it is difficult to meditate on his formless aspect. Devotees can use his names, forms, and manifestations to fill their minds with his thoughts and strengthen their faith and devotion. He has countless known and unknown or manifested and unmanifested aspects. His unknown and unmanifested aspects are more than his manifested aspects. As the Lord implied here, his numerous manifestations constitute but a fraction of his unmanifested Self. His absolute formless aspect is invisible, imperceptible, and indefinable, and cannot be known by any means. Therefore, trying to know everything about him mentally or intellectually will be a futile exercise.

Further, even the manifested Supreme Lord cannot be known objectively through study, imagination, or contemplation. We may think of him or form a mental opinion of him, but it will not be sufficient to comprehend his immensity or essential nature. He is known only by self-knowing, as oneself, in a subjective state of unity and nonduality when the mind is silent, and the duality of the knower and the known is absent. His creation itself is endless. Even modern science concurs that knowing everything about the manifest universe is humanly impossible. The visible material universe, which is vast and infinite, is but a tiny fraction of the unknown, invisible, and subtle universe. We still do not know whether we live in a universe or a multiverse and whether there are more dimensions than the four we know. Because of the advances in recent times, we are gradually waking up to the hidden secrets of the universe while grappling with its many riddles, such as the nature of dark matter or the behavior of particles in a quantum field. We are still in the early stages of knowing its inner workings, vastness, or laws that govern its movements and functions. Since existence is such an enigma, the great Buddha remained silent about esoteric subjects such as the causes of creation or the role of God in it. He felt that speculating upon such indeterminate subjects would hinder Nirvana and would not lead to the right understanding or discernment.

Conclusion

iti srīmadbhāgavadgītāsupanisatsu brahmavidyāyām yogasāstre srikrisnārjunasamvāde vibhūtiyogaḥ nāma dasamo 'dhyayah

iti = thus; srīmadbhāgavadgītā = in the sacred Bhagavadgita; upanisatsu = in the Upanishad; brahmavidyāyām = the knowledge of the absolute Brahman; yogasāstre = the scripture of yoga; srikrisnārjunasamvāde = the dialogue between Sri Krishna and Arjuna; vibhūtiyogo nāma = by the yoga of divine manifestations; dasama = tenth; adhyayah = chapter;

Thus ends the tenth chapter, named Vibhuti Yoga (the Yoga of Divine Manifestations) in the Upanishad of the divine Bhagavadgita, the knowledge of the Absolute, a treatise on Yoga, and the debate between Arjuna and Lord Krishna.

11 – Visvarupa Darshana Yoga

The Yoga of the Vision of the Universal Form

Sloka 1

arjuna uvāca
madanugrahāya paramaṃ guhyam adhyātmasaṃjñitam
yat tvayoktaṃ vacas tena mohoyaṃ vigato mama

arjunah uvaca = Arjuna said; mat-anugrahaya = as a favor to me, for my sake; paramam = supreme; guhyam = secret; adhyatma = the inner Self; samjnitam = known as; yat = by which; tvaya = by You; uktam = said; vacah = words; tena = by that; mohah = delusion; ayam = this; vigatah = is gone; mama = My.

Arjuna said, "The utmost supreme secret, known as the inner Self, was spoken by you to me as a favor, by which words this delusion of mine has gone."

Arjuna said, "O Lord, you have been kind enough to reveal to me the supreme secret of the Self. By knowing from you that I am an eternal and indestructible Self, I have overcome the delusion that I am merely a physical being. I am now fully established in my spiritual identity as the Self. My eyes are opened to the reality of who I truly am." However, this is just the first part of his statement. The remaining part is in the next verse.

What is delusion (moha)? It is having and accepting the mistaken notion that the physical self is the true Self and the mind is the seat of one's true consciousness. It arises due to the lack of discernment and persists as long as one does not realize that the Supreme Lord is present in all beneath the impurities of their minds and bodies as their true Self and supports them just as he supports the whole creation. It does not matter whether the Lord divides himself into numerous individual selves and appears in each jiva, or the same indivisible Supreme Self appears as the witness Self in all. What is more important is to know with conviction that you are not a physical entity subject to death and rebirth but a spiritual being. Knowing that the Lord lives in each of us as our very Self is the first step to our spiritual rebirth. Therefore, one should find time to reflect on this truth and look inward to find the Lord, who is seated in the cave of the heart and never separate or distant from the seeing one.

A devotee becomes established in the eternal, stable, and indestructible Self and qualifies for liberation when his delusion disappears. Where there is delusion, there is no true devotion. They cancel each other. In the second chapter, Lord Krishna taught Arjuna the distinction between the impermanent, physical self and the indestructible, eternal Self. He told him that the Self was the dweller of the body, distinct from the body and unlike the body, and that he was impervious to death and destruction. He further told him that those who thought that it could be killed or it would kill were deluded and did not know the truth. Thus, knowing the distinction between the Self and the not-self (the body), he said, was the first step to overcoming the delusion of the mind and body and realizing one's eternal, indestructible, essential nature. This awareness is fundamental to the seeker's spiritual awakening. In this verse, Arjuna alluded to this realization.

The pure consciousness of the Self, which is eternal and unchanging, and the impure consciousness of the mind, which is the source of ignorance and delusion, do not coexist except in the twilight zone of the objective reality which Nature induces in the jivas with the help of the triple gunas. In that temporary construct of the mind-driven reality, the Self remains in a passive state of withdrawal as the witness (sakshi), enveloped by a veil of maya. When the mind is silenced and the veil is removed, the brilliance of the Self shines through its consciousness (citta), declaring its presence and divinity just as the sun appears on the horizon and declares its presence when the darkness of the night recedes into the background. In that transformative state or the spiritual rebirth of the jiva, the witness Self hidden in the depths of inner silence (susupti) becomes the wakeful Self (chaitanya atma).

The knowledge of the Self is supreme because there is no other knowledge that is as liberating and enlightening. It is the utmost secret that is not readily available to all but known only to a few who renounce the world and engage in the austere practice of yoga or earn the grace (anugraha) of the Supreme Lord through exclusive devotion. It happened to Arjuna on the battlefield of Kurukshetra. In today's world, knowledge of the Self is available in books and other sources. However, intellectual knowledge may inspire one to pursue liberation, but it does not purify or transform. Only those who realize it experientially or directly through self-knowing or self-absorption reach the highest Goal.

Sloka 2

bhavāpyayau hi bhūtānāṃ śrutau vistaraśo mayā
tvattaḥ kamalapatrākṣa māhātmyam api cāvyayam

bhava = creation, existence apyayau = dissolution; hi = surely; bhutanam = of the beings; srutau = heard; vistarasah = in detail; maya = by Me; tvattah = from You; kamala-patra-aksa = O lotus-eyed one; mahatmyam = greatness; api = more so; ca = and; avyayam = inexhaustible.

"The creation and dissolution of beings was heard from You by me in detail, O Lotus-eyed, and so also your inexhaustible greatness."

This and the previous verse summarize the knowledge Arjuna learned from Lord Krishna. In the previous verse, he said that he overcame delusion by knowing his true identity as the eternal Self. In this verse, he acknowledged that he learned about creation and dissolution in detail from him. It may be recalled that in the ninth chapter, Lord Krishna explained to him how, at the end of each cycle of creation, he withdrew beings and things into his eternal Nature and brought them forth at the beginning of the next. Apart from describing his most important manifestations, he also told him that he was the Self of all and the beginning, the middle, and also the end of them. Thus,

Arjuna learned many secrets from Lord Krishna about his inexhaustible greatness, which he acknowledged here with gratitude. This was a prologue to the wish he was going to express next. That wish is rarely granted by the Supreme Lord, who is unknown and invisible even to gods and the beings of the highest realms.

Sloka 3

evam etad yathāttha tvam ātmānaṃ parameśvara
draṣṭum icchāmi te rūpam aiśvaraṃ puruṣottama

evam = moreover; etat = this; yatha = just as; attha = spoken; tvam = You; atmanam = yourself; parama-isvara = Supreme Lord; drastum = to see; icchami = I wish; te = You; rupam = form; aisvaram = supreme, sovereign; purusa-uttama = O best of purushas.

"Moreover, just as You speak about Yourself, O Supreme Lord, I wish to see Your Supreme Form, O best of the Purushas."

Arjuna said, "O Lord, I heard of your divine manifestation from you. I realized your greatness. I also heard that you control this gigantic universe with just a fraction of yourself. Now, I want to see with my eyes that enormous universal form that upholds all this and extends beyond."

Most of the time, you rely upon your mind and senses in your search for truth. It helps you know the world and objective reality. Even then, you may not know sufficiently, and your knowledge may not help to know the entire truth. This is especially true when you want to know metaphysical truths without doubts and confusion. The knowledge of the Supreme Lord is even more difficult to ascertain since he cannot be known in duality or entirely. If you are not conversant with the scriptures, you may perceive his numerous manifestations as different from him and fall into further confusion and delusion. Even if you know them to be his manifestations, it may not help you much or know him fully. Hence, Arjuna wanted to see the Lord's universal form in one glance to comprehend his opulence and true dimensions. He wanted to see him objectively, not as an idea but in person, right in front of him in duality.

It is rather an unusual and paradoxical wish since infinity cannot be perceived entirely by the human senses from any perspective. In the past, we have instances where he appeared before humans, but this was an unusual situation. Arjuna was familiar with Lord Krishna's incarnated form. Having realized that he was indeed the Supreme Lord of the universe, he wanted to see his universal form. It was not because he doubted his universality or lordship but because he wanted to see him in that form, maybe due to curiosity or excitement. He requested him by calling him Purushottama, which means the best of all Purushas. The individual Self, the embodied Self, and all the divinities in creation are also known as Purushas. Isvara, the Lord of the Universe, is the best of them. Hence, he is Purushottama.

The Purusha in the body does not participate in creation or actions. The invisible, formless, and absolute aspect of Brahman also does not participate in creation, preservation, etc. However, Isvara, his manifested form (sambhuta), is the Lord of the universe and the source of all creation, actions, and their results. Arjuna wanted to see the totality of that Supreme Being. In some schools of Hinduism, the material universe, consisting of all the material things, energies, divinities, and individual selves (in short, the whole creation), is considered his cosmic body, and Brahman his pure Self.

Sloka 4

manyase yadi tac chakyaṃ mayā draṣṭum iti prabho
yogeśvara tato me tvaṃ darśayātmānam avyayam

manyase = you think; yadi = if; tat = That; sakyam = possible; maya = by me; drastum = to be seen; iti = thus; prabho = O Lord; yoga-isvara = lord of yoga; tatah = then; me = to me; tvam = You; darsaya = show physically; atmanam = self; avyayam = inexhustible.

"O Lord, if you think that it can possibly be seen by me, then O Lord of Yoga, show me physically your inexhaustible Self."

In this verse, Arjuna requested Lord Krishna to show him physically his endless universal form if it was possible for him to see it. He did not ask the Lord to show his universal form if it was possible for him to show it, since he knew the Lord had no bounds. He asked him to show it if he could see it physically. By qualifying his statement thus, Arjuna showed humility and left the decision entirely to the divine will. God's devotees are free to pray and make their wishes known to him, but the final decision should be left to him since he knows what is appropriate for each occasion. Sometimes, devotees feel frustrated if their prayers and wishes are not answered. It is a sign that their faith has not yet reached perfection. A devotee may place an intention (samkalpa) before him, but should leave the result to God. It is the essence of karma-sannyasa yoga. Even though devotees are expected to renounce all desires, they may still desire for the good of others or for something that is not about them or their welfare. However, they should not be attached to them or their results. Arjuna desired to see the universal form of the Lord. It was not due to any selfish desire. As this verse affirms, he left the result entirely to Lord Krishna. It is the right approach. We can always ask and pray, but the result should be left to him. As we know from the subsequent verses, Lord Krishna fulfilled his wish and showed him his universal form.

While requesting him, Arjuna addressed Lord Krishna as the Lord of Yoga (yogisvara). He did it probably because he wanted him to show his universal opulence or his highest state (yoga) as the Lord and Creator of all. One may wonder how the Lord could show his universal form to Arjuna only while standing in the middle of the battlefield. It is doubtful that anyone on the battlefield saw it since, as we will see later, the Lord revealed to Arjuna the outcome of the war and the fate of all those standing there. He showed him that they were about to march in a single file into the mouth of Death. If Kauravas or others knew what would happen to them, they would not have been so inclined to fight. It is possible that Lord Krishna showed his universal form only to Arjuna by granting him a special vision. Others could not see it because they lacked it. This seems to be the most plausible reason. Physically, it is impossible to see any universal form in its entirety with human eyes.

Especially, no one can see the Supreme Brahman from the outside because He is without a second. No one can see him from outside, just as we cannot see the physical universe by standing apart from it. In other words, no one can see the Universal Lord standing apart from him. Lord Krishna probably showed him a smaller version of himself for Arjuna to see. It is similar to the models we use to make sense of complex phenomena that cannot be seen physically.

Sloka 5

śrībhagavān uvāca
paśya me pārtha rūpāṇi śataśotha sahastraśaḥ
nānāvidhāni divyāni nānāvarṇākṛtīni ca

sri-bhagavan uvaca = the Blessed Lord said; pasya = see; me = My; partha = O Partha; rupani = forms; satasah = hundreds; atha = and; sahasrasah = thousands; nana-vidhani = numerous types; divyani = divine; nana = innumerable; varna = colors; akrtini = shapes; ca = and.

The Supreme Lord said, "O Partha, see my hundreds and thousands of divine forms of various types in innumerable colors and shapes."

Lord Krishna had already revealed to him his numerous manifestations, which were illustrative but not exhaustive. After hearing them, Arjuna wanted to see the totality of his opulence, omnipotence, and manifestations in one universal form. Since he was dearer to him, Lord Krishna obliged and showed him his universal form, consisting of his innumerable manifestations in different forms, shapes, and colors. He probably showed him his cosmic form as Purusha, who is described in the Rigveda as the Being 'with a thousand eyes and feet, who pervades the earth from every side and fills the space ten fingers wide.' He showed him the form of 'the Lord of immortality who expands further in size with food.' The Upanishads describe him as Kala (Death), the Lord of the mortal world, who rules over all the jivas. They also describe him as the first manifestation of Brahman in the world and a great devourer for whom all the jivas and all that exist in the world become food. The verse also conveys that no one can see that form except by the Lord's will. At the same time, through exclusive devotion, one can win him over and earn an opportunity to see him thus.

Sloka 6

paśyādityān vasūn rudrān aśvinau marutas tathā
bahūny adṛṣṭapūrvāṇi paśyāścaryāṇi bhārata 11.6

pasya = see; adityan = the Adityas vasun = Vasus; rudran = the Rudras; asvinau = the Asvinis; marutah = the Maruts; tatha = and; bahuni = many; adrsta = not seen; purvani = before; pasya = see; ascaryani = incredible wonders; bharata = O best of the Bharatas.

See the Adityas, the Vasus, the Rudras, the Asvins, and the Maruts. See many incredible wonders not seen before, O best of the Bharatas.

The Adityas, the sons of Aditi, are solar deities mentioned in several texts, including the Vedas. They put their number from six to twelve. Aditya is also an epithet of Surya, the sun god, and Lord Vishnu. The twelve Adityas, as listed in the Mahābhārata, are Dhatr, Mitra, Aryaman, Indra, Varuna, Amsha, Bhaga, Vivsvat, Pushan, Savitr, Tavsthtr, and Vishnu. Symbolically, they refer to the sun (Brahman) in each of the 12 months of the year or 12 hours of the day. Lord Vishnu is the brightest of them all. The Vasus are the gods of commonality, born to Dharma and his wife, Vasu. They represent fire, light, and other aspects of Nature. The Mahābhārata states they were born to Ganga to be sacrificed by her as per a curse, except Bhishma, the last of them. In some accounts, Drona is also mentioned as a Vasu. The Rudras are storm gods. They are called Rudras because they follow the commands of Rudra (Shiva) and produce howling and weeping sounds during violent storms and tempests. Their number varies from 11 to 33 in different texts. The Asvins are the twin gods of medicine with great healing powers and surgical skills. The Maruts are also storm gods or wind gods. They are forty-nine, divided into seven groups of seven each. They are mentioned in many hymns of the Vedas.

These Vedic deities are not mere forces of Nature but divinities of the heavenly region with specific names, forms, and powers. They uphold Dharma and serve God in ensuring order and regularity. When invoked and nourished through sacrificial ceremonies, they precipitate rains, nourish the earth, prevent calamities, death, and destruction, help humans fulfill their desires, protect them from evil, and contribute to peace and prosperity. Lord Krishna addressed Arjuna in this verse as the best of the Bharatas. Just as he mentioned groups of gods, he identified Arjuna as a part of the group of warriors called Bharatas and called him the best among them.

Sloka 7

ihaikasthaṃ jagat kṛtsnaṃ paśyādya sacarācaram
mama dehe guḍākeśa yac cānyad draṣṭum icchasi

iha = here eka-stham = in one place; jagat = the universe; krtsnam = entire; pasya = see; adya = now; sa = with; cara = moving; acaram = not moving; mama = My; dehe = body; gudakesa = O Gudakesa; yat ca anyat = so also anything else; drastum = to see; icchasi = you wish.

See here now in one place the entire universe in My body, O Gudakesa, both moving and unmoving, and anything else you wish to see.

Lord Krishna asked Arjuna to see the whole universe in him in one place (ekastam). This meant that he presented him with a unified vision of his material body (the universe) and wanted him to see its moving and unmoving parts and anything else he wished to see at one glance, such as the outcome of the war or the fate of the people who participated in it. His words convey that he spoke these words just before he transformed into his universal form and before Arjuna could see it. The universal aspect of the Supreme Lord has moving and unmoving parts, just like the human body. Hence, it is often compared to a human body. In the Svetasvatara

Upanishad, it is described as the wheel of Brahman. The moving and unmoving parts constitute the fundamental duality of our existence and the objective reality we experience. At the highest level, Prakriti is the moving part, and Brahman, or the Supreme Self, is the unmoving part. Within Prakriti, the jivas are the moving parts, and the inanimate things are the unmoving parts. In each jiva, the body is the moving part, and the Self is the unmoving part. In our world, the earth and the mid-region are the moving parts, and the sky (akasa) is the unmoving part. You can discern this fundamental duality even at the atomic and subatomic levels. Within the human body, breath, blood, the heart, the senses, the mind, intelligence, etc., are the moving parts, while the bones are the unmoving parts.

Thus, the whole universe is made up of these two. The moving parts of creation represent impermanence, instability, mutability, transformation, and evolution, whereas the unmoving ones represent stability, immutability, continuity, and permanence. The unmanifested Brahman is formless, fixed, and eternal. However, in the universal body of Manifested Brahman (Isvara), the moving and unmoving parts coexist, enabling the whole existence (creation) to work as a unified system despite the divisions and diversity. Out of his pure consciousness, which is permanent and fixed, emerges the dynamism of Prakriti like a wave. She is the source of all the mutable and moving parts of creation, pervaded and inhabited by the Self as its unmoving part. Within the Lord himself, his higher and lower nature constitute the moving parts, and his pure consciousness, the unmoving part.

Sloka 8

na tu māṃ śakyase draṣṭum anenaiva svacakṣuṣā
divyaṃ dadāmi te cakṣuḥ paśya me yogam aiśvaram

na = not; tu = but; mam = Me; sakyase = able; drastum = to see; anena = with; eva = surely; sva-caksusa = your own eyes; divyam = divine; dadami = I give; te = you; caksuh = eyes; pasya = see; Me = My; yogam = state; aisvaram = supreme sovereignty.

But surely you would not be able to see Me with your own (ordinary) eyes. I will give you divine eyes. See the state of My supreme sovereignty.

We cannot see the whole universe, but only its parts. Similarly, no one can see the Supreme Lord but only his manifestations and qualities that appear in creation. At most, we can find his unmistakable presence in the beauty, divinity, harmony, peace, radiance, intelligence, and abundance of the things we perceive. They are signs of his hidden presence and universality. It is beyond our ability to see his whole universal form or comprehend its infinity or immensity since we do not possess that power or reach. The physical universe is too vast and complex to be seen by the naked eye. Even the models we have about it do not adequately convey its true dimensions. Lord Krishna gifted Arjuna with a divine eye (divya drishti) to see his universal body. We do not know how it helped Arjuna to perceive the infinity, universality, and immensity of the Supreme Being in one continuous view. Probably, he understood whatever his mind and intelligence allowed him to see in that

Supreme Vision. We are subject to selective perception. Although the world presents us with its unending spectacle, we see only what interests us or draws our attention. Arjuna must have done the same. He did not see him as a physicist or astronomer but as a devotee. As we will learn later, upon seeing his supreme state with the divine eyes, he felt a surge of emotions and experienced great fear.

Yoga aisvaram refers to the supreme state of majesty, supremacy, might, lordship, or sovereignty. It is the natural state of Brahman in his highest manifested form as Isvara. According to the Vedas, the cosmic form of Brahman is known as Purusha, Saguna Brahman, or Isvara (Universal Lord). He is the highest aspect of Brahman who manifests in Prakriti with her tattvas and modes in their purest and subtlest form. He also appears variously in creation as Brahma, Vishnu, Shiva, and numerous other divinities in varying degrees of purity and subtlety and in association with diverse energies and powers (shaktis) to perform various functions and uphold creation. However, rarely does anyone see his complete, cosmic form as Arjuna did. The epic Mahabharata and Shrimad Bhagavatam suggest that Lord Krishna previously showed his universal form to a few others, but not in such great detail. He did it probably because the occasion warranted it.

Solka 9

sañjaya uvāca
evam uktvā tato rājan mahāyogeśvaro hariḥ
darśayām āsa pārthāya paramaṃ rūpam aiśvaram

sanjayah uvaca = Sanjaya said; evam = thus; uktva = having said; tatah = thereafter; rajan = O King; maha-yoga-isvarah = the great Lord of Yoga; harih = Hari; darsayam asa = showed; parthaya = to Arjuna; paramam = supreme; rupam = form; aisvaram = divine.

Sanjaya said, "Having said thus, O King, after that, Hari, the great Lord of Yoga, showed Arjuna His supreme divine form."

In this verse, Sanjaya described Lord Krishna as Hari and the great Lord of Yoga (maha yogisvara). According to Moksha Dharma, the Lord is known as Hari because he receives all the sacrificial offerings and represents the blue shade in Nature's greenery. Hari means yellowish green. The name is used in the early Vedic texts as the epithet of several gods: Indra, Yama, Shiva, Brahman, Surya, Chandra, Agni, and Vayu. Subsequently, it became synonymous with Lord Vishnu and all his incarnations, including Lord Krishna. Since green and yellow represent vigor, vitality, purity, divinity, and auspiciousness, the materials containing these colors are frequently used in Hindu sacrifices and domestic rituals as offerings or to decorate the deities or ritual places. The epithet is appropriate for Lord Vishnu since he represents all the auspicious qualities mentioned here. As the merciful Lord, he grants various auspicious abundances to his devotees, such as the abundance of wealth, knowledge, name, fame, strength, intelligence, children, courage, etc. As the preserver, nourisher, and upholder, he upholds Dharma and ensures the order and regularity of all the worlds. The other epithet, Supreme Lord of Yoga (maha-yogisvara), is also apt because, as the Lord of all (Isvara), he is the source and controller of all auspicious states and conditions (yogas) in creation. As the thread that connects all, he facilitates the union (yoga) of the embodied selves (jivatmas) with the Supreme Self, removing their darkness and delusion and granting them liberation. The knowledge of all the yogas and yoga practices flows from him only. He is a true yogi endowed with infinite powers and perfections (yoga siddhis) and, as the embodied Self, remains untouched and undisturbed in samsara amidst dualities, bondage, and suffering.

Sloka 10

anekavaktranayanam anekādbhutadarśanam
anekadivyābharaṇaṃ divyānekodyatāyudham

aneka = innmerable; vaktra = mouths; nayanam = eyes; aneka = numerous; adbhuta = wonderful; darsanam = sights; aneka = many; divya = divine; abharanam = ornaments; divya = divine; aneka = many; udyata = uplifted state of readiness; ayudham = weapons.

Of innumerable mouths, eyes, numerous wonderful sights, many divine ornaments, holding many weapons in a state of readiness.

Arjuna saw the Cosmic Person, the universal Purusha, who is described in the Rigveda as the deity with a thousand heads, a thousand eyes, and a thousand feet, and who pervades the earth from all sides, filling the space ten fingers wide. He is the manifested Brahman, known as Isvara, Hiranyagarbha, Viraj, Kala (Time and Death), and by a thousand other names. That Purusha who stood before him represents all that has been and will ever be, being the Lord of all creation and the source and support of all. He is so vast and expansive that all the beings in creation constitute one-fourth of him, while the rest is filled with heavenly worlds. Endowed with the divine vision (divya drishti) granted by Lord Krishna, Arjuna saw that wondrous being having innumerable mouths and eyes, wearing divine ornaments, and holding many weapons in a state of readiness indicative of his duties as the protector, upholder, and destroyer. The description suggests that the Purusha he saw was not a passive being or witness but the Supreme Lord and Controller of all. They also point to his omniscience, omnipotence, and universality. His innumerable mouths suggest his all-devouring nature as the Lord of Death. His numerous eyes convey his all-knowing and all-grasping omniscience. The wonderful sights Arjuna saw in him refer to his supreme forms, creations, and manifestations. The divine ornaments refer to his opulence, abundance, and materiality, while the weapons he held in readiness denote his power and supremacy.

Sloka 11

divyamālyāmbaradharaṃ divyagandhānulepanam
sarvāścaryamayaṃ devam anantaṃ viśvatomukham

divya = divine; malya = garlands; ambara = garments; dharam = wearing; divya = heavenly; gandha = perfumes; anulepanam = anointed with; sarva =

all kinds of; ascarya-mayam = filled with wonderful things; devam = radiant; anantam = unending, infinite; visvatah-mukham = faces everywhere.

Wearing divine garlands and garments, anointed with heavenly perfumes, filled with all kinds of wonderful things, radiant, infinite, with faces everywhere.

The descriptions used in this verse convey both the microcosmic and macrocosmic aspects of the Supreme Being. Malya means garlands and mountain ranges. Ambaram means garments, clothes, or the sky. Gandham means perfume or air laden with the smell of the earth or earth's greenery. The incredible and infinite radiant things refer to the stars, heavenly bodies, divinities, celestial worlds, and all the bright and beautiful things in creation. The multiple meanings hidden in each description convey Brahman's infinity, divinity, diversity, and multidimensional grandeur in his manifested aspects at various levels, from the highest to the lowest.

Sloka 12

divi sūryasahastrasya bhaved yugapad utthitā
yadi bhāḥ sadṛśī sā syād bhāsas tasya mahātmanaḥ

divi = in the sky; surya = suns; sahasrasya = thousands; bhavet = present; yugapat = simultaneously; utthita = risen, rising, born; yadi = as if; bhah = splendor; sadrsi = similar, like; sa = that; syat = might be; bhasah = effulgence; tasya = was; maha-atmanah = the Great Self, Being.

As if thousands of suns had arisen simultaneously in the sky, similar to that splendor might be the effulgence of the Great Being.

The opulence and grandeur of the Supreme Being that manifested before Arjuna in a universal form dazzled with the brilliance of a thousand suns. It was probably not all, but just a little aspect of him. Our scriptures declare Narayana as the Supreme Light (paramjyoti). His brilliance is self-luminous and infinitely radiant, especially when it manifests with supreme purity (suddha sattva). It reflects his infinite power (tejas) and energy (shakti) and cannot be seen with the naked eye. Infinitely greater than all the shining bodies of the universe combined, it is also different from the brightness of a star or a celestial body. Unlike them, it is also self-luminous. As the Kaushitaki Upanishad declares, the light of Brahman glows when the sun is seen and not seen, when the moon is seen and not seen, and when the lightning is seen and not seen. The same idea is found in the following verse from the Katha Upanishad, "The sun does not shine there, nor do the moon and the stars. The lightning does not flash there; what can one then say about the earthly fire? Only when he shines does everything else shine. By his light only, all this shines."

Sloka 13

tatraikastham̩ jagat kṛtsnam̩ pravibhaktam anekadhā
apaśyad devadevasya śarīre pāṇḍavas tadā

tatra = there; eka-stham = as one; jagat = universe; krtsnam = whole, entire; pravibhaktam = was divided; anekadha = into numerous things; apasyat = saw; deva-devasya = God of the gods; sarire = in the body; pandavah = Arjuna; tada = then, at that moment.

There, at that moment, the Pandava saw the entire universe in one place, divided into numerous things, in the body of the God of the gods.

At that moment, Arjuna saw the diversity of creation and its underlying unity in the universal body of the Supreme Being. He saw many in One, and the One supporting many. He saw unity in diversity and the interconnectedness of things, with the Supreme Lord serving as their creator, container, connector, and support. Things do not exist in isolation. They either depend upon something or exist in something that must be independent and superior to them while supporting them. Beneath the apparent diversity of the whole creation, there is the power of Brahman that is common to them and connects them all as facets of the same reality. It may not immediately be perceptible to the human mind, but it becomes evident through knowledge, purity, and discernment. The Supreme Lord's numerous manifestations, which exist in him as different entities, are interconnected to one another in mysterious ways by his power. He upholds and pervades them all with a fraction of himself.

Creation is like a tree with numerous branches, leaves, and flowers, but at the base of it all, it is connected to one main trunk and a primary root system. The Upanishads describe it as an inverted Asvattha Tree with its roots in heaven and branches below. Everything that manifests here is a part of that eternal tree. Behind the illusion of movement, coming and going, and separation, there is an underlying thread of stability and connectivity. Things exist in creation, like the atoms in a lake. They are one as the lake, but at the same time, as individual atoms and particles, they are different and have an existence of their own. You disturb one part of the universe, and its ripples will be felt elsewhere. It is what physicists call the butterfly effect. In that exalted state, Arjuna saw the diverse manifestations of the entire universe as numerous parts of the universal body of Brahman. He saw him as the God of gods, the One universal Being appearing as many and controlling them all. We do not have complete control of our bodies, but unlike us, the Supreme Being controls every aspect of his.

The world is pervaded by his ubiquitous presence. He may not be in them since he is not a part of their essential nature, but they arise from him, exist in him, and reflect one or more of his aspects and attributes. Since everything exists in his universal body, everything in the universe demands our respect and consideration and must be seen with equanimity and sameness as his creation without judgment. The world will be a better place if we live with the sacred feeling that we live inside the body of the Supreme Lord, and that we must live responsibly and do our part, just as the organs in our body do, and contribute to our well-being.

Sloka 14

tataḥ sa vismayāviṣṭo hṛṣṭaromā dhanaṃjayaḥ
praṇamya śirasā devaṃ kṛtāñjalir abhāṣata

tatah = then; sah = he; vismaya-avistah = astonishment, bewildered; hrsta-roma = hairs standing on end due to excitement; dhananjayah = winner of wealth, Arjuna; pranamya = bowing down; sirasa = his head; devam = to the supreme being; krta-anjalih = with folded hands; abhasata = said.

Then, overwhelmed with great astonishment, his hair standing on end due to excitement, bowing down his head to the Supreme Being, Dhananjaya said with folded hands.

If ordinary people ever see God face to face, even in their mystic vision, they will experience extreme emotions and lose consciousness because they cannot withstand the power and joy arising from that extremely rare and supernatural encounter. Those who are exclusively devoted to him (ananya bhaktas) and ever absorbed in his contemplation enter rapturous states of joy just by imagining that they are in communion with him or standing in his presence. Such is the captivating power of the Supreme Being, which is more powerful than the gravitational force or any magnetic force we know. Here, Arjuna saw with his own eyes the universal form of the Supreme Being because of the mystic vision (divyadrishti) granted to him by Lord Krishna. His seeing was not a mystic experience. He was not dreaming or lost in a trance but was fully awake in the presence of a Mighty Being who contained within himself everything a seer could conceive or comprehend. You can imagine his physical and emotional state as he tried to process that great spectacle and make sense of it. He withstood the fieriness and force of that splendor and brilliance because he was a brave warrior who fought many wars and had the strength and resilience to see Death in its fiercest form. Besides, he was destined to see the Lord's universal form and undergo a great transformation from a simple karma yogi to an enlightened spiritual warrior or Kshatriya Bhagavata, a true follower of the Lord. However, he could not control his emotions upon seeing that universal form. He was overwhelmed with great astonishment, and his hair stood on end due to excitement. The wondrous joy, gratitude, humility, and fear combined with devotion he experienced at that moment were marks of true devotion. He was born to be a devotee, and Lord Krishna was destined to teach him with the right knowledge and lead him in the right direction as his friend, philosopher, and guide. Arjuna was Nara, and Lord Krishna was Narayana. Theirs is an eternal relationship that manifests in the world at different times in different forms for different purposes. In this particular instance, their purpose was to reveal to humanity the sacred knowledge of the Bhagavadgita.

Sloka 15

arjuna uvāca
paśyāmi devāṃs tava deva dehe sarvāṃs tathā bhūtaviśeṣasaṃghān
brahmāṇam īśaṃ kamalāsanasthaṃ ṛṣīṃś ca sarvān uragāṃś ca divyān

arjunah uvaca = Arjuna said; pasyami = I see; devan = all the gods; tava = Your; deva = O Divine Being; dehe = in the body; sarvan = all; tatha = also; bhuta = living beings; visesa-sanghan = various classes and groups of things; brahmanam = Brahma; isam = Lord; kamala-asana-stham = seated in the lotus flower; rsin = great seers; ca = and; sarvan = all; uragan = serpents; ca = and; divyan = divine.

Arjuna Said, "O Divine Being, I see all the gods in your body, also all living beings, various classes and groups of things, Brahma, the Lord seated in the lotus flower, and all the divine serpents."

Arjuna saw the universal form of the Supreme Being, containing all the gods, living beings, Brahma seated in a lotus flower, and all the divine serpents. He mentioned Brahman separately and particularly to denote his exalted status among gods. In the Vedic times, Brahma was a supreme deity, the creator god. He lost his prominence subsequently and yielded that place to Shiva and Vishnu as they gained prominence due to the developments in Hinduism, as the Vedic religion spread eastward. However, within the traditional Vedic rituals, Brahma is still revered along with other Vedic gods. He is not worshipped in the temples because it has been the practice to worship the Vedic gods through sacrifices and invocations rather than in temples. However, he still enjoys prominence as a Trinity god. He also enjoys an exalted position in the Buddhist and Jain pantheons.

The whole creation, both the subtle and the gross, is the body of the Supreme Being. Hence, Arjuna saw all the gods, beings, and other things in him. Gods exist as organs and tattvas in our bodies also. It is our obligatory duty to nourish them through the actions we perform, the food we eat, and the pleasures we enjoy by offering them daily to the Supreme Lord as an internal sacrifice. Unfortunately, many people do not take it seriously. These offerings are helpful to cleanse the mind and body. The human body is a divine temple where gods reside as organs, and the Supreme Lord reigns as the Self. We have an obligatory duty to keep our bodies clean. The best way to do it is by offering our actions, food, and other enjoyments to the Supreme Lord. Whatever is offered to him will go to them also.

Arjuna's descriptions confirm that he did indeed see the Supreme Purusha with his divine eyes from the ground up as a gigantic universal body that stretched into the sky as far as his eyes could reach. By God's grace, he could see the whole creation compressed into a form that could fit into his vision. He not only saw him but was also able to describe what he was seeing. It meant that he was fully conscious and in his senses. He saw the Supreme Being filled with diverse things, worlds, and beings. He saw his infinity as well as unity contained in that singular vision. Because of the limitations Nature imposes upon us and the impurities in and around us, we can only see things from a limited perspective as separate and distinct within themselves. We cannot see them as connected, contained within one reality, or supported by an invisible force beneath the apparent diversity. We may guess or speculate, but we cannot see the Lord spanning across all creation as one Being.

Arjuna saw the whole existence being contained within the universal form of the Supreme Lord. Apart from gods and beings of several kinds and Brahma, the Lord of creation, he also saw several divine serpents in that exalted state. One may wonder why serpents are specially mentioned. In Hinduism, serpents have great significance. Serpents symbolize death and infinity. Hindu texts mention several well-known divine serpents such as Vasuki, Ananta or Adishesha, Astika, Nagaraja, Manasa, Takshaka, etc. Apart from inspiring awe and wonder, they possess mystic powers to grant wealth, protection, and progeny to those who worship them. Symbolically, they represent creation, royalty, death, life, movement, time, the power to give or take away life, mystic powers (siddhis), coiled energy or kundalini, prana, healing, the senses, breaths, fear and fearlessness, desire, infinity, immortality, chaos, control, and self-mastery. Serpents are also associated with knowledge, wealth, diversity, and abundance. Hence, the prominent gods of Hinduism appear with snakes in images and icons to denote their control over death (serpents) and their power to grant life to the dying or the dead..

Sloka 16

anekabāhūdaravaktranetraṃ paśyāmi tvāṃ sarvatonantarūpam
nāntaṃ na madhyaṃ na punas tavādiṃ paśyāmi viśveśvara viśvarūpa

aneka = many; bahu = hands; udara = bellies; vaktra = mouths; netram = eyes; pasyami = I see; tvam = You; sarvatah = everywhere; ananta-rupam = infinite form; na antam = without an ened; na madhyam = without the middle; na punah = nor again the end; tava = Your; adim = beginning; pasyami = I see; visva-isvara = O Lord of the universe; visva-rupa = of universal form.

"I see your infinite form everywhere with many hands, bellies, mouths, eyes. I see neither the end nor the middle nor the beginning of you, O Lord of the Universe of universal form."

The Supreme Being is Visveswara, Lord of the universe. His form is universal, which means it contains everything in creation and is found everywhere. It is not the usual form of gods and goddesses we see in temples, paintings, and images with pleasant visages, standing or seated on high pedestals, holding various objects in their hands, and surrounded by opulence and colorful ensembles of pomp and pageantry. The form he saw was unfamiliar, grotesque, overwhelming, and somewhat terrifying. He saw a form that had numerous hands, bellies, mouths, and eyes without a beginning, middle, or end. God's creation has similar characteristics. We see it from the inside but cannot comprehend its true form, immensity, or infinity. We cannot fathom its beginning, middle, or end. Even though we possess a rich imagination, it does not fit our imagination. The disturbing and terrifying reality of it is always hidden from us because we either refuse to acknowledge it or remain preoccupied with our selective perceptions, seeing what we want to see.

The universal form of Brahman is even more complex and mysterious than the physical reality in which we live. We may understand its physical dimension partially through perception, but its subtle and transcendental dimensions are beyond our comprehension. The material universe is just one aspect of his universality. His other dimensions are largely unknown and beyond our imagination. Some occultists and mystics may see them in their inner minds or altered states of consciousness, but we may best compare their attempt metaphorically to using a small lamp to describe the brightness of the sun. The reality of Brahman is indeterminate, indefinable, and inexhaustible. Hence, nothing is certain about him. You may reduce him to a being or a form, but that will not truly represent him or his reality. As the omniscient, omnipresent, and omnipotent being with unfathomable secrets, he is greater, farther, and beyond all the frontiers we know and the knowledge we can ever possess. Lord Krishna affirmed it while speaking about his manifestations, saying he upholds the whole manifested universe with just a fraction of himself.

One cannot experience the Supreme Reality of Brahman entirely, even after overcoming duality and individuality or experiencing transcendence. Perhaps Brahman himself knows it or does not, since he is free from time, conscious memory, and the division and duality of subject and object. They do not exist in his pure consciousness. Arjuna was still in a state of duality. Otherwise, he would not have objectively seen those eyes, hands, and bellies or the infinite forms of Brahman and spoken about it. He could do so because the Supreme Lord manifested his transcendental reality in a form his human mind and senses could envision and understand without becoming overwhelmed or lost by its immensity, diversity, or infinity.

Sloka 17

kirīṭinaṃ gadinaṃ cakriṇaṃ ca tejorāśiṃ sarvato dīptimantam
paśyāmi tvāṃ durnirīkṣyaṃ samantād dīptānalārkadyutim aprameyam

kiritinam = with a crown; gadinam = with a mace; cakrinam = with a disc; ca = and; tejah-rasim = rays of light; sarvatah = in all directions; dipti-mantam = glowing; pasyami = I see; tvam = You; durniriksyam = difficult to see; samantat = from all sides; dipta = blazing; anala = fire; arka = sun; dyutim = radiance; aprameyam = immeasurable.

"I see You with a crown, with a mace, with a disc, and with rays of light spreading in all directions, which is difficult to see from all sides, having immeasurable light of the blazing fire (and) the sun."

In the previous verse, Arjuna saw the universal form everywhere with numerous hands, eyes, mouths, bellies, etc. Here, he saw him wearing a crown and holding a mace and a disc, with his blazing aura spreading from him in all directions into infinity. Perhaps his eyes were moving, and he was speaking these words as he examined the various aspects of the universal form. The crown denotes his royalty, lordship, and supremacy. The mace and disc represent his strength and power as the creator, preserver, and destroyer. The immeasurable effulgent aura radiating from him symbolizes his purity, which arises from his suddha sattva and self-luminous nature. Now, one may wonder whether what Arjuna saw was the definitive and only form of the Universal Lord or whether he was shown a form that was relevant to his discourse. We have to presume that the Lord must have shown Arjuna a form that he needed at the time to clear his moral confusion about death and destruction and prepare himself mentally to fight. By showing him that form, he probably wanted Arjuna to know the true face of Death and be prepared for it. Like a skillful teacher, He transmitted the knowledge according to the latter's mental and perceptual abilities.

Some scholars may argue that the form Arjuna saw was Lord Krishna's true and fixed form. Devotees tend to become attached to the deities they worship and to their names and forms. If you try to present to them the same deities in different forms or colors, they may feel upset. Therefore, we do not want to disturb their faith. We presume that the form of Isvara appears differently to different people in different contexts. We know that he has pleasant as well as fierce forms. He may appear in pleasant forms to his devotees and in fierce forms to his enemies or to those he wants to reform or jolt them up from delusion or inertia. He definitely chose the latter option for Arjuna, who was in a depressive mood and reluctant to fight his relatives on the battlefield due to moral fears. We know that in the past, the Lord appeared differently to different people in different times and circumstances. The Puranas confirm that he appeared as a pillar of fire, a dwarf, a yaksha, a man-lion, a boar, a light, a fish, etc., and imparted different teachings. We may also presume that Arjuna witnessed a living and dynamic form, not a static one. He also witnessed him in his dynamic state performing various duties in his universal aspect. It was probably meant to convey that even the Lord was not free from duties and performed them continuously.

Sloka 18

tvam akṣaraṃ paramaṃ veditavyaṃ tvam asya viśvasya paraṃ nidhānam tvam avyayaḥ śāśvatadharmagoptā sanātanas tvaṃ puruṣo mato me

tvam = You; aksaram = imperishable; paramam = supreme; veditavyam = to be known; tvam = You; asya = of this; visvasya = of the universe; param = supreme; nidhanam = source of abundance; tvam = You are; avyayah = inexhaustible; sasvata-dharma-gopta = protector of the everlasting dharma; sanatanah = eternal; tvam = You; purusah = person, being; matah me = is my opinion.

"You are the imperishable, supreme One to be known. You are the supreme source of abundance and support for the entire universe. You are the protector of the everlasting Dharma. You are the eternal Being. This is my opinion."

After seeing the universal form blazing like a thousand suns, Arjuna came to the firm opinion (matah) that the Cosmic Person (Purusha) he saw was indeed the imperishable Supreme Being, the one who was meant to be known by the seekers of liberation. He also recognized him as the supreme source of abundance (paraṃ nidhānam), the everlasting support of the universe, and the protector of the eternal Dharma. The supreme reality of Brahman is the exact opposite of the objective reality, which arises from him as a projection or superimposition. While Brahman is eternal and indestructible, his manifestations are not. They appear and disappear just as the clouds in the sky. Eventually, everything in the objective realm would be withdrawn and dissolved.

Although he is the Supreme Lord and the controller of all, he does not directly govern creation, but through the forces of Nature and universal laws of Dharma, which he sets in motion at the beginning of each cycle of creation to ensure its progression, balance, order, and regularity. As he declared before, whenever the eternal order and regularity decline due to the decline of Dharma and the rise of evil, he intervenes or even personally incarnates upon earth to restore it. While his manifestations have a beginning and an end, his absolute supreme aspect is eternal, and so is Prakriti. At the beginning of creation, he reveals the divine knowledge of creation, duties, liberation, etc., through Brahma. In the end, when Brahma goes to sleep, he withdraws everything into himself.

In a broader sense, Dharma means faith, religion, or a set of religious and moral laws one must follow. However, it is difficult to accurately translate it into English because the concept of Dharma is unique to the Sanatana Dharmas of India. Since it has traditionally been used in different contexts by different faiths, it also has multiple meanings. For example, in Buddhism, Dharma means the doctrine or the teachings of the Buddha, consisting of the Four Noble Truths and the Eightfold Path. In Hinduism, it may mean religious duty, obligatory duty, moral duty, divine law, religion, moral obligation, morality, righteousness, virtue, moral conduct, etc. It also means essential nature, inherent property, or the distinguishing characteristics and natural properties and functions of things and beings. Thus, the dharma of fire is to glow and burn, water is to be aqueous and flow, air is to be gaseous, invisible, and free-flowing, and the earth is to be hard, claylike, and earthen. The essential nature of Brahman and the individual Self is bliss at its highest level, which manifests in the creation as sattvic enjoyment or pure pleasure, devoid of evil intentions or impurities.

Although Brahman has no particular interest in anything, he takes upon himself various obligatory duties as the Creator, Regulator, Controller, Concealer, Revealer, and Destroyer to ensure the orderliness and regularity of the worlds and beings he creates. These duties constitute his eternal (sanatana) Dharma, which he performs in association with Nature. He also reveals and enforces our essential Dharma (duties upon earth) directly through his manifestations and incarnations and indirectly through natural laws and revelatory scriptures.

Sloka 19

anādimadhyāntam anantavīryam anantabāhuṃ śaśisūryanetram
paśyāmi tvāṃ dīptahutāśavaktraṃ svatejasā viśvam idaṃ tapantam

anadi = without beginning; madhya = without middle; antam = without end; ananta = infinite; viryam = valor, power, energy; ananta = unlimited; bahum = arms; sasi = moon; surya = sun; netram = eyes; pasyami = I see; tvam = You; dipta hutasa-vaktram = with a mouth spouting fire; sva-tejasa = self-effulgence; visvam = universe; idam = this; tapantam = heating up.

"I see you without a beginning, middle, and end, with infinite power, unlimited arms, with the sun and the moon as your eyes, with a mouth emitting fire, your self-born effulgence heating this universe."

Arjuna saw a rapidly changing universal form before him as he tried to make sense of the numerous objects that floated before him as if on a screen. Probably, Lord Krishna wanted him to see as much of his universal form as he could in a short time and grasp whatever he could. We can also find in these descriptions the signs of an active God engaged in different tasks. For example, Arjuna previously saw numerous mouths and eyes in the universal form. Here, he saw a bigger face, probably the central one, with its mouth emitting fire and the sun and the moon glowing as his two eyes. Although the sun and moon are compared here to his blazing eyes, in the Upanishads, the sun is compared to the eye and the moon to the mind. These descriptions confirm that instead of a pleasant form that devotees usually see in meditation, Arjuna saw the fierce form of the Supreme Lord, described in the Upanishads as Kala or the Lord of Death. The form was appropriate for the occasion since they were in the middle of the battlefield, and the war meant death and destruction on a large scale, which Arjuna would be witnessing soon from a short distance.

Brahman manifests numerously in the field of Prakriti. No one can be definitive about his projected forms or eternal and infinite realities, even at the highest level. Arjuna saw numerous hands of Kala and his self-induced spiritual energy (tejas) heating the entire universe with its brilliance. His numerous hands suggest that he is the source of all actions and the real Karta (doer). The tapah (body heat) that is emitted from him denotes that he is ascetic and austere by nature, and the source of all spiritual energy. In the physical universe, light and heat arise from Isvara, his highest manifestation, and in the body from the Self. His fiery mouth reminds us of his devouring nature as the Lord of Death and the sacrificial pit as the Lord of sacrifices. As Kala, he consumes the worlds and beings to facilitate renewal and rebirth. As the Lord of sacrifices, he is the ultimate recipient of all the actions we perform as our obligatory duties.

Sloka 20

dyāvāpṛthivyor idam antaraṃ hi vyāptaṃ tvayaikena diśaś ca sarvāḥ dṛṣṭvādbhutaṃ rupam ugraṃ tavedaṃ lokatrayaṃ pravyathitaṃ mahātman

dyau = of the sky; a-prthivyoh = of the earth; idam = this; antaram = the space between; hi = surely; vyaptam = pervaded; tvaya = by You; ekena = alone, as one; disah = directions; ca = and; sarvah = all; drstva = having seen; adbhutam = marvellous, wonderful; rupam = form; ugram = fierce, terrible; tava = Your; idam = this; loka = worlds; trayam = three; pravyathitam = filled with fear; maha-atman = O Great Self.

Surely, the space between the sky and the earth and all directions is pervaded by You only; seeing this, your wonderful (and) fierce form, the three worlds are filled with fear, O Great Self."

Lord Krishna showed Arjuna his fierce form (ugra rupam) so that he would overcome fear and doubt in all its forms, including the fear of the sin that would arise from the death and destruction caused by fighting in the war. He wanted him to realize that the Supreme Lord was the controller and source of all, and he (Arjuna), as an actor in the cosmic drama, was meant to play his role dutifully as a warrior without worrying about the consequences. He wanted to assure him that he was with him in this effort and helping him as his teacher, guide, mentor, and charioteer.

Brahman is the unifying and connecting power (sutratman) that pervades and upholds all. He pervades the world, the earth, heaven, and the space between them. The worlds tremble at the thought of him because he is the fiercest Lord of Death and destruction. Gods and other beings rarely see him, and if they do, it means something terrible is about to happen. The Taittiriya Upanishad declares that the earth (bhuh), the middle space (bhuvah), and the heaven (suvah) are the three worlds. The fourth one is the Great one (maha), often described as the radiant world of the sun. All these are projections of Brahman, who manifests in the beings as the Self. The other divinities (devatas) who arise from him with a vast array of powers are akin to his limbs. If Brahman is the sun (Aditya) as described in the Upanishads, his manifestations are like his rays. Just as the sun fills the space between the earth and heaven, Brahman pervades the space between the worlds and fills them with his effulgence.

Arjuna probably projected his fear into what he saw, and felt that the worlds were filled with fear at the sight of him. Or he actually saw the beings of all three worlds in his universal form, trembling with fear at the sight of his fierce visage (ugra rupam). It is difficult to assume that everyone saw it since they were not endowed with divine eyes, which were granted to him only. He probably saw the fear everyone experiences at the thought or sight of death. The Supreme Lord does not show his fierce form to everyone, especially to his devotees, unless there is a divine purpose. Therefore, by all means, it was a rare and unfamiliar sight. Whoever saw it would have been filled with intense fear. Every mortal being fears Death (Kala). It is the most common fear. People are either afraid of their death or of causing death. Therefore, if they see Death itself standing before them in all its fierceness, they would be even more frightened. Faith (sraddha), fear (bhayam) of sin and God, and devotion (bhakti) are considered virtues in Hinduism. They are the hallmarks of true devotion. Fear is healthy when it prevents people from falling into evil ways or engaging in self-destructive actions. Fear of God keeps the worlds and beings under control. As the Katha Upanishad (2.3.2-3) states, whatever exists in this world and all that breathes follow the commands of the Supreme Brahman obediently out of great fear, as if they heard a rolling thunder. Due to fear of him, the fire burns, the sun blazes, and gods such as Indra, Vayu, and Death go forth in five different ways. That fear of him, says the Taittiriya Upanishad (2.9.1), will go away only when we gain the knowledge of Brahman and realize his essential nature as pure love and infinite bliss.

Sloka 21

amī hi tvāṃ surasaṃghā viśanti kecid bhītāḥ prāñjalayo gṛṇanti svastīty uktvā maharṣisiddhasaṃghāḥ stuvanti tvāṃ stutibhiḥ puṣkalābhiḥ

ami = those; hi = surely; tvam = You; sura-sanghah = groups of gods; visanti = are entering; kecit = some of them; bhitah = out of fear; pranjalayah = with palms joined; grnanti = offering you prayers; svasti = benediction; iti = thus; uktva = uttering; maha-rsi = great seers; siddha-sanghah = groups of perfect beings, siddhas; stuvanti = praise; tvam = You; stutibhih = with hymns; puskalabhih = elaborate.

"Surely those groups of gods are entering you. Some of them, out of fear, are offering you prayers of obeisance with folded hands. Great seers are uttering swasti, wishing the welfare of all, and groups of perfect beings are praising you with elaborate hymns of praise."

This verse affirms that humans and beings from other worlds worship the Supreme Being continuously. He is feared and loved. Even the perfect ones who attained liberation remain his devotees and offer prayers and salutations. All are drawn to him in devotion, whether they are gods, humans, wise ones, or ignorant. They continue to worship him even as liberated souls (muktas). Devotion is the bond that draws the embodied souls to the Supreme Being and the path of liberation. Arjuna's words do not mean that they were doing this because they were also witnessing him, along with Arjuna. It only means his devotees are everywhere in all the worlds. They worship him continuously with devotion and pay him homage.

Sura sangha means the community of pure souls and liberated souls who live in the immortal world and the gods who live in the celestial world (bhuva). Whenever humans perform sacrificial rituals, the gods descend upon earth and participate in them to accept their share of sacrificial offerings and fulfill the wishes of the worshippers. In the Brihadaranyaka Upanishad (3.9.1), Yajnavalkya mentions their number first as three hundred and three Visvadevas and in all three thousand and three. Then, he reduces the number further, saying there are only thirty-three gods, and the rest are their manifestations. The thirty-three gods are the eight Vasus, eleven Rudras, twelve Adityas, Indra, and Prajapati. These gods are the principal divinities of the Vedic pantheon. The number increased as many new traditions gained ascendence within the Vedic fold. Thus, Hinduism currently has innumerable gods and goddesses whose number is difficult to determine. A popular saying puts them at 30 million (mukkoti), which may be an exaggeration. Their number may exceed the number of villages in India since each village has one or more village deities who protect its inhabitants. However, it is true that popular Hinduism has numerous deities, apart from several seers, saints, and gurus who are also worshipped as divinities or demigods. Apart from them, Hindus also worship rivers, trees, mountains, spirits, sacred places, sacred symbols, icons, etc. Their number keeps increasing as people take a liking to religious teachers or yogis who catch their imagination and add them to the list.

According to this verse, Arjuna saw groups of gods bowing down to the Supreme Self in fear. Although the gods are pleasure-loving beings of light, they also experience different emotions like us, such as fear, love, anger, envy, compassion, etc. Gods offering prayers to Isvara or Narayana in fear or submission is one of the common themes of the Puranas. They do it whenever they are troubled by demons or engage in sinful or unethical actions. Although the gods are a step above humans in the cosmic hierarchy, they are not entirely blemishless. They have weaknesses and often engage in questionable behavior, which results in problems for themselves and humans. Therefore, they are also subject to the same desires and emotions when they worship the Lord with love or fear.

Swasti is a blessing or benediction conferred by priests, elders, seers, etc., upon others, wishing them good health, well-being, peace, prosperity, happiness, etc. Devotees and priests also utter it in sacrifices, expiatory rites, and religious ceremonies to spread positive vibrations, secure divine blessings for the welfare of the worshippers, drive away evil forces, or create an atmosphere of peace and harmony.

Siddhas are the perfect ones who absorb their minds in the Supreme Lord and attain oneness. Since they attain the highest purity and remain established in the boundless state of pure consciousness, they also possess many supernatural powers. Upon departing from here, they live in the highest plane of Brahman in proximity to him. The seers are the mind-born sons of Brahma. They share the intelligence of Brahma and have the power to create and destroy things with their mystic power, which is sustained by their austerities (tapas) and inner brilliance.

Sloka 22

rudrādityā vasavo ye ca sādhyā viśveśvinau marutaś coṣmapāś ca
gandharvayakṣāsurasiddhasaṃghā vīkṣante tvāṃ vismitāś caiva sarve

rudra = Rudras; adityah = Adityas; vasavah = Vasus; ye = those; ca = and; sadhyah = the Sadhyas; visve = the Visvedevas; asvinau = Asvins; marutah = Maruts; ca = and; usma-pah = Usmapahs; ca = and; gandharva = Gandharvas; yaksa = Yaksas; asura-siddha = asura siddhas; sanghah = groups, congregations; viksante = behold,see; tvam = You; vismitah = with amazement; ca = and; eva = indeed; sarve = all.

"Those Rudras, Adityas, Vasus and Sadhyas, Visvadevas, Asvins, Maruts, and Usampahs, and groups of Gandharvas, Yakshas, Asura Siddhas, all indeed behold you with amazement."

Rudras, Adityas, Vasus, Sadhyas, Visvadevas, Asvins, Maruts, Usampahs, Gandharvas, Yakshas, and Asura Siddhas are groups of gods and celestial beings who are endowed with the light of Brahman. Many of them possess supernatural powers and participate in heavenly wars and weather phenomena. Even they look upon Brahman with amazement because their love for him is boundless, and they are never tired of watching his glories and opulence and declaring their love and devotion. The immensity and sovereignty of Brahman are such that they invoke awe and wonder in all, including the highest gods, when they see him, worship him, or contemplate him. We have previously discussed the Rudras, Adityas, Vasus, Asvins, and Maruts. We will briefly speak about others. The Visvadevas are gods of universality endowed with omniscience and omnipresence. In the Vedas, they are extolled as gods of commonality, about 12 in number, who act in unison as a group for the welfare of the worlds and beings. They are entitled to their share of offerings in all Vedic sacrifices, including the daily sacrifices.

The Usmapahs are mentioned in the Mahābhārata (2.8.350) as one of the five classes of ancestors, the other four being Agniswattas, Fenapa, Swadhavat, and Verhishada. They accept offerings of hot food. The Gandharvas are a class of celestial beings from the mid-space (antarisksha). They excel in music and art and serve the gods and yakshas as singers and dancers. According to the Atharvaveda, their number is in the thousands. They live in a world of their own (Gandharvalok) and frequent Indra's heaven (Indralok) to serve as divine musicians and artists in his court. Their king is Chitraradha. In the Mahābhārata, some forest dwellers and worshippers of Shiva are also described as Gandharvas. Asura siddhas are the demon-yogis who excel in yoga and possess supernatural powers. By nature, they misuse their powers and cause trouble. All these groups of beings exist in different planes and participate in God's creation according to his will.

Sloka 23

rūpaṃ mahat te bahuvaktranetraṃ mahābāho bahubāhūrupādam
bahūdaraṃ bahudañṣṭrākarālaṃ dṛṣṭvā lokāḥ pravyathitās tathāham

rupam = form; mahat = great; te = Your; bahu = many; vaktra = faces; netram = eyes; maha-baho = O mighty-armed one; bahu = many; bahu = arms; uru = thighs; padam = feet; bahu-udaram = many bellies; bahu-damstra = many teeth; karalam = terrifying; drstva = seeing; lokah = all the worlds; pravyathitah = disturbed tatha = and so; aham = I am.

"Seeing Your great form with many faces, eyes, many arms, thighs, feet, many bellies, and many terrifying teeth, O Mighty Armed, all the words are disturbed, and so am I."

In the universal form of Lord Krishna, Arjun saw many wonders. He saw worlds and beings who were disturbed by his fierce form of universal dimensions. We are not sure whether they felt disturbed at the sight of him or Arjuna projected his mental condition upon them. Whatever the truth, the sight of Death in its full fury will unsettle even the bravest of the brave. The very thought of Death unsettles many. One can imagine the consternation when Death stands before any mortal in his universal form with blazing fury, just as he stood before Arjuna on that occasion. It is not the usual form in which the Supreme Lord usually appears before his devotees or even gods. Only a few might have seen the true form of Kala, the Lord of Death. Arjuna still did not know whose form he witnessed. That would be revealed to him shortly. In the next verse, he explains the reason for his terror.

Sloka 24

nabhaḥspṛśaṃ dīptam anekavarṇaṃ vyāttānanaṃ dīptaviśāla netram dṛṣṭvā hi tvāṃ pravyathitāntarātmā dhṛtiṃ na vindāmi śamaṃ ca viṣṇo

nabhah-sprsam = touching the heaven; diptam = shining, glowing; aneka = with many; varnam = colors; vyatta = wide open; ananam = mouth; dipta = blazing; visala = wide; netram = eyes; drstva = seeing; hi = surely; tvam = You; pravyathita = terrified; antaratma = in myself or my heart; dhrtim = stability; na = not; vindami = find; samam = equanimity; ca =and; visno = O Vishnu.

"O Vishnu, seeing you touching the heaven, shining with many colors, with a wide-open mouth, with blazing wide eyes, I am terrified in myself and find neither stability nor equanimity."

A profound experience such as Arjuna's would have a lasting effect on anyone. Arjuna was not just afraid; he was terrified of what he saw. Lord Krishna's frightening universal form filled him with trembling fear. It was extremely disturbing for a warrior of such stature because he had never seen a universal Being of such dimensions or ferocity. He did not see Isvara, but Kala, Death himself, rarely seen by anyone. It must have profoundly and permanently changed his thinking, consciousness, and outlook. Whatever hesitation he might have had until then about death and immortality must have vanished from his mind. Until then, he knew the familiar and friendly form of Lord Krishna. He knew him as a friend, philosopher, and mentor, but on that day, he saw another side of him that was hugely different and emotionally challenging. The Lord of Death is no one's friend. He is duty-bound and does not appear or speak pleasantly. Even the most advanced yogis and the highest of the divinities would have felt unnerved if they saw him so closely. The very thought of death unsettles many. Although it is inevitable for mortal beings, we rarely think about it or prepare for it. No wonder, at the sight of him, Arjuna was filled with terrible fear and lost his stability and poise. Probably, he would no longer complain or worry about the death and destruction he would soon witness on the battlefield.

Sloka 25

daṃṣṭrākarālāni ca te mukhāni dṛṣṭvaiva kālānalasaṃnibhāni diśo na jāne na labhe ca śarma prasīda deveśa jagannivāsa

damstra = with the teeth; karalani = terrible; ca = and; te = Your; mukhani = faces; drstva = having seen; eva = indeed; kala-anala = the fire of final destruction; sannibhani = resembling similar to; disah = directions; na jane = do not know; na labhe = not find; ca = and; sarma = comfort; prasida = be kind; deva-isa = O lord of the gods; jagat-nivasa = abode of the universe.

"Indeed, having seen your terrible teeth and faces resembling the fire of the final destruction, I no longer know the directions, nor find any comfort, O Lord of the gods, O Abode of the Universe."

In the presence of Lord Krishna's universal form, which he did not expect to see, Arjuna was filled with fear and amazement. As he lost his balance and discernment, his anxiety grew, and he fell into confusion. As a warrior, he was familiar with the images of death and destruction. However, in the universal form of Lord Krishna, he saw the terrifying vision of Death magnified a million times. It must have reminded him of how the world might look in the final moments of its destruction. One may wonder why Lord Krishna chose to show him his most dreadful and terrifying form of Death. He could have shown him a friendlier and agreeable form. Arjuna was his close friend and a devotee. Why was he put through such a harrowing experience? The ways of the Lord are mysterious. True, he had many options. However, he chose this particular form because the subject of their discussion was the death and destruction that would result from the war and whether Arjuna should be a part of that gruesome event. He wanted to show him that even the Lord of the Universe engages in destruction as an obligatory duty. Someone must cleanse the world and facilitate the transmigration of souls. A warrior has a similar duty to uphold Dharma. He should fight and should not be afraid of the death and destruction that might follow from his actions. Lord Krishna's central teaching is about performing obligatory duties, however difficult, challenging, or disturbing they may be. Karma yogis should not hesitate to perform them to escape from their consequences. If they offer those actions to the Lord along with their fruit, they will have the same result as not doing them. Therefore, Lord Krishna decided to show him the true form of Death and drive away his doubts and hesitation about the moral consequences of fighting in the war and causing death.

If the all-knowing Lord is the source of death and destruction and the cause of all actions and their consequences, a warrior like Arjuna should not have to worry about fighting and discharging his duty. He should not have to assume any moral or personal responsibility for the consequences. We ignore that we owe the Lord a karmic debt for living in his world. We can only pay it by performing our duties selflessly as a sacrifice and leaving the results to him. We also ignore life's transience, although we see it happening all around us. Lord Krishna wanted to show Arjuna that death and destruction were a part of Nature's functions and inherent to mortal life. They cannot be wished away or ignored. One may escape from actions but not from death, which is inevitable for all. He wanted him to see that the Lord of Death would eventually devour everything. While we may ignore or delay our duties, he would never. Therefore, by appearing before Arjuna as the Lord of Death, he wanted to shake him out of his delusion that he would be responsible for the death and destruction arising from his actions. He wanted him to know that, ultimately, it would be Isvara, as the Lord of Death, who would do all the fighting and defending from both sides and decide the fate of all those who participated in it.

Sloka 26

amī ca tvāṃ dhṛtarāṣṭrasya putrāḥ sarve sahaivāvanipālasaṃghaiḥ
bhīṣmo droṇaḥ sūtaputras tathāsau sahāsmadīyair api yodhamukhyaiḥ

ami = those; ca = and; tvam = You; dhrtarastrasya = Dhrtarastra; putrah = sons; sarve = all; saha = along with; eva = importantly, chiefly; avani-pala = kings, rulers of the earth; sanghaih = multitude; bhismah = Bhisma; dronah =

Dronacarya; suta-putrah = Karna, son of Suta; tatha = and; asau = that; saha = including; asmadiyaih = our; api = even; yodha-mukhyaih = warrior chiefs.

"And into you all those sons of Dhritarashtra, along with multitudes of kings, importantly Bhīshma, Drona, and that son of Suta, including even our own warrior chiefs ...

In the universal form, Arjuna saw the Kauravas (the sons of Dhritarashtra) and several kings (avani palas) from both sides marching toward death. Among them, he also saw Bhīshma, Drona, and Karna, great warriors, each with a long history of victories and conquests. From what he saw, he must have realized that their death was imminent and predetermined. Previously, he was concerned that he might be responsible for the deaths of Bhishma, Drona, etc. After seeing it, he might have realized that the Lord of Death had already destined them to die, and even if they died in his hands, he would not be responsible for their deaths.

Sloka 27

vaktrāṇi te tvaramāṇā viśanti daṃṣṭrākarālāni bhayānakāni
kecid vilagnā daśanāntareṣu saṃdṛśyante cūrṇitair uttamāṅgaiḥ

vaktrani = mouths; te = Your; tvaramanah = in great speed; visanti = entering; damstra = teeth; karalani = blood curdling; bhayanakani = very fearsome, terrible; kecit = some; vilagnah = being stuck; dasana-antaresu = between the teeth; sandrsyante = are seen; curnitaih = crushed; uttama-angaih = with their head.

"In great haste (they) are entering your mouths, which are lined with very fearsome blood, curdling teeth. Some are seen stuck between teeth, with their heads crushed.

Arjuna saw all those who were going to die in the war. He saw in advance what was going to happen in the coming days and weeks of the war. He saw that many warriors and kings were destined to die, and the Lord of Death had already sealed their fate. He saw them marching into the mouth of Death, and some becoming stuck between his dreadful teeth with their heads crushed. In short, he saw Death devouring the Kauravas and a multitude of kings and warriors. It meant the fate of the war and of all those who were participating in it were already sealed. It would not matter whether Arjuna would participate in it or not. Even if he did not participate, they would die anyway, and he would have to live with the dishonor that he abandoned his duty and left the battlefield in fear.

The Upanishads describe Death as Brahman's first manifestation in the mortal world. They describe him as the devourer of all things with an insatiable hunger. He rules the world as its Lord, and no one can escape him unless they achieve liberation. Everything here serves as his food. All the sacrificial food is also ultimately devoured by him alone. He is the fire in the body and the fire in creation. That hunger of his manifests in us as desires. Through them, he makes sure that everyone becomes his food. He acts as the funeral pyre during cremation, the final sacrifice (antyeshti), and accepts the offerings. He is also the Lord of the elements. Through them, he consumes the jivas, causing their death, and leaves the embodied souls to continue their journey. Every jiva dies at its destined time. Therefore, they are interlinked. Hence, in Hinduism, the name Kala refers to both Time and Death. The Lord of Death is a functional manifestation of Isvara. He is also known by other names, such as Ghora, Aghora, Kapala, Bhairava, Virabhadra, Mahakala, etc. His consorts also have multiple names, such as Kali, Karali, Bhairavi, Chandi, etc.

Sloka 28

yathā nadīnāṃ bahavombuvegāḥ samudram evābhimukhā dravanti
tathā tavāmī naralokavīrā viśanti vaktrāṇy abhivijvalanti

yatha = as; nadinam = of the rivers; bahavah = many; ambu-vegah = swift currents of waters; samudram = ocean; eva = only; abhimukhah = towards in the direction of; dravanti = flow; tatha = so does, in the same manner; tava = Your; ami = all those; nara-loka-virah = heroes of the mortal world; visanti = passing, entering; vaktrani = mouths; abhivijvalanti = blazing, glowing.

"As the swift currents of the waters from many rivers flow towards the ocean only, so are all those warriors of the mortal world passing into Your blazing mouth."

Just as the rivers culminate in the ocean, the lives of all the jivas end up in the blazing mouth of fearsome Death. Just as the river swiftly flowed towards the ocean, Arjuna saw the warriors swiftly rushing towards Death. Through that spectacle, he was probably forewarned that the war would result in large-scale bloodshed and destruction, and there would be no victors or vanquished at the end of it. Only a few survivors would be left to grieve for the dead. The blazing mouth of Death denotes the unpleasantness associated with the experience of death. In whatever way it may happen, dying is not a pleasant experience. No one likes to die or spend much time thinking about death. The speed with which the warriors were rushing towards Death denotes their death was certain, and they had no control over it.

Sloka 29

yathā pradīptaṃ jvalanaṃ pataṅgā viśanti nāśāya samṛddhavegāḥ
tathaiva nāśāya viśanti lokās tavāpi vaktrāṇi samṛddhavegāḥ

yatha = as; pradiptam = blazing; jvalanam = fire; patangah = moths; visanti = enter; nasaya = for destruction; samrddha = with great; vegah = speed; tatha eva = in the same manner; nasaya = for destruction; visanti = entering; lokah = all people; tava = Your; api = and; vaktrani = mouths; samrddha-vegah = with great speed.

"Just as moths enter the blazing fire and are quickly destroyed, in the same manner, all the people are entering your mouths with great speed for their own destruction."

Moths are instantly attracted to the blazing fire, not knowing that their actions will lead to their destruction. Their ignorance and attraction to fire and light drive them to that end. Human beings are also subject to a similar fate due to ignorance and delusion. Just as moths are attracted to fire, humans are attracted to the blazing fire of worldly pleasures. As they engage in desire-ridden actions to enjoy worldly pleasure, not knowing that it will lead to bondage and suffering, they incur sinful karma and become food for Death. Arjuna saw people rushing toward the blazing mouth of Death and falling into it at great speed. It was as if they were rushing towards it in a hurry. Birth, death, and rebirth are inevitable for most jivas. However, human beings have a choice. They do not have to rush towards Death. They can escape from him by controlling their desires, cultivating discernment, and engaging in nishkama karma.

Sloka 30

lelihyase grasamānaḥ samantāl lokān samagrān vadanair jvaladbhiḥ
tejobhir āpūrya jagat samagraṃ bhāsas tavogrāḥ pratapanti viṣṇo

lelihyase = licking lips; grasamanah = devouring; samantat = from all sides; lokan = world, beings, people; samagran = all; vadanaih = by mouthfuls; jvaladbhih = with flaming, blazing; tejobhih = with vigorous heat; apurya = filled; jagat = the universe; samagram = enitre; bhasah = with effulgent rays; tava = Your; ugrah = terrible; pratapanti = scorched; visno = O Vishnu.

"Licking your lips, with flaming mouths, you are devouring the whole world from all sides. The glowing rays of Your vigorous heat, O Vishnu, are scorching the entire universe."

Arjuna saw Death devouring the whole world from all sides. He also saw abundant light and heat scorching everything. Death is responsible for the renewal of life, and so is heat. Excess heat burns everything, but without the sun heating the Earth, life would also not be possible. However, in Death, such dualities do not exist. It is the opposite of life. Everything in the mortal world is food (annam) for the Lord of Death. He does not spare anything or anyone. His hunger is insatiable. Therefore, the Vedas describe him as the destroyer and voracious eater of impermanent things. Once he performs his duties and devours things, Vishnu, the Supreme Lord, ensures that the departed souls return to the earth and start their journey afresh. As the preserver, he makes sure that the world progresses as ordained. Thus, he performs his duties as the Creator, Preserver, and Destroyer. As the Creator, he brings forth beings in each cycle of creation and ensures their continuity in samsara. As the Preserver and source of heat and light, he fills the world with his radiance (tejas) to uphold it and ensure its continuation. As Death, he destroys life and purifies the world. Arjuna addressed the universal form of Lord Krishna as Vishnu. As the sun and the solar deity (Aditya), Lord Vishnu spreads heat and light in all the worlds. He is the source of all the external and internal heat (tapah). Without him heating the worlds, life would not be possible. Hence, he rightly addressed him as Vishnu.

Sloka 31

ākhyāhi me ko bhavān ugrarūpo namostu te devavara prasīda
vijñātum icchāmi bhavantam ādyaṃ na hi prajānāmi tava pravṛttim

akhyahi = please tell; me = to me; kah = who; bhavan = are You; ugra-rupah = in this fierce form; namah astu = my salutations; te = to You; deva-vara = best of the gods; prasida = be gracious; vijnatum = to know; icchami = I wish; bhavantam = You; adyam = primal, first; na = never; hi = certainly; prajanami = I know; tava = Your; pravrttim = disposition, actions, natural tendencies, basic nature.

"Please tell me who you are in this fierce form. My salutations to you, O Best of the Gods, be gracious to me. I want to know you, the first among all. Surely, I do not know your natural tendencies."

Arjuna knew that he was seeing Lord Krishna's universal form, and he himself requested it. However, after seeing the universal form, he was unsure of whom he saw. He did not know who appeared before him. He knew Lord Krishna very well, but the Being who appeared before him was totally different and had nothing in common with the Lord he knew. He was also unsure whether the Supreme Being he saw was friendly or hostile, and whether he would be as gentle and compassionate as Lord Krishna or different. By no means was the form he saw pleasant, friendly, or comforting. It also filled him with great horror. He himself was born of a god, but the great Being he saw was fierce, infinitely large, and devoured life from all sides while people rushed toward his blazing mouth in a great hurry. He saw them falling into his blazing mouth, becoming stuck between his blood-curdling teeth, and being crushed. Although he was a warrior, the sight of the universal form of Death filled him with great fear. Hence, he addressed him with humility as the best of the gods (deva-vara), confessed his ignorance, and expressed his wish to know him and his nature.

Sloka 32

śrībhagavān uvāca
kālosmi lokakṣayakṛt pravṛddho lokān samāhartum iha pravṛttaḥ
ṛtepi tvāṃ na bhaviṣyanti sarve yevasthitāḥ pratyanīkeṣu yodhāḥ

sri-bhagavan uvaca = the Supreme Lord said; kalah = Kala; asmi = I am; loka = worlds; ksaya-krt = destroyer; pravrddhah = mighty; lokan = worlds; samahartum = destroy; iha = in this world; pravrttah =manifest; rte = without; api = even; tvam = you; na bhavisyanti = will not exist; sarve = all; ye = who; avasthitah = standing; prati-anikesu = on opposing sides; yodhah = warriors.

The Supreme Lord said, "I am Kala, the vast and mighty Destroyer of the worlds. I manifest to destroy the worlds. Even without you, all the warriors standing on the opposing sides will cease to exist."

The universal form said, "I am Kala, the destroyer of the worlds. I am vast and mighty and manifest in creation to destroy all animate and inanimate forms. I have already decided the fate of those participating in this war on both sides. They are all destined to die, whether you fight or not." By saying these words, he conveyed to Arjuna that he should not worry about killing anyone on the battlefield since they were destined to die, and he would be instrumental in making that happen.

The manifestations of the Supreme Lord are numerous. Vishnu Purana lists four main manifestations: Purusha or Isvara, Pradhana (also referred to as Prakriti) or the Primal Substance, Vyakta or the Visible Substance, and Kala or Time. Purusha is the first. He is the Cosmic Being who manifests from Brahman as a reflection in Nature with a pure body of the finest sattva and acts as the Self of all. Pradhana and Vyakta, the second and the third, are the visible and invisible, or the manifested and unmanifested, aspects of the same Primal Nature (Mula Prakriti). Kala, or Time, is the fourth, which moves all these and the Wheel of Time. The creation begins when Purusha, the Cosmic Male, pervades the domain of the Pradhana, the Cosmic Female (Mother Goddess). Their union results in the flowering of tattvas (the five elements, the fifteen senses, mind, ego, and intelligence) in the manifested Prakriti, resulting in the appearance of things and beings. Intelligence is the highest of the tattvas, appearing as Mahat on the cosmic scale and as buddhi in the beings. It manifests fully in gods and humans but remains clouded by impurities in humans due to Maya. Thus, names and forms arise due to the union of Purusha and Prakriti and due to the intermixture of the gunas and tattvas within Prakriti.

Time binds Purusha and Prakriti at the beginning of creation and, in the end, separates them to complete the cycle of creation. According to the Puranas, as an aspect of Brahman, Time is eternal and infinite. No one knows his beginning or end. At the beginning of each cycle of creation, he becomes the Creator and brings into existence all things. After the worlds and beings are set in motion, he acts as their sustainer and preserver, regulating and controlling things. In the end, when the cycle of creation completes its full circle, he becomes the destroyer and withdraws everything. The great Kala (Time) is responsible for the progression of events (niyati), the modifications (parinama), and the impermanence that result in the death, destruction, and renewal of things. Thus, in making Prakriti visible (vyakta) or invisible (avyakta), the Lord of Death as Time acts as the catalyst, with himself as the source and witness.

In this verse, Lord Krishna, in the form of Kala, stated that he had already decided the fate of all the people participating in the war on both sides. Their destruction would happen even without Arjuna fighting. He had already seen them marching in great haste into the fiery mouth of Time. Therefore, if he decided to fight, he would play an instrumental role in their death and serve the aims of creation. Lord Krishna appeared before as the Lord of Death to deliver this message and encourage him to fight. He wanted him to know that he (Arjuna) should not assume doership or ownership or take responsibility for his actions. Instead, he should perform them as a karma-sannyasa yogi, offering the fruit of his actions to the Lord.

Sloka 33

tasmāt tvam uttiṣṭha yaśo labhasva jitvā śatrūn bhuṅkṣva rājyaṃ samṛddham
mayaivaite nihatāḥ pūrvam eva nimittamātraṃ bhava savyasācin.

ṭasmat = therefore; tvam = you; uttistha = stand up; yasah = fame; labhasva = to gain; jitva = conquering; satrun = enemies; bhunksva = enjoy; rajyam =

kingdom; samrddham = vast and prosperous, flourishing; maya = by Me; eva = surely; ete = these; nihatah = killed; purvam = already, before, eva = indeed, surely; nimitta-matram = mere instrument, cause; bhava = are; savya-sacin = ambidextrous archer.

Therefore, you should stand up to gain fame. Conquering your enemies, enjoy a vast and prosperous kingdom. Indeed, they have already been killed by me. You are but instrumental only, O Savyasachi.

After showing him the images of warriors marching into the blazing mouth of Death, Lord Krishna told him that he should fight since his enemies were already destined to die in the war. By performing his actions as a karma-sannyasa yogi, he should gain name and fame and enjoy the riches of a prosperous kingdom as his true devotee, offering the fruit of his actions to him and incurring no karma. He particularly mentioned name, fame, and kingdom because, in the first chapter (32 & 33), Arjuna wondered what use there could be of desiring a kingdom and enjoying peace and prosperity after killing his friends and family members. Here, he conveyed that the best way to enjoy the riches of the world was by performing one's duties and offering them to the Lord as a sacrifice. Those who enjoy the remains of a sacrifice would not incur any sin or suffer from the consequences of their actions, even if they were troublesome. Speaking thus, he reaffirmed that he should focus on his duties rather than their consequences. He addressed Arjuna as Savyasachi (ambidextrous archer) to remind him he should perform his duties as a skillful archer and fulfill his obligations to himself, his family, his King Dharmaraja, and God.

This verse raises a few important philosophical questions about divine will and free will, and whether any distinction exists between them. If everything is predetermined, do we have free will and any freedom to make choices and perform actions? Is free will an illusion or real? If it is an illusion, why should anyone perform any action or pursue any goal willfully, including the goal of liberation? These are pertinent questions. If we do not know their answers correctly, we will remain confused and deluded and will not truly understand the teachings of Lord Krishna. The fact is, at the highest level, everything is predetermined. Due to delusion, divine will appears as free will and gives us the illusion of freedom to live freely and independently, and to interfere with our lives and destinies. If we exercise it, assuming ownership and doership, we will become responsible for our actions and incur the sin of interfering not only with our lives but with God's creation and progress. Therefore, the best option is to renounce ownership and doership and offer the fruit of our actions to him so that even if we interfere with our lives and destinies or his creation due to our ignorance or delusion, he will take responsibility for them, and protect us from their consequences. Karma does not arise because we exercise our so-called free will or perform our actions, but because of the attitude or the nature with which we exercise that free will or perform our actions. This is an important revelation of the Bhagavadgita, which Lord Krishna spoke previously while distinguishing action and inaction.

We are not separate from God. The duality we perceive between the individual will and the divine will is due to delusion and egoism. Free will is a trap. It is meant to keep us bound to samsara. Exercising it for one's selfish enjoyment is like swimming in a turbulent river against the flow rather than flowing with it. The whole creation runs according to the divine will. It manifests continuously through various agencies. We are his numerous eyes, ears, faces, hands, and legs, and we are here to manifest his will through our actions as his trusted soldiers in the sacrifice of life. Free will is not separate from divine will unless we assume ownership and doership and fight with God for control and independence, or act as if he does not exist or does not matter. When we do that, we become responsible for our actions, incur karma, and suffer from the consequences. If we renounce egoism, delusion, ownership, and doership and become his true devotees, the duality between God and us disappears. His will and actions become ours, and our actions and will become his. That will give us the freedom to enjoy the riches of the world, peace, and happiness. This is the essence of karma-sannyasa yoga. The adept yogis (yuktas) who practice it with self-control and exclusive devotion excel in it. They renounce desires and attachments, overcome the duality and delusion between their individual will and the divine will, surrender to the Lord unconditionally, and engage in nishkama karma, offering the fruit of their actions to him. For them, every action arises from the divine will only. Through karma-sannyasa yoga, renouncing their free will and desires, they attain sameness (samsiddhi) and freedom from karma (naishkarmya siddhi).

Thus, all karma and the fruit of karma are manifestations of divine will only. Karma afflicts us when we assume ownership and doership and act as if we have free will and we are independent of the Supreme Lord. It liberates us when we renounce ownership and doership and perform actions without desires, accepting that the will that manifests in us is indeed the divine will. Thus, the notion that we have free will is but an illusion and a trap set by Maya to bind us to samsara. In deluded humans, the distinction or duality between divine will and individual will arises. In them, divine will appears as free will due to Maya, tainted by egoism, desire, and delusion. However, when they are removed, the duality disappears, and only divine will remains unimpeded by the impurities. Those who attain it become the Lord's true instruments. They become his eyes, ears, faces, hands, and feet and manifest his will through their actions. Their words become his words, and their actions become his actions. Suffering arises when we assume ownership and doership, mistake the divine will as the individual will due to delusion, and act accordingly. Lord Krishna wanted Arjuna to overcome this delusion and perform his duties, knowing that he was acting as his instrument and manifesting his will through his actions.

Sloka 34

droṇaṃ ca bhīṣmaṃ ca jayadrathaṃ ca karṇaṃ tathānyān api yodhavīrān mayā hatāṃs tvaṃ jahi mā vyathiṣṭhā yudhyasva jetāsi raṇe sapatnān

dronam ca = and Drona; bhismam ca = and Bhisma; jayadratham ca = and Jayadratha; karnam = and Karna; tatha = so also; anyan = other; api = more over; yodha-viran = heroic warriors; maya = by Me; hatan = killed; tvam =

you; jahi = slay; ma = never; vyathisthah = feel disturbed; yudhyasva = fight; jeta asi = you should be victorious; rane = in the battle; sapatnan = enemies.

Drona, Bhīshma, Jayadratha, Karna, and other valiant warriors have already been killed by Me. Therefore, you shall fight and emerge victorious in the battle against your enemies without feeling distressed.

Previously, Arjuna was distressed at the thought of incurring sin and infamy and bringing ruin upon his family by killing these great warriors. Hence, Lord Krishna assured him that he had already willed their deaths. Therefore, without worrying about the consequences, he should fight and emerge victorious in the battle against them. Bhīshma, Drona, Karna, and Jayadratha were great warriors endowed. They were also God's devotees and earned his blessings through their conduct and devotion. Without the Lord's will, it would be humanly impossible for anyone to defeat them in a battle or emerge victorious. Therefore, Lord Krishna comforted him and boosted his morale by saying that he had already willed them to die, and he should execute his will without assuming ownership and doership and feeling distressed.

Sloka 35

sañjaya uvāca
etac chrutvā vacanaṃ keśavasya kṛtāñjalir vepamānaḥ kirīṭī
namaskṛtvā bhūya evāha kṛṣṇaṃ sagadgadaṃ bhītabhītaḥ praṇamya

sanjayah uvaca = Sanjaya said; etat = thus; srutva = having heard; vacanam = the words; kesavasya = of Kesava; krta-anjalih = with hands folded; vepamanah = trembling; kiriti = Arjuna; namaskrtva = offering obeissance, bowing down; bhuyah = again; eva = and; aha krsnam = spoke to Krsna; sa-gadgadam = in a choked voice; bhita-bhitah = fearfully; pranamya = with reverence.

"Said Sanjaya, "Having heard the words of Kesava, Arjuna, with hands folded, trembling, and bowing down, spoke again to Krishna, in a voice choked with fear and reverence."

Sanjaya narrated to Dhritarashtra how Arjuna was filled with fear and trembling after seeing the universal form of Lord Krishna and hearing his words. Dhritarashtra had already seen the universal form of Lord Krishna when the latter went to his court on behalf of the Pandavas to settle the dispute. Kauravas also saw it. However, they ignored his divine opulence and wise counsel, thinking he was an ordinary human who tried to play magic on them. The words of Lord Krishna still left no impact on Dhritarashtra. He merely listened and ignored them. It shows that divine will is inviolable. The Kauravas were destined to die in the war, and Dhritarashtra could do nothing about it. He was fated to ignore Lord Krishna's words and the fate of the warriors who were destined to become a sacrifice to the Lord of Death. Due to his delusion and desire to see his son on the throne, he could not see what was coming to happen to his family and children.

Sloka 36

arjuna uvāca
sthāne hṛṣīkeśa tava prakīrtyā jagat prahṛṣyaty anurajyate ca
rakṣāṃsi bhītāni diśo dravanti sarve namasyanti ca siddhasaṃghāḥ

arjunah uvaca = Arjuna said; sthane = rightly; hrsika-isa = O Hrisikesa, Master of the senses; tava = Your; prakirtya = supreme glory; jagat = the world; prahrsyati = gladdened, invigorated, encouraged; anurajyate = drawn, attracted; ca = and; raksamsi = the demons; bhitani = with fear; disah = directions; dravanti = fleeing; sarve = all; namasyanti = offering obeisances; ca = and; siddha-sanghah = the perfect human beings.

Said Arjuna, " O Master of senses, the world is gladdened and energized by your supreme glory. The demons are fleeing in all directions, and all the perfect ones are offering you their obeisance with great reverence."

According to this verse, Arjuna saw different entities reacting differently to the universal form of Death. He saw the world was gladdened and energized by his supreme glory (prakīrti), and the enlightened ones (siddhas) offering him prayers, delighted by his presence, while the evil ones were fleeing in all directions in great fear, just as the darkness of the night flies away at the sight of the morning light. This is a supreme example of how different people react to divine truths or manifestations in different ways, according to their karma, essential nature, and destiny. The same applies to any situation, happening, or circumstance. Due to their karma and essential nature, people approach him and worship him differently. In response to their devotion and to fulfill their wishes, he appears to them in the forms they think of him or worship him, according to their likes and dislikes and inherent nature. Some forms of God are uplifting and assuring, while others invoke fear or anxiety. As the indweller and knower of all and as the universal witness, he helps them according to their devotion. Mirroring our consciousness and essential nature, he appears in pleasant forms to those who worship him and serve him with pure devotion and in fierce forms to those who are inherently evil and hostile to him or who need a wake-up call. Arjuna saw the Siddhas worshipping him reverently, unaffected by what was happening around them. They are liberated souls with pure consciousness and saintly nature, exclusively devoted to the Supreme Lord and forever absorbed in his contemplation. Hence, they are undisturbed by names and forms, the turmoil of the worlds, or the pleasant and unpleasant aspects of the Supreme Being.

Sloka 37

kasmāc ca te na nameran mahātman garīyase brahmaṇopy ādikartre
ananta deveśa jagannivāsa tvam akṣaraṃ sad asat tatparaṃ yat

kasmat = why; ca = and; te = to You; na = not; nameran = offer obeisance; maha-atman = O Great Self; gariyase = dearer, greater, superior; brahmanah = Brahma; api = even; adi-kartre = the first creator; ananta = infinite; deva-isa = God of the gods; jagat-nivasa = abode of the universe; tvam = You are;

aksaram = imperishable; sat-asat = both existence and non-existence; tat = That; param = highest; yat = which is.

"And why should they not offer obeisance to You, O Great Self, who is greater than even Brahma, the first creator? You are infinite, God of the gods, abode of the universe, imperishable, both existence and non-existence (and) That which is the Highest."

The great Siddhas are knowers of Brahman. They know that he is the highest and the most supreme, the creator and indweller of all, the source of all sources, eternal and inexhaustible, and existence and nonexistence. He is the Great Self because he is the Self of all and greater than Brahma, since the latter manifests from him and is supported by him. He is the Lord of the gods (devesa) because all the divinities worship him and look to him for support and protection. He is also both existence (Sat) and nonexistence (Asat). Sat means real, truth, existence, the presence of something, state of being, or that which manifests or comes into being. It also refers to the Supreme Reality of Brahman, which is eternal, indestructible, and unchanging, and which yogis experience in samadhi. At the highest level, Sat refers to the unknown absolute aspect of Brahman that never manifests or comes into existence, including the unmanifested aspect of Prakriti (asambhuta). In creation, it refers to all his manifestations, manifested worlds, things, and beings, and the objective reality projected by him. Asat means unreal, absent, falsehood, nonexistence, unreality, untruth, negative state of condition, etc. In creation, it refers to the impure states of existence, including negative and evil conditions and dark worlds. Hence, from a philosophical perspective, creation is also considered Asat since it is not real but a temporary formation or projection riddled with impurities and darkness.

The absolute Brahman is Sat. However, since he is imperceptible, incomprehensible, unreal, and inconceivable to the human mind, he is nonexistent perceptually but existent through knowledge, discernment, and liberation. Isvara, his manifested aspect, is Sat and Asat, Sat representing his pure Self (Purusha) and Asat representing his body or materiality (manifested Prakriti). In human consciousness, the wakeful state represents existence, whereas the dream and deep sleep states represent nonexistence. The transcendental state is nonexistent (Asat) for the mind and senses but existent (Sat) for the Self. In terms of action, Sat and Asat refer to the active (prvritti) and inactive (nivrtti) states of the mind and senses. From the moral perspective, Sat is Dharma, and Asat is Adharma. For the jivas, life is existence, and death is nonexistence. For the liberated soul (jivanmukta), the liberated state is Sat, and the bound state is Asat. For the ignorant ones, the bound state is Sat, and the liberated state is Asat. Thus, one can see that Sat and Asat are relative to our knowledge, understanding, and perspective. Brahman is the controller and liberator in his manifestation as the Supreme Being. The siddhas who attain him transcend Asat and remain absorbed in Sat, his pure consciousness, without duality and division.

Sloka 38

tvam ādidevaḥ puruṣaḥ purāṇas tvam asya viśvasya paraṃ nidhānam
vettāsi vedyaṃ ca paraṃ ca dhāma tvayā tataṃ viśvam anantarūpa

tvam = you; adi-devah = First God; purusah = person, purusah; puranah = ancient; tvam = you; asya = this; visvasya = universe; param = final, supreme, transcendental; nidhanam = resting place, place of dissolution; vetta = knower; asi = you are; vedyam = the one who is to be known; ca = and; param = highest, absolute; ca = and; dhama = abode, place; tvaya = by you; tatam = is pervaded; visvam = universe; ananta-rupa = infinite forms.

"You are the First God, the most ancient Purusha, the final resting place of all, the knower of all and the one to be known, and the highest abode. The entire universe is pervaded by You, O Lord of infinite forms."

Arjuna continued his adoration of the Supreme Lord, justifying why he was worthy of worship by enlightened beings (siddhas). His words convey that he was deeply absorbed in devotion and expressed it by praising him as the First God, the most ancient Purusha, the highest abode, the knower of all, and the one to be known. In short, he recognized him as Brahman. As the highest, absolute, supreme reality, containing Sat and Asat within himself, Brahman is the beginning and end of everything in creation. He is before all and remains untouched even after the creation is dissolved. Even the highest gods, such as Brahma, Vishnu, and Shiva, manifest from him only, partaking in his pure nature. He is the womb of all and existence itself, where everything begins and ends according to his will. Therefore, he is truly the First God (adideva) and the final resting place (nidhanam), in whom the diversity of creation is resolved into its primordial state. He is also the most ancient Purusha, the Cosmic Self, who manifests in all as the individual Self. The same Cosmic Being is described in the Vedas as the divinity who manifests all beings and worlds by performing a great sacrifice, using his cosmic body as the sacrificial material and the sacrificial ground, employing ancient gods as priests. As the indweller, pervading Self, and universal witness, he is also the knower (vetta) in whom knowledge, consciousness, and intelligence self-exist and knowing happens without the help of any external agency or medium. Arjuna also extolled Lord Krishna as vedyam, the one to be known, because without knowing him, one cannot overcome ignorance or attain liberation. Brahman is Parandhama, the highest abode. According to the Vishistadvaita, he is the lord of his immortal world where the eternally immortal souls (nityamuktas), liberated souls (muktas), siddhas, and other enlightened beings reside near him, enjoying his company and ever-absorbed in his contemplation and devotion. Ananta Rupa means the Lord with infinite forms. The name is perfectly justified since he has numerous manifestations and appears differently to his devotees according to their faith and devotion. Lord Krishna already spoke about them and revealed the important ones.

Sloka 39

vāyur yamognir varuṇaḥ śaśāṅkaḥ prajāpatis tvaṃ prapitāmahaś ca namo namas testu sahastrakṛtvaḥ punaś ca bhūyopi namo namas te

vayuh = Vayu; yamah = Lord Yama; agnih = Agni; varunah = Varuna; sasa-ankah = Sasanka; prajapatih = Prajapati; tvam = You; prapitamahah = great-grandfather; ca = and; namah = salutations; namah = salutations; te = to You; astu = are; sahasra-krtvah = a thousand times; punah ca = and again; bhuyah = again; api = also; namah = salutations; namah te = salutations to You.

"Vayu, Yama, Agni, Varuna, Sasanka, Prajapati, and the Great Grandfather, You are. I offer salutations and salutations to You a thousand times. Salutations and Salutations to You again and again."

Agni (fire), Vayu (air), Yama (death), Varuna (water), Sasanka (moon), and Prajapati are extolled in the Vedas as manifestations of Brahman. They are created for the welfare of the world and the preservation and continuation of life and Dharma on earth. They are responsible not only for rain, crops, seasons, harvest, and granting their worshippers' wishes but also for the transmigration of souls and their rebirth. They also protect the Earth from evil and demonic forces. They are also present in our bodies as our organs and faculties. As the Creator of all, Brahman is their source. In their highest aspect, they are but different manifestations of Brahman only, although they may or may not be aware of it. Hence, in the sacrificial ceremonies, the offerings made by the worshippers to various gods ultimately reach him only, just as the food shared by all the organs in the body ultimately reaches the person who eats it. Sasanka is an epithet of Chandra (the moon), also known as Soma, the Lord of the Dream and Ancestral worlds. The moon in the Upanishads is considered an eye of Brahman. Prajapati was the original creator god of the Vedas. He was later substituted by Brahma, who is known as pitamaha, the grandfather. The Vedas and Puranas mention several Prajapatis. They are born from Brahma to perform various functions. They include several sages such as Angira, Bhrigu, Narada, Kashyapa, Marichi, etc. Prapitamaha, meaning the great-grandfather, is the father (or creator) of Brahma, the grandfather or the ancestor of all. It refers to Isvara, the lord of the universe. In the cosmic hierarchy, Isvara is the first to manifest from Brahman. Hiranyaharbha (the Golden Germ) is the second. Purusha, the World Soul, is the third, and Viraj, the manifested world (Jagat), is the fourth. The last one is also known as Brahma in some descriptions.

Sloka 40

namaḥ purastād atha pṛṣṭhatas te namostu te sarvata eva sarva anantavīryāmitavikramas tvaṃ sarvaṃ samāpnoṣi tatosi sarvaḥ

namah = salutations; purastat = from the front; atha = and; prsthatah = from behind; te = You; namah astu = salutations; te = to You; sarvatah = from all sides; eva = indeed; sarva = O All; ananta-virya = infinite power; amitavikramah = infinite valor; tvam = You; sarvam = everything; samapnosi = envelop; tatah = therefore; asi = are; sarvah = everything.

"My salutations to You from the front and back. Indeed, O All, I offer my salutations from all sides. You are infinite in power and infinite in valor. You envelop everything. Therefore, you are everything."

Purasta means standing before or at the front. It also means facing the east or eastward. Many Hindus offer morning prayers to the gods and the Supreme Lord, turning eastwards and facing the morning sun. Later in the day, they offer evening prayers, turning westward and facing the evening sun. When they are in the presence of deities, they offer circumambulatory salutations (pradakshina), turning around themselves or moving around the images. By these, they offer salutations to the deities before them and to the Lord who is seated in them. Arjuna offered these salutations to Lord Krishna in deep devotion. He offered him salutations from all sides, realizing that he existed everywhere and in all directions. By offering salutations in every possible way and calling him sarva (all) and anantavirya (infinite power), he acknowledged his omnipresence, omnipotence, and his Lordship as the source of all actions and manifestations.

Sloka 41

sakheti matvā prasabhaṃ yad uktaṃ he kṛṣṇa he yādava he sakheti
ajānatā mahimānaṃ tavedaṃ mayā pramādāt praṇayena vāpi

sakha = friend; iti = thus; matva = thinking, considering; prasabham = impetuously; yat = whatever; uktam = said; he krsna = O Krsna; he yadava = O Yadava; he sakhe iti = O dear friend; ajanata = without knowing; mahimanam = greatness; tava = Your; idam = this; maya = by me; pramadat = carelessly; pranayena = out of love; va api = either or.

"Because of carelessness or love and without knowing your true greatness, whatever I might have impetuously said, calling you 'O Krishna, O Yadava, O dear friend,' treating you thus as a friend..."

Lord Krishna and Arjuna had been good friends and relations for a long time. Lord Krishna supported Arjuna and helped the Pandavas on many occasions. Their relationship was cemented further by Arjuna's marriage to Subhadra, Lord Krishna's younger sister. After realizing that Lord Krishna was the Supreme Lord, Arjuna apologized for treating him like an ordinary human being and calling him by his first name, his caste name, and as a friend. When we are with friends, we speak to them freely, ignoring the social norms and usual courtesies. However, in the Mahabharata, we do not find any instances where Arjuna misbehaved with Lord Krishna, ignored common courtesies, or questioned his judgment.

Sloka 42

yac cāvahāsārtham asatkṛtosi vihāraśayyāsanabhojaneṣu
ekothavāpy acyuta tatsamakṣaṃ tat kṣāmaye tvām aham aprameyam

yat = whatever; ca = and; avahasa-artham = in jest; asat-krtah = disrespect; asi = done to You; vihara = during recreation, walking for pleasure; sayya = while resting; asana = sitting; bhojanesu = while eating; ekah = along in private; atha va = or; api = even; acyuta = O infallible one; tat-samaksam = in public in front of others; tat = that; ksamaye = seek forgiveness; tvam = from You; aham = I; aprameyam = incomprehensible.

"Whatever was done to you either in jest or in disrespect, during recreation, while resting, while sitting, while eating, alone or in front of others, for that, I seek your forgiveness, O incomprehensible One."

The Supreme Lord is always forgiving, more so if we pray to him and seek his forgiveness, repenting for our failures and sinful actions. Since we are subject to ignorance and delusion, he knows that we are bound to make mistakes and fall into the trap of Maya. Inadvertently or unknowingly, we commit many mistakes or behave carelessly with others, with gods, or with God, as Arjuna mentioned here. Whenever we realize that we are at fault, it is humility to seek forgiveness and unburden ourselves of guilt and remorse. It is a transformative practice that cleanses our minds and makes us more responsive and responsible towards others and even ourselves. For a devotee, it is even more important. It helps us clear our minds and live in the present. Here, Arjuna sought forgiveness for his inadvertent past actions toward Lord Krishna in their long relationship. By saying it, he showed humility, devotion, and a newfound awareness about himself. In their ignorance, devotees often blame the Lord for their problems and difficulties, even though the Lord is in no way responsible for them and has no reason to resolve them. In difficulties, one should ask for forgiveness for past sins and seek the Lord's help instead of blaming him. Rewards and punishments arise from our karma. They can be mitigated through righteous conduct, exclusive devotion, and nishkama karma, and by seeking forgiveness.

Sloka 43

pitāsi lokasya carācarasya tvam asya pūjyaś ca gurur garīyān
na tvatsamosty abhyadhikaḥ kutonyo lokatrayepy apratimaprabhāva

pita = father; asi = You are; lokasya = of all; cara = moving; acarasya = nonmoving; tvam = You are; asya = of this; pujyah = worthy of worship, venerable; ca = and; guruh = master; gariyan = still greater; na = not; tvat-samah = equal to You; asti = there is; abhyadhikah = greater than; kutah = how can there be; anyah = other; loka-traye = in the three worlds; api = even; apratima = immeasurable; prabhava = power.

"You are the father of all things of this world, both moving and non-moving. You are worthy of its worship and greater than any guru. None is equal to you or greater than you. How can there be in the triple worlds, O Immeasurable Power?"

There can be only one Supreme Lord and Controller of all creation. There cannot be two or three performing the same duties. As this verse affirms, Purusha or Isvara alone is the Supreme Lord of all creation. Prakriti is his dynamic aspect. She should not be viewed as a separate entity or a rival force, but an inseparable part of him, worthy of worship and adoration, and responsible for all his dynamic functions and duties. Guru means one who drives away darkness from the minds of his disciples. The Supreme Lord is greater than any guru because he is the source of the Vedas and the knowledge the gurus seek and preach. He illuminates all the worlds through his brilliance and removes darkness from our minds. He is worthy of worship because he is the ancestor or father (pita) of all. No one is equal to him in the triple worlds because he is the source and support of all.

Sloka 44

tasmāt praṇamya praṇidhāya kāyaṃ prasādaye tvām aham īśam īḍyam
piteva putrasya sakheva sakhyuḥ priyaḥ priyāyārhasi deva soḍhum.

tasmat = therefore; pranamya = offer salutations; pranidhaya = prostrating or laying down completely; kayam = the body; prasadaye = seek mercy or grace; tvam = to You; aham = I; isam = God, the Lord; idyam = venerable; pita iva = like a father; putrasya = of a son; sakha iva = like a friend; sakhyuh = of a friend; priyah = lover; priyayah = of the beloved; arhasi = You should; deva = O God; sodhum = forgive, bear with, tolerate.

"Therefore, prostrating my body completely, I offer my salutations to you. The most venerable Lord, I seek your mercy. May you forgive me, O God, the way a father (forgives) his son, a friend (forgives) his friend, (or) a lover his beloved."

Arjuna offered a full salutation to Lord Krishna's universal form, prostrating before him. In Hinduism, offering a salutation with prostration and the eight limbs of the body touching the ground is called shashtanga namaskaram. Sashta means eight, anga means limbs, and namaskaram means salutation. Devotees customarily offer it to the deities they worship in temples and domestic rituals. By offering it to Lord Krishna with humility and surrender, Arjuna asked him to forgive him just as a father, friend, or lover would forgive his son, friend, or lover. He wanted him to treat him kindly with love and forgiveness. God's exclusive devotees renounce worldly relationships and depend upon him entirely. They see in him the relationships they left behind and make him their sole support. Through unwavering devotion, they remain in his company and feel assured and protected.

Sloka 45

adṛṣṭapūrvaṃ hṛṣitosmi dṛṣṭvā bhayena ca pravyathitaṃ mano me
tad eva me darśaya deva rūpaṃ prasīda deveśa jagannivāsa

adrsta = not seen; purvam = before, in the past; hrsitah = happy, delighted; asmi = I am; drstva = having seen; bhayena = with fear; ca = and, but; pravyathitam = disturbed, agitated; manah = mind; me = my; tat = that; eva =

very; me = to me; darsaya = show; deva = O God; rupam = form; prasida = be gracious; deva-isa = O God of gods; jagat-nivasa = dweller of the universe.

"I Am Delighted to have seen what I had never seen before. However, my mind is stricken with fear. Please show me that very (familiar) form and be gracious, O God of gods and Dweller of the Universe."

Arjuna sought forgiveness because he was afraid. It is human to be afraid of unknown situations, forms, or objects. Our fear on such occasions arises from our self-preservation instinct. We do not fear speaking to people, friends, and relations we know, and do not worry about visiting familiar places. However, we experience anxiety if we have to visit unknown places or meet total strangers in unfamiliar situations. Even when we meet known people, we may experience fear or anxiety if they behave abnormally or unusually and show us a different side of themselves. It is like stepping out of your comfort zone and entering an unfamiliar territory. Arjuna wanted to see the universal form of Lord Krishna. He knew him as a friend and mentor, but not as the Supreme Lord of the Universe or the Lord of Death. Therefore, when he showed him his terrifying universal form, he was afraid and requested him to revert to his pleasant and familiar form.

Sloka 46

kirīṭinaṃ gadinaṃ cakrahastaṃ icchāmi tvāṃ draṣṭum ahaṃ tathaiva
tenaiva rūpeṇa caturbhujena sahastrabāho bhava viśvamūrte

kiritinam = with crown; gadinam = with mace; cakra-hastam = disc in hand; icchami = I wish; tvam = You; drastum = to see; aham = I; tatha eva = verily as before; tena eva = that very; rupena = form; catuh-bhujena = with four arms; sahasra-baho = he who has a thousand arms; bhava = be, become, visva-murte = O Universal Being.

"I wish to see you very much as before, wearing a crown, carrying a mace, and holding a disc in (your) hand. O thousand-armed One, O Universal Being, please be the four-armed One."

Arjuna wanted to see Lord Krishna in the familiar form of Lord Vishnu, which he and his family probably worshipped. He might have also seen that form in the images or heard about it. Hence, to appease the fierce form before him and escape from that scary situation, he wanted to see the Lord's familiar and pleasant form with four arms, wearing a golden crown, and carrying the mace and the disc. The Supreme Brahman is both with form (murtam) and without form (amurtam). He is both the Universal Self and Universal Being. The whole creation is his body, which he pervades as its very Self and remains concealed in all. As the Universal Being (visvamurthy), he has numerous pleasant, unpleasant, finite, and infinite forms. He manifests them to appear as many in his universal Play (lila). Kala is one of them. In the Kurukshetra War, he showed it to Arjuna to teach him important lessons about destiny, duty, death, and destruction. He wanted Arjuna to know that the latter had the right to perform his obligatory duties and leave their result to the Lord since he would determine their outcome. He should not worry about the consequences of his actions but focus on performing them. The results and the consequences should be left to him since he, as the Lord of Death, had already destined the outcome of the war and those who would die in it.

Sloka 47

śrībhagavān uvāca
mayā prasannena tavārjunedaṃ rūpaṃ paraṃ darśitam ātmayogāt
tejomayaṃ viśvam anantam ādyaṃ yan me tvadanyena na dṛṣṭapūrvam

sri-bhagavan uvaca = the Blessed Lord said; maya = by Me; prasannena = pleased; tava = with you; arjuna = O Arjuna; idam = this; rupam = form; param = supreme; darsitam = shown; atma-yogat = by my self-illumined power; tejah-mayam = filled with brilliance; visvam = the universal; anantam = infinite; adyam = the first; yat me = of Mine; tvat anyena = none other than you; na drsta-purvam = saw previously.

The Supreme Lord said, "Pleased by you, O Arjuna, this Supreme Form has been shown to you through My self-illumined power, which is fully illuminated, universal, infinite, the first. No one, other than you, saw that (form) of Mine previously."

Arjuna saw the universal form of Kala with the mystic vision granted to him by Lord Krishna. Pleased by his devotion and curiosity, Lord Krishna revealed to him through his self-illumined, sovereign power (atma yoga) the whole creation in a universal form. His universal form, by whatever name one may recognize it, is brilliant, infinite, eternal, indestructible, universal, and endowed with all the perfections (siddhis) and powers one can imagine. However, he showed a fiercely terrifying form because the situation demanded it.

Ordinary humans will never get an opportunity to see the Supreme Lord in a physical form; forget about his universal form. Even among his best devotees, only a few were ever allowed to see him in their deepest meditative states. Arjuna was given a glimpse of the universal form of Death because he was destined to see death and destruction on a large scale in the Kurukshetra war, and the Lord wanted to prepare him for it. He wanted him to fight with equanimity, knowing that he was not the cause of anyone's death, and he was fighting against those who were already fated to die due to divine causes (adhidaivika) beyond his control. By revealing to him this supreme secret about human actions, life and death, and the importance of karma-sannyasa or renouncing desires, ownership, and doership of all actions, he wanted to open his eyes to the role of God in human life and become indifferent to the results of his actions.

Persistent individual effort (abhyasa) is necessary in spiritual practice (sadhana). However, it is insufficient to reach the supreme Goal without renouncing desires, egoism, attachment, and the fruit of one's actions. There is no such thing as free will or individual will. It is a delusion that arises due to duality and ignorance. The Supreme Being is the source of all. Everything in creation arises and subsides in him due to his inviolable will alone. Those who seek liberation or wish to live happily on earth should recognize this eternal truth and surrender themselves to the Supreme Lord, letting him take responsibility for their lives and actions. The whole creation is controlled by divine will only. Deluded people take ownership of it and engage in actions, which result in karma and bondage. Those who surrender their will to the Lord and engage in nishkama karma, offering the fruit of their actions to him, acknowledging him as the source of all, escape from it by his grace and attain his immortal realm. In this verse, the Lord reaffirms this supreme secret, conveying that Arjuna could see his universal form because he let it happen through his self-willed illumination. It was his personal choice. The last sentence of the verse reaffirms our argument that none other than Arjuna saw it.

Sloka 48

na veda yajñādhyayanair na dānaiḥ na ca kriyābhir na tapobhir ugraiḥ evaṃrūpaḥ śakya ahaṃ nṛloke draṣṭuṃ tvadanyena kurupravīra

na = not; veda = knowledge of the Vedas; yajna = sacrifice; adhyayanaih = study; na danaih = by charity; na = not; ca = and; kriyabhih = by actions; na = not; tapobhih = even by austerities; ugraih = severe; evam = thus; rupah = form; sakyah = can be seen; aham = I; nr-loke = human world; drastum = see; tvat = you; anyena = by another; kuru-pravira = O best among the Kurus.

Neither by the study of the Vedas, sacrifices, acts of charity, pious actions, nor severe austerities could I ever be seen in this form in the world of humans by anyone other than you, O most valiant among the Kurus.

The study of the Vedas, sacrifices, charity, pious actions, or austerities - they are all desirable and helpful to achieve liberation. However, none of them qualify them to see his universal form with their own eyes. Spiritual practices mentioned by him may lead to self-purification and liberation, but not a direct vision of the thousand-armed Universal Being. Arjuna could see his radiant, universal, infinite, and original form because the Lord chose to show him using his divine power (yoga-maya). It means it happened not because of adhyatmika (internal), adhibhautika (external), or adhidaivika (fortuitous) reasons but because the Lord personally willed it. It does not happen in the mortal world (nara loka) except in the rarest of circumstances. He also implied that it would not happen again. One may see him in imagination, dream states, or meditation, or attain his state in samadhi (self-absorption). Arjuna was able to see it because of divine grace (daiva prasadam).

Sloka 49

mā te vyathā mā ca vimūḍhabhāvo dṛṣṭvā rūpaṃ ghoram īdṛṅ mamedam vyapetabhīḥ prītamanāḥ punas tvaṃ tad eva me rūpam idaṃ prapaśya

ma = not; te = you; vyatha = worry, suffer; ma = not; ca = and; vimudha-bhavah = become deluded; drstva = seeing; rupam = form; ghoram = terrible; idrk = such as; mama = My; idam = this; vyapeta-bhih = becoming free from fear; prita-manah = cheerful mind punah = again; tvam = you; tat = that; eva = even; me = of Mine; rupam = form; idam = this; prapasya = see.

Do not be worried or fall into delusion after seeing the terrible form of Mine, such as the one you saw. Free from fear and with a cheerful mind, see that (pleasant) form of Mine again.

Lord Krishna wanted Arjuna not to fall into delusion after seeing his universal form of Death and develop misconceptions about him or the war due to fear. Therefore, he quickly showed him his pleasant form as the Supreme Lord, upholder, and protector of all the worlds to help him regain his courage, composure, and discernment. He also wanted him to wake up from the unusual state he had fallen into after seeing him as Kala and return to the reality of his present moment. The forms of the Supreme Lord are numerous. They are impermanent and illusory. The Lord manifests them for different reasons. They are like random pieces in a gigantic puzzle on the canvas set by Maya under his will and should not be mistaken for real or the Supreme Lord. The forms arise due to his association with Prakriti in her manifested state. They may appear differently on different occasions. They also disappear with creation. He shows his pleasant forms to his devotees and fierce forms to the evil ones or those who despise him. However, occasionally, as in the case of Arjuna, he may show his fierce forms to his devotees to awaken them from ignorance and delusion or unsettle their rigid beliefs. Having achieved that end in the case of Arjuna, he withdrew his universal form and appeared to him in his pleasant form.

Sloka 50

sañjaya uvāca
ity arjunaṃ vāsudevas tathoktvā svakaṃ rūpaṃ darśayām āsa bhūyaḥ
āśvāsayām āsa ca bhītam enaṃ bhūtvā punaḥ saumyavapur mahātmā

sanjayah uvaca = Sanjaya said; iti = thus; arjunam = to Arjuna; vasudevah = Vasudeva; tatha = thus; uktva = speaking, saying; svakam = personal, own, natural; rupam = form; darsayamasa = showed; bhuyah = again; asvasayamasa = pacified, revived the spirits; ca = and; bhitam = frightened, fearful; enam = this; bhutva punah = returning, becoming again; saumya-vapuh = pleasant form; maha-atma = the Great Self.

Sanjaya said, "Thus speaking to Arjuna, Vasudeva showed again his personal (svakam) form. Returning to his pleasant form, the Great One revived the spirits of the frightened one."

To comfort Arjuna, Lord Krishna reverted to his original, divine form. From the subsequent verses, we may presume that he appeared to him in this distinct form as the transcendental, divine Krishna, or the Lord of the Universe, whom the Vaishnavas identify with Narayana or Maha Vishnu. According to our scriptures, the divinities we worship have standard and distinct forms (svarupas) that define them and establish their specific identities. The svarupas (personal forms) personify their duties, qualities, and potencies and help them stand apart in the Lord's creation, ritual worship, and in the minds of their devotees. They also help devotees identify them, relate to them, worship them, or contemplate them. Only a few ever happen to see them physically or ethereally in their true svarupas. Some may see them but do not recognize them since they may appear before them, concealing their svarupas to test their faith or devotion. Some may see them in their subtle minds and feel ecstatic, confused, or fearful since our minds tend to color our thoughts and emotions and create a self-induced reality. People may also form set opinions and expectations about the svarupas of various divinities and miss the truth in their deluded notions about them. The Lord may also appear to his devotees according to their mental projections since he does not want to displease them. For example, archeological evidence shows that the forms people envisioned about their beloved gods a thousand years ago are very different from how people imagine them or depict them today. In other words, the forms of the deities we worship are essentially our personal creations, partly influenced by the images we see, the descriptions we read in the scriptures, or the popular notions we acquire from others. To argue that they should be universal or that everyone should envision and worship them uniformly is sheer ignorance.

While the divinities we worship have specific svarupas, it is difficult to say the Supreme Lord who manifests from Brahman as Purusha or Isvara in his manifested, dynamic aspect has any definitive svarupa. Devotees worship him variously as Brahma, Vishnu, Shiva, Shakti, etc., and call him by different names. We may, therefore, say that nothing is definitive about his svarupa since, by nature, he is indeterminate, complete, and without limits. We may also say his svarupas are as numerous and diverse as his manifestations and vary according to the qualities, modes, functions, and circumstances in which he manifests in the creation or before his devotees. The Vedas describe him as a being with numerous hands, feet, faces, ears, eyes, etc., and with the brilliance of a thousand suns. Some of his forms are also temporary and time-bound since they are withdrawn once the purpose is served. Some may last for a short period, some for a long time, and some for the duration of a time cycle. The universal form as the Lord of Death, which he showed Arjuna, probably lasted for a few moments, his incarnated human form for a lifetime, and his transcendental divine form (svakam) personifying his qualities and duties as the Supreme Lord may last for a time cycle or appear differently to different people according to their mindset, expectations, purity, and devotion. Even among gods, only a few might have seen the svarupa (if any) of the Supreme Being. That day, Lord Krishna showed Arjuna his transcendental divine form (svarupa) to calm him and revive his morale.

Sloka 51

arjuna uvāca
dṛṣṭvedaṃ mānuṣaṃ rūpaṃ tava saumyaṃ janārdana
idānīm asmi saṃvṛttaḥ sacetāḥ prakṛtiṃ gataḥ

arjunah uvaca = Arjuna said; drstva = seeing; idam = this; manusam = human; rupam = form; tava = Your; saumyam = plesant; janardana = O chastiser of the enemies; idanim = now; asmi = I have; samvrttah = become sa-cetah = peaceful, mindful, conscious; prakrtim = nature; gatah = returned.

Said Arjuna, "Seeing this pleasant human form of yours, O Janardana, I have become peaceful and returned to my natural disposition."

Upon seeing the pleasant form (saumya svarupa) of Lord Krishna, Arjuna recovered from fear and regained his natural disposition. It was as if he woke up from a nightmare and felt reassured by seeing his pleasant and glorious form. He became sachetah, meaning right-minded, conscious, mindful, rational, peaceful, normal, or properly balanced. Sometimes, when we are disturbed or anxious, we feel reassured by seeing familiar faces and sights. It revives our sagging morale and helps us regain our composure. We may also experience the same when we see a close friend or relative who has been highly disturbed or agitated for some reason, returning to his normal, pleasant state after a while. Upon seeing Lord Krishna's pleasant form, Arjuna felt the same. The form of Kala frightened him, but that of Janardana as the savior of people reassured him. Janardana means one who agitates, frightens, or excites evil people but assures and calms those who are pious, pure, and devoted by mitigating their cries of suffering.

Sloka 52

śrībhagavān uvāca
sudurdarśam idaṃ rūpaṃ dṛṣṭvān asi yan mama
devā apy asya rūpasya nityaṃ darśanakāṅkṣiṇaḥ

sri-bhagavan uvaca = the supreme lord said; su-durdarsam = very difficult to see; idam = this; rupam = form; drstavan asi = you have seen; yat = which; mama = of Mine; devah = the divinities; api = indeed, even; asya = of this; rupasya = form; nityam = always, daily; darsana-kanksinah = yearn to see.

The Supreme Lord said, "This form of Mine that you have seen is very difficult to see. Even the divinities are always eager to see this form."

Lord Krishna said that his pleasant form was rarely seen even by gods, and seeing him thus by Arjuna was a blessing. Madhavacharya felt that it was a blessing because his pleasant form was delightfully pleasing to the eye (su), but, at the same time, rare and difficult (durdasa). Even gods rarely succeed in seeing him in that mood. It means that the status in the hierarchy of creation does not matter. The Supreme Lord shows his agreeable svarupa only to a few qualified devotees according to their merit and purity of devotion. The Kena Upanishad contains an episode about this. It states that the Supreme Lord once appeared to Indra, Agni, and Vayu as a Yaksha and asked about them. They did not know who he was. In their arrogance, they tried to show off their powers to him, but they failed in his presence. When he disappeared, after showing them that their powers would not work before him, Uma Haimavathi appeared in the sky and told them about the Supreme Lord they had just seen. In the cosmic hierarchy, the gods are a step above humans. However, they are not qualified to know Brahman or attain liberation. Humans only enjoy that privilege. Through self-effort and self-transformation, they can overcome their impurities and enter the pure state of Brahman.

Sloka 53

nāhaṃ vedair na tapasā na dānena na cejyayā
śakya evaṃvidho draṣṭuṃ dṛṣṭavān asi māṃ yathā

na = not; aham = I; vedaih = through the Vedas; na = not; tapasa = by austerity; na = not; danena = by gifts, charity; na = not; ca = and; ijyaya = by sacrifices; sakyah = possible; evam-vidhah = in this manner; drastum = to see; drstavan = have seen; asi = you; mam = Me; yatha = as.

Neither through the Vedas nor by austerity nor by gifts nor by sacrifices can I be seen in this manner as you have seen Me.

The study of the Vedas, the practice of austerities such as celibacy, fasting, etc., and charity, such as giving gifts of cows, land, gold, etc., are recommended for householders to overcome desires and selfishness and serve the Lord and his eternal Dharma. They promote sattva (purity) and divine qualities necessary to achieve liberation. Studying the Vedas, a practice of jnana yoga, helps us acquire the right knowledge and discernment. Austerity, a part of sannyasa yoga, helps us develop self-control, detachment, and renunciation. Charity, a part of karma yoga, also leads to the same beneficial ends. By these means, one accumulates enough merit (punyam) to attain a good birth in the next life and advance spiritually toward the highest goal. Those who excel in these practices and attain perfection qualify for God's grace and liberation. However, they do not grant them the blessing to see the Supreme Lord's divine form (svarupa) or communicate with him directly as Arjuna did. As suggested in the next verse, it is possible through single-minded and undivided devotion (ananya bhakti), but not guaranteed. Human beings are deluded and ignorant. Even if an incarnation or pious soul is born amidst them, they do not recognize him, doubt his divinity and mystic wisdom, cast aspersions, view him with suspicion, and deny themselves an opportunity to learn from them. It is due to divine Maya, God's will, and karma.

Sloka 54

bhaktyā tv ananyayā śakya aham evaṃvidhorjuna
jñātuṃ draṣṭuṃ ca tattvena praveṣṭuṃ ca paraṃtapa

bhaktya = by devotion; tu = but; ananyaya = not another or no other; sakyah = can be; aham = I; evam-vidhah = in this manner; arjuna = O Arjuna; jnatum = known; drastum = seen; ca = and; tattvena = reality; pravestum = enter; ca = and; parantapa = O destroyer of foes.

Only by devotion, but by no other means, O Arjuna, can I be known or seen in this manner, or can My divine reality be entered, O destroyer of foes.

Until now, Lord Krishna spoke about his manifestations, essential nature, divine qualities, and duties as the Lord of the universe. From here on, he will focus on devotion and speak about it. The first six chapters of the Bhagavadgita are primarily about knowing the individual Self, overcoming delusion, and cultivating discernment and the knowledge of the Self. In the next six chapters, we learn mainly about the Supreme Brahman and his numerous glories and manifestations. In the next six chapters, for which this one is introductory, we will learn about the relationship between him and his devotees or between the Supreme Self and the individual Self. Their relationship is established, sustained, and strengthened through devotion of the highest kind.

In this verse, Lord Krishna emphasizes the importance of devotion in attaining divine grace and liberation, describing it as ananya, meaning exclusive or nothing else. It is also known as single-minded devotion (kevala bhakti). Thus, this verse sums up the essential practice of bhakti yoga, which is considered the highest of all yogas. Although it seems simple and easy, it is not. Devotees of the Supreme Lord who practice kevala bhakti or ananya bhakti have a unique opportunity to know him, see him directly, and enter his supreme reality or immortal abode. Followers of Dvaita and Vishistadvaita believe that they are uniquely qualified to enjoy his company and live blissfully in his presence after death, establishing with him an everlasting, internal connection through their pure consciousness. However, according to the Advaita, those who attain liberation cease to exist individually after death as they become dissolved in His pure consciousness without a trace. Whatever the truth, without exclusive devotion, one cannot attain liberation or the Supreme Brahman.

True devotion is the gateway to eternal life and liberation. It is the royal path by which pure souls ascend to the highest heaven. There is no better way to enter the reality of Brahman (brahma tattva) than through pure and unmixed devotion, which is free from desires and worldly attachments. However, it does not arise without self-purification and perfection in yoga. The devotion that is tinged with selfishness and desires is a poor shadow of it. It may lead to a better life in the next birth, but not liberation. In this journey, faith and knowledge are important because true devotion arises from the right knowledge acquired through jnana yoga and the firm faith that is strengthened by that knowledge. The knowledge of Brahman arises from the study of scriptures and association with mahatmas (great souls). Without it, true devotion (bhakti) does not arise as one remains deluded, impure, and ignorant. Liberation is not possible without the grace of the Supreme Lord, and his grace can be attained only when the mind is free from egoism, desires, and attachments and filled with pure devotion.

Ananya bhakti is not the simple devotion many people practice in temples and homes to fulfill their desires or for worldly reasons. Renunciation, purity, detachment, and discernment are important aspects of it. It arises only when you are absent from your consciousness and fully establish your mind in the thoughts of the Lord. Exclusive devotion means devotion that is free from the duality between you and God. True devotees do not think of themselves but only of the Lord. They worship him without seeking, desiring, expecting, or claiming attention, ownership, or doership. For them, devotion is an act of sacrifice, renunciation, and an opportunity to serve others by seeing him in them. For them, life becomes a great sacrifice in which they pour everything they have as a sacrificial offering, becoming the sacrificer and the sacrificed, as a mark of their purity, divinity, love, and devotion.

What happens to the devotees who attain Brahman in the embodied state? According to the descriptions available in our devotional literature, when a devotee attains liberation through the grace of the divine couple (Maha Lakshmi and Maha Vishnu) while he is alive and when he leaves this world, he passes through many planes and worlds of light, meeting on the way many divinities. They rejoice in his liberation and take great delight in seeing him and helping him. After meeting them, he finally reaches the river called Viraja, which reflects the beauty, splendor, and illumination of the Supreme Lord. The liberated soul takes a plunge into its radiant waters and becomes invigorated and perfected by its cleansing and illuminating power. When he emerges from the river, a strange being named Amanava appears on the banks of the river and greets him. He is a personal messenger, or ambassador of Lord Vishnu, meant to accompany the liberated souls and acquaint them with the landmarks and the wonders they will see on the way. Accompanied by him, they enter the immortal world of the Supreme Lord, where he takes leave of them.

Continuing their journey further, they interact with many divine beings and witness divine splendors. Then, they enter the Golden City of Vaikuntha and pass through many golden palaces and halls, where many divinities and souls of the highest order come forward to welcome them, showering them with great love and affection as if they have met their long-lost companions. Marching further, they pass through a Golden Hall studded with precious stones and gems of all kinds, where the aura of the Supreme Lord enters them and pervades them, filling them with supreme bliss. Passing further, they meet with the deputies of Lord Vishnu, divinities of the highest order. They assist him personally. Finally, at the end of that long and delightful journey, they come into the presence of the Great Lord himself, decked in his divine splendor and resting on the coils of the mighty serpent, Adishesha, surrounded by his close attendants and the purest beings, with the Divine Mother, Goddess Maha Lakshmi, seated by his side. Upon seeing his divine form (svarupa), the devotee who traveled thus far becomes fully saturated with infinite love and bliss. The sight of his kevala bhaktas in his close presence fills the Lord with great delight since he enjoys their company and keeps them close to his heart. From that moment of reunion onwards, the liberated soul (mukta atma), who entered his direct presence, remains eternally connected to him through an internal channel and experiences the same consciousness and potency as his.

According to the Vishistadvaita School (qualified dualism), the liberated souls who enter Vaikuntha through exclusive devotion to Lord Vishnu earn an honorable place in his court. They enjoy proximity, direct access, and a direct connection with him through their inseparable, infinite consciousness, while the Lord enjoys their delightful presence. Thus, in the liberated state, they enjoy three great blessings that are rarely achieved by gods or celestial beings, namely nearness (samipya), same form (sarupya), and eternal unity (sayujya).

Sloka 55

matkarmakṛn matparamo madbhaktaḥ saṅgavarjitaḥ
nirvairaḥ sarvabhūteṣu yaḥ sa mām eti pāṇḍava

mat = for Me; karma = actions; krt = perform; mat-paramah = Me as the Supreme; mat-bhaktah = with devotion to Me; sanga-varjitah = abandoning attachment; nirvairah = without enemity; sarva-bhutesu = all living beings; yah = who; sah = he; mam = to Me; eti = comes; pandava = O son of Pandu.

O son of Pandu, whoever performs actions for Me, accepting Me as the Supreme, with devotion to Me, abandoning all attachment, without enmity towards all living beings, he comes to Me.

Here are a few marks of God's devotees who exemplify single-minded devotion (kevala bhakti) or exclusive devotion (ananya bhakti), which leads to liberation (mukti). Their first distinguishing quality is that they perform actions exclusively for God. They engage in selfless actions as an offering or sacrifice to God and exemplify karma-sannyasa yoga. Most people live for themselves and perform actions for themselves. Since they cannot take themselves out of their thinking or actions, their devotion remains weak, divided, and fluctuating, just like their faith. Kevala bhaktas think of their beloved Lord only. Transcending their self-interests and selfishness, they perform actions for him and live for him without desiring any personal reward or benefit from their actions or devotion. They exemplify bhakti yoga and serve him through desireless actions (nishkama karma) out of love and devotion rather than as an obligatory duty or due to desires or fear.

Bhakta means an offering (prasada). Bhakti means an act of offering. Kevala bhaktas consecrate their lives as an offering to the Supreme Lord. They give themselves up to the Supreme Lord as an offering and remain ever-engaged in the sacrifice of their lives. They focus on liberation or union with the Lord rather than any other goal. They love none but the Supreme Lord and spend their time serving him or worshipping him. Awake or asleep, they soak their minds with his thoughts, names, and forms, oblivious to the world and its attractions. Ordinary people pursue dharma, artha, and kama and worship different gods to attain worldly ends or fulfill their endless desires. Kevala bhaktas aim for oneness or nearness to the Supreme Lord. They are not drawn to worldly pleasure or material things and prefer to visit places where like-minded devotees spend their time speaking, listening, hearing, or contemplating God's names and glories.

Another mark of kevala bhaktas is their unwavering devotion even in pain, suffering, and adversity. Since they cultivate purity (sattva), cleansing their hearts and minds, they attain sameness (samsiddhi), indifference (vairagyam), and freedom from karma (naishkarmya siddhi). With such enduring qualities, they remain indifferent to their circumstances or physical or mental states, accepting their pain and suffering as God's will. Devotion shines in them uninterruptedly, just as the brilliance of the sun remains undiminished by the presence of clouds in the sky. In the previous chapters, Lord Krishna already emphasized this form of bhakti. He compared the devotion of those who approach him due to suffering, curiosity, or to fulfill their desires, and those who worship him exclusively without any other thought, concern, or intention. The mind remains disturbed and scattered when the senses are in their outward mode, searching for happiness and fulfillment amidst transient objects. True devotion does not arise in such minds since their devotion is for worldly enjoyment, and their primary loyalty is to themselves, not the Lord. Kevala bhaktas do not divide their devotion or energies between the four aims of human life (dharma, artha, kama, and moksha). They withdraw their minds and senses into themselves and remain exclusively absorbed in contemplating the Self. Since they excel in atma-samyama and dhyana yogas, they excel in selfless devotion and desireless actions and qualify for God's eternal love, protection, and grace.

Kevala bhaktas have no material goals. They see the Self in all and treat everyone as an embodiment of the Supreme Lord. Since they overcome attraction and aversion to transient things and cultivate sameness and purity, they do not entertain enmity or hatred toward anyone. Although they renounce their families, friends, relationships, wealth, and possessions, they are ever willing to help others as a service to the Lord. Seeing him in everyone and everywhere, they develop universal reverence or friendliness, treat others with humility, reverence, and sameness, and exemplify the virtue of nonviolence.

Conclusion

iti srīmadbhāgavadgītāsupanisatsu brahmavidyāyām yogasāstre srikrisnārjunasamvāde visvarupadarsana yogo nāmaikadasopa 'dhyayah

iti = thus; srīmadbhāgavadgītā = in the sacred Bhagavadgita; upanisatsu = in the Upanishad; brahmavidyāyām = the knowledge of the absolute Brahman; yogasāstre = the scripture of yoga; srikrisnārjunasamvāde = the dialogue between Sri Krishna and Arjuna; visvarupadarsana yogo nāma = by name yoga of the vision of the universal form; nāmaikadasopah = eleventh; adhyayah = chapter;

Thus ends the eleventh chapter, named Visvarupa Darshana Yoga (the Yoga of the Vision of the Universal Form) in the Upanishad of the divine Bhagavadgita, the knowledge of the Absolute, a treatise on Yoga, and the debate between Arjuna and Lord Krishna.

12 – Bhakti Yoga

The Yoga of Devotion

Sloka 1

Arjuna uvāca
evaṃ satatayuktā ye bhaktās tvāṃ paryupāsate
ye cāpy akṣaram avyaktaṃ teṣāṃ ke yogavittamāḥ

arjunah uvaca = Arjuna said; evam = thus; satata = always; yuktah = engaged; ye = those; bhaktah = devotees; tvam = You; paryupasate = devotional service, religious meditation; ye = those; ca = and; api = others; aksaram = imperishable; avyaktam = unmanifested; tesam = of them; ke = who; yoga-vit-tamah = the most perfect in yoga.

Arjuna said, "Thus, always engaged (in devotion) those devotees who worship you, and others (who worship) the imperishable and the inexhaustible, of them who is the most perfect in yoga?"

This chapter is about bhakti yoga. Arjuna started the conversation with an important question about it. What is the best practice, worshipping the Manifested Brahman, who is the Lord of the universe with forms and essential nature, or the Unmanifested Brahman, who is invisible, indescribable, imperishable, and beyond the reach of the mind and senses? In Hinduism, both approaches are valid, although those who worship the formless, imperishable, and unmanifested Brahman are rare. These two aspects of Brahman are also known as sambhuta and asambhuta (with and without Nature) or as Sat and Asat (existence and nonexistence or being and non-being). Arjuna wanted to know which of the two the Lord considers better, since he is the one who grants liberation. Most people prefer to worship the Supreme Being with names and forms since they can relate to him, meditate on him, and emotionally connect to him. Image worship or idol worship is widespread in Hinduism because devotees see the Supreme Lord, Isvara, hidden in every aspect of creation and feel his ubiquitous presence near them. Some devotees worship the images of the Lord as Arcas or his living incarnations. They believe the idols are energized and brought to life by devotion and sacred rituals and become the living and breathing manifestations of the Lord, possessing mystic powers to alleviate their suffering or fulfill their wishes. Some jnana yogis and sannyasis prefer to worship the formless Brahman by meditating on him since they believe that the Lord does not have a specific form and should be worshipped as the infinite and eternal Self rather than a Being. However, it is difficult to worship the formless Brahman or meditate on him since the mind cannot easily rest on abstract notions or transcendental states. Further, the moment you think of Brahman or concentrate on an idea, concept, or notion of him, it automatically becomes his manifested aspect and cannot truly be considered unmanifested. The unmanifested Brahman is ungraspable to the human mind, even as a thought or idea. Hence, most people prefer to worship the Supreme Lord or his manifestation rather than his unmanifested aspect.

Special note: Sambhuta and asambhuta are more commonly used for Prakriti. They apply to Brahman because he manifests in creation by joining her.

Sloka 2

mayy āveśya mano ye māṃ nityayuktā upāsate
śraddhayā parayopetāḥ te me yuktatamā matāḥ

sri-bhagavan uvaca = the Blessed Lord said; mayi = to Me; avesya = by fixing, concentrating; manah = the mind; ye = those who; mam = Me; nitya = always; yuktah = absorbed; upasate = worship; sraddhaya = with faith; paraya = supreme upetah = endowed; te = they; me = Me; yukta-tamah = skillful, accomplished; matah = opinion, thinking.

The Supreme Lord said, "By fixing their minds upon Me, ever absorbed in Me, those who worship Me, endowed with supreme faith, in My opinion, they are the most skillful or accomplished."

Lord Krishna gave a clear answer to Arjuna, stating that in his opinion (matha), those who worshipped him (as the Universal Lord) personally with utmost devotion, supreme faith, and unwavering concentration were most skillful and accomplished in yoga. It means they have better chances of earning his grace and achieving liberation. The word yukta is used in this verse twice: nitya-yukta, one who is ever absorbed in his devotion, and yukta-tama, one who is skillful or accomplished (in yoga or devotion). In other words, he is pleased with the devotees who venerate him as the Supreme Lord or the Universal Lord, ever absorbed in his contemplation and devotion, and find a way into his heart and eternal Abode. Ritual worship is an outer and inferior aspect of it. However, one cannot excel in devotion by merely engaging in outward ritual practices. Those who indulge in them may still be considered bhaktas and accumulate good karma, but they cannot attain liberation or qualify as kevala bhaktas. This teaching must be read in conjunction with his previous statement that those who worship gods and demigods go to them, but those who worship him (as the Supreme Lord) attain him only.

In bhakti yoga, devotees engage their minds and bodies to practice devotion. Devotion pervades all aspects of their lives and becomes the guiding factor of their thoughts and actions. Absorbed in His devotion and contemplation, such a devotee gives up everything, including himself, and puts himself at His feet. He loves Him without a motive, surrendering his will and ego and offering Him his actions, decisions, and the fruit of his actions. He prefers His company since the world or the people do not excite him or draw his interest. Through exclusive devotion, surrendering his will, ego, and independence, like a creeper twisting around a tree trunk or a post, and making himself vulnerable and helpless, the exclusive devotee attaches himself to the Lord and finds his way into his heart. His devotion is selfless, unconditional, and yielding. In his unyielding love for the Lord, he becomes an offering and sacrifice like the fuel that burns itself to spread radiance and serve some mysterious purpose.

Ignorant people are conditioned to worship the Lord for worldly reasons. They remember him when they need something and return to their habitual ways once their wishes are fulfilled or their purpose is served. It is devotion, but of an inferior kind. It helps them develop an emotional connection with the Lord, but it does not earn them his grace to attain liberation. In his divine order, they are rewarded with a better life in the next birth and nudged gently on the path since they are still superior to those who despise him or do not worship him. Unlike them, his kevala bhaktas worship him as the one and only God. Their devotion does not diminish or waver by place or circumstance. It is not conditioned or influenced by results or responses. In happiness and sorrow, they remain steadfast with unflinching faith. Through their continuous devotion, loyalty, dependence, and persistence, they leave no option to the Lord, who is otherwise indifferent and disinterested, but to pay them attention and answer their prayers.

Sloka 3

ye tv akṣaram anirdeśyaṃ avyaktaṃ paryupāsate
sarvatragam acintyaṃ ca kūṭasthaṃ acalaṃ dhruvam

ye = those; tu = but; aksaram = imperishable; anirdesyam = indefinable, indescribable, indeterminate; avyaktam = unmanifested; paryupasate = worship; sarvatra-gam = omnipresent; acintyam = inconceivable, beyond thought; ca = and; kuta-stham = the highest, standing at the top, occupying the highest place; acalam = immovable, constant; dhruvam = fixed.

However, those who worship the Imperishable, the Indefinable, the Unmanifested, the Omnipresent, the Inconceivable and the Highest, the Immovable, the Fixed ...

This is an incomplete verse and should be read in conjunction with the next. Previously, Lord Krishna spoke about worshipping him as the manifested Brahman. Here, he spoke about the other approach, the worship of the formless, imperishable Brahman. Paryupasana may mean worship or contemplation, or both. Usually, the formless Brahman is worshipped mentally through contemplation since it is not possible to worship him physically. Avyaktam means that which is not manifested or differentiated into a personality or being (vyakti). Although we loosely use the terms Manifested Brahman and Unmanifested Brahman, the truth is that Brahman is immutable and has no states. He does not manifest or unmanifest. He is always the same, absolute, Supreme Self. What manifests or unmanifests is Prakriti. She has manifested and unmanifested aspects. In the absolute state of Brahman, Prakriti is always unmanifested (asambhuta) and remains in the primal, indistinguishable state in which the gunas remain in perfect equilibrium. When she manifests in association with the immutable, imperishable Brahman, we call that state the Manifested Brahman.

When Prakriti manifests, embodying Brahman with distinct tattvas and active modes, the Universal Being who appears from that union is called variously Purusha, Isvara, Narayana, Maheswara, Saguna Brahman, or Manifested Brahman. Thus, the Avykta Brahman is Brahman in his absolute, pure state without active modes and tattvas, and the Vyakta Brahman is the same absolute, pure Brahman in his embodied State with active modes and tattvas. Brahman (Self or the Supreme Self) remains immutable in both situations. He is immutable and indistinguishable before and after creation and dissolution. In other words, the manifested Brahman is the Universal Being, such as Kala or Isvara, who appears with a distinct personality due to his association with Prakriti and her modes and tattvas. In his manifested and unmanifested states, he is always immutable, indescribable, transcendental, and indefinable. For our knowledge and understanding, we may rely upon words to describe him, but he is beyond names, forms, speech, and our limited intelligence.

The words used in this verse to describe Brahman have multiple meanings. For example, aksharam means indestructible, firm, and fixed. It also means water, sky, and any sound or letter in the alphabet. The sacred syllable Aum is extolled as aksharam, meaning the indestructible and eternal sound. Anirdesyam means indeterminate, indescribable, and indefinable. It appropriately points to the indescribability, indeterminacy, and unknowability of absolute Brahman and the difficulties we have in knowing him or expressing him. Sarvatragam means the ability to be simultaneously present everywhere or go instantly everywhere. In our world, wind (vayu) is sarvagata. In the body, space, sky (akasa), or the universe, it is the subtle energy, Prana (breath). Achintyam means that which cannot be thinkable, conceivable, abstracted, theorized, or beyond the mind and thought. Our thoughts do not adequately convey the transcendental nature of Brahman. Therefore, he is inconceivable (achintyam). Kutastha means exalted, lofty, standing at the top or highest. It also means immovable and unchangeable. These words appropriately describe the transcendental reality of Supreme Brahman.

Sloka 4

saṃniyamyendriyagrāmaṃ sarvatra samabuddhayāḥ
te prāpnuvanti mām eva sarvabhūtahite ratāḥ

sanniyamya = restraining; indriya-gramam = all the senses; sarvatra = everywhere; sama-buddhayah = with equanimity, even minded; te = they; prapnuvanti = attain; mam = Me; eva = also, surely; sarva-bhuta-hite = in the welfare of all beings; ratah = devoted to, takes delight.

Restraining all the senses, remaining the same everywhere, taking delight in the welfare of all beings, they also attain Me only.

The meaning of this and the previous verse is that those who worship the imperishable, Supreme Brahman also attain him, just as those who worship the Supreme Lord. In other words, anyone who worships or meditates on the Supreme Lord with exclusive devotion, be it his manifested or unmanifested aspect, will attain him, even if they choose different paths and practice different methods. All paths lead to him only. The devotees must worship him with firm faith and exclusive devotion, establishing their minds in his thoughts (nitya-yukta), cultivating sameness and selflessness, and taking delight in the welfare of all beings instead of thinking about themselves or their families. In the previous verse, Lord Krishna emphasized the virtues of concentration (mano āveśya) and supreme faith (śraddha). In this, he mentioned sameness or undisturbed intelligence (samabuddhi) and selflessness or taking delight in the welfare (hita) of all. All living beings represent Brahman only in their essence. He pervades them and remains hidden in them as their very Self. Therefore, serving others with love and devotion is equal to serving the Supreme Lord. In the end, the worshippers of Brahman attain Brahman only. Their devotion may take several forms. It may manifest as love for God, humanity, or all living beings. Our scriptures state that serving others (manava seva) is the same as serving God (Madhava seva). The very idea of daily sacrifices (nitya karmas) is rooted in this principle. Through them, we serve gods, ancestors, saints, seers, needy people, and other living beings. However, in all such actions, one should practice nishkama karma with detachment and self-restraint.

Sloka 5

kleśodhikataras teṣāṃ avyaktāsaktacetasām
avyaktā hi gatir duḥkhaṃ dehavadbhir avāpyate

klesah = obstacles, afflictions; adhika-tarah = very, greater, excessive; tesam = for them; avyakta = unmanifested; asakta = is drawn to; cetasam = mind; avyakta = unmanifested; hi = indeed; gatih = path, goal; duhkham = suffering, struggle, pain, sorrow; deha-vadbhih = by the embodied souls; avapyate = attained.

Obstacles and afflictions are more for those whose minds are drawn to the Unmanifested. Indeed, the goal of the Unmanifested is attained with great suffering by the embodied souls.

Here, Lord Krishna said that worshipping the formless, invisible, and imperceptible Brahman is difficult for humans, and those who do so attain liberation through great suffering. The reasons are not difficult to discern. First, it is difficult to concentrate or meditate on an unknown, invisible, intangible, and imperceptible state of Brahman. Second, it is difficult for devotees to form an emotional bond with an abstract notion of God and experience devotion. Third, the unmanifested Brahman is indifferent and uninvolved by nature and does not reciprocate or respond to devotion or supplications. It is much like praying to a stone or a wall. Karma yoga, karma-sannyasa yoga, and even bhakti yoga are mostly ineffective in his worship since he keeps no personal relationship with anyone or anything. He is attained mainly by those who practice jnana and sannyasa yogas, which necessitate rigorous self-discipline, austerities, and penances for self-purification and cultivate the highest purity. It was why Lord Krishna said that the path was painful. Lastly, the Unmanifested Brahman does not participate in creation but remains a witness to it. Therefore, those who worship him must rely upon themselves without any help from the deity they worship. They may receive help from the Supreme Lord (Isvara) if he takes pity on them, since he experiences no duality between himself and Brahman. These problems do not arise when one worships Isvara, the Supreme Lord and Controller, who takes great delight in helping his devotees and reciprocating their love. As the preserver and supporter of all, with inviolable will and limitless potencies, he actively helps his devotees cross the ocean of samsara. His devotees are never lost to him, and he is never lost to them.

We have already stated that Brahman, the Supreme Self, is always formless, invisible, imperceptible, unmanifested, and beyond the mind and body. The Purusha or Isvara, who manifests from him in association with Prakriti, has names, forms, and several manifestations. He is the Lord of the Universe, Universal Being, Creator, Preserver, Concealer, Revealer, and Destroyer, and is known by several names. Worshipping him is easier since the mind can easily be engaged in his thoughts and established in him. It is difficult for the mind to concentrate upon the impersonal, unimaginable, indescribable, and indefinable state of Brahman. Since the mind is subject to duality and objectivity, it cannot grapple with the indeterminate, formless, intangible, and unknowable reality that cannot be objectified, quantified, or visualized. Hence, to worship him and attain liberation, one has to withdraw the mind and senses completely, cultivate detachment and indifference by overcoming egoism, desires, and attachments, and keep the body under firm control. They are difficult to practice and produce a lot of pain and suffering. Further, it is almost impossible to please and obtain any help from the invisible, imperceptible, and formless Brahman. In contrast, a devotee's relationship with the Supreme Lord is reciprocal. The Lord takes particular interest in his devotees. He reciprocates their exclusive devotion and actively helps, guides, protects, and liberates them. Thus, worshipping the Unmanifested Brahman is more arduous and painful than worshipping Isvara, the Manifested Supreme Lord.

Sloka 6

ye tu sarvāṇi karmāṇi mayi saṃnyasya matparaḥ
ananyenaiva yogena māṃ dhyāyanta upāsate

ye = those who; tu = but; sarvani = all; karmani = actions; mayi = to Me; sannyasya = renouncing; mat-parah = having accepted Me; ananyena = without any distraction; eva = only, alone; yogena = by practicing yoga; mam = to Me; dhyayantah = meditating; upasate = worship.

But those who worship Me alone, renouncing all actions, accepting Me alone without any other thought, meditating upon Me by practicing yoga ...

Indeed, it is difficult to attain the unmanifested Brahman since it is hard to please him and earn his grace even after subjecting oneself to rigorous austerities, self-control, pain, and suffering. However, those who worship the manifested Supreme Lord with exclusive devotion (ananya bhakti), renouncing the ownership, doership, and fruit of all actions, acknowledging and meditating on him only and without any distraction, earn his grace and attain liberation. They do not have to strive that hard through rigorous austerities and self-control for self-purification or endure that much pain and suffering. For such people who take refuge in him only, dedicate their lives to him only, offer him only their actions, meditate upon him only, and thus practice kevala bhakti, he becomes their liberator. As they surrender their egos and will and depend upon him exclusively with faith and devotion, he will make their task easier, overlook their imperfections, forgive their mistakes and failures, and grant them liberation. Although Lord Krishna suggested here how he should be worshipped with devotion, one should not misconstrue his words, especially his use of the first-person "Me," to mean that everyone should worship Lord Krishna only and no one else. In this discourse, Lord Krishna personifies Brahman, the Self or the Supreme Lord. He delivered the discourse in a unified state of consciousness, without duality or division.

Therefore, one should not see him as a specific deity or incarnation but as Isvara, the Lord of Creation only. Those who are devoted to him may worship him exclusively. However, it is not obligatory. Devotees may worship him in any form or with any name they choose. They may worship him as Brahma, Vishnu, Shiva, Rama, Ganesha, Shakti, Lakshmi, Parvathi, Durga, etc. There is no taboo on which divine personality or name they should choose to express their love and devotion. As long as they worship him in any of these forms as the Supreme Lord of the Universe, they obtain the same results and attain the immortal world of Brahman. The Lord has numerous names and forms. All are equally worthy of worship and devotion. In their highest and purest aspect, they are considered Isvara only. We learned in the previous three chapters that all the divinities at the highest level of creation are his manifestations only. Devotees may worship them or meditate on them exclusively as Isvara or Brahman. However, one should not worship them as separate entities or worship multiple deities. Doing so is a sign of delusion and wavering faith. Lord Krishna already stated that those who worship gods go to them, and those who worship him reach him and attain immortality. One should, therefore, choose one deity as the Supreme Isvara and worship him without distractions. Other essential requirements emphasized here are kevala bhakti, karma sannyasa, and uninterrupted dhyana.

Sloka 7

teṣāṃ ahaṃ samuddhartā mṛtyusaṃsārasāgarāt
bhavāmi na cirāt pārtha mayy āveśitacetasām

tesam = them; aham = I; samuddharta = lift up, liberate; mrtyu = death; samsara = birth and death, mortal world; sagarat = ocean; bhavami = become; na cirat = not long, without delay; partha = O Partha; mayi = in Me; avesita = absorbed, drawn; cetasam = mind.

For those whose minds are absorbed in Me, O Partha, I become, without delay, the Liberator from the death-ridden ocean of samsara.

Lord Krishna said, "Those who worship Me exclusively, offering their actions to Me, and whose minds are drawn to Me and absorbed in Me, I quickly uplift them from the ocean of Samsara ruled by the Lord of Death." It means that his exclusive devotees do not have to exert excessively or subject themselves to much pain and suffering. Their devotion shields them from their failures and weaknesses. Since they live in his heart, the Lord takes the initiative and saves them from the jaws of Death. Uddharata, meaning lifting, taking out, or rescuing, conveys the active and personal involvement of the Lord in their liberation. Generally, he remains passive until the devotees achieve perfection and excellence in yoga and qualify for his grace. However, in the case of exclusive devotees, he takes the lead and quickly grants them liberation. In this verse, he explicitly gave that assurance, speaking from the depths of unified consciousness as the liberator and the Supreme Goal (parandhama) of liberation. Hence, the path of devotion (bhakti marg) is considered the best and easiest of all the paths, especially since the Lord makes many exceptions for his exclusive devotees and compensates for their failures and shortcomings. According to some, on the path of devotion, one does not have to perform even obligatory duties or pursue Dharma, Artha, and Kama. Their caste, family background, and profession also do not matter since they are measured by their devotion rather than their birth or other considerations. Devotion becomes the purifier and liberator for the kevala bhaktas, whose lives and actions revolve around the Supreme Lord.

Death is certain for those born here, and rebirth for those who leave this world without resolving their karma. You may try to escape from the ocean of life entirely through self-effort, as those who worship the Unmanifested Brahman or the Unmanifested Prakriti, or engage their minds in meditating on abstract notions. To them, his advice is, "Worship Me with exclusive devotions, soaking your mind with my thoughts. If you do so, and even if you have not fully purified yourself or resolved your karma, before you even realize, I guarantee liberation and rescue you from the death-ridden waters of samsara." Thus, exclusive devotees of God have a clear advantage over others. He becomes the raft and carries across those who take refuge in him with pure devotion and solely depend upon him.

How should a devotee absorb his mind in contemplation and soak his mind with pure devotion? The Bhagavata Purana lists nine practices through which devotees can stabilize their minds in contemplation and cultivate ananya-bhakti. They are listening (sravana), chanting (kirtana), remembering (smarana), serving the Lord (pada sevana), worshipping (arcana), revering (vandana), serving (dasya), becoming a friend (sakhya), and offering oneself (atma nivedana). Through them, a devotee gradually transcends his lower nature, egoism, and delusion, empties his mind and heart, and fills them with divine thoughts. Advaita Vedanta prescribes three methods: hearing (sravanam), remembering (mananam), and meditation (nidhidhyasana).

Sloka 8

mayy eva mana ādhatsva mayi buddhiṃ niveśaya
nivasiṣyasi mayy eva ata ūrdhvaṃ na saṃśayaḥ

mayi = on Me; eva = alone; manah = mind; adhatsva = fix; mayi = in Me; buddhim = intelligence; nivesaya = rest, repose, establish; nivasisyasi = you live; mayi = in Me; eva = alone; atah urdhvam = after that; na samsayah = without any doubt.

Fix your mind on Me only. Rest your intelligence in Me. After that, without any doubt, you will live in Me alone.

Lord Krishna said, "Since I quickly deliver from the ocean of Death and impermanence those devotees who are exclusively devoted to Me and dedicate their lives to Me, you too should fix your mind on Me, rest your intelligence in Me only, and become My exclusive devotee." Fixing your mind on Me means you should always think of Me, whether you are active or inactive. Resting your intelligence in Me means you should surrender your will and discernment to Me and let yourself be solely guided by My instructions and teachings. If you do that, you will undoubtedly live in Me, meaning you become a part of My consciousness, and we both enjoy the same pure consciousness without duality or division."

Thus, in this verse, Lord Krishna explicitly instructed his devotee, Arjuna, on how he could become absorbed in his consciousness and attain oneness through exclusive devotion. This is a reiteration of his previous assurance that he would personally look after the welfare (yoga kshema) of those who worship him selflessly, with their minds established in his devotion and contemplation. Such a privilege is not granted to those who approach him to fulfill their desires or to those who worship his unmanifested aspect, which is difficult and produces pain and suffering.

Ignorant people live for themselves, think of themselves, and use their intelligence to fulfill their desires, assuming ownership and doership while performing actions and pursuing the four aims of human life to achieve selfish ends. They may worship him or pray to him to overcome their suffering, out of curiosity, or fulfill their desires. For them, God is the means, not the end. Their actions do not qualify as true devotion. God may listen to them and grant them their wishes in abundant mercy. However, he does not grant them liberation. That privilege is reserved for his exclusive devotees who devote themselves to him unconditionally and live for him, renouncing everything. Since they engage in nishkama karma, worship him with unwavering devotion, and secure his love and mercy, he washes away their sins, ignoring their faults and defects, and grants them liberation.

However, although devotion seems to be the easiest option, it is not easy to practice exclusive devotion, renouncing worldly things, letting go of the ego, and absorbing the mind in devotional contemplation. Devotion must arise naturally as the spontaneous expression of one's essential nature. It cannot be affected, contrived, or forcefully induced. It is similar to falling in love, in which one is helplessly drawn to the object of love. It manifests only when the gunas are subdued, one is free from impurities, worldly things, passions, and desires, and the mind is filled with unwavering devotion to God. It is said that it arises when one attains purity, naishkarmya siddhi (freedom from desire-ridden actions), samsiddhi (sameness), and atma-samyama (self-control) as a natural consequence of excellence in jnana, karma, and sannyasa yogas.

According to some, bhakti manifests when God personally shows mercy and induces it in his devotees and is pleased with their effort, devotion, and sincerity. Whatever may be the truth, only a few people achieve perfection in exclusive devotion and earn divine grace to reach the immortal world.

Ordinary people cannot practice it since their devotion remains clouded with impurities, just as their essential nature. However, from a spiritual perspective, it is better to be a God's devotee, even if one's devotion is inferior or imperfect, rather than living in denial of him or questioning his existence. His devotees always have the chance to worship him and earn his grace. Even if they do not succeed in fixing their minds on him or resting their intelligence in him, they will still earn his love and protection and a good life in the next birth. Surely, the Lord notices the spark of devotion in them and gently nudges them towards the cherished goal. Therefore, it is better to be a God's devotee and worship him rather than worshipping worldly things and remaining bound.

Sloka 9

atha cittaṃ samādhātuṃ na śaknoṣi mayi sthiram
abhyāsayogena tato mām ichāptuṃ dhanaṃjaya

atha = now; cittam = mind; samadhatum = stabilize, fix; na = not; saknosi = able; mayi = upon Me; sthiram = steadily, firmly; abhyasa = regular practice; yogena = by yoga; tatah = then; mam = Me; iccha = seek, wish, desire; aptum = to attain; dhanam-jaya = O Dhananjaya.

Now, if you are unable to fix your mind steadily upon Me, then, O Dhananjaya, try to attain Me through constant practice.

The word abhyasa, meaning regular practice, appears at least ten times in the Bhagavadgita. In this verse, abhyasa yoga may also be translated as the regular practice of yoga, but the meaning of constant practice seems to be appropriate. It implies that one should practice devotion constantly to fix the mind upon the Lord. Previously, in the eighth chapter, Lord Krishna stated that stabilizing the restless mind was difficult but could be done through constant practice and detachment. Here, he reiterated the same principle. The best alternative is to practice exclusive devotion with an unwavering mind. If it cannot be done for any reason, the next best alternative is to persevere in fixing the mind upon the Lord through abhyāsa yoga and reach the goal. Abhyasa yoga is the adjunct of every yoga and successful endeavor. Through constant practice only, one achieves perfection and excellence in any yoga, skill, or action. He addressed Arjuna as Dhananjaya, the conqueror of wealth, to remind him that just as one accumulates wealth gradually through perseverance, one should strive to attain the wealth of devotion and the Lord's grace, step by step, through constant practice. The mind is fickle and restless by nature. It can be tamed through constant effort only, repeatedly withdrawing the mind and senses from the sense objects and restraining them whenever they regress into their habitual outgoing mode (prvritti).

In the Yogasutras, we find similar advice, where Patanjali states (1.12) that by regular and constant practice (abhyasa) of dispassion (vairagyam), one can control the fluctuations of the mind and experience peace and equanimity. In the subsequent verse (1.13), he further defines abhyasa as the effort (yatnah) to remain fixed in concentration. In another verse (1.32), he declares that the mind's interruptions or obstacles (antarayahs) can be overcome only by practicing contemplation upon Isvara, the inner Self, as Aum. Lord Krishna suggested a similar approach in this verse to absorb the mind in contemplation and exclusive devotion, stating that if Arjuna was unable to fix his mind upon him or stabilize it in divine contemplation, he should accomplish it by the regular practice of withdrawing his mind and senses and suppressing all distractions, thinking of him only. People cannot easily control or concentrate their minds. However, with regular and persistent practice of sense withdrawal (pratyahara), they can control them and attain peace and stability. Constant and persistent practice (abhyasa) is the means to achieve perfection in any discipline. The same holds true for yoga. Through persistent practice, devotees can absorb their minds in the contemplation of the Lord and attain him.

Sloka 10

abhyāsepy asamarthosi matkarmaparamo bhava
madartham api karmāṇi kurvan siddhim avāpsyasi

abhyase = to practice; api = even; asamarthah = unable; asi = you are; mat-karma = My actions; paramah = supremely devoted; bhava = happen, manifest, happen, become; mat-artham = for Me; api = even, also; karmani = actions; kurvan = by performing; siddhim = perfection; avapsyasi = attain.

If you are unable to practice even (this), let My Supreme actions come to fruition through you. Even by performing actions for Me, you will attain perfection.

Here, Lord Krishna suggested the third alternative: to perform actions for the Lord to attain perfection in devotion. Everyone cannot practice exclusive devotion (ananya bhakti) or persevere in regular practice (abhyasa) to stabilize their minds with self-control in devotional worship or in the contemplation of his names and forms. Exclusive devotion is the final stage in a devotee's spiritual journey and manifests when one cultivates purity and excels in jnana, karma, sannyasa, and atma-samyama yogas. One requires a different mindset to practice exclusive devotion, which arises after several births or when one perseveres for a long time in self-transformation through austerities and yoga practice. Kevala bhaktas are bhagavatas (servants of the Lord) in human form, born to exemplify his higher nature and manifest his divine qualities in them. Those who excel in it are not required to pursue knowledge or perform obligatory duties. They are also not required to trouble their bodies, practicing austerities, renunciation, and painful methods of self-discipline. Some become so absorbed in their devotion that they become indifferent to their circumstances and self-care and ignore their health and hygiene. Exclusive devotees are also not obligated to perform traditional devotional services such as visiting temples or performing daily or occasional sacrifices since they are forever (nitya) bhaktas who continuously remain engaged in devotional worship only and exemplify devotion through their actions. Those who practice contemplation, fixing their minds on the Lord, are also exempt from obligatory duties and devotional service. If they do, it is their personal choice. Instead of engaging in rituals and sacrifices or worshipping the images and idols of the Lord, they internalize them through contemplative practices, fixing their minds on him and becoming absorbed in his thoughts.

Hence, Lord Krishna suggested the next alternative for his devotees: to perform His duties as theirs and let them come to fruition through them. In other words, he prescribed karma yoga for those who are not yet ready for the highest form of devotion or do not possess the purity or resolve to cultivate it through regular practice (abhaysa). However, they should continue to practice some form of bhakti while serving the Lord and doing his work (matkarma) until they attain purity and develop exclusive devotion. By such actions, they can gradually stabilize their minds in divine thoughts, spend time in religious and devotional activities, and progress on the path of devotion. Lord Krishna offers this third alternative to those who lack self-control and cannot practice exclusive devotion or fail to cultivate it through persistent practice.

True devotion is a rare gift. It happens only when the mind and body are filled with the purity and radiance of divine love, which does not happen in everyone's case. Just like the diversity of the world, devotion is of different kinds. In human beings, due to the influence of the gunas (sattva, rajas, and tamas), it is colored by the impurities of desires, attachments, ignorance, egoism, delusion, etc., and produces sinful consequences. For such people, karma yoga is the best option to develop a religious or spiritual mindset and strengthen their devotion. Apart from doing their obligatory duties, they can also practice it by engaging in devotional activities such as cleaning the temple grounds, carrying water, arranging flowers, cooking food for distribution, administering in temples, helping devotees, teaching religious knowledge, reciting scriptures, singing God's glories, spending time in the company of devotees, giving charity, helping the poor and needy, supporting religious causes, going on pilgrimages, visiting temples and sacred places, offering worship, performing sacrifices, honoring gods and guests, etc.

The scriptures suggest a few important practices to cultivate a devotional mindset: sravanam (listening to the glories of the Lord), mananam (remembering his names and glories), kirtanam (singing his glories), and nidhidhyasanam (contemplating upon them). Even practicing karma-sannyasa by performing one's obligatory duties selflessly is doing God's work only, and highly beneficial to cleansing and stabilizing the mind in devotion and contemplation. These activities help novices and karma yogis to transcend their selfishness, egoism, and delusion and cultivate nearness to the Lord. By spending more time in divine thoughts (daiva chintana) and devotional service, they can prepare for the next stage in their spiritual evolution. When you do God's work and dedicate yourself to serving him and performing tasks that are pleasing to him, you will earn his grace and progress on the path of liberation.

Sloka 11

athaitad apy aśaktosi kartuṃ madyogam āśritaḥ
sarvakarmaphalatyāgaṃ tataḥ kuru yatātmavān

atha = again; etat = this; api = even; asaktah = not interested; asi = you are; kartum = doing; mat = My; yogam = divine state; asritah =taking refuge;

sarva-karma = all actions; phala = fruit; tyagam = renunciation; tatah = thereafter; kuru = do; yata-atma-van = keeping mind under control.

Again, if you are not interested in doing even this, taking refuge in My Divine State, thereafter, renounce the fruit of all actions, keeping your mind under control.

So far, Lord Krishna suggested three methods to practice devotion: kevala bhakti (exclusive devotion), cultivating exclusive devotion (antarbhakti) through persistent practice (abhyasa), and devotional service, or performing pious deeds to please him and earn his love and grace. In the third approach, the reference to mat-karma (my duties) and matartham (for my sake) is important. They imply that one should perform God's duties or tasks to fulfill the aims of creation, namely fulfilling obligatory duties, practicing virtuous conduct, supporting righteous causes, serving gods and others, promoting Dharma, and ensuring the order and regularity of life on earth. Although in the previous verse, he did not explicitly suggest that they should perform their duties without desires, by using 'matartham,' He intended them to perform His eternal duties (mat karma) for His sake, not for themselves. In other words, he suggested that karma yogis should perform obligatory duties (nitya karmas) as ordained for them, but not kamya karmas. However, he did not specifically insist on them to practice nishkama karma (desireless actions) by renouncing the fruit of their actions.

In this verse, he suggested the fourth approach. He said that if his devotees were not interested in performing their obligatory duties, they should take refuge in him and perform all their actions (sarva karma) by renouncing the fruit of their actions (karma-phala tyaga) and keeping their minds under control. In other words, he prescribed karma-sannyasa yoga for those who are not interested in performing their householder duties or those who take up sannyasa by renouncing worldly life. He said that such people should engage in desireless actions (nishkama karma) for his sake and leave the result to him. Since he mentioned sarva karma (all actions), apart from obligatory duties and devotional activities, devotees should perform even mundane actions such as eating and sleeping in his name and for his sake without desiring their fruit. Thus, according to this verse, those who are incapable of practicing exclusive devotion should practice karma sannyasa yoga and live for the sake of the Lord, offering him all their actions and renouncing their fruit. By that austere path of selfless actions, they can purify and transform their actions into sacrificial offerings and devotional service. By that, the devotee remains ever engaged in his service. This is another royal approach to practicing self-purification and cultivating exclusive and selfless devotion.

When you become a divine instrument and manifest God's will through your actions, without desires and without claiming ownership or doership, you join the special class of devotees who dedicate their lives to him and earn his love. Selfless devotion expressed through action and renunciation is superior in some respects to devotion expressed solely through devotional activities. Those who practice the former combine the merit of sacrifice and devotion. People with the predominance of rajas and tamas cannot practice exclusive devotion due to desires and passions and their restless and unyielding nature. They are wired to live for themselves due to the impurities of egoism, desires, passions, delusion, etc. For them, karma yoga is the best solution until they are ready to practice karma-sannyasa yoga. The latter is ideal for those who have the predominance of sattva and are willing to renounce their desires and passions for the sake of the Lord or liberation.

Matyoga-asritah means taking refuge in the supremely stable and pure state of the Lord or consecrating oneself to him without any distractions. It is the act of becoming divine-centered or establishing the mind in the Lord, renouncing everything, and surrendering to him unconditionally with firm faith. In that state, the devotee dissolves his will and identity in him and attains oneness. In that supreme state of yoga, the Lord speaks through him, lives in him, and acts through him. When a devotee becomes skillful (yukta) in karma-sannyasa and devotion, becoming a conqueror of himself by himself, the Lord incarnates in him as his living Self and takes care of his well-being (yoga kshema). Hence, Lord Krishna qualified his advice at the end of the verse, stating that one should practice it with the mind under control (yatatma). It means one should always control desires and cultivate detachment and indifference while performing duties and actions.

Sloka 12

śreyo hi jñānam abhyāsāj jñānād dhyānaṃ viśiṣyate
dhyānāt karmaphalatyāgas tyāgāc chāntir anantaram

sreyah = better; hi = surely; jnanam = knowledge; abhyasat = than practice; jnanat = than knowledge; dhyanam = meditation; visisyate = excel; dhyanat = than meditation; karma-phala-tyagah = renunciation of the results of actions; tyagat = by renunciation; santih = peace; anantaram = follows, subsequent to.

Surely knowledge is better than practice; better than knowledge is meditation; better than meditation is renunciation of the fruit of action. From renunciation, peace follows next.

Knowledge is better than practice means knowledge is better than the practice of karma yoga or the performance of obligatory duties. Alternatively, it may also mean the practice of the three alternatives that Lord Krishna suggested in the previous verses to cultivate exclusive devotion. Jnanam means the knowledge of the Self. It may also mean the knowledge by which one may realize the Self. According to Shankara, knowledge means the knowledge of the Self or the Supreme Self, and practice means the repeated study of the Vedic scriptures to ascertain their true meaning. The right knowledge is gained from the study of the scriptures or the teachings of an enlightened master.

Knowledge is better than practice because it gives us discernment and purpose and helps us improve the practice and attain perfection in it. With knowledge, a karma yogi becomes a karma-sannyasa yogi, and a karma-sannyasa yogi becomes an exclusive devotee. Meditation is better than knowledge (jnana) because meditation helps us establish the mind in the Self and see the Self directly (pratyaksha) as a seer. It quickly leads to oneness.

With the knowledge we gain from the scriptures, we can only draw inferences (anumana) about him, but not see him directly.

Renunciation of the fruit of action cleanses our minds and bodies and sets us free from karma. It is superior to meditation, knowledge, and the pursuit of knowledge (abhyasa) because, without the renunciation of desires, they produce impurities and sinful karma and keep the yogis bound. Hence, Lord Krishna said that giving up the fruit of actions was better than meditation. In other words, a seeker of liberation should not spend his full time performing obligatory duties, pursuing knowledge, or practicing meditation. He should simultaneously practice karma sannyasa while engaged in these pursuits and performing mundane actions such as eating, walking, or speaking. The pursuit of knowledge and the practice of meditation are actions only, and they need to be practiced by renouncing desires so that they will not produce karma.

Finally, a note on why peace follows renunciation. When you renounce desires and the fruit of your actions, you cease to worry about the results or the karma that may arise from them. You focus on the actions rather than on their outcome, as you become indifferent to success and failure and to other such pairs of opposites. You treat all outcomes alike and accept everything as the play or will of God or a part of your fate. Further, when you perform actions giving up the desire for their outcome, you also become free from samsara, or the cycle of births and deaths. Therefore, by renouncing desires and attachments and surrendering to the Lord's will, you will experience great peace.

Lord Krishna made this comparison to point out the relative importance of karma, jnana, atma-samyama, and karma-sannyasa yogas in cultivating exclusive devotion. He hinted that one should not feel despair for not being able to experience or practice exclusive devotion or engage in devotional service. Some people are not made to experience exclusive devotion, and they should not feel discouraged. They should acquire the right knowledge and practice meditation and karma-sannyasa yoga to attain perfection in devotion. When exclusive devotion does not arise naturally, this is the alternative to cultivating it.

Sloka 13

adveṣṭā sarvabhūtānāṃ maitraḥ karuṇa eva ca
nirmamo nirahaṃkāraḥ samaduḥkhasukhaḥ kṣamī

advesta =without envy; sarva-bhutanam = for all the living beings; maitrah = friendly; karunah = compassionate; eva = even; ca = and; nirmamah = without the feeling of me and mine; nirahankarah = without egoism; sama = same; duhkha = sorrow; sukhah = happiness; ksami = forgiving.

Without envy and hatred, with friendliness and compassion for all living beings, also without self-love, without egoism, remaining the same in sorrow and happiness, forgiving...

In this and the subsequent seven verses, Lord Krishna describes the qualities of his dearest devotees. This knowledge is helpful in cultivating exclusive devotion. Divine love is not ordinary love, ridden with desires, attachments, delusion, and egoism. It is the love of the purest kind, which manifests when one is free from them and when the duality between the devotee and the Lord is weak or absent. Exclusive devotion manifests in those who establish their minds in him and make him the center of their lives. As they absorb their minds in him continuously with unwavering faith, divine qualities strengthen and become part of their essential nature. The qualities that are mentioned in this verse are the earliest signs of their progress, namely freedom from envy and hatred, friendliness, compassion, egolessness, selflessness (nirmama), sameness in sorrow and happiness, and forgiveness. These and the other qualities mentioned in the next few verses are necessary to stabilize the mind and cultivate exclusive devotion and an abiding relationship with the Lord. The qualities are also interrelated, meaning they reinforce each other and stabilize the mind in devotion.

Lord Krishna previously stated that he had no favorites, likes, or dislikes and would not discriminate against anyone. As the Lord and Protector of Dharma, he enforces his laws equally and universally. However, he also established the law that whoever strives for oneness with him and lives in his service and contemplation without any other thought or avocation will surely earn his love and grace. Devotees who practice exclusive devotion to him and excel in yoga earn the right to enter his Abode and enjoy his company. He is indifferent to those who do not worship him, but helps those who worship him or engage in his devotional service. To help them, he listed here the qualities they can develop to strengthen their divine nature and stabilize their minds. According to the tenets of his eternal Dharma, human beings are meant to live and serve the Lord as his true representatives upon earth, performing his duties and actions for the order and regularity of the world without egoism and selfishness. Those who exemplify it in their lives instantly earn his love and grace.

Ananya bhaktas, who excel in exclusive devotion, are a class apart. They embody the living presence of God in them. Free from egoism, selfishness, envy, or hatred, they remain content within themselves with whatever they have, surrendering their will to him and accepting their lot as divine providence. Nothing breaks or weakens their faith or resolve. Suffering, cruelty, the wickedness of the world, or the difficulties they face do not disturb or distract them or their devotion. His devotees, such as Prahlada, Tukaram, and Ramadas (who built the temple at Bhadrachalam), exemplified this attitude. They saw him everywhere and in everyone, extended their love and reverence to others, and revered the whole creation as his manifestation. Many devotees spend their lives serving others, thinking that serving them is serving others. The feelings of 'me and mine' are also absent in them. They are happy and content with any opportunity they find to worship the Lord and serve him. Since they renounce worldly life and see the living presence of the Lord in everyone, they are free from enmity and hostility, do not bear grudges, and forgive those who are inimical to them.

Sloka 14

saṃtuṣṭaḥ satataṃ yogī yatātmā dṛḍhaniścayaḥ
mayy arpitamanobuddhir yo madbhaktaḥ sa mepriyaḥ

santustah = satisfied, contended; satatam = ever, always; yogi = yogi; yata-atma = self-controlled; drdha-niscayah = strongly determine; mayi = Me; arpita = offered; manah = mind; buddhih = intelligence; yah = he who; mat-bhaktah = devotee of Mine; sah me priyah = is very dear to Me.

The yogi who is ever contented, self-controlled, firmly determined, who has offered his mind and intelligence, that devotee of Mine is very dear to Me.

Lord Krishna listed additional qualities of his dearest devotees in this verse. They are primarily meant for those who renounce worldly life and practice sannyasa. According to Shankaracharya, they are meant for those who practice Akshara Upasana or the worship of the imperishable Brahman. Qualities such as adveshta (freedom from envy), universal friendliness, absence of the feelings of 'me or mine,' etc., cannot easily be cultivated by those who practice kama-yoga or karma-sannyasa yoga, but by those who renounce worldly life and practice exclusive devotion. Ananya-bhakti means worshipping the Supreme Lord exclusively without any other interest, focus, or attachment. It is difficult for householders to persist in it since they have to perform many duties and responsibilities apart from looking after their families.

God's love for his devotees is not the same as the love of humans for their children, friends, relations, or the things to which they are attracted. Human love is primarily selfish, judgmental, and conditional. It is influenced by desires and expectations. Hence, it is also unstable and impermanent and may result in suffering and conflicts. The love between God and his devotees is also conditional since it depends on the nature of devotion and relationship. It is also not an equal relationship since the Lord is the controller of it and its outcome. We cannot definitively say it is a relationship between two distinct entities because, beneath the surface, it is between the Supreme Self and the individual Self or between one Self and another. A devotee attains perfection in it only when he becomes a friend of his true Self by cultivating purity and divine qualities, and ends up dissolving himself in Him. In that relationship, God is the recipient of the devotion and the offerings, while the devotee is the recipient of his unending love and grace.

A devotee's unwavering devotion (kevala bhakti) is like an ethereal fragrance. It manifests in pure hearts directly from the Self as the outpouring of the Lord's love and touches others like the sweet fragrance of a flower, uplifting and comforting those who come near it. The qualities specified here are also divine qualities arising from the higher nature in the absence of impurities and modes: lasting contentment, self-control, determination, and dedication to the Lord. Contentment arises from the absence of egoism, desires, and attachments. Ananya bhaktas are not merely content. They are always (satatam) content, which means their contentment is not affected by circumstances or the presence or absence of dualities. They are always happy, whether they have basic comforts and necessities or whether their prayers are answered or unanswered. Due to self-control and firm resolve (dridha nischaya), they overcome their desires and excel in sameness and detachment. These qualities help them maintain peace and stability and practice uninterrupted and exclusive devotion.

Sloka 15

yasmān nodvijate loko lokān nodvijate ca yaḥ
harṣāmarṣabhayodvegair mukto yaḥ sa ca me priyaḥ

yasmat = by whom; na = not; udvijate = disturbed; lokah = the world; lokat = by the world; na = not; udvijate = disturbed; ca = and; yah = he who is; harsa = joy; amarsa = impatience; bhaya = fear; udvegaih = distress; muktah = freed; yah = who; sah = he; ca = also; me = Mine; priyah = very dear.

By whom the world is not disturbed and he who is not disturbed by the world, who is free from joy, impatience, fear, and distress, he is also dear to Me.

God expects his devotees to be peaceful, stable, and gentle. However, sometimes, you may meet devotees who are violent, wicked, destructive, mentally unstable, or hyperactive. Even if they excel in devotion like Ravana, they cannot be considered his best devotees unless they renounce their evil nature and cultivate purity. An exclusive devotee who earns God's love and mercy is, by nature, gentle and nonviolent. He does not disturb others and is not disturbed by them because he remains centered in divine thoughts and indifferent to the world. He is ever-content, firmly under control, free from desires and attachments, devoid of ego, compassionate, and ever-forgiving. He does not retaliate or seek vengeance even if treated unjustly or cruelly. Instead, he uses those situations as opportunities to practice self-control. Amidst people and society, he lives as if he does not exist at all, minimizing his interaction with the world without becoming a burden to others, even while depending upon them for food and occasional help. Since he gives up the world and worldly desires and lives on the fringes of society, he does not create any ripples around him or negative consequences for himself or others. Practicing self-control and restraining his mind and body (atma-samyama), he remains undisturbed amidst the dualities and disturbances of life. Thus, as the lotus in a pond, he lives a pure and peaceful life without touching the world or being touched by it.

Ordinary people cannot live in this world without disturbing others or being disturbed by them. They constantly interact with the world and leave ripples of karma all around them and in themselves. In the process, they disturb others and are disturbed by them. When you live for yourself, your family, or your selfish interests, it is inevitable that you clash with others, hurt them, and are hurt by them. Violence is the norm for most beings on Earth as a survival strategy. Human beings are no exception. They have the potential to unleash destruction and violence. The multitude of wars fought on Earth reflects the violence and destruction to which humans can succumb. Even in matters of religion, violence plays a key role. The world witnessed many wars fought in the name of God and religion. Even today, religions have the potential to incite passions, conflicts, and violence and destabilize the world. Here, Lord Krishna clearly stated that he expects his devotees to remain peaceful and gentle and excel in compassion and universal friendliness towards all. God exemplifies these qualities, and those who want to cultivate nearness and oneness with him must also exemplify them. To be a part of the pure consciousness of Brahman, one has to be pure physically, mentally, emotionally, and rationally. In these verses, Lord Krishna conveyed that he does not approve of any behavior that leads to suffering within oneself or in others. Spiritually or morally, it is repugnant to engage in evil behavior.

A true devotee is free from desires, egoism, delusion, attraction, and aversion. He is indifferent to the dualities and distractions of life and has no expectations from himself or others. Therefore, he is not disturbed by what happens or does not happen, how he is treated or ill-treated, and whether the path on which he walks is decked with flowers or thorns. Since the world or external factors do not influence him, he is free from joy, impatience, fear, and distress. With his mind and body firmly under his control and his mind engaged in the contemplation of God, he lives upon the earth without being repulsed by it or attracted to it. The world ceases to disturb him or make any difference to his thinking and attitude, just as he ceases to control it or make any difference to it by his actions. To the extent possible, he tries to cultivate nearness to God while distancing himself from the world, which he considers illusory and a source of desires and delusion. Self-giving and unassuming, he neither claims self-importance nor indulges in any actions that would disturb others or their lives. He may help others find peace or teach them the knowledge of liberation, but does so without expecting any favors or appreciation in return. His motivation to engage in selfless actions or help others arises from within himself due to his divine nature or these divine qualities, not due to any external or worldly causes.

Sloka 16

anapekṣaḥ śucir dakṣa udāsīno gatavyathaḥ
sarvārambhaparityāgī yo madbhaktaḥ sa me priyaḥ

anapeksah = without expectation; sucih = pure; daksah = skilful, capable; udasinah = impartial; gata-vyathah = free from sorrow; sarva-arambha = all undertakings; parityagi = who has renounced; yah = he who; mat-bhaktah = that devotee of Mine; sah = he; me = to Me; priyah = very dear.

That devotee of Mine who is without expectations, pure, skillful, indifferent, and without sorrow, and who has renounced all his undertakings, is very dear to Me.

The qualities described here are not meant for householders who engage in obligatory duties (although there is no explicit restriction) but for those who renounce worldly life and practice exclusive devotion to achieve liberation. They remain absorbed in the contemplation of God, with oneness as their supreme goal. Householders have difficulty practicing exclusive devotion since they are obligated to engage in worldly actions to achieve the four aims of human life. Only sannyasis have a good opportunity to give up worldly life and work for liberation. They can live without any expectations (anapeksha), anticipation, regard, or consideration for anything or from anyone for their actions or service. Those who practice it and excel in it do not desire or expect anything, even from God.

Devotees who earn God's love are pure souls. They possess physical and mental purity by overcoming egoism, desires, and delusion through self-purification (suci). They practice outward cleanliness (bahya suci) by living in clean surroundings and inward cleanliness (antar suci) by keeping their minds and bodies clean, knowing that cleanliness is another name for godliness. They eat sattvic food, take regular baths, avoid unclean people and places, and restrain their minds and senses with discernment from impure thoughts and objects. They also focus on cultivating spiritual purity by overcoming egoism, ignorance, and delusion, knowing one cannot unite with the Self without resolving them.

Mental purity helps them strengthen the quality of daksha, which means to be skillful, intelligent, wise, balanced, capable, qualified, dexterous, or diligent in thinking and actions. It also arises from the purity of their intelligence and discernment. Due to detachment and absence of desires, these pure souls can discern things clearly without being influenced by external considerations. Because of their knowledge and discernment, they perform their actions skillfully with detachment, stability, and sameness and remain untainted by worldly desires or prarabdha (accumulated) karma.

Sloka 17

yo na hṛṣyati na dveṣṭi na śocati na kāṅkṣati
śubhāśubhaparityāgī bhaktimān yaḥ sa me priyaḥ

yah = he who; na = not; hrsyati = rejoices; na = not; dvesti = hates; na = not; socati = laments; na = not; kanksati = desires; subha = good, auspicious; asubha = bad, inauspicious; parityagi = he who renounces; bhakti-man = filled with devotion; yah = who; sah = that one; me = Me; priyah = dear.

He, who does not rejoice, does not hate, does not lament, does not desire, who renounces the auspicious and inauspicious, who is filled with devotion, that one is dear to Me.

These qualities denote control, restraint, equanimity, sameness, detachment, dispassion, universal love, and exclusive devotion. Rejoicing when we are happy, hating someone or something that we intensely dislike or detest, desiring things to which we are strongly attracted, and preferring to live in auspicious circumstances, these are common human reactions. In worldly life, they make our lives meaningful and purposeful and help us align with the world and form a mutually convenient relationship with it. However, from a purely spiritual perspective, they indicate deluded behavior. The qualities Lord Krishna specified here are not found in worldly people but among those who practice exclusive devotion. They indicate the absence of ego, envy, hatred, pride, greed, fear, and passion. It is natural for people to react differently to different situations and circumstances. We try to cling to things we love and run away from those we dislike. When circumstances are favorable or when our desires are fulfilled, we rejoice and feel positive. However, when things go against our expectations or when we find ourselves in difficult or hostile situations, we feel disturbed, unhappy, or disappointed. As we are drawn into the whirls of life by our indulgences, desires, or attachments, we suffer from afflictions and mental instability.

Exclusive devotees who renounce worldly life for the sake of union with God free themselves mentally from life's externalities and desire for things or dependence on them. They remain absorbed in the thoughts of the Self, controlling their emotions and reactions. They renounce the world not because they detest it but because they love God and are intensely drawn to him. Since they sacrifice everything to earn his love and grace, including their closest relationships and personal attachments, he lives in their heart and grants them liberation.

Sloka 18

samaḥ śatrau ca mitre ca tathā mānāpamānayoḥ
śītoṣṇasukhaduḥkheṣu samaḥ saṅgavivarjitaḥ

samah = equal, same; satrau = to foe; ca = and; mitre = to friend; ca = also; tatha = so; mana = in honor; apamanayoh = dishonor; sita = cold; usna = heat; sukha = happiness; duhkhesu = sorrow; samah = eaual; sanga-vivarjitah = giving up attachment, association, contact, relationships.

Equal to friend and foe and honor and dishonor as well, equal to cold, heat, happiness, and sorrow, free from attachment ...

Samah, or sameness, is the highest state in yoga. It is also the pure state of the Self. Hence, in the second chapter (48), Lord Krishna defined yoga as sameness (samatvaṃ yoga ucyate). A yogi reaches that stage by overcoming the impurities of egoism, attachments, and delusion. In that state, he renounces judgment, likes, and dislikes, and looks upon the world with an equal eye. Free from desires, attachments, and external influences, without friends and foes, and undisturbed by the presence or absence of anything, he remains equal to cold and heat or sorrow and happiness. He treats all things (visaya), circumstances (samaya), and relationships (sambandha) with indifference and with an attitude of renunciation and sameness. When he is firmly established in it, he mirrors (samapatti) the world around him in his consciousness without being touched by it. Free from passions, emotions, and distractions, he practices exclusive devotion and effortlessly enters the state of self-absorption (samadhi) wherever he finds himself. When the yogi is free from attraction and aversion or likes and dislikes and becomes equal to all dualities and circumstances, with his mind firmly under control, he excels in yoga, especially in the practice of dharana (concentration), dhyana (meditation), and samyama. With a purified mind and intelligence and becoming firmly established in sameness and nonjudgmental awareness, he does not disturb others or is disturbed by them. As he excels in self-control, the modifications of his mind cease to interfere with his thinking, perceptions, and discernment, and he sees things as they are in their purest essence. In the early stages of yoga, the yogi may rely upon his intelligence to shield himself from the attractions of the world and contemplate the Self. However, in the later stages, as he silences everything in himself, including his buddhi, and becomes detached from all notions of otherness, he enters the purest state of stateless and seedless (nirbija) samadhi. When he excels in it, sameness becomes his natural and abiding state.

Sloka 19

tulyanindāstutir maunī saṃtuṣṭo yena kenacit
aniketaḥ sthiramatir bhaktimān me priyo naraḥ

tulya = equal; ninda = blame, accusation; stutih = praise, adulation; mauni = silent; santustah = satisfied, contended; yena kena cit = with anything, whatever; aniketah = without fixed abode, homeless; sthira = stable, fixed; matih = mind; bhakti-man = full of devotion; me = Me; priyah = dear; narah = the person.

Equal to blame and praise, silent, satisfied with anything; without a fixed abode, with a stable mind, full of devotion, the person (of such qualities) is dear to Me.

The virtues described in these verses arise from the absence of egoism, desires, attachments, and the conditioning to which humans are subject. The world influences our thinking and actions. We are bound to it in many ways. The need for belongingness, acceptance, approval, recognition, and appreciation arises from it. We want to fit into the world and be a part of it rather than live alone or in seclusion. Many people are frightened by the prospect of living alone or being ignored. These early influences condition our behavior and make us look to the world with desires and attachments. From a spiritual point of view, it is a problem since we cannot withdraw our minds and senses and remain equal in all conditions and situations. The Lord's exclusive devotees are different. Since they overcome worldly desires and attachments and absorb their minds in divine contemplation, they are indifferent to the dualities of the world, including blame (ninda) and praise (stuti). Unlike worldly people, they are not elated by praise or depressed by criticism. If they are unjustly judged, slandered, or criticized, they accept it as fate or divine will and let it go. They also practice silence of the highest kind, silencing speech and all desires and attachments. Having renounced worldly life and worldly possessions, they avoid living in fixed abodes and keep wandering from place to place, seeing the world as God's Abode, feeling comfortable wherever they find themselves, and remaining absorbed in his devotion. Most of them stay in secluded places, abandoned homes, temples, or ruins to practice quietude and avoid places where worldly people live or congregate, except when they go for alms. The remaining two qualities, stable mind and devotion, arise due to self-purification and perfection or excellence in yoga.

Sloka 20

ye tu dharmyāmṛtam idaṃ yathoktaṃ paryupāsate
śraddadhānā matparamā bhaktās tetīva me priyāḥ

ye = those; tu = however, but; dharma = dharma, religious duty; amrtam = liberating, immortal; idam = this; yathoktam = as prescribed or stated; paryupasate = honor, practice with devotion, worship; sraddadhanah = with faith; mat-paramah = Me as the Supreme Goal; bhaktah = devotees; te = such; ativa = exceedingly, extremely; me = Me; priyah = dear, lovable.

However, those who practice with devotion and faith this liberating immortal Dharma in the right manner as prescribed, with Me as the Supreme Goal, such devotees are exceedingly lovable to Me.

With this, Lord Krishna concludes his discourse on bhakti yoga and the endearing qualities of his dearest devotees, who earn his grace through exclusive devotion and attain liberation. The Supreme Lord is indifferent and impartial. Yet, his devotees enjoy a special place in his heart by practicing pure devotion (suddha bhakti) in the right manner as prescribed by him, with him as the supreme goal. The Dharma he mentioned here refers to the principles he laid down in this chapter to practice exclusive devotion. The qualities he mentioned are secondary since they are strengthened by devotion only through practice. The focus is on earning a special place in his heart through devotion. As he suggested in this chapter (verse 9), devotees who cannot practice exclusive devotion must cultivate it in one or more of three ways: through persistent effort (abhyasa yoga), by serving him through selfless actions, or by taking refuge in him and renouncing the fruit of their actions. As he said in verse 13, those who renounce the fruit of action are better suited to practice it than those who perform obligatory duties, pursue knowledge, or practice contemplation.

Here, the words yathoktam and ativa are important. The first one suggests that devotees must practice exclusive devotion as instructed by Lord Krishna correctly. The second word suggests that those who practice it strictly are closest to him. Impure souls or those who pursue worldly desires cannot practice it. To practice it perfectly, one must give up all desires and attachments, stabilize the mind in his contemplation, and remain exclusively devoted to him, with no other thought, aim, or interest. Devotion can be of many types. The devotion ridden with the gunas is impure and inferior since it is motivated by desires and passions. Even sattvic people may not attain pure devotion since sattva also induces desires and attachments. Hence, devotees must transcend the triple gunas and fully subdue their influence. Only then do they attain perfection in pure devotion and earn the grace of the Lord. Exclusive devotion requires renunciation of all undertakings (sarvarambha parityaga), surrendering the mind and intelligence (arpita mano-buddhi), and the absence of 'me and mine' and egoism (nirmama and nirhankara). Devotees who excel in it reach that stage only after they excel in other yoga.

Conclusion

iti srīmadbhāgavadgītāsupanisatsu brahmavidyāyām yogasāstre srikrisnārjunasamvāde bhaktiyogo nāma dvādaśo 'dhyayah.

iti = thus; srīmadbhāgavadgītā = in the sacred Bhagavadgita; upanisatsu = in the Upanishad; brahmavidyāyām = the knowledge of the absolute Brahman; yogasāstre = the scripture of yoga; srikrisnārjunasamvāde = the dialogue between Sri Krishna and Arjuna; bhakti yogo nāma = by name yoga of devotion; dvādaśah = twelfth; adhyayah = chapter.

Thus ends the twelfth chapter, named Bhakti Yoga (the Yoga of Devotion) in the Upanishad of the divine Bhagavadgita, the knowledge of the Absolute, a treatise on Yoga, and the debate between Arjuna and Lord Krishna.

13 – Kshetra Kshetrajna Vibhāga Yoga

The Yoga of the Division of the Field and Knower of the Field

Sloka 1

arjuna uvāca
prakṛtiṃ puruṣaṃ caiva kṣetraṃ kṣetrajñam eva ca
etad veditum icchāmi jñānaṃ jñeyaṃ ca keśava

arjunah uvaca = Arjuna said; prakrtim = Nature; purusam = Purusa; ca = and; eva = also; ksetram = the field; ksetra-jnam = knower of the field; eva = so also; ca = and; etat = these; veditum = to know; icchami = wish; jnanam = knowledge; jneyam = what is to be known; ca = and; kesava = O Keshava.

Arjuna Said, "Prakriti and Purusha, also (known as) the Field and the Knower of the Field, so also knowledge and what should be known, these I wish to know, O Keshava."

From this chapter onwards, we enter the third and concluding part of the Bhagavadgita. As already stated, the first six chapters of the scripture describe the predicament of Arjuna as the Jiva (the individual Self) caught in the ocean of samsara and how he can attain liberation through self-purification by practicing the various yogas. The next six chapters describe the glory and the manifestations of Isvara, the Supreme Lord, and how devotees can cultivate exclusive devotion (ananya bhakti) and worship him to become absorbed in his contemplation and attain liberation. The third part, from this chapter until the last, explains the division or the distinction between Purusha and Prakriti and how devotees can overcome impurities and reach the supreme goal by knowing them with faith and resolve.

Arjuna wanted to know the concepts he had heard previously from Lord Krishna: Purusha and Prakriti, the Field and the Knower of the Field, and Knowledge and its Goal. The main theme of this chapter is the distinction between Purusha and Prakriti. They represent the fundamental duality of creation personified by Isvara, the Supreme Lord and the highest manifestation of Brahman in creation, and represented by Lord Krishna in this discourse. In the seventh chapter, Lord Krishna spoke about the eightfold division of his lower nature, contrasting it with his higher nature, consisting of all the embodied souls (jivbhutam). The earth, water, fire, air, space, mind, intelligence, and ego constitute his lower nature. The living Self hidden in all beings constitutes his higher nature. In human beings, they are represented by the body, which is made up of the tattvas of Prakriti, and the Self, which resides in the body and supports it as its lord and knower. This duality exists in all creation and beings. Prakriti means Nature or the natural state of things.

It is the opposite of vikruti, which means change or effect. When Prakriti becomes active due to the disequilibrium in the gunas and is associated with the Self, she undergoes change or transformation (vikrti), resulting in the diversity of forms (akrtis).

In some schools of Hinduism, Prakriti is considered the material cause of creation, while Brahman, the Supreme Self, is the efficient cause. Although Prakriti is translated as Nature in English, it is more than Nature. It is the sum of all life, materiality, energy, and dynamism. Prakriti is the dynamic aspect of Para Brahman and the mirror-self or the not-self of all existence. Life and objectivity arise from her only. She is not only responsible for the evolution and transformation of all things but also the sole source of matter, energy, and intelligence required to create animate and inanimate forms and sustain them with life energy. Purusha is the Cosmic Lord or the Universal Being. He is Brahman in the active mode in the field of Prakriti and revered variously as God, Isvara, Narayana, Maheswara, Pati, or the Supreme Lord of the Universe. Brahman's manifestations arise only because Primal Nature, which is unmanifested (asambhuta), becomes manifested (sambhuta) in association with Brahman, who is immutable and has no states.

In human beings, Prakriti is the physical self or the mind and body, made up of the eightfold division of the Lord's lower nature. Purusha is the embodied Self (jivatma), the divine representing His higher nature. Prakriti is Kshetra, the field or the playground of Purusha, where he enjoys the drama of life (lila). He resides in all as the witness and the enjoyer of their interactions with the world. Life happens as long as he is present in the field as its Lord. Hence, he is known as Kshetrajna, the knower of the field. The Purusha in the body is a passive witness. However, according to the Bhagavadgita, the Purusha of the manifest creation is the Supreme Lord and Controller of all the worlds and beings, and performs numerous duties to uphold them and ensure their continuity and progress. He is not the same as Brahman, who is described in the Upanishads as the highest, absolute, transcendental, and indestructible reality, but a dynamic aspect of him, who manifests in creation in union with Prakriti and performs different functions as its creator, preserver, destroyer, lord, and witness.

Just as the divine nature is divided into higher and lower, the divine knowledge or the knowledge of the Manifested Brahman (Isvara) is also divided into higher and lower. Knowledge of Prakriti's eightfold division constitutes the lower knowledge (vijnanam), while the knowledge of the Self constitutes the higher knowledge (jnanam). When dissociated from its true purpose, which is liberation, lower knowledge is considered ignorance (ajnanam) or a force of Maya. However, when used in self-purification for liberation, it serves as an instrument of higher knowledge and a bridge to reach the supreme Brahman. Whether it is the lower or higher knowledge, its object (jneeyam) is always the Self (Brahman), by knowing which one becomes liberated from samsara, the cycle of births and deaths. Arjuna wanted to know them all.

Sloka 2

śrībhagavān uvāca
idaṃ śarīraṃ kaunteya kṣetram ity abhidhīyate
etad yo vetti taṃ prāhuḥ kṣetrajña iti tadvidaḥ

sri-bhagavan uvaca = the Blessed Lord said; idam = this; sariram = body; kaunteya = O son of Kunti; ksetram = the field; iti = thus; abhidhiyate = is called; etat = this; yah = who; vetti = knows; tam = he; prahuh = call; ksetra-jnah = knower of the field; iti = thus; tat-vidah = the learned.

The Supreme Lord said, "This body, O son of Kunti, is called the Field. He who knows it thus, the wise call him the Knower of the Field."

The body is the Field of Prakriti. The Self is the Knower of the Field. The Self has an awareness of the body, but the body has no awareness of the Self. Though they coexist in each jiva, they belong to different planes and have no direct connection. Kshetra means a field, a designated place, or a piece of land. In spiritual terms, it represents the creation, body, materiality, objective reality, or not-self. It is the playground of the Lord (the Self) where he witnesses life and movements (chaitanyam) happening. Kshetrajna means the knower of the field. In your body, which is the field, you are Kshetrajna, or the knower of the field or the body. You can feel it and relate to it. However, according to this verse, you become a true knower only when you realize that your body is distinct from you and is not you or your true Self. In the last part of the verse, Lord Krishna emphasized this using the word thus (ity). He meant that he who knows with clarity and conviction that the body is Prakrit's domain and he is distinct from it is the true Knower of the Field.

Endowed with that discernment, the jnani, the true knower, lives in his body with detachment and indifference, knowing that it is impermanent and subject to aging, sickness, and death, and he, as the Knower and the eternal Self, is free from them. The material universe is a Field, a playground of Prakriti. The world is also her Field. So is the human body, where deities (devas) reside in their respective spheres as organs and perform their respective functions. The body or the organs have no knowledge or awareness of the Self, the Knower of the Field. They perform their functions according to their Dharma (duties) as ordained by Nature or propelled by the gunas present in them. Therefore, neither the body nor its organs can be considered the knower. Only the Self, who resides in the body and pervades all as the Cosmic Self, has the distinction of being the knower.

In the body, you are the knower. Since you are aware of your embodied state, you have the opportunity to practice detachment and renunciation, suppressing the modes, desires, and attachments, and achieve freedom from its hold. The purpose of any yoga is to help you cultivate this discernment and detachment from your body and become established in the Self. The deluded ones identify themselves with their bodies and mistake them for their true Selves. In the awakened state, as you overcome ignorance and delusion and detach yourself from your body, you become centered in your pure Self and lay the foundation for your liberation. The Self is always the

Knower of the Field, whether he is in the body of a deluded one or a self-realized one. In theistic philosophies, the Self is the Knower of the Field. However, in materialistic and atheistic philosophies, the mind is the knower of the field, and the body is an aggregation of parts. Both schools of opinion exist in Hinduism.

Sloka 3

kṣetrajñaṃ cāpi māṃ viddhi sarvakṣetreṣu bhārata
kṣetrakṣetrajñayor jñānaṃ yat taj jñānaṃ mataṃmama

ksetra-jnam = the knower of the field; ca = and; api = and; mam = Me; viddhi = know; sarva = all; ksetresu = in the fields; bharata = O descendent of Bharata; ksetra = the field; ksetra-jnayoh = the knower of the field; jnanam = knowledge; yat = which; tat = that; jnanam = true knowledge; matam = opinion; mama = that.

And, O Bharata, know Me as the Knower of the Field in all fields. The knowledge of the Field and the Knower of the Field, that, in my opinion, is the true knowledge.

Two important Vedantic concepts are mentioned in this verse. Both are essential to understanding the nature of the perceptual reality, the supreme reality, and ourselves. Each living entity is a combination of the knower and the known, the subjective and objective realities, or the Self and the not-self. The mind, the ego, or intelligence should not be mistaken for the knower since they belong to the domain of Nature and, thereby, to the Kshetra. The Self in all the jivas, distinct from the body or the mind, is the Kshetrajna, the Knower. These two are also known as Prakriti and Purusha, respectively.

This understanding leads to an interesting philosophical conundrum if we accept the individual Self and the Supreme Self as different entities. In that case, you have to envision the presence of at least three supreme realities in each being, namely Nature as the body or the field (kshetra), the individual Self as the Knower of the Field (ksehtrajna), and the omniscient Supreme Self as the Knower of all the fields (Sarvajna). This contradicts the fundamental premise of Advaita (nondualism), according to which the same Self (Brahman) resides in all the bodies and represents the only supreme reality everywhere in the whole existence. Dvaita (dualism) and, to some extent, Vishistadvaita (qualified nondualism) acknowledge the duality between the individual Self and the Supreme Self. Each of these three schools uses verbal testimony from the same scriptures to justify their respective arguments. Since our purpose is not to expound them, we leave the matter here and settle with Lord Krishna's statement that the body is the Field, the Self is the Knower of the Field, and it is the same Self in all.

The Field of Brahman is vast and infinite, and so are its infinite forms and types. Everything here and hereafter is a field of Brahman, be it the world of Brahma, Vishnu, or Shiva, or the body of a tiny insect, a bird, or an animal. As Lord Krishna stated here, Purusha is the indweller of all the jivas and the Knower of the Field in all the fields. The Unmanifested Brahman does not have a body. However, for the Manifested One, the universe is his body. As the indweller of all, he knows all the fields, whether they are the bodies of the jivas, constellations, planetary systems, or the entire universe. He witnesses everything from within and without, untouched and unmoved by the happenings in and around them.

For the seeker of liberation, knowledge of both Kshetra and Kshetrajna is essential to overcome delusion and stabilize the mind in the Self with discernment. Knowledge of the Kshetra (the mind and body) is not as important as that of Kshetrajna (Knower of the Field). However, its importance in achieving liberation cannot be undermined. As the Isa Upanishad declares, into blinding darkness enter those who worship the Unmanifested (Kshetrajna) and into still greater darkness those who delight in the Manifest (Kshetra) only. Hence, one should pursue the knowledge of both to cross the world of delusion and reach the other side. Knowing kshetra helps us restrain the mind and senses and overcome the impurities. Knowing the Self helps us overcome desires and delusions and cultivate detachment, discernment, sameness, and equanimity.

Sloka 4

tat kṣetraṃ yac ca yādṛk ca yadvikāri yataś ca yat
sa ca yo yatprabhāvaś ca tat samāsena me śṛṇu

tat = that; ksetram = field; yat = what; ca = and; yadrk = what like; ca = and; yat = what; vikari = modifications, changes; yatah = from which cause; ca = also; yat = which; sah = he; ca = and; yah = who; yat = what; prabhavah = powers; ca = and; tat = that (body); samasena = briefly, in brief; me = from Me; srnu = hear, listen.

What that Field is and what it is like, what (its) modifications (are) and from which causes, who (He is) and what (His) powers are, briefly hear all that from Me.

Krishna stated that he would speak briefly about the five aspects of the Field and the Knower of the Field. Using the word "and" (ca) five times, he conveyed that they are all important and must be known to understand their significance. They are what that Field is like in itself ('tat kshetram yat'), what its nature is like or what its properties are (yadrik), what changes or modifications arise from it (yad vikari), and from which causes they arise (yatah). Also, who that (yah) Knower of the Field (Kshetrajna) is and what his powers are (yat prabhavah). Through them, he wanted to explain how diverse forms, natures, and properties of the jivas arise due to the union between the Kshetra (Prakriti) and Kshetrajna (Purusha), and what powers and modifications manifest in them.

Sloka 5

ṛṣibhir bahudhā gītaṃ chandobhir vividhaiḥ pṛthak
brahmasūtrapadaiś caiva hetumadbhir viniścitaiḥ

rsibhih = by the seers; bahudha = variously; gitam = sung, extolled; chandobhih =by Vedic meters; vividhaih = numerous; prthak = distinct separate; brahma-sutra = Brahma sutras; padaih = words, statements; ca =

and; eva = surely; hetu-madbhih = by the followers of reason; viniscitaih = ascertain conclusively.

Sung variously by the seers in numerous, distinct Vedic meters and even ascertained conclusively by the followers of reason in the words of the Brahmasutras.

The knowledge of the Kshetra and Kshetrajna was already known to the Vedic seers and followers of the Brahmasutras. The seers preserved it in distinct Vedic meters for future generations. Subsequently, the hetuvadins (logicians) ascertained it and recorded it in the Brahmasutras. That knowledge today serves as a verbal testimony to verify truths regarding Purusha and Prakriti or Brahman and his creation. Thus, quoting them, Lord Krishna suggested that their existence is corroborated by both sources of metaphysical knowledge: Sruti and Smriti. The former refers to the indisputable knowledge (sruti) heard from a divine source such as Brahma, which requires no further validation. The latter refers to the memorial knowledge (smriti) derived from the study of the Sruti and codified in scriptures by scholars and intellectuals through analysis, reasoning, and discernment. The Vedas are considered Sruti, and all the derivative works, such as the Brahmasutras, Vedangas, Grihyasutras, or the Dharmasutras, are considered Smriti. The Brahmasutras, ascribed to Badarayana and a text of great antiquity, is the logical starting point (nyaya prastana) of the Vedantic philosophy, where you will find the logical and intellectual interpretation of the knowledge found in the Upanishads and the Bhagavadgita regarding Brahman and Atman, the nature of ultimate reality, and the methods and meaning of liberation. The Upanishads, Brahmasutras, and the Bhagavadgita are collectively known as Prastana Traya or the triple (traya) sources of knowledge for final liberation or the ultimate journey. Much of the Vedic philosophy and doctrine, even the teachings of the Bhagavadgita, are derived from the Vedas. Whatever knowledge, conclusions, or interpretations we find in the Smritis or contemporary intellectual works are but recantations of the knowledge in them. Therefore, if any metaphysical theory or school of philosophy needs validation or repudiation, it is customary for scholars to look for evidence in the Vedas to validate their statements.

Sloka 6

mahābhūtāny ahaṃkāro buddhir avyaktam eva ca
indriyāṇi daśaikaṃ ca pañca cendriyagocarāḥ

maha-bhutani = the five great elements; ahankarah = ego; buddhih = intelligence; avyaktam = the unmanifested; eva = very, itself; ca = and; indriyani = the senses; dasa-ekam = eleven; ca = and; panca = five; ca = and; indriya-go-carah = objects of the senses.

The five great elements, ego, intelligence, and that which is unmanifested, senses, and the eleventh, and the five objects of the senses...

In this and the following verse, Lord Krishna described the tattvas (evolutes, formations, or finite realities) of Nature or Kshetra (the Field). They are responsible for the forms and shapes of the jivas, objects, and their diversity in Creation. Unlike the Self (Kshetrajna), which is eternal, indestructible, fixed, and infinite, Nature (Kshetra) is dynamic and subject to change (parinama), modifications, divisions, and differentiation. Nature itself is indestructible, but her forms and manifestations are destructible. The permutations and combinations of the various tattvas and gunas serve as the basic modules to produce the diversity of life and activity and fulfill the aims of creation.

The mahabhutas (great elements) are five: fire, water, air, earth, and space. They are responsible for the elemental bodies (bhuta-deham) of both the animate and inanimate objects in the manifested universe. Ahamkara is the ego, the ego-self, or the ego-sense, which arises due to the coagulation of thoughts, emotions, feelings, desires, and attachments around an illusory notion of 'me and mine." It creates the delusion that the jivas are different and distinct from each other and should strive to ensure their survival and continuity by pursuing their desires and living for themselves and those that are necessary for their survival. The intelligence found in the jivas is called buddhi. It arises as the first evolute or formation in creation from Mahat (the great one, and is responsible for discernment (vivekam), reasoning, and logical thinking. Mahat is another name for the manifested Prakriti. It is responsible for the "intelligent design" hidden in Creation. The unmanifested (avyaktam) refers to the triple gunas, Sattva, Rajas, and Tamas. Madhavacharya concurs with this definition of the unmanifested. The gunas are unmanifested (avyaktam) because they are invisible, immutable, and present in the unmanifested Prakriti also. However, they pervade everything in creation, exert their influence, and induce diverse propensities, qualities, modes of behavior, and natural functions in things and beings.

The senses (indriyas) are ten, grouped into two sets of five each: the organs of action (karmendriyas) and perception (jnanendriyas). The objects of the senses are also five, associated with the five organs of perception: form or light, taste, smell, touch, and sound. The eleventh one (dasekam) is the mind (manas), considered the eleventh sense since it controls the senses and acts as the receptacle to store the information they gather. Desires and attachments arise due to the movement of the senses among the sense objects. Their constant interaction results in attraction and aversion, leading to desires and attachments. Hence, withdrawal of the mind and senses is recommended in yoga to overcome them. The words avyakta and asambhuta are also used to refer to the Primal Nature, or that aspect of Nature that remains uninvolved or undifferentiated in its original and pure state. In that state, Prakriti does not participate in creation. The triple gunas (sattva, rajas, and tamas) remain in her in an indistinguishable state of equilibrium. They become active only when Prakriti becomes active in creation in her dynamic role and manifests things and beings.

According to the classical Sankhya, Prakriti means the original state or that which is not produced from anything. Whatever arises from it is Vikriti, the transformed one. The first evolute (vikriti) to manifest in the Field of Prakriti is Mahat. It manifests in the jivas as buddhi (intelligence). From buddhi arises egotism (aham). Egotism, which is the product of buddhi, acts as the source of the five objects of the senses: form, taste, smell, touch, and sound. The five objects of the senses, which are products of egotism, produce the five great elements: fire, water, earth, air, and space. Fire arises from form, water from taste, earth from smell, air from touch, and space from sound. The remaining tattvas, namely the mind, the five senses of perception, and the five senses of action, also arise from egotism. Thus, the total number of tattvas according to this school is 23. However, some scholars include the Mahat and the Self in the list and make the number 25. According to them, the Self is also a pure tattva, although different from the tattvas of Prakriti, and is neither a product nor the producer of anything.

Special note: Shankaracharya thought that Mahat meant the Lord's divine Maya, mentioned in verse 14 of the seventh chapter.

Sloka 7

icchā dveṣaḥ sukhaṃ duḥkhaṃ saṃghātaś cetanādhṛtiḥ
etat kṣetraṃ samāsena savikāram udāhṛtam

iccha = attraction, desire; dvesah = hatred, dislike; sukham = pleasure, happiness; duhkham = sorrow; sanghatah = the aggregate; cetana = liveliness; dhrtih = resolve, determination, firmness; etat = this; ksetram = field; samasena = briefly; sa-vikaram = along with modication; udahrtam = is said.

Desire, hatred, pleasure, sorrow, the aggregate, liveliness, determination, briefly speaking, this is the field with its modifications.

Prakriti is the original state. She is asambhuta in her unmanifested state and sambhuta in her manifested state. Vikritis are the evolutes (tattvas) that arise from her in her Field. This verse lists the modifications (vikaras), such as desire, hatred, pleasure, etc., that manifest from her due to the influence of the triple gunas. We experience them as states, feelings, emotions, sensations, etc., as they induce egoism, delusion, desires, attachments, attraction, and aversion. Their presence or absence creates the illusion of change, duality, and impermanence. Desire is described here as a modification of Prakriti. However, desires may also induce or influence all other modifications. Collectively, they all represent the impure, ignorant, and deluded state of the jivas. Chetana means aliveness, liveliness, awareness, responsiveness, dynamism, reactiveness, etc. In the jivas, it arises from the union of Purusha and Prakriti and pervades the mind and body, imparting to them the quality of being alive, active, or responsive and distinguishing them from all inanimate things. In the higher jivas, including humans, it is responsible for sentience, consciousness, or self-awareness. Some scriptures define it as chit-shakti, consciousness infused with shakti or energy. The dynamism of the jivas is self-induced, whereas that of the inanimate things is automated. Sanghatah refers to any object, organ, or organism comprised of parts. The mind is an aggregate of parts, like the body and the internal organ (antahkarana). Each jiva is also an aggregate, as are the world and the universe. Dhritih, meaning resolve or determination, arises due to will, courage, faith, and desires. It is responsible for the will to endure suffering and persevere against obstacles. The modifications mentioned here arise in the body, the Field. They also give rise to other modifications, such as aging, sickness, suffering, and death.

Sloka 8

amānitvam adambhitvam ahiṃsā kṣāntir ārjavam
ācāryopāsanaṃ śaucaṃ sthairyam ātmavinigrahaḥ

amanitvam = humility, absence of pride; adambhitvam = without vanity, unpretentiousness; ahimsa = nonviolence, non-injury, without cruelty; ksantih = tolerance, patience, endurance, forgiveness; arjavam = sincerity, straightforwardness; acarya-upasanam = service to teacher; saucam = cleanliness; sthairyam = resoluteness, determination or steadfastness; atma-vinigrahah = self-control.

The absence of self-pride, humility, nonviolence, tolerance, sincerity, service to the teacher, cleanliness, resoluteness, and self-control ...

Having listed the evolutes and modifications of the Field, Lord Krishna turned his attention to the qualities arising from the reflection or light of the Self (Kshetrajna) in the Field that would help a yogi to exemplify virtues, knowledge, discernment, etc., and attain nearness, sameness, and oneness. The qualities that are mentioned in this verse have multiple meanings. Amanitvam means lack of concern for one's name, pride, image, status, respect, importance, or fame. It is the absence of self-pride or self-esteem (manam). A true devotee does not take pride in his knowledge, purity, or divinity. Instead, he treats others with respect, compassion, and understanding, seeing the Self in them and empathizing with their suffering in samsara. Adambhitvam means the absence of dambhikam (deceit, vanity, hypocrisy, showiness, exaggerated self-importance, etc.) It is the quality of being unpretentious, simple, sincere, humble, and straightforward. Ahimsa means mental and physical nonviolence. It should be practiced in word and deed, meaning even the thought of causing injury or harm to anyone should be absent. In Hinduism and Yoga traditions, it is the highest virtue or the virtue of virtues. Kshanti means patience, tolerance, endurance, forbearance, or the ability to withstand suffering, disappointments, insults, or setbacks. Without it, a yogi cannot endure or remain indifferent to the hardships of spiritual life. Arjavam means simplicity, sincerity, austerity, frankness, or being truthful, honest, transparent, or straight. Acharya-upasanam means serving the teacher with reverence and respect. It is necessary to earn the trust and confidence of the teacher and acquire the secret knowledge of liberation from him. Saucham means cleanliness. It refers to both physical and mental cleanliness. For liberation, one must remove the impurities of the mind and body for personal cleanliness and keep the surroundings also clean. Sthairyam means steadfastness, resoluteness, willpower, or determination. It is the ability to persevere in the face of difficulties and not succumb to fear, anger, greed, or temptations. Atma-vinigraha means self-control or self-restraint. It is necessary for self-control (atma-samyama) or controlling the mind, body, and their modifications (vikaras).

Sloka 9

indriyārtheṣu vairāgyam anahaṃkāra eva ca
janmamṛtyujarāvyādhiduḥkhadoṣānudarśanam

indriya-arthesu = with regard to the sense objects; vairagyam = dispassion, detachment; anahankarah = egolessness; eva ca = so also; janma = birth; mrtyu = death; jara = old age; vyadhi = disease; duhkha = sorrow; dosa = defect, impurity, fault, harm, injury, evil; anudarsanam = seeing, reflecting.

Dispassion towards sense objects, absence of egoism, so also reflecting on the suffering arising from the impurities of birth, death, old age, (and) sickness...

On the path of liberation, a yogi must cultivate divine qualities through internal purification (parisuddhi) to cultivate devotion and stability and absorb his mind in the Supreme Lord. As Lord Krishna declared in the second Chapter, desires and attachments are responsible for delusion and passions such as anger, envy, pride, etc., which prevent one from achieving liberation. As long as one is subject to them, one cannot practice detachment or renunciation, attain sameness, or establish the mind in the Lord with unwavering devotion. It is equally important even for exclusive devotion. "Indriya arthesu vairagyam" means dispassion or indifference to the sense of objects and the like. Raga means passion, feeling, or emotion. Vairagyam means absence of passion (viragam). The phrase means a dispassionate state of disinterest and indifference to material things, such as wealth, name and fame, sensual pleasures, wife, children, family, etc., as well as to their relationship, ownership, and enjoyment. Birth, death, disease, old age, and the sorrow arising from them are defects (dosas) and modifications of the Field (the body). People accept them as facts of life and endure them in their respective ways without permanently resolving them or addressing their root causes. Those who know the distinction between the Field and the Knower of the Field know that they are limited to the Field and do not exist in the Self. Therefore, they practice detachment towards their minds and bodies and take refuge in the Self or the Lord to experience peace. Anahamkaram means the absence of egoism or the feeling of "me and mine." Egolessness and dispassion for sense objects go together and arise in the absence of desires and passions. When the ego is subdued and surrendered to the Self, the yogi remains humble, nonviolent, without deceit, upright, etc. He does not indulge in desire-ridden actions to promote himself or pursue Dharma, Artha, and Kama for selfish enjoyment. With his ego out of the way and free from desires, passions, and attachments, he remains contented, peaceful, and equal to all.

Solka 10

asaktir anabhiṣvaṅgaḥ putradāragṛhādiṣu
nityaṃ ca samacittatvam iṣṭāniṣṭopapattiṣu

asaktih = absence of attachment or interest; anabhisvangah = absence of intense attachment or clinging; putra = sons; dara = wife; grha-adisu = home and the like.; nityam = always; ca = and; sama-cittatvam = sameness, equanimity; ista = like, desirable; anista = dislike, undesirable; upapattisu = attainment.

Non-attachment, the absence of intense attachment to sons, wife, home, and the like, sameness in what is attained, whether it is desirable or undesirable...

Asakti means having no interest, passion, enthusiasm, inclination, or curiosity in anything or any desire-ridden action. It is usually translated as detachment, disinterest, or non-attachment. Attachments manifest in the Field or Nature as modifications due to egoism, desires, and delusion. Because of them, the deluded jivas cling to material objects, names, and forms. The most common attachments of householders are attachment to children, wives, home, wealth, etc., which they find challenging to renounce or pursue liberation. Compelling habits and passions such as anger, envy, pride, and greed arise due to attachments only, resulting in birth and rebirth. They are also responsible for our self-preservation instinct and the need for belongingness, love, approval, and recognition.

The Field is a playground of the Self. However, for the deluded ones caught in the grip of Nature, it is very much like a prison where her Maya Shaktis hold them in control and keep them bound. We love our children, families, friends, and the things we cling to because we find in them an extension of our egos or ourselves. We like those who mirror our qualities, nature, behavior, desires, likes, and dislikes. Through them, we extend our minds and senses into objective reality and create a world or reality that is very much an extension of our consciousness. If anything happens to it, we feel as if it happened to us. When we are at odds with the world or helplessly forced to live in a world we dislike, we experience negativity, pain, and suffering.

Attachments define and influence our relationships, thinking, and behavior towards others and ourselves. We cling to those with whom we feel an affinity or emotional connection and feel repelled by those who seem to challenge the constructs we build in our minds to define ourselves and safeguard our interests. Even extraneous factors such as name, appearance, gender, race, nationality, language, religion, and caste influence our thinking, behavior, and relationship with others. Thus, our attachments and relationships represent in many ways our egos, desires, and attachments. Whether we know it or not, we like to see reflections of ourselves in others and the world around us. We love those who mirror our thoughts, opinions, choices, and preferences, and stay away from those who represent their opposites. While they may help us to survive and succeed in the world, they also limit our ability to transcend our limitations and experience the world with sameness and equanimity.

For the yogi who is intent on liberation, the body is a prison from which he aims to escape forever. He knows it is the source of impurities and is responsible for his bondage and suffering. Therefore, he renounces his relationship with his mind and body, his children, his family, his wife, the world, and all material things and practices detachment and indifference (asakti). Giving up attachments, attraction, and aversion (raga and dvesha), he remains the same in all situations, neither liking what is desirable nor disliking what is undesirable. Surrendering himself unconditionally, he accepts the Lord's will as his command and embraces life without choice, preference, likes and dislikes. Established in sameness, he does not engage in willful actions to control, change, or escape from what happens or does not happen.

Sloka 11

mayi cānanyayogena bhaktir avyabhicāriṇī
viviktadeśasevitvam aratir janasaṃsadi

mayi = to Me; ca = and; ananya-yogena = exclusive, unswerving; bhaktih = devotion; avyabhicarini = not wandering or transgressing or seeking pleasures; vivikta desa sevitvam = inclined to retreat into solitary places; aratih = without taking delight; jana = people; samsadi = company.

With unwavering and exclusive devotion to Me, without transgressing or seeking pleasures, inclined to retreat into solitary places, without taking delight in the company of people...

Unwavering devotion (ananya bhakti) means devotion with a mind that is undistracted or undisturbed by any internal or external factors or by devotion or loyalty to another deity, object, or interest. Bhakti yoga is the best path to liberation. Contrary to popular opinion, although it looks simple to practice, it is not. Bhakti is of several types. They are all pleasing and acceptable to the Lord, but do not lead to liberation. Only ananya bhakti or kevala bhakti has the potential to earn divine grace. In the Bhagavadgita, Lord Krishna repeatedly emphasized its importance, stating that it is attainable only through constant practice (abhyasa yoga) or by his mercy (anugraha). It is especially difficult for worldly people, even if they practice their obligatory duties and show devotion, unless they remove their impurities.

Since they must perform obligatory duties, ordinary people cannot exclusively devote themselves to the Lord until they empty their minds, renounce worldly desires and attachments, and fill them with his thoughts. Ananya bhakti arises naturally after many births in those who cultivate the qualities mentioned in the previous two verses, starting with dispassion (vairagyam) and ending with sameness (sama-chittatvam). Only through renunciation of desires and attachments and cultivating such qualities can a devotee restrain himself, keep his mind from wandering or falling into licentious modes (vyabhichara), and establish it in unwavering and exclusive devotion.

Thus, perfection in ananya bhakti requires an extraordinary mindset characterized by desirelessness, selflessness, and willingness to let go of everything. Those who practice it prefer to live alone in solitary places. When they find themselves in the company of people, they do not delight in them, for they delight in the Lord's thoughts and their imaginary association with him. Since their minds are filled with devotion and devotional thoughts, they are comfortable wherever they are, whether alone or in the company of others. They know that the Lord is the only raft and support in their journey across the ocean of Samsara and stays with them until the last moment.

Liberation is a solitary journey where you have to fight your battles alone. Others may help you and guide you, but you have to reach the finish line all by yourself, overcoming all the obstacles. Liberation itself means aloneness (kaivalyam) because, in the state of liberation, you remain alone, independent, and self-existent without a second. The yogi, who has established his mind in the Lord with firm resolve, self-discipline (atma-samyama), and exclusive devotion, is not deluded or distracted by the promise of anything or any teaching in which the Lord is not the goal or the support. Rather than seeking the company of people, he seeks the company of God. Rather than relying upon his will, he relies upon the Lord's will without worrying about his prarabdha karma or liberation or how the world perceives him or judges him, and lives with the conviction that the Supreme Lord will take care of him and ensure his wellbeing. His strength and resolve to continue against difficulties and obstacles arise from his unwavering faith and devotion to him.

Thus, in this verse, Lord Krishna emphasized the ideal practice of exclusive devotion for those drawn to devotion and fit to practice it. He suggested the need to become detached from the Field to remain established in the Self or the Knower of the Field. In the embodied state, the Self is bound to the body (Kshetra). To be free from it, the yogi has to cultivate detachment (vairagyam), disinterest (anasakti), egolessness (anahamkaram), equanimity, sameness, renunciation of worldly relationships, and the awareness that mortal life is full of impurities, misery, and suffering. When they manifest in a devotee, exclusive devotion manifests in him naturally. The senses and the gunas are responsible for desires and attachments, and the modifications arising from them. In secluded places, it will be easier to withdraw the mind and body and practice self-control (atma-samyama) and discipline. Therefore, exclusive devotees are naturally drawn to places conducive to their practice. They do it not because of desires or attachments but because of their love and devotion to the Lord.

Sloka 12

adhyātmajñānanityatvaṃ tattvajñānārthadarśanam
etaj jñānam iti proktam ajñānaṃ yad atonyathā

adhyatma = the Self; jnana = knowledge; nityatvam = constant, always; tattva-jnana = knowledge of tattvas; artha = object, purpose, goal; darsanam = insightful inquiry, seeing the truth of; etat = this; jnanam = knowledge; iti = thus; proktam = declared; ajnanam = ignorance; yat = that which is; atah = from this; anyatha = others.

Constantly established in the knowledge of the Self, seeing the truth of the knowledge of the tattvas, this is declared to be knowledge. Ignorance is that which is other than this.

Knowledge (jnanam) is important for exclusive devotion. Ignorant people remain deluded and cannot practice it. Hence, jnana yoga is considered preparatory for bhakti yoga by many scholars. Lord Krishna declared here two types of knowledge as true knowledge (jnana) and the rest as ignorance or other than knowledge. They are vijnana, or the knowledge of the tattvas and gunas that are exclusive to the Field (Prakriti), and jnana, or the knowledge of the Knower of the Field or the Self (adhyatma jnana), without which one cannot overcome the delusion of the mind and body or practice devotion. Since this is a continuation of the previous verses, it is implied that these two types of knowledge arise in those who have cultivated the virtues stated in them. A devotee must cultivate them to withdraw his mind and senses into the Lord and practice exclusive devotion without distractions.

Adhyatma jnana refers to the knowledge of the Knower of the Field, and tattva jnana refers to the knowledge of the Field. The former refers to the knowledge of the Self, and the latter to the knowledge of the not-self. The tattvas are the primordial realities or components of Prakriti, which serve as the building blocks of the Field (Kshetra), its diversity, and objectivity. They are responsible for the objective reality we perceive through our minds and senses. By seeing the truth of the tattvas through inquiry, reflection, and observation, and knowing how they bind the jivas, a yogi cultivates discernment and dispassion and resolves to achieve liberation. Thus, tattva jnana is the starting point to develop constancy in the knowledge of the Self.

Self-knowledge is gained through self-purification and devotion to God. When you strengthen in yourself the divine qualities Lord Krishna enumerated before, you will overcome delusion and settle permanently in the knowledge that the Self is your true Self. Knowledge of the tattvas is gained through insightful study, philosophical inquiry, knowledge of the scriptures, and the teachings of those who have already gained insight into them. It refers not only to the knowledge of the tattvas but also to the knowledge of the world and all its objects, since they are all made up of tattvas and represent the not-self or objective reality. Hence, on the path of liberation, tattva jnana is considered as important as atma jnana. They are like the two facets of true knowledge (vidya). The former serves as the foundation for the latter. Gaining through them the right views, right perceptions, right awareness, and right discernment, the yogi sees the truth of the tattvas and the Self.

Indeed, the goal of tattva jnana (knowledge of realities) is atma jnana (knowledge of the Self) only. By knowing the tattvas and their true purpose and realizing that the field of Prakriti is an illusion or a temporary projection of the Self, one becomes firmly established in the transcendental knowledge of the Self (adhyatma jnana). However, tattva jnana alone does not lead to adhyatma jnana unless one uses the knowledge to cultivate the virtues Lord Krishna described in the previous verses. Tattva jnana is an adjunct to adhyatma jnana, but on its own, it is empty knowledge and a source of delusion. Both types of knowledge are necessary for liberation, and they should always be attained on the firm foundation of nishkama karma (desireless actions) through karma-sannyasa (renunciation of the desire for the fruit of actions), and samsiddhi (sameness) through naishkarmya siddhi (freedom from karma.

Sloka 13

jñeyaṃ yat tat pravakṣyāmi yaj jñātvāmṛtam aśnute
anādimat paraṃ brahma na sat tan nāsad ucyate

jneyam = what is to be known, knowable; yat = that; tat = which; pravaksyami = I shall now speak; yat = which; jnatva = knowing; amrtam = immortality; asnute = tastes, attains; anadi = without beginning; mat= considered, thought of, believed; param = Supreme; brahma = Brahman; na = not; sat = being; tat = that; na = nor; asat = non-being; ucyate = is said.

That which is to be known, I shall now speak to you, knowing which immortality is attained. The Supreme Brahman, believed to be without beginning, is said to be neither being nor non-being.

What is to be known (jneyam) is Brahman because only by knowing him can one gain liberation from the cycle of births and deaths. Upon liberation, an embodied Self returns to its original state of pure consciousness, which is immortal, blissful, indestructible, and all-knowing. In an embodied state, knowing the Self is the same as knowing Brahman because, in their essential nature, they are either the same or, as the dualists proclaim, represent the same reality. However, even if we accept the latter argument, we have to acknowledge that the Universal Self is more expansive, pervasive, and completely independent, while the individual Self is dependent upon Him and in some way connected to Him. Now, who is this Brahman, knowing whom, we transcend our limitations and gain immortality? How do we know that the reality we experience in a transcendental and non-dualistic state is Brahman only? Here, Lord Krishna, an incarnation of the Supreme Self, made a somewhat paradoxical statement about the absolute state of Brahman, saying that it is neither Sat nor Asat.

If Brahman is neither of them, then what else is he? Indeed, there is no ambiguity about what he said in this verse. Lord Krishna quoted the Vedas to describe himself, saying that he was infinite and 'believed' to be neither Sat nor Asat. "Sat" means existence, truth, reality, beingness, goodness, purity, and virtue. It represents the manifested aspect of Prakriti in association with Brahman. Asat means non-existence, falsehood, unreality, non-beingness, or impurity. It refers to the unmanifested or undifferentiated aspect of Prakriti in association with Brahman. Brahman remains unmanifested, invisible, formless, and hidden in both states because he is eternal, indestructible, immutable, and fixed. What manifests (sambhuta), unmanifests (asambhuta), or transforms is Prakriti. Sat and Asat, known as existence and nonexistence or manifested and unmanifested, are her states. When she becomes active at the beginning of creation, Brahman manifests as Isvara in association with her. His higher and lower natures represent Sat, while he is other than them. When he withdraws from her at the end of creation and reverts to his pure state, she reverts to her primordial and unmanifested state and becomes Asat. Thus, Brahman is the connecting link between the Sat and Asat aspects of Prakriti. He is their support as well as their cause. Some scholars, however, describe the Purusha (the Cosmic Self) or the Supreme Lord (Isvara) as Sat, his creation as Asat, and Brahman's supreme and absolute Reality as different and distinct from both.

The truth is that Brahman has no states, qualities, or modes. He is eternally the same and beyond all known methods of knowing him objectively. Hence, he is considered indeterminate and ungraspable. He cannot be known by the known methods of knowing: study, perception, analysis, comparison, imagination, learning, etc., however pure and stable the internal organ (antahkarana) is. Absolute reality cannot be known by these methods but only absolutely through oneness, in which awareness is not a process or state but reality. In the absolute state of Brahman, (perhaps) knowing is not a movement driven by desires or modes or the knower and the known but spontaneous self-knowing. We cannot know Brahman by negation, affirmation, comparison, analysis, or imagination. The Upanishads suggest the neti-neti (not this, not this) approach to know him. However, that knowing is not true knowing but an approximation or, at best, an intellectual speculation. Brahman is beyond names and forms and everything we define and describe in our consciousness. To the human mind, he is knowable and unknowable, real and unreal. We cannot say conclusively whether he is this and that or not this and not that. He is always the same in parts and the sum of parts, whether present or absent in creation, or whether Prakriti is active or inactive. He is all this. At the same time, he is not them or in them.

Sat and asat are also translated as being and non-being. Some interpret them as Brahman with form (murtam) and without form (amurtam). Beingness implies individuality, objectivity, materiality, and specificity. Non-beingness, which is devoid of them, transcends all known realities, states of existence, modes, modalities, and consciousness. While with some difficulty, we may draw a few conclusions about his qualities, names, forms, potencies, and manifestations, the Supreme Non-Being is unknowable in a knowable state of duality and perhaps even in the transcendental state. The Reality of Brahman is neither emptiness nor fullness, neither existence nor non-existence, neither consciousness nor unconsciousness. Entering its absolute and perfect state, one becomes nothing and, at the same time, everything. One ceases to exist as a limited being and (perhaps) becomes all. The skepticism is intended because what can we say about that which is the object of knowing but cannot truly or definitively be known in specific terms?

Since it is so difficult to grasp the essential nature of Brahman or intellectualize it with the known interpretations and definitions of our conditioned knowledge, the Kena Upanishad declares that Brahman is other than the known and so also above the unknown. If you think you have understood him, you have known him but little. If you think you do not know him, you probably know him. Brahman is other than all that we know or envision. It is difficult to say what he is and is not. We can only speculate about him, but we cannot be sure. We must, therefore, surrender our knowledge, intelligence, and discernment to the Supreme Lord and let him decide how far he will make himself known.

Sloka 14

sarvataḥ pāṇipādaṃ tat sarvatokṣiśiromukham
sarvataḥ śrutimal loke sarvam āvṛtya tiṣṭhati

sarvatah = everywhere; pani = hands; padam = legs; tat = that which; sarvatah = everywhere; aksi = eyes; sirah = head; mukham = mouths; sarvatah = everywhere; sruti-mat = ears; loke = in the world; sarvam = everything; avrtya = pervading, enveloping; tisthati = exists.

That which has hands (and) feet, everywhere, which has eyes, head, (and) mouths everywhere, which has ears everywhere; (and) exists in the world enveloping everything.

The Being described in this verse is the knowable Brahman or Isvara, the Supreme Being, who represents Sat and is also known as Kshetrajna or the Knower of the Field. Arjuna had already witnessed one aspect of his universal form. His power of knowing has been illustrated in three expressions in this verse, indicating that he is everywhere (sarvatra) and all this or all that exists (sarvam). All the jivas are a part of the Field he creates, manifesting his Nature. He is also present in all as the Knower of the Field. Our bodies are a part of his universal form (visvākāram). Hence, along with countless other beings in other worlds, the jivas constitute his hands, feet, heads, eyes, mouths, and other organs. Through them, he witnesses and enjoys the Play of Prakriti enacted under his will. Even without the Kshetra in active mode and without hands, feet, eyes, ears, etc., he is omniscient and omnipresent. The following three phrases describe his all-pervading universal presence and all-knowing and all-grasping supreme power. Shankaracharya commented that they are metaphorical and used to indicate his existence.

Sarvatah Panipadam means the Supreme Being has hands and legs everywhere and is omnipresent. In other words, he participates in all actions and movements. The limitations of time and space do not apply to him because he is unbound, limitless, and independent. Although unmoving and fixed, he moves freely like the wind or space and is found in every aspect of creation. He is also supremely powerful as the controller of all the universal forces. He is the real doer (karta) of all actions, movements, and events in creation, including those we assume are ours. All the organs in our bodies obey his will, are supported and controlled by him, and work for and belong to him only. The whole creation constitutes his universal body (Kshetra). Arjuna already saw it in the universal form of Lord Krishna and understood his significance as the Lord who controls all destinies, the beginning and end of all actions.

Sarvatokṣiśiromukham means having heads, mouths, and eyes everywhere. Because of these instruments of knowing present in his Field, he is known as the all-knowing (sarvajna), universal witness (sarva sakshi) as the all-seeing Eye. As our inner witness and ultimate enjoyer, and through our minds and senses, he watches the drama (lila) unfolding in and around us. With his universal presence and numerous ways of knowing and perceiving, he watches over the worlds as their controller, protector, and upholder, ensuring their progression, order, and regularity. Since he is the Lord of Time and all the energies in creation, he is the controller and regulator of what happens and does not happen, and what moves and does not. As the source and impeller of Time but himself timeless, he knows the past, present, and future and has the power to alter at will the course of any movement, event, action, or outcome.

Sarvatah srutimat means having ears everywhere and listening to all sounds and speech. The Supreme Being has ears everywhere, meaning he is the all-hearing Ear. He is not only the silent witness and enjoyer of all, but also the universal listener. With ears everywhere, he listens to all sounds that manifest in creation. Nothing escapes him. He is the Lord of all sounds (nada), subtle and gross. He also supports our speech when it travels through space, carrying the sounds to their intended target. The Upanishads proclaim that Brahman is verily speech. He is the source of all letters, syllables, and speech, carries them from one place to another, and presides over the potencies hidden in them. As the merciful Lord, who listens to our prayers, supplications, and gross and subtle thoughts, he helps us according to our nature and destinies. Hence, we are advised to think carefully since they also produce the fruit of karma.

Sloka 15

sarvendriyaguṇābhāsaṃ sarvendriyavivarjitam
asaktaṃ sarvabhṛc caiva nirguṇaṃ guṇabhoktṛ ca

sarva = all; indriya = senses; guna = qualities or functions; abhasam = appearing, looking like, shining; sarva = all; indriya = senses; vivarjitam = without, devoid of; asaktam = unattached, independent; sarva-bhrt = upholding all; ca = and; eva = really surely; nirgunam = without modes, attributes or properties; guna-bhoktr = ruler, user, enjoyer; ca = but.

Appearing to possess all the senses along with their qualities, (but) without senses; unattached and independent, (but) supporting all; and without modes, but really the ruler and enjoyer of the modes ...

In this and the next verse, Lord Krishna distinguished the Knower of the Field (Kshetrajna) from the Field (Kshetra). With all its organs and faculties, the body appears to be the Self but not the Self. It appears to have senses but without them. It seems to be attached to the body but is unattached and supports all organs. It is without modes but the enjoyer of all the desires and actions arising from them. Thus, although the Knower of the Field appears to be a part of the Field endowed with tattvas and modes, he is completely without them and detached from them. The Field (body or creation) is his ornament, but he is not in it. This is the meaning.

The Knower of the Field represents the subjective reality, and the Field represents the objective reality (the not-self). The objective reality of the Field is knowable and perceptible to the mind and senses, but the reality of the Self is unknowable and imperceptible to them. They exist in their respective dimensions and do not overlap. The Field is a dependent aspect of the Self and cannot exist without it. However, when they are united, they create the illusion of a third reality or dimension, the state of liveliness (chaitanyam), movement, and beingness in which the Knower of the Field (Purusha or the Self) appears (abhasa) to be endowed with the modes, tattvas, qualities, divisions, and organs of the Field (Prakriti). In reality, he is without them.

The very presence of the Self in the Field illuminates it with life and imparts to its dynamism, consciousness, formations, and modifications. Since he is all-knowing, self-knowing, and self-aware, he knows without any instruments of knowing, such as the senses or the mind. Yet, in the body, he appears connected to them and enjoys sense objects. As the Upanishads suggest, he is not the senses; they all work for him and exist because of him.

Another truth about him is that although he is independent and self-existent, he appears to be connected to everything as the supporter of all (sarvabhrt). He supports the material universe (the Field or Prakriti), which manifests in him as his essential duty (Dharma). He upholds it and all the jivas without being interested in them or attached to them. In each being, the individual Self is detached and uninterested in the Field of Prakriti or the physical self, consisting of all the tattvas of the mind and body. Yet, it cannot sustain itself without the Self. It is alive so long as the latter supports it. So is the case with the world. The world will collapse into chaos if Isvara, the lord of the universe, withdraws from it. He is, therefore, rightly the upholder of all. Brahman (or Atman) has no qualities, functions, or modes (gunas). He appears in the Field of Prakriti as the owner and enjoyer of the gunas and tattvas, although he has no direct connection with them and is devoid of them.

Sloka 16

bahir antaś ca bhūtānām acaraṃ caram eva ca
sūkṣmatvāt tad avijñeyaṃ dūrasthaṃ cāntike ca tat

bahih = without; antah = within; ca =and; bhutanam = of the living being; acaram = unmoving; caram = moving; eva = similarly; ca = and; suksmatvat = because of subtle nature; tat = that, It; avijneyam = unknowable; durastham = far away; ca = and; antike = near; ca = and; tat = that.

Without and within all beings, unmoving, yet moving also, it is unknowable because of its subtle nature. That is also far away and near.

'Tat' refers to the Self in the Vedic texts since it is gender-neutral and devoid of qualities and modes. Some scholars translate this verse as "That is without and within in the moving and the unmoving beings..." However, 'acaram caram' seems to describe Brahman or the Self rather than the beings (or perhaps both). The Self is situated within the body of each jiva as its Lord and support. It is also outside all of them and envelops them as their Supreme Lord. In the jivas, it seems to move as they move, but it has no movement of its own, whether in or outside them. Further, since it is everywhere, it may appear to move or accompany us wherever we go, just like the wind or space, but in truth, it is eternally fixed and immovable. Similarly, it is fixed and unmoving in the wakeful state but said to move and wander in the astral or dream worlds.

The moving and unmoving aspects of Brahman can be compared to the wheel and its axis. Just as the wheel moves around its fixed and immovable axis, the Wheel of Life, carrying the world and the jivas, moves around the Self, its axis and support. Another aspect of the Self is its unknowability because of its subtle nature. It is subtler than the subtlest and smaller than the smallest. Hence, it is invisible to the senses and unknowable to the mind. It is also unknown because we are subject to ignorance, delusion, and the duality of the knower and the known. However, it can be known in subjectivity and oneness, free from duality and delusion. Lastly, the Self is far away because it is beyond the mind and senses. It is also very near since it exists in all beings as their very Self.

Sloka 17

avibhaktaṃ ca bhūteṣu vibhaktam iva ca sthitam
bhūtabhartṛ ca taj jñeyaṃ grasiṣṇu prabhaviṣṇu ca

avibhaktam = undivided, indivisible; ca = and, yet; bhutesu = in living beings; vibhaktam = divided; iva = similarly; ca = and; sthitam = remains, exists, seated; bhuta-bhartr = supporter or upholder of beings; ca = and; tat = that; jneyam = known grasisnu = absorbing, devouring; prabhavisnu = creator, originator; ca = and.

Undivided, yet (he) exists in the beings as divided. Similarly, That One, who is known as the upholder of beings, is also the devourer and creator.

The apparent contradictions of Brahman that are described here arise not because Brahman is inconsistent but because of our duality and delusion. They do not exist in him since he represents one indivisible and immutable reality. Due to our ignorance and delusion, it is how we think or perceive him. He is indivisible, yet he appears to be divided because he is present in all. He is the supporter of all. Yet he seems to be devouring the things he creates because, as the Lord of all, he performs different functions, including destruction. Therefore, we are bound to see some apparent (but not real) contradictions in him. In his absolute and pure state, Brahman is indivisible, indistinguishable, and without a second. Yet, he projects himself in creation as different beings and Selves. The One becomes many or, as some think, appears as many in the Field of Prakriti.

Is the indivisible Supreme Self different from the individual Selves (atmas) who appear in creation as the embodied Selves (jivatmas)? To repeat what we already stated before, there is no unanimity about this among scholars. The Dvaita philosophy holds that they are eternally different, although they both possess similar qualities, such as omniscience, omnipresence, and omnipotence. Despite such similarities, the duality between them is permanent, continuous, and real. In the Dvaita worldview, duality exists at every level of creation and is fundamental, not illusory. In contrast, the Advaita philosophy holds that Brahman is one and only. He alone is real, and everything else is false or an illusion caused by the superimposition of Maya on the Truth of Brahman. The appearance of individual Selves in creation is also a part of that illusion. When jivas attain liberation, the apparent duality between them disappears. According to this school, Brahman is unmanifested, indivisible, eternal, indestructible, fixed, and so on. However, in Prakriti (Field), enveloped by her modes and tattvas, he appears as Isvara,

Hiranyagarbha, Viraj, gods, goddesses, worlds, beings, and so on. They all, including the highest gods, are temporary creations. They manifest at the beginning of creation and are withdrawn at the end. Thus, the unmanifested Brahman is indivisible, but in creation, numerous forms manifest from him to create the illusion of diversity and distinction.

Apart from them, other schools, such as the Vishistadvaita, hold an intermediary position, suggesting they are different but not very different, etc. However, these schools agree that the Supreme Lord, Isvara, is the source of all. As Isvara, the Universal Lord, he performs three vital functions: creation, preservation, and destruction, represented in creation by Brahma, Vishnu, and Shiva, respectively. In addition, he also acts as the Concealer and Revealer. In the deluded beings, he conceals his knowledge, consciousness, and radiant presence beneath layers of Prakriti's modes, tattvas, and impurities. When they are removed or purified, he reveals himself, letting the jivas know him and experience his pure state. He performs these functions universally in the jivas and the whole creation in each cycle of creation. Thus, even from the perspective of Dvaita, the apparent contradictions of Brahman are illusory. The one Supreme Lord is behind all the drama. As the creator of all, he unleashes the effects hidden in their causes and manifests worlds and beings. As the preserver, he upholds them and protects them. As the lord of Death, he devours them all in their due time. In worldly life, he accepts our sacrificial offerings and fulfills our desires. In spiritual life, when we surrender to him, serve him, and seek his protection and guidance, he devours our ignorance and delusion, delivers us from samsara, and leads us toward truth, light, and immortality.

Sloka 18

jyotiṣām api taj jyotis tamasaḥ param ucyate
jñānaṃ jñeyaṃ jñānagamyaṃ hṛdi sarvasya viṣṭhitam

jyotisam = of the shining objects; api = verily; tat = that; jyotih = the light; tamasah = darkness; param = beyond; ucyate = said to be; jnanam = knowledge; jneyam = knowable; jnana-gamyam = the end of knowledge; hrdi = in the heart; sarvasya = of all; visthitam = situated.

That Light of the shining objects is said to be beyond darkness. As knowledge, the knowable and the goal of all knowledge, (he) is situated in the heart of all.

The light of the Supreme Self illuminates all objects in Prakriti and is beyond ignorance, duality, and delusion. Tamasa param means it is beyond or on the other side of darkness. It also means you cannot find him in an ignorant and deluded state. The knowledge of Brahman is true knowledge that should be known to attain liberation. It is hidden in the heart of all, accessible to all, and is the end of all knowing and learning. The absolute state of Brahman is the ever-shining transcendental light (parama jyoti). It is self-illumined (svayam prakasi) and the shining Self in all (atma jyoti). The objective reality is not self-illumined. It is illuminated by the Self or Brahman and arises as his reflection in intelligence. So is the liveliness (chaitanyam) of our consciousness or our minds, and bodies. All the objects in Prakriti, and

Prakriti herself, are illuminated by the light (consciousness) of Brahman only. Just as the sun illuminates all the objects in its domain, the Self illuminates all objects in creation. He is the source of light and movement in all objects, including the sun and moon. Because he illuminates our consciousness (mind and intelligence), we can perceive things and make sense of them. The internal organ (antahkarana) is also illuminated by him only. Thinking, reasoning, discerning, speaking, knowing, understanding, etc., arise because of his illumination only.

The distinction between the gunas (modes) arises because Brahman illuminates them differently in manifested Prakriti to ensure that they produce distinct qualities and tendencies in creation. He is essentially Nirguna, without modes. Hence, he is beyond the light and darkness that the gunas reflect in creation. He is not in the tattvas and gunas he illuminates, but they exist in him. However, Prakriti has chaitanyam (consciousness, dynamism, and sentience) because of His illumination only. He is brightly reflected in sattva, partially reflected in rajas, and hardly reflected in tamas. Darkness has no place (astitva) in the effulgence of the Supreme Self. It is but the absence of his light and cannot prevail in his presence. Hence, in darkness or in the predominance of tamas, we cannot reflect things or perceive truths as they are. The world appears to be what it is because of the mode of sattva, which has the natural tendency to illuminate and brighten things with the least obstruction or resistance. Hence, when sattva predominates, we know and understand better. We see things as they are and discern their distinctions better. When rajas and tamas prevail and predominate, we lose that clarity and objectivity and succumb to passions, delusion, and ignorance.

Brahman is knowledge (jnanam) because all things exist in him and arise from him. He is pure consciousness, omnipresent, omniscient (sarvajna), and the source of all. Since creation arises from him as an effect and he is its source, its knowledge is always hidden in him. There is also no limit to his knowing, which is self-illumined and self-existent. He is the one to be known (jneyam) because there is nothing better to know and because by knowing him, one becomes liberated. He is the goal of all knowledge because all knowledge arises, subsides, and leads to him only. He is also the end of all knowledge because there is nothing other than him or beyond him. He is the final destination (param gati) and the end of all seeking and searching. The Upanishads state that he is located in the heart of all, meaning he is the center and supporter of all. They further declare that the knowledge about him is true knowledge (vidya), and the rest is ignorance (avidya). Hence, by knowing him, one is purified and liberated with his knowledge and becomes a self-illuminated, adept yogi.

Sloka 19

iti kṣetraṃ tathā jñānaṃ jñeyaṃ coktaṃ sanāsataḥ
madbhakta etad vijñāya madbhāvāyopapadyate 13.19

iti = thus; ksetram = the field; tatha = also; jnanam = knowledge; jneyam = the knowable; ca = and; uktam = explained; samasatah = briefly; mat-bhaktah = My devotee; etat = this; vijnaya = By knowing; mat-bhavaya = My state; upapadyate = qualify to attain.

Thus, the Field, so also knowledge, and the knowable are explained briefly. By knowing this, My devotee is qualified to attain My state.

The Field (body or the world) is Prakriti. The knowable (jneyam) is the Self or the Knower of the Field (Kshetrajna), and the knowledge mentioned here refers to the knowledge of both. The Field refers to the physical composition of the jiva, its nature, identity, functions, and objective consciousness. It is the not-self, in contrast to the Self or the Knower of the Field. Because of delusion and ignorance, we accept the Field (the body) as our true identity rather than the Knower of the Field (the Self), who remains hidden. When we gain the right knowledge and understand that the Self is the one to be known and the body is to be renounced and controlled, we become qualified to attain the supreme state of Brahman. How is it accomplished? It is by cultivating detachment towards the mind and body, suppressing the modes through self-control to overcome desires and attachments, renouncing the fruit of our actions, and practicing exclusive devotion to the Lord by taking refuge in him. Ignorance does not mean ignorance in an academic sense. It is ignorance of the Self and the distinction between the Field and the Knower of the Field, or how to escape permanently from the control of Prakriti to gain mastery and independence. Because of ignorance, delusion arises. It is mistaking the body (Field) for the Self and the universe for Brahman. When we remove the darkness of ignorance and delusion from our minds by resolving the modes, the light of the Self shines in us, and we discern the truths regarding ourselves and our essential purpose. When we are free from these twin evils and endowed with knowledge and discernment, we know clearly what needs to be known and what needs to be renounced. With that discerning wisdom, we qualify to attain true knowledge (vidya) and enter the supreme state of Brahman. Thus, the right knowledge of the Self (jnanam) is essential to dispel our ignorance and delusion and choose the right path to immortality. It is also the foundation to practice karma-sannyasa yoga and self-control, and cultivate exclusive devotion.

Sloka 20

prakṛtiṃ puruṣaṃ caiva viddhy anādi ubhāv api
vikārāñś ca guṇāṃś caiva viddhi prakṛtisaṃbhavān 13.20

prakrtim = Prakriti, Nature; purusam = Purusha, Cosmic Person; ca = and; eva = surely; viddhi =know; anadi = without beginning; ubhau = both; api = also; vikaran = modifications, changes; ca = and; gunan = gunas; ca = and; eva = surely; viddhi = know; prakrti = Nature; sambhavan = profrom.

Know that both Purusha and Prakriti are indeed without a beginning; also, know that modifications and gunas surely arise from Nature.

Prakriti and Purusha represent the fundamental duality of creation. The Bhagavadgita identified them as the Kshetra (the Field) and Kshetrajna (Knower of the Field). In the jivas, they correspond to the body and the Self, respectively. Some schools believe that the Supreme Self (Paramatma) is distinct from them and beyond them. In other words, they regard Manifested

Brahman or Isvara, who embodies Prakriti and Purusha, as distinct from the absolute Brahman. According to them, duality exists eternally between the Unmanifested Brahman, who is free from the modes, modifications, divisions, and attributes, and the Manifested Brahman, in whom Prakriti and Purusha coexist in their purest state. All the worlds and beings manifest from the latter due to the activity of the gunas and the differentiation of tattvas. The Vedas affirm that Purusha, the Cosmic Being, manifests from Brahman at the beginning of creation and is withdrawn into him at the end. Creation is his universal body, and Brahman is his Supreme Self.

In some schools, Purusha and Prakriti are considered eternally independent, while in some, Prakriti is viewed as an eternal but dependent aspect of the former. In many Shakta and Shaiva traditions, Prakriti is regarded as the material cause of creation and Purusha as the efficient cause. Some schools regard Prakriti as the sole cause of creation and Purusha as the passive witness. Most Vedic traditions, including the Bhagavadgita, regard Prakriti as an eternal but dependent aspect of Purusha. The latter is not a mere witness but an active Lord and Controller of the whole creation, who is the cause of all, including the liberation of his devotees. This chapter concurs with this view and considers Prakriti an eternal aspect of Brahman. She executes his will to bring forth creation and its diversity. These speculations do not dispute that Prakriti is primarily responsible for all creation, whether by herself or under the will and command of Isvara. Further, if Purusha (Brahman) is eternal, his energy or materiality cannot be otherwise. It also makes sense that there can be only one primary and ultimate source of creation. Otherwise, chaos will ensue.

Another important distinction between the two is that Purusha is eternally indivisible and unchangeable, whereas Prakriti is divisible and changeable in her manifested aspect (sambhuta). Before the beginning of creation, she remains dormant, undifferentiated, and unmanifested (asambhuta) in a Primal state. However, at the time of creation, she becomes active, illuminated by Brahman, and executes his will. In her manifested aspect, she becomes the material cause of creation, while he remains in the background as the efficient cause. In her unmanifested state, the triple gunas remain in equilibrium. In her manifested state, that balance is lost as they become active in the tattvas such as Mahat, Buddhi, egotism, elements, etc., resulting in a vast diversity of beings and objects. They all arise along with their states, forms, and modifications in the Field of Prakriti only. The Self remains as the witness, untouched, immutable, and indestructible. However, nothing will happen in the Field of Prakriti if he is not present.

Sloka 21

kārya kāraṇa kartṛtve hetuḥ prakṛtir ucyate
puruṣaḥ sukhaduḥkhānāṃ bhoktṛtve hetur ucyate 13.21

karya = action; karana = cause of action; kartrtve = the agent or producer of action; hetuh = reason, primary cause; prakrtih = Nature; ucyate = said to be; purusah = purusha; sukha = of happiness; duhkhanam = sorrow; bhoktrtve = enjoyment or experience; hetuh = the means; ucyate = is said to be.

With regard to the actions, the cause of actions (and) the producer of actions, Nature is said to be the primary source. With regard to the enjoyment or the experience of happiness and sorrow, Purusha is the primary cause. They arise from the organs or the tattvas in the body, which act as their cause (kārana).

Kārya primarily means actions, but is also used to mean effects since an action may be the effect of a cause or the cause of an effect. Kārana (with long a) means a cause, reason, or motive. If the word is read as karana (with short a), it means an action, instrument, organ, or agency. However, these meanings are often used interchangeably since an organ (karana) may cause (kārana) or produce actions. Hence, commentators tend to consider both meanings of kārana, and we have followed the same. Actions and effects (kārya) in this context refer to the movements and modifications arising from the body or in the body due to the activity of the gunas and the organs present in it. Since the body is the Field of Prakriti, where all actions happen, she is considered their producer and primary cause of all actions and dynamic states. Shankara interpreted the effect (kārya) as the body (kaya) and the cause (kārana) as the thirteen tattvas of Prakriti, which make up the body and act as its instruments (or organs) to produce causes and effects (kārana) in it. The agent of such actions and effects is the jiva, a temporary formation created by Prakriti with her tattvas in which the Self does not participate except as a witness. Although Shankara referred to 13 tattvas, the Samkhya School identifies 23, and the Shaiva traditions 36.

Each living being (jiva) is a combination of these two fundamental realities of Creation. The body is the sum of the tattvas and gunas and the causes, actions, and effects produced by them. As the agents or instruments of Prakriti, the tattvas produce actions propelled by the desires induced by the gunas. Purusha is their witness and enjoyer. The body with the organs, the tattvas, and all actions arising from them constitute the enjoyed. Prakriti is the actor, and Purusha is the spectator. The jivas are active and alive only when they are present together. Prakriti imparts to them their essential nature, movements, organs (karana), and liveliness, and the Self provides support, continuity, and consciousness. The name (nama), form (ākara), actions (kārya), modifications (vikāra), nature (svabhāvam), and the beingness (jivatvam) of each jiva arise from Prakriti due to the admixture of the gunas with the tattvas in different permutations and combinations and due to the actions and effects they produce. Thus, each jiva is a marvel of Prakriti created by her parts (tattvas), which are collectively mentioned here as the agencies (karana) or causes (kārana). Each living being is a playground of Prakriti's dynamic actions and effects (kāryas) witnessed by the Self, who resides in the body as its ultimate enjoyer (bhokta). In the sacrifice of life, the body of each jiva (bhakta) is the devotional offering (bhakti) for the Self, the enjoyer who resides in them. Due to the influence of Maya, all the actions, causes, effects, and modifications arising from these agencies create the delusion in the jivas that they are responsible for them and affected by them.

Sloka 22

puruṣaḥ prakṛtistho hi bhuṅkte prakṛtijān guṇān
kāraṇaṃ guṇasaṅgosya sadasadyonijanmasu

purusah = purusa, person, self; prakrti-sthah = established in Prakriti; hi = indeed; bhunkte = enjoys; prakrti-jan = arising, produced from Nature; gunan = gunas, modes; karanam = cause; guna-sangah = attachment with the qualities; asya = of his; sat-asat = good and evil; yoni = womb; janmasu = birth.

Indeed, established in Prakriti, Purusha enjoys the modes arising from Nature. His attachment to the modes is the cause of his birth in good and evil wombs.

Without Purusha, the Self, there is no liveliness, activity, movements, causes, or effects. Indeed, the real cause of all these is Purusha since Prakriti is a dependent aspect of him, and he is the ultimate cause of whatever actions she performs or the effects she produces. However, due to delusion and attachment, jivas enjoy the fruit of their actions, believing that they are responsible for them. Thereby, they incur karma and take birth in good and evil wombs according to their actions. According to the Bhagavadgita, Prakriti is a dependent aspect of the Supreme Lord. By herself, she has no dynamism or activity. All actions (kāryas), gunas, agencies, and causes (kāranas) remain latent in their seed form in her until they materialize in the presence of the Self. Prakriti is the source of all material manifestations, but Prakriti cannot manifest them without the Self. Their association or coming together is the key to all creation. The mortal world and all its beings and objects are products of these eternal principles. The sun is essential to sustaining life on Earth. Several biological, chemical, and physical processes happen on Earth because of him alone. Just as the earth depends upon the sun, Nature depends upon Purusha to sustain itself and perform its actions.

Purusha, the Self, is pure and independent. Yet, seated in Nature, he becomes bound to her modes and remains embodied in the jivas during their existence on earth. While remaining embodied, he develops an attachment to names and forms, and likes and dislikes that are induced by his gunas, and engages in desire-ridden actions. It results in karma and his rebirth in good and evil wombs. What holds the Self inside the body is the jiva's attachment to the modes of Nature and the desires that arise from them. They are responsible for the jivas' existence in samsara. In Hinduism, diverse opinions exist about the relationship between Purusha and Prakriti and their relative importance. The Bhagavadgita represents one such opinion. However, even that is interpreted differently by different scholars.

Sloka 23

upadraṣṭānumantā ca bhartā bhoktā maheśvaraḥ
paramātmeti cāpyukto dehesmin puruṣaḥ paraḥ

upadrasta = overseer, witness; anumanta = permitter; ca = and; bharta = supporter; bhokta = enjoyer; maha-isvarah = great lord; parama-atma =

supreme self; iti = thus; ca = and; api uktah = is described, spoken of; dehe = in the body; asmin = this; purusah = purusha; parah = highest, supreme.

The Overseer, Permitter, Supporter, Enjoyer, and Great Lord, described as the Supreme Self, is Purusha, the Highest in the body.

The Knower of the Field is the Overseer (updadrashta), the One who watches over the Field as its overlord. In Vedic terminology, the Brahman priest performs similar functions. He watches over the proceedings of complex sacrificial ceremonies silently as an overseer and passive witness without participating in them. Like him, the Purusha in a jiva watches over the actions of the organs of the mind and body as a passive witness. The mind and intelligence are the seers (drashta) who witness whatever happens in their field, while the Self is the overseer (upadrashta) who watches over them and their actions from a distance. As the Witness, he observes everything from within and without. However, untouched and unaffected by them or their actions and modes, he remains passive and indifferent. The mind, body, and senses are also witnesses in the Field, but they are subject to modifications and impurities. Since they lack self-illumination, they cannot be considered true knowers. Unlike them, the Self is the knower and overseer of the Field and remains above them, unchanged and unaffected by its modifications.

The Self is also the Permitter (anumanta) because he does not interfere with the lives and actions of the jivas and allows the karma and fate of each of them to unravel themselves. He lets Nature perform her functions as ordained. Nothing can happen without his permission. Therefore, whatever happens must be because he willfully allows that to happen. Although he witnesses the activities of the mind, body, and the tattvas in them, he does not obstruct or interfere with them. He remains passive in the Kshetra so Prakriti can perform her duties according to the prevailing modes. He supports the whole creation. Hence, he is the supporter (bharta) of all. The mind, body, world, and jivas cannot exist or perform their functions without his support or presence in them. They perform their duties for his sake only to manifest his will and ensure the order and regularity, and well-being of the jivas and the world. He is the enjoyer because he enjoys the fruit of all actions and sacrifices. Residing in the jivas as their embodied Self, he witnesses their pleasures and pains and enjoys the play of Prakriti. Seated in the Field of Prakriti as the Knower, he enjoys her company, just as Shiva enjoys the company of Parvathi or Vishnu, that of Lakshmi.

The great Lord (Maheshwara) is the Lord of all the lords of the earth, heaven, and other realms. He protects the gods and helps them in conflicts against the Asuras (demons). Even the gods, Brahma, Vishnu, and Shiva, are considered his manifestations only in their supreme aspect. Presiding over everything in the Field of Prakriti, he controls all with his inviolable will. The Knower of the Field is none other than you in your purest aspect, or that part of you that is not created by your mind and body, but the pure consciousness that exists beyond them in the deeper core of your being. That pure Self, which is the same in all, is the Purusha, the Cosmic Person in the body, the world, and the universe. According to Advaita, he is 'one and only.' The rest is a projection, reflection, superimposition, or illusion. According to the Dvaita, the Cosmic

Person in the body is eternally different from the One who presides over the whole creation as its Supreme Lord. He is Paramatma, the Lord of the Lords. The individual Self is Drshta (the seer), and the Supreme Self is Updadrasta (the overseer). They may share similar consciousness, but their duality is not an illusion but real and permanent.

Soka 24

ya evaṃ vetti puruṣaṃ prakṛtiṃ ca guṇaiḥ saha
sarvathā vartamānopi na sa bhūyobhijāyate

yah = he who; evam = thus; vetti = knows; purusam = purusa; prakrtim = prakriti, nature; ca = and; gunaih = gunas; saha = with; sarvatha = in all ways; vartamanah = in the present; api = even; na = not; sah = he; bhuyah = again; abhijayate = is born.

He who knows thus Purusha and Prakriti, along with the gunas, will not be born again, whatever may be his present (way of life).

Purusha is the Self. Prakriti is the body. Because of delusion and ignorance, beings cannot distinguish them within themselves and fall into the trap of identifying themselves, their names and forms, and the world with Prakriti. When they know the distinction between them, they become established in their pure nature and achieve liberation, irrespective of their current behavior and disposition, even if they have strayed from the path of Dharma. This is the essence of this verse. To teach Arjuna their distinction, Lord Krishna explained their distinguishing features. He said he was the Knower of the Field in all Fields. The body is the Field, consisting of tattvas and the triple gunas. It is subject to modifications such as desire, repulsion, happiness, sorrow, etc. The jiva, in his ignorant state, represents Prakriti or the Field.

The Self residing in him represents Purusha. Unlike the Field, the Purusha is eternal, indestructible, and free from modifications. It is the one to be known (jneyam). What keeps the jiva bound to samsara is its ignorance, delusion, and its failure to know the Self hidden in it. The jiva can overcome its ignorance and delusion through the right knowledge and become established in the Knower of the Field without duality and delusion. Lord Krishna also defined knowledge as the everlasting knowledge of the Self, its purpose, and the qualities (in verses 8-11) by which one could attain it. Any knowledge other than that, he said, was ignorance. From verses 14 to 23, he described Purusha's essential nature and qualities. This knowledge is thus useful for the Bhagavatas, who serve the Lord, or those who strive to attain liberation with unwavering devotion. Knowing the distinction between Purusha and Prakriti, cultivating the qualities he listed, and practicing exclusive devotion to him, as he suggested in Verse 11, one can overcome ignorance and delusion and attain the Supreme State of Brahman.

The jiva begins its state of existence in the mortal world with ignorance, egoism, desires, and other impurities. At this stage, a human being remains entirely under the control of Prakriti and her Maya and is bound to Samsara. When he realizes the distinction between Purusha and Prakriti or between the Self and his body and knows through insight and observation that the Purusha is the overseer, supporter, and enjoyer in the body, he renounces his physical nature and identity and withdraws into himself. With discernment and insight into the nature of reality, he sets himself on a new journey to achieve liberation from Prakriti and her tattvas and gunas and attains the Self. However, this knowledge regarding the distinction between them should arise from direct experience, not from the study of the scriptures or the teachings of a spiritual guru. Only then is liberation guaranteed. In the following two verses, Lord Krishna suggested how one may attain that knowledge through meditation, etc., and what other options are available for those who do not attain it.

Rebirth is inevitable for those who are attached to Prakriti, her tattvas, and modes, and seek fulfillment through desire-ridden actions. While it may temporarily help them find solace and comfort, it does not guarantee lasting peace or liberation. Indeed, it may even prolong their suffering and delay their liberation. The yogi who discerns the distinction between the Self and the body through self-realization is not deluded again. As Shankaracharya stated, he dissolves his ignorance (avidya) with knowledge (vidya), attains Brahman, and becomes Brahman. His deeds perish without bearing fruit as he practices exclusive devotion, performs selfless actions (nishkama karma), and attains freedom from karma (naishkarmya siddhi). As his ignorance is burnt in the fire of knowledge, and his nature (Prakriti), along with the tattvas and gunas, is purified through exclusive devotion or devotional contemplation, he attains samsiddhi or samadhi (sameness) and freedom from death and rebirth.

Sloka 25

dhyānenātmani paśyanti kecid ātmānam ātmanā
anye sāṃkhyena yogena karmayogena cāpare

dhyanena = by meditation; atmani = in oneself; pasyanti = see; kecit = some; atmanam = the Self; atmana = by oneself; anye = others; sankhyena = by Sankhya; yogena = yoga; karma-yogena = by karma yoga; ca = and; apare = others.

Some see the Self in oneself by oneself by meditation, others by Samkhya Yoga, and some others by Karma yoga.

To escape from Samsara, one must directly see the Self as the Knower of the Field and know the distinction between them. Direct knowledge (pratyaksha anubhava) of the Self may arise from exclusive devotion (bhakti), contemplation (dhyana), knowledge of Purusha and Prakriti (samkhya), selfless actions (karma-sannyasa yoga), or simple devotion. The first three are mentioned in this verse, and the last in the next. Through any of these approaches, a yogi may attain a direct vision (darshana) of the Self within himself and become liberated.

In the previous chapter (12.12), Lord Krishna said that meditation (dhyana) was better than knowledge. Through dhyana only, one gains direct knowledge and insight into the nature of things. The Yogasutras defines dhyana as thinking or meditating on anything towards which the mind is naturally drawn (1.39). It further declares that through meditation, one can overcome the afflictions of the mind (klesas) and stabilize it (2.11). Dhyana means letting the mind (dhi) travel (yana) freely or in the desired or intended direction. In Yoga, it is the practice of meditating with a purpose. The purpose is usually to stabilize the mind and keep it focused on the object of our concentration. Some people choose an image, a symbol, or a material object for meditation and concentration. Adept yogis meditate upon the Self. Whatever the method is, in dhyana, one comes closest to the Self as the witness or observer.

While many meditation techniques are available, the most classical one is concentrated meditation on an object of attention, withdrawing the mind and the senses into oneself. Patanjali defines meditation as one-pointedness (eka tanata) of the mind upon a single object. When meditation becomes intense, and the mind stops reflecting, letting the object of meditation alone shine, one enters the state of self-absorption (samadhi). When meditation is practiced upon the Self and reaches its ultimate perfection, the object of meditation, the Self, alone remains, reflecting its effulgence in the pure consciousness (suddha citta), while the Field (the body) with its modifications disappears from the field of awareness leaving the Self to abide in its eternal, indestructible, pure nature.

Seeing the Self in oneself by oneself (atmani atmanam) means seeing the Self directly within oneself or one's consciousness through meditation and devotion. It is seeing the Self as distinct from the body and realizing that it is independent, has its own radiance and existence, and is untainted and unaffected by the mind or body. Although we keep saying "one sees the Self," it is metaphorical. The truth is one cannot see the Self with the senses or the mind, but can intuit or experience it directly as oneself without duality or the aid of any external agent. That experience leaves its impression on the internal organ and is subsequently recollected by the seer with conviction. By that realization, recollection, discernment, or direct knowledge, the yogi remains established in the Self, identifying himself with it without doubt or delusion.

Thus, meditation is the best means to realize the Self and attain liberation. However, you cannot practice meditation effectively without purifying the mind and body and suppressing the gunas. For that, one has to practice self-restraint (yamas), discipline (niyamas), breath control (pranayama), and sense-withdrawal (pratyahara). Concentration and meditation lead to purification, and the prolonged practice of samyama (meditation with resolve) burns away the latent impressions of past lives and dissolves the mind in self-absorption. Hence, Classical Yoga is viewed as a holistic system in which all the limbs are essential to achieve purification and perfection. Meditation cannot be practiced in isolation without corresponding improvement in other areas. It is easier to practice samyama when one is free from desires and attachments and the mind is stabilized in devotional contemplation. Meditation becomes natural for those who overcome impurities and resolve the gunas. Yuktas or dhiras exemplify it.

However, meditation is not the only means to realize the Self or the distinction between Purusha and Prakriti within oneself. Everyone is not suited to practice it due to the differences in their modes and essential nature. For them, Lord Krishna suggested samkhya yoga and karma yoga. In the context of the Bhagavadgita, samkhya yoga refers to theistic Samkhya or the yoga of divine knowledge. It is not the same as the classical Samkhya of Kapila, but they share many similarities. In this yoga, one studies the scriptures or receives instruction from an enlightened teacher to acquire the right knowledge (vidya) and contemplates that knowledge to become absorbed in the Self and experience it directly. In classical Samkhya yoga as well, meditation is recommended as an essential practice to know the Self. Indeed, it is the heart of many spiritual practices. One may also pursue knowledge and practice meditation with exclusive devotion. In Ashtanga Yoga, Patanjali called it devotion to Isvara (isvara paridhana) and suggested that one should practice it by meditating on Aum. By knowing the truth regarding the Self (Purusha) and the not-self (Prakriti) through such means, the yogi becomes liberated on this path.

The third approach Lord Krishna suggested is karma yoga, or, more appropriately, karma-sannyasa yoga, which we have already discussed. On this path, householders wishing to attain liberation perform their duties without desiring their fruit and offer it to the Lord. By renouncing the fruit of karma and giving it to the Lord, they are absolved of all karma arising from their actions. This approach is best suited for those not inclined to acquire knowledge or practice renunciation but want to stay with their families and perform their obligatory duties to serve God without desiring their fruit. Karma-sannyasa is difficult to practice but equally effective in liberating people from samsara.

The three methods suggested in this verse are equally effective. They become even more effective when combined with exclusive devotion. We cannot say which of them is superior since their efficacy and suitability depend upon the nature of those who practice it. For example, contemplative practices (atma-samyama yoga) are ideal for those who are introverted and prefer to live in solitary places or avoid the company of worldly people; samkhya yoga is better suited for those who are curious and inquisitive and prefer to use knowledge and reason to ascertain truths, and karma yoga is appropriate for those who are disinterested in contemplation or knowledge but want to serve the Lord and practice devotion through dutiful and virtuous living.

Sloka 26

anye tv evam ajānantaḥ śrutvānyebhya upāsate
tepi cātitaranty eva mṛtyuṃ śrutiparāyaṇāḥ

anye = others; tu = however, but; evam = thus; ajanantah = without knowing, not knowing; srutva = by hearing; anyebhyah = from others; upasate = worship; te = they; api = also; ca = and; atitaranti = go beyond, transcend, overcome; eva = surely; mrtyum = death; sruti-parayanah = constantly reciting or hearing.

Others, however, who do not know thus, may worship Me by hearing (about Me) from others. They will surely go beyond death by constantly hearing the Lord's words, knowledge, or glories.

Knowledge, meditation, and karma-sannyasa yoga are effective in knowing Brahman or the Purusha in the body and attaining oneness. However, devotees may also achieve liberation by cultivating devotion and worshiping him through the constant practice of hearing (sravanam) about him, his words, glories, manifestations, teachings, etc., from others. Many devotees practice it by attending religious discourses or listening to the speeches of spiritual masters and religious teachers. This is especially useful for those who do not have opportunities to study scriptures, live amidst spiritual people, or practice meditation, yoga, etc. Sruti means hearing, any knowledge acquired through hearing, or any sacred text such as the Vedas, which are believed to have been rendered into verbal form after hearing them from Brahma.

Previously, Lord Krishna suggested that in whichever way people worshipped him, he would stabilize their faith in that. According to this verse, if it is not possible to acquire religious or spiritual knowledge directly by studying the scriptures or taking initiation from a guru, one can acquire it and cultivate devotion by listening to those who possess that knowledge. Upasana means paying respect, homage, or adoration by sitting nearby. It may involve ritual worship, devotional service, contemplative practice, and other similar methods to cultivate exclusive devotion. In this approach, the devotee engages his mind and body to express his devotion and loyalty and opens himself to his divine grace. This method of worship is beneficial to those who are, by nature, ignorant and deluded and depend upon the knowledge, authority, and wisdom of others to pursue liberation.

In this approach, Lord Krishna specifically suggested shruti-parayana, the repeated listening, recitation, or remembrance of the Vedas or any sacred text. He also said that they would 'surely' go beyond death. It may mean that liberation is guaranteed for them only after death, not when they are alive. In the eighth chapter (8.6), he said that in whatever state of mind or with whatever thoughts one departed from the body at the time of death, one would attain that. Therefore, by offering his mind and intelligence to the Lord, constantly thinking of him or hearing about him from others, and saturating his mind with his thoughts, a yogi will surely attain the transcendental Supreme Purusha after death. Although he specifically mentioned Sruti (the Vedas) for the purpose, devotees may choose any standard scripture, including the Bhagavadgita. The Vedas are suggested because they are held in the highest esteem as the most reliable source of divine knowledge. However, they are voluminous, difficult to understand, and not easily accessible to everyone. Teachers endowed with their knowledge are also rare. Hence, one may choose any sacred scripture or teaching recommended by their teachers for the purpose and continue their practice. In the subsequent three verses, Lord Krishna explains why the knowledge of Purusha and Prakriti is essential for liberation and what purpose it serves.

Sloka 27

yāvat saṃjāyate kiṃcit sattvaṃ sthāvarajaṅgamam
kṣetrakṣetrajñasaṃyogāt tad viddhi bharatarṣabha

yavat = whatever; sanjayate = takes birth; kincit = any; sattvam = living being, existence; sthavara = unmoving; jangamam = moving; ksetra = the field; ksetra-jna = knower of the field; samyogat = union; tat viddhi = know that; bharata-rsabha = O chief among the Bharatas.

Whatever comes into existence, moving or unmoving, know that it is due to the union between the Field and the Knower of the Field, O the mighty among the Bharatas.

Every living being, without exception, is a combination of spirit and matter, Purusha and Prakriti. Nature, of which matter is a part, is subject to modifications while the Self remains eternally constant and unchangeable. The Self is the Knower or the subject, and the Field is the known or the object. Jiva, the being, is the fruit of this union, and none, including gods, are free from this union. The gods (*devas*) may not possess gross bodies, but they do possess subtle bodies of pure *sattva*, because of which they radiate the light of the Self and wield supernatural powers.

The higher the beings in the cosmic hierarchy, the greater their ability to control Nature and its modifications. Because of their power and control over Prakriti and her tattvas, divinities can manipulate causes and effects and make things happen, alter reality, or fulfill our wishes. They can produce different results from existing causes or initiate new events, such as rain falling or storms receding. Thus, what we consider miracles are divine interventions or effects manifested differently or randomly from their causes by the divinities of higher realms.

Purusha and Prakriti represent the fundamental duality of creation. They have little in common. Both are eternal and indestructible. Life exists and is possible because of them. Their union results in birth and disunion in death. Their permanent separation or dissociation in a jiva leads to liberation. Although Purusha is seated in Prakriti, he remains detached, independent, and untouched. Even though they coexist in the jivas, they remain disconnected and separate without any contact (samyoga) between them. Shankara interpreted their relationship in the jivas as an illusion arising from mutual superimposition (adhyasa), like the union between a snake and a rope or silver and the mother of pearl when we mistake the latter for the former. In the jivas, Prakriti and her higher faculties remain in control, and the Self remains passive and hidden, whereby beings suffer from delusion and mistake the body (not-self) as the Self and the Self as nonexistent. The illusion of being a physical entity arises in the jivas because of the impurities arising from Maya. Although beings seem to be in control of themselves and their destinies, they are not truly independent or free. They are bound to their delusion, desires, karma, and fate. They become aware of their divine nature only when they overcome delusion with the right knowledge and cultivate purity and discernment. Their association with Prakriti ends only when they attain liberation and depart from the body.

Sloka 28

samaṃ sarveṣu bhūteṣu tiṣṭhantaṃ parameśvaram
vinaśyatsv avinaśyantaṃ yaḥ paśyati sa paśyati

samam = equally; sarvesu = in all; bhutesu = living beings; tisthan-tam = established, ensconced; parama-isvaram = the Supreme Lord; vinasyatsu = in the destructible; avinasyantam = indestructible; yah = who; pasyati = sees; sah = he; pasyati = sees really.

He who sees the Supreme Lord established in all living beings equally as the Indestructible in the destructible, he sees really.

In verse 24, Lord Krishna said that those who know Purusha and Prakriti, along with the gunas, are not born again, irrespective of their present condition or way of life. In the subsequent two verses, he said the two could be known through dhyana, samkhya, karma, or bhakti yogas. In this, he stated that those who see the Self in themselves and all living beings as the indestructible in the destructible (matter, the body, or the jivas) have the right knowledge and discernment. Those who see him situated in all develop sameness towards all. They extend that vision and reverence and feel connected to all, seeing him in everything and feeling devotion to him. If we see the Purusha in all and become established in the vision of sameness and oneness, our attitude towards the world and other beings undergo a fundamental transformation. We accept all creation as an integral and important part of God's creation.

Animals, insects, etc., may not possess the same intelligence as we do, but that does not make them any less important than us. Life in all its forms is important for the existence of life itself on this planet. They are but his numerous forms and should be treated as such. It is what seeing unity in diversity really means. It is seeing the Purusha in all, not notionally, speculatively, or superficially, but as one sees oneself or an image of the Lord in a temple or sacred place, with knowledge and conviction and free from doubt. Deluded people see the diversity in creation. They mistake their bodies for themselves. Unlike them, the wise one sees with clarity the distinction between themselves and their bodies. They see the imperishable Self hidden in the bodies and supporting the whole creation. Thus, seeing them both, knowing their difference with direct awareness, and feeling connected to the Self in them, they remain free from delusion and wrong attribution (adhyaropa). Neither from studying nor from learning nor from hearing from others, but through a direct experience (pratyaksha anubhava) of oneness or seeing the Self in them, they attain this state.

Sameness, universal friendliness, compassion, and nonviolence are the hallmarks of devotees and adept yogis who see the Self in all and feel connected to them. They extend their devotion equally to all things in creation and reflect it in their thinking, attitude, conduct, and actions. Although detached from everything, they remain connected to the Lord hidden in them and extend the same reverential humility towards them. Their relationship is not with them, with the things they possess, or with the Prakriti that embodies them, but with the Purusha only as they see his universal presence and are drawn to him. Thus, as this verse affirms, those who discern the indestructible Self as residing in the destructible not-self see really and are forever freed from delusion and ignorance.

Sloka 29

samaṃ paśyan hi sarvatra samavasthitam īśvaram
na hinasty ātmanātmānaṃ tato yāti parāṃ gatim

samam = equally; pasyan = seeing; hi = indeed; sarvatra = everywhere; samavasthitam = established alike or similarly; isvaram = the Lord; na = not; hinasti = harm or injure; atmana = by the self; atmanam = the Self; tatah = therefore; yati = attains, goes; param = the highest; gatim = goal.

Indeed, equally seeing the Lord, who is established alike everywhere, he does not harm the Self by the Self. Therefore, he attains the Highest Goal.

The highest goal here may mean liberation, sameness, or nonviolence. Sameness is oneness only. It is the highest perfection and goal of yoga. Nonviolence is considered the highest virtue and the culmination of utmost purity. Ignorant people harm themselves and others by their desire-driven and deluded actions, incurring sinful karma and delaying their liberation. They remain bound to the cycle of births and deaths and prolong their suffering. This is harming the Self by the Self. Shankara said that ignorant people are slayers of the Self. They harm themselves with their egoism, ignorance, desires, and delusion. Those who see the Self in all overcome such impurities. Seeing the Self in themselves and others and knowing that the Self is the same in all and untainted by Prakriti, they attain oneness and sameness. They also attain perfection in nonviolence. Seeing the Self in all, knowing that the same Lord is seated in all as the witness and the enjoyer, and feeling connected to them through oneness, they do not wish to harm or disturb anyone. They also empathize with others. Seeing their suffering in their suffering and feeling compassion for them, they serve others with compassion. Whoever perceives the Self in all and the world as a divine manifestation treats others with equanimity and sameness. He eschews all forms of violence. The world may be filled with impurities, but it is a creation of the Lord and is his abode. For the enlightened ones who see the Self in all, it is a sacred ground and temple of God. Wherever they go and whatever they see, they find themselves in his company and extend the same love and reverence to others without judgment, choice, or discrimination. Since they restrain their desires and modes and practice sameness, nonviolence becomes their natural state and way of life. They practice it effortlessly. In many yogic traditions, including Classical Yoga, nonviolence is considered the highest virtue. All other virtues lead to it only. It is said that in the presence of those who practice nonviolence, one does not think of hurting or harming anyone, and even the most dangerous animals remain peaceful and gentle.

Sloka 30

prakṛtyaiva ca karmāṇi kriyamāṇāni sarvaśaḥ
yaḥ paśyati tathātmānam akartāraṃ sa paśyati

prakrtya = by Nature; eva = alone; ca = and; karmani = actions; kriyamanani = being done; sarvasah = in all respects; yah = he who; pasyati = sees; tatha = and; atmanam = the Self; akartaram = non-doer; sah = he; pasyati = sees.

He who sees that actions are performed by Prakriti only in all respects and the Self is the non-doer, he (truly) sees.

Here, seeing is not seeing physically but seeing with knowledge and insight into the nature of actions, their causes, and effects. It means seeing beyond the apparent reality and the veil of delusion and making sense of them and their ultimate cause with discernment. The wise ones know that all actions arise from Prakriti or the body and its modes and tattvas, and the Self does not participate in them. Therefore, they do not become involved or entangled with them. The deluded human attributes actions to himself as the doer (karta) and incurs sinful karma. Although the Self and Prakriti are together in each jiva, they exist as separate entities without any relationship or connection. The Self does not participate in the actions of Prakriti or become involved with her modifications. He remains a passive witness. He is the akarta, the non-doer, and the body is the karta or the doer. In verse 21, Lord Krishna already stated that in the jivas, Nature is the cause of actions, the means of actions, and the agent of actions, and Purusha is the cause of enjoyment only. Established in the Field, he enjoys the modes and modifications arising from Prakriti without participating in them. Yogis who understand this withdraw from their minds and bodies and remain established in the Self. Seeing the same Self residing in all, they do not harm themselves or others through desire-ridden action. Lord Krishna reiterated the same idea in the fifth chapter (5.14), stating that he does not create doership or actions and has no attachment to the fruit of actions. All actions arise from Prakriti only.

These statements can be confusing when we read the descriptions of Isvara as the Creator or the Supreme Lord of all creation. The Self in the jivas should not be confused with the Supreme Self in creation. We do not know with certainty whether they are the same or different. However, we know that functionally, they are different and perform different roles in creation. The Self in the jivas is passive, but the Supreme Self is the Lord and controller of all. According to the Bhagavadgita and many schools of Hinduism, as the Isvara, he is the Lord, source, and controller of all, including Prakriti. She is his dependent aspect and acts according to his will. The Vedas confirm it. They distinguish between the Unmanifested Brahman or the pure Self in his absolute state and the Manifested Brahman or the Supreme Being in his role as the Creator and Upholder of all. The Pure Self is the universal witness. He is not a being per se but represents the highest, absolute, supreme reality and pure consciousness, which is also the state of the Self in the body. He does not engage in any actions but is the center and support of all. All actions arise from the manifested Prakriti in Isvara according to his will. Endowed with the diverse Shaktis, potencies, and possibilities, he acts as the Lord and controller of all creation.

As the Supreme Lord of all, Isvara is responsible for creation, preservation, destruction, delusion, bondage, and liberation. The jivas are modeled on him only, although in them, he remains passive. Each of them is a combination of Purusha and Prakriti. Their existence arises from the former, but their actions from the latter. However, unlike him, who controls and directs his nature, the jivas remain under the control of Prakriti (who in turn remains under the control of Isvara) until they attain liberation. The union of Purusha and Prakriti in Isvara is symbolically well represented by Ardhanariswara, a supreme manifestation of Shiva, who is half-male and half-female. Due to their relationship at the highest level, almost all the manifestations of the Supreme Lord in the Hindu pantheon have different Shaktis serving them in their duties and actions as their companions. However, even in the case of Isvara, all actions arise in the field of Prakriti only according to his will. By remaining disinterested and indifferent and performing his duties without desires and attachments, he exemplifies inaction in action (akarma in karma) and produces no consequences for himself.

Sloka 31

yadā bhūtapṛthagbhāvam ekastham anupaśyati
tata eva ca vistāraṃ brahma saṃpadyate tadā

yada = when; bhuta = living beings; prthak-bhavam = diversity, diverse existence; eka-stham = centered, situated or rooted in one; anupasyati = discerns with certainty; tatah = from there or that; eva = also; ca = and; vistaram = manifested; brahma = Brahman; sampadyate = attains; tada = then.

When one discerns with certainty that the diverse existences of all living beings are centered in One and spread out from that One only, then one attains Brahman.

The Self is the hub of all creation, described in the Svetasvatara Upanishad as the Wheel of Brahman. Everything in the creation arises and subsides in Brahman and is connected to the rest by its connection with Brahman. The Brihadaranyaka Upanishad aptly describes him as the spider (Death) and creation as the web he weaves to keep the beings bound to it. The wise ones see Brahman as the center and circumference of the whole creation. They see unity in the diversity of creation. Prakriti may appear to be a distinct entity in charge of creation, but she is his dependent aspect and follows his will. The deluded ones do not perceive that unity or his lordship. They only see the diversity of the apparent reality and become deluded and distracted. They identify themselves with their names and forms and ignore their spiritual nature and their hidden connection with the Supreme Lord. Due to the impurities of egoism (anavatvam), attachments (pasas), and delusion (moha), they see themselves as separate from others and engage in selfish and desire-ridden actions. Those who see that all existence is centered in Brahman, arises from Brahman, and dissolves in Brahman are not deluded and escape from samsara.

Brahman represents the eternal constant. He is imperceptible. The jivas mistake His creation for Him and become deluded, just as they mistake their bodies and physical identities (or names and forms) for the Self in them. They see actions but not their true cause, and assume ownership and doership. As Lord Krishna stated before, all actions in the jivas arise in the Field of Prakriti only. The Self (Kshetrajna) does not participate in them. However, in creation, Isvara is at the center of the whole creation. Prakriti is his dependent reality. Without his presence, she cannot perform actions in the jivas or engage in creation. Just as all the tattvas in the jivas become active and spread out from the Self like the sun's rays, the whole creation spreads out from Brahman as his effulgence, projection, or energy field. It arises and subsides in him, just like the ocean waves or the lotus flowers in a pond. All existence is established in him only. He pervades, envelops, and supports it from within and without. Nothing exists beyond him, external to him, or without him. As the Upanishads declare, the sky, the earth, the heavens, the sun and the moon, the five elements, the aspects of Nature, gods, demons, humans, and the rest of the beings arise from Brahman only, and in the end, are withdrawn by him into himself only.

Sloka 32

anāditvān nirguṇatvāt paramātmāyam avyayaḥ
śarīrasthopi kaunteya na karoti na lipyate

anaditvat = because without beginning; nirgunatvat = because without modes or gunas; parama = supreme; atma = Self; ayam = this; avyayah = indestructible, inexhaustible; sarira-sthah = situated in the body; api = although; kaunteya = O son of Kunti; na = not; karoti = does, perform; na = not; lipyate = touched or affected.

Because he is without a beginning and without gunas, this Supreme Self is indestructible. O son of Kunti, although he is present in the body, he does not act and is not tainted.

In the Jivas, Brahman is without a beginning, without modes, indestructible, passive, and untouched by the body. These attributes pertain to the Self in the body (atma), not the Supreme Lord (Paramatma), who rules the whole creation as its Creator and Controller. We will not debate whether they are different, the same, or notionally different. We leave that to other scholars. We presume that the same Self performs different functions in creation in different roles. Brahman is without a beginning because He is uncreated or unborn. He is eternally self-existent (Svayambhu). Therefore, the question of his beginning or end does not arise. He is also free from the triple modes (sattva, rajas, and tamas), their influence, and the modifications they induce. He is the Lord of all, including Prakriti and her modes, but in the body of a jiva, as the Self, he remains passive and untouched by Prakriti.

The Vedas reaffirm the same and validate the truths which are mentioned here. They state that Brahman is imperishable (aksharam), inexhaustible (avyayam), and without a beginning (adi) and an end (antam). What holds good for Brahman also holds good for the individual Self since they are essentially the same, except for the one difference mentioned before. In the jivas, the triple gunas are responsible for desires and desire-ridden actions and the modifications arising from them, such as karma, bondage, birth, aging, sickness, death, etc. Brahman is devoid of them and does not participate in any of the actions they induce. Therefore, he is untouched by them. Although he is established in the body, he is neither the cause nor the effect of anything that happens to it or in it. Hence, he is also free from karma. All actions in the jivas arise from Prakriti only. The Self exists in them as the sole witness (kevala). This knowledge is useful to become firmly established in the Self and practice detachment towards the mind, the body, and all material things.

Sloka 33

yathā sarvagataṃ saukṣmyād ākāśaṃ nopalipyate
sarvatrāvasthito dehe tathātmā nopalipyate

yatha = as; sarva-gatam = all-pervading; sauksmyat = because of subtlety; akasam = space, sky; na = not; upalipyate = touched, tained; sarvatra = everywhere; avasthitah = present, situated; dehe = in the body; tatha = similarly; atma = the Self; na = does not; upalipyate = touched, entangled.

Just as the all-pervading space is not touched or tainted because of its subtlety, so is the Self, which is present everywhere in the body, is not touched or tainted.

Just as Purusha and Prakriti in the creation, the Self (Kshetrajna) and the Body (Kshetra) in each jiva represent opposite realities. Although they are equally vital for the jivas' existence and the jivas are born from their union, no physical or spatial relationship or contact exists between them. The Self absorbs nothing from the body, and the body gains nothing from the Self, physically or otherwise. Just as space is untouched by the impurities of clouds or the earth that float in it, the Self is untouched by the impurities of the mind and body. Just as space (akasa) is imperceptible to our minds and senses, the Self in the body is also imperceptible. Because of his subtlety, he is unknown and imperceptible to the jiva. Also, he has no relationship with the body where he dwells and is unaffected by the body's actions, movements, desires, or attachments. In other words, the Self is eternally the same, whether he is free or associated with Prakriti or is present in a tiny organism, a human, or a celestial being. Since he is untainted by their actions, he remains pure and blemishless, whether he is embodied in a sinner or a pious person. The sins of the jivas do not accrue to him. The jiva's actions may prolong his existence in samsara, but the jiva cannot cause him any harm since he remains the same when bound or free. The suffering or the bondage is for the minds and bodies of the jivas, but not for the Self. He is eternally blissful, self-absorbed, self-existent, and indestructible.

Sloka 34

yathā prakāśayaty ekaḥ kṛtsnaṃ lokam imaṃ raviḥ
kṣetraṃ kṣetrī tathā kṛtsnaṃ prakāśayati bhārata

yatha = just as; prakasayati = illuminates; ekah = one, single; krtsnam = the whole; lokam = world; imam = this; ravih = the sun; ksetram = the field; ksetri = the lord of the field; tatha = similarly; krtsnam = all; prakasayati = illuminates; bharata = O descendent of Bharata.

Just as the one sun illuminates the whole world, so does the Lord of the Field illuminate the Field, O descendent of Bharata.

Brahman is self-illuminated. Prakriti has no illumination of her own. The tattvas and organs in the body receive their illumination from the Self only. The Self illuminates them according to their modes and purity. It is the brightest in the pure beings and great souls (mahatmas), but the dimmest in the ignorant, deluded, and sinful souls. Just like the body, the Supreme Lord, who controls all, illuminates the whole creation. The Vedas compare Brahman to the sun physically and symbolically. They state that his immortal world is located in the sun. Upon liberation, liberated souls travel to his world by the path of the gods (devayana), never to return. Just as the sun illuminates all the planets and beings, Brahman illuminates all. Just as the sun is untouched by darkness, the Self in the body is untouched by darkness or impurities. The Self is described in this verse as Kshetri, meaning the occupier or owner of the field. The Self may not be the owner, since ownership denotes control, but is surely the indweller. Kshetrajna, the Knower of the Field, is more appropriate since he is the all-knowing (sarvajna) and all-seeing witness of the Field. The Self does not radiate physical illumination. Its illumination is also imperceptible to the senses. In this context, illumination (prakasa) means liveliness, vitality, sentience, or awareness (chaitanyam). In the body, it becomes reflected as dynamism, knowledge, awareness, intelligence, or consciousness. The body is essentially a field of impurities with no self-illumination. Liberation happens only when the mind and the body are purified, and the radiance of the Self illuminates the jiva without any hindrance.

Sloka 35

kṣetrakṣetrajñayor evam antaraṃ jñānacakṣuṣā
bhūtaprakṛtimokṣaṃ ca ye vidur yānti te param

ksetra = of the field; ksetra-jnayoh = of the knower of the field; evam = thus; antaram = difference; jnana-caksusa = through the eye of knowledge or wisdom; bhuta = living beings; prakrti =Nature; moksam = liberation; ca = and; ye = those who; viduh = know; yanti = go; te = they; param = Supreme.

Those who know thus through the eye of knowledge the difference between the Field and the Knower of the Field and the liberation of beings from Prakriti, they go to the Supreme.

With the knowledge of Purusha and Prakriti, devotees can cultivate discernment and avoid the trap of Maya, which keeps people bound to the mortal world. Prakriti is responsible for desires, attraction, aversion, attachments, and the happiness and sorrow that arise from them. She is the cause, source, means, and agent of all actions and modifications. The Purusha is self-luminous, pure, the Self of all, free from modifications, all-pervading, without a beginning and an end, neither being nor non-being, undivided, fixed, and devoid of actions and senses. He is the enjoyer, overseer, permitter, and the Great Lord, who does not participate in the actions and modifications of Prakriti and remains pure even while bound to samsara and the Field of

Prakriti. In verse 19, Lord Krishna already said that by knowing this knowledge, his devotees would be qualified to attain his state (madbhava).

The immediate benefit of this knowledge is knowing the distinction between the body and the Self, or the not-self and the Self, and overcoming the delusion that the body is the real Self. Endowed with that knowledge and discernment, a yogi knows where to focus his attention and spend his energies to escape from the cycle of births and deaths. He realizes that he can control his restless mind and body and experience peace and equanimity, freeing himself from the influence of the gunas. He gives up desires and attachments, practices detachment and renunciation towards his mind and body and all worldly things, and seeing that the same Lord is situated in all, he does not harm others by his words or actions. As Lord Krishna suggested in verses 26 and 27, devotees can surely transcend death through dhyana, jnana, or karma yogas, by learning about him from the Vedas and worshipping him with devotion. Thus, the knowledge of Purusha and Prakriti helps his devotees attain the highest goal. With that knowledge, they can overcome the fear of death (knowing that the Self is immortal) and transition from darkness to light, untruth to truth, and death to immortality. As the last part of this verse implies, the knowledge may not grant them immediate liberation when they are alive. However, they will surely go to the immortal world of Brahman upon departing from here.

Conclusion

iti srīmadbhāgavadgītāsupanisatsu brahmavidyāyām yogasāstre srikrisnārjunasamvāde kṣetrakṣetrajñavibhāgayogo nāma trayodaśo 'dhyayah.

iti = thus; srīmadbhāgavadgītā = in the sacred Bhagavadgita; upanisatsu = in the Upanishad; brahmavidyāyām = the knowledge of the absolute Brahman; yogasāstre = the scripture of yoga; srikrisnārjunasamvāde = the dialogue between Sri Krishna and Arjuna; kṣetrakṣetrajñavibhāgayogo nāma = by name the yoga of the distinction between the Field and the Knower of the Field; trayodasah = thirteen; adhyayah = chapter.

Thus ends the thirteenth chapter, named Kshetra Kshetrajna Vibhāga Yoga (the Yoga of the Distinction Between the Field and the Knower of the Field) in the Upanishad of the divine Bhagavadgita, the knowledge of the Absolute, a treatise on Yoga, and the debate between Arjuna and Lord Krishna.

14 – Gunatraya Vibhāga Yoga

The Yoga of the Division of the Triple Gunas

Sloka 1

paraṃ bhūyaḥ pravakṣyāmi jñānānāṃ jñānamuttamam
yaj jñātvā munayaḥ sarve parāṃ siddhim ito gatāḥ

sri-bhagavan uvaca = the Supreme Lord said; param = supreme; bhuyah = again; pravaksyami = I shall speak; jnananam = of all types of knowledge; jnanam = knowledge; uttamam = superior, the best; yat = which; jnatva = knowing; munayah = the silent ones; sarve = all; param = the highest; siddhim = attaining; itah = here; gatah = departed, gone.

The Supreme Lord said, "I shall speak again about the supreme knowledge, the best of all types of knowledge, knowing which the silent ones attained the highest perfection when they departed from here.

As the title of this chapter suggests, this chapter is about the distinction between the triple modes and the actions and nature they induce in the jivas according to their predominance. It is the best (uttama) knowledge because by knowing them and how they induce desires and desire-ridden actions, one can overcome them and attain purity, which is essential for attaining liberation. Lord Krishna already spoke about it in the second chapter, stating that the Vedas are about the triple gunas. In the third chapter, he said that all actions arise from the gunas, but deluded by the ego, the ignorant one would think he is the doer. In the seventh chapter, he said the triple modes would arise from him only, but he would not be in them. Deluded by them, he said, people would not know him as the inexhaustible Self. In the previous chapter, distinguishing between Purusha and Prakriti, he suggested that all actions would arise from Prakriti only in which the Self would not participate or cause them to happen. Hence, in this verse, he said that he would speak about them again (bhuya). He also said that the silent seers (munis) attained liberation by knowing them. As he said, the gunas delude beings and prevent them from knowing the Self. Therefore, by knowing them and their influence, the Munis overcome their delusion, establish their minds in the Self, and attain the highest perfection, which is sameness and freedom from karma and rebirth. Munis are a special category of ascetics who practice silence of the highest kind. They silence not only their minds and senses but also their modes and, thereby, their desires and attachments. Withdrawing from their minds and bodies, overcoming impurities, and remaining established in the Self, they exemplify inaction in action (naishkarmya siddhi) and sameness. The last line suggests that they attain siddhi (perfection) only when they depart from this world.

Sloka 2

idaṃ jñānam upāśritya mama sādharmyam āgatāḥ
sargepi nopajāyante pralaye na vyathanti ca

idam = this; jnanam = knowledge; upasritya = taking refuge, following; mama = My; sadharmyam = essential nature, state; agatah = attain; sarge api = even during creation; na = never; upajayante = reborn; pralaye = during dissolution; na = not; vyathanti = suffer; ca = and.

By taking refuge in this knowledge, those who attain My essential Nature are not reborn during creation and do not suffer during the dissolution of the worlds.

Liberated souls have neither birth nor death. However, to reach that stage, a yukta has to excel in self-control and exclusive devotion. Transcending his lower nature, which is influenced by the triple gunas, he has to become established in the higher nature whose essence is pure consciousness and which is free from Prakriti and the triple gunas. Lord Krishna already spoke about the two types of nature and stressed the importance of overcoming the lower one to abide in the higher. To become firmly established in it, devotees must acquire the knowledge of the Self through study or by learning from a teacher and engage their minds in its inquiry and contemplation. Knowledge of the transcendental Self is central to achieving liberation. Once a bound soul (baddha) is freed from the hold of Nature, it is never subject to delusion or rebirth. This has been stated in several scriptures and is repeated here.

In this verse, Lord Krishna clearly said that the liberated souls survive the dissolution of the creation without suffering. It implies that they do not dissolve in the Supreme Self upon liberation but continue their existence as divine entities, untouched by the cyclical events of creation and dissolution. However, one may also conclude that since they become dissolved in him and cease to exist as separate entities, they do not have to face the same predicament as the bound souls during the end times. According to Hindu theories of creation, during the dissolution of the world, Brahman (Isvara) withdraws all into himself, including the divinities. The bound souls experience great suffering during this period as they witness the cataclysmic events and perish in a violent conflagration. As the night of Brahma approaches, both the liberated souls and bound souls go into a temporary resting mode while Brahma himself falls into a deep sleep. Prakriti becomes unmanifested (asambhuta) as she is withdrawn by Primal Nature (Mula Prakriti) into herself, where the triple gunas resolve themselves into perfect equilibrium and cease to be active. They become active again when Prakriti becomes manifested (sambhuta), and Brahma as Isvara begins a new cycle of creation. During these upheavals, the Supreme Lord himself shields and protects the liberated souls.

During creation, Time (Kala) is one of the earliest manifestations of Brahman. In the world of Brahman, Time does not exist since it remains absorbed in Him. He may exist in Brahman as an idea, but even that we are not even sure. Hence, all the freed souls (muktas) and eternally free souls (nitya muktas) who enter the immortal world of Brahman are not subject to Time or

Death, which is another name for Time. They remain there eternally blissful in the company of Brahman or the deity they worshipped as Brahman, even as the great Brahma, the creator god, goes into a long sleep for billions of years. However, in the Field of Prakriti, Time becomes an inviolable force as the Lord of Death and subjects everyone to impermanence, death, and destruction. Thus, Time, which becomes unmanifested and ceases to be a force in Brahman, becomes the Lord of Death and the source of change, impermanence, and suffering in creation.

Sloka 3

mama yonir mahad brahma tasmin garbhaṃ dadhāmyaham
saṃbhavaḥ sarvabhūtānāṃ tato bhavati bhārata

mama = My; yonih = womb; mahat brahma = the great expansive Prakriti; tasmin = in this; garbham = the seed, embryo; dadhami = place, offer; aham = I; sambhavah = ensues; sarva-bhutanam = of all living beings; tatah = from that; bhavati = arise; bharata = O descendent of Bharata.

Mahat Brahma is My womb. In that, I place the seed. From that ensues the birth of all living beings.

In this verse, Lord Krishna explained how Purusha (Ksehtrajna) and Prakriti (Kshetra) come together in the jivas and creation. He described Prakriti as Mahat Brahma and compared her to his womb. Thus, he confirmed that Prakriti is his essential aspect and under his control. Prakriti is known as Mahat. This world is often described as Mahat only since it is the Field where the Self resides as its Knower. In this verse, creation is compared to reproduction. The world manifests in the Lord's womb due to the presence of his seed (Kshetrajna). Both Kshetra and Kshetrajna are Brahman's aspects only. Purusha represents his higher nature or pure consciousness, which is self-existent and free from associations (upadhis). Prakriti, with her modes and tattvas, represents his lower nature. She is divisible, impermanent, and subject to modification. The Self is the seed (the efficient cause), and Prakriti is the womb (the material cause) of all manifestation. The jivas who arise from their union represent both. Isvara, the Lord of the universe, also manifests from the same union. When Purusha (the Pure Self) enters Prakriti and is enveloped by her tattvas and gunas, he becomes the cosmic germ or the golden embryo (Hiranyagarbha). From that arises the diversity of all living beings (jivas), including gods and celestial beings. Mahat means the Great One or Prakriti. Its highest tattva is intelligence (buddhi) in the jivas and cosmic intelligence in Isvara. The former is tainted with impurities due to the gunas, and the latter remains untainted since the gunas remain under the control of the Supreme Lord and act according to his will. Prakriti is the sum of all material manifestations or the energy of Brahman. She remains unmanifested (asambhuta) in the absolute state of Brahman and becomes manifested (sambhuta) in creation as the Lord's womb.

Sloka 4

sarvayoniṣu kaunteya mūrtayaḥ saṃbhavanti yāḥ
tāsāṃ brahma mahad yonir ahaṃ bījapradaḥ pitā

sarva-yonisu = of all the wombs; kaunteya = O son of Kunti; murtayah = forms; sambhavanti = are born; yah = which; tasam =of them; brahma = Brahma; mahat = great; yonih = the womb, source; aham = I am; bija-pradah = the giver of seed; pita = father.

O Son of Kunti, whatever forms are born from all the wombs, Mahat Brahma is their womb. I am the Seed-Giving Father.

Mahat means great, and Brahma means the creative god. Mahat Brahma means the Great Brahma, the Great One, or Prakriti. It is the first tattva to emerge from Prakriti in her manifested state, just as Brahma is the first divinity. It becomes buddhi (intelligence) in the evolved jivas. In some ancient descriptions, the materiality of creation is attributed to Brahma. The Vedas extol Brahma as Purusha also. Indeed, Brahma is the original Great God (Isvara) in the Vedic tradition, who manifests in creation as the First due to the union of Purusha (Brahman) and the manifested Prakriti (sambhuta). We do not have a proper understanding of him or his significance because the Vedic tradition underwent many changes in its long history during its expansion into various parts of the Indian subcontinent. In the early Vedic period, Brahma was the highest god, revered as the creator of all, the great grandfather, the all-knowing teacher, and the highest and most exalted deity. The earliest incarnations of fish and tortoise, which are attributed now to Lord Vishnu, were originally attributed to him. The ancient Kshatriya clans and the earliest proponents of the Upanishadic philosophy, who pursued the path of wisdom (jnana), worshipped him as the highest god of the Vedic pantheon. Subsequently, for unknown reasons, he lost his significance and yielded his exalted position to Shiva and Vishnu. The description of Brahma as Prakriti and the source of all is reminiscent of the times when Brahma was venerated as the highest god and the Lord of Creation. In the current symbolism, the Supreme Being who manifests from Brahman is Isvara. Brahma represents his Cosmic Body or manifested Nature. Hence, in some texts, he is extolled as Viraj, the shining one or the ruling one. If Isvara is Lord of the Universe, Brahma is the Lord of the triple worlds, who is illuminated by the light and consciousness (chaitanyam) of Isvara. This was before he lost his significance in the Hindu pantheon.

Sloka 5

sattvaṃ rajas tama iti guṇāḥ prakṛtisambhavāḥ
nibadhnanti mahābāho dehe dehinam avyayam

sattvam = sattva; rajah = rajas; tamah = tamas; iti = thus; gunah = qualities, modes of nature; prakrti = nature; sambhavah = arise, are born; nibadhnanti = bind; maha-baho = O mighty-armed one; dehe = in this body; dehinam = dweller, embodied self; avyayam = inexhaustible, imperishable.

Sattva, rajas, tamas, thus are the qualities which are born of Nature, O the mighty-armed one, which bind the inexhaustible dweller of the body.

Lord Krishna spoke about the gunas or modes before. They are different from the tattvas. There are no equivalent words for the guna or tattva in English.

The tattvas represent the primal formations, aspects, categories, or divisions of Nature. They manifest in the jivas as organs or parts. Classical Samkhya puts their number at 23 or 24, and Shaiva traditions at 36. The triple gunas, Sattva, Rajas, and Tamas, represent the modes of Prakriti or the light, gray, and dark natures or divine, human, and demonic natures found in the jivas. Human beings may display a variety of behaviors, tendencies, and personality types due to their intermixture and predominance. They pervade all the tattvas in the body. Therefore, their influence is pervasive. They are primarily responsible for desires, attachments, and desire-ridden actions. Both tattvas and gunas are unconscious or inanimate (achetana) and lack illumination and activity of their own. In the jivas, the embodied Self illuminates them all, thereby imparting to them liveliness (chaitanyam), modes, qualities, activity, and inertia according to their specific roles and functions in Nature.

The tattvas are found only in living beings, while the gunas are universally present in all animate and inanimate objects. While we can identify the tattvas in bodies, we cannot discern the gunas by their location. They are discernible only through their effects. The intermixture of the gunas and the five great elements, or the mahabhutas, is responsible for the diversity and multiplicity of the manifested creation. Both the tattvas and gunas are inherently present in Prakriti in her manifested and unmanifested states. They remain dormant in her unmanifested state and become active in her manifested state due to her association with Purusha or the Self. They are primarily responsible for the impurities of the mind and body, such as ignorance, delusion, desires, etc., and subject the beings to birth and death. Hence, Lord Krishna said in the first verse that their knowledge was important, and by knowing it, the silent ones attained perfection.

According to Advaita, the gunas are unreal, like all the tattvas and functions of Prakriti. Their activity is an illusion due to Maya. They exist only because of the Self and disappear when it is withdrawn from the body. The dualistic schools hold the opposite view that they are real and eternal, just as Prakriti is. They may be suppressed or rendered inactive, but cannot be destroyed. Whatever the truth, the gunas are primarily responsible for all the activity and diversity in creation. They are present in every entity and object in creation, from the lowest organism to the highest, including the divinities and the triple gods (Trimurthis). In the primordial Nature (mula Prakriti), which is unmanifested (asambhuti) and undefined (avyakta), they remain in equilibrium. In creation, when Prakriti becomes active and alive (sambhuta and vyakta) due to the presence of Purusha, they become active and animated, having lost their equilibrium, and produce diversity as they permeate the tattvas in different permutations and combinations.

Although guna means quality, property, virtue, etc., in philosophical terms, it means a mode of behavior or natural propensity. All the qualities, properties, and features of the animate and inanimate objects arise from them only. They are why objects have properties, functions, and predictable reactions, and why beings experience various behaviors, feelings, emotions, desires, passions, tastes, likes, and dislikes, and become bound. According to the Yogasutras, the gunas are responsible for the modifications (guna vrittis) of the citta (consciousness), which results in suffering. In sentient beings, they are the chief instigators of desire-ridden actions whereby they incur karma and become bound. The impurities arising from their intermixture cloud the consciousness and delude the beings, because of which they cannot discern their true nature and become bound. By establishing their minds in the Lord and performing actions without desires, devotees can remove those impurities, still their minds, and enter the deeper states of meditative self-absorption. Patanjali states that cultivating indifference to the triple gunas (gunavitrasnyam) is essential for liberation, and it is higher than practicing renunciation. A yogi excels in it when he develops the awareness of the Self (purusha-khyati) in him through self-purification and practices concentration and contemplation to become centered in it.

Patanjali further states (2.18) that the tattvas and organs in the body are characterized by illumination, activity, and inertia due to the presence or absence of the gunas in them. Based on their qualities and particularities, they can be grouped into four categories: particularized (vishesa), unparticularized (avishesa), distinctive (linga), and indistinctive (alinga). The particularized tattvas are the final evolutes. They do not produce any further evolutes and arise from the unparticularized tattvas. For example, the five elements, ether, air, fire, water, and earth, are final evolutes. They arise from the unparticularized tattvas: sound, touch, sight, taste, and smell. Alinga refers to the unmanifested aspects of Prakriti, which cannot be discerned with the mind or the senses. Linga refers to those tattvas which can be discerned or sensed. For example, the undifferentiated primal Nature is alinga, and intelligence (buddhi), which manifests from it and can be sensed, is linga.

Sloka 6

tatra sattvaṃ nirmalatvāt prakāśakam anāmayam
sukhasaṅgena badhnāti jñānasaṅgena cānagha

tatra = of them; sattvam = the quality of sattva, purity; nirmalatvat = being pure and tranquil in nature; prakasakam = illuminating, reflector of light; anamayam = healthy, sound; sukha = pleasure, happiness; sangena = through attachment, association; badhnati = binds; jnana = knowledge; sangena = through attachment ca = and; anagha = O sinless one.

Of them, being pure and tranquil in nature, sattva is illuminating (and) healthy; it binds through attachment to pleasure and through attachment to knowledge, O sinless one.

Sattva may be comparatively better than the other two modes. However, all three gunas produce impurities through desire-ridden actions, causing bondage and suffering. Hence, cultivating sattva should be viewed as a means, not an end in itself. It is helpful to purify the mind and intelligence. However, in the end, one should suppress and transcend them all to attain the Self, which is nirguna (free from the gunas) and beyond the gunas (gunatita). The mode of sattva is described in the scriptures as pure and transparent, with the ability to reflect the light of the Self and illuminate the mind and intelligence. When it predominates, the mind discerns things and objects with greater clarity and understanding. Because of sattva only, the mind overcomes delusion and ignorance and knows the distinction between

Dharma and adharma. Because of it, we perceive things and reflect them well in our consciousness. Without it, one remains deluded and ignorant and mistakes the body for the Self. Hence, sattva is often equated with discerning intelligence (buddhi) in yoga. The purity of consciousness is directly proportionate to the predominance of sattva in humans. The same is true about the worlds and all the objects in them. The brighter worlds are filled with sattva, while the darker ones are filled with tamas. The demonic worlds are dark and sunless (asuryanam), not because Brahman is absent in them, but because the grossness of tamas does not let any light enter them and reflect the objects.

Those who live in those worlds also possess that darkness due to the absence of sattva. Their intelligence remains enveloped by impurities and does not let them think clearly or discern truths. Hence, they remain deluded, ignorant, sinful, and bound. As this verse implies, sattva contributes to health and happiness by removing impurities (doshas) and invigorating the mind and body with life-enhancing qualities. The practice of yoga is beneficial and contributes to good health because it promotes sattva and purifies the mind and body. It also improves one's essential nature. Sattvic people are gentle, relaxed, contented, humble, and detached. Therefore, they are healthier and happier. Although sattva is a positive mode, being an aspect of Prakriti, it tends to bind people through attachment to pleasure and happiness. The Yogasutras (2.42) concurs with this opinion, stating that when the mind is filled with sattva, it leads to happiness, concentration, sense-control, and the ability to see the Self directly (atma darsana yogatvam). Attachment to happiness is an obstacle to liberation since it creates attraction to things that produce happiness and aversion to those that do not. It binds, inducing desire-ridden actions, ignorance (avidya), and attachments. Therefore, although sattva is a positive mode and produces an agreeable nature, one must eventually overcome it to attain liberation.

Sloka 7

rajo rāgātmakaṃ viddhi tṛṣṇāsaṅgasamudbhavam
tan nibadhnāti kaunteya karmasaṅgena dehinam

rajah = the quality of rajas; raga-atmakam = nature of passion; viddhi = know; trsna = thirst or craving for things, hunger; sanga = attachment; samudbhavam = born of, produced from; tat = that; nibadhnati = binds; kaunteya = O son of Kunti; karma-sangena = through attachment to action; dehinam = the embodied beings.

Know that rajas has the nature of passion, born of attachment and thirst for things. It binds the embodied beings, O son of Kunti, through attachment to action.

Rajasic mode induces desire-ridden actions and intentions, inciting passions and attachment to worldly pleasures and strengthening egoism, delusion, ignorance, attachments, etc. Under its influence, people exert themselves excessively and restlessly to fulfill their desires or cravings (trishna) and succumb to materialism and worldliness. Rajasic people tend to be pragmatic, selfish, ambitious, and self-centered. They pursue Dharma, Artha, and Kama through desire-ridden actions (kamya karmas) to achieve success, peace, and happiness. The qualities of rajasic people are aptly described by Lord Krishna in verses 42, 43, and 44 of the second chapter, saying that they take delight in the superficial aspects of religious knowledge and flowery words, solely focusing on the rites and rituals recommended by the Vedas with the desire to attain heaven or wealth and enjoyment. Thus, through attraction and aversion (raga and dvesha) and desire for sense objects and worldly pleasures, rajas binds people to samsara. It induces evil passions, namely lust, anger, pride, envy, and greed, and drives people to pursue sinful ends. Under its influence, people experience an excessive craving for material wealth and worldly enjoyment or the egoistic need to establish their superiority, dominance, and control.

In verses 62 and 63 of the second chapter, Lord Krishna describes how desires ruin people and lead to their downfall. He says that desires and attachments arise when the mind constantly dwells upon sense objects. Desires and attachments produce passions such as anger. From them arises delusion; from delusion, confusion of memory, and loss of discernment. When discernment is lost, one engages in indiscriminate actions and ruins oneself. Knowing it, a disciplined yogi controls his desires and attachments and attains sameness. Thus, the mode of rajas binds people to actions that strengthen materialism and worldliness. It induces aggression, dominance, and passion for success, name, and fame, making people selfish, self-centered, and blind to their ambition and egoism. Under its influence, people aggressively pursue materialistic goals and worldly actions, often at the cost of their values, morals, comfort, and happiness. The unbridled materialism of the present-day world is due to the prevalence of rajas only. When it rules our consciousness, we become restless with worldly desires and lose discernment. Although it is responsible for vitality and activity, it is considered an impurity because it promotes sinful nature, evil passions, attachments, and desire-ridden actions.

Sloka 8

tamas tv ajñānajaṃ viddhi mohanaṃ sarvadehinām
pramādālasyanidrābhis tan nibadhnāti bhārata

tamah = tamas; tu = but; ajnana-jam = born of ignorance; viddhi = know; mohanam = delusion; sarva-dehinam = of the embodied beings; pramada = negligence; alasya =sloth, laziness; nidrabhih = sleep; tat = that; nibadhnati = binds; bharata = O descendent of Bharata.

But know that tamas is born of ignorance, which deludes the embodied beings. That binds, O descendent of Bharata, through negligence, sloth, and sleep.

Sattva increases through peace and happiness, rajas through desire-ridden actions and attachments, and tamas through ignorance, inertia, and delusion. Sattva binds people through knowledge, peace, and happiness, rajas through worldly actions, and tamas through laziness, inertia, or sloth. The triple gunas are responsible for illumination, activity, and inertia in the beings, apart from the particularized, unparticularized, distinctive, and indistinctive effects they produce. Of them, tamas is primarily responsible for inertia, sloth, and sleep. It is an inhibitive force that suppresses the purity, illumination, and discernment of sattva and the vitality, strength, and dynamism of rajas and fills the beings with delusion, apathy, and ignorance. Hence, from a spiritual perspective, it is a more formidable force and requires special attention. It is also the densest of the three and difficult to purify.

However, we cannot undermine its importance in Nature. It is as essential as the other two to create and sustain the diversity in Nature. Together, they play an important role in producing diverse forms, states, qualities, and tendencies. Sattva and tamas represent the two extremes in the spectrum of life, with rajas standing in between as the balancing force, each being distinguished by its contrasting influence. Sattva illuminates and enlightens, and tamas obscures and darkens. Sattva leads to knowledge, peace, and happiness, and tamas to ignorance, delusion, restlessness, and suffering. Sattva is transformative, pure, and subtle. Tamas is destructive, gross, and impure. Sattva promotes divine qualities, and tamas, demonic qualities. Rajas is also an impure quality. However, it promotes activity, strength, vitality, passion, and self-preservation rather than inertia, brutality, apathy, perversion, and self-destruction, which tamas induces. The spiritual intensity of sattva and the inertia of tamas are matched by the worldliness and vitality of rajas. Thus, the three gunas, in their separate ways, contribute to the balance, equilibrium, diversity, and predictability found in the world of opposites and dualities. They also tend to compete and suppress each other to establish their dominance.

However, they are not found in Nature in their pristine state. They cannot be distilled, isolated, or extracted through any process since they are subtle, permeate the tattvas or matter, and have no physical location. They can be discerned only through the effects they produce. Except for Isvara, the highest manifestation of Brahman, they are found in different permutations and combinations in all other objects and beings of creation, including the highest divinities. Every aspect of human behavior, including devotion, choice of gods, methods of worship, food, friends, and other preferences, is colored by them. For example, sattvic people prefer to achieve liberation through conventional methods of yoga and self-purification; rajasic people through the practice of Dharma (obligatory duties) and the pursuit of the four aims of human life, and tamasic people who are rebellious, delusional, disobedient, and stubborn by nature through unconventional, perverse, and prohibited methods.

Sloka 9

sattvaṃ sukhe saṃjayati rajaḥ karmaṇi bhārata
jñānam āvṛtya tu tamaḥ pramāde saṃjayaty uta

sattvam = sattva; sukhe = through pleasure, happiness; sanjayati = binds; rajah = rajas; karmani = through actions; bharata = O descendent of Bharata; jnanam = knowledge; avrtya = enveloped; tu = but; tamah = tamas; pramade = through negligence; sanjayati = binds; uta = it is said.

Sattva binds through pleasure; rajas binds through actions; but O descendant of Bharata, it is said that tamas binds through negligence by enveloping knowledge.

Knowing how the gunas influence our thinking and actions is helpful to contain their influence and practice self-control. The gunas tend to attract things of their nature and strengthen our attachment to them. Prakriti relies upon them to induce desire-ridden actions in the beings and keep them bound and deluded. Through them, she enforces Maya and moves the Wheel of Creation, keeping the jivas in her control. The gunas induce attraction and aversion according to their nature and keep the mind restless and unstable. They are responsible for all the modifications arising in the Field of Prakriti and our physical, mental, and emotional states. Since they act as Nature's forces and are pervasive, they are difficult to control. As we have seen, sattva binds people through peace and happiness, rajas through desires and attachment to worldly actions, and tamas through negligence and slothfulness. Hence, they are troublesome and unwholesome and must be controlled or suppressed to limit their influence.

The triple gunas have spheres of influence in the body. The dense physical body is more vulnerable to the influence of tamas, the restless mental body to the passions and desires induced by rajas, and the breath and intelligent bodies are where the illumination and purity of sattva shine the most. Of the three, the consequences arising from the actions induced by tamas are more painful and, in many ways, regressive. It strengthens evil nature and sociopathic and psychopathic behavior and keeps the beings deluded, ignorant, and irrational. Pramada means negligence or carelessness. When people are negligent, they will be careless, make mistakes in their thinking and actions, disregard their duties and responsibilities, resort to unconventional practices, or engage in reckless actions disproportionate to their strength, resources, or abilities. The three gunas are troublesome in their specific ways. Of them, however, tamas is more troublesome and difficult to suppress. Therefore, those who seek liberation should strive hard to suppress it and minimize its influence by cultivating sattva or worshipping the Lord with supreme devotion.

Sloka 10

rajas tamaś cābhibhūya sattvaṃ bhavati bhārata
rajaḥ sattvaṃ tamaś caiva tamaḥ sattvaṃ rajas tathā

rajah = rajas; tamah = tamas; ca = and; abhibhuya = by subduing; sattvam = mode of goodness; bhavati = increases, prevails, predominates; bharata = O descendent of Bharata; rajah = rajas; sattvam = sattva; tamah = tamas; ca = and; eva = similarly; tamah = tamas; sattvam = sattva; rajah = rajas; tatha = thus.

Sattva prevails by subduing rajas and tamas, O descendent of Bharata; rajas by (subduing) sattva and tamas; and similarly, tamas (by subduing) sattva and rajas.

The gunas tend to prevail in Nature by suppressing each other. Their struggle for dominance keeps the beings and the entire creation in flux and a restive and chaotic mode. When sattva prevails over the other two, beings experience peace, happiness, stability, and harmony. When rajas prevails, it induces passions, cravings, and attachment to worldly actions. When tamas prevails, it clouds and perverts the mind and intelligence, promotes demonic tendencies, and deludes beings. Thus, by observing people's nature, actions, behavior, likes, and dislikes, we can infer which guna is at work in them. Spiritual teachers do the same when they admit students or when they guide them on the path. They prescribe methods and solutions that work well with their predominant nature. The knowledge also helps spiritual people know which gunas they need to weaken or strengthen to overcome their impurities and stabilize their minds. The gunas are responsible for much of what happens to us, the actions we form, and the goals we pursue. The dynamism and diversity of Nature arise from the modes and their internal struggle to suppress each other. They are also responsible for much of our suffering. The predominance of each mode leads to different outcomes. How those effects manifest in the beings is explained in the following verses.

Sloka 11

sarvadvāreṣu dehesmin prakāśa upajāyate
jñānaṃ yadā tadā vidyād vivṛddhaṃ sattvam ity uta

sarva-dvaresu = through all the doors; dehe asmin = in the body; prakasah = illumination; upajayate = radiate; jnanam = knowledge; yada = when; tada = then; vidyat = one should know; vivrddham = increased; sattvam = sattva; iti = thus; uta = said, declared.

When the illumination of knowledge radiates through all the doors in the body, then one should know that sattva has increased profusely. Thus, it is declared.

Sattva illuminates all the openings in the body (the senses, mouth, mind, anus, and reproductive organs) and makes living a pleasant experience. When you see a gentle and intelligent person who has knowledge and discernment, practices Dharma as a service or offering to God, is drawn to the knowledge of the Self and devotion to God, virtuous, serene, indifferent to worldly desires, practices detachment and renunciation, and spends time in contemplation or in the company of God's devotees or seekers of liberation, it is mainly due to the predominance of sattva. Sattvic people practice nonviolence, truthfulness, self-restraint, and other virtues. The mode shines brightly as physical vigor, grace, erudition, and mental brilliance in people. Those with its predominance excel in knowledge, intelligence, and spirituality. Those whose minds and bodies are purified by its presence discern the Self in them and remain established in it through contemplation and devotion. They surrender their egos and will to the Supreme Lord, put themselves at his mercy with humility, and remain satisfied and happy with whatever they have and whatever happens. Devotion arises in them naturally, and truths become self-evident to their discerning minds. Their knowledge, wisdom, and pure sattvic nature become reflected in their words, actions, decisions, and relationships. Since they overcome impurities such as egotism and delusion, they remain in the present, observe with insightful awareness, and empathize well with others by seeing their suffering as their own. Hence, they are also good at counseling, helping, and guiding others without any expectations or desires. Just like the sunlight that bursts through the crevices and openings of a roof, cloud, or wall, the illumination of the sattva bursts through the cloud of impurities and radiates through the mind and body once it gains strength.

However, those with the predominance of other gunas will have different temperaments and attitudes and react differently, even if they are engaged in similar pursuits or possess similar interests. Knowledge and intelligence are not exclusive to sattvic people only. Rajasic and tamasic people also possess them. However, their knowledge, wisdom, actions, interests, and pursuits will be colored by their impure gunas. Hence, the fruit of their actions or the karma that arises from them will also be different. For example, sattvic people's minds and bodies are illuminated by purity and virtue and the desire for peace and happiness; those of rajasic ones by passions and the desire for selfish gains; and those of tamasic ones by delusion and ignorance and the desire to prevail at any cost. In other words, each of these categories of people uses their knowledge, intelligence, mental brilliance, and other possessions with different motives and temperaments and for different purposes. Those with impure gunas may also worship gods or engage in religious and spiritual activities for different reasons. Hence, they do not succeed much in attaining perfection or overcoming their impurities. If sattvic people work for righteous causes with their knowledge and intelligence, rajasic people use their resources to fulfill their passions and desires, while those with tamas use them to hurt and harm others or achieve evil ends. It is why, in ancient gurukulas, teachers used to observe their students closely before imparting to them sacred knowledge.

The mind, the senses, the organ of speech (vak), and intelligence (buddhi) are vulnerable to the influence of gunas and the play of Maya. Through them, the gunas reflect the light of the Self. When the mind is pure and shines with mental brilliance, cleansed by the fire of sattva, a yogi perceives the world with greater awareness and understanding. He sees things from a broader perspective, without judgment or the weight of knowledge and authority. Hence, yogis whose minds are free from impurities and selfish desires grasp truths with greater clarity and understanding. Unlike the rajasic and tamasic people, they are not driven by selfish desires or evil passions. They also remain peaceful and serene with their minds and senses under control. Therefore, they can perceive things without confusion, cognitive biases, and perceptual errors. They use their knowledge and intelligence for righteous causes, to serve the Lord, uphold Dharma, help others, or spread peace and happiness. Even though they may seek happiness or enjoy comforts and luxuries, they do so without compromising their values or duties. They remain steadfast in their devotion to the Lord, taking refuge in him and establishing their minds in his contemplation.

Sloka 12

lobhaḥ pravṛttir ārambhaḥ karmaṇām aśamaḥ spṛhā
rajasy etāni jāyante vivṛddhe bharatarṣabha

lobhah = avarice, greed; pravrttih = exertion, activity; arambhah = undertaking, enterprise, initiative; karmanam = desire-ridden actions; asamah = absence of sameness, restless; sprha = hankering, craving, coveting; rajasi = in rajas; etani = all these; jayante = develop, manifest, arise; vivrddhe = grows, increases; bharata-rsabha = O chief among the Bharatas.

Greed, activity, the undertaking of desire-ridden actions, absence of sameness, and craving - all these manifest when the mode of rajas increases, O Chief among the Bharatas.

These qualities of rajasic people indicate their restless and unstable nature, vulnerability to cravings, passions, and emotions, and tendency to engage in desire-ridden actions for enjoyment or personal gain. They are always busy, resourceful, enterprising, and motivated by gain. However, they cannot accept failure or tolerate people who criticize them, disagree with them, or seem to threaten or oppose their interests, goals, success, and progress. Hence, unlike sattva, the mode of rajas is impure and poses a significant problem to people pursuing spiritual or material goals. However, it can be suppressed or countered through self-purification and self-control by overcoming desires and attachments. Rajasic people are attracted to actions to secure things for themselves or others and satisfy their egoistic, deluded need for approval, acceptance, and appreciation. They pursue goals to experience peace and fulfillment, but rarely achieve them since their intentions are selfish and impure. Due to desire-ridden actions, they incur sinful karma and remain bound. Lacking discernment and self-control, they bring their worldliness, pragmatism, desires, and attachments into their religious and spiritual practice and delay their liberation. Some may even use religion and spirituality to fulfill their desires or further their selfish interests. Hence, the rajasic mode is not conducive to purity, discernment, equanimity, sameness, or liberation.

In this verse, Lord Krishna emphasized the distinguishing qualities of this mode: avarice, activity or the tendency to remain active in pursuit of something, enterprising nature, desire-ridden actions, restlessness due to likes and dislikes, and craving. Lobha means avarice. It is the egoistic desire to accumulate things beyond the basic needs to overcome fear, doubt, insecurity, inferiority, or uncertainty, to be superior to or ahead of others, or to feel good about oneself. Its side effects are negative thoughts (vitarka) such as fear, anxiety, violence, selfishness, egoism, and envy. Because of this, even if they achieve grand success and become the richest people in the world, they remain perpetually unhappy, insecure, and dissatisfied with themselves and their self-worth.

Pravritti means the natural inclination for activity due to the outgoing nature of the mind and senses, and one's preoccupation and involvement with the world, its values, and attractions. The rajasic mode makes people extroverted and pursue worldly goals at the cost of their spiritual well-being. Hence, they remain restless, self-centered, egoistic, greedy, and ambitious.

Arambha means enterprise or initiative in undertaking actions or performing tasks. Rajasic people are action-oriented, so they undertake many activities, sometimes beyond their means or capacity, to fulfill their desires or earn appreciation and recognition. Hence, they are vulnerable to stress, restlessness, and poor health.

Asama means not being equal to or not being the same toward the dualities of life, such as success and failure, pleasure and pain, honor and dishonor, or fame and infamy. It arises due to attraction and aversion (raga dvesha) to sense objects, due to passions such as pride, lust, greed, envy, etc., or due to craving for material things and worldly pleasures, thereby keeping people restless, unhappy, and unstable. It is a common trait of rajasic people since they habitually engage in desire-ridden actions and lead stressful lives. It is further aggravated by their passions and the impermanence and uncertainty of worldly life.

Sprha means longing, endless craving, or covetousness, which is an offshoot of greed, lust, and other evil passions. It keeps rajasic people actively engaged in some pursuit or the other, irrespective of the consequences they produce.

People with the predominance of rajas are the main drivers of our civilization and are responsible for much of the material progress the world has achieved so far. Since they are this-worldly, creative, enterprising, and pragmatic, they rely mostly upon themselves and their ingenuity to solve their problems or make progress. It results in an imbalance in their personal lives as they ignore their spiritual well-being and focus on their actions and achievements, or worldly gains. In today's world, sattvic people are rare, while there is no shortage of the rajasic ones. In this mode, people are good at performing their duties and fulfilling their obligations with or without any reference to God or Dharma. However, the qualities associated with it expose them to many personal problems and keep them restless, unhappy, and distracted from their spiritual goals and fulfillment.

Sloka 13

aprakāśopravṛttiś ca pramādo moha eva ca
tamasy etāni jāyante vivṛddhe kurunandana

aprakasah = darkness; apravrttih = inactivity; ca = and; pramadah = carelessness, negligence; mohah = delusion; eva = even; ca =and; tamasi = of tamasa; etani = these; jayante = manifest, prevail; vivrddhe = predominate; kuru-nandana = O son of Kuru.

Darkness, inactivity, carelessness, and delusion - they surely manifest when tamas predominates, O son of Kuru.

Tamas is a force of darkness, ignorance, and delusion. It is the opposite of sattva, a force of light, knowledge, and discernment. Hence, they produce opposite tendencies in jivas and try to cancel each other. Even rajas produces contrasting effects when they are associated with it and are predominant. For example, in the predominance of sattva, rajas induces positive and righteous actions, desires, and attachments. However, in association with tamas, it induces harmful and destructive actions, desires, and attachments. Of the three modes, tamas is the most impure. When it is the strongest, it produces dark and demonic qualities in humans, which Lord Krishna will explain in the sixteenth chapter. As stated before, the gunas do not have self-illumination. They are illuminated by the Self and induce different qualities, natures, desires, and actions according to their strength relative to the other two. Being transparent, sattva is the least obstructive. Tamas, which is the densest, is the most obstructive. Hence, when tamas predominates, the Self remains obscure and hidden beneath the grossness of tamas, creating the illusion that it does not exist and the body is the self.

Darkness, inactivity, carelessness, and delusion of the most stubborn type arise from tamas. They manifest differently in the jivas relative to the strength of the sattva and rajas. For example, ignorance of the sattvic type arises due to the lack of knowledge and can be overcome with effort, but ignorance of the tamasic type arises mostly due to erroneous beliefs and irrational thinking and is difficult to overcome. Darkness means the absence of light (aprakasah). It arises when the light of the Self is obstructed primarily by tamas or rajas. Just as darkness prevails on earth when clouds obstruct the sun, the internal organ (antahkarana) becomes enveloped in the darkness of impurities arising from tamas or rajas. However, unlike light and darkness, sattva and tamas are not dualities. The three modes work differently, but in the end, keep the jivas bound to the world. Of them, tamas is the most troublesome and difficult mode to overcome.

In the darkness of night, we cannot see objects clearly and have to fumble our way out. A similar situation happens when tamas predominates and clouds our thinking and judgment. Many unhappy situations arise because of this, making it difficult for the jivas to escape from the darkness of samsara. Due to the lack of balance and moderation, tamasic people go to extremes to resolve their problems or reach their goals. For example, in spirituality, they indulge in extreme austerities, torturous yogas, and prohibited actions to achieve their goals. However, as Lord Krishna stated, even those with the predominance of tamas qualify for divine grace by cultivating sattva and practicing self-control, desireless actions, and exclusive devotion.

Sloka 14

yadā sattve pravṛddhe tu pralayaṃ yāti dehabhṛt
tadottamavidāṃ lokān amalān pratipadyate

yada = when; sattve = sattva; pravrddhe =increases, predominates; tu = completely; pralayam = dissolution, death, end time; yati = goes, travels, reaches, enters; deha-bhrt = embodied self; tada = then; uttama-vidam = those who know the highest; lokan = the worlds; amalan = pure, without impurities; pratipadyate = attains.

If sattva is predominant when the embodied one goes into dissolution, then he attains the pure worlds of those who know the highest.

Since the modes are primarily responsible for desires, attachments, and desire-ridden actions, they also produce consequences for the jivas and influence their lives and destinies. They tend to attract and associate with the things of their nature. Thus, sattvic people are attracted to sattvic people, things, and objects. When they depart from here, they attain the pure worlds of the wise ones, such as siddhas and muktas. If they do not attain liberation, they will be born in good families amidst sattvic people. The tamasic ones go to the sunless worlds of impure souls, and the rajasic ones attain the middle worlds of light and darkness. The gunas are ubiquitous in the whole creation and at every level. They permeate the worlds in the cosmic hierarchy and determine their nature and progression. The highest worlds are made up of pure sattva, inhabited by the purest souls. The lowest ones are permeated with pure tamas, inhabited by dark and demonic beings. The middle worlds, of which ours is one, are inhabited by beings of mixed nature. Therefore, in these worlds, the spiritual progress of the jivas depends upon how quickly they overcome their impurities and qualify for liberation.

Since the three modes compete with and suppress each other, their conflict is reflected in various aspects of our lives and the whole creation. They are responsible for much of what happens to us here and hereafter. They influence our thinking, actions, decisions, likes and dislikes, or the choice of professions, friendships, relationships, food, etc. Since they tend to attract things of their nature, they also influence our social behavior and the company we keep. By inducing desire-ridden actions, they determine our essential nature, karma, and fate. As this verse suggests, they determine the transmigration of the jivas after they depart from here. Because of them only, we experience moral and mental dilemmas and conflicts. The conflict between gods and demons, which the Puranas depict, also arises due to their influence only. The gods are made of sattva, and the demons are made of tamas and rajas. Hence, conflicts between them are inevitable. Within our world, the conflict between good and evil, morality and immorality, or Dharma and Adharma, happens because of them. The caste system was founded on the same principle. In the Vedic age, humans were divided first into three and later into four groups according to the predominance of gunas. Brahmanas represented sattva, Kshatriyas represented rajas, and the other two classes (Vaishyas and Shudras) represented rajas and tamas.

Sloka 15

rajasi pralayaṃ gatvā karmasaṅgiṣu jāyate
tathā pralīnas tamasi mūḍhayoniṣu jāyate

rajasi = rajasic person; pralayam = death, dissolution; gatva = journeying; karma-sangisu = those attached to action; jayate = takes birth, is born; tatha = thsu, in the same manner pralinah = upon death, dissolution; tamasi = tamasic person; mudha = deluded, ignorant; yonisu = wombs; jayate = take birth.

He who is predominantly rajasic, upon going to dissolution, is born among those who are attached to actions; in the same manner, he who is predominantly tamasic takes birth in the wombs of the deluded.

In the eighth chapter, verse 6, Lord Krishna said that in whatever state one left the world, he would attain that. That statement is relevant here since the gunas influence one's state of mind at the time of death. Upon death, sattvic people go to sattvic worlds and return from there to attain birth in the families of pious people. Rajasic ones go to the mixed worlds and, upon returning from there, are born in the families of worldly people who engage in desire-ridden actions. Tamasic ones go to the lower worlds. Upon rebirth, they are born with impure bodies in the families of deluded ones. Thus, the predominant gunas determine our essential nature, which, in turn, influences our current actions and future lives. They are responsible for our thoughts, desires, actions, habits, and latent impressions (samskaras) and, thereby, our karma and future births. As is one's essential nature (svabhavam), so is one's karma. It determines one's character, conduct, and future. The jivas are bound to the world because of the gunas and the consequences they produce through desire-ridden actions. The fruit of such actions follows them into their future lives. Mortal beings cannot escape this loop until they transcend the gunas through spiritual transformation and stabilize their minds in equanimity and sameness.

Sattvic people attain liberation if they do not stumble on the path. They will surely go to the highest world of pure beings, while rajasic and tamasic people are less fortunate. Upon exhausting their karma in the ancestral world or a lower world, they return to the earth and take birth among those who are closer to them in their temperament and attitude. Rajasic people love action and take pride in their achievements. Therefore, they are born into families that are attached to actions and materialistic goals. Since tamasic people are ignorant and deluded, they take birth amidst people of a similar nature. Lord Krishna mentioned wombs (yonisu) in this verse. Hence, we have to assume human birth is not guaranteed for them. They may also be born from the wombs of animals and other creatures.

However, there can be exceptions to these possibilities since life is unpredictable, and even the best of sages and spiritual people can falter on the path and fall, or the worst of sinful people can redeem themselves by earning the Lord's grace. In normal circumstances, Nature balances things and establishes order and regularity. She makes sure that the gunas work as designed and beings act according to their predominant nature under the influence of Maya and reinforce it through their desire-ridden actions, attracting and accumulating things to satisfy the desires they induce. Since they do not have self-illumination, the modes cannot be transformed or made to act differently. One can suppress or balance them by cultivating opposite modes or practicing self-control, withdrawal, renunciation, detachment, and exclusive devotion. Sattva does not necessarily guarantee a place in the mortal world since it also induces desires and attachments. One should, therefore, suppress the modes by earning the Lord's grace through self-control and exclusive devotion.

Sloka 16

karmaṇaḥ sukṛtasyāhuḥ sāttvikaṃ nirmalaṃ phalam
rajasas tu phalaṃ duḥkham ajñānaṃ tamasaḥ phalam

karmanah = of actions; su-krtasya = of good; ahuh = they say; sattvikam = pure, virtuous; nirmalam = spotless, sinless, pure; phalam = fruit; rajasah = of rajas; tu = but; phalam = fruit; duhkham = sorrow; ajnanam = ignorance; tamasah = of tamas; phalam = fruit.

They say the fruit of good actions is pure and sinless, but the fruit of rajas is sorrow, (and) the fruit of tamas is ignorance.

Sukruta means righteous actions or sattvic actions. They produce peace and happiness and lead to liberation. Pain and suffering (dukkha) are the fruit of desire-ridden actions induced by rajas. Ignorance (of the Self) and delusion are the fruits of actions that arise from tamas. Just as a fruit inherits its qualities from the tree that produces it, consequences partake in the nature of actions that produce them, and the nature of actions depends upon the nature of those who perform them. Thus, the gunas extend their sway through the chain of cause and effect and create ripples in the ocean of life. Karma arises from kamya-karmas (desire-ridden actions) only. The fruit of such actions (karma phalam) leads to further causes and effects, keeping the wheel of Dharma moving. The sinful karma, which arises as the cumulative effect of desire-ridden actions, serves as a self-correcting mechanism to help them learn valuable lessons from their suffering and past mistakes and improve themselves.

Karma in Sanskrit means both action and its consequences. Good actions lead to good ends when sattva is predominant. Sattva strengthens sattva. It transforms, purifies, and produces peace, happiness, stability, and other positive states in one's consciousness. One becomes pure and holy, and virtues such as discernment, nonviolence, truthfulness, etc., arise when the mind is filled with sattva. Divine qualifies manifest. One experiences cheerfulness, one-pointedness, stability, self-control, knowledge, contentment, discernment, etc. They produce the highest happiness (anuttama sukha). In that serene state, the yogi becomes pure and transparent and reflects the intelligence of his divine nature. Subduing his desires and cravings and the modifications of his mind through continued practice (abhyasa), he succeeds in attaining insight into the nature or essence of things without conceptualization, imagination, or any mental notion or formation (nirvitarka samāpatti). In that expansive state, with the mind, the modes, and the body completely resting, he experiences supreme peace and discerning wisdom.

Thus, sattva is conducive to self-transformation, dissolution of impurities, stability, knowledge, wisdom, and selfless devotion. In contrast, rajas and tamas are considered impurities because they induce desires and attachments and keep the mind and senses in their outgoing mode (prvritti) and a restless state. They are also agents of transformation, but in a retrogressive sense, since they keep the beings distracted and deluded and produce impure qualities such as ignorance, delusion, egoism, selfishness, inertia, etc., resulting in sinful karma, suffering, and bondage. Most of the ills in the world and unwholesome behaviors and attitudes in people arise from them only. They also reinforce evil passions such as lust, anger, pride, vanity, fear, and envy. As this verse states, actions and the consequences they produce lead to ignorance, sorrow, and suffering. By ignorance, we mean the ignorance of the Self, which produces the mistaken notion that the mind and body constitute the real self. In this context, suffering means suffering from repeated births and deaths and the afflictions and modifications such as mental turbulence, aging, sickness, and death to which beings are subject due to their desires and attachments.

The fruit of sattva is nearness to Isvara (the Self) through purification and devotion. The fruit of rajas is attachment to the world and its objects through desires and passions. The fruit of tamas is attachment to egoism, the mind, and the body due to deluded notions and evil actions. According to The Yoga Vasishta, predominantly sattvic people do not act indiscriminately. They study sacred scriptures, consult holy ones, and enquire into the nature of reality and the world's appearance. With the knowledge thus gained, they understand the truths about themselves and the world and avoid the mistakes that delay their liberation or prolong their delusion, bondage, and ignorance. Therefore, the scripture says that one should aim to cultivate sattva to escape from samsara quickly. It does not mean rajasic and tamasic people cannot attain liberation. They must find appropriate methods to offset their impure modes and rescue themselves from the ocean of samsara. As stated before, in the end, one has to transcend the triple modes to attain the Self.

Sloka 17

sattvāt saṃjāyate jñānaṃ rajaso lobha eva ca
pramādamohau tamaso bhavatojñānam eva ca

sattvat = from sattva; sanjayate = is born; jnanam = knowledge; rajasah = from rajas; lobhah = greed; eva = verily; ca = and; pramada = negligence; mohau = delusion; tamasah = from tamas; bhavatah = arises; ajnanam = ignorance; eva = surely; ca = and.

From sattva is born knowledge, and from rajas surely greed; from tamas arise negligence, delusion, and indeed ignorance.

By nature, sattvic people are drawn to the knowledge of the Self and the truths of our existence. They are driven by the desire to know their essential nature through study, service, and inquiry, and master what they learn. When sattva predominates, intelligence (buddhi) shines like the sun in a cloudless sky. Hence, sattvic people are considered mentally brilliant and ripe for liberation. They serve as a good example to others because of their righteous conduct, knowledge, wisdom, and skillfulness in yoga. However, sattvic people are rare to find, first because sattva is difficult to cultivate, second because sattvic people lead contemplative lives and avoid public attention, and third because others may not immediately recognize their sattvic nature. Further, since they withdraw from the external world and seek the company of like-minded people who have the predominance of sattva, they are not known to many who are predominantly rajasic or tamasic.

In contrast, rajasic and tamasic people are the most common and found everywhere and in every culture. Most humans are of mixed nature, with the predominance of rajas or tamas. Perhaps the world is intended to be this way so that most jivas remain bound to the cycle of births and deaths to ensure its orderly progression. The scriptures also suggest the number of sattvic people keeps falling from one epoch (yuga) to another until the world becomes increasingly filled with rajasic and tamasic people. In Kaliyuga, their number will increase exponentially as evil nature (asura prvritti) takes hold. Ideally, jivas are supposed to progress from the tamasic nature to rajasic and, finally, to sattvic nature. However, according to our scriptures, the opposite happens in creation due to the deluding force of Prakriti and the gradual decline of Dharma.

Rajas promotes passions such as greed due to excessive attachment to worldly things. In the pursuit of wealth, power, prestige, social status, name, fame, etc., rajasic people may lose balance and become excessively involved with the world, ignoring their spiritual well-being. They may still engage in religious and spiritual activities and perform their obligatory duties, but mainly to fulfill their desires. Hence, they rarely achieve peace, happiness, or fulfillment. The problem with tamasic people is even more acute. They prefer to live according to their whims and avoid exerting themselves physically or performing obligatory duties. They may also engage in spiritual and religious activities, but mostly in their ignorant and deluded ways against the established norms and conventions. Spiritual darkness permeates their minds and thinking. Therefore, they are the most difficult to reform.

Sloka 18

ūrdhvaṃ gacchanti sattvasthā madhye tiṣṭhantirājasāḥ
jaghanyaguṇavṛttisthā adho gacchhanti tāmasāḥ

urdhvam = upwards; gacchanti = go; sattva-sthah = who are established in sattva; madhye = in the middle; tisthanti = sit, remain, reside; rajasah = who are rajasic; jaghanya = lowest; guna = guna, mode; vrtti-sthah = settled, occupied; adhah = down; gacchanti = go; tamasah = tamasic people.

Those who are established in sattva go upward; those who are rajasic remain in the middle; tamasic people who indulge in the activities of the lowest kind go downwards.

In sattvic people, the upper body (the mind and intelligence) is more active; in rajasic people, it is the middle part, and in tamasic people, the lower body. Hence, in this verse, the tamasic ones are described as jaghanya-guna-vrittishtā, meaning those who indulge in the actions of the lower body, which are mostly impure. Sattvic people engage in obligatory duties, study, recitation of the scriptures, serving others, prayers, worship, devotion, meditation, etc. They are primarily interested in intellectual and spiritual pursuits, the knowledge of the Self, and the means to attain it. Hence, they wisely use the higher tattvas of Prakriti in them (the senses, the mind, ego, and intelligence) to cultivate discernment and realize their spiritual and material goals. In them, the higher chakras in the heart, the throat, and the head (Sahasrara, Ajna, Vishuddha, and Anahata) remain open and active and facilitate the upward movement of pranas and kundalini. Rajasic people are driven by passions, egoism, and desires. They rely upon the lower and middle tattvas of their bodies to pursue desire-ridden actions. In them, the middle chakras in the middle body (Anahata, Manipura, Svadhishtana) are active. Tamasic people suffer from delusion and ignorance. Their higher tattvas remain clouded and impure. Hence, the lower chakras (Svadhishtana and Muladhara) remain active in them. Of the five sheaths (kosas) in the body, the subtle bodies are active in sattvic and rajasic people, while the gross, food body (annamaya kosam) is mostly active in the tamasic ones. The gunas determine the nature of beings and their fate or destinies. Sattvic people attain the higher worlds, rajasic people attain the middle worlds, and tamasic people go to the darker or sunless worlds due to their evil actions. The gunas are responsible for our karma and essential nature. Sattvic people have better chances of attaining liberation. However, rajasic and tamasic people can reverse their nature and destinies through self-purification and attain the higher worlds. Karma-sannyasa, Jnana, Bhakti, and even Sannyasa yoga are suitable for them to overcome their modes and impurities and qualify for liberation.

Sloka 19

nānyaṃ guṇebhyaḥ kartāraṃ yadā draṣṭānupaśyati
guṇebhyaś ca paraṃ vetti madbhāvaṃ sodhigacchhati

na anyam = none other; gunebhyah = than the gunas, modes; kartaram = doer; yada = when; drasta = seer; anupasyati = sees, perceives; gunebhyah = than the guans, modes; ca = and; param = beyond, higher, superior; vetti = knows; mat-bhavam = My State, essential nature; sah = he; adhigacchati = goes, attains.

When the seer sees none other than the gunas as the doer and knows That, which is beyond the gunas, he attains My State.

In this and the next verse, Lord Krishna suggests how one can achieve liberation by knowing how the gunas are behind all actions and transcending them. When a yogi realizes that the gunas helplessly drive beings into actions, he cultivates discernment and overcomes their influence and the desires they induce. He cultivates discernment and sees that the body, the seat of the gunas, is the doer, and he, the Self, is the non-doer. Knowing that gunas are the agents of all actions and he is not responsible for them, he turns to the Lord in him with exclusive devotion and attains the supreme state of oneness, which is beyond the modes and tattvas. Thus, this verse emphasizes two critical steps to self-transformation: cultivating the discernment that the gunas are the agents of actions and becoming established in the Self as Isvara through renunciation, meditation, and exclusive devotion.

The gunas are the drivers of actions and agents of change, instability, and impermanence. Because of them, the tattvas are transformed into functioning parts of the jivas. They are why the jivas engage in actions and keep the world moving. They also determine the cosmic hierarchy of the world and beings and the jivas' progress and transmigration. Since they are ubiquitous, none can escape them or their influence. Since they permeate our internal organs, they also cloud our consciousness and delay our liberation.

On the spiritual path, one must see the gunas as agents of action and obstacles to liberation. They are responsible for the suffering, ignorance, and delusion the jivas experience. When yogis realize that the gunas are the root cause of all the desires and attachments and the problems and suffering that arise from them and that they are not in them and not responsible for them, they attain the Supreme State of Brahman. The various techniques of yoga, such as the yamas, niyamas, dharana, and dhyana, or the karma-sannyasa, jnana, bhakti, and sannyasa yogas, help us suppress or neutralize the gunas and shift our attention from the world and our bodies to the Self within. They bring a fundamental shift in our thinking, knowledge, and awareness and draw our minds and senses from their outgoing mode into ourselves and the Lord, who resides in us.

In this verse, Lord Krishna emphasizes the need to transcend the three gunas to attain him. Mat-bhavam (my state) refers to his transcendental state of pure consciousness, which can be attained only by transcending all the gunas, including sattva. The gunas, without exception, induce desires and attachments. Sattva may help devotees in the early stages to cultivate purity and discernment and stabilize the mind and body. However, in advanced stages, it becomes an obstacle since it also induces desires and creates the delusion of ownership and doership. However worthy or auspicious they may be, desires produce karma. Therefore, yogis should not be content with their sattvic nature but become free from all three by transcending them (gunatita). The seers who realize that desires and desire-ridden actions are induced by the gunas silence them, practicing detachment and renunciation, and overcoming attraction and aversion. With their minds stabilized in the Self, they attain oneness and supreme peace.

Sloka 20

guṇān etān atītya trīn dehī dehasamudbhavān
janmamṛtyujarāduḥkhair vimuktomṛtam aśnute

gunan = gunas; etan = these; atitya = by transcending; trin = three; dehi = the embodied self; deha = body; samudbhavan = origin, birth; janma = birth; mrtyu = death; jara = old age; duhkhaih = sorrow; vimuktah = freed from; amrtam = immortality; asnute = attains.

Going beyond these three modes that spring from the body, the embodied Self becomes free from birth, death, old age, and sorrow and attains immortality.

A yogi who transcends the triple gunas in his body by overcoming desires and attachments and practicing exclusive devotion attains liberation. Shankaracharya felt he would attain liberation while still in the body and become a liberated, living soul (jivamukta). This verse identifies the root cause of our suffering and bondage. It goes directly to the solution, without wasting time, suggesting how to resolve them and attain liberation. The body is subject to birth, death, old age, and sickness. As long as the gunas are active, the jiva is not free from desires and attachments; as long as it is not free from desires and attachments, it is not free from the influence of the gunas and samsara. Thus, in the wheel of life, the gunas become both the causes and effects, and those who are caught in it keep revolving from one birth to another. Because of the delusion and desires induced by them, the jivas mistakenly accept the suffering and modifications of their bodies as theirs, thinking that they are responsible for them and that the modifications are happening to them. In reality, all the modifications arise and subside in the mind, body, or the physical self, in which the Self does not exist. The body is the Field, and the Self is the knower of the Field. He is not a part of the Field but only a witness. Knowing that distinction, the wise ones mentally detach themselves from their minds and bodies and become indifferent to the desires, attachments, and suffering they induce. In other words, to escape from samsara and attain the Self, one must become detached from the body and transcend the gunas and their influence. Instead of becoming involved with the Field and its modifications, and through self-effort and devotion to the Supreme Lord, one must focus on silencing or suppressing the gunas in it and the desires they induce. The Self is free from the gunas. Therefore, anyone who wants to attain oneness with him must resolve the gunas and neutralize their influence. Even a little impurity can hinder that goal, which can happen for many reasons. Birth, death, aging, and sickness are the modifications of the body. They are caused by the gunas only. When a yogi realizes it, he restrains his mind and body and renounces desires and attachments to suppress and silence the gunas. Upon attaining liberation, he enjoys the nectar of immortality (amritam), available only to gods.

Sloka 21

arjuna uvāca
kair liṅgais trīn guṇān etān atīto bhavati prabho
kimācāraḥ kathaṃ caitāṃs trīn guṇān ativartate

arjunah uvaca = Arjuna said; kaih = by what; lingaih = signs, marks; trin = three; gunan = modes; etan = theses; atitah = transcendence, going beyond; bhavati = manifest, become; prabho = O Lord; kim = what; acarah = behavior; katham = how; ca = and; etan = these; trin = three; gunan = modes; ativartate = overcome, transcend.

Asked Arjuna, "By what marks, O Lord, does one happen to go beyond the triple gunas? What is his behavior, and how does he transcend the triple gunas?"

The gunas have no physicality. They cannot be extracted from the body or quantified. Their presence can only be known through the effects they produce or the marks they leave on the jivas' nature and conduct. For example, the influence of sattva can be discerned from a person's mental brilliance or peaceful disposition. Wherever you find passions such as pride, anger, envy, etc., or intense desire for worldly things, you can be sure that rajas is at work. If you come across people who are deluded, ignorant, lazy, aggressive, lustful, irrational, perverted, evil, or violent, it may be because tamas is predominant. These are indicative and sometimes may be misleading since one cannot deny the role of circumstances in inducing a person's behavior or responses. Further, in real life, you will not come across people who are exclusively sattvic, rajasic, or tamasic. Almost all humans possess the three modes in different combinations and respond according to situations and circumstances. For example, when performing religious or spiritual activities, sattva bhava may come to the fore; in worldly activities. In worldly life, rajasic nature may come to the fore and influence a person's thinking and actions. When people are tired, drunk, confused, or intoxicated, they may be influenced by tamas. Thus, in most situations, people display a wide range of behaviors according to the gunas that become active in them. In this verse, Arjuna wanted to know how one would overcome the triple gunas, what distinguishing qualities manifested when it happened, and what would be the behavior of those who achieved it. In other words, he wanted to know whether it would be possible to recognize it in people by any outward signs. In the previous verse, Lord Krishna stated that only those who transcended the modes would attain liberation. In the next four verses, he will explain their distinguishing qualities.

Sloka 22

Śrībhagavān uvāca
prakāśaṃ ca pravṛttiṃ ca moham eva ca pāṇḍava
na dveṣṭi saṃpravṛttāni na nivṛttāni kāṅkṣati

sri-bhagavan uvaca = the Supreme Lord said; prakasam = light, radiance, illuminatin; ca = and, pravrttim = activity, passion for action; ca = and; moham = illusion; eva = even; ca = and; pandava = O son of Pandu; na = not; dvesti = hates, resents, dislikes; sampravrttani = present, prevail; na nivrttani = cease to exist; kanksati = desires, seeks.

The Supreme Lord said, "O Son of Pandu, not disliking when illumination, sense activity, and delusion arise nor desiring when they cease to exist."

Illumination refers to the illumination of sattva in people and objects. It may also refer to the sun's illumination or the wakeful state when the eyes perceive objects clearly. Prvritti refers to any physical or mental activity, especially the outgoing activity of the mind and senses. Delusion refers to the delusion of ignorant jivas. A yogi who transcends the gunas treats these temporary modifications alike, thinking it is the way of Nature. He is not disappointed when they are present or absent. He does not desire them when he withdraws his mind and senses from worldly objects and practices meditation, or dislikes them in any way when he wakes up from meditation and looks at the world. The beauty, oddity, purity, or impurity of the things and beings he witnesses in his daily life do not disturb him. Free from attraction and aversion, with his cravings, desires, and attachments under control, he excels in sameness and indifference to the ever-changing dualities and circumstances. He remains in harmony with himself and the world around him, neither wishing to change anything nor desiring to control anything, neither liking nor disliking people for their actions and inaction nor the qualities and virtues they possess or do not possess. He is indifferent to the illumination (prakasam) of sattva, the outgoing nature (prvritti) of rajas, or the delusion of tamas he finds in others. He treats them alike, irrespective of their predominant gunas, without judgment, approval, or disapproval.

Those who are subject to the modes have likes and dislikes. They hold firm opinions, judgments, desires, attachments, and entrenched beliefs and act accordingly, whether they are rational or irrational and justified or not. In contrast, those who transcend the gunas (gunatita) remain equal to dualities and conditions. Our suffering and problems arise due to the cravings, choices, likes, and dislikes induced by our predominant gunas. Because of them, we form expectations about how we should live, what we should do, or how others should behave or treat us. We are attached to things we strongly desire and become dependent upon them for peace and happiness. We also develop negative attachments towards things we dislike and feel repelled by their presence. Thus, the union with what we dislike and separation from what we like is a major source of instability, anxiety, pain, and suffering. They also make it difficult for people to be impartial, indifferent, or equal, or contain their emotions, feelings, and passions when life happens to them against their wishes. Those who understand the play of the gunas and how they influence their actions and conduct know how to resolve their suffering and restlessness and attain peace, happiness, or even liberation. Indeed, if the gunas are active, no one can escape suffering, bondage, or karma. To achieve equanimity and sameness, one must transcend the modes through detachment, dispassion, renunciation of desires, and devotion.

Sloka 23

udāsīnavad āsīno guṇair yo na vicālyate
guṇā vartanta ity eva yovatiṣṭhati neṅgate

udasina-vat =as if indifferent; asinah = seated; gunaih = by the gunas; yah = one who; na = not; vicalyate = is disturbed or distracted; gunah = the gunas; vartante = act; iti evam = knowing thus; yah = one who; avatisthati = remains firmly established; na = not; ingate = flickering.

Seated as if indifferent, undisturbed by the gunas, knowing that the gunas alone act, he remains firmly established and does not waver.

All actions in the body arise from the gunas only. The Self does not act or participate in any action. Our attachments and involvement with the world and worldly things also arise from the gunas only. They draw us deep into the whirls of life and keep us busy in our struggle for preservation, security, acceptance, and recognition. The source of our suffering is not external. It is hidden within us in our essential nature, although we keep searching for its causes and solutions in the outside world. As a result, we never fully succeed in resolving our suffering or attaining lasting peace. The source of the problem is within us, and we must focus there to find and resolve it. We may escape from the world with temporary distractions, but we cannot escape from ourselves. Therefore, unless we address the internal causes, we will never be free from our suffering, instability, and dependence upon the world for peace, fulfillment, and happiness. This is not an inescapable or insurmountable problem since it is within the realm of possibility. We can have the knowledge and wisdom to address the hidden causes and resolve our suffering. By creating physical or mental distance from everything that does not constitute the Self, we can become established in the tranquil state of our higher nature or in the silence of the Self. For that, we must give up everything within ourselves and the world, which constitutes the Field of Prakriti, and become physically and mentally empty. Only in the emptiness of the mind, when the gunas are fully at rest and when the mind is coiled into itself in infinite silence and cannot conceptualize, objectify, or ideate, does a yogi enter the realm of the Supreme Lord or the pure state of self-absorption (nirvikalpa samadhi).

The gunas are an essential part of the not-self or Prakriti. Since they are the prime cause of our desires and attachments and cannot be discerned physically, our efforts must begin with the effects they produce. By controlling or suppressing them, we can make the gunas and their influence ineffective. This verse suggests the same. A yogi learns to stay free from the influence of the gunas by controlling the desires, disturbances, and attachments they induce. Through self-control, he willfully avoids the actions, the behavior, and the tendencies they induce, knowing that they are responsible for them and that he is not their cause. Thus, by distancing himself from the world and the causes or agents of his actions, remaining indifferent and uninvolved, and withdrawing from the external world, he remains firmly established in the Self and does not waver. Practicing sameness with an unwavering mind, even when his body is active, he exemplifies the supreme state of inaction in action. Ordinary people react and respond to people and situations according to their gunas. They experience strong passions and emotions such as anger, fear, pride, and envy. The wise ones know that all the actions, desires, and troubles arise from the gunas. Therefore, they practice self-control and self-purification and neutralize the gunas. They remain indifferent and silent to the commotion they create.

Sloka 24

samaduḥkhasukhaḥ svasthaḥ samaloṣṭāśmakāñcanaḥ
tulyapriyāpriyo dhīras tulyanindātmasaṃstutiḥ

sama = same, equal; duhkha = pain, sorrow; sukhah = pleasure, happiness; sva-sthah = self-absorbed, established in the Self; sama = same, equal; losta = a lump of earth; asma = stone; kancanah = gold; tulya = same; priya = pleasant; apriyah = unpleasant; dhirah = steady and unwavering; tulya = balanced; nindatma = in being censured, blamed, criticized; sam= equal; stutih = praised or appreciated.

Equal in pain and pleasure, established in himself, equal to a lump of earth, stone, or gold, equal to what is pleasant or unpleasant, with a steady and unwavering mind, balanced and equal when praised or criticized...

This verse should be read with the next to understand its whole meaning. It describes the state of exclusive devotees (ananya bhakta) who transcend the gunas (gunatita). These qualities manifest when the gunas are dormant or suppressed. The yogi who transcends them (gunatita) remains equal to the dualities. Knowing that the body and the tattvas act according to the gunas, he does not willfully cause them to act or participate in them. Thus, transcending the gunas and his lower nature, with his mind firmly established in the Lord, he becomes stable-minded, balanced, and equal (sthithaprajna) to all dualities, and looks upon everything with sameness, be it a gold nugget, a lump of clay, criticism, or admiration. There are many ways to accomplish this austere goal. However, as Lord Krishna will explain later, the best way to accomplish it is through selfless service and exclusive devotion. Jnana and sannyasa yogis accomplish it by cultivating discernment through the right knowledge and practicing detachment and renunciation. Through uninterrupted contemplation and devotion, they become established in the Lord and attain oneness. Karma yogis accomplish it through nishkama karma, and bhakti yogis through exclusive devotion. In all cases, one must earn the Lord's grace through devotion since any yoga is effective only with devotion and faith.

The yogi who transcends the gunas and is firmly established in his higher nature with the awareness that he is the pure Self does not participate in the actions and movements of his mind and body. In him, detachment, devotion, sameness, and equanimity manifest naturally as he becomes indifferent to the play of the gunas and Maya and remains satisfied within himself. He attains samadhi as he becomes firmly established (svastha) in the thoughts of the Lord within himself. Sameness or oneness (sama+adhi) becomes his natural state as he excels in it and sees his pervading presence in all things he perceives. We find similar ideas in the Ashtavakra Gita also. In one of the chapters, Ashtavakra states that the knower of truth, who is free from attraction and aversion, becomes indifferent towards religious duty (dharma), wealth (artha), sensual pleasure (kama), and even liberation (moksha). He neither accepts them nor rejects them and is neither attached nor unattached. Free from desires, he lives like a child.

Sloka 25

mānāpamānayos tulyas tulyo mitrāripakṣayoḥ
sarvārambhaparityāgī guṇātītaḥ sa ucyate

mana = in honor; apamanayoh = in dishonor; tulyah = equal; tulyah = equal; mitra = friend; ari = enemy; paksayoh = in supporting, taking sides; sarva = all; arambha = beginning, initiating; parityagi = the one who has given up or renounced; guna-atitah = the one who has transcended the gunas; sah = he; ucyate = said to be.

Equal in honor and dishonor, equal to friend and foe in taking sides, who has given up initiating works, he is the one who is said to have transcended the gunas.

A yogi who transcended the gunas remains the same amidst the dualities and disturbances of life. Since he is free from egoism, desires, attachments, and delusion, he is indifferent to honor and dishonor. He treats his friends and foes alike and does not take a stand for them or against them. He also loses interest in initiating any actions due to desires or to achieve anything. He gives up everything, including his name, family name, status, past, present, and future. Renouncing them, he becomes free from the pulls and pressures of the world and how others may think of him or treat him or what may happen to him. Free from the influence of the gunas, he abides in his divine nature, with his mind firmly established in the thoughts of the Lord and his divine qualities, which he aspires to reflect in his thoughts and actions.

Any sign of physical or mental disturbance in response to any external or internal situation is a sign that the ego is still active and not fully subdued. Spiritual gurus and yogis who emotionally react to the opinions of others or the events of the world and make public statements to defend themselves or their actions are not the best examples of those who have transcended the gunas or excel in equanimity or sameness. Their actions suggest that the gunas are still active in them, and they have to overcome the last vestiges of impurities in them. The gunatita, who has transcended the gunas, is always impartial, indifferent, undisturbed, and equal. He does not take sides in disputes or discussions since he has neither friends nor foes. He is non-judgmental in his thinking and attitude. Hence, he neither supports nor condemns anyone or any actions. Being free from desires and worldly attachments, he has no specific aims or goals and no desire to initiate actions or undertake works. If he does, it is only at the behest of others or as an act of sacrifice or offering to God. He may engage in actions for the maintenance of his body or for the sake of Dharma or the welfare of others, as willed by fate or circumstances, but in doing so, he is not motivated by personal gain or loss.

The gunas are responsible for desire-ridden actions. They promote selfishness and egoism in their specific ways. When they are absent, the ego becomes passive, and its influence wanes, letting life take its course and destiny unravel itself. Hence, for the one who transcends the gunas, renunciation becomes an effortless journey. He lays his will and intention at the feet of God and surrenders them to his will. Free from the gunas, desires, attachments, likes, and dislikes, he gives up making choices and judgments and lets things happen to him. Materialistic and ignorant people pursue goals and desires for success and happiness. They spare no effort to seize opportunities, succeed against others, or in their effort, or gain wealth, name, fame, etc. In spiritual life, the priorities are different. Yogis and devotees who seek liberation must pursue different values and ideals. They have to give up everything, including their egos and the need for self-preservation and self-promotion, and surrender themselves to the divine will. It means they should live with unwavering faith, devotion, and trust in the Lord, giving up the urge to control, compete, and strive.

Sloka 26

māṃ ca yovyabhicāreṇa bhaktiyogena sevate
sa guṇān samatītyaitān brahmabhūyāya kalpate

mam = Me; ca = and; yah = who; avyabhicarena = without distraction; bhakti-yogena = by the yoga of devotion; sevate = serves; sah = he; gunan = gunas; samatitya = transcends; etan = these; brahma-bhuyaya = the Self or the State of Brahman; kalpate = fit, suitable, qualified.

Whoever servers Me without distraction and by the yoga of devotion transcends these gunas, he is fit for the State of Brahman.

The importance of ananya bhakti (exclusive devotion) is reemphasized here. It is the best way to transcend the gunas and qualify for liberation. One can serve God in many ways, but of them, devotional service is the best. Devotion to God can be practiced in many ways. It may take the form of worshipping the Lord, contemplating upon him, singing his glories, hearing about him, working for religious causes, teaching spiritual knowledge, promoting Dharma, helping the poor and needy, serving spiritual masters, saints, and great souls, showing compassion to animals, etc. Whatever it may be, it must be done as a sacrifice or offering without expecting anything in return. It must be done solely to declare one's love and devotion to the Supreme Lord. Apart from pure devotees, jnana, karma, and sannyasa yogis also have the opportunity to transcend the triple gunas through exclusive devotion and selfless service. The inclination to worship God and serve others happens mostly due to divine grace when one excels in these yogas. Yogis and devotees may develop it by studying the scriptures, learning from wise people, practicing yamas and niyamas, charity, good deeds, etc., and cultivating discernment, which may lead to the predominance of sattva and suppression of rajas and tamas. As they continue such practices, they will gradually overcome the gunas and the desires and attachments they induce. The Yogasutras of Patanjali states that when intelligence becomes pure as the Self, liberation (kaivalyam) follows. However, to attain liberation, one must transcend the triple gunas. Only then will one be qualified to attain Brahman, who is nirguna (devoid of gunas). Avyabhicarena means not indulging in wayward activities, especially worldly activities that will distract, disturb, and pollute the mind. Brahmabhuta means the Supreme Being or the Cosmic Self (Purusha). Brahman exists in active and passive or manifested and unmanifested states. The passive and unmanifested states are without form (amurtam) and attributes (nirgunam). It is the ultimate state one attains in oneness or liberation.

Sloka 27

brahmaṇo hi pratiṣṭhāham amṛtasyāvyayasya ca
śāśvatasya ca dharmasya sukhasyaikāntikasya ca.

brahmanah = in Brahman; hi = surely; pratistha = established; aham = I am; amrtasya = immortal; avyayasya = inexhaustible; ca = and; sasvatasya = eternal, permanent; ca = and; dharmasya = Dharma; sukhasya = bliss; aikantikasya = highest and absolute; ca = and.

Surely, I am verily established as Brahman, the immortal, inexhaustible, and eternal, the Dharma and the highest bliss.

The Bhagavadgita is a Vedantic text. Its teachings are rooted in the Vedas, especially in the Upanishads and the philosophies of Mimansa and Vedanta. Neither the Mahābhārata nor the Bhagavadgita, which forms a part of it, belongs to any particular Hindu sect, although traditionally Vaishnava teachers used it to propagate their doctrines. One can see its Upanishadic and Vedantic roots from verses such as these, where Lord Krishna identifies himself with Brahman. The idea that he is an incarnation of Lord Vishnu is a subsequent, historic development whose origins are shrouded in history. It might have gained popularity with the development of Vaishnavism as an important sect of Hinduism. However, the Bhagavadgita was not a sectarian text, nor is the Mahabharata in which it is found. Shankaracharya, one of the early commentators of the scripture, was not a Vaishnava. From the earliest times, it was identified as an important Vedantic text. Identifying oneself with Brahman or establishing oneself in the identity of Brahman or the Self is also one of the core concepts of Vedic religion, Vedanta, and the popular belief system of modern Hinduism. The Supreme State of Brahman represents the absolute state of universal oneness, characterized in our terms as the absence of duality and division, which can be attained by one through self-absorption or transcendence. Lord Krishna delivered the discourse in the state of oneness or nonduality. He spoke in the first person as the Lord of the Universe and as if he delivered the discourse to Arjuna from the highest and purest state of Brahman himself. However, at the same time, he showed him his universal form of Kala rather than his pleasant form of Isvara because he needed to prepare Arjuna to fight in the war and fulfill his destiny.

A yogi transcends the triple qualities by practicing undistracted devotion to the Supreme Lord and engaging his mind in contemplation. This dissolves his lower nature and limited identity and establishes him in oneness, which is the immortal, imperishable, eternal state of the Self or Brahman, whose essential nature is absolute bliss. One may worship Brahman directly, but as Lord Krishna stated before, worshipping his unmanifested aspect is difficult for humans. Hence, ideally, devotees should worship the manifested forms of Brahman. Since Lord Krishna declared himself as Brahman in this verse, devotion to Lord Krishna is the same as devotion to Supreme Brahman, Isvara, Narayana, Maha Vishnu, or any other higher manifestation. Through exclusive devotion and earning his grace, a yogi can transcend his lower nature and attain the supreme state of Brahman, which is pure and infinite consciousness.

Several commentators translate brahmaṇo hi pratiṣṭhāham as "I am verily the abode of Brahman." It means I embody Brahman (the Self), or I am the abode of Brahman (the Self). The body is the abode of the Self. All the jivas, without exception, embody the Self in them. If we accept this interpretation, it creates the wrong impression that Lord Krishna embodies Brahman just as all other jivas and is not different from them. Hence, to convey that Lord Krishna is a direct and extraordinary manifestation of Supreme Brahman, not a mere jiva, I translated it as "I am verily established as Brahman" rather than "I am verily the abode of Brahman." The use of 'pratishta' strengthens this argument.

Conclusion

iti srīmadbhāgavadgītāsupanisatsu brahmavidyāyām yogasāstre srikrisnārjunasamvāde guṇatrayavibhāgayogo nāma caturdaśo 'dhyayah.

iti = thus; srīmadbhāgavadgītā = in the sacred Bhagavadgita; upanisatsu = in the Upanishad; brahmavidyāyām = the knowledge of the absolute Brahman; yogasāstre = the scripture of yoga; srikrisnārjunasamvāde = the dialogue between Sri Krishna and Arjuna; guṇatrayavibhāgayogo nāma = by name the yoga of the division of the triple gunas; caturdasah = fourteen; adhyayah = chapter.

Thus ends the fourteenth chapter, named Gunatraya Vibhaga Yoga (the Yoga of the Division of the Triple Gunas) in the Upanishad of the divine Bhagavadgita, the knowledge of the Absolute, a treatise on Yoga, and the debate between Arjuna and Lord Krishna.

15 – Purushottama Yoga

The Yoga of the Supreme Person

Sloka 1

śrībhagavān uvāca
ūrdhvamūlam adhaḥśākham aśvatthaṃ prāhur avyam
chandāṃsi yasya parṇāni yas taṃ veda sa vedavit 15.1

sri-bhagavan = the supreme lord; uvaca = said; urdhva-mulam = roots above, upwards; adhah = below, downwards; sakham = branches; asvattham = asvattha tree; prahuh = said; avyayam = unending; chandamsi = Vedic hymns; yasya = of which; parnani = the leaves; yah = who; tam = that; veda = knows; sah = he; veda-vit = the knower of the Brahman.

The Supreme Lord said, "With roots above, branches below, the Asvattha tree is said to be unending, of which the Vedic hymns are the leaves. He who knows that is a knower of Brahman."

The Asvattha tree (the holy fig tree) symbolizes creation or the manifested Prakriti (sambhuta). It is described here as the tree in an inverse position, with its roots in the sky and the branches below. Its roots are above or in the highest heaven because Brahman is its source and support. He nourishes the earth, the heaven, and all creation. He is also the source of all knowledge and whatever happens or does not happen. Its branches are below, meaning his creations are spread everywhere in the worlds below. The inverse Asvattha tree also symbolizes the human body. In the human body, the head is the root, and the limbs are the branches below. The symbolism can be extended to the four worlds of the Vedic cosmology. The sun, which is considered the immortal world of Brahman, is the root, and the rays emanating from it are the branches. They are spread in the three worlds below: bhur (earth), bhuva (middle world), and suva or swaha (heaven). In the cosmic hierarchy, Brahman, the highest, is the root. Prakriti is the trunk, and her manifestations (worlds and beings) are the branches below, with the brighter ones inhabiting the higher planes and the darker ones the lower planes. The Earth is in the middle. However, it is not at the center of creation but plays an important role in the spiritual evolution and liberation of jivas. The mortal world is dependent and impermanent. So are all the worlds, including the world of Indra and the ancestral world. They constitute the branches, while the beings or the souls who inhabit them are comparable to the leaves.

Thus, in a very symbolic sense, the Asvattha tree represents Brahman and creation or his numerous manifestations. It is unending because Brahman is infinite and ever-expanding. Structurally, it fits the description of a Banyan tree, considered sacred in Hinduism and found commonly in various parts of India. In the Vedas, Brahman is compared to numerous things such as fire, air, horse, sun and moon, breath, speech, intelligence, sky, space, knowledge, brilliance, etc. Of them, his comparison to the Asvattha tree is the most descriptive. It is probably appropriate to say that it represents Creation rather than Brahman himself. Brahman is not in the Asvattha tree, but it arises from him and exists in him. The tree represents Prakriti. Brahman is its source and soul. We may also say that the Asvattha tree represents samsara, the impermanent world, with its source in heaven and its branches upon earth.

The 15th chapter is about Purusha or the Cosmic Person (Purushottama). In the Vedic tradition, he is compared to the human personality. The Great Purusha is symbolically represented here as the source of the Tree of Life, or Life itself. He is its source and support and pervades every aspect of it. Its roots are in the Purusha's head or pure consciousness, from where light and the life-breath flow into every aspect of his cosmic body. The tree itself is the work of Prakriti. It represents his universal body or the Field, made up of the tattvas and pervaded by the triple gunas. From them arise all the modifications which characterize our impermanent and unstable world. The word "vedavit" is translated by most as the knower of the Vedas. Veda means sacred knowledge. The Vedas contain the sacred knowledge of Brahman, of his numerous manifestations, and the means to attain him through ritual and spiritual practices. Vedic hymns contain his power and the secrets to invoke it. When the Vedic mantras are chanted correctly and loudly, the vibrations release Brahman's power hidden in them, propelling it to spread into the universe through space, energizing and cleansing everything it touches. Thus, Vedic hymns awaken Brahman's power, purify the worshippers, and connect the earth with the heavens, humans with gods, the mind and the body with the Self, and the yogis and siddhas with Isvara, the Supreme Being. The Asvattha tree is also mentioned in the Katha Upanishad (2.61), the Taittiriya Upanishad (7.4), the Mahābhārata (47.12-15), and the Puranas.

Each living being is a replica of the universal Asvattha tree only. The body, with all its limbs, represents the tree. Its roots are high above the head in the highest heaven or the Sahasrara Chakra, the highest chakra in the body and the seat of pure consciousness. The tree represents the body, and the aerial roots are all the attachments and entanglements the jivas form upon earth. As they grow deeper, the jivas' liberation becomes increasingly complicated. It is important to remember that our source is Brahman, and our roots are in heaven. Brahman connects us all and is present in all as our pure consciousness and divine nature. We may belong to different countries, families, races, castes, creeds, and backgrounds, but ultimately, we are all connected to one ultimate, universal source and belong to one family, the family of Brahman.

Sloka 2

adhaś cordhvaṃ prasṛtāstasya śākhā guṇapravṛddhā viṣayapravālāḥ
adhaś ca mūlāny anusaṃtatāni karmānubandhīni manuṣyaloke

adhah = downward; ca = and; urdhvam = upward; prasrtah = spread, extending; tasya = of its; sakhah = branches; guna = gunas; pravrddhah = nourished, strengthened; visaya = sense objects; pravalah = young shoots, sprouts; adhah = downward; ca = and; mulani = roots; anusantatani =

extended, spread; karma anubandhini = following the actions; manusya-loke = in the world of human beings.

Downward and upward are spread the branches of that (Tree), nourished by the gunas. The sense objects are its sprouts. Downward are spread (its aerial) roots, following the actions in the world of human beings.

The Asvattha tree is the Tree of Life. It symbolizes creation itself and is comparable to a living being (jiva) who arises from the union of Prakriti and Purusha, also known as Kshetra and Kshetrajna. The body, consisting of the tattvas and gunas, represents the Field (Kshetra), and the Self or pure consciousness represents the Owner of the Field (Kshetrajna). These two entities are present in all the jivas and all the manifestations of Brahman, including Isvara. The tree's origin is in the highest heaven, but its development and modifications happen here in the world of mortals. The banyan tree has a peculiar structure. It has primary roots like any other tree and secondary roots, which grow downward from branches into the base and provide support to the branches. Its branches spread out in various directions and provide shelter to many jivas. Sometimes, they grow so big that the tree occupies several acres, supported by the secondary roots acting as the pillars. The tree is an excellent example of the diversity and complexity of life on Earth and in the heavens, and how life here is inseparably connected to the source above. The branches of the tree are said to spread in both directions, upward and downward, meaning creation is spread out in all directions in the worlds above and below. In the Vedic descriptions of creation, things and beings exist in all the worlds, from the highest to the lowest. The difference is mainly about their purity, divinity, and brightness. The Earth is in the middle plane, while the darker worlds exist below, inhabited by sinful and evil beings.

The triple gunas play an important role in shaping the nature of things in all the worlds. Everything in creation, except Brahman, is subject to their influence. In this verse, the sense objects are compared to sprouts, which will eventually grow into leaves or branches. They symbolize the seeds of karma, which arise from the activity of the senses and our desires and attachment to sense objects, which are, in turn, induced by the gunas. Because of that, beings are deluded and bound as they become entangled with the world and find it hard to escape. The secondary roots are comparable to the attachments and deep bonds we develop in this world through our predominant desires (vasanas), familial and personal relationships, and likes and dislikes. They make it difficult for us to practice renunciation or leave the world or the things we desire or cling to. Thus, symbolically and functionally, each living being is an inverse Asvattha tree bound to the world through countless roots that grow in the soil of our karma bhoomis.

The symbolism of the Asvattha tree has an important hidden message for all humans. It conveys that you are the tree of life. Your roots are supposed to be in heaven, but you grow them in this world through desires and attachments and refuse to leave it. With each birth, you grow illusory roots and become entangled in samsara through friends, family, relationships, ownership, and possessions, which severely restrict your freedom to know or be yourself. Through renunciation, you have to disentangle yourself and return to your source.

Sloka 3

na rūpam asyeha tathopalabhyate nānto na cādir na ca saṃpratiṣṭhā
aśvattham enaṃ suvirūḍhamūlaṃ asaṅgaśastreṇa dṛḍhena chittvā

na = not; rupam = form; asya = of this; iha = here, this; tatha = also; upalabhyate = seen, available, found; na = not; antah = end; na = not; ca = and; adih = beginning; na = not; ca = and; sampratistha = foundation; asvattham = asvattha tree; enam = this; su-virudha = well developed; mulam = roots; asanga-sastrena = by the sword or weapon of detachment; drdhena = strong; chittva = by cutting.

The form of this is not seen here, nor is its end, beginning, or foundation. By cutting the well-developed roots of this Asvattha tree with the sword of detachment...

No one can see the whole creation symbolized as the Asvattha tree, just as no one can see the beginning or the end of the material universe at a glance. It is too big for the human eye to see all at once. Besides, it arises from the union of Purusha and Prakriti, who are infinite, without a beginning or an end. You can, however, separate yourself from it and become free from it by practicing detachment and renunciation and developing a distaste for all worldly things. This is the essence of this verse, which should be read in conjunction with the next. The Tree of Creation arises from Brahman as a projection or illumination. He is not in, remains distinct from it, and supports it as its controller and protector. We cannot see it because we exist in it and are never separate from it. This is true even about gods. We may see it partially as far as our senses permit. The gods may see a little more, but none can see it fully except Isvara. This has been amply illustrated in the Puranas and the Upanishads. It is doubtful whether even self-realized yogis can fully comprehend its dimensions. By overcoming desires and cutting the roots of attachments and the karmic bond with detachment, one may go beyond the limits of creation and unite with Brahman, the source itself. The aerial roots, which are compared to the consequences or the fruit of our actions, must be cut with detachment and renunciation, performing actions without desiring their fruit and preventing the mind from developing roots in the mire of samsara. By withdrawing the mind and senses, overcoming attraction and aversion, and cultivating detachment, one can stabilize it in the Self and attain sameness and oneness.

Sloka 4

tataḥ padaṃ tatparimārgitavyaṃ yasmin gatā na nivartanti bhūyaḥ
tameva cādyaṃ puruṣaṃ prapadye yataḥ pravṛttiḥ prasṛtā purāṇī

tatah = thereafter; padam = place; tat = that; parimargitavyam = has to be sought; yasmin = where; gatah = going; na = no; nivartanti = returns; bhuyah = again; tam = in That; eva = only; ca = and; adyam = the first, primeval;

purusam = purusa, person; prapadye = take refuge; yatah = from whom; pravrttih = manifestation, creation, activity; prasrta = issued forth, spread out, extended; purani = remote past.

After that, that Place has to be sought by going where there is no return again (saying), "I take refuge in that Primeval Purusha only from whom issued forth this ancient creation."

According to the Rigveda, the Primeval Purusha manifests from Brahman before all. This may confuse some people since Purusha has multiple meanings in Hinduism. Purusha means a person or, more specifically, a male or a man. It is also used to denote the individual Self, the Cosmic Being, the Supreme Self, or any divine manifestation. Irrespective of whether they are male or female, the Purusha who resides in the Jivas refers to the embodied Self (jivatma) only. He is gender neutral but identified in the scriptures as the archetypal universal male to distinguish him from Prakriti, the archetypal universal female. The Vedic society was patriarchal. Men had the upper hand in all matters and acted as the lords of their households. They had the obligatory duties to uphold Dharma and serve Isvara, the Cosmic Male, as his representatives on earth. However, in the jivas, the individual Self remains passive, and all the functions are performed by Prakriti only.

The Purusha mentioned here is the first Cosmic Being (adya purusha) to appear in creation. According to some descriptions found in the Vedas, in the beginning, three Purushas emerged from Brahman, namely Hiranyagarbha (the golden germ), Isvara (the universal lord), and Viraj (the material universe which Brahman illumines). Hiranyagarbha is the Cosmic Self. Isvara is the Cosmic Being. Viraj is his alter ego or reflection. The last one is also known as Brahma, the creator god. He was the first divinity (deva) to manifest from Isvara. As the hymns suggest, he performed a sacrifice using parts of his own body or the body of another Purusha he created from himself as the sacrificial material. From that sacrifice, he manifested all beings. Isvara (the Supreme Being) is the first Purusha (adyapurusha) who emerges from Brahman before all, with Prakriti acting as his dynamic force and Brahma as his active agent. He is the archetypal supreme God, who goes by several names and forms and, together with Prakriti, acts as the efficient and material cause of all creation. The Vedas extol him as Saguna Brahman or Brahman with modes (gunas). The material universe is his gross outer body. Bliss, Prana, intelligence, and consciousness are his subtle bodies, in which he resides and pervades as the pure Self. He illuminates Prakriti and all her tattvas and gunas and facilitates the whole creation. The divinities who manifest in creation and participate in it as the upholders of Dharma are his names and forms only.

Here, Lord Krishna suggested that those who seek liberation or want to attain the highest immortal heaven should take refuge in that Supreme Purusha and contemplate upon him, renouncing all desires and attachments, knowing that they should not become bound to the world (the Asvattha tree) since it is a temporary projection and has no real existence. With these words, he gives hope to his devotees that although the Asvattha tree is infinitely large and spread everywhere, they can still escape from it by taking refuge in him and worshipping him with single-minded devotion. In the next verse, he explains who can do it.

Sloka 5

nirmānamohā jitasaṅgadoṣā adhyātmanityā vinivṛttakāmāḥ dvandvair vimuktāḥ sukhaduḥkhasaṃjñaiḥ gacchhanty amūḍhāḥ padam avyayaṃ tat

nir = without; mana = pride, egoism; mohah = delusion; jita = victorious; sanga = attachment; dosah = impurity; adhyatma = absorbed in the Self; nityah = always; vinivrtta = withdrawn, turned away, disengaged; kamah = desires, lust; dvandvaih = dualities; vimuktah = free from; sukha-duhkha = pleasure and pain; samjnaih = such as; gacchanti = attains; amudhah = undeluded, one without delusion; padam = state, path, goal; avyayam = indestructible, inexhaustible; tat = that.

Without pride (and) delusion, conquering the impurity of attachment, always absorbed in the Self, withdrawn from all desires, free from the dualities such as pleasure and pain, the undeluded one attains that indestructible state.

This verse describes the qualities that lead to the highest and most indestructible state of liberation. Nirmānamoha means freedom from pride (mana) and delusion (moha). One may also say freedom from the delusion of pride or egoism. Māna means pride, arrogance, self-respect, etc. It is an offshoot of egoism, which arises due to the deluded identification of oneself with the name and form or with the mind and body under the influence of the triple gunas. Self-love, or love for oneself or one's name and form (namarupa), which people manifest in different ways, indicates that the gunas are still active and exerting influence on actions. Yogis who excel in exclusive devotion must renounce their physical selves, desires, and attachments and remain established in the thoughts of the Lord, subduing their egos, pride, delusion, etc. When they are under control, they remain disinterested in worldly matters and indifferent to their physical identities, names, and forms, and how people perceive them, think about them, accept them, approve them, or disapprove them. In other words, they give up their egotism completely and remain satisfied within themselves.

An adept yogi may engage in selfless actions due to altruistic considerations rather than winning the approval of others or earning their appreciation. He does not give any importance to the values the world holds in esteem to measure people or control them. Free from attraction and aversion, he remains established in the sameness, without any selfish notion or interest, and equal to the dualities such as pleasure and pain. Ananya bhaktas renounce desires and attachments, which means they do not act upon them or let them influence them. Worldly people let their minds wander in all directions to fulfill their desires. Their outgoing nature is attuned to the world and its values. The enlightened withdraw into themselves, keeping their minds and senses under firm control. Since they subdue the gunas, desires, and attachments, they radiate divine qualities.

Sloka 6

na tad bhāsayate sūryo na śaśāṅko na pāvakaḥ
yad gatvā na nivartante tad dhāma paramaṃ mama

na = not; tat = that; bhasayate =illuminates; suryah = the sun; na = not; sasankah = the moon; na = nor; pavakah = fire; yat = where; gatva = going; na = not, never; nivartante = return; tat = that; dhama = abode; paramam = supreme; mama = My.

Neither the sun nor the moon nor the fire illuminates That. Where, by going, one never returns. That is My Abode.

The highest and most effulgent Abode of Brahman is not illuminated by the sun and the moon but by Brahman, who is self-luminous. According to the Vedas, he illuminates the sun and the moon, all his manifestations, all the objects that we perceive in our consciousness, all the knowledge and awareness, liveliness, sentience, and the whole creation that manifests in the Field of Prakriti. Unlike our world, the immortal word of Brahman is free from dualities such as heat and cold or pleasure and pain. The limitations of form, divisions, time, space, knowledge, power, or illumination do not exist in his realm. Liberated souls who attain him enter the same state of absolute freedom. They are not born again or subject to many modifications. They are also not affected by the recurring cycles of creation and destruction. In contrast, those who do not reach him remain bound to the cycle of births and deaths. They keep coming and going until they attain liberation.

Sloka 7

mamaivāṃśo jīvaloke jīvabhūtaḥ sanātanaḥ
manaḥṣaṣṭhānīndriyāṇi prakṛtisthāni karṣati

mama = My; eva = only; amsah = fraction, portion, part; jiva-loke = world of beings; jiva-bhutah = living Self, embodied Self; sanatanah = eternal; manah = mind; sasthani = six; indriyani = senses; prakrti = nature; sthani = abiding, established; karsati = draws, attracts.

The embodied Self, a fraction of Me only, in the world of beings draws to itself the senses of which the mind is the sixth, established in Prakriti.

According to this verse, the embodied Self (jiva bhuta), which resides in the jivas, is a part of the Supreme Self. Entering the Field of Prakriti (the body or creation), it draws to itself the materiality required to become a living entity. Although the senses and the mind are mentioned, we have to assume that it draws to itself different tattvas for the formation of the jiva. Some jivas contain all the tattvas, and some only a few. The Vedas concur that the individual Self is an aspect of the Universal Self only. However, it is unclear whether the individual Self exists as an independent entity distinct from the Supreme Self or whether the same Self appears in each being (jiva) as an individual Self. This verse gives the impression that the embodied Self is a fraction or part (amsa) of the Supreme Self.

The mind (manas) is considered the sixth sense because it is their lord and controller and receives all the offerings (perceptions) they gather and bring in. However, in Vedic terminology, manas (the memorial mind) is not equivalent to the mind as understood in modern science but a receptacle of all the thoughts, knowledge, feelings, perceptions, memories, etc., the jiva experiences. The knowledge thus accumulated and stored is processed and retrieved by the ego with the help of intelligence. The senses, the mind, the ego, and intelligence constitute the internal organ (antahkarana). It is well-formed and fully functional only in humans.

The individual Self is distinct from the tattvas and has no relationship with them. It is self-luminous. The tattvas do not possess their own illumination. They are, instead, illuminated by the Self only. Hence, they are active only when the Self is present in the body. Although the verse says that the Self attracts or draws to itself the senses, that action is carried by Nature only. Lord Krishna said so because he spoke without duality and did not distinguish between himself and his Nature. The tattvas are drawn to the Self by the force of Nature. Just as a lamp attracts insects or just as a lump of sugar attracts ants, the Self attracts the tattvas of Nature by its very presence and becomes enveloped by them. The next verse explains the fate of the body or the beingness of a jiva when the Self departs from it.

Sloka 8

śarīraṃ yad avāpnoti yac cāpy utkrāmatīśvaraḥ
gṛhitvaitāni saṃyāti vāyur gandhān ivāśayāt

sariram = body; yat = when; avapnoti = acquired; yat = when; ca = and; api = even; utkramati = departs; isvarah = the Lord, the Self; grhitva = taking; etani = these; samyati = goes away; vayuh = air; gandhan = fragrance; iva = like; asayat = from abode, retreat, resting-place.

When the Lord acquires the body and when he departs, he goes away taking these, like the wind (carries away) the fragrance from their abodes.

After drawing the tattvas to himself and acquiring a body and after thus becoming a living Self, the Lord lives in the mortal world as a jiva, bound to Prakriti and Samsara. When the jiva dies, he departs from here carrying with him the essences of life (breaths, senses, etc.), just as the wind carries away fragrances from flowers, etc. The tattvas, including the mind and senses, perish with the body. The analogy of wind carrying away fragrance makes the relationship between the Self and the jiva's essences coincidental. When the wind carries away fragrances from their sources, it does not carry them forever or is tainted by them, but leaves them behind and moves on. Similarly, when the embodied Self departs from here, carrying with it the breaths and the deities in the organs, it leaves them behind in the mid-region (Antariksha) and travels alone to the next world. The Self participates in it passively and does not become involved with it. Thus, there is no permanent connection between the Self and any activities associated with the birth and death of the jivas, including their transmigration. However, in the body, he is the support. The tattvas are bound to him and function only when he is present. As the Upanishads declare, the Self does not depend upon the senses, but because of him and for him only they work. He does not depend upon the mind, but because of him only, it works. Prana, the life-sustaining force in the body, remains active and flows in the subtle channels (nadis) because of him, and when he is present. Once he departs from the body, prana also departs and accompanies him to the mid-region, where they part their ways.

Sloka 9

śrotraṃ cakṣuḥ sparśanaṃ ca rasanaṃ ghrāṇam eva ca
adhiṣṭhāya manaś cāyaṃ viṣayān upasevate

srotram = ears; caksuh = eyes; sparsanam = skin; ca = and; rasanam = tongue ghranam = nose; eva = even; ca = also; adhisthaya = presiding over; manah = mind; ca = and; ayam = this; visayan = sense objects; upasevate = enjoys.

Presiding over the ears, eyes, skin, nose, tongue, and even the mind, this One enjoys sense objects.

In the body, the Self is the enjoyer. He presides over it as the enjoyer while remaining passive. As Lord Krishna said before, the individual Self is a fraction of the Supreme Lord. Although he is ensconced in the web of life and witnesses its myriad hues, he is untouched by them or the impurities of samsara. His presence in the Field of Prakriti is temporary, during which he remains unchanged and untainted. He presides over the organs of the body as their Lord (Adhidaiva) and enjoys the fruit of their actions. However, he does not control them, their actions, or modifications. When he departs from the body, he carries with them all the deities present in the organs.

According to the Vedas, the human body comprises five sheaths (kosas), corresponding to the five elements (pancha bhutas). The outermost sheath is formed by the food the jiva consumes. Hence, it is known as the food body. It is gross and dense. Next to it is the breath body, made up of prana. The mental body is the next, made up of all mental objects or consciousness. Beneath it is the intelligence body, made up of pure intelligence. The innermost sheath is known as the bliss body. It is permeated with the bliss flowing from the Self. The food body constitutes the gross outer body, while the other four constitute the subtle body. All the tattvas in the body, including the mind and the senses, have functional aspects corresponding to these five sheaths. They have their own subtle and subtlest aspects. The Self, the subtlest of all, does not participate in their activities but remains a silent witness, absorbed in itself. We say the Self is the enjoyer because enjoyment is a subjective experience arising from the feeling of "I-am-ness," which is the closest approximation to the Self. In truth, the Self is self-absorbed and blissful and has no connection with the world or its sense objects. The Self is the enjoyer because it has no suffering and eternally enjoys bliss as its natural state.

The idea behind this is that one should not seek enjoyment through the senses because that privilege belongs to the Self only. You may enjoy the world and its objects with self-awareness or by remaining established in the Self, but not in the body or the ego. Therefore, a yogi who pursues liberation should practice self-restraint (atma samyama) and remain indifferent to sense pleasures. When the body is engaged in actions, he must know that the body is engaged in actions for him, but he is not in them. He must practice exclusive devotion (ananya bhakti) to the Supreme Lord of the Universe as well as the Lord who dwells in him as his very Self. As the Kaushataki Upanishad declares, a seeker should not let himself be distracted by his senses but try to know the Person behind them, who is responsible for their actions. In other words, if liberation is your aim, you should not be interested in the actions of your mind and body or senses but focus on the one who enjoys them and for whom they work. Similarly, one should be indifferent to the dualities such as pain and pleasure, day and night, or heat and cold, knowing that the Self is untouched by them and indifferent to them.

Sloka 10

utkrāmantaṃ sthitaṃ vāpi bhuñjānaṃ vā guṇānvitam
vimūḍhā nānupaśyanti paśyanti jñānacakṣuṣaḥ

utkramantam = in the end; sthitam = present, situated, located; va = or; api = also; bhunjanam = enjoying; va = or; guna-anvitam = adorned with qualities; vimudhah = deluded people; na = not; anupasyanti = see; pasyanti = see; jnana-caksusah = eyes of knowledge.

Deluded people do not see him when he departs in the end or when he is present (in the body), enjoying or adorned with qualities. Those with the eyes of wisdom see.

The Lord in the body can only be seen with the eye of discernment when one is free from delusion and the ignorance that the body represents one's true Self. You will know the Self only when you are free from all attachments, associations, formations, qualities, modes, and expressions, see your body as distinct from you, and enter the subjective state of I-am-ness, which is free from duality. You become aware of it only when your internal organ falls into absolute silence, and you alone remain. Until you dissolve your ego in that pure state of self-awareness, you do not truly possess the eye of discernment (jñānacakṣu) and should not consider yourself the knower of the Self. The physical self is visible and tangible. Hence, the deluded ones readily accept it as their true Self and fail to discern the invisible and imperceptible Self hidden in them. The Self is known only when the senses are inactive, the surface consciousness is tranquil, and the mind is fully absorbed in itself without awareness or otherness. The ignorant ones remain stuck in their physical identities and all the associated identities arising from them, such as the identities associated with their families, communities, genders, castes, nationalities, regions, religions, languages, professions, etc. As they cling to them and remain stuck in them, they cannot hope to know anything about themselves or their essential nature beyond them.

Thus, veiled by Maya and ignorant of the Lord who resides in them as their very Self, the deluded ones remain bound to their chaotic surface consciousness, seeking fulfillment, peace, and happiness through sense-gratification and desire-ridden actions and accepting only that which their minds and senses validate as true and real. The Charvakas of ancient India followed a similar philosophy. They were materialists who believed in the objective reality they could validate through their senses, mind, and intelligence. According to them, there was no rebirth; death was the final salvation, and when beings died, their bodies returned to the elements, and they ceased to exist. Buddhists also do not acknowledge the existence of a permanent and indestructible Self. According to them, existence is impermanent and unstable, and everything in the phenomenal existence, including the Self, is subject to change and dissolution. However, they believe in the physical self or the not-self (mind and body), karma, and rebirth, and hold that beings remain bound to samsara until they extinguish the not-self, are free from births and deaths, and attain Nirvana.

Despite these divergent theories, the Bhagavadgita is unequivocal about the existence of the eternal and indestructible Self and its liberation from the mortal world. As Lord Krishna stated, a portion of the Supreme Self manifests in the Field of Prakriti as the embodied Self. It goes through the cycle of births and deaths due to the influence of the gunas and desire-ridden actions until it is liberated from the impurities of the Field through self-control and exclusive devotion. Only the wise ones who cultivate discernment or the self-realized ones who possess the eye of wisdom perceive the Self. They qualify for liberation. The deluded ones who solely rely upon their minds and senses and perceptual reality do not perceive it as they remain centered in their physical nature, trapped by maya. Hence, they keep revolving from birth to birth in samsara.

Sloka 11

yatanto yoginaś cainaṃ paśyanty ātmany avasthitam
yatantopy akṛtātmāno nainaṃ paśyanty acetasaḥ

yatantah = with intense effort, striving, yoginah = yogis; ca = and; enam = this; pasyanti = see; atmani = in themselves avasthitam = present, established; yatantah = striving; api = but; akrta-atmanah = imperfect or incomplete beings; na = not; enam = this; pasyanti =see; acetasah = without discernment or intelligence.

And with intense effort, the yogis see this (Self) established in themselves, but the ignorant ones with impure minds, lacking in discernment, cannot see it even with striving.

Liberation is a difficult journey. One has to endure arduous effort (yatana), hardships, obstacles, and suffering on the Path to reach the Goal. In the context of the Bhagavadgita, yoga means the state of sameness or equanimity attained by withdrawing and restraining the mind and senses and suppressing desires and attachments. It is the same state that classical yoga aims to achieve by suppressing the modifications of the mind through the eightfold practice. In either case, one has to cultivate knowledge, detachment, and discernment and practice renunciation to transcend the gunas and overcome desires and attachments. Only a few accomplished yogis, such as the siddhas (perfect ones) and yuktas (skillful ones), who possess transparent minds and pure intelligence and excel in exclusive devotion, succeed in it by discerning the Lord in them. Overcoming duality and division and dissolving their surface consciousness in him, they attain oneness. If liberation is difficult to attain even for striving yogis who endure the hardships of abhyasa, what can be said about those who are impure and engage in sinful actions (akṛtātmās)? With unrestrained and unstable minds, driven by the gunas and desire-ridden actions, how can they stabilize their minds in the Self and attain oneness? Even if they strive hard, they fail because, veiled by Maya and the impurities of ignorance, egoism, delusion, and desires, they lack the discernment to know the Lord in them or establish their minds in him.

Thus, instead of taking their liberation for granted, yogis must strive to excel in self-restraint, karma-sannyasa, and exclusive devotion to purify themselves, transcending the gunas, desires, and attachments. Through renunciation, devotion, detachment, and indifference, they must persevere to overcome desires and attachments and establish their minds in exclusive devotion. When they attain the highest perfection through these efforts, their internal organs (antahkarana) become illuminated with the light of the Self just as the earth is illuminated by the sun that shines brightly in a cloudless sky. It does not happen if the gunas are still active or if the mind is still clouded and subject to impurities and disturbances. Hence, Lord Krishna emphasized that impure people cannot perceive the Self even if they strive. They may read scriptures, acquire the knowledge of liberation, or seek the guidance of gurus, but do not experience sameness or oneness with the Self.

Sloka 12

yad ādityagataṃ tejo jagad bhāsayatekhilam
yac candramasi yac cāgnau tat tejo viddhi māmakam

yat = that; aditya-gatam = in the sun; tejah = brilliance, light; jagat = the world; bhasayate = illuminates; akhilam = whole; yat = that which; candramasi = in the moon; yat = that which; ca = and; agnau = in the fire; tat = that; tejah = splendor; viddhi = know; mamakam = Mine.

That brilliance in the sun which illuminates the whole world, which is in the moon as well as in the fire, know that brilliance is Mine.

The Supreme Lord is the support of all creation. He is the source of the life-sustaining prana, energy, and consciousness in the jivas. Whatever shines in the manifested worlds, its source is the Lord only. When he enters the body, all the tattvas in it come to life, and when he departs from it, the body dies. The Vedas affirm that neither the sun nor the moon nor any fire shines in Brahman, but shines by himself since he is self-effulgent. In a previous verse (15.6), Lord Krishna also said the same to convey that the world of Brahman is self-luminous, independent of external causes, and free from dualities like day and night or light and darkness. All the brilliance in creation arises from him. The same brilliance shines within all the jivas due to the presence of the Lord in them. The light in the macrocosm and the light within the jivas arise from him only. It radiates in the jivas as liveliness (chaitanyam) and is experienced in self-absorption as pure consciousness. Without him, the mind will not be illuminated by consciousness, intelligence will not function, and knowing, knowledge, and awareness will not arise.

Of the triple gunas, the mode of sattva has the power to reflect the Lord's brilliance. According to the Yogasutras, we perceive sense objects when they are illuminated in our consciousness (chitta) by sattva. We owe that illumination (mental brilliance) and the knowledge and discernment arising from it to the Self in us, the life-support, not to our bodies or the tattvas. The illumination of the sun, the moon, and the stars also arises from Brahman only. Isvara, the Supreme Being, is illuminated by his own light. His body, unlike ours, is pure and untainted. Hence, his effulgence radiates from him without obstructions and can illuminate and awaken even the darkest minds. In the jivas, delusion arises when Prakriti (maya) veils his illumination. When impurities are removed, and the light of the Self shines through the internal organ without interruptions and hindrances, one develops mental brilliance, knowledge, and wisdom, and discerns the Self. Yoga is meant to accomplish this transformation and facilitate purity so that yogis can radiate the self-luminous light within them without interruptions and abide in sameness and oneness.

Sloka 13

gām āviśya ca bhūtāni dhārayāmy aham ojasā
puṣṇāmi cauṣadhīḥ sarvāḥ somo bhūtvā rasātmakaḥ

gam = the earth; avisya = entering; ca = and; bhutani = living beings; dharayami = support, sustain; aham = I; ojasa = by My vigor, energy; pusnami = nourish; ca = and; ausadhih = herbs, plants; sarvah = all; somah = soma; bhutva = becoming; rasa-atmakah = filled with juice, juicy, succulent.

And entering the earth, I sustain all beings with My vigor and nourish all the plants by becoming the juicy Soma.

The manifestations of the Brahman are numerous. He manifests fully or partially, and sometimes, only his functional aspects manifest in the places, images, icons, or jivas to denote his presence and influence. The power to sustain and nourish life upon earth and elsewhere arises from Brahman only. He is called the bearer or husband (bhartha) because he bears the burdens of life and creation as the upholder of all. The earth is called Dharitri because she also bears the burden of all the jivas and the brunt of Nature when calamities strike. She nourishes all life as the Universal Mother, supported by the Lord, the ultimate nourisher and upholder of all. Due to him, the sun, the moon, the gods, and humans perform their functions to ensure the order and regularity, and the progression of the world. When gods are nourished through sacrifices, they nourish the earth with rains, fertility, natural abundance, cattle, and food. Thus, the Lord sustains all beings and exemplifies sacrifice and selfless duty. As the source of food, he becomes the nourisher, and as the food, he becomes the nourished. The Vedas declare Brahman as food, nourisher, and devourer of all as he engages in the triple duties of creation, preservation, and destruction. They also declare that all that exists here is food for Brahman. As the Lord of Death, he devours everything and facilitates their renewal and rebirth. A part of the food consumed by humans becomes reproductive material (retas) or the seed for the continuation of life on Earth. Lord Krishna specifically said here that he sustains all plants by becoming their sap (juicy Soma) because plants are the primary sources of food and energy for all life forms. Without them, life on Earth cannot be sustained. The sap in the earth (water and nutrients) directly nourishes plants. The rest of the jivas depend upon them or those who derive their food from them.

Sloka 14

ahaṃ vaiśvānaro bhūtvā prāṇināṃ deham āśritaḥ
prāṇāpānasamāyuktaḥ pacāmy annaṃ caturvidham

aham = I; vaisvanarah = Vaisvanarah, the digestive fire; bhutva = becoming; praninam = in the living beings; deham = body; asritah = residing, taking refuge; prana = prana, upward breath; apana = apana, downward breath; samayuktah = union, association; pacami = digest; annam = food; catuh-vidham = four kinds of.

Residing in the body of living beings (and) becoming the digestive fire, together with upward and downward breaths, I digest four kinds of food.

The Lord, who resides in us as our very Self, is the ultimate enjoyer of all actions and functions, including digestion. He is also the ultimate source of the digestive fires in the body. Becoming the digestive fire, he digests the food. It is important to remember that the Lord does not perform any functions directly in the body. All actions are performed by his Prakriti. Since she is an integral and dependent aspect of him, he is considered the ultimate cause. Vaisvanara is the divine fire that shines brightly in heaven as an aspect of Agni. It collectively belongs to the gods. Through it, they receive all the sacrificial offerings when humans perform sacrifices and pour offerings into the sacred fire. Its subtle version is present in the jivas as the digestive fire, which is responsible for digestion and the warmth in the body. In the macrocosm, it becomes the sun's rays, nourishes plants, and keeps the world warm and bright. In beings, it transforms food into life-sustaining and reproductive energies. Hence, in the Upanishads, it is extolled as the life-supporting and life-giving fire.

In the previous verse, Lord Krishna said that he was the life-sustaining Soma Juice (sap) in plants. It is a reference to his association with the water element. In this verse, he describes himself as Vaisvanara, which is a reference to his association with the fire element. Together, the two represent Agni-Soma (the sun and the moon), the presiding deity of digestion. Thus, by associating himself with fire and water in the digestive tract, he supports and sustains all life forms. The Mandukya Upanishad describes Vaisvanara as the jiva (living being) in a wakeful state who enjoys gross material things with seven limbs and nineteen mouths. According to Chandogya Upanishad, the seven limbs are the head, feet, bladder, chest, hair, heart, and mouth. The nineteen mouths are the five sense organs, five organs of action, five vital breaths, mind, ego, intelligence, and dynamic consciousness (citta). Thus, Vaisvanara is the personification of the Lord as the Lord of Fire in the body, who presides over it as its controller (Adhidaiva), enjoyer, breath, and life-sustaining digestive power.

Fire is an essential aspect of Vedic ritualism and symbolism. It has numerous forms. Just as there are many types of sacrificial fires, the human body contains many types of internal fires responsible for many life-sustaining functions, including birth, death, breathing, digestion, and procreation. The gods in the body are nourished by the food digested through the Vaisvanara fire and carried to different organs by prana through the nerve channels. Thus, the survival of life on earth depends upon the internal fires kept alive by Prakriti, the Lord's agent. Symbolically, in the Vedas, digestion is compared to an internal fire sacrifice, in which, knowingly or unknowingly, jivas nourish the gods who preside over their organs with the food they consume. In that sacrificial ritual, food is poured into the digestive fires of the body, which serves as the sacrificial pit. From the offering thus made, manifest the life and destiny of the sacrificer as its fruit (prasadam). Pleased by the offering, the divinities help the jivas in their survival and well-being and enjoy peace and happiness as the rewards of their sacrifice.

In this verse, Lord Krishna states that he digests four kinds of food in the jivas with the help of prana and apana. Prana is the upward or inward breath, and apana is the downward or outward breath. The air we breathe is prana, whereas the air that flows downwards and goes out of the body through the digestive system is apana. The breaths in the body also distribute the energy generated from the food to various organs in the body. According to Shankaracharya, the four kinds of food mentioned in this verse are the foods consumed by chewing, sucking, swallowing, and licking.

Sloka 15

sarvasya cāhaṃ hṛdi saṃniviṣṭomattaḥ smṛtir jñānam apohanaṃ ca
vedaiś ca sarvair aham eva vedyo vedāntakṛd vedavid eva cāham

sarvasya = of all; ca = and; aham = I; hrdi = in the heart; sannivistah = seated, situated; mattah = from Me; smrtih = memory; jnanam = knowledge; apohanam loss, removal; ca = and; vedaih = from the Vedas; ca = and; sarvaih = all; aham = I am; eva = alone; vedyah = which is to be known, knowable; vedanta-krt = the creator of the Vedanta; veda-vit = knower of the Vedas; eva = also, even; ca = and; aham = I.

And I am seated in the heart of all. From Me, memory, knowledge, and even their loss. I alone am the object to be known from the Vedas. I Myself am the creator of the philosophical wisdom and the knower of the Vedas also.

These verses describe the glories of the indwelling Lord (Paramatma) and the Supreme Lord (Parabrahma) of all. He is also the Self of all (Adhyatma), the Lord of all materiality (Adhibhuta), and the Supreme Lord of all creation (Adhidaiva). Previously, Lord Krishna said that a fragment of him becomes the indwelling Self in the jiva and draws to itself the mind and senses. He also said that he was the enjoyer, illuminator, supporter, nourisher, and energizer, who could be discerned only by adept yogis through striving but not by the undisciplined and deluded ones, even if they strived. In this verse, he added that he was indeed the source of all knowledge, learning, memory, their loss, the source of the Vedas, the knower of the Vedas, and the one to be known. Although the senses, the mind, and intelligence, which belong to Prakriti, are responsible for the memorial knowledge and our mental faculties, they are illuminated by the Self only. Hence, it is rightly concluded here that memory, knowledge, and even their loss arise from the Lord only.

This verse affirms that the Self is seated in the heart of all, not just humans. He is the source of dynamism or sentience (chaitanyam) in all beings. Because of his illumination only, we experience liveliness or the feeling of being alive and active. His presence lights up our internal organs (antahkarana) and keeps our minds illuminated and active with mental brilliance. All the modifications of the mind, knowledge, memory, etc., arise from him only when he is present. He is responsible for all the dualities. Light and darkness, knowledge and ignorance, and memory and memory loss arise from him and subside in him only. Apoha means loss of memory or knowledge. Apoha also means confusion, misunderstanding, or having wrong or false opinions. It may arise from the absence of right knowledge, faulty reasoning, or lack of discernment when the mind and intelligence are clouded by ignorance and delusion. When the Self illuminates the internal organ uninterruptedly, people discern the Self and work for their liberation. When it is interrupted by impurities, they suffer from delusion and mistaken notions about themselves and remain bound. As the grantor of liberation and wielder of Maya, he is responsible for both conditions.

The Vedas affirm that Brahman is the source and personification of the Vedas. Just like him, they are eternal and uncreated and were transmitted by Brahma through his mind to his seven mind-born sons or the seven seers. Hence, the Vedas are also known as apaurusheya, meaning not created by humans. As Lord Krishna states here, Brahman is also the goal and the purpose of the Vedas. They reveal the knowledge and practice of Dharma (obligatory duties) so that humans may practice God's eternal duties (Sanatana Dharma) in the world as theirs and ensure its orderly progression. The Vedas help the seekers of truth, and the wise ones (jnanis) know the secrets of Brahman. They help the householders achieve the four aims of human life (purusharthas), namely Dharma (performing obligatory duties), Artha (attaining wealth), Kama (fulfilling desires), and Moksha (achieving liberation).

Lord Krishna also stated that he is the source of the Vedanta. Vedanta means the end of the Vedas or the knowledge and wisdom contained in the end part of the Vedas, which is a reference to the Upanishads since they constitute the end parts. The Upanishads are numerous and composed at different times over a long period. They are, at best, fragments of esoteric knowledge about Brahman and the Self. The Bhagavadgita is also considered a Upanishad, although it is not a part of the Vedas and belongs to a different category. Each Veda is associated with several of them. Their collective wisdom is called the Vedanta. It is further divided into several schools, such as Advaita, Dvaita, Vishistadvaita, Dvaita Advaita, etc. However, Vedanta also means the knowledge, wisdom, or philosophy that arises from the Vedas or from knowing Brahman. From this perspective, it means any philosophical knowledge or school of philosophy that is derived from the Vedas and accepts the Vedas as the inviolable and ultimate authority.

Sloka 16

dvāv imau puruṣau loke kṣaraś cākṣara eva ca
kṣaraḥ sarvāṇi bhūtāni kūṭasthokṣara ucyate 15.16

dvau = two; imau =these; purusau = purusas; loke = in the world; ksarah = perishable; ca = and; aksarah = imperishable; eva = only indeed; ca = and; ksarah = the perishable; sarvani = all; bhutani = living beings; kuta-sthah = unchangeable, standing at the top, occupying the highest place, the ancestor of all; aksarah =indestructible; ucyate = is said.

These are the only two Purushas in the world: the imperishable and the perishable. All living beings are perishable, but the unchangeable one who stands above all is said to be imperishable.

Lord Krishna began this chapter by describing creation as the Tree of Life (Asvattha), whose roots are in the highest heaven and whose branches and leaves are spread below. Then he revealed that a portion (amsa) of him becomes the living Self in the beings (jivas) and draws to himself the senses and the mind. In this verse, he brought these two divergent aspects of samsara, describing them as the two Purushas, one perishable, consisting of all the living beings, and the other, the imperishable, who is without a second, unchangeable, and stands above all. The jiva is also a god, but a perishable god. He has a false Self, the ego, which is also perishable. His body with the impurities is perishable, but his pure consciousness, which is independent of his mind and intelligence, is imperishable. Although they are mentioned here as Purushas, they are but Purusha and Prakriti, his immutable and mutable aspects. The imperishable Purusha is the presiding deity of all jivas (jiva bhutam), but he is not the highest. He is an aspect (amsa) of Isvara, the highest in creation. Beings are bound to samsara and subject to modifications, death, rebirth, and maya or delusion. They have a beginning and an end and experience impermanence and suffering due to dualities, desires, and attachments. The indwelling, imperishable Self is unchangeable, imperishable, and without a beginning or an end. The modifications of Prakriti arising from impermanence do not affect him.

Kutastha means unchangeable, highest, standing at the top, etc. In the material world, it is represented by the sun. In the body, it refers to the Self. In creation, it refers to Isvara, who is above all and represents the roots in the upside-down Asvattha tree. The whole creation, consisting of all the jivas, divinities, objects, worlds, states, and finite realities, constitutes the perishable Cosmic Reality or the Field. The imperishable Self resides in them as their support and illuminator. Even though he is situated amidst the impurities and modifications, he remains immutable. Thus, Purusha and Prakriti, as the perishable and the imperishable Purushas, represent the most fundamental duality of creation. They are also known as his higher and lower natures. This and the following verse support the argument that there is a fundamental duality between the Supreme Self and the individual Self and between Brahman and his creation. However, the school of nondualism (Advaita) refutes the whole idea with a different interpretation.

Sloka 17

uttamaḥ puruṣas tv anyaḥ paramātmety udāhṛtaḥ
yo lokatrayam āviśya bibharty avyaya īśvaraḥ

uttamah = the highest, supreme; purusah = purusha; tu = but, however; anyah = different, another; parama = supreme; atma = self; iti = thus; udahrtah =said to; yah = who; loka = worlds; trayam = three; avisya = pervading; bibharti = upholds; avyayah = inexhaustible; isvarah = the Lord.

However, the highest Purusha, who is said to be the Supreme Self, the imperishable Lord who upholds the three worlds, pervading them, is different.

This verse distinguishes between Isvara, the Lord of the Universe, and the embodied Self (Purusha) in the jivas. Both are imperishable, but are different. They also have different functions and roles. Isvara is the Creator, Preserver, Concealer, Revealer, and Destroyer. He is also the supreme controller and the presiding Lord of Prakriti. The embodied Self performs no such functions and remains a passive witness and enjoyer. The Supreme Lord of the Universe, variously known as Isvara, Parameswara, Sada Shiva, Narayana, etc., has a hidden aspect also: the unmanifested Brahman. He is the First, before all, and the beginning of all, because everything emerges out of him. The Upanishads describe him as the unmanifested (avyaktam) and formless (amurtam) absolute reality. He is also the non-being, who is incomprehensible and known only to a few seers who attained the highest purification through jnana, karma, sannyasa, and bhakti yogas. Lord Krishna mentioned him in the previous chapters as the deity who was difficult to worship and realize. The unmanifested and mysterious Brahman, who is not a Being but the eternal, indestructible, and immutable Reality and whose nature is pure consciousness, does not participate in creation or engage in any actions. Prakriti remains dormant in him. Isvara is indeed the source and support of the Asvattha tree, which spreads out from him as a projection into the three worlds and upon which rests his creation, including the worlds, jivas, divinities, and his highest manifestations. He pervades it and envelops it, apart from illuminating it, upholding it, and nourishing it. The three worlds mentioned here refer to the three cosmic planes: the lower world (bhuh), the middle world (bhuva), and the upper world (svah).

Thus, the Bhagavadgita envisages a cosmic reality consisting of three supreme entities: Purusha, the embodied and imperishable Self; Prakriti, the perishable not-self; and Isvara, the Supreme Lord of the Universe. The Supreme Self or the unmanifested Brahman remains hidden. Purusha (the individual Self), Isvara (the Cosmic Self), and Brahman (the absolute Self) all have pure consciousness as their essence or essential nature. We do not know whether they are the same or different or notionally different. We can only speculate about him since they are eternal and beyond the knowable reality. Prakriti is an integral part of all the Purushas. She is a part of Brahman also as the unmanifested, primal Prakriti (asambhuta). The state of Brahman is always absolute and unmanifested. His manifested and unmanifested states arise because of Prakriti only. She is the Field (Kshetra) where the divine drama (lila) unfolds. She serves all the Purushas in creation and sustains them as their force and dynamic energy. In the Vedas, Brahma, the highest god in the original Vedic pantheon, is identified with all these purushas - as the embodied Self, as the creator god, as Isvara, and as Brahman. He is also identified with Prakriti (the world).

Sloka 18

yasmāt kṣaram atītoham akṣarād api cottamaḥ
atosmi loke vede ca prathitaḥ puruṣottamaḥ

yasmat = since; ksaram = the perishable; atitah = higher, beyond; aham = I; aksarat = the imperishable; api = even; ca = and; uttamah = above or better than; atah = thereby; asmi = I am; loke = in the world; vede = in the Vedas; ca = and; prathitah = known; purusa-uttamah = as the Supreme Person.

Since I am beyond the perishable and above even the imperishable, I am, therefore, well known in the world and the Vedas as the Supreme Person.

The perishable and the imperishable aspects of Brahman constitute his jiva bhutam, the living being. Isvara is the highest Purusha (purushottama). Although they exist in him as a part of his creation, he is beyond and different from them. The pure Self is always imperishable. The unmanifested Prakriti (asambhuta) is also imperishable. The manifested Prakriti (sambhuta), which constitutes the Field, is the only perishable reality. Isvara is the highest Purusha because no manifestation of Brahman is higher than him. All the higher divinities, such as Brahma, Vishnu, and Shiva, are also considered and revered as Isvaras by their respective traditions, with Brahman as their hidden, unmanifested, and absolute aspect. Lord Krishna is also accorded the same status and revered by his devotees as Isvara and the personification of Brahman. While we may call him by different names according to our beliefs, the indisputable fact validated by the Vedas is that Brahman is the highest, absolute, supreme reality. He is the first, the most ancient, and far beyond all known and unknown manifestations, dualities, and qualities projected by him. The Upanishads extol him as indefinable, indescribable, and incomparable. Everything manifests or unmanifests in him and from him due to his association and disassociation with Prakriti. Since he encompasses and upholds all and represents all here and above, he is truly qualified as the best among the Purushas. In the next verse, Lord Krishna explains the importance of knowing Brahman without duality.

Sloka 19

yo mām evam asaṃmūḍho jānāti puruṣottamam
sa sarvavid bhajati māṃ sarvabhāvena bhārata

yah = he who; mam = Me; evam = thus; asammudhah = without delusion; janati = knows; purusa-uttamam = the Supreme Person; sah = he; sarva-vit = all knowing; bhajati = worships; mam = Me; sarva-bhavena = with complete devotion; bharata = O descendent of Bharata.

He who knows Me thus without delusion as the Supreme Person—he, the all-knowing one, worships Me with complete devotion, O descendant of Bharata.

He who knows Me without delusion (asammudha) means whoever knows the Lord of all without duality and confusion as the highest, Supreme Purusha, the Lord of the Universe, or the Self of all who has both perishable and imperishable aspects and manifests differently for different purposes. It means he knows that even though he appears differently in different manifestations and performs different functions, he knows that they are all his manifestations. He knows that he is the One and Only Supreme Lord who should be worshipped and to whom one should make all the offerings. Such a devotee is the all-knowing one (sarvavit) because he knows all aspects of Brahman without confusion. Delusion arises due to ignorance and mistaken notions about the Self or the Supreme Self. It may also arise when you find conflicting statements about him and his manifestations in the scriptures. As Ashtavakra says, the knowledge found in the scriptures or the teachings of wise masters can be confusing if you solely depend upon them because they speak differently and express different opinions about the absolute reality or the nature of the Self. Only when you worship the Supreme Purusha with exclusive devotion and take shelter in your pure consciousness, silencing your gunas, mind, and senses, will you transcend them and find the truth. When they finally enter Brahman's purest and highest state, without duality and divisions, they become the all-knowing jnanis and attain omniscience in oneness.

Thus, whoever overcomes the delusion caused by Maya and dissolves all the divisions, dualities, and disturbances in the pure consciousness of oneself attains true knowledge through self-knowing and abides in sameness and oneness forever. Any knowledge that deludes the mind and keeps it involved with the world is ignorance, and the knowledge that leads to the Self through withdrawal, discernment, detachment, devotion, and one-pointedness is true knowledge. Without that, the mind will not stabilize, and true devotion will not arise. All the qualities that strengthen concurrently through self-purification and devotional practices form the foundation for exclusive devotion (ananya bhakti), which is the doorway to liberation. Lord Krishna affirmed this truth. Deluded people worship him and practice devotion, but with duality and delusion. They worship him externally as if he were distinct and different from them. Since they cannot overcome the deluding power of the Maya, they do not excel in devotion or attain perfection. The Lord must be worshipped as the Lord of all and one's very Self with an unwavering mind. The mind, with all its modifications and impurities, must be dissolved in the pure consciousness that surfaces when the mind and senses are fully asleep, and all disturbances disappear. Only then, your devotion, duality and distinction will culminate in oneness.

Sloka 20

iti guhyatamaṃ śāstram idam uktaṃ mayānagha
etat buddhvā buddhimān syāt kṛtakṛtyaś ca bhārata

iti = thus; guhya-tamam = the most secretive; sastram = teaching, doctrine, percept, scripture; idam = this; uktam = described, revealed; maya = by Me; anagha = O sinless one; etat = this; buddhva = understanding; buddhi-man = wise; syat = one becomes; krta-krtyah = successful, accomplished; ca = and; bharata = O descendent of Bharata.

Thus, this most secretive teaching has been revealed by Me, O sinless one; understanding this, the wise one becomes successful (in his effort), O descendent of Bharata!

Shastra means a scripture, book, manual of instruction, teaching, doctrine, perspective, theory, etc. It can be secular, religious, or spiritual. Shastra is also a weapon (astra) against ignorance, delusion, and evil nature. Here, Lord Krishna said he revealed the most secret teaching to Arjuna because he was sinless and fit to know the Supreme Lord through exclusive devotion. Indeed, the Bhagavadgita is a collection of many ancient philosophies, with the Vedas as their basis. Its teachings can be found in the Upanishads and the Darshanas of Hinduism, especially those which are theistic and acknowledge the truths of the Vedas. Lord Krishna incorporated many of them in this discourse to present a cohesive and practical philosophy for attaining liberation, with Brahman at the center and the source of all. The Lord of his teachings is the supreme controller and upholder, who, in his aspect as Isvara, dwells in all, rules over all, and performs many eternal duties to ensure the order and regularity of the worlds. Through his actions, he sets an example to all, especially to his devotees, to live righteously, overcome their impurities, and achieve liberation. He cautions them against desires and attachments and prescribes renunciation of desires as the solution to overcome suffering.

The advantage of studying the Bhagavadgita is that it presents a cohesive and practical philosophy that is easy to know and follow. Students who aspire for liberation do not have to study several scriptures or worship numerous gods. They can establish their minds in him, worship him exclusively, offer him the fruit of their actions, and earn his grace to escape from the world. Since it is both an Upanishad and a treatise on Yoga, it is surely a valuable source of secret (guhya) and utmost secret knowledge (atiguhya), which can be taught to people of all backgrounds, not only to those who excel in Dharma and are intent upon liberation but also to those who pursue knowledge or practice renunciation. While devotees traditionally acknowledge it as a book of utmost secret knowledge requiring a teacher to reveal its secrets and hidden truths, in this verse, Lord Krishna declared that the knowledge which is contained in this particular chapter also qualifies as the most secretive knowledge (guhyatamam). He said it because the chapter, as its title implies, contains the knowledge of the highest Purusha (Purushottama) and his highest perishable and imperishable aspects. It begins with a description of the Asvattha tree and ends with the knowledge of the transcendental, eternal, and absolute Brahman. The teaching contained in it strengthens a seeker's faith and devotion and helps him stabilize his mind in his contemplation. In this verse, Lord Krishna addressed Arjuna as Anagha, meaning one who is sinless, blameless, or blemishless. Its use here conveys that this knowledge is fit for those who are sinless, innocent, pure, and righteous, as Arjuna was.

Undoubtedly, by knowing the Supreme Purusha as one's inner Self, a pure and sinless yogi, whose intellect is illuminated with the right knowledge within and whose mind is exclusively devoted to the Supreme Lord, would quickly progress on the path and achieves liberation whether he continues to perform his obligatory duties or renounces them completely and devotes himself to him.

Conclusion

iti srīmadbhāgavadgītāsupanisatsu brahmavidyāyām yogasāstre srikrisnārjunasamvāde puruṣottamayogo nāma pañcadaśo 'dhyayah.

iti = thus; srīmadbhāgavadgītā = in the sacred Bhagavadgita; upanisatsu = in the Upanishad; brahmavidyāyām = the knowledge of the absolute Brahman; yogasāstre = the scripture of yoga; srikrisnārjunasamvāde = the dialogue between Sri Krishna and Arjuna; puruṣottamayogo nāma = by name the yoga of the supreme person; pancadasah = fifteen; adhyayah = chapter.

Thus ends the fifteenth chapter, named Purushottama Yoga (the Yoga of the Supreme Person) in the Upanishad of the divine Bhagavadgita, the knowledge of the Absolute, a treatise on Yoga, and the debate between Arjuna and Lord Krishna.

16 – Daivāsura Sampadvibhāga Yoga

Yoga of the Division of Divine and Demonic Properties

Sloka 1

śrībhagavān uvāca
abhayaṃ sattvasaṃśuddhir jñānayogavyavasthitiḥ
dānaṃ damaś ca yajñaś ca svādhyāyas tapa ārjavam

sri-bhagavan uvaca = the supreme lord said; abhayam = fearlessness; sattva-samsuddhih = with predominance of sattva; jnana = knowledge; yoga = yoga; vyavasthitih = established in; danam = charity; damah = self-restraint; ca = and; yajnah = sacrifice; ca = and; svadhyayah = self-study of the scriptures; tapah = austerity; arjavam = simplicity.

The Supreme Lord said, "Fearlessness, the predominance of sattva, well established in the yoga of knowledge, (engaged in) charity, self-restraint, self-study of the scriptures, austerity and simplicity ...

This and the following two verses describe the qualities of those who purified their minds and bodies on the path of yoga and are endowed with the knowledge of Brahman. If you want to find Brahman, you have to mirror his qualities, erasing the boundaries that limit you and prevent you from achieving oneness with him. You have to become godlike, an enlightened yogi, in whom divine qualities and the light of the Self shine. Brahman is absolute, pure consciousness, not a Being with a universal form. Although he is often equated with a Cosmic Being or Universal Being, such descriptions are symbolic to denote his all-pervasive universality and omniscience. He represents the Supreme Reality, the sum of all that there is here and hereafter, rather than any corporeal manifestation or incarnation. His appearances are temporary, while the absolute reality, his purest state, is permanent and indestructible. Since he is beyond the mind and intelligence, no one can truly grasp his essential nature or describe it. As the Upanishads affirm, he is what we know and do not know, is and is not, existence and nonexistence, everything and nothing, and fullness and emptiness.

However, you can discern him in the qualities and attributes that manifest in creation, reflecting his true glory and unmistakable presence. He already spoke about them in the tenth chapter. In the ninth chapter, he said that those with vain hopes and demonic nature would disregard him, while great souls (mahatmas) who possessed his nature would constantly worship him and remain united with him forever. In this chapter, he distinguished between the divine and the demonic nature so that his devotees could discern and cultivate the qualities that reflect him and lead them towards their release from births and deaths. Since he is the source of all, demonic nature also manifests from him only. Both these manifest in creation in his perishable Self

(Prakriti), although they may exist in Brahman's unmanifested Nature (asambhuta) also as potencies.

The jivas who are subject to birth and death cannot escape from the duality of divine and demonic natures. They contain both potentials as part of their composite nature. If they want to progress spiritually, they have to suppress their lower nature, which is primarily demonic, and illuminate their higher nature, which is primarily divine, so they can reflect his qualities and attain him. This is the purpose of spiritual transformation and all the yogas. They have to cultivate sattva in which divine qualities shine brightly, and demonic qualities arising from rajas and tamas become suppressed. Liberation is attainable for those in whom the Lord's divine nature shines brightly, which is free from sin, imperfection, mortality, change, impermanence, ignorance, time, delusion, and desires. It is said that when your consciousness becomes as pure as the consciousness of the Self in you, you will reflect his divine nature and merge into him. Those who possess it excel in stability, sameness, calmness, exclusive devotion, and liberation.

Having understood the importance of cultivating the divine qualities, let us now turn our attention to the qualities mentioned here.

The first one is fearlessness. Fearfulness is a demonic quality, while fearlessness is divine. Fear is one of the most dominant emotions that afflict the mind. It arises due to desires, attachments, egoism, and delusion. It assails our minds when we are disconnected from God and feel lonely and helpless against the forces of Nature, fate, or those who wish to harm us. Lord's exclusive devotees are fearless since they live with the conviction that he will protect them and take care of their well-being. Fear also goes away when they overcome desires and attachments and cultivate sameness towards all dualities, such as loss and gain, happiness and sorrow, or fame or ill-fame. Becoming equal to the dualities and circumstances, they embrace their lives and circumstances unconditionally without fear or envy.

The second quality is the predominance of sattva. Sattva is essential for self-transformation and purification and is also at the root of many divine qualities. It is also necessary to cultivate knowledge, discernment, and sameness and practice detachment, renunciation, and self-control. Hence, it is a very important requirement for overcoming ignorance and delusion, cultivating divine nature, and achieving liberation. When it is predominant, yogis experience peace and stability within themselves and stabilize their minds in exclusive devotion or uninterrupted contemplation. Sattva is the essence of many advanced yogis, divinities, and beings of higher worlds. However, it is still an impurity that disturbs the mind, inducing desires and attachments for pleasure and happiness or comforts and luxuries. Hence, eventually, on the path of liberation, one has to transcend it.

The inclination to pursue the knowledge of the Self (jñānayoga vyavasthita) is another important divine attribute to overcome delusion and ignorance and cultivate discernment, and know oneself or establish the mind in the Lord with exclusive devotion. One does not have to be educated or intellectual to practice it or excel in it. It is easier for those whose minds are empty, who are free from the intellectual clutter and worldly knowledge, who have a natural distaste for worldly life, and who are naturally drawn to contemplation and devotion. By knowledge, we mean the knowledge of the Self or Brahman. Without it, one cannot stabilize the mind, overcome the delusion of the mind and body, or pursue liberation with conviction. It is also necessary to practice karma-sannyasa, buddhi, and atma-samyama yogas. Jnana yoga helps seekers cultivate sattva and suppress rajas, tamas, and the impurities they create. For those who excel in its practice, the restraint of the mind and senses becomes easier and more spontaneous. It also leads to exclusive devotion.

Charitable quality is divine. The Supreme Lord exemplifies it when he liberates his devotees or listens to their prayers for help. Purity, selflessness, forgiveness, and compassion are its associated qualities. Danam refers to the act of giving gifts freely and selflessly, without expectations. People may practice it to expiate for their sins, invoke the gods to fulfill their desires, or engage in meritorious actions (punya karma). The Hindu lawbooks (Dharmashastras) state that the charity given to Brahmanas, seers, and renunciants is the most beneficial. However, the best charity is that which is given without desires and expectations as a service or sacrifice. Only the most pious and virtuous excel in its practice since they exemplify egolessness, freedom from desires, and exclusive devotion to the Supreme Lord. It is easier for those who overcome their desires and attachments and see God in all and pervading all. When you see that the same Lord in you as your Self is also present in everyone, in that state of oneness, you will feel love and empathy for all beings, especially those in distress, and generously help them. Hinduism identifies charity as one of the most important virtues and an essential practice of Dharma. Brahma recommended it for humans since selfishness is a common trait in them. The daily sacrifices (nitya karmas) are meant to promote selflessness, charity, and the welfare of the world through sharing and caring. Charity does not have to be of the material kind. The law books identify the charity of spiritual knowledge as the best charity. Manu states that one should "perform works of charity with faith since offerings and charitable works made with faith and lawfully earned money bring endless rewards." He also states that one should always give to a worthy recipient according to one's ability, even if it is little, without grudging, and with a cheerful heart.

Damah means self-restraint or especially controlling the mind and physical responses. People who have the predominance of sattva need to practice the restraint of their senses since they are pleasure-oriented. Those with the predominance of rajas should practice it to restrain their egoism, passions, and selfish desires. It is even more important for tamasic people since they tend to overreact in most situations and are subject to delusion and ignorance. The Brihadaranyaka Upanishad states that Lord Brahma taught the virtue of damah to the gods. The practice of damah is central to all forms of yoga, especially atma-samyama yoga, to achieve balance, peace, and stability. In Ashtanga yoga, it is essential to practice the eight limbs, especially the five restraints, withdrawal of the senses, and controlled meditation (samyama). Manu states that a student shall bring his organs under control before beginning his study. By that, he succeeds in reaching all his aims. When control is lost, wisdom slips away. He also suggests that self-control is more important than the knowledge of the Vedas for students, householders, women, ascetics, and renunciants.

Yajna, or sacrifice, is central to Hindu ritual and spiritual practices. It is also foundational to the essential practice of Dharma, which involves performing obligatory duties as stipulated by the Vedas and adhering to the code of conduct as approved by tradition and scriptures. Through sacrifices, a householder practices his Dharma and fulfills his obligations. The Vedas do not disapprove if they are performed to fulfill one's desires, although ideally, they should be performed as an obligatory duty without desires and expectations. Symbolically, any action performed selflessly without desires and without desiring its fruit to serve God constitutes a sacrifice. According to Manu, the Vedas were created by God from fire, wind, and sun for the sake of sacrifices only. They proclaim that God's creation itself was an act of sacrifice. According to them, sacrifice is even superior to the gods because it is through sacrifices that the world is sustained, and through sacrifices, Dharma is upheld upon earth. The law books also state that sacrifices should not be performed for impure and unworthy people.

Svadhyaya means self-study. It is an important aspect of kriya yoga (YS 2.1) and one of the five niyamas listed by Patanjali in the Yogasutras (YS 2.32). Vyasa, one of the traditional commentators of the Yogasutras, defined svadhyaya as the study of scriptures and the relentless practice of japa or chanting of Aum or specific mantras. The purpose of svadhyaya is to saturate the mind with the scriptural and spiritual knowledge concerning Brahman, the Self, and liberation so that one's awareness and understanding vastly improve and the practice of meditation and concentration becomes easier.

Tapah means austerity, which involves various practices such as the restraint of the mind and senses, celibacy, detachment, renunciation, yogic postures, breath control, contemplation, etc., for self-purification, transformation, and augmentation of physical and mental energies. It is a form of internal sacrifice to cleanse the mind and body, which is believed to generate internal body heat and transform sexual energy (retas) into spiritual energy (ojas), bodily vigor (tejas), and mental brilliance (medhas). Tapah was an earlier form of yoga, which renunciants, hermits, and ascetics used to practice in ancient times to achieve liberation or invoke gods and obtain boons from them. Manu states that austerity and sacred learning are the best means by which a Brahmana secures supreme bliss. By austerities, he destroys guilt; by sacred learning, he overcomes births and deaths. He also states that righteous conduct is the root of all austerity. He also lists obedience to teachers and parents, the study of the Vedas, contemplation upon the syllable Aum, breath control, silence, and truthfulness as the best austerities. By performing austerities, a sinner overcomes guilt and sinful karma.

Arjavam means honesty, simplicity, righteousness, open-mindedness, or straightforwardness. This quality is found predominantly in virtuous people who are pure in heart, with selfless thoughts and intentions, and always willing to help others or perform actions for a divine cause. It naturally manifests in those who perfect the practice of the five yamas: nonviolence, truthfulness, non-stealing, celibacy, and non-possession of material wealth.

Sloka 2

ahiṃsā satyam akrodhas tyāgaḥ śāntir apaiśunam
dayā bhūteṣv aloluptvaṃ mārdavaṃ hrīr acāpalam

ahimsa = non-injury; satyam = truthfulness; akrodhah = freedom from anger; tyagah = sacrifice or renunciation; santih = peace, serenity; apaisunam = non-slandering, absence of fault-finding; daya = compassion; bhutesu = living being; aloluptvam = non-covetousness; mardavam = gentleness; hrih = modesty; acapalam =unwavering.

Non-injury, truthfulness, freedom from anger, renunciation, peace and tranquility, non-slandering, compassion towards all living beings, non-covetousness, gentleness, modesty, unwaveringness...

Ahimsa means non-injury, nonviolence, not causing cruelty, injury, or violence (himsa) in any form, or not showing hostility to living beings, including oneself. In the yogic tradition, it is considered the most important niyama (restraint or abstention). Perfection in its practice denotes victory over the reptilian nature to which human beings are vulnerable due to their instinctual nature to defend themselves against real or imaginary threats. All the niyamas lead to nonviolence only. Many people equate it with not eating meat. However, its practice is not as much about eating or not eating meat but about the thinking, attitude, and conduct toward others. It must be reflected in every aspect of our lives and personal conduct, which requires perfection in other virtues. Hence, it is considered the highest and the ultimate virtue or the virtue of all virtues.

A truly non-violent person does not seek anything that will hurt or inconvenience others, even if it means he has to sacrifice his comfort or convenience and undergo pain and suffering. He excels in its practice by freeing himself from anger, fear, violence, cruelty, and deception and refrains from even thinking of causing hurt or harm to anyone. The attitude of nonviolence should be grounded in righteous thinking, love for God, and the conviction that life is a divine gift, sacred and inviolable. The practice of nonviolence was exemplified to its extreme in the ancient world in the Sannyasa Ashrama of the Vedic Varnashrama Dharma, in which householders and ascetics who took the vows of sannyasa gave up using fire or cooking food. They refrained from intentionally or unintentionally harming any living being, including plants. Hence, they subsisted exclusively on discarded plant and tree parts such as fruit, seeds, dried roots, bark, wild plants, and vegetables.

Truthfulness is a universal virtue. By truthfulness, we mean to be truthful, transparent, and honest, and refrain from falsehood and deception in thinking or actions. It is the defining aspect of the Supreme Lord, who personifies it through his highest manifestations. Therefore, those who wish to attain oneness with him through liberation should reflect it in their actions and conduct. They should speak and stand for the truth. The only exception they have been allowed is if its practice harms or hurts others and violates the principle of nonviolence. In worldly life, truthfulness is difficult to practice in all situations. It is even more difficult for those who wish to live righteously and attain liberation. Yet, its importance cannot be ignored since it is the foundation for self-purification and overcoming ignorance and delusion. The practice of any yoga or moral code is futile without it. The doors of immortal heaven are open only to those who are truthful in their thinking and actions. It is the highest virtue, and its practice is the best form of austerity. When you practice truth, the supreme and absolute Brahman, who personifies Truth, will manifest in your consciousness and open the gates of immortality.

Freedom from anger (akrodha) arises when desires and attachments are suppressed, and the impurities, such as ignorance, egoism, selfishness, fear, and delusion that afflict the mind are removed. Anger is one of the chief evils (maha pataka) since it impairs one's discernment and mental stability and leads to many other evils. It is also an obstacle to peace and happiness. In the second chapter, Lord Krishna explained how, from desires and attachments, anger would arise due to the repetitive contact of the senses with the sense objects, from anger delusion, from delusion confusion of memory, and from the confusion of memory loss of discrimination. When discernment is lost, one will perish as he engages in sinful actions. Thus, knowing that anger is self-destructive, spiritual aspirants should guard themselves against it. The absence of anger is a nonviolent attitude. It is also reflected in other virtues such as universal love, compassion (karuna), fearlessness, friendliness, forgiveness (kshama), mercifulness (daya), humility, etc.

Tyaga means giving up desires, name and fame, family, relationships, wealth, and other possessions. A yogi who practices atma-samyama and ananya bhakti renounces desires and attachments for liberation, knowing that the world is impermanent and nothing lasts forever. Being aware that all this is for the Lord's habitation and nothing belongs to anyone else, he, giving up ownership and doership, performs his duties as a sacrifice without desiring their fruit. Withdrawing his mind and senses into himself, clinging to nothing but oneness with the Self in him with love and adoration, and using his devotion as the raft, he crosses over the turbulent ocean of samsara to the shore of liberation. One must practice renunciation to transcend the gunas and their influence and abide in the Self, which is gunatita, meaning beyond the gunas.

Santih (peace) arises from the absence of desires and attachments, which in turn arises from self-restraint and stability of the mind. It is an associated quality of the predominance of sattva, contentment, knowledge, discernment, tolerance, understanding, detachment, and sameness towards the pairs of opposites. The purpose of Yoga, as Patanjali declared, is to overcome the turbulences of the mind so that one abides in peace and self-absorption. The gunas are responsible for the restlessness and instability of the mind. When they are overcome, by withdrawing the mind and senses from sense objects and excelling in yoga with perfection in detachment, renunciation, self-control, and devotion to the Lord within, the yogi attains freedom from attraction and aversion, peace and tranquility.

Apisunam means the absence of fault-finding, vengefulness, slander, or hateful nature. It is an important requirement for the right speech and closely related to other virtues such as nonviolence, sameness, absence of anger, pride, egoism, and freedom from desires, judgment, and attachment. The practice of restraints, self-control, detachment, and renunciation is foundational to its cultivation. When the yogi sees the Lord in him as the Lord in all and feels an affinity towards all beings, he overcomes negativity towards others and accepts them as they are.

Compassion (daya) towards all living beings is closely related to the qualities mentioned in this and the previous verse, especially nonviolence and the absence of anger. A spiritually awakened person feels compassion for all living beings, knowing they all suffer, are caught in an impermanent world, and are subject to the cycle of births and deaths. He knows that they engage in sinful actions not because they are inherently sinful or evil but because they are subject to Maya and the play of Prakriti. Therefore, he feels compassion for them and helps them with counsel and blessings. The other qualities mentioned in this verse - non-covetousness, gentleness, modesty, and unwaveringness - are also related to the previous ones. They denote the absence of ego, desires, delusion, duality, and ignorance. The unwavering mind, which is the foundation for self-absorption and self-realization, arises from perfection in self-restraint and sameness towards the pairs of opposites.

Sloka 3

tejaḥ kṣamā dhṛtiḥ śaucam adroho nātimānitā
bhavanti saṃpadaṃ daivīm abhijātasya bhārata

tejah = vigor; ksama = forgiveness; dhrtih = fortitude; saucam = cleanliness; adrohah = freedom from treachery; na = not; ati-manita = self-importance; bhavanti = manifest; sampadam = properties, qualities; daivim =divine; nature abhijatasya = born in consequences of, out of; bharata = O descendent of Bharata.

Vigor, forgiveness, fortitude, cleanliness, freedom from betrayal, and absence of self-importance (these) are the qualities of those who are born as a result of their divine nature, O descendent of Bharata!

In this verse, Lord Krishna mentioned six additional divine qualities, thus making the qualities of the purest souls who radiate them a total of 26. The first of the six mentioned here is tejas, meaning brightness, vivacity, or vigor. It manifests in the yogis who are predominantly sattvic and excel in celibacy, self-control, and other austerities. Madhavacharya defined it as the commanding spirit of a person that "strikes fear in others and prevents them from slighting him." Shankara interpreted it as "energy, not brightness of the skin." Tejas is the physical, mental, and spiritual power of a yogi or ascetic who engages in austerities, controlling his sexual passions and base desires. By that austerity, he sublimates and transforms his physical and mental energies into strength and vigor.

Forgiveness (kshama) arises from discriminating awareness, non-violence, detachment, and compassion. It is a defining expression of egolessness, nonviolence, compassion, renunciation, or letting go, and the absence of desires and anger. When you forgive others without expectations, you cleanse your heart and unburden yourself of any sinful karma that may arise from harboring inimical and hurtful thoughts against others. It is that when you indulge in inimical thoughts towards others or criticize them, their negative karma will accrue to you. It is, therefore, important to cultivate tolerance and forgive others for their transgression and hurtful behavior. As you overcome desires, attraction and aversion, egoism, anger, and critical nature through detachment and renunciation, forgiveness becomes your natural response towards others. The Supreme Lord is ever-forgiving. He readily forgives our sins and transgressions and uplifts the fallen souls who relent and seek forgiveness with devotion and willingness to change. By forgiving others, a devotee reflects his divine nature and cultivates nearness to the Supreme Lord.

Shuchi means pure, spotless, clean, etc. The Yogasutras describes uncleanliness as a manifestation of ignorance, leading to pain and suffering (dukkha). Cleanliness extends beyond physical cleanliness and encompasses all aspects of life and ethical conduct. The Vedas identify it as a virtue, equating cleanliness with holiness and uncleanliness with evil. According to the Hindu Vastu Shastras, the places chosen to construct buildings, structures, and ritual places (yajnasthala) must be clean and worthy of gods and holy people. Cleanliness is also a prerequisite for spiritual practice and divine worship. Spiritual people must maintain the highest standards of cleanliness in their lives. They must keep themselves and their surroundings clean to cultivate nearness to the Lord and achieve liberation. The body is the abode of the Lord, where he lives as the Self. Therefore, it must be treated like a temple and kept clean. As mortal beings, we cannot avoid contacting the impurities of the world. Therefore, as our scriptures suggest, one must live like a lotus plant in the impure waters of samsara, untouched by them, practicing detachment and renunciation, and performing actions without desires. A yogi becomes pure as a crystal by transcending the gunas through self-purification.

Adroham means the absence of treachery or malice. It is an associated quality of truthfulness, non-covetousness, purity, and absence of anger, pride, greed, and selfishness. It is strengthened by the continued practice of renunciation, detachment, and other divine qualities mentioned by Lord Krishna. Atimanita, meaning freedom from excessive pride and self-importance, also strengthens in the same circumstances when purity and virtue reign supreme. Excessive pride is an evil quality. Taking pride in oneself for appearance, personality, power, position, family, knowledge, or influence is an obstacle to learning, knowing, improving, and progressing. In spiritual practice, it is an obstacle to self-purification and liberation. Yogis who attain divine powers (siddhis) through perfection in their practice must also remain on guard, since they can make them feel self-important and exceptional.

Sloka 4

dambho darpobhimānaś ca krodhaḥ pāruṣyam eva ca
ajñānaṃ cābhijātasya pārtha saṃpadam āsurīm

dambhah = hypocrisy, pretentious, deceit, fraud; darpah = arrogance; abhimanah = excessive pride; ca = and; krodhah = anger; parusyam = harshness, rude, harsh, insulting behavior; eva = even; ca = and; ajnanam =

ignorance; ca = and; abhijatasya = born out of or in consequence of; partha = O Partha; sampadam = possessions, qualities, endowments; asurim = demoniac nature.

Hypocrisy, arrogance, excessive pride, anger, harshness, and even ignorance are the qualities of those who are born due to the demonic nature.

So far, Lord Krishna has mentioned divine qualities. From here on, he listed a few important evil qualities that manifest in those who are predominantly demonic or those who frequently interact with them and develop a similar nature. According to the Vedas, Brahma created three classes of beings to keep the wheel of life moving and balanced: devas (gods), asuras (demonic beings), and manavas (humans). The gods are beings of light and possess a divine nature. The demonic ones are beings of darkness and personify evil nature. Humans are beings of light and darkness. They are good or evil according to their gunas and may serve gods, the evil ones, or both.

The qualities mentioned in this are self-destructive and harmful to one's spiritual and material well-being. Hence, they should be suppressed by all means to avoid suffering and spiritual downfall. Some are born with an evil nature (asura prvritti) due to their past karma, while some become evil due to their actions, circumstances, and evil influences. Whatever the cause, it does not bode well for those who possess them. When evil qualities predominate in humans, the world falls into chaos. Dharma declines. People lose common sense and discernment and fall into evil ways. They value worldliness, ignore or discredit righteous conduct, question the existence of God, and uphold evil conduct, justifying it with irrational arguments and convenient logic.

While divine qualities arise from the predominance of sattva, evil qualities arise from the predominance of rajas and tamas. The Vedic tradition prescribes Dharma, Artha, Kama, and Moksha as the chief aims of human life for those engaged in household duties. The problem is that they can be pursued righteously or unrighteously according to the Vedic injunctions or against them. Ideally, they must be practiced strictly as prescribed by the Vedas and the law books. Therefore, performing obligatory duties does not guarantee liberation or a good life in the next birth unless one adheres to the righteous path and stays away from evil influences. Whatever the goal or purpose, householders must practice nishkama karma through karma-sannyasa, controlling their lower nature and evil tendencies. In the cosmic hierarchy, humans have a unique opportunity to transcend their natural drives and perform actions selflessly and intelligently to escape from samsara. They can rise to the heights of spirituality, cultivate divine nature, and reach the immortal heaven, which is not accessible to even gods, or descend into the depths of dark and demonic worlds, succumbing to evil nature and prolonging their suffering and bondage. They can either nourish the gods within them through righteous actions and strengthen their divine nature or strengthen evil qualities and serve the aims of evil forces. They must fulfill their obligation to practice Dharma and serve the Lord who lives in them as their Self, nourishing the gods and divine nature, which assist them in their actions and protect them from evil.

Dumbah means hypocrisy, deceit, vanity, or showiness. It is characteristic of those who resort to trickery and deceit to fulfill their desires or reach their goals. Tricksters draw innocent people into their nefarious schemes and cause them harm, preying on their weaknesses. The Puranas illustrate how the wicked have no qualms about deceiving even the gods, misusing the boons they secure from them through prayers and austerities. They also show how they engage in deceptive methods and misleading tactics to defeat their enemies in wars and conflicts.

Darpa means conceit, arrogance, or impudence, which makes people feel self-important, vain, imprudent, and blind to their faults and weaknesses. It is an offshoot of egotism and delusion common among those who take excessive pride in their achievements, abilities, wealth, family, group (jati), identity, etc.

Closely related to darpa is abhimana, meaning having excessive pride, which arises from having undue attachment to material things such as one's self-identity (svabhimanam), family (kulabhimanam), race or community (jatyabhimanam), etc., and makes people act insolently or vindictively if they feel that they or the things in which they take pride are slighted or insulted. When Duryodhana felt that Draupadi had insulted him in the hall of illusions (Mayasabha), he decided to take revenge. It set in motion a chain of events that led to the Mahabharata war and great destruction.

Krodha, meaning anger, is a self-destructive quality recognized as one of the chief evils (maha pataka). Under its influence, people lose discretion and engage in violent and destructive actions, often with tragic consequences for themselves and others.

Parushya means harshness and rudeness. It is a sign of insensitivity or lack of empathy and compassion due to excessive selfishness and egotism. Evil people show little restraint in using force or choice of words toward others to achieve their ends. Hence, they tend to be cruel, brutal, violent, and relentless in their actions and relationships.

Ajnanam, or ignorance, is a universal trait of all the jivas deluded by Maya. However, the ignorance of demonic people is denser since they are too deluded and impatient to open their minds to the truth of things. Light, knowledge, and reason cannot penetrate their clouded consciousness. Ignorance and delusion reinforce each other. The Chandogya Upanishad illustrates a legend about how the demons came to accept the body as the true Self. It is said that once, Vairochana, their leader, went to Brahma to learn about the Self. Indra, the leader of the gods, also went at the same time to learn the same. Brahman taught them the first lesson by showing them their reflections in the water and telling them that they represented the Self in them. After hearing it, Vairochana concluded that the form or the body was the true Self and went away, thinking that he understood the true nature of the Self. Upon returning to his world, he taught the same to other demons. Hence, it is said that until this day, the demons remain deluded, thinking that the body is the true Self. On the other hand, Indra, the Lord of Heaven, remained unconvinced and kept asking Brahma to teach him more until he taught him fully and revealed the true nature of the Self.

Sloka 5

daivī saṃpad vimokṣāya nibandhāyāsurī matā
mā śucaḥ saṃpadaṃ daivīm abhijātosi pāṇḍava

daivi = divine; sampat = qualities, virtures; vimoksaya = for liberation; nibandhaya = for bondage; asuri = demonic; mata = thought of, considered, opined; ma = do not; sucah = worry; sampadam = nature; daivim = divine; abhijatah = born as a result of; asi = you are; pandava = O son of Pandu.

Divine qualities are thought to be for liberation (and) demonic (ones) for bondage. Do not worry, O Pandava! You are born with the divine nature.

Divine qualities bring us closer to the divine nature within us and facilitate nearness and oneness. As we are purified and transformed through persistent practice and self-restraint, they gain strength and set us firmly on the path to liberation, strengthening our devotion, faith, and resolve to overcome obstacles and persevere on the path. When the Lord shines with pure brilliance in the internal organ of a devotee without any hindrances, divine nature becomes his natural state, and divine qualities radiate through him and become self-evident. No one can attain liberation without purity and divinity or manifesting the divine qualities through self-effort or divine grace, since only the purest can enter the pure consciousness of the Supreme Brahman. When the divine qualities fully manifest and the devotee becomes pure and godlike, he experiences oneness and immortality.

Divine qualities appear in our surface consciousness when we are pure, and divine nature becomes our natural state. Therefore, devotees should focus on cultivating them, restraining their minds and senses, resisting evil thoughts, and suppressing the impurities and the demonic qualities arising from them. On the spiritual path, aspirants must endure this internal and ongoing conflict between good and evil within themselves. For them, it is like a personal Kurukshetra war on the battlefield of their consciousness, which they must fight with faith and resolve, taking refuge in the Lord and seeking his help until they achieve perfection and the qualities fully manifest in them.

The purpose of yoga is to achieve this end and manifest the divine qualities until they become an integral part of our essential nature and facilitate oneness with the pure consciousness of the Self. They strengthen when one renounces desires and attachments and practices exclusive devotion with unwavering faith. Human life is sacred because we have the rare opportunity to manifest the divine qualities that lie dormant within us and express them through our thoughts and actions, becoming, in the process, a living and breathing personification of the very divinity in us who is their source. The goal of spiritual transformation and the journey from death to immortality, from untruth to truth, and from darkness to light depend upon this singular achievement and the effort, resolve, and commitment that are required to achieve it. Those who persevere with exclusive devotion accomplish it with divine help. Others may have to wait until they succeed.

As Lord Krishna stated here, demonic qualities are for bondage. They delay liberation, strengthening the impurities, prolonging suffering, and delaying liberation. Overcoming demonic influence is particularly difficult when the impurities of samsara persist and the gunas are active, since, under their influence, the mind and senses are vulnerable to evil desires and temptations. Because of them, most people remain stuck in their lower nature and do not even think of liberation as an option or an achievable goal. For spiritual aspirants, it is a constant battle until they attain perfection in nishkama karma and self-purification. Just as the sun shines when the clouds are removed, divine qualities manifest as soon as the impurities are removed.

Sloka 6

dvau bhūtasargau lokesmin daiva āsura eva ca
daivo vistaraśaḥ prokta āsuraṃ pārtha me śṛṇu

dvau = twofold; bhuta-sargau = creation of beings; loke = in the world; asmin = this; daivah = divine; asurah = demonic; eva = surely; ca = and; daivah = divine; vistarasah = in detail; proktah = described; asuram = demonic; partha = O Partha; me = from Me; srnu =hear.

Twofold is the creation of beings in this world, the divine and the demonic. The divine has been described in detail; O Partha, (now) hear from Me about the demonic (nature).

According to the Vedic texts, the devas (gods), the asuras (demons), and the jivas (humans) are all children of Brahma only. The devas are beings of light and delight. They possess the divine nature, represent the pleasure principle, participate in the good works of humans, and help them when they are pleased with their offerings and devotion. The asuras are dark and demonic beings, possess the quintessential demonic nature, and represent the pain principle. They are divided into various categories, such as daityas, danavas, rakshasas, etc. They influence and misuse vulnerable humans for their evil ends. Humans possess the propensities of both. Since they have intelligence and free will, they have the potential to become better or worse by their choices and actions. Since they stand between the two groups, they possess both divine and demonic natures and are vulnerable to their influences. As a result, they unwittingly draw themselves into the conflict between the two and witness it within themselves. Their divine and demonic natures constitute their higher and lower natures, respectively. Those who take refuge in the former, living righteously with discipline and control, progress on the path of liberation, but those who take refuge in the latter let the evil forces pervade their consciousness and become increasingly evil and self-destructive.

The Supreme Lord is impartial and indifferent to all three groups of beings. He helps them according to their nature, actions, and devotion. The Puranas show that even when he helps the Asuras and grants them boons, they misuse their powers and invite their own destruction. In our lives, we have a clear choice. We can either worship and nourish the gods and pious human beings through sacrificial and noble actions, and let divine qualities strengthen in us, or side with the demonic and evil people and participate in their wicked actions. We can cultivate divine qualities and ascend to the higher heavens, or we can reflect evil qualities and prolong our bondage and suffering. Once humans fall into the trap of wicked forces, there is no turning back. They have to pay a heavy price for the evil propensities if they nourish the demons within them and outside. Those who choose the path of the gods overcome their impurities and progress towards light and immortality, but those who choose the path of evil fall into the deluded ways of their evil nature and descend into demonic worlds.

Both groups bring their respective attitudes, religiosity, and spirituality into their actions. The righteous ones withdraw into themselves and pursue the four chief aims of human life (purusharthas). They engage in karma yoga and serve the aims of creation. The pious ones among them surrender to God and his inviolable will and strive for liberation, restraining their minds and bodies and renouncing desires and attachments. In contrast, the impure ones engage in evil actions, fall into sinful ways, and perish. As the Isa Upanishad states, "The worlds of the demons are enveloped in binding darkness. To them go after departing from the body those who harm themselves." The battle between divine and demonic forces continues at several levels within oneself and outside. It intensifies exponentially when one resolves to achieve liberation, renouncing desires and attachments, and overcoming the impurities. They experience a lot of resistance within themselves as they try to restrain their lower nature, silencing the gunas that are associated with it. Some give up, but the discerning ones resolve it by taking refuge in the Lord and persevering in their effort.

Sloka 7

pravṛttiṃ ca nivṛttiṃ ca janā na vidur āsurāḥ
na śaucaṃ nāpi cācāro na satyaṃ teṣu vidyate

pravrttim = tendency to do, what should be done; ca = and; nivrttim = tendency to avoid, what should not be done; ca = and; janah = people; na = not viduh = know; asurah = demonic; na = not; saucam = cleanliness; na = not; api = also; ca = and; acarah = customary or formal behavior; na = not; satyam = truth; tesu = in them; vidyate = there is.

Demonic people do not know what should be done or what should not be done. They do not know about cleanliness and customary behavior. Truthfulness does not exist in them.

This and the subsequent 11 verses describe the evil qualities of the demonic beings, such as the Asuras or Rakshasas, Daityas, etc., or humans who succumbed to their influence. Since they induce delusion and ignorance, those who possess them lack discernment and balance. They do not know which qualities they should strengthen, avoid, or suppress, which actions they should or should not perform, which attitudes and tendencies they should strengthen or weaken, or which goals they should pursue or not pursue. They also do not care much about the distinction between approved actions and prohibited actions, rules and restraints, action and inaction, or right knowledge and wrong knowledge due to delusion and ignorance. Driven by evil passions such as lust, fear, anger, pride, and envy, yielding to their demonic nature and lacking in discipline and self-control, they pursue their desires and impulses with complete abandon. Since they are, by nature, impure and unclean both physically and mentally, they do not give much importance to observing cleanliness or personal hygiene in their personal conduct, surroundings, religious observances, eating habits, or the practice of Dharma. Naturally rebellious, they disregard established norms and traditions (acharas), rites and rituals, and the code of conduct ordained by the Vedas or the lawbooks. They also ignore the teachings of enlightened masters, seers, and saints and resort to any means or methods, however harmful or self-destructive, to achieve their ends or justify their actions.

Prvritti and nivrtti have multiple meanings. Pravritti means natural tendency, inclination, preference, propensity, or behavior, reflected in one's nature, character, thinking, and actions. Nivritti is the opposite. It is the tendency reflected in what one avoids, suppresses, withdraws, or abstains. They are used mostly in connection with the activities of the mind and senses. Prvritti is the tendency of the mind and senses to wander among worldly things and objects. Nivrtti is their tendency to withdraw from them and remain restful or absorbed. Prvritti increases desires and attachments, and one's involvement and attachments to worldly things. Nivrtti does the opposite and is helpful in practicing self-control. The evil ones do not know which tendencies they should strengthen or suppress or how and when they should be used to cultivate the right knowledge and discernment. They do not know when to control their minds and senses and when to let them go. Hence, they remain ignorant, deluded, and bound to their evil ways.

Sloka 8

asatyam apratiṣṭhaṃ te jagad āhur anīśvaram
aparasparasaṃbhūtaṃ kim anyat kāmahaitukam

asatyam = unreal, false; apratistham = without a basis, support or foundation; te = they; jagat = the world; ahuh = they say; anisvaram = devoid of or without Isvara; aparaspara = by mutual union; sambhutam = comes into existence; kim anyat = what else; kama-haitukam = because of sexual passion.

They say, "The world is unreal, without foundation (and) devoid of Isvara, which comes into existence because of mutual union and caused by what else but sexual desire."

Those with the evil mindset hold the belief that the world is devoid of truth (Satyam), support (aprathishtam), and a Lord (anaisvaryam). They believe the world is a product of the mutual union of things (paraspara sambhar) and is driven by lust (kama hetukam). These five beliefs empower them to commit evil acts without fear or remorse. However, it is crucial to understand that these beliefs are contrary to the path of Dharma, which advocates for truth, support, and a higher power. By rejecting these beliefs, we can avoid descending into a demonic mindset.

The belief that the world is without truth means they believe that there are no eternal, universal, permanent, or fixed truths that are dependable or trustworthy. It may also mean, according to them, that there are no absolute truths, such as God, but only relative ones that keep changing according to place, time, and circumstances. In other words, you cannot take any truth for granted, rely upon it, or build your life around it. Because of this belief, the demonic ones have little regard for any truths, for the knowledge and wisdom found in the truth-based scriptures such as the Vedas, or for the guidance or teachings of enlightened masters. With that mindset, they follow whatever they perceive to be true, and whatever suits them is acceptable to them, or is convenient for them on the spur of the moment.

The belief that the world is without foundation (aprathishtam) means the world does not have any lasting support or basis, such as God, a Supreme Being, a Controller, an eternal Dharma, morality, truth, or any indestructible or invincible entity, power, or force. For them, the world is unstable, destructible, unreliable, ever-changing, illusory, and worthy of enjoyment while it lasts. Since they do not believe in any cosmic hierarchy, divine authority, the individual Self, or the Supreme Self, they think that anyone with enough power and strength can conquer it, take control of it, become its overlord, challenge its current institutions and authority figures, or enjoy its riches and resources.

The belief that the world is without an Isvara or Supreme Lord (anisvaryam) emboldens them to act according to their whims, set their own rules and code of conduct, claim ownership and doership of their actions and possessions, pursue selfish and evil desires, or satisfy their evil passions without fearing their consequences. It makes them believe that they are on their own; they have to depend upon themselves for their survival and continuity, and no mysterious, supernatural, or invisible power or entity will judge, control, punish, or reward them for their actions or conduct. Hence, in their view, whatever happens, or does not happen, is due to fate, circumstances, individual actions, decisions, or random events. Accordingly, they believe that they are responsible for their lives and actions and masters of their fate or destinies.

The belief that the world comes into existence due to the union or coming together of things and beings (paraspara sambhutam) is a materialistic belief that refutes the idea that the creation is caused by an intelligent, supernatural force or entity such as God or Nature. The theistic philosophies of Hinduism also assume that the creation of things and beings happened because of the union, aggregation, admixture, permutation, or combination of tattvas, gunas, elements, qualities, categories, substances, causes, and effects, or the union between male and female entities. However, it also affirms that Isvara, the Supreme Lord, is their ultimate cause. The demonic ones, however, believe that there is nothing magical or supernatural about the creation. Life happens because of random events or because of the union of things made possible by the inherent laws or forces of Nature, and Nature itself is an automaton with no illumination or intelligence of its own.

The belief that the world and beings exist because of lustful desires or for the sake of enjoying sexual pleasures (kama hetukam) puts Kama (sexual desires) as the sole aim and purpose of human life. Hence, the demonic ones give no importance to the pursuit of Dharma, Artha, or Moksha and solely focus on fulfilling their lustful desires, as if it is the purpose for which all are born. Accordingly, they hold that humans should not worry about studying the Vedas, worshipping gods, performing sacrifices, nourishing the ancestors, or engaging in spiritual practices, austerities, etc., to achieve liberation. They seek the bliss of sexual union rather than the eternal bliss attained through oneness with Brahman or the Self.

Because of these beliefs, demonic people do not worship God, follow any established scriptures, respect any traditions, or pursue spiritual goals. They rely solely on their minds and senses for knowledge, apprehension, and understanding. Their truths are limited and relative to their knowledge, experience, observation, and understanding, as are their beliefs and worldviews. According to them, the world is without a moral or ethical foundation, and people can follow whatever they think is true, moral, or valid. The Puranas show that although the asuras often worship gods and practice austerities, their loyalty or devotion cannot be taken for granted since they are slippery, do not believe in fixed notions, change their positions quickly, and act according to their convenience.

It is wrong to assume that whoever denies the existence of God or his role as the creator and upholder of the world is evil by nature. In Hinduism, evil nature is characterized by selfishness, evil intentions, and egoism. Mere disbelief in the existence of God or his role in creation is not a sign of demonic nature. It can be a sign of ignorance or delusion. People may deny the existence of God for various reasons, but that alone does not make them evil. Many atheists and rational people possess discernment and excel in righteous conduct and spirituality. The demonic ones are different. They engage in evil actions, pursue evil ends, and inflict pain and suffering upon others with their evil conduct without fear, remorse, fear, compassion, or empathy. They are evil because they abandon Dharma, truthfulness, righteousness, and humanity to fulfill their selfish desires or attain their selfish goals.

Sloka 9

etāṃ dṛṣṭim avaṣṭabhya naṣṭātmānolpabuddhayaḥ
prabhavanty ugrakarmāṇaḥ kṣayāya jagatohitāḥ

etam = this; drstim = view, observation, perspective, opinion; avastabhya = accepting, holding; nasta = depraved, wasted, lost; atmanah = souls; alpa-buddhayah = of poor intelligence; prabhavanti = flourish, prevail; ugra-karmanah = in terrible activities; ksayaya = for the destruction; jagatah = of the world; ahitah = enemies, ill-wishers, adversaries.

Holding on to this view, the depraved souls of poor intelligence prevail as enemies for the destruction of the world.

Demonic people work for their own good. They do not wish to work for the welfare of anyone or the world unless they have some ulterior motive. They are also opposed to anyone practicing Dharma or worshipping the Lord. Hence, they are considered the enemies of the righteous. They are not interested in performing obligatory duties or righteous actions or helping others, and do not hesitate to engage in terrible and destructive deeds (Agra karma), if it suits them, to disturb the order and regularity of the world or inflict pain and suffering upon others. Because of their delusion, ignorance, and poor intelligence (alpa buddhi), even gods have trouble dealing with them and often land themselves in trouble by helping them. They are destructive as well as self-destructive. By their reckless actions, they delay their own liberation. Hence, Lord Krishna called them destructive souls (nashtatmas). Holding on to erroneous beliefs described in the previous verse, taking refuge in their demonic nature, and ignoring the Self in them, they become a source of suffering for themselves and others. As the Isa Upanishad suggests, because of their demonic nature and destructive actions, and seeing no other possibility to redeem themselves, they fall into sunless worlds and enter blinding darkness. Most of them rely upon their deluded thinking and perceptual knowledge and put little faith in the scriptures or the words of enlightened beings. Hence, they are not usually drawn to spiritual practice or knowledge. Due to their delusion and evil nature, they oppose righteous actions and question the existence of God. Some of them may contain virtues, as in the case of Ravana, but in the end, their evil nature prevails. Hence, pious people and God's devotees are advised to avoid them and their destructive influence. The Puranas illustrate how they act as enemies of God and disturb the world even with the best of their intentions. They are certainly not a good example for humans to follow.

Sloka 10

kāmam āśritya duṣpūraṃ dambhamānamadānvitāḥ
mohād gṛhītvāsadgrāhān pravartanteśucivratāḥ

kamam = lust; asritya = yielding, taking refuge, surrendering; duspuram = insatiable; dambha = vanity; mana = pride; mada = arrogance; anvitah = filled with; mohat = because of delusion; grhitva = seeking, grasping, taking recourse; asat = illusory, false, wrong; grahan = things; pravartante = engage or indulge in actions, behave; asuci vratah = the worshippers of the unclean.

Yielding to insatiable lust, filled with vanity, pride, (and) arrogance, seeking false or illusory things because of delusion, the worshippers of the unclean engage in actions.

Demonic people yield to insatiable (duspuram) lust since they believe that beings and the world exist to enjoy sensual pleasures (kama hetuakam) and there is no other higher purpose. We already heard from Lord Krishna that, according to them, the world came into existence because of the union of opposite sexes and the aggregation of things (aparaspara sambhutam). Hence, they repeatedly engage in sensual activities and pursue pleasures as if it were the sole aim of human life. The qualities of dumbha (vanity, conceit), māna (pride), and mada (arrogance, recklessness), which arise due to egotism and deluded nature, make them vengeful, aggressive, self-centered, eccentric, and toxic. Since they do not believe in the possibility of rebirth or liberation and consider the body to be the Self, they go after impermanent and illusory things such as power, prestige, name, fame, wealth, worldly enjoyment, etc., which do not give them lasting happiness or peace. Lord Krishna described them as the worshippers of unclean things (asuch vratah) because they do not observe cleanliness (suchi) or personal hygiene in their activities. They also engage in unconventional rituals, austerities, and methods of worship, which are considered unclean and perverted by traditional wisdom.

Sloka 11

cintām aparimeyāṃ ca pralayāntām upāśritāḥ
kāmopabhogaparamā etāvad iti niścitāḥ

cintam = worry, cares, anxieties; aparimeyam = countless, immeasurable; ca = and; pralaya-antam = until the end or until death; upasritah = taking refuge; kama-upabhoga = enjoyment of desires or carnal pleasures; paramah = the highest; etavat = this is all; iti = thus; niscitah = concluding.

With countless worries and fears that will last until the last breath, and taking refuge in the enjoyment of desires or sensual pleasures as the highest goal, concluding thus that it is all...

Demonic people suffer from many fears. They cannot overcome them easily as they experience fears of different kinds, such as the fear of sin, retribution, hostility, and the loss of power, prestige, wealth, etc., due to desires and attachments. Life becomes uncertain for them as they indulge in evil actions and create many enemies for themselves in their lust for power, wealth, and sensual enjoyment. They know that, eventually, they have to pay the price for their cruel and wicked actions. Evil attracts evil. Evil actions produce evil consequences. For those who are neck-deep in evil, there is no escape from this loop until they see reason and mend their ways. They live in constant fear since they do not know when their enemies will attack them, harm them, or take revenge against them. Their fears are further aggravated due to their distrustful nature and lack of faith in themselves, others, or God. They suffer even more as the fruit of karma arising from their evil actions begins to manifest. The thought of going to hell and suffering there for their misdeed also worries them. Worldly desires and temptations contain seeds of sorrow, which bear fruit in their own time. For evil people, there is no escape from the seeds of evil they sow and the suffering they create for themselves.

Logically, sense gratification is seemingly the easiest solution to distract the mind from worries and anxieties. However, those who pursue it for a long time realize that it does not deliver the promise. The pursuit of worldly pleasures leaves behind a trail of rewards and punishments. The rewards may be immediate, but they contain the seeds of sin hidden in them. The punishments mostly appear slowly over time as karma begins to bear fruit. Therefore, the wise ones are not disturbed when they see evil people enjoying worldly pleasures or gaining wealth, name, and fame. They know that they will not last long. Even after they succeed in their aims, fear and worry are common for those who engage in worldly pursuits and desire-ridden actions through evil means. Their suffering is self-inflicted. Since they are lost to darkness and refuse to embrace light or follow reason, a darker fate awaits them in the abysmal depths of their evil nature.

On the surface, it seems that life has no purpose other than enjoying what we have or what we can acquire according to our abilities and opportunities, ignoring the consequences or repercussions arising from it. The wicked embrace that idea due to their erroneous beliefs and self-destructive nature. The discerning ones know that true happiness lies within oneself, not in the things and pleasures of the world. They know that they should stay away from fires of desire and attachments rather than jumping into them and destroying themselves. Sense gratification does not lead to lasting peace or fulfillment but to more suffering, fear, and anxiety due to its very unstable nature. This is explained in the next verse.

Sloka 12

āśāpāśaśatair baddhāḥ kāmakrodhaparāyaṇāḥ
īhante kāmabhogārtham anyāyenārthasaṃcayān

asa-pasa = the bonds of hopes and expectations; sataih = innumerable, many, hundreds; baddhah = caught, bound; kama = lust; krodha = anger; parayanah = devoted to, absorbed in, given over; ihante = strive; kama = lustful; bhoga = enjoyment of material objects; artham = for the sake of; anyayena = unjust or unlawful means; artha = wealth; sancayan = amass, accumulate.

Bound by hundreds of hopes and expectations, devoted to lust and anger, they strive to amass wealth by unjust means for lustful enjoyment.

Driven by endless hopes and desires and by the chief evils of lust and anger, evil people amass wealth to enjoy worldly pleasures. They do not accumulate wealth through righteous means or by practicing Dharma, but through unjust means by stealing from others or forcibly taking what does not belong to them. They also use that wealth for selfish enjoyment rather than to nourish the gods or help others. Thus, they defy the Lord's command at every step and turn themselves into his enemies and forces of darkness.

In pursuing goals or performing obligatory duties, means are as important as the ends. Since actions produce karma through consequences, one should consider where those actions will lead and what fruit they bear. Ends and means become more important for those who are caught in the web of desires and expectations and perform actions for worldly reasons or selfish enjoyment, using whatever means they can find and ignoring their consequences. They may justify their actions to feel good by suppressing their moral judgment or the sense of morality and immorality. However, they cannot escape from the fruit they bear and the suffering they produce in time. Both ends and means are indispensable if the purpose is to live righteously and achieve liberation or freedom from bondage and suffering. The ideals of Dharma and its purpose must be the sole support in performing obligatory duties or pursuing liberation. They cannot be ignored even in worldly life or in the pursuit of the four chief aims. Of the four, Dharma (righteous actions) comes first since it is the foundation of all the pursuits, actions, peace, and happiness.

When people ignore righteousness (Dharma) in their eagerness to secure wealth or worldly pleasures (Kama), they give themselves to demonic influences and harm themselves. When they fall into evil ways and become enemies of themselves, they destroy their chances of peace and happiness. The Bhagavadgita is clear on this. If you want to be a friend to yourself and be the source of peace and happiness, you must live in harmony with the ideals of Dharma. If liberation is the ultimate purpose, you should not ignore the importance of righteousness in your actions or goals. For the sake of Dharma and your own material and spiritual welfare (Moksha), you cannot compromise your ideals or your allegiance to God. Without the Lord guiding you and leading you from within and Dharma showing you the path, you cannot strengthen your divine nature or protect yourself from evil influences. This is the ideal guiding principle for those who wish to excel in ananya bhakti and atma samyama and achieve liberation. It is also an effective way to suppress evil tendencies and keep oneself free from demonic nature (asura prvritti).

Evil minds ignore the means, even when they pursue righteous goals. They use everything, even God, Dharma, and spirituality, to achieve their selfish or egoistic ends. Wealth is divine, but usually, it is evil people who mostly succeed in securing it or controlling it. Because of their erroneous beliefs, they misuse their resources and their natural abilities and talents for their selfish ends. The ideal pursuit of Dharma demands that the discerning ones must be righteous in all possible ways and aim for only righteous goals to become the living embodiments of the Lord and express him through their character and conduct. In the purity of a devotee's mind and body and the righteous aspirations of his heart and soul, the Lord must shine naturally and spontaneously as his very radiant nature. Those who are drawn to evil ways do not recognize the centrality of Dharma in their actions or conduct. They do not mind using unjust means to achieve their ends. For them, winning is more important than whether their actions and choices are ethical or unethical. In their worldview, achieving their goals is more important than every other consideration. Thereby, they succumb to evil temptations and bring ruin upon themselves.

Sloka 13

idam adya mayā labdham imaṃ prāpsye manoratham
idam astīdam api me bhaviṣyati punar dhanam

idam = this; adya = today; maya = by me; labdham = gained; imam = this; prapsye = I shall gain; manah-ratham = hidden desire, secret desire, wish; idam = this; asti = it is; idam = this; api = also; me = mine; bhavisyati = in future; punah = again; dhanam = wealth.

This has been gained by me today; this hidden desire of mine I shall fulfill (next); this (wealth) is (mine); and in the future, this wealth too shall be mine.

Evil people focus on gaining wealth to fulfill their desires and passions. They are not easily satisfied with what they have, since they want to have more and enjoy more. With each gain or success, their lust for power and wealth keeps increasing, as does their compulsion to fulfill more desires. Therefore, they are always on the lookout to gain more, flouting all rules, morals, and principles if necessary. In their insatiable desire to acquire endless wealth and power and improve their social and economic standing, they do not care whether their actions will hurt them or others or what consequences may arise from them. Of the four aims of human life, they focus mainly on Artha and Kama, which they pursue without caring for Dharma and Moksha.

Nothing pleases them more than the possibility of gaining wealth, power, and prestige, even if it means suffering and misery for countless others. In reaching their goals or fulfilling their desires, they solely focus on themselves and their achievements, ignoring how their actions may affect others or cause them suffering. Due to their evil propensities, they tend to be aggressive and destructive and are easily provoked. Aparigraha (non-possession) and asteya (not-stealing) are considered the highest restraints (yamas) in many spiritual traditions. Evil people violate them habitually and enjoy doing it. One of the ideals of Dharma is that this whole existence belongs to the Supreme Lord since he creates and supports it. Hence, humans are not to crave anything or claim ownership of anything but live on earth as a sacrifice or service to the Lord (Isa), offering him their actions and the fruit arising from them. Evil people do not believe in that or in righteous actions or virtuous living. They live for themselves and take credit for their actions and abilities. What matters to them most is what they have gained today and what else they can have tomorrow.

Sloka 14

asau mayā hataḥ śatrur haniṣye cāparān api
īśvaro.aham ahaṃ bhogī siddhohaṃ balavān sukhī

asau = that; maya = by me; hatah = has been slain; satruh = enemy; hanisye = I shall harm; ca = and; aparan = others; api = also; isvarah = the lord; aham = I am; aham = I am; bhogi = the enjoyer; siddhah = perfect; aham = I am; balavan = powerful; sukhi = happy.

That enemy has been slain by me; I shall harm others also; I am the lord; I am the enjoyer; I am perfect, powerful, (and) happy.

Evil people have no shortage of enemies since they hurt and harm others indiscriminately to achieve their ends with little regard for the suffering their actions cause to others. In achieving their goals, they are driven by the chief evil passions (maha patakas): lust, anger, pride, envy, and greed. These evils are common to humans also but are more pronounced in demonic beings. As they repeatedly act upon them, they keep fueling their demonic nature. As they continue on this retrogressive path to perdition, they reach a point of no return. They have no compunction in harming others or exploiting their weaknesses or trust. Because of their extreme nature, they are not content with small victories. As the Puranas illustrate, in their eagerness to prove themselves, they do not mind challenging even the Supreme Lord. They act with great vengeance against those who they feel are in their way. The propensity to do evil exists in humans as well. However, most people keep it under control for one reason or another. It is well evident in those who are prone to excessive cruelty, aggression, anger, delusion, and lust. From their actions, one can see that the evil nature has taken hold of them, and they are difficult to reform.

Demonic people do not believe that the all-pervading Lord is the Self and controller of all. Hence, they act as if they are the lords of their minds and bodies and masters of their fate and as if they have a right to fulfill their desires and enjoy their lives. With that deluded thinking, they take credit for their actions and achievements. They also dislike those who criticize them or give them the right advice that is not good for their goals or intentions. The pious ones are inclined to help others, serve the Lord, or work for the welfare of the world. Because of their sattvic nature, they practice nonviolence and other virtues. The evil ones are the opposite. They show no empathy and do not care whether their actions hurt others or cause them suffering. Hinduism is not averse to competing with others, fighting enemies, or defending oneself against evil people. The Bhagavadgita itself is an excellent example in this regard. Even gods fight battles, slay enemies, display anger, and compete with humans or among themselves. However, they differ from the evil ones in their temperament and attitude. They engage in such actions to uphold Dharma, protect the world, serve the Lord, or help their pious ones. The demonic ones are driven by evil desires and passions.

Sloka 15

āḍhyobhijanavān asmi konyosti sadṛśo mayā
yakṣye dāsyāmi modiṣya ity ajñānavimohitāḥ

adhyah = wealthy; abhijana-van = from a superior lineage; asmi = I am; kah anyah = who else; asti = is there; sadrsah = like; maya = me; yaksye = I offer sacrifices; dasyami = I give charity; modisye = I shall rejoice; iti = thus; ajnana = by ignorance; vimohitah = deluded.

"I am wealthy; I belong to a superior lineage; who else is there like me? I will offer sacrifices; I will give charity; I will rejoice," thus (they) are deluded by ignorance."

These attitudes denote egoism, attachment, ignorance, and delusion. The wise ones have no ego, no vanity, and no attachment to their birth, family lineage, status, or acclaim. They act selflessly and perform sacrifices as an obligatory duty to God and Dharma. When they give charity to Brahmanas and others, they do so out of compassion, duty, reverence, and discipline to help them, not to show off their wealth or feel superior. The egoistic ones do it for egoistic and selfish reasons to fulfill their selfish desires or achieve some ulterior goal. In the end, their vain actions lead to their downfall. The ego is a major problem in overcoming the impurities of ignorance and delusion or the influence of the gunas. Egoistic people consider themselves superior to others and act accordingly. Sometimes, they slight others or make them feel inferior or unworthy to feel good about themselves, or prove their superiority. The wise ones believe in equality and sameness, as they see the same Lord residing in all as their very Self. Therefore, they do not claim distinction or superiority or take pride in their virtues and possessions. Since they are free from the delusion that arises due to ignorance (ajnana vimoha), they do not give any importance to their births, families, lineages, names, forms, etc., and renounce them as impermanent and sources of bondage. In contrast, the evil ones take pride in their families, family lineages, castes, professions, nationalities, races, cultures, place names, possessions, etc. These extended identities strengthen their egotism, involve them deeply with the world and illusory things, and make them even more deluded.

Sloka 16

anekacittavibhrāntā mohajālasamāvṛtāḥ
prasaktāḥ kāmabhogeṣu patanti narakeśucau

aneka = many, numerous; citta vibhrantah = bewildered or perplexed by thoughts; moha = delusion; jala = snare, net; samavrtah = caught, surrounded; prasaktah = excessively attached, addicted, engrossed; kama = sensuous desires; bhogesu = in the enjoyment; patanti = fall down; narake = into hell; asucau = those who are unclean.

Bewildered by many thoughts, caught in the snare of delusion, excessively attached to the enjoyment of sensual desires, (they) fall into the unclean hell.

'Chitta vibhranta' means delusion, confusion, or bewilderment, which arises from restlessness, conflicting thoughts, and endless desires, coupled with unbridled egoism, delusion, and ignorance. It is common to those who are prone to demonic nature and such egoistic thoughts as, "I am wealthy; I belong to a superior lineage; who else is there like me? I will perform sacrifices and give charity to show the world my superiority and rejoice in my victories." Lord Krishna compared delusion to a snare or net (jala) because it is difficult for anyone who is caught in a net to escape, especially from the net of worldly desires and temptations. The Lord himself casts the net with his deluding power of Maya to keep the mortal beings bound to the world and ensure its orderly progress. Those who are caught in it remain bound to Samsara and cannot escape easily. The demonic ones find it even more difficult as they become deeply involved with the world due to delusion, egoism, and excessive attachment to lustful enjoyment (kama bhoga) and invite their destruction (patanam).

From Lord Krishna's teachings, it is obvious that divine qualities contribute to peace, happiness, and liberation. Demonic qualities induce restlessness, delusion, and confusion and lead to self-destruction. A similar fate may also await those who pursue Artha and Kama to the exclusion of Dharma and Moksha. There is no sin in pursuing worldly goals, but one must adhere to the righteous path and live responsibly with Moksha as the ultimate goal. When the mind is driven by conflicting desires in different directions due to impurities and evil nature, one becomes bewildered about one's purpose and priorities in life. People often pay a heavy price for it, as the consequences do not immediately manifest or become known. Demonic people erroneously believe themselves to be the lords of their lives, whereas they have little control over themselves or their desires and actions. Until they realize their faults and correct themselves, they have no escape from the abyss into which they descend by their willful and self-destructive actions.

Sloka 17

ātmasaṃbhāvitāḥ stabdhā dhanamānamadānvitāḥ
yajante nāmayajñais te dambhenāvidhipūrvakam

atma-sambhavitah = self-conceited, egoistic; stabdhah = stubborn; dhana = wealth; mana = self-importance; mada = arrogance, intoxication; anvitah = filled with; yajante = perform sacrifices; nama yajnaih = namesake only; te = they; dambhena = out of vanity; avidhi-purvakam = against the established practices.

Self-conceited, stubborn, and filled with pride and the arrogance of having wealth, they perform sacrifices for the namesake only, out of vanity and against established practices.

Demonic people are self-conceited (atma-sambhavita), meaning they have an exaggerated sense of self-importance and think that the world should revolve around them and everything, including religion and scriptures, should serve them. They are stubborn (stabdha), meaning you cannot change them or reason with them unless the world or circumstances fit into their thinking. They are filled with pride (mana) and the arrogance (mada) of having wealth (dhana), meaning they entertain a different value system in which having wealth is more important than having character and integrity. They are also insincere. Hence, they perform sacrifices insincerely due to vanity and according to their convenience, ignoring the rules and procedures (vidhis) or the restrictions (nishedhas) prescribed by the scriptures or the tradition. Since they are stubborn, they do not think of the consequences of their actions or how they may affect them or others. Their devotion is also conditional. Hence, they worship gods and make offerings only when it suits them or when they have to fulfill desires.

When devotion or religious practices are mixed with egoism, delusion, selfishness, or evil intentions, they become counterproductive and produce unintended consequences. The gods are rarely pleased by the devotion of evil people or the methods they follow since they know that they are unreliable, dangerous, and deceptive. The wise ones also distrust them, knowing that they are insincere and mischievous and misuse the knowledge of the scriptures or the rites and rituals for selfish gains. Due to vanity and conceit, the demonic ones think they are no less important than gods and worthy of worship and adoration. Hence, they practice Dharma not to serve God or the world but to strengthen themselves or show off their power and wealth. Thus, filled with pride (mana) and arrogance (mada), they practice Dharma in name only, following perverted methods, creating their own rules, and ignoring the scriptural injunctions, established procedures, or the words of enlightened masters. With their eccentric and unconventional methods, they cause confusion in the minds of others, contribute to chaos and the decline of Dharma, and ruin themselves. Unfortunately, evil influences predominate in Kaliyuga. People are vulnerable to the demonic nature. Hence, the Lord's devotees must be careful and avoid the company of evil people.

Sloka 18

ahaṃkāraṃ balaṃ darpaṃ kāmaṃ krodhaṃ casaṃśritāḥ
mām ātmaparadeheṣu pradviṣantobhyasūyakāḥ

ahankaram = egoism; balam = brute power, strength; darpam = arrogance, air of superiority, pride; kamam = lust; krodham = anger; ca = and; samsritah =

abiding, taking shelter, indulging, resorting to; mam = Me; atma = own; para = other; dehesu = in bodies; pradvisantah = hating; abhyasuyakah = the excessively envious.

Resorting to egoism, brute power, arrogance, lust, and anger, these excessively envious ones hate Me in the bodies of their own and others.

Ahankaram (egoism) means feeling excessively proud of oneself or one's real or imaginary qualities, achievements, and possessions. It arises due to ignorance (avidya), delusion (Maya), and attachment to one's name and form. According to Shankaracharya, it is a source of many evils and is difficult to overcome. Balam means physical strength. When associated with evil, it becomes a source of evil and destruction, but in association with good people, it becomes a source of strength and support. According to Shankara, it is physical strength mixed with lust and passion that aims to hurt or humiliate others. Darpam is pride or arrogance mixed with vanity, conceit, and self-importance. Shankara stated that it is located in the internal organ, and it is a destroyer of virtue or righteousness. Those who are full of it cannot take refuge in the Lord or practice surrender and exclusive devotion. Kama is the unbridled sexual passion, ranked as the first of the chief evils. Anger is the second most potent chief evil. As Lord Krishna said before, it is the destroyer of discernment and is self-destructive. All these evil qualities not only strengthen demonic nature but also make those who possess them turn against God and become his enemies.

These qualities lead those who possess them on the downward path to their destruction and distance them from their divine nature and the Supreme Lord. Those who give themselves to them are averse to everything divine. They hate gods, their actions, opulence, and glory. They also trouble the worshippers who make sacrifices for them or worship the Supreme Lord. Their actions intensify their evil nature and keep them bound to dark and demonic worlds. Envy is another evil passion that is characteristic of them. It is well expressed by the word abhyasuyaka, which means envy tinged with anger and resentment. Humans also experience envy, but it rarely becomes destructive or evil. The envy of evil people induces anger and makes them think of destroying the source of their envy. Envy can be a positive force if it is controlled. It can make the right-minded ones engage in constructive actions and improve themselves or better their conditions. In evil people, it becomes a negative and destructive force and prompts them to harm those they envy. It may also make them divert their anger towards God and blame him for their plight. The evil ones cannot bear the thought that someone is superior to them or more powerful than them. God, being the highest of all, they hate him even more. The Puranas show that asuras who secure boons from him use those very powers against him or the gods to prove their superiority.

This verse states that the evil ones hate God in their bodies, as well as in others' bodies. It means they hate the Lord wherever they find him, whether in their own bodies or others' bodies, since he is hidden in all as their true Self. The battle between good and evil is universal and happens at various levels and forms. It happens within the world and in the minds and bodies of all people who are vulnerable to desires and outside influences. Due to their mixed nature, humans are susceptible to both divine and demonic influence. Both tendencies exist equally in all humans. Depending upon what they nurture within themselves, they can become divine or demonic. Hence, God's devotees should use discretion and cultivate divine qualities only, nourishing the gods in them through righteous actions, taking refuge in the Lord, and seeking his protection. Those who abide in divine nature strengthen the gods in them through virtuous living and radiate their presence. In contrast, those who strengthen their demonic nature through evil actions and let the demons in them feed upon their evil nature join the ranks of those who are opposed to the forces of light and righteousness. Thus, devotees must be careful about which way they lean, what they worship, and whom they nurture within themselves with their thoughts, desires, and actions. Those who nurture gods, live righteously, and overcome their impurities through spiritual practice strengthen their divine nature. However, the opposite will happen if they let evil nature take hold of their consciousness and control their actions.

Sloka 19

tān ahaṃ dviṣataḥ krurān saṃsāreṣu narādhamān
kṣipāmy ajasram aśubhān āsurīṣv eva yoniṣu

tan = these; aham = I; dvisatah = haters; kruran = cruel; samsaresu = into samsaras the cycles of births and deaths, existence; nara-adhaman = the lowest of the humans; ksipami = cast, throw; ajasram = forever; asubhan = impure, inauspicious; asurisu = demonic; eva = surely; yonisu = in the wombs.

I cast forever these cruel haters, the lowest of humans, into various cycles of births and deaths and inauspicious and demonic wombs.

Lord Krishna described here the fate of those who possess an evil or demonic nature. He called them cruel haters of God, the lowest humans (naradhama), and said that he would cast them into impure and inauspicious demonic wombs and repeated cycles of births and deaths (samsaras), birth after birth. The use of 'samsaras' instead of 'samsara' denotes that he would ensure their births in different worlds or different forms or classes of jivas. Thus, for example, upon death, evil people may fall into the lowest hells and undergo punishment or wander in the mortal world as ghosts or evil spirits and continue to indulge in evil actions until they find redemption. When their next birth is due, they may be reborn as animals, worms, insects, asuras, or humans. Thus, the law of karma inexorably applies to everyone, including the evil. However, these souls are not eternally condemned to hell. Redemption is possible for them if they change their ways and return to the righteous path.

These words of Lord Krishna should not be inferred to mean that the Lord of the Universe deals with the sinners cruelly. It happens because of the laws he establishes. He has no personal stake in what they do or do not do, is equal to all, and ensures that his laws are applied equally without discrimination. He rewards devotees according to their actions and devotion, just as he punishes the evil ones according to their actions and demonic nature. The law of karma applies to all, and he has no direct involvement in how the karma of each jiva bears fruit. According to the same law, humans are responsible for their actions and their consequences. Previously, Lord Krishna affirmed that everyone is his best friend or worst enemy. Righteous people are their own best friends. The evil ones are their own worst enemies. Through their deluded actions and evil nature, they harm themselves. Many people blame God for their problems and suffering, ignoring their personal responsibility for it. The truth is that happiness and suffering arise from one's actions and conduct. If they have problems and difficulties, they must look within themselves, examine their actions and conduct, and try to change them. The Lord of the Universe does not hurt or harm anyone. That part rests with each being. The suffering or the punishment is always the fruit of one's karma. However, he does help those who pray to him and seek his help or protection. If he is ignored or if someone acts as if he does not exist, he will remain silent and indifferent.

In the tenth chapter, Lord Krishna said he was the punishing rod (danda) of the punishers. The analogy applies here also. The punishing rod merely dispenses punishment. The decision to punish arises from the authority, which determines the appropriate punishment according to the crime or the misdeed. The punishing rod is a nonmaterial cause. The punishing authority is the material cause. The law that determines the punishment is the efficient cause. The Supreme Lord does the same in creation. As the efficient and material cause of all, he sets the Wheel of Dharma in motion by establishing universal laws. Through those who are vested with the authority to dispense justice, he acts as the instrumental cause and facilitates rewards and punishments according to the laws he established. As the Self of all, he witnesses all punishments without becoming the subject or the object of the punishment or the suffering. However, as the Supreme Lord and source of all, he is the cause, effect, source, subject, and object of all actions and happenings in the Play he enacts. In punishments, he becomes the punisher, the punished, the laws governing the punishment, and the punishing instruments. All the power and authority to reward or punish anyone arises from him only and for him only while he remains indifferent, uninvolved, and untainted.

Like Isvara, the Supreme Lord, he abides in sameness and tranquility. As the Witness Self and the source of all, he lets each jiva participate in his Play according to its actions (karma). Although he does not directly interfere or involve himself with anyone or anything, he does respond to love and devotion. If pious souls worship him or pray to him with exclusive devotion, he helps them cross the ocean of samsara. He does it even when the asuras worship him through their demonic devotion (asura bhakti). He takes care of his dearest devotees, even if they indulge in evil actions, but remains indifferent to those who ignore him or do not worship him. He does not seek loyalty or devotion from anyone, or discriminate against anyone because they are opposed to him, ignore him, or do not worship him. Thus, remaining equal to all and without becoming involved with the ways of samsara, he lets the jivas live their lives according to their choices and actions. Only in exceptional cases, when the world is in chaos and near destruction, may he be directly involved or interfere to restore balance and uphold Dharma. He declared the same in the second chapter of the Bhagavadgita.

Sloka 20

āsurīṃ yonim āpannā mūḍhā janmanijanmani
mām aprāpyaiva kaunteya tato yānty adhamāṃ gatim 16.20

asurim = demoniac; yonim = wombs; apannah = obtaining, acquiring; mudhah = the deluded; janmani janmani = in birth after birth; mam = Me; aprapya = without reaching, attaining; eva = ever; Kaunteya = O son of Kunti; tatah = thereafter; yanti = fall, go; adhamam = lowest, downward, lower; gatim = movement, direction, path.

Obtaining demonic wombs, deluded beings, birth after birth, without reaching Me, O son of Kunti, fall by the downward path.

Obtaining demonic wombs, the wicked ones keep falling into lower worlds repeatedly by the downward path (adhogati). It means that in each birth, it becomes increasingly difficult for them to attain a good birth or achieve liberation. Human beings have the unique opportunity to purify themselves and achieve liberation. Other jivas (animals, birds, insects, etc.) do not have this opportunity. Their transmigration is solely shaped by circumstances (adhibhautika) and fate (adhidaivika). Until they attain human birth, external causes decide their progress and spiritual evolution. Redemption is also not possible for them, and so is it for gods, celestial beings, asuras, daityas, danavas, yakshas, etc., unless they are born as humans and work for their liberation. Demonic beings have no path to liberation unless they die at the hands of a divinity or due to a divine cause. Lord Krishna said that by attaining demonic wombs, they would perish by the downward path without attaining him (mama aprapya), meaning they would fall into hell without attaining him or his higher nature.

For humans, life offers two choices, each with a different destiny, direction, and goal. One is the upward path (paramagati). It leads them to the highest and supreme Abode of Brahman, meant for those who live righteously and worship the Lord with exclusive devotion. The purest of souls (shuddhatmas) qualify for it. It is the path of the pure, the liberated, the practitioners of Dharma, and the knowers of Brahman. In the Upanishads, it is described as the Northward Passage (Uttarayanam) or the Path of the Immortal Gods (Devayana) since on that path, various divinities (devas) help the liberated souls who are on their way to the immortal world of Brahman to reach their destination. The other one is the downward path (adhama-gati or adhogati), a path reserved for the most sinful and evilest humans. It is a path filled with darkness and suffering, a stark contrast to the light and liberation of the upward path. Those who fall into them have limited opportunities to attain human birth or liberation, a reflection of the severity of their actions.

Hinduism does not believe in the eternal condemnation of sinners to eternal fires. It does not hold that the Supreme Lord, Isvara, is a wrathful God who sends sinners into an eternal hell for not obeying him or acknowledging him. He may assume fiery forms and perform destructive roles as a part of his duties, but his natural state is always pleasant (saumya). It suggests that those who do not attain liberation but perform their duties and live righteously will go to the ancestral heaven and return from there after their due time. They are not lost to God or denied redemption. They can restart from where they left off and work for their liberation. However, if they continue to engage in evil actions, their chances of reaching the highest heaven become increasingly remote.

Sloka 21

trividhaṃ narakasyedaṃ dvāraṃ nāśanam ātmanaḥ
kāmaḥ krodhas tathā lobhas tasmād etat trayaṃtyajet

tri-vidham = three types; narakasya = of the hell; idam = this; dvaram = gate, door; nasanam = destruction; atmanah = for self; kamah = lust; krodhah = anger; tatha = and; lobhah = greed; tasmat = therefore; etat = these; trayam = three; tyajet = must renounce.

Triple is the gate to this hell that leads to the destruction of the Self, lust, anger, and greed. Therefore, these three must be renounced.

The spiritual traditions of India, including those of Buddhism and Jainism, identify five chief evils (pancha patakas) that are responsible for evil actions, namely lust, anger, pride, greed, and envy. They lead humans on the harmful and self-destructive downward path to hell. This verse identifies only three of them, probably because the other two, pride and envy, are induced by them only. By controlling these three, one may subdue the other two. All these evil qualities exist in humans in different intensities according to the modes. They exist even in yogis, jnanis, gurus, and those who have advanced on the path of liberation but remain under control. They may even lose control in weak moments and succumb to them. Those who are predominantly rajasic or tamasic are most vulnerable to them. However, the good thing is that humans can overcome them by resolving the modes and strengthening their divine nature. Some people may never succeed in overcoming their evil nature due to karma, or are meant to be born that way.

Kama (sexual desire) has many shades. It is a positive force as sexual pleasure or enjoyment, and a negative force as lust and perversion. As a positive force of Nature, it is recognized as one of the four aims (purusharthas) of human life since it gives meaning and purpose to life and since it is a part of the right to enjoy life and the obligatory duty to raise children and continue life upon earth. Therefore, it is not prohibited for householders and even for yogis, seers, and sages who live as householders. However, kama, as lust, is always a negative force and decidedly evil. Hinduism identifies it as an evil quality and prohibits it universally. The positive force of kama is conducive to happiness and fulfillment and leads to a holistic life when it is pursued as an obligatory duty, in conjunction with other chief aims of life, and with righteousness (Dharma) as the foundation of all actions. In contrast, the negative force of kama (lust), which is pursued purely for selfish pleasure in disregard of the aim of Dharma and approved conduct, leads to sinful karma and unhappy consequences.

Just like Kama, krodha (anger) has many shades. In humans, it may be mild or moderate. Even gods are prone to anger when they show their displeasure. Hence, almost all the gods of Hinduism have fiery forms. They personify righteous anger, which leads to change, renewal, and improvement through death and destruction. However, the anger that arises when desires are thwarted is decidedly evil. Actions induced by it produce evil consequences and lead humans to the gates of hell. Anger that results in violence (himsa) and cruelty also falls into this category. Greed is also a human trait. It is common to most humans since human beings are selfish by nature. It may arise due to fear or insecurity, which is the case with humans, or purely due to the evil nature, which is the case with asuras or those who are predominantly evil. Greed, which induces people to engage in desire-ridden actions or commit violent or unethical actions such as stealing from others, deceiving others, or indulging in some cardinal sin, is surely an evil quality. However, greed in any form arises primarily due to selfishness. Hence, it cannot be anything but evil.

Kama, krodha, and lobha constitute the triple path to the gate of hell because those who succumb to them have no other destiny. Whether people act for themselves or on behalf of others under their influence, the result is the same. It means that one should not work for evil people who are driven by these passions or help them to achieve their evil ends. Evil actions produce multiple consequences, create many ripples in the ocean of samsara, and touch many people at many levels. Hence, the karma that arises from them will be difficult to overcome. Lust arises from attraction to pleasure, anger arises from aversion to pain, and greed arises from excessive attachment to sense objects. They all lead to ignorance and delusion. They are considered chief evils because they induce people to indulge in wrong actions and leave strong impressions upon the consciousness, which collectively become the seed for repeated births and deaths. If these obstacles to liberation are not promptly overcome, they lead the beings into the worlds of darkness. They can be overcome only through discipline, detachment (vairagya), and exclusive devotion (ananya bhakti).

Sloka 22

etair vimuktaḥ kaunteya tamodvārais tribhir naraḥ
ācaraty ātmanaḥ śreyas tato yāti parāṃ gatim

etaih = by these; vimuktah = free; kaunteya = O son of Kunti; tamah-dvaraih = from the gates of darkness; tribhih = triple, three; narah = a person; acarati = acts; atmanah = self; sreyah = welfare; tatah = thereafter; yati = reaches, goes; param = supreme; gatim = goal.

A person who is free from these triple gates of darkness, O son of Kunti, acts for the welfare of the Self and reaches the highest goal.

Lust (kama), anger (krodha), and greed (lobha) are the chief evils that surely lead one to hell. Hence, whether one pursues liberation or not, is spiritual or materialistic, it is better to stay away from them and not act under their influence. If one is free from them and pursues liberation, one's chances of achieving it increase greatly. These evils exist internally and externally and reinforce each other. Together, they make it increasingly difficult for humans to practice Dharma, live righteously, and escape from samsara. Under their influence, the lower maya shaktis gain strength and lead their victims to self-destruction. The wise ones know that the senses and the mind are inherently vulnerable to evil thoughts and desires. They know that they can afflict even the most advanced souls and even gods, as is illustrated in the Puranas and epics. Therefore, they practice self-control, take refuge in the Lord, and establish their minds in him with exclusive devotion. Devotees can overcome them by renouncing desires and attachments, performing desireless actions (nishkama karma), and worshipping the Lord with exclusive devotion.

As far as the chief evils are concerned, divine help is surely needed to overcome them since many evil forces may be lurking behind those evil passions. In a world that is increasingly becoming evil, it is essential to live righteously, like a lotus in the muddy waters of samsara, suppressing evil qualities and tendencies and strengthening divine nature by worshipping the Supreme Lord and leading a divine-centered life. One should strive to overcome kama through detachment, renunciation, and brahmacharya (celibacy); krodha through nonviolence (ahimsa), forgiveness, freedom from malice (adroha), and excessive pride (atimana); and lobha through self-restraint, contentment (trpti), non-stealing (asteya), and non-covetousness (aparigraha or aloluptam), all the while taking refuge in the Lord and offering all actions to him. Even those who fall into evil ways can escape from these gates of hell by taking refuge in the Lord and becoming his exclusive devotees. Lord Krishna assured it before in a previous verse.

Sloka 23

yaḥ śāstravidhim utsṛjya vartate kāmakārataḥ
na sa siddhim avāpnoti na sukhaṃ na parāṃ gatim

yah = he who; sastra-vidhim = scriptural injunctions; utsrjya = discarding, ignoring; vartate = acts; kama-charatah = acts under the influence of desire or lust; na = not; sah = that one, he; siddhim = perfection; avapnoti = attain; na = not; sukham = happiness; na = not; param = the supreme; gatim = goal.

He who, discarding scriptural injunctions, acts under the influence of desire, that one attains neither perfection nor happiness nor the Supreme Goal.

Scriptures, such as the Upanishads, Brahmasutras, and the Bhagavadgita, are meant for guidance for those who want to overcome suffering through liberation. They contain valid knowledge, accepted by seers and sages as truthful and dependable, to attain Brahman. Hence, they are ideal for self-study (svadhyaya) to know conceptually Brahman and the means to attain Him before one can put them into practice. The scriptures are the best way to establish the mind in divine thought and activate our divine nature. When you study them, you are in communication with God himself. One of the beliefs of Trika Shaivism is that a sacred text is a transcendental thought manifested as speech by the Shaktis who govern vocal sounds, speech, and the alphabets (matrka chakra). The material universe also manifests similarly from Isvara as an objectified reality of his supreme will expressed in sounds and words. In that aspect, he is known as Para Vak (transcendental Word) or Shabda Brahman, symbolized in the Upanishads as Aum or Pranava.

According to the Vedic theories of epistemology, scriptures are helpful to confirm or validate justified beliefs and transcendental truths and experiences (yathartha anubhava) or overcome mistaken notions (ayatartha anubhava) that arise due to doubt or ambiguity (samsaya), misapprehension (viparyaya), logical errors (tarka), or false memory (smriti). Therefore, the wise ones treat the scriptures as repositories of sacred knowledge containing the words of the Lord or his Shaktis and accept them at face value without disputing them. They can be considered teachers (gurus) in word form. When real gurus are unavailable, they serve as teachers and reliable sources of trustworthy knowledge to purify oneself and cultivate discernment. They teach the right-minded how to live righteously, perform their obligatory duties, and escape from samsara by taking refuge in the Supreme Lord.

Demonic people do not respect the scriptures or follow the methods they prescribe. They take pleasure in doing things according to their whims or desires, disregarding the words of wise people or the sacred knowledge of the scriptures. For them, the ends only matter, and the means can be whatever fits into their plans. As long as they reach their goals, it does not matter how they accomplish them or what methods they follow. They regard morals and scriptural injunctions as inconvenient obstacles which must be ignored or broken. As a result, they may achieve their ends but not peace, happiness, or liberation. Truth eludes them as they gradually lead themselves towards the gates of hell.

Sloka 24

tasmāc chāstraṃ pramāṇaṃ tekāryākāryavyavasthitau
jñātvā śāstravidhānoktaṃ karma kartum ihārhasi

Tasmat = therefore; sastram = scriptures; pramanam = testimony, standard, proof; te = your; karya = what should be done; akarya = what should not to be done; vyavasthitau = in ascertaining, establishing, determining; jnatva = by knowing; sastra = of scripture; vidhana = methods, instructions, procedures; uktam = as described; karma = duty; kartum = perform; iha = here; arhasi = must, should.

Therefore, let the scripture be your testimony in ascertaining what should be done and what should not be done. Knowing the methods proclaimed by the scriptures, you must perform your duty here.

The scripture in this verse primarily refers to the Vedas, but it can be any scripture in which one has faith and which does not contradict the Vedas. For centuries, the Vedas have been considered the final authority in spiritual knowledge. They served as the standard texts to ascertain metaphysical truths and methods that are useful to attain liberation or self-realization. They uphold both Vidhi and Vidhanam in performing sacrificial rituals or worshipping the Lord. Vidhi refers to the rules and regulations, or the laws that should be followed strictly. If they are ignored or violated, sin will result. Vidhanam refers to the methods one must follow or practice to ensure intended outcomes. For the practitioners of Dharma and seekers of liberation, both Vidhi and Vidhanam are important. Lord Krishna used the word arhasi (must) to convey that the methods as proclaimed by the scriptures must be learned and performed. This is especially true about sacrificial rituals, obligatory duties, moral injunctions, and certain social observances. They should be strictly practiced as laid down by the scriptures (sastram). Texts like the Grihya Sutras and many lawbooks (smritis) also contain rules regarding domestic rituals and code of conduct. However, they are optional because they are memorial works (smritis), and their knowledge does not constitute valid knowledge. One may use discretion while following them. Truths may be ascertained in several ways through perception, inference, expert knowledge, etc. However, as far as metaphysical truths are concerned, scriptures are the most reliable authority until one has a direct experience of them. They help us know how to live righteously, practice Dharma as prescribed by them, and pursue our spiritual goals without making mistakes or falling into sinful ways. By studying them, we cultivate discernment and develop the right knowledge, right thinking, and right understanding.

Conclusion

iti srīmadbhāgavadgītāsupanisatsu brahmavidyāyām yogasāstre srikrisnārjunasamvāde daivāsurasaṃpadvibhāgo nāma ṣoḍaśo 'dhyayah.

iti = thus; srīmadbhāgavadgītā = in the sacred Bhagavadgita; upanisatsu = in the Upanishad; brahmavidyāyām = the knowledge of the absolute Brahman; yogasāstre = the scripture of yoga; srikrisnārjunasamvāde = the dialogue between Sri Krishna and Arjuna; daivāsurasaṃpadvibhāgo nāma = by name the yoga of the division of the divine and demonic properties; ṣoḍaśah = sixteenth adhyayah = chapter.

Thus ends the sixteenth chapter, named Daivāsura Saṃpada Vibhāga Yoga (The Yoga of the Division of Divine and Demonic Properties) in the Upanishad of the divine Bhagavadgita, the knowledge of the Absolute, a treatise on Yoga, and the debate between Arjuna and Lord Krishna.

17 – Shraddhā Traya Vibhāga Yoga

The Yoga of the Triple Division of Faith

Sloka 1

arjuna uvāca
ye śāstravidhim utsṛjya yajante śraddhayānvitāḥ
teṣāṃ niṣṭhā tu kā kṛṣṇa sattvam āho rajas tamaḥ

arjunah uvaca = Arjuna said; ye =who; sastra-vidhim = scriptural injunctions; utsrjya = ignoring giving up; yajante = worship; sraddhaya = with faith; anvitah = endowed; tesam = of them; nistha = condition, devotion, state; tu = however, but; ka = what; krsna = O Krishna; sattvam = sattva; aho = said; rajah = rajas; tamah = tamas.

Said Arjuna, "However, ignoring the scriptural injunctions, those who worship with complete faith, what is their devotion, O Krishna? Is it of sattva, rajas, or tamas?"

Some people may have faith in the Lord but not in the scriptures. Arjuna wanted to know the nature of their devotion and whether they should be considered sattvic, rajasic, or tamasic. In other words, he wanted to know whether devotion and faith were superior to the knowledge or the Vidhi and Vidhanam of the scriptures, and whether sin would accrue if they were not followed. This question is critical to know whether we should mechanically adhere to the scriptures and their instructions, or we can rely upon faith and devotion to attain liberation. Indeed, the Vedas may not appeal to everyone because of their emphasis on several outdated customs and practices. Many spiritual teachers in the past questioned them and advised people to ignore them. Even Lord Krishna said that the statements in the Vedas can be confusing to those who lack discernment. Apart from them, Hinduism has several scriptures. Many of them claim divine authority as their source for approval and acceptance. If we exclusively adhere to the scriptures, it can lead to confusion since they prescribe different methods and approaches to worshiping the gods or attaining liberation. The Bhagavadgita itself offers numerous yogas and approaches to stabilize the mind and attain oneness. The Vaishnavas emphasize bhakti. The Shaivas emphasize knowledge and renunciation. These divergent approaches and teachings of various scholars, teachers, and scriptures can be very confusing to novices.

Therefore, Arjuna raised an important question about the nature of faith and devotion and whether that should be based on the scriptures or the love for the Lord. The answer is critical for the seekers of liberation. People may not follow the scriptures for various reasons due to circumstances or their inherent nature. They may study them and know them, but still ignore them while worshipping the Lord with supreme devotion. Many great devotees in the past exemplified bhakti but did not acknowledge the Vedas or the ritual practices they prescribed. It did not diminish their importance in the esteem of their followers. In this chapter, Lord Krishna addresses these issues by focusing on the nature and importance of faith (shraddha) in devotion and self-purification.

Sloka 2

śrībhagavān uvāca
trividhā bhavati śraddhā dehināṃ sā svabhāvajā
sāttvikī rājasī caiva tāmasī ceti tāṃ śṛṇu 17.2

sri-bhagavan uvaca = the supreme lord said; tri-vidha = three ways; bhavati = manifest; sraddha = faith; dehinam = of the embodied selves; sa = that; sva-bhava-ja = according to inherent nature; sattviki = sattvic; rajasi = rajasic; ca = ando; eva = certainly; tamasi = tamasic; ca = and; iti = thus; tam = about it; srnu = hear.

The Supreme Lord said, "In three ways does manifest the faith of the embodied, according to their inherent nature, (namely) sattva, rajas, and tamas. Hear about it."

Shraddha generally means faith or trust in something. In religious terms, it means the conviction or the belief that God or some supreme power or intelligence exists beyond our cognitive experience and controls our lives and destinies, which the mind, the senses, or intelligence cannot grasp. In a secular sense, it also means having respect, reverence, trust, interest, or loyalty. In this verse, Lord Krishna said that shraddha manifests in humans naturally (svabhavaja) in three ways from the triple modes. Human nature (svabhavam) arises from birth-related factors and circumstances: the modes, past life impressions (samskaras), karma, fate, environment, current life experiences, etc. It is responsible for desires, beliefs, likes, and dislikes. The same is true about shraddha (faith) since it is also determined by one's nature. These factors can be changed or mitigated through self-effort. Hence, it is possible to change one's nature and faith through transformative yogas and purification practices.

The essence of this teaching is that people express their faith and choose their methods of worship according to their predominant nature. It determines their goals, thoughts, actions, attitudes, mindset, and their faith or the lack of it. They act according to their gunas. The mode of Sattva strengthens divine qualities and inculcates faith and exclusive devotion to the Supreme Lord. Hence, the faith of the sattvic people tends to be pure and unwavering. They pursue spiritual knowledge and liberation with discernment, contentment, detachment, and renunciation, and develop a distaste for worldly things and pleasures. The mode of rajas induces passion and emotions even in matters of faith and religious practice. Hence, the faith of rajasic people runs in different directions and remains wavering. They worship many gods with devotional passion and perform their actions and obligatory duties to fulfill their desires and enjoy material things. They may also engage in elaborate rituals to show off their wealth and status or please the gods and win their favors. In spirituality, they pursue knowledge out of curiosity or to improve their health, wealth, and spiritual powers. Tamasic people are deluded and ignorant. Hence, their faith is driven mostly by delusion and ignorance. They may worship gods of a similar nature and practice their faith ignorantly or with half knowledge, disregarding rules (vidhis) and restraints (nishedhas). They may engage in worship or spiritual practice to control others or their destinies by gaining psychic powers (siddhis). For that, they worship gods, demigods, spirits, etc., rather insincerely or selfishly, but mostly with ulterior motives. They also perform unconventional methods, such as the left-hand tantras, which are shunned by the majority. Some practice extreme methods of self-mortification and painful austerities to appease the gods or develop spiritual powers.

If people stick to their inborn nature, which is mostly impure, they will remain bound to the cycle of births and deaths. They will continue to engage in desire-ridden actions, propelled by their gunas, and do not seek any improvement. The gunas belong to Prakriti. They bind people, inducing various types of desires, attachments, and behaviors. Although sattva is comparatively better, it is still an impurity since it binds people to worldly things and delays liberation. Therefore, one should transcend the gunas and abide in the Self, which is free from the gunas and their influence. Lord Krishna has already suggested this.

Sloka 3

sattvānurūpā sarvasya śraddhā bhavati bhārata
śraddhāmayoyaṃ puruṣo yo yacchraddhaḥ sa eva saḥ

sattva-anurupa = according to sattva; sarvasya = in everyone; sraddha = faith; bhavati = manifests; bharata = O descendent of Bharata; sraddha = faith; mayah = made up of; ayam = this; purusah = personl; yah = who; yat = that; sraddhah = faith; sah = that; eva = surely; sah = he.

O descendant of Bharata, faith manifests in everyone (or everywhere) according to sattva. A person is made up of his faith only. He is surely what his faith is.

According to this verse, shraddha or faith arises from essential nature. It is pure when it is induced by sattva, but when mixed with rajas and tamas, it becomes mixed and impure. In other words, sattva is necessary to cultivate pure devotion and establish the mind in the Self or divine thoughts. When sattva prevails, ananya bhakti (exclusive devotion), discernment, mental stability, vairagya (detachment), and the attitude of sannyasa (renunciation) arise naturally. When the other two modes predominate, devotion becomes mixed with desires, passions, worldliness, ignorance, and delusion. Hence, one must cultivate sattva to achieve liberation. However, in the advanced stages, one must transcend all the gunas to abide in sameness. In the following discussion, we examine the three important statements of Lord Krishna.

Sattvānurūpā sarvasya śraddhā bhavati. It means as is sattva, and so is faith. According to some, it means that, as is the essential nature, so is faith. The latter translation is indeed true since essential nature arises from the three modes, not just sattva. However, since sattva is specifically mentioned, we have to understand that it was done to refer to pure faith. Pure faith is essential to establish the mind in divine thoughts, practice exclusive devotion, and absorb the mind in the Self. It arises from the predominance of sattva only. There is no contradiction here since only unwavering faith qualities as true faith. Mixed faith that is prone to doubt and distraction is not true faith at all. From the spiritual or devotional perspective, sattva is absolutely important since it illuminates and purifies one's faith and devotion, while the other two weaken them and serve as obstacles. When sattva prevails, faith becomes pure and unwavering and strengthens devotion. Devotees with the predominance of sattva are naturally drawn to the Supreme Lord. Faith becomes weak when it is polluted or clouded by the impurities of egoism, lust, selfishness, delusion, ignorance, etc., which arise mainly from rajas and tamas. If sattva is fully suppressed, it leads to erroneous beliefs and demonic tendencies. Those under their influence misuse their faith for evil purposes and perish. In the real world, purely sattvic people are very rare due to karma and other factors. Most people are born with the predominance of rajas and tamas. Their faith, devotion, and commitment to Dharma remain mixed, just as their essential nature. They worship gods and perform obligatory duties, but do not achieve perfection because of their vacillating faith. When sattva is predominant, devotion, detachment, self-restraint, and obedience to the teacher or the teaching arise naturally. Hence, sattvic people are more inclined to worship the Supreme Lord and are qualified to attain liberation. Saints, seers, sages, partial incarnations, and enlightened masters fall into his category. They set an example for others through their actions and conduct.

Śraddhāmayoyam puruso. It means a person is made up of his faith. His behavior, thinking, beliefs, likes and dislikes, attitudes, etc., arise from faith, which is, in turn, determined by his nature. As is his faith, so are his actions and pursuits. Therefore, it leads to the conclusion that if one wants to change oneself, one must focus on one's beliefs and cultivate the right faith or the right beliefs, interests, and pursuits. For that, one must improve one's knowledge and discernment and cultivate sattva by purifying one's mind and body. Scriptural knowledge or the study of scriptures like the Bhagavadgita is useful in this regard. They provide valuable guidance to help devotees overcome their impurities and cultivate pure and unwavering faith. Faith serves as one's moral and spiritual compass. Judging by how a devotee practices his faith, which gods he worships, or methods he follows, one can ascertain his true nature and where he stands in relation to himself, the world, and the Supreme Being. With that knowledge, he can make informed decisions about improving himself and his spiritual practice. Faith is foundational to achieving progress on all fronts. It is foundational to one's morality, character, conduct, knowledge, wisdom, devotion, and relationship with God, the world, and oneself. Therefore, to change himself and progress in the right direction materially and spiritually, a devotee must change his beliefs (faith), what they tell about him, and what he can do about them.

Yacchraddhah sa eva sah. It means a person is certainly what his faith is. Faith does not mean only religious faith. It includes the sum of beliefs that influence one's thinking, actions, personality, and behavior. Although we are rational beings, we depend more on our beliefs, accepting them as facts without validating them rationally. We rely upon them, consciously or unconsciously, in making decisions or performing actions and in dealing with the ambiguity and uncertainty of our complex lives. From a philosophical perspective, our beliefs are the residue of our past, to which we cling because they are deeply interwoven into the fabric of our nature and consciousness. Without discernment, beliefs can fuel our illusions and erroneous or irrational thoughts, and lead us in the wrong direction or create confusion and conflicts. Facts can be verified and validated, but you cannot do the same with beliefs or assumptions. A belief or an assumption is what you accept as a fact without valid proof. It becomes problematic if you are attached to it and refuse to see the truth when evidence is presented. Many people cling to their erroneous perceptions and beliefs because of their essential nature. Unless they improve, their faith or beliefs will not improve. Therefore, self-purification is necessary to cultivate knowledge, right faith, right beliefs, right thinking, and right actions. Faith also influences our transmigration from one birth to another through our beliefs, desires, thoughts, and actions. They leave their residues in our consciousness as latent impressions (samskaras), which become the seed for our future births. Therefore, to escape from samsara by overcoming injurious and irrational beliefs and the desires and actions they induce, a devotee must cultivate sattva. When his essential nature shines with sattva, his faith becomes the raft by which he can cross the ocean of Samsara. When he is purified by faith and devotion, the Lord illuminates his intelligence and shows him the safest way to achieve liberation.

Sloka 4

yajante sāttvikā devān yakṣarakṣāṃsi rājasāḥ
pretān bhūtagaṇāñś cānye yajante tāmasā janāḥ

yajante = worship; sattvikah = sattvic people; devan = devas, gods, divinities; yaksa-raksamsi = yakshsas and rakshasas; rajasah = rajasic people; pretan = ghosts; bhuta-ganan = hosts of elemental spirits; ca = and; anye = others; yajante = worship; tamasah = tamasic; janah = people.

Sattvic people worship Devas; Rajasic people worship Yakshas and Rakshasas; and other people of Tamasic nature worship ghosts and hosts of elemental spirits.

Our religious or spiritual activity and choices depend upon our beliefs (faith), which are, in turn, shaped by our essential nature. Thus, our nature, as determined by the gunas, is at the heart of our religious inclinations, methods, and the deities we worship. It may be noted that most of our gods have numerous aspects. Some are sattvic, some rajasic, and some tamasic. Therefore, people may worship the same gods but in different ways or worship different aspects of them according to their nature or predominant modes. For example, the Vedas contain rituals that are meant to help and those that are meant to inflict pain and suffering upon others. Our gods have pleasant and fiery forms, and worshippers choose them according to their nature or inclination.

As Lord Krishna stated here, sattvic people worship the purest aspects of Brahma, Vishnu, Shiva, Indra, Agni, Vayu, Varuna, Mitra, etc., and nourish them with sacrificial offerings through rituals as ordained by the scriptures. The purest among them worship the Supreme Lord with exclusive devotion. The gods extolled in the Vedas as the lords of heaven are, by nature, pleasure-loving. They are primarily sattvic deities who serve Isvara, the Supreme Lord, as the guardians of Dharma, performing their ordained duties and ensuring the order and regularity of the world. They reciprocate the worshipper's ritual offerings by fulfilling their wishes. They also protect them and assist them in performing their duties and upholding Dharma.

Due to their passionate nature, rajasic people choose deities who agree with their nature. They worship deities that are powerful, fierce, and passionate like them and are known for their wealth, beauty, power, strength, and status with sacrificial offerings to fulfill their desires, enjoy worldly pleasures, or destroy their enemies. They may also do it for vanity and to show off their wealth and importance. In the past, rajasic beings such as Ravana, Bali, or Banasura practiced spirituality to obtain boons from the gods, gain control over the triple worlds, and extend their sway.

Tamasic people are delusional, ignorant, and extreme in their choices, thinking, and actions. They bring the same attitude to their religious and spiritual practice. They worship dark powers, spirits, gods, and demigods of the lower realms or the tamasic aspects of the higher gods to acquire destructive powers, fulfill their extreme desires, or establish their sway or control over others. They engage in ritual or spiritual practices against approved methods, rules, and restraints. Some resort to extreme austerities, penances, and painful methods to obtain higher powers and use them for deluded ends. Since they lack discipline, balance, and moderation, they are careless or insincere in their worship and practice. As a result, they fail in their methods, attain unexpected results, or cause trouble for themselves. Their methods of worship are described in the next verse.

Sloka 5

aśāstravihitaṃ ghoraṃ tapyante ye tapo janāḥ
dambhāhaṃkārasaṃyuktāḥ kāmarāgabalānvitāḥ

asastra = not by the scriptures; vihitam = instructed, approved; ghoram = severe, painful; tapyante = perform penances; ye = those; tapah = austerities, penances; janah = people; dambha = vanity, conceit; ahankara = pride, egoism; samyuktah = filled with; kama = lust; raga = passion; bala = force, power, strength; anvitah = impelled by.

Those people who are filled with vanity (and) egoism perform severe penances not sanctioned in the scriptures, propelled by the force of lust and passion.

Here, "those" refers to the tamasic people, who are mentioned as the "other people" in the last part of the previous verse and who are described as worshiping ghosts and elemental spirits. This verse describes their faith, stating that they perform penances and austerities filled with vanity, pride, lust, and passion. Tamasic people bring these deluded attitudes into many aspects of their lives, including their faith. Their nature remains concealed by the predominance of tamas. Hence, they succumb to dark and demonic desires and engage in evil actions in their pursuit of Dharma, Artha, Kama, and Moksha. Deluded by tamas, they perform extreme penances, austerities, and sacrifices, causing misery to themselves and others. For them, yoga and spirituality are convenient tools to manipulate others or achieve their selfish goals. Since they are unpredictable and difficult to discipline, lack balance, discernment, and moderation, and do not know where to stop and begin, they resort to extreme forms of austerity and penance, ignoring the scriptural injunctions, traditional wisdom, and the words of wise masters.

Severe penances that test the limitations of the mind and body and lead to extreme pain and suffering are not encouraged or recommended by the devotional traditions of Hinduism. They encourage the worship of sattvic gods according to established beliefs and practices. Some people practice left-hand methods (vamachara), but they constitute a small minority. Right-hand methods (sadachara) are ideal for self-purification, renunciation, and devotional worship to overcome desires, attachments, and other impurities. Most devotees follow standard procedures only, even though some of them may not strictly be considered sattvic. In any case, the methods must adhere to the prescribed code of conduct and be in harmony with the highest ideals. For example, nonviolence is considered the highest virtue in almost all spiritual traditions. The methods and practices to attain liberation must adhere to that norm. It means one should avoid hurting and harming oneself, others, or animals in devotional worship or spiritual practice. Similarly, one should follow other virtues also, such as celibacy, truthfulness, non-stealing, and non-possession during worship or while making sacrificial offerings. The rules (vidhi), procedures (vidhanam), and prohibitory actions ordained by the Vedas are meant to ensure that the devotees follow righteous practices and the code of conduct.

Sloka 6

karṣayantaḥ śarīrasthaṃ bhūtagrāmam acetasaḥ
māṃ caivāntaḥśarīrasthaṃ tān viddhy āsuraniścayān

karsayantah = torture, torment; sarira-stham = in the body; bhuta-gramam = organs; acetasah = without discrimination; mam = Me; ca = and; eva = surely; antah = within; sarira-stham = in the body; tan = them; viddhi = know; asura = demons; niscayan = resolve, determination.

Who foolishly torture the organs in the body, and Me also, who is in the body, know them to be of demonic resolve.

Tamasic devotees ignore balance and moderation in their methods and practices because they do not follow prescribed methods and invent their own rules and methods. Without discipline, balance, and control, one cannot achieve a wholesome life, peace, tranquility, or sameness. By going to extremes to reach their goals or fulfill their desires, most people end up suffering or facing failure. This is a common trait of those who possess demonic resolve and faith. One may occasionally spend sleepless nights completing a task or fasting for days to expiate for sins or impress the gods. It is not considered tamasic. It becomes tamasic if it is done with vanity, anger, delusion, or egoism. Almost all spiritual practices produce some discomfort, pain, and suffering, at least in the initial stages, until the mind and body adapt to them. The Vedas also prescribe some extreme penances that are not presently practiced. Since they are prescribed by the scriptures for self-purification and do not arise from tamasic resolve, they should not be treated as avidhi (against the injunctions) or achetasa (foolish).

As a precaution, householders must follow the methods and practices prescribed by the scriptures for self-purification, performing obligatory duties, renunciation, pursuit of knowledge, or devotional worship to avoid unintended or harmful consequences and suffering. It is better to follow the same approach in worldly life. The wise know that when the organs in the body experience pain and suffering, the divinities presiding over them also suffer. Hence, they develop discernment and practice moderation in their methods to avoid hurting themselves and putting themselves at risk. The Buddha suggested the Middle Path for the same reason. Lord Krishna also suggested the same in a previous chapter, stating that yoga is not for the one who sleeps excessively or does not sleep at all. Following extreme methods to compel the gods to pay attention or pull the force of Shakti into an unprepared mind and body is tamasic and delusional. Therefore, one should avoid such methods and let the divine will manifest itself.

Egoistic people want their way in worldly life and do not consider the suffering they cause others or themselves. They resort to shortcuts and evil methods to achieve their selfish goals or fulfill their desires if necessary. The evil ones go a step further. They act with demonic resolve to achieve their ends, ignoring the harm they cause to themselves or others with their torturous methods. As Lord Krishna stated here, they torture not only their minds and bodies but also the Lord in them.

Sloka 7

āhāras tv api sarvasya trividho bhavati priyaḥ
yajñas tapas tathā dānaṃ teṣāṃ bhedam imaṃ śṛṇu

aharah = food; tu = verily; api = also; sarvasya = of all; tri-vidhah = three types; bhavati = is; priyah = dear; yajnah = sacrifice; tapah = austerity; tatha = and; danam = charity; tesam = their; bhedam = distinction; imam = thus; srnu = hear.

Even the food, which is dear to all, is also of three types, just as the sacrifices, austerity, and charity. Hear now about their distinction.

Understanding the significance of the three types of food in Hinduism-sattvic, rajasic, and tamasic-can enlighten us about our dietary choices. Just as with everything, the food we eat or offer to the gods is also of these three types. In the devotional and ritual practices of Hinduism, it is customary to offer food to the gods that the devotees worship. The Vedas extol food as Brahman and declare that every object in creation is food for Brahman in his aspect as the Lord of Death. The food we eat is the main source of our energy. Like everything else in the universe, it is also of three types: sattvic, rajasic, and tamasic, according to the gunas present in them. Depending upon the food we eat, the triple gunas gain or lose strength. Sattvic food strengthens sattva, rajasic food rajas, and tamasic food tamas. The physical body is made up of five sheaths, known as kosas. They are permeated by the gunas we derive from food. The outermost one is known as the food body (annamaya kosa) since it is formed by food only. The inner layers are the breath body, the mind-body, the intelligence body, and the bliss body (anandamaya kosa). The last one is made up of sattva only.

The wisdom of accepting food without desires is a practice that can inspire us all. The human body reflects the gunas we consume through food. The essential nature of a jiva also depends upon the food it consumes. Lord Krishna will teach more about this in the subsequent verses. This knowledge is useful for making intelligent food choices and overcoming impurities. Worldly people choose food according to their desires, likes, and dislikes. Most of them prefer tasty food that appeals to their palate. It is not a wise choice. The wise ones who have given up worldly life accept whatever food is offered to them without desire and eat it with indifference. They also offer it to God before eating it. Therefore, whatever impurities are present in it become neutralized. With discernment, devotees can make food an important part of their self-purification. The human body is a living and breathing universe in itself, ruled over by Isvara (the Self) as its Lord. Many divinities are present in it, presiding over the organs and regulating their functions in the sacrifice of life. They receive their share of the food the jiva consumes, just as they share the food offered to them in the sacrificial ceremonies. In both cases, Agni is the carrier. Acting as the heat-generating fire (jatharagni) in the digestive organs, he carries them to various organs with the help of prana that flows in the nerve channels.

Sloka 8

āyuḥsattvabalārogyasukhaprītivivardhanāḥ
rasyāḥ snigdhāḥ sthirā hṛdyā āhārāḥ sāttvikapriyāḥ

ayuh = lifespan, duration of life; sattva = purity; bala = strength; arogya = health; sukha = happiness; priti = satisfaction; vivardhanah = increasing; rasyah = tasty; snigdhah = oily; sthirah = firm, stable; hrdyah = agreeable to the heart; aharah = foods; sattvika = sattvic people; priyah = dearer.

The foods that increase lifespan, purity, strength, health, happiness, (and) satisfaction, which are tasty, oily, firm, (and) agreeable, are dear to sattvic people.

Sattvic foods, beyond being tasty and wholesome, hold a profound spiritual significance. They contribute to health, vitality, happiness, and spirituality, making them a preferred choice for devotees seeking purity, self-control, and devotion to achieve liberation. The gunas are responsible for our essential nature (svabhava), thinking, and behavior. They are also responsible for our desires, attachments, likes, dislikes, and food choices. At the same time, they are greatly influenced by the food we eat since the body is largely made up of the food we eat. One should, therefore, pay attention to dietary habits. From the spiritual perspective, sattvic food is the best choice. It promotes sattva and all the associated qualities that are essential to achieve equanimity and sameness.

This verse mentions the qualities that are strengthened by sattvic food and its connection to health and happiness, or contentment. It states that the food that is well-cooked, fresh, juicy, sweet, nourishing, non-toxic, and tasty (rasya), with medicinal and curative properties, is agreeable to sattvic people. These foods do not excite our passions. They are not hard on our palate, do not lead to indigestion or drowsiness when eaten in moderation, and do not destabilize the mind or the body. Since vegetable oil or ghee is used in their preparation, they contain fatty acids and other minerals the body requires for building strength, memory, and vitality. Fatty acids reduce inflammation and, thereby, pain and suffering, which is another health benefit. These foods are firm and stable, meaning they stay fresh and do not quickly decay, ferment, lose flavor, or cause lethargy or intoxication. In other words, sattvic foods are freshly prepared and cooked, and not stored for a long time. They increase one's lifespan because they are prepared with fresh and healthy ingredients and are free from toxins and harmful substances.

All these qualities make sattvic foods healthy and life-sustaining and contribute to good health (arogya). Since they are prepared for sattvic people by sattvic people with love, care, and attention as if they were made for the Lord himself, they also contain a lot of positive energy and increase purity (sattva). Because of these positive aspects, sattvic foods are recommended for the purification of the mind and body and for suppressing impurities. They help yogis on the path of liberation by strengthening qualities such as detachment, equanimity, contentment, sameness, endurance, etc. Most vegetarian foods are sattvic if they are well-cooked without using rajasic or tamasic ingredients such as spices or excessive salt and sauces. Foods that are oily, tasty, or pleasing to the heart are not necessarily healthy if made solely for taste, using oily and sugary substances without considering their adverse health effects. They can lead to obesity, addiction to oily foods, imbalance, and illnesses. Therefore, one should practice moderation.

Sloka 9

kaṭvamlalavaṇātyuṣṇatīkṣṇarūkṣavidāhinaḥ
āhārā rājasasyeṣṭā duḥkhaśokāmayapradāḥ

katu = bitter; amla = sour; lavana = salty; ati= very; usna = hot and spicy; tiksna = pungent; ruksa = dry; vidahinah = burnt; aharah = food; rajasasya = of rajasic nature; istah = desired, liked, preferred; duhkha = pain; soka = suffering; amaya = disease; pradah = cause, produce.

Foods that are very bitter, sour, salty, hot and spicy, pungent, dry, and burnt, which cause pain, suffering, (and) disease, are dearer to those of rajasic nature.

The main difference between sattvic and rajasic foods is that sattvic foods calm the mind and promote purity, peace, stability, and happiness, while rajasic ones promote passions such as pride, anger, lust, etc., and destabilize the mind. Another important difference is that they are prepared mainly for taste and enjoyment rather than to develop spiritual qualities or stabilize the mind. As a result, they may taste good but produce many side effects or complications. The difference between sattvic, rajasic, or tamasic foods arises mainly due to their methods of preparation. In other words, the same food can be sattvic, rajasic, or tamasic, depending upon how they are made and what ingredients are used in its preparation. For example, sattvic foods become rajasic if they are mixed with excessive quantities of spices, salt, chilies, onions, tamarind, etc., for taste. They excite the taste buds, incite passion, or the fickleness of the tongue (jihad chapalyam). The same foods become tamasic if they are allowed to ferment or decay or mixed with substances that induce sloth, sleep, or intoxication.

Thus, the nature of food depends upon many factors, including how the ingredients are used and how the food is prepared. Lord Krishna used the word excessive (ati) to describe the characteristics of rajasic foods. He said foods that are very bitter, sour, salty, hot, spicy, dry, and burnt are of rajasic nature. Because they lack balance and moderation and are made solely to appeal to the raw senses, they promote rajas rather than sattva. Instead of promoting health and well-being or a stable mind, they strengthen egoism, pride, desires, and passions. They also produce pain and suffering by causing many health problems, such as stress, anxiety, indigestion, flatulence, sleeplessness, high blood pressure, high cholesterol, and problems associated with the kidneys, heart, lungs, liver, etc. Since they induce passions, desires, and attachments, they keep the senses wandering and the mind restless and unstable. Rajasic foods are suitable for people like warriors, sportspeople, guards, etc., who rely upon strength, vigor, and vitality to perform their duties. However, they must be taken in limited quantities and must be avoided by spiritual people who pursue liberation or practice renunciation.

Sloka 10

yātayāmaṃ gatarasaṃ pūti paryuṣitaṃ ca yat
ucchiṣṭam api cāmedhyaṃ bhojanaṃ tāmasapriyam

yata-yamam = not freshly cooked; gata-rasam = lost taste; puti = foul smelling; paryusitam = putrefied, stale, stored overnight; ca = and; yat = which; ucchistam = eaten and left over by others; api = even; ca = and; amedhyam = unfit for sacrifice; bhojanam = food; tamasa =tamsic; priyam = pleasing, dear.

Food that is not freshly made, without taste, foul-smelling and putrefied, eaten and left over by others, and unfit for sacrifice, is pleasing to those of the tamasic nature.

Tamasic foods are not freshly made. They are half-cooked, stored, or left in the open for a long time, whereby they become toxic and harm the mind and body. As the adjectives used here convey, any food that is improperly prepared, stored for a long time, or has lost its natural properties and become rancid or foul-smelling, etc., due to prolonged storage or decay, is tamasic. Even foods that were originally sattvic or rajasic become tamasic under these conditions. One should, therefore, eat food on time or take proper precautions to safeguard it from decaying or fermenting. Yata-yamam means food that has been cooked and stored for more than three or four hours. Gatarasam means food that has lost its freshness of taste (rasa) because it has been stored for a long time and has become stale. When foods are stored in the open and left unattended, they become toxic due to contamination with dust, microorganisms, and chemical reactions. With continued decay and fermentation, they develop a rancid or putrid smell. Intoxicating and fermented foods or foods that induce sleep or slothfulness are all tamasic. They make one slow, sluggish, and dull-witted. In today's world, better storage techniques increase the shelf life of several foods and food products. They should not be considered tamasic unless their shelf life has expired, they are improperly stored, or they are inherently tamasic.

Frozen foods may still retain their freshness and sattvic or rajasic properties unless they are stored for a long time or allowed to decay. However, for some people, any stored food, whether it decays or not, qualifies as tamasic only. One should, therefore, use caution and discretion. Even the best foods become tamasic over time due to negligence or carelessness. They become tamasic if cooked improperly or left in the open for too long. Tamasic foods should not be served to guests, used in sacrifices, or given to others as alms (bhiksha). It is sinful. According to our lawbooks, half-eaten and leftover foods should not be served to anyone, especially to alms seekers and renunciants who depend upon others for food. Since the Vedic gods prefer pure and clean food, nitya karmas (daily sacrifices) should not be performed with stored or leftover food. One may offer it to animals, but certainly not to those who follow the Vedic way of life (vedachara) and pursue liberation. Tamasic foods reinforce tamasic nature and promote evil qualities. Hence, one should not eat it or serve it to others.

Sloka 11

aphalāṅkṣibhir yajño vidhidṛṣṭo ya ijyate
yaṣṭavyam eveti manaḥ samādhāya sa sāttvikaḥ

aphala-akanksibhih = without the desire for the fruit; yajnah = sacrifice; vidhi drstah = dutifully according to the established practice; yah = which; ijyate = performed, offered; yastavyam = obligatory; eva = surely, certainly; iti = that; manah = mind; samadhaya = firm conviction; sah = that; sattvikah = sattvic nature.

Without seeking the fruit, the sacrifice, which is performed dutifully according to the established practice, with the firm conviction in the mind that it is surely obligatory, is sattvic in nature.

Sacrifices are also sattvic, rajasic, or tamasic, depending upon how they are performed and for what purpose. Sattvic people are disciplined and duty-bound. They perform sacrifices as an obligatory duty according to the rules and restraints prescribed by the scriptures or the tradition. The Vedas prescribe three types of sacrifices: obligatory (baddha), prohibited (nishiddha), and optional sacrifices (kamya). The first ones are compulsory for householders and must be performed dutifully as an obligation to God to avoid the sinful consequences of neglecting the Dharma (duty). Hence, Lord Krishna advised householders to uphold Dharma and do their part in creation. He also advised that if they wanted to pursue liberation, they must practice karma-sannyasa yoga and perform the sacrifices without desires and attachments, offering their fruit to him. As the name implies, prohibited sacrifices should not be performed under any circumstances. Not performing them is also an obligatory duty for the householders since by doing so, they will uphold Dharma. The optional sacrifices are meant to fulfill one's desires. Hence, they are known as desire-ridden actions (kamya karmas). Although they are not prohibited, householders are urged not to perform them since they produce sinful karma and bind them to the mortal world.

Thus, householders must perform only the obligatory sacrifices and avoid the other two. These distinctions do not arise if they renounce desires and attachments and achieve perfection in karma-sannyasa yoga, performing their actions without desires and offering the fruit of such actions to the Supreme Lord. Technically, all Vedic sacrifices must be performed selflessly, without desires, to serve the Supreme Lord. Householders must uphold Dharma and live righteously, devotedly, and selflessly. Only a few succeed in that. The word yajna (sacrifice) itself means an offering or an act of giving. Although the One does it not for oneself but for others or God as a mark of gratitude or obligation. Vedic sacrifices are primarily meant to ensure the order and regularity of the world. All other considerations are secondary. When they are performed without desires, expectations, selfishness, and egoism, they lead to liberation or freedom from karma and bondage. Hence, in the Bhagavadgita, we see Lord Krishna repeatedly asking Arjuna to perform them without desiring their fruit.

Even ordinary actions become sacrifices if they are performed selflessly to serve God. It is the ideal way to uphold Dharma and live righteously, devotedly, and selflessly. It is what is known as living life as a sacrifice or becoming a sacrifice to God through actions. According to our scriptures, sacrifice does not mean ritual sacrifices only. It can be any action one performs with the mind and body. Every action we perform as an offering to the Supreme Being qualifies as a sacrifice. When devotees surrender to God and perform actions, giving up desires and attachments, their every action becomes a sacrifice. When they give up the fruit of such actions, they become sacrificial offerings poured into the fire of renunciation. When they live that way, they engage in continuous sacrifice and devotional worship, in which they become the sacrificers and the sacrificed. The Vedas envisage sacrifice not just as a ritual but as a way of life. They declare that creation itself is an act of sacrifice performed on a universal scale by the Supreme Brahman, in which he uses himself (his energies and matter) as the sacrificial offering and over which he presides as the Priest, the Host, and the Guests. When actions are performed without selfish desires but with the intention to perform one's obligatory duties and serve the Lord with devotion, even mundane actions such as walking, talking, sleeping, or eating become sacrificial actions and do not produce karma.

Sloka 12

abhisaṃdhāya tu phalaṃ dambhārtham api caiva yat
ijyate bharataśreṣṭha taṃ yajñaṃ viddhi rājasam

abhisandhaya = with an eye for; tu = but; phalam = fruit, result; dambha = vanity; artham = for the sake of; api = so also; ca = and; eva = even; yat = which; ijyate = performed; bharata-srestha = O the best among the Bharatas; tam = that; yajnam = sacrifice; viddhi = know; rajasam = of the rajasic nature.

However, that sacrifice performed with an eye for the fruit, so also for the sake of vanity, O the best among the Bharatas, know that to be of rajasic nature.

We have previously discussed the three types of sacrifices mentioned in the Vedas. Sattvic people perform obligatory sacrifices for others or the world without selfish desires and expectations. Out of obligation, devotion, and reverence to the Supreme Lord, they perform his duties selflessly as ordained by the Vedas as their own. By doing that, they fulfill their obligation to him as his ardent devotees (Bhagavatas) and upholders of his eternal Dharma and earn his love and protection. Their actions lead to liberation, peace, and happiness. Rajasic people do not entertain those lofty ideals. They are driven by desires and passions and put themselves before God. Unlike the sattvic devotees, they do not perform actions as a selfless duty to God, but to fulfill their desires (kamyartha phala siddhi), for the welfare of their families and children (putra pautrabhi vriddhi), for vanity (dambha), or some personal gain such as name, fame, wealth, or happiness. Since their actions and sacrifices are desire-ridden, selfish, delusional, and egoistic, just as they are, they incur karma and remain bound to samsara. They do not attain liberation but attain either a good birth or a worse one in their next lives according to their deeds. Those who die while performing their duties, such as the warriors who die on the battlefield, may attain heavenly life and return to the earth after their due time.

Selfless actions and sacrificial actions with their fruit offered to God lead to liberation. Any other action produces karma and binds the jivas to the cycle of births and deaths. The sacrificial food offered to the gods in sacrifices nourishes and energizes them and helps them protect the world from evil beings by performing their duties vigorously as the guardians of the world. In the ancestral world, it helps the ancestors stay nourished and strong until they return to the earth. On earth, it helps humans and other creatures square their karmas and improve their chances of liberation. Thus, selfless sacrifices performed by the sattvic people ensure the orderly progression of all three worlds. However, since sattvic people are rare, sattvic sacrifices are rare. Most sacrifices are performed primarily for worldly reasons, personal gain, vanity, pride, or egotism. While sattvic people keep the wheel of dharma moving, the rajasic and tamasic ones keep the wheel of karma moving. Of the four aims of human life, they focus primarily on Artha and Kama rather than Dharma and Moksha. They desire to achieve freedom through possessions and worldly gains, and when they engage in religious or spiritual activities, it is mainly to fulfill their desires or gain some advantage. Hence, the world does not benefit much from their actions.

Sloka 13

vidhihīnam asṛṣṭānnaṃ mantrahīnam adakṣiṇam
śraddhāvirahitaṃ yajñaṃ tāmasaṃ paricakṣate

vidhi-hinam = devoid of rules; asrsta-annam = in which blessed food is not distributed or shared; mantra-hinam = devoid of mantras; adaksinam = without giving sacrificial fees; sraddha = faith, dedication; virahitam = without; yajnam = sacrifice; tamasam = of tamasic nature; paricaksate = they declare.

They declare the sacrifice to be tamasic, which is devoid of rules, in which blessed food is not distributed, in which mantras are not chanted, in which sacrificial fees are not given to the priests, and which is devoid of faith.

Tamasic sacrifices, although performed wrongly, for wrong reasons and purposes, or against established and approved practices, are not a reflection of the entirety of Hinduism. Hinduism, in its essence, is not rigid about its methods and practices, allowing for a certain degree of flexibility and adaptation. This is particularly true for those practices that do not involve Vedic rituals and sacrifices, which must be performed strictly according to established practices by informed priests. When people deviate from established practices due to ignorance, delusion, or lack of discernment, they become karmically accountable for their actions.

Hinduism emerged on the world stage as a major religion in compelling circumstances due to the amalgamation of numerous faiths, which originated in India and shared many common beliefs and practices. They constitute its core. Over time, for historical reasons, these disparate faiths were given a collective name, Hinduism. Due to its organic growth and assimilation of divergent beliefs and practices over a long period, Hinduism contains many contradictions and contradictory approaches, which can be confusing for those who do not know much about it. Its complex knowledge, beliefs, and practices also give rise to many myths and false notions about its beliefs and practices. One such popular notion is that it can be practiced freely, in whatever way one chooses, or whatever is convenient, ignoring its traditions, scriptures, and established practices. While it is true that Hinduism is not definitive or dogmatic, its sectarian faiths and teacher traditions have their dogmas, codes of conduct, beliefs, and practices. Those who intend to follow them should know them and follow them. When they are ignored or followed incorrectly, the practice becomes tamasic. Followers of popular Hinduism should not take too many liberties with their faith. They should adhere to the prevailing customs and traditions that are commonly approved and accepted by the majority and not explicitly prohibited.

The idea of Dharma is central to Hinduism and common to all its sects and philosophies. It binds the diverse aspects of Hinduism and gives it the semblance of a monolithic religion, with many ideas from the Vedas and other texts forming its core. Fundamentally, Dharma, which has multiple meanings, refers to a set of duties and morals or virtues a householder must practice as his obligatory duty on earth. These duties arise from God, who practices them at the highest level to ensure the orderly progression of creation. Householders must practice them as an obligation and service to him, adhering to the prescribed methods. If they are ignored or defied, the practice becomes tamasic with unpleasant consequences. One does not have to follow them literally as people did three thousand years ago, but one must follow them in essence. If there is ambiguity or uncertainty, one may use discretion without explicitly violating any known injunctions. Dharma is the first chief aim (purusharthas) of human life because it is foundational to cultivating the right knowledge and practicing it correctly without falling into delusion or confusion. When one has the right knowledge and understanding, one is free to choose the right methods and practices with the right discernment.

Thus, although Hinduism has no central authority, it is not a free-for-all dogma or belief system. The freedom it offers is not without boundaries or conditions. The followers have obligations, duties, and responsibilities for their own sake and for the good of the world in which they live. They must be respected dutifully so that order and regularity will prevail, and the tradition does not fall into the wrong hands. Tamasic people may think that they have unlimited freedom to express their faith and invent unconventional methods and practices. Since there is no regulating authority, they may even get away with it, but they will pay the price. This verse reiterates that sacrifices are deemed tamasic if householders do not follow the rules, if sacrificial food is not distributed correctly, if sacrifices are not performed with faith according to the mantras chanted, and if the performing priests are not adequately rewarded. In other words, deluded people filled with tamas may worship God or practice Hinduism, ignoring the conventional wisdom. They may ignore the traditional methods and practices (sampradayas) of ritual worship and set new trends. However, there will be consequences. Sattvic and rajasic people follow approved methods and practices, although for different purposes and with different attitudes. Tamasic people follow them incorrectly or inappropriately or follow the prohibited ones, incurring sinful karma. By their actions, they set in motion a chain reaction that will follow them into their future lives.

Sloka 14

devadvijaguruprājñapūjanaṃ śaucam ārjavam
brahmacaryam ahiṃsā ca śārīraṃ tapa ucyate

deva = gods; dvija = the twice-born; guru = spiritual teacher; prajna = wise ones; pujanam = worship, veneration; saucam = cleanliness, purity; arjavam = simplicity, straightforwardness; brahmacaryam = celibacy; ahimsa = non-injury; ca = and; sariram = of the body; tapah = austerity; ucyate = said to be.

Worshipping gods, the twice-born, spiritual teachers, and wise ones, cleanliness, simplicity, celibacy, and non-injury are said to be the austerity of the body.

Austerity (tapas) is of three types: the austerity of the body, the speech, and the mind. Tapas means a heat (tapah) producing penance or rigorous spiritual activity involving self-control through celibacy and other restraints.

It is one of the most ancient ascetic practices of the Vedic times (before Yoga), which is mentioned frequently in the epics and Puranas. Vedic seers, sages, and those who took the vows of celibacy and renunciation (sannyasa) practiced it by retiring into forests and living secluded lives. They subjected themselves to rigorous discipline and self-control, renouncing desires, holding their minds steady on the object of concentration, performing penances, and living in harsh conditions. Through them, they produced internal heat (tapah) and kept their bodily fires alive. The belief is that its prolonged practice will help the practitioners accumulate and transform their bodily heat (energy) into spiritual power (taposhakti) and develop supernatural powers to control the elements (bhutas), tattvas, and natural functions of their bodies and prolong their lives. Yogis who excel in it can endure the harshest living conditions, pain, and suffering, and even help those in need. This practice of austerity is not just a physical or mental exercise but a profound spiritual journey towards the ultimate goal of Dharma and Moksha.

In this verse, Lord Krishna defined the austerity of the body as the purification of the body through self-control. Sattvic people practice it by worshipping pure souls, such as the twice-born, spiritual teachers, and wise ones who abide in Dharma. They also practice other austerities, namely cleanliness, simplicity, and nonviolence. In the context of the Bhagavadgita, tapah should be understood as an exercise in self-restraint (atma samyama) or controlling the mind and body to establish the mind in the Supreme Lord with devotion and concentration. It is somewhat different from the ancient ascetic practice of transforming bodily energies to generate bodily heat and accumulate spiritual or supernatural powers. The austerity mentioned here is primarily prescribed for householders and devotees, but ascetics and renunciants who give up worldly life and obligatory duties may also practice it. This chapter mentions three main types of austerity: body, speech, and mind. They encompass all practices for self-control.

The human body performs many functions or karmas. The austerity of the body includes those that are meant for its purification. Although this verse mentions a few practices, the austerity of the body includes any action that purifies and prepares it for the pursuit of Dharma and Moksha. They help the yogis to transcend their modes and establish their minds in divine nature (daiva-svabhava) with sameness and equanimity, free from desires and attachments. Since the body is where the gunas are active and compete with each other for dominance, with the austerity of the body, they can be neutralized to purify and transform the body into a vehicle fit for liberation. In this verse, Lord Krishna suggested benign forms of austerity only, such as showing respect to gods, Brahmanas, teachers, and seers, keeping the body clean and simple in itself, without ornaments or expensive clothing, and practicing celibacy and nonviolence. The last one implies that one should practice nonviolence with the body, speech, and mind toward oneself and others. Tradition holds that while practicing austerities, one should avoid hurting or harming the body with extreme penances such as self-mortification. Such methods are considered to be tamasic. The transformation of the body into a pure vessel of divinity is a testament to the power and potential of sattvic tapas.

Sloka 15

anudvegakaraṃ vākyaṃ satyaṃ priyahitaṃ ca yat
svādhyāyābhyasanaṃ caiva vāṅmayaṃ tapa ucyate

anudvega = dispassion or without excitement; karam = causing; vakyam = speech; satyam = truthful; priya = pleasant; hitam = beneficial; ca = and; yat = which; svadhyaya = self-study; abhyasanam = practice; ca = and; eva = so also; van-mayam = of speech; tapah = austerity; ucyate = said to be.

Speech that incites no passion, which is truthful and beneficial, and so also, the practice of self-study, is said to be the austerity of speech.

The austerity of the body is meant to neutralize the gunas and purify the body, using the energy (taposhakti) produced during the austerity as internal heat (tapah). The austerity of speech is meant to gain control over speech and stabilize the mind. It consists of practicing the right speech and self-study to cultivate the right vocabulary, use the right language, chant the sacred hymns correctly, develop comprehension, and avoid misunderstandings and misapprehensions in the study and understanding of the scriptures or gaining the right knowledge. Speech can transform and purify a person's thinking, character, and conduct. Lord Krishna defined soft, impassionate, truthful, wholesome, and beneficial speech as the right speech. We know that karma arises from speech also. It is an important aspect of a person's conduct and behavior and reflects their virtues or qualities. Divine qualities such as truthfulness, peace (santih), non-slandering (apaisunam), compassion (daya), contentment (tripti), freedom from anger (akrodha), non-covetousness (aloluptam), gentleness (mardavam), and nonviolence (ahimsa) manifest through the austerity of speech only. Speech should not be harsh, deceitful, hurtful, untruthful, insincere, vain, or violent. Lord Krishna included svadhyaya (self-study) in the austerity of speech because it is an auspicious and salubrious activity that purifies the mind and body and strengthens righteous conduct. It requires initiative, faith, and interest (shraddha) and involves studying and reciting scriptures, listening to spiritual people, and chanting mantras or the names of God, Japa, etc. It is helpful to cultivate thoughtful speech, correct pronunciation, and the knowledge necessary for performing ritual worship and engaging in conversations without making mistakes.

There is a profound connection between the mind and speech. The mind and intelligence find their expression and manifestation through speech alone. As the Brihadaranyaka Upanishad proclaims, at the time of creation, Brahman united speech with the mind and, utilizing both, brought forth all that exists here. The organ of speech (larynx) in the throat acts as the conduit between the mind and the body, between oneself and another, and between humans and gods. The Upanishads identify speech as Brahman himself. It is a divine faculty that extends the reach of the mind and intelligence, connecting them to other minds, gods, and the rest of the world. Through speech, we assert our presence, articulate our thoughts, and seek fulfillment of our desires. Speech is also a transformative force. With the right speech, at the right time, and in the right manner, we can transform ourselves and others. Speech has the power to inspire people to be divine or demonic, creative or destructive, and change themselves for the better or worse. By aligning their minds with sacred utterances and supplications, devotees can practice pure devotion and experience ecstatic states of self-absorption.

Through the practice of austere speech, characterized by gentleness, softness, and humility, one can become a harbinger of peace and happiness. When wise people speak, even the most aggressive and violent individuals are compelled to become peaceful and reflective and listen to them. People may not always speak the truth, but they hold in high regard those who do. Gentle speech is a noble quality. Auspicious words, blessings, inspiring words, and kind words do not inflict harm, create conflicts, or incite passions. Instead, they open our minds to truth, light, peace, and harmony. We should strive to speak kind words in a sattvic manner to the extent possible, spread peace and happiness, and avoid wrong, false, harsh, and deluded speech. Through harmful, deceptive, and destructive speech, one may hurt others, create conflicts and disharmony, or invoke negative emotions such as fear, greed, envy, anger, pride, etc. Rajasic speech filled with passions and emotions can incite ego clashes, conflicts, and negativity. Tamasic people, who are violent, careless, and deluded by nature, bring similar attitudes into their speech. They speak with extreme emotions, ignorance, and delusion to control or intimidate others or cause pain, suffering, confusion, and conflicts.

In Hinduism, speech is regarded as divine because worlds and beings are created and sustained through it. The Brihadaranyaka Upanishad declares that every sound in creation is a form of speech. The source of all the sounds is the Supreme Lord. Hence, speech is also known as "Isvara," which means the Lord who is the source or Lord of all sounds or vibrations (svara). The Vedas are sacred because they unleash Brahman's mysterious power through the sounds hidden in the sacred hymns. The most revered of all syllables is Aum because it is the seed of all sounds (bijaksaram). Speech distinguishes human beings from other mortal beings. Yet, speech is the source of noise and many other problems. It is because, as the Upanishads affirm, speech is vulnerable to evil influences and can be taken over by them. Therefore, it must be safeguarded and free from evil thoughts, desires, and attachments.

Ascetic people and those who enter sannyasa (renunciation) should practice the austerity of speech by restraining it. They should speak only when necessary or when they are addressed or approached. Otherwise, they should remain silent for days and months if necessary. They should not use speech to defend themselves, voice their egotism, express their desires, or draw attention to themselves. As they conserve energy by practicing it with greater restraint, they develop the power to manifest their thoughts or actualize their speech. The Puranas illustrate how seers and sages possessed that power and often used it against evildoers and even gods. Householders should practice the austerity of speech for self-purification and self-control. It also helps them gain control over their actions and reactions, become mindful, and experience peace and tranquility. If they keep at it, it will become their natural state and help them in old age (during vanaprastha) live in seclusion and establish their minds in contemplation.

Sloka 16

manaḥprasādaḥ saumyatvaṃ maunam ātmavinigrahaḥ
bhāvasaṃśuddhir ity etat tapo mānasam ucyate

manah-prasadah = mental peace or serenity; saumyatvam = gentleness, mildness, friendliness; maunam = silence; atma vinigrahah = self-control; bhava = thoughts, feelings, emotions; samsuddhih = purity; iti = thus; etat = this; tapah = austerity; manasam = of the mind; ucyate = said to be.

Mental peace, gentleness, silence, self-control, and purity of mental states; thus, it is said to be the austerity of the mind.

The common impression about tapas or tapah is that it is a meditative practice to obtain boons from the gods. In common folklore, this is how tapah is depicted. However, contrary to popular belief, tapas is not a mere mental exercise but a comprehensive set of austere practices that aim to activate the higher powers of the mind and body through discipline and self-control. The effort purifies the whole body and all the sheaths (kosas) in it and awakens the hidden spiritual powers that do not naturally manifest. In this chapter, Lord Krishna identified three types of tapas: the austerity of the body, speech, and mind. In this verse, he suggested how the austerity of the mind should be practiced. These suggestions are meant for householders who do not renounce worldly life and cannot go to forests or live in secluded places to practice sannyasa or intense asceticism. What he described here is a milder version, which they can practice without much discomfort according to their convenience and prepare themselves for the last two stages of varnashrama dharma: vanaprastha (retreat into forests) and sannyasa (renunciation).

This austerity involves the practice of keeping the mind calm and composed, gentleness or good-naturedness, silence, self-control, and having pure and positive thoughts, feelings, and emotions or mental states (bhava samsuddhi). It is the highest and most difficult of the three. One can control the body and its organs, except perhaps those under the control of the autonomous nervous system. One can control and limit one's speech with discipline, spending more time listening rather than speaking, speaking when necessary, thinking before speaking, or practicing silence. However, controlling the mind and senses requires greater effort since it is unstable and inconsistent and does not yield easily. However, it becomes easier with the simultaneous practice of the other two austerities. For liberation, the three austerities are very important. However, success is not achieved until the mind is completely controlled because it is necessary to practice the other two. Hence, it is of the utmost importance. By succeeding in it, one can restrain the movements of the mind and senses and establish them in the Self with vigorous concentration and control (atma-samyama). With its continued practice, devotees can keep their minds tranquil and free from afflictions and impure mental states (asuddhi bhavas) such as egoism, delusions, and ignorance, and enter the tranquil state of oneness.

The austerity of the mind can be understood by breaking it down into its components. Manah-prasada refers to the stable, peaceful, and noble state of mind that radiates divine qualities and is not subject to frequent disturbances.

It is both a cause and an effect. By remaining peaceful and serene, you can control your mind. With the mind under control, you can experience peace and tranquility. With that, you will also experience bhava-suddhi or mental cleanliness. Saumyatvam means good-naturedness. It is characterized by gentleness, softness, friendliness, compassion, and other divine qualities. It is indicative of having a good heart and a friendly and humble nature. It arises naturally with the predominance of sattva when you control your body, speech, and mind. By cultivating it, you can neutralize or minimize the adverse effects of egoism, attraction, and aversion. One should practice it by keeping calm, being friendly, gentle, and nonviolent, avoiding harsh words, and cultivating sattva. Maunam or silence arises from the austerity of speech. From a spiritual perspective, its practice leads to control over one's speech, thinking, and actions. Seers, sages, and ascetics invariably practiced it in the past to control their minds and purify themselves. Those who attained perfection in it were known as munis, meaning the silent ones. Silence becomes easier when the mind is calm and impurities such as egoism, desires, and attachments are inactive or absent. Atma-vinigraha means self-control. It is practiced by withdrawing and controlling the mind and senses to attain stability and equanimity. In the austerity of silence, you restrain speech only. In self-control, you must control your desires and attachments by overcoming attraction and aversion and using all three austerities mentioned. Bhava-samsuddhi manifests when the gunas are silent and self-control is perfected, whereby the yogi remains indifferent to their binding influence.

Sloka 17

śraddhayā parayā taptaṃ tapas tat trividhaṃ naraiḥ
aphalākāṅkṣibhir yuktaiḥ sāttvikaṃ paricakṣate

śraddhaya = with faith and sincerity; paraya = supreme, highest; taptam = performed, undertaken; tapah = tapas, austerity; tat = that; tri-vidham = three types, three kinds; naraih = by men; aphala-akanksibhih = without the desire for the fruit of actions; yuktaih = skillful yogis; sattvikam = of sattvic type; paricaksate = they say, declare.

When the three kinds of austerities are performed with supreme faith, without any desire for the fruit of their actions by those skillful in yoga, they speak of it as the sattvic kind.

Having explained the three types of tapas, Lord Krishna suggested that each could be practiced in three ways according to the modes. Thus, for example, the austerity of the body, speech, or mind can be practiced in a sattvic, rajasic, or tamasic manner. The gunas influence all actions. Austerities are not an exception. Here, he described the austerities of the sattvic type. He said that they become sattvic when they are performed by adept yogis with supreme faith, without any desire for their results. In other words, sattvic austerities purify the mind and body but do not produce karma. Consequences arise only when they are performed with desires. It means one should not even think of controlling or avoiding the pain and suffering, or discomfort that may arise from them. Supreme faith, desirelessness, and skillfulness in yoga are sattvic qualities. Hence, only those who have cultivated sattva can practice them successfully. Sraddha means faith.

The faith which is mentioned here is not the simple kind. It is boundless and intense (apara), free from doubt and conflicting thoughts. When you have it, you perform actions sincerely and strictly according to the established norms ordained by the scriptures, with conviction, devotion, dedication, and discipline. You set your mind on performing the austerities rather than their result and commit yourself to the goal of liberation with no other thought. Sraddha becomes pure and intense when sattva predominates. Sattvic people perform austerities for the sake of God and the welfare of the world. They do it to uphold Dharma and serve the Lord rather than gain something out of it for themselves. Since they practice self-control and possess discernment, they maintain balance and do not go to extremes or indulge in experimental and unconventional methods. Hence, they are called yuktas, those who are skillful in yoga. With their minds established in the Self, they practice the austerities with supreme faith and endure the suffering that may arise from them with equanimity.

Sloka 18

satkāramānapūjārthaṃ tapo dambhena caiva yat
kriyate tad iha proktaṃ rājasaṃ calam adhruvam

sat-kara = fame, recognition; mana = honor; puja = worship, adoration; artham = for the sake of; tapah = austerity; dambhena = ostentatious display; ca = and; eva = so also; yat = which; kriyate = performed, undertaken; tat = that; iha = this worldly; proktam = said to be; rajasam = of rajasic nature, of the nature of rajas; calam = wavering; adhruvam = unstable, uncertain.

The austerity that is performed for fame, honor, and adoration, and for ostentatious display - this is said to be rajasic, this-worldly, wavering, and unstable.

In performing obligatory duties or spiritual actions, intentions are important. Sattvic are pure, desireless, and selfless, and so are their intentions. Those of rajasic people are impure and riddled with desires, passions, and egoism. They perform austerities not to serve God or fulfill the aims of Dharma but to satisfy their desires or achieve worldly gains. Hence, their austerities produce karma. As this verse states, they perform austerities for name, fame, honor, vanity, or to gain the attention and appreciation of others. In other words, they practice austerity not for self-purification or to fulfill their obligation to God but for self-promotion, egoistic satisfaction, or some selfish gain. Their austerity is this worldly because they perform them for worldly ends. It is wavering because they cannot concentrate, control their minds and bodies, or stick to their resolve (sankalpa). It is unstable or uncertain (adhruvam) because it produces transient effects that do not last long. In today's world, you will find many devotees falling into this category. Spiritual people should examine their intentions to know why they want to pursue spirituality or practice austerities, whether they want to do it due to curiosity, conformity, or to achieve some worldly aims. Without knowing it and correcting themselves, they would remain deluded. If the intentions are impure, whatever worldly goals they seek through spirituality, such as peace, happiness, or good health, will remain temporary or elusive. Some people also practice penances to gain spiritual powers or to control or attract others. They produce negative karma and lead to bondage and suffering.

Sloka 19

mūḍhagrāheṇātmano yat pīḍayā kriyate tapaḥ
parasyotsādanārthaṃ vā tat tāmasam udāhṛtam

mudha = foolish, stupid, ignorant; grahena = intentions, desires; atmanah = to oneself; yat = which; pidaya = pain; kriyate = performed, undertaken; tapah = austerity; parasya = another; utsadana-artham = for the destruction; va = or; tat = that; tamasam = tamasic in nature; udahrtam = said to be.

Austerity, which is performed with foolish intentions, causing pain to oneself or the destruction of another, is said to be tamasic in nature.

Tamasic people practice austerities with foolish intentions and deluded beliefs, thinking that they will increase their wealth, bring them luck, give them supernatural powers, make them physically attractive, irresistible, or desirable, cure incurable diseases, change their destiny, destroy their enemies, etc. Their methods produce pain and suffering since they resort to extremely painful and harsh methods to achieve quick results. Religious penances cause some degree of pain and discomfort since they are meant to purify the mind and body through fasting, sexual abstinence, withdrawal of the mind and senses, etc. Tamasic people ignore their limits of tolerance while practicing them, thereby causing themselves great pain and suffering. They also engage in evil practices and dark methods to hurt and harm others or invoke evil powers to find shortcuts or achieve quick results. They engage in such methods due to ignorance, delusion, and poor discernment. They choose faulty methods or invent their own since they possess little knowledge of liberation, the scriptures, or the traditions. With false notions and beliefs, they practice them in their ignorant ways. The Vedic sculptures prescribe specific rules and procedures to perform sacrifices and penances. They also suggest the sins that may arise if they are improperly performed. Tamasic people disregard them and practice unconventional methods, ignoring the consequences that may arise from them. While austerities are prescribed for self-purification and liberation or upholding Dharma, tamasic people use them for wrong purposes. It is why the secret knowledge of liberation is not taught to everyone, but to those who are virtuous and intelligent.

Sloka 20

dātavyam iti yad dānaṃ dīyatenupakāriṇe
deśe kāle ca pātre ca tad dānaṃ sāttvikaṃ smṛtam

datavyam = what is to be given; iti = thus; yat = that; danam = charity; diyate = given; anupakarine = from whom no help is expected; dese = in place; kale = in time; ca = and; patre = suitability; ca = and; tat = that; danam = charity; sattvikam = of sattiv nature; smrtam = lawbooks.

The charity that is given to the one from whom no help is expected, with due consideration for place, time, and suitability, that charity is declared in the Smritis (lawbooks) as sattvic in nature.

According to the gunas, charity is also of three types: sattvic, rajasic, and tamasic. Sattvic charity is the best and the ideal. Rajasic and tamasic charities are problematic and should be avoided since they produce consequences and bind people. However, in real life, you rarely find people who practice sattvic charity. Because of the mixed nature of gunas, people may practice it once in a while but not always. The three gunas are universally active in almost everyone, and their influence may vary according to circumstances. However, comparatively, we may say rajasic and tamasic type charities are more common.

This verse identifies sattvic charities. While one may occasionally engage in them in moments of heightened spirituality, ideally, one should practice them as an obligatory duty and part of one's Dharma. The most notable feature of sattvic charities is that they are given without desires and expectations, and appropriately to the right person at the right time and place. In other words, giving charity to a person who does not deserve it or not giving to someone who deserves it should be avoided. Vedic tradition puts teachers, seers, sages, Brahmanas, guests, servants of the Lord, and those who seek alms or depend upon others for food as the most worthy recipients of charity.

Giving charity or gifts to the deserving is one of the highest virtues in Hinduism. The law books (smritis) encourage householders to give charity and bestow gifts upon others to ensure their own material and spiritual welfare. Manu declares that charitable works given with faith and "lawfully earned" wealth bring endless rewards. In other words, charity should be given from what is lawfully earned or owned. He also identified charity as one of the six duties of a Brahmana. According to him, in the four orders of humans delineated by the Vedic varnashrama-dharma, the order of householders is the highest because they are uniquely positioned to bestow knowledge and food to others and thereby serve the highest cause of Dharma. Helping others through charity and sharing their wealth for the good of the world is their obligatory duty and an essential part of their householder's Dharma. The underlying principle is that those who pursue Dharma should not be selfish. They should think of others beyond their selfish desires and immediate families and try to help them. By serving others, they will be serving the Supreme Lord since all the jivas belong to one universal divine family (Vasudeva Kutumbam).

The law books identify three types of charity: obligatory, optional, and prohibited. The first category includes charities such as giving gifts to teachers, offering food to gods and ancestors, paying fees to the priests when they perform sacrifices, and giving gifts to the guests when they visit or attend a sacrifice. They are obligatory because they are gifts of gratitude. Through them, a householder can discharge his karmic debt and expiate for his sins. The lawbooks identify paying taxes to the rulers or the protectors and enforcers of the law as an act of charity only, which is obligatory. Optional charities include donations to temples, community service, helping the poor, the sick, and the needy, teaching for free, honoring religious teachers and ascetics, spreading the knowledge of the scriptures, or offering money or helping for a righteous cause such as building temples, shelters, community projects, digging wells, lakes, etc.

The law books also prohibit certain types of charity. For example, householders are prohibited from giving gifts to those who commit crimes or indulge in evil actions. Charity should be in accordance with Dharma and moral values. They should be given to protect and preserve the eternal good (dharma) upon earth so that the order and regularity of the world are not disrupted, and the evil ones do not get any incentives for their actions. Suitability is also important. If evil people are given charity due to fear, pity, or coercion, one becomes complicit in their evil and shares their evil karma. One should, therefore, be judicious in offering help or giving gifts. There is no limit to what one can give. Charity should not have to be given only when one has excess wealth. Anyone can practice charity within their means by sharing whatever one has. It is more beneficial if given by sacrificing one's comforts and needs.

Brihadaranyaka Upanishad contains a story in which Brahma gives specific suggestions to the three classes of beings he produced: gods, humans, and demons, according to their nature and considering their weaknesses. He advises humans to practice charity (dana), gods to practice restraint (dama), and asuras to practice compassion (daya), respectively. He prescribed charity for humans because they are, by nature, selfish and, due to desires and attachments, do not easily part with their possessions. They can overcome selfishness, desires, and attachments to material things through charitable works and excel in selflessness, gratitude, friendliness, detachment, and renunciation.

Sloka 21

yat tu prattyupakārārthaṃ phalam uddiśya vā punaḥ
dīyate ca parikliṣṭaṃ tad dānaṃ rājasaṃ smṛtam

yat = which; tu = but; prati-upakara-artham = for reciprocating the help received; phalam = fruit; uddisya = with the desire; va = or; punah = again; diyate = given; ca = and; pariklistam = grudgingly, with difficulty; tat = that; danam = charity; rajasam =rajasic in nature; smrtam = is declared in the lawbooks.

However, charity given for the sake of reciprocating the help received, or again with a desire for its fruit, or given grudgingly, that type of charity is declared in the lawbooks as rajasic in nature.

Charity given with selfish desires and expectations is rajasic. Anything that is given with an expectation, ulterior motive, or for hidden personal gain is rajasic. The person who gives may expect something in return, and the person who receives it may reciprocate with a return gift in some form. One can see examples of this in the business world, where money is donated for publicity or brand recognition. Bribing someone for personal favors is also rajasic. These kinds of charity or gift-giving produce karma. Worldly people are accustomed to making deals or exchanging gifts for personal gain. Some bring the same attitude to their worship and try to make deals with God. The motive here is not to help or show kindness but to secure maximum advantage at the minimum cost. It is more like buying a favor in the guise of gifting. Since this type of charity is motivated by desires, it is not conducive to spiritual growth or purification and does not even qualify as a virtue. Ideally, charity should be selfless and without egoism, desires, and expectations. The Hindu lawbooks are clear on this. They state that charity should always be given selflessly or as a reward without selfish motives. It is the norm, which is obligatory for householders who uphold Dharma. When done with desires and expectations, it becomes a kamya karma (desire-ridden action) and a binding action. In Hinduism, giving charity is a sacrificial duty. It strengthens detachment, renunciation, and selflessness. When it is done with selfishness or desires, it becomes a barter, a desire-ridden action, and loses all merit. The same is true when charity is given grudgingly or under compulsion. In today's world, rajasic charities are common. However, many also give charity due to compassion and devotion. There is still some virtue in rajasic charities since they may still do some good to others or promote righteous causes.

Sloka 22

adeśakāle yad dānam apātrebhyaś ca dīyate
asatkṛtam avajñātaṃ tat tāmasam udāhṛtam

adesa-kale = improper place and time; yat = which; danam = charity; upatrebhyah = unworthy or undeserving people; ca = and; diyate = is given; asat-krtam = without respect; avajnatam = with contempt; tat = that; tamasam = tmasic in nature; udahrtam = said to be.

That charity, given at an improper place and time to undeserving people and given without respect and with contempt, is said to be tamasic in nature.

Rajasic people give charity with desires and expectations. At least, they do not give it with contempt or disrespect. Tamasic people do it with contempt and without respect for the person who receives it. They also give to people who do not deserve it while ignoring those who deserve it, since they go by their deluded judgment and mostly act against the prevailing norms and customs. In other words, their charity does not serve the intended purpose, does not promote Dharma, and cannot be considered a virtue. Any gift given freely to another out of compassion or in appreciation of a service rendered is considered charity (danam) in Hinduism. It must be given with the right attitude to the right person at the right place and time. For example, the fee paid to a priest who performs a sacrifice or ritual worship is charity. It must be given immediately after the sacrifice is completed, not after three months or with reluctance. The charity of this kind is an obligation. If it is given with gratitude and respect, and in time, it is a sattvic charity. If it is given after haggling, grudgingly, and conditionally, or because some intended aim or desire is fulfilled, it is rajasic. If it is not paid at all, paid less, paid after a long delay, with contempt and disrespect as if the person who rendered the service is inferior or unworthy, it is tamasic. If you hire an unqualified priest and pay him with contempt, thinking that he does not deserve it, but you are giving anyway, it is also tamasic charity. Similarly, the sacrificial food served to guests at home or after a sacrificial ritual or worship is also considered charity only. If you serve them selflessly without any expectations, it is sattvic. If you serve them expecting that you will be appreciated or invited to their functions in the future, it is rajasic. It becomes tamasic if you invite to religious ceremonies those who do not practice Dharma or believe in God, serve them inappropriate food, or treat them with contempt. Thus, intentions and conduct are important in giving charity.

The law books provide numerous guidelines for giving charity or gifts. They stipulate that charity should be given only from rightfully or lawfully earned money. Only pure and freshly cooked food with the right ingredients, pleasing to the gods, and worthy of sacrifices should be served to guests. The Grihyasutras further prescribe that the materials used as sacrificial offerings in a fire sacrifice (agnihotra) should be clean and fresh and should not be mixed with pungent materials or salt. Before using them, they must be purified and sanctified with proper rituals and pure water like the water from a sacred river. They prohibit using leftover materials or burnt offerings from a previous sacrifice. They also specify that gifts must be made during auspicious periods only and at places worthy of religious worship or devotional service. Those who want to give charity at the end of a religious observance or activity should do so at an auspicious time and place after consulting an almanac. Similar rules apply when gifts are given at marriage to the bride, the bridegroom, and their parents. These rules are not mere suggestions; they are meant to regulate human behavior and ensure ethical or lawful conduct. When they are sincerely and selflessly followed, it is sattvic. When they are sincerely but selfishly followed, it is rajasic, and when they are wrongly, delusionally, or inappropriately followed, it is tamasic.

Indeed, the code of conduct may vary according to circumstances, time, and place, influenced by local or regional customs and traditions. However, some fundamental principles remain constant. Basic human morality should not change. For example, the law books state that charity must be given only from the rightfully earned wealth. This standard applies even today. It is a misconception to believe that charity, however it is given, will absolve one's sins. In any moral conduct, the basic virtues remain the same. The attitude with which it is given is also important. It is incorrect to regard those who ask for charity or receive charity as inferior or to treat them with contempt or disrespect. In the eyes of the Lord, all are equal. The one who gives merely discharges his duty and obligation to the Lord, the source of all. Devotees must be grateful for the opportunity to serve others or give them charity because it helps them practice Dharma and overcome impurities. It is especially beneficial to householders. They must uphold Dharma by helping ascetic people who depend upon them for food, since they renounce worldly life and give up cooking. By helping them, they fulfill their obligation to God, accumulate good karma, and progress spiritually.

Sloka 23

oṃ tat sad iti nirdeśo brahmaṇas trividhaḥ smṛtaḥ
brāhmaṇās tena vedāś ca yajñāś ca vihitāḥ purā

Om =Aum; tat = tat, that; sat = sat, truth, existence; iti = thus; nirdesah = instruction, description; brahmanah = of Brahman; tri-vidhah = three ways, threefold; smrtah = mentally reciting or recollecting or remembering; brahmanah = Brahmanas; tena = by this; vedah = the Vedas; ca = and; yajnah = sacrifices; ca = and; vihitah = ordained, prescribed; pura = in the past.

"AUM TAT SAT"- thus were instructed the three ways of mentally reciting or recollecting Brahman. By this, the Brahmanas, the Vedas, and the sacrifices in the past were decreed.

Brahman, the universal Supreme Self, manifests in creation with numerous names and forms. He is the presiding deity, driving force, giver, recipient, and upholder of every sacrificial act. The scriptures describe him as the source of all, the Lord of all, and the real mover and doer in all deeds. One may meditate on him or remember him in several ways in ritual and spiritual practices. Devotees can recite his names, contemplate his glory, or envision his universal forms. All the divinities in creation are his numerous manifestations and represent him in their purest and highest aspect. While you can worship him or meditate on him in many ways, the most standard method approved by the Vedas is to remember him as "Aum Tat Sat." It can be translated variously as "Aum! That (Brahman) is the Reality or "Aum is That and the Reality" or "He is Aum, That and Reality." It is a powerful mantra representing his three names or aspects, on which devotees and yogis meditate, and the three supreme manifestations that make up the whole existence. They reveal to us his true essence and supreme reality.

Thus, Aum, That, and Sat are three ways to reflect on him or remember him. First, meditate on him as Aum, the eternal sound and the source of all the sounds and the entire alphabet. Second, remember him as That, not this (the body or the being). Third, accept and worship him as Sat, the eternal reality in contrast to his creation, which is an illusion or unreal (asat). As this verse states, by remembering and reflecting on Brahman in this manner, the ancient rishis could bring to light the Brahmanas (books of rituals), the Vedas, and the yajnas (sacrifices) in the remote past. The mantra has the purifying and manifesting power. It helps one remain established in the contemplation of Brahman as one's very essence. When you mentally recite it with concentration and meditate on its parts, it will purify your mind and nullify any mistakes or errors you might have committed in performing your sacred duties. As you keep remembering the word or mentally reciting it, it will elevate and extend your consciousness, whereby you develop detachment from your physical self and become established in the realization that you are the eternal Self. When your mind is fully saturated with it, you will frequently experience the turiya (transcendental) consciousness and, finally, develop the vision of oneness in your wakeful consciousness as well.

The mantra has three parts. As we already noted, they represent the three aspects of Brahman. Aum is the sacred syllable, considered the source of all sounds, letters (matras), words, and languages. It is known as sabda brahma, meaning Brahman in sound form, or nada, the eternal, subtle sound that flows uninterruptedly. When you prefix it to any mantra, as done in this one, it becomes supremely auspicious and powerful. Aum multiplies its potency and reach. Tat means That. In the Vedic tradition, it is used to refer to Brahman in his purest and absolute state since he is beyond all the labels, genders, words, and forms with which we are familiar. It denotes that Brahman is indescribable and indefinable. It is also used to distinguish Him from His creation or materiality. The pronouns 'That' and 'this' are often used to refer to Brahman and Atman (the individual Self), to the Self and the body, or the Lord (Shiva) and the being (jiva). Sat has multiple meanings. It means truth, reality, or existence itself, in contrast to untruth, unreality, or non-existence (asat), which refers to Brahman's creation or our names and forms. Sat is eternal (sada) and immutable, while asat is temporary and destructible. This mantra, "Aum Tat Sat," is used in contemplation and sacrificial ceremonies and added at the beginning of many spiritual writings and discourses as a reminder that Brahman is the ultimate truth and the source of all knowledge and wisdom. It is said that adding these sacred words before any hymn, mantra, or sacred writing imparts to it the power of Brahman. When not added, they lose their potency and effectiveness or become vulnerable to asuric influence. Knowing their meaning is equally important. If uttered without knowing their meaning, they do not protect those who recite them.

Sloka 24

tasmād om ity udāhṛtya yajñadānatapaḥkriyāḥ
pravartante vidhānoktāḥ satataṃ brahmavādinām

tasmat = therefore; om = Aum; iti = thus; udahrtya = after uttering; yajna = sacrifice; dana = charity; tapah = austerity; kriyah = acts of; pravartante = begin, start; vidhana-uktah = as ordained in the Vedas; satatam = always; brahma-vadinam = those who teach or proclaim the knowledge of Brahman.

Therefore, those who proclaim the knowledge of Brahman always begin acts of sacrifice, charity, (and) austerity as ordained in the Vedas after uttering Aum.

In this and the next two verses, Lord Krishna explains the importance of the sacred words (Aum Tat Sat) in sacrifice, charity, and austerity. Here, he stated how those who teach or proclaim the true knowledge of Brahman (Brahmavadis) utter Aum before engaging in these triple acts according to the rules (vidhi) as ordained in the Vedas. They begin by uttering Aum because it is one of Brahman's triple names. It represents Brahman in sound form. Hence, it is sacred. Whenever uttered, it reverberates with his power. Several Upanishads emphasize its importance in the ritual and spiritual activities householders perform as their duties (dharma) to pursue the four chief aims of human life (Dharma, Artha, Kama, and Moksha). It is said that the knowledge one ever needs to know to achieve liberation is hidden in Aum. When infused with the power gathered through tapas, it reveals its secrets. Aum is the teacher, the guide, and the secret one needs to know to realize the Self.

According to Chandogya Upanishad, one should always sing the hymns of the Vedas (during sacrifices) beginning with Aum. Just as the stalk extends into all leaves as the midriff, so does Aum extend into all speech and all syllables. Hence, Aum is all this. It further states, "Aum is pronounced to declare compliance, for whenever we comply with anything, we say Aum." The Taittiriya Upanishad (1.8) extols its importance elaborately, saying, "This Aum is Brahman. This Aum is all this. This word, which is Aum, invokes obedience. Moreover, when told, 'Aum, recite,' they recite. Uttering Aum, they sing the Samans. Uttering, 'Aum, Som,' they recite scriptures. Uttering Aum, the Adharvayu priest responds with praise. Uttering Aum, the Brahman priest indicates approval. Uttering Aum, the Agnihotri priest gives permission (to the sacrificer) to make offerings (in the fire sacrifice). A Brahmana says, 'Aum,' when he is about to begin the recitation (of the Vedas), wishing, 'May I attain Brahman.' Thus (wishing) he attains Brahman."

According to the Mundaka Upanishad (2.2.4), one can attain liberation by using the syllable Aum as the bow, the Self as the arrow, and Brahman as the target. The Yogasutras declares that by repeating Aum and contemplating upon it, one can attain the knowledge of the Self (pratyak chetana) and freedom from disturbances (antaraya bhava). When we begin our actions and utterances with Aum, our actions do not produce karma since they become infused with the light and power of Brahman. By constantly remembering it or reflecting on it, one becomes divine-centered and naturally inclined to practice karma-sannyasa yoga with mindfulness, offering all thoughts and actions to the Supreme Self. Since it is also a purifier, it purifies our minds and bodies and strengthens our resolve to live righteously and achieve liberation. By chanting it, yogis become free from the afflictions of their minds and bodies and stabilize their minds. The scripture further suggests that one should constantly meditate upon Aum to practice devotion to the Self (Isvara paridhana) and remain established in it.

The symbolic significance of Aum is also well-known. The triple letters in Aum and the silence that follows their utterance represent the four states of consciousness, Jagrat, Svapna, Susupta, and Turiya, in which the jiva abides. They also denote the four worlds of Vedic cosmology, namely Bhur, Bhuva, Swaha, and Maha. The Taittiriya Upanishad (1.5) states, "Bhur, bhuvah, suvah, these, certainly, are the three mystic utterances. Besides them, there is the fourth, Mahah, made known by the son of Mahacamasa. That is Brahman, that is the Self." The four syllables also represent the triple gods (Brahma, Vishnu, and Shiva) and Brahman himself. It is further said that those who meditate on it transcend the physical and subtle worlds and attain the immortal world of Brahman. Aum is also known as Pranava because it is the sustaining force of life-energy (prana). It purifies the mind, the senses, breath, and speech so that intelligence (buddhi) shines. Thus, Aum has great significance in Hinduism. In rituals, it is used to initiate actions, recite mantras, purify names and places, and empower our thoughts, prayers, and invocations. By chanting it, sacrifices, charity, and austerity become auspicious. Because of its association with Brahman, it serves as a pathfinder and doorway to the world of immortality. By using it in meditation and concentration, yogis dissolve their minds in the pure consciousness of the Self and abide in self-absorption and deeper states of tranquility and bliss.

Sloka 25

tad ity anabhisaṃdhāya phalaṃ yajñatapaḥkriyāḥ
dānakriyāś ca vividhāḥ kriyante mokṣakāṅkṣibhiḥ

tat = that; iti = thus; anabhisandhaya = without desiring, seeking; phalam = the fruit; yajna = sacrifice; tapah = austerity; kriyah = acts; dana = charity; kriyah = acts; ca = and; vividhah = various; kriyante = perform; moksa = liberation; kanksibhih = those wishing or hoping.

(Uttering) TAT, thus, those wishing for liberation perform various acts of sacrifice, austerity, and charity without desiring the fruit (of karma).

The expounders of Brahman (brahmavadis) utter Aum before performing sacrifices, austerities, and acts of charity according to the rules and injunctions (vidhi) of the Vedas. Remembering Brahman as the purest and the most auspicious syllable, Aum or Tat, they become grounded in the knowledge of the Vedas and Brahman and serve him by teaching those who wish to know him. Those who wish to seek liberation (moksha kanksha) perform the same activities after remembering Brahman as Tat. The syllable Tat (That) aptly describes Brahman, who is without gender, identity, or duality. No other word better describes him, who is indescribable, indefinable, and beyond the mind, senses, and intelligence. It is also used to remember Brahman or the Self as the transcendental reality, in contrast to idam (this), meaning this world, the objective reality, the jiva, or the mind and body. Tat also objectifies Brahman as the distant goal or ideal yet to be achieved. It appropriately reminds the seekers of the liberation of their goal and the need to achieve it without ignoring their duties and obligations. Sacrifices, austerities, and charity are the means to bridge the distance between That (tat) and them. Using it as the golden brick, they must lay the path to liberation and immortality.

Tat also reminds the seekers of liberation to engage in actions not for themselves, but for the Supreme Lord. As Lord Krishna already emphasized, seekers of liberation should be selfless, free from desires and attachments, and perform actions as their obligatory duty for the sake of God, without desiring their fruit, knowing that they must live in the service of God and perform his duties on earth as theirs to ensure the order and regularity of the world. The welfare of the world is the ultimate fruit of our selfless actions rendered in service to God. It rightly belongs to him and should be offered to him. We should value the opportunity given to serve him and express our gratitude to him for that. Having any other expectation will undermine the divine purpose and the sacred goal for which we are born. Those who know Brahman and the Self, and liberation as their true purpose upon earth, perform their duties devotionally and selflessly, with their minds established in him. They know that by performing actions in this manner, they will be free from the consequences of their actions and attain eternal freedom.

Sacrificing egoism, selfishness, and desires, and performing sacrifices for the Supreme Lord, they engage thus in the highest form of sacrifice, the sacrifice of karma-phala (the fruit of actions). Giving themselves entirely to him and living for him, they also practice the best form of austerity and charity. With their minds focused on him, they overcome their sins and impurities and attain nearness and oneness with Brahman.

Sloka 26

sadbhāve sādhubhāve ca sad ity etat prayujyate
praśaste karmaṇi tathā sacchabdaḥ pārtha yujyate

sat-bhave = reality, the state of reality; sadhu-bhave = the state of righteousness, virtuous nature; ca = and; sat = sat, Brahman, truth; iti = thus; etat = this; prayujyate = is used, is spoken; prasaste = commendable, praiseworthy; karmani = actions; tatha = so also; sat-sabdah = truthful words; partha = O Partha; yujyate = is spoken, is used.

The (word) Sat is fit to denote reality and goodness, O Partha. Also, the word Sat is used for praiseworthy action.

Sat means truth, reality, existence, what is, etc. Here, Lord Krishna said, Sat is the truth that denotes reality, goodness, or saintliness, and any praiseworthy or auspicious karma. Sadbhāvam means the state of truth or reality. It is the reality of things in existence or who you are in your purest and natural state. It is the reality of Brahman, which manifests in Prakriti or human consciousness as the higher nature with resplendent qualities such as right thinking, right state of mind, right attitude, truthfulness, saintliness, goodness, etc. When you are established in it and perform righteous actions purely for the sake of that Supreme Being, we may say you are established in the reality of Sat or the truthful state of Brahman (sadbhāvam). When you excel in the restraints (yamas) such as nonviolence, truthfulness, non-covetousness, and non-stealing, follow the rules (niyamas) of righteous conduct and engage in actions as ordained by the scriptures, or when you renounce the world and lead a purely divine-centered life just as the ascetics do, you are considered to possess the highest and purest sadbhāvam. In general usage, whenever anyone displays right-mindedness or acts with the right attitude in a sattvic manner, it is called sadbhāvam. Sadbhavam is the state of sattvic people or those exclusively devoted to the Supreme Lord without any desire or distraction.

Aum represents Brahman in speech. Tat refers to Brahman as the goal or the ideal. Sat denotes his pure state of reality in its absolute aspect as the eternal, endless, indestructible, unchanging, pure consciousness. It is his higher nature, which Lord Krishna mentioned in the previous chapters. Sat is the reality or the truth Brahman represents, which manifests in human consciousness when all the impurities are removed, as a divine quality representing purity, positivity, right-mindedness, friendliness, gentleness, selflessness, saintliness, holiness, and so on. All these qualities are represented by sādhubhavam, which manifests in sadhus, the pious ones, as the divine nature. A sadhu is a monk, saint, or holy person who has no ill will, is free from delusion and ignorance, and is firmly established in his higher nature and the contemplation of Brahman with no other thought, interest, or desire. All good and virtuous actions, such as obligatory duties, sacrifices, speaking truth, practicing nonviolence or truthfulness, devotional worship, self-restraint, helping others, charity, etc., qualify as Sat only. All actions arising from positive thoughts and noble intentions (sadbhavam) and saintliness (sādhubhavam) also qualify as Sat since they uphold God's eternal Dharma and contribute to the welfare of the world. Hence, they are praiseworthy and ideal for householders to follow.

In the Vedic tradition, the Supreme Self is considered Sat in contrast to his creation, which is considered asat, meaning false or illusory. It arises from Brahman as a temporary projection, reflection, or formation. Since it appears briefly and temporarily, with a beginning and an end, and like a cloud in the sky or a ripple in the ocean, it is unlike Brahman, who is truth consciousness and represents absolute Reality, which is eternal, imperishable, and infinite. In contrast, the phenomenal world is illusory and perishable. Hence, it is considered asat or unreal. In the Vedas, the word Sat denotes the pure state of Brahman or Truth itself, which is transcendental, largely unknown, and untouched by Nature (Prakriti) and the objective reality of the senses. The word is used as a noun to describe the state of Brahman and as an adjective to denote his qualities, manifesting in the phenomenal world as goodness or righteousness (sadbhāvam). In logical terms, Sat represents the truths that can be proven or validated with the Pramanas (valid methods of knowing) in contrast to asat or falsehood arising from the impurities of ignorance and delusion.

Sloka 27

yajñe tapasi dāne ca sthitiḥ sad iti cocyate
karma caiva tadarthīyaṃ sad ity evābhidhīyate

yajne = sacrifice; tapasi = in austerity, dane = charity; ca = and; sthitih = steadfastness, perseverance, firmness, established practice; sat = sat; iti = thus; ca = also; ucyate = referred to; karma = work; ca = and; eva = eeven; tat = that; arthiyam = for the sake of, meant for; sat = truth; iti = thus; eva = verily; abhidhiyate = is described as.

Steadfastness in sacrifice, austerity, and charity is also referred to as Sat, and even the work done for that sake is also described as Sat.

Sat represents not only the highest state of Brahman but also his purest and highest reflections, manifestations, or projections in the diversity and duality of creation. They include his divine qualities and appearances (vibhutis) in the objective reality of Nature enumerated in the tenth chapter. The Vedas are Sat since they arise from Brahman as speech or sounds reflecting the Truth of his absolute state and how to attain him. Sacrifices, austerities, and charitable actions mentioned in them are also Sat. They yield intended results if practiced correctly according to the established tradition (sthithi). By practicing them truthfully, consistently, and perseveringly according to the rules (vidhi), one can attain Brahman. Thus, Sat is situated (sthithi) in various aspects of creation as the hidden Truth, including our actions and obligatory duties. Through them, householders can practice their duties (dharma) and abide by them. Sthithi has different meanings. In the context of this verse, it means persistence or resoluteness in following the established rules and procedures as approved by the Vedas while performing the sacrifices. As an aspect of Sat, it ensures their efficacy and purity.

Brahman is distinct from material things (asat) that appear in creation. Although he is distinct from them and does not exist in them, he pervades and remains hidden in them. Depending upon their purity and divinity (sadbhāvam), they partake of his nature and reflect his glory and potency. In the beings, he is the individual Self, which, according to some schools, is a distinct entity, according to some, not so distinct, and according to others, the same as Brahman. The Vedas state that only those endowed with knowledge and wisdom discern the truth (Sat) hidden in creation from asat (untruth). They see his footprints in its divine aspects, including meritorious actions such as sacrifices, austerities, and acts of charity. Since they manifest from Brahman, reflecting his higher nature and potency, they represent Sat (truth), promote Sat, and lead to Sat. By performing them with devotion and detachment, devotees become established and dissolved in Sat. Meritorious and virtuous actions contribute to the predominance of sattva, which is a manifestation of Sat in the waters of life.

Vedic rituals and sacrifices symbolize the creative and manifesting power of Brahman through sounds and human actions. Through them, we invoke and manifest his power in desirable ways for the welfare of the world and the preservation of Dharma (duty) and Rta (the natural order of creation or existence). His power remains coiled in the syllables and chants of the Vedas until they are unleashed through utterances during sacrifices, austerities, devotional worship, and prayers. If invoked properly through them according to the norms (vidhi), it connects the worshippers with their highest nature and with the corresponding potencies of Brahman. The union, which is the final goal of all yoga practices, leads to their material and spiritual transformation, welfare, and liberation. Although Brahman is not directly invoked in the Vedic sacrifices, it is the hidden intent and ultimate purpose since he is the presiding deity (Adhidaiva) of all sacrifices. The hymns of the Vedic Samhitas are intended to invoke various divinities, such as Indra, Varuna, and Agni, to seek their help. However, he is their Lord and the source of their divinity and potency. Hence, through them, he also partakes in the offerings. All actions arising from Sat are sacrifices. The Vedas proclaim that being the Lord of all and hidden in all, he is the sacrifice, the sacrificed, and the sacrificer. The knowledge to perform sacrifices also arises from him. According to the Vedas, Brahman manifests all the worlds through sacrifice only. Through them only, he establishes order and regularity and preserves and upholds creation. Through them only, he destroys and renews it afresh from one epoch to another. Sacrifices are thus rooted in Sat (truth) and represent Sat. Hence, the Mimansikas believed that there was no need to invoke Brahman. The yajnas themselves represented Sat and were endowed with its indomitable power. Hence, if worshippers performed them strictly as ordained by the Vedas, Sat would manifest as a result (karma phalam) and grant their wishes.

In the Vedic symbolism, sacrifices do not necessarily mean sacrificial ceremonies or rituals. They include all selfless actions, either offered to

Brahman along with their fruit or performed to serve him by partaking in his duties. In other words, all our thoughts, words, prayers, and actions to uphold, promote, and protect righteousness (dharma) or serve the Lord constitute sacrificial actions. It means austerities such as penances like sexual abstinence and fasting, and charitable actions also qualify as sacrifices, in which actions become the offerings, the body becomes the sacrificial pit, the organs become the witnessing deities, and the Self becomes the Lord of all, and the final recipient. Brahman is the subject, object, and connecting link in these actions. Through them, the worshippers serve the Lord, attain their aims, uphold Dharma, and enjoy peace and happiness. They help them invoke the power of Brahman to purify themselves and qualify for liberation. Through them, they abide by Sat, uphold Sat, reflect Sat, and attain Sat. They overcome asat, the samsara, transcend the impurities of selfishness, covetousness, egoism, greed, and envy, and reflect Sat in their detachment, renunciation, selflessness, and sacrificial attitude. If lust, anger, and pride are the triple gates of darkness, sacrifice, austerity, and charity are the triple gates of light and purity. They open the doors of immortal heaven for the pious and the pure. Sat is the final truth that awaits its manifestation in all through virtuous and pious actions. Those who are steadfast in their performance realize it and become one with it.

Sloka 28

aśraddhayā hutaṃ dattaṃ tapas taptaṃ kṛtaṃ ca yat
asad ity ucyate pārtha na ca tat pretya no iha

asraddhaya = without faith; hutam = oblation, offering made in sacrifice; dattam = given in charity; tapah = austerity; taptam =suffered, heated; krtam = performed; ca = and; yat = that which; asat = false; iti = thus; ucyate = said to be; partha = O Partha; na = not; ca = and; tat = that; pretya = next world or ancestral world; no = not; iha = here.

Without faith, whatever offering is made in a sacrifice, given in a charity, suffering endured in austerity, and any action performed is thus said to be asat (false), O Partha. It has no consequence here or in the next world.

Any action performed without faith lacks the purity of intention. Hence, it is imperfect or defective even if precisely performed. Sraddha (faith or belief) arises from having trust, conviction, interest, or inclination to believe in something. In matters of faith, it refers to the belief in the existence of the Lord or the deity worshipped by devotees. It is the empowering force that drives them into action. In willful actions, reinforced by desires, it becomes impure; in spiritual actions, reinforced by devotion, it becomes pure. Lord Krishna emphasized its importance a few times previously. For example, in the third chapter (31), he said that those who followed his teachings with great faith would be freed from the consequences of their actions. In the fourth chapter (39), he said that those who had faith (sraddhavan) and control over their senses would gain knowledge and quickly attain supreme peace. In the sixth chapter (47), he said that the yogis who worshipped him with great faith, with their minds fixed on him, would be considered by him as the most skillful yogis (yuktatma). There are other examples, but it is sufficient to say that the Scripture regards faith as an essential requirement for liberation. Without it, one cannot stabilize the mind, practice self-control, or develop exclusive devotion. Without it, householders cannot persevere in practicing sacrifices, austerities, or charity. Faith gives us the strength to endure suffering and persevere in obligatory duties according to the injunctions of the Lord found in the scriptures. Hence, it is synonymous with truth or sat.

When our actions are rooted in faith and committed to the truths of Brahman as declared in the Shrutis, they lead us to Dharma, Rta, and union with the Truth of Brahman. Faith, which is sattvic and devoid of desires and expectations, should be the driving force behind all our actions. If faith is impure and tainted with desires, it is false and does not lead to liberation. Lord Krishna has clarified that even virtuous actions are insignificant and do not qualify as Sat if they are not grounded in faith. Therefore, householders must perform their obligatory duties with unwavering faith and without desires and attachments to realize Sat. The steadfastness or firmness in sacrifices, austerities, and charity, which he equated with Sat, can only arise from unwavering faith. Hence, faith is the key to realizing the Truth or Reality of Brahman.

Faith implies a harmonious alignment between intentions and actions. Actions that lack sincerity and purity, even if performed strictly according to established procedures, do not count as Sat. All actions, including sacrifices, austerities, and charity, should be grounded in truth, based on truth, and performed with faith and purity. They should be carried out with faith for the sake of the Lord as a selfless service, without desires and expectations. Only then can we say that they are established in Sat and lead to Sat. In this context, truth, faith, and pure devotion are synonymous with Brahman's absolute Reality (Sat). Shraddha, or faith, is the foundation of all yogas and righteous actions. It is the catalyst in self-transformation and the raft by which devotees cross the oceans of samsara.

Conclusion

iti srīmadbhāgavadgītāsupanisatsu brahmavidyāyām yogasāstre srikrisnārjunasamvāde śraddhātrayavibhāgayogo nama saptadaso 'dhyayah.

iti = thus; srīmadbhāgavadgītā = in the sacred Bhagavadgita; upanisatsu = in the Upanishad; brahmavidyāyām = the knowledge of the absolute Brahman; yogasāstre = the scripture of yoga; srikrisnārjunasamvāde = the dialogue between Sri Krishna and Arjuna; śraddhātrayavibhāgayogo nama = by name the yoga of the threefold division of faith; saptadasah = seventeenth; adhyayah = chapter.

Thus ends the seventeenth chapter, named Shraddhā Traya Vibhāga Yoga (The Yoga of the Triple Division of Faith) in the Upanishad of the divine Bhagavadgita, the knowledge of the Absolute, a treatise on Yoga, and the debate between Arjuna and Lord Krishna.

18 – Moksha Sannyasa Yoga

The Yoga of Liberation by Renunciation

Sloka 1

Arjuna uvāca
saṃnyāsasya mahābāho tattvam icchāmi veditum
tyāgasya ca hṛṣīkeśa pṛthak keśiniṣūdana

arjunah uvaca = Arjuna said; sannyasasya = of renunciation; maha-baho = O mighty-armed; tattvam = truth; icchami = I want, wish; veditum = to know; tyagasya = of sacrifice; ca = and; hrsikesa = O master of the senses; prthak = in detail, severally; kesi-nisudana = O slayer of Kesi.

Said Arjuna, "O Mighty Armed, Master of the Senses, Slayer of Kesi, I want to know in detail the truth about renunciation and sacrifice."

The eighteenth chapter briefly reviews the main teachings Lord Krishna delivered in the previous chapters. At best, it is a conclusion or recantation of the whole scripture. The chapter is titled, 'moksha sannyasa yoga.' Some translate it as the yoga of liberation, and some as the yoga of liberation through renunciation. One may also translate it as the yoga of renunciation and liberation, the yoga of renunciation for liberation, or the yoga of liberation by renunciation. It focuses on renunciation, the true meaning of sacrifice, and the correlation between the two. Arjuna wanted to know the truth about both.

With renunciation and liberation as central themes, this chapter sums up the teachings of the Bhagavadgita, presenting it as a liberation theology with the ritual model (sacrifice) superimposed upon it. It suggests how to attain liberation, the highest end, rather than a better life in the next birth, which the sacrifices promise to householders. It combines the best of both themes, bringing renunciation into householders' sacrificial duties and guaranteeing liberation to those who practice it with exclusive devotion. The various yogas discussed in the previous chapters are meant to help the yogis adopt this approach and escape from sin and karma. The chapter emphasizes giving up desires in actions and obligatory duties (sacrifices), or worldly life and spiritual life. Hence, it is appropriately called moksha sannyasa yoga. Desireless actions are the support. Sannyasa is the shield. Moksha is the goal. This holds for all the yogas Lord Krishna taught to Arjuna in this discourse. Whether one pursues knowledge (jnana), actions (karma), renunciation (sannyasa), or devotion (bhakti), the ultimate goal is liberation through the renunciation of desires. The same holds for householders. They must pursue Dharma, Artha, or Kama by giving up desires in their actions and offering the fruit of their actions to the Lord to attain the fourth and the ultimate goal of Moksha (liberation). In pursuing liberation, all the yogas, pursuits, and actions become sanctified by the practice of sannyasa.

The practice of renunciation is as old as India's religious history. The Indus Valley people (3500 BCE to 1500 BCE) probably practiced archaic forms of yoga and asceticism. They became a common feature of Indian spirituality by the sixth century BCE when the Buddha was born. Ascetic practices and traditions were well known even during the early Vedic period before the Vedas were fully rendered into their current form. The ascetic groups held different beliefs and belonged to divergent faiths, sects, and traditions. Hindu, Jain, and Buddhist texts mention their names, such as Sramanas, Rishis, Munis, Siddhas, Pasupathas, Kevalins, and Kesins (the long-haired ones). These groups admitted people of all backgrounds from both Vedic and non-Vedic traditions. Some of them also admitted women, although it was not viewed favorably. For them, sannyasa meant giving up worldly life and living a solitary life to purify themselves and overcome desires and attachments. They practiced various techniques to control their minds and bodies and purify themselves.

Kesins, the long-haired ones mentioned in the Rigveda, were probably the oldest renunciants known to the Vedic people. The ancient Rishis practiced tapah, an ancient ascetic practice that combined meditative and purification practices with Vedic penances and observances. Ascetic people outside the Vedic fold might have also practiced similar methods. The Vedic tradition incorporated the idea of sannyasa in their varnashrama dharma and prescribed it for householders in their old age to pursue Moksha (liberation) by renouncing worldly life. Householders who discharged their obligatory duties as ordained for them had the option to retire from active worldly life and take the vows of renunciation to pursue liberation as their sole aim. They internalized sacrifices and brought the idea of sacrifice (tyaga) into sannyasa. In the Vedic tradition, sannyasa originally meant giving up using fire for sacrifices and domestic purposes and living solely at the mercy of fate or Nature. Later, it assumed spiritual connotations.

The Vedic model of sannyasa is still followed in India by many ascetic traditions, minus the extremely harsh methods of giving up life through self-starvation. It involves taking strict vows of celibacy, etc., and renouncing worldly life to pursue liberation. Renunciants must sever all mental, emotional, and physical connections with the world, including their families, names, identities, material possessions, and relationships. Those who take the vows of renunciation must adhere to their vows, follow the discipline, and pursue the highest goal. In ancient times, ascetic people lived in secluded places away from the din of worldly life. The Bhagavadgita added a new element to its practice (although it may not be the first to do it), suggesting that true renunciation means renouncing desires and attachments rather than actions or duties. As we have seen in the chapter on Karma-sannyasa, householders can practice renunciation, just like the ascetics, by giving up desires in their actions and the desire for the fruit of their actions without the obligation to give up worldly life or their duties.

In this verse, Arjuna wanted to know the difference between sannyasa and tyaga. The traditional meaning of tyaga is offering or giving away the sacrificial materials to the gods who are worshipped in a sacrifice. According to the Vedic formula of yajnas, each yajna has three components: (1) dravya, the material that will be used as an offering; (2) Devata, the deity who will be worshipped; and (3) tyaga, the act of giving away the offering. In the Bhagavadgita, Lord Krishna used it to mean giving up the desire for the fruit of one's actions, whether they are sacrificial duties or otherwise. As we will learn in the subsequent verses, it elevates all actions into sacrifices by introducing the element of renunciation into them. As we have already seen, Lord Krishna does not recommend the renunciation of actions but the renunciation of desires in all actions, including mundane actions such as eating and sleeping. He puts karma-sannyasa yoga (giving up the desire for the fruit of actions) one step above ordinary karma yoga, which householder perform to fulfill their worldly desires through sacrificial rituals. The distinction between renunciation and sacrifice is subtle. We will come to know more about it in the subsequent verses. Giving up the fruit of actions (tyaga) is an act of renunciation (sannyasa) only, even if one has not renounced duties and responsibilities. Thus, the Bhagavadgita brings renunciation into the householders' practice of Dharma. Giving up their desires, a householder can still perform his sacrificial duties and pursue Dharma, Artha, and Kama to attain Moksha. By giving up desires and attachments in all actions, he becomes a friend of the Self and attains sameness (samasiddhi), the highest yoga. In the Brihadaranyaka Upanishad, Yajnavalkya lovingly explained the importance of living for the sake of the Self to his wife Maitreyi before he retired to the forests to practice Sannyasa.

Sloka 2

srībhagavān uvāca
kāmyānāṃ karmaṇāṃ nyāsaṃ saṃnyāsaṃ kavayoviduḥ
sarvakarmaphalatyāgaṃ prāhus tyāgaṃ vicakṣaṇāḥ

sri-bhagavan uvaca = the Supreme Lord said; kamyanam = desires; karmanam = of actions; nyasam = resigning, giving up; sannyasam = renunciation; kavayah = the learned; viduh = know; sarva = of all; karma = actions; phala = result, fruti; tyagam = giving up; prahuh = call; tyagam = sacrifice; vicaksanah = the discerning ones.

The Supreme Lord said, "The learned ones know that giving up the desires in the actions is renunciation. The discerning ones call the giving up of the fruit of all actions a sacrifice."

This verse distinguishes between renunciation and sacrifice. It declares renunciation as the act of giving up desire-ridden actions (kamya-karmas) and tyaga as the act of giving up the fruit of obligatory actions. As stated before, the Vedas identify three types of actions: baddha karmas, kamya karmas, and nishiddha karmas. The first ones are obligatory. Householders are bound to perform them, whether they like it or not. The second ones are optional. Householders should avoid them if they want to avoid rebirth. The third type includes sacrifices that are completely prohibited. Householders should abstain from them totally to avoid sinful consequences and self-destruction. This verse suggests that householders should give up kamya-karmas but perform their obligatory duties, renouncing desires as a service, obligation, and sacrifice to the Lord without desiring their fruit. By that renunciation and sacrifice (tyaga), they cleanse themselves and earn the Lord's grace.

Sattvic people perform their baddha karmas without desires. They offer the fruit of their actions to the Lord and live with their minds fixed in devotion and his contemplation. They are, therefore, most qualified for liberation. Rajasic people perform both baddha and kamya karmas to fulfill their desires. They do not renounce desires or the desire for the fruit of their actions. Therefore, they remain bound to samsara until they overcome their egoism, delusion, and desires. Tamasic people ignore the scriptural injunctions and engage in all types of actions, including the prohibited ones, ignoring the consequences. Thereby, they destroy themselves and fall into demonic wombs. This chapter is meant for all types of people, especially those who want to remain householders and pursue liberation without ignoring their duties and obligations or their purity and morality.

Desires in actions and the desire for the fruit of one's actions both lead to bondage. In worldly life, they are the norms. Desires ensure the continuation of the world. They move the wheel of creation, the cycle of births and deaths, and the progression of jiva from one birth to another. Because of them, samsara exists, death rules, and souls transmigrate. Driven by their nature (svabhavam), people engage in desire-ridden actions and pursue their goals. The world will end if everyone renounces worldly life, desires, and desire-ridden actions. The Vedas recognize this predicament. Hence, they accommodate kamya-karmas in the householder's Dharma, making them optional and allowing them to pursue the four aims of human life or only liberation. The Creation Hymn in the Rigveda hints at desire as the driving force of creation, suggesting that the desire manifested in Brahman set the whole creation in motion. We know that life in this world cannot be sustained without desires. People will not engage in actions if they are not motivated by the desire to pursue Dharma, Artha, Kama, and Moksha. The Bhagavadgita suggests that instead of pursuing them to fulfill desires, one should pursue them due to devotion and obligation to God.

Since desires are responsible for bondage and suffering, at some stage in their progress, householders must give them up and work for their liberation. They must bring sannyasa into sacrifices without abdicating their duties, responsibilities, or chief aims. When we perform actions for action's sake, with God as our witness, support, and goal, we become free from the impurities of worldly life. It is hard for householders to overcome desires or avoid desire-ridden actions. Only a few wise ones succeed through sustained practice (abhyasa). Endowed with discernment (vicaksanah), they do not renounce actions but perform them selflessly without desires and expectations, offering their fruit to the Lord in devotion. They excel in tyaga and sannyasa.

Sloka 3

tyājyaṃ doṣavad ity eke karma prāhur manīṣiṇaḥ
yajñadānatapaḥkarma na tyājyam iti cāpare

tyajyam =should be given up; dosa-vat = as evil or faulty; iti = thus; eke = some; karma = actions; prahuh = said; manisinah = thinkers, wise ones; yajna = sacrifice; dana = charity; tapah = austerity; karma = actions; na = not; tyajyam = to be renounced; iti = thus; ca = and; apare = others.

Some wise ones say that actions should be given up as evil; others say that actions such as sacrifice, charity, and austerity should not be renounced.

This verse reflects two fundamental beliefs regarding renunciation. The first one holds that actions are faulty or evil since they lead to bondage and suffering. Hence, people should shun worldly actions and live passively like hermits or recluses, with their minds established in the Self. Ascetic traditions in ancient India followed this belief. The second school holds that while actions do lead to bondage and suffering, householders should not abandon their duties since the aims of Dharma do not intend the jivas to live passively and renounce actions. Their duties arise from their nature (svabhavam). They are meant to uphold the world and ensure its orderly progression. Hence, they should perform their duties and fulfill their obligation. The Mimansikas supported this view and advised people to engage in sacrificial duties as ordained by the Vedas. They believed that sacrifices, austerities, and charity were meant to grant people's wishes and help them attain the heavenly life, which they considered Moksha.

The Bhagavadgita makes a slight deviation from these contrasting approaches. It imparts a new meaning to the idea of renunciation, suggesting that true renunciation means renouncing desires, not actions. While we do not know whether the idea existed before the Mahabharata period, Lord Krishna's teachings might have contributed to its popularity. He has clarified that actions are neither good nor evil and do not produce karma by themselves. They become sinful or evil and produce karma due to desires. The desires in actions produce consequences for those who act upon them. Therefore, one should not renounce actions but desire-ridden actions or desires in actions only. This is especially true for householders who have a duty to God and Dharma. Desires produce karma and bind people when they are acted upon with the selfish intent to enjoy their fruit. Karma also arises if people renounce actions and neglect the duties and responsibilities they are supposed to perform according to their background. Hence, to escape from karma and samsara, one must abandon desires in actions and desire-ridden actions (kamya karmas) and perform the obligatory duties by sacrificing the fruit of such actions to God without desiring it. This advice is meant for householders, not for the ascetics or the knowers of the Self (atma-jnanis) who renounce worldly actions and pursue liberation, taking refuge in the Lord. However, they must also practice renunciation and sacrifice simultaneously, but under no circumstances renounce actions that are necessary for their practice or keeping themselves alive.

As we heard from Lord Krishna before, inaction is not a viable solution to the problem of karma. No one can remain inactive for long or achieve freedom from karma (naishkarmya siddhi) by avoiding actions. The organs in the body continue to function whether we are awake or asleep. The mind remains active even in sleep, dreaming, and resetting its memory. Breathing, blood circulation, and subtle energies continue to flow, and the autonomous nervous system remains active. The triple gunas also remain active. Therefore, inaction is not a solution for householders or renunciants. Instead, both should strive to achieve the ideal state of inaction in action by renouncing desire-driven actions and performing duties without expectations as an offering to God. The Bhagavadgita defines the renunciation of desires as true renunciation and the relinquishment of the fruit (the burnt offering) of actions as the true sacrifice (tyaga). Ideally, everyone should follow these principles, regardless of their paths.

Sloka 4

niścayaṃ śṛṇu me tatra tyāge bharatasattama
tyāgo hi puruṣavyāghra trividhaḥ saṃprakīrtitaḥ

niscayam = firm conclusion; srnu = hear; me = from Me; tatra = regarding that; tyage = renunciation; bharata-sat-tama = O best of the Bharatas; tyagah = sacrifice, giving up; hi = surely; purusa-vyaghra = O tiger among human beings; tri-vidhah = three kinds; samprakirtitah = is stated to be.

Hear from Me, My firm conclusion regarding that sacrifice, O Best of the Bharatas. Surely, O Tiger, among men, sacrifice is said to be of three kinds.

In this verse, Lord Krishna wanted Arjuna to hear from him the truth about sacrifices. Who can better speak about it with authority and certainty than the Lord himself, who is firmly established in the Supreme Reality and is the source of all knowledge, including the Vedas and Shastras? He conveyed it by saying, 'nischayam srunu me,' meaning 'hear My firm conclusion without doubt and confusion.' Previously, he distinguished the difference between renunciation (sannyasa) and sacrifice (tyaga), saying that renouncing desire-ridden actions or the desires in actions is renunciation and renouncing their fruit or result is sacrifice. This is an improvement over the traditional meaning of tyaga, which means giving away or offering sacrificial material to the deity.

In other words, renunciation means giving up desires, and sacrifice means giving up results, hopes, and expectations associated with actions and consecrating them to the Lord. When householders perform sacrifices without desires and without desiring their fruit, they earn the distinction of practicing both karma yoga and sannyasa yoga. By bringing renunciation and sacrifice into their practice of Dharma, they transcend their selfishness, egoism, and delusion and progress quickly towards samsiddhi (sameness), naishkarmya siddhi (freedom from karma), and liberation. In this approach, householders have an advantage over the hermits and ascetics, who renounce their obligatory duties (their Dharma) and retire to secluded places to practice self-control and austerities. They, too, will benefit if they observe their vows strictly and practice renunciation without desires, offering the fruit of their actions to the Lord without expectations.

In this verse, Lord Krishna said that the sacrifices were of three kinds. Sacrifices (yajnas) are of various kinds. We have Paka, Soma, and Havir yajnas. We have daily sacrifices, occasional sacrifices, and seasonal sacrifices. The Vedas divide them into obligatory, optional, and prohibited sacrifices. They are also divided according to the purpose, occasion, the deities worshipped, and the materials and mantras used. Therefore, we do not know which three types of sacrifices Lord Krishna had in mind. Most commentators believe he divided them according to the offering or sacrifice made. Madhavacharya identified them as giving up the fruit, ownership, and doership of actions. Ramanuja held them to be (1) sacrificing the fruit or result of actions, (2) sacrificing desires and attachments, knowing that the Self is not responsible for them, and (3) sacrificing the doership to the Lord, acknowledging him to be the doer in all actions. Shankara felt that it referred to the threefold abandonment (sattvic, rajasic, and tamasic), and by using the single word tyaga for both renunciation and sacrifice, the Lord implied that they meant the same.

Since the gunas are found in every aspect of creation, we may divide sacrifices into three kinds according to the mode in which they are performed and the type of offering made. Sacrifices are sattvic when performed by pure and selfless devotees, rajasic when performed with desires and passions without relinquishing doership and ownership, and tamasic when performed with ignorance and delusion, without faith, self-knowledge, discipline, or self-control. Sattvic sacrifices are rooted in purity and righteousness, rajasic sacrifices in egoism, passion, and delusion, and tamasic sacrifices in delusion, ignorance, and dark and demonic desires. One may also divide them depending on the nature of the offering. For example, when sattvic people offer the fruit of their obligatory duties to the Lord with exclusive devotion, it is a sattvic sacrifice. When worldly people devotedly offer the fruit of their desire-ridden actions to the Lord, it is a rajasic sacrifice. When tamasic people devotedly offer the fruit of their ignorant and deluded actions to the Lord, it is a tamasic sacrifice. Each of them leads to the worshippers' purification, although it may involve extra effort in the case of rajasic and tamasic people.

Sloka 5

yajñadānatapaḥkarma na tyājyaṃ kāryam eva tat
yajño dānaṃ tapaś caiva pāvanāni manīṣiṇām

yajna = sacrifice; dana = charity; tapah = austerity; karma = doing, practicing; na = not; tyajyam = given up; karyam = should be performed; eva = certainly; tat = that; yajnah = sacrifice; danam = charity; tapah = austerity; ca = and; eva = even; pavanani = purifiers; manisinam = for the wise.

Performance of sacrificial rituals, charity, (and) austerity should not be given up but certainly be performed. Sacrifice, charity, and austerity are surely purifiers for the wise.

Here, Lord Krishna extended the idea of renunciation and sacrifice to sacrifices, charity, and austerity, stating that the wise and discerning ones should not abandon them since they are purifiers, meaning they suppress rajas and tamas and all the impurities from them, resulting in the predominance of sattva. When sattva prevails, the mind becomes stable and pointed, intelligence shines, and exclusive devotion and equanimity become the natural states. Obligatory duties constitute Dharma. Traditionally, sacrificial rituals, charity, and austerity are considered obligatory for householders. They are obligated to perform them for their and others' welfare strictly according to the rules prescribed by the scriptures. Even ascetics have to perform austerities and pious actions without desires and stabilize their minds in contemplation and austere practices to attain stability and sameness.

Brahman is the source of the eternal Dharma humans must uphold on earth as their personal and collective obligation to the Lord of creation. If they protect and uphold it, it will uphold and protect them and the other jivas. Chaos and evil will prevail if they are neglected. In Hinduism, Dharma is the foremost pursuit (purusharthas) of human life, although many people are unaware of it due to ignorance. Dharma does not mean duty only. It also means morality, code of conduct, natural laws, religious and spiritual teachings, faith, truthfulness, righteousness, divine laws, etc. Actions meant to serve and uphold it on the righteous path and in harmony with the aims of creation are considered obligatory and constitute one's Dharma. They are ordained by God and contribute to our spiritual and material well-being. As the controller and preserver of the world, the Lord not only performs them without desires as his eternal duty to set an example, but also assigns them to the gods in the heavens and humans upon the earth as their duties to assist him in that task.

By the very design inherent in God's creation, performing obligatory duties selflessly by offering their fruit to the Lord as a sacrifice is a mark of devotion. It leads to peace and happiness for those who practice it and liberation for those who excel in it. The Vedas encourage people to perform their obligatory duties for the welfare of all. Because of them, we fulfill our chief aims, and gods receive nourishment from humans, gain strength and vigor, and perform their duties effectively. By upholding Dharma, householders ensure their spiritual growth, secure divine love, and qualify for liberation. Thus, pious householders have the moral and religious obligation to live responsibly, personifying the highest virtues and honoring the code of conduct established by the Lord. Performing sacrificial actions without desires ensures their spiritual growth and brings them closer to liberation.

Sloka 6

etāny api tu karmāṇi saṅgaṃ tyaktvā phalāni ca
kartavyānīti me pārtha niścitaṃ matam uttamam

etani = these; api = even; tu = however, but; karmani = actions; sangam = attachment; tyaktva = by renouncing, giving up; phalani = fruit, result; ca = and; kartavyani = to be performed; iti = thus; me = My; partha = O Partha; niscitam = firm conclusion, definite; matam = opinion; uttamam = the best.

However, even these actions should be performed by renouncing attachment and the fruit. O Partha, this is my firm conclusion and the best opinion.

Sacrifice does not mean giving up actions but giving up attachment to them and their fruit. The expression 'even these' refers to the three activities mentioned before as purifiers: sacrifice, charity, and austerity. They should not be renounced because they are obligatory and conducive to self-purification. However, attachment to them and desire for their results should be sacrificed. Actions alone are neither good nor bad and do not bind us to samsara. Attachment to them and the desire for their fruit are the problems. Hence, one should renounce them rather than actions. As this verse implies, sacrifice, austerity, and charity must not be abandoned. It is the sacred duty (kartavyam) of all householders to practice them as their obligatory duty in God's creation. They do not apply to ascetics and renunciants since they renounce worldly life. However, the principle does apply to them. They must perform their bodily-related actions and any austerity or charity without attachment and desiring their fruit. Whether a householder or a renunciant, the principles of sacrifice and renunciation apply to all. Sacrifice means giving up the desire for the fruit of one's actions. This is the essence of karma-sannyasa yoga, which is the ideal for everyone to overcome impurities and achieve mental stability and detachment.

Sloka 7

niyatasya tu saṃnyāsaḥ karmaṇo nopapadyate
mohāt tasya parityāgas tāmasaḥ parikīrtitaḥ

niyatasya = obligatory or assigned duties; tu = therefore; sannyasah = renunciation; karmanah = actions; na = not; apapadyate = is not justified; mohat = by delusion; tasya = of that; parityagah = giving up, renunciation; tamasah = tamas; parikirtitah = is declared.

Therefore, renunciation of obligatory actions is not justified. The giving up due to delusion is declared tamasic.

Householders should not renounce obligatory duties because the wise ones found through experience that they were purifiers and helpful in expediting liberation. Besides, they are obligatory for the householders. The Vedas prescribed them for the welfare of all, including gods, ancestors, and all living beings. Therefore, householders must perform them and take no chances. Even ascetics and renunciants should continue actions that are necessary to purify and maintain their bodies. They should uphold the sannyasa dharma ordained by their tradition or teachers, practicing austerities (tapah), observing vows, controlling their minds and bodies, and giving up desires, attachments, and the fruit of their actions. They require actions and should not be abandoned. In any case, giving up actions, thinking erroneously that one can escape from karma by abandoning them, is tamasic. Sometimes, people take up sannyasa to escape from duties and responsibilities and the suffering inherent in worldly life. It is also tamasic. Sannyasa is meant for liberation and to find a lasting solution to suffering. Taking up sannyasa to escape from the duties and burdens of life is sinful and counterproductive. No one can escape from suffering by avoiding suffering. One must either learn to endure it gracefully by developing an inner fortitude or achieve liberation by renouncing desires and taking refuge in the Lord. Human life is a rare opportunity for householders to purify themselves, clear their karmic debt, and escape from samsara. By performing their duties, they can discharge their debt to parents, family, elders, teachers, gods, ancestors, etc. They can also strengthen their faith, cultivate divine qualities, earn the Lord's grace, and qualify for liberation. Even ascetic people and recluses who renounce worldly life incur karmic debt due to their dependence upon others for nourishment. Therefore, they should not abandon actions or the practice of karma yoga and sannyasa.

Sloka 8

duḥkham ity eva yat karma kāyakleśabhayāt tyajet
sa kṛtvā rājasaṃ tyāgaṃ naiva tyāgaphalaṃ labhet

duhkham = painful; iti = thus; eva = merely; yat = whatever, which; karma = actions; kaya = bodily; klesa = suffering, affliction; bhayat = because of fear; tyajet = give up; sah = he; krtva = having done; rajasam = rajasic quality; tyagam = sacrifice; na = not; eva = certainly; tyaga = sacrifice; phalam = fruit; labhet = gain.

Whoever gives up any action, thinking that it is painful or fearing that it will cause bodily afflictions, having thus performed the sacrifice of a rajasic kind, will certainly not gain the fruit of sacrifice.

Tamasic people, driven by delusion, laziness, and lethargy, avoid their duties and difficult actions. For instance, they might procrastinate on important tasks or choose to sleep in instead of going to work. They mistakenly believe that they can escape from karma or find happiness by renouncing actions or doing nothing. Rajasic people, on the other hand, are motivated by desires and passions. They do what they like and avoid what they dislike. This leads them to choose the easy tasks that bring them pleasure and happiness and avoid the difficult ones that cause pain, discomfort, and suffering. They may engage in actions due to passions like lust, anger, pride, greed, or envy, and avoid them due to fear of failure, loss, criticism, or loss of reputation. In other words, they are driven mostly by desires and passions that are induced by rajas. Since they perform actions selectively due to desires and attachments, they do not attain a wholesome life or achieve happiness and fulfillment. They may achieve material success but may fail to achieve peace and tranquility or happiness and fulfillment here and hereafter. If tamasic people are driven by ignorance and delusion and prefer to avoid actions to remain inactive and lethargic or intoxicated, rajasic ones prefer to be active and perform actions to pursue worldly desires such as gaining wealth, strength, name, power, fame, merit (punya), etc. They reflect the same attitude in performing their obligatory duties, sacrifices, austerities, and charities, performing those that are convenient, profitable, or favorable and avoiding the rest. As a result, they may gain wealth and enjoyment from their desire-ridden actions but will not achieve purification or liberation.

Sloka 9

kāryam ity eva yat karma niyataṃ kriyaterjuna
saṅgaṃ tyaktvā phalaṃ caiva sa tyāgaḥ sāttvikomataḥ

karyam = obligatory duty; iti = thus; eva = verily; yat = whatever; karma = action, duty, work; niyatam = prescribed; kriyate = is performed; arjuna = O Arjuna; sangam = attachment; tyaktva = giving up; phalam = fruit, result; ca = and; eva = even; sah = that; tyagah = sacrifice; sattvikah = sattvic nature; matah = considered.

Whatever action is performed thus verily as an obligatory duty, O Arjuna, giving up attachment and even the fruit (of such actions), that sacrifice (tyaga) is considered sattvic in nature.

Performing actions carelessly or against the established rules (avidhi-purvakam) is tamasic. They produce sinful consequences, pain, and suffering. Avoiding actions because they are painful or produce suffering is rajasic. It does not bring any rewards but may lead to sinful consequences. When actions are performed as an obligatory duty to God, giving up desires and attachments, and without desiring their fruit, is sattvic. The same person may exhibit these three tendencies since most humans are a mixture of the triple gunas. Thus, when actions exemplify renunciation (sannyasa) and sacrifice (tyaga), it is sattvic. People with the predominance of sattva perform all actions as obligatory duties (niyata-karmas). They perform them dutifully according to the established norms without desires and attachments and offer them and their result to the Lord in devotion, service, and surrender and without expectations. Hence, every sattvic action becomes an offering to God and an act of renunciation, devotion, and true sacrifice. Thereby, they do not produce karma and lead to self-purification and liberation. Being free from desires and attachments, the wise ones endowed with sattva perform all actions as if they are obligatory and necessary for Dharma, even if they produce pain and suffering or cause them personal loss. Their happiness lies in serving the Lord and declaring their love, loyalty, and devotion through actions. Thus, abandoning the fruit of actions and attachments rather than the actions themselves to serve the Lord is sattvika. When actions are performed with the sattvic bhava, even kamya-karmas become niyata-karmas since they are performed without desires and expectations and offered to the Lord without expectations.

Sloka 10

na dveṣṭy akuśalaṃ karma kuśale nānuṣajjate
tyāgī sattvasamāviṣṭo medhāvī chinnasaṃśayaḥ

na = not; dvesti = hate; akusalam = evil, sinful, inauspicious; karma = actions; kusale = good, meritorious, auspicious; na = not anusajjate = becomes attached; tyagi = the person of sacrificial actions; sattva = the quality of sattva; samavistah = established in; medhavi = wise; chinna = cut off, cut asunder, dispelled; samsayah = doubts.

He neither hates evil actions nor becomes attached to good actions. The wise one, who, established in sattva, has given up (the fruit of actions) - his doubts are all cut off.

Sattvic individuals, the enlightened ones who perceive the Self, comprehend the true essence of renunciation (sannyasa) and sacrifice (tyaga). They execute actions without any personal desires, considering all actions as obligatory and a part of their Dharma. They perform these actions selflessly as if they are engaged in a lifelong sacrifice. They transcend ignorance about dharma (duty), karma (actions), and liberation (moksha) and nurture unwavering faith and devotion. By practicing self-control and overcoming attraction and aversion, they rise above the concepts of good and evil and the relative morals and values, becoming equal to both. They perform actions dutifully, whether they are proper or improper, evil or good, auspicious or inauspicious, as if they are under an obligation by the will of the Lord to live according to his wish. In contrast, tamasic individuals have strong likes and dislikes and distrust established procedures and scriptural norms. Rajasic individuals possess strong passions and desires and are attracted to worldly enjoyment. For the sattvic individuals, actions are neither desirable nor undesirable, neither good nor evil, but dutiful and obligatory. They do not avoid them since they are free from judgment, preference, and consideration. Instead, they perform them dutifully with sameness, devotion, and equanimity, without judgment and without desiring their fruit. Akusala karma refers to inauspicious or impure actions that lead to ignorance, bondage, and suffering. Kamya-karmas (desire-ridden actions) fall into this category. Kusala karma, on the other hand, denotes auspicious or pure actions that lead to health, happiness, cleanliness, perfection, progress, and liberation. Obligatory duties, ordained by the Vedas, are considered pure (kusala) and do not produce karma when performed without desires.

For those seeking liberation, it is crucial to renounce all judgments, preferences, and prejudices. They should strive to be equal to the dualities of life, including good and evil, as their ultimate goal is to transcend personal likes and dislikes and attain the highest yoga, which is oneness, sameness, or completeness. This 'sameness' does not imply being equal to heat and cold or pain and pleasure alone. The yukta should be equal to all dualities, including good and evil, and accept unconditionally whatever life offers without desires and expectations. It is living without choice, with the awareness that the Lord is in all and pervades all. If one is faced with a choice between duty and morality, duty should be chosen and performed, no matter how difficult or painful it may be. Despite the fact that wars cause destruction and violence, and violence is morally reprehensible, Lord Krishna advised Arjuna to fight because it was his obligatory duty as a warrior to uphold righteousness and manifest the Lord's will. Householders are encouraged to practice karma-sannyasa yoga for this reason. They are obligated to serve God through selfless service and accept everything as his manifestation. By cultivating the right knowledge and discernment and practicing karma-sannyasa, they must excel in true sacrifice (tyaga) by giving up desires and the fruit of their actions. True renunciation is the renunciation of desires; true sacrifice is giving up the fruit of one's actions. If they remember this and persist in karma sannyasa yoga, it will lead to their liberation. However, achieving perfection in karma-sannyasa or tyaga is not easy. It requires considerable effort to attain purity at all levels. It is possible only when one dissolves all impurities in the fire of knowledge, duty, and devotion, and the mind is firmly established in exclusive devotion to the Lord as one's Self, free from doubts and confusion.

Sloka 11

na hi dehabhṛtā śakyaṃ tyaktuṃ karmāṇy aśeṣataḥ
yas tu karmaphalatyāgī sa tyāgīty abhidhīyate

na = not; hi = surely; deha-bhrta = embodied one, who carries a body; sakyam = possible; tyaktum = to give up, renounce; karmani = actions; asesatah = all, completely; yah = who; tu = however, but; karma = actions; phala = fruit; tyagi = who renounces; sah = he; tyagi = sacrificer; iti = thus; abhidhiyate = is called.

Indeed, it is not possible for the embodied one to give up all actions completely. However, he who renounces the fruit of his actions is called a (true) sacrificer.

According to these teachings, you may renounce all your possessions, but if you do not renounce desires, it does not count as true renunciation (sannyasa). Similarly, if you do not give up the fruit of your actions, it does not count as a true sacrifice (tyaga). Renunciation ends in sacrifice when desireless actions culminate in the offering of their fruit (karma-phalam) to the Supreme Lord without expectations. Knowing these definitions and distinctions is essential to excel in karma-sannyasa yoga, which is the starting point of liberation for householders. It is why Lord Krishna advises his devotees to acquire knowledge and practice jnana karma-sannyasa yoga instead of just karma-sannyasa yoga. However, knowledge is not the only requirement. One must also practice buddhi yoga to sharpen the intellect and cultivate the right discernment.

Chaitanyam (liveliness), which is the chief characteristic of all life, itself means movement and activity. All organisms are subject to movement and activity. They cannot remain inactive for long. Even when they seem to be inactive, cellular activity keeps happening continuously in all living beings, including one-celled organisms. Much of this liveliness arises from the gunas. They propel the beings into actions, movements, and seeking things to survive by inducing desires. Repetitive actions to fulfill desires lead to attachments, habit formation, and the reinforcement of the gunas that induce them. In the process, the beings develop distaste or aversion for certain actions, things, and situations, resulting in unpleasant, painful, or negative emotions and reactions. Caught between attraction and aversion, the jivas become bound to samsara. This is more so in the case of humans. While our actions are responsible for our suffering and emotional instability, we cannot mitigate suffering by avoiding them. It is because the effort to avoid actions is also induced by the gunas and desires only.

Life has to be lived, however unpleasant it may be, but with an attitude of detachment and dispassion. Our scriptures clearly state that we cannot escape from karma by escaping from actions. Actions are necessary for our existence on Earth and the continuation of the world. The very process of living requires effort by those caught in the web of samsara. Even routine activities such as thinking, breathing, eating, walking, and sleeping are also karma only. They produce positive or negative consequences depending on how and with what attitude they are performed. Our minds and bodies are always active, even when we are asleep, and their actions, willful or otherwise, keep producing the fruit of karma and seeds of our future actions and births. One cannot, therefore, refrain from actions or physically renounce them. However, with effort, a devout householder devoted to the Lord and practicing Dharma can renounce the fruit of his actions and become a karmaphala tyagi. Only then does he become a true sannyasi and qualify for liberation.

Sloka 12

aniṣṭam iṣṭaṃ miśraṃ ca trividhaṃ karmaṇaḥ phalam
bhavaty atyāgināṃ pretya na tu saṃnyāsināṃ kvacit

anistam = unpleasant, dislike; istam = pleasant, like; misram = mixed; ca = and; tri-vidham = three kinds; karmanah = actions; phalam = result; bhavati = manifest, happens; atyaginam = those who do not give up the fruit of their action; pretya = after death; na = not; tu = but; sannyasinam = those who practice renunciation; kvacit = at all.

Unpleasant, pleasant, and mixed are the threefold fruit of actions manifest for those who do not renounce, but not at all for those who practice true renunciation.

Three types of results or consequences arise from actions: pleasant, unpleasant, and mixed. One may also call them enjoyable, painful, and mixed. Sattvic actions produce pleasant experiences; tamasic actions produce painful experiences; rajasic ones, mixed or partly positive and partly negative experiences. Through good actions, sattvic people attain the ancestral world, serve the gods, and live in their company. Upon returning, they attain a good birth in this world and find another opportunity to improve their lot. Tamasic people do not go to heaven or attain a good birth upon return because of their sinful and evil karma. When they die, they go to the underworld and experience pain and suffering. After a prolonged spell of suffering, they return to the earth and take birth in unfavorable circumstances to experience pain and suffering. Because of their karma, they continue their deluded ways until they reform and take refuge in the Lord. Rajasic people accumulate mixed karma due to their desire-ridden actions. Upon departing from here, they go to the ancestral world. However, when they return from there, they are reborn in mixed circumstances. Hence, the consequences arising from their actions are considered mixed.

These distinctions do not matter for those who practice true renunciation and sacrifice by giving up (tyaga) desire-ridden actions (kamya karmas) and the fruit of their obligatory duties (kusala karma). Since they perform actions selflessly or to serve the Lord, they attain naishkarmya siddhi (freedom from karma) and samatva siddhi (sameness). With their desires under control and the gunas neutralized, they endure life's hardships and remain undisturbed and absorbed in devotion and contemplation. In the end, they attain the highest, immortal world where neither pleasure nor pain exists, but only oneness and endless bliss.

In the supreme state of Brahman, or oneness, things are neither pleasant nor unpleasant. All the dualities and divisions dissolve into indistinguishable oneness. It is why the path to Brahman is through sameness or oneness only. Without overcoming dualities, one cannot absorb the mind in Brahman and experience the indistinguishable state of nonduality. Distinctions arise in our awareness because we are bound to the objective reality, which does not make sense without being the subject. The distinctions inherent to objective reality arise from our desires, thinking, and attitude, which are, in turn, influenced by our senses and our perceptual and cognitive experiences. So is the case with the results of our actions. Since actions have consequences, we may reap the rewards of our actions depending on our choices and desires. If we remove desire and attachment from our thinking, our minds become tranquil and stable. We cease to react and respond to external or internal events. As we are mentally detached from the world and our suffering ceases, we let things be as they are without the desire to change them, control them, or use them according to our desires and expectations. Hence, sattvic people who practice renunciation and sacrifice with the right attitude, giving up the desire for the fruit of their actions, attain the highest good. Seeing the same Lord in everyone as the Self of all, they abide in sameness and treat everything as his manifestation.

Sloka 13

pañcaitāni mahābāho kāraṇāni nibodha me
sāṃkhye kṛtānte proktāni siddhaye sarvakarmaṇām

panca = five; etani = these; maha-baho = O mighty-armed; karanani = causes; nibodha = know; me = from Me; sankhye = in the Samkhya; krta-ante = the end or culmination of actions; proktani = declared; siddhaye = reaching success, accomplishment, excellence; sarva = all; karmanam = actions.

Know from Me these five causes, O Maha Bahu, declared in the Samkhya for attaining the end of all actions.

Lord Krishna was about to explain to Arjuna the underlying causes of all actions, which would lead to the end of all actions. The end of any action is the result, which is pleasant, unpleasant, or mixed. For worldly people who engage in desire-ridden actions, the result is suffering. For the enlightened ones who transcend desires, the result is liberation or freedom from suffering. Many factors influence actions and their results. There is no guarantee of how they end. Hence, karma-sannyasa yoga is prescribed for humans to help them overcome the fear and anxiety arising from their actions and obligatory duties. In all the actions performed by the Jivas, the Lord remains as the witness Self, without participating in them or the causes responsible for them. In the next few verses, Lord Krishna will identify the factors or agents (kartas) responsible for actions (kriya) and the karma arising from them. In worldly life, desire-ridden actions lead to sinful karma and suffering. In spiritual practice, when actions are performed without desires, they lead to purity, knowledge, discernment, sameness, self-knowledge, liberation, etc. In spiritual actions, the highest end (siddhi) refers to sameness or oneness (samsiddhi). Lord Krishna wanted Arjuna to know the causes or agents responsible for attaining such perfect ends in actions.

In this verse, he addressed Arjuna as Maha Bahu, which means long-armed or mighty-armed. It is appropriate in this context since a warrior like Arjuna, an archer, performs his obligatory duties on the battlefield mainly with his hands. The Samkhya, which is mentioned here, refers to the classical philosophy that originally identified the agents of actions, namely the tattvas and forces of Nature. Many aspects of it found their way into other philosophies and scriptures, including the Upanishads and the Vedanta. Some commentators identify it as the Vedanta-Samkhya rather than the traditional Samkhya Darshana of Kapila. Whatever may be the truth, in this verse, Lord Krishna probably referred to a popular notion of his times, which dealt with the agents (kartas) that operated in the field of Prakriti, propelled beings into actions, and subjected them to karma. They are listed in the next verse.

Sloka 14

adhiṣṭhānaṃ tathā kartā karaṇaṃ ca pṛthagvidham
vividhāś ca pṛthakceṣṭā daivaṃ caivātra pañcamam

adhisthanam = the field, the body; tatha = and; karta = the doer, the ego; karanam = instruments, causative organs; ca = and; prthak-vidham = several kinds; vividhah = numerous; ca = and; prthak = several, various; cestah = actions, movements, effort, behavior; daivam = fate or providence; ca = and; eva = surely; atra = here; pancamam = five.

The Field, so also the doer, instruments of several kinds, actions which are numerous and of several kinds, and surely fate or providence is here the fifth...

The five agents or causes of actions are the (1) body, (2) the ego, (3) internal or external instruments of several kinds which the jivas use to perform various actions, (4) actions themselves, which are also numerous and of various kinds, and lastly (5) fate or providence. Adhistana means the seat of authority, dwelling, or the place where the Self is established and where life happens and actions take place when it is present. It refers to the physical body or the Field of Prakriti, which Lord Krishna previously described while distinguishing it from the Self. He said that the body is the Field (kshetra), and the Self is the owner or the knower of the field (Kshetrajna). The body of a living being is a small universe in itself. Without it, existence in the mortal world is not possible, and neither are all the actions and movements (chestas). It is where all desires and physical and mental activities manifest and where creation happens on a small scale. Hence, Lord Krishna mentioned it first to signify its importance.

Karta is the second. Karta means the doer. The ego (aham) assumes the doership in the body, although the Supreme Lord is the real doer, and all actions arise from him. However, in the body, as the Lord (Self), enjoyer, and witness, he does not directly participate in any actions. Instead, his shadow, the ego or the false self, a tattva of Nature, takes control of it as the doer and performs various desire-ridden actions. Even this happens due to His Maya only. Hence, even deluded actions arise from the Lord only, although the ego assumes doership. In Shaivism, the ego is considered one of the triple impurities of Nature. The other two are attachments (pasa) and delusion (moha). Collective, they cause the bondage of jivas. Delusion means mistaking the ego-self as the Self. It arises due to ignorance and is chiefly responsible for the suffering and bondage of the jivas in the mortal world.

Karanas are the causative instruments or organs in the body performing actions of various kinds. They also refer to the tools used in sacrifices to perform actions, such as the sacrificial fire, coals, cooking pots, pans, ladles, water, milk, spoons, bricks, wood, sacrificial altars, axes, ropes, kusa grass, etc. All karanas (instruments) are made from Nature's materials (drayvyas). They are internal to the body and responsible for perception and cognition. They are collectively known as the internal organ (antahkarana), consisting of the five organs of action (karmendriyas), the five organs of perception (jnanendriyas), the mind (manas), and the intellect (buddhi). It is responsible for sentience, memorial knowledge, intelligence, and self-awareness. We are not mentioning here other organs, such as the limbs or the digestive organs, since they are already accounted for as body parts (adhistana). Cestas refer to various actions, behaviors, and movements the jivas perform to survive or fulfill their desires. Daivam refers to the fate or providence (adhidaivika). It includes acts of God and spontaneous or unexpected events that happen due to chance or divine will without human intervention.

Sloka 15

śarīravāṅmanobhir yat karma prārabhate naraḥ
nyāyyaṃ vā viparītaṃ vā pañcaite tasya hetavaḥ

sarira = body; vak = speech; mana = mind; abhih = and with; yat = whatever; karma = action; prarabhate = performs; narah = a human being; nyayyam = lawful, just, right; va = or; viparitam = opposite, perverse; va = or; panca = five; ete = these; tasya = of it; hetavah = causes.

Whatever action a person performs with the body, speech, and mind, whether lawful or the opposite, these five are its causes.

The five causes of any action, whether just or unjust, right or wrong, are the body, the doer, various organs, various types of efforts, and fate or providence. They are said to be the agents that propel beings into action. They all belong to the domain of Prakriti only. The Lord is the ultimate cause because Prakriti is an integral and essential aspect of him. The five causes work through three agents: the body, speech, and mind, and the actions they induce through them are either lawful or unlawful. Lawful actions are righteous or ethically correct and approved by the Lord or the law books. Unlawful actions are those that are unethical, harmful, or evil and prohibited by the scriptures or the Lord. The fruit of karma from the five agents is also expressed or experienced through them. Actions arising from the body are physical actions such as eating, sleeping, walking, etc. They are perceptible to the mind and senses. Bodily actions such as digestion or the flow of prana through the nerve channels (nadis) may not be visible, but they are physical actions nonetheless. Actions that arise from the mind are different. They are subtle and remain hidden unless expressed through speech or physical actions. Those arising from speech fall in between the two. They have a physical aspect that manifests as sounds and a subtle aspect that remains hidden in the mind in thought form or a subtle current. Physically, the source of speech is in the throat. The mind, intelligence, senses, and some organs in the body also participate in the formation of speech.

However, according to the Vedic scriptures, speech is divine in origin. Both the gods and humans possess the power of speech. Brahman himself is said to have gifted it so that through speech and sacrifices, we can invoke gods, communicate with them, and nourish them by offering food. It manifests in us primarily due to the divinities presiding over the organs in our bodies. They help us perform our obligatory duties and communicate with others, ensuring the order and regularity of the world and the welfare of all. Speech and related actions differ from the actions of the body and mind in that they extend our reach beyond our bodies and physical reach, carrying our thoughts, prayers, desires, and aspirations as sounds through space to the worlds beyond and the Lord of the sacrifice himself. The scriptures constitute sacred speech. They give us the power to manifest our thoughts and desires through the sacred chants and the sounds hidden in them. Speech connects us to the world, other people, gods, and ancestors, and helps us participate in God's eternal play. Hence, due to its connecting ability, speech is considered more powerful than the abilities we have in the physical realm. Since sounds can travel through space and manifest things, the Vedas greatly emphasize correct pronunciation and usage of the right mantras in pursuing Dharma, Artha, Kama, and Moksha, and performing sacrifices and obligatory duties. Speech also produces the fruit of karma. Speech can be used for good and evil purposes since, as the Chandogya Upanishad (1.2.3) declares, it can be pierced by the evil of selfishness and used for harmful purposes, such as cheating, lying, hurting, etc. Hence, the Dharma Shastras emphasize the importance of right speech or ethical speech, which is nonviolent, truthful, selfless, and free from lust, anger, pride, greed, envy, etc.

Sloka 16

tatraivaṃ sati kartāram ātmānaṃ kevalaṃ tu yaḥ
paśyaty akṛtabuddhitvān na sa paśyati durmatiḥ

tatra = that; evam = so; sati = being; kartaram = doer, the cause; atmanam = the self; kevalam = alone; tu = but; yah = who; pasyati = sees; akrta-buddhitvat = due to perverted intelligence; na = not; sah = he; pasyati = sees; durmatih = of foolish mind or ignorant mind.

That being the case, whoever sees, due to perverted intelligence, the Self alone as the doer or the cause, he of such an ignorant mind, does not see.

Understanding that actions arise from the five causes in the Field of Prakriti, not from the Lord (Self) or the person in the body, is a crucial realization. To believe that actions stem from oneself is a misconception, a sign of ignorance, and a distortion of intelligence (akrta-buddhi). Those who are deluded due to indiscriminate intelligence identify themselves with their minds and bodies (the five causes) and consider themselves the agents of their actions. Lacking scriptural knowledge or the guidance of an enlightened master, they assume ownership and doership and think, "I have done this. I have achieved that." They fail to recognize their distinctness from their physical personalities and the fact that actions arise from the latter but not from them. Believing they are the kartas or agents of all actions, they accumulate karma and become accountable for them. In contrast, the wise ones understand the true causes of actions. They know that actions arise in the Field of Prakriti, and they are not in it, and they should not become entangled with them or with the world and prolong their suffering. Therefore, they dutifully perform actions, renouncing ownership and doership of their actions and their fruit. By practicing true renunciation (sannyasa) and sacrifice (tyaga) by giving up desires in actions and the fruit of such actions, they remain untainted by them. Taking refuge in the Lord, who is the Self in the body, and practicing self-control, discernment, and exclusive devotion, they remain detached from all actions, happenings, and movements in it and escape from samsara, leading to self-realization.

Sloka 17

yasya nāhaṃkṛto bhāvo buddhir yasya na lipyate
hatvā.api sa imāṃl lokān na hanti na nibadhyate

yasya = he who; na = not; ahankrtah = egoism; bhavah = state, thoughts, feelings; buddhih = intelligence; yasya = whose; na = not; lipyate = attached, involved, affected; hatva api = even killing; sah = he; iman = this; lokan = people, humankind; na = not; hanti = killing; na = not; nibadhyate = is bound.

He who does not have egoistic thoughts, whose intelligence is not attached, even if he kills people, he does not kill and is not bound.

He who is free from the egoistic thoughts of "Me" and "Mine" or doership and ownership, whose intelligence is not attached to likes and dislikes, that yogi of excellent attitude does not engage in actions even if he engages in them, and is not bound by them. In other words, those who truthfully engage in karma-sannyasa yoga do not produce karma by their actions. Thereby, they become free from the cycle of births and deaths. 'Ahamkara bhava' means having the egoistic notion or the sense of being a distinct entity, which makes one mistake the physical self for the real Lord and develop the notions of individuality, self-importance, and attachment to name and form. How can one be free from egoism? It is through the power of self-purification, through study and knowing the truths of oneself. Ego (aham) is a Prakriti tattva, which is present in all embodied beings and manifests as the longing for life, identity, individuality, and continuity. It is essential for one's existence and self-preservation in the mortal world. However, excessive egoism is a demonic or asuric quality. Asuras, the evil ones, act under its powerful influence and engage in acts of wickedness.

Egoism makes you think and act as if you are an individual entity, different and distinct from the rest of the world, and solely on your own. It is also known as anavatva (atomicity). It makes you rely upon yourself and your resources and build walls of defenses around yourself to control your life, destiny, and well-being, and ensure your continuity. Under its influence, the bound jiva cannot easily relinquish ownership and doership, cultivate devotion to the Self or the Lord in the body, or surrender to the divine will. Identification with name and form or the physical self leads to desire-ridden actions, selfishness, ownership, attachments, and delusion. Ahamkara does not produce feelings of pride (abhimana) only, although it is one of its manifestations. It manifests in various ways as the desire to extend itself into material things and possess them to enjoy, own, or control them. It exists in all the sentient beings of the earth who are endowed with intelligence or self-sense. At the physical or mental level, the very beingness or individuality of those jivas who possess intelligence produces the feeling of 'I am' and compels them to engage in self-preservation and propagation. It becomes weak or strong to the extent one is pure or impure. Only the highest gods, such as Indra, Rudra, or Vishnu, in their purest aspect, are free from it from the beginning of their manifestation. Others are born with it. They must subdue it through practice to achieve liberation.

The second quality mentioned here is unattached intelligence, which is free from attraction and aversion or likes and dislikes. When bound to worldly objects, it cannot discern truths, being tainted by desires and attachments. Without discernment or pure intelligence, one cannot perceive the true Self or distinguish it from the false self or the ego. To be free from delusion and egoism or desire and attachments, one has to purify intelligence by cultivating sattva. When intelligence is pure, the Self shines in its self-illuminating brilliance and becomes self-evident. Intelligence is the highest aspect of Prakriti. It is the bridge between the body and the Self that leads to transcendence. It is where the light and bliss of the Self are cognized in deeper states of self-absorption. A yogi of pure intelligence, whose ego is subdued, discerns the truths of himself with impeccable clarity. Knowing that he is pure consciousness distinct from his body, he cultivates detachment and dispassion (vairagya) and abides in the pure Self. Practicing self-control and exclusive devotion, he becomes an adept (yukta) in karma-sannyasa. He performs actions without desiring their fruit and arrests the flow of karma. Thereby, even if he indulges in actions, he remains untainted.

Sloka 18

jñānaṃ jñeyaṃ parijñātā trividhā karmacodanā
karaṇaṃ karma karteti trividhaḥ karmasaṃgrahaḥ

jnanam = knowledge; jneyam = object of knowledge, the knowable; parijnata = the knower; tri-vidha = three kinds, threefold; karma = action; codana = inducement, impetus; karanam = the cause; karma = the fruit of action; karta = the doer; iti = thus; tri-vidhah = three types; karma = work; sangrahah = components, collection.

Knowledge, the knowable or the object of knowledge, and the doer are the threefold inducements to actions. The cause of inducement, the fruit of action, and the doer are the threefold components of actions.

This verse explains the mechanism of actions and how they arise and are executed. The first part explains the impulse or the impetus behind actions (karanachodana), and the second part explains the process (karana samgraha) that leads to its completion. In every action, we find three basic factors that lead to its fruition or completion: (1) the knowledge that an action can be performed in certain ways to reach the intended object, thing, or goal, (2) the goal or object that is knowable or attainable due to a known or perceived cause, desire, or purpose, and (3) the doer or the actor who has to pursue the goal to fulfill its purpose or intent. You may call them the impelling agents of any action. Without them, actions and the need to perform them will not arise. This is the phase where desires, intentions, or aspirations arise. In yogis who have renounced worldly desires and conquered their minds and bodies, karanachodana arises from the Lord's will only since all the inducements (desires) to perform them willfully and the five causes mentioned before (verse 14) remain subdued and exert no influence. The organs participate in actions but without desires.

Knowledge, a cornerstone of the spiritual journey, refers to the awareness that some desirable object exists within or without. We seek things we know through perception, inference (drawn from the knowledge of others or circumstantial evidence), or conjecture. This knowledge may arise from studying scriptures, learning from others, observation, or experience. For instance, the knowledge of the Self prompts aspirants to seek liberation to escape from suffering and bondage. It is only when we are aware of something's existence that we begin to contemplate attaining it. Thus, knowledge of the object or goal is the first inducement to action. Our knowledge of the world and things primarily comes through our senses. However, the knowledge of metaphysical truths and transcendental states arises from studying scriptures or knowing from enlightened masters. It may manifest in great souls (mahatmas) due to the merit (punya) accumulated in past lives. In some cases, negative inducements may arise to prevent people from performing actions and attaining the right knowledge.

The knowledge we gain thus should also help us know what we should or should not do or how we may do it correctly according to the established norms (vidhi). Without that knowledge, actions may produce unintended consequences. Once we know that something exists and feel the desire or purpose to attain it, and once we ascertain the right knowledge and methods to succeed, we begin to think about how to reach it and what resources and actions are needed. Thus, the object of knowledge, meaning the knowable, attainable, or enjoyable goal or purpose, is the second inducement to action. Knowledge of the object and the object itself is useless unless a willful agent acts to obtain it. This is where the doer, the third inducement, comes into play. The doer uses his knowledge to perform actions and attain the knowable goal or object. Thus, to put it simply, to perform any action, first, you must know or be aware that something desirable exists. Second, you must know that it exists in reality and is knowable, attainable, or within your reach. Third, the agent or the karta (you) must be present at the right time and place to perform a suitable action to attain it. This is the usual process in which humans perform actions to fulfill their desires or attain desired goals. However, when devotees surrender to the Supreme Lord and practice exclusive devotion, the Lord becomes the doer (karta) and inducer of all actions and takes care of their welfare.

As we gleaned from verses 14-15, all actions stem from the five causes, such as the body, the organs, etc., and are categorized into three types (those of the body, the mind, and speech). Karma-chodana is the initial stage where the idea of the action takes shape as an intention, desire, or expectation. Karma samgraha refers to the process or the execution of action where different components converge and act in harmony. The three components of any action that lead to its fruition are the organs that act as the cause, the fruit of the action or the end of it, and the doer who performs it. The organs may be one or more of the tattvas, such as the organs of action, perception, or the internal organ (antahkarana). The fruit of karma, or the end of action, is the reason to perform or achieve it. Lord Krishna classified them in verse 12 as pleasant, unpleasant, and mixed. The organs are, in turn, influenced by the triple gunas. The doer (karta) is the one who engages in actions to attain the desired ends induced by the triple impellers. Thus, actions come to fruition when the three components (samgraha) are present. These triple inducements and triple components of karma apply to both desire-ridden (kamya-karmas) and desireless actions (nishkama-karma)—the desire-ridden actions lead to bondage, and the other to liberation.

Sloka 19

jñānaṃ karma ca kartā ca tridhaiva guṇabhedataḥ
procyate guṇasaṃkhyāne yathāvac chṛṇu tāny api

jnanam = knowledge; karma = action; ca = and; karta = doer; ca = and; tridha = threefold, three kinds; eva = only; guna-bhedatah = because of the differentiation of the gunas; procyate = declared said; guna-sankhyane = in the teaching about the gunas; yatha-vat = exacts or truthfully as they are; srnu = hear; tani = about them; api = also, and.

Knowledge, action, and the doer are declared to be of three kinds in the teachings concerning the gunas due to the distinction of the gunas. Hear about them also exactly as they are.

Now, Lord Krishna is going to explain how knowledge, actions, and doers are of three kinds due to the influence of the triple gunas. As he stated, this teaching is drawn from the Samkhya, which may be a reference to the original Samkhya Darshana of Kapila or the theistic Vedanta Samkhya, which was subsequently derived from it. The three gunas are present in all material things. They are responsible for the distinct effects they produce in the Field of Prakriti. Diversity manifests in creation because of them. Because of them, we experience different emotions, feelings, and physical and mental states. Knowledge, actions, and the beings or agents (kartas) are no exception. Their influence manifests in them also, whereby each of them can be divided into pure, impure, and mixed. The gunas are responsible for all actions and modifications in Prakriti. Sattva is responsible for purity, light, and stability; rajas for passions, emotions, and liveliness or vitality; and tamas induces darkness, inertia, and extremity. Thus, the permutations and combinations of the triple gunas make the diversity of Nature (prakriti vaividhyam) possible. Nature goes into a dormant or withdrawal phase, and all actions and movements enter a restful mode when they remain in equilibrium. All the activity and dynamism arise when they are in disequilibrium and compete with each other for their predominance.

Sloka 20

sarvabhūteṣu yenaikaṃ bhāvam avyayam īkṣate
avibhaktaṃ vibhakteṣu taj jñānaṃ viddhi sāttvikam

sarva-bhutesu = in all living being; yena = by which; ekam = one; bhavam = being, state, condition; avyayam = inexhaustible; iksate = one sees; avibhaktam = undifferentiated, indivisible; vibhaktesu = differentiated, divisible, ; tat = that; jnanam = knowledge; viddhi = know; sattvikam = of the nature of sattva.

Know that knowledge to be of the nature of sattva by which one perceives the inexhaustible state of oneness in all living beings, the undifferentiated in the differentiated.

The supreme reality of Brahman does not change from one being to another, from one place to another, or from one object to another object. It is the same everywhere, even if the objects are different and possess different properties and characteristics. From the highest unmanifested (avyakta) state to all the manifested (vyakta) states, it remains immutable, imperishable, and indivisible. The changes arise from Prakriti, not from Purusha. The verse refutes the idea that the Self, who is the Lord in the body, changes according to the size and form of beings, a belief supported by Jains and Vaisheshikas. It also leads to the conclusion that the Self (the Lord) is different from the Jiva and has no physical relationship with it. The Self and the Jiva represent distinct realities. This knowledge or realization helps the yogis see the eternal truth of the indivisible and inexhaustible Self who dwells in all living beings as their embodied Self. Although beings appear to be different and distinct, the Self that resides in them all is the same. Through him, they represent the unity or oneness of the Cosmic reality. This knowledge, which is real and liberating, arises from the mode of sattva only. When the mind and body are pure, and consciousness is filled with sattva, yogis perceive the Self as the all-pervading, eternal Lord. Seeing the same, undifferentiated reality within themselves, they attain supreme knowledge and bliss. They enter that pure, undifferentiated, eternal, and infinite oneness, dissolving their divided and differentiated consciousness. The state of oneness (ekabhavam) or unity in diversity arises when beings (karta) and their actions (karma) are also pure and illumined by sattva. It does not manifest if the other two gunas are active or if any impurities are present. When intelligence is imbued with the predominance of sattva, the yukta (an adept yogi) becomes aware of the Self as the Lord himself. In that unified state of oneness, he sees himself in all and all in himself. He overcomes desires, duality, and delusion and discerns the presence of the universal Lord as the all-pervading, absolute reality, hidden in every aspect of creation but different from it. Sattvic knowledge opens our eyes to the supreme reality of Brahman and the impermanence of things. It is attained through self-purification and the practice of virtues such as truthfulness, non-injury, non-covetousness, etc.

Sloka 21

pṛthaktvena tu yaj jñānaṃ nānābhāvān pṛthagvidhān
vetti sarveṣu bhūteṣu taj jñānaṃ viddhi rājasam

prthaktvena = by separateness, distinction; tu = but; yat = which; jnanam = knowledge; nana-bhavan = numerous entities, states; prthak-vidhan = of different kinds; vetti = perceives; sarvesu = in all; bhutesu = living beings; tat = that; jnanam = knowledge; viddhi = know; rajasam = rajasic in nature.

But know that knowledge to be of the rajasic nature, which, because of separateness, perceives all beings as numerous entities of various kinds.

Sattvic knowledge helps us see the hidden reality beyond the appearance of things. When intelligence is pure, the mind becomes stable and enters the pure state of sameness (samsiddhi), where one can discern truths without distortions, free from attraction and aversion or likes and dislikes. With rajas, it is difficult to stabilize the mind or practice self-control. The mind filled with rajasic knowledge sees only the superficial reality and accepts its apparent diversity and division as real. When you focus on names and forms and accept them for real, you will see only their diversity and seek them according to your desires and passions. In other words, rajasic knowledge does not introduce us to transcendental truths or the reality of Brahman, who is one, indivisible, eternal, and immutable. Hence, rajasic people have a confused understanding of the Self, reality, God, and themselves. Despite their lack of knowledge, they believe that they are justified in their beliefs and actions. They mistake the jiva as the doer and thereby do not relinquish the fruit of their actions.

Thus, the mode of rajas strengthens duality, division, passions, individuality, egoism, desires, and delusion. It induces worldliness and delusion, making people mistake the apparent reality as real and perceive things as desirable or undesirable. Reinforcing such mistaken notions with deluded arguments (mayavada), they engage in desire-ridden actions according to their likes and dislikes. Under its influence, they may also perceive the Self as different in different beings, mistake the physical self as the real self, or not acknowledge the existence of the Self at all. Since they are drawn to materiality and the enjoyment of worldly pleasures, they do not experience exclusive devotion but devotion that is tinged with desires, egoism, and selfishness. Therefore, they may worship the Lord or his different forms, but do not relinquish their desires, attachments, or passion for worldly enjoyment. They may perform sacrificial duties, but with selfish intentions to impress others or fulfill their desires. Rajas and tamas are the predominant modes of today's world. Therefore, these behaviors are common.

Sloka 22

yat tu kṛtsnavad ekasmin kārye saktam ahetukam
atattvārthavad alpaṃ ca tat tāmasam udāhṛtam

yat = which; tu = but; krtsna-vat = as if it were all; ekasmin = in one; karye = in action; saktam = occupied with, interested, attached, interested, attached; ahaitukam = without reason, irrational; atattva-artha-vat = without grounded in reality; alpam = insignificant. little, small; ca = and; tat = that knowledge; tamasam = tamasic in nature; udahrtam = is said to be.

But that knowledge is said to be of the nature of tamas, which is attached to one action only as if it were all, which is irrational, impractical (or unrealistic), and insignificant.

Tamasic people are delusional, irrational, impractical, and unrealistic. Hence, they resort to extreme and unreasonable behavior and perform actions with stubborn resolve according to their convoluted thinking. They are also prone to binary or polarized thinking and acknowledge only those truths or falsehoods that fit into their constricted worldview. They refuse to acknowledge anything that does not agree with them or make sense to them. Hence, they cannot easily be persuaded or dissuaded from their imprudent actions. They bring the same attitude into their relationship with God, the world, and others. Their choices are driven by their constricted thinking and limited knowledge. They are also fickle, do not stick to a particular viewpoint or approach, and act impulsively and unpredictably according to their convenience or intentions. Since they see the world in terms of polarities and extremities, they cling to their points of view as if it were all and other possibilities or alternatives do not exist. For example, they may argue that what is true for one Jiva or entity is true for all or that what holds in a particular instance is universally true. Because of such polarized thinking, troublesome attitudes, rigid thought patterns, and antisocial behavior, which often verges on self-destructive, they do not get along well with others and end up being hostile or troublesome. Since they are close-minded, they are also easily baffled by the unknown, unfamiliar, ambiguous, or uncertain truths and situations.

These attitudes are also reflected in their religious practice. For example, in performing sacrifices and austerities, they may focus on nonessential or nonsensical aspects and ignore the important ones. They may focus on fulfilling their desires, as if it is the most important thing, and ignore the importance of renunciation, sacrifice, duty, discipline, procedure, cleanliness, self-control, etc. In their eagerness to obtain quick results, they may resort to unconventional methods and shortcuts or devious practices prohibited by the scriptures or the tradition. They may practice Dharma selectively, according to their convenience, ignoring the obligatory duties and performing those that are optional or avoidable. In sacrifices, they may focus on their expectations rather than making the offering or giving up selfishness. In spiritual practice, they may focus on particular restraints, ignoring the rest, as if it is sufficient to attain desired results and acquire spiritual powers. In practicing austerities and penances, they may exclusively focus on extreme and painful methods as if that is all. Since they do not study the scriptures, possess the right knowledge, or pay adequate attention to the truths they validate, their actions produce pain and suffering and do not lead to peace and tranquility. Usually, wherever they are, chaos, confusion, controversy, and disorder prevail.

Sloka 23

niyataṃ saṅgarahitam arāgadveṣataḥ kṛtam
aphalaprepsunā karma yat tat sāttvikam ucyate

niyatam = obligatory; sanga-rahitam = without attachment; araga-dvesatah = without attraction or aversion; krtam = performed, done; aphala-prepsuna = one who does not seek the fruit; karma = actions; yat = which; tat = that; sattvikam = sattvic in nature; ucyate = is called.

That action is said to be sattvic in nature, which is obligatory, performed without attachment, without attraction or aversion, by one who does not seek its fruit.

Sattvic people perform their duties and actions without desires, attachments, likes, and dislikes. They perform them dispassionately and devotedly without desiring their fruit. Since they possess the right knowledge and discernment, they know the distinction between the physical self and the eternal Self and between that which is eternally true (Sat) and that which is its temporary projection (asat) or between reality and illusion. Knowing that the same Self is the Lord and is the source of all and that the mind and body, or Prakriti, perform all actions, they renounce doership and ownership and exemplify the virtue of inaction in action. Hence, their actions do not bind or taint them but lead to liberation and oneness.

The gunas, which influence our actions, also influence our knowledge and essential nature through the same desires. Just as our knowledge can be pure, impure, or mixed, our actions also fall into these categories based on the gunas and the desires they induce. It is our human nature to perform actions to fulfill desires or achieve specific goals. However, the scriptures advise those seeking liberation to perform actions selflessly, renouncing desires and the desire for the outcome. The nature of the jivas is dynamic and remains in flux, driving them into seeking and striving. This dynamism and essential nature arise from the gunas and vary based on their predominance. The ability to perform actions consciously and intelligently is a blessing, but it also poses a trap set by Nature to keep the jivas in bondage, inducing egoism, desires, and delusion. When we detach desires from actions, actions become the means to our liberation. We succeed in this endeavor when our actions arise from sattva rather than rajas and tamas.

In sattvic actions, the motivation to perform actions for selfish causes is either suppressed, weak, or absent. According to the rules prescribed in the revelatory scriptures, actions should be performed with sameness, free from dualities, as an obligatory duty or service to the Supreme Lord. Only those who perform sattvic actions can become Bhagavatas, the true servants of the Lord. They dedicate their lives to his service with exclusive devotion and earn his grace. Since they surrender their will and consecrate their actions to him with devotion as an act of sacrifice or renunciation, he becomes their doer and takes responsibility for them. As they exemplify renunciation (sannyasa) and sacrifice (tyaga), their actions do not produce karma, and even if it does, it is neutralized by the Lord himself. Actions of this kind, arising from sattva, promote Dharma and the welfare of the world. They also lead to peace, happiness, knowledge, and liberation.

Sloka 24

yat tu kāmepsunā karma sāhaṃkāreṇa vā punaḥ
kriyate bahulāyāsaṃ tad rājasam udāhṛtam

yat = that which; tu = but; kama-ipsuna = desire for the result; karma = action; sa-ahankarena = with egoism; va = or; punah = again; kriyate = performed; bahula-ayasam = with strenuous effort; tat = that; rajasam = rajasic in nature; udahrtam = is said to be.

But that action is said to be rajasic in nature, which is performed with the desire for the result, with egoism, and again with strenuous effort.

Rajasic mode does not let you see the unity or universality of the pure Self. Rajasic people acknowledge the diversity of creation but not its underlying unity. They see all living beings as different entities with different souls or soul-nature and consciousness. For them, the Self represents the beingness or the essential nature of each jiva, but not its eternal, indestructible, and unchanging pure consciousness. They see the physical aspect of the jivas, their names, and forms, but not their spiritual aspect. In their worldview, each being is a separate entity and must live by its own rules, actions, and intelligence. They attribute the same beliefs personally and see themselves in competition with others for survival and living at the mercy of Nature, chance, fate, or their self-effort and intelligence.

This attitude or way of looking at life makes them vulnerable to delusion, egoism, selfishness, desires, passions, and restlessness. Hence, actions arising from the rajasic mode characterize selfishness, egoism, and eagerness to secure and enjoy their fruit. Those under its influence are prone to worldliness and materialism. Rajasic mode also makes beings think and act selfishly and aggressively and seek things through egoistic striving and strenuous effort (bahula ayasam), often disregarding the moral consequences arising from them, scriptural injunctions, or others' welfare.

Since actions are performed with pride or vanity, with an end in mind and desire for their fruit, rajasic people seldom experience peace, mental stability, or pure devotion. Since they see themselves as separate entities and their faith falters, they feel insecure and vulnerable to external threats. It also makes it difficult for them to give up seeking and striving and stabilize their minds in exclusive devotion with unwavering faith. Their faith remains unstable with endless desires and attachments, just as their minds do. They may worship one God or numerous, mainly to secure their lives or fulfill their desires. While their actions may yield them the rewards of a good life and worldly enjoyment, they do not lead them toward liberation or freedom from bondage, pain, and suffering. As they assume ownership and doership of their actions, they become prisoners of their karma.

Rajasic mode is cherished and promoted in the materialistic world, which values merit-based reward systems or excellence in individual effort. The progress of the world greatly depends upon those who act under its influence and exemplify distinction in personal success. While they are effective in manifesting their desires and intentions, from a spiritual perspective, they become enemies of themselves and the eternal Dharma of God. Ultimately, communities that thrive on rajasic values of success and achievement experience instability and disruptions due to increasing inequalities and conflicts fueled by greed, envy, and corruption.

Sloka 25

anubandhaṃ kṣayaṃ hiṃsām anapekṣya ca pauruṣam
mohād ārabhyate karma yat tat tāmasam ucyate

anubandham = relationship, bondage; ksayam = loss, destruction; himsam = violence, injury, pain; anapeksya = without consideration; ca = and; paurusam = ability, capacity; mohat = delusion; arabhyate = undertaken; karma = action; yat = which; tat = that; tamasam = tamas; ucyate = said to be.

That action is said to be of tamasic mode, which is undertaken out of delusion without the consideration for relationship, loss, violence or injury, and ability.

Actions create their ripples in the world and probably in the higher worlds. They affect our lives and the lives of others and may even change the course of the world, our transmigration, or future generations. We do not live in isolation. Our actions do not affect us alone. They touch others with whom we may or may not interact, since we are all interconnected through various visible and invisible relationships. The same Self residing in all as the Lord also connects us to the rest of creation. Hence, whether we are aware or not, we are always connected to others, and our thoughts and actions produce ripples in the waters of life, bringing joy or suffering through them to the multitude of beings with whom we share this world and existence. We are, therefore, ordained by the scriptures to live responsibly, performing our obligatory duties and ensuring that we do not disturb others or disrupt the natural order of things. In one of the previous chapters, Lord Krishna stated that he who does not disturb others or is not disturbed by them is dearest to him. The same principle applies here also. Those who violate it are considered the enemies of God. They do so because of the mode of tamas.

Tamasic people live under the delusion that the world is created for them and that they only matter, and others do not. Hence, they perform actions ignoring how they affect others and how they will eventually backfire and hurt them. In pursuing goals and performing actions, they work with a single-track mind and excessive zeal, ignoring reality, their limitations, well-being, and the moral or social implications. Since they are narrow-minded and possess a very constricted and lopsided view of the world, they stick to their rigid opinions and extreme methods, ignoring other possibilities and rational choices. Due to the same factors, they are frequently prone to engage in irrational exuberance and extreme or reckless exertion in their actions, ignoring the important tasks, rules, and restraints and spending their energies on unimportant or irrelevant ones without considering how they may affect others, impair relationships, cause loss, harm, or injury, or produce unintended consequences. Hence, they seldom succeed in their actions, reaching goals or fulfilling their desires without resorting to shortcuts and unjust and evil methods.

Sloka 26

muktasaṅgonahaṃvādī dhṛtyutsāhasamanvitaḥ
siddhyasiddhyor nirvikāraḥ kartā sāttvika ucyate

mukta-sangah = free from attachment; anaham-vadi = who speaks without egoism; dhrti-utsaha = resolve and enthusiasm; samanvitah = endowed with; siddhi = success, perfection; asiddhyoh = failure; nirvikarah = undisturbed; karta = doer; sattvikah = sattvic in nature; ucyate = is said to be.

The doer, who is free from attachment, speaks without egoism, endowed with resolve and enthusiasm, undisturbed by success and failure, is said to be of the mode of sattva.

We heard from Lord Krishna the three modes of knowledge and action. Now, he speaks about the three modes of actors or doers (karta) who engage in actions. Knowledge influences actors or agents and, thereby, their actions. By improving knowledge, one can improve one's nature and actions. By changing and improving one's knowledge and purity, one can suppress the impure gunas, change one's way of thinking and actions, and cultivate sattva. Only then will a yogi progress on the path of liberation. Detachment, egolessness, dispassion, and sameness amidst the dualities, such as success and failure, are the distinguishing marks of sattvic people. Their actions reflect purity, intelligence, selflessness, devotion, and sameness. It is difficult to find people in today's world who predominantly possess these qualities and excel in selflessness and renunciation. Sattvic people perform actions without desires and egoism, but retain their resolve and enthusiasm while performing them. Although they renounce desires and attachments and are indifferent, they remain committed to obligatory duties and responsibilities. Even if they give up the fruit of their actions, they perform them diligently for the sake of God due to their devotion to him.

In worldly life, people need motivation to perform tasks. In worldly life, success or failure depends upon the strength of motivation and desire-driven effort. Sattvic people are self-motivated and do not require any impetus or motivation to perform their tasks. They are motivated by duty, devotion, allegiance to the Lord, and commitment to serve him through selfless actions. For rajasic people, the desire for the fruit of actions serves as the motivation. However, tamasic people are not easily motivated to perform actions since they are naturally obstinate, lazy, careless, and prone to procrastination. They are motivated by their egoistic and deluded desires or by evil passions such as pride, lust, anger, fear, envy, or greed. Hence, their actions and inaction cause more harm than good and produce negative consequences for them and others.

In spiritual life, we must transcend our desires and cravings and strive hard to stabilize the mind in unwavering contemplation or devotion. The most effective way to do it is by cultivating sattva and removing the impurities of rajas and tamas. Sattvic people are committed to their duties without external motivation. For them, devotion to duty or God is the main motivating factor. It strengthens their faith and resolve and allows them to remain focused on performing their actions. They engage in selfless actions or pursue auspicious goals approved by the scriptures, renouncing desires and exemplifying sacrifice. It is difficult to reach that level of purity in actions. However, through self-purification and jnana karma-sannyasa yoga, one can gradually stabilize the mind in sattvic mode and become free from karma.

Sloka 27

rāgī karmaphalaprepsur lubdho hiṃsātmakośuciḥ
harṣaśokānvitaḥ kartā rājasaḥ parikīrtitaḥ

ragi = who is passionately attached; karma-phala = the fruit of the actions; prepsuh = who desires; lubdhah = greedy; himsa-atmakah = cruel by nature; asucih = unclean, impure; harsa-soka-anvitah = subject to joy and sorrow; karta = doer rajasah = rajasic in nature; parikirtitah = is declared to be.

The doer who is passionately attached, who desires the fruit of his actions, who is greedy, cruel by nature, unclean, and subject to joy and sorrow, is declared to be of the mode of rajas.

Human nature is essentially a mixture of light and darkness, with a mixture of the three modes. However, rajas is the most common mode, followed by tamas and sattva. As Kaliyuga advances, tamas will probably take over and influence human actions, thereby completing the cycle. Rajasic nature is a step above the lower nature found in evil people and a step below the divine nature exemplified by enlightened masters. Lord Krishna mentioned them previously while contrasting his two natures. Rajasic nature is conditioned by egoism, delusion, passions, and desires, and promotes individuality, independence, and the desire for self-preservation and self-promotion. Rajasic people are passionately attached to worldly actions and perform them with the desire to enjoy their fruit, pursuing those that make them happy and avoiding those that are painful and difficult. Because of greed, envy, pride, or anger, they may engage in the relentless pursuit of Artha (wealth) and Kama, even at the cost of their health and happiness. They may also seize others' wealth or property unlawfully to enrich themselves. They are cruel by nature, meaning they are ruthless and predatory and do not hesitate to hurt and harm others to fulfill their desires or achieve their goals. They are unclean or impure (such), meaning they do not observe physical, mental, or spiritual purity in their living, behavior, conduct, thinking, or actions. They are subject to joy and sorrow (harsa-soka-anvitah) due to attraction and aversion, happy when they fulfill their desires and enjoy success and fulfillment, and unhappy when they do not.

Due to these tendencies, those with Rajasic nature are particularly drawn to desire-ridden actions (kamya karmas) rather than obligatory duties, performing them to enjoy worldly success, wealth, power, status, name, and fame. While these actions may promote material progress, they also lead to sinful karma, bondage, and suffering. The conflicting desires and motives that drive them often result in conflicts, disharmony, social injustice, and inequalities. This constant competition for the same resources can make people stressed and insecure. It is a struggle not to be passionate about what we do and stay free of passions such as pride or envy. However, if Rajasic nature is not controlled or sublimated through self-purification, it will not be easy to find peace and balance in our lives or cultivate equanimity.

Sloka 28

ayuktaḥ prākṛtaḥ stabdhaḥ śaṭho naiṣkṛtikolasaḥ
viṣādī dīrghasūtrī ca kartā tāmasa ucyate

ayuktah = imbalanced, imperfect, unskillful; prakrtah = unnatural, crude; stabdhah = stubborn; sathah = deceitful; naiskrtikah = malicious, evil; alasah = lazy, indolent; visadi = prone to sadness, depression or dejection; dirgha-sutri = procrastinating; ca =and; karta = doer; tamasah = tamasic in nature; ucyate = said to be.

The doer, who is imperfect or unskilled, unnatural, stubborn, deceitful, malicious, lazy, prone to sadness, depression, or dejection, and procrastinating, is said to be tamasic in nature.

The qualities mentioned in this verse describe the predominantly tamasic doers. They represent impure qualities, which in many ways offer a strong contrast to those of sattvic people. If sattva is light, rajas is gray, and tamas is pure darkness. Tamas induces the baser human nature and demonic qualities, which Lord Krishna enumerated in the sixteenth chapter. Tamasic people are ayuktas, meaning they are imperfect, untrained, unskillful, unsteady, or imbalanced. Yukta means united, joined, perfect, balanced, skillful, and self-absorbed. It refers to a yogi who has achieved perfection in yoga and stabilized his mind in equanimity, steadiness, sameness, balance, and exclusive devotion. Yuktas are predominantly sattvic and excel in controlling their minds and bodies through renunciation and sacrifice to remain centered in the Self, the Lord in the body. Auyktas are the opposite. They are wayward, careless, and distracted because they lack discipline and are erratic or eccentric in their behavior and actions. Their minds run in all directions. Hence, their actions reflect their lack of stability, control, and balance.

Prakrtah means one who is crude, uncivilized, vulgar, unnatural, or has given to wild behavior. Tamasic people are uninhibited and lack civilized and refined behavior, unlike the sattvic people, who are more civilized and refined (sanskritah). Stabdha means stupefied, hard-hearted, rigid, senseless, or blocked. The foolishly unrelenting and stubborn quality characteristic of the tamasic people prevents them from knowing the reality of the world or their essential nature, making the right decisions, or performing the right actions. Under its influence, they focus their energies upon inconsequential matters, ignoring the more consequential ones, and remain preoccupied with them. Because of their stabdhibhava (stubbornness), it is difficult to persuade them or appeal to their common sense with logical arguments. They stick to their opinions, actions, and choices, even if they hurt them or create problems and obstacles for them. Satha means deceitful, cheating, or cunning. Deceptiveness is a common trait of tamasic people, which makes it difficult for others to know them correctly or anticipate their actions and behavior. They may appear differently to the world to gain an advantage or achieve a nefarious goal, concealing their true power, strength, or intentions. Since they are slippery and dishonest, you cannot trust or rely upon them or their promises. If you are careless or naive, they can mislead you, expose you to harm or loss, or involve you in their wicked schemes. Naiskrtikah means dark, malicious, or wicked. Tamasic people are evil by nature. They engage in hurtful and destructive actions without showing any remorse or compunction. The other qualities mentioned here to describe this mode are indolence (alasa), despondence (viṣādī), and procrastinating habit (dīrghasūtrī). These and the qualities mentioned above point to the demonic nature. They are not conducive to the best human behavior or achieving liberation. They are responsible for the impurities that darken the mind and intelligence with delusion, whereby one cannot see the truth of things and remains bound to the mortal world.

Sloka 29

buddher bhedaṃ dhṛteś caiva guṇatas trividhaṃ śṛṇu
procyamānam aśeṣeṇa pṛthaktvena dhanaṃjaya

buddheh = of intelligence; bhedam = division; dhrteh = resolve, firmness; ca = and; eva = also; gunatah = due to or arising from the gunas; tri-vidham = threefold, three types; srnu = hear; procyamanam = as described; asesena = fully, in detail; prthaktvena = separately, particularly; dhananjaya = conqueror of wealth.

Hear now, the three-fold differentiation of intelligence and resolve or firmness, arising from the gunas, which will be described comprehensively and separately (for each guna), O Dhananjaya.

Like other aspects of the human personality, intelligence and resolve manifest in humans differently as pure, impure, and mixed according to the modes. Intelligence (buddhi) is the highest tattva. It represents the higher mind or the reasoning mind, which gives the ability to think, analyze, discern, and distinguish things and the dualities of the experiential world. The intelligence found in the jivas is an objectified aspect of Brahman's pure intelligence, which is also found in the jivas as the Self, the Lord in the body. Its ability to discern truths from untruths depends upon its purity or the predominant gunas pervading it. Oneness with the Self becomes possible when the mind and intelligence and pure and without modifications. Resolve (dhriti) is the fortitude or the willpower to remain firm in performing actions or reaching goals despite challenges and obstacles. Its strength depends upon one's commitment to actions, duties, and tasks, which again depends upon motivation, desires, and attachments. It is difficult to say how it manifests in our consciousness, but it may be due to desires, attachments, and latent impressions from past lives (samskaras) and is colored by the modes. However, we can experience it consciously and strengthen it willfully with knowledge, discipline, faith, and devotion. The resolve arising from our nature strongly influences our thoughts and actions and is, in turn, influenced by the gunas and the desires and attachments they induce. Hence, it varies according to the modes and desires people possess. For example, a person may strongly resolve to earn wealth but may not be much interested in performing obligatory duties, serving gods, or helping others. A devotee may resolve to practice self-control and exclusive devotion, but may not be interested in other matters. Thus, the nature of intelligence and resolve depends upon the gunas, which, in turn, influence the goals and desires people pursue. With pure intelligence or discernment, devotees must cultivate the right resolve to engage in righteous actions, cultivate a divine nature with the Lord serving as the goal, and pursue liberation.

In life, resolve and intelligence are both necessary. Resolve gives us the strength to endure suffering. Intelligence gives the wisdom to overcome it. Both determine the nature of our actions and the karma arising from them. Intelligence helps us know truths about ourselves and others, make the right choices, overcome obstacles, and determine where to be firm and where to let go. In spiritual practice, it serves as the rudder to overcome delusion and ignorance, distinguish the Self from the not-self or the reality from the unreality, pursue the right path, or make the right decisions. It also helps us distinguish obligatory duties from desire-ridden actions (kamya-karmas), which are meant to fulfill desires and produce karma. Mortal life is riddled with many problems and difficulties. Without the right discernment or purified intelligence, it is difficult to navigate through them and remain stable and firm amidst the impermanence and uncertainty of life. Resolve also gives us the strength to practice self-purification and renunciation until perfection is attained. It helps us restrain the outgoing nature of the mind and senses and withdraw them from worldly objects to remain established in the Self. If the senses wander, the mind is unstable, or the body is weak or sick, one cannot attain sameness, stability, or freedom from karma. Resolve is necessary, but one should strictly avoid the extreme forms of resolve (stabdah), especially the delusional or the egoistic kind, which is foolish and detrimental to one's well-being. Most importantly, in the advanced stages, one must also renounce resolve and surrender to the divine will without desires and expectations.

Sloka 30

pravṛttiṃ ca nivṛttiṃ ca kāryākārye bhayābhaye
bandhaṃ mokṣaṃ ca yā vetti buddhiḥ sā pārtha sāttvikī

pravrttim = the path of action, going forth; ca = and; nivrttim = the path of withdrawal; ca = and; karya = obligatory action as ordained by the scriptures; akarye = action which is forbidden or prohibited by the scriptures; bhaya = what causes fear or what should be feared; abhaye = what causes fearlessness or what should not be feared; bandham = bondage; moksam = liberation; ca = and; ya = that; vetti = knows; buddhih = intelligence; sa = that; partha = O Partha; sattviki = sattvic in nature.

That intelligence, by which is known the path of action which leads to bondage and rebirth and the path which leads to the cessation of karma and liberation, what action is obligatory and what action is forbidden, what should be feared and should not be feared, what causes bondage and what causes liberation, is sattvic, O Partha.

The human mind is subject to many cognitive distortions and perceptual errors. They are resolved when it is pure and transparent, without egoism, delusion, desires, and attachments. When intelligence is pure and pointed without disturbances, it discerns things better and distinguishes binding actions from liberating ones, permitted actions from prohibited ones, what should be feared or not feared, and what leads to bondage or liberation. When intelligence is free from the modifications of the mind, it perceives truths without delusion, hindrances, or distortions. It becomes pure with the predominance of sattva and excels in purity, stability, harmony, and balance when it is free from desires, etc. A 'sattvic' person who embodies these qualities, endowed with discerning wisdom, possesses the right knowledge, common sense, and discretion. He knows which paths to choose, which qualities to develop, which to suppress, to what extent he can involve himself with the world, and where to draw a line and protect himself from harmful distractions and influences.

Prvritti, the predisposition or basic tendency of the mind to move among sense objects and enjoy life, is the natural inclination of the jivas to act, express, or engage in desire-ridden actions for self-preservation. On the other hand, Nivrtti is the opposite tendency, motivating people to retire or withdraw from the mortal world, give up worldly and sinful activities, and remain indifferent and absorbed in the Self, practicing rules and restraints, such as brahmacharya and ahimsa. Prvritti is extroverted dynamism, and nivrtti is introverted indifference and affected inertia arising from renunciation and detachment. In a philosophical or spiritual sense, prvritti refers to the path of desire-ridden actions which lead to karma and bondage. Nivrtti refers to the path of knowledge or renunciation, which leads to detachment, sameness, and liberation.

Karya, in the context of this verse, signifies not just any action, but the importance of right action or obligatory duty. This duty is essential for preserving Dharma and the natural order of things and crucial for one's own spiritual and material well-being. On the other hand, Akarya represents any action or inaction that is frivolous, unnecessary, incorrect, or prohibited, and is spiritually self-destructive. Devotees must avoid such actions to escape from negative and unhappy consequences. For instance, the Vedas prescribe certain duties as obligatory, which one cannot avoid for the sake of Dharma. They also prohibit certain actions, which one should avoid, to escape from sinful consequences. The latter constitutes akarya.

Bhaya refers to the actions, situations, qualities, causes, results, consequences, or developments one should fear or cause fear. Abhaya means the opposite. For example, engaging in sinful, egoistic, or deluded actions is the cause of fear since those actions determine the course of one's transmigration or next birth or transition to the next world. One should also fear evil actions and avoid them. Similarly, japa, dhyana, or archana are reason enough to be fearless since they strengthen one's faith and devotion and stabilize the mind in contemplating the pure Self.

Bandham signifies the bondage to samsara (the cycle of births and deaths) together with its causes, such as egoism, desires and attachments, ignorance, and delusion. Moksha, on the other hand, represents the ultimate liberation of the Self from this bondage, achieved through purification, discernment, resolve, devotion, and skillfulness in yoga. These practices lead to the suppression of negative tendencies and freedom from egoism, ignorance, delusion, desires, and attachments. The awareness of these distinctions arises when intelligence shines with the predominance of sattva. Those who possess it, the wise ones, know what causes bondage and suffering and what one should avoid or practice to achieve final liberation. They know how to perform actions without becoming bound by them, leading to a state of ultimate liberation.

Sloka 31

yayā dharmam adharmaṃ ca kāryaṃ cākāryam eva ca
ayathāvat prajānāti buddhiḥ sā pārtha rājasī

yaya = by which; dharmam = dharma; adharmam = adharma; ca = and; karyam = obligatory action as ordained by the scriptures; akaryam = action which is forbidden or prohibited by the scriptures; eva = so also; ca = and; ayatha-vat = wrongly, incorrectly, falsely, untruthfully; prajanati = knows; buddhih = intelligence; sa = that; partha = O Partha; rajasi = rajasic mode.

That intelligence by which one wrongly knows dharma and adharma, and even obligatory action and forbidden action, is of rajasic mode, O Partha.

Sattvic intelligence is filled with the brilliance of the Self, whereby one gains the right knowledge and understanding. Rajasic people are swayed by passions and emotions and do not possess the holistic vision of pure souls who are mentally stable, free from desires, and abide in self-control and exclusive devotion. Since they are materialistic by nature and rely upon their minds and senses, their knowledge is limited to perceivable reality and gross material things. As their intelligence remains colored by passions and emotions and filled with impurities, they cannot discern the Self or the need to cultivate the right knowledge or pursue liberation. Hence, even though they may be drawn to spirituality and yoga, they do not readily accept or comprehend metaphysical truths or the truths validated by the scriptures.

Karya refers to obligatory and righteous actions, and akarya refers to forbidden, inappropriate, or unrighteous actions. Dharma refers to the moral and sacrificial duties that are obligatory for householders and ordained by God. Due to their clouded intelligence, rajasic people do not have a proper understanding of Dharma and adharma or obligatory and prohibited actions. They may mistake Dharma for morality, ritual worship, kamya karmas, sacred teaching, the words of their gurus, or their tradition. Due to desires and passions and the lack of resolve and faith, they may selectively perform obligatory duties according to their convenience or half-knowledge, choosing the popular or convenient ones and ignoring those that are difficult or painful to perform. Hence, they do not attain liberation.

In today's world, rajasic nature is the most prevalent. Hence, materialism, ignorance of scriptures and spiritual knowledge, evil passions, and immoral conduct are rising. Ignorance and delusion are evident in how people practice their faith or speak about it, worship the gods, respect the tradition, treat others, or conduct themselves in public. Self-destructive habits and evil passions such as lust, anger, pride, fear, envy, and greed are commonplace. The situation is well described in the Mahanirvana Tantra when Parvathi describes Kali Yuga in the following words, "Men pursue evil ways. The Vedas have lost their power, the Smritis are forgotten, and many of the Puranas, which contain stories of the past and show the many ways to liberation, will, O Lord! be destroyed. Men will become averse to religious rites, without restraint, maddened with pride, ever given over to sinful acts, lustful, gluttonous, cruel. heartless, harsh of speech, deceitful, short-lived, poverty-stricken, harassed by sickness and sorrow, ugly…" When the world is viewed through a narrow prism of passions and emotions characteristic of the rajasic mode, and actions are performed for instant sense gratification, unhappy consequences follow for those who fail to discern correctly the truths of Dharma and karma.

Sloka 32

adharmaṃ dharmam iti yā manyate tamasāvṛtā
sarvārthān viparītāñś ca buddhiḥ sā pārtha tāmasī

adharmam = adharma; dharmam = dharma; iti = thus; ya = which; manyate = perceives, thinks; tamasa = darkness; avrta = enveloped; sarva-arthan = all things; viparitan = twisted, inverse, perverse, extreme; ca = and; buddhih = intelligence; sa = that; partha = O Partha; tamasi = tamasic mode.

That intelligence is of tamasic mode, O Partha, which, enveloped in darkness, perceives thus adharma as dharma and all things in a twisted manner.

Dharma refers to the body of knowledge about duties and morals ordained by God for the righteous to serve God and fulfill the aims of creation. Adharma is the opposite, which, although not prescribed for anyone, is the refuge of evil and wicked people. In other words, whatever is unholy, unrighteous, harmful, and destructive for the welfare of the world and human beings is adharma. Dharma is passed down to us by our ancestors and guardians through tradition, teachings, and scriptures. It is considered a divine instruction. Manyate means what we think, consider, believe, or regard as true, correct, or right. Viparītā means extreme, opposite, inverse, perverse, or twisted. Viparita is characteristic and symptomatic of the extreme, eccentric, unusual, or atypical tamasic nature. These descriptions appropriately characterize the tamasic mode.

People under tamasic influence see the world differently and delusionally, holding on to their perverted beliefs and unpopular opinions, usually shunned by the mainstream. They view the world with cynicism, rejecting its values and ethos, holding on to their profane and absurd views and beliefs, and ignoring reality. As a result, they view dharma as adharma and adharma as dharma. Since their intelligence is clouded, they cannot discern truths, think rationally, or make intelligent choices. When you interact with them, you will find it difficult to communicate your ideas or deal with their evil nature. They will push back if you try to convince, correct, or reason with them. If you persist, you may incur their displeasure or risk your peace and tranquility. They may even confuse you and temporarily draw you into their mode of thinking to trick you or mislead you. The worst part is that they do not know they are wrong, which makes the task of changing, correcting, or improving them even more difficult.

Sattvic intelligence gives us purity of knowledge, wisdom, and discernment. Rajasic mode clouds intelligence with passions and desires, whereby one cannot distinguish between what leads to bondage and what leads to liberation, or what is to be done or not done to avoid karmic consequences. The mode of tamas clouds judgment even further and makes matters worse. Under its negative influence, one develops an abnormal and irrational way of thinking and perceiving the world with a cognitively distorted mind. As a result, tamasic people see things indiscreetly and pursue inappropriate goals using questionable methods, ignoring the conventional wisdom and the consequences arising from their methods and actions. In pursuing goals, including the practice of spirituality, tantra, or yoga, they may resort to extreme methods and torture their minds and bodies, even if it would cause them pain and suffering or bodily harm. Their faith is clouded by ignorance and delusion. Hence, they either refuse to acknowledge God or hold him in contempt. They may also worship spirits and gods of the lower realms, usually feared or shunned by others, using dark and obscure methods.

When tamas predominates, people become irrational and negative in their thinking and actions. They find fault with conventional truths, beliefs, and practices that are upheld by the scripture or accepted by most people. Because of their biases and distorted thinking, they rarely make correct decisions or follow proven methods and practices. Without proper knowledge or intelligence, they question the knowledge and wisdom of the wise ones and take pleasure in defying the prevailing social norms, moral values, and code of conduct. Due to their stubborn nature, know-all attitude, and consuming intoxicating substances and tamasic food, they stick to their rigid views and cannot be persuaded or reasoned with. They are also deceptive and destructive. Therefore, one should avoid tamasic people, tamasic substances, and activities, which fill the mind with darkness and impair judgment.

Sloka 33

dhṛtyā yayā dhārayate manaḥprāṇendriyakriyāḥ
yogenāvyabhicāriṇyā dhṛtiḥ sā pārtha sāttvikī

dhrtya = resolve, firmness or steadiness; yaya = by which; dharayate = stabilizes; manah = mind; prana = prana; indriya = senses; kriyah = actions; yogena = through the practice of yoga; avyabhicarinya = without distractions, unwaveringly; dhrtih = such firmness; sa = that; partha = O Partha; sattviki = sattvic in nature.

The resolve or firmness with which one stabilizes the activities of the mind, prana (and) the senses through the practice of yoga, that resolve or firmness, O Partha, is of sattvic mode.

Dhriti means firmness, steadiness, or resolve, which arises from willpower and self-control. In this context, it refers to the firmness of the unwavering mind, which arises in the advanced stages of yoga practice. Yoga, in this specific case, means the practice of dharana (concentration) or samyama (controlled and concentrated meditation), which results in stillness and mental absorption or self-absorption. However, firmness or steadiness does not arise from these two methods only. It arises as a culmination of the various techniques described in this text, the Yogasutras of Patanjali, and several yoga texts and Upanishads. They define yoga variously as the control of the mind and body and their modifications, actions, and movements whereby the body becomes strong and supple, the mind becomes stable and tranquil, and the yogi experiences a deeper state of turiya (transcendence) in samadhi or mental absorption. The exalted state is attained through self-transformation in which rajas and tamas are suppressed while sattva is augmented to fill the mind and the body with purity and brilliance. The various yamas and niyamas (restraints and observances), prescribed for self-purification and stabilizing the mind, promote sattva and prepare the yogi for higher states of consciousness.

With the predominance of sattva, yoga becomes easier, and the yogi attains skillfulness (yukti). Breathing becomes slower and regular; prana flows smoothly through the nadis as the blockages in them are dissolved by its purity; the senses remain withdrawn and restrained, and the mind becomes firm and stable. These developments eventually lead to atma-samyama (self-control), ananya bhakti (exclusive devotion), and oneness or absorption in the Self. In the Yogasutras, Patanjali affirms that when the mind is purified and stabilized, one experiences cheerfulness, single-mindedness, control of the senses, and the ability to perceive the Self (atma darsana yogyatvam). Sattvic resolve is unwavering in achieving inner purification, balance, and self-absorption through austerities and yoga practice. It helps one remain undisturbed and firm on the path of liberation, enduring the pressures, problems, and difficulties life or fate puts on one's path. A person with the resolve or firmness of the sattvic kind is not easily disturbed or distracted by frivolities. Surrendering himself to the divine will, he excels in sameness and equanimity as sthithaprajna (he who is contended and whose mind, senses, and intelligence are firm, unflinching, and stable).

Sloka 34

yayā tu dharmakāmārthān dhṛtyā dhārayaterjuna
prasaṅgena phalākāṅkṣī dhṛtiḥ sā pārtha rājasī

yaya = by which; tu = but; dharma-kama-arthan = dharma, artha and kama; dhrtya = by firmness; dharayate = upholds, sustains; arjuna = O Arjuna;

prasangena = out of attachment; phala-akanksi = desiring the fruit of actions; dhrtih = firmness; sa = that; partha = O Partha; rajasi = rajasic in nature.

But the firmness by which one upholds Dharma Artha and Kama, O Arjuna, out of attachment and desire for the fruit of actions, that firmness, O Partha, is rajasic in nature.

Sattvic people use firmness or resolve without desire to practice yoga and attain liberation. Rajasic people use it to perform desire-ridden actions with passion and attain the chief aims of Dharma, Artha, Kama, and Moksha. Sattvic people pursue the same goal to help others and serve God, with Moksha (liberation) as their ultimate aim (paramartha). Therefore, they stoically perform their actions in the pursuit of these aims with detachment, renouncing their fruit. Rajasic people pursue them selfishly for their enjoyment or name and fame, desiring the fruit of their actions and ignoring the ultimate aim of liberation. Since they are subject to attraction and aversion and cling to material things, they engage in desire-ridden actions and accumulate karma, which keeps them bound to samsara. Further, the firmness of the sattvic people is strong and unwavering as they practice self-control and establish their minds in peace, tranquility, and devotion to the Lord. Rajasic people remain restless, distracted, and disturbed by passions and emotions. Their minds keep wavering, wandering, and unsteady as they perform actions to fulfill their desires and enjoy worldly pleasures.

This is the main distinction between the firmness arising from the two modes. The resolve of sattvic mode sets you free, whereas that of rajasic mode keeps you bound to the mortal world. It is not that rajasic resolve is weak or lacks strength. It drives people in different directions, away from the goal of liberation and deep into the thick of the world and sensory enjoyment. In pursuing Dharma, Artha, and Kama, when the rewards of their actions are attractive, they act resolutely with zeal. However, they do not show the same firmness in the pursuit of liberation since it does not offer them immediate results or material rewards. Even in worldly actions, their resolve varies due to the fluctuating nature of nivrtti or the outgoing mode of the mind and senses, which are by nature restless. It is difficult for rajasic people to be free from worry and anxiety since they pursue transient goals through desire-ridden actions, and their outcome cannot be predicted or foreseen. Hence, their resolve is mixed and unsteady by nature.

Sloka 35

yayā svapnaṃ bhayaṃ śokaṃ viṣādaṃ madam eva ca
na vimuñcati durmedhā dhṛtiḥ sā pārtha tāmasī

yaya = by which; svapnam = sleep, dreaming, drowsiness; bhayam = fear; sokam = grief, sorrow; visadam = despair, dejection; madam = lustfulness, virility, arrogance; eva = so also; ca = and; na = not; vimuncati = give up; durmedha = imprudent, ignorant or foolish person; dhrtih = firmness; sa = that; partha = O Partha; tamasi = tamasic in nature.

That by which excessive sleep, fear, grief, despair, and lustfulness are not given up, the firmness of that imprudent person, O Partha, is of the tamasic mode.

A tamasic person is described here as durmedha, which means one who is not in his right mind and whose intelligence or mental brilliance (medhas) is obscured by darkness and sinful nature. A tamasic person's resolve to do good, practice yoga, overcome evil qualities, or achieve liberation is weak. However, it is stronger when indulging in sinful passions and immoral actions, practicing adharma, or troubling others. When tamas predominates, one does not see sinful thinking (durmedha) as a problem or feel the need to address it. Tamasic people may even consider it a virtue and show little inclination to resolve it. As a result, they remain bound to their deluded, ignorant, and sinful ways, with little determination to change themselves, improve their conduct, or cultivate discernment. The mode of tamas also does not let them give up the qualities mentioned in this verse: excessive sleep, fear, grief, despair, and lustfulness. They are illustrative only but give us an insight into how it is difficult, if not impossible, to overcome the tamasic nature or resolve the problems and consequences arising from it.

Svapnam means sleep, dream, or idle reverie. Here, it denotes the drowsy condition, a dreamlike reverie, or a lethargic state, a chief characteristic of the tamasic mind. Tamasic ones are apathetic about overcoming their inertia, sleepiness, laziness, or drowsiness since they are habituated to consuming sleep-inducing food, chemicals, and intoxicants and since they prefer to remain inactive and passive when they are not engaged in sinful actions. Fear (bhayam) in this context refers to the fear of enemies, sin, divine retribution, suffering, bondage, etc. Although tamasic people experience it, their resolve to overcome it is weak due to excessive pride (mada), self-denial, and their inclination to hurt and harm others or engage in hostile acts. Sokam refers to the affliction, grief, or sorrow that arises from bondage to samsara and sinful karma. Visdam is the state of despair or mental depression that arises in evil people due to their negativity and self-destructive actions. Vanity, pride, ignorance, delusion, etc., prevent them from resolving these negative feelings or their causes. Mada means excessive pride, arrogance, virility, lustfulness, or drunkenness. It makes tamasic people excessively aggressive, proud, violent, and vengeful. Their evil nature does not let them overcome this evil quality.

Sloka 36

sukhaṃ tv idānīṃ trividhaṃ śṛṇu me bharatarṣabha
abhyāsād ramate yatra duḥkhāntaṃ ca nigacchhati

sukham = pleasure, happiness, joy, comfort; tu = about; idanim = now; tri-vidham = three types; srnu = hear; me = from Me; bharata-rsabha = O the best among the Bharatas; abhyasat = by persistent practice; ramate = takes delight in, rejoices at, enjoys; yatra = at which place; duhkha = sorrow; antam = end; ca = and; nigacchati = attains, acquires.

Now hear from Me, O the Best among the Bharatas, about the three kinds of happiness, in which one takes delight by persistent practice and at which point attains the end of sorrow.

Sukham means happiness, pleasure, joy, delight, or ease of comfort, created by favorable circumstances arising from internal or external factors. People derive their happiness from different sources according to their nature. Sattvic devotees are happy worshipping the Lord or spending time in his contemplation. Worldly people are happy if they gain wealth, name, or fame. Evil people are happy if they destroy their enemies or cause harm to them. Some people are happy when they are successful after enduring much pain and effort. Some are happy when they fulfill their worldly desires. Some are happy when they engage in sinful or evil actions. Thus, people derive their happiness in different ways according to their nature, goals, and desires.

The quality of happiness depends upon the predominant gunas or essential nature. The next three verses describe how it varies in people according to the modes. Abhyasa, in this context, means repetitive or habitual actions or the persistent practice of self-discipline and self-purification. Both meanings are relevant – the first one is relevant to worldly people, and the other to those who practice yoga and reach the end of sorrow. The happiness quotient, or the potential to be happy or unhappy, varies from person to person. How optimally people can be happy or unhappy in different situations depends upon their essential nature and how they restrain their minds and senses or control their desires and emotions. Some people are easily satisfied and content with whatever they have or what happens to them. Some cannot be happy even if they have everything since their desires are endless, or they always compare their wealth and achievements with those who are better off than they are. Some are unhappy if their neighbor buys an expensive car or hosts a party and does not invite them.

Thus, experience, habitual thought patterns, karma, and inherent nature determine how people seek and experience happiness. Those who seek it through external things may not enjoy lasting happiness due to the instability of their minds and the impermanence of the world itself, while those who withdraw their minds from the world and resolve the causes of sorrow within themselves, strengthening their will and stabilizing their minds, enjoy enduring happiness. The onset of happiness signifies the end of sorrow. However, one cannot predict how long that cycle will last since, in the mortal world, both happiness and sorrow are transient. One follows the other. The permanent end of sorrow is reached only when one finds the Lord in oneself and enters His consciousness, whose essential nature is enjoyment and supreme bliss. For them, happiness is permanent, and so is the ending of sorrow or suffering.

Sloka 37

yat tadagre viṣam iva pariṇāmemṛtopamam
tat sukhaṃ sāttvikaṃ proktam ātmabuddhiprasādajam

yat = which; tat = that; agre = in the beginning; visam iva = very much like poison; pariname = in the end; amrta = nectar; upamam = like; tat = that;

sukham = happiness, pleasure; sattvikam = sattvic in nature; proktam = declared by the prauktas or the wise ones; atma-buddhi = pure intelligence of the self; prasada-jam = produced by, arising from.

That which in the beginning is very much like poison, but in the end is like nectar, that happiness arising from the pure intelligence of the Self is declared by the wise as sattvic.

There is a saying in Telugu that if you eat the bitter leaves of neem or margosa (Azadirachta indica) every day, they begin to taste sweet, and their bitterness will no longer trouble you. Sattvic happiness is similar. It is attained through effort and endurance. Life teaches us many valuable lessons as we go through many hardships and unpleasant situations. As the adage goes, there is always light at the end of a long and dark tunnel. The Lord always keeps some doors open when others are shut. Nothing lasts forever in this world. When the light comes, darkness recedes; when happiness arises, sorrow ends. It is said that when God loves his devotees, he first gives them suffering or sorrow as a gift so they can learn from it and be cleansed. True happiness is that which lasts and is not affected by transient causes. Some experiences produce instant happiness or gratification, but ultimately, they may lead to problems and suffering. Sometimes, we experience great relief and happiness after enduring a lot of adversity, pain, and suffering, and come out of it successfully.

No wonder most medicines taste bitter, and most sugary, tasty, and sweet things lead to many health problems. It takes time to cultivate clean habits, but in the end, they produce health and happiness. Certain harmful addictions produce happiness and fulfillment in the beginning, but end up causing a lot of suffering. The same is true about exercise, discipline, self-study (svadhyaya), yoga, dieting, etc. They require effort and some discomfort in the early stages, but eventually lead to peace and happiness. Sattvic happiness arises similarly. Self-purification practices in the early stages of spirituality also produce a lot of pain and suffering. However, if one persists, it results in oneness with the Self (yoga) and lasting happiness. When gods and demons churned the ocean, the first thing that emerged from the ocean was a dangerous poison (halahal). After that, many auspicious things emerged gradually, with Amrit (immortality) as the final blessing. In spiritual practice, halahal symbolizes the suffering arising from the churning of the mind and body, and Amrit symbolizes liberation, immortality, and endless happiness. Thus, the final fruit of sattvic effort is the sweet nectar of enduring happiness, which is indestructible and arises from the grace of God or the Self. One can also see this happening in worldly life. Those who spend the early part of their lives with discipline, focus, and hard work have better chances of enjoying more comfortable lives later in life than those who waste their childhood and adolescence in frivolous activities. The sweet fruit of success is enjoyed by those who earn it by working hard.

Detachment, renunciation, self-restraint, obligatory duties, and selfless actions are difficult to practice. They require unwavering resolve and supreme faith. However, if one persists, it will lead to lasting happiness, peace, and tranquility. Through their persistent practice (abhyasa) of self-control and exclusive devotion, sattvic people reach the permanent culmination of sorrow. They attain the highest happiness, which is everlasting, unchanging, and independent of causes and circumstances. Thus, the happiness of the enduring kind, as the culmination of yoga, is experienced by sattvic people only. Just as right means lead to right ends, sattvic actions eventually lead to sattvic pleasures and happiness, although in the beginning, they may appear to be different. It arises from the predominance of sattva and freedom from desires and attachments, untouched by the dualities, impermanence, and modifications of the mind. Yogis and devotees subject themselves to rigorous discipline and harsh conditions during their practice and initially experience great suffering and discomfort. However, as they progress on the path and stabilize their minds, they experience deeper states of consciousness, peace, and happiness. When they dissolve their minds in the Self and experience oneness with its intelligence (atma-buddhi), the Self becomes the source of their happiness.

Sloka 38

viṣayendriyasañyogād yat tad agremṛtopamam
pariṇāme viṣam iva tat sukhaṃ rājasaṃ smṛtam

visaya = sense objects; indriya = senses; samyogat = from contact, attachment, union; yat = which; tat = that; agre = in the beginning; amrta-upamam = just like nectar; pariname = in the end; visam iva = like poison; tat = that; sukham = pleasure, happiness; rajasam = rajasic in nature; smrtam = is declared.

That which arises from the contact of the senses with the sense objects and is like nectar in the beginning, but in the end is like poison, that happiness is declared by the wise ones as of rajasic mode.

Rajasic pleasures are essentially physical or sensual pleasures. They arise from the contact of the senses with sense objects due to passions and desire-ridden actions. In the beginning, they produce happiness and instant gratification, but in the end, they act like poison and prove detrimental to one's health, strength, stamina, vigor, wealth, happiness, and intelligence. Their actions and choices lead to sinful karma, pain and suffering, and bondage to the cycle of births and deaths. One of the examples quoted by scholars for rajasic pleasure is the enjoyment one derives from adultery or infidelity. Initially, adulterous relationships produce pleasure and happiness, but ultimately complicate life and cause many problems, including suffering, broken relationships, sinful karma, and loss of reputation, trust, peace, and harmony.

Rajasic people do not enjoy lasting happiness since they perform actions to fulfill their desires and enjoy their fruit, which is happiness or fulfillment. They pursue Dharma, Artha, and Kama for selfish enjoyment without thinking much about Moksha. Lord Krishna has already explained in the previous chapters the consequences of pursuing sensual pleasures. For example, in the second chapter (62-63), he explained how suffering arises when one constantly dwells upon sense objects. Due to the repeated outgoing mode of the senses, he said, one develops an attachment to them. From attachments arise desires, which produce passions such as anger, envy, greed, etc. Because of them, one suffers from delusion, confusion of memory, and loss of discernment. When discernment is lost, one is lost to the possibility of liberation and enduring happiness. According to the Yogasutras, the outgoing nature of the mind and senses and desire-ridden actions draw the mind deeply into the world and strengthen one's involvement with it. When one is caught in the samsara thus, it leads to physical and mental afflictions such as ignorance (avidya), delusion (moha), egoism (asmita), attraction (raga), aversion (dvesha) and intense clinging (abhinivesa), which keep the mind increasingly restless and outgoing.

Another problem with the rajasic mode is that it makes people perceive the diversity of the world rather than its oneness or unity and mistake the physical self for the real Self. Hence, in the pursuit of happiness, rajasic people focus on their selfish desires and interests, names and forms (nama rupa), birth (jati), status, lifespan (ayuh), and the enjoyment (bhogah) of pleasures. In the end, their actions and pursuits produce halahal, the poison of suffering. Rajasic pleasures are, therefore, transient, pain-producing, and harmful. Although they appear to be sweet and nectar-like (amrta-upamam), they produce poisonous effects on one's mind and body, causing aging, sickness, and death.

Sloka 39

yad agre cānubandhe ca sukhaṃ mohanam ātmanaḥ
nidrālasyapramādotthaṃ tat tāmasam udāhṛtam

yat =which; agre = in the beginning; ca = and; anubandhe = subsequently; ca = also; sukham = pleasure; mohanam =delusion; atmanah = the self; nidra = sleep; alasya = laziness; pramada = negligence; uttham = arise from; tat = that; tamasam = born of tamasic nature; udahrtam = is said to be.

That pleasure or happiness, which is self-deluding in the beginning and subsequently also arises from sleep, laziness, and negligence, is said to be in the tamasic mode.

Tamasic pleasures delude jivas in the beginning and subsequently. This means tamasic people remain continuously deluded, oblivious to whether the pleasures or happiness they pursue are good for them or not, and whether they produce sinful karma and harm them in the long run. They think it is the best way to live and do not like to change, or if challenged, they rationalize their actions, thinking there is no other way. They are happy if they can avoid hard work and remain passive in a stupor or intoxication, with their minds lost in delusion and ignorance. Their resolve (dhriti) to engage in sinful actions and pursue evil passions is stronger, while their resolve to change themselves or follow the righteous path is weaker. With deluded minds and perverse thinking, they do not feel any guilt or remorse for their actions, lifestyles, or sinful pursuits. Due to their preference for inactivity and intoxication, they prefer to neglect their duties and obligations and remain irresponsible. Discipline and duty make them unhappy, while unrestricted freedom to do whatever they like makes them happy. Some derive happiness by engaging in criminal actions, defying authority, and challenging established social and moral values. In the sattvic mode, the mind and senses remain withdrawn and stable. In the rajasic mode, they run in all directions and actively pursue sense objects and worldly pleasures. In the tamasic mode, they remain dull and inactive. As a result, tamasic people do not pay much attention to themselves or others. They act by instinct and primitive passions and sleepwalk through their lives, paying little attention to what goes on within themselves or around them and how their actions are going to harm them. Tamasic pleasures are, therefore, self-destructive and addictive and produce far-reaching consequences for one's physical, mental, and spiritual well-being. The saying, "Ignorance is bliss," applies to tamasic people perfectly.

Sloka 40

na tad asti pṛthivyāṃ vā divi deveṣu vā punaḥ
sattvaṃ prakṛtijair muktaṃ yad ebhiḥ syāt tribhirguṇaiḥ

na = not; tat = that; asti = there is; prthivyam = on earth; va = or; divi = in the heavenly world; devesu = among the gods; va = or; punah = again; sattvam = being, entity, thing; prakrti-jaih = born of Nature; muktam = free; yat = which; ebhih = from these; syat = can be; tribhih = three; gunaih = gunas.

There is no being on earth or again in the heavenly world among gods, who, born of Prakriti, is free from these triple gunas.

The three gunas are universally present in all objects and beings and the whole manifestation of God. They are responsible for the diversity, duality, qualities, and inherent nature of all creation. No one is free from them or their influence. Like humans, the gods are also born of Prakriti and are subject to these modes. The gods are not much different from us, except that they have ethereal bodies, possess supernatural powers, belong to a superior class, and are free from births and deaths. According to the Bhagavata Purana, they lack individuation or egoism. It is strong in humans and extreme in Asuras, and so is the influence of the gunas. The mind and senses are drawn to sense objects due to their influence only. Our desire-ridden actions are also caused by them. Life is permeated with their influence and interplay. If they are silent, all activity and dynamism will end. Since they induce desires and desire-ridden actions in us, they are responsible for our karma, bondage, ignorance, intelligence, delusion, and, indirectly, even liberation. They permeate the tattvas (realities), the building blocks of creation, from which all forms and their specific qualities, propensities, and behavioral tendencies arise.

Only the Supreme Brahman is nirguna, meaning he is free from the gunas. However, whatever manifests from him, including the highest Isvara, the triple deities of Brahma, Vishnu, and Shiva, and all the other gods and goddesses, are subject to them. They also exist in the unmanifested, primordial Prakriti, but in a state of equilibrium and inertia. When she wakes up and enters a dynamic mode, as that equilibrium is disturbed, the gunas become active. The Paingala Upanishad explains how the diversity of things, gross and subtle bodies, manifests in creation from the admixture of the tattvas and the gunas in varying proportions. If the gunas are present in everything, the question that arises is whether it is possible at all for anyone to be free from them, and if so, how. In the following verses, Lord Krishna will teach how we can resolve them and overcome the problem of samsara, which is essentially a work of Prakriti and her modes.

Sloka 41

brāhmaṇakṣatriyaviśāṃ śūdrāṇāṃ ca paraṃtapa
karmāṇi pravibhaktāni svabhāvaprabhavair guṇaiḥ

brahmana = the brahmanas; ksatriya = the ksatriyas; visam = the vaisyas; sudranam = the sudras; ca = and; parantapa = O subduer of the enemies; karmani = duties, actions; pravibhaktani = are divided; svabhava = essential nature; prabhavaih = born out of; gunaih = by gunas.

O conqueror of the enemies, the duties of Brahmanas, Kshatriyas, Vaishyas, and Sudras are divided according to the gunas arising from their essential nature.

Knowledge of the gunas is useful to cultivate self-awareness and live in harmony with our essential nature. By paying attention to our predominant gunas, we can know a great deal about ourselves and our natural propensities, live in harmony with our essential nature, or change it if necessary. Although we may not always succeed in it, we can still adapt to it within the natural constraints we are subject to, choosing our goals according to our nature, expressing our natural talents and abilities, and living in harmony with ourselves. If you have the predominance of sattva, you can devote your life to intellectual and spiritual pursuits. If you have the predominance of rajas, you can control your passions and emotions and lead a balanced life, tempering your material desires and worldly pursuits with spiritual practice and selfless service. If you have the predominance of tamas, you can set definitive and time-oriented goals to overcome your procrastinating habits, delusion, and lethargy and become an active, intelligent, and energetic person.

The gunas are present in every aspect of creation. Even those life forms without a nervous system or consciousness are propelled by them. Physically, they are imperceptible but can be discerned in people through their actions, choices, behavior, and natural propensities. You can know which of them are active by observing others and their predominant behavior and actions. The Vedic caste system was founded on them only. The Vedas identify four classes (chaturvarnas) of humans according to their predominant modes: Brahmanas, Kshatriyas, Vaisyas, and Sudras. The Brahmanas are considered predominantly sattvic in nature. In the past, they took upon themselves the duty of practicing, protecting, and preserving the Dharma and the knowledge associated with it. They studied the Vedas, performed obligatory duties, mediated as priests, substituted for gods during sacrificial ceremonies, served as teachers and spiritual gurus to pass on the knowledge to future generations, and advised the rulers in State matters. They enjoyed the patronage and protection of kings and rulers to whom they gave counsel on important matters. The law books held them in the highest esteem since they were the closes to gods in purity, acted as the guardians of the Dharma, and excelled in the knowledge of the scriptures and religious doctrine.

Kshatriyas formed the ruling elite. The law books entrusted them with the duties of warriors, rulers, chieftains, and administrators. Their duty was to protect people, dispense justice in civil and criminal matters, and fight wars, if necessary, against enemies for conquest or in self-defense. They were believed to possess the predominance of rajas, with sattva as their secondary mode. Vaisyas and Sudras were in the mixed category. The Vaisyas belonged to the merchant class. They were supposed to practice trade, commerce, and agriculture, participate in the distribution of wealth, and support good causes and charitable works. They were believed to possess the predominance of rajas, with sattva and tamas in varying proportions. The Sudra class included land-owning gentry, farmers, and workers believed to possess the predominance of tamas, followed by rajas and sattva in varying proportions. This verse mentions Brahmanas, Kshatriyas, and Vaisyas in one compound word (brāhmaṇakṣatriyaviśāṃ), but Sudras separately because they were believed to have originated subsequently from the Cosmic Purusha. In ancient times, they were precluded from studying the Vedas or performing sacrificial duties. The Brihadaranyaka Upanishad (1.4.15) extends this classification even to gods.

The four-fold caste system of the Vedic times does not exist anymore, although the beliefs associated with it still exist. The purity of the original fourfold caste system is also extinct now. However, some people still cling to it and justify it with elaborate arguments. The original fourfold social structure has been replaced currently by a vestigial social order consisting of thousands of castes, with their origins unknown or vague. Their equation with the original four varnas is also ambiguous. Some scholars superimpose it upon today's castes and draw parallels, but it is a stretch. Many of today's castes originated subsequently due to the complex history of India and the many developments that happened in the wake of internecine wars and foreign conquests. Some castes might have existed as independent communities, tribes, army units, or cultural groups outside the Vedic fold in ancient times before they were gradually integrated into mainstream Hinduism. Castes still exert influence on the social fabric and add to the cultural diversity of India. The fourfold division of people is justified if we group them according to their essential nature (gunas) rather than their birth. We know that humans vary in their behavior and nature according to their predominant modes. However, it would be unfair to group them exclusively according to birth or genetics. The essential nature, purity, impurity, or propensity of humans they are not static. They can change according to circumstances or one's actions. Therefore, the argument that people belong to rigid social groups or castes from birth is untenable, at least in today's world. We can cite many examples to prove it. The same holds for women and their changing status roles in today's world. They can no longer be treated as subservient to men in religious or household duties.

Sloka 42

śamo damas tapaḥ śaucaṃ kṣāntir ārjavam eva ca
jñānaṃ vijñānam āstikyaṃ brahmakarma svabhāvajam

shamah = serenity, tranquility, equanimity; damah = self-control; tapah = austerity; saucam = cleanliness, purity; ksantih = endurance, tolerance, forgiveness; arjavam = uprightness; eva = so also; ca = and; jnanam = knowledge; vijnanam = wisdom; astikyam = faith, belief; brahma = of a brahmana; karma = obligatory duties; svabhava-jam = born of nature.

Equanimity, self-control, austerity, cleanliness, endurance, also uprightness, knowledge, wisdom, and faith, are the obligatory duties of a Brahmana born of his natural disposition.

Shama means serenity, peace, and tranquility. Dama means self-restraint or self-control. Both are interrelated. Shama arises from dama only when the mind and senses are withdrawn and desires and attachments are suppressed. Both are essential for self-purification. When dama is practiced, and shama is firmly established through renunciation and detachment, one experiences sameness or equanimity. From that arises the ability to practice samyama (restraint of the mind and senses and the influence of the gunas), which leads to exclusive devotion and absorption in the Self or the chosen deity. Tapah means the practice of generating bodily heat (tapah) through austerities to purify, increase, and conserve the energies in the body for spiritual purposes. It is a form of yoga only, which seers and saints practiced in ancient times before yoga became the standard spiritual practice. Some practices of tapah were subsequently incorporated into yoga. For example, tapo-yoga combines the best of both practices, such as renunciation, fasting, restraint of speech, mind, and senses, and techniques such as dharana, dhyana, samyama, and samadhi.

Saucham refers to physical cleanliness. It is how one should maintain the surroundings and living place. Without cleanliness, godliness does not arise. It is important to keep the mind free from impure thoughts and awaken the deities in our subtle bodies to assist us in our internal sacrifices, self-purification, and inner awakening. Kshanti means endurance, tolerance, forgiveness, or forbearance, which arises due to the predominance of sattva, absence of desires and expectations, self-control, nonviolence or absence of enmity, firm resolve, and faith in God. Jnanam and vijnanam are often used to mean the same. However, from a philosophical perspective, jnanam refers to the knowledge contained in the scriptures. It is essential to practice self-study and spirituality. Vijnanam refers to the knowledge that arises from experience, observation, reflection, analysis, and discernment. Some translate them as knowledge and wisdom, or scriptural and experiential knowledge. Brahmanas are supposed to maintain utmost purity and live righteously and selflessly, performing their obligatory duties. The Dharma Shastras affirm that the Brahmanas who do not live righteously, study the Vedas, or perform the sacrifices ordained by the Vedas should not be considered Brahmanas.

The qualities or attributes mentioned here should naturally manifest in Brahmanas if they live according to their natural sattvic disposition and perform their obligatory duties as ordained by the Vedas. It is also obligatory on their part to cultivate or strengthen them through their actions (karma), serving the aims of Dharma as a sacrifice to God. In other words, Brahmanahood is not a birthright. One does not become a Brahmana by birth but by actions (karma), conduct, and the preponderance of sattva (svabhava). Either these qualities must manifest in him, or he must cultivate them.

Sloka 43

śauryaṃ tejo dhṛtir dākṣyaṃ yuddhe cāpy apalāyanam
dānam īśvarabhāvaś ca kṣātraṃ karma svabhāvajam

sauryam = valor; tejah = vigor; dhrtih = resolve, firmness, determination; daksyam = dexterity, ability; yuddhe = in battle; ca = and; api = also; apalayanam = not fleeing or running away or deserting; danam = generosity; isvara bhavah = lordliness; ca = and; ksatram = ksatriya; karma = obligatory duties; svabhava-jam = born of nature.

Valor, vigor, firmness, dexterity, also not running away in the middle of a battle, generosity, and lordliness are duties of a Kshatriya born of his natural disposition.

The qualities mentioned here are the ideal characteristics of Kshatriyas with the predominance of rajas. As we have seen before, the mode of rajas induces passions and emotions, materiality, desires, attachments, etc. If they are controlled and channeled properly with righteous intentions, the ideal Kshatriya nature will manifest in humans. The Kshatriyas originally belonged to the warrior class and formed the ruling elite. However, in today's world, these qualities are not limited to warriors alone. They are equally relevant in various other professions, including business and agriculture. Some Brahmanas may also possess Kshatriya nature, as is evident from the Puranas like Parasurama and Dronacharya. Kshatriya nature is prevalent in all humans, however, to different degrees. Every living being on Earth is engaged in a battle for survival. The willingness to fight and take risks arises from the Kshatriya nature only. It is beneficial when tempered by divine qualities and destructive when tempered by asuric qualities.

This verse mentions six qualities of Kshatriyas: shauryaṃ, tejam, dhriti, dakshya, apalayanam, danam, and isvarabhava. They arise from the combination of rajas and sattva and manifest in those who protect and uphold God's eternal Dharma, whether they serve as householders, warriors, village heads, tribal chiefs, commanders, kings, rulers, administrators, judges, or enforcers of law and order. These duties were not just assigned but were commanded by God himself. The Baudhayana Sutras state that God placed strength in Kshatriyas and entrusted them with the duties and privileges of studying the Vedas, sacrificing, generosity, knowledge of weapons, and protecting the wealth and life of beings.

Shauryam, the quality of courage, bravery, or heroism, is a defining characteristic of Kshatriyas. It is the heroic quality of acting courageously against enemies and facing adverse situations without giving up until the end. Dhriti, the quality of resolve or firmness, is equally important. A warrior is nothing without bravery and resolve. In ancient times, Kshatriyas were born to die fighting. They were taught to face death on the battlefield without fear. The teachings of the Bhagavadgita were primarily meant for warriors like Arjuna to deal with the fear of death and the moral problem of causing death and destruction in wars, which used to be brutal in the past.

Dakshyam means skill, hard work, dexterity, or capability. A Kshatriya should be firm and resolute and muster all his strength, courage, intelligence, knowledge, and skills on the battlefield or in competitive work. He should persevere even if the odds are stacked against him and never turn his back on his enemy, run away from the battlefield (apalayanam), or leave the task unfinished. He must also vigorously train himself in martial arts and various combative techniques, besides studying warcraft and statesmanship (rajanīthi) if he was born in a royal family or was destined to serve as a minister, commander, general, or nobleman. Manu says, "Not to turn back in battle, to protect the people, to honor the Brahmanas, is the best means for a king to secure happiness." Those who fight on the battlefield with utmost exertion until the end, without turning back, go to heaven.

Tejam means speed, vigor, or fieriness arising from excessive vitality, strength, and stamina. A warrior's life and actions depend on them. He needs mental vigor to outsmart his enemies in strategy and physical vigor to outlast them in fighting. He must exude fieriness (tejam) to strike terror in the hearts of his enemies.

Danam, the quality of generosity, is a fundamental trait of a Kshatriya. A warrior must be generous and kind-hearted, forgive his enemies, and spare their lives if they surrender or admit defeat. He should generously give gifts to the Brahmanas who perform sacrifices for him, give him counsel or guidance, approach him for help, or work for the cause of Dharma. He should also be charitable towards his subjects and those who fight along with him or serve him. This generosity, coupled with his leadership, forms the backbone of a Kshatriya's character.

Isvara bhava means to think and act like a lord, ruler, or leader (Isvara) or act as God's representative upon earth. The Gautama Sutras state that the king is the master of all except Brahmanas, and everyone, including the Brahmanas, shall obey him. In dispensing justice, he shall follow the Vedas and use reason to arrive at the truth. Tradition empowers Kshatriya rulers to act as the lords of the land, claim the lands they conquer by force, and punish those who disobey them or their lordship, indulge in criminal or treasonous conduct, or ignore their duties. As lords and rulers, they have the right to impose taxes justly upon the people they rule and collect them by force, if necessary. This concept of 'Isvara bhava' highlights the leadership role of Kshatriyas and their authority in maintaining law and order.

A Kshatriya has the right and obligation to protect and uphold his dignity, nobility, humanity, pride, righteousness, and self-esteem through his actions and righteous conduct. He should be a valiant and resolute fighter and a good human being, devoted to God and his duty. In prosperity or adversity, he shall be a resourceful leader and commander with a generous heart and an intelligent mind, and perform his duties in war and peace as ordained by the Vedas or the laws of his land. These qualities manifest in him if he abides in the Kshatriya dharma and performs his obligatory duties without succumbing to evil passions such as pride, fear, anger, greed, envy, etc.

Sloka 44

kṛṣigaurakṣyavāṇijyaṃ vaiśyakarma svabhāvajam
paricaryātmakaṃ karma śūdrasyāpi svabhāvajam

krsi = agriculture; go = cows; raksya = protection; vanijyam = trade and commerce; vaisya = vaisya; karma = duty; svabhava-jam = born out of his own nature; paricarya = service; atmakam =in the form of; karma = obligatory duties; sudrasya = of the sudra; api = and; svabhava-jam = born of nature.

Agriculture, protection of cows, trade, and commerce are the duties of a Vaisya born of his essential nature. Work in the form of serving others is the duty of a Shudra, arising from his natural disposition.

Agriculture, cattle rearing, trade, and commerce are the prescribed duties of a Vaishya. Serving others is the obligatory duty of a Shudra. Although these two classes were placed in the social hierarchy after the Brahmanas and Kshatriyas, Manu (8.418) recognized their importance, stating that the world would fall into chaos if they did not perform their respective duties. The Vedas entrusted the Vaishyas with the duty of generating wealth through farming, trade, and commerce. Their main duty was the creation and distribution of wealth for the good of society. According to Manusmriti (1.90), Vaishyas should tend to cattle, bestow gifts, offer sacrifices, study the Vedas, trade, lend money, and cultivate land. Due to many historical reasons, these duties were subsequently shared by several other castes. The main difference between the two classes is that in the original Vedic tradition, Vaishyas had the privilege to study the Vedas and perform sacrificial ceremonies, while Shudras were precluded. They were also denied the opportunity to hear the Vedas, which meant they were barred from hosting or participating in the Vedic sacrifices. Another difference is that rajas is the predominant mode of Vaishyas, whereas it is tamas in the case of Shudras. However, due to the presence of the other two modes, it is often difficult to draw a clear line between them, and for that matter, between any castes.

In the Vedic tradition and around the Mahabharata times, Vaishyas were superior to the Shudras and played a vital role in producing and distributing wealth. They were expected to be experts in their professions and ascertain the quality and value of various goods, materials, metals, and precious stones. Ideally, they were ordained to pursue the four aims of human life with Dharma as the foundation and Moksha as the ultimate goal. For a long time in the history of India, they did their part. They also propagated Dharma by generously contributing to charitable works such as constructing temples, stupas, memorials, and monuments. In war times, they supported their kings by lending them money or supplying food and other materials. Today, Vaishyas are no longer confined to trade, commerce, or business. They are now in almost every profession, including politics. Many also live abroad.

The Shudras formed the fourth and the lowest class in the fourfold varna system (chaturvarna) of the Vedic tradition. All the mixed castes, outcasts, foreigners, etc., were lumped into this group. The Vedas entrusted them with the duty of serving the other three classes. Historically, they were subject to discrimination and many social disabilities. The law books discriminated against them even in marriage, inheritance, and punishment. However, it is doubtful how far the caste system was rigidly followed due to the heterogeneous nature of India's population and culture and the fact that the country's rulers came from different social and religious backgrounds. Many kings of ancient India came from the lower rungs of the social ladder and theoretically belonged to this class. Their social status did not preclude them from ruling large kingdoms and establishing powerful dynasties. Since the sixth century B.C., India witnessed the rise of many religious faiths, sects, schools, philosophies, teacher traditions, and ascetic movements. Most of them, especially those outside the Vedic fold, scoffed at the idea of the caste system and did not support caste-based discrimination. Even within the Vedic religion, there were contrary opinions about the hereditary caste system, like the ones mentioned in the Vajrasuchika Upanishad. However, wherever the system prevailed, the lower castes faced discrimination and social inequality. For a long time, they were at the receiving end of discrimination and exploitation. Remnants of that discrimination still exist in some parts of India as a reminder of the past, especially in remote and inaccessible areas where the government's reach is limited or traditional panchayats are still in control.

Sloka 45

sve sve karmaṇy abhirataḥ saṃsiddhiṃ labhate naraḥ
svakarmanirataḥ siddhiṃ yathā vindati tac chṛṇu

sve sve = one's own; karmani = duty; abhiratah = following, taking delight; samsiddhim = absolute perfection, excellence, success; labhate = attains; narah = a person, human being; sva-karma = by his own duty; niratah = following; siddhim = perfection, success; yatha = how, in what manner; vindati = attains; tat = that; srnu = hear, listen.

By following one's own duty, a human being attains absolute perfection. Listen to how that perfection is achieved by following one's own duty.

Svakarma means the duty that arises from one's essential nature. It is the duty ordained by God for humans according to their natural propensities or predominant modes. The idea is that one should follow one's natural inclinations to attain perfection in life and fulfill one's obligation to God and others. Siddhi means perfection. It refers to the serene state of purity and sameness, which is completely free from the impurities of ignorance, delusion, desires, duality, attachments, egoism, evil qualities, and mental disturbances. It begins with the practice of jnana karma-sannyasa yoga, in conjunction with other yogas such as adhyatama and buddhi yogas, which lead to the purification of the mind and body and the firmness of the mind, faith, and resolve. In whatever way one may begin the practice, the ultimate aim is to abide in the Self with unwavering devotion and attain liberation.

This verse clearly states that perfection is attained only by following one's duty (svakarma). The duties are specific to one's essential nature as determined by the predominance of the modes. Sattvic people attain purification and perfection by selflessly performing the duties listed in verse

42: serenity, self-control, austerity, cleanliness, endurance, uprightness, knowledge, wisdom, and faith. Rajasic people (Kshatriyas) attain it by performing their duties as listed in verse 43: acting with bravery, vigor, firmness, skill, generosity, and lordliness, and not fleeing from the battlefield. Lastly, Vaishyas and Shudras should attain it by selflessly practicing their duties as stated in the previous verse, namely agriculture, cattle rearing, trade and commerce, business, arts and crafts, and service.

When the three classes of people perform their duties in this manner, without desiring their fruit, the predominant gunas in them strengthen, and the weaker modes are suppressed or weakened. When karma-sannyasa yogis reach a certain level of optimum perfection in their practice, and their minds and bodies are purified through sacrificial duties, mystic powers (siddhis) manifest in them as the outward expression of their growing perfection and spiritual progress. However, such developments on the path of liberation are not as important as the ultimate goal of attaining liberation, sameness, or oneness. Hence, without being distracted by them, yogis should remain focused on reaching the ultimate goal, transcending the gunas. Although they play an important role in practicing obligatory duties, in the advanced stages, the gunas should be transcended since they induce desire-ridden actions and attachments. If they are active, one is always vulnerable to their influence. Therefore, ideally, householders must advance from practicing karma-sannyasa to transcending the gunas and entering the pure state of self-absorption.

The journey of liberation is long and arduous. Householders must begin their pursuit of Moksha by performing duties selflessly according to their essential nature (karma svabhavajam) and sacrificing (tyaga) their fruit. When duties are performed and obligations are met through jnana karma-sannyasa yoga, they must attain the modeless state of self-awareness, transcending the gunas and becoming a gunatita, one who is beyond the modes. According to the Yogasutras, it is achieved when the gunas retire into their original, latent state and stop inducing desires and attachments or causing mental modifications (chitta vrittis). However, one should not stop there but continue practicing self-control (samyama) and exclusive devotion until the final state of absolute perfection (samsiddhi) is attained. However, it cannot be attained through duty and devotion only. The grace of the Supreme Lord is also essential. This is explained in the next verse.

Sloka 46

yataḥ pravṛttir bhūtānāṃ yena sarvam idaṃ tatam
svakarmaṇā tam abhyarcya siddhiṃ vindati mānavaḥ

yatah = from whom; pravrttih = issue forth, manifest, emerge; bhutanam = of living beings; yena = by whom; sarvam = all; idam = this; tatam = is pervaded; sva-karmana = by own duty; tam = Him; abhyarcya = by worshipping; siddhim = perfection; vindati = achieves; manavah = a human being.

He from whom issue forth all the living beings (and) by whom all this is pervaded, by worshipping him through one's own duty, a human being achieves the highest perfection.

The best form of devotion for a householder is devotion through obligatory duties, sannyasa (renouncing desires), and tyaga (sacrificing the fruit of karma). All actions are elevated and purified by the last two. In a broader sense, karma means all actions, but in karma yoga, it refers to obligatory duties or any action that is sacrificed to the Supreme Lord. One does not live by performing duties only. One has to perform several actions to ensure self-preservation. Since they also produce karma, one has to extend the practice of karma yoga to include all actions, even the mundane ones, and consecrate them to the Supreme Lord from whom all this manifests and by whom all this is pervaded. In the ultimate sense, all actions also arise from the Supreme Lord only. Although he remains passive in the beings, since all actions arise from Prakriti, which is an inseparable aspect of him, we must consider that he is the source of all actions. Hence, this verse clearly states that the key to attaining liberation is by worshipping the Lord through one's duty and actions without desires and attachments and without desiring their fruit. When you worship him thus, the higher shaktis in your body awaken and help you in self-transformation and purification.

The seeker of liberation must be completely selfless and free from the influence of desires and gunas in his thinking and actions, with God as the center of his life and consciousness. He must put himself at his feet and under his will, establish his mind in his contemplation, and make himself, his life, and his actions a sacrificial offering to him. He may worship him ritually or spiritually, but by performing his duties and offering them to him, he elevates his actions into a superior form of renunciation and sacrifice. By that consecration or sacrifice, his actions become worship, and his life a way of expressing faith, devotion, offering, and surrender. When you perform actions for the Lord, suppressing your desires and attachments and leaving your cares to him, you open yourself to his eternal love, inner awakening, and purification. Whether you are a Brahmana, Kshatriya, Vaisya, or Shudra, as a householder, your path to liberation is through duty or actions only. Knowledge, wisdom, discernment, purity, morality, righteous conduct, detachment, renunciation, self-control, etc., prepare you for that journey, but ultimately, devotion is the raft, and God's love is the wind that gently moves you across the ocean of samsara.

You may worship the Supreme Lord ritually or spiritually, but the best form of worship is through your actions, which you must perform for his sake and to fulfill the aims of his creation. Performing them according to your predominant nature, you must fulfill your obligations not only to the Supreme Being but also to all others in your life, including your family members, ancestors, gods, seers, and sages, those who seek your help or live in your protection, animals, and other living beings. This is the path ordained by the Vedas for the householders unless or until they renounce their duties and take up sannyasa. Jnana karma-sannyasa yoga is the prescribed path. However, by itself, it does not lead you to liberation. You must also practice it with devotion to the Lord in you, establishing your thoughts in his contemplation. Devotion to him (Isvara paridhana) is the ultimate duty. It burns your desires and purifies your actions. Patanjali states that one can attain the state of uninterrupted self-absorption (sampradaya samadhi) or the awareness of the Self through devotion to Isvara. The Katha Upanishad (2.20) affirms the same by stating that the Self, which is greater than the great and smaller than the small, can be realized through divine grace (anugraha). You earn his grace through duty and devotion. Whatever your duty, profession, or background, devotion to the Lord who resides in you as your true Self is necessary to shield yourself from the uncertainties of life. It is the best way to earn his grace. Without it, one cannot attain the highest perfection (samsiddhi).

Sloka 47

śreyān svadharmo viguṇaḥ paradharmot svanuṣṭhitāt
svabhāvaniyataṃ karma kurvan nāpnoti kilbiṣam

sreyan = better; sva-dharmah = one's own dharma; vigunah = devoid of merits; para-dharmat = another's duty; suanusthitat = well performed; svabhava-niyatam = according to one's nature; karma = actions; kurvan = performing; na = not; apnoti = attains; kilbisam = sin.

Better is one's duty, even if devoid of merits, than another's duty well performed. By performing actions according to one's nature, one is not tainted by sin.

This verse contains the simple truth: you must be true to yourself and live accordingly. A householder should perform his obligatory duties arising from his essential nature (svabhavajam) rather than following another's duty, however superior or better it may be. It means you must be true to yourself, be yourself, and live in harmony with yourself, choosing your actions according to your essential nature. You must not imitate others just because you like them, consider them superior, or feel inspired by them, not at least until you improve, purify, or change your nature, and it is in harmony with what you intend to do.

Some people interpret this verse to mean that obligatory duties must be according to one's caste, and one must stick to them instead of dabbling in the duties of another caste, even if they are superior, convenient, or excellent. It would have been true a few centuries ago when the ancient, fourfold varna system was strictly followed, and people strictly adhered to their family traditions and vocations. It does not hold in today's world, where we have thousands of castes, and people have the freedom to choose different occupations and lifestyles according to their preferences and circumstances. Therefore, ideally, people will be better off if they make informed decisions about their duties and occupations according to their essential nature, paying attention to their deepest aspirations, talents, and skills. It would be good for them and their ancestors if they stick to their ancestral faith and do not convert to another faith. Hindu householders have obligatory duties towards several entities, especially gods, ancestors, seers, and sages, who depend upon them for nourishment. If they convert to another faith and abandon their gods and ancestors, they will break the transmigratory cycles of several souls, including their own, and disrupt the order and regularity of their evolution and progression. That is sinful and adharma.

Apart from the above, one should stick to one's essential nature and perform duties accordingly, for other reasons. For example, each obligatory duty is an offering or an obligation to God. By performing it, you not only uphold his eternal duties and ensure the order and regularity of the world but also grow mentally and spiritually and progress towards a better future, light, and liberation. Svadharma is the means to svarajya, independence, or liberation from dependence upon the world and its conditioning. Further, it is always good to follow one's natural inclinations and aspirations according to one's nature rather than trying to be someone else. No one will be happy by being pretentious or living a lie. One must choose a profession, vocation, or occupation according to one's predominant modes, deepest aspirations, and natural talents and perform actions as an offering or sacrifice to the Lord. All this belongs to the Lord of the Universe. By performing their obligatory duties and serving him with devotion, using their wealth of talents and abilities, householders can repay their debt to him and attain the ultimate freedom. They will remain bound, accumulating sinful karma, if they neglect them or ignore their deeper calling and fail in their duties.

All animate and inanimate things in the universe are endowed with certain natural propensities (prvritti) born out of their modes and properties or essential nature. For example, it is the nature of fire to burn, water to flow, air to move swiftly, and earth to stay firm and support. The world will be in chaos if they do not perform their duties or if beings ignore theirs. For the natural order to prevail and life to progress as ordained, all things must function according to their nature. Only then will balance, peace, and harmony prevail. If you are naturally inclined to be an artist or philosopher but choose another profession hoping to earn more, you will not do justice to it, your duties, or yourself. When things and people perform their duties in harmony with themselves, they express their uniqueness and contribute to the diversity and richness of life. If everyone wants to be a doctor, lawyer, or engineer, who will perform other tasks? For their happiness and the world's progress, people should pursue different occupations according to their predominant nature or mode.

How can people choose what is good for them or give them happiness and fulfillment? In such matters, one should listen to the deepest longing or the soul's yearning. When we listen deeply and pay attention, we will know what is good for us, what profession suits us, what talents and skills are inherent, and how we can excel in our actions. Ideally, one must choose whatever one likes doing, enjoy peace, happiness, and fulfillment, or an opportunity to be true to oneself, serve others, or God himself. When we follow our essential nature and perform duties accordingly, we align with our goals, aspirations, and spiritual destinies and become skillful in our actions. In today's world, your discernment, buddhi, or intelligence, is your best guide. If you are in harmony with yourself and perform your actions, you have better chances of manifesting your highest vision. Irrespective of what others think about it, you will have better chances and opportunities to achieve peace and happiness and fulfill your obligations to yourself, your family, the world, and God.

Sloka 48

sahajaṃ karma kaunteya sadoṣam api na tyajet
sarvārambhā hi doṣeṇa dhūmenāgnir ivāvṛtāḥ

saha-jam = innate, inborn or inherent nature; karma = duty; kaunteya = O son of Kunti; sa-dosam = faulty, with faultu; api = even if; na = not; tyajet = give up; sarva-arambhah = all actions, undertaking; because = surely; dosena = by fault, defect, error; dhumena = with smoke; agnih = fire; iva = as; avrtah = enveloped, covered.

O Son of Kunti, one should not give up one's duty, which arises from the inherent nature, even if it is faulty, because all actions are enveloped by faults just as fire is by smoke.

Some scholars interpret sahaja karma as the duty particular to the caste as determined at birth. The interpretation supports the hereditary caste system and the belief that duties and castes are genetically predetermined at birth due to karma. If we believe in karma and rebirth, we must accept that this interpretation has some validity. However, the world is now more complex. Many factors interfere with the birth of humans and their transmigration. It is difficult for every soul to obtain the right womb. The current caste system has little resemblance to the Vedic caste system of ancient times. The Vedic religion itself disappeared, and what we have now hidden in Hinduism is its remnant. Therefore, while we may accept that a person's inherent nature and circumstances are predetermined at birth, we cannot say they can be correlated to that person's caste, social, or economic status. We must also accept the fact that apart from genetics, environmental factors, cultural influences, and circumstances also play an important role in the development of human personality, character, and behavior.

Yet, we come across many educated scholars who still believe in the hereditary caste system and justify it using outdated arguments. For example, we still have people who believe that a Brahmana might perform the duties of a Shudra in adversity, but that Shudras should never undertake the duties of a Brahmana or Kshatriya. Such interpretations find their support in the ancient laws prescribed by the Manusmriti. However, in today's world, law books like the Manusmriti are not mandatory for Hindus. They may help us cultivate discernment and make good choices about conduct and morality, but one should not follow them mindlessly, ignoring the current reality. The ancient fourfold varna system is extinct and cannot be revived or applied to the present world. Hence, it is safe to stick to the premise that people must choose their duties and occupations according to their inherent nature and best judgment rather than what people followed 2000 years ago.

Dosha means an impurity, consequence, or defect. Doshas are inherent to our existence. Everything is enveloped by impurities. The same is true about actions also. They can be unpleasant, difficult to perform, or morally repugnant. In every profession, one has to perform unpleasant tasks. A Brahmana may perform the last rites for a deceased person sitting on the floor at the cremation grounds, surrounded by the stench of burning bodies. A Kshatriya has to slay people on the battlefield and walk through piles of injured and dead people. A manager in an enterprise may have to fire people to keep the Company profitable. One cannot avoid such tasks because they are unpleasant or create moral dilemmas. Lord Krishna says that one should not abandon actions because they are faulty, meaning difficult, routine, inferior, boring, unpleasant, painful, destructive, or objectionable. The Lord himself performs many unpleasant tasks as the Lord of Death and Destroyer to keep the worlds in balance or restore Dharma. The gods of heaven often unleash terrible storms and other natural calamities to help Nature renew and recycle. As God's representatives upon earth, humans must follow the same example. By transcending likes and dislikes and remaining equal and indifferent, and without desires and expectations, they should perform their duties and fulfill their obligations, however difficult they are.

Sloka 49

asaktabuddhiḥ sarvatra jitātmā vigataspṛhaḥ
naiṣkarmyasiddhiṃ paramāṃ saṃnyāsenādhigacchati

asakta-buddhih = detached, disinterested intelligence; sarvatra = universally everywhere; jita-atma = self-conqueror, self-subdued yogi; vigata-sprhah = without desires; naiskarmya-siddhim = attains the state of inaction; paramam = supreme; sannyasena = by renunciation; adhigacchati = attains.

With his intelligence detached from everything (and) everywhere, the self-conqueror, who is without desires, attains the supreme state of Naishkarmya Siddhi.

When the mind is always detached from everything and everywhere, the conqueror of the mind and body, who is without desires and expectations, attains naishkarmya siddhi, which means the supreme state of inaction in action. It is also the supreme state of stillness, which is free from prvritti (the outgoing mind), parinama (changes arising from causes and effects), niyama (the obligation to perform duties and actions), and sprha (the longing or desire to attain any end). Naishkarmya means the state of absolute freedom from actions, duties, and obligations. According to the ideal code of conduct, Hindu householders must perform obligatory duties such as daily sacrifices (nitya) and occasional (naimittika) sacrifices, sacraments (samskaras), austerities, and other rites and rituals as prescribed by the Vedas. These duties, while necessary for maintaining the social and spiritual order, can also be seen as potential obstacles to attaining naishkarmya siddhi. They cannot be avoided, whether they are pleasant or unpleasant. In the mortal world, karma arises from both action and inaction as long as they are performed with desires and attachments, wishing to enjoy their fruit. Upon liberation, the conqueror of the mind and body (jitatma) becomes the conqueror of action and inaction. He becomes the actionless Self. The supreme state is attained through knowledge, detachment, self-conquest, and renunciation of desires.

This verse directly refutes the earliest Mimansika belief that the jivas are bound to actions and never attain liberation or freedom from obligatory duties, and that upon completing their obligations, they go to heaven to return and continue their duties from where they left. It presents the Vedantic concept that humans can qualify for liberation through Naishkarmya Siddhi, or freedom from obligatory duties. The jivas are subject to causes and effects (karma). They cannot be free from movements and actions. Dynamism (chaitanyam) is the essential nature of the life and consciousness of the jivas. When humans subdue their minds and senses and perform actions without desiring their fruit, they attain freedom from karma (naishkarmya). This is the highest perfection (siddhi) they can ever attain while they are still embodied. If they falter on the path, they go to heaven, but if they succeed, they attain oneness with Brahman or go to the immortal heaven and live there forever in bliss.

The state of liberation is also the supreme state of inaction in action (karmani akarma). In that state, karma (actions) becomes akarma (inaction) and ceases to produce consequences. It is as if you have not engaged in any action, even when awake and actively engaged. Lord Krishna presented these ideas in the fourth chapter (18-19) of the Bhagavadgita, where he stated that the wise ones who saw action in inaction and inaction in action would be free from karma, even when they performed actions. In the previous verse, we heard how difficult it was for people to remain free from the consequences of their actions because all actions were faulty and enveloped by impurities (dosas). In this verse, he stated that those defects or consequences could be removed by attaining naishkarmya siddhi, the highest perfection, through detachment, the conquest of the mind and senses, and the renunciation of desires.

Sloka 50

siddhiṃ prāpto yathā brahma tathāpnoti nibodha me
samāsenaiva kaunteya niṣṭhā jñānasya yā parā

siddhim = perfection; praptah = achieved, attained; yatha = just as; brahma = Brahman; tatha = so is; apnoti = attained, reaches; nibodha = understand; me = from Me; samasena = in brief; eva = indeed; kaunteya = O son of Kunti; nistha = steadfast dedication, devotion or commitment, ; jnanasya = of knowledge; ya = which; para = the highest.

Understand from Me in brief, O son of Kunti, how just as perfection is achieved, in the same way, Brahman is attained through steadfast dedication to knowledge, which is the highest.

In the previous verse, Lord Krishna expounded how a self-restrained and detached self-conqueror could attain perfection through renunciation. Here, he wanted Arjuna to understand how, after attaining the actionless state of naishkarmya siddhi, Brahman could be attained through steadfast dedication (jnana nishta) to knowing the highest knowledge about him. This highest knowledge is the knowledge of the highest and absolute state of Brahman, by knowing which nothing else needs to be known. According to these verses, naishkarmya siddhi precedes or leads to the attainment of Brahman or his absolute reality, and freedom from karma should not be mistaken for the supreme state of Brahman, as some schools of Vedanta hold. Actions are for the mind and body only, not for the Self. Even in the embodied state, the Lord, who is the Self in the body, is not bound by any duties or actions. However, the Siddha who attains that perfection still needs to perform actions to keep himself alive. Therefore, we may safely assume that naishkarmya siddhi is the highest perfection a devotee can achieve in the embodied state through detachment, freedom from desires, and the conquest of his physical self (jitatma). Having attained that freedom or perfection in this way, he must focus on attaining the highest perfection of oneness through the relentless pursuit of the supreme knowledge of Brahman (brahmajnanam). Thus, Para (transcendental) Brahman is attained through naishkarmya siddhi and jnana nishta. The former is attained through karma-sannyasa yoga, and the latter through jnana and bhakti yogas. The last one is crucial because all yogis, despite their achievements, need divine grace to escape from samsara.

Sloka 51

buddhyā viśuddhayā yukto dhṛtyātmānaṃ niyamya ca
śabdādīn viṣayāṃs tyaktvā rāgadveṣau vyudasya ca

buddhya = intelligence; visuddhaya = purest, completely pure; yuktah = endowed with, filled with, united to; dhrtya = by resolve; atmanam = in oneself; niyamya = restraining; ca = and; sabda-adin = such as sound etc.; visayan = sense objects; tyaktva = giving up; raga = attraction, attachment; dvesau = aversion; vyudasya = setting aside; ca = and.

Endowed with the purest intelligence, restraining himself with resolve, giving up sense-objects such as sound, etc., setting aside attraction and aversion...

This and the next three verses explain how to achieve Brahman's absolute state. This verse mentions four requirements: pure intelligence, self-restraint, giving up sense objects, and overcoming attraction and aversion. Visuddhi buddhi (purified intelligence) means intelligence free from delusion, doubt, and confusion. The unwavering control of the mind and body with firm resolve or fortitude (dhriti) is attained through withdrawing the mind and senses and practicing atma-samyama with yamas and niyamas. The third requirement is the renunciation of sense objects, starting with sound. etc., meaning one has to separate the senses from the mind by arresting all the incoming perceptual information through withdrawal (nivrtti) and inward-looking. Although only sound is mentioned, one has to give up all worldly objects and sensual pleasures except those required to keep the body alive and healthy and practice detachment, self-control, and renunciation. Sound is emphasized because sounds can be very distracting. We can control the perceptions arising from sights, smells, touch, and taste by moving away from their sources. However, most sounds like thunder, the noises of people talking, birds chirping, water flowing, wind blowing, rain falling, etc., are not in our control, and we cannot wholly avoid or shut them down. They can be restrained through resolve only by becoming indifferent to them and drawing the mind and senses into oneself. The fourth requirement is overcoming attraction and aversion to the pairs of opposites and sense objects, including those necessary for maintaining the body. It is achieved by overcoming desires through detachment and renunciation and offering actions and their fruit to the Lord. We may presume that the requirements are mentioned in the order of their importance. Purified intelligence is the foremost because it is necessary for other practices.

Sloka 52

viviktasevī laghvāśī yatavākkāyamānasaḥ
dhyānayogaparo nityaṃ vairāgyaṃ samupāśritaḥ

vivikta-sevi = dwelling in solitude; laghu-asi = eating little; yata = controlling; vak = speech; kaya = body; manasah = mind; dhyana = dhyana yoga = yoga of meditation and concentration; parah = as the highest; nityam = ever, always; vairagyam = dispassion; samupasritah = having taken refuge.

Dwelling in solitude, eating little, controlling speech, body, and mind, practicing dhyana yoga on the highest, and always taking refuge in dispassion...

This verse mentions four more requirements: solitude, eating little, controlling speech, body, and mind, and dispassion. Vivikta means seclusion, solitude, or isolation. Viviktasevin means one who prefers solitude or renders devotional service in solitary places. It was customary in ancient times for householders who gave up their obligatory duties to retire to forests and practice their vows of renunciation (sannyasa), living in secluded or abandoned places to avoid contact with worldly people. Solitude leads to purity, clarity, discernment, and mental stability. Staying alone, yogis can reflect upon themselves, their purpose, and their essential nature. They can minimize distractions and practice austerities and self-purification without interruptions. The restraint of the mind and speech, detachment, and renunciation also become easier in solitude, staying away from worldly people and crowded places. Laghvasi means eating in small quantities or as much as is necessary to keep oneself alive. Lord Krishna previously said that yoga is not for the one who overeats or does not eat at all. On the path of liberation, one has to practice moderation in eating, speaking, and sleeping. In the advanced stages, one should eat even less to purify the body. It will not only strengthen the resolve to overcome hunger and craving for food but also suppress the tamasic mode, which is responsible for excessive sleep, lethargy, lust, etc. The control of speech becomes easier in seclusion when one avoids human contact and practices solitude. By restraining speech even amidst people, one can avoid disturbing others or oneself. Restraining the body and mind is necessary for self-control, stability, peace, and tranquility. Controlling the speech, body, and mind helps the yogis in dhyana yoga (concentration and meditation) to fix their minds on Brahman (para) without distractions. Some commentators interpret 'dhyana-yoga' as two words, 'dhyana and yoga,' and some as one. We prefer the latter since yoga encompasses all the yogic practices, including the ones mentioned here, whereas dhyana yoga refers to a specific yoga, the practice of meditation or meditation with concentration, which leads to samyama (stillness) and samadhi. All these practices help the yogi excel in the fourth practice: vairagya, or the practice of dispassion, detachment, or indifference to material things. With its uninterrupted and regular practice (nityam), the other practices mentioned here and before also become easier.

Sloka 53

ahaṃkāraṃ balaṃ darpaṃ kāmaṃ krodhaṃparigraham
vimucya nirmamaḥ śānto brahmabhūyāya kalpate

ahankaram = egoism; balam = strength; darpam = pride, arrogance; kamam = lust; krodham = anger; parigraham = covetousness; vimucya = becoming free; nirmamah = without the thought of 'me' or 'mine'; santah = peaceful; brahma-bhuyaya = abide in Brahman; kalpate = becomes qualified, fit.

Freeing himself from egoism, strength, pride, lust, anger, (and) covetousness, without the feeling of mine or ownership, (and) peaceful, he becomes fit to abide in Brahman.

This verse must be read in conjunction with the previous two (51 & 52) to comprehend fully the practices and qualities required to attain the absolute state of Brahman. The three verses collectively emphasize the strengthening of divine qualities and the suppression of negative ones. The current verse specifically addresses six negative qualities: egoism, strength, pride, lust, anger, and covetousness. These qualities, originating from rajas and tamas, must be relinquished to achieve purity and liberation. Just as rajas and tamas can be subdued through knowledge, discernment, renunciation, detachment, and dispassion, so can these negative qualities be subdued so that one can overcome desires and attachments.

Ahamkaram is egoism or the feeling that "I am different and separate from others, and I am important and responsible for my actions and achievements. Therefore, I deserve importance, recognition, and respect." In a spiritual sense, it is the belief that the physical self is real, distinct, and different from others. It is the strongest among the tamasic people, with an asuric nature, and comparatively weaker in rajasic ones. Egoistic people live for themselves, engaging in selfish and desire-ridden actions. They may ignore their obligatory duties or perform them to fulfill their desires. Its associated qualities are ignorance, delusion, desires, and attachments.

Balam usually means strength, but in this context, it has a negative connotation. Here, it means animal strength, brute power, or strength mixed with the impurities of rajas and tamas. According to Shankara, it is different from the physical or natural strength of the body that cannot be renounced. So, we may consider it excessive strength that can be controlled or channeled for good or bad. Darpa means vanity, false pride, an inflamed ego, or arrogance arising from poor self-image or self-esteem. It makes one put on false appearances or engage in showy behavior. Kama (lust) and krodha (anger) are included in the six evilest passions (mahapatakas). They strengthen evil nature, egoism, and delusion. Hence, they should be controlled vigorously to avoid self-destruction.

Parigraham means coveting ownership or trying to seize things that do not lawfully belong to one but to others. A renunciant must give up everything and should not entertain the thought of owning or having anything. According to Shankara, he must give up the ownership of even the few belongings necessary for maintaining his body, including its life, to become a Paramahamsa, Parivrajaka, or the Sannyasin of the fourth or the highest order.

These impurities, if left unchecked, can hinder self-purification, peace, and happiness. However, when they are successfully removed, as Patanjali states (2.41), the yogi attains cheerfulness, one-pointedness, sense-control, and readiness to perceive the Self. The yogi, free from them, including the notion of 'me' and 'mine' (nirmama), gains control over his mind and body (kāyendra siddhi) and attains peace and tranquility (sāntih). With a still mind absorbed in uninterrupted silence or exclusive devotion, and with all the impurities suppressed, he becomes fit to enter the absolute state of Brahman, experiencing ultimate freedom and peace.

Sloka 54

brahmabhūtaḥ prasannātmā na śocati na kāṅkṣati
samaḥ sarveṣu bhūteṣu madbhaktiṃ labhate parām

brahma-bhutah = Brahman; prasanna-atma = blissful within oneself; na = not; socati = grieves, laments; na = not; kanksati = desires; samah = same, equal; sarvesu = all; bhutesu = living beings; mat-bhaktim = devotion to Me; labhate = gains; param = supreme.

He who has attained Brahman and become blissful within himself neither grieves nor desires. Becoming equal to all beings, he gains Supreme devotion to Me.

He who attains Brahman is complete and perfect like Brahman. Therefore, he neither grieves nor desires and has nothing to gain or lose. Prasanna means pure, delighted, blissful, or peaceful. Prasannatma means a happy and contented soul who is satisfied and blissful within himself. A self-realized yogi who attains Brahman's absolute state of wholeness remains cheerful and blissful internally. He neither grieves for nor desires anything. Having attained the highest and absolute fulfillment, he becomes equal to all dualities and remains contended and fulfilled within himself. His state of happiness does not arise from worldly pleasures or from having or not having material things, but from his oneness with Brahman and his blissful consciousness. Even if he is awake and not absorbed in meditation, the bliss of Brahman or the Turya (transcendental) state keeps flowing into him continuously. Having attained that highest state, he remains established in him, with his mind and body completely under his control. Seeing him everywhere and in everyone, he looks upon all beings as equal. Established in that pure consciousness, he reflects upon their actions, happiness, sorrow, and suffering as the undulating waves of samsara without feeling disturbed by them. He regards all events and experiences as the play of Maya, knowing that amidst all the commotion of the world, the Lord in them remains untouched, untainted, and blissful. Having established an unbroken, inseparable, and permanent connection internally with his highest and purest state, immersed in his pure consciousness without distinctions and seeing the Lord in his body as himself or as his very Self (atmanubhuti), he experiences oneness or sameness while remaining detached from the external world. He attains the devotion of the highest kind, which Lord Krishna mentioned in the seventh chapter (7.16) as the selfless and unwavering devotion of the wise one (jnani). The human mind is difficult to control and unstable by nature. In normal conditions, it experiences pain and pleasure through union with and separation from sense objects. It also mirrors the things it perceives within itself and stores them in its layers as fragments of memory (smriti). They keep disturbing it, causing further instability even when the senses are asleep, and the sense objects are absent. When it is dissolved in the supreme consciousness of the Self, the yogi attains peace and bliss and experiences oneness. Patanjali called it 'drashta svarupa avasthanam' (the seer abiding in his own, true nature).

Sloka 55

bhaktyā mām abhijānāti yāvān yaś cāsmi tattvataḥ
tato māṃ tattvato jñātvā viśate tadanantaram

bhaktya = by devotion; mam = Me; abhijanati = know; yavan = comprehensively; yah ca asmi = who I am; tattvatah = in truth; tatah = then; mam = Me; tattvatah = by truth; jnatva = knowing thus; visate = enters; tat-anantaram = afterwards.

Through devotion, he knows Me comprehensively as to who I am in truth. Then, knowing Me in truth, afterward, he enters (My State).

You become that which prevails in your thoughts and with which you devotedly and wholeheartedly identify yourself. If you think of God, you will cultivate divine qualities and reflect godliness in your conduct and actions. If you think of the world, you become materialistic and reflect worldliness, selfishness, or even the evil nature. Accordingly, the gunas - the three fundamental qualities of nature, namely sattva (purity), rajas (activity), and tamas (inertia) - gain or lose strength in you. It is the nature of the mind's consciousness to mirror the things upon which it dwells. Hence, we have to be careful where our senses wander and which thoughts, memories, and feelings prevail in our minds and dominate our thinking and actions. Bhakti (devotion) drives a devotee's mind toward God and fills it with his thoughts, reminding him of his oneness with him. However, before he reaches that stage, first, he must know through study and devotion that his pure Self or his absolute reality, which is other than his mind and intelligence, is eternal, indestructible, complete, without duality, self-existent, all-pervading, pure, unborn, etc., and by attaining That he will attain the absolute, final freedom. Having cultivated that awareness, he must persevere in yoga through devotion, contemplation, renunciation, and self-control until he severs all bonds and enters the supreme state of oneness or pure consciousness. Thus, the knowing of Brahman, the ultimate reality, through study and contemplation precedes liberation or his direct knowing through oneness. In the liberated state, knowledge becomes self-existent, meaning it no longer depends upon knowing through the mind, senses, or intelligence.

It is well known that duty, knowledge, renunciation, and devotion are foundational to practicing yoga and achieving liberation. Knowledge of one's essential nature, the duties associated with it, and the knowledge of the means to attain the Self are equally important. This knowledge may arise spontaneously due to fate and karma of previous lives, by intense intellectual and spiritual effort, or intuitively by divine grace. In most cases, knowledge is attained by learning through discernment, for which purity and devotion to knowledge (jnana nishta) are essential. Jnana nishta, or devotion to knowledge, is a state of unwavering commitment to the pursuit of spiritual wisdom and understanding. It involves studying the scriptures, reflecting upon their great truths, and learning from the teachings of reverent masters who have known Brahman through self-realization. When firmly established, it strengthens his faith, establishes his mind in his contemplation with exclusive devotion, and prepares him to know the supreme reality (Isvara tattva) directly through oneness.

Thus, the path to liberation or Brahman is paved by three types of devotion. First is the devotion to duty (dharma nishta); second is the devotion to knowledge (jnana nishta); and third is the exclusive devotion to the Supreme Lord (brahma nishta). When perfection is attained in all three endeavors, one becomes skillful (nishnata) in knowledge and practice and attains the highest and absolute perfection. The wise ones attain this supreme state by abiding in the Self with the highest devotion, dedicating their minds and bodies to him, and transforming their way of living into a continuous form of sacrifice, devotion, and worship. They devote themselves to performing duties through karma yoga, sacrificing their fruit and doership. Through jnana yoga, they offer their egoism, desires, ignorance, delusion, and internal organs (antah karanas) to the fire of knowledge and achieve self-purification. Through renunciation, they sacrifice their lives, actions, desires, attachments, modes, and possessions as a mark of their supreme devotion. Thus, becoming empty, putting themselves at his mercy, and earning his grace through exclusive devotion, they enter his supreme reality and dissolve themselves. As Lord Krishna declared previously, the knower of the Self, who is always self-absorbed with single-minded devotion, is like his very Self and is supremely dearer to him. He reciprocates their devotion, becoming their path-finder and supreme teacher.

Sloka 56

sarvakarmāṇy api sadā kurvāṇo madvyapāśrayaḥ
matprasādād avāpnoti śāśvataṃ padam avyayam

sarva = all; karmani = actions; api = even, although; sada = continuously, always, forever; kurvanah = engaged; mat = I am; vyapasrayah = shelter; mat = My; prasadat = grace, mercy; avapnoti = attains, obtains; sasvatam = eternal; padam = abode; avyayam = imperishable.

Even if continuously engaged in all actions, he, to whom I am the refuge, attains by My grace the eternal, imperishable Abode.

The karma-sannyasa yogi who is established in the Lord within himself with supreme devotion through jnana-nishta, dharma-nishta (devotion to knowledge and duty), and bhakti-tatpara (devotion to the Supreme Self), taking refuge in him with abiding faith and resolve, attains his eternal and indestructible Abode by his grace. 'Sarva karmani api' means even all actions. In this context, it denotes that it does not matter what actions the devotee performs. If he takes refuge in him and earns his grace through supreme devotion, the Lord will free him from the consequences of all his actions (sarva karma) and ensure his liberation. It does not matter whether he follows or ignores the instructions of the Vedas and performs or does not perform obligatory, desire-ridden (kamya karmas), or prohibited actions (nishiddha karmas). In other words, although desireless actions, knowledge of the Self, and renunciation are necessary, devotion to the Lord, taking refuge in him, and earning his grace are critical in the later stages and should not be ignored. Those who take refuge in him and attain his grace do not have to worry about anything and live freely. However, the devotion must be exclusive and the purest kind arising from unwavering faith (shraddha).

The term 'prasadam' holds a multitude of meanings in Hindu rituals. It signifies favor, kindness, gift, or gratuity, as well as purity, calmness, well-being, remainder, and brightness. In the context of traditional Hindu sacrifices and rituals, prasadam refers to any sacrificial food offered to the gods or the Lord for nourishment and left behind. This food, believed to have been partaken by the gods, is considered sacred, divine grace, and beneficial. Devotees believe it is infused with divine love and contains healing and purifying properties. The act of distributing prasadam to the worshippers after a ritual or sacrifice is an integral part of Hindu ritual and sacrificial worship. Divine grace (prasadam) also manifests in various forms in a devotee's life, such as luck, favorable circumstances, peace, prosperity, divine love, etc. God's mercy is limitless and selfless and flows abundantly, reciprocating his devotees' love and devotion with abundant love, accepting readily whatever offerings they make, answering their sincere and ardent prayers, and fulfilling their wishes according to their faith.

In this verse, Lord Krishna also emphasized taking refuge in him (vyapasraya). By surrendering to the Lord unconditionally, giving up his independence, and taking refuge in him, a devotee consecrates his ego, desires, attachments, and will to the Lord as a sacrifice. He cuts all his bonds, burns his egoism in the fire of renunciation, and remains devoted to the Lord as the sole refuge or support. Devotion without true surrender is tamasic, which is practiced by deluded people. They worship gods to fulfill their wishes without consecrating their egos or will. Therefore, they may earn boons from the gods they worship, but do not qualify for liberation or divine mercy. A devotee must be a vyapasraya, meaning he must unconditionally surrender himself to the Lord and exclusively depend upon him for his liberation and existence. Lord Krishna previously assured his devotees that he would take care of those who renounced everything and absorbed their minds in him with exclusive devotion. He reaffirmed the same here in a different way. How to secure his grace and enter forever the Brahmic consciousness of Isvara is explained in the next two verses.

Sloka 57

cetasā sarvakarmāṇi mayi saṃnyasya matparaḥ
buddhiyogam upāśritya maccittaḥ satataṃ bhava

cetasa = mentally, by mind; sarva-karmani = all actions; mayi = to Me; sannyasya = giving up, renouncing; mat-parah = treating Me as Supreme;

buddhi-yogam = the yoga of intelligence; upasritya = taking shelter in; mat-cittah = with your mind or consciousness fixed in me; satatam = always; bhava = exists.

Mentally renouncing all actions to Me, treating Me as the Supreme, taking shelter in buddhi yoga, with your mind always fixed on Me...

This and the next verse elucidate the significance of exclusive devotion to the Supreme Lord. The Supreme Reality of formless Brahman (para) is impersonal. However, the Supreme Being (Parameswara), who manifests from that Absolute State, is endowed with modes, forms, qualities, powers, and attributes due to his association with the manifested (sambhuta) Prakriti. Worshipping the formless and transcendental Brahman is a challenging task, as the mind is naturally drawn to names and forms rather than to formless and indescribable states and abstract notions. A deity who can be visualized, conceptualized, and described or envisioned in concrete terms allows the devotees to establish their minds in him and practice devotion, concentration, and contemplation without distractions, thereby earning the love and grace of the Supreme Lord.

Therefore, the Vedas do not encourage the direct worship of Brahman but only the worship of his manifestations. Of them, as Lord Krishna said, one should worship him only, meaning Isvara or the Supreme Lord. He also cautioned his devotees, saying that those who worshipped them would go to them, but those who worshipped him would come to him only. Therefore, ideally, devotees who pursue liberation should worship Isvara only, the Supreme Lord, with exclusive devotion to earn his grace. It does not matter which Isvara you choose to worship as long as you consider him the Lord of the Universe and the direct and immediate manifestation of Brahman. This Isvara with names and forms is approachable, knowable, relatable, and attainable. As the Lord of creation and as the Knower of the Field, he has an inseparable connection with Prakriti. Since he is actively associated with Prakriti, without being tainted by her, and much different from the jivas, he possesses corporeality, names, and forms to which devotees can relate and worship.

Four requirements or conditions are prescribed here to worship him and earn his grace. The first one is renouncing actions to the Supreme Lord and their fruit as an offering. The second one is holding him alone in the highest esteem as the transcendental Being (para). The third requirement is taking shelter in discerning intelligence through buddhi yoga to overcome the impurities of the mind, such as ignorance and delusion, and see the Lord within as the Self, distinct from the mind and body. The fourth condition is fixing the mind in his contemplation with pure and unwavering devotion. These four practices help the devotees transcend the triple impurities of egoism (ahamkara), desires and attachments (pasa), and delusion (moha), and practice atma-samyama (self-control) and ananya bhakti (exclusive devotion) without interruptions. Together, they lead to self-absorption, sameness, and oneness.

On the path of liberation, the ego (aham) is the root of all problems. As long as it controls and influences thoughts and actions, one cannot restrain the mind and the body or suppress the modes and the modifications arising from them. When you take shelter in it, your vision, thinking, and awareness remain clouded and deluded, and you remain bound to duality, desires, and desire-ridden actions. Only when you subdue your ego and dissolve your limited and fragmented identity and individuality in the silence of your mind, breaking the walls that you build to protect your self-interests, vulnerabilities, and weaknesses, will you enter the pure consciousness of the Self and experience the Supreme Reality or the pure essence (shuddha tattva) of the Supreme Lord, which is indivisible, all-pervading, limitless, self-knowing, self-existing and pure intelligence (prajna). Devotion and renunciation are the supports in this journey. One guides you, and the other keeps you free from the burden of your past and the influence of your modes. Both are emphasized in this verse. In devotion, you surrender the ego. In renunciation, you give up desires and attachments and become empty. When you achieve perfection through them, you attain naishkarmya siddhi.

Sloka 58

maccittaḥ sarvadurgāṇi matprasādat tariṣyasi
atha cet tvam ahaṃkārān na śroṣyasi vinaṅkṣyasi

mat = My; cittah = mind, thoughts; sarva = all; durgani = obstacles; mat = My; prasadat = kindness, mercy; tarisyasi = overcome, pass through, transcend, cross over; atha = however, otherwise; cet = if; tvam = you; ahankarat = because of egoism; na = not; srosyasi = do not listen, pay heed, hear; vinanksyasi = will perish.

Fixing your mind on Me, you should overcome all obstacles by My grace. However, because of egoism, if you do not listen, you will perish.

A devotee should overcome problems and obstacles through devotion to the Supreme Lord, whether about his practice, life, or some other difficulty, fixing his mind upon him and seeking his help. Through unconditional surrender, love, devotion, and dependence, he should earn his grace and attain oneness. It means that in the face of problems or adversity, a devotee should not lose faith or become distracted. He should not resort to his egoistic and delusional thinking or engage in the actions induced by his desires and modes to solve his problems. He should let go of his fears and wait patiently to let the divine will to take care of them. Each difficulty or problem is a test of faith. When faith falters, it is a sign that the ego has gained strength and is trying to reassert itself. If liberation is the aim, the devotee should become indifferent to his difficulties and circumstances and remain steadfast in his practice, fixing his mind on the Lord. He should cultivate exclusive devotion, withdrawing his mind into himself and becoming equal to all dualities. When problems arise, he should always look to him for solutions, accepting whatever happens or whatever guidance he receives as his will. If they become insurmountable or if the suffering is unbearable, he may, at best, pray to him and wait for his response. In all matters and every aspect of his life, he should control the urge to act willfully or independently and let the Lord respond, do his part, and keep his promise. This is the essence of exclusive and unconditional faith, devotion, and surrender, which should inspire and encourage the devotees to continue on the path.

The ego, as the main obstacle to exclusive and abiding devotion, is a challenge that every devotee must confront. It resists all efforts towards self-purification, surrendering to the Lord, or establishing the mind in him. The Lord reminds his devotees that if they cannot renounce their desires and egos and abide in exclusive devotion and contemplation, they will not earn his grace and achieve liberation. The truth is that devotion must be exclusive, unconditional, and undivided. A devotee cannot simultaneously share his loyalties, faith, or devotion with God, the world, or himself. He should not be loyal to two or three masters concurrently. The same logic applies to why Lord Krishna advises devotees to worship the highest Supreme Lord only. True devotion will not arise without renunciation or letting go. Devotees must sacrifice their possessions, names, forms, egos, desires, and attachments and put themselves at the feet of the Lord with the faith of a child in her mother. They should not worship many gods or divide their loyalties and devotion to many pursuits. Through pure and exclusive devotion only, they earn the Lord's grace and enter his immortal Abode.

No threat is implied in this approach or Lord Krishna's words. This is not a vengeful God delivering a dire message to his devotees that if they do not worship him exclusively or surrender to him, they will be destroyed. Instead, he offers a promise of security and protection. He said it to let them know they would be alone if they depended upon themselves to overcome their problems, but they would have his help, support, and protection if they turned to him with devotion and took refuge in him with abiding faith. In the mortal world, karma shapes one's life and destiny. It determines the transmigration and future births of all jivas until their karma is fully resolved. Devotees whose karmas are not fully resolved and who still have impurities are always vulnerable to the vagaries of Nature and the possibility of rebirth and suffering. For them, the best option is to surrender to the Lord and hand over their care and comfort to him entirely. By surrendering their egos and taking refuge in him, they can enjoy his assured protection. By renouncing desires and attachments and sacrificing the fruit of their actions to him, they can also escape from karma and samsara.

Surrender, renunciation, and sacrifice are foundational to purity, stability, self-control, and exclusive devotion. Through them, you transfer your actions and their consequences to the Lord as a mark of your self-sacrifice or self-annihilation, which is the essence of bhakti, and let him take care of them and you. Lord Krishna's words in this verse should be viewed from this perspective. It is meant for those who wish to practice exclusive devotion and cross the ocean of samsara on the raft of faith. It is worth remembering since it offers a way to achieve liberation even without performing duties or practicing yoga. It is relevant to all devotees, irrespective of their nature, methods, and practices, and whether they perform their obligatory duties with or without desires. They should remember that perfection in any yoga or devotional practice is possible only when they fully subdue their egos and overcome their attachment and identification with their minds and bodies. The ego keeps exerting its influence in countless ways. It remains restless and fights for its survival until the end. It is also an obstacle to unconditional surrender and self-control. Hence, devotees must surrender it to the Lord and practice pure devotion to him so that he will help them subdue it and earn his grace. By that act of total surrender, a devotee can make Him the karta, karma, and kriya of his life and liberation.

Sloka 59

yad ahaṃkāram āśritya na yotsya iti manyase
mithyaiṣa vyavasāyas te prakṛtis tvāṃ niyokṣyati

yat = if; ahankaram = egoism; asritya = taking shelter; na = not; yotsye = fight; iti = thus; manyase = think; mithya = false, untrue, illusory, deluded; esah = this; vyavasayah = resolve, effort, determination, resolution; te = your; prakrtih = nature; tvam = you; niyoksyati = force or regulate you.

Taking shelter in egoism, if ever you think, 'I will not fight,' your resolve or effort will be delusional. Nature will force you (to fight).

In verse 45, Lord Krishna said that by following one's duty (svakarma), one should attain absolute perfection (samsiddhi). One verse later (47), he said that sin would not arise if actions were performed selflessly according to one's own nature (svabhava niyatam), even if they were inferior or unpleasant. Following the same argument, in the next verse (48), he further said that one should not abandon duties that arise from one's essential nature (sahaja karma) just because they were defective, since all actions were enveloped in defects of one kind or another. In these verses, the common theme is that devotees should not listen to their egos and abandon their duties but must perform them without fail. If they do, their attempts to avoid them will be delusional since their essential nature will somehow compel them to perform them. In other words, it is difficult to live against one's essential nature for long.

Arjuna was born into a royal family with the blessings of Indra, the Lord of heaven, and a warrior (Kshatriya). Therefore, his essential nature was that of a Kshatriya, and his svakarma (main duty or occupation) was fighting, which he was obligated to perform to attain purity and perfection (samsiddhi). Therefore, Lord Krishna said that because of delusion, if he thought that his duty was problematic for any reason and wanted to abandon or decided to live like a beggar or an ascetic, which he previously wished to do in the second chapter, he would not continue for long against himself and will eventually return to his original occupation by the force of his nature. In summary, no one can go against one's inherent nature until the modes are suppressed or neutralized. This is the essence of this teaching.

The ideal Lord Krishna suggests in these verses is that one should live and act according to one's inborn nature (sahaja svabhavam), as determined by his predominant modes (gunas) and past karma. The modes may arise from various external and internal causes and induce desires and attachments, forcing people to live and act accordingly. Lord Krishna cautions us that even if we want to go against our essential nature due to our egos or any other reason, we will suffer from the consequences and eventually return to it, settle with it, and make peace with it. This cautionary tale is often seen in many people's lives when they choose occupations that do not suit their nature, talents, or temperament because of family, social, or economic pressures and compulsions. Eventually, they find themselves unhappy and unfulfilled, even if they are successful, unable to enjoy their work or adapt to its demands. Therefore, Lord Krishna's advice to Arjuna not to succumb to his ego and withdraw from fighting is a powerful reminder of the consequences of going against one's essential nature.

Sloka 60

svabhāvajena kaunteya nibaddhaḥ svena karmaṇā
kartuṃ necchasi yan mohāt kariṣyasy avaśopi tat

svabhava-jena = arising from inherent or essential nature; kaunteya = O son of Kunti; nibaddhah = bound; svena = by one's own; karmana = actions, duty; kartum = to do; na = not; icchasi = like; yat = that; mohat = by delusion; karisyasi = you will do; avasah = uncontrollably, involuntarily, independent of will; api = even; tat = that.

Bound by the actions arising from your inherent nature, O son of Kunti, whatever you would not like to do due to delusion, even that you will do against your will.

It is obvious by now that no one can go against the force of Nature, although it does not mean that people must remain forever bound to their essential nature. A yogi can change his nature by practicing yoga and self-control to change himself. Through effort, he can contain the modes and the predominant desires and attachments they induce. Until then, he must follow his natural inclinations that are in harmony with his spiritual goals and obligatory duties to fulfill the purpose of his life and serve the Lord. If he neglects them, he will suffer the consequences and continue to do so until he realizes his mistake. Lord Krishna advised Arjuna to fight since he was born to fight in the war and fulfill his destiny. This advice has significant implications for all of us. We must pay attention to our hearts and minds and live and act according to our inherent nature, choosing goals and duties that are in harmony with it and performing our actions to fulfill our obligation to the Lord, ourselves, and others. We must take note of our strengths and weaknesses, know what comes to us naturally and what we enjoy doing, listen to our intelligence (buddhi) or intuition, accept it as the will of God, and follow it sincerely, reposing our trust in him with the faith that he will show us the way and guide us in the right direction. This is best accomplished by renouncing egoism, desires, attachments, and delusions and living in harmony with oneself. If desires and attachments are overcome, one becomes indifferent to the world and its values, listens to oneself, and acts according to his inner calling. We have different yogas, paths, and yogas because people can choose them according to their nature and temperaments, using their knowledge and discernment.

Sloka 61

īśvaraḥ sarvabhūtānāṃ hṛddeśerjuna tiṣṭhati
bhrāmayan sarvabhūtāni yantrārūḍhāni māyayā

isvarah = the Supreme Lord; sarva-bhutanam = of all living beings; hrt-dese = heart region; arjuna = O Arjuna; tisthati = seated; bhramayan = move around; sarva-bhutani = all living beings; yantra = mechanical device, machine; arudhani = mounted; mayaya = by the power of Maya.

O Arjuna, seated in the heart region of all living beings, the Supreme Lord moves around all the beings by the power of Maya as if they are mounted on a mechanical device.

This verse is meant to correct any misconception that may arise from the previous one. Lord Krishna stated in them that everyone was bound by their essential nature and compelled to engage in actions even against their will. Here, he stated that seated in the hearts of all beings, he controlled them through maya and moved them as if they were helpless without any will or intelligence of their own. Although the two verses seem to be contradictory, there is no contradiction. Deluded beings are compelled by their essential nature (sahaja svabhava) to act in particular ways like automatons. It is a natural design inherent in creation and applies to all beings. Although maya is enforced by Prakriti, its source is the Supreme Lord only since Prakriti is an aspect of him and works under his control. Therefore, though he does not directly control or micromanage our lives and actions, he does it indirectly through Prakriti. In the jivas, he does it through their essential nature. Since he is present in all, Prakriti spreads the net of maya (delusion) and ensures that he remains hidden in them, and beings do not know him. The idea is that whatever we do or think is due to Maya, and the Lord is responsible for it. Deluded people think they are responsible for their thoughts and actions and, by that misconception, incur karma and fall into bondage.

In the context of Lord Krishna's teachings, Maya refers to Prakriti. She is an inseparable aspect of the Supreme Lord, executing his will and manifesting things through her, including his aspects, duties, and functions. She is his force and inseparable companion at each level of creation. Nothing happens without her. Through the modes (gunas) and the essential nature arising from them, she regulates our lives, actions, and destinies. Even in the case of Isvara, the Lord of the universe, she is responsible for his actions, modes, and manifestations. When he is not associated with her or when she is in her primordial and undifferentiated state (asambhuta), he remains unmanifested and without attributes (Nirguna). He becomes manifested as the Supreme Lord (Isvara) with pure modes (saguna) when she joins him in her awakened state (sambhuta) and imparts qualities and attributes to him. However, Prakriti is not the source of maya only. She has higher aspects and manifests as her destroyer in devotees who earn the grace of the lord and qualify for liberation. She moves the wheels of creation, dharma, and karma.

Prakriti, also known as Maya, is responsible for all the modifications in her domain and the transmigration of the jivas. Our minds and bodies are but machines (yantras). They belong to the domain of Prakriti and function mechanically as machines according to the laws she sets in motion. Through her, the Supreme Lord controls all the worlds and beings without moving or acting. Again, when devotees practice yoga or spirituality to purify and transcend their nature, he responds according to their devotion and grants liberation to the deserving ones. Deluded by the power of Maya and compelled by our inherent nature, the ignorant ones engage in actions, assuming they have a will of their own and can act freely according to their choices. It does give them the illusion of being free-willed and independent, but they are not truly in control of their actions. (This fact is partially admitted by molecular and neurobiologists based on recent findings that much of human behavior is predetermined by how they are born, how their brain is structured, how feelings, emotions, and desires arise, and how the neurons or nerve cells communicate). Until we are bound to Prakriti and her deluding influence, we are subject to the forces of Nature and the will of God. All the beings caught in the whirl of samsara are thus comparable to the dancing selves in the playground of Maya, with God as the witness, enjoyer, controller, and dance master (Nataraja).

The Isavasya Upanishad declares that all this is for the habitation of the Lord. He lives in everything, envelops everything, and moves everything. All this and the whole existence belong to him only. Hence, it says we should not covet things that do not belong to us. By selflessly performing our duties only, we should wish to live on earth and escape from karma. Whether the Supreme Self is the same as the individual Self or not, and whether Prakriti is his dependent or independent aspect, it is imperative to know that he is the source of all. His will and grace are necessary for our existence and liberation. He is responsible for all the movements and happenings in creation, while he remains unmoved and unchanged as the hub of everything. By taking shelter in him as the unmoving and unchaining reality, we must strive to attain stability and perfection (naishkarmya siddhi) and qualify to enter his pure consciousness. When we take shelter in him, Prakriti becomes a positive and cleansing force in our liberation. She becomes Kali, the destroyer of delusion.

Sloka 62

tam eva śaraṇaṃ gaccha sarvabhāvena bhārata
tatprasādāt parāṃ śāntiṃ sthānaṃ prāpsyasi śāśvatam

tam = to Him; eva = certainly, truly; saranam = sanctuary, shelter, refuge; gaccha = go; sarva-bhavena = with entire being, wholeheartedly; bharata = O Bharata; tat-prasadat = by his mercy, grace; param = supreme; santim = peace; sthanam = place, abode; prapsyasi = attain; sasvatam = eternal.

Go to him certainly for refuge with your entire being, O Bharata; by His mercy, you will attain supreme peace and the eternal Abode.

Here, Lord Krishna advised Arjuna to earn God's mercy (prasada) by surrendering to him and taking shelter in him wholeheartedly and unconditionally. He also hinted that the supreme abode of eternal peace is attained only by his mercy. Thus, he affirmed that he is the supreme controller of all beings, and they can escape from samsara through his intervention. He is responsible for our delusion, bondage, and liberation. He controls our lives and actions by subjecting us to our modes and essential nature (Prakriti). When we unconditionally surrender to him and engage our minds in his exclusive devotion, he also liberates us from his Maya. Through him, and in him alone, we will find supreme peace and the highest heaven.

When a devotee surrenders to him and takes shelter in him, seeking his help and protection, his energies transform from being deluding forces of Maya (maya shaktis) into higher, purifying forces of Prakriti (daiva shaktis). They purify the devotee and prepare him for liberation.

Hence, surrendering to God and seeking the help of Parashakti is the easiest and quickest method to practice self-purification and attain liberation. If yogis want to attain it by themselves, they may have to spend several years or even several lives without the certainty that they will succeed. The Supreme Mother, who is an inseparable aspect of the Supreme Lord, deludes all the jivas with her nature. When her purpose is served and when the jiva wakes up from delusion and takes refuge in the Lord, she helps him and sets him free.

In worldly life, we seek comfort and happiness through worldly possessions. Although the approach looks promising, it does not guarantee lasting peace or happiness. If liberation is the goal, a yogi should withdraw into himself and take shelter in the Lord who resides in him as his Self, surrendering his will, possessions, desires, and attachments and absorbing his mind in supreme devotion. Through devotion and surrender, he should let Him awaken the Parashakti in him and do her work. In the Yogasutras, Patanjali suggests that to attain the inner Lord, a yogi should envision him as Aum and continuously meditate on its meaning. If he perseveres, he enters the supreme consciousness (pratyak cetana) of the Lord (Isvara) and attains freedom from obstacles and disturbances (antaraya abhava).

Sloka 63

iti te jñānam ākhyātaṃ guhyād guhyataraṃ mayā
vimṛśyaitad aśeṣeṇa yathecchasi tathā kuru

iti = thus; te = to you; jnanam = knowledge; akhyatam = revealed; guhyat = than any secret guhya-taram = more secret; maya = by Me; vimrsya = contemplating; etat = this; asesena = fully, deeply; yatha = as you; icchasi = wish, desire, like; tatha = so shall you; kuru = perform.

Thus, this knowledge has been revealed to you by Me, which is more secretive than all that is secret. Contemplating upon it fully, do whatever you wish to do.

This is the concluding verse of the part (56-62) in which Lord Krishna emphasizes the importance of devotion in performing duties (karma yoga). The word 'iti' (thus) suggests that he concluded the main teaching here, and we are nearing the end of this long, sacred dialogue called the Bhagavadgita. The teaching is considered the 'utmost secret' because it is not revealed to all householders but only to those who study it on their own or with the guidance of an enlightened master and take shelter in the Lord himself. Anyone can read it because the scripture is freely available nowadays, but its hidden secrets or insights will be known only through his grace. Hence, it is known as the utmost secret (guhyatiguhyam). The scripture occupies a significant place in Hinduism as one of the three most sacred scriptures of the liberation (prastanatraya), along with the Upanishads and the Brahmasutras.

Its knowledge is considered the secret of secrets (guhyat guhyataram) because its true message is hidden from the deluded minds and known only to a few exceptional devotees who cultivate discernment and devotion through the grace of God. Each instruction he imparted to Arjuna on the battlefield is a secret within the greater secret, the discourse itself. The transformative power of the Bhagavadgita's knowledge inspires a sense of awe and reverence in the readers, making them more receptive to its teachings. This explanation may not convince today's readers since the knowledge is in the public domain, and people, even the most ignorant, can access it from various sources. Anyone can now read it and make something out of it according to their knowledge, ignorance, wisdom, or delusion. However, there was a time when it was inaccessible to most, was relatively unknown, and was taught to a few lucky ones by their teachers in secrecy. Even today, although the knowledge is readily available, many cannot truly understand it or gain insight, even with all the commentaries and helpful guidance. It is understood differently by different people according to their essential nature. Only through the Lord's grace does one understand it without confusion and attain liberation.

Its deeper knowledge helps us understand the significance of the various yogas and their importance in the journey of liberation. Only a few understand this knowledge through study, devotion, and divine grace. Arjuna personifies an ideal devotee who was not only a devotee but also a friend, a dutiful householder committed to Dharma and his family. Hence, Lord Krishna chose him for the revelation. The other two who also participated in the discourse, though indirectly, Sanjaya and Dhritarashtra, were also God's devotees, well-versed in the Vedas and excellent karma yogis. The Lord also manifested in his universal form as Kala before Arjuna because the occasion demanded it, and it was crucial to the teaching and its import. Arjuna represents all ideal devotees, who are at times emotional and fall into despair or elation, overwhelmed by the conflicting situations life presents to them. Arjuna means a sattvic person with a pure mind and heart. Arjuna also means white color, which stands for the purity of sattva. Lord Krishna imparted to him this sacred knowledge because he was pure and sattvic, an excellent devotee who exemplified duty, discipline, knowledge, and devotion, yet was a human to the core. Further, he was destined to play a critical role in the battle of Kurukshetra, and his participation was crucial for its outcome.

The knowledge of the Bhagavadgita contained in the 18 chapters can be divided into three parts of six chapters each. The first part deals with the embodied soul (jivatma) and the jiva's obligatory duty in this world to serve God and uphold Dharma through the six yogas mentioned in the first six chapters. They essentially deal with the obligatory duties or actions (karma) assigned to them by God and how one should perform them dutifully to avoid the sinful karma that may arise from them if they are performed incorrectly. Hence, the first part is also known as Karma Kanda (the part that deals with duties or actions). It helps the devotees practice karma-sannyasa yoga and stabilize their minds in the Lord or the Self with detachment and sameness. The second part deals with the Supreme Self (Paramatma), his duties, manifestations, and attributes, and how humans are obligated to serve him and others in this world to fulfill his aims of creation. The knowledge serves as the foundation to cultivate devotion to the Supreme Lord through an integrated approach involving jnana, karma, buddhi, and sannyasa yogas. Hence, it is also called the knowledge part (jnana kanda). The third part deals with liberation (moksha) or the union between the embodied soul (jivatma) and the Supreme Being (Paramatma), how a devotee (jiva) can attain freedom from karma (naishkarmya siddhi) arising from action and inaction, and how he can attain oneness with the Supreme Lord, following the knowledge contained in the first two parts, while practicing renunciation and exclusive devotion to the highest Lord (Purushottama). Atma-samyama, ananya bhakti, jnana karma-sannyasa, and moksha yogas are its dominant themes. The first part is considered the secret, the second part is very secret, and the third part is the utmost secret.

Another interpretation is that the first part deals with the duties of a Bhagavata or servant of God who is caught in samsara and how he may overcome delusion and other impurities to attain the exalted states of samsiddhi (sameness) and parama siddhi (oneness) through various yogas. The second part deals with the sovereign knowledge of the Bhagavan (Supreme Lord), his glories, and manifestations, and the third part deals with the union of the two through knowledge, duty, devotion, and renunciation.

The knowledge of the Bhagavadgita was considered the utmost secret for other reasons also. First, it is a yoga shastra, which contains the knowledge of several largely unknown yogas. Second, it is a Upanishad. Hence, by definition, it contains the secret knowledge of the Self or Brahman, which is meant to be taught by teachers to students secretively by sitting near them. Third, the knowledge was unknown. Until it was composed, or until Lord Krishna taught it, no one knew it. Even the great sages such as Narada did not know of it. Fourth, the scripture contains the knowledge of Brahman (brahma vidya), which is the highest secret and about which even the gods do not know clearly. Fifth, by studying the ritual portion of the Vedas, which is the most popular aspect of it, householders will not gain the true knowledge of karma or liberation. The Vedas may help them perform their duties as ordained by them and abide in Dharma. However, they do not reveal how one may perform sacrifices, rituals, and actions without incurring sin or how one may achieve liberation from the suffering caused by karma and one's existence in samsara. Only in the Bhagavadgita can we find a comprehensive approach to overcoming suffering and escaping from samsara by securing God's grace through knowledge, duty, and devotion. For these and probably other reasons, Lord Krishna considered his teaching the utmost secret. Having taught him the knowledge, he told Arjuna to do whatever he wished, knowing that Arjuna would eventually act according to his inborn Kshatriya nature and perform his duties with devotion and resolve.

Sloka 64

sarvaguhyatamaṃ bhūyaḥ śṛṇu me paramaṃ vacaḥ
iṣṭosi me dṛḍham iti tato vakṣyāmi te hitam

sarva-guhya-tamam = the utmost secret of all; bhuyah = again; srnu = listen; me = My; paramam = supreme; vacah = teaching, utterance, words; istah asi = you are dear; me = to Me; drdham = steadfast, firm; iti = since; tatah = therefore; vaksyami = I speak; te = for your; hitam = benefit, wellbeing.

Listen to Me again, My supreme teaching, the utmost secret of all, which I speak for your own good since you are very dear to me (and) steadfast (in devotion).

Having revealed to Arjuna the utmost secrets of various yogas and liberation, Lord Krishna wanted to repeat the most important secret of all for Arjuna's good (hitam) since he was a dear devotee and steadfast in his devotion. At the beginning of this discourse, Arjuna wavered in performing his duties due to moral doubts, but his devotion was pure and firm, just like his faith in his teachings. Lord Krishna knew Arjuna had the faith, devotion, and discernment fit enough to be his exclusive devotee and follow his teachings. He also knew that soon he would march onto the battlefield and would be deeply involved and distracted by the fighting and commotion. Therefore, he wanted him to remember the most important teachings to fight with resolve and sameness like a true karma-sannyasa yogi, putting to use his knowledge of renunciation and sacrifice. The Supreme Lord communicates with his devotees in mysterious ways according to their nature, devotion, and commitment. Sometimes, he may send the same message to reinforce it or ensure that they understand it clearly without doubt or confusion.

Sloka 65

manmanā bhava madbhakto madyājī māṃ namaskuru
mām evaiṣyasi satyaṃ te pratijāne priyosi me

mat-manah bhava =fix your mind on Me; mat-bhaktah = be My devotee; mat-yaji = My worshiper; mam = to Me namaskuru = offer your salutations; mam = to Me; eva = only, alone; esyasi = come; satyam = truth; te = to you; pratijane = I promise; priyah = dear; asi = you are; me = to Me.

Fix your mind upon Me. Be My devotee. Be My worshipper. Offer Me your salutations. You will come to Me only. I promise you this is true. You are very dear to Me.

This verse contains the most straightforward approach to attain liberation through exclusive devotion (ananya bhakti), offering contemplation, worship, surrender, and abiding faith as the best means to practice it. The Yogasutras (1.23) also suggests that samprajnata samadhi (undistracted self-absorption) arises from abiding devotion (pranidhana) to the Lord in the body (Isvara), who is omniscient and free from karma and other impurities. Patanjali says he should be worshipped by constantly meditating on him as Aum, the sacred syllable. From that effort arises the realization of pure consciousness (pratyak chetana) and freedom from disturbances. According to the Bhagavadgita, of all known yogas, bhakti yoga is the culminating point in one's spiritual journey. It leads the yogi on a straight path towards liberation. However, devotion is of different kinds since it also arises in the

Field of Prakriti (mind and body) and is subject to the influence of the gunas. For instance, there can be devotion driven by passion (rajas), devotion driven by ignorance (tamas), and devotion driven by purity (sattva). Each of these types of devotion leads to different ends. One has to cultivate the highest and the purest devotion, which the wise ones (the jnanis) practice and which is free from desires and expectations. It leads to the highest goal (parandhama).

One may spend a lifetime performing complex rituals and feel good about it, or pursue spiritual knowledge and analyze the finer nuances of religious and spiritual philosophies to saturate the mind with the intellectual knowledge of Brahman and earn a good reputation as a scholar (pandita) or even a guru. These efforts are futile unless practiced with true devotion, cultivating purity. This verse may give the impression that one can attain liberation by devotion only. It is not entirely true. True devotion does not arise in a vacuum or an impure, desire-ridden mind. The devotion that Lord Krishna spoke here is of the purest kind, in which only the wise ones excel. It does not arise without prior preparation but as the culmination of an enduring effort (abhyasa) that frees the mind and body from the impurities of egoism, delusion, ignorance, desires, and attachments. In the journey of liberation, all the yogas mentioned in the scripture are important. Each has a significance of its own and helps the yogis at different stages in their spiritual development. Their cumulative effect is the unconditional devotion by which they attain naishkarmya siddhi (freedom from duties), samsiddhi (freedom from attraction and aversion), and anubhava siddhi (the direct seeing of the Self). Some people may be born with the seed of pure devotion in their hearts due to the progress achieved in past births. They may develop exclusive devotion spontaneously. However, such instances are rare.

In this verse, Lord Krishna outlines four practices that would bring his devotees closer to him and facilitate their liberation. He delivers a straightforward message with a clear assurance that they will be liberated if they follow these practices. The first requirement is to fix their minds on him without distractions. Second, they must become his exclusive devotees in word and deed. Exclusive here means they should not worship any other god or demigod and should dedicate their lives to him. Through this devotion and selfless service, they become offerings to the Lord in the sacrifice of their lives. Third, they must worship him and express their devotion continuously, not just through ritual worship or sacrifices but in every possible way. In chapter 7 (verse 16), Lord Krishna identifies four types of people who worship him and declares that the knowers of the Self (jnanis) are the best among them. God's exclusive devotees embody the highest form of devotion. They worship him continuously with knowledge and discernment through rituals, obligatory actions, study (svadhyaya), charity (dana), and by hearing (shravanam), remembering (mananam), uttering his names, singing his glories, praying, meditating, serving (seva), and expressing gratitude. Through such methods, they remain internally connected to him always and everywhere. Fourth, they offer him salutations before the images they worship physically or mentally as a declaration of their faith and devotion. Through these actions, they exemplify renunciation, sacrifice, reverence, humility, divinity, and devotion.

The word eva (meaning only) is also important. It means that if you worship Isvara, you will reach him only. It also implies that if you seek liberation, you must completely focus on the Supreme Lord and should not entertain any other interest, desire, or expectation. If you are devoted to worldly things such as wealth, fame, name, etc., and worship them, you may attain them, but not the Abode of Brahman. Lord Krishna said the same when he said that those who worshipped the gods and demigods would go to them, whereas his devotees would return to him only. Therefore, exclusive devotion to the Supreme Lord is critical to yoga.

Sloka 66

sarvadharmān parityajya mām ekaṃ śaraṇaṃ vraja
ahaṃ tvā sarvapāpebhyo mokṣyayiṣyāmi mā śucaḥ

sarva-dharman = all obligatory duties; parityajya = giving up, renouncing; mam = to Me; ekam = alone, only; saranam = shelter, surrender; vraja = go, take; aham = I; tvam = you; sarva = all; papebhyah = from sins; moksayisyami = liberate; ma = do not; sucah = grieve, worry.

Renouncing all obligatory duties, in Me alone take shelter. I will liberate you from all sins. Do not grieve.

At the beginning of this scripture, Arjuna expressed concerns for the consequences that might arise from his actions for him and his family's reputation if he fought in the war and killed his relatives and reputed warriors. He thought that by his actions, his name and his family's standing in society would be ruined, and he would incur the sin of killing great souls like Bhīshma and Drona. The whole discourse of the Bhagavadgita happened because of the turmoil he experienced upon reaching the battlefield and the despair into which he had fallen. In many ways, this verse can be considered the concluding verse of Lord Krishna's long discourse given to Arjuna in these 18 chapters and 600 verses. The reference to 'not to worry' (mā śucaḥ) connects this verse to the beginning of Arjuna's grief (vishada yoga) in the first chapter, suggesting that, having heard all that, he should stop worrying now and prepare for the battle. After explaining how sin could be avoided by performing his duties without desires and attachments and with devotion and renunciation, he assured him that there was no cause for worry even if he engaged in fighting and killed his enemies. He did not advise him to renounce fighting and become a devotee, renunciant, or seeker of knowledge. He wanted him to perform his duties first through karma-sannyasa yoga, a practice that involves renouncing the fruits of one's actions and dedicating them to the Lord, with resolve, faith, and devotion, using the knowledge he imparted to him and offering the fruit of his actions to him, knowing that the Lord would take care of the rest.

In the context of the Bhagavadgita, renunciation means giving up the desire for the fruit of one's actions. It means performing selfless actions as an offering to the Lord in total devotion and surrender. We have learned from this discourse that for a householder, duty (karma), renunciation (of desires), knowledge of the Self (jnanam), and devotion (bhakti) are necessary for liberation, and one must practice them with detachment, surrender, purity, and sameness. When perfection is attained in that practice, the skillful karma yogi earns divine grace and attains liberation. The transformation and purification of the mind and body require enduring effort, discipline, persistence, and perseverance. True devotion manifests in him only in the later stages when he attains perfection in the various disciplines. Thus, a devotee's spiritual journey normally begins with duty. He starts as a householder and karma yogi and advances through the practice of various yogas to break the fetters that keep him bound to his ignorance and delusion. When he cultivates purity and discernment with self-control, giving up desires and attachments through renunciation and practices contemplation (dhyana) to establish his mind in the Lord, he enters the final phase of liberation as an exclusive devotee. From there, the Lord will take care of his final journey to the immortal Abode of Brahman. Self-knowledge (jnana) plays a crucial role in this journey, as it is through this knowledge that one can understand the true nature of the Self and the world, and thereby attain liberation.

Shankaracharya expressed a different opinion in his commentary. He felt that 'sarvadharmān parityajya' meant a yogi should abandon all actions, meaning both good and evil (dharma and adharma) actions, and take shelter in the Lord to overcome his ignorance and achieve liberation. When he persisted in that pursuit with firm faith that he indeed was the Lord and attained self-knowledge, the Lord would release him from the karma arising from dharma and adharma. According to him, liberation is not possible through actions alone or actions and knowledge combined. Only through pure self-knowledge (jnana) can one attain liberation. When ignorance (avidya) is removed in this manner, one gains self-knowledge and attains the highest bliss through oneness. This may hold in the case of those who renounce worldly life and obligatory duties, take up sannyasa, and pursue jnana, the knowledge of Brahman. However, it may not apply to householders who perform their obligatory duties as a sacrifice or practice exclusive devotion. In verse 56, Lord Krishna advised Arjuna to perform actions by taking refuge in him. If actions were unnecessary and only self-knowledge ensured liberation, there was no need for the discourse on karma yoga or karma-sannyasa yoga. Lord Krishna would not have repeatedly advised Arjuna to follow his Kshatriya dharma and fight. He would have initiated him into sannyasa and advised him to abandon his duties and pursue self-knowledge. Shankara's argument is justified only when a householder performs his duties and takes up sannyasa to pursue self-knowledge and liberation.

Sloka 67

idaṃ te nātapaskāya nābhaktāya kadācana
na cāśuśrūṣave vācyaṃ na ca māṃ yobhyasūyati

idam = this; te = you; na = never; atapaskaya = irreligious, uncontrolled; na = never; abhaktaya = who is not a devotee; kadacana = at any time; na = not; ca = and; asusrusave = disinclined or reluctant to serve; vacyam = spoken; na = not; ca = and; mam = to Me; yah = who; abhyasuyati = acts enviously.

This should never at any time be spoken by you to one who does not practice his dharma, who is not a devotee, who is not disinclined to serve and envious of Me.

In this verse, Lord Krishna has provided crucial guidelines, laying down four criteria to admit students for the teaching of the Bhagavadgita. These criteria serve as a litmus test to identify and exclude unworthy individuals to whom the profound knowledge of the Bhagavadgita should not be taught. He emphasized that this knowledge should not be imparted to those who neglect their duties, lack devotion to their teachers or God, and are disinclined to serve him or other great souls. He also included those who envy him. According to Sri Shankaracharya, these four criteria are of utmost importance and should be applied simultaneously to determine the qualification and worthiness of a student to receive this knowledge. The teacher traditions of Hinduism discourage the teaching of spiritual knowledge or the knowledge of the scriptures to those who are irreligious, unprepared, lack faith and devotion, do not assist others, and disrespect their teachers or God or speak ill of them. This is particularly true when it comes to teaching the knowledge of Brahman or liberation. They may accept lay disciples who do not meet the criteria prescribed by Lord Krishna to prepare them for progress or purification, but do not bestow upon them advanced knowledge.

He used 'kadacana' (at any time) specifically because students chosen for the teaching must have been free from the four disqualifications since birth. For example, if a person was an atheist in the past but is now a devotee, he is still not qualified. The same applies to those who did not practice Dharma, were not devotees, did not participate in charity or religious and devotional service, and envied the Lord. By this injunction, Lord Krishna gives precedence to the students' purity or essential nature (svabhavam) rather than their birth, caste, family, or profession, which were traditionally used as the criteria since the Vedic times to determine the worthiness of students to receive the knowledge of the Vedas. In today's world, people who are completely free from all four criteria from birth are indeed rare, a testament to the high standards set by Lord Krishna. It is also true that those who practice exclusive devotion and pursue liberation, renouncing desires and attachments, are equally rare. Perhaps a guru may accept anyone as a student who approaches him and may teach him the knowledge, without desires and attachments, as service or offering to the Lord. Then, by that karma-sannyasa, no sin will accrue to him for violating this injunction.

Sloka 68

ya idaṃ paramaṃ guhyaṃ madbhakteṣv abhidhāsyati
bhaktiṃ mayi parāṃ kṛtvā mām evaiṣyaty asaṃśayaḥ

yah = he who; idam = this; paramam = supreme; guhyam = secret; mat = My; bhaktesu = to devotees; abhidhasyati = explains, teaches; bhaktim = devotion; mayi = to Me; param = supreme; krtva = having practiced; mam = to Me; eva = only; esyati = come; asamsayah = without doubt.

He who teaches this supreme secret to My devotees, having practiced supreme devotion to Me, will come to Me only without any doubt.

The supremely secret (parama guhyam) knowledge of the Bhagavadgita can be taught to all the devotees except those who are irreligious and undisciplined, do not possess faith and devotion, are disinclined to serve God and others, and are envious of him. It is clear from this verse that only a devotee who is not otherwise disqualified can teach it to other devotees who are also free from the four disqualifications mentioned in the previous verse. Lord Krishna also stated that the teacher should teach with supreme devotion, having practiced it. By that selfless and devotional service (seva), he undoubtedly attains the highest Goal. However, as we learned in the previous verse, having devotion to the Supreme Being is not a sufficient qualification to teach the scripture. The teacher must be free from the other disqualifications mentioned before.

Devotees worship the Bhagavan for different reasons. Teachers also teach the knowledge for different reasons, some with and some without desire. Lord Krishna identified (7.16) the wise ones who worship him with knowledge and pure devotion as the best. They are most qualified to teach or receive his teachings since they meet all the criteria. Teachers who find worthy students and teach them are blessed. Students who find worthy teachers and learn from them are also equally blessed. In both situations, karma or divine grace brings them together. By teaching and preparing them for the journey of liberation and rendering meritorious service (seva) without desiring any reward or gain, the teachers earn divine grace and qualify for liberation. The word 'asamsayah' suggests that liberation is guaranteed for them.

In short, the knowledge of the Bhagavadgita should be taught mainly to the purest souls by the purest souls who are exclusively devoted to the Lord. Teaching them without expectations and out of love and devotion is an act of devotion and sacrifice in itself. By that act of supreme devotion and selfless service, a teacher excels in his actions and exemplifies jnana, karma, sannyasa, and bhakti yogas. Through his selfless and sacrificial service, he strengthens the faith and resolve of his students to become God's exclusive devotees and work for their liberation. By his desireless actions, he serves the Lord and his creation with devotion, engaged in the sacrifice of knowledge and wisdom.

Sloka 69

na ca tasmān manuṣyeṣu kaścin me priyakṛttamaḥ
bhavitā na ca me tasmād anyaḥ priyataro bhuvi

na = not; ca = and; tasmat = than he; manusyesu = among people; kascit = anyone, even one; me = to Me; priya-krt-tamah = who performs a supremely dearer service or action; bhavita = will be; na = not; ca = and; me = My; tasmat = than him; anyah = other; priya-tarah = dearer; bhuvi = in this world.

And among all the people, there is none whatsoever who performs a supremely dearer service to Me than he; nor will there be anyone in this world who is dearer to Me than he.

Teaching or propagating the knowledge of the Bhagavadgita is the most excellent service in the cause of Dharma, peace, and happiness, especially if it is done with supreme devotion without desiring or expecting any reward or return. By that action, the teacher will earn God's love and grace and attain liberation. The best teachers master the knowledge of the scripture and practice it in word and deed. They cultivate purity and excel in jnana, karma, atma-samyama, sannyasa, and bhakti. With supreme devotion, they spread the word of God to other devotees to help them in their journey of devotion. By that selfless service, they uphold the eternal Dharma, set an example for others to follow, and contribute to the welfare of the world. A teacher who purifies himself and dissolves his ego in the silence of his mind, controlling his desires and expectations, suppressing the modifications of his mind, and cultivating discernment, becomes the voice of God and personifies the saying that a guru is indeed equal to Brahman (guru sakshat para brahma).

The knowledge of the Bhagavadgita is useful to devotees who want to achieve liberation or escape from the mortal world. It helps karma yogis, jnana yogis, bhakti yogis, and sannyasis to practice self-purification, acquire the right knowledge, and permanently escape from this world. It is also helpful to those pious souls who want to overcome their sinful karma and improve their chances of liberation through devotion, service, and righteous conduct. You will find in it answers to overcome your problems, heal your past, change your thinking and actions, or learn to endure suffering with detachment and indifference. Devotees can find inspiration in it to live wholesomely, integrating their goals and actions into a holistic approach to experience peace and happiness, or achieve material and spiritual well-being, or liberation. The teaching can help you cultivate sattva, overcome ignorance and delusion, and witness life from a spiritual perspective without becoming involved. It has the potential to teach and inspire everyone if they suspend their judgment, renounce their egos, and cultivate faith and devotion. Teaching the Bhagavadgita knowledge to God's beloved devotees is an opportunity to elevate our consciousness by establishing communion with the Lord. It is like having the Lord himself as our guru, living in his company (Satsang), and enjoying his friendship and nearness. Teaching the Bhagavadgita is an act of devotion, sacrifice, and selfless service. By serving the Lord through teaching, the teacher becomes a Bhagavata.

Sloka 70

adhyeṣyate ca ya imaṃ dharmyaṃ saṃvādam āvayoḥ
jñānayajñena tenāham iṣṭaḥ syām iti me matiḥ

adhyesyate = will study; ca = and; yah = he who; imam = this; dharmyam = sacred; samvadam = dialogue; avayoh = of ours; jnana = knowledge; yajnena = through sacrifice; tena = by him; aham = I; istah = worshiped; syam = shall be; iti = this; me = My; matih = opinion.

And he who shall study this sacred dialogue of ours, I will be worshipped by him through the sacrifice of knowledge. This is my opinion.

Apart from teaching its knowledge to others, it is equally beneficial to study the scripture or learn it from others. This verse affirms that studying the Bhagavadgita is an act of worship and devotion, and a sacrifice of knowledge. It is a form of active contemplation (dhyana) or establishing the mind in the Lord. By studying it, one harnesses the austere power of jnana, and by practicing it, one engages in karma-sannyasa, bhakti, and atma-samyama yogas. It becomes a liberating force if one does it without any desire or expectation. Lord Krishna said in his opinion (me mat), it will be considered the sacrifice of knowledge (jnana yajna). It is because studying a sacred scripture is indeed a part of jnana yoga, only because the student pursues the highest knowledge. Lord Krishna also said that it is equal to worshipping him because the sacrifice of knowledge is a devotional activity only, which strengthens the student's resolve, faith, and devotion. By studying it, the student engages his mind in the thoughts of the Lord, overcomes his ignorance, and cultivates discernment. It also strengthens his faith, devotion, and resolve to purify himself and escape from samsara. It amounts to pouring the oblation of sacred knowledge into the fire of his consciousness with devotion as an offering to the Lord. With that, he acquires the right knowledge, overcomes delusion, practices nishkama karma, self-control, and devotion, and cultivates purity, stability, and sameness. The knowledge will activate Prakriti's higher forces (divine Shaktis). They will assist him in his purification and overcoming the Maya shaktis. The Bhagavadgita has been rendered as a dialogue on Dharma (dharma samvadam) between the Lord and his devotee, Arjuna. It is a Yoga Shastra (treatise on yoga) because it contains the knowledge of several yogas, and every chapter in it has yoga in its title. It is also a discourse on the secret knowledge of Brahman and how to attain it, which is meant to be imparted to qualified and advanced yogis in close proximity. Hence, it is called a Upanishad.

Sloka 71

śraddhāvān anasūyaś ca śṛṇuyād api yo naraḥ
sopi muktaḥ śubhāṃl lokān prāpnuyāt puṇyakarmaṇām

sraddha-van = he who is full of faith; anasuyah = without envy; ca = and; srnuyat = happens to hear; api = even; yah = any; narah = human being; sah = he; api = also; muktah = liberated from sin; subhan = auspicious; lokan = worlds; prapnuyat = attains; punya-karmanam = of those who perform meritorious actions.

Anyone who is full of faith and without envy happens to hear this, even he, liberated from sin, also attains the worlds of those who perform meritorious actions.

The knowledge of the Bhagavadgita acquired either by studying or hearing from others liberates the devotees, who do not envy the Lord, from sin. They attain the higher worlds of those who perform righteous actions (punya karmas). However, neither of them will achieve liberation unless they practice it and achieve perfection. To achieve liberation, they must put that knowledge into practice and excel in it. They must become skillful yogis (yuktas), giving up desires and attachments and engaging in nishkama karma with exclusive devotion. Thus, nothing much is gained by merely reading the scripture. The superficial effort may have some benefit, but it does not take the devotee far on the path. One must study it with the right attitude and excel in its practice.

This and the previous two verses mention three types of people who benefit from knowing and understanding the Bhagavadgita through study or listening. Teachers come first. They study the Bhagavadgita, understand it, and teach it to others selflessly. By that meritorious act (punya karma) of teaching, with faith and devotion, they earn the grace of God and go straight to the immortal world. The students come next. They earn his grace and attain liberation if they study it and practice karma-sannyasa, engaging in actions (nishkama karma) with exclusive devotion and giving up egoism, delusion, desires, and attachments. If they do not attain liberation for some reason, they will earn the merit of engaging in a pious deed and attain a good birth in their next lives, from where they can continue their effort to progress further on the path. Those who learn the scripture by listening or hearing from others without malice or ill will come next. If they use that knowledge for righteous purposes and become skillful karma yogis, perform their obligatory duties, and serve the Lord, they will accumulate good karma and go to the ancestral heaven like the previous ones. Upon returning, they will attain a good birth and continue from there.

Sloka 72

kaccid etac chrutaṃ pārtha tvayaikāgreṇa cetasā
kaccid ajñānasaṃmohaḥ pranaṣṭas te dhanaṃjaya

kaccit = whether; etat = this; srutam = heard; partha = O Partha; tvaya = by you; eka-agrena = one-pointed, concentrated; cetasa = with mind; kaccit = whether; ajnana = ignorance; sammohah = delusion; pranastah = destroyed; te = of you; dhananjaya = O Dhananjaya.

Has this been heard by you, O Partha, with a one-pointed mind? Has this delusion of you, caused by ignorance, been destroyed, O Dhananjaya?

After completing his discourse and explaining its importance, Lord Krishna asked Arjuna whether he had listened to him with concentration and whether the delusion caused by his ignorance had been destroyed. A good teacher wants to know from his students whether they understand his teaching and whether their doubts and confusion are cleared. By their response, he decides whether he can conclude his discourse. Lord Krishna did the same. He asked Arjuna whether he listened to him with one-pointedness (ekagrata) and whether his moral confusion about duty and morality caused by his ignorance was removed. When knowledge is imparted orally, students may miss some parts of the teaching due to lapses in attention. Therefore, the teacher has to make sure that they listened and understood correctly.

The ignorance and delusion that Lord Krishna mentioned in his question were the ignorance of the hidden Self and the delusion that the body is the real self. One may also possess ignorance and delusion about the difference between action and inaction and what truly constitutes renunciation and sacrifice. At the beginning of the discourse, Arjuna had many doubts, which led to his despair and sorrow. He had mistaken notions about duty, morality, death, destruction, and the sinful consequences of his actions. He was ignorant of many spiritual truths and what led to sinful karma. He did not know that the Self was eternal, indestructible, represented his true identity, and would not participate in any action or modification of Prakriti. He was unaware that actions would not produce consequences, but the desires hidden in them and the desire for their fruit, and that by renouncing them, he could avoid sinful karma.

Because of that ignorance and delusion, he thought that killing his elders and relatives on the battlefield would ruin his reputation and his family's fortunes. Lord Krishna had to teach him that destruction was for the body but not for the Self, and the latter could not be killed or would kill anyone. He also revealed to him that the fate of all those who were going to fight in the war was already predetermined by him, and Arjuna would be instrumental in the death and destruction of those he feared to fight. Due to these misconceptions and deluded notions, and fearing that he would incur sin by killing his enemies in the battle, Arjuna wanted to abandon his duty and leave the battlefield. Lord Krishna cleared those misgivings and helped him know the importance of achieving liberation through knowledge, discernment, selfless actions, renunciation, contemplation, and devotion.

Sloka 73

naṣṭo mohaḥ smṛtir labdhā tvatprasādān mayācyuta
sthitosmi gatasaṃdehaḥ kariṣye vacanaṃ tava

arjunah uvaca = Arjuna said; nastah = destroyed; mohah = delusion; smrtih = knowledge; labdha = gained; tvat-prasadat = by your mercy; maya = by me; acyuta = Achyuta; sthitah = firm, steady; asmi = I am; gata = gone; sandehah = doubts; karisye = I shall act; vacanam = words; tava = according to you.

Arjuna said, "My delusion has been destroyed, O Achyuta, and by your mercy, I gained knowledge. I am now steady, with my doubts all gone. I shall now act according to your words."

Arjuna responded by saying that he understood the teaching, his delusion was destroyed, and he gained the right knowledge and discernment. With his doubts and confusion cleared, he was now mentally stable and ready to perform his duty according to the knowledge he had learned. He showed signs of improvement by speaking like a true devotee and karma-sannyasa yogi, acknowledging that by the grace of his teacher (tvatprasad), Lord Krishna, he overcame delusion and gained the knowledge of liberation. He seems to have realized that by performing actions without desires and sacrificing their fruit to the Lord, he could overcome whatever fear and guilt he experienced before at the thought of fighting his enemies. He was convinced that by performing his obligatory duties as a devotional offering without desires, upholding Dharma, and participating in a divine cause the Lord himself willed, he could serve him and enjoy his company forever. He realized that without attraction and aversion, hatred, or ill will, and serving the Lord as his devotee, he could remain untainted from the actions he feared to perform. After witnessing the universal form of Kala, he must have realized that the Supreme Lord of the universe had already predestined the result of the war and the destiny of all those who were fighting in it from both sides. Therefore, it would not be prudent on his part to claim ownership or doership of his actions. Having heard the importance of karma-sannyasa, jnana, and bhakti yogas and knowing the distinction between the Self and the not-self, Arjuna must have also understood that his right was to his obligatory duties only, but not to their fruit. As God's dutiful devotee, he must surrender to the Lord's will and offer his actions and possessions to him as a sacrifice, renouncing their fruit. Here, he acknowledged that by the Lord's mercy and will, he heard the Lord's teaching with unwavering devotion and concentration and understood that he was born to fulfill his destiny as the Lord wished. With his impurities now dissolved and his mind and senses firmly under control, he was now prepared to do the Lord's bidding.

Sloka 74

sañjaya uvāca
ity ahaṃ vāsudevasya pārthasya ca mahātmanaḥ
saṃvādam imam aśrauṣam adbhutaṃ romaharṣaṇam

sanjayah uvaca = Sanjaya said; iti = thus; aham = I; vasudevasya = of Vasudeva; parthasya = of Partha; ca = and; maha-atmanah = great souls; samvadam = dialogue; imam = this; asrausam = heard; adbhutam = wonderful; roma-harsanam = make hair standing on end.

Sanjaya said, "Thus, I heard this dialogue of Vasudeva and the great soul, Partha, which is wonderful and makes one's hair stand on end...

We know that Sanjaya and Dhritarashtra were remotely listening to the dialogue that went on between Lord Krishna and Arjuna. They did not participate in the conversation directly but listened to the whole conversation and its contents. Sanjaya was the Lord's devotee. Therefore, he was fully qualified to listen to it. Dhritarashtra must have accumulated enough good karma in his current and previous births to receive it by providence. Thus, by God's will, both became the earliest recipients of the Bhagavadgita after Arjuna. From the words of Sanjaya, we can see that he was apparently thrilled by the opportunity to witness the events, listen to the discourse, and even see the universal form of Lord Krishna, which no one had ever seen before. We cannot say the same about Dhritarashtra since he only heard what Sanjaya told him. Besides, he was more interested in events on the battlefield and the activities of his children. We are not sure whether he understood the full ramifications of the war since he had no faith in Lord Krishna or his words. Otherwise, he would have stopped the war before it even began.

The conversation between Lord Krishna and Arjuna is known as samvad, meaning a dialogue, interaction, or discussion between two or more people. Bhagavadgita is a dialogue (samvad), not a monologue, debate, or argument. It is also a teaching, a treatise on yoga, an Upanishad, and a study on Brahman (Brahma vidya), by knowing which, without delusion, one attains liberation. Four people participated in the dialogue, and two conversations happened, one between Lord Krishna and Arjuna on the battlefield and the other between Dhritarashtra and Sanjaya in the royal palace far from the battleground. Traditionally, samvad has been an approved method of instruction in Hinduism for a long time. Through constructive dialogue, teachers transmitted knowledge to their students, and the latter developed insights into it by asking questions, raising doubts, and clearing their confusion. The two-way dialogue helped the teachers ascertain their students' progress while helping them reinforce their knowledge. The method helped Arjuna overcome his confusion and delusion, know the importance of his obligatory duties, and fulfill his destiny in the Lord's divine play. The dialogue survived the ravages of time and still inspires millions of devotees to escape from samsara by performing desireless actions (nishkama karma) to uphold their obligatory duties and participate in the Lord's eternal sacrifice.

Sloka 75

vyāsaprasādāc chrutavān etad guhyam ahaṃ param
yogaṃ yogeśvarāt kṛṣṇāt sākṣāt kathayataḥ svayam

vyasa-prasadat = by the blessings of the sage Vyasa; srutavan = heard; etat = this; guhyam = most secret; aham = I; param = supreme; yogam = yoga; yoga-isvarat = from the Lord of Yoga; krsnat = from Krishna; saksat = directly; kathayatah = as he was delivering; svayam = personally.

"By the grace of sage Vyasa, I heard this most secretive and sacred yoga directly from the Lord of Yoga, Krishna Himself, as he was personally delivering it...

Sanjaya remembered his teacher, Vyasa, with gratitude because he had this rare opportunity to witness an epochal event because of him. Hence, he remembered him saying, "By the grace of sage Vyasa." He was grateful because he heard the sacred teaching of Moksha Yoga from the Lord of Yoga, Lord Krishna, himself. In this context, Yoga means the body of knowledge and techniques to achieve liberation or union with the Self. The Bhagavadgita is considered a Yoga Shastra, a sacred text on Yoga, since it deals with Yoga comprehensively, presenting several yogas and yoga techniques and their relative importance in the journey of liberation. Traditionally, yoga means a state or condition and a system of philosophy and practice. In the context of the Bhagavadgita, both meanings are appropriate. The knowledge imparted by Lord Krishna is the utmost secret (guhyam) because it is truly grasped by only the wisest and the purest souls. Others may understand it only partially or remain ignorant even after receiving it. It is supreme (param) because it leads to the transcendental knowledge of Brahman. Sanjaya was thankful because he gained direct knowledge from the Lord himself. While he was fully qualified to receive it, we cannot say the same about Dhritarashtra. Although he was well-versed in the Vedas and had many good qualities, he had some weaknesses and was deluded by desires, ambition, and attachments. Still, the Lord might have had his reason to let him hear it. Maybe he gave him a final opportunity to learn from it and stop the war. However, Dhritarashtra seemed to have learned nothing from it.

Sloka 76

rājan saṃsmṛtya saṃsmṛtya saṃvādam imamadbhutam
keśavārjunayoḥ puṇyaṃ hṛṣyāmi ca muhur muhuḥ

rajan = O King; samsmrtya samsmrtya = remembering again and again; samvadam = the dialogue; imam = this; adbhutam = wonderful; kesava = Kesava; arjunayoh = and Arjuna; punyam = meritorious, pious; hrsyami = rejoice in my heart; ca = and; muhuh muhuh = minute by minute.

"O King, remembering again and again this wonderful, pious dialogue between Kesava and Arjuna, I am rejoicing in my heart, every minute ...

These words convey that Sanjaya was ecstatic after listening to the conversation and lost in that memory like a true devotee. Sravanam (listening) and mananam (remembering) are important devotional practices. Combined with contemplative practices (nidhidhyasana), they can lead to permanent peace and liberation. Sanjaya was a true devotee, and he knew exactly what to do with the knowledge he received.

Sloka 77

tac ca saṃsmṛtya saṃsmṛtya rūpam atyadbhutaṃhareḥ
vismayo me mahān rājan hṛṣyāmi ca punaḥ punaḥ

tat = that; ca = also; samsmrtya samsmrtya = remembering again and again; rupam = form; ati adbhutam = supremely wonderful; hareh = Hari; vismayah = filled with wonder; me = my; mahan = great; rajan = O King; hrsyami = rejoicing in my heart; ca = and; punah punah = again and again.

"O King, remembering that supremely wonderful form of Hari again and again, I am filled with great wonder. I am rejoicing in my heart again and again...

Sanjaya kept reminiscing, with his mind filled with devotion and memories of what happened and what he witnessed. He kept remembering the wonderful form of Lord Krishna. It meant that, like a true devotee with a pure heart, he focused on his pleasant form as Hari or Maha Vishnu rather than his fierce form of Kala. Vaishnavas and Lord Krishna's devotees revere him as an incarnation of Maha Vishnu, who is also known more popularly as Hari, meaning green or the one responsible for all the greenery. Both the epithets, Hari and Vishnu, are used in Chapter 11 to describe his universal form (visvarupam). The Bhagavadgita also supports the view that he is an incarnation of Lord Vishnu and is indeed Hari. For example, in verse 9, Sanjaya tells Dhritarashtra, "Having said thus, O King, thereafter Hari, the great Lord of Yoga showed Arjuna his supreme divine form." In verse 24, Arjuna says, "O, Vishnu, seeing you touching the heaven, glowing with many colors...I am terrified in my heart and not finding stability and equanimity." In verse 46, he wishes to see his pleasant and original form. The description of the form he saw fits that of Maha Vishnu's pleasant form (saumya rupam). As described in the scripture, Vishnu has four arms, wears a crown, and holds a mace in one hand and a disc in the other. With the third arm, he holds a conch shell, while he holds the fourth one in an assuring mode (abhaya mudra). The objects in his hands may change according to his mood or functions, but the description perfectly fits him. After showing him the pleasant form, in verse 52, Lord Krishna says, "This (pleasant) form of mine which you have seen is difficult to see. Even the gods are always eager to see it." It may be possible that the pleasant and peaceful form (saumya rupam) Sanjaya witnessed was not his fearful, universal form, but that of Maha Vishnu. It may be recalled that before showing him his universal form, Lord Krishna said that no one with ordinary eyes could see it. Therefore, he granted him supernatural vision (divya chakshu). Therefore, we cannot be sure whether Sanjaya saw the universal form of Kala just as Arjuna saw. However, from his narration to the King, it appears that he did see it, perhaps in a trance, but could not remember it in the wakeful state. Whatever may be the truth, he focused on his pleasant form as Hari and remembered him now because he worshipped him in that form only.

Sloka 78

yatra yogeśvaraḥ kṛṣṇo yatra pārtho dhanurdharaḥ
tatra śrīr vijayo bhūtir dhruvā nītir matir mama

yatra = wherever; yoga-isvarah = Lord of Yoga; krsnah = Krishna; yatra = wherever; parthah = Partha; dhanuh-dharah = the bearer of the bow and arrows; tatra = there; srih = wealth, abundance, opulence; vijayah = victory; bhutih = happiness; dhruva = sure, certain; nitih = justice, righteousness, morality; matih mama = is my opinion.

"Wherever is Krishna, the Lord of Yoga, and wherever Partha, the bearer of the bow and arrows, there will surely be wealth, victory, happiness, and righteousness. This is my opinion."

Wherever the dialogue between Lord Krishna and Arjuna is remembered and revered, peace and prosperity will prevail. By knowing it, a devotee can secure wealth and victory by living righteously, performing obligatory duties (Dharma) without desires (nishkama karma), and worshipping the Lord with exclusive devotion. By his grace, he achieves peace and equanimity and lives happily. This is the essence of Sanjaya's words.

Within the bounds of the Bhagavadgita, the epic Mahābhārata, and Vaishnava literature, Lord Krishna and Arjuna are not mere historical figures or characters in a divine drama. They were born with a divine purpose to restore righteousness, order, and regularity when the times were bad, the Dharma was in decline, evil was ascending, and the world was about to transition from Dvapara Yuga to Kali Yuga. The two symbolize the ideal and sacred relationship between the Lord and his devotee and between the

Supreme Self (Brahman) and the individual Self (Atman). The thread of righteousness, love, and devotion binds their relationship. One may even say that the Supreme Being creates the world to experience the love and devotion of himself in the form of a living and breathing devotee. Through the jivas, he experiences life's numerous aspects and the duality and delusion of his limited and conditioned existence in the mirror of his creation. As the Upanishads declare, being one and alone, out of the desire to have company, he created the worlds and beings. As if it is not enough, occasionally, he incarnates upon earth to live amidst his own created forms to feel their suffering in mortal bodies or rescue them from Maya or suffering. The relationship between God and the Jivas is significant in the spiritual destiny of the world and the mental, material, and spiritual progress or evolution of all beings on earth. We do not know whether lower life forms are conscious of him or experience him. However, surely, human beings are capable of feeling his presence and seeking his help and support to further their spiritual growth and transformation.

Some schools of philosophy believe in the possibility of achieving liberation through self-effort without God's intervention or grace. They do not believe he is the controller and the cause of all. They think he is either passive or nonexistent. In devotional theism, we do not accept it. We believe that the Supreme Lord is the source of all and Controller of all and is central to our lives and destinies. We believe that he is responsible for all actions and outcomes in all endeavors, and the jivas are merely instrumental in that divine drama. In other words, nothing happens without him, his will, or force. Everything arises from him and subsides in him according to his will. All this belongs to him and is inhabited by him. Therefore, it is wise and safe not to claim ownership or doership but to live in devotion, offering all actions to him and performing his duties as he ordained.

The Bhagavadgita affirms these beliefs and gives us the hope that by renouncing desires, attachments, ownership, and doership and taking refuge in him, we can escape from samsara and from the suffering we experience due to karma and rebirth. It shows us sacred pathways so we can cultivate knowledge and devotion, escape from karma, and attain the highest perfection, which even gods cannot achieve. It teaches us how to escape from karma and rebirth without abandoning our duties or suffering from the consequences of our actions, giving us a radically new definition of karma and sacrifice and a new approach to living righteously and responsibly as God's exclusive devotees and loyal soldiers in the battle of life. The scripture is a treasure house of knowledge and practical wisdom. It reveals itself to the extent we study it and contemplate it. It helps us become skillful yogis with stable minds and firm resolve to the extent we assimilate and practice its knowledge and wisdom as a devotional offering and service to him without selfishness or egoism. The scripture immortalizes the sacred dialogue between Lord Krishna and Arjuna and the eternal relationship between God and his dearest devotees with the promise to rescue them from samsara. Therefore, wherever it is revered, remembered, and practiced, wealth, victory, happiness, and righteousness are bound to manifest as sacred gifts from the Lord's bountiful love.

The Bhagavadgita begins with the words of Dhritarashtra and ends with the words of Sanjaya. The dialogue between Lord Krishna and Arjuna appears in between as a conversation within a conversation. Indeed, the scripture itself is a scripture within another scripture, the epic Mahābhārata. Veda Vyasa is the author of both. He presents the Bhagavadgita as a conversation between Sanjaya and Dhritarashtra, with Sanjaya overhearing the dialogue between Lord Krishna and Arjuna. Since Vyasa received that knowledge intuitively or indirectly from Sanjaya rather than directly from Lord Krishna, we have to consider it a memorial text (smriti) rather than a directly heard text (shruti).

Conclusion

iti srīmadbhāgavadgītāsupanisatsu brahmavidyāyām yogasāstre srikrisnārjunasamvāde mokshasanyasayogo nama astadaso 'dhyayah.

iti = thus; srīmadbhāgavadgītā = in the sacred Bhagavadgita; upanisatsu = in the Upanishad; brahmavidyāyām = the knowledge of the absolute Brahman; yogasāstre = the scripture of yoga; srikrisnārjunasamvāde = the dialogue between Sri Krishna and Arjuna; mokshasanyasayogo nama = by name the yoga of liberation by renunciation; astadasah = eighteenth; adhyayah = chapter.

Thus ends the eighteenth chapter, named Moksha Sannyasa Yoga (the Yoga of Liberation by Renunciation), in the Upanishad of the divine Bhagavadgita, the knowledge of the Absolute, a treatise on Yoga, and the debate between Arjuna and Lord Krishna.

The Greatness of the Bhagavadgita

Although Bhagavadgita emphasizes the importance of performing actions without desiring their fruit, tradition declares the beneficial results of studying and practicing it. This is meant to encourage the devotees to study it and understand its knowledge and wisdom to achieve liberation. The following is a free translation of the greatness of the Bhagavadgita, as revealed by Lord Vishnu to Mother Earth and proclaimed by sage Suta in the sacred Varaha Purana.

1. He who practices the teachings of the Bhagavadgita assiduously is freed from the stain of prarabdha karma. He lives happily in this world and, upon death, becomes liberated.

2. He who studies the Bhagavadgita with devotion is not stained by sin, just as the lotus leaf is untouched by water.

3 & 4. Wherever the Bhagavadgita is kept and wherever it is read regularly, there is the holiness of all the holy places and all gods, seers, yogis, celestial beings, and even Narada, Uddhava, and their followers.

5. Where the Bhagavadgita is recited regularly, help comes swiftly from God. Where the Bhagavadgita is discussed, recited, and taught, God resides there doubtlessly.

6. God dwells in the Bhagavadgita. It is His best abode. With the wisdom of the Bhagavadgita, He protects the three worlds.

7. The Bhagavadgita is God's Supreme Knowledge. It is undoubtedly Brahman Himself. It is the dot (bindu) in the Aum symbol and the eternal and inexhaustible Self.

8. It is spoken by Lord Krishna, the Supreme Lord, in his own words to Arjuna, containing the wisdom of the Vedas and the knowledge of the tattvas.

9. Whoever constantly studies the eighteen chapters of the Bhagavadgita with an undistracted mind will gain perfect wisdom and reach the supreme goal.

10. If one cannot complete all eighteen chapters, at least by studying even half the chapters of the Bhagavadgita, one gains the merit equal to gifting a cow.

11. By reading only one-third of it, he obtains the merit of bathing in the waters of the Ganga. By reading only one-sixth or three chapters, he gains the merit of performing the Soma sacrifice.

12. A single chapter read daily with devotion makes one a member of a Shivagana and obtains the world of Rudra.

13. He who reads daily one-fourth of a chapter is assured of human birth in every reincarnation for a manvantara.

14 &15. He who reads ten, seven, five, four, two, three, one, or a half verse securely obtains the world of the moon or the ancestral world for ten thousand years. Forever reading the Bhagavadgita and completing his stay there, he will take a human birth when he returns to the mortal world.

16. Upon his return, if he continues to practice its teachings, he will attain the final liberation. At the time of death, by uttering "Gita," he reaches the Immortal Path.

17. By regularly listening to the wisdom of the Bhagavadgita, even sinners can attain the Abode of God (Vaikuntha) and rejoice with the Supreme Lord.

18. He who meditates on the meaning of the Bhagavadgita, having dutifully performed his obligatory duties, becomes a liberated soul (jivanmukta) even while in the body. Upon leaving the body, he attains the Highest Goal.

19. In the past, great kings such as Janaka and others took refuge in the knowledge of the Bhagavadgita. Having been cleansed of all their sins, they attained the immortal world.

20. Whoever completes the study of the Bhagavadgita without reading this description of its greatness, his reading shall remain in vain, and his effort shall be lost.

21. He who practices the Bhagavadgita and reads this eternal greatness of it, which has been declared by Lord Vishnu and proclaimed by Suta, will gain the fruit described above.

Image Credits:

Front cover image: Adobe Stock License No: #358517756
Back cover Image: Adobe Stock License No: #575718363
Book Cover Design by Jayaram V

www.ingramcontent.com/pod-product-compliance
Lightning Source LLC
Chambersburg PA
CBHW080750300426
44114CB00020B/2684
* 9 7 8 1 9 3 5 7 6 0 2 7 6 *